Contemporary
Literary Criticism

Guide to Gale Literary Criticism Series

When you need to review criticism of literary works, these are the Gale series to use:

If the author's death date is: **You should turn to:**

After Dec. 31, 1959
(or author is still living)

CONTEMPORARY LITERARY CRITICISM

for example: Jorge Luis Borges, Anthony Burgess,
William Faulkner, Mary Gordon,
Ernest Hemingway, Iris Murdoch

1900 through 1959

TWENTIETH-CENTURY LITERARY CRITICISM

for example: Willa Cather, F. Scott Fitzgerald,
Henry James, Mark Twain, Virginia Woolf

1800 through 1899

NINETEENTH-CENTURY LITERATURE CRITICISM

for example: Fedor Dostoevski, Nathaniel Hawthorne,
George Sand, William Wordsworth

1400 through 1799

LITERATURE CRITICISM FROM 1400 TO 1800
(excluding Shakespeare)

for example: Anne Bradstreet, Daniel Defoe,
Alexander Pope, François Rabelais,
Jonathan Swift, Phillis Wheatley

SHAKESPEAREAN CRITICISM

Shakespeare's plays and poetry

Antiquity through 1399

CLASSICAL AND MEDIEVAL LITERATURE CRITICISM

for example: Dante, Homer, Plato, Sophocles, Vergil,
the Beowulf Poet

Gale also publishes related criticism series:

CHILDREN'S LITERATURE REVIEW

This series covers authors of all eras who have written for the preschool through high school audience.

SHORT STORY CRITICISM

This series covers the major short fiction writers of all nationalities and periods of literary history.

POETRY CRITICISM

This series covers poets of all nationalities, movements, and periods of literary history.

ISSN 0091-3421

Volume 67

Contemporary Literary Criticism

Excerpts from Criticism of the
Works of Today's Novelists, Poets,
Playwrights, Short Story Writers, Scriptwriters,
and Other Creative Writers

Roger Matuz
EDITOR

Cathy Falk
Sean R. Pollock
David Segal
ASSOCIATE EDITORS

Gale Research Inc. • DETROIT • LONDON

STAFF

Roger Matuz, *Editor*

Cathy Falk, Marie Lazzari, Sean R. Pollock, David Segal,
Robyn Young, *Associate Editors*

Jennifer Brostrom, John P. Daniel, Christopher Giroux, Ian Goodhall, Grace N. Jeromski,
Susan M. Peters, Bruce Walker, Debra A. Wells, Janet M. Witalec, *Assistant Editors*

Jeanne A. Gough, *Production & Permissions Manager*
Linda M. Pugliese, *Production Supervisor*
Lorna Mabunda, Maureen A. Puhl, Jennifer VanSickle, *Editorial Associates*
Donna Craft, Paul Lewon, Camille P. Robinson, Sheila Walencewicz, *Editorial Assistants*

Maureen Richards, *Research Supervisor*
Mary Beth McElmeel, *Editorial Associate*
Kathleen Jozwiak, Amy Kaechele, Julie Karmazin, Tamara C. Nott, Julie Synkonis,
Editorial Assistants

Sandra C. Davis, *Permissions Supervisor (Text)*
Josephine M. Keene, Denise M. Singleton, Kimberly F. Smilay, *Permissions Associates*
Maria L. Franklin, Michele Lonoconus, Shalice Shah, Nancy K. Sheridan,
Rebecca A. Stanko, *Permissions Assistants*
Shelly Rakoczy, *Student Co-op Assistant*

Margaret A. Chamberlain, *Permissions Supervisor (Pictures)*
Pamela A. Hayes, *Permissions Associate*
Karla Kulkis, Nancy Rattenbury, Keith Reed, *Permissions Assistants*

Mary Beth Trimper, *Production Manager*
Shanna Heilveil, *External Production Associate*

Art Chartow, *Art Director*
C. J. Jonik, *Keyliner*

Contents

Preface   vii

Acknowledgments   xi

Preface

Named "one of the twenty-five most distinguished reference titles published during the past twenty-five years" by *Reference Quarterly,* the *Contemporary Literary Criticism (CLC)* series provides readers with critical commentary and general information on more than 2,000 authors now living or who died after December 31, 1959. Previous to the publication of the first volume of *CLC* in 1973, there was no ongoing digest monitoring scholarly and popular sources of critical opinion and explication of modern literature. *CLC,* therefore, has fulfilled an essential need, particularly since the complexity and variety of contemporary literature makes the function of criticism especially important to today's reader.

Scope of the Series

CLC presents significant passages from published criticism of works by creative writers. Since many of the authors covered by *CLC* inspire continual critical commentary, writers are often represented in more than one volume. There is, of course, no duplication of reprinted criticism.

Authors are selected for inclusion for a variety of reasons, among them the publication or dramatic production of a critically acclaimed new work, the reception of a major literary award, revival of interest in past writings, or the adaptation of a literary work to film or television.

The present volume of *CLC* includes Kate Millett, widely acknowledged as a pioneering figure of the contemporary feminist movement; Derek Walcott, an acclaimed West Indian poet whose 1990 epic poem *Omeros* reinvents Homer's *Odyssey* to explore the Caribbean people's influence on world culture; Oliver Sacks, English neurologist and author of the best-selling *The Man Who Mistook His Wife for a Hat* and *Awakenings,* the latter of which was adapted into an award-winning film; and John Guare, whose Tony-nominated play *Six Degrees of Separation* achieved great popularity on Broadway.

Perhaps most importantly, works that frequently appear on the syllabuses of high school and college literature courses are represented by individual entries in *CLC*. James Baldwin's *Go Tell It on the Mountain* and William Carlos William's *Paterson* are examples of works of this stature appearing in *CLC,* Volume 67.

Attention is also given to several other groups of writers—authors of considerable public interest—about whose work criticism is often difficult to locate. These include mystery and science fiction writers, literary and social critics, foreign writers, and authors who represent particular ethnic groups within the United States.

Format of the Book

Each *CLC* volume contains about 500 individual excerpts—with approximately seventeen excerpts per author—taken from hundreds of book review periodicals, general magazines, scholarly journals, monographs, and books. Entries include critical evaluations spanning from the beginning of an author's career to the most current commentary. Interviews, feature articles, and other published writings that offer insight into the author's works are also presented. Students, teachers, librarians, and researchers will find that the generous excerpts and supplementary material in *CLC* provide them with vital information needed to write a term paper, analyze a poem, or lead a book discussion group. In addition, complete bibliographical citations note the original source and all of the information necessary for a term paper footnote or bibliography.

Features

A *CLC* author entry consists of the following elements:

• The **author heading** cites the form under which the author has most commonly published, followed by birth date, and death date when applicable. Uncertainty as to a birth or death date is indicated by a question mark.

• A **portrait** of the author is included when available.

• A brief **biographical and critical introduction** to the author and his or her work precedes the excerpted criticism. The first line of the introduction provides the author's full name, pseudonyms (if applicable), nationality, and a listing of genres in which the author has written. Since *CLC* is not intended to be a definitive biographical source, cross-references have been included to direct readers to these useful sources published by Gale Research: *Short Story Criticism* and *Children's Literature Review,* which provide excerpts of criticism on the works of short story writers and authors of books for young people, respectively; *Contemporary Authors,* which includes detailed biographical and bibliographical sketches of more than 98,000 authors; *Something about the Author,* which contains heavily illustrated biographical sketches of writers and illustrators who create books for children and young adults; *Dictionary of Literary Biography,* which provides original evaluations and detailed biographies of authors important to literary history; and *Contemporary Authors Autobiography Series* and *Something about the Author Autobiography Series,* which offer autobiographical essays by prominent writers for adults and those of interest to young readers, respectively. Previous volumes of *CLC* in which the author has been featured are also listed in the introduction.

• A list of **principal works,** arranged chronologically and, if applicable, divided into genre categories, notes the most important works by the author.

• The **excerpted criticism** represents various kinds of critical writing, ranging in form from the brief review to the scholarly exegesis. Essays are selected by the editors to reflect the spectrum of opinion about a specific work or about an author's literary career in general. The excerpts are presented chronologically, adding a useful perspective to the entry. All titles by the author featured in the entry are printed in boldface type, which enables the reader to easily identify the works being discussed. Publication information (such as publisher names and book prices) and parenthetical numerical references (such as footnotes or page and line references to specific editions of a work) have been deleted at the editor's discretion to provide smoother reading of the text.

• A complete **bibliographical citation** designed to help the user find the original essay or book follows each excerpt.

• A concise **further reading** section appears at the end of entries on authors for whom a significant amount of criticism exists in addition to the pieces reprinted in *CLC.* In some cases, this annotated bibliography includes references to material for which the editors could not obtain reprint rights.

Other Features

• An **Acknowledgments** section lists the copyright holders who have granted permission to reprint material in this volume of *CLC.* It does not, however, list every book or periodical reprinted or consulted during the preparation of the volume.

• A **Cumulative Author Index** lists all the authors who have appeared in the various literary criticism series published by Gale Research, with cross-references to Gale's biographical and autobiographical series. A full listing of the series referenced there appears on the first page of the indexes of this volume. Readers will welcome this cumulated author index as a useful tool for locating an author within the various series. The index, which lists birth and death dates when available, will be particularly valuable for those authors who are identified with a certain period but whose death date causes them to be placed in another, or for those authors whose careers span two periods. For example, Ernest Hemingway is found in *CLC,* yet a writer often associated with him, F. Scott Fitzgerald, is found in *Twentieth-Century Literary Criticism.*

• A **Cumulative Nationality Index** alphabetically lists all authors featured in *CLC* by nationality, followed by numbers corresponding to the volumes in which they appear.

• A **Title Index** alphabetically lists all titles reviewed in the current volume of *CLC.* Listings are followed by the author's name and the corresponding page numbers where the titles are discussed. English translations of foreign titles and variations of titles are cross-referenced to the title under which a work was originally published. Titles of novels, novellas, dramas, films, record albums, and poetry, short story, and essay collections are printed in italics, while all individual poems, short stories, essays, and songs are printed in roman type within quotation marks; when published separately (e.g., T.S. Eliot's poem *The Waste Land*), the title will also be printed in italics.

• In response to numerous suggestions from librarians, Gale has also produced a **special paperbound edition** of the *CLC* title index. This annual cumulation, which alphabetically lists all titles reviewed in the series, is available to all customers and will be published with the first volume of *CLC* issued in each calendar year. Additional copies of the index are available upon request. Librarians and patrons will welcome this separate index: it saves shelf space, is easy to use, and is disposable upon receipt of the following year's cumulation.

A Note to the Reader

When writing papers, students who quote directly from any volume in the Literary Criticism Series may use the following general forms to footnote reprinted criticism. The first example pertains to material drawn from periodicals, the second to material reprinted from books:

[1]Anne Tyler, "Manic Monologue," *The New Republic* 200 (April 17, 1989), 44-6; excerpted and reprinted in *Contemporary Literary Criticism,* Vol. 58, ed. Roger Matuz (Detroit: Gale Research, 1990), p. 325.

[2]Patrick Reilly, *The Literature of Guilt: From 'Gulliver' to Golding* (University of Iowa Press, 1988); excerpted and reprinted in *Contemporary Literary Criticism,* Vol. 58, ed. Roger Matuz (Detroit: Gale Research, 1990), pp. 206-12.

Suggestions Are Welcome

The editors welcome the comments and suggestions of readers to expand the coverage and enhance the usefulness of the series.

ACKNOWLEDGMENTS

The editors wish to thank the copyright holders of the excerpted criticism included in this volume, the permissions managers of many book and magazine publishing companies for assisting us in securing reprint rights, and Anthony Bogucki for assistance with copyright research. We are also grateful to the staffs of the Detroit Public Library, the Library of Congress, the University of Detroit Library, Wayne State University Purdy/Kresge Library Complex, and the University of Michigan Libraries for making their resources available to us. Following is a list of the copyright holders who have granted us permission to reprint material in this volume of CLC. Every effort has been made to trace copyright, but if omissions have been made, please let us know.

COPYRIGHTED EXCERPTS IN *CLC,* VOLUME 67, WERE REPRINTED FROM THE FOLLOWING PERIODICALS:

Agenda, v. 21, Autumn, 1983 for "Another Look at Edith Sitwell" by Jean MacVean. Reprinted by permission of the author.—*America,* v. 135, September 11, 1976. © 1976. All rights reserved. Reprinted with permission of America Press, Inc., 106 West 56th Street, New York, NY 10019.—*American Notes & Queries,* v. XVI, September, 1977. Reprinted by permission of University Press of Kentucky.—*The American Poetry Review,* v. 16, January-February, 1987. Copyright © 1987 by World Poetry, Inc.—*Ariel: A Review of International English Literature,* v. 17, October, 1986 for "Beyond the Myth of Confrontation: A Comparative Study of African and African-American Female Protagonists" by Ebele Eko. Copyright © 1986 The Board of Governors, The University of Calgary. Reprinted by permission of the publisher and the author.—*The Atlantic Monthly,* v. 253, March 1984 for "A New American Master" by Lloyd Rose. Copyright 1984 by The Atlantic Monthly Company, Boston, MA. Reprinted by permission of the author.—*The Bloomsbury Review,* v. 11, March, 1991 for "Mourning the Loss of a Generation" by Mark Hummel. Copyright © by Owaissa Communications Company, Inc. 1991. Reprinted by permission of the author.—*Booklist,* v. 76, June 15, 1980. Copyright © 1980 by the American Library Association. Reprinted by permission of the publisher.—*Book World—The Washington Post,* March 24, 1968 for "In the Shadow of Megadeath" by Josh Greenfeld; October 20, 1968 for "A Psycho-History of Mao Tse-tung" by John K. Fairbank; August 9, 1970 for "The Wrong Lessons About Life" by Clara Claiborne Park. © 1968, 1970 Postrib Corp. All reprinted with permission of *The Washington Post* and the respective authors./ June 24, 1973; July 7, 1974; May 16, 1976; October 5, 1986; November 15, 1987; March 20, 1988; July 17, 1988; November 5, 1989; May 13, 1990; October 7, 1990; October 21, 1990; January 6, 1991; February 17, 1991. © 1973, 1974, 1976, 1986, 1987, 1988, 1989, 1990, 1991, *The Washington Post.* All reprinted with permission of the publisher.—*Callaloo,* v. 12, Summer, 1989. Copyright © 1989 By Charles H. Rowell. All rights reserved. Reprinted by permission of the publisher.—*Chicago Tribune,* April 9, 1989 for "Brazilian Saga" by Thomas Christensen. © copyrighted 1989, Chicago Tribune Company. All rights reserved. Reprinted by permission of the author.—*Chicago Tribune—Books,* July 10, 1988 for "Cantata for Three Female Voices" by Alan Cheuse; June 3, 1990 for "Spilling the Beans" by Joy Williams. © copyrighted 1988, 1990, Chicago Tribune Company. All rights reserved. Both reprinted by permission of the respective authors.—*The Christian Century,* v. LXXXVII, December 9, 1970. Copyright 1970 Christian Century Foundation. Reprinted by permission from *The Christian Century.*—*The Christian Science Monitor,* January 29, 1986 for a review of "Rum and Coke" by John Beaufort. © 1986 the author. All rights reserved. Reprinted by permission of the author.—*Chronicles: A Magazine of American Culture,* v. 14, June, 1990 for "Hell Is Other People" by Florence King. Copyright © 1990 by The Rockford Institute. All rights reserved. Reprinted by permission of the author.—*CLA Journal,* v. XIX, December, 1975. Copyright, 1975 by The College Language Association. Used by permission of The College Language Association.—*Commentary,* v. 85, June, 1988 for "Arabs as Jews" by Edward Alexander; v. 88, July, 1989 for "A Major Israeli Novel" by Alan Mintz. Copyright © 1988, 1989 by the American Jewish Committee. All rights reserved. Both reprinted by permission of the publisher and the respective authors.—*Commonweal,* v. 113, March 28, 1986; v. 115, May 20, 1988. Copyright © 1986, 1988 Commonweal Foundation. Both reprinted by permission of Commonweal Foundation.—*The Commonweal,* v. LVIII, May 22, 1953. Copyright 1953, renewed 1981 Commonweal Publishing Co., Inc. Reprinted by permission of Commonweal Foundation.—*Contemporary Literature,* v. 17, Autumn, 1976. © 1976 by the Board of Regents of the University of Wisconsin System. Reprinted by permission of The University of Wisconsin Press.—*Daily News,* New York, November 9, 1990. © 1990 New York News Inc. Reprinted with permission.—*The Denver Quarterly,* v. 15, Spring, 1980. Copyright © 1980 by the University of Denver.—*Encounter,* v. XXI, August, 1963 for "Dark Angel: The Writings of James Baldwin" by Colin MacInnes. © 1963 by Encounter Ltd. Reprinted by permission of the Literary Estate of Colin MacInnes./ v. XLI, November, 1973 for "A Linking of Disciplines: Prospects in Neuro-Psychiatry" by Anthony Storr. © 1973 by Encounter Ltd. Reprinted with the permission of Peters, Fraser & Dunlop Group Ltd.—*The Hispanic American Historical Review,* v. 59, August, 1979. Copyright © 1979, Duke University Press.

of Power' " by Joyce Johnson. © copyright 1985 *WLWE-World Literature Written in English*. Reprinted by permission of the publisher and the author.

James Baldwin

1924-1987

(Full name: James Arthur Baldwin) American novelist, essayist, playwright, scriptwriter, short story writer, and author of children's books.

The following entry presents criticism on Baldwin's novel *Go Tell It on the Mountain* (1953). For further information and commentary on his career, see *CLC*, Vols. 1, 2, 3, 4, 5, 8, 13, 15, 17, 42, 50.

Baldwin is considered among the most prestigious writers in post-World War II American literature. Beginning with the publication of his first and most highly respected novel, *Go Tell It on the Mountain*, he garnered praise for exposing the racial and sexual polarization of American society and for challenging readers to confront these differences. Critics have reserved their highest acclaim for his essays, yet Baldwin's novels, plays, and short stories have also consistently generated commentary, and most reviewers concur with the opinion of Robert Bone: "The best of Baldwin's novels is *Go Tell It on the Mountain*, and his best is very good indeed. It ranks with Jean Toomer's *Cane*, Richard Wright's *Native Son*, and Ralph Ellison's *Invisible Man* as a major contribution to American fiction."

Like the protagonist of *Go Tell It on the Mountain*, Baldwin was born into poverty in Harlem, a predominantly black district of New York City, and was raised in a strict religious household headed by his stepfather, an often abusive storefront preacher who had migrated from New Orleans. After experiencing an extreme religious crisis at fourteen years of age, Baldwin entered a ministry and began to preach at the Fireside Pentecostal Church in Harlem, where his sermons emphasized the vision of the apocalypse described in the Book of Revelation. Baldwin attended De Witt Clinton High School and served on the staff of the school's literary magazine, *The Magpie*. He graduated in 1942 and renounced the ministry to become a writer. After a brief stint working in defense factories in New Jersey and following the death of his stepfather, Baldwin returned to Harlem in 1943. Over the next five years, he held a succession of menial jobs and began publishing book reviews in such periodicals as the *Nation* and the *New Leader*. Shortly after the publication of his first essay, "The Harlem Ghetto," in 1948, Baldwin moved to Paris, where he suffered a mental breakdown. While recovering, however, he recognized his frustrations with racial prejudice and completed what was to become his first published novel.

Go Tell It on the Mountain dramatizes events leading up to the religious confirmation of John Grimes, a sensitive youth trying to come to terms with his confusion over his sexuality and his religious upbringing. Central to the novel is John's relationship with his stepfather, Gabriel Grimes, a fundamentalist preacher whose overweening pride and insecurities concerning his own religious commitment re-

sult in his abusive treatment of John and the emotional neglect of his family. Many reviewers have interpreted *Go Tell It on the Mountain* as an exercise in confessional autobiography. Michel Fabre, who saw the primary theme as the conflict between fathers and sons, called *Go Tell It on the Mountain* "a barely fictionalized account of James Baldwin's own life," and David Littlejohn concurred by characterizing the book as "the testament of [Baldwin's] coming to terms with, his defining and transcending, the experience of his boyhood—his family, his religion, his Harlem youth." Although most commentators agree that the book's ambiguity allows for multiple interpretations, the view of Baldwin's novel as autobiography was supported by Baldwin himself: "*Mountain* is the book I had to write if I was ever going to write anything else. I had to deal with what hurt me most. I had to deal, above all, with my father. He was my model. I learned a lot from him. Nobody's ever frightened me since."

Following the publication of *Go Tell It on the Mountain*, Baldwin was commonly linked to the tradition of black protest fiction exemplified by the works of Ralph Ellison and Richard Wright. Baldwin had met Wright, author of *Native Son*, while working on a novel that he later abandoned. Although he briefly embraced Wright as his mentor, Baldwin felt he had to break with the older writer in order to complete *Go Tell It on the Mountain.* In his influential essay "Everybody's Protest Novel," Baldwin asserted that writers like Wright who overtly espouse social causes such as racial justice are essentially sincere propagandists. According to Stanley Macebuh, Baldwin later stated that he was "not about to become another Richard Wright, and his early efforts at writing had proved unsuccessful because he had listened to too many advisers who expected only a certain kind of writing from black writers." Baldwin declared in *Nobody Knows My Name* that he and Wright "were about as unlike as any two writers could possibly be." While Wright's purpose had been to express rage against racial oppression, Baldwin sought to create a highly personal literature dealing less with racial conflict than with the complexity of human motivations: "Only within this web of ambiguity, paradox, this hunger, darkness, can we find at once ourselves and the power that will free us from ourselves." While some commentators, such as Therman B. O'Daniel, have continued to categorize Baldwin as a protest writer in the tradition of Wright, others have concurred with Granville Hicks, who judged Baldwin's avoidance of polemicism successful because "there is no danger that [*Go Tell It on the Mountain*] will be pigeonholed as a novel of protest, [as] it neither expresses indignation nor seeks to arouse it, and we do not think of the characters as victims of injustice or as anything else than human beings."

Much critical debate has surrounded the issue of Baldwin's treatment of race in *Go Tell It on the Mountain.* Although some acknowledge that the novel subtly portrays the white world as a remote and abstract force that is somehow responsible for the dehumanizing conditions of the Harlem ghetto, most commentators agree that the issue of racial conflict is generally deemphasized. Baldwin stated that the book represents "a fairly deliberate attempt to break out of what I always think of as the 'cage' of Negro writing. I wanted my people to be people first, Negroes almost incidentally." Some initial reviewers, such as T. E. Cassidy, felt that Baldwin had failed to achieve his goal "because there is always the absolute feeling of injustice toward a people, not as people, but as a race of people." Most early reviewers, however, found the issue of race to be of secondary importance. Houston A. Baker, Jr. supported this conclusion by remarking that *Go Tell It on the Mountain* is "far more than the chronicle of the experiences of a single black boy in a Harlem environment. The novel is a *Bildungsroman* (a novel recording the development of a young man) of universal appeal, and it speaks eloquently of the terrors and hopes of youth as a whole, while at the same time it portrays the very special terror of being young and black in America."

Later commentators who have faulted Baldwin's attempt to transcend racial issues have frequently based their arguments on the author's later essays, which often describe the poverty of his early life in Harlem. Norman Podhoretz, for instance, declared that the reader senses that "Baldwin is trying to persuade you that there is no real difference between the situation of [John] Grimes and that of any other sensitive American boy who is at odds with

his environment. But there *is* a difference, and it is not merely one of degree—as any reader of *Notes of a Native Son* can tell you." Colin MacInnes felt that Baldwin failed to transcend the racial issue in *Go Tell It on the Mountain* because the "misery and drama" of the novel "are, by implication, a consequence of the Negro situation in the United States." Robert Bone stated that "Baldwin sees the Negro quite literally as the bastard child of American civilization" and asserted that the author had implied racial conflict in his depiction of religious and family strife. Bone further contended that Baldwin's portrayal of John as the innocent victim of his father's incoherent rage "approaches the very essence of Negro experience. That essence is rejection, and its most destructive consequence is shame."

Some critics believe that the primary significance of *Go Tell It on the Mountain* lies less in its treatment of race than of religion. Shirley S. Allen, for example, demonstrated "that John is struggling against forces more universal than white persecution of blacks in America," and MacInnes contended that the novel presents "a story saturated with religious feeling" and "would simply not exist at all without it." Most critical controversy surrounding the religious theme of Baldwin's novel has centered on whether or not the author's treatment of religion is reverent or critical. Baldwin's portrayal of black religion was initially considered sincere and respectful; Richard K. Barksdale, for example, called the book "essentially a religious novel" free of "mockery," and Harvey Curtis Webster stated that "[Baldwin's] penetration of the mind of John, especially in the scene of his conversion, is as valid as anything in William James's *Varieties of Religious Experience* and as moving as the interior monologues in Faulkner's *As I Lay Dying.*" Critics who view Baldwin's novel as a sympathetic treatment of black religion contend that religious faith offers black Americans in *Go Tell It on the Mountain* a moral and political means to bridge the gap between their previous communal experience in the South and existence in the individualized North. Richard A. Courage, for example, noted that *Go Tell It on the Mountain* "highlights the role of the black church in maintaining a sense of communal identity in the face of socially and psychologically destructive pressures."

In contrast to critics who accept Baldwin's portrayal of religion as sincere, many have read *Go Tell It on the Mountain* as an ironic critique of religion. This group views John's faith as a means by which white society inflicts guilt and self-hatred upon blacks—citing, for example, John's obsession with the Biblical association of blackness with dirt and evil, and whiteness with cleanliness and goodness. John experiences his spiritual conversion to Christianity as a violent, convulsive seizure on "the threshing floor" of his father's church, during which his mind is flooded by hallucinatory images. While some reviewers have interpreted this scene as signifying his salvation and rebirth, Howard M. Harper has contended that John's acceptance of religious ecstasy results falsely from his need for fatherly acceptance. Bone, while insisting that John's conversion is genuine, believes that "he is too young, too frightened, and too innocent to grasp the implications of his choice." Critics have also remarked that John's rebirth represents his acceptance of his blackness or his awareness of his own artistic nature; others, such as Stanley Macebuh and C. W. E. Bigsby, have expanded on Baldwin's statements in various essays concerning his own attitude towards his sexuality as a youth. Suggesting that John's religious transcendance results from his recognition of his homosexuality, Bigsby commented: "John's conversion is not the result of spiritual revelation but of a homosexual attraction for Elisha, a young Negro convert. . . . While setting out to establish the desirability and viability of compassion, Baldwin can only visualize this love in terms of sexual alliances, more particularly in terms of homosexual relationships."

Most initial critics commended *Go Tell It on the Mountain* as the achievement of an up-and-coming young novelist rather than a work of lasting significance. Wallace Graves later suggested that "these praises may well have been clouded by a politeness engendered by Caucasian guilt or by the confusion of the reviewers between one's conventional education being broadened into a relatively untilled field (the experience of the Negro) as opposed to a true engendering of one's understanding and forgiveness which is native to the novel irrespective of its topic." However, the diverse and continuing interpretations surrounding *Go Tell It on the Mountain* have served to reflect the complexity and ambiguity of the work. As Stanley Macebuh noted, "*Go Tell* may be seen as a very subtle essay on the effects of social oppression on a minority group, as an attack on the excesses and snares of black inspirational worship, or as a passionate plea for love in personal relationships. . . . The essential achievement of this novel is ultimately not that there are so many perspectives from which it may be seen to have meaning, but that these perspectives coalesce into an astutely integrated vision."

(See also *Contemporary Authors*, Vols. 1-4, rev. ed, Vol. 124 [obituary]; *Contemporary Authors New Revision Series*, Vols. 3, 24; *Contemporary Authors Bibliographical Series*, Vol. 1; *Black Writers; Concise Dictionary of American Literary Biography, 1941-1968; Dictionary of Literary Biography*, Vols. 2, 7, 33; *Dictionary of Literary Biography Yearbook: 1987;* and *Something about the Author*, Vols. 9, 54.)

PRINCIPAL WORKS

NOVELS

Go Tell It on the Mountain   1953
Giovanni's Room   1956
Another Country   1962
Tell Me How Long the Train's Been Gone   1968
If Beale Street Could Talk   1974
Little Man, Little Man: A Story of Childhood   1976
Just above My Head   1979
Harlem Quartet 1987

ESSAYS

Notes of a Native Son   1955
Nobody Knows My Name: More Notes of a Native Son
   1961
The Fire Next Time   1963

Black Anti-Semitism and Jewish Racism   [with others]
   1969
Menschenwürde und Gerechtigkeit [with Kenneth Kaunda]   1969
No Name in the Street   1972
The Devil Finds Work   1976

PLAYS

The Amen Corner   1955
Giovanni's Room   1957

Blues for Mister Charlie   1964
A Deed from the King of Spain   1974

OTHER

Autobiographical Notes   1953
Going to Meet the Man   (stories)   1965
This Morning, This Evening, So Soon   (novella)   1967
A Rap on Race [with Margaret Mead]   (dialogue)
   1971
One Day, When I Was Lost: A Scenario Based on 'The Autobiography of Malcolm X' [adaptor; from Alex Haley's novel of the same title]   (screenplay)   1972
A Dialogue [with Nikki Giovanni]   1973
Jimmy's Blues: Selected Poems   1983
The Evidence of Things Not Seen   (nonfiction)   1985
The Price of the Ticket: Collected Nonfiction, 1948-1985
   1985

J. Saunders Redding

[In *Go Tell It on the Mountain*], James Baldwin has used the familiar story-within-a-story device to produce good entertainment—and something more; even the most insensitive of readers will put the book down with a troubled feeling of having "looked on beauty bare."

It is not, however, the kind of beauty to which lazy senses respond—no honeysuckle and moonlight, no pastoral charm or urban elegance, no pure young love, no soft, sweet lostness of the brave and the damned. Its beauty is the beauty of sincerity and of the courageous facing of hard, subjective truth. This is not to say that there is nothing derivative—of what first novel can this be said?—but James Baldwin's critical judgments are perspicacious and his esthetic instincts sound, and he has read Faulkner and Richard Wright and, very possibly, Dostoevski to advantage. A little of each is here—Faulkner in the style, Wright in the narrative, and the Russian in the theme. And yet style, story and theme are Baldwin's own, made so by the operation of the strange chemistry of talent which no one fully understands.

Baldwin's style is lucid and free-running but involved. It is a style that shows the man to be keenly sensitive to words. The frame story of ***Go Tell It on the Mountain*** is relatively slight. It is a simple account of what frustration does to an adolescent boy named John Grimes. The fact of his being a Negro has little significance other than as description. John could have been any susceptible fifteen-year-old, illegitimate boy, hated by his stepfather, estranged by younger children from his mother, and forced to live within himself. But living within oneself is unnatural for a physically healthy boy in Harlem, and John, in a violent burst of seeking for he knows not what, finds another world.

If this frame story is slight, the narratives that fill it are not. In them we are made acquainted with the separate stories of John's mother. Elizabeth, and his father, Gabriel. These are expository narratives, interesting as drama, significant as foreshadowing. The theme of them is frustration. They take the reader out of Harlem to Georgia and Baltimore, and throw a searching light into the murky depths of marginal existence. These stories are two long short stories embodied in the novel, but they are as essential to it as the novel's theme itself. They tell not only the how but the why, and the reader, through them, is brought flush to an understanding of young John's life.

The theme is an old one—the search for a father. What James Baldwin seems to be saying is that the human being's need for identification with others is one of the major drives in life. Though one may quarrel with James Baldwin's explication of this theme—and, indeed, the embodied narratives make quarreling inevitable—one cannot deny that the author has explored the theme with a maturity surprising in a new, young writer.

It is a cliche to say that a first novel shows promise. But what does one say when a first novel is fulfillment?

> *J. Saunders Redding, in a review of "Go Tell It on the Mountain," in* New York Herald Tribune Book Review, *May 17, 1953, p. 5.*

Donald Barr

[*Go Tell It on the Mountain*] is about pietism in Harlem— and, of the three sorts of novel (string, wind and percussion), it belongs to the first. It does not produce its story as an accumulation of shocks (as most novels of Negro life do), or by puffing into a rigid metaphysical system (as most novels about religion do); it makes its utterance by tension and friction.

The organizing event of the book is a 14-year-old boy's first religious experience. This experience is a fit, a brutal, unexpected seizure; for poor little John Grimes is the son, or thinks he is, of a deacon in one of the stomping, moaning, falling sects that ululate in converted stories around Harlem, the metropolis of grief. As a matter of fact, John and his real father had never known of each other's existence; Gabriel Grimes, a preaching widower up from the South, hard, without laughter, with a touch of the Messianic in his nature and a good deal of the trapped animal, had married John's mother and accepted John in expiation of his own carnal sins.

While John is in the holy spasm, Mr. Baldwin (who has really unusual substantive powers but conventional ingenuity in form) passes through three generations to find the antecedents of that hour. He has a curious attitude toward religion. He respects it. He does not find it comical, or anthropological, or pathetic. At its most grotesque, he will still have us know it in its own terms.

It is easy to explain. When the slaves, bred like animals and denied an equity in their own lives, were sent forth into monogamy, civil existence and the labor market, they received both freedom and the Law in the same instant. They then had the need of religion. In the religion that was most available (a vulgar export-model Puritanism) the notion of sin was central and fearfully inclusive. It included all but the most joyless releases of human needs. Guilt, guilt, guilt chimes through the book. Gabriel is guilty. His first wife Deborah is guilty, though she was the victim of rape. His second wife Elizabeth is guilty, though she loved much. Guilt is visited on his children. Hypocrisy will not sweeten the tragic dissonance. And guilt could not be removed not by everyday contrition or penance—only by being born again altogether, as in baptism, but with huge pangs and convulsions. So it is writhing on the floor of "The Temple of the Fire Baptized" that John is saved.

Judicious men in their chairs may explain the sociology of guilt, and so explain Negro religion away. Mr. Baldwin will not have it away. In this beautiful, furious first novel, there are no such reductions.

> *Donald Barr, "Guilt Was Everywhere," in* The New York Times, *May 17, 1953, p. 5.*

T. E. Cassidy

[*Go Tell It on the Mountain*] is a novel about Harlem's store-front churches, seen through the eyes of the people who go to one of them. These people have blood and flesh in their church, and in their past in the South, and it would seem that, therefore, their story would be of wonder, strength, tragedy, and sometimes beauty. The story is of all these things, partly. But it is not what the author hopes it will be, when he says of his intentions: "It is a fairly deliberate attempt to break out of what I always think of as the 'cage' of Negro writing. I wanted my people to be people first, Negroes almost incidentally."

He has not really accomplished that in this book, because there is always the absolute feeling of injustice toward a people, not as people, but as a race of people. The disasters that occur are those that occur only, or largely, because these are Negro people. Their feelings may be those shared in other circumstances by others, but these, here, are clearly marked 'Negro.' Yet the mark of the spirit is here, that which can be seen in any experience of men who have a sense of sin and a sense of repentance.

This is the mark that is upon the Grimes family, in one way or another. The tale of John's childhood and growth is the tale of his awakening to his role in the life of the Harlem church where his father is head deacon. The "Temple of the Fire Baptized" is the scene of a revival meeting. During the course of the meeting, the author goes back over the lives of the Grimes family—their individual journeys from the South to the North. The first part ("The Seventh Day") sets the scene and gathers all the family into present focus. In part two, the lives of Florence, Gabriel, and Elizabeth—sister, brother, and wife—are recorded in relation to each other and to the children, John and Roy. Each of these is a story that leads to a prayer for salvation and hope for the children, especially for John who is marked for the elect. The last part is "The Thresh-ing Floor," the wrestling arena where John meets the Lord and the sword-test of the soul.

Temptation stalks everyone, and wins and loses alternate-ly. Gabriel, for example, "hated the evil that lived in his body, and he feared it, as he feared and hated the lions of lust and longing that prowled the defenseless city of his mind." Elizabeth had been told by her father to "weep, when she wept, alone; never to let the world see, never to ask for mercy; if one had to die, to go ahead and die, but never to let oneself be beaten." And Florence, as she finds her way to the Lord, was "as though she had been hurled outward into time, where no boundaries were, for the voice was the voice of her mother, but the hands were the hands of death."

There are many strong and powerful scenes in this work. Mr. Baldwin has his eye clearly on the full values that his sincere characters possess, though these values often are tossed aside and trampled. His people have an enormous capacity for sin, but their capacity for suffering and repen-tance is even greater. I think that is the outstanding quali-ty of this work, a sometimes majestic sense of the failings of men and their ability to work through their misery to some kind of peaceful salvation. Certainly, the spark of the holy fire flashes even through their numerous external misfortunes.

> *T. E. Cassidy, "The Long Struggle," in* The Commonweal, *Vol. LVIII, No. 7, May 22, 1953, p. 186.*

Granville Hicks

[*The essay below was originally published on June 1, 1953 in* The New Leader.]

There is a new name to be added to the list of serious and talented young writers—that of James Baldwin. Born in Harlem in 1924, Mr. Baldwin was the son of a preacher, and, he tells us, was a preacher himself from the age of fourteen to the age of seventeen. Shortly after ceasing to preach, he turned to literature, and, in the next few years, he had two fellowships and wrote two books, neither of which was published. Now he has a book in print, *Go Tell It on the Mountain,* and a very fine book it is.

Readers of the *Partisan Review* may remember Mr. Bal-dwin as the author of two interesting and disturbing arti-cles, **"Everybody's Protest Novel"** and **"Many Thousands Gone."** In these articles he discussed the dangers of indig-nation in fiction, the problem of stereotypes in fiction about Negroes, and the place of the Negro in American life. Re-reading them now, after reading his novel, one sees them as the statement of a personal and pressing di-lemma: acknowledging the bitterness he felt as a Negro, he was putting on record his determination not to allow that bitterness to dominate his work as a novelist.

Go Tell It on the Mountain is the result of that struggle and the proof of Baldwin's victory, for there is no danger that it will be pigeonholed as a novel of protest, it neither expresses indignation nor seeks to arouse it, and we do not think of the characters as victims of injustice or as any-thing less than human beings.

> One writes out of one thing only—one's own ex-perience. [Baldwin has said] Everything depends on how relentlessly one forces from this experi-ence the last drop, sweet or bitter, it can possibly give. This is the only real concern of the artist, to recreate out of the disorder of life that order which is art. The difficulty then, for me, of being a Negro writer was the fact that I was, in effect, prohibited from examining my own experience too closely by the tremendous demands and the very real dangers of my social situation.

In other words, the Negro problem was there in the fore-ground, and he had to get behind it to find the kind of real-ity that seems to him to be the artist's proper concern.

Two other talented Negro novelists, Ralph Ellison and Richard Wright, have recently written about Negroes without writing novels of protest. They have done so, however, by demonstrating that the Negro problem is at bottom merely a variant of the human problem: We are all "invisible men," we are all "outsiders." In the long run, we begin to forget that their heroes are Negroes, and that is what they want us to do. Their strategy is excellent, but Baldwin's is even subtler. His novel centers in a character-istic Harlem institution, the storefront church, and we never lose the awareness that we are reading about Ne-groes. The fact that his characters are Negroes is impor-tant, but increasingly we are made to feel that its impor-tance is secondary.

What happens in the novel is that John Grimes gets reli-gion on his fourteenth birthday, and perhaps the most re-markable thing Mr. Baldwin has done is to give this expe-rience an intense reality. In the first part of the novel we see John in his normal range of activities. He is afraid of his father, devoted to his mother, alienated from and wor-ried about his "bad" younger brother. He makes a birth-day excursion into the sinful world of Times Square, re-turns to a family crisis, and helps to prepare for Saturday evening services at the Temple of the Fire Baptized. In the second section, we learn about his father and mother, and then, in the third section, comes the conversion.

"In the context of the Negro problem," Mr. Baldwin has written, "neither whites nor blacks, for excellent reasons of their own, have the faintest desire to look back; but I think that the past is all that makes the present coherent, and further, that the past will remain horrible for exactly as long as we refuse to assess it honestly." In his novel, he looks steadily at that segment of the past that is relevant to his story. Through the recollections of Gabriel Grimes, John's supposed father, and those of Gabriel's sister Flor-ence, as they take part in the Saturday-evening service, a dramatic and significant story unfolds. Their old mother, born in slavery, links them with the more remote past. They themselves are, in different ways, products of the mi-gration northward. Gabriel's story is marked by violence and sin and the struggle for righteousness, and violence has touched the life of Elizabeth, his wife and John's mother.

The adroitness with which Mr. Baldwin sets these dramas

within the framework of John's conversion is evidence of his skill as a novelist. Yet he never seems obsessed with form, as some of the other young novelists do; it is something that he knows how to make serve his purpose. Indeed, his technical skill, which is remarkable in many ways, is most remarkable for its unobtrusiveness. His narrative is assured and straightforward, and the description of John's seizure achieves its great emotional effect without any fireworks. Best of all is the dialogue, with its strong, authentic rhythms. Everything about the book bears witness to a mastery that is astonishing in so young a novelist.

The strange and fatal conflict between ideal and reality is the theme of this book, as it is of much of the world's greatest literature. The principal characters of the novel are sustained by their peculiarly dogmatic and violent interpretation of Christianity. The faith of Gabriel and Deborah and Elizabeth, and of Praying Mother Washington and Sister McCandless and Brother Elisha, is grotesque but dignified. They are the saved, set apart from the rest of the world, and their lives have meaning; but for this high privilege they pay by their adherence to a code of morality that puts a heavy burden on weak human flesh and may result, as it has resulted with Gabriel, in sins worse than those against which the saints preach.

Mr. Baldwin makes us fully aware of the meaning of religion for these people, and, because we have seen enough of Gabriel and Elizabeth to understand the tensions of John's childhood, his conversion becomes a climax for us as well as for him. Mr. Baldwin wisely drops the story there. There are intimations that there will be other climaxes for John, but it is enough that we understand why the conversion has happened and what, for the moment, it means to him.

Mr. Baldwin has said that he wants to be "an honest man and a good writer." It is obvious that he has had a tremendous struggle against attitudes on the part of others, and emotions within himself, that might have made him a more or less dishonest propagandist; but he has achieved his goal, and he has also achieved, as a consequence of the struggle, a phenomenal maturity. (pp. 87-90)

> *Granville Hicks, " 'Go Tell It on the Mountain', " in his* Literary Horizons: A Quarter Century of American Fiction, *compiled with the assistance of Jack Alan Robbins, New York University Press, 1970, pp. 87-90.*

"[*Go Tell It on the Mountain*] is a fairly deliberate attempt to break out of what I always think of as the 'cage' of Negro writing. I wanted my people to be people first, Negroes almost incidentally."

—*James Baldwin, 1953*

Colin MacInnes

[The essay excerpted below was originally published in August, 1963 in Encounter.]

This [*Go Tell It on the Mountain*] is a densely-packed, ominous, sensual, doom-ridden story, lit by rare beauty, love and human penetration. The theme is life and religion and how both, wonderful and terrible, can create and destroy. The scene is the Temple of the Fire Baptized in Harlem during two days and a long night; from which place the writer leads us back and forth in time among the lives of worshippers in the congregation.

The prime figures are Gabriel the deacon, proud, passionate, violent and unforgiving as Satan, yet taking none of Satan's sweets (unless perhaps the love of power), and still wrestling inexorably with his God; and his adoptive son John, aged 14 (who believes Gabriel to be his father), torn between hatred of his parent and the wish to love him, and between the force of his own animal and mental life, and the hope of submission to salvation.

Gabriel, who is from the South, is twice married: first to Deborah, a sad sterile saint who was once raped by whites, and then to Elizabeth, whose bitter and beautiful lover Richard was killed himself leaving her the infant John. Gabriel has thus taken two "fallen" women—and is, we learn, responsible himself for yet another "fall"—that of Esther, a southern beauty who gives him a son, Royal, whom he rejects with shame and yearning.

By Elizabeth, his second wife, Gabriel has three children, the first-born being the defiant and irreligious Roy whom he beats and secretly adores. Gabriel's sister Florence who is, so to speak, the deacon's human—if not religious—conscience, has also lost her charming wastrel husband Frank. The chief remaining character is Brother Elisha, a sweet-natured, fervent young pastor of the church who stands in relation to young John as a true brother.

All this may seem something of a mouthful—as indeed it sometimes does even in the novel, where the author makes severe demands on our attention. We may also notice that, among these blasted and determined lives, there are three disastrous marriages, two tragic love affairs, three rapes or seductions, and that four of the most adjusted and potentially happy characters meet violent ends; also that the sole other unself-torturing personage in the book, the young pastor Elisha, is the only one who is not, as all the others are, related.

This bald synopsis may conjure up the notion of a melodrama, but the book is not like that at all. In the first place Baldwin never makes his characters suffer—or even die—unless they, so to say, "have to": unless, that is, the tragedy both arises from their inner natures and explains them. (A sure sign, incidentally, of an able writer is that he will never do violence to his creations unless this is, artistically, quite inevitable; whereas inferior writers strike their characters arbitrarily down for superficial effect—thereby throwing the whole story out of human balance.) The next reality about this misery and drama is that these are, by implication, a consequence of the Negro situation in the United States. For though this novel is less overtly a declaration of the doom that haunts Negro lives than other books of Baldwin's are, the social pressures impelling to destruction are suspended over almost every page. The third redeeming feature lies in the interplay of the obsessive religious instincts of the characters—or the lack of these—with their spiritual and even physical lives. Religion, whatever its quality, is not for them a mere matter of "worship" detached from normal daily existence: it is a fierce and constant compulsion that never abandons them a second.

To give a clue to the nature and omnipresence of this religious feeling, one might mention books entirely different from it—*Pilgrim's Progress,* say, or *The Scarlet Letter.* The point is that this is not a religious book in the sense of religion being an accessory theme grafted on to the plot—as so often turns out to be the case with the Roman Catholic novelists—but a story saturated with religious feeling, and which simply would not exist at all without it. As for the quality of this religious instinct that inexorably impels the characters, one might describe it as that of early prehierarchical Christianity, but transformed in three ways by its Negro nature. In the first place, it is *sensual* as white Christian religion so rarely has been, even to the extent of physical paroxysms in the church amounting to a kind of holy orgasm—not so much hysterical, as in equivalent white ecstasies, as in the sense of the flesh made spirit. Bodily sin may be rejected, but by no means the body (the fervent Elisha, we notice, is an accomplished and graceful athlete). Next, their faith is the characters' chief form of *social* life, as well as religious: most of them only begin to operate, or to do so intensely, as social beings, in the religious context of their lives. And last, their religion is unquestionably—though the author does not stress this fact unduly—one of moral protest. We know at once who the Egyptians are, and who the Israelites that their God will lead out of bondage.

As for the effects of their religion on their lives, these are, in human terms, usually repellent. One may admire the pride and utter devotion to their faith of the devouter characters; but scarcely the cruelties to themselves and others to which their beliefs command them. To meet, the "sinners" (as Esther, Royal, Frank or Richard) would certainly be more endearing; and even Gabriel's sister Florence, who comes to God in the end by fear of death, not by devotion, or his second wife Elizabeth, who refuses to deny the earlier joy of her "sinful" fondness for her dead lover Richard, are infinitely more humane—and, one may say, Christian—than the relentless deacon or his coldly saintly first wife Deborah. Yet I should make it clear Baldwin is far too subtle an artist to reverse the conventional roles and make the good bad, and the bad good. For there is a lack of profundity in some of the "good" sinners, and the author can equally suggest that the holy Elisha is, in human terms, most lovable.

What Baldwin's own views on all this are—I mean his views as James Baldwin, and not as the creator of these persons—it is difficult to tell, and indeed it is scarcely our business to try to guess. All one can say with certainty is that he has been marked forever by his own early religious experience, and that he understands this theme as do few

writers of our day. Also that his understanding is informed throughout with hope and pity; two qualities, I would like to add, that few writers are entitled to make manifest, since one must earn one's right to bestow them on mankind. (We are surely all tired by now of reviewers who tell us the most commonplace authors are "compassionate": you must be a fine kind of man or woman to be worthy to show compassion.)

We see this best in his portraits of the two chief characters of the book—in the Lear-like Gabriel, and in young John, reaching eagerly his whole being out to life from what imprisons it. Gabriel, like Lear, is in most senses a monster; and, tougher in spirit than the mad king, he does not even crack when his will comes close to madness. He has sinned with Esther, yes, but no man—still less any woman—may tell him so: God has forgiven him, for God is Gabriel's god, and to mankind he is unrepentant. Even when young John bends, at the book's end, to his overpowering will (or seems to), Gabriel cannot love John: his inexorable suspicion in fact redoubles. To those who have served him, or his body—Deborah, Esther and Elizabeth—he remains a demanding tyrant. Because he is God's elect, his hatred for any of God's creatures who do not bow before him is vengefully malevolent.

And yet . . . how is it that it is impossible to loathe—even to despise—Gabriel? Firstly, because he suffers and—worst of all suffering—endures its agonies without enlightenment. And then, though pride in a general way may be detestable (and spiritual pride, as Gabriel never knows, the ultimate of sins), one cannot but respect—if not admire—his pride: it is so total and so terrible in its effects on him. Most touching of all, this puritan who denies the flesh is hopelessly attached to it: his agony at the death of his bastard son Royal, and his love for the son Roy who denies him, give to this grim prophet feet of common clay.

But Gabriel's love for his own flesh makes him hate the son John who is not of his flesh. It is not that John is illegitimate, for so was his own loved son Royal—but that he, Gabriel, did not create him. And John, whose infant will is no less violent than his adoptive father's—and whose intelligent introspection is incomparably greater—knows this, curses Gabriel in his heart, and even hopes, when his half-brother Roy is stabbed, "that Roy, to bring his father down, would die."

But John is also possessed, partly by example and partly by inner light, of religious yearnings. I am not quite sure how authentic James Baldwin intends us to believe John's religious instinct may be—for John's is not, for instance, a "natural" religious temperament like Elisha's or even, in terms of charity, his mother Elizabeth's. And since John is but fourteen, and undergoes, in the final pages of the book, an ecstatically terrifying conversion, my feeling is the writer intends this to be a reality for an adolescent boy but not, perhaps, an ultimate, enduring reality. Indeed, the final cryptic sentences of the book suggest this, when John says to his mother: "I'm ready . . . I'm coming. I'm on my way." This "way," one can feel, will never cease to be in some sense religious, but surely not as the Temple of the Fire Baptized—let alone the deacon—would understand this term.

The description, in the last chapter, of young John wrestling with religion, beholding eternity and death, plummeting into darkness, soaring to the dazzling light, is one of the most convincing accounts of a conversion I have read. It is unbearably harrowing, profoundly imaginative, and psychologically exact. The reader's sensation of being physically present in the Temple—and of entering John's soul stretched out on the spiritual rack—is so compelling as to make one wish to flee this holy place. And curiously, one has a strong sensation of *noise*—of hectic music, rushing winds, agonized hosannahs, tortured hallelujahs: so much so that, at this moment of the book, Baldwin seems suddenly to become a blues or gospel singer.

Among what are known as "technical" felicities of the novel, I would mention first the language. Of possible influences on his style Baldwin himself has written, "I hazard the King James Bible, the rhetoric of the store-front church, something ironic and violent and perpetually understated in Negro speech . . ." and all this is accurate; though I would especially insist on the last item as opposed to the first, since any Semitic floridity that may linger in the Authorized Version is attenuated by that chiselled, *lethal* quality of prose which, as we shall see later on, is one of the glories of Baldwin's essays: words of a measured passion, like a healing knife. Though most of the book is in "author's narrative," rather than in dialogue, I would add that speech, when it does come, is marvellously economical, accurate and revealing. The scene, for instance, in which Gabriel tries to extricate himself from responsibility for his own and Esther's child makes me suppose that Baldwin will one day be a playwright—if he is not, as I suspect, already one.

As for the "flashback" device—so immediately effective and comprehensible in the cinema, but often troublesome in print—this does sometimes leave the reader rather up in the air but, in compensation, it permits of horribly effective ironies when the past abruptly clicks back to the present whose actions it has determined. In final praise, I would mention Baldwin's consummate gift for evoking what I believe to be the most elusive of emotions to any writer—that of pure animal love; and not of mere "sex," but a tender, erotic passion. And deeply as the dramatic and religious elements of the book impress me, I find even more wonderful his gift for persuading me beyond possibility of doubt that Elizabeth adored Richard, Elisha does love John—and even that poor Gabriel yearns for dead Royal and for living Roy. (pp. 121-26)

> *Colin MacInnes, "Dark Angel: The Writings of James Baldwin," in* Five Black Writers: Essays on Wright, Ellison, Baldwin, Hughes, and LeRoi Jones, *edited by Donald B. Gibson, New York University Press, 1970, pp. 119-42.*

Robert Bone

[The essay excerpted below was originally published in 1958 and revised in 1965. A small portion of Bone's commentary was previously excerpted in CLC, Vol. 1.]

James Baldwin was a product of the Great Migration. His father had come North from New Orleans; his mother, from Maryland. James was born in Harlem in 1924, the first of nine children. His father was a factory worker and lay preacher, and the boy was raised under the twin disciplines of poverty and the store-front church. He experienced a profound religious crisis during the summer of his fourteenth year, entered upon a youthful ministry, and remained in the pulpit for three years. The second crisis of his life was his break with this milieu; that is, with his father's values, hopes, and aspirations for his son. These two crises—the turn into the fold and the turn away—provide the raw material for his first novel and his first play.

Baldwin graduated from De Witt Clinton High School in 1942, having served on the staff of the literary magazine. He had already discovered in this brief encounter a means of transcending his appointed destiny. Shortly after graduation he left home, determined to support himself as best he could while developing his talent as a writer. After six years of frustration and false starts, however, he had two fellowships but no substantial publications to his credit. This initial literary failure, coupled with the pressures of his personal life, drove him into exile. In 1948, at the age of twenty-four, Baldwin left America for Paris, intending never to return.

He remained abroad for nine years. Europe gave him many things. It gave him a world perspective from which to approach the question of his own identity. It gave him a tender love affair, which would dominate the pages of his later fiction. But above all, Europe gave him back himself. Some two years after his arrival in Paris, Baldwin suffered a breakdown and went off to Switzerland to recover:

> There, in that absolutely alabaster landscape, armed with two Bessie Smith records and a typewriter, I began to try to recreate the life that I had first known as a child and from which I had spent so many years in flight. . . . I had never listened to Bessie Smith in America (in the same way that, for years, I would not touch watermelon), but in Europe she helped to reconcile me to being a "nigger."

The immediate fruit of self-recovery was a great creative outburst. First came two books of reconciliation with his racial heritage. *Go Tell It on the Mountain* and *The Amen Corner* represent a search for roots, a surrender to tradition, an acceptance of the Negro past. (pp. 216-17)

The best of Baldwin's novels is *Go Tell It on the Mountain* (1953), and his best is very good indeed. It ranks with Jean Toomer's *Cane*, Richard Wright's *Native Son,* and Ralph Ellison's *Invisible Man* as a major contribution to American fiction. For this novel cuts through the walls of the store-front church to the essence of Negro experience in America. This is Baldwin's earliest world, his bright and morning star, and it glows with metaphorical intensity. Its emotions are his emotions; its language, his native tongue. The result is a prose of unusual power and authority. One senses in Baldwin's first novel a confidence, control, and mastery of style that he has not attained again in the novel form.

The central event of *Go Tell It on the Mountain* is the religious conversion of an adolescent boy. In a long autobiographical essay, which forms a part of *The Fire Next*

Time, Baldwin leaves no doubt that he was writing of his own experience. During the summer of his fourteenth year, he tells us, he succumbed to the spiritual seduction of a woman evangelist. On the night of his conversion, he suddenly found himself lying on the floor before the altar. He describes his trancelike state, the singing and clapping of the saints, and the all-night prayer vigil which helped to bring him "through." He then recalls the circumstances of his life that prompted so pagan and desperate a journey to the throne of Grace.

The overwhelming fact of Baldwin's childhood was his victimization by the white power structure. At first he experienced white power only indirectly, as refracted through the brutality and degradation of the Harlem ghetto. The world beyond the ghetto seemed remote, and scarcely could be linked in a child's imagination to the harrowing conditions of his daily life. And yet a vague terror, transmitted through his parents to the ghetto child, attested to the power of the white world. Meanwhile, in the forefront of his consciousness was a set of fears by no means vague.

To a young boy growing up in the Harlem ghetto, damnation was a clear and present danger:

> "For the wages of sin were visible everywhere,
> in every wine-stained and urine-splashed hall-
> way, in every clanging ambulance bell, in every
> scar on the faces of the pimps and their whores,
> in every helpless, newborn baby being brought
> into this danger, in every knife and pistol fight
> on the Avenue."

To such a boy, the store-front church offered a refuge and a sanctuary from the terrors of the street. God and safety became synonymous, and the church, a part of his survival strategy.

Fear, then, was the principal motive of Baldwin's conversion: "I became, during my fourteenth year, for the first time in my life afraid—afraid of the evil within me and afraid of the evil without." As the twin pressures of sex and race began to mount, the adolescent boy struck a desperate bargain with God. In exchange for sanctuary, he surrendered his sexuality, and abandoned any aspirations that might bring him into conflict with white power. He was safe, but walled off from the world; saved, but isolated from experience. This, to Baldwin, is the historical betrayal of the Negro Church. In exchange for the power of the Word, the Negro trades away the personal power of his sex and the social power of his people.

Life on these terms was unacceptable to Baldwin; he did not care to settle for less than his potential as a man. If his deepest longings were thwarted in the church, he would pursue them through his art. Sexual and racial freedom thus became his constant theme. And yet, even in breaking with the church, he pays tribute to its power: "In spite of everything, there was in the life I fled a zest and a joy and a capacity for facing and surviving disaster that are very moving and very rare." We shall confront, then, in *Go Tell It on the Mountain,* a certain complexity of tone. Baldwin maintains an ironic distance from his mate-

rial, even as he portrays the spiritual force and emotional appeal of storefront Christianity.

So much for the biographical foundations of the novel. The present action commences on the morning of John Grimes' fourteenth birthday, and before the night is out, he is born again in Christ. Part I, "The Seventh Day," introduces us to the boy and his family, his fears and aspirations, and the Temple of the Fire Baptized that is the center of his life. Part II, "The Prayers of the Saints," contains a series of flashbacks in which we share the inmost thoughts and private histories of his Aunt Florence, his mother Elizabeth, and his putative father, Gabriel. Park III, "The Threshing-Floor," returns us to the present and completes the story of the boy's conversion.

Parts I and III are set in Harlem in the spring of 1935. The action of Part II, however, takes place for the most part down home. Florence, Elizabeth, and Gabriel belong to a transitional generation, born roughly between 1875 and 1900. *Go Tell It on the Mountain* is thus a novel of the Great Migration. It traces the process of secularization that occurred when the Negro left the land for the Northern ghettos. This theme, to be sure, is handled ironically. Baldwin's protagonist "gets religion," but he is too young, too frightened, and too innocent to grasp the implications of his choice.

It is through the lives of the adults that we achieve perspective on the boy's conversion. His Aunt Florence has been brought to the evening prayer meeting by her fear of death. She is dying of cancer, and in her extremity humbles herself before God, asking forgiveness of her sins. These have consisted of a driving ambition and a ruthless hardening of heart. Early in her adult life, she left her dying mother to come North, in hopes of bettering her lot. Later, she drove from her side a husband whom she loved: "It had not been her fault that Frank was the way he was, determined to live and die a common nigger." All her deeper feelings have been sacrificed to a futile striving for "whiteness" and respectability. Now she contemplates the wages of her virtue: an agonizing death in a lonely furnished room.

Elizabeth, as she conceives her life, has experienced both the fall and the redemption. Through Richard, she has brought an illegitimate child into the world, but through Gabriel, her error is retrieved. She fell in love with Richard during the last summer of her childhood, and followed him North to Harlem. There they took jobs as chambermaid and elevator boy, hoping to be married soon. Richard is sensitive, intelligent, and determined to educate himself. Late one evening, however, he is arrested and accused of armed robbery. When he protests his innocence, he is beaten savagely by the police. Ultimately he is released, but half hysterical with rage and shame, he commits suicide. Under the impact of this blow, Elizabeth retreats from life. Her subsequent marriage to Gabriel represents safety, timidity, and atonement for her sin.

As Gabriel prays on the night of John's conversion his thoughts revert to the events of his twenty-first year: his own conversion and beginning ministry, his joyless marriage to Deborah, and his brief affair with Esther. Deborah had been raped by white men at the age of sixteen. Thin, ugly, sexless, she is treated by the Negroes as a kind of holy fool. Gabriel, who had been a wild and reckless youth, marries her precisely to mortify the flesh. But he cannot master his desire. He commits adultery with Esther, and, informed that she is pregnant, refuses all emotional support. Esther dies in childbirth, and her son, Royal, who grows to manhood unacknowledged by his father, is killed in a Chicago dive.

Soon after the death of Royal, Deborah dies childless, and Gabriel is left without an heir. When he moves North, however, the Lord sends him a sign in the form of an unwed mother and her fatherless child. He marries Elizabeth and promises to raise Johnny as his own son. In the course of time the second Royal is born, and Gabriel rejoices in the fulfillment of God's promise. But John's half brother, the fruit of the prophet's seed, has turned his back on God. Tonight he lies at home with a knife wound, inflicted in a street fight with some whites. To Gabriel, therefore, John's conversion is a bitter irony: "Only the son of the bondwoman stood where the rightful heir should stand."

Through this allusion, Baldwin alerts us to the metaphorical possibilities of his plot. Gabriel's phrase is from Genesis 21:9-10, "And Sarah saw the son of Hagar the Egyptian, which she had born unto Abraham, mocking. Wherefore she said unto Abraham, Cast out this bondwoman and her son: for the son of the bondwoman shall not be heir with my son, even with Isaac." Hagar's bastard son is of course Ishmael, the archetypal outcast. Apparently Baldwin wants us to view Gabriel and Johnny in metaphorical relation to Abraham and Ishmael. This tableau of guilty father and rejected son will serve him as an emblem of race relations in America.

Baldwin sees the Negro quite literally as the bastard child of American civilization. In Gabriel's double involvement with bastardy we have a re-enactment of the white man's historic crime. In Johnny, the innocent victim of Gabriel's hatred, we have an archetypal image of the Negro child. Obliquely, by means of an extended metaphor, Baldwin approaches the very essence of Negro experience. That essence is rejection, and its most destructive consequence is shame. But God, the Heavenly Father, does not reject the Negro utterly. He casts down only to raise up. This is the psychic drama that occurs beneath the surface of John's conversion.

The Negro child, rejected by the whites for reasons that he cannot understand, is afflicted by an overwhelming sense of shame. Something mysterious, he feels, must be wrong with him, that he should be so cruelly ostracized. In time he comes to associate these feelings with the color of his skin—the basis, after all, of his rejection. He feels, and is made to feel, perpetually dirty and unclean:

> John hated sweeping this carpet, for dust arose, clogging his nose and sticking to his sweaty skin, and he felt that should he sweep it forever, the clouds of dust would not diminish, the rug would not be clean. It became in his imagination his impossible, lifelong task, his hard trial, like that of a man he had read about somewhere, whose curse it was to push a boulder up a steep hill.

This quality of Negro life, unending struggle with one's own blackness, is symbolized by Baldwin in the family name, Grimes. One can readily understand how such a sense of personal shame might have been inflamed by contact with the Christian tradition and transformed into an obsession with original sin. Gabriel's sermons take off from such texts as "I am a man of unclean lips," or "He which is filthy, let him be filthy still." The Negro's religious ritual, as Baldwin points out in an early essay, is permeated with color symbolism: "Wash me, cried the slave to his Maker, and I shall be writer, whiter than snow! For black is the color of evil; only the robes of the saved are white."

Given this attack on the core of the self, how can the Negro respond? If he accepts the white man's equation of blackness with evil, he is lost. Hating his true self, he will undertake the construction of a counter-self along the line that everything "black" he now disowns. To such a man, Christ is a kind of spiritual bleaching cream. Only if the Negro challenges the white man's moral categories can he hope to survive on honorable terms. This involves the sentiment that everything "black" he now embraces, however painfully, as his. There is, in short, the path of self-hatred and the path of self-acceptance. Both are available to Johnny within the framework of the Church, but he is deterred from one by the negative example of his father.

Consider Gabriel. The substance of his life is moral evasion. A preacher of the gospel and secretly the father of an illegitimate child, he cannot face the evil in himself. In order to preserve his image as the Lord's anointed, he has sacrificed the lives of those around him. His principal victim is Johnny, who is not his natural child. In disowning the bastard, he disowns the "blackness" in himself. Gabriel's psychological mechanisms are, so to say, white. Throughout his work Baldwin has described the scapegoat mechanism that is fundamental to the white man's sense of self. To the question, Who am I?, the white man answers: I am *white,* that is immaculate, without stain. I am the purified, the saved, the saintly, the elect. It is the *black* who is the embodiment of evil. Let him, the son of the bondwoman, pay the price of my sins.

From self-hatred flows not only self-righteousness but self-glorification as well. From the time of his conversion Gabriel has been living in a world of compensatory fantasy. He sees the Negro race as a chosen people and himself as prophet and founder of a royal line. But if Old Testament materials can be appropriated to buttress such a fantasy world, they also offer a powerful means of grappling with reality. When the Negro preacher compares the lot of his people to that of the children of Israel, he provides his flock with a series of metaphors corresponding to their deepest experience. The Church thus offers to the Negro masses a ritual enactment of their daily pain. It is with this poetry of suffering, which Baldwin calls the power of the Word, that the final section of the novel is concerned.

The first fifteen pages of Part III contain some of Baldwin's most effective writing. As John Grimes lies before the altar, a series of visionary states passes through his soul. Dream fragments and Freudian sequences, lively fantasies and Aesopian allegories, combine to produce a generally surrealistic effect. Images of darkness and chaos, silence and emptiness, mist and cold—cumulative patterns developed early in the novel-function now at maximum intensity. These images of damnation express the state of the soul when thrust into outer darkness by a rejecting, punishing, castrating father figure who is the surrogate of a hostile society. The dominant emotions are shame, despair, guilt, and fear.

An excerpt from *Go Tell It on the Mountain*

He knew, without knowing how it had happened, that he lay on the floor, in the dusty space before the altar which he and Elisha had cleaned; and knew that above him burned the yellow light which he had himself switched on. Dust was in his nostrils, sharp and terrible, and the feet of the saints, shaking the floor beneath him, raised small clouds of dust that filmed his mouth. He heard their cries, so far, so high above him—he could never rise that far. He was like a rock, a dead man's body, a dying bird, fallen from an awful height; something that had no power of itself, any more, to turn.

And something moved in John's body which was not John. He was invaded, set at naught, possessed. This power had struck John, in the head or in the heart; and, in a moment, wholly, filling him with an anguish that he could never in his life have imagined, that he surely could not endure, that even now he could not believe, had opened him up; had cracked him open, as wood beneath the axe cracks down the middle, as rocks break up; had ripped him and felled him in a moment, so that John had not felt the wound, but only the agony, had not felt the fall, but only the fear; and lay here, now, helpless, screaming, at the very bottom of darkness.

He wanted to rise—a malicious, ironic voice insisted that he rise—and, at once, to leave this temple and go out into the world.

He wanted to obey the voice, which was the only voice that spoke to him; he tried to assure the voice that he would do his best to rise; he would only lie here a moment, after his dreadful fall, and catch his breath. It was at this moment, precisely, that he found he could not rise; something had happened to his arms, his legs, his feet—ah, something had happened to John! And he began to scream again in his great, bewildered terror, and felt himself, indeed, begin to move—not upward, toward the light, but down again, a sickness in his bowels, a tightening in his loin-strings; he felt himself turning, again and again, across the dusty floor, as though God's toe had touched him lightly. And the dust made him cough and retch; in his turning the center of the whole earth shifted, making of space a sheer void and a mockery of order, and balance, and time. Nothing remained: all was swallowed up in chaos. And: *Is this it?* John's terrified soul inquired—*What is it?* —to no purpose, receiving no answer. Only the ironic voice insisted yet once more that he rise from that filthy floor if he did not want to become like all the other niggers.

At the depth of John's despair, a sound emerges to assuage his pain:

> He had heard it all his life, but it was only now that his ears were opened to this sound that came from the darkness, that could only come from darkness, that yet bore such sure witness to the glory of the light. And now in his moaning, and so far from any help, he heard it in himself—it rose from his bleeding, his cracked-open heart. It was a sound of rage and weeping which filled the grave, rage and weeping from time set free, but bound now in eternity; rage that had no language, weeping with no voice—which yet spoke now, to John's startled soul, of boundless melancholy, of the bitterest patience, and the longest night; of the deepest water, the strongest chains, the most cruel lash; of humility most wretched, the dungeon most absolute, of love's bed defiled, and birth dishonored, and most bloody, unspeakable, sudden death. Yes, the darkness hummed with murder: the body in the water, the body in the fire, the body on the tree. John looked down the line of these armies of darkness, army upon army, and his soul whispered, *Who are these?*

This is the sound, though John Grimes doesn't know it, of the blues. It is the sound of Bessie Smith, to which James Baldwin listened as he wrote *Go Tell It on the Mountain.* It is the sound of all Negro art and all Negro religion, for it flows from the cracked open heart.

On these harsh terms, Baldwin's protagonist discovers his identity. He belongs to those armies of darkness and must forever share their pain. To the question, Who am I? he can now reply: I am he who suffers, and yet whose suffering on occasion is "from time set free." And thereby he discovers his humanity, for only man can ritualize his pain. We are now very close to that plane of human experience where art and religion intersect. What Baldwin wants us to feel is the emotional pressure exerted on the Negro's cultural forms by his exposure to white oppression. And finally to comprehend that these forms alone, through their power of transforming suffering, have enabled him to survive his terrible ordeal. (pp. 218-25)

Robert Bone, "James Baldwin," in his The Negro Novel in America, *revised edition, Yale University Press, 1965, pp. 215-39.*

Edward Margolies

One of the few cultural institutions the Southern Negro transplanted to Northern soil with a modicum of success was his church. Initially its principal purpose was to serve the spiritual needs of the community, but as time went on the Church came to function as a kind of community newspaper linking the new migrants to their Southern past. In this respect the importance of the ghetto churches cannot be overestimated.

Migration to the cities constituted the most abrupt break in the Negro cultural experience since the days of the African slave trade. It was not simply the anxieties of the passage from a rural to an urban way of life—these, after all, were the afflictions of most Eastern and Central European immigrants around the turn of the century—it was more that the racial mores, prejudices, and barriers of the North were ill-defined, vague, and elusive so that the Negro felt he stood on ever-shifting grounds whose pitfalls were at once invisible and treacherous. Negro votes were courted in some parts of the country and discouraged in others. In New York, service trades such as barbering and catering, which at one time had been the almost exclusive province of Negroes, seemed suddenly to pass out of their hands and become the domain of Caucasian foreigners, while neighborhoods such as Greenwich Village, the Hell's Kitchen area, and the mid-Sixties of the West Side were suddenly theirs and almost as suddenly not, all in the passage of forty years or so after the Civil War. In the South, at least, a Negro knew where he stood, however barren and bitter his place. Above all, there existed in the South a pattern of interpersonal relationships among whites and Negroes—rooted, to be sure, in racial preconceptions, but for all that occasionally warm and recognizable—so closely interwoven had been the lives of both races over the centuries. But the white Northerner, when he was not downright hostile, treated Negroes with cold and faceless indifference. If he granted them greater self-expression, he seemed at the same time to be saying, "You may amuse me from time to time with your quaint and primitive antics, but in all significant areas of my life please keep away." For the Southern Negro migrant, the emotional stresses must have been intolerable.

It was precisely in this area that the Negro church functioned so effectively as an integrative force. It connected the Southern Negro with his former life, and gave him a socially acceptable outlet for his rage, his terror, and his frustrations—in its thinly veiled apocalyptic warnings, its evangelical fervor, and its promises of a better life to come. It also functioned as a political force, drawing together persons of diverse Southern origin and directing them toward goals which did not seem threatening to the established white power structure. Negro ministers were approached by white politicians who requested their support in elections, in return for favors to their communities and especially to themselves. This afforded the more successful Negro clergy—those with large congregations—some bargaining power. It never amounted to much, the way the world reckons these affairs, but it did provide a foothold of sorts in the great world beyond the ghetto.

The pluralistic and anarchic aspects of city life wrought their disintegrative forces on the Negro church just as they did on churches outside the Negro community. First-and second-generation urban Negroes tend, on the whole, to look less and less to evangelical Christianity as the source of their spiritual and emotional salvation. Still, the Messianic strain, the apocalyptic vision, the imagery and the fervor of the church, live on in the Negro community, fashioned now to more material and worldly ends. Indeed, the transfer of religious energies to political and social causes has swept along many Negro clergymen into what has since been called the Negro Revolt. The spirit of evangelism still permeates all areas of Negro culture.

Nowhere has this been so apparent as in the works of James Baldwin. In a sense, Baldwin is himself a symbol

of this change. He was born in Harlem in 1924, the stepson of an evangelical minister, and was brought up in an atmosphere suffused with piety and puritanical rigor. His stepfather, stern, distant and authoritarian, insisted that his children devote as much spare time as they could to his views of Christian teachings. The evangelical church demanded much of the emotional and intellectual energies of its members, and it is a measure of Baldwin's commitment that he became a Young Minister at the age of fourteen. Baldwin's Christian ardor began to cool in favor of literature when he attended high school, but his writing career has been shaped by the rhetoric of evangelism and by his childhood understanding of the nature of the Christian's experience. (pp. 102-04)

The prototypical church experience is related in Baldwin's first novel, *Go Tell It On The Mountain* (1953). Essentially it is the story of fourteen-year-old John Grimes's conversion, but the truly major figure of interest is John's father, Gabriel—and it is Gabriel, chiefly, around whom all the other characters' difficulties are centered. This is in a sense Baldwin's most ambitious book, in that he endeavors here not only to interconnect the lives and psychology of all the characters but also to relate these to the Southern Negro experience and the consequent shocks of urban slum living. The church, naturally, somewhat softens the impact—indeed makes their lives endurable, but it becomes clear in this novel that Baldwin regards the church as only a kind of temporary palliative and that dangerous trials lie ahead.

The novel is divided into three parts. The first part, "The Seventh Day," establishes the attitudes of John, his mother Elizabeth, and his Aunt Florence toward Gabriel—whom they alternately hate, fear, or distrust. Gabriel is a stern, aloof, self-righteous man with a scarcely concealed animosity toward John. He is a deacon of his church and commands his family in an imperious, hostile, arrogant manner. John is a sensitive, brooding boy, troubled with a sense of sin, distressed at his worldly desires, yearning guiltily to break free from the bounds of the ghetto into the exotic white world beyond. After a particularly dreadful scene with his father in which the whole family participates, he goes to the family church to perform some janitorial duties in preparation for the Saturday night "tarry" services. Here he meets Elisha, a seventeen-year-old Young Minister. John feels a strange physical attraction toward Elisha, and they tussle playfully. Later, several of the elders of the Church—the Saints, as they call themselves—enter to sing and worship and contemplate their souls. As the section closes, John's mother, father, and aunt join them.

The tone of "The Seventh Day" is one of futility, of unyielding frustration that permeates the lives of all the characters, indeed of the Harlem community itself—and the reader is made to feel that they and their posterity are doomed to an existence of shabby poverty and soured dreams. A significant passage details John's household chores. His mother has asked him to clean the rug and John thinks of Sisyphus pushing his boulder up the hill.

> He had John's entire sympathy, for the longest
> and hardest part of his Saturday mornings was

his voyage with the broom across this endless rug; and, coming to the French doors that ended the livingroom and stopped the rug, he felt like an indescribably weary traveler who sees his home at last. Yet for each dustpan he so laboriously filled at the doorsill demons added to the rug twenty more; he saw in the expanse behind him the dust that he had raised settling again into the carpet; and he gritted his teeth, already on edge because of the dust that filled his mouth, and nearly wept to think that so much labor brought so little reward.

The narrowness of their lives compels each character to seize his identity where he may, however senseless and self-defeating it may appear. Thus Gabriel maintains an authoritarian righteousness as head of his family even though he knows that his lack of charity has alienated him from their love. John cherishes his intelligence and his hatred of his father as being his own unique identity, and longs for the time he can emulate the white actress he had seen in a film that very day, who seemed to be telling the entire appalled and nasty world it could go to hell. But John knows in his heart that it is a fantasy, and that in some profound and mysterious way over which he has had no control, his fate has been long settled.

The stage has been thus set to examine the lives of Florence, Gabriel, and Elizabeth, in whom the seeds of John's fate are buried. In the second part of the novel, "The Prayers of the Saints," the three are seen at their prayers, each seeking the causes of his misery as he wanders back and forth over memories of the past.

It develops that Gabriel and Florence were brought up in the deep South by a pious mother whose other children had been taken from her during the bitter days of slavery. Despite their mother's constant prayers for their salvation, both Gabriel and Florence rejected her in her lifetime—Florence seeking a better life for herself in the North, while Gabriel stayed behind, sunk deep in sin, whisky, and disreputable women. Florence eventually married in the North, but her attempts to elevate her husband to bourgeois status failed utterly—and he left her for another woman, declaring that he wanted to remain the kind of common "nigger" she despised. Gabriel, meanwhile, experienced a religious conversion after his mother's death, and shortly thereafter became a preacher whose renown spread quickly throughout the region. He married a plain, sickly woman, Deborah, who bore him no children—a disappointment that bitterly rankled. At the height of his fame and despite himself, he had a brief liaison with a younger woman, Esther, whom he afterwards sent away when she told him she was going to have his baby. Esther died after the birth of their son, Royal, but Royal was brought up in Gabriel's town, and Gabriel silently watched him grow into a cocky and arrogant young man. Just prior to her own death, Deborah tells her husband that Royal has been murdered in Chicago, and that she has always suspected Gabriel of being his father. Her dying words to Gabriel are that he had better repent.

Elizabeth met Florence when they both worked as scrubwomen in a downtown New York office building. Elizabeth, too, had suffered a severe, puritanical upbringing,

under the guardianship of an unloving aunt in Maryland. When she was nineteen she came north to Harlem, following a young man with whom she had fallen in love. Richard, sensitive, tormented, and angrily bitter at the white world, committed suicide, ignorant of the fact that he had sired her baby. Florence introduced Elizabeth to Gabriel after the latter had come North following the death of his wife. Gabriel, evidently desiring to atone for his neglect of Esther and Royal, regarded the unwed Elizabeth and her infant, John, as a kind of second chance God had revealed to him. But Gabriel is incapable of giving Elizabeth and John the kind of love and protection they need. He is too full of his own sense of cosmic importance, and lavishes all ardor on his own blood son, Roy (Elizabeth has borne him three other children as well), whom he regards as being part of God's strange designs.

Florence, in turn, has hated Gabriel since childhood. It was she who had been ambitious and desired an education to improve herself, but her mother unaccountably devoted all her attention to Gabriel, whose worthlessness and selfishness were patently obvious to all. It is interesting to note that Florence attempted to manage her husband in much the same way her mother had attempted to manage Gabriel—and, like her mother, failed utterly. Florence cannot understand where she was mistaken. She has endeavored to emulate the middle-class life, but the results are quite the same as if she had never tried. She is old and alone now, living in abject poverty in a miserable Harlem room. Her greatest residual passion is simply to inflict pain on Gabriel, whom she blames for all her wretchedness. She wants as well to protect Elizabeth, whose marriage to Gabriel she feels partially responsible for.

It is clear, then, that the prayers of the Saints are not quite so spiritual as one might expect, but Baldwin, with nice irony, suggests that prayer is the only thing they have. And underlying their prayer is an immense anger, scarcely concealed, at a universe that has suppressed and choked them.

Part Three, "The Threshing Floor," is once more John's story. Falling prey unconsciously to a variety of emotions, John suddenly experiences a lengthy religious conversion, flinging himself prone on the floor of the church. It clearly festers in Gabriel that his bastard stepson—and not one of his own blood descendants—is now one of the elect. Florence, sensing her brother's bitterness toward John, threatens to reveal the contents of a letter that Deborah had sent her just before she died, which tells of Gabriel's dalliance with Esther and his subsequent neglect of his illegitimate son. Florence hopes, in so doing, to exact revenge on the brother she has hated all her life. John feels immense and mysterious forces at work in his life, and in an intensely passionate scene at the end of the service, he asks Elisha to remember him at these moments of his splendor regardless of what may happen to him in later years.

Each of the actors in Baldwin's drama has thus somehow "ritualized" the dominant passions of his life in the externals of religious worship. Gabriel remains embittered and righteous, Florence hating and wretched, Elizabeth bewildered and tormented, and it is suggested that John has now discovered and recognized his homosexuality. Religion has not liberated them from themselves permanently, but it has "objectified" their misery momentarily, and so has helped them to survive. This is especially true of John, whose fear and guilt and desire and despair and hatred have all been converted into a kind of meaningful delirium as he lies thrashing about the floor.

Ordinarily revelations of this nature produce an ability to cope better with the tragic conditions of one's life; an enhanced self-awareness implies an enhanced possibility of human action to adjust to the conditions of existence. But unfortunately for Baldwin's characters, they are as utterly hopeless at the end of the novel as at the beginning. This is their private hell—and perhaps the Negro's; they know but they cannot act. From time to time their misery will be alleviated in the communal act of prayer but ultimately their despair is immovable. And one's final impression is of Baldwin's characters frozen in tableaux, arrested in prayer while a host of furies play about their heads and hearts. (pp. 109-14)

> Edward Margolies, "The Negro Church: James Baldwin and the Christian Vision," in his Native Sons: A Critical Study of Twentieth-Century Negro American Authors, *J. B. Lippincott Company, 1968, pp. 102-26.*

"[*Go Tell It on the Mountain*] may be seen as a very subtle essay on the effects of social oppression on a minority group, as an attack on the excesses and snares of black inspirational worship, or as a passionate plea for love in personal relationships. . . . [The] essential achievement of this novel is ultimately not that there are so many perspectives from which it may be seen to have meaning, but that these perspectives coalesce into an astutely integrated vision."

—*Stanley Macebuh, 1973*

Stanley Macebuh

It was Lionel Trilling who, in 1963, cautioned us against the tendency to think of Wordsworth mainly as the poet who defined poetry as the spontaneous overflow of powerful feelings or as emotion recollected in tranquility. In the context of Black literature in this country, it was a timely and salutary reminder that such easy explanations could be quite misleading if not adequately qualified. The decade of the Sixties was both the decade of Black rage and of the flowering of Baldwin's talent, and particularly after the publication of *Another Country,* there was a general tendency to employ the argument from anger as both justification and permanent dynamic in the latter's writings. But Baldwin's beginnings were nothing so simple. The desper-

ate months in Europe when he laboured with *Go Tell It on the Mountain* were certainly not memorable for their tranquility, nor was the labour of gestation itself a particularly spontaneous one. Rather, the novel was the result of almost ten years of false starts, shattered hopes and numbing frustrations, and we must therefore look elsewhere for the sources and origins of this important novel.

In a certain sense, his beginnings as a writer were quite typical. He actively participated in the production of his High School newspaper, some of his teachers willingly recognised his promise, and he himself had quite made up his mind, by the time he was sixteen, that he was going to become an important writer. By 1944 when he had his first crucial meeting with Richard Wright, he had been writing for some time, and had in fact produced the first sixty pages of his first abortive novel, a fact which was the main justification for his meeting with Wright. And for those who are inclined to see political rage as the primary motivation in Baldwin's writings, it is instructive to recall the reasons why this novel was never published. Richard Wright was, in the forties, the major literary light in the black community, and a good many of the young black writers who began their careers during this period felt in some way pressed to follow his example and write in accordance with the standards he had set, especially in *Native Son.* Baldwin was later to discover, and to announce his discovery in a quite spectacular manner, that admiration for an older writer did not necessarily imply the obligation to indiscriminately imitate him. He was not, he later contended, about to become another Richard Wright, and his early efforts at writing had proved unsuccessful because he had listened to too many advisers who expected only a certain kind of writing from black writers.

It was not unusual that Baldwin should have failed to get his first novel accepted for publication, and as he himself was later to admit, this early failure did give him the opportunity of reassessing his own objectives and of discovering his abilities and limitations. He could not be another Richard Wright precisely because the sources of his discontent were fundamentally different from Wright's. Where Wright was driven to write by a *political* rage of uncomplicated intensity, Baldwin brought to his ambition of becoming a writer an intricate web of psychological complexes that were distinguished more by fear than by anger. If the urge to express his rage against social oppression was for Wright the primary necessity, Baldwin could not arrive at this stage destroying, first, his theological dread, his sense of personal corruption, and his fear of his father. To begin, as he had tried, and as he had been advised to do, by dealing with the public aspects of his alienation, was inevitably to court failure, since such a start seemed to presuppose that the sources of the individual talent were identical in all respects, in all writers of the same colour; and it was of crucial importance that he should discover this false assumption at the very beginning of his career. Six months after the failure of his first novel, he gave eloquent notice of his discovery in **"Everybody's Protest Novel"**, and if the sentiments expressed in this essay could hardly be accepted as a permanent or definitive refutation of the literature of social protest, it had the more limited value of indicating the direction in which his more immediate preoccupations were likely to lead him.

Baldwin's dilemma was threefold. By the time *Go Tell* was ready for publication, he had formally broken away from the Church in Harlem, but this formal renunciation of the ministry was by no means a reliable indication that he had truly won that freedom from the terror of sin which the break was meant to imply. He was indeed by 1954 no longer a member of any church, but the habits of thought formed over a period of twenty years were not to be legislated away merely by a formal declaration of separation. Writing became for him at this time primarily, therefore, a means of personal therapy, a medium, as it were, of exorcism through confrontation. We shall see how the need to destroy the apocryphal vision of life which the church had taught him, how the necessity to rid himself of that sense of personal corruption that had been impressed upon him in his early years, was to lead, in *Go Tell,* to a compassionate but nonetheless heretical presentation of the religious life in this novel.

If it is objected that there was something quaintly meretricious in Baldwin's quarrel with God (since such a quarrel could only with great difficulty be made the essential theme of a successful novel) the matter was for him of real and crucial importance. He could not live the life that he so passionately desired, he could not claim for himself that freedom of imagination that was so essential if he was to become a serious artist, so long as his vision of life was so inextricably bound to his medieval sense of dread and sin. But if God was far away in his heaven, if his rebellion against Him was so tragically impractical, there was the memory of his own stepfather—that most formidable of Old Testament patriarchs—against which the would-be writer could vent all his fury, all his rebellion. And it is for this reason that Gabriel Grimes becomes, in *Go Tell,* not simply a reluctant stepfather whose ironically questionable claim to redemption turns him into an egocentric villain, but, more significantly, a personification of the vengeful God of Baldwin's fundamentalist Christian imagination. John Grimes both hates and fears God, but he fears and hates his father with even greater intensity. But within this pathological relationship there is a touching but unavailing need on his part for love and recognition, from his stepfather who for him is not just God's self-proclaimed spokesman on earth but a veritable incarnation of God himself. John's quarrel with God is, then, rendered dramatically plausible through his quarrel with his stepfather, and the creative justification for this painful relationship is provided through the suggestion that the failure of Love is at the root of John's alienation. But if the desperate need for love is a function of John's theophobic predicament in this novel, we must be careful to recognise that there is nothing dogmatic or unduly constricting about the definition of love in this first novel. Homosexuality was in Baldwin's latter novels to be presented often as the exclusively valid category of love, but here its meaning is as much more ramified as it derives ultimately from the Pauline notion of Christian feeling. . . . [We] may here distinguish four major categories of love int his first novel. There is the 'erotic' definition (Elizabeth and Richard) that is presented with some degree of sympathy but as

having also the least chance of success. (It is conceivable that Baldwin's dark puritan imagination felt rather uneasy about so carnal a love.) There is also the homosexual definition (John and Elisha), the familial definition (Gabriel and John; Gabriel and Elizabeth; Gabriel and Florence), and finally, what may be termed social love—much closer to 'agape' but dealing specifically with the failure of human relationships in society.

If the various categories of love we have here identified are plausible, it becomes clear that *Go Tell* possesses a degree of structural unity that is a fitting testimony to the lessons Baldwin learned during his prolonged apprenticeship. The apparent simplicity of mood that is sometimes seen as the source of this novel's success is, clearly, quite misleading, for its achievement derives not so much from the simplicity of voice or theme, as from the powerful control which Baldwin here exercised over a broad range of thematic concerns. *Go Tell* may be seen as a very subtle essay on the effects of social oppression on a minority group, as an attack on the excesses and snares of black inspirational worship, or as a passionate plea for love in personal relationships. In addition to these perspectives of meaning, the novel can even more significantly be seen as an eloquent record of Baldwin's struggle to break away from his ties to his stepfather's God, from the bondage of theological terror, and the essential achievement of this novel is ultimately not that there are so many perspectives from which it may be seen to have meaning, but that these perspectives coalesce into an astutely integrated vision in which the fear of God and the despair of love are the fundamental forces. John Grimes is afraid of God because he has been persuaded of his own personal corruption (and the God of this novel is a vengeful one)—an equivalent, incidentally, of the black view of whiteness implicit in this novel. But God is ultimately an abstraction against which rebellion can at best be fanciful, and so his stepfather, who in many significant respects *is* God, becomes the actual and visible object of John's fear and hatred. He, however, is not an Iago, and he fears and hates precisely because he so desperately wishes to be loved and recognised. His fear and hatred consequently become intense in proportion to his conviction that love is a real, conceivable possibility, one that he discovers to his chagrin appears to be negated by the ironic power of theological fate. And finally, the negation of the possibility of love on the personal plane, when extended to its communal level, becomes the source both of the pathetic despair of the 'saints' and of racial oppression in American society. Let us examine in some detail the manner in which fear and despair serve as the basic symptoms of Baldwin's rebellion in *Go Tell It on the Mountain.*

Just as love is construed in this novel from varying perspectives, so also does the definition of sin continuously change. Of all the major characters who pray in the Temple, there is not one of them who is not, in some way, guilty of sin, though of course, the enormity of their sins varies from venial to cardinal. If Florence's sin is that of egocentric unbelief and hateful malice against Gabriel, Gabriel's is both carnal and spiritual, for, despite his pretentions to moral rectitude, he is basically incapable of loving anyone. Where Sister McAndless and Praying

Mother Washington are presumably guilty of the relatively venial sin of taking themselves too seriously and denying the fulness of life, Elisha's sanctity is apparently contaminated by his innocuous affair with Ella Mae and his apparently sexually motivated love for John. The guilt of sin, however, is not limited merely to the Saints. Indeed, they at least are aware of the promise of redemption, while the rest of 'the world', as represented by the 'sinners along the avenue', is doomed to suffer God's vengeance on the day of reckoning. Part of the dark and critical irony in this situation derives, of course, from the consideration that whereas all the other characters in the novel are guilty of sins of commission, sins that are at any rate subsequent to their existential recognition of the distinction between virtue and vice and over which they therefore have some measure of control, John's sin indeed precedes his birth. It is as though the very circumstances of his conception, let alone his birth, are sufficiently sinful to forever damn him, and there is nothing he can do about his fate. It does not appear to matter that his birth is the one labour of mutual love in the novel, nor that he is the one character for whom love is an absolute necessity. From his first day, it appears, the enormity of this 'sin' is forcefully impressed upon him, and it is hardly surprising that he should grow up both convinced of, and angry over, his fated damnation. Waking up on the morning of his fourteenth birthday, his sense of guilt climaxes in an oppressive feeling of doom. The wages of sin is death, and John convinces himself that nothing can save him. . . . The immediate cause of this desperate fear of damnation is, it is true, a harmless enough act of masturbation in the school lavatory, but it is in the nature of Baldwin's concerns here for us to suppose that John's guilt is not merely a putative guilt of the flesh but a more fundamental one that has to do with his desire to disturb the proper relationship between God and man. His sin is not only that he had become aware of his flesh, nor even that he had been born out of wedlock, but that, in refusing to admit his guilt by falling at the feet of God, he had put himself in opposition to God:

> The darkness of his sin was in the hardheartedness with which he resisted God's power; in the scorn that was often his while he listened to the crying, breaking voices, and watched the black skin glisten while they lifted up their arms and fell on their faces before the Lord. For he had made his decision. He would not be like his father, or his father's fathers. He would have another life.

Despite this rebellion, this determination to have another life, John Grimes remains nevertheless as much a victim of his fear of God as those who more willingly concede His power. He cannot, for all his scepticism, entirely rid himself of the suspicion that the penalty for his rebellion is the burning in hell for a thousand years, and because he cannot deny this, he hates even more intensely the vengeful God who so capriciously seeks to confine him to hell.

There is, then, the element of ineluctable fate in John's relationship to his father's God. The one weapon he could employ against this malice was his rebellious imagination, yet this very weapon serves finally only to compound his sense of sin, and in the end God, however unjustly, remains the victor. And so his pathological dread was always to remain more powerfully real than his dreams of escape, even in those brief moments, as in the movie house scene, when he was vividly aware of other possibilities. If his bondage to God is one primarily characterised thus by fear, so also is fear the basic element in his complex relationship to his stepfather Gabriel. Just as John is convinced that God hates him, so also are we given a graphic account of Gabriel's hatred. For the latter, John, with his far from immaculate conception, his bulging devil's eyes, his taciturnity and his rebellious imagination, is the incarnation of the devil. Further, John is not really his son; he is the son of a bondswoman who now threatens to become his heir, since his own true son, Roy, appears to have chosen for himself the path of perdition. Elsewhere in the novel Baldwin does draw the character of Gabriel with appreciably greater compassion, but in the scene in which he describes Gabriel's reaction to Roy's wound, there is no mistaking the searing hatred with which he reenacts his painful life with his own stepfather. Roy is lying on the sofa, having been injured in a street fight. Gabriel returns home from his job and finds him bleeding; and out of his concern for this wayward son he vents his rage on his wife and John:

> More than his words, his face caused John to stiffen instantly with malice and fear. His father's face was terrible in anger, but now there was more than anger in it. John saw now what he had never seen before . . . a kind of wild, weeping terror that made the face seem younger, and yet at the same time unutterably older and more cruel. And John knew, in the moment his father's eyes swept over him, that he hated John because John was not lying on the sofa where Roy lay.

The point to be made here is that in John's mind there is hardly any distinction between the capriciousness of God's threat to his existence and the intensity of his father's hatred for him. If God had preordained him to burn in hell even before he was born, his father's hatred appears equally to have little to do with whatever sin he may be deemed to have committed; and just as the only defence he has against God is his rebellious imagination, his refusal to concede the power of hell without struggle, so also his only defence against his father is his 'intelligence', the freedom he arrogates to himself to dream at will of the most harrowing revenge:

> That moment gave him, from that time on, if not a weapon at least a shield; he apprehended totally, without belief or understanding, that he had in himself a power that other people lacked, that he could use this to save himself; and that, perhaps, with this power he might one day win that love which he so longed for . . . His father's arm, rising and falling, might make him cry, and that voice might cause him to tremble; yet his father could never entirely be the victor, for John cherished something that his father could not reach. It was his hatred and intelligence that he cherished.

It is truly remarkable the way in which Baldwin appears in these passages to recognise hardly any distinction between his heavenly and terrestrial fathers. Gabriel, whose very name has obvious significance, is not only John's father but also 'God's minister, the ambassador of the King of Heaven'. To fear and hate him is therefore tantamount to challenging God, as John himself clearly sees: "and John could not bow before the throne of grace without first kneeling to his father"; and precisely because the collusion between these two terrible deities is one against which imaginative rebellion is but specious and ineffective, he is forever doomed to pay the price for his 'sin', a sin doubly compounded by his very attempt to break away from its thrall:

> On his refusal to do this had his life depended, and John's secret heart had flourished in its wickedness until the day his sin overtook him.

Part of the chilling effect that this novel has on the reader derives from the fact that in John's mind, as in Baldwin's, the objects of his fear are ultimately indivisible. In terms of their threat to his existence, there is no significant difference between God, Gabriel, and as we shall see later, the racist society that threatens to destroy him. And in terms of the limited responses available to Baldwin's fictional surrogate in this novel, it is hardly surprising that John's imaginative rebellion against God and Gabriel belongs in the same category as Baldwin's own choice of creative writing as his weapon against the pain of life. Just as God and Gabriel appear to insist on John's corruption, so also does a racist society insist more on his bestiality than on his humanity (and here, we see the manner in which Baldwin manages to draw attention to the theological foundations of racism without at the same time converting this insight into an article of dogma). And if his refusal to kneel before the throne of grace is in the end a specious defence, it is also clear that creative freedom can hardly be seen as the most effective weapon against social injustice. John's dilemma is, then, a vicious one, and the intensity of his hatred is in precise proportion to the enormity of his apparently ineluctable predicament. (pp. 49-58)

[In *Go Tell It on the Mountain,* Baldwin asserts] that one hates precisely because one cannot love or be loved. And in this regard it may be said that a fundamental theme in *Go Tell* is the absurd irrationality of John's undeserved predicament, given, especially, the real possibilities there are for love. The failure of love may then be seen as being at the root of John's despair. The God of this novel is vengeful because he does not truly love; Gabriel is driven by insane and self-consuming hatred because he is incapable of love, and by the same token, the root cause of racism is the failure of love in society: But Baldwin does not merely present these ideas in a dogmatic, rhetorical or polemical manner but rather succeeds in conveying them through the lives and interrelations of his characters. Let us examine, then, the many faces of love, its possibilities and its failures in *Go Tell.*

In the context of Baldwin's despair, the failure of love in this novel in respect of human relationships has its complement in the failure of love with respect to man's relationship to God. The God of this novel is not a long-suffering one. His essential attribute is neither infinite con-

cern nor forbearance. Rather, He is a vengeful and jealous deity whose kingdom is the realm of fear. The saints, when they pray, do so not out of their love for Him but out of fear that he might otherwise hurl his thunderbolts at them. He is not the compassionate God of the New Testament; He does not love. He holds before his worshippers the threat of damnation and the burning in hell for a thousand years, and as has been suggested, Gabriel is not merely God's ambassador on earth; he is indeed God's very incarnation. One does not love Gabriel. One either hates or fears him in proportion to the power he has of punishment over one. Perhaps the only character in the novel who dares to love Gabriel is his mother, who prays to live only for as long as it takes him to realise his potential as a man of God; and it is perfectly ironic that the very realisation of this potential results in Gabriel's denial of his humanity, of his need and capacity for love. . . . He hates his sister, Florence, because she refuses to admit that he is any more virtuous than she is. When he sees her kneeling in tortured prayer in the Temple, he is gratified not because she has at last opened up her heart to God, but because God's vengeance has finally caught up with her and brought her low:

> Gabriel turned to stare at her, in astonished triumph that his sister should at last be humbled. . . . She knew that Gabriel rejoiced, not that her humility might lead her to grace, but only that some private anguish had brought her low.

And because Florence knows that the saints are happy over her sudden appearance in the Temple not from love or christian solicitude but from the desire to see her suffer, her prayer is ultimately meaningless, for she dares to believe that those who now stand in gloating judgment over her are no more sinless than she is. Is not Gabriel himself guilty of murder? Had he not stood by in his saintliness while the son of his adulterous passion lived and died in sin? And did he not now hate Elizabeth and John precisely for that sin of which he himself stood guilty? Gabriel is, then, both incapable of love and of charity. He cannot love, nor can he forgive those who dare to love. But it is not that love is impossible of realisation in the world of this novel, though it is difficult enough to achieve and perpetuate. Rather, in the case of Gabriel, the failure of love is a failure in the case of a specific individual, and not one that is attributable to the objective impossibility of it.

But if Gabriel's essential selfishness is an individual limitation rather than the result of an objective dilemma, the relationship between Elizabeth and Richard suggests that there is perhaps a certain arbitrariness in the manner in which Baldwin disposes of the relationships that fall within his various categories of love. If Gabriel does not love because he does not wish to, Richard and Elizabeth fail to perpetuate their love in spite of their desire to do so. Apart from John's love for Elisha, Elizabeth's brief affair with Richard is the one relationship that is presented with less irony than tenderness. They are selfless and considerate, each accepting the other as a human being in his own right. They dream of marital happiness, but Richard dies by his own hand all too soon because society would not have him live. On the one hand, then, it may be argued that Baldwin here intended to dramatize the objective dilemma of being black in America, a dramatization that appears to us so much more plausible because it is illustrated in so private a relationship as the love affair between two young people. On the other hand, however, it is quite possible that Baldwin is here concerned not so much with the racial dimensions of black tragedy as he is preoccupied with his puritan discomfiture over sexual love. . . . Gabriel despises Elizabeth, as he did Deborah, his first wife, because she is in his eyes a 'fallen' woman, and in a certain sense Baldwin is himself as much an inheritor of his father's prejudices as he is a rebel against them. In any case, when we consider the love affair between John and Elisha—and that is what it clearly is, in spite of all the cautiousness of description—it becomes apparent that the argument from social determinism, from racism, is inadequate as an explanation for Richard's untimely death. Elisha and John love each other as much, if more discreetly, as Richard and Elizabeth do, and they are both black and young. Yet their love does not terminate as abruptly as Richard's love for Elizabeth. Indeed, there is the suggestion at the end of the story that their love grows rather than dies. More significantly, if in Gabriel's dreadful theology premarital sex is a sin (and there is no question about this—Elisha is himself admonished for his little harmless affair with Ella Mae), then homosexual love should be even more abominable, since it does not have even the extenuating potential of procreation, and particularly as it seeks to play itself out in the Temple of God. (It is true that Gabriel does not know of the wrestling incident in the Temple, but it is perhaps part of his own obtuseness that he fails to see the erotic element in Elisha's evangelical zeal.) One would expect the God of this novel then to avenge himself on Elisha and John as he presumably did on Richard and Elizabeth. But then, there is the little matter of actual intercourse, and of the innate bestiality of woman. The history of sexual attitudes in Christian thought is a most confusing one indeed, and there is little that is unambiguous to be gained by referring to it for illustration. Nevertheless it is worth observing that Gabriel's (and Baldwin's) attitude to women is little different, for instance, from that of Saint John Chrysostom, who though that "among all savage beasts none is found so harmful as woman." . . . Gabriel's disgust with women—with Deborah, with Florence, with the mother of his illegitimate son, and with Elizabeth—does have quite respectable antecedents in Christian thought, and in this specific respect his attitude appears to coincide with Baldwin's. Elisha and John survive, and Richard's love for Elizabeth terminates, because despite the 'heresy' implicit in homosexuality, the female involvement in heterosexuality makes it equally, if not more, nauseating. It is not without reason therefore that heterosexual copulation in this novel, as in Baldwin's other novels, is described often as a brutal, indecent spectacle. When Deborah is raped, or when Gabriel makes love to her later; when he sleeps with Esther or the woman from the North, and when John observes his parents in bed, it is always as though we are watching an ugly, distasteful show. The beauty of John's love for Elisha lies, then, apparently in the absence of copulation, and it is possible that Baldwin's puritan imagination saw in this minor distinction a useful alibi for what

ultimately appears to be a mere prejudice. The distinction is so obviously absurd that we can only conclude that the author was here denoting a personal preference rather than making an objective comment on the merits of homosexuality.

In view of this confusion with respect to sexuality (a confusion in which Baldwin is clearly not alone) it is more meaningful to see these different dimensions of love—John's love for Elisha, Richard's abortive love for Elizabeth, and Gabriel's rejection of love—primarily as indications of Baldwin's recognition of the possibilities of love. And it is in this sense that *Go Tell It on the Mountain* may be said to be a powerfully idealistic novel, one in which the writer's despair is seen to derive not from the impossibility of an ideal and perfectly blissful relationship between God and man, and among men, but from the corruption of this ideal. In the love between Richard and Elizabeth, between John and Elisha, we are offered glimpses of the ideal relationship, and if, in the end, these intimations do not appear to us to be presented with as much force as the frustrated lives of Florence and Gabriel are, it is less because of a lack of faith on Baldwin's part than because our ideals have a way of often being corrupted by the humdrum reality of our every day lives. Equally, in terms of the broader social perspective of the novel, racism may also be seen as another illustration of the failure of love. If love is in part the willingness to accept the validity of another's life, so is racism the denial of another's humanity. If love implies the ability to forgive, to be charitable, in the Christian sense of the term, racial bigotry is equally and inability to show charity and compassion. And it is therefore not surprising that for John Grimes there is ultimately no meaningful distinction between theological and social malice. The God who threatens to consign him to hell is no different from the father who hates him and the society that refuses to concede his right to live. (pp. 58-63)

In a very basic sense, *Go Tell* is a painfully sad novel, a novel in which Baldwin testifies to the limitations imposed upon his vision of the infinite possibilities of life by that vengeful triad of loveless forces consisting of God, his father and white society. We may also see the novel as a tenderly lyric celebration of the struggles of such puny mortals as Richard and Elizabeth, John and Elisha, to realise through love their true potential in life. Even Gabriel, who for the most part is presented with an ambiguous feeling of resentment and pity, is occasionally shown as striving in his own fumbling way to love and be loved. Colin McInnes probably overstates the case when he implies that there is more love than sheer egocentric narcissism in Gabriel's relationship to Roy [see excerpt above], but he does draw attention to the crux of the matter when he remarks that

> . . . deeply as the dramatic and religious elements of the book impress me, I find even more wonderful (Baldwin's) gift for persuading me beyond possibility of doubt that Elizabeth adored Richard, Elisha does love John—and even that poor Gabriel yearns for dead Royal and living Roy.

It is part of the tragedy of this novel that love should be

so unconsummated or aborted, yet it is also a mark of Baldwin's provisional triumph over theological and social circumstance that he should thus have even conceived of the possibility of love, given the nature of his experience at the time this novel was written. But it is precisely out of this juxtaposition of hope and despair that true tragedy is made, for to hope in the midst of such formidable sanctions is indeed to testify to one's faith in man's ability to rise above them. Yet this hope, this faith is, if we may believe Baldwin here, in itself an act of rebellion, since it seeks to invalidate the power which external forces, especially theological, have over man. And where the individual who dares thus to dream is one whose mind is consumed, as John's is, by fear of God's vengeance, the rebellion is likely to express itself in primarily theological terms. In this sense then, God, that implacable deity who appears to equate the acceptance of life with sin, is the villain of the piece, with Gabriel, his terrestrial spokesman, and white society—the children apparently created in his image—coming in for secondary condemnation. If God is the villain of this novel, then to dare to love is to rebel against him, and this presumably, is what makes Gabriel such a perfect candidate for God's Kingdom—the fact that he is incapable of loving anyone.

It is not surprising that for Baldwin, in this novel, homosexual love—especially when it seeks to express itself in the Temple of God—is the highest form of rebellious heresy he can conceive of. The body, the Bible tells us, is a temple consecrated to God, and since homosexuality is in this novel expressed for the most part in terms of physical attraction, John apparently sins by trying to substitute Elisha for God. On the occasion of their first meeting in the Temple, it is as though John consciously, if uneasily, exchanges his fear of God for his admiration and love of Elisha:

> But he was distracted by his new teacher, Elisha . . . John stared at Elisha all through the lesson, admiring the timbre of Elisha's voice, much deeper and manlier than his own, admiring the leanness, and grace, and strength, and darkness of Elisha in his Sunday suit . . . But he did not follow the lesson, and when, sometimes, Elisha paused to ask John a question, John was ashamed and confused, feeling the palms of his hands become wet and his heart pound like a hammer. Elisha would smile and reprimand him gently, and the lesson would go on.

When, much later, John is lying in psychic pain on the 'threshing floor', it is Elisha's intervention that rescues him from the abyss, and there is an exquisite irony at the end of the story, in the manner in which Elisha's certainty that John has been saved unto God is indeed the very indication of John's conditional release from the power of God's vengeance. Elisha's parting kiss is, to be sure, a holy one, but holy more in the sense that it consecrates a new life, a new beginning, a new religion than that it attests to John's arrival at the throne of grace. The novel ends, then, with Baldwin giving notice of his provisional liberation, of his discovery of a new, more congenial religion, the religion of love. Homosexuality will, for a long time after *Go Tell*, be the medium through which he conveys his alien-

ation from God and society—an alienation, we shall later see, of questionable significance. But apart from the structural achievement of this novel, Baldwin's more limited triumph here is the manner in which, by objectifying the details of his past, he succeeds in making apparent his preliminary liberation from theological terror. (pp. 65-7)

Stanley Macebuh, in his James Baldwin: A Critical Study, *Third Press, 1973, 194 p.*

Shirley S. Allen

[*For information concerning critical studies referred to in the essay below, see Further Reading list at the end of entry.*]

James Baldwin's first novel, **Go Tell It on the Mountain,** deserves a higher place in critical esteem than it has generally been accorded. Although critics have recognized its widespread appeal, often asserting that it is Baldwin's best work, and although teachers of literature have incorporated it into the standard curriculum, they assume that the work is primarily important as an interpretation of "the black experience," comparing it with *Invisible Man, Native Son,* and Baldwin's own essays. Certainly, **Go Tell It on the Mountain** is an authentic and convincing presentation of a wide range of that experience from the days of slavery in the South to the Harlem of Baldwin's youth, and obviously Baldwin weaves the black-versus-white theme into the central conflict as inextricably as it is woven into the daily consciousness of the characters; but the major conflict of this novel, unlike *Invisible Man* and *Native Son,* is not black against white, but the more universal problem of a youth achieving maturity, with literary parallels in *David Copperfield, Great Expectations, The Brothers Karamazov,* and Hawthorne's "My Kinsman, Major Molineux." Its excellence as a "Negro novel" has obscured its relevance to other human concerns, particularly the process described by the psychiatrist Rollo May in *Man's Search for Himself* (which appeared in the same year as Baldwin's novel) as "cutting the psychological umbilical cord." The central action of the novel is John's initiation into manhood—a ritual symbolization of the psychological step from dependence to a sense of self; but most critics describe the conversion as the acceptance of his blackness.

A contributing factor to the misinterpretation of the novel is Baldwin's extensive use of Biblical allusion and Christian ritual for symbolic expression of the psychic realities he wishes the reader to experience. Although critics have commented on the religious setting, they have generally missed its symbolic importance. Colin MacInnes, for example, remarks that the story is "saturated with religious feeling" like *The Scarlet Letter* and *Pilgrim's Progress,* but discusses the religion's effects—"usually repellent"—on the lives of the characters rather than its symbolic use [see excerpt above]. John R. May finds evidence of an apocalyptic theme and D. E. Foster of the theme of the Fall, but in both cases the tendency to look for themes typical of black writers obscures insight into the pervasive religious symbolism peculiar to this novel, just as for other critics the symbolism is obscured by their effort to describe the novel as a typical illustration of the Adamic myth in American literature. Howard M. Harper speaks of the specific use of Biblical symbolism when he points out the identification of the hero with John the Baptist, but he fails to see the relevance of "The Seventh Day"—the title of Part One—perhaps because he is unaware that in Biblical terms Saturday, not Sunday, is the seventh day. Because the symbolism is essential to understanding *Go Tell It on the Mountain,* critics, missing the clues, have found fault with Baldwin's art. So, Marcus Klein writes

> In fact, the dark that John goes through is not so substantial as the scheme of the novel hopes for. Much of it is just Biblical reference. John doesn't really know the lives of his aunt, his stepfather, and his mother. Only the reader does. And that is a technical fault.

Perhaps a better understanding of the symbolism will lead to critical re-evaluation, since Baldwin's most serious "technical fault" may be his assumption that most readers are as familiar with the Bible as the members of his childhood Harlem community were.

From the very beginning of the novel Baldwin clearly indicates the central importance of religious symbolism. The title, taken from a Negro spiritual, suggests not only the basic Christian setting of the action, but also the kind of symbolism we are to expect. In different versions of the folk hymn the command, "Go tell it," refers to the good news (gospel) that "Jesus Christ is born" or to the message of Moses to the Pharaoh, "Let my people go." The ambiguity of the allusion in the title is intentional and also suggests the unity of Old Testament and New Testament faith that is characteristic of the Christian belief described in the novel—the teachings of a sect formed from Baptist practices and Calvinist doctrines, grounded in frequent reading of the King James translation of the Bible, and influenced by the needs, hopes, and artistic expression of Negro slaves. A poignant example of the perfect blending in Baldwin's novel of the Old Covenant with the New occurs in the old black woman's prayer for her daughter Florence as the family huddle in their dark cabin listening for the hoofbeats of white riders intent on rape and arson: "Lord, sprinkle the doorpost of this house with the blood of the Lamb to keep all the wicked men away." The doctrine of the Paschal Lamb is intuitively grasped by a people who identify themselves with the children of Israel in Egypt and the suffering Christians in the early Roman empire.

This same coupling of Exodus with the Book of Revelation occurs in the song "Go Tell It on the Mountain" when the speaker asks, "Who's that yonder dressed in white?" and is answered, "Must be the children of the Israelites." The question is an echo of the question put to John of Patmos in Revelation 13:14. "Who are these robed in white?" and therefore suggests the identification of the children of Israel with the "saved" in John's apocalyptic vision. The cry, "Go tell it!" thus becomes the cry of all the faithful from the beginning of history to the judgment day; and the phrase "on the mountain" further links Moses' Mount Sinai and John's Mount Zion with one of the best known passages in scripture: the second Isaiah's

exhortation to the Jewish exiles, "O Zion, that bringest good tidings, get thee up into the high mountain; O Jerusalem, that bringest good tidings, lift up they voice with strength."

By this multiplicity of Biblical allusion, the cry "Go tell it on the mountain" is much more than the announcement of good news: it is a shout of faith in ultimate victory while the struggle and suffering are still going on. Jesus is born, but he has still to face the cross. The Israelites still have to survive the wilderness and conquer the promised land, the freed captives have to cross the desert and rebuild Jerusalem, and the seventh seal has yet to be opened before God will "wipe away all tears from their eyes." Because of the allusions, all of which Baldwin reiterates in the course of the novel, the title becomes symbolic of the specific human situation when a costly break with the past has been made and a new road, beset with dangers but promising salvation, has been undertaken. This is clearly the situation of the protagonist at the end of the novel.

Immediately after the title Baldwin has placed a quotation from the same chapter of Isaiah alluded to in the title:

> They that wait upon the Lord shall renew their strength; they shall mount up with wings like eagles; they shall run and not be weary, they shall walk and not faint.

This epigraph reinforces the symbolism of the title by making specific its allusion to the situation in Isaiah 40 where the prophet is promising the Lord's help to the released captives in their effort to cross the desert and shout from the mountain top the good news to the cities of Judah. Their release is thus symbolically identified with the main action of the novel, John's release from childish dependence on his parents; and therefore, the prophet's promise of the Lord's protection applies also to John in his hazardous journey through the wilderness of life. On the last page of the novel as John stands on the threshold of his family's house, shaken by the emotional trauma of his release and trembling with fear that he may fail in his new role of adult, Elisha says to him, "Run on, little brother. . . . Don't you get weary." Those who find the novel's ending ambiguous fail to catch in Elisha's words the echo of Isaiah's promise, "They shall run and not be weary," as well as the shout of faith in ultimate victory which is implied symbolically by the title.

Baldwin's use of Biblical allusion in the title and the first epigraph to give symbolic meaning to John's conversion and to interpret the event is typical of his use of symbolism throughout the novel. Each of the three parts has a title and two epigraphs referring to the Bible or Christian hymns, and each of the prayers in Part Two begins with a quotation from a hymn. . . . The doctrines, ritual, songs, and visual symbols of the Baptist church are equally pervasive in the words and events of the novel. But all this religious apparatus, like the central scene of the tarry service itself, is used not simply as psychological and social milieu for the action, but also to give symbolic expression and archetypal meaning to the characters and events. Biblical allusion in *Go Tell It on the Mountain* serves some of the same purposes as the Homeric myth in *Ulysses* and the Olympic paraphernalia in *The Centaur,* but Baldwin's use of the religious apparatus is more like that of Dostoyevsky in The *Brothers Karamazov* than that of Joyce and Updike in one important respect: the symbolism arises naturally out of the setting. This very integration of symbolic apparatus and milieu is perhaps the reason critics have missed the symbolism—a case of not seeing the forest for the trees.

In Part One, Baldwin uses Biblical allusion to set the major conflict in much larger dimensions than the specific situation of the fourteen-year-old John Grimes confronting his stepfather in problems of family relationships, Christian belief, and racial attitudes. The title of this part, "The Seventh Day," gives a more universal significance with its double allusion to the creation myth in Genesis and the holiness of the Sabbath in Mosaic law. John's fourteenth birthday is like the seventh day of creation in that it marks the end of the creative process for him—the moment at which a completed, whole individual emerges from the process that begins in his mother's womb and continues through the nurtured years until the psychological umbilical cord is cut. His birthday falls on Saturday, the Biblical Sabbath, a day set apart for making one's account with God. (pp. 173-78)

The effect of this religious symbolism is to keep the reader aware of the universal elements in John's struggle so that its significance will not be lost amid the specific details and particular persons complicating his conflict. The symbolism prevents us, for example, from mistaking John's peculiar problem as a black taking his place in a society dominated by whites for the more basic problem, common to all humanity, of a child taking his place in adult society. The symbolism also keeps us from being sidetracked by the specific personality of Gabriel or the fact that he is not John's real father, since he is named for the angel of the Annunciation and therefore symbolically is the agency of fatherhood. We are to see John in the larger view as a human child struggling against dependency and finding a sense of his own selfhood through the initiation rite practiced in his community, even though Baldwin has fully realized that struggle in the specific circumstances of Harlem, the fully rounded human characters of the Grimes family, and the particular heritage of American Negro religion.

Even the aspects of John's struggle that are peculiar to his situation—racial persecution, his father's preference of his younger brother, and the ritual practices of the Baptist sect—are carefully linked to archetypal patterns by means of Biblical allusion and religious symbolism.

The racial situation is lifted to a more universal plane by equation of the Negroes' sufferings in America with those of the children of Israel in Egypt and the early Christians in the Roman Empire. This symbolic identification is not only implied by many allusions throughout the novel, but also specifically stated in Florence's account of the days of slavery.

Moreover, John himself is identified with the saint John who was on Patmos in the time of Roman persecution. Although the names Gabriel and Elizabeth and the allusion in the novel's title to the herald of the advent of the Messi-

ah suggest symbolic linking of John Grimes with John the Baptist, Baldwin has more clearly identified him with the John of Revelation. For example, when John setting off to celebrate his birthday emerges from Harlem into midtown Manhattan, he runs up a hill of Central Park "like a madman" and looks down with a feeling of exultation on the "shining city which his ancestors had seen with longing from far away." The parallel with John of Patmos glimpsing the New Jerusalem could hardly be missed—"And he carried me away in the spirit to a great and high mountain, and showed me that great city"—but Baldwin makes identification sure by using a turn of speech characteristic of the Book of Revelation in the King James translation, the repetition of the name "John" after the personal pronoun. "Then I John saw the holy city" is deliberately mimicked in Baldwin's "Then he, John, felt like a giant." . . . Through such symbolic identification Baldwin lifts his hero's problem of being a victim of persecution out of his particular racial situation in twentieth-century United States and places it in a larger historical and religious context.

He gives a still more universal significance to the black-versus-white problem by another device of religious symbolism. During the first major episode of the novel, Harlem and, by implication, the black race are linked with dust and dirt. First he describes the kitchen that is constantly scrubbed but which "no labor can ever make . . . clean;" then he gives John's inner cry against his father, "He who is filthy, let him be filthy still;" and immediately afterward he describes John's Saturday morning task of dusting and sweeping the front room. When we remember that the family name is Grimes, we accept this symbolic identification of John's environment and heritage with dust. But the dust itself is described in highly connotative words that link it symbolically with sin. The dirt "triumphs" beneath the sink; it lives behind the stove 'in delirious communion with the corrupted wall;" and it is piled on the rug by 'demons." John's cry against his father echoes John of Patmos, speaking of sinners not to be saved on the judgment day. Before the tarry service can begin, the church must be dusted, swept, and mopped; but even so when John is lying on the floor before the altar, there is dust in his nostrils, and he must be lifted out of the dust to be saved. So, symbolically, as John's salvation will come only by rising above the innate or inherited sinfulness of man, so his achievement of maturity or self-identity will come only by rising above the innate and inherited conditions of race, locality, and family. The linking of Harlem with dust and of dust with sin makes clear that John is struggling against forces more universal than white persecution of blacks in America.

Similarly, Baldwin takes pains to set John's relationship to Gabriel against archetypal patterns in order to emphasize the universal aspects of their conflict. Critics who have accused Baldwin of sentimentality and lack of artistic distance for making Gabriel John's stepfather, like those who find it a technical fault that the true relationship is never revealed to John, have overlooked the symbolism. With consummate artistry Baldwin has reversed the usual situation of an adolescent searching for his own identity: whereas it is fairly common for a fourteen-year-old to wish that his parents were not his real parents—a psychological result of the incompatibility he feels between himself and them, John never suspects that his father is not his real father. John finds the strength (or is given the grace) to stand up to his father without having a basis for questioning Gabriel's right to authority over him, and therefore Baldwin is not guilty of providing an easy way out for his hero. At the same time the reader, knowing Gabriel's history, sees John's conviction that his father doesn't love him as something more than a projection of adolescent insecurity. This ironic inversion suggests that the psychic reality of an Oedipal situation may reflect external reality.

Baldwin, by means of Biblical allusion, substitutes Hebrew archetypes for the Freudian Greek myth in interpreting the father-son confrontation. Gabriel sees the situation in terms of Abraham and Ishmael when he thinks, "Only the son of the bondwoman stood where the rightful heir should stand." He has already used as a text for one of his sermons Paul's translation of the story (in Galatians 4:21-31) into an analogy to explain the difference between those bound by the law and the "children of promise." To Gabriel, John is Ishmael, "born after the flesh," and so must be exiled in order to protect the inheritance for Roy, the true son of the promise, Isaac.

But Baldwin does not allow us to accept Gabriel's view of the father-son conflict. In this case as in several others, he shows us by use of the very religious faith Gabriel professes that Gabriel has misconceived his own relationship to scriptural paradigms. John is not Ishmael, but Jacob, who supplanted his brother Esau as the accepted heir against the wishes of his father and with his mother's encouragement. The symbolic identification is prepared for in the early episodes of the novel, where John is encouraged by his mother and Roy is clearly regarded by his father as his true heir; and it is made explicit before the end of Part One in the wrestling scene before the beginning of the tarry service. Before Jacob could claim the birthright, won on the human level by "buying" it from Esau and by tricking his father into giving it, he had to wrestle with an angel of the Lord. So John on the night of his initiation into the community of saints wrestles with a strong and holy young man who represents the Lord. Baldwin describes John's wrestling with Elisha in language that identifies it as more than a playful encounter and makes it a serious test of John's strength. John sees his victory as a manifestation of his power and is "filled with a wild delight." Baldwin has already prepared the reader for Elisha's role as John's guardian angel by giving some history of their friendship and emphasizing Elisha's holiness, but more explicitly he identifies Elisha after the wrestling match as a "young man in the Lord; who, a priest after the order of Melchizedek, had been given power over death and Hell"—recalling the words and Messianic connotations of Psalm 110. Throughout John's ordeal on the threshing floor Elisha continues his symbolic role as the angel of the Lord: his interposed body prevents Gabriel from striking his stepson; his voice guides John through the dark; and his parting kiss is called "the seal ineffaceable forever" like the seal of God on the foreheads of the saved in the Book of Revelation. Like Jacob, John wrestles with an angel of the Lord to win his place as the recipient of his father's reluc-

tant blessing and as the heir to leadership of the chosen people in spite of his brother's birth-based claim. Like Jacob, who received the new name Israel, John wins his Christian (baptismal) name:

> "He come through," cried Elisha, "didn't he, Deacon Grimes? The Lord done laid him out, and turned him around and wrote his *new* name down in glory."

Baldwin's italics, besides emphasizing the identification with Jacob and the relation to Christian doctrine, remind us that John's real name is not Grimes, although he may never know it. By use of the Jacob archetype, Baldwin suggests that as the spirit has triumphed over the flesh in John's conversion, so in psychic terms his consciousness of self has overcome adverse family circumstances.

Similarly, the sectarian ritual of the Temple of the Fire Baptized becomes symbolic of a more universal human experience through association with Biblical patterns. The ritual colors of the store-front church are given their full Biblical significance by careful use of suggestive language in the first part of the novel. The red altar cloth is called "scarlet," and the golden cross glows "like smothered fire." The saints are dressed in white "from crown to toe," and their white caps seem "to glow in the charged air like crowns." Such metaphors and connotative words give the colors the symbolic meaning they have for Isaiah— "Though your sins be as scarlet, they shall be as white as snow"—and for John of Patmos in his vision of the golden Jerusalem. (pp. 179-83)

In Part Three the colors are used to express both John's religious experience and his psychic perceptions about his parents. He sees the cross on the altar as a "golden barrier" keeping his father, mother, aunt, and friend from coming down to help him. Thus it becomes a symbol for both the religious salvation and the adulthood that separate them from him while suggesting the isolation felt both by a soul in the presence of God and by a youth who must throw off childish dependence. John then thinks of the "mountaintop, where he longed to be, where the sun would cover him like a cloth of gold. This deliberate echo of Gabriel's dream symbolizes John's need to take his rightful place as an adult by receiving the covenant traditionally handed down by father to eldest son, at the same time suggesting that this is God's promised salvation. That he sees "his mother dressed in scarlet and his father dressed in white" indicates his psychological perception of the relationship between his parents. And finally, his salvation is achieved when he grasps the Christian doctrine that God accepts and dwells with *sinful* man—an understanding that comes to him through the symbolic colors of the ritual of the Lord's Supper:

> Now this service was in a great, high room, a room made golden by the light of the sun; and the room was filled with a multitude of people, all in long, white robes, the women with covered heads. They sat at a long, bare, wooden table. They broke at this table flat, unsalted bread, which was the body of the Lord, and drank from a heavy silver cup the scarlet wine of His blood. Then he saw that they were barefoot, and that their feet were stained with this same blood.

That the blood of salvation is scarlet, the color of sin, reveals to John the possibility of his own eligibility; and then he sees the Lord, and the darkness is filled with light: "The light and the darkness had kissed each other, and were married now, forever, in the life and vision of John's soul."

On the religious level, the colors express [John's] conversion—his understanding and acceptance of the central Christian belief. On the psychological level, the colors express his growth into maturity through the perceptions that his sexual impulses are common to humanity (even his parents), that both black and white men share the heritage of sin in the "army of darkness," and that the golden cloak of manhood belongs to him in spite of his father's opinion.

Besides color, another type of imagery relates John's experience in the tarry service to more catholic Christian ritual and through it to universal human experience. Because John has reached the age at which he is expected to make his commitment to the church, to be "saved," in the presence of the community, this ritual performance is the equivalent of confirmation, bar mitzvah, and the initiation rites of many other religious communities. In Christian doctrine, however, the true initiation rite is baptism, and therefore the practice of confirmation, becoming a member of the congregation, or "making your witness"—made necessary by the long-established practice of infant baptism—is considered a completion of the baptismal rite. Baldwin gives John's experience its basic Christian significance by describing it in terms of the imagery of birth and thus emphasizing the traditional concept of baptism as regeneration accomplished after symbolic death by drowning. From the moment John begins to face his decision, his descent into darkness is described as drowning. . . .

As the tarry service goes on, Baldwin makes the birth metaphor an explicit analogy for Christian conversion:

> With this cry, and the echoing cries, the tarry service moved from its first stage of steady murmuring, broken by moans and now and again an isolated cry, into that stage of tears and groaning, of calling aloud and singing, which was like the labor of a woman about to be delivered of her child. On this threshing-floor the child was the soul that struggled to the light, and it was the church that was in labor, that did not cease to push and pull. . . . For the rebirth of the soul was perpetual.
>
> (pp. 184-86)

In the third part John's mental and physical anguish on the threshing floor is described in birth imagery. The rhythmic chanting of the saints and the beating of their feet are like throbbing blood vessels and muscular contractions; sudden silences are like the intermission of labor, which he knows will resume; and the voice that calls, "Go through," is the final push through the narrow passage. His painful struggle to face subconscious knowledge matches this physical pattern of crescendo and intermission as each new climax of insight is followed by utter exhaustion and fear. And at the end of his ordeal John is told to rise up and "talk about the Lord's deliverance." His heart is "newborn and fragile," and he speaks "in the new

voice God had given him." This figurative language enables us to see John's conversion as a second birth both in the Christian sense of regeneration and in the psychological sense of stepping from childhood into maturity, becoming fully separated from the parental womb and speaking in a manly voice instead of a childish treble. Although the second birth is only symbolically accomplished in a particular event and we are aware that John's new state is not the end of the struggle—the "terrors of the night" are not finished—we are given assurance of his victory in both the religious and psychological spheres by the reiteration in the speeches of Praying Mother Washington and Brother Elisha of Isaiah's promise: "They shall run and not be weary."

The main action of *Go Tell It on the Mountain* is thus clarified and linked with universal human experience through the use of religious symbolism; but even more remarkable, perhaps, is Baldwin's use of Biblical allusion to explain the psychic realities of three other characters: Florence, Gabriel, and Elizabeth—the older generation from which John must differentiate himself to find his own identity. Some critics have objected to the extensive use of flashbacks in this novel and to the tenuousness of their connection with the main action. Many of these objections can be removed, I believe, by a better understanding of the religious symbolism that links the events recounted in "The Prayers of the Saints" with the psychological perceptions John attains on the threshing floor. The use of colors discussed above is only one of several devices that integrate the facts of his parents' lives, which he does not know, with his new awareness of the true relationships, which he grasps psychologically during his ritual initiation into manhood.

In the basic structure of the novel the prayers of the saints are linked with the threshing floor in that all four characters are kneeling before the same altar in hopes of obtaining the same boon—salvation. Florence, Gabriel, and Elizabeth, who have all participated in the family crisis brought on by Roy's injury, are seeking divine help in a desperate situation just as John is. For them, to be sure, this occasion is not the ritual conversion nor initiation into adulthood; but just as the rebirth of the soul is perpetual, according to the doctrine of the Grimeses' church, so the struggle to attain maturity is continual, according to psychological theory. The rules for successful prayer, which are given at the beginning of Florence's prayer, apply to all four supplicants:

> Her mother had taught her that the way to pray was to forget everything and everyone but Jesus; to pour out of the heart, like water from a bucket, all evil thoughts, all thoughts of self, all malice for one's enemies; to come boldly, and yet more humbly than a little child, before the Giver of all good things. . . . And God did not hear the prayers of the fearful, for the hearts of the fearful held no belief.

The successive attempts by Florence, Gabriel, and Elizabeth to win salvation by qualifying under these rules prepare us for John's encounter and increase the tension as each one fails to meet the test. Florence cannot empty her heart of malice, against "niggers," against men, and especially against her brother Gabriel; so she falls back with the hand of death on her shoulder. Gabriel cannot come humbly, but only with proud confidence in his own righteousness; so he remains in fiery darkness. Elizabeth cannot come boldly, but only in fear of her own unworthiness; so she ends in weeping and struggling through darkness still.

On the psychological plane the situation is analogous. The rules for successful prayer are easily translated into criteria for maturity, so that as each character re-thinks the events of his life, we see how each failed to find his own identity in growing from dependency to self-reliance. Florence, filled with the sense of unworthiness that is typical of children who are deprived of parental love, reacted with fierce determination to prove her own worth by leaving home, going north, and finding a husband who would amount to something. Her fear of her mother, hatred of her family and race, and her proud facade (compare the account of her marriage she gives Elizabeth with the facts as she privately remembers them) are evidence of the rebellion that masks continuing dependency. Gabriel, spoiled and dominated by a mother who was as strong as a man, shows the characteristics of the typical Oedipal victim: his guilt feelings drove him to harlots, who were safely unlike his mother, and prevented him from loving Deborah, whom he married as a surrogate mother. In his conversion, which is carefully described as an antithesis to John's, he could not go through the darkness alone, but only with the aid of his mother's spiritual presence and her voice singing. His career as a preacher was devoted to her: "If only, he felt, his mother could be there to see—her Gabriel mounted so high!" That he had to marry Deborah in order to achieve a sense of reality is evidence that he never achieved selfhood.

Elizabeth, neglected by her mother and separated from the father she adored, is unable to emerge from childish dependency on men. She fell into Richard's arms— "waiting for her since the day she had been taken from her father's arms"—when he called her "little girl." She was afraid to tell him of her pregnancy, and after his death she was unable to make her way alone. She married Gabriel without loving him, as an escape from the struggle, "like a hiding-place hewn in the side of the mountain."

The prayers of the saints, then, function as prototypes for John's ordeal on the threshing floor, setting both the religious and psychological conditions for salvation. When John's turn comes, the reader is fully aware of the dangers and the seriousness of the test. The basic structure of the novel thus emphasizes the central importance of John's experience and suggests a parallel between him and the archetypal hero of myth who must face a crucial test of strength or grace or wit—the riddle of the Sphinx or the sword in the stone—which other men fail. (pp. 187-90)

Structurally the prayers of the saints are linked to "The Threshing Floor" by another device, which also increases the tension felt by the reader. In the course of each prayer there is a return to the scene before the altar so that we are reminded of John's progress while we are still involved with the older generation. The very facts of his parents' lives, juxtaposed to his present crisis, increase our fears

that John will fail as they do to reach the top of the mountain, since we see that their attitudes toward him resemble those of the previous generation toward them and therefore are likely to produce the same result: fear, guilt, and hatred that prevent the child from attaining psychological independence. We wonder if it is an endless chain of psychological cause and effect—the sins of the fathers visited upon the children for endless generations, and with John we ask, "Could a curse come down so many ages?"

John's negative answer to this question, which is his salvation, evolves from his new perception of his parents as separate from himself with their own sins and psychological problems. This perception, at once allowing him to empty his heart of evil thoughts, malice, and fear and giving him a sense of his own identity, comes to him (mystically) and to the reader (explicitly) through symbolism based on Biblical allusion. Like the mythical hero undergoing the trials of his initiation, John's experience resembles the dreams and hallucinations of a patient in psychoanalysis. . . . But the dream landscape of John's mind is inhabited by religious symbols of the Hebrew-Christian tradition, so the reader does not have to be a psychoanalyst to interpret them. Although the symbolism is complex, Baldwin carefully alerts the reader by pinpointing the Biblical sources early in the novel and by repeating his texts in different situations so that they run through the three parts as themes that link characters and events. Much of the poetic intensity and psychological subtlety of Part Three derives from the use of these themes, with all their acquired symbolic meaning, to illuminate John's psychic experience on the threshing floor by relating it to the events of the morning and the past lives of his family.

As the first example of Baldwin's technique, let us look at his use of the last chapter of the Book of Revelation to give John insight into Gabriel's character. He first draws the reader's attention to this chapter by using a quotation from it as the epigraph of Part One. Almost immediately afterward he uses another passage from it for John's first expression of hatred toward his father: "He which is filthy, let him be filthy still." With remarkable economy Baldwin uses this allusion for several purposes. It at once connects the dirt of Harlem with John's family heritage and with sin. Since the passage is a pronouncement of damnation at the last judgment on those who are currently sinful, it is in John's mouth a child's curse of his father. Psychologically it expresses the childish trick of turning against a parent the very punishment the parent normally uses against the child, since Gabriel is always warning his children of their imminent damnation with such texts as "Set thine house in order." But there is also a latent irony in this inversion which becomes explicit when Gabriel repeats the quotation in his guilty despair after the affair with Esther. The reader, as Marcus Klein points out, wants John to know Gabriel's guilt, forgetting or not believing the promise John's mother gave him that morning: "The Lord'll reveal to you in His own good time everything he wants you to know." At the moment John needs to know the truth about Gabriel a wind blows over him reminding him of another verse of the same chapter: "Whosoever loveth and maketh a lie." The wind, whether of the Holy Spirit or psychic inspiration, imparts the necessary insight into Gabriel's hypocrisy and enmity by re-calling to his memory a Biblical text juxtaposed to one he has recently applied to his father. (pp. 190-92)

Baldwin's most important use of Biblical symbolism to express the psychic realities of the older generation and to interpret John's sudden comprehension of them centers in the theme of God's covenant with Abraham. The theme is suggested in the first pages of the novel by parallels between Gabriel and the patriarch who holds the covenant on behalf of the whole tribe and passes this power to his son with his blessing. Gabriel has spiritual as well as temporal authority, so John must kneel to his father before he can kneel to the Lord. It is "his father's church" as well as "his father's house," and John's rebellion against him includes rebellion against the whole race: "He would not be like his father, or his father's fathers." Later his father's fathers, the Negro slaves, are identified with Abraham's tribe in Egypt. In John's dreams of escaping his father, he sees himself as "the Lord's anointed," an epithet Florence uses of Gabriel in expressing her reluctance to bow before Gabriel's God.

In Gabriel's prayer the theme becomes more explicit. Before his conversion he wants to become "the Lord's anointed," and his fear of dying in a state of sin is expressed in terms of God's covenant with Abraham—the promise of an heir "out of thine own bowels" and "seed" that shall outnumber the stars—given in Genesis 15. Gabriel feared that

> where he had been would be silence only, rock, stubble, and no seed; for him, forever, and for his, no hope of glory. Thus when he came to the harlot, he came to her in rage, and he left her in vain sorrow—feeling himself to have been, once more, most foully robbed, having spent his holy seed in a forbidden darkness where it could only die.

His first important sermon is concerned with sexual sin and paternity, based on a text from St. Paul: "and if ye be Christ's, then ye are Abraham's seed, and heirs according to the promise." He marries Deborah to "continue the line of the faithful, a royal line" after waking up one night to find himself "covered with his own white seed" and then dreaming that God called him to the top of a mountain, showed him the elect, and promised (in the words of the Lord to Abraham), "So shall thy seed be." His reaction to Esther's pregnancy is horror that "the seed of the prophet would be nourished" in the womb of a harlot. His sons are named (ironically by Esther and in most religious earnestness by Gabriel) Royal and Roy to preserve their symbolic identification with the kings of Israel from Saul, who was anointed by the Lord, to Jesus, whose title is Christ or Messiah, "the anointed One."

For Gabriel salvation is connected with lawful paternity. When Roy calls him a bastard, he considers it a curse. His hatred of John is doubly inspired by this religious conviction: first, because the "son of the bondwoman" might stand in the place of the "rightful heir," and second, because Elizabeth, mother of the prophet, might have contaminated Roy by not thoroughly repenting the conception of John. The Covenant theme expresses both Gabri-

el's psychological motivation—his thirst for power and his feeling of sexual guilt—and its result—his behavior toward Deborah, Esther, Elizabeth, Roy, and John. Through this symbolic identification with Abraham we understand Gabriel.

But Baldwin, using the same symbolism, takes us a step farther and leads us to forgive him, for this novel is more like *Great Expectations* than *David Copperfield* in that the child-parent conflict is set in a larger social context. If Gabriel is Abraham, his people are the children of Israel in the wilderness. As he makes a preaching tour in penitence for his treatment of Esther, he sees how white oppression has driven the blacks away from the Lord into the wilderness of lechery, gambling, drinking, and jazz:

> There seemed . . . no woman . . . who had not seen her father, her brother, her lover, or her son cut down without mercy; who had not seen her sister become part of the white man's great whorehouse; . . . no man whose manhood had not been, at the root, sickened, whose loins had not been dishonored, whose seed had not been scattered into oblivion, into living shame and rage, and into endless battle. Yes, their parts were all cut off, they were dishonored, their very names were nothing more than dust blown disdainfully across the field of time—to fall where, to blossom where, bringing forth what fruit hereafter, where?—their very names were not their own. Behind them was the darkness, nothing but the darkness, and all around them destruction, and before them nothing but the fire—a bastard people, far from God, singing and crying in the wilderness!

Gabriel's mother had seen her older children sold out of her house and one taken into her master's house where she could not go. Deborah had suffered rape and mutilation which Florence barely escaped. Elizabeth's mother and father were both "part of the white man's great whorehouse," and her Richard was "cut down" by the white man. Like the Israelites in the wilderness their only salvation must be strict obedience to the Lord's commandments in an effort to fulfill the covenant that promised them their own land and a name of their own.

Understanding this, who could not forgive Gabriel's mother her fierce determination to establish Gabriel in the covenant, even at the cost of her daughter's happiness; or Elizabeth's parents their neglect born of despair; or Gabriel his decision that he "would not go back into Egypt for friend, or lover, or bastard son"? The question that remains is whether the curse must be passed down. Is there no way to prevent Gabriel's understandable concern to establish his royal line and Elizabeth's understandable refusal to climb to the top of the mountain from warping a new generation? John's ordeal on the threshing floor is the crucial test, and the reader approaches it with the feeling that only a miracle can save him.

The miracle, whether it comes from the Holy Spirit visiting the two or three gathered in his name or from the evocation of subconscious knowledge by the group therapy of the tarry service, happens through the agency of Biblical passages. First John sees the relation of racial persecution to sexually based father-son hatred through the story of Noah and his son Ham. His father's accusing stare of hatred makes John feel naked and reminds him of the only serious sin he is conscious of—masturbating in the bathroom. (Here the critics go wildly astray, both those who assume that his masturbation is an indication of homosexual tendencies induced by Oedipal love and those who assume that his labeling the act as sin indicates religious neurosis.) By association of ideas he remembers that he, like Ham, has seen his father naked. Religious symbolism interprets the experience: the bathtub is dirty, suggesting sin, and his father's penis reminds him of the serpent and the rod, both symbols of Moses, the lawgiver. He recognizes the source of his hate and understands Noah's reason for cursing Ham: sexual rivalry between the father-king and the son-subject—the Biblical parallel to the Oedipus situation.

The curse on Ham—"A servant of servants shall he be unto his brethren"—suggests racial persecution since John is aware of modern use of the ancient Jewish excuse for enslavement of the Canaanites as justification for white enslavement of blacks. For a desperate moment he considers the possibility that the passage really means that "all niggers had been cursed," as he listens to the mocking voice of the unbelief within him, which has been urging him to get up off the floor and walk out of the church. But the anger expressed in his father's approaching footsteps resounding "like God's tread in the garden of Eden, searching the covered Adam and Eve" gives him the insight that this curse is common to all men—all the sons of Adam, not just the sons of Ham—and that it is "renewed from moment to moment, from father to son"—not by God's fiat.

After a short rest another labor pain begins, signaled by a crescendo of sound that John identifies as the rage and weeping he has heard around him all his life. It is the sound "of boundless melancholy, of the bitterest patience, and the longest night; of the deepest water, the strongest chains, the most cruel lash; of humility most wretched, the dungeon most absolute, of love's bed defiled, and birth dishonored, and most bloody, unspeakable, sudden death." To leave childhood is to join the ranks of unprotected adults who suffer all the ills that flesh is heir to, and in John's case, adults who suffer the additional ills of being despised, rejected, and spat upon by other men, the "armies of darkness." There will be no one in those armies to take care of him, to heal him and lift him up. He is terrified and dreads leaving the womb.

Just as in the first crisis Biblical passages gave him the insights needed to see his fear and hatred of his father as a universal problem, so again they lessen the terrors of adulthood by calling up the testimony of the ages. Looking on the armies he asks, "Who are these? Who are they?" and so becomes John of Patmos looking at the persecuted who will be saved. He thinks of their sufferings in the words of Paul: "Thrice was I beaten with rods, once I was stoned, thrice I suffered shipwreck . . . " These quotations forge the link in his chain of understanding so that he sees the love of God specifically offered to the persecuted, whether they are victimized by Egypt, Babylon,

Jerusalem, Rome, or New York. Their robes "stained with unholy blood" and their feet "blood-stained forever" relate them to the sacrificial Lamb of God. John then sees that all men are both persecutors and victims, trampling over each other in the struggle of life: "the strong struck down the weak, the ragged spat on the naked, the naked cursed the blind, the blind crawled over the lame." In accepting manhood he is accepting the human condition, which is redeemed by the love of God.

The love of God becomes, in the end, the cloak of manhood, which is golden like the cross. After seeing the light, John stands up as an adult. He is no longer dependent on his mother, who he senses is claimed by the dead even though he knows nothing of Richard. And he is able to stand up to Gabriel, sensing that he is the "enemy . . . that wants to cut down my soul," although he suspects nothing about his true paternity. God by baptism has given John a new name, independent of the name Gabriel has fought so hard to keep from him in defending his own earthly kingdom of "royal" lineage. John has gone a step beyond Gabriel's lament for American Negroes, that "their very names were nothing more than dust blown disdainfully across the field of time;" he sees that all earthly names are "Grimes"—dust and sin—that all men are subject to the curse renewed from moment to moment from father to son. In becoming a man he has rejected not only childish dependency on his mother and fear of his father, but also racial bondage. When the light and the darkness kissed each other, he became no longer a child of the bondwoman but an heir according to the promise—not Ishmael but Isaac, not bound by the racial law of circumcision or Noah's curse on Ham, but redeemed from Adam's sin and justified by faith. Through religious symbolism Baldwin suggests that the conversion which frees John from sin is also his psychological initiation into maturity, which frees him from the umbilical cord, and racial hatred. "He was free . . . he had only to stand fast in his liberty. He was in battle no longer, this unfolding Lord's day, with this avenue, these houses, the sleeping, staring, shouting people, but had entered into battle with Jacob's angel." (pp. 194-99)

Shirley S. Allen, "Religious Symbolism and Psychic Reality in Baldwin's 'Go Tell It on the Mountain'," in CLA Journal, *Vol. XIX, No. 2, December, 1975, pp. 173-99.*

Rolf Lundén

[*For information concerning critical studies referred to in the essay below, see Further Reading list at end of entry.*]

Critics have been uncomfortable with the religious theme of James Baldwin's *Go Tell It on the Mountain.* They have found it confusing that a serious writer, and an unbeliever at that, has devoted so much space and intensity to the various stages of a young man's conversion. The conclusion they have drawn is that the novel depicts, not what it seems to depict, but something very different. Some scholars have deduced that the religious theme stands for some other aspect of life that Baldwin wants to focus on.

"[*Go Tell It on the Mountain*] is not a Christian novel, in the sense that it tries to convince the reader to come to Christ, but it is a novel about Christian experiences and Christian values. One may ask oneself why Baldwin, no longer a believer, would go to such pains to give a sympathetic rendition of religious experience. One answer may be that Baldwin had to understand what had taken place in his own conversion, an event which had shaken him so fundamentally that it had marked him forever."

—*Rolf Lundén, 1981*

Others have become convinced that Baldwin's picture of John's conversion is ironic, and have thus come to terms with the disconcerting fact that Baldwin seems sympathetic in his treatment of the conversion.

Shirley S. Allen pays much attention to the religious symbolism of the novel, but finds that Baldwin's primary message, hidden beneath a religious superstructure, is psychological [see excerpt above]. "The central action of the novel", she writes, "is John's initiation into manhood—a ritual symbolization of the psychological step from dependence to a sense of self." Others have seen the spiritual enthusiasm of the book merely as an expression of physical love. Stanley Macebuh, for instance, suggests that John is not saved in the end, but rather finds a new religion of homosexual love [see excerpt above]. David E. Foster puts forward a racial interpretation of John's conversion. John is made free, not as a human being, but as a black man. He "finds grace not in rejecting blackness but in seeking it the only way it is available to him—as a black man". Wallace Graves discerns still another reading of John's religious experience: the conversion stands for John's sense of moral energy as an artist. At the end of the novel, Graves proposes, "John emerges into a golden dawn symbolizing the emergence of the artist from his chrysalis".

In addition to these psychological, sexual, racial, and birth-of-artist readings, several critics declare that Baldwin's treatment of religion, and the "coming through" in particular, is ironic. According to Marcus Klein, John is "not initiated but victimized". The primary psychological motivation for John's search for salvation is "his search for a father who will love and forgive him". Drawing the parallel with Baldwin's own experience, Klein implies that John's conversion is to be seen as a "spiritual seduction". Howard M. Harper, Jr. holds that it is not God who lays John low, but an obscure sense of sexual guilt. John assumes a false identity. His experience has not really changed anything. Baldwin reveals in the novel "the awe and innocence and idealism which motivate the boy's acceptance of the illusions of the Temple. And through the creation of this very subtle double vision Baldwin achieves powerful dramatic irony". Robert A. Bone adds that Baldwin maintains an ironic distance from his material [see excerpt above]. The young protagonist " 'gets religion', but he is too young, too frightened, and too innocent to grasp the implications of his choice". Michel Fabre comes to a similar conclusion when he states that Johnny's rediscovery of Gabriel is fake and that no relation of equality is established between them [see *CLC,* Vol. 3]. "The conversion is carried out for other ends than the Lord's service; it becomes a trick to escape the ghetto and his father, what Baldwin calls 'a gimmick' in *The Fire Next Time*."

However, to borrow Klein's phrase about John, most of these critics have not been initiated but victimized. They have fallen victim to their own reluctance to believe that a writer of Baldwin's caliber could write seriously about religion, to their knowledge of Baldwin's career after his conversion, and most significantly to their reading of *The Fire Next Time*. All the critics who have seen *Go Tell It on the Mountain* as an ironic depiction of Christianity use *The Fire Next Time* as a starting-point for their discussion. They have consciously, or subconsciously, come to Baldwin's novel to secure evidence that John's conversion, like Baldwin's, is a "gimmick" and a "spiritual seduction". But they have found little support in the text of the novel for their theories.

It is interesting to notice that the interpretations of *Go Tell It on the Mountain* as an ironic account of religion appeared only after *The Fire Next Time* had been published. All the reviewers back in 1953 failed to detect any irony. On the contrary, most critics then pointed to Baldwin's sympathetic treatment of religion. Harvey Curtis Webster wrote that Baldwin made the Holy Roller religion "plausibly sympathetic" and that his "penetration of the mind of John, especially in the scene of his conversion, is as valid as anything in William James's *Varieties of Religious Experience* and as moving as the interior monologues in Faulkner's *As I Lay Dying*" [see excerpt in *CLC,* Vol. 17]. . . . Richard K. Barksdale was even more explicit. He was convinced that *Go Tell It on the Mountain* is "essentially a religious novel. Hence, there is no mockery in his description of the almost Dionysian revelry of the 'Saints' of the 'Temple of the Fire Baptized'—no mockery of their songs and of their wordless religious ecstasy in their storefront church, no mockery of their emotional gyrations before the altar of deliverance" [see excerpt above]. He further found John's mystical experience a "beautiful climax": "When John Grimes sees the Lord and envisions the marriage of light and darkness, the misery and folly of his elders are forgotten. The storm of their lives is over, and the reader sees the blue sky of the young man's mystical affirmation."

Embarrassingly simple as it may seem, *Go Tell It on the Mountain* is a novel about Christianity. Its major theme is not the relations between father and son, or between black and white. Nor is the book chiefly about homosexuality or innocence being replaced by maturity. Baldwin's work is not a Christian novel, in the sense that it tries to convince the reader to come to Christ, but it is a novel about Christian experiences and Christian values. One may ask oneself why Baldwin, no longer a believer, would go to such pains to give a sympathetic rendition of religious experience. One answer may be that Baldwin had to understand what had taken place in his own conversion, an event which had shaken him so fundamentally that years later he confessed that it had marked him forever. His absolute demand for honesty and truth, so often recorded, made him tell this story about a conversion as he himself had lived through the same experience, not as he had rationalized and psychologized it from a distance. He must consciously have returned to his own youth, and it is one of the admirable aspects of the novel that Baldwin can refrain from ridiculing or explaining away the feelings of the young protagonist.

Go Tell It on the Mountain is not only depicting the complex progress of a conversion, but Baldwin is also concerned with an exposition of false and true Christianity. Colin MacInnes finds the novel religious, but entirely different in kind from such a work as [John Bunyan's] *Pilgrim's Progress*. However, *Go Tell It on the Mountain* is closer to Bunyan's book than we might at first suspect. Not being openly allegorical, Baldwin's account still depicts characters representing more than themselves; they take on universal meaning. As Bunyan's work is a picture not only of a Christian's life but also of a person's way to conversion, so is Baldwin's. Bunyan uses the technical device of the journey with stations along the road, stations which elicit different sides of true and false Christianity. Baldwin uses a similar structure. The concept of travel, journey, and voyage runs like an undercurrent through John's story. This journey is interrupted by the prayers of the Saints, which can be likened to stations along the road showing what Christianity is and, in particular, what it is not. The goal of Christian's and John's journey is the top of the mountain. Moreover, in a few instances, which will be pointed out later, it seems as if Baldwin actually had Bunyan's writings in mind when composing *Go Tell It on the Mountain.*

The characters of *Go Tell It on the Mountain* are not allegorical like those of Bunyan. Still they come to perform roles which make them shed light on various aspects of Christianity in general. Florence can be seen as the straying lamb returning to the fold. Because of her mother's injustice to her, she leaves home and whatever faith she has, and moves north. She refuses to accept God's authority and sets out to find an earthly salvation through her own efforts. She puts her trust in material goods and in social status. She constantly urges her husband, Frank, to get ahead and persuades him to come with her to Uplift meetings where they hear "speeches by prominent Negroes about the future and duties of the Negro race". Florence wants to be in charge of her own destiny, and God has no say in her life, even though she continues to refer to Him in a general way. But Florence's ambition helps her little; she does not reach her goals. She never gets the house she so eagerly desires. She is humiliated again and again by Frank's irresponsible behavior. She gains no sense of identity and no peace of mind. In the midst of this disillusionment she is dealt the ultimate blow of a fatal disease. At that point Florence realizes that she should turn to God, but "she had thought to evade him", as she says, and tries every other conceivable cure, even demonic powers.

It has been implied that Florence's quest is insincere, because she seeks the Lord as a last resource and out of fear. She escapes into the illusion of religion, as it were, because she can no longer cope with life. But Baldwin does not present Florence in such simplistic light. She seeks God primarily because of her fear of death, it is true, but, like so many proud people, she refuses to take Him into consideration until her own power has come to nil. Florence wants to "walk in peace"; she wants relief not only from her illness, but also from the "sixty groaning years" which have made up her life. She realizes that she stands "in need of prayer"; her thoughts are "all on God". At last the "stony ground of her heart" breaks up, and she weeps.

Critics have come to different conclusions as to whether Florence is saved or not. Baldwin gives no definite answer himself. First he indicates that she does come through. Florence surrenders before the altar. After the service she is changed. Her voice is gentler than John "had ever known it to be before". She says to her nephew with conviction: "I *know* the Lord's done laid His hands on you", which seems to indicate that Florence has truly come to know the Lord. A few pages later, however, Baldwin has her say that God has never spoken to her and that she has not changed, proof of which is that she still nourishes her hatred for Gabriel and her wish for revenge. When Florence became ill, God had given her the same message that He gave to Hezekiah: "Set thine house in order, for thou shalt die and not live". It is not clear whether Baldwin wants us to extend the parallel between Florence and the Old Testament king. If we do, Florence's prayer, like that of Hezekiah, has been heard, and God has given her a few more years to live. But Baldwin leaves the question unresolved, thereby suggesting that Florence will continue her quest until her death, whenever it comes.

Many have erroneously believed that Baldwin presents Gabriel as a representative of Christianity. Stanley Macebuh even goes so far as to state that Gabriel is "a personification of the vengeful God of Baldwin's fundamentalist Christian imagination" and that Gabriel is not merely God's ambassador on earth but "indeed God's very incarnation" [see excerpt above]. Nothing could be further from Baldwin's intention. In Gabriel, Baldwin gives a picture of a man who, because of pride and fear, abandons God, in spite of his rabid insistence to the contrary. To return to the Bunyan analogy, Gabriel becomes Mr. Badman, the hypocrite of *The Life and Death of Mr. Badman,* or Talkative of *Pilgrim's Progress,* who talks of his faith, but who does not live it, "a saint abroad, and a devil at home".

We have no reason to doubt the sincerity of Gabriel's conversion. He is born again and saved from his earlier life of "silence", "darkness", and "stinking corruption". Not only his outward life, but also his heart, is changed. However, even in his conversion we can detect what will later cause his fall. Gabriel is proud. The idea of being a humble servant of the Lord does not appeal to him. He confesses: "Yes, he wanted power—he wanted to know himself to be the Lord's anointed. His well-beloved, and worthy, nearly, of that snow-white dove which had been sent down from Heaven to testify that Jesus was the son of God. He wanted to be master, to speak with that authority which could only come from God".

A few pages later Baldwin has Gabriel utter the first of a series of ironic statements which foreshadow or shed contrastive light on his career. Speaking about Florence, Deborah and Gabriel agree that "the Word sure do tell us that pride goes before destruction".—"And a haughty spirit before a fall". And Gabriel is drawn deeper into his pride during the Twenty-Four Elders Revival Meeting. He prays for days and nights "that God might work through him a mighty work and cause all men to see that, indeed, God's hand was on him, that he was the Lord's anointed". He is more interested in the acclaim of the people than in the will of the Lord.

As Albert Gérard has pointed out, Gabriel marries Deborah to affirm his humility. But soon he feels superior to her; she becomes "wholly undesirable" to him and he hates her. He meets Esther and persuades her to come and listen to his memorable sermon about "all those who failed to wait on the counsel of the Lord; who made themselves wise in their own conceit", another ironic comment by Baldwin on what is soon to characterize Gabriel himself.

Gabriel's sin in his relation to Esther is not so much the adulterous act as his refusal to take responsibility for this act. His pride and his fear of what others might say lead him to deny his Christian faith. His words to Esther, "I got God's work to do—my life don't belong to you", mean a definite disobedience to God's commandment. Ironically enough, it is precisely because he does not take care of Esther that he will not be able to do "God's work" in the future. On the contrary, one sin leads to another. His hatred for Deborah grows daily; he lies, and he steals Deborah's money. Gabriel does not truly repent, he does not take the consequences of his sin, and his heart is hardened. But Gabriel starts feeling his guilt and finds peace nowhere. He gets another chance to do right by Esther. But tragically enough he believes that he is doing the will of the Lord. He must keep his faith. "He would not go back into Egypt for friend, lover, or bastard son: he would not turn his face from God, no matter how deep might grow the darkness in which God hid His face from him". Again Baldwin's irony is biting. God has not hidden His face from Gabriel; it is Gabriel who has hidden his face from God. The only way for him to keep his faith is to go back into Egypt and face his responsibility. But he is so filled with pride and self-righteousness that he no longer knows the will of God.

Gabriel believes that Elizabeth and John have been sent to him as a sign of God's forgiveness. Taking care of them may also give him a sense of being a good Christian, since he is fulfilling what is written in James 1:27: "Pure religion and undefiled before God and the Father is this. To visit the fatherless and widows in their affliction, and to keep himself unspotted from the world." But again Gabriel deceives himself. He is not changed. He treats Elizabeth and John as shabbily as he treated Esther and Royal. He hates them as he hated Deborah. He is unjust in his treatment of his children. He is the perfect exemplification of 1 Corinthians 13:1: "If I speak in tongues of men and of angels, but have not love, I am a noisy gong or a clanging cymbal".

Gabriel looks upon himself as a deliverer, but is in reality a stumbling-block. As Esther has vowed concerning her son that "I ain't going to read to him out of no Bibles and I ain't going to take him to hear no preaching", Florence feels that "if Gabriel was the Lord's anointed, she would rather die and endure Hell for all eternity than bow before His altar". The tragedy of Gabriel is that he has so deceived himself that he does not see how petrified his heart has become. He cannot rejoice even at the salvation of his stepson John. And still he believes that he has been doing the will of the Lord and that he has put his hand in Jesus' hand and gone where He has told him to go. When Florence tells him the truth in the end that he has "caused souls left and right to stumble and fall", Baldwin has Gabriel utter his last ironic phrase: "The Lord . . . He sees the heart—He sees the heart". Yes, the Lord sees Gabriel's heart—its unrelenting pride, hatred, hypocrisy, and self-righteousness. Gabriel ultimately comes to stand for everything that comprises false Christianity.

As foils to Gabriel, Baldwin presents the preacher's two wives, Deborah and Elizabeth. Even though their Christian lives are not depicted in detail, they come to stand for what in Baldwin's view is essential to true Christianity. Neither of these women enjoys an untroubled faith, and yet they have understood, what Gabriel has not, that God is love. And they live their faith instead of talking about it.

It is not fair to call Deborah "coldly saintly", as Colin MacInnes has done [see excerpt above]. If one considers the sufferings she has lived through, she is rather a surprisingly compassionate, loving woman. She has for a long time been the considerate, "faithful visitor" not only to Gabriel's mother but to many others in her community: "She seemed to have been put on earth to visit the sick, and to comfort those who wept, and to arrange the last garments of the dying". She devoted her life not to gossip and backbiting but to prayer and reading the Bible. In the eyes of her community, but not necessarily in the eyes of Baldwin, she is seen as "a terrible example of humility" or "a holy fool". Her "unquestioning faith in God" causes some men to ridicule her. But they are ill at ease in their mockery, because "they could never be certain but that they might be holding up to scorn the greatest saint among them, the Lord's peculiar treasure and most holy vessel".

In one crucial scene Baldwin draws attention to the difference between Gabriel's and Deborah's faith. As the tragedy of Esther reveals Gabriel's lack of faith, it highlights Deborah's active trust in the Lord. When she suspects the ruinous consequences of her husband's sin, she remains loyal to him. She continues to keep his house and to share his bed. Maybe it would have been even more in line with her faith, if she had faced him with her suspicions and let him have "the healing humility of confession" that he is longing for. But Deborah has been hoping that he would confess himself. To make up for Gabriel's sin, Deborah starts to befriend Esther's family. She wants to take responsibility, and she says later to Gabriel:

> If you'd said something even when that poor girl was buried, if you'd wanted to own that poor boy, I wouldn't nohow of cared what folks said,

or where we might of had to go, or nothing. I'd
raised him like my own, I swear to my God I
would have—and he might be living now.

These are no empty words. Baldwin's portrayal of Deborah is such that one believes she would have sacrificed everything to keep her faith.

Gabriel is equally convinced that Elizabeth is damned
whereas he himself is saved. Baldwin strongly indicates,
however, that the opposite is true. Like Deborah, Elizabeth comes to serve as a powerful contrast to Gabriel's
hollow religiosity. In her youth Elizabeth is bitter and
proud, and as in Gabriel's case, pride causes her to fall.
Glorious as it is, life together with Richard means a god-
less, blasphemous environment. Elizabeth's love for Richard is stronger than her love for the Lord, but still she
keeps Jesus on the backburner, praying for Richard and
timidly speaking of the love of Jesus. Later she believes
that God punishes her for her worldly life by taking Richard away from her. Her fear of God is great; God is "terrible" and cannot be escaped. But in her fear she also realizes that "only the love of God could establish order in this
chaos".

Meeting Gabriel, Elizabeth is ready to "embrace again the
faith she had abandoned, and walk in the light again from
which, with Richard, she had so far fled". She feels great
joy "that the hand of God had changed her life, had lifted
her up and set her on the solid rock, alone". Elizabeth is
really changed, and she becomes a counterpoint to her
husband. Her newfound humility is contrasted to Gabriel's pride. Now she advises her children to "walk humble
before the Lord". Gabriel calls Elizabeth names and accuses her of neglect; in spite of her ill-treatment Elizabeth
remains loyal to Gabriel and defends him repeatedly
against Roy's accusations. Gabriel is impatient and reckless; Elizabeth makes real, at least to John, "that patience,
that endurance, that long suffering, which he had read of
in the Bible and found so hard to imagine". Gabriel's favorite biblical text is "Set thine house in order"; he sits in
judgment of others. Elizabeth's text shows a humble trust
in the Lord: "All things work together for good to them
that love the Lord". Gabriel does not want John to be
saved: Elizabeth weeps for his deliverance, that "he might
be carried, past wrath unspeakable, into a state of grace".

As was the case with Deborah, Baldwin introduces a key
scene in which he is able to put a particular emphasis on
the differences between Gabriel's and Elizabeth's faith.
Roy has been stabbed and is only to be blamed himself.
Gabriel's reaction is anger and injustice. He blames the
whites and John, rather than Roy, for what has happened.
He slaps Elizabeth, and he whips Roy. Although so deeply
humiliated, Elizabeth still wants reconciliation between
Florence and her brother and between Roy and his father.
She is just when Gabriel is unjust; she points out Roy's
guilt and defends John against Gabriel's groundless accusations. She is grateful to the Lord that Roy is alive, and
suggests four times that the answer to this crisis is prayer:
"Hush now . . . ain't no need for all this. What's done is
done. We ought to be on our knees, thanking the Lord it
weren't no worse".

Together Deborah and Elizabeth come to represent an active Christian faith of humility, devotion, brotherly love,
responsibility, righteousness and thankfulness. They per-
sonify what Baldwin believes is the core of Christianity,
and they make the pharisaism of Gabriel's faith stand out
in glaring contrast.

The unifying element in *Go Tell It on the Mountain* is the
story of John's conversion. The "prayers" of the Saints are
interrupted by glimpses of how far John has progressed on
his spiritual journey toward Mount Zion. As Albert Gérard has noted, it would be a mistake to believe that John's
religious experience is presented as an exceptional one. In
the Church of the Fire Baptized this kind of conversion
is a common event. It would also be a mistake to see it as
the hysterical reaction of an emotionally unstable boy.
Baldwin does not intend to depict only a black or adolescent phenomenon. His interest is more universal. He
wants to investigate what takes place at a conversion, irrespective of the person's age or cultural background.

And even then John's conversion does not become exceptional. The fourteen-year-old boy goes through the same
development as countless other Christians have done.
Even the emotional level reached that Saturday night is
not unusual. One may only study the numerous conversion accounts from all times to see that Baldwin describes
a much more universal experience than one might at first
suspect. To give a few examples, [in his *Out of Darkness
into Light* (1876)], Rev. Asa Mahan, the first president of
Oberlin College, expresses his pre-conversion throes as an
agony of suspense which "deepened at length into the ray-
less midnight of blank despair". After days in this "blackness of darkness" all his sensibilities seem to fail, and he
descends into "a state of almost emotionless despondency
cy". At the point of conversion he is so "overshadowed
with a sense of the manifested love of a forgiving God and
Saviour, that [his] whole mental being seemed to be dissolved, and pervaded with an ineffable quietude and assurance". Charles G. Finney, the major figure of the Second
Awakening, believes that God has given him up and experiences such an "overwhelming sense of [his] wickedness"
that he cries at the top of his voice. [In his *Memoirs* (1876),
Finney] describes his salvation in the following manner;
"No words can express the wonderful love that was shed
abroad in my heart. I wept aloud with joy and love, and
I do not know but I should say, I literally bellowed out the
unutterable gushings of my heart." The most interesting
conversion account in this context is John Bunyan's *Grace
Abounding to the Chief of Sinners*. There are remarkable
similarities between Bunyan's and Baldwin's descriptions
of the different stages of the soul's progress from darkness
to light and in the emotional language used by both. For
instance, Bunyan depicts his sufferings like this:

> Then I was struck into a very great trembling,
> in so much that at sometimes I could for whole
> days together feel my very body as well as my
> minde to shake and totter under the sence of the
> dreadful Judgement of God, that should fall on
> those that have sinned that most fearful and un-
> pardonable sin. I felt also such a clogging and
> heat at my stomach by reason of this my terrour,
> that I was, especially at some times, as if my
> breast-bone would have split in sunder.

One can consequently assume that Baldwin is not ridiculing an aberrant phenomenon, but rather sets out to delineate almost a standard pattern in conversions. Perhaps John's emotional abandon is not standard, but among Christian believers it is not extraordinary.

To show that John's religious crisis is not singular. Baldwin lets Gabriel go through a corresponding conversion. Not only are their prostration and exultation equally high-pitched, but the individual phases of their deliverance are the same and are presented in the same order; awareness of sin, conviction of sin, silence of God, contrary forces raging within, fear of damnation, total helplessness, coming through, exultation, and new creation.

Long before his fourteenth birthday John has been aware of sin. Every time he has encountered the vices of the street or of the "harlot's house downstairs", he has been embarrassed or afraid. He has long been conscious of his evil nature, of the scorn he feels towards the worshippers and the hatred he nourishes towards his father. His heart has become "hardened against the Lord". Like numerous others he might have continued to live in this awareness of sin without ever becoming a Christian.

Around the time of his fourteenth birthday, however, John is convicted of the sin he has only been aware of before. He realizes the "darkness" of his sinful nature. What brings this revelation about is the act of masturbation, but the menace he feels in the air and the panic that lurks in his heart are much more than mere "sexual guilt", as has been suggested. His whole being feels condemned and unworthy before God. He feels filthy "in his false pride and his evil imagination". All of a sudden it is of the utmost matter to him, though it was not before, whether his relationship with the Lord is right. What had earlier seemed the peculiarity of his parents and the other members of the church, now becomes a question of life and death. Words which have meant little before, now become personal messages from God. Elizabeth's everyday warning to Roy, "It'll be too late when you come to be . . . sorry", is taken by John to be "dictated by Heaven" and meant for him. "He was fourteen—was it too late?"

To underline the universality of John's feelings Baldwin introduces a passage, the sweeping-the-carpet-scene, which most critics have understood to be symbolic. Edward Margolies takes this to mean that the blacks and "their posterity are doomed to an existence of shabby poverty and soured dreams". Robert A. Bone sees it as an image of how John is made to feel "perpetually dirty and unclean" [see excerpts above]. What is so remarkable about the carpet is that the more John sweeps it the more dust there is: "Yet for each dustpan he so laboriously filled at the doorsill demons added to the rug twenty more". He nearly weeps "to think that so much labor brought so little reward". Shirley S. Allen comes closer to an understanding of this scene when she identifies the dust as sin. But why are twenty more dustpans added to the rug for each one filled by John? Baldwin presents a symbolic rendition of what happens to most people who have been convicted of their own sin. They try to eradicate their flagrant sin, only to discover twenty more beneath it. John has turned to the Law to get rid of his sense of condemnation, but the

Law has only made things worse. It has shown him his total depravity. All his labor has brought little reward.

To support this kind of interpretation one may again turn to Bunyan, this time to *Pilgrim's Progress*. When Christian arrives at the house of the Interpreter, the latter shows him a parlor full of dust, a setting that strikingly resembles that of Baldwin. The Interpreter calls for a man to sweep: "Now when he began to sweep, the dust began so abundantly to fly about that Christian had almost there with been choked" (cf. John). The Interpreter explains that the parlor is the heart, that the dust is original sin and that the sweeper is the Law, and he continues:

> Now whereas thou sawest that so soon as the first began to sweep, the dust did so fly about that the room by him could not be cleansed, but that thou wast almost choked therewith: this is to show thee that the law, instead of cleansing the heart (by its working) from sin, doth revive, put strength into, and increase it in the soul, even as it doth discover and forbid it, for it doth not give power to subdue.

In this particular instance, one has special grounds to suspect that Baldwin was familiar with Bunyan's allegory, and that he used it for his own ends.

But Baldwin's symbolism does not end with the sweeping of the carpet. He has John clean the mirror, and the youth ransacks himself in a new way: "In the eye there was a light that was not the light of Heaven, and the mouth trembled, lustful and lewd, to drink deep of the wines of Hell". What John sees is not his face, but his soul. On the mantelpiece is a photograph of John as a naked baby, which makes him feel shame and anger. Baldwin again lets an object reflect the state of John's soul, naked and helpless before God. Close to the photograph on the mantelpiece is also a green metal serpent, "perpetually malevolent", "biding the time to strike", an obvious allusion to Satan as a threat to naked John. As an opposing force stands one of the mottoes on the mantelpiece, the offering in John 3:16 of everlasting life through Jesus Christ. With small but effective means Baldwin introduces the fight that will characterize the rest of John's spiritual journey, the fight between Satan and God over his soul.

From this point in the story John's soul becomes the object of an increasingly fierce battle between two antagonistic forces. John is torn between lust and purity, hatred and love, scorn and devotion, Satan and God. During his walk through New York he vacillates between a desire "to throw himself headlong into the city" and a dream of being the "Lord's anointed" who might "crumble this city with his anger".

He is attracted by the whisky, cars, and jewelry of city people, only the next moment to be repelled because "their thoughts were not of God, and their way was not God's way. They were in the world, and of the world, and their feet laid hold on Hell". He is drawn into the moviehouse even though it reminds him of Hell. He sees the film as a personal message to him and struggles to pacify the battling forces, "to find a compromise between the way that led to life everlasting and the way that ended in the pit", a typical reaction for a person in his predicament.

When the Saturday evening service starts, John feels hostile towards Sister Price and Sister McCandless. His mind is paralyzed, and his heart tells him "that he had no right to sing or rejoice". The next appearance of John occurs in the middle of Florence's prayer. His depression has deepened. He feels, expressed in common Christian images, as if he were in a valley, or a dungeon like Peter and Paul, or in the "endless, swelling water, and no dry land in sight, the true believer clinging to a spar". In his desolation John is longing for "a light that would teach him, forever and forever, and beyond all question, the way to go; for a power that would bind him, forever and forever, and beyond all crying, to the love of God". He wishes that God would take free will away from him, and forcibly expel all doubts. At the bottom of his being dwell an "awful silence" and a "dreadful weight" which give him a "terror he had never felt before". He is torn between a desire for deliverance and a suspicion that God, if He exists, does not care: "Why did they [the worshippers] come here, night after night, calling out to a God who cared nothing for them—if, above this flaking ceiling, there was any God at all?"

The next step in John's conversion is when he tries to pray. Two voices start speaking in him. The first voice says to him that "God is real", that the hand of God would surely lead him through darkness only to raise him up. It further convinces him that he wants to be reconciled to his father: "He could speak to his father then as men spoke to one another—as sons spoke to their fathers, not in trembling but in sweet confidence, not in hatred but in love". But the other voice in him says that this is not what he really wants. He wants to hate his father, "to cherish that hatred, and give his hatred words one day". He wishes his father eternal damnation.

When the threshing-floor section opens, John to his surprise is lying on the floor, gagging from the symbolic dust of sin. He is filled with "an anguish that he could never in his life have imagined", and he lies there "helpless, screaming, at the very bottom of darkness". The two forces battling over his soul have intensified their efforts. Satan's "malicious, ironic voice" tells him to get up from the floor and leave. God's voice is silent at this stage, but His power is speaking instead. John cannot get up; he is "turning, again and again, across the dusty floor, as though God's toe had touched him lightly". Satan insists once more that he get up, but to no avail.

John feels as if he were going down, farther and farther from the joy and the light. He struggles in his own power to rise, but "his struggles only thrust him downward". His attempts to save himself are futile. He is torn between the bottomless darkness and the sunlit mountaintop, between his wish to be loved and accepted by his father and his desire to hate him. The ironic voice urges him to stand up and rebel against Gabriel. This voice is "terrified . . . of no depth, no darkness" simply because these are its true elements. John has a vision in which his hatred makes him identify his father with the devil, while his longing for fellowship with his father makes him see himself as the unjustly rejected Ishmael and Isaac. Like Christian in *Pil-*

grim's Progress, John is here walking through the Valley of Humiliation, doing battle with Apollyon, the foul fiend.

Having successfully passed through this tribulation, John gets temporary relief. "Irony", or Apollyon, has left him, and he can see clearly that he is "searching something, hidden in the darkness, that must be found". But again like Christian, John has to travel through another valley, the Valley of the Shadow of Death, which follows immediately after the Valley of Humiliation. John feels as if he were wandering in a grave, full of "icy mist". Here is no speech or language, no love, no forgiveness, no healing, no redemption. The darkness begins to murmur and John gets a vision of hellish suffering:

> It was a sound of rage and weeping which filled the grave, rage and weeping from time set free, but bound now in eternity; rage that had no language, weeping with no voice—which yet spoke now, to John's startled soul, of boundless melancholy, of the bitterest patience, and the longest night; of the deepest waters, the strongest chains, the most cruel lash; of humility most wretched, the dungeon most absolute, of love's bed defiled, and birth dishonored, and most bloody, unspeakable, sudden death.

John struggles to flee out of this darkness. He finally comes to the bottom, where he realizes that he is "the lowest among these lowly" and that he cannot save himself. He starts to shout for help; "Oh, Lord, have mercy on me". And immediately God's voice, which has been silent as long as John has tried to redeem himself, answers: "Go through, Go through", and the murmuring of the grave ceases. But the battle is not over. One minute he is almost overwhelmed by "the sharp fumes of Hell", while the next he remembers "Jesus saves". Again he is drawn towards the fire "burning in a night eternal", only to once more recall "Jesus saves".

Again John calls for mercy, and now the darkness is filled with "a light he could not bear". Then, in a moment, he is set free, and his tears spring as from a fountain. He feels that his drifting soul has been "anchored in the love of God, in the rock that endured forever". He cannot speak for joy. John feels that he has been given "a new life", a "new voice". He cannot speak of his great gladness, and he does not know how he moves, because his hands and his feet are new and he moves "in a new and Heaven-bright air". John's hatred for his father is gone; he wants to "conquer the great division between his father and himself". He feels the need to testify about "the wonders he had seen". There is no irony whatever in this description of John's deliverance.

John's eyes are also new. He sees the world in a new light. He has been walking in a storm, but now "the storm was over. And the avenue, like any landscape that has endured a storm, lay changed under Heaven, exhausted and clean, and new. Not again, forever, could it return to the avenue it once had been". Yet the houses are still there, the sin of the street is still there. What has changed is that John is still in the world but not of the world. He has been set free, and his battle is no longer with this avenue or with his father, but with "the princes and the powers of the air", that is the devil. He realizes that the devil has many faces, that he will go through temptations, and that he may fall temporarily, and he prays to the Lord to make him strong, to sanctify him and keep him saved. John's request that Elisha pray for him has no homosexual overtones as has been suggested [by James R. Giles (see Further Reading)]; nor has Elisha's holy kiss which glows on John's forehead "like a seal ineffaceable forever". Even though Gabriel may see it differently, John's smile towards him in the last lines of the novel is not a smile of mockery, as critics have suggested, but a smile of holy love which has conquered his father's hatred. (pp. 113-26)

> Rolf Lundén, "The Progress of a Pilgrim: James Baldwin's 'Go Tell It on the Mountain'," in Studia Neophilologica, *Vol. LIII, No. 1, 1981, pp. 113-26.*

FURTHER READING

Campbell, Jane. "Retreat into the Self: Ralph Ellison's *Invisible Man* and James Baldwin's *Go Tell It on the Mountain.*" In her *Mythic Black Fiction: The Transformation of History,* pp. 87-110. Knoxville: The University of Tennessee Press, 1986.
> Analyzes confessional elements and Baldwin's "fictionalizing" of history in *Go Tell It on the Mountain* to challenge Robert A. Bone's speculation that black "assimilationist" novels such as Ralph Ellison's *Invisible Man* resulted from a decrease in racial oppression in the 1940s and 1950s.

Courage, Richard A. "James Baldwin's *Go Tell It on the Mountain:* Voices of a People." *CLA Journal* 32, No. 4 (June 1989): 410-25.
> Assesses Baldwin's use of narrative voice and point of view in *Go Tell It on the Mountain.*

Foster, David E. " 'Cause My House Fell Down': The Theme of the Fall in Baldwin's Novels." *Critique* XIII, No. 2 (1971): 50-62.
> Explores the theme of humanity's fall from grace "to illuminate Baldwin's changing vision" and to "suggest that the successively poorer quality" of his novels "results as much from the stress of this change as from a failure in imagination."

Gérard, Albert. "James Baldwin et la religiosité noire." *La revue nouvelle* 33 (February 1961): 177-86.
> Evaluates religious elements in *Go Tell It on the Mountain.*

Giles, James R. "Religious Alienation and 'Homosexual Consciousness' in *City of the Night* and *Go Tell It on the Mountain.*" *College English* 36 (November 1974): 369-80.
> Examines the themes of religion and homosexuality in *Go Tell It on the Mountain* and John Rechy's *City of the Night.*

Graves, Wallace. "The Question of Moral Energy in James Baldwin's *Go Tell It on the Mountain.*" *CLA Journal* VII, No. 3 (March 1964): 215-23.
> Negative assessment attempting to put aside liberal politeness toward racial distinctions in order "to determine . . . whether the reader's involvement in *Go Tell It on the Mountain* is genuinely one of understanding and forgiveness, or whether it is merely an enlargement of his conventional education."

Harper, Howard M., Jr. "James Baldwin: Art or Propaganda?" In his *Desperate Faith: A Study of Bellow, Salinger, Mailer, Baldwin, and Updike,* pp. 137-61. Chapel Hill: University of North Carolina Press, 1967.
> Describing *Go Tell It on the Mountain* as a "remarkable first novel and a considerable achievement," Harper identifies the book as a "powerful account of the bleak physical environment and the lacerating emotional tensions of Negroes in the Harlem ghetto."

Kinnamon, Keneth, ed. *James Baldwin: A Collection of Critical Essays.* Englewood Cliffs, N.J.: Prentice-Hall, Inc., 1974, 169 p.
> Collection of reprinted essays on Baldwin's works by critics such as Irving Howe, Eldridge Cleaver, and Michel Fabre. Includes an overview of opinions on Baldwin's work, a summary of recurring themes, and two pieces specifically devoted to *Go Tell It on the Mountain.*

Klein, Marcus. "James Baldwin: A Question of Identity." In his *After Alienation: American Novels in Mid-Century,* pp. 147-95. Cleveland: The World Publishing Company, 1962.
> Addressing the anonymous status of many black individuals in American society, Klein explores the theme of recovering one's identity as a means of achieving maturity in *Go Tell It on the Mountain.*

May, John R. "Images of Apocalypse in the Black Novel." *Renascence* XXIII, No. 1 (Autumn 1970): 31-45.
> Demonstrates how "the outstanding contributions of recent black authors to American literature have been dominated by the mood and images of apocalypse."

Mootry, Maria K. "Baldwin's *Go Tell It on the Mountain.*" *The Explicator* 43, No. 2 (Winter 1985): 50-2.
> Examines Baldwin's use of "ironic voices and situational irony" to interpret whether or not the protagonist is saved at the novel's conclusion.

O'Daniel, Therman B. "James Baldwin: An Interpretive Study." *CLA Journal* VII, No. 1 (September 1963): 37-47.
> Brief analysis of such topics as homosexuality and the racial dilemma in Baldwin's novels.

——, ed. *James Baldwin: A Critical Evaluation.* Washington, D.C.: Howard University Press, 1977, 273 p.
> Collection of eight reprinted pieces and fifteen previously unpublished essays by such commentators as Shirley S. Allen and John S. Lash. Includes a detailed bibliography of articles by and about Baldwin.

Porter, Horace A. "The 'Bitter Nourishment' of Art: The Three Faces on James Baldwin's Mountain." In his *Stealing the Fire: The Art and Protest of James Baldwin,* pp. 97-121. Middletown, Conn.: Wesleyan University Press, 1989.
> Detailed study asserting that by providing a counterpoint to the literary techniques of Richard Wright and Henry James in *Go Tell It on the Mountain,* "Baldwin renders what is arguably the most complex and reveal-

ing portrait of a black youth in the history of American fiction."

Pratt, Louis H. "Love Denied, Love Fulfilled." In his *James Baldwin*, pp. 50-81. Boston: Twayne Publishers, 1978.

Examines characters in *Go Tell It on the Mountain* from the perspective of "two Baldwinian prerequisites for self-discovery: the understanding necessary for an acceptance of the past and the ability to establish genuine interpersonal relationships among humanity."

Shawcross, John T. "Joy and Sadness: James Baldwin, Novelist." *Callaloo* 6, No. 2 (Spring-Summer 1983): 100-11.

In response to critics who treat Baldwin's novels as sociopolitical or autobiographical tracts, Shawcross attempts to evaluate the author's fiction from a purely literary perspective.

Standley, Fred L., and Burt, Nancy V. *Critical Essays on James Baldwin*. Boston: G. K. Hall & Co., 1988, 312 p.

Collection of new and reprinted essays on Baldwin's fiction. Includes two pieces on *Go Tell It on the Mountain*.

Standley, Fred L., and Standley, Nancy V. *James Baldwin: A Reference Guide*. Edited by Ronald Gottesman. Boston: G. K. Hall & Co., 1980, 310 p.

Descriptive bibliography of writings by and about Baldwin from 1946 to 1978.

Sylvander, Carolyn Wedin. " 'I'm Ready,' 'I'm Coming,' 'I'm on My Way': *Go Tell It on the Mountain*." In her *James Baldwin*, pp. 27-44. New York: Frederick Ungar Publishing Co., 1980.

Asserts that the religious imagery and structure of *Go Tell It on the Mountain* serve to illustrate "the impact of history—personal and collective—on an individual, whether or not that individual is aware of the history."

Werner, Craig Hansen. "Joyce Hero: Sylvia Plath, Jack Kerouac, James Baldwin." In his *Paradoxical Resolutions: American Fiction Since James Joyce*, pp. 50-68. Urbana: University of Illinois Press, 1982.

Contends that the religious conversion of John Grimes in *Go Tell It on the Mountain* parallels that of James Joyce's Stephen Dedalus and illustrates that "the very terms of transcendence derive from the environment ostensibly left behind."

Wilson, Robert N. "James Baldwin: Relationships of Love and Race." In his *The Writer as Social Seer*, pp. 89-104. Chapel Hill: The University of North Carolina Press, 1979.

Explores "the interior sense of race and class" in Baldwin's novels *Go Tell It on the Mountain* and *Another Country*.

Eavan Boland

1944-

Irish poet and critic.

Boland's poetry often focuses on the central experiences of ordinary women. Presenting such activities as motherhood and domestic life as vital elements of the Irish nation and civilization in general, she challenges the opinion that such topics are mundane or inappropriate for literature. Many of her poems express a sense of anger and imprisonment associated with the constricted or unrealistic expectations placed upon women by Irish society. Marilyn Hacker asserted: "Boland has set herself no less a task than giving words, giving music to that half of human endeavor which has been routinely erased, silenced, or passed by word of mouth, not by word of text; from mother to daughter, neighbor to neighbor, friend to friend. . . ."

The youngest of five children, Boland was born in Dublin. She has acknowledged her parents' influence on her artistic development: her father was a medievalist in law and the classics at Trinity College in Dublin and a diplomat who served in London and with the United Nations, and her mother was a painter who abhorred the academic in art. When Boland was six years old, her family moved to London, where she attended a convent school. Her childhood experiences in England, where she often encountered anti-Irish hostility, strongly influenced her perception of her homeland: "My image-makers as a child were just refractions of my exile: conversations overheard, memories and visitors. I listened and absorbed. Long before Ireland was my country, therefore, it had become my nation." Her sense of isolation continued when her family moved to New York City in 1956, where she attended another Catholic school. Several years later, she returned to Dublin to attend the Holy Child Convent, where she found the solitude and peace of her surroundings beneficial for writing poetry. After graduating, she worked as a housekeeper and self-published a pamphlet titled *23 Poems.* Most critics (including Boland herself) consider the work ambitious but far inferior to her later collections. Following her completion of an English degree at Trinity College, she held a position as a lecturer there, but resigned when she found the highly structured academic environment threatening to her creativity. However, she has continued to teach at the School of Irish Studies in Dublin, and frequently contributes reviews and articles to the *Irish Times.*

Boland's early poems are formal in structure and tone and frequently focus on political and academic subjects. In her collection *The War Horse,* for example, Boland addresses political turmoil in Northern Ireland and comments on such literary figures as Horace, Herodotus, and Vladimir Mayakovsky. Although some critics considered the work overly mannered and restrained, many praised the collection's title poem, in which Boland compares her

perception of a distant war to the vision of a horse trampling flowers outside a window: "You might say, only a crocus, its bulbous head / Blown from growth, one of the screamless dead. / But we, we are safe, our unformed fear / Of fierce commitment gone; why should we care?" *The War Horse* also examines the theme of entrapment—a central motif of Boland's work. In "Ode to Suburbia," she laments the passivity and lethargy of a housewife confined by her culture's limited expectations of women: "By this creature drowsing now in every house, / The same lion who tore stripes / Once off zebras, who now sleeps / Small beside the coals. . . ." Her following collection, *In Her Own Image,* also focuses on themes of limitation, but departs from the subdued tone of *The War Horse,* addressing the victimization of women in an angry, often shocking manner in such poems as "Mastectomy," "Menses," and "Anorexic." "In His Own Image" graphically depicts domestic violence: "He splits my lip with his fist, / shadows my eyes with a blow, / knuckles my neck to its proper angle. / What a perfectionist!" Amy Klauke observed: "[These] poems are at times confessional, jumping into an uncomfortable intimacy with the reader, who is both repelled and fascinated with their revelations of the degraded self."

Boland's poetry often reflects her effort to restructure a poetic tradition that has largely simplified or excluded the genuine experiences of women. In her essay "The Woman Poet in a National Tradition," she explained: "Inexorably, I wrote my way into my own reality. Inevitably, Irishness, womanhood, things which had remained safely at the edges of the poem moved dangerously to its centre." Much of her collection *Night Feed* focuses on motherhood, emphasizing nurturance and growth. In an interview, Boland explained her decision to write poetry about familiar domestic experiences: "I was there with two small children in a house and I could see what was potent and splendid and powerful happening everyday in front of me and I wanted to express that." Her following book, *The Journey,* also presents a heightened perspective on routine household work through detailed images of color and texture, as reflected in such poems as "The Bottle Garden": "I decanted them—feather mosses, fan-shaped plants, / asymmetric greys in the begonia— / into this globe. . . . " Many critics praised the collection's blending of common experience with elements of myth. The title poem, for example, begins with the mother of an ill child contemplating the need for a poem to the antibiotic. The traditionally-structured verse of "The Journey" then diverges into a mythical dream sequence descending into the underworld and building into a dark vision of "the children of the plague." Commending the poem's understated depiction of the suffering of mothers and children throughout history, Anthony Libby asserted, "I have a feeling that this moving poem may be one for the ages."

(See also *CLC,* Vol. 40 and *Dictionary of Literary Biography,* Vol. 40.)

PRINCIPAL WORKS

POETRY

23 Poems   1962
New Territory   1967
W. B. Yeats and His World   [with Michael MacLiammoir]   1970
The War Horse   1980
In Her Own Image   1980
Introducing Eavan Boland   1981
Night Feed   1982
The Journey   1983
Selected Poems   1990

Anthony Libby

The Irish poet Eavan Boland lives in a different world, one from which she can see not only "the Dublin mountains," but a looming poetic tradition and the wastes of European history. Though her long title poem, **"The Journey,"** also concerns the suffering of mothers and children, its meditation on that suffering has a radically different tone from that of the American poets, in part because these are mothers and children not out of the poet's past but out of our collective past. Eavan Boland's actual childhood appears in the collection, but recollected in something like

tranquillity, not as a time of turmoil. Her language has a tranquil control as well, for which it sacrifices nothing in grace or expressive power in any number of tones, from the colloquial to the very aureate. And all convinces; a poem like **"The Oral Tradition,"** an account of a stranger's birth, achieves what it promises: "a sense / suddenly of truth, / its resonance."

The wealth of Eavan Boland's language is complemented by a visual wealth in her metaphors, especially those involving color. She writes occasionally about the process of painting ("light unlearning itself, / an infinite unfrocking of the prism"), about paintings themselves, or about memories of her mother painting. [The poems in *The Journey*] are full of the names of colors, usually rendered in terms that imply metaphor: almond, flax, oyster, kingfisher blue, seedy green, cinnabar. These are often the colors of household things; Ms. Boland insists, perhaps too much and too defensively, on her status as a poet of the common.

At her best she reaches very far from the common into the realms of history and myth, but her beginnings are resolutely plain. **"The Journey"** is a traditionally structured account of a descent into the underworld, inspired by a quotation from Virgil and featuring Sappho as mother and guide. But it begins with a contemporary mother's musing on the need for "a poem to an antibiotic." Language shifts through a variety of tones as mythic experience penetrates the ordinary. Ultimately the lines develop an almost Victorian elegance as the dream builds to a terrifying vision of "the children of the plague." Suffering is more piercing for being understated, hardly stated at all; as Sappho tells her, "what you have seen is beyond speech." But not beyond love and terror, as this mother finds the depths of her own present experience in the darks of history:

I have brought you here so you will know forever
the silences in which are our beginnings,
in which we have an origin like water.

The sense of history here is appropriate; I have a feeling that this moving poem may be one for the ages.

> *Anthony Libby, "Fathers and Daughters and Mothers and Poets," in* The New York Times Book Review, *March 22, 1987, p. 23.*

Eavan Boland

[Excerpted below is Boland's essay discussing the tenuous relationship between Irish women writers and their national tradition.]

Early on as a poet, certainly in my twenties, I realized that the Irish nation, as an existing construct in Irish poetry, was not available to me. It was not a comfortable realization. There was nothing clear-cut about my feelings. From the first they were composed of tribal ambivalences and doubts. Nevertheless, even then, I had a fairly clear perception of the conflict which awaited me: as a poet I could not easily do without the idea of a nation. Poetry in every country draws on that reserve. On the other hand, as a woman I could not accept the nation formulated for me by Irish poetry and its traditions. Therefore it looked as if I must remain outside that poetry and that tradition, cut off from its energy, at a distance from its archive, unless, in some sense, and by some means I could re-possess it. This essay is about that conflict and that re-possession. (pp. 148-49)

Like many children born after the foundation of the Free State and before the establishment of the Republic, the national question was a pervasive, elusive part of my childhood. But with a difference. In my case distance exacerbated everything. My father was a diplomat. The starched collars and the dislocations of an official childhood distorted my image of Ireland. There was no Irish landscape outside my window. We went to London at the end of the 40s. My image-makers as a child were just refractions of my exile: conversations overheard, memories and visitors. I listened and absorbed. Long before Ireland was my country, therefore, it had become my nation. That nation, then and later, was a session of images: of defeats and sacrifices, of individual defiances happening just out of sight. The songs enhanced the images: God save Ireland. Down by the Glenside. The Croppy Boy. No-one proposed those songs to me. I doubt if anyone in my immediate environment listened to or approved of them. I did not care. To me they were soundings of the place I had lost: drowned treasure.

And there were human images. Men and women, acquaintances of my parents, who seemed almost incarnations of the songs. When they walked out of a room, the conversation followed them. They were gossiped about with a mixture of ambivalence and wonder: they had or they had not been out on Bloody Sunday. They did or they did not shoot the British agent point-blank as he shaved in front of his mirror in Northumberland Road. It would take me years to rid myself of the virulence of these impressions; to transit the difficult, necessary distance between violent perceptions and perceptions of violence.

I entered Trinity to study Latin and English. Dublin was a different world then, a city for which I can still feel Henry James's 'tiger-pounce of homesickness'. The old ways held good. In Bewley's they poached eggs in a rolling boil and spooned them onto thick, crustless toast. There were no discos. The lights went on at twilight. The Autumn brought a constant, violent drizzle. After the day's lectures I took a bus from outside College. It was a short journey. Home was an attic flat on the near edge of a town that was just beginning to sprawl. There in the kitchen, on an oilskin tablecloth, I wrote my first real poems. Derivative, formalist, gesturing poems.

They were derivative because I asked too few questions of the world around me and myself as a poet. I was Irish; I was a woman. Yet night after night, bent over the table, I wrote in forms explored and sealed by English men hundreds of years before. I saw no contradiction. Inasmuch as I thought about it at all, I believed that ethics and aesthetics could only be guaranteed by the technical encounter. Perhaps this was not surprising. It was the mid-60s, the heyday of the Movement in Britain. The neat stanza, the well-broken line were the very stuff of poetic identity. I never queried it. I doubt if I knew how to. In my absorp-

tion, in my lack of any sense of implication, I might have been a scientist in the 30s, bombarding uranium with neutrons.

I changed. For the sake of argument and space I must make those two words do the work and take up the slack of several years. The reasons for change are too many and look too simple. Time, marriage, children. None of these exactly account for it. All of them are implicated in it. Inexorably, I wrote my way into my own reality. Inevitably, Irishness, womanhood, things which had remained safely at the edges of the poem, moved dangerously to its centre. 'Perhaps a simple way of putting it' says Adrienne Rich of her own work 'would be to say that instead of poems about experience I am getting poems that are experiences'.

By that time other things had changed as well. The oilskin tablecloth was gone. The sprawling town had become a rapacious city. The attic flat was a house in the suburbs. I was older and more realistic. I had to accept that I was a woman and a poet in a culture which had the greatest difficulty associating the two ideas. 'No poet' says Eliot 'no artist of any kind has his complete meaning alone'. I existed, whether I liked it or not, in a mesh, a web, a labyrinth of associations. Of poems past and present. Contemporary poems. Irish poems.

Irish poetry was predominantly male. Here or there you found a small eloquence, like "After Aughrim" by Emily Lawless. Now and again, in discussion, you heard a woman's name. But the lived vocation, the craft witnessed by a human life, that was missing. And I missed it. Not in the beginning, perhaps. But later, when perceptions of womanhood and Irishness began to redirect my own work, then I greatly missed the voice of a woman in Irish poetry. Apart from any poems she might have written, what I regretted most of all was the absence of an expressed poetic life which would have dignified and revealed mine.

I cut my cloth. Whatever dignity and revelation a woman poet might have offered me I was willing to find, to any extent I could, in the work of Irish male poets. But here I ran into difficulties. I thought of myself as an Irish poet. I wanted to locate myself within the Irish poetic tradition. The dangers and stresses in my own themes gave me an added incentive to discover a context for them. I would have relished the sense of community which came early and easily to male contemporaries. I did not find it. The reasons are not easy to describe. If I say my rapport with Irish poetry faltered because of the simplifications of women in Irish poems that makes it sound more symmetrical and more conscious than it was. At first I felt only a sense of unease. Later, as my own womanhood moved toward the centre of my work, this hardened into a critique. And this is the basis of that critique: the women in Irish male poems tended to be emblematic and passive, granted a purely ornamental status. Not in every case. There were exceptions, distinctions. When male poets wrote about women in a private dimension the images were often warm and convincing. Once the feminine image in their poems became fused with a national concept then both were simplified and reduced.

This happened all too often. Most Irish poets depended on women as motifs in their poetry. Most used women to explore their own ideas about Irishness. The fusion of the national and the feminine, the interpretation of one by the other, was common practice in Irish poetry. . . . It was also hallowed custom. Both practice and custom reached back, past the songs and simplifications of the 19th century, into the Bardic tradition itself. Daniel Corkery in *The Hidden Ireland* has written about this, in his own analysis of the Aisling convention. 'The vision the poet sees' he writes there 'is always the spirit of Ireland as a majestic and radiant maiden'.

The more I looked at these images in Irish poetry, the more uneasy I became. I did not recognize these women. These images could never be a starting point for mine. There was no connection between them and my own poems. How could there be? I was a woman. I stood in an immediate and unambiguous relation to human existences which were only metaphors for male poets. As far as I was concerned, it was the absence of women in the poetic tradition which allowed women in the poems to be simplified. The voice of a woman poet would, I was sure, have precluded such distortion. It did not exist. In the meantime, I could only formulate my rejection of these images as they stood. I did not accept such strategies as my truth. I would not consider them as my poetic inheritance. (pp. 150-53)

This essay is not about the simplification of women in Irish poetry. Certainly that is part of it. Those simplifications isolated and estranged me as a young woman and poet. But the real issue goes deeper than that. All good poetry depends on an ethical relationship between the imagination and the image. It is essential to the integrity of the poem. That relationship for me, as woman and poet, was violated by the simplification of women in Irish poetry. But it was the violation more than the simplification which alienated me.

The poetic imagination can never afford to regard the image as a temporary aesthetic manoeuvre. It must always see it as integral to the truth of the poem. Once the image is distorted the truth is demeaned. That was the heart of the matter as far as I was concerned: in availing themselves of an old convention, in using women as ornamental icons and figments of national expression, Irish poets were not just dealing with emblems. They were also evading the real women of an actual past. Women whose silence their poetry should have broken. There was an inseparable connection between the ornaments they used and the human truths those ornaments belied. The real women with their hungers, their angers, endured a long struggle and a terrible subsistence. Those women are in all our pasts. We are the heirs of their survival. They exist in history and in family archives as spectres and victims, memories and ghosts. Their suffering is our common possession. How then did they re-emerge in Irish poetry as queens, as Muses, as convenient fictions of a hollow victory? How could that happen? Only if Irish poets complied with the wishful thinking of Irish nationalism. Only if such women could be seen as ornaments, as aesthetic conventions rather than human lives.

Yet it was impossible, I believed, to have as a poet an exclusively aesthetic relationship to those women and that past. There must also be an ethical one. Neither could exist in isolation. Irish poets had no licence to make those women elements of style rather than expressions of a truth. Yet, in several cases, this is exactly what had been done. They had allowed the reflexes of their national tradition to turn a terrible witness into empty decoration.

If I seem to be accusing Irish poetry of deficient ethics, at least in one respect, I make no apology for it. Those simplified women, those conventional reflexes and reflexive feminizations of the national experience; those static, passive, ornamental figures do no credit to a poetic tradition which has been, in other ways, radical and innovative, capable of both latitude and compassion. But how do such simplifications occur? They happen, I believe, because national traditions—the Irish one is just a single example of it—have the power to edit out human complexities which do not suit its own programme.

'I am invisible' begins the eloquent prologue to Ralph Ellison's novel *The Invisible Man*. 'I am invisible, understand, because people refuse to see me. Like the bodiless heads you see sometimes in circus side shows it is as though I have been surrounded by mirrors of hard, distorting glass. When they approach me they see only their surroundings, themselves or figments of their own imagination—indeed everything and anything except me'.

A society, a nation, a literary tradition is always in danger of making up its communicable heritage from its visible elements. Women, as it happens, are not especially visible in Ireland. They are very indistinct indeed in its literary canon. Years ago I came to realize when I published a poem that what was seen of me, what drew approval, if it was forthcoming at all, was the poet. The woman, by and large, was invisible. It was an unsettling discovery. Yet I came to believe that my invisibility as a woman was a disguised grace. It had the power to draw me, I sensed, towards a greater invisibility; towards the suffering which lay below the surface of Irish history and out of reach of its tribalism.

Marginality within a tradition, however painful, confers certain advantages. It allows the writer clear eyes and a quick critical sense. That critical perspective, in turn, may allow him to re-locate himself within the tradition which alienated him in the first place. I wanted to re-locate myself within the Irish poetic tradition. I felt the need to do so. A woman poet is rarely regarded as an automatic part of a national poetic tradition. There has been a growing tendency, in the past few years, for academics and critics to discuss women's poetry as a sub-culture within a larger tradition, thereby depriving both of a possible enrichment. I felt it vital that women poets such as myself should establish a discourse with the idea of a nation, should bring to it a sense of the emblematic relationship between the feminine experience and a national past.

The truths of womanhood and the defeats of a nation. An improbable intersection? At first sight perhaps. Yet the more I thought of it, the more it seemed to me if I could find the poetic truth of the first then, by virtue of that alone, I would re-possess the second. If so, then Irishness and womanhood, those tormenting fragments of my youth, would at last become metaphors for one another. (pp. 155-57)

My particular darkness as an Irish poet has been the subject of this piece. It proceeded from a number of things. I was a woman in a tradition which simplified them. I was a poet lacking the precedent and example of previous Irish woman poets. Both these circumstances displaced my sense of relation to the Irish past and its present in Irish poetry. All of these things forced me into a series of re-evaluations. These in turn and by almost infinite indirections brought me to new beliefs and fresh starts.

There are writers for whom the concept of a nation is meaningless. They argue out their identity and context in terms of social and historical symmetries which are altogether different. They are able to dismiss the suggestions of a national tradition as irrelevant to them. I was not so free. For all my quarrels with the concept of a nation, and no doubt partly because of them, I needed to find and re-possess that idea at some level of repose, compromizing neither my poetry nor my womanhood in the process. But why? Why do poets, in this country and others, return to nourish themselves within that idea? In my case, the answer grew clearer to me as time went on. I needed to re-possess my nation because, in some subterranean way, I felt myself to be part of its ordeal; because its fragmentations extended into mine. Therefore, for me, as for others, it became an act of self-possession.

That is not to say I lost sight of the difficulties. It will always be an uneasy truce. Writers do not make their home in any comfort within a national tradition. However vigilant the writer, however enlightened the nation, the dangers persist. As a woman and a poet I took issue with the idea of the nation. For that reason, more of my time than I would have liked as a young writer was spent in confusion and division; in an ethical dusk. Even when that cleared, my sense of the precariousness of the situation remained.

There is a recurring temptation for any nation and for any writer who operates within its sphere of influence to make an ornament of the past; to turn its losses to victories; to restate its humiliations as triumphs. In every age language holds out narcosis and amnesia for this purpose. But such triumphs, in the end, are unsustaining.

It all comes back to ethics. If a poet does not tell the truth about time, his or her work will not survive it. Past or present, there is a human dimension to time, human voices within it and human griefs ordained by it. Our present will become the past of other men and women. We depend on them to remember it with the complexity with which it was suffered; as others, once, depended on us. (pp. 157-58)

> *Eavan Boland, "The Woman Poet in a National Tradition," in* Studies, *Vol. 76, No. 302, Summer, 1987, pp. 148-58.*

Lachlan Mackinnon

There are two kinds of poem in Eavan Boland's ***The Jour-***

ney and other poems. The first deals directly with the poet's own experience as a woman, as a mother, and as an Irish girl brought up in England. In the opening poem, **"I Remember"**, she recalls her mother painting a portrait in the drawing-room, and coming down herself that morning to find, as

> a nine-year-old in high, fawn socks—
> the room had been shocked into a glacier
> of cotton sheets thrown over the almond
> and vanilla silk of the French Empire chairs.

One sentence blocked into six quatrains, the poem comes to rest on those familiar "chairs" as though to anchor an unspoken desperation. Secretly it is the child who is "shocked", but the frequently violent enjambment lets that emotional pressure pervade the entire poem, barely reining it in. As an adult, Eavan Boland is saddened by the loss of such transformations:

> The last dark shows up the headlights
> of the cars coming down the Dublin mountains.
>
> Our children used to think they were stars.

The adult knows better, as **"Suburban Woman: A detail"** shows, but is still afraid to walk to a neighbour's house at dusk, fearing that

> something
> which may be nothing
> more than darkness has begun
> softening the definitions
> of my body.

An object in nature, she is subject to dissolution, leaving only her fears to remain "crying 'remember us' ".

Boland is fascinated by materials: "almond / and vanilla silk", lace, crêpe de Chine, denim, muslin, worsted are just a few random examples; and her emphasis on women's work reminds us of a younger poet, Medbh McGuckian, although she is much less unyieldingly hermetic. The first stanza of **"The Bottle Garden"** has that timbre, for instance:

> I decanted them—feather mosses, fan-shaped plants,
> asymmetric greys in the begonia—
> into this globe which shows up how the fern shares
> the invertebrate lace of the sea-horse.

"Lace", though, has earlier suggested the sort of language Boland is seeking, and acts as a pointer to what follows the turn of the poem, "And in my late thirties, past the middle way, / I can say how did I get here?" The question would be embarrassing if the "signs" it found were not in the subject of the poem—"Earth stars, rock spleenwort, creeping fig / and English ivy". The "English ivy" looks back to the childhood of **"Fond Memory"** in which she hears her father play "the slow / lilts of Tom Moore":

> I thought this is my country, was, will be again,
> this upward-straining song made to be
> our safe inventory of pain. And I was wrong.

"The Bottle Garden" describes her as "a gangling school-girl" reading the *Aeneid* in "the convent library". Her own entrapment finds an emblem in that poem's Stygian seclusion, but she will here escape through the "open weave", tellingly clothy, of "harbour lights" from the uniform she is already outgrowing. Implicitly, she will slip out like an "invertebrate", like a sea-horse or the oldest, toughest of plants with which she shares her "lace" of language. This poem moves well beyond McGuckian's privacies, for **"Mise Eire"** has already told us how she fears Ireland, "the small farm, / the scalded memory"—burned and poeticized—where "songs / . . . bandage up history". Boland's "poetic of imprisoned meanings" is much less "improvised" than it looks, as shown by the unpunctuated leap between stanzas in **"The Bottle Garden"**, and in the way so many of the poems in this book feed into one another by the lightest allusive touches. The domestic can be brushed by the political, the erotic by the commonplace.

Of the other kind of poem there are three examples, **"The Journey"**, **"Envoi"** and **"Listen. This is the Noise of Myth"**. **"Envoi"** invokes a muse, a female Christ:

> If she will not bless the ordinary,
> if she will not sanctify the common,
> then here I am and here I stay and then am I
> the most miserable of women.

Such an open statement of intent, blurred by inconsequential myth-making, wrecks all three poems. Instead of an artful "open weave" we have willed effort. When she conceals her art, Eavan Boland can be memorable and unnervingly honed, but when she does not she is hardly an artist at all. This is a generous, if slim, volume, though, and for the most part furtive and deadly.

> *Lachlan Mackinnon, "A Material Fascination," in* The Times Literary Supplement, *No. 4403, August 21, 1987, p. 904.*

Eavan Boland [Interview with Amy Klauke]

[Klauke]: *We were discussing silences.*

[Boland]: Yes, and what poetic traditions are really made out of. If you're a woman, you have two inheritances. First, like all poets, you inherit a powerful tradition coming from the Romantic movement which subliminally dictates which experiences and languages are poetic, which approaches you should take as a poet to your material. All young poets have to work through that to find their own voice. But for women it's a particularly disturbing aesthetic to deal with because it's built on realities, like the elegy or the war poem, that have little to do with the daily life of women. So it's disturbing to have on the one hand this powerful Romantic aesthetic and on the other hand the awareness of women that behind them is a tradition not articulated in poetry, but in the silences of other women, the fact that other women didn't write.

So in your workshops do you teach women who haven't been writing to find a subject they can express artistically?

No, the workshops are at a more modest level. They simply give to women certain of the amenities which are very difficult to get if you're a woman, especially living outside Dublin. You forget that in America you have great libraries open at all hours. There aren't such libraries in this country, such places of congregation. There's a great deal more of people being closed in and questioning their own talents. Workshops bring people together. They can air certain views, short circuit certain critical processes, that's all.

There's an essay in the collection Irish Women: Image and Achievement *suggesting that part of Irish women's reticence stems from the fact that the male literary tradition in Ireland has been so outstanding; women are almost afraid to enter that arena.*

A lot of women simply didn't read Yeats and Joyce, it wouldn't be a matter of being intimidated by them. Funnily enough, in this country we have a tradition very favorable to women in terms of the fact that men here often wrote out of types of silent humiliation with which women feel an intimate rapport. It's not a cerebral or suffocating tradition at all, it's a sympathetic one.

There was also the suggestion that women portrayed in Irish literature were alien to the woman writer who found it hard to express herself or describe her experience in terms of stereotypes such as the hag, the virgin, the whore.

Yes, but I think most people take a Brechtian view of stereotypes. They know that they are fictions of a time and place, metaphors, transparencies through which other truths come. I don't think they're binding upon anybody. What is important is what these metaphors or images are used for. Often in the case of Joyce or Yeats or Patrick Kavanagh they are simply transparencies, profound obsessions which are anything but intimidating for women.

Could you speak more about Irish women's silence, which you mentioned earlier?

The Irish experience is much concerned with the silence of the past. One of the important questions that still has to be aired is the whole complicated area of societal permissions that are given to (or denied) women to write. Look at Eastern Europe: the tragic lack of permission given to writers to be truly creative, to do more than conform. In Ireland, with its conservative Catholicism, the image and perception of women as artists is more restrictive than for men. Therefore what you're trying to do here in workshops, discussions, seminars, contacts over years is to equalize the societal permission, which I think in the States has been accomplished.

When we were talking before the interview you mentioned that a lot of Irish women are afraid to acknowledge themselves as feminist writers.

Yes. Feminism is a word that's come into Ireland with a pretty powerful sense of threat behind it. I'm not a separatist. I would regret separatism especially in poetry. The division of men and women makes little sense in the poetic tradition of our country, where a person like Patrick Kavanagh, who came from a poor rural area, spoke with incredible power. He touches on a lot of feminine themes. Why should we divide a tradition like that? We should have as wide a poetic transaction as we can.

Nevertheless, women are genuinely wary of being called

feminist. They're afraid of labels, afraid they'll be categorized, without seeing that they're already categorized. For good or ill, women are categorized as women.

Are the same women reading feminist work?

There's no avoidance of feminist work here, but it's very hard to get hold of. Adrienne Rich's work is not nearly widely enough circulated in this country.

Can you talk about how the strong Catholicism of this country affects its literature?

Yes. It's a legacy. I think that the view of women and their duties imposed by the Catholic church has been restrictive, understandably so, considering the people's history, their poverty and danger. The Catholic church would have perceived not the danger that people wouldn't write poetry, but that people wouldn't survive, wouldn't eat, wouldn't be Catholic. Yes, the history of Catholicism has been fascinating, sometimes rich, but finally restrictive for women.

Do you see elements of Ireland's pagan history, its goddess religion, surfacing in women's writing? Is anyone rediscovering or recreating that mythology?

A number of women here do have an interest in it. The goddess culture is very much a European phenomenon, and in Ireland it lies behind the fact that women, although restricted in some ways, finally become figures of great power within the home. Ireland herself is represented as a woman, although this can be exploited for poetic purposes.

Do women have political power as well?

They do, but it's important to remember that Ireland has a deeply chauvinistic political tradition. Very few women have entered the republican movement.

How does the political situation in northern Ireland affect you as a writer?

It has to affect the way you think of yourself as an Irish poet. It is a situation of eroding tragedy, where people are quarrelling over the name Irish, the whole concept of Irishness. It's a constant sadness and an impoverishment of the word Irish.

I'd like to talk to you about your work. Is there a writer you've been significantly influenced by?

I am a lyric poet and that's the Yeatsian heritage. I see poetry as a passionate witness to one's own life. That is its mode of truth. Obviously there are people who have a lot more complex view of what language does, but if language renders the truth of a life, and renders it within poetry, then I'm satisfied. I mean, Yeats has long ceased to have any linguistic influence on anyone, but his aesthetic is powerful and he made poetry a great construct of reality.

I'm also impressed by Adrienne Rich and a number of American poets. I like Lowell and Berryman. Although I like Sylvia Plath's work, I feel that, contrary to what is thought about her, she was a very literary writer. She's like Dylan Thomas, a stylist, somebody whose sound has a bit

more meaning than her sense. You wonder about Plath and Thomas: In the end, did they have an awful lot to say?

I recognized her influence in your third book, **In Her Own Image,** *a Plath-like pain and anger.*

Strangely enough, I can see why you say that. The book is much more of an attack on the male tradition of the muses, something which I don't think Plath would ever have done. It's an attack on things like the mimic muse and a belief that experiences which haven't been given a voice are degraded. But I don't glamorize the states I write about there: I regard them as tragic states. (pp. 55-8)

Has your latest book, **Night Feed,** *in any sense arisen out of* **In Her Own Image***?*

To be radical as a poet, as a woman poet, it it is essential to break away from that Romantic aesthetic. In the seventeenth century there was a painter, Jean-Baptist Chardin, who, in the middle of his century of court paintings and religious triptychs, painted the ordinary, the articulation of the ordinary, of the woman coming back from market or the loaf of bread. In so doing he didn't invent a meaning, but revealed it. In *Night Feed* I was interested in a poetry that would reveal the meaning of something ordinary and everyday and that would turn around this great unwieldy poetic aesthetic with all its powerful implications of what language should be and make it do the work it ought to be doing. I was there with two small children in a house and I could see what was potent and splendid and powerful happening every day in front of me and I wanted to express that.

A lot of women poets who went to university, who taught in university, have a powerful and, in many cases, prohibitive intellectual tradition saying these things are not important, they're ordinary, they're commonplace. That's always the voice at your ear you have to resist.

Did you find it necessary to change your form or voice to approach these realities?

No. What seems a change of tone is actually a change of focus. You're moving the lyrical persona closer to the material. (pp. 58-9)

I noticed in your first book the speaker is more distant, omniscient almost, and in **In Her Own Image** *the speaker is much more personal and speaks to a she or a her, seemingly a part of the self. Could you talk about this fragmented speaker?*

In Her Own Image was very liberating to write. It allowed me to look at the anti-lyrical aspects of experience, which is terribly necessary for a lyric poet who is always in danger of sentimentalizing, simplifying, prettifying. To examine domestic violence, for example, that fortified me for going into the other areas.

You see, women are the carriers of unresolved areas in human nature. They attract violence because they are the images of what men have rejected: intuition, softness. That's how the violence comes upon them. To take those unresolved areas and put them into a poetic tradition takes a vulnerable, violent area and reincorporates it, reintegrates it, you see.

Would you describe the speaker in **Night Feed,** *then, as expressing an affirmation of self?*

I suppose a more limited self, human and limited. The great dangers for poets are always the hidden dangers. For example, the temptation to write as poets, as people made special by their powers to articulate, not as human beings. But of course they are only special as long as they can give articulation to the ordinary human reality. Once you begin to believe that you are what you are able to express, once you believe that you are the created object not the creator, you begin to lose that power. It seemed to me that *Night Feed* would be as good, not as the poetry that was written (I thought that might look after itself if I worked hard at it and was careful), but as my human rapport with the subject, my human suffering within that situation.

You've discussed your "persona" coming closer to home through your work. Would you say that your audience has also changed?

Yes, strangely enough, I have quite a populist streak. I love to have readers who are not within the church of poetry. I mean, **"Night Feed"** would be a poem that people might know because it's within their experience, not because it's a poem. There's a famous story told about Byron and Moore sitting on the Thames in London. When on one of the boats coming down the Thames they were singing a song by Tom Moore, Byron tapped him and said, "Ah, Tom, that's fame." I think that one of the great dreams of the poet, although he can't compromise in favor of it, is to live in the hearts of the people. Most poets manage it with one poem, or two poems. Living in the hearts of the people is a pretty dangerous place for anybody to live, but it's nice to touch there just for a moment.

Would you talk about the genesis of your latest piece, **"The Journey,"** *where you communicate with Sappho and travel, with her, into hell.*

Yes, it's the title poem for my next book. When I was in Iowa, our baby, who was then a year and a half old, got meningitis. She went to Mercy Hospital, which I often think about with gratitude, and she recovered. But she was very ill for those few days. I used to go to see her in the evening, and I was terribly aware of the differences in levels of reality. I used to think to myself: Nobody's ever written a poem to an antibiotic; nobody has, in fact, faced these issues of losing children and of the terrible infant mortality rate. They haven't been deemed to be poetic. I wanted to write in the terms of the poetic tradition, inverting it, you see.

One poetic tradition is the dream sequence, as in Dante's *Divina Comedia.* Also in the *Aeneid,* in the sixth book, Aeneas goes down to the underworld. He crosses the river. There's a little aside by Virgil, something like, "Well, there are all the babies who never saw the light of day." It's a mere aside, but that becomes the center of my poem. I go down to the underworld with Sappho, and she shows me these silences and these sufferings and says these should be at the center of a poetic tradition, and I believe they should be. (pp. 59-61)

Eavan Boland and Amy Klauke, in an inter-

view in Northwest Review, *Vol. 25, No. 1, 1987, pp. 54-61.*

Eavan Boland

Let us say, for argument's sake, that it is a wet, Novemberish day in a country town in Ireland. Now, for the sake of going a bit further, let us say that a workshop or the makings of one has gathered in an upstairs room in a school perhaps, or an Adult Education Centre. The surroundings will be—as they always are on these occasions—just a bit surreal. There will be old metal furniture, solid oak tables, the surprising gleam of a new video in the corner. And finally, let us say that among these women gathered here is a woman called Judith. I will call her that as a nod in the direction of Virginia Woolf's great essay "A Room of One's Own." And when I—for it is I who am leading the workshop—get off the train or out of the car and climb the stairs and enter that room, it is Judith—her poems already in her hand—who catches my eye and holds my attention.

"History," said Butterfield, "is not the study of origins; rather it is the analysis of all the mediations by which the past has turned into our present." As I walk into that room, as Judith hands me her poems, our past becomes for a moment a single present. I may know, she may acknowledge, that she will never publish, never evolve. But equally I know we have been in the same place and have inherited the same dilemma.

She will show me her work diffidently. It will lack almost any technical finish—lineation is almost always the chief problem—but that will not concern me in the least. What will concern me, will continue to haunt me, is that she will be saying to me—not verbally, but articulately nonetheless—I write poetry but I am not a poet. And I will realize, without too much being said, that the distance between writing poetry and being a poet is one that she has found in her life and her time just too difficult, too far and too dangerous to travel. I will also feel—whether or not I am being just in the matter—that the distance will have been more impassable for her than for any male poet of her generation. Because it is a preordained distance, composed of what Butterfield might call the unmediated past. On the surface that distance seems to be made up of details: lack of money, lack of like minds and so on. But this is deceptive. In essence the distance is psycho-sexual, made so by a profound fracture between her sense of the obligations of her womanhood and the shadowy demands of her gift.

In his essay on Juana de Asbaje, Robert Graves sets out to define that fracture: "Though the burden of poetry," he writes, "is difficult enough for a man to bear, he can always humble himself before an incarnate Muse and seek instruction from her. . . . The case of a woman poet is a thousand times worse: since she is herself the Muse, a Goddess without an external power to guide or comfort her, and if she strays even a finger's breadth from the path of divine instinct, must take violent self-vengeance."

I may think there is a certain melodrama in Grave's commentary. Yet, in a subterranean way, this is exactly what many women fear. That the role of poet added to that of woman may well involve them in unacceptable conflict. The outcome of that fear is constant psycho-sexual pressure. And the result of that pressure is a final reluctance to have the courage of her own experience. All of which adds up to that distance between writing poems and being a poet, a distance which Judith—even as she hands me her work—is telling me she cannot and must not travel.

Eavan Boland, "The Woman Poet: Her Dilemma," in The American Poetry Review, Vol. 16, No. 1, January-February, 1987, pp. 18-19.

Amy Klauke

Against the fiercely heroic tradition of Irish nationalist poetry, a number of women are expressing a new perspective which is at once personal and political. Foremost among these writers is Eavan Boland, who has published several books of poetry in Ireland and the U.S. Her work traces the growth of a personal poetry, a radical development in the literature of Ireland since Yeats set a political stage with "Easter, 1916."

The War Horse, Boland's second book of poetry, works within political and academic realms, with poems responding to the present turmoil in Northern Ireland, to literary figures such as Horace, Herodotus and Mayakovsky, or recreating Irish folklore, as in **"Elegy for a Youth Changed to a Swan"** and **"From the Irish of Pangur Ban."** In this collection, the poems are structured and formal, the tone reserved and contained. We sense the writer hidden behind her themes and observations. In her best pieces, she combines a rhythmic but restrained style with personal experiences that suggest universal concerns. For example, in the title poem a horse passing outside her window, trampling everything, becomes emblematic of wars which happen within our sphere but which don't immediately affect us:

> Only a rose which now will never climb
>
> The stone of our house, expendable, a mere
> Line of defence against him, a volunteer
>
> You might say, only a crocus, its bulbous head
> Blown from growth, one of the screamless dead.
>
> But we, we are safe, our unformed fear
> Of fierce commitment gone; why should we care.

We sense at once her confidence and linguistic finesse, similar to Mary Oliver's tight-knit, early verses or Adrienne Rich's first poems, such as "Storm Warnings," where something portentous and feral circles an otherwise tame poem. Overall, these poems are well crafted, clear and commentarial, more intellect than emotion, as in **"Naoise at Four,"** written to a boy named after one of three slain brothers in Irish folklore, a poem which addresses the current violence in her country:

> As each suburban, modern detail
>
> Distances us from old lives.
> Old deaths, but nightly on our screen
> New ones are lost, wounds open.
> And I despair of what perspective

> On this sudden Irish fury
> Will solve it to a folk memory.

Her radicalism begins to emerge when these poems focus not on "a cause," but rather on the human tragedy of the conflict itself. In the above example, the speaker undercuts the tendency to "solve" this child's death into another Irish legend. Instead, these young victims incite her to protest, as in these lines from **"Child of Our Time"**:

> yesterday I knew no lullaby
> But you have taught me overnight to order
> This song, which takes from your final cry
> Its tune, from your unreasoned end its reason;
> Its rhythm from the discord of your murder,
> Its motive from the fact you cannot listen. . . .

>   . . . Child
> Of our time, our times have robbed your cradle.
> Sleep in a world your final sleep has woken.

Often, as in the last line quoted above, Boland repeats a word or phrase with a slightly different stress and meaning. The repetitions such as, "And living, learn, must learn from you, dead" from the same poem, work themselves into the reader's memory. With skill and judiciousness, she employs slant rhyme, as in, "The bare rowan tree / berries rain" (**"The Muse Mother"** from *Night Feed*), and other lyrical techniques to create a momentum which carries each poem to resolution, as in **"Prisoners,"** a poem inspired by two lovers' visit to the zoo:

> You can no more free yourself from the bars
> Of your arms around me than can over
> Us the lion flee, silently, his stars.

This poet is unafraid to use end-rhyme or direct sentiment. She doesn't mind luxuriating in long sonorous sentences, allowing them to sift and settle in. These poems play on ambiguity and allusion, but always with extreme control. The speaker uses precise language and careful, if sometimes complex, syntax, extending metaphor and parallelism: "with rhymes for your waking, rhythms for your sleep."

The War Horse contains several poems which explore the condition of being trapped, whether literally as the lion is in the previous example, or figuratively. **"Ode to Suburbia"** recalls the lion image, but refers this time to a spiritually sleepy housewife, someone confined socially by living out her culture's limited image of women:

> By this creature drowsing now in every house,
> The same lion who tore stripes
> Once off zebras, who now sleeps
> Small beside the coals and may
> on a red letter day
> Catch a mouse.

In this ode, the final line in each stanza is truncated, hinting at the sparser style Boland develops in her following collection, *In Her Own Image,* where the lion roars and rattles its cage, and the poetic structures change.

The speaker of *In Her Own Image* is at once cynical and chastising, the language stark, sharp and colloquial. Hear a bit of **"Tirade For the Mimic Muse"**:

> "The more primitive a truth gets, the more difficult it gets to formalize, and the real radicalism for me has been to bring the very sophisticated apparatus of poetry nearer to the less easily articulated human experience."
>
> —*Eavan Boland*

In a nappy stink, by a soaking wash
Among stacked dishes
Your glass cracked, your nerve broke.

In contrast to the comfortable distance in the earlier book, these poems are at times confessional, jumping into an uncomfortable intimacy with the reader, who is both repelled and fascinated with their revelations of the degraded self. Spoken in the first person, these poems are written with alarming sass, the lines are crisper, shorter; "I raddle / and I prink / pinking bones." The poet's level-headed certainty has been replaced by vulnerability and bewilderment:

She is not myself
anymore, she is not
even in my sky
anymore and I
am not myself.

("In Her Own Image")

In this collection, Boland speaks from inside the cage. Here, the body is what confines, or more specifically, society's attitude towards women's bodies which compels the speaker to starve or hide or deform her natural physical self. But in contrast to the more passive voice in *The War Horse,* the speaker here is not resigned to her confinement. She feels angry and cornered. Her voice lifts from personal pain and spills into sarcasm:

He splits my lip with his fist,
shadows my eyes with a blow,
knuckles my neck to its proper angle.
What a perfectionist!

("In His Own Image")

The most beguiling poems in this collection allow a moment of quiet sorrow, an eye in the storm, such as this whispering lament in "Mastectomy":

So they have taken off
what slaked them first,
what they have hated since:

blue-veined
white-domed
home.

In "Anorexic," the speaker describes thinning herself into a rib, an indirect reference to Eve, and a particularly poignant metaphor for this debilitating disease:

Only a little more,
only a few more days

sinless, foodless,

I will slip
back into him again
as if I had never been away.

We can recognize her natural lyricism in this collection, although the focus and tone have become more personal. There is still the formal control, and an even livelier rhyme. For example, in "Menses" she virtually hums:

I am sick of it,
filled with it,
dulled by it,
thick with it.

As her titles in this collection suggest—"Anorexic," "Menses," "Witching," and "Making Up"—Boland here addresses women's experience, in poems both bold and liberating. The speaker rejects convention, as she rejects the "mimic muse" and burns what she cannot use in her life or poetry:

Yes it's my turn

to stack
the twigs
and twig the fire
and
smell
how well

a woman's
flesh
can burn.

("Witching")

> "I was very interested in a poetry that would reveal the meaning of the ordinary and everyday and that would turn around this great unwieldy poetic aesthetic with all its powerful implications of what language should be and make it do the work it ought to be doing."
>
> —*Eavan Boland*

In Her Own Image, then, appears as a transitional book, one which frees Boland to explore and struggle with subjects nearer to home, subjects which counter the nationalistic trend in Irish poetry, and to speak with a decidedly woman's voice. *Night Feed,* her latest book, maintains this woman's perspective, but the sense of confinement is replaced by an acceptance and even celebration of the boundaries presented by parenthood. In the title poem we recognize qualities from both her earlier books, her distinctive cadence coupled with intimacy of voice and subject:

This is your season, little daughter:
The moment daisies open,
The hour mercurial rainwater
Makes a mirror for sparrows.
It's time we drowned our sorrows. . . .

> . . . Poplars stilt for dawn
> And we begin
> The long fall from grace.
> I tuck you in.

This collection celebrates the nurturing instinct, with images of flowers and children, experiences of planting, feeding and tending. She explores the emotions of motherhood especially, and devotion to her two daughters:

> Then it's over—
> The pride
> However slight
> In giving life.
>
> **("Before Spring")**

The strident voice from *In Her Own Image* is missing here; instead the voice is looser, deeper, expressing a warm sanity. Two poems especially explore the necessary distances between parent and child, and the loss intrinsic to growth:

> If I lean
> I can see
> what it is the branches end in:
>
> the leaf,
> the reach,
> the blossom,
> the abandon.
>
> **("Endings")**

and:

> You are my child and your body is
> the destiny of mine and between us are
> spaces, distances, growing to infinities.
> **("Fruit on a Straight-Sided Tray")**

Discoveries and possibilities characterize these poems. Moving from the omniscient speaker in *The War Horse* toward a more vulnerable position as one among many, Boland casts inquisitive looks to other women, seeking to understand their shared experiences. While observing a neighbor's face she wonders:

> she might teach
>
> me a new language,
> to be a sybil
> able to sing the past
> in pure syllables,
>
> limning hymns sung
> to belly wheat or a woman,
> able to speak at last
> my mother tongue.
>
> **("The Muse Mother")**

Without being didactic or moralistic, Boland's poems are gentle chidings, and without painting a bleak or hopeless landscape, she presents issues to be addressed and responded to. Judging from the preceding selections from her new book, *The Journey,* Eavan Boland continues to express public realities through her uniquely personal perspective. In a voice both tender and intelligent, she is successfully widening the arena of viable poetry in Ireland.

> And I had distances
> ahead of me; iron miles
> in trains, iron rails

> repeating instances
> and reasons; the wheels
>
> singing innuendos, hints,
> outlines underneath
> the surface, a sense
> suddenly of truth,
> its resonance.
>
> **("The Oral Tradition")**
> (pp. 73-80)

Amy Klauke, "Toward Her Own Image," in Northwest Review, *Vol. 25, No. 1, 1987, pp. 73-80.*

Neil Corcoran

Eavan Boland's *Selected Poems* is one of those carefully pruned volumes in which a poet of quiet, meticulous, patient craft stands revealed as something more interesting and integrated than her individual books had led one to anticipate. She is, like Richard Murphy, an Irish poet, and her feminism, radical but undoctrinaire, takes its particular edge from its political refusals: **"Mise Eire"** opens 'I won't go back to it— / my nation displaced / into old dactyls,' and offers an adversarial role as self-definition:

> I am the woman—
> a sloven's mix
> of silk at the wrists,
> a sort of dove-strut
> in the precincts of the garrison . . .
>
>   who neither
> knows nor cares that
> a new language
> is a kind of scar
> and heals after a while
> into a passable imitation
> of what went before.

So much for 'the language question' and its nationalist context, as far as Eavan Boland is concerned, even if the matter of Irish history sounds at the edge of earshot throughout this collection. Secular, convinced, sceptical, haughty, the lines are very much inscribed with her signature, as is the sudden aggressive humour of the historical identification.

Sylvia Plath is clearly the major presence behind Boland's evolution from an early rather inert anecdotal and emblematic manner, but the influence never swamps her. She has, throughout, her own individual fix on certain central preoccupations and motifs. There are many assured, flexible and provocative readings of male painters' readings of women, with especially fine poems on Degas and Ingres; and there are numerous suburban interiors of her own. If they lack the fraught mythologising of Plath, Boland's interiors nevertheless have their terrors of confinement, the 'lethal/rapine of routine'; and her work painfully recounts some of the most intimate womanly experiences. The 'radical but undoctrinaire feminism' I have referred to is not merely a matter of disconcerting material, however, but an ingenious, cunning fictionalising, particularly in some of the poems towards the close of this volume. **"The Journey"**, for instance, is a poem written because there are no poems in praise of the antibiotic. It takes its epigraph from *Aeneid VI,* on the dead infants at the entrance to Hades, and opens up into a dream-vision journey through the underworld in which the poet is accompanied by Sappho. I don't know whether this is written in any direct response to Seamus Heaney's *Station Island,* but its final depiction of the fading Sappho's poetic laying-on of hands may be read as an oblique riposte to that poem's all-male cast. **"The Journey"** and the book's final poem, **"The Glass King",** in which the mad Charles VI of France and his wife Isabella of Bavaria become emblems of Boland's sense of the place of lyric poetry in domestic life, are complex, self-reflexive and sharply affecting; they indicate a fine poet moving onto a new plateau of achievement.

> Neil Corcoran, *"Neil Corcoran Confronts the New Recklessness,"* in London Review of Books, *Vol. 11, No. 18, September 28, 1989, p. 14.*

R. T. Smith

In her recent poem, **"Listen. This is the Noise of Myth,"** Eavan Boland describes her own work as the product of modest strategies of abandonment and illumination— "This is mine. / This sequence of evicted possibilities. / Displaced facts. Tricks of light. Reflections." The reader of her *Selected Poems* is likely to concur with the surface of this ironic proposition, while noting that candor and generosity also play a role. Her culling and "eviction" of received truths is crucial, as Boland's work has from the start been a manifesto of skepticism towards "those who touch the Grail and bring no proof," as well as a voyage of discovery. Guided and often freed by Horace, old Irish poems, Keats, H. D., Plath, and Heaney, Boland has become the imitator of none, is instead a complex sensibility equally attuned to a variety of subjects such as Catholicism, feminism, Irish history, personal experience, the serenity and flux of art, all of which she explores with a precise eye and carefully pitched voice in the five volumes her *Selected Poems* has been drawn from.

The more than seventy poems in the collection testify to two decades of authentic attention to the inner and outer worlds whose points of intersection shape her carefully controlled language. In her first volume, *New Territory,* she suggests that poets "with their own hands quarried from hard words / A figure in which secret things confide," and she has proceeded to pursue that mission herself, whether the secrets are concealed in paintings of the masters (Degas, Ingres, Van Eyck, Chardin, Renoir), the Irish past (**"The Flight of the Earls," "The Famine Road,"** the more urgent **"Mise Eire"**), her personal predicaments (**"Night Feed"** or **"An Irish Childhood in England: 1951"**) or the oddities of myth and history (**"The Glass King"** and **"Athena's Song"**).

Titles such as **"Anorexic," "Menses,"** and **"Mastectomy"** combine with the sinuous syntax, jagged edges and thin-lipped oracular pitch of many of Boland's poems to point to the influence of Plath, and indeed she shares some of her predecessor's awareness of woman-as-victim and some of her bitterness. But Boland's poems inevitably achieve

an equilibrium, a sense of rebirth out of the punishingly claustrophobic and into a charged and engaging world. She never demonstrates the lack of extensive sympathy that diminishes some of Plath's work, and when she reveals that twilight is "My time of sixth sense and second sight," one understands that these gifts are not hermetic, never solipsistic or sybilline. She can still, nevertheless, construct those thickets of syllables that seem to ignite on the tongue and recall the hard processes of Plath or the Heaney of *North:*

> It's a night
> white things ember in:
> jasmine and the shine—
> flowering, opaline—
> of the apple trees.
>
> **"Endings"**

> "and they too like you
> stood boot deep in flowers once in summer
> or saw winter come in with a single magpie
> in a caul of haws, a solo harlequin."
>
> **"The Journey"**

The ultimate value of these poems, however, lies not in optical and auditory pyrotechnics but in the insatiable yearning to see mysteries as clarities, to encircle the strange and to tend the quiet light of the familiar. Boland brings an exuberant imagination to the commonplace, yet approaches the remarkable with reserve.

This is not to say, however, that her work is without flaws. In the poems from *The War Horse,* when she has begun to focus with a new immediacy on the nuances of suburban life, Boland occasionally forces a form, and her poems containing dialect seldom digest it comfortably. In her next collection, *In Her Own Image,* a renewed sense of humor emerges in collaboration with those image-rich, blade-shaped poems of womanly suffering. The bulk of *Night Feed* serves to refine those elements in poems as various in subject matter as a Degas laundress, a snake woman, an ironing housewife, Daphne, a model of Ingres, and a fish woman. Here her imagination extends and embraces tones and flavors that prepare the reader for the dual excellence of *The Journey,* where the terse, wiry poems mingle with more rhetorically dense ones. In this last score of poems she reaches a peak of sustained performance, and the reader is little inclined to share her doubt when she wonders in **"Envoi"** about the name and nature of her muse:

> If she will not bless the ordinary,
> if she will not sanctify the common,
> then here I am and here I stay and then am I
> the most miserable of women.

This muse has, as the poet had hoped earlier, confided some of her secrets in these figures, and Boland, only in her mid-forties, orchestrates the secrets with the complete mastery upon which the beauty of dressage depends: as the horse responds gracefully to almost imperceptible commands, one never forgets the mass and muscle involved, the power that is ruled and restrained. This combination confers on Boland's art the aura of the necessary. (pp. 236-38)

> *R. T. Smith, in a review of "Selected Poems,"*

in Poetry, *Vol. CLVI, No. 4, July, 1990, pp. 236-38.*

FURTHER READING

Reizbaum, Marilyn. "An Interview with Eavan Boland." *Contemporary Literature* XXX, No. 4 (Winter 1989): 471-79. Boland discusses women's poetry and the relationship between feminism and nationalism.

Kate Braverman

1950-

(Full name Katherine Braverman) American poet, novelist, short story writer, and editor.

Braverman is known for poetry and fiction reflecting the physical and social environment of Los Angeles, California. Although Braverman primarily considers herself a poet, critical attention has focused on her fiction, which draws from her verse for its fluid, suggestive language. Characters in such works as *Palm Latitudes* and *Squandering the Blue* are predominantly women who employ highly descriptive language, a distinctive feature of Braverman's fiction. For these characters, the freedom to express themselves through language is often the greatest means of liberation from their highly structured, urban surroundings.

Braverman's first novel, *Lithium for Medea,* addresses problems of drug addiction and illness, topics which often arise in her works. The protagonist, Rose, is involved in a relationship with a manipulative drug addict who keeps her on a cocaine high for most of the novel. Memories and fears surrounding Rose's childhood and a previous marriage provide the central focus of the work as she contemplates the imminent death of her father, who lies in a hospital with cancer, and must interact with her overpowering, successful mother. Although several reviewers found *Lithium for Medea* overwritten and sentimental, many noted that Braverman successfully developed the evocative, urban imagery that marks her later fiction.

In *Palm Latitudes,* Braverman portrays the lives and environments of three Mexican-American women struggling to maintain their femininity in the male-dominated Los Angeles barrio where they now live. Francisca Ramos is a prostitute who feels she cannot contact the family she longs for in Mexico, and Gloria Hernández, who came to Los Angeles as a teenage bride seventeen years earlier, has yet to learn English. Gloria's increasing feelings of isolation from her husband and two sons lead her to stab a neighbor whom she suspects of having an affair with her husband. Unlike the other women, Marta Ortega, a willful matriarch, is connected with the members of her family and community, who come to her for advice and wisdom. Some critics argued that Braverman's depiction of the Los Angeles barrio is oversimplified, casting all Hispanic men as abusive and placing women in the stereotypical roles of mother, wife, and whore. Most reviewers, however, commended Braverman for the rich, imagistic language spoken by her characters. Alan Cheuse observed: "We've had few fiction writers in our tradition who hold an entire book together out of such moonspun inebriation with English [as does Braverman]."

Centering around female characters as well, the stories in *Squandering the Blue* build upon Braverman's earlier themes of illness and isolation. Many of the women deal with drug or alcohol addiction, attempt to reestablish fa-

milial relationships, and encounter AIDS and cancer. The stories are unified by Braverman's characteristic voice, recurring images of the sea and the sky, and descriptions of color and mood. Critics were particularly impressed by *Squandering the Blue*'s evocation of Los Angeles scenery, which is often bleak and harsh in its realism. Sarah Ferguson wrote of the collection: "Never have the gaudy tropical flora of Los Angeles and Hawaii produced such gorgeously poisonous fruit."

(See also *Contemporary Authors,* Vols. 89-92.)

PRINCIPAL WORKS

POETRY

Milk Run   1977
Lullaby for Sinners: Poems   1980
Hurricane Warnings   1987
Postcard from August   1991

NOVELS

Lithium for Medea: A Novel   1979
Palm Latitudes   1988

OTHER

Squandering the Blue   (short story collection)   1990

Katha Pollitt

"I am twenty-seven years old," thinks Rose, the narrator of this first novel [*Lithium for Medea*] by a young California poet, "and a pine tree my age knows more." It certainly does. Rose takes drugs and is in her seventh year of being exploited by Jason, the hippie slumlord and pseudo-painter who replaced her husband, an impotent near-psychotic whose major interest in life was watching *Star Trek*.

"I do more in a day than you do in a year," says Rose's mother, a successful television producer exasperated by her daughter's apparent willingness to spend her life contemplating the weeds in the canals of Venice, Calif.

What is Rose's problem? The disruption of her childhood by her father's cancer and her mother's consequent struggle to support the family? The terrible fights that ended in her parents' divorce? The fact that they talk about her in her presence as though she were not there? The corrupting influence of Los Angeles? All of the above. And Jason and Gerald are no help. When Rose's father is stricken with cancer again, his illness becomes a catalyst for her own enlightenment. The nature of her revelation was not entirely clear to me, but never mind. At least it gets her into her car and out of town.

Unlike her heroine, Miss Braverman clearly has energy to burn. It was passion and a sense of urgency, I think, that led her into the overwriting that clots her pages: cancer is always roots and dark tangles; Los Angeles is "the terminal ward of the world"; Rose, when elated or high, is prone to remarks like, "I am windsong." We make fun of Victorian bombast, but our modern incantatory prose can be just as bad. I found myself skimming many histrionic tributes to the sun, ocean, trees or "that maniac, that cold-hearted, one-white-eyed bitch, the moon."

I had trouble, too, with Rose herself. Her self-pity gets wearisome, and I thought her hippie-mystic search for "blood truths" was way off base. What she needs is more rational intelligence, not less, and when she strangled Jason's cat to placate the god of death and save her father, I felt myself blushing for her. Under the veneer of counter-cultural hip—the drugs, the cool and hot sex, the idleness—is a romanticism that verges on sentimentality.

What saves Rose's story is her parents. They are marvelous. Rose's upwardly mobile mother is shrewd, tough, a survivor; her capacity for love may have been blighted by a Dickensian childhood of orphanages and foster homes, but at least she's game, she's vital. She *does* do more in a day than her daughter does in a year, and she doesn't accept for a minute the truckload of guilt Rose would like to leave at her door. Rose's father, the aging hipster, gambler and sports fanatic, is good, too. There is a wonderful moment toward the end when Rose visits him in the hospital. He is weak, possibly dying, unable to speak. "Lifes [sic] gone so bad," he writes on his pad, to which Rose replies: "Once the gray-haired man was sage. A dispenser of wisdom, revered. . . . That was before industrialization, decay, rot, drugs, free sex." His response: "I was born 30 years too soon. I would have been a hippie."

The vigor with which Miss Braverman has endowed Rose's parents undermines what little sympathy one might otherwise have felt for Rose's attempts to indict them or, worse, "understand" them. While that may not have been the effect Miss Braverman was seeking, it suggests a latent gift for naturalism that I hope she won't neglect. Angst is easy. Only a novelist of real perception and wide sympathies could have invented this pair. (p. 23)

> *Katha Pollitt, "Parables and Problems," in*
> The New York Times, *August 5, 1979, pp. 10,*
> *23.*

Joseph Parisi

Kate Braverman's [poetic] concerns are central—love, sex, and spiritual and mental sustenance, or rather, the lack thereof—but the luscious backgrounds of sunshine and flowers in Los Angeles (that "rented city") belie the profound sadness these poems convey. Incorporating poems from previous works published, [*Lullaby for Sinners: Poems, 1970-1979*] again uses the quasi-autobiographical persona who recalls an unsettling girlhood of neglect, resentment, and self-denigration. The latent self-pity of the unloved child becomes the hard edge of the still-vulnerable woman, trying to escape into drugs, travel, and joyless sex with faithless men who leave her hurt and unsatisfied. Fortunately, Braverman's brilliant imagery raises this material above the clinical, capturing the scene and sense of loss amid the all-too-real grotesqueries of life lived on the edge of madness and despair. There is thus some redemption in this "lullaby," as the self-inflicted wrongs are turned into surreal art.

> *Joseph Parisi, in a review of "Lullaby for Sinners: Poems 1970-1979," in* Booklist, *Vol. 76, No. 20, June 15, 1980, p. 1485.*

Suzanne Juhasz

[The poems in *Lullaby for Sinners: Poems, 1970-1979*] give us a world where lovers are gone and never loved, anyway; where parents, too, are gone, dead, or occupied—their past love irrevocably clumsy. Poems from L.A., a world violent and empty. Violent color, where "Bougainvillaea pushes insistent burgundy / crepe faces snaking up fences and roofs." White emptiness, where "you drift past the last reefs naked / in silk stockings. / Your lungs unfurl white / canvas across white caps / as you sail." Unremittingly, these are poems of the self stripped down to its own isolation, and to words. If all this sounds a little like Sylvia Plath, it is. At times, Braverman echoes both Plath's bravura surrealism and her dry-eyed misery. Yet often enough Braverman has her own images of decay, danger, survival; and they are elegant, unerring, fierce. "Fall rain, fall wind and leaf. / Bring the sudden cold / and abandonment, the loss / of trust, the rush of a shapeless / hungry black space drunk on itself."

Suzanne Juhasz, in a review of "Lullaby for Sinners: Poems, 1970-1979," in Library Journal, *Vol. 105, No. 13, July, 1980, p. 1520.*

Alan Cheuse

Kate Braverman has produced in *Palm Latitudes* an anomalous creation, a novel that proceeds almost solely on the heat generated by its language, by the way in which each of her three major speakers—we should call them oracles rather than characters—delivers her sentences and paragraphs, and sometimes lists of nouns, about the world of La Ciudad de los Angeles, the City of the Angels, where each of them resides. Their city is on fire—"ash . . . falls from the sky" almost constantly—but their city smoulders only because the language of this poet's novel burns.

Consider this cast of characters: a Latin prostitute named La Puta de la Luna ("Moon Whore"), Gloria Hernandez, a housewife driven mad by her husband's supposed adulterous lust for a white social worker who lives next door in the barrio, and Marta Ortega, a grandmother near the end of her life with the gift of speech that seems almost pure imagery.

Where's the plot that comes of this? Nowhere. La Puta de la Luna stalks her street corner, Gloria Hernandez broods a while and then stabs her neighbor, and Marta Ortega exhorts her daughters and their children to see the world as lyric metaphor. Here's a poet's novel then, and a poet in the surrealist tradition, whose women have tongues of silk and sky-rockets.

Hear now the voice of one of Marta's daughters, brooding on her fate in the City of the Angels:

> I am nameless, limbless. It is ice I grown in daggers and sheet and I am a web of gashes and salt is offered me . . . this is a city of dogs, of half-buried bones and anger, of a mean wind aggressive as a lover drunk and thwarted, stumbling where alleys collapse. And I will die without love in this haunted obscure hour of lamplit leaves fallen in deserted culs-de-sac where loss is deafening. . . .

We've had few fiction writers in our tradition who hold an entire book together out of such moon-spun inebriation with English. James Agee did, and so did William Goyen. Among the living writers who call so much attention to the way that they speak that what they say becomes of lesser importance? Cormac McCarthy, for one. And Nicholas Delbanco. But these are lapidary writers, whereas Braverman works with material more evanescent than stone. It's soul she seems to want to make manifest in her vast array of pages filled with lyric lament, the souls of three Chicanas to be exact. And beyond that, the soul of La Ciudad de los Angeles, or at least a major part of it, and the soul of a region she defines as the "palm latitudes"

of her title, "a realm of texture and fragrance where no passport is required" that "stretches from Mexico City and El Salvador, through Havana and Miami, across the islands of the Caribbean, from Caracas to Los Angeles." Its inhabitants appear mainly to be women, and its language is Spanish, which itself, as Gloria Hernandez asserts, is feminine. "English," she muses,

> hurt my lips, the soft fibers of my tongue . . . Spanish flows like the ocean, aware of cycles, waves, completion and return . . . Spanish is the earth were she to choose to grow a mouth. Her lips are as clouds, volcanoes and jungles. Her gestures are as natural as the wind, as the dance of branches and fronds caught in breezes and shadows . . . The border did not lie at Juarez or Mexicali or Tijuana. The border sat at my mouth. . . .

Palm Latitudes is not so much a novel as it is the text of a cantata for three female voices, one of the strangest, bravest, and, depending on your taste, possibly one of the most appealing inventions in recent years. (pp. 6-7)

Alan Cheuse, "Cantata for Three Female Voices," in Chicago Tribune—Books, *July 10, 1988, pp. 6-7.*

Jesús Salvador Treviño

Kate Braverman's second novel, *Palm Latitudes,* is likely to be compared to Latin American "magical realist" writing, since it is filled with rich, surreal imagery and haunting Latino characters. Yet upon closer reading, the novel is more reminiscent of the tradition of North American writers such as John Steinbeck who have chosen the Chicano experience as a vehicle for the expression of their own persona.

Braverman's novel focuses on the limitations placed on women's lives in a male-dominated society and the options open to women who would be masters of their own future. She has narrowed her focus to the Chicano barrio and three Latina archetypes to explore these themes: the disaffected whore, the long-suffering housewife, the earthy, prescient matriarch.

Francisca Ramos is a mid-30-ish prostitute known as *la puta de la luna,* the "whore of the moon." She plies her trade by day and night near the Echo Park lake in Los Angeles. Years ago, she was the kept mistress of a wealthy Mexican businessman. When this *patrón* dismissed her, she began a series of empty encounters with abusive men.

The taste for the high style that she acquired from her worldly *amante* and her unwillingness to work at other jobs have doomed her to a life of prostitution. She survives the repeated abuses of her clients by withdrawing into herself; she has become numb—alienated from her own emotions.

Gloria Hernandez, the mother of two *Chicanitos,* is married to Miguel, a Vietnam veteran with whom she crossed illegally into the United States many years ago. Now, after 17 years of marriage, she has become emotionally estranged from her husband and her children. Miguel's enthusiasm for the English language, which Gloria cannot or will not learn, and his love of sports have erected a wall between them.

Gloria's two sons, José and Carlos, are accomplices to this painful alienation as they assimilate into mainstream American culture. Gloria is the stereotype of the long-suffering housewife enduring in silent anguish, until her husband's overtures to an attractive white neighbor push Gloria over the edge. Her muted disguise of seeming complacency explodes in a frenzy of violent passion. She murders the woman with a kitchen knife.

Completing this barrio triad is the most memorable of Braverman's characters, Marta Ortega, a 75-year-old matriarch known as *la bruja del barrio,* the witch of the neighborhood.

All three women experience pivotal moments when their lives are changed irrevocably. Braverman writes: "You enter a bus, or a plane. You answer a doorbell, a letter, a telephone, and the course of your entire life is changed." In *Palm Latitudes,* abusive men are the ones who usually orchestrate these fundamental life changes. The results are as varied as the spectrum of women's lives. For Francisca, it leads to prostitution. For Gloria it leads to murder. But there is another option. Iconoclastic Marta Ortega is symbolic of women who take their lives into their own hands.

Unlike the other two protagonists of *Palm Lattitudes,* Marta Ortega survives quite well without men. She has opted to rear her two daughters, Angelina and Orquidea, by herself. She dedicates her time to her garden and to reading great literature systematically—by author, from A to Z. Marta Ortega is the strong, accepting and consoling mother-confessor to her daughters and granddaughters.

She is the embodiment of feminine consciousness that refuses to accept men as arbiters of women's lives. It is through her character that the values of independence, sisterhood and mother-daughter bonding are affirmed.

Stylistically, *Palm Latitudes* is a masterfully crafted literary work. It is rich in lyrical, poetic passages, full of sensual metaphors and of evocative, challenging similes.

Braverman's descriptions are often stark and vivid, as in her depiction of the oppressive, windowless environment in which Gloria Hernandez is forced to work:

> A window might tempt a woman to look up for an instant from her work, glance at an escaped sunbeam, an aberrant passing sea gull or a falling brick. A window could beacon attention. They were a danger. A woman might leave her thin, gray metal chair, smash the glass with her fist and scratch an opening wide enough for a body to jump through.

At other times, the images are evocative and sensual, as in the advice that Marta Ortega gives to a granddaughter: "You are freed from the cold geometry of absolute direction, which is an illusion. Let this be a time where time fills itself in, in dogs barking, in drugged insects between hot flowers and the songs of worms and the sweet gossip of stars in a pure black night."

Unfortunately, and what a shame, *Palm Latitudes* is also a novel with serious flaws.

Latino men *and* women are likely to find Braverman's characterizations one-dimensional, offensive and perhaps even racist. Her Manichaean rendering of barrio male-female relations into a struggle between stupid, lazy, abusive, womanizing, drunken Mexican men and alienated, powerless and inarticulate Mexican women fails to grasp the complexities of their three-dimensional humanity.

It also overlooks the subtleties of love, compassion and bonding that have sustained Mexican men and women in the barrio for more than 400 years of colonization. By showing only exaggerated portrayals of Mexican men as *machos,* Braverman diminishes the power of her poetic vision to the level of anti-male rhetoric. By singling out Marta Ortega as the only positive Chicana figure, she overlooks the strength, vitality and love that resides in so many other Chicano life styles.

But despite Braverman's limited insight into the life of barrio women, *Palm Latitudes* is an impressive testament to the magic of language and a powerful rendering of the struggles, defeats and victories of women on their own. (pp. 2, 7)

> *Jesús Salvador Treviño, "Whore, Wife, Matriarch: Three Latinas of the Barrio," in* Los Angeles Times Book Review, *August 7, 1988, pp. 2, 7.*

Alexander Coleman

For some American fiction writers, Los Angeles has for a long time now been thought of as providing a definitive opportunity to describe uprooted characters struggling to survive humanely amid a geography of asphalt, aluminum and glass, made all the more deadening by the notorious blanket of smog. In her second work of fiction [*Palm Latitudes*] the poet and novelist Kate Braverman plunges us into this world with savage intensity, giving us portraits of three Chicana women who live on Flores Street in a barrio of East Los Angeles.

Their lives are depicted as symptomatic of the final destiny of all women condemned to live in what the author calls the "palm latitudes," stretching "from Mexico City and El Salvador, through Havana and Miami, across the islands of the Caribbean, from Caracas to Los Angeles. It is that particular air of slow rotting, that special scented steaming poison masquerading as emeralds, spice, clouds." These latitudes are a specifically Hispanic province of the planet.

In this still heavily *macho* world, Ms. Braverman's Francisca Ramos, Gloria Hernández and Marta Ortega share illusions related to the varying fidelity and reliability of their respective lovers or husbands, Ramón, Miguel and Salvador, among others. But since these men fall away from their cultural heritage (and for many other reasons fail as people), they lurk throughout *Palm Latitudes* as shadowy and sometimes treacherous good-for-nothings.

It is the women who speak to us, telling the story of their

stunted lives on Flores Street. At times they take note of one another's existence, as when Francisca and Marta, with tragic consequences, see Gloria's husband dallying with a gringa social worker. Over too many pages, they express their passionate state of anguish and rage at their outcast state. As different as the three are from one another, they all speak in a heightened, overwrought language intended to contrast dramatically with their physical subjugation to their men, wayward children and alien Anglo surroundings.

The catalogue of their woes can be decidedly repetitious. For instance, early in the book Francisca contemplates an old woman who "has been married, has been installed like an appliance, has been ordered when to speak and when to remain mute." Later, Gloria will complain of the treatment accorded her by her husband and sons, feeling that "I was an appliance they were switching on. They were hungry. They wanted food wrapped in plastic to take to the park . . . where they practiced sports." On another occasion, she notes that "my nerves were the frayed cord of a worn-out appliance, subject to eruptions and sparks. I was obviously short-circuiting."

For these women, imaginative salvation is found in the close but still safely distant Hispanic language and culture—a verbal realm unleashed from the objective demands of the world around them. They think that Spanish is the language of myth, of wholeness, of a possible existence freed from grubby actuality. It is the way out, but to what? Using it, they argue for a vision more human than the brutalities of unbridled male-dominated ambition in an Anglo world. As Gloria says, "I could not bear the sheer weight of the city, its American vastness, and its assertion that the ground was insignificant, obsolete, and that all breathing entities, from the tendrils of infant plants to things winged or limbed, could be eradicated."

In Ms. Braverman's exalted imagination, this world and its agent, the English language, generate the desiccation and sterility the women see all around them. In spite of the misdeeds of the Hispanic male characters, the remembered (or often only imagined) Hispanic milieu and the Spanish language itself are fondly evoked as remnants of a pastoral Eden. As Gloria tells us,

> English hurt my lips, the soft fibers of my tongue. When I repeated English phrases, my mouth embraced unnatural American objects, appliances, concrete, steel girders and electric lights in abnormal abundance and force. I felt violated by traffic, pollution and the abuse of sirens and neon. English was absolute as a world where the forests have been felled, rivers dammed, and each inch of earth parceled, labeled and sold. It was an offense to my aesthetics.

On the other hand, she contends,

> Spanish flows like the ocean, aware of cycles, waves, completion and return. It sculpts the air with tenderness, with the fronds of palms, with moss and beds of vines. It is delicate and discreet, speaking in whispers, incantations and chants. Spanish dances across the tongue, inti-

mate and accomplished, composed of moonlight, cliffs unnamed and lush, moist earth, dusk skies and the arcs inscribed by serpentine migrating stars.

As a concerned reader and teacher of Spanish, however, I must attest that the Hispanic imagination and the Spanish language of the New World are *not* automatically poetic, despite the argument of *Palm Latitudes.* No surprise, then, if Ms. Braverman's novel gives the indelible impression of factitious cultural romanticism. (pp. 22-3)

> *Alexander Coleman, "English Hurt Her Lips," in* The New York Times Book Review, *August 21, 1988, pp. 22-3.*

"I believe a great feminist achievement is to experiment with the language. It was my revolutionary intention in *Palm Latitudes* to rearrange the language, to tropicalize and feminize it. My second goal was to create a world in which there were only women, and only non-Anglo women, and to give these women a mythology, to have the city understood through them."

—Braverman in an interview with Cristin Garcia (*Time,* November 20, 1989)

Michael Harris

The women in Kate Braverman's first collection of short stories [*Squandering the Blue*] seem to have stepped from the works of Joan Didion into another color scheme. The "hard white empty core of the world" in **"Play It as It Lays"** has given way to the green of money, the red of tropical flowers and sunsets, and, above all, blue. Blue is the sea and the sky and the swimming pools of Beverly Hills. Blue also is the blues, the flames of the gas with which poets commit suicide, even the fallout from Chernobyl tinkling down on California as "a kind of blue ice."

Still, we recognize these women. They aren't the Latinas of Braverman's most recent novel, *Palm Latitudes.* They are Didion women: WASPy and skinny and neurotic, prone to nervous breakdowns and chemical dependencies, so overwhelmed with sensibility that they fumble at life's ordinary tasks. They go to AA meetings, wreck cars, agonize over Christmas shopping, write in the Hawaiian jungle, picket a nuclear installation in Nevada, tour Eastern Europe with an alienated daughter, dread cancer and AIDS and being exiled by divorce to live in some shabby apartment. (The men in their lives are creeps who bully and manipulate, deal drugs and take them for rides on the wild side, but don't truly matter.)

Still, color schemes count. There are differences. Didion came to fiction from journalism, Braverman from poetry. Didion's prose has the poise of exhaustion. Her Los Angeles is where the American journey ended; her women draw what strength they have from fading memories of frontier grit. Braverman's Los Angeles is where something corrupt but vital, no longer exclusively American, is being born: "not an absence but a seizure of competing postures and rituals." Her women, despite all their problems, are on the trail of that something; her prose makes sudden jumps into the florid and the visionary.

In fact, Braverman's voice in these 12 stories is quite distinct from Didion's: more inward, less political, symbolically rather than explicitly sexual. What makes them comparable is their authority. As a book, ***Squandering the Blue*** is uneven, and also too much of the same thing. It has too many creative-writing teachers, too much vodka and cocaine, too much *Angst* about turning 40. The color imagery wears on the nerves. Some of the dialogue is impossible. The best stories are those the Braverman woman has to share with someone else: another woman, or one of the creeps, or a child, or her own childhood. But all of them have the Braverman voice, which has become one of L.A.'s most compelling, even when it goes overboard, into the blue.

> *Michael Harris, in a review of "Squandering the Blue," in* Los Angeles Times Book Review, *October 14, 1990, p. 6.*

Kate Braverman   (Interview with Joyce Jenkins)

[Jenkins]: *Just to open up the discussion, you live in Los Angeles; and the colors and landscapes of L.A. form an interior as well as an exterior texture for your work—I want to say background, but it's not background; it's a state of reality, a primary means of perception, for your characters. It's a pretty deep topic to start out with, but could you tell us about that?*

[Braverman]: Well, I love the tropics, and I'm working with the Tropical Princess of Danger motif, as a friend of mine called it. I do see Los Angeles as a ruined tropical kingdom, and I love it in that way. I love the heat; I love the color of Los Angeles; I love the sense of corruption and vitality. And I do believe that geography is destiny, in certain ways, and it ties into how I want to tropicalize and feminize the language. So I think of the landscape in that way. (p. 1)

Kirkus Review *once wrote, "In a bravura performance, Braverman writes of women who drink, drug, and finally turn to A.A. And she makes their stories grippingly fresh and insistent. Language, itself, which tempts and mocks her characters, also becomes the one permitted intoxication." And I find that "one permitted intoxication" note really powerful, the fact that, in your stories, these women have struggled with so much substance abuse, but yet language is what they have left.*

Well, I do still have language. I'm in love with language, I must tell you. I always felt that, as a woman writer—as a writer from Los Angeles, as a latchkey girl child of the shabby streets of Los Angeles, of a city that did not exist in literature, in a region that did not exist, I wanted something to validate my experience when I was younger. And

the only literature that I could find was about boys on fishing trips, or playing polo in Connecticut. And that did not validate my experience. I've always had a sense that, in order to validate your landscape, you must attack language. Language is fire. That's what you must take, particularly as a woman writer, or a writer from a region in exile. (p. 11)

One thing that strikes me about your short stories, in particular, is the frequency with which poetry surfaces—references to poets—does that come primarily from your own background and experiences? Or is there something about that that appeals to you as a vehicle for your fiction?

Well, I'm not sure exactly how to deal with that question. But I did want to write stories about more recognizable characters. I'm just sick and tired of reading these novels and listening to these stories about professors' wives having lunch. I think that every professor's wife having lunch in an American story should be taken out and shot to death, slowly.

I love to read stories about poets, so I'm not complaining. I'm just fascinated by it, and I appreciate it, because real-life writers, not writers that have perfect sets of circumstances, aren't the subjects of fiction very often. Writers as we know them, writers that I would run across at Poetry Flash, *for example . . .*

. . . don't exist. No, because all the writers that exist in American fiction are all women who accept the status quo; they're all women who are successful within the parameters of bourgeois thinking and lifestyle, which repels me. I want to enlarge the scope of characters possible for women. That's why I love my Diana Barrington character. She's a poet, and a single parent—as if things are not tough enough—trying to keep her sanity in Los Angeles and other places. That fit into my idea of the other book I have; a sorceress, Marta Ortega, a Latina sorceress, was the main character in ***Palm Latitudes.*** In the book before that, Rosa is a junkie on the Venice canal. We just expect our women to be middle class, in our fiction. I think that's why women in American fiction are bankrupt.

I am really impressed with your writing. The frequency with which certain words come up over and over again. I see it in your poetry. Words like "architecture," "light," "blue" come up a lot as an abstract concept, not as a description. And that is echoed in your new book of short stories. Of course, it organically happens. But is that intentional at all? You were talking about your poems being sketches, in a sense, for your short stories.

Well, nothing's really intentional. My work is totally organic. But I don't keep a journal. I don't keep a diary. I don't take notes. I just write poetry. That's the primary medium by which I entertain myself in this incarnation. So, later, I'm able to take the poems, and they're compacted, dense masses, like black stars, and I'm able to look at them and see entire stories. Because they are little, condensed universes. I've done novels where I arbitrarily picked up poems written in the same voice and arbitrarily put them down and said, "Okay, this is the spine of the novel." I did that with ***Lithium for Medea*** and then just wrote a narrative between poems. Also, when I'm lost in a longer work, a story, or a novel, and I don't know what to do, I just take a poem, and I throw it in, and it flares up, illuminating the path to take in the infinite, wretched, ghastly, don't-ever-do-it darkness of longer works. (pp. 11, 19)

[You] seem to me, at heart, to be involved, still, with poetry as an art form.

I don't see that there's any line between poetry and prose. I think that that's an arbitrary distinction. I think that's one way the poet is ghetto-ized. Then reviewers are able to say, "Well, it's a poetic novel." So then you don't have to review it, and you don't have to read it, and you don't have to take it seriously. I think, you know, I write poetry; I write short stories; I write novels; I write essays. So I'm here to tell you, you do it one good line at a time. That's all there is. And whether these things in this ultimate fabric become nailed into poems, or expanded into stories, I don't think it's the issue. I think the issue is finding moments. For instance, *Squandering the Blue* is something that I look at as being an unconventional novel. It is a novel without the conventional exists and entrances. It's just going from points of energy along a spectrum. It's a molecular novel, in a way.

Even though you've mentioned that calling **Squandering the Blue** *a 'poetic novel' is an easy way out, it's also very true. What was so moving to me, reading it, was how intuitively, strongly poetic it was. The sensibility is poetic. Your poetry has always, for me, had a very narrative quality—a straightforward, direct, certainly not prosaic, but prose-like quality. I thought that was fascinating, because in some ways your prose is a mirror image of your poetry.*

I was talking to Peter Schneidre of Illuminati Press; he publishes my poetry, and he said, "You know, you're a fascinating writer, because your novels are epic poems, and your poems are mini-novels." And I was really struck. I instantaneously saw the truth of that. I just have got to find forms and then de-conventialize them. I don't know what it is; I just have this flair, to take forms and reinvent them: I think that my talent is just not comfortable in any of the forms. That's probably why I do all of them. Now, in that respect, I though that short stories really were a lot of fun for me to do. Because they have that wonderful quality that a poem does, which is that you feel you're going to live through it. And yet it also has the sustained layerings that a novel has.

I'll tell you something that's interesting. As I began to write them, the short stories that were written piece by piece, I began to understand who and what I was writing about. And when I had about half of them, I began to be consciously aware that they began to talk to each other. They begin inventing their own connections. They begin consorting when you're not looking; they start dating, and doing things. So that's what happened with these people. It always happens. Stuff starts glowing in the dark, and kissing, and talking dirty. Who knows? Anyway. I then consciously knew that I could make them work as bigger works. Some of those stories in the collection only make sense in terms of the larger work of the collection. I think *Squandering the Blue* is an experimental work, and I think

maybe I'm being punished in the reviews a little bit, because it's experimental. Because I think people read it, and they have a sense, 'there's a resonance here.' And there's a subliminal coherence here, but they don't really get what, exactly, it is. Then, there's a tendency to want to deprecate the writer. Even though we're at the end of this millennium, people are still not comfortable with ambiguity.

And poetry is sometimes about ambiguity.

That's all my work is ever about. It's about other things, of course, but I'm deeply comfortable with the ambiguous nature of life on this planet. (p. 19)

What about performing, your work yourself, as I've seen you do before? Is reading your prose an entirely different experience than reading your poetry? Does a more performative aspect come in when you read your poetry? . . .

I read at the punk clubs before there were punk clubs. First I read at the rock clubs, and then later they called them punk clubs. I liked the sense that writing is not something that occurs in a library setting. I like the idea that writing has a kinetic component. For years I would edit my poems at readings. Because your audience never lies. You can hear where they're fading out. You know what works, because you feel an intake and outtake of breath. I love doing that. That's one reason I write everything for the ear. I would much rather be led along by the sound of something than by the logic of something. I think that's a great discovery I made. But that comes from the fact that a writer my age comes out of the rock-and-roll tradition. Now, a writer a little older than me, I think the great innovations that would have affected them would be cinema—flash cuts, and flash forwards, and the image, and the different manipulations that could go on with images. For a writer coming out of the sixties, it certainly seems to me that the art form that would inform our work, on a subliminal level, has certainly gotta be the drive and cadence of rock-and-roll. . . .

Let's talk about "Squandering the Blue" the story, not the entire collection. It is a deeply moving story. As a single mother, poet, divorced person, myself, it had a lot of resonances for me. Are we part of your constituency, part of who you wrote the story for? Women alone, young women poets?

I don't know if you read the story where the woman, her husband is always threatening to divest her of everything. And she has to go out looking for apartments. And she sees that there are no dining rooms anymore, when she leaves her big house. There are just living rooms. Because we don't eat as families, together, anymore. We just stand; we grab food out of refrigerators, or we sit on the floor in front of television. It's a world where you don't need a dining room, 'cause you don't cook and you have no families. It's just a world of women, alone with children.

It's about the legacy of the sixties. I had no idea that the kind of stamina and integrity that I was going to need to be a true woman writer was going to have the cost that it has had, in my life. And that to build the new world that we talked about building, in Berkeley, in the sixties, was going to have to be built with your fingers bleeding, by yourself, under an abscess of moon. I didn't know it was going to be like that. I think that my characters have some of that residue. So there is that sense, I think. Are these my people, women alone with children, who read books? Women who write poetry? Women who live in Northern and Southern California? Women who have loved mad hippies, like the Derek character—mad, mad, drug addict, drug dealer, alcoholic, hippie guys smelling of the jungle. Oh, I think that's part of my constituency. I think that all these women are incarnations of all of us, and that what I wanted to do in this book was write about everyday women. These women were not supposed to be brilliant women, like my sorceress, in *Palm Latitudes.* These are the women I know, [who come] out of the collective mythology of AA, out of the collective mythology of my experience as an American woman. What interests me is the resistance that there is to this, to the times in which we live. I think there's a lot of denial. (p. 20)

> *Kate Braverman and Joyce Jenkins, in an interview in* Poetry Flash, *No. 213, December, 1990, pp. 1, 11, 19-20.*

West Coast Review of Books

In the mood for a rollicking, upbeat comedy? Then [*Squandering the Blue*] is not for you. But if you wish to savor the written word at its very best, try reading Kate Braverman. Long known for her magnificent and relevant poetry, Braverman has hitherto produced two compelling (if not "commercial") novels. Now she groups together a series of short stories that cannot fail to move.

Emphasis, as always, is on women, young and not so young. Themes of drug and alcohol addiction, psychotic episodes, terminal cancers, run through the stories, yet the overall mood leaves one not so much depressed as impressed. Impressed with Braverman's use of the English language, her ability to create haunting mood pieces, her

unforgettable descriptive passages. As in her novels, the scene is mainly the one the author knows so well—the City of Angels. There are repeated images of Hawaii, the blue of the ocean, of the sky, of the fauna, and occasionally we are taken abroad, but it is images of Los Angeles that linger most vividly.

Admittedly, these are not upbeat pictures, but they are full of jarring reality and insight. A curious thread runs throughout; at times we are uncertain who is speaking until well into the story. There are grandmothers, mothers, daughters and, above all, friends. These relationships endure the most difficult times, see their victims through crisis after crisis.

It will be difficult for this critic to erase the images of a lower class, "cement" apartment building in Palms during the fifties, where (surely) the author grew up. Here in West Los Angeles, schoolchildren were divided into two groups—those whose mothers stayed at home, and the latchkey children, whose mothers went to work. Fathers stayed behind in wheelchairs, trying to recover from chemo treatments. And who could fail to be moved by the affluent housewife, trading an upper-class life in a splendid hillside home for a dreary apartment complex in the San Fernando Valley, in her effort to escape a loveless marriage? Or the mother trekking through the Russian plains with her uncaring daughter, in her fruitless effort to bring meaning and bonding into their lives?

This is powerful stuff, a joy to read. And if occasionally Ms. Braverman gets carried away by her sheer love of language (she must have her wrists slapped for overworking the word "stasis," to mention but one), she is surely to be forgiven. (pp. 28-9)

> *A review of "Squandering the Blue," in* West Coast Review of Books, *Vol. 16, No. 1, February-March, 1991, pp. 28-9.*

David Grossman

1954-

Israeli novelist, nonfiction writer, journalist, and short story writer.

Considered one of Israel's most promising young authors, Grossman is an inventive writer whose work has been compared to that of Gabriel García Márquez and Günter Grass for its complexity and self-reflexiveness. While some critics fault Grossman for verbose and overmannered prose, most concur that he deals imaginatively with such important topics as the Arab-Israeli conflict and the aftereffects of the Holocaust among surviving Jews and their families. Grossman, who writes in Hebrew, first attained prominence in English-speaking countries with *The Yellow Wind,* a nonfiction account of his travels and interviews primarily with Palestinians in the Israeli-occupied territories on the West Bank of the Jordan River. Originally conceived as an article for the liberal newsweekly *Koteret Rashit* on the twentieth anniversary of the occupation, the piece was expanded by Grossman into a book that became a best-seller in Israel. *The Yellow Wind* documents the profound hatred and grief the occupation has ingrained in the Palestinians as well as their unyielding belief that only destructive force can help them reclaim their avowed homeland. The book's title refers to the yellow wind, or *rih asfar*—the hellish east wind that reputedly comes every few generations to annihilate those who have committed cruel and wrongful acts. Grossman concludes that the occupation has damaged Israel as much as it has harmed the Palestinians. *The Yellow Wind* provoked controversy among Israelis for its sympathetic depiction of the Palestinians' plight; some commentators maintained that Grossman had presented a distorted picture of the situation by comparing the Arabs' exile to the persecution of Jews throughout history.

Written prior to *The Yellow Wind,* Grossman's first novel, *Hiyuch ha-gedi (The Smile of the Lamb),* is a political fable based on the modern predicament of Arabs living under the domination of Israel's military government. *The Smile of the Lamb* portrays the complex interrelationships of four distinct narrators as they attempt to distinguish truth from falsehood and right from wrong. The story concerns Uri, an idealistic Israeli soldier stationed in an Arab town who doubts the morality of his country's policies; his wife Shosh, a psychotherapist responsible for the suicide of one of her adolescent patients, who leaves Uri and has an affair with Katzman, a cynical Holocaust survivor; and Khilmi, an Arab mystic-storyteller whose son is killed by Israeli troops. After the death, Uri abandons his unit and joins Khilmi to tell him the news but is held hostage by Khilmi, who threatens to kill Uri if the occupiers do not leave the town. Joseph Coates commented: "Grossman's expert deployment of delayed revelations by a chorus of different voices makes his moral search for meaning as suspenseful as a thriller—and as chilling."

Grossman's second novel, *See Under: Love,* is an intricate, metafictional work about the effects of the Holocaust on the human psyche and the difficulty of writing about this atrocity. Initially set in Israel in the 1950s, *See Under: Love* first focuses on nine-year-old Momik Neuman's attempts to alleviate his parents' traumatization after their experiences in concentration camps. Each of the volume's four sections is written in a different style: childlike fantasy; the overly formal nineteenth-century Hebrew style as practiced by such authors as Avraham Schlonsky and Natan Alterman; magic realism; and the literary encyclopedia. The plot follows Momik as he matures into a writer and travels to Gdansk, Poland to search for the ghost of Jewish author Bruno Schulz, who was murdered by Nazis in 1942. In Gdansk, Momik learns of his deranged great-uncle Anshel Wasserman, a famous children's author. The novel's most successful section is generally considered to be Momik's reinvention of Wasserman's life, in which he is portrayed as a storyteller to Nazi Commandant Neigel in the manner of Scheherazade. After each story, Wasserman asks to be killed, but neither bullets nor poison gas have any effect on him. By writing this allegory, Momik, and by extension Grossman, illustrates the redemptive power of art and that individuality can exist despite genocide. In a review of *See Under: Love,* Alan Mintz observed: "Throughout all of the stories-within-stories and multiple frames of reference in this complex and complicated work, one challenge is presented again and again, and it has to do with the attempt of the imagination . . . to redeem the suffering of the past by, in a sense, rewriting it."

PRINCIPAL WORKS

NOVELS

Hiyuch ha-gedi   1983
  [*The Smile of the Lamb,*   1991]
*See Under: Love   1989

OTHER

The Yellow Wind   (nonfiction)   1988

*Originally published in Israel in 1986.

Christopher Lehmann-Haupt

Early last year, the young Israeli novelist David Grossman received an enviable assignment. He was commissioned by the newsweekly *Koteret Rashit* to undertake a seven-week journey on the West Bank of the Jordan River, and, in recognition of the 20th anniversary of Israel's occupation of the territory, to write an issue-length report on his findings and impressions.

He would visit Palestinian camps and Jewish settlements. He would talk to old people and children, soldiers and students, storekeepers and laborers. He would weigh objectively the conflicting claims of all sides in what has become one of the world's greatest social tragedies.

He went, as he puts it near the end of *The Yellow Wind* because "the worn sentences that I used like so many other people, though true, seemed now to be something else: like the walls of a penitentiary that I built around a reality I do not want to know; like jailers I stationed in order to protect myself from a gray world now repugnant to me."

He continues: "Suddenly I discovered that some jailers and criminals create—after years of living together and becoming accustomed to each other—unholy alliances. But I am in great danger from this, too, so I wanted to go to the places which most haunted me." He wanted to go, as he concludes somewhat uneuphoniously, into "the heart of the harsh clash between Jew and Arab."

The result of his undertaking, like the diction of that last sentence, strikes dissonant notes. To Mr. Grossman's credit, his report opens our eyes to certain perceptions. He reveals the double-mindedness of many refugees: how the beauty of their memories of the land grows as the squalor of their present living conditions deepens, and how the widening of that split serves to feed their desire for violence. ("Understand," a young schoolteacher tells the au-

thor. "We are against Arafat, because Arafat wants peace. We want a solution by force. What was taken by force will be returned by force. Only thus.")

He dramatizes the subtle ways in which, he believes, the experience of occupation is corrupting Israelis, although the most eloquent passages he quotes on this subject come from George Orwell's famous essay on colonialism, "Shooting an Elephant."

Best of all, he shows that on both sides of the conflict there are thoughtful, sensitive, intelligent human beings. And he puts us readers directly [in] touch with them. Yet he does not finally believe such people can resolve the crisis simply by their existence. "There are those who say," he writes, that "over the years the 'fabric of life' (mutual acquaintance, economic links, and so on) will overcome enmity. That is idiocy, and reality proves it even now. As long as the present 'fabric of life' continues, it is wrapped around an iron fist of hate and revenge."

Some solution must be imposed, he implies, otherwise, as one old Arab tells him, the yellow wind will come from the gate of hell—

> *rih asfar,* it is called by the local Arabs, a hot and terrible east wind which comes once in a few generations, sets the world afire, and people seek shelter from its heat in the caves and caverns, but even there it finds those it seeks, those who have performed cruel and unjust deeds, and there, in the cracks in the boulders, it exterminates them, one by one.

Unfortunately, as must be evident from this sentence, even Mr. Grossman's more lyrical passages have a tendency to stumble and grope, lending the whole of his book an oddly unfocused quality, where it wants the clarity of an Albert Camus or a V. S. Naipaul. This may simply be a matter of translation. . . .

Yet there are other passages that even a decent translation would not have saved. . . .

And in his chapter on the harassment of Arabs by Israelis at one of the bridges that cross between the West Bank and Jordan, Mr. Grossman visits the site on a relatively tension-free day, describes a scene of bureaucratic oppression not much worse than what goes on at Manhattan's motor vehicles bureau, and concludes with a sense of outrage that we ought to have seen it when it's bad, or words to that effect. Just lazy reporting.

If gravity of subject were the sole criterion of a book's merit, then *The Yellow Wind* would be a masterpiece. But though he provides food for thought on a tragic theme, Mr. Grossman fails to mobilize the energy, resourcefulness and language that the Israeli-Palestinian impasse deserves. The result is an ordinary book that is all the more disappointing given the high expectations its grave subject creates.

Christopher Lehmann-Haupt, in a review of "The Yellow Wind," in The New York Times, *March 3, 1988, p. C29.*

Walter Reich

If the startling power of the riots in the West Bank and Gaza can teach us anything, it is that the conflict that produced them can't be understood merely in political, diplomatic or military terms.

For decades, Middle East specialists, reporters and commentators told us who was meeting with whom, who was refusing to meet with whom, which faction of which party had rejected which item of which proposal and how much support one group or government was getting from another group or government. The information flowed in torrents into minds long numbed by claims and counterclaims, by rumors of initiatives and deadlocks and by partisans offering positions already fossilized many years, and many wars, ago.

But in all this hectic flood of fact and opinion, we learned only the form of the conflict, its size and status. We didn't learn much about its meaning, and even less about its likely fate. That fate, and the meaning from which it derives, can only be learned from the hearts of those enmeshed in the struggle. In the reporting during the recent riots, we began to get some glimpses of those hearts. But it's only the appearance of *The Yellow Wind* by David Grossman that enables us, finally, to enter those hearts, peer inside and learn their terrible secrets.

To be sure, there are reasons for caution in reading this book. For one thing, it's only some of the relevant hearts—those of the Palestinians, and especially those of the Palestinian refugees—that Mr. Grossman really enables us to enter. Also, Mr. Grossman wrote his book with an Israeli audience in mind. In addition, as brilliant and evocative as he is, Mr. Grossman stands toward the left end of the Israeli political spectrum, and his book presents what is, in fundamental ways, only a partial vision. Still, even the most cautious readers—and even the most hostile—are bound to learn something about the conflict that they never knew before, something that illuminates the news and the reality that produces it, something that explains what is and may yet be, something deep and achingly, damningly, true. (pp. 1, 26)

The title Mr. Grossman chose for [*The Yellow Wind*] was given to him by an old Arab who, in 1972, together with other Arabs, was invited by the Israeli Government, after a quarter of a century as a refugee in the West Bank, most of it spent under Jordanian occupation, to resettle the site of his original village in Israel. The Arab's life as a refugee had been hard, but, back in his village, he felt once again like a human being. Mr. Grossman wonders whether the return might have made him and his fellow returnees hate Israelis any less. As if in answer, the old Arab, Abu Harb, tells Mr. Grossman about *rih asfar,* the yellow wind, which, as Mr. Grossman explains, is

> a hot and terrible east wind which comes once in a few generations, sets the world afire, and people seek shelter from its heat in the caves and caverns, but even there it finds those it seeks, those who have performed cruel and unjust deeds, and there, in the cracks in the boulders, it exterminates them, one by one. After that day, Abu Harb says, the land will be covered with bo-

dies. The rocks will be white from the heat, and the mountains will crumble into a powder which will cover the land like yellow cotton.

Thus is presented the book's central image, an image of fiery, total, endless, implacable, apocalyptic hatred, an image built, in one way or another, stated or unstated, in interview after interview, chapter after chapter.

And right from the start. The book opens in Deheisha, a refugee camp in the West Bank, between Jerusalem and Hebron, the home of some 12,000 souls and the site of recent rioting. Most of the residents have lived their entire lives in the camp, with only their parents, or grandparents, remembering firsthand the villages in Israel they fled during the 1948 fighting between the newly established Jewish state and the Arab countries that invaded to destroy it.

But if there's little firsthand memory, there's much that's secondhand and thirdhand, memory turned into pining, keening myth. Nothing is as good now as it was then, back *there.* (p. 26)

For the refugees from the part of Palestine that became Israel—a minority of the Palestinians in the West Bank but a majority of those in Gaza—reality stopped at the moment of Palestinian exodus in 1947 and 1948; generations continued, and time, but, Mr. Grossman suggests, not real, living life, even for those born decades later. For those who fled—for those who were not absorbed by the Arab countries but were kept by them in refugee camps as a reproach to the world and told constantly that they must wait there until Israel was destroyed and they could return—waiting was everything. And waiting became everything for their children as well, and for their grandchildren, and now, under Israeli occupation, their great-grandchildren—waiting, holding on and, Mr. Grossman repeatedly shows us, hating. "We will not change," is their message, as Mr. Grossman read it during his visit early last year. "We will remain before you like a curse cast in cement."

The static quality of that curse may have undergone a transformation in recent months, a change prodded not only by the recognition that their salvation won't come from their fellow Arabs, but also that it won't come from waiting. We can see, from Mr. Grossman's account, that these lessons are absorbed early in the refugee camps. Visiting a Deheisha kindergarten, Mr. Grossman asks one of its two young refugee teachers, "And who will help you return to your village—Arafat?"

"Arafat? Arafat is bourgeois," one says. "He drives a Mercedes. He doesn't feel the suffering of the refugees. All the Fatah commanders have houses in Syria and the Gulf states. Arafat has no supporters here. Only we can represent ourselves."

"And if Arafat achieves a political settlement?" Mr. Grossman asks. "There is talk now of an international conference, you know."

"Understand," a teacher replies. "We are against Arafat, because Arafat wants peace. We want a solution by force. What was taken by force will be returned by force. Only thus."

Little wonder, then, that a 2-year-old child should get up suddenly in that class, point a plastic stick at Mr. Grossman and shoot him. " 'Who do you want to shoot?" the teachers ask, smiling, like two mothers taking pride in a smart child. 'Jews.' " It is these children, or their slightly older siblings, who have learned that through rocks and gasoline bombs they may yet achieve their own salvation. And it is such children, and their parents and teachers, who may have developed political conclusions regarding who should represent them, or who should not, that may be more widely held than the positions articulated by the Palestinian intellectuals to whom most reporters usually speak—positions that almost invariably identify the P.L.O. as the sole, legitimate representative of the Palestinians in the West Bank and Gaza.

But Mr. Grossman goes beyond kindergarten. He enters zones of ordinary Palestinian life under occupation and recounts the griefs and humiliations of a people whose hatred for the Israelis has grown as the occupation has dragged on.

Mr. Grossman's capacity to make this journey—indeed, the energy that mobilizes him to make it—stems, in large measure, from his readiness to see in the Palestinian experience parallels to the Jewish one. The refugees' all-powerful dream of the return reminds him of the vow, "Next year in Jerusalem," uttered by Jews through two millenniums of exile. (pp. 26-7)

Little wonder, then, that Mr. Grossman, the Israeli Jew, is able to sustain, with such determination and fidelity, his empathy for Palestinians, even those who wish to kill him—and little wonder, too, that he finds the refusal to adopt such empathy a flaw in the West Bank Jewish settlers with whom he engages in rancorous disputation. For him, one of the greatest ironies of the Zionist experience is the fact that it has reversed the Jews' traditional role, consistent through thousands of years, of being the powerless and victimized figures in world history.

Another irony of the Zionist experience for Mr. Grossman is that it has resulted in an occupation that has damaged the occupier no less, perhaps, than it has the occupied. By maintaining control over unwilling Palestinians without granting them political rights, by employing a two-level system of justice, one for its citizens and one for the Palestinians under occupation, by having to repress them with force in order to stop their violent opposition, Israel, Mr. Grossman says, is destroying its own democratic soul.

But perhaps the greatest irony is one that Mr. Grossman doesn't note but that emerges from every chapter—the irony that, if he's right, then he has undermined the solution to the problem that most of us will deduce from his writing.

To be sure, Mr. Grossman doesn't spell out a solution, and some readers might object to any effort to draw political conclusions from a novelist's impressionistic reportage. Still, whatever his professional identity, Mr. Grossman has written a nonfiction work about a real and acute political situation, a book designed to teach and to affect the reader's perspective; and it's therefore a political work, no matter how he might want it to be read, has political impli-

cations and must be read from a political as well as artistic perspective. Ultimately, it becomes evident that Mr. Grossman believes that the occupation has already deeply damaged what is best in Israel and that if it goes on it may well destroy what is left. Based on this logic and these observations, many readers, desperate for a solution, will conclude that ending the occupation now, perhaps by almost any means, is, whatever the danger, preferable to allowing the damage to go on.

But such a solution—whether or not Mr. Grossman is willing to take responsibility for favoring it is simply unrealistic if everything that he shows us is correct. For if the refugees among the Palestinians will never be satisfied, or even feel like real people, unless they can return *to their original villages,* and if it's really true that they are as full of hate for Jews as Mr. Grossman depicts, and so willing to wait forever to achieve their revenge, then *no* solution that the Israelis can devise, including a fast and complete march out of the West Bank, would be enough. Even after such a unilateral action, the refugees, the reader becomes convinced by Mr. Grossman's descriptions of them, would devote their lives, and make use of the new opportunities available to them, to liberating their homeland, which is to say pre-1967 Israel. And in this effort they would, presumably, be aided, and led, by the much larger group of refugees outside of Palestine, in Syria, Jordan and elsewhere—the group that, even before Israel occupied the West Bank and Gaza, produced the P.L.O. in order to liberate not the West Bank and Gaza but Jaffa, Haifa and Lydda.

And it is, finally, Mr. Grossman's unwillingness to see the problem whole, and to imagine the possibilities in all their parts, that give *The Yellow Wind* both its greatest power and its most crippling limitations.

To many Israelis, the nightmare comes easy: a Palestinian state is established in the West Bank and, on the other side of Israel, Gaza. Israel's exquisite geographic vulnerability returns. Hundreds of thousands of Palestinian refugees flow into the new state, including all of the Palestine Liberation Organization fighters. Calls grow ever louder for the sacred liberation of the rest of Palestine. Constant shellings, infiltrations and terrorism ensue. Israeli Arabs, who form the majority of the population in the western Galilee, which was not assigned to Israel by the 1947 United Nations partition plan but was won by it during the 1948 war, mount incessant riots, demanding self-determination and union with the Palestinian state—a demand supported at the United Nations by the third world and the East bloc. Shellings and infiltrations from the Palestinian state grow worse. Beirut-style chaos develops there as factions of the P.L.O. massacre one another. The Syrians intervene. A massive war follows, involving a panoply of Arab powers. And tens of thousands of deaths, perhaps hundreds of thousands, result on both sides, with Israel, if it wins, ultimately re-occupying the West Bank and Gaza—an occupation greeted by worldwide condemnation, including that of America, since what is now being occupied are not disputed territories but a state.

If Mr. Grossman had been inclined to be driven by such a nightmare—a nightmare that is, in several of its parts, no more unlikely than many other possible outcomes of an Israeli withdrawal from the West Bank and Gaza—then his imagination would have been as seared by fright as the imaginations of many other Israelis, and his readiness to empathize and become the harp of the Palestinians' terrible song would have been rendered impossible. By not succumbing to that nightmare, Mr. Grossman was able to summon up the extraordinary human capacity—evident in one segment of the Israeli population but not yet developed, perhaps for understandable reasons, among the Palestinians—of being able to step into the enemy's shoes and feel his fears and his pain. But in doing so, he has also chosen to embrace feeling and humanity and art, and to let go of, to what may be a fatal extent, at least to his own people, a full appreciation of brutal, even deadly, reality.

In the end, it is both capacities—the capacity for empathy as well as the capacity to accept the cataclysmic possibilities of reality—that the Israelis will have to have, as well as the Palestinians, if they are ever to find some way of living alongside each other without endless fear and endless rage. So far, a decisive portion of neither side has managed to achieve both capacities. Whether *The Yellow Wind* will help the Israelis achieve them is unclear. We can at least hope that it will—and hope, too, that a Palestinian David Grossman, capable of feeling the Israelis' predicament as keenly as the Jewish David Grossman feels that of the Palestinians', will someday emerge to lead his people on the dangerous, imaginative and necessary journey to empathy and reconciliation. (p. 27)

> Walter Reich, "Endless Fear and Endless Hate?" in The New York Times Book Review, *March 6, 1988, pp. 1, 26-7.*

Glenn Frankel

[*The Yellow Wind*'s] publication in the United States is as timely and important as its appearance in Israel was [in 1987]. Instead of shining a searchlight on a forgotten corner of Israeli society, it now fills in for outsiders some of the blanks and gaping holes between the headlines on what has again become one of the world's most important and troubling stories—the struggle between Arab and Jew in the hallowed, bloodstained, unyielding ground that both claim for a homeland.

David Grossman wandered the West Bank for seven weeks last year, long before the Palestinian uprising began in December, and his strengths are his novelist's eye for detail, his ability to tell a story through his characters and his passionate need to grope with the human dimension of an occupation that he sees as a cancer on his beloved country. For those of us who regularly visit and write about the West Bank, there are many familiar faces—the angry young stone throwers, the refugee camp dwellers, the workers, the collaborators, the human rights lawyer, the middle-aged moderate, the innocent Jewish victim of terrorism. And familiar stories—the indignity inflicted on the prominent family man body-searched by smart-mouthed young soldiers at a checkpoint, the agonized cries of a small girl whose doll is confiscated at a customs station even after it has been thoroughly dismantled and

checked for explosives because, as an Army officer puts it, "We cannot make exceptions."

Sometimes the book is a simple human cry of pain, sometimes a roaring diatribe. Its best moments are both. "Start thinking about us not as your Arabs, asses that anyone can ride, people without honor," pleads Taher, the moderate businessman. "Start thinking about us as your future neighbors."

What Grossman attempts to do here is similar to what Amos Oz, an older and more experienced Israeli novelist, succeeded in doing in his *In the Land of Israel*—to tell the story of where his country stands today through the mouths and experiences of those he meets. Oz was more successful because his eye was even sharper than Grossman's and because he was able to capture accurately but with great empathy the visions and attitudes of all his characters, even those whose views he clearly found outrageous.

Grossman often succeeds, but he sometimes fails to get as close to his Arab characters as Oz got to his Israeli ones, nor does he always have the patience. The fanaticism and lack of self-doubt among Jewish settlers, for example, so annoys Grossman that he simply cannot keep himself from lecturing us about them and from making clear his own sense of moral superiority to them.

His best chapter is about Gidi, an agent of the Shin Bet security service who returns to the Arab village he oversees a few days after the birth of his first son. Gidi seeks to find someone in the town in whom he can confide his news. But no one fits. Either he has no respect for those he meets or, in the case of the one aloof villager he decides to tell, the resident holds him in barely concealed contempt. He leaves, telling no one.

It is a complex moment. Beyond the simple theme of mutual dependency and contempt, it is also about the gradual loss of innocence of both the agent and his subjects and about the ways the occupation has destroyed some of the humanity of both ruler and ruled. "Gidi wondered who was guilty, he or other people, in that he could no longer believe in anybody, or in anything visible, or in the simple emotions which had become in his trained hands handles to be pulled and pushed."

In the end, for Grossman as for Gidi, the occupation remains above all a personal matter. That is ultimately the richness and meaning of the book. One can debate endlessly the security merits of the territories for Israel, one can sketch dry, lifeless political scenarios on legal pads. But the personal cost, the vertigo of conquest, is undeniable and terribly sad.

"We have lived for 20 years in a false and artificial situation, based on illusion, on a teetering center of gravity between hate and fear, in a desert void of emotion and consciousness, and the passing time turns slowly into a separate, forbidding entity hanging above us like a suffocating layer of yellow dust," writes Grossman. "From this point of view, nothing matches the occupation as a great personal challenge. As a personal crossroads demanding action and thought."

Glenn Frankel, "Heartbreak at the Edges of Israel," in Book World—The Washington Post, *March 20, 1988, p. 5.*

Gregory Baum

[In *The Yellow Wind*] David Grossman reveals what life is like in the occupied territories, for Palestinians and for Jews, by recording in a simple, reflective style his own encounters and conversations with ordinary people. His brilliant prose makes readers feel that they have been there, that they know these people and have heard their voices.

This beautiful book is deeply disturbing. What Grossman discovers is that the occupation of the territories is producing a destructive, self-damaging transformation of Palestinians and Israelis. The memory of repeated military violence and the daily humiliations created by the occupation—a humiliation that affects all, from the simple peasants to the successful merchants—has produced in the Palestinians an abiding hatred for Israel and all it stands for. The Israelis are seen as the foreign invaders who govern with the instruments and weaponry of the West.

The occupation transforms the Israelis into conquerors, sometimes unwilling and reluctant conquerors, who impose military rule according to military justice. Grossman shows how Israelis are changed almost against their will. The occupied have power over the occupier. They, the powerless, not only make the army brutal but also gradually turn its beloved Israel into a racist society. (pp. 309-10)

David Grossman believes in Israel. That is why he has written this book. But he fears the ongoing occupation of the territories has created a dynamic that leads to the self-destruction of two peoples. This dynamic is "the yellow wind." At certain times, according to an Arab legend, a yellow wind comes from the gates of Hell, a hot and terrible east wind that sets the world afire: and even when people seek shelter from the heat in underground caves, the yellow wind will find its way to them, seek those who have performed cruel and unjust deeds, and suffocate them one by one.

The Palestinians believe that the unjust treatment inflicted on them by the Israeli government is intended to make them want to leave and seek refuge elsewhere. Against this policy the Palestinians have adopted the policy of "sumud," which means hanging on and hanging in, steady and patient resistance. What they fear is that if the present Israeli policy turns out to be unsuccessful, the government will look for a final solution of the Palestinian problem, that is mass expulsion of the entire people. David Grossman allows us to meet Israelis who already dream of this final solution. Will their number grow?

Grossman's conclusion is dark. He fears that the status quo will continue. It is perhaps too painful for Israelis to look reality in the face and recognize the self-destructive dynamism produced by the occupation.

This message has certainly been heard by a number of prominent American and Canadian Jews. They argue that it is time for North American Jews, in solidarity with Isra-el, to denounce the occupation and support those groups in Israel who stand against the present government's policy. . . .

Conscious of the history of Christian anti-Semitism and the church's silence during the Holocaust, many Christians have tended to refrain from criticizing Israel. More than that, the Jewish establishment has often denounced critics of Israeli policies as anti-Semites. Yet today many Jews recognizing the present danger plead with North Americans, be they Jewish or Christian, to defend the human rights of Palestinians and speak out against the occupation in solidarity with Israel's best interests. This, as I see it, is the historical context of David Grossman's moving book. (p. 310)

Gregory Baum, "No Shelter from Scorn," in Commonweal, *Vol. 115, No. 10, May 20, 1988, pp. 309-10.*

Marshall Berman

David Grossman's *The Yellow Wind* belongs to [a] literary genre that has flourished in Israel over the past decade: something we might call the search for self through dialogue. Amos Oz, Lesley Hazleton, Haim Chertok and the Egyptian Sana Hassan, among others, have written impressively in this vein. This is a literature of existential crisis, experienced from the left. After reading [Mitchell Cohen's] *Zion and State,* we can see it as a return of the passionate quest for identity that the official left has long repressed. In this genre, cracks and conflicts in Israel's identity are fused with the author's uncertainty about his or her own. The author/narrators hope to find themselves through encounters with Israelis and Arabs who are defined as the religious, cultural, ideological Other—often, as their mortal enemy. The resonance of this quest in Israeli culture derives from its connection with one of the creators of that culture, the existentialist philosopher Martin Buber. According to Buber, honest, penetrating, open-ended dialogue between "I" and "thou" is the act that makes us human. The refusal of dialogue, the denial that there is anything to say, is a primary way for an individual or a society to stop being human. For obvious reasons, works in this genre tend to feature dialogue, or attempts at dialogue, between Jews and Palestinians. But many of the most anguished attempts, and the most brutal rejections, take place between Jew and Jew. (p. 742)

The Yellow Wind is a study, made in early 1987, of Israel's occupation of the West Bank and what it has done to people, occupied and occupier alike. Grossman starts with the occupied, and visits the Deheisha refugee camp near Hebron. He finds a family who will talk with him, and a remarkable conversation takes place. The old lady of the family, proud in her fatalism after a life of work and suffering, reminds him of his Polish grandmother. This situation could be dissipated in a sentimental blur, but he has the chutzpah to say it, and the old lady sees the connection immediately and reflects on it, and goes on to speak almost as if the grandmother were there with them. She, and many other Palestinians he encounters, express an impressive range of feelings toward him and other Israelis. She gets angry about how little Israelis—but also, perhaps, her own grandchildren—know of her people and her past: "Culture! You people don't know that we have culture! You can't understand this culture. It's not a culture of television!"

> Suddenly she is completely emptied of her anger: once again her face takes on an expression of defeat, of knowing all, the ancient signs written on the faces of the old: "The world is hard, hard . . . " She nods her head in bitter sorrow, her eyes close themselves off from the small, dark room: "You can't understand. You can't understand anything. Ask, maybe, your grandmother to tell you."

Apart from the literary talent that enables Grossman to bring this old lady to life, he has a gift for empathy, a sweetness and openness that enables him to get close to people at the point where their life comes flowing out of them. (Anyone who has ever done interviews, a frustrating activity in which, so often, nothing is revealed, can appreciate this gift.) Grossman goes on to argue, as Israeli doves often argue, that Jews are now doing to Palestine what a legion of oppressors through the ages have done to Jews. But he doesn't have to argue the point, because he has made it live. The old lady has become part of our families, whether we want her around or not.

Many of the book's scenes present the occupation in searing detail: a family's home blown up by the Israeli Army because someone in the family has been arrested, even though the man was released immediately without charge; the soldiers on Allenby Bridge conducting strip-searches of old people, opening every baby's diaper to search for hidden explosives (once they actually found some), confiscating every toy and doll, even those that have passed inspection, who knows why, it's policy; a court-martial in which it is obvious to everyone in the room, including the prosecutor and judge, that the prisoner is innocent, but he has to be found guilty of something lest his false imprisonment embarrass the government. So it goes. These scenes are said to have created a sensation when Grossman presented them in a series of newspaper articles last spring. In recent months we have seen many scenes like them, and worse, on television. But they have deeper resonance when told in an author's voice that fuses a prophet's passionate anguish with a novelist's precision of detail. (pp. 742-43)

The Yellow Wind is full of great dialogue. But many of the most poignant moments in the book are about the failure of dialogue. At the kindergarten of the Deheisha refugee camp, the smiling young teachers encourage their 2-year-olds to play at shooting Jews, and tell them that this is what they will do when they grow up. When Grossman asks them if there couldn't be another way, beyond bringing up generation after generation in hatred, they insist passionately that there cannot, must not, be another way. They pour out venomous abuse against Yasir Arafat because they believe he wants peace. And they say they have a responsibility to the suffering of the past, to make sure that there will be no reconciliation in the future.

But the failures of dialogue are not with Arabs alone. Grossman asks [a Palestinian named] Taher whether he

isn't afraid that there will be a Beirut-style bloodbath on the West Bank after Israel leaves. Taher admits that this might well happen, and he knows that he would be a likely victim if it does. However, he adds, "there will be a second Beirut among you as well, because your debate over us, about the territories, is what keeps you from the real disagreements you have among you, which you haven't pursued for twenty years." Here Grossman's Arab friend touches on his deepest fear: The struggles between Jews and Arabs may turn out to be more soluble and less tragic than the gulf between Jews and Jews.

This conclusion is suggested in Grossman's account of his futile attempts to enter into dialogue with West Bank settlers and followers of the Gush Emunim. His great gift for empathy and his desire for communication can't get to first base in their ball park.

Grossman pays a visit to the Ofra settlement. Amos Oz was there in the early 1980s (he describes his visit in *In the Land of Israel*), when Ofra was an outpost of messianic frenzy: "redemption of the land" was under way, the time of the Third Temple seemed to be at hand. Last spring, with the momentum of the settler movement stopped cold (thanks to Peres), with Ofra's own young terrorists in jail and their vision in disgrace (these were the yeshiva boys who were going to blow up the Dome of the Rock and start a world war—or was it an end-of-the-world war?), the settlers were depressed and confused, but just as implacable as ever. Grossman describes an evening with them, trying to get them to "imagine themselves in their Arab neighbors' places" and to feel what the occupation must feel like. They receive him politely, but he might as well be talking Gaelic. The sounds of silence are deafening. Finally one settler says that he can't afford even a minute of empathy, because if he allowed himself to pity and identify, it would weaken his will to carry on a total war. The others nod agreement, and this is as close to dialogue as they get.

The book's last scene is terrifying. A young mother and her 5-year-old son have been killed by a Molotov cocktail thrown into her car by terrorists hidden in a grove of trees. Settlers have rampaged through the neighboring Arab village, smashing and burning. The army has come to cut down the trees and prevent mob violence. Grossman attends the funeral. As the family huddles and weeps silently, suddenly ideologues of the Gush Emunim appear, including Meir Kahane; they seize control of the ceremony and turn it into a kind of Nuremberg rally, shaking their fists and shouting for revenge and blood. . . . "I knew them all," Grossman says, "and I could speak with all of them"—settlers, villagers, soldiers, survivors, even terrorists—"as well as find similarities and sympathy between us. But now every eye is bloodshot, they are all possessed, the slaves of a single power, tyrannical and cruel, leading them, blinded, one into the other." For the first time in the book, Grossman, whose empathy and good spirits seem boundless, has come to despair of his capacity to feel and to heal. We want to reassure him and shore up his faith, but who knows? There are times and places where no amount of faith or hope or love will be enough.

If there is one word for Grossman's faith, it is humanism.

This word is in some disrepute today; it is rare and awesome to come across the real thing. "I do not seek pure justice," Grossman says, "nor the settling of historical accounts, but rather possible life, no more than imperfect and tolerable, causing as little injustice as possible." He says that this means limiting our aspirations: "I fear life among people who have an obligation to an absolute order. Absolute orders require, in the end, absolute deeds, and I, nebbish, am a partial, relative, imperfect man who prefers to make correctible mistakes rather than attain supernatural achievements." But the modesty is deceptive. For people in the Middle East, perpetrators and victims of so much hate and murder, to settle for acceptance of themselves and one another would itself be close to a supernatural achievement. We must hope that the humanists in Israel and in Palestine can find more kindred spirits soon. (pp. 744-45)

Marshall Berman, "Humanism and Terror," in The Nation, *New York, Vol. 246, No. 21, May 28, 1988, pp. 740-46.*

Edward Alexander

George Eliot once said that, since opinions are a poor cement between human souls, the novelist's task should be the creation and diffusion of imaginative sympathy among those who differ from each other in everything except their shared suffering and their human status. [In *The Yellow Wind*, David] Grossman too eschews opinions and aspires "to display wide-hearted humanism," but he does so by means of an inversion that directs all sympathy to one party while turning the other into a metaphor. Grossman leaps across the divide between Jews and Arabs by making his Arabs into Jews. . . .

Grossman maintains that the Palestinians "are making use of the ancient Jewish strategy of exile, and have removed themselves from history. They close their eyes against harsh reality, and . . . fabricate their Promised Land." Like the Jews in exile, they are "not willing to compromise" or to "try to improve [their] lives." Where, in this licentious equation between Palestinian Arabs and Diaspora Jews (by no means original with Grossman), is the Jews' belief that they were exiled because of their *own* sins? Where, in this desperate attempt to decorate the Arabs with the tattered coattails of Jewish suffering, is the equivalent of the Jews' enrichment of their life in exile by the elaborate pretense that they were already living in the Holy Land? Where, among the Arabs of Deheisha and Balata, is the equivalent of the Torah that sustained the Jews in exile—unless it be what Grossman refers to as "the oral law" of hatred now passed from Arab mouth to Arab ear in the absence of anti-Semitic textbooks confiscated by Israeli soldiers?

When Grossman—who was born in 1954—claims that Arab children who chant, "By throwing stones and burning tires we will free the motherland," remind him of Jewish children "who sang patriotic songs when British soldiers passed by," he does not merely mock memory and history, he comes perilously close to those Israelis (like the fifteen who signed up for passage on the PLO ship intend-ed "to echo the voyage of the *Exodus*") who can discover their Jewish identity only by pretending to be Arabs who are themselves pretending to be Jews. When Grossman walks down the Ben Yehuda mall in Jerusalem, he succumbs to the illusion that he sees behind every Jew "a sort of double peeking out . . . his double from Nablus." (p. 58)

Grossman is a model of self-effacement as he listens submissively to Arabs who tell him that "the Jordanians took only our national identity from us, and you took everything," or expound on "Israeli rudeness, cynicism, idiocy, and arrogance," or regale him with the tale of the yellow wind that comes hot from hell to seek out "those who have performed cruel and unjust deeds"—by which they mean his Israeli countrymen—and "*exterminate* them, one by one" (emphasis added). Raj'a Shehade tells Grossman that although the Arab world is one of oppression, he is confident that the emergent Palestinian nation can be entirely free of the faults of Israel because he has seen that such great nations as England, America, and France are proud and nationalistic without oppressing their minorities. To such arrant nonsense, the author, a graduate of the Hebrew University of Jerusalem, cannot find the means to reply.

Susceptibility to balderdash disappears, however, and self-effacement turns to strident self-assertion when Grossman finds himself among the Jews. Among the Arabs, even when he sees children receiving "education in blind hatred," he tries "to be neutral. To understand. Not to judge." He entered Deheisha as if returning to the land of his ancestors. But he comes to the Jewish settlement of Ofra fully armed with suspicion, hostility, and partisanship, a "wary stranger" among people who remind him neither of his grandmother nor of anything human, especially when they are "in the season of their messianic heat." . . . In Ofra, Grossman does not want "to let down his guard" or be "seduced" by the Sabbath "warmth" and "festivity" of these wily Jews.

Whereas most of Grossman's remarks to Arabs in conversations recounted in the book are the perfunctory gestures of a straight man to whom his interlocutors pay no serious attention, he angrily complains that the Jewish settlers do not listen to or "display a real interest" in him. He asks them to "imagine themselves in their Arab neighbors' places," and is very much the angry schoolmaster when they decline to dance to his tune or accept his pretense that such an act of sympathetic imagination is devoid of political meaning. Neither are the settlers, despite their experience in creating a "well oiled publicity machine" (a rich joke, this), nimble enough to make the appropriate reply: "All right, we will imagine ourselves as Arabs if you will imagine yourself as a Jew." But Grossman has no intention of suspending his own rhythms of existence long enough to penetrate the inner life of these alien people: "What have I to do with them?" Although in the publicity for this book Grossman has been likened to the great modern Hebrew novelist S. Y. Agnon, one would do better to compare this chapter with its analogue called "Judea" in Philip Roth's *The Counterlife* to see the real meaning of imaginative sympathy in a novelist.

Grossman's resentment of the Jewish settlers is at least as much "cultural" as it is political. In Deheisha he had been much taken with the elderly Arab woman who told him: "We are people of culture! . . . You can't understand this culture. It's not a culture of television!" But in Ofra he complains that the settlers have "little use for culture," speak bad Hebrew, indulge in "old Diaspora type" humor, and own no books, "with the exception of religious texts." And these, far from mitigating the barbarity of their owners, aggravate it. The final image of the Jews in this long chapter is of "potential terrorists now rocking over their books."

The succeeding chapter also treats of culture and books, including religious ones. Grossman has come to Bethlehem University, one of several universities in the territories that have been punningly described as branches of PLO State. Here Grossman, though he acknowledges the school to be "a stronghold of the Democratic Front for the Liberation of Palestine," sees no terrorists rocking over books, but rather idyllic scenes that remind him of "the pictures of Plato's school in Athens." Bubbling with affection, eager to ascribe only the highest motives, Grossman is now willing to forgive even readers of religious books. He has not so much as a snort or a sneer for the Bethlehem English professor who ascribes Arabs' supreme sensitivity to lyric rhythm in English poetry to the "rhythm of the Koran flow[ing] through their blood." The author's ability to spot racism at a distance of twenty miles when he is among Jews disappears when timeless racial categories are invoked in Bethlehem.

The Yellow Wind is by no means lacking in harsh criticisms of Arabs; but these are almost always made by other Arabs. A schoolteacher is "against Arafat, because Arafat wants peace." . . . One Arab moderate, a businessman educated at Hebrew University, seconds the view of another Arab that if the Israelis were to leave the territories there would be a "second Beirut." This man speculates compellingly on the likely consequences of Israeli withdrawal: "There will be a great slaughter. . . . First they will kill whoever had any connection with Israel, and those who did business with Israel. . . . And after they kill half of the population here, they will begin killing each other in a struggle for power."

Grossman himself remains aloof from such vulgar imaginings of the years to follow the realization of "peace now," though it seems clear that a "second Beirut" in the immeditate vicinity of Jerusalem and Tel Aviv would be a catastrophe for Israel infinitely greater than the original Lebanese version, a very hot yellow wind indeed. Despite the obvious political implications of what he writes about the Israelis and those Arabs who make themselves "a partner in my crime," Grossman does not wish to appear to assign his own, explicitly political meaning to the people and events he describes. Therefore he talks with no politicians, Jewish or Arab, and claims that "it is not a question of who is right," but strictly of "facts and numbers." As it happens, many of the "facts" that he does not get from personal observation come from sources that are profoundly entangled in politics. (On three separate occasions he reports that he "checked the facts with Dr. Meron Ben-

venisti," confidently withdrawing from the latter's "data bank" some of the most debased currency in Israel.) Yet there is also much evidence that Grossman really is as innocent of politics as he claims to be.

It is characteristic of *The Yellow Wind* to remove facts from their history in such a way as to suggest the author is either massively ignorant of politics or fiendishly mischievous. After describing the terrible conditions of the Deheisha camp he casually remarks that "It doesn't matter at all who is really guilty of the refugee camps. . . ." For Grossman to have explained how and why the Arab nations are responsible for the existence of the camps might have been boring work for a novelist, and might have made the book less palatable to the *New Yorker,* which published excerpts from it after the riots began in December; but it would have been appropriate for someone who professes to believe that "to become human" is to pass "from speech to moral action." Grossman is guilty of similar irresponsibility when he declares that "the hard kernel of the entire conflict" is "two nations which still don't recognize each other's legitimacy." But the UN plan of 1947 envisaged a Jewish state and an Arab state in western Palestine; the Jews recognized the Arab state, but the Arabs did not recognize the Jewish state—or, for that matter, the Arab state (any more than they had done in 1937, when the Peel Plan would have given the Arabs all of Palestine except for the coastal plain between Tel Aviv and Haifa). Whatever the reasons for which the Arabs started the war on November 30, 1947, Israel's refusal to recognize Palestinian Arab sovereignty was not one of them. (pp. 58, 60-1)

The Yellow Wind concludes with two chapters ostensibly about the murders of Jews, members of a family named Moses whose car was firebombed near the settlement of Alfei Menashe and two couples killed by a gang of Arab terrorists. These terrible stories afford Grossman an opportunity to display his wide-ranging "humanism" and generous inability to curb his benevolence. But the benevolence is directed toward the father of the captured terrorist because his house has been destroyed, and the anger reserved for Gush Emunim activists accused of exploiting the sorrow of the Moses family and friends. And what of the families of the victims? Grossman says that he cannot begin to measure their sorrow. Yet he also cannot resist the itch to speculate darkly about these people whom he has not bothered to meet: "I do not know if the families of the victims find any comfort in fostering hatred of the murderer, his family, his nation. How can we judge them if that is how they feel?" How generous, to forgive these people for sins they have yet to commit! There is such a thing as a heart too full for weeping, a silence more eloquent than speech; but David Grossman cannot, in *The Yellow Wind,* demonstrate these qualities of the sympathetic imagination when he is dealing with Jews. (pp. 61-2)

Edward Alexander, *"Arabs as Jews,"* in Commentary, *Vol. 85, No. 6, June, 1988, pp. 58-62.*

Michiko Kakutani

In *The Yellow Wind* (1988), his widely debated report on

the occupied West Bank, the Israeli novelist David Grossman created a sympathetic portrait of the Palestinians as a people obsessed by the past, a people who live within their memories of a vanished homeland. Now, in *See Under: Love*, his first novel to be published in America, Mr. Grossman looks at another people unable to escape the past—the generation of Israelis whose parents survived the Holocaust, a generation for whom history remains an almost palpable reminder of mankind's capacity for radical evil, its vulnerability and grief. The result is a remarkable and important novel, a novel that in taking on the daunting subject of the Holocaust also tackles the pivotal literary and philosophical issues spawned by this sad, tormented age.

> **"[*See Under: Love*] is perhaps one of the most profound meditations upon the meanings of the Holocaust because [Grossman] recognizes that we need a new language (and shape) to explain and capture the Abyss."**
>
> **—*Irving Malin***

If there is a God, how could He countenance the existence of an Auschwitz or a Dachau? How, in the wake of such terrible events, is one to live a "normal" life, enjoy the ordinary pleasures of love and work? Of what use are the tools of reason and imagination in the face of history's brutality? Was T. W. Adorno, in fact, correct, when he suggested that after the Holocaust, language is inadequate, poetry impossible? Though it addresses each of these questions, *See Under: Love* never becomes didactic or portentous; rather, these issues are shrewdly embedded in the life and work of its hero, a novelist by the name of Momik Neuman. Indeed, it is one of Mr. Grossman's many achievements in this novel that he makes Momik's banal day-to-day life in contemporary Israel utterly recognizable and real, and that he's able, at the same time, to plunge us—through Momik's own writings—into the phantasmagorical world of history, giving us a fiction as magical and as resonant as works by García Márquez or Grass.

When we first meet Momik, he is an earnest 9-year-old boy, devoted to getting good grades and making his parents happy. But as hard as Momik tries, his parents and their friends remain haunted by the horrors of the war: they are afraid of the doorbell and the phone, and at night they are troubled by bad dreams. No one will tell Momik exactly what happened "Over There" in Europe, and Momik, who writes down all his observations in a secret notebook, vows to free his parents somehow from their fears. To him, the dread "Nazi Beast" is some sort of mythical creature, and armed with boyish courage, he sets about trying to exorcise the Beast in his parent's basement.

Conjuring up the secretive world of childhood with hand-

fuls of tiny details, Mr. Grossman makes Momik's attempts to grasp the idea of the Holocaust in fairy tale terms both touching and disturbing; and he proves equally adept at delineating Momik's subsequent loss of innocence, his decision, as an adult, to cloak his horror of the world with chilly detachment. In fact, the next time we meet him, Momik has become a cold and bitter man, obsessed with death and afraid to love. He tells his wife it's dangerous to become "attached to any one place, or any one person," and he chastises his young son, Yariv, for not being strong enough to survive in such a hostile and violent world. . . .

There's something self-indulgent about Momik Neuman's willingness to sacrifice his family's happiness to his own historical despair, his reluctance to submit to the ebb and flow of everyday life, and his wife and mistress eventually force him to go off on his own, to sort out his obsessions in private. There, in the solitude of a lonely room, he will begin writing a series of stories, and through them, he will take a small step toward redemption, toward becoming a New Man.

The first story, given to us by Mr. Grossman in florid, looping sentences that feel like a parody of post-Joycean prose, concerns the Polish writer Bruno Schulz, who was killed by the Nazis in 1942. In Momik's telling, however, Bruno miraculously escapes to plot his own death and rebirth as a fish, who talks of living in world devoid of memory—a world as horrific, in its own way, as Momik's memory-obsessed one.

If this tale of Momik's seems rather mannered and forced, his second—conceived as a re-creation of his great-uncle Wasserman's experiences during the war—succeeds as an imaginative tour de force. In this tale, the Nazis send Wasserman, a former writer of children's stories, to the gas chambers, but the old man finds that for all his weariness of life, he is unable to die. He is summoned by Neigel, the camp commandant, who discovers his storytelling gifts and orders him, like Scheherazade, to tell him a story every night; in return, Wasserman asks that he be relieved of his seemingly eternal life.

The story that Wasserman proceeds to tell is half fairy tale, half modernist myth—a story about a band of friends who discover an orphan child, cursed with a strange disease that causes him to age an entire lifetime in the space of a single day. It is a story that entrances Neigel, causing him to re-evaluate his Nazi credo; and it is a story that will have lasting reverberations in Momik's own life.

In giving us Wasserman's life as it has been transformed by Momik's fanciful imagination, Mr. Grossman asks us to look at the elusiveness of historical truth, the difficulties of conveying the horrors of the modern world. Yet at the same time he testifies to the powers of fiction, for he has created in this volume a dazzling work of imagination that forces us not only to examine the consequences of history but also to recognize the possibility of their transcendence.

Michiko Kakutani, "Wrestling with the Beast of the Holocaust," in The New York Times, *April 4, 1989, p. C19.*

Richard Eder

David Grossman, a gifted young Israeli novelist, has found some startling new light in his massive and complex novel about the Holocaust [*See Under: Love*]. He has tacked up a dazzling circuitry between nightmare and hope.

See Under: Love possesses moments of hair-raising beauty and discovery. They are knotted into forms and styles that sometimes obscure them and leave them accessible only at a price. We struggle to get through; in that struggle, we are exercised, illuminated, and perhaps resentful at the same time.

See Under: Love is divided into four sections, each written in a drastically different style. In the first, Momik, a frail and gifted child, lives with his parents in Israel and tries to explain to himself the nature of the terrible events that have left his family and their friends broken and fearful, and with tattooed numbers on their arms.

Momik's childhood is narrated in a thick, rich patois that, in translation, comes across as Yiddish-inflected English. It is the speech that Momik's Polish-born parents have taught him, drawn out into a child's associative stream of consciousness that can run a single sentence for two pages.

It can be heavy going, but the story is astonishing and infinitely touching. Nobody wants to tell Momik about the past. Using his imagination, the scraps of information and misinformation he picks up, the children's adventures he reads, he constructs his own theory about the "Nazi Beast."

It lives in his cellar, he decides, invisibly. It is up to him, Momik, "to find the Nazi Beast and tame it and make it good and persuade it to change its ways." It is a battle he pursues, using all kinds of childish means, on behalf of his parents. "He's fighting like a partisan. Undercover. All alone. So that finally they'll be able to forget and relax a little, and stop being so scared for once in their lives."

Momik will have a breakdown. In the second section of the book he reappears, grown up and a writer. He is on the same quest but now he takes a byway. He comes to Gdansk, on the Baltic Sea, to pursue the ghost of Bruno Schulz, a Polish writer killed by the Nazis.

He stands on the shore and engages in a dialogue with the sea. It tells him of Schulz being adopted by a giant school of salmon, conducted through various piscine adventures and transformations, and finally becoming a fish himself. The language is surreal and lush; the fantasy churns along with great energy and dim purpose. The sea talks; the sea is a bore.

After this watery detour, things pick up. Momik now uses everything he has ever known—his childhood, his wanderings, his studies—to pursue his Nazi Beast quest in still another form. Now, as a mature artist, he will devise a fable that will indeed tame it, if not exactly make it nice.

The fable tells of Anshel Wasserman, Momik's great-uncle and author of a vastly successful prewar series of children's adventure stories. Anshel is thrown into a death camp, but after a while the guards bring him before Nei-

gel, the camp commandant. Neigel's men have tried to kill Anshel three times—by shooting, gas and a truck—but he doesn't die. Anshel is apologetic; it is some kind of disorder, he explains; perhaps a doctor should be called.

Neigel is the emotionless bureaucrat-butcher. Anshel's problem infuriates him, but it intrigues him too. He is further intrigued to learn that the prisoner is the author of the adventure series he used to read as a child.

Accordingly, Neigel proposes that Anshel shall live in Neigel's attic, work his garden and, like Scheherazade, tell him a story each night. Anshel objects that, far from wanting to live, he wants to die. They agree that after each story, Neigel will shoot him. It will do no good, of course, since Anshel is unable to die.

The story he tells is a strange updating of his old children's adventures. Those were about a band of super-kids, of various races and nationalities, who traveled around the world doing good and righting wrongs. The band called itself The Children of the Heart.

In Anshel's nightly telling, the Children have grown old and formed an underground community in the Warsaw zoo. There they raise Kazik, a doomed and miraculous child who lives an entire life, up to age 65, in the space of 22 hours and 20 minutes.

Anshel gradually gains an ascendancy over the Nazi boss by means of his extended story. A chaotic human sensibility begins to awaken in this inhuman figure. And Grossman shifts into a new narrative device in the form of entries in an encyclopedia. It is a post-modern usage, intended to deconstruct the proprietorial narrator. It is briefly irritating, but Grossman has too much to tell for it to matter one way or the other for very long.

The breaking down of Neigel, who tries to bully the story his way, only to submit each time to Anshel's artistic dictatorship, the portrait of Anshel himself, with his artist's vanity and his redemptive mission, and the marvelously varied stories within Anshel's narrative, are an imaginative bonfire that light up the book's final sections.

Sometimes the fire smokes. The reader will not be transported; he must bring his own boots and use them. The book's oddly radiant theme must be worked for; the author contorts himself to earn the right to speak plainly.

The characters in Anshel's story—the saintly Children of the Heart, now in their 70s and conducting a kind of anti-Nazi resistance; Kazik with his tragic and instant life and death—all these gradually take Neigel over. He will kill himself, but before he does, he begs to be allowed to create a fictional character of his own to join the Children.

Anshel has his characters argue the point. Albert, one of the children, finds Neigel's fictional personage "too raw." But Otto, the leader, says that he must be allowed in.

"Even when we seek the greatest and most humanitarian motives, Albert, we must never for a single moment forget to have mercy because otherwise we're no better than they are, may their names be blotted out."

A blessing and a curse in the same sentence. Neigel, the

butcher, hangs in the extraordinary eschatological half-light that Grossman has come upon. Even for the damned there can be mercy. In the context of the Holocaust, this is an astonishing, perhaps a scandalous, and certainly an extraordinary and valiant message. (pp. 3, 14)

Richard Eder, "The Circuitry of Nightmare and Hope," in Los Angeles Times Book Review, *April 6, 1989, pp. 3, 14.*

Edmund White

Undoubtedly *See Under: Love* is one of the most disturbing novels I've ever read. When I was already well into it, I'd circle it warily before picking it up again, as though it were a thing capable of hurting me in some vicious, seductive and permanent way. I'd take it up reluctantly, then fall instantly under its spell, for it is wickedly readable.

It crackles with sparks of artistic invention. It scrambles art and life together. It tells its multiple tales of memory and suffering and degradation and courage with a Dostoyevskian compulsiveness. I refer to Dostoyevsky advisedly, since David Grossman seems to have learned from him how to release a wild voice and let it wail, how to remove all impediments before a flood of obsessive, self-incriminating narrative that embarrasses us, maddens us—and touches us profoundly.

Best of all, worst of all, this is a book that tricks us into thinking once more about the most painful subject of modern times, one we thought we'd exhausted or that had exhausted our capacity to suffer, to remember, to relive—the Holocaust. (I keep saying "we" instead of "I" because a novel of such epic strength commands a collective, not a personal, response). An advance comment about this book tells us it's not just a "novel of the Holocaust," but in fact it is the supreme Holocaust novel, because it is precisely an investigation of the difficulty of imagining pure horror; talking about hell-on-earth requires a re-examination of narration itself.

It turns out that the real problem of such narration is how to make a story out of suffering, how to stretch the skein of fable over the ghastly remains—the charred bits of bone, the extracted gold fillings, the lampshades of human skin, the soap made from human fat—as well as over the nightmares of the survivors. Mr. Grossman, an Israeli in his thirties who writes in Hebrew, starts with a family of survivors in the 1950's in Israel, a mother and father who barely make a living selling lottery tickets but who eat supper every night with savage determination, as though they were undertaking the most painful and onerous task imaginable. They keep their son Momik ignorant of the truth about the death camps, but the child is sensitive to their screams in the night, their insatiable hunger, their fear of other people, their fierce love of him. Momik canvasses the neighbors, other adults who bear blue numbers on their arms, and slowly he constructs his own version of the Nazi Beast, which he comes to believe is living in his cellar and can be made to come out only when presented with its favorite food: a Jew.

One day the child's great-uncle is delivered to the house

by authorities who have finally tracked down the senile old man's only surviving relatives. Uncle Wasserman keeps up a constant murmur, which everyone else ignores but which Momik reconstructs and records (the boy is bilingual in Hebrew and Yiddish, which his family speaks at home, though the language is frowned on by the new state). Momik discovers that his great-uncle was a famous children's book writer, the inventor of the serialized adventures of a youthful band called the "children of the heart."

The second section of this long and ambitious novel (ambitious in its form as well as its content) is a first-person account by a young Israeli writer, the adult Momik, who visits Poland in search of traces of Bruno Schulz, the great Jewish writer who was shot by a Nazi during the war. (In fact Schulz was working for one Nazi officer and was shot by another, the first officer's rival and enemy.) Schulz left behind an unpublished manuscript, *The Messiah,* and Momik attempts to imagine what it might have been. . . .

At the same time Momik is writing a reconstruction of the story his great-uncle was always humming to himself, the further adventures of his ecumenical band of do-gooding Jewish kids. Momik has several other projects going as well. He wants to launch a children's Encyclopedia of the Holocaust, but he's unable to find sponsors or collaborators. Then he wants to write the story of his great-uncle in the death camp and of his strange relationship with Neigel, an SS officer.

Along the way we learn about Momik's amorous conflicts and his frustration as a writer. His Holocaust researches have plunged him into a depression over the extinction of all individuality in the camps, the total erasure of personality.

The third section, by far the most gripping, is obviously the story that Momik has decided to write as a resolution of his conflicts. Neigel, the commander of the death camp, discovers that one of the Jewish prisoners is Anshel Wasserman, the author of the stories he read and loved as a child. Like Scheherazade, Wasserman must tell the tyrant another new episode of the "children of the heart" every night, but with this difference: where Scheherazade told stories to save her life, Wasserman bargains for death. Neigel must promise to shoot Wasserman after each session. More than anything else, Wasserman wants to die, but bullets just glance off his skull and even repeated gassings leave him hale and hearty.

Wasserman hopes his stories will infect Neigel with humanity. By immersing the Nazi in the intimacy of Jewish lives, Wasserman is scheming to teach him how to look at Jews as human beings. The Nazi has his own reasons to listen to the story; he is copying out each episode in letters to his estranged wife and presenting the adventures as his own fabrications. Neigel hopes to convince his wife that despite his profession as murderer he's still a decent guy.

The tangled and tragic conclusion of the plot gets told in a fourth and final section, which is set up as a glossary complete with vocabulary items and cross-references (whence the title of the book). In this highly original piece of writing, the lives of Mr. Grossman's characters are mixed in with the destinies of Wasserman's children's book heroes—and Momik's ambition to write an Encyclopedia of the Holocaust is at least partially realized.

Without a doubt Wasserman is the novel's greatest achievement, the proof that even the camps could not erase all individuality. In the camp we hear him as a voice by turns humble and complaining—the Yiddish voice of suffering—and then angry and proud, the denunciatory voice of an Old Testament prophet. We see him as a fabulist who, like Bruno Schulz, is caught in the cross fire of rival Nazi officers. We discover the old man's tenderness for his wife (whom Neigel has already killed). We overhear the strangely complicitous conversations between victim and executioner. We soar with Wasserman during his homely but exhilarating night flights of imagination.

The usual thing to say about the Holocaust is that it defies fictional treatment because no narrative can equal this event's horror and any invention trivializes it. How appropriate, then, that this book should be both an examination of the art of storytelling and of the Holocaust. We start with Momik as a child putting together a story based on hints about what went on "Over There." Then we watch the adult Momik invoking the spirit of perhaps the greatest modern Jewish writer after Kafka, Bruno Schulz. The most traditional narrative occurs in the death camp itself—could this be Momik's reconstruction of the lost "Messiah" of Schulz? This surrender to straightforward storytelling breaks down completely in the final section, the glossary. In coming to grips with the Holocaust, then, Mr. Grossman gives us a compendium of narrative strategies—as if to say that no one approach is sufficient. . . .

In a few nearly mythic books, such as Faulkner's *Sound and the Fury,* Günter Grass's *Tin Drum,* Gabriel García Márquez's *One Hundred Years of Solitude,* large visions of history get told in innovative ways. *See Under: Love* may be a worthy successor to this small but awesome canon.

> *Edmund White, "Imagining Pure Horror," in*
> The New York Times Book Review, *April 16,*
> *1989, p. 7.*

Alan Mintz

See Under: Love commands attention . . . because of the very large ambitions which are most evident in the series of big ideas it seeks to float aloft. These ideas tend toward the metaphysical: can the effects of the Holocaust on survivors and their children be undone? Can love survive under conditions of adversity? Is it possible so to be transformed as to see the world through the intelligence of another? Can the past be altered by being retold? Is evil susceptible to the powers of art?

The last is the crux of Grossman's undertaking. Throughout all of the stories-within-stories and multiple frames of reference in this complex and complicated work, one challenge is presented again and again, and it has to do with the attempt of the imagination—by which Grossman means the storytelling faculty of invention—to redeem the

suffering of the past by, in a sense, rewriting it. The audacity of this challenge is patent, and one might be tempted to dismiss it out of hand were it not for Grossman's genuine achievement and the many pleasures afforded in the reading. That in the end the attempt is impossible perhaps goes without saying

See Under: Love is made up of four discrete sections which, though interconnected, tell separate stories. There is a puzzle quality here. The connections are not always obvious, and, in the often annoying manner of postmodernist fables, the reader is obliged to participate in the game by searching for elusive correlations. Grossman's most daring move is to make the difference among the stories hinge on style. Each of the four sections is written (*à la* Joyce in *Ulysses*) in a radically different Hebrew style, ranging from the stilted locutions of the 19th-century Haskalah ("Enlightenment") to the spare pseudo-precision of modern scientific description. At times the chosen style is of a piece with the story being told, at other times ironically at odds with it—the point being that style is not merely surface texture but a mode of perceiving the world.

Grossman's manipulation of these varieties of discourse is brilliant, though it often leaves the reader groping for a stable point of literary and even moral reference behind, or within, the play of voices. In any case, the emphasis on style, and on features of style highly peculiar to the history of modern Hebrew, poses significant problems of translation. Happily, Betsy Rosenberg has met these problems with flair and a virtuoso range of effects; in order to suggest the texture of the original, she has also wisely chosen to leave in her text bits and pieces of Hebrew and Yiddish.

The first section of *See Under: Love* is the most accessible, and in it the ratio of aspiration to achievement is the most satisfying. The section is named for Momik (a diminutive of Shlomo), the nine-year-old only child of two survivors, Gisella and Tuvia Neuman; the story, set in the mid-50's, takes place over a period of five months in an immigrant neighborhood in Jerusalem. It is told from the perspective of Momik himself, a perspective captured not only in the lilt of childhood speech with its run-on sentences but also in the immigrant inflections of a child who speaks Yiddish at home and Hebrew at school.

Like many survivors, the Neumans say very little about their ordeal during the war. Momik knows that his life is different in a thousand ways from that of other children—he is not encouraged to have friends, he is not allowed to go on an overnight class trip, his father never says more than a few words to him—and he further knows that all these differences are the consequences of what happened Over There (as his parents call it). Yet because of his parents' silence, precisely that which would explain his life is kept from him.

Being a boy of methodical intelligence and adventuresome spirit, Momik treats this blank as a mystery to be solved, or (as he quotes Sherlock Holmes), "what one man invents another can discover." Arthur Conan Doyle, Jules Verne, *Emile and the Detectives* are in fact just some of the boyhood reading through which Momik absorbs his terms for understanding the world. For Grossman, the fantasies expressed in juvenile adventure literature are not merely a passing point of reference; here and in the third and fourth sections of the novel they become the central vehicle for weightier explorations of the redemptive capacities of art.

The literature of childhood adventure is embodied here and later in the novel in the figure of Anshel Wasserman, Momik's senile and demented great uncle. At the beginning of the century Wasserman had been famous as the author of an immensely popular series of adventure tales, written in Hebrew and translated into many European languages. Now, reduced by his experiences in the Nazi camps to mumbling the same few incomprehensible words, Wasserman has suddenly been deposited with the Neumans, and is put in Momik's charge. It is Wasserman's arrival that sets off Momik's quest to solve the mystery of his parents' life by keeping secret "spy notebooks" in which he records clues unwittingly dropped by grown-ups—including the words his father screams in sleep at night—about life Over There. The passages reproducing his decodings of this mystery derive their skewed pathos from the childish, almost comical innocence of Momik's approach to the macabre. . . . (pp. 56-7)

Like the heroes of all good mystery stories, Momik seeks not only to put together the pieces of the puzzle but also to save the hapless victims of evil: "Who else can save Mama and Papa from their fears and silences and krechtzes?" His rescue efforts revolve around the elliptical allusions his parents have often made to something called the Nazi Beast, which he imagines literally as an actual creature imprisoning his parents. He sets out "to find the Beast and tame it and make it good, and persuade it to change its ways and stop torturing people and get it to tell him what happened Over There and what it did to those people." But beyond this self-appointed mission, which takes the practical form of keeping a menagerie of captive animals in his basement, there is the sad fact that the person Momik most needs to rescue is himself, and the inevitable failure of his campaign leads to something more than a loss of innocence. It is too much for him; he collapses, defeated by the Beast.

The second section of *See Under: Love* is titled "Bruno," for the Polish-Jewish writer Bruno Schulz, and is the most difficult. The real Schulz was shot by a Gestapo officer on the streets of the Jewish quarter in his native Drohobycz, Poland in November 1942. In Grossman's telling, however, he does not die; escaping to Danzig, he jumps into the sea, and instead of drowning he is embraced by the ocean and becomes a fish, developing fins and gills and learning to roam the oceans swept along by the currents with great shoals of sea creatures.

All these events are related in that surrealistic or "magic-realist" mode familiar from the works of Günter Grass and Gabriel García Márquez and, of course, Bruno Schulz himself, in which the remarkable and the fantastic, described in minute naturalistic detail, are made to seem part of the ordinary scheme of things. The Hebrew style Grossman adopts for this section evokes the lushly figurative diction of Avraham Shlonsky and Natan Alterman, the preeminent modernist poets of the Jewish community of Palestine between the two world wars, whose verse, char-

acterized by musicality and a penchant for neologism, draws deeply upon French and Russian symbolism. Here, however, the novel's stylistic experimentalism is overextended; what may be evocative in conception turns out to be tedious in practice.

Not all is watery depths, fortunately. We meet Momik, now in his late twenties, as a published poet of "thin-lipped," ironic Hebrew verse. He has put aside his poetry in order to try to write, with little success, the story of Anshel Wasserman's experiences during the Holocaust, for he has been assailed by "visions of the old man locked inside the story for so long, a ghostly ship turned away at every port," while he, Momik, remains "his only hope of liberation, of salvaging his story." It is not only Wasserman he is trying to rescue but, again, himself as well. Momik's life as an adult has not been a success. He has not been able to drive away the ghosts his parents brought from Europe; he can neither trust nor love nor extend empathy. After his long-barren wife Ruth gives birth to a son, he helplessly watches his anger begin to poison his offspring as well.

The way out comes via Schulz's *The Street of Crocodiles,* given to him as a parting gift by a woman; a kind of all-in-one Holocaust groupie and muse, with whom Momik has had an affair. The experience of reading Schulz is a revelation. The constriction of Momik's imagination is overcome by Schulz's passion for language, the "veritable stampede of panting, perspiring words." He becomes obsessed with Schulz, seeking not merely to write like him but to become him. He wants, in short, to submerge himself in Schulz, and it is this desire that provides the link to the oceanic passages here.

Going off to Poland to swim in the waters off contemporary Gdansk—which, he is certain, embraced and enveloped Schulz forty years earlier—Momik receives there reassuring news of Bruno through long conversations with the sea, personified as a knowing, world-weary vamp of marvelous and constantly changing polymorphous possibilities. What happens to Momik in the bosom of the ocean—it involves a vision of Bruno's messianic Age of Genius—cannot, as one might imagine, be easily summarized. Enough to say that the ocean serves as a mythic representation of the unconscious, a realm in which transformations are possible and one can push through to become another.

The prize Momik wins for his descent into the unconscious is the capacity to tell the story of his great-uncle Anshel Wasserman as well as the story told by Wasserman to a concentration-camp commandant by the name of Neigel. This tale-within-a-tale occupies the remainder of the novel (the "Wasserman" and "Kazik" sections), and it is more straightforward than what has come before—but no less fantastic.

Wasserman's wife and daughter have been shot upon arrival at the camp, but Wasserman is not allowed to die; by some decree of fate, he *cannot* die. It comes to the attention of the camp commander that Wasserman is the author of tales which he, Neigel, had hugely enjoyed as a child; he therefore installs Wasserman as his "house Jew" (much as was Bruno Schulz in Drohobycz) with Scheherezade-like orders to amuse him when the day's work is done. Wasserman consents, but, in a reversal of the Scheherezade motif, on condition that Neigel shoot him at the end of each evening's telling.

Even in this section of the book, Grossman does not permit Momik to break out of his solipsism. As the story is conceived, Momik is actually physically present in the camp—no one but Wasserman can see him, presumably—standing over Wasserman's shoulder and frequently being addressed by him. Not for a moment are we allowed to forget that it is Momik who has brought Wasserman back to life—in every sense, reinvented him—and given him a chance to live his life over again.

The figure of Wasserman moves the theme of juvenile literature to the center of *See Under: Love.* Although his children's stories were penned in the 20th century, their ethos and style hark back to an earlier era, and Wasserman himself writes in the antique modern Hebrew of the Enlightenment—this is the style of the entire section. Furthermore, like the literature of the Haskalah, his stories are deliberately universal and didactic in their concerns. They narrate the adventures of the Children of the Heart, a band of young people from different backgrounds and lands who join together to fight for right all over the globe and, through their trusty time machine, in earlier eras as well, rescuing a runaway American slave, assisting a scientist in his battle against cholera, lending support to Robin Hood, and so forth.

The twist comes with Wasserman's resurrection as a storyteller. What the Nazi commandant wants from him is more of the same: benevolent, childlike tales that will divert his overwrought mind. What Wasserman gives him instead is something very different. He again conjures up the Children of the Heart, but now, instead of the brave adolescents Neigel knew and loved as a child, they are forty years older, not broken exactly but ragged and disillusioned. He places them, furthermore, not in the eternal land of youth but squarely within the world the Nazis have made in Eastern Europe. Neigel complains bitterly: he is being cheated. But Wasserman invokes against him the sacred principle of the inviolability of art; a story, he avers, cannot depart from its own truth. Given his elaborate second chance, Wasserman succeeds in rising above juvenile fantasies and in placing his gift for invention within the constraints of historical actuality.

The final section of *See Under: Love,* no less exorbitantly inventive than those preceding, is titled "The Complete Encyclopedia of Kazik's Life." Kazik is a newborn baby, discovered by the aging Children of the Heart in the abandoned Warsaw zoo. The baby is found to suffer from a rare disease which causes it to experience the entire human life cycle within the course of twenty-four hours. This miniaturized life provides the unique occasion for Momik, posing now as the voice of a complete editorial staff, "to compile an encyclopedia embracing most of the events in the life of a single individual, as well as his distinctive psychosomatic functions, orientation to his surroundings, desire, dreams, etc." The encyclopedia is of course organized al-

phabetically, with numerous cross references, the title of the novel being one of them.

This section, preoccupied with definition and classification, is written in stiff and hyper-rational social-sciencese, which plays in counterpoint to the horrible irrationality of the fate that awaits Kazik. The key here is suggested in words used earlier about Bruno Schulz: "For him the Holocaust was a laboratory gone mad, accelerating and intensifying human processes a hundredfold." Kazik represents the freak intensity of human experience under conditions of the greatest extremity. Although the Children of the Heart do their best to educate Kazik under these conditions and to guide him as he rapidly progresses through his life, their efforts come to naught. Kazik requests to see the world beyond the zoo; what he is shown are the electrified barbed-wire fences of Neigel's concentration camp. Horrified, he commits suicide two hours short of his allotted twenty-four.

Yet Kazik's fate triggers Neigel's own suicide, and this death represents a triumph of the storyteller's art. By locating his nightly tales in the present reality, and by involving Neigel in the telling, Wasserman has managed to lure the commandant into an emotional identification with the victims of persecution. The death of Kazik in a world he has helped to create—Neigel has by now ceased to distinguish between story and life—is too much for him. Not that he has been morally regenerated, but the story has unmanned him, made him hateful to himself, and the taking of his own life becomes the only way out. So *See Under: Love* is brought to a close.

Though the lengthy description I have offered may seem to tell too much, it fails to touch on dozens of this novel's motifs and characters. For example, all of the deranged survivors Wasserman meets on the public benches of his neighborhood in the "Momik" section are in the "Kazik" section amplified into full-fledged characters with individual life histories. One wonders, indeed, whether the whole conception of an encyclopedia may have come into being as a brilliant "solution" for these many tangential narratives, which could thereby simply be filed as entries without being integrated into a narrative fabric. Here and in many other instances, at any rate, one yearns for a sober editorial hand.

But the problems of *See Under: Love* go deeper than what could have been solved by judicious pruning and disciplined restraint. Grossman is endowed with literary genius, but the particular models he has chosen to follow are precisely of the sort that fan the flames of his native extravagance rather than lending it structure and purpose.

The novel imitates two key features of the "postmodernist" sensibility in contemporary fiction: self-conscious literary borrowing and the solipsistic preoccupation with literary artifice. As to the first, it must be said that Grossman's decision to narrate each of the four sections in a different Hebrew style succeeds completely; in its own context, each style is consistently sustained and thematically supported. Yet within this canny architectonic design, Grossman has opened the door to a swarm of other influences. Reading through the novel is like making one's way down the halls of a museum: look, here's a Grass, there's a García Márquez! And, for the Hebrew reader, there is Sholem Aleichem, Mendele Mocher Seforim, Yoram Kaniuk, and many others. The possibility of total derivativeness is parodied in Wasserman's pulp adventure tales, with their indebtedness to Karl May, Jack London, James Fenimore Cooper, *et al.*

Nice distinctions might be made here among literary concepts of allusion, homage, and imitation, but they are swept aside by the riveting, monumental figure of Bruno Schulz. Schulz has exerted a pull on other writers, . . . and it would take a reader with intimate knowledge of Schulz's Polish-language stories to say just how Grossman has appropriated him. But the dominant impression is that, to adapt the oceanic metaphor of the "Bruno" section, Grossman has been sucked under by this material. If Momik, as the novel's narrator, seems to understand thematically the difference between being influenced by someone and *becoming* that person, for Grossman the novelist this boundary at times disappears altogether.

Which brings us to Grossman's preoccupation with the mechanics of storytelling. After the relatively "straight" description of Momik's boyhood, the focus of the novel shifts to the question of how one *writes* about the Holocaust. We are given an account of Momik's case of writer's block, then of his search for inspiration from Bruno Schulz; finally there is the re-invention of Wasserman as a writer and, to cap it all, the completed encyclopedia. In the story of Wasserman and the Nazi commandant Grossman puts together his most involved arrangement of Chinese boxes. It is Momik who has conjured up Wasserman, who in turn tells the story to Neigel, who, for his part, is not only morally overcome by the story—thus changing historical reality retroactively by means of fiction—but steals Wasserman's story and retells it to his wife as his own. All the while Momik, the conjuror, is present inside the frame, and is addressed by Wasserman in direct discourse. The result is a constant cutting back and forth between narrative contexts as the devices by which the story is told are deliberately exposed to view.

The deep purpose of these games, one supposes, is to make a statement about the ineluctable interdependence of reality and illusion, event and story. Grossman's maneuvers, however, end by producing the opposite effect. Instead of becoming interwined, the realms of art and life seem to proceed along separate and ever diverging tracks. In *See Under: Love* the realm of "life," in the sense of reality represented fictively without magical transformation, is unrelievedly bleak: the deformed emotions of Momik's parents, the murder of Bruno Schulz in the streets of Drohobycz, the shooting of Wasserman's wife and daughter, Wasserman's own hard labor in the latrines and crematoria. This unbearable sadness is summed up in an aside Momik utters about his Aunt Idka, who came to his wedding wearing a Band-Aid over the number on her arm. "All evening I couldn't tear my eyes away from her arm. I felt as if under that clean little Band-Aid lay a deep abyss that was sucking us all in: the hall, the guests, the happy occasion, me."

Yet although this cosmetic bandage is occasionally re-

moved in *See Under: Love* to reveal the horror beneath, most of the novel takes place in the realm of art and storytelling, a much happier place by far. Thus, not only is Bruno Schulz brought back to life, and Wasserman too given a second chance, but, in an ultimate compliment to the power of art, an SS officer is conquered by the enchantments of story.

What is most startling about *See Under: Love* is the moral vision implicit in this divergence, most strikingly embodied in the tales Wasserman tells to snare his prey. Wasserman's own moral code is a direct transcription of the naive universal values which his children's tales were designed to inculcate. All men are brothers. Band together to work for the useful and the good. Be faithful and courageous in the face of evil. Amazingly, Wasserman's vision stands here unmolested and unreconstructed, as if to say that *this* is the truth of art, everywhere and always.

Through the figure of Momik, Grossman had an opportunity to project a subtler and deeper understanding of the links between his dissociated realms of art and life. We could have been shown, for instance, how Momik's life is affected by his success in telling Wasserman's story and in compiling his encyclopedia. What would it mean to return to the business of everyday life after writing about such horror? But Grossman, apparently unwilling to renounce the consolations of story, passes the opportunity by.

The limitations of this vision stem from a fantasy of rescue which Grossman seems not to want to relinquish. Integral to the juvenile literature invoked so extensively in the novel is the notion that the weak and defenseless can be saved by the courage and secret intelligence of others. For Grossman the magic ring is not action but language. As a child, Momik works to deliver his parents from the clutches of the Nazi Beast through the words in his spy notebooks. As an adult, he seeks salvation from terminal embitterment by submersion in Bruno Schulz, himself saved from death as a reward for his luminous prose. Wasserman is rescued from mediocrity as a literary hack and given the chance to practice true art; and it is that art which saves Neigel from his bestiality. While in the early, "Momik" section such fantasies of rescue are deployed to great ironic and pathetic effect, later the novel seems drawn to a disturbingly close identification with the figure of Wasserman, who, despite his marvelous vividness as a character, remains fixed in the adolescent world of his literary creations.

Does Grossman's work mark a new, third-generation response to the Holocaust in Israeli literature? It is, of course, too soon to say. But two issues that emerge from *See Under: Love* are worth bearing in mind in this connection. The first is the book's relationship to the Jewish past. Historically, the Jewish literature of response to catastrophe has consciously invoked the models of the Bible and midrashic legend and exegesis, even if in modern times the relationship has been one of parody and rebellion. In *See Under: Love,* this literary tradition simply does not figure. Grossman's imagination is engaged by certain universal questions raised by Jewish suffering, and his literary models are correspondingly alien to the Jewish canon.

A second, more delicate issue touches on what might be termed the uses of the Holocaust. What this novel has to teach us about the Holocaust itself, in any of its dimensions, is in the end quite limited. The description of Momik's childhood is an exception: a brilliant and genuine contribution to our understanding of the effects of the catastrophe on children of survivors. But after this initial point *See Under: Love* moves off in another direction, becoming absorbed in the drama of the writer's soul, the virtuoso manipulation of narrative, the redemptive potentialities of art. The novel's ostensible subject is reduced to a backdrop on which the adventures of the artistic ego are projected.

The Holocaust presents a singular temptation to the artist: on the one hand, its bleakness as a subject acts as a discipline, giving little scope for grandiosity or revery; on the other hand, to the undisciplined or narcissistic imagination, that very bleakness may spur fantasy and ostentation without end. Grossman's daring novel may, indeed, thus betoken a disturbingly wider impatience with the intractability of the Holocaust as a subject—and by extension (as his more recent, "soft" political writings would suggest) with the tragic element in human conflict altogether. (pp. 57-60)

Alan Mintz, "A Major Israeli Novel," in Commentary, *Vol. 88, No. 1, July, 1989, pp. 56-60.*

Denis Donoghue

Unless I am much mistaken, David Grossman's *See Under: Love* is an extraordinary novel. If I were to guess the source of the book, the impulse that has taken this form, I would choose one incorrigible conviction: that the Holocaust is an event about which nothing useful can now be said, and yet that this nothing must continue to be said.

The novel has four related sections. The first is set in Jerusalem, where Momik, a boy of nine, has to cope with his father and mother, his grand-uncle Anshel Wasserman (once a famous author of children's stories who wrote under the name Scheherazade) who is now senile. The boy takes on the further responsibility of destroying the Beast—adults call it Nazism—which is hiding in a cellar and must be outwitted by the resources of detection and espionage.

In the second part, Momik is grown up. He and his wife, Ruth, have had a child, Yariv. There is another woman, Ayala, with whom Momik has had an affair. His marriage is collapsing. He goes to Warsaw to try to understand his grand-uncle's life, and to commune in some way with a writer, Bruno Schulz, who means much to him. The official records say that Schulz lived and wrote in Drohobycz in southeast Poland, and that on November 19, 1942, he was shot dead by a Gestapo officer. Momik persuades himself that Schulz committed suicide, "escaped" by drowning. Gradually, he imagines Schulz's life under the waves, in the company of salmon. He identifies himself sometimes with Schulz, sometimes with the sea, speaking of Schulz in the sea's voice. . . . Sometimes Momik thinks of his life in communion with the lives of various characters in Schulz's stories, especially in certain chapters of *Sanatorium Under the Sign of the Hourglass* (1937) and *The Street of Crocodiles* (1934).

The third section is the life of Wasserman, so far as Momik has been able to reconstruct it. In 1943 Wasserman was in a concentration camp, run by Herr Neigel, who had read and enjoyed Scheherazade's stories as a boy. (Neigel seems to me to resemble Reinhard Heydrich, whom Goering appointed to effect the Final Solution; except that Heydrich was drawn to music, not literature.) Neigel will spare Wasserman's life, so long as he keeps telling him, every night, new stories as sequels to the old ones. Meanwhile Neigel continues his work of extermination. . . . Wasserman would much prefer to be dead, and he bargains with Neigel for his death, but Neigel refuses: the storytelling must continue. Running short of invented characters, Wasserman enters into league with the unseen but ever-present Momik and together they drag into his stories many of the people they knew in Israel. Though busy with his daily chores, Neigel is alert to Wasserman's narrative procedures. If he doesn't like a new style, he orders Wasserman back to the old one:

> "I don't like this new style one bit." "Ai, would that you blessed me with your patience, sir." And Neigel, weary, almost whining, says, "I like simple stories!" To which the writer, with a trace of cruelty, replies, "There are no simple stories anymore."

The fourth and last section is called "The Complete Encyclopedia of Kazik's Life," Kazik being the hero of one of Wasserman's stories. I take it that the entries in this encyclopedia are meant to draw all the stories together, Momik's as well as Wasserman's and Schulz's and, by inescapable implication, every story that might be told of Hitler, Himmler, and the Jews.

One of the many remarkable features of *See Under: Love* is Grossman's control of the multiplicity of styles and emotional tones his several stories require, from the demotic to the sublime. Some of the episodes between Wasserman and Neigel show a rich and uncruel comedy in an otherwise appalling dance of death. Many of Grossman's transitions, especially in the "Encyclopedia," are so daring that a question of tact arises; but on every questionable occasion his sense of the issues involved is exact; his moral taste seems impeccable.

"A million stories, a million troubles," Momik says to himself in the heartbreaking section called "Bruno." It doesn't take one iota away from Grossman's achievement in this section if I say that it could not have been written if Melville had not written *Moby-Dick* and Joyce the "Proteus" chapter of *Ulysses,* merging Stephen Dedalus with the sea—"Their blood is in me, their lusts my waves." Nor does it take anything from *Sanatorium Under the Sign of the Hourglass* to say that it required the example of Kafka's *Metamorphosis.* Later writers are not parasites upon earlier ones. The life and work of Bruno Schulz incited David Grossman to feel with emphasized reiteration and intensity what he might have felt under his own auspices but in less measure. What Grossman makes of Schulz, as a source of further feeling in Momik, is his own moral and artistic achievement. Schulz is to Momik what, in Christianity, the life of a saint is to a Christian who feels special devotion to it. (pp. 42-3)

Denis Donoghue, "Haggling Presences," in The New York Review of Books, Vol. XXXVI, No. 14, September 28, 1989, pp. 39-43.

Barbara Probst Solomon

[From the very first pages of *The Smile of the Lamb*]—one is aware of Grossman's potential range and originality. On one level the author shows us how the Israeli-Palestinian conflict feels closeup in Andal, a small town in the occupied West Bank: Only when war is at a safe remove and becomes abstract does any of it make sense. On another level—and here is where Grossman truly excites as a novelist—he is informing his readers that the Israeli novel is no longer the child of only European literature. Through his graceful use of very different voices, each bearing a distinctly different music, he has given birth to a new hybrid form more true to the Middle East. The European novels that Grossman mentions in *The Smile of the Lamb* are heterodoxal, concerning a mixed culture. He evokes Camus, who was in continual conflict about his mixed French and Algerian heritage, and Cervantes, whose universe was created by the mixture of Spanish, Arab and Jewish cultures.

Uri, who serves as Grossman's alter ego, is a soldier in an Israeli army unit patrolling Andal. While he is stationed there the fabric of his life is permanently altered. His wife, Shosh, whom he formerly perceived to be a dedicated child therapist, causes the suicide of Mordy, a mute adolescent at her clinic, whom she has seduced. Shosh's incestuous interest in her charges, masked as love, ends up as a sordid tragedy. She and Uri drift apart, she starts an affair with his commander, the worldly realist, Katzman.

Grossman's novel poses the question: What went wrong with Shosh? Everything in her background prepared her to become the natural flowering (her name means rose in Hebrew) of the best in Israel. Her parents, Abner and Leah, are depicted as well-meaning progressives, deeply rooted in the pioneering, humanist tradition of early Israel. Abner is one of several story-telling shadow voices that Uri, in his moral quest, must come to terms with; for many years Shosh's father had been secretly publishing poems in the Israeli newspapers.

But it is Khilmi, an Arab storyteller who lives in a cave in Andal near the terebinth and lemon trees, who is the novel's great imaginative narrative achievement; Grossman creates his voice and story in the Arabic mode. He insists that in order for us to understand Khilmi and his notions of truth and justice, we must enter his head, which has been informed by centuries of Arab storytelling. Just as Uri needs to become Khilmi's spiritual heir, so does Grossman, the Israeli novelist, need to borrow from the Arabic to complete his Israeli novel. Khilmi's sense of timelessness, his notion of a past which curls in and over a fluid present becomes the crucial part of Uri's journey. (pp. 1, 10)

It becomes Uri's fate to tell Khilmi that his adopted son, Yazdi, had been killed by the Israelis. Katzman, Uri's superior, follows him into Khilmi's cave in order to save him from Khilmi's suffering wrath; at the novel's end the Israeli commander and the Arab storyteller fight each other for possession of Uri's soul.

Though Grossman's portrait of Khilmi works novelistically, and Khilmi's stories are the best passages in the novel as a political parable—which Grossman also means the book to be—the book works less well. I always get a bit queasy at literary searchings for the exotic which involve perceiving the "other" as a sort of noble savage. Grossman seems not so much in quest of love, as in flight from modernity, which he sees Israel personifying in the Middle East. But the real opposite of his Israeli intellectuals with feet of clay, are Palestinian intellectuals, who are abundant, and who presumably also have feet of clay. Khilmi's true counterpart is the Northern African blue-eyed Berber Jews transplanted into Israel from the Atlas mountains; they also smell of lemon trees and have a desert sense of storytelling, the only difference being their occasional cry: *torah! torah!* Is it really true that doctors and hospitals are agents of child murder, while the man who sits in the olive grove has his children torn from him? Is it not more complicated than this simple equation?

As I read the novel, I said to myself, I bet Grossman will evoke the music of Um Kultum, the great maternal Egyptian singer, worshipped by the masses. Sure enough, Khilmi invites Uri to listen to her music on his radio. . . .

But, amidst the plants, leaves and lemon trees, Khilmi can listen to Um Kultum, because he, like everyone else, has a radio. And I know what her music sounds like because her records were sold in the '70s in Paris and New York: Modernity is not merely the wicked province of the culture you happen to be born into. Ironically, Grossman is doing just the opposite of his idol, Cervantes. *Don Quixote* was a break with the past, a rebellion against the static love-mores of the middle-ages, our first great modern novel. But despite my quibbles, what a rare pleasure to read a novel in which the novelist's narrative and ideas are so gripping, they are worth arguing about! Here we have authentic talent. (p. 10)

Barbara Probst Solomon, "In the Cave of the Storyteller," in Book World—The Washington Post, January 6, 1991, pp. 1, 10.

"[*The Smile of the Lamb*] is a story about falsehood and fantasy, about the way a lie invades a simple and sincere life. It is also the story of the Jewish people in Israel, champions of humanistic morality and justice turned subjugators of another people, causing the erosion of their own values."

—David Grossman, 1981

Donna Rifkind

Dreams and metaphors are seductive artistic choices for any novelist trying to capture the stony realities of life in Israel. So it is easy to see why David Grossman's first novel [*The Smile of the Lamb*], originally published in Hebrew in 1983, is as full of allegorical weight as a drowning man's pockets are full of rocks. . . .

The central conceit in *The Smile of the Lamb* is woven around the expression Arabs use to begin a story, *kan-ya-ma-kan,* which means "there was or there was not," or "once upon a time." Mr. Grossman uses *kan-ya-ma-kan* as a refrain to suggest the loss of boundaries between truth and falsehood, justice and injustice in the Israeli Army's control of the occupied territories.

"We're all *kan-ya-ma-kan* around here, and the only real thing about us is the pain we bring," reflects Uri Laniado, a young soldier tormented by doubts about the legitimacy of his country's domination of the West Bank. During a raid in Juni, the large Arab town where Uri is stationed, three teen-age Palestinian terrorists are killed. When Uri learns that one of the boys was the son of his friend Khilmi, a half-crazed old Arab, he abandons his unit in disgust and hides in the cave where Khilmi lives.

Meanwhile, Uri's wife, Shosh, who works in an institution for juvenile delinquents, is wrestling with guilt of her own. In trying to help a particularly difficult patient, a deranged Israeli teen-ager, she has inadvertently caused his suicide; to make matters worse, she has also been having an affair with Uri's commander, a Holocaust survivor named Katzman. Uri's discovery of his wife's betrayal, together with his growing doubts about the army's morality, leads to a final murderous showdown with Katzman and Khilmi in the old Arab's cave.

The book's four main characters—Uri, Khilmi, Shosh and Katzman—take turns narrating chapters, so the reader must unravel the facts of the story from a tangle of lies, justifications, omissions and fanciful exaggerations. All of the characters are hopelessly stuck in the half-dream world of *kan-ya-ma-kan,* of "there was and there was not." As Shosh says, "The road from truth to falsehood is the same dirt path you tread each day. . . . But if you come from the opposite direction, you may discover that there never was a path."

Despite all the confusion, we can be sure that Uri's apprehensions echo those of Mr. Grossman himself. It was he, after all, who wrote in *The Yellow Wind*: "I could not understand how an entire nation like mine, an enlightened nation by all accounts, is able to train itself to live as a conqueror without making its own life wretched." Whether or not one agrees with the author's point of view, it is plain in this novel that his decision to cloak his sentiments in a dreamy, insubstantial atmosphere was not the best choice.

The hard issues Mr. Grossman tries to address—the limits of power, the role of conscience in a country at war—would have had much more force had they been confronted more straightforwardly. . . .

Why, moreover, have Mr. Grossman's publishers chosen this moment to issue a somewhat dated first novel about the Arab-Israeli conflict on the West Bank? The book was, after all, written back in 1982, five years before the intifada began and eight years before the Palestinians' demand for statehood would be cynically annexed to Iraq's *casus belli* during the most recent Gulf crisis.

One might answer that Mr. Grossman's three books are so closely related that they form a kind of trilogy. Here and there, between the unsure outlines of this early venture, are traces of the descriptive power that American readers found so absorbing in *See Under: Love* and *The Yellow Wind.* On its own, *The Smile of the Lamb* is not much more than a curiosity; but if viewed as the first work of a distinguished young writer's career, it compels some genuine literary interest.

> Donna Rifkind, "Doubt and Betrayal on the West Bank," in The New York Times Book Review, *January 13, 1991, p. 14.*

Irving Howe

The Smile of the Lamb is, by contrast [with *See Under: Love*], relatively modest in conception, but it is also, I fear, an unsatisfying piece of writing. Grossman set his first novel in the West Bank, and he deserves credit for scouting a terrain that most Israeli writers find difficult. He has written, he says, "the story of the Jewish people in Israel, champions of humanistic morality and justice turned subjugators of another people, causing the erosion of their own values." This statement of intention seems to me admirable; but the book itself is something else again.

As a convenience let me separate two elements of the novel: its situation and its story. The situation turns on the twisted relationships among three Israelis, Uri, Shosh, and Katzman. Uri is a young soldier stationed in the West Bank, one of Israel's "gentle folk," soft and idealistic, and marked, as his wife, Shosh, puts it, by "the smile of the lamb." Shosh herself is an equally familiar type, ravenously neurotic, a virtuoso of *kvetching.* If "the smile of the lamb" strikes her as acceptable in a husband, she prefers as her lover someone more wolfish, the cynical and battered Katzman, Uri's friend and superior officer.

This triangle, if not exactly brimming with freshness, is probably no worse than many others in modern fiction: all depends on what the writer can make of it. It is a situation that cries out for narrative development, but mostly Grossman vibrates emotionally with his characters, so that again and again we share the self-lacerations of his trio—perhaps true to life, but like many things that are true to life, soon wearisome in a novel.

It may be argued in Grossman's defense that the entanglements of these characters should be seen as a neurotic refraction of the circumstances in which they find themselves, that is, the struggle in the West Bank. That may indeed have been Grossman's intention. Still, the troubles of his trio seem so uncontrolled and ingrown, so much a consequence of their own character disorders, that the neurotic aura too often gets in the way of the depicted circumstances.

The story, by contrast, is absorbing, especially if one trips past the allegorical suggestions. Uri has become the friend of Khilmi, a wise old Arab who serves a little as the Karataev to his Pierre Bezhukhov. When Khilmi's son is killed in a clash with Israeli troops, Uri has to break the news to the old man; and then, overcome not just by his own pain but by a sense of how insufferable life has become in the West Bank, Khilmi issues an "ultimatum": either the Israeli occupiers get out immediately or he will kill his beloved friend Uri, whom he has managed to entrap. The tense denouement comes when Katzman leads a squad to rescue Uri and the novel reaches a violent, necessarily ambiguous conclusion.

Even with its stereotyped characters (idealistic young Israeli, mythmaking old Arab), *The Smile of the Lamb* might have been a tolerable novel if Grossman had not been so intent on loading his pages with verbal and symbolic weight. Perhaps sensing that his matter is fairly thin, he compensates through a nervous strategy of verbal intensification, somewhat like a musician in a fever of vibrato. The result is wanton.

When old Khilmi screams in despair over the death of his son, Uri "groans. Ripping me right down the middle. No, that's not a groan, that's a blind drill press." Exactly what a *blind* drill press might be, Grossman does not tell us. He ought to have been content with the introductory groan. At another point, Uri examines a picture of the dead Arab boy and sees in him

> the infinite loneliness of one who has been bereft of life, whose body is but an empty hull stuffed full of cotton-wooly words by strangers, and just then he resembled one of the animal trophies hanging by the tail in the tent of Sha'-aban Ibn Sha'-aban, the mirthless hunter.

The first of these clauses would have sufficed, but a mania for accumulation drives Grossman to the bad prose of the second clause and the opaque comparison with "the mirthless hunter." (p. 40)

Grossman's overreaching can lead to embarrassment, as in Shosh's reflection that she "had known what she was getting into by allowing [Katzman] to resonate inside her." Some of this may be the fault of the translator—I am not equipped to check the original Hebrew—but I doubt it, since Betsy Rosenberg is quite capable of writing disciplined prose when Grossman's text asks her to. . . .

By now [Grossman] must be thoroughly sick of critics, especially this one, who nevertheless wishes to repeat that in the marred pages of his two novels there lurks a large talent waiting to emerge. (p. 41)

> *Irving Howe, "Contested Terrain," in* The New Republic, *Vol. 204, No. 17, April 29, 1991, pp. 40-1.*

John Leonard

Of the four voices who tell us alternating stories in *The Smile of the Lamb,* three belong to characters who would be comfortable in any serious European novel. Uri, the smiling lamb himself, is an idealistic young Sephardic Jew who hopes to bring hospitals and electricity to an Arab village on the West Bank in 1972. Katzman, a Polish survivor of the Holocaust, is the military commander of this zone of the occupied territories; he brought Uri into his service, ostensibly to help do "justice" but in fact to "contaminate" Uri with Katzman's own cynicism and hopelessness. Shosh, an unorthodox psychotherapist working with juvenile delinquents in Tel Aviv, may be married to Uri but she's sleeping secretly with Katzman. While the Israeli military demolishes houses so that arrested Palestinians will have no place to come home to, cut down trees to eliminate snipers' nests, put on the thick skin and the uniforms of the bully, Katzman, Shosh and Uri talk a lot, to themselves and to each other, about their motives and illusions. My, how they talk, with theories on everything, as though on loan from Malraux or Camus, tending to the oracular.

Katzman thinks of consciousness as "a kind of sponge that can absorb the most voluminous fictions and intricate lies, and then wring them out again as fresh truth." He thinks of justice not as a social or ethical convention but as "a hormone secreted at varying levels of intensity. Something a sensitive brain produces as a response to injustice, the way it does in response to sexual stimuli." He believes Uri to be "one of those holy fools . . . rash enough to let the world filter through to him"; can anyone so vulnerable survive in "this disaster area"?

Shosh spends a good portion of her time, when she isn't engaged with her delinquents in a "love" therapy that's part Trojan horse and part Stanislavsky method, theorizing into her tape recorder: "The human inclination to deceive will use anything, even love, as a lethal weapon." And: "The pretty names we give emotions are like the names that sailors give approaching typhoons in the vain hope of appeasing them, of making them easier to understand." To Uri, she lays down "the law of indemnity for dreams and fantasies," and accuses him of being a "do-gooder" only because he doesn't "have the guts to hurt anyone."

Uri—well, Uri suffers. All he ever wanted to do was good, among earthquake victims in Italy on his vacation, among Arabs on the West Bank. But he's subverted by superior theorizers. "I'm going through what you might call a reverse conversion right now," he says; "I'm learning not to believe." And: "It's only anguish, calling me louder than the other voices. Like a craving. Like a passion. For a woman, let's say. Yes." Finally, he hasn't much strength left, "not enough to take revenge, and not enough to forgive either. Only enough to sleep and not to be."

Now meet Khilmi, the novel's fourth storyteller and its afflatus. At last: an Arab. Perhaps conveniently, he is also mad, a one-eyed humpback in a silk robe and a black beret, who goes on too much, in his grape bower, his cave, his magic barrel, the cleft of his terebinth tree, about "his patron and protector," the hermit Darius and a hunter "who draws lions in the sand." Khilmi belongs to another literature entirely, the Koran and *Arabian Nights.* In place of our "once upon a time" he substitutes an Arabic equivalent, *kan-ya-ma-kan:* "there was or there was not." In "splashes of color and points of memory," he dreams an epic of panthers and dervishes; of lanterns from Bethlehem and candles from Nablus; of harvest songs, locust plagues, donkeys with samovars, the awful English and the awful Turks, the Emir Abdullah and King Hussein, "whose soldiers slaughtered us without mercy." We hear about rababa, darbekas and the singing of the prophets Noah and Mussa; about beloved Job, and the twenty-eight stations of the moon, and Sha'aban with his bottles of powdered hyena testicles and jars of ravens' blood and jackal claws, off to kill a Syrian bear. What Khilmi, flying over his "invisible village," sees through the blue tunnel of his blind eye is Palestinian history. What he listens to on his transistor radio, from Fayruz in Beirut, from Um Kultum in Cairo, is a lamentation of "the weeping, fallen and forsaken people."

Against the logic of power, the instrumentalism and the bad faith of the Israelis, Khilmi is the embodiment—and the levitation—of the repressed: memory, history, landscape.

See him grow up speechless and unwanted, tethered like a dog to a courtyard tree. See him take in Arab children as unwanted as he was. See one of these "moonchildren" join Al Fatah, and die in a skirmish with Israelis. Khilmi believes in nonviolence: "Softer than a feather. More fragile than an egg . . . stubborn patience and infinite weakness. They will not be able to bear it." And: "We should have drawn into ourselves. Each person to his house and village in silence, to wait. . . . Then you would be struck with terror. Perhaps you would resort to violence. Think of it: a million people never touching you at all. Silence growing. . . . In the beginning you may shoot us, but we will kick a hole through our killers. And you are not made of very hard stuff." But his adopted son is dead. And so Khilmi takes a hostage: the ever-willing Uri.

Causing Katzman to think: "You have to be as crazy as Uri to step out of your life and view it from the outside, to rub your eyes and wonder how such a thing had happened. How we had all been turned into hostages." Whereas Uri, as always, sees things differently: "We're all *kan-ya-ma-kan* around here, and the only real thing about us is the pain we bring."

Besides *kan-ya-ma-kan,* Khilmi speaks another language he's taught his moon-children, an "infant tongue" with only a word or two of human speech ("longing," "caress"); stories "carved in water," "quarried in the wind"; "shadowplay" and bird-gibber; parables of plants, "of crushed leaves or twisted stalks, or perhaps," "to cure sadness," a broken thistle. Compare this speech with what a therapized Shosh talks into her tape recorder: "magnetic residue." Or the hateful scribblings of Al Fatah: words "so hot [they] did not see whose blood had been spilled in the ink." Or the infant tongue that Katzman, like Khilmi,

spoke only to his father, in the pit where they hid from the Germans, "a private language" based on Ariosto, about whom his scholar father was writing—a book the son was forced to memorize. Shosh thought Katzman was "the person who could translate me into a foreign language" but he's only "the steam that reveals the invisible ink spilled on the page long ago." She's also furious to find that her own father, the liberal hypocrite Abner, is the very poet who under the pseudonym Aviv Raz "named the names, who kneaded me into words—no, not words—but shattered syllables, swollen letters that sank into me with a cold flame."

Lamb is an anthology, a Rosetta stone, of secret languages, symbolic systems of communication. Kites talk, "long-tailed paper bats, colorful rhomboids with crosses of nickel and bamboo." And so do military orders, when you do harm: "How convenient military language was for such occasions. Sometimes Katzman felt it was his mother tongue, having lost his Polish and never mastered Hebrew." And so does a game of Scrabble, spelling out, like a Ouija board, words like "timely," "victim" and "yearning." There's even a sign language for lovers: Katzman and Shosh devise "a sly language of signals and insinuations" to use in Uri's presence. When she kisses Uri on the nose, it means she'll be waiting for Katzman the next day, when Uri has gone to the West Bank to do good. (If this sounds like the Judas kiss, well, "lamb" also has a Christian resonance. Maybe Christ was the first Middle Eastern hostage.) And *against* all these languages, there are a surprising number of mutes, as well as suicides: a sign language that speaks of nothing left to say. If, sometimes, the fathers are assisted in their suicides by their sons, almost as often the children kill themselves, feeling betrayed by their parents and their surrogate parents.

Obviously, Grossman intends his occupation to stand as a metaphor for a whole range of distorted relationships: for power and deceit and betrayal; for violations of privacy and intimacy in the bedroom, at the therapist's, wherever there's a West Bank; for the fictions we invent to excuse and suppress those violations and betrayals; *kan-ya-ma-kan.* Just as obviously, Khilmi is an imaginary Arab—too fantastical, too much a literary construct of exotic bric-a-brac and secondhand *Sumud* (long-suffering, endurance) to represent a Palestinian reality with its own fair share of innocent Uris, cynical Katzmans, deracinated Shoshes. . . . But at least, in an enormously ambitious first novel, he demanded of himself meaningful answers to the hard questions. (pp. 703-06)

John Leonard, "Tongue-Tying in Israel," in The Nation, *New York, Vol. 252, No. 20, May 27, 1991, pp. 705-09.*

John Guare

1938-

American playwright and screenwriter.

Guare's plays often satirize elements of American society, including the power of media images, the "American dream" of individual success, and a pervasive lack of human understanding aggravated by constrictions of church, state, and class. He develops his characters with both humor and pathos; obsessed with fame and wealth, they are simultaneously the victims and the supporters of superficial cultural myths. Praising the dichotomous style of his plays, Michael Malone observed: "Guare has the nimbleness to run up and down the scaffold of gallows humor, cap and bells on his head, the comic sock on one foot, the tragic buskin on the other, without tripping into either burlesque or bathos."

Guare was born in Queens, New York. In an interview, he described his childhood: "My parents were very bright, very unhappy people. Loners. They lived intensely but separately in their own little worlds. Eventually so did I." Guare nourished his vivid imagination by reading avidly, attending the theater frequently, and studying the structure of musicals. At the age of eleven he produced his first play for family and friends. After graduating from Georgetown University in 1960, he attended the Yale Drama School, where he earned an M.F.A. degree despite his dissatisfaction with the program's emphasis on traditional dramatic structure. Guare later wrote several one-act plays while serving in the Air Force reserves, and also worked as a reader for a London publishing house. It was during a hitch-hiking trip through Europe in 1965 that Guare began his first full-length drama *The House of Blue Leaves.* Completed in 1971, the work won both an Obie Award and a New York Drama Critics Circle Award upon its revival in 1986.

Many critics have interpreted *The House of Blue Leaves* as an admonishment of the American public's obsession with celebrities at the expense of meaningful relationships and moral values. Michael Malone stated: "Its characters are all dreamers; they dream of fame and of the famous. . . . This unending American dream (American tragedy)—[is] that we all could have been, should have been, contenders for the only spot there is, the number one spot." The main character of the work, Artie Shaughnessy, is a middle-aged zookeeper who dreams of making his fortune as a pop songwriter in spite of his blatant lack of talent. Increasingly frustrated by failure and consumed by resentment, he resorts to violence, murdering his mentally unbalanced wife, Bananas. Throughout the play, Bananas has watched helplessly as her husband and his girlfriend plot their elopement. Lonely and starved for love, she develops a pathological affection for glamorous celebrities—a fixation reflecting a national psychosis, according to some reviewers. Critics also view Bananas as a symbol of moral integrity and human need, victimized by the self-

ish ambitions of others. Frank Rich observed: "As Bananas nuzzles helplessly against her husband, Mr. Guare's inspired image of the all-American loser acquires a metaphorical force. . . . Where once there was a woman with stars in her eyes, we see a battered mutt, the forgotten underdog that the bright lights of our national fairy tales always pass by."

Six Degrees of Separation also depicts self-absorbed characters obsessed with images of fame and dissatisfied with the artificiality of their relationships. Based on an actual series of events, this Tony-nominated work portrays a young black man named Paul who poses as a mugging victim and as the son of actor Sidney Poitier, deceiving several wealthy New Yorkers by claiming to be a friend of their children. They invite him into their homes, impressed by his sophistication and tempted by his offer of bit parts in his "father's" upcoming movie version of *Cats.* An ambiguous and mysterious figure, Paul appeals to his victims' longing for genuine experience. Through his conversation, a woman senses the authentic relationship she has failed to develop with her children. Paul's monologue on the importance of the imagination exposes the detachment of an art-dealer whose fascination with art has been reduced to the materialistic attitude of a salesman toward his product. Frank Rich observed: "[Paul] becomes the fuse that ignites a larger investigation of the many degrees of separation that prevent all the people in the play from knowing one another and from knowing themselves."

Guare frequently portrays violence as a symptom of alienation within American society. In *Landscape of the Body,* he presents a dark, brutal image of urban America, focusing on the deterioration of a young mother and her child when they move to New York City; she sinks into prostitution while her son joins a murderous gang. Guare's works also link estrangement from community with the American longing for a perfect society. Set in the nineteenth century, *Gardenia* and *Lydie Breeze* are part of a planned but unfinished cycle of three plays depicting the idealization, corruption and rebirth of a commune created by three Civil War veterans and a nurse who dream of a utopia. Critics noted that the plays' incorporation of such nineteenth-century philosophies as transcendentalism and the Emersonian belief that the emotional rebirth of individuals must precede social politics are particularly relevant to contemporary America. Lloyd Rose asserted: "*Gardenia* and *Lydie Breeze* are not only the finest and most sophisticated response to the dashed ideals of the sixties by any American filmmaker or dramatist but also a majestic fulfillment of the themes and obsessions that Guare has been spinning across the stage for the past eighteen years."

(See also *CLC,* Vols. 8, 14, 29; *Contemporary Authors,* Vols. 73-76; *Contemporary Authors New Revision Series,* Vol. 21; and *Dictionary of Literary Biography,* Vol. 7.)

PRINCIPAL WORKS

PLAYS

Did You Write My Name in the Snow? 1962
To Wally Pantoni, We Leave a Credenza 1964
The Loveliest Afternoon of the Year 1966
Something I'll Tell You Tuesday 1966
Muzeeka 1967
Cop-Out 1969
Home Fires 1969
A Day for Surprises 1971
The House of Blue Leaves 1971
Two Gentlemen of Verona 1971
Marco Polo Sings a Solo 1973
Optimism, or The Adventures of Candide [with Harold
          Stone, adapted from Voltaire's *Candide*] 1973
Rich and Famous 1976
Landscape of the Body 1977
Bosoms and Neglect 1979
Gardenia 1982
Lydie Breeze 1982
Six Degrees of Separation 1990

OTHER

Altantic City (screenplay) 1981

Lloyd Rose

To create a masterpiece and have it go unrecognized is the artist's nightmare. John Guare has been living that nightmare for nearly two years, ever since *Gardenia* and *Lydie Breeze* opened in New York, almost back to back, in early 1982, met with mixed reviews and small audiences, and closed after four weeks. These two plays of his as-yet-unfinished Lydie Breeze cycle . . . can be taken together, as two parts of one great theatrical whole. As such, they are an extraordinary memory-drama of our country's past, as personally and luminously vivid as any autobiographical play, part farce, part tragedy, part parody, part dream. *Gardenia* and *Lydie Breeze* are not only the finest and most sophisticated response to the dashed ideals of the sixties by any American filmmaker or dramatist but also a majestic fulfillment of the themes and obsessions that Guare has been spinning across the stage for the past eighteen years.

Of the three major American dramatists of the seventies—the other two are generally acknowledged to be Lanford Wilson and Sam Shepard—Guare is the odd man out. Where Wilson is sentimental and lyrical and Shepard visceral and mythic, Guare is cerebral, a little abstract. He writes music (he did the songs for his most popular play, *The House of Blue Leaves*), and his plays feel like librettos set to some manic melody he can't get out of his head. Certainly they give the sense, as John Stuart Mill wrote of poetry, of having been *overheard.* Guare is in love with language, and the American dreamers of his plays revel in talk. They tell long, marvelous stories. They give long, impassioned monologues. And they never really listen to one another. As a playwright, Guare is the heir of Chekhov, whose comedy lies in his characters' self-involvement.

Guare's people are not paying any attention to one another because they're focused on their dreams, wherever those may lie: in the future, in the past, inside their heads. They have had images of what they would become, the lives they would lead, but somehow none of it is working out and they can't understand why. In his foreword to *The House of Blue Leaves,* Guare equates this situation with living in Queens (where the play is set and where Guare was born, in 1938, and spent his Irish Catholic boyhood). Each is a temporary stopover until things get better and one can move on and up, "the pay-off that [is] the birthright of every American." But no one moves on and up. Chekhov's three sisters never got to Moscow; Guare's characters never get to Manhattan. In their collective voice, he writes:

> Why don't I get the breaks? What happened? I'm hip. I'm hep. I'm a New Yorker. The heart of the action. Just a subway ride to the heart of the action. I want to be part of that skyline. I want to blend into those lights. Hey dreams, I dreamed you. I'm not something you curb a dog for. New York is where it all is. So why aren't I here?

Guare's characters are desperate to avoid reality, so it falls on them and smashes their heads. In the course of their farcical, selfish scrambling they meet terrible fates: a boy is decapitated; two analysands stab each other; a man strangles his crazy wife; lovers are shot; suicides are committed; nuns explode. "Why shouldn't Strindberg and Feydeau get married, at least live together . . . ?" Guare writes in the foreword to *The House of Blue Leaves.*

The majority of Guare's protagonists, in their single-minded fixation on what they think will make them happy, are in the mainstream tradition of farce. But most of Guare's plays aren't structured as farce. His comedy isn't generated primarily by plot but through words. Guare has the ear of a poet-vaudevillian. In this respect, he is like Beckett, but he's less self-consciously poetic and more fun-loving. He hears the underlying patterns of speech and understands the comic surprises to be had from putting a spin on the expectations that a sentence's form arouses in a listener. What is probably Guare's most famous line (owing to its being in a movie, *Atlantic City,* rather than a play) is a perfect example of his comic sense of language at work: Lou, an aging, second-rate mobster, what few days of glory he has had long gone, gazes at the sea and tells a young punk, "The Atlantic Ocean used to be something. You should have seen the Atlantic Ocean in those days."

Guare appears to love language not just because it can render his ideas but for its own sake. Words arouse his curiosity: he bats them around to see what will happen. A hint of this objective fascination shows up in the opening lines of his early one-act play, *The Loveliest Afternoon of the Year.* A young woman feeding pigeons in Central Park is confronted by a frantic young man:

> HE. (*Terror-stricken.*) I don't want you feeding pigeons because I just saw pigeons at the Seventy Ninth Street Entrance and the covey of them— the whole bunch of them—whatever you call a bunch of pigeons—a gaggle—all those pigeons had *foam*—(*She stops rummaging through her purse.*) Were foaming at the mouths.
>
> SHE. (*Simply.*) I'll scream.
>
> HE. At the *beaks?* Pigeons were foaming at the beaks—all of them.

Bunch. Covey. Gaggle. Mouths. Beaks. In the very act of warning, he is searching for the exact word to convey the odd reality of pigeons foaming like mad dogs.

Rabid pigeons are tame stuff for Guare; his plays are full of much stranger happenings. A man has a sex-change operation and then, through artificial insemination, fathers his/her own child. A woman stuffs her cancerous wound with Kotex and, to cure herself, stands by a window in the night air, waving a statue of Saint Jude. One of the lions outside the New York Public Library comes alive and eats a member of the staff. . . .

But the action of the plays is not as wild as these events, which the audience is told about rather than shown. It's the extraordinary, language-drunk monologues that burst with craziness. The static nonconnecting predicaments of Guare's people translate directly into his dramatic style. Large portions of his plays are taken up with discussions of what has happened or what will happen; the present of the drama is the characters' relating to the past and the future. One can crudely describe the structure of a Guare

play as a series of monologues thrown together by a more-or-less arbitrary plot: the monologues bounce against one another until something cracks. This is a peculiar method of constructing plays. But although Guare may break all the rules of dramatic structure, he still commands the only talent a playwright really needs: he makes an audience ask "What next?"

They may often have asked more in vexation than in eagerness. Guare has written his share of plays that simply don't work. *Marco Polo Sings a Solo,* which is set in the Arctic Circle, is chock full of one nutty thing after another—not only the transsexual who fathers his/her own child but also gestation-shortening rays and plants that sprout out of a character's hands. *Bosoms and Neglect* attempts to connect neglected lives with neglected authors and to juggle this conceit with cancer. But Guare is frequently most brilliant when he is most off the wall. His mad, glittering failures, whatever their faults as plays, are always unmistakably the work of a great writer.

Beginning with *Atlantic City,* after five years or so of plays in which he experimented with the relationship between form and theme, Guare found new assurance and control. *Atlantic City* is tightly plotted, and its characters' dreams, rather than humiliating or destroying them, are magically, rightly fulfilled. Every one of the characters gets what he or she deserves and some of them get what they want. Violent, funny, and amoral, *Atlantic City* affirms the strength of the American dream, which rises in all its acquisitiveness and hopefulness, along with the new casinos, from the rubble of buildings torn down and days gone by.

Before *Atlantic City,* Guare hadn't made much use of time and place. His plays are mostly set in a rather featureless New York City, which is really Queens-as-a-state-of-mind. But much of the success of *Atlantic City* derives from the metaphorical perfection of its setting. Atlantic City itself is an extension of the characters, who derive their identities and drive from its bold, greedy new world. And in *Gardenia* and *Lydie Breeze* (which he was working on at roughly the same time as *Atlantic City:* the movie was released in 1981 and both plays were first staged in 1982), he links his characters' dreams and the ruin of those dreams to the idealism and the corruption of American society in the last quarter of the nineteenth century.

The characters in *Gardenia* and *Lydie Breeze* are an organic part of the America they live in. They are destroyed by forces in our history, and their corruptibility—the fragility of their idealism—is what makes that history destructive. They're not just society's victims; they're its shapers, too. The sophistication, toughness, and breadth of this social vision lifts *Gardenia* and *Lydie Breeze* above Guare's other work and to the pinnacle of American drama.

Guare interweaves personal and social history, using American transcendentalism, that idealistic nineteenth-century philosophy that postulated a mystical unity among all things in the universe, and which had its most concrete expression in the utopian community of Brook Farm ([Nathaniel] Hawthorne's Blithedale, in *The Bli-*

thedale Romance). Guare's utopians are three Civil War veterans and the woman who nursed them in the hospital, Lydie Breeze. They set up their commune, which they whimsically name Aipotu, on Nantucket Island at the war's end, rejecting the America being formed by the likes of Andrew Carnegie and Jay Gould and led by Ulysses S. Grant, and vowing to find the transcendental purpose of their lives.

Taking Lydie's husband, Joshua Hickman, as his focal character, Guare presents the corruption, ruin, and final regeneration of Aipotu, by dramatizing four days in its history: one in 1875, when the book Joshua has worked on for seven years is rejected by William Dean Howells, and when Lydie's lover, Dan Grady, brings into the community money acquired by graft; one in 1884, when Joshua, imprisoned for murdering Dan, destroys his new book, which Howells has greeted as an American masterpiece; and two days in 1895, when all the threads of the plot and all the guilt and horror work themselves into a final pattern of healing and rebirth.

Guare's decision to set *Gardenia* and *Lydie Breeze* in the nineteenth century, which might seem as if it would have restricted him, turns out to be a master's choice. The history and thought of the nineteenth century mirror and give form to his themes of isolation and connection. He lays the foundations of the plays solidly in nineteenth-century American literature. [Ralph Waldo] Emerson, who believed, as Irving Howe put it, that "individual regeneration must precede social politics . . . " is the infusing spirit of *Gardenia. Lydie Breeze,* which opens in a Gothic dawn with Lydie dead and her namesake daughter trying to communicate with her, is haunted by [Edgar Allan] Poe; the girl's eventual final acceptance by Joshua (she is Dan's daughter, not his) and her own acceptance of her coming womanhood are a healing variant of Poe's neurotic obsession with the dead beloved who rises from her grave. *Gardenia* opens and *Lydie Breeze* closes with Joshua reading lines from [Walt] Whitman that express the soul and hope of the plays:

> A vast similitude interlocks all.
> All spheres, grown, ungrown, small, large, suns,
>   moons, planets,
> All distances of time. All souls
> All lives and deaths, all of the past, present, future,
> This vast similitude spans them, and always has spanned
> And shall forever span them and compactly hold and enclose them.

Whitman, Emerson, and Poe shape and integrate these plays as they shaped and expressed the America about which Guare is writing.

Guare also makes a concession to the nineteenth century in his language. He shapes his dialogue more formally than usual, and it has a new purity and beauty: it's lyrical, yet steely. It is not really like nineteenth-century language as we know it from books and letters of the time. Stylized and reduced to its essential rhythms, it has an archaic, haunted sound. And because we don't actually know what casual American speech was like then, its strangeness

makes it begin to seem real. It transports us fully into Guare's nineteenth century, at the same time that it distances us, reminding us by its alien tone that we are looking into a world buried forever beneath the wars, technology, and politics of our own century.

In a very basic sense, *Gardenia* and *Lydie Breeze* are nineteenth-century plays. Guare takes as his model [Henrik] Ibsen, in whose dramatic territory of social disintegration and sexual misalliance he is working. In *Lydie Breeze,* we follow the story by the movement of syphilis through the characters. The transmission of the infection is our clue to the play—who had it first? who had it when?—and our efforts to track it become a macabre game. This brilliant gloss on *Ghosts* (a perfect alternate title for *Lydie Breeze*) fulfills Guare's dramatic purposes; at the same time, it both acknowledges Ibsen's mastery of plot and turns him on his head.

Guare jams the plays with adultery, murder, madness, theft, injury, mistaken identity, blackmail. These are the same melodramatic clichés from which Ibsen built his dramas. But whereas Ibsen transcended them through superb craftsmanship and the force of his moral sensibility, Guare merrily piles them one atop the other until they tumble over, a satiric abundance of misfortunes that explodes the conventions of nineteenth-century melodrama through overcrowding.

"One can crudely describe the structure of a Guare play as a series of monologues thrown together by a more-or-less arbitrary plot: the monologues bounce against one another until something cracks. This is a peculiar method of constructing plays. But although Guare may break all the rules of dramatic structure, he still commands the only talent a playwright really needs: he makes an audience ask 'What next?' "

And each horror is dramatized with a deft and startling eccentricity. Just after we have heard a terrible and graphic account of Lydie's suicide (she hanged herself), Guare gives us that dawn séance, in which young Lydie is instructed to tell her mother's spirit what she has learned. She recites a recipe, getting most of the quantities wrong and leaving out the salt and the nutmeg.

This tonal shift is so abrupt it's disorienting; it's as sudden and frightening (yet mysteriously right) as the dislocations we experience in dreams. We're watching peoples' lives and hopes, and our country's idealism, collapse. We have every reason to expect sober austerity. What we get is jokes, looniness, images that seem to have been thrown in from the wings. It's as if Ibsen had been translated by Lewis Carroll.

Not that Guare can't be straightforward enough when he

pleases. The center of the plays lies in a simple conversation Lydie and Joshua have when she visits him in prison. "We wanted perfection," she says. "So we thought we were perfection." He confesses to her that he murdered Dan not from fierce, romantic passion but for small reasons, ending ruefully, "Oh Christ—in all our dreaming, we never allowed for the squalid, petty furies. We lived on a beach in a vast landscape. We mistook the size of the ocean, the size of the sky, for the size of our souls."

But Guare prefers to work elliptically, skidding past the dangers of pretension and dullness. Toward the end of *Lydie Breeze,* he puts forward the idea that perhaps the only possible connection between people is forgiveness. Where a lesser playwright might have given us a long and boringly message-ridden soliloquy, Guare uses a Ouija board. Gussie, Joshua and Lydie's daughter, is playing with it, and it keeps spelling out FORG. Joshua tells her it means she should "Forget here. Forget your father. Forget Nantucket." Gussie retorts that it means "forge ahead. For Gussie. Forget me not. Forgo any bad thoughts." Neither of them figures out what the letters are actually spelling, but during this scene they forgive each other. And by the play's end, Joshua has forgiven young Lydie, whom he has brought up as his own but never truly accepted, for being Dan's child.

It's this tension between Guare's bizarre sense of invention and the dramatic and social conventions of the nineteenth century that sets the plays spinning like a top: the core may sleep on an axis of loss and dreams, but the surface is whirling. Guare's refusal to tell his story straight, his commitment to the unexpected and the berserk, gives *Gardenia* and *Lydie Breeze* a giddy exhilaration. They're a screwball epic.

Yet for all their whirligig plotting and crazy humor, they're graceful where his other plays were frenetic, sustained in their power rather than explosive. Their American past is as much Guare's invention as his Queens or Arctic Circle, but whereas those settings seemed like nutty dreams, his Nantucket colony has the glow and the distortion of memory. The plays roll through lives and years from the Civil War to the edge of the twentieth century, from hope to ruin to hope again, held and enclosed by that visionary fragment from Whitman.

But Guare has reached further back than Whitman for his underlying literary structure. It is late Shakespearean comedy, with its vision of healing and continuance in the reconciliation of fathers and daughters (*Lydie Breeze,* in particular, has its roots in *The Tempest*) that accounts for the mysterious serenity of Guare's plays. By their final scene, all scores have been settled, all lovers have found each other, the father and his daughters have made peace. Young Lydie, waiting on her first suitor and her approaching menstruation, sits beside Joshua, and he teaches her to read: "All spheres, grown, ungrown, small, large. . . ."

At the beginning of *Gardenia,* Guare has Howells write to Joshua, "Let the brisk air of America blow through your vigorous imagination." Guare has taken his own advice. That air blows through *Gardenia* and *Lydie*

Breeze—the bracing air we breathe only rarely, and then only on the heights. (pp. 120-22, 124)

Lloyd Rose, "A New American Master," in The Atlantic Monthly, *Vol. 253, No. 3, March, 1984, pp. 120-22, 124.*

John Simon

Names, alas, make a big difference in our society. I cannot think of anything but the signature "John Guare" to explain why *Landscape of the Body* was done even once. . . . Despite the odd clever line and some bedraggled bits of poignance, this is a play as pointless as it is odious. Not funny enough for a cartoon, not authentic enough to justify its horror and shock effects, not beautifully enough written to stand on its language, not saying anything beyond that people—even children—can be corrupted (and saying *that* in a way that does not make even absurdist sense), *Landscape of the Body* is really an inscape of the mind gone stale and desperately trying to dredge up something, anything, with which a stage can be cluttered up.

It is not pleasant to have to say this, for John Guare once held genuine promise as a dramatist, and as recently as in *Atlantic City* gave us a screenplay of savory eccentricity. But, in play after pretentious play, Guare has been turning our theater into a kind of disused rumpus room. Here we have an innocent young woman from Bangor, Maine, come to New York with her teenage son to reclaim her wayward sister, who proves irredeemable. She herself sinks rapidly into prostitution as her son forms a murderous youth gang. Violent, mostly meaningless deaths are everywhere as heads, quite literally, roll.

There is studied brutality and wheezing whimsy as the heroine's now dead sister comments, in narration and inept and irrelevant songs (also by Guare), on the progress of the shallowly attitudinizing and deeply distasteful action. And what facile verbal flummery: "Boy, oh girl, I said"; "You're the fruit of my loins or the fruit of the loom" (a mother to her son); "To settle my estate along with my hash"; "The moon, like a little Turkish flag waving in the sky" (from a character who couldn't have seen a Turkish flag—and an author who apparently hasn't, either); "These golden days, the clear gold of cough drops that rescue you in the middle of the night," and so on through this topper: "My life is a triumph of all the things I don't know." No comment.

The attempts to join absurdism to naturalism, poetic prose to street talk, psychology to symbolic arbitrariness, manage to fail each in both directions. (pp. 105-06)

John Simon, "Bangs and Whimpers," in New York *Magazine, Vol. 17, No. 21, May 21, 1984, pp. 104-06.*

Edith Oliver

The mercurial, bleak, fanciful, humorous, gritty imagination of John Guare is unique in the American theatre, and it is nowhere more evident than in his puzzling, grisly comedy *Landscape of the Body*. . . . When the play opened originally, in 1977, I remember enjoying it in spite of some rather sizable reservations; this time, although a number of scenes worked well, I didn't laugh at all. The story, which is told in flashbacks, songs (by the playwright), fantasy, and even one spectacular break dance, opens aboard a ferry from Cape Cod to Nantucket, where a young woman is engaged in conversation by a fellow in a Groucho Marx false face. She recognizes him as the detective who has been querying her for months about the murder of her fourteen-year-old son, hoping to trap her into a confession. Back we go to her arrival with the boy in New York, some months before, from Maine, and then, in episode after episode, to the death of her sister, to getting a job at a crooked tourist agency and another making porn films after she moves into the sister's apartment on Christopher Street, where the boy joins a trio of juvenile delinquents and becomes one himself, and eventually to the murder by decapitation when she leaves him alone in the city with a thousand dollars. All through this sordid tale, there should be evidence of the dramatist's irrepressible high spirits and wayward humor, but there wasn't much.

Edith Oliver, in a review of "Landscape of the Body," in The New Yorker, *Vol. LX, No. 14, May 21, 1984, p. 98.*

Frank Rich

Returning to *The House of Blue Leaves* 15 years after its Off Broadway premiere, one expects to find a musty, archetypal artifact of late 1960's black comedy. Set in Sunnyside, Queens, on that 1965 day when Pope Paul VI visited New York, John Guare's early, breakthrough play features mockingly observed nuns, a lethal (but farcical) political bombing, a G.I. earmarked for Vietnam and, as a protagonist, a zookeeper who dreams in vain of making it big in Hollywood as a songwriter. As if that weren't enough countercultural loopiness, the zookeeper, Artie Shaughnessy, has a wife named Bananas who really is bananas. In the period's R. D. Laing-Ken Kesey tradition, Bananas, a schizophrenic destined for a cuckoo's nest (the house of Mr. Guare's title), is the sanest character in the work.

Yet a funny thing has happened to *Blue Leaves* in the loving revival. . . . The play no longer seems all that funny, and it's none the worse for the shift in tone. While some of Mr. Guare's jokes are indeed dated remnants of the 60's, his characters and themes have gained the weight and gravity so lacking in his more pretentious recent plays. Time hasn't healed the wounds described in *Blue Leaves*—it's deepened them. One still leaves the theater howling at Mr. Guare's vision of losers at sea in a materialistic culture, but the howls are less of laughter than of pain. . . .

[Much of that pain derives from the character of Bananas. She] wears a ragged, misbuttoned cardigan over a faded nightgown; her hair is a dark, silver-tinged mop, framing a pallid face with bulging, swimming eyes. Making her first entrance in silence, she stands in the gloomy fringes of her threadbare cage of a living room, watching her husband, Artie, and his mistress, a platinum-haired downstairs neighbor named Bunny, plot their elopement to California. Powerless to do anything to halt the plan—which will place her in the loony bin—the spectral . . . [Bananas] exits as quietly as she entered, a catatonic ghost. And without a single line, she casts the entire play in tragic shadows.

Blue Leaves can accommodate that darkness. Mr. Guare has found the terror as well as the absurdity in working-class Queens nobodies who aspire to be somebodies; at its best, his play often seems like *The Day of the Locust* as rewritten by Tennessee Williams. Certainly . . . [Bananas] seems as lost as Blanche DuBois in her climactic Act I speech, in which Bananas madly recalls having been at Forty-second Street and Broadway, "the crossroads of the world," on a day when Jacqueline Kennedy, Cardinal Spellman, Bob Hope and President Johnson were all at that intersection hailing cabs. Bananas explains that she gave the celebrities a lift—only to discover later that night that the disastrous results were recounted as comic anecdotes on the Johnny Carson show. Recalling her humiliation before 30 million television viewers, Bananas wonders why stars can't "love" fans like herself. . . . [The] monologue is not just a surreal shaggy joke: Bananas' pathological relationship to glamorous American myths becomes grotesquely symbolic of a national psychosis.

> **"[Guare] sees his characters sympathetically [in *The House of Blue Leaves*], as helpless victims of a society in which movie stars and the Pope are indistinguishable media gods, in which television is a shrine, in which assassins are glorified in headlines."**

This isn't to say there is no humor left in *Blue Leaves*. When those wayward nuns appear in Act II, they fly like bats into the iron window bars of the Shaughnessy living room. We meet a deaf Hollywood starlet . . . whose hilarious confusions include what must be the single funniest gag ever sparked by the word "Unitarian." There are also Artie's many failed Tin Pan Alley songs—would-be Hoagy Carmichael ditties with titles like "Where Is the Devil in Evelyn?" . . .

What makes these comic twists closer in spirit to Nathanael West than the 1960's is Mr. Guare's refusal to condescend. The playwright sees his characters sympathetically, as helpless victims of a society in which movie stars and the Pope are indistinguishable media gods, in which television is a shrine, in which assassins are glorified in headlines. In such an icon-ridden landscape, the best hope is the pathetic one stated by the brash Bunny: "When famous people go to sleep at night," she wistfully posits, "it's us they dream of."

Bunny also claims, apropos of the Pope's visit, that

"there's miracles in the air." But the miracles she and the others long for are either spiritually bankrupt or unobtainable. Mr. Guare's Sunnyside denizens believe that a neighborhood boy turned filmland big shot will bring them instant fame and fortune; they even believe that the Pope, by addressing the United Nations, can end the war in Vietnam. Such starry-eyed fantasies do little but drive everyone bananas. The blue spotlight of stardom craved by the songwriting Artie may be as much of a nuthouse as the blue-leaf-shaded asylum where he would dispose of his wife. When the Shaughnessys' son auditions for the role of Huckleberry Finn in a Hollywood movie, his various stunts (all learned from the Ed Sullivan show) are pointedly mistaken for the behavior of a "mental defective." . . .

By evening's end, Bananas has actually become one of her husband's animals. Bananas likes animals, she has explained, because they're not famous and because they represent to her the buried feelings that her fit-regulating pills usually restrain. . . . [Bananas's] metamorphosis brings the theater to a shocked hush. Her slender hands become paws dancing in the air, her voice trails off into a maimed puppy's whimper. As Bananas nuzzles helplessly against her husband, Mr. Guare's inspired image of the all-American loser acquires a metaphorical force as timeless as West's locusts. Where once there was a woman with stars in her eyes, we see a battered mutt, the forgotten underdog that the bright lights of our national fairy tales always pass by.

> *Frank Rich, in a review of "The House of Blue Leaves," in* The New York Times, *March 20, 1986, p. C21.*

Edith Oliver

The revival of John Guare's *The House of Blue Leaves* is infinitely better than its original production, fifteen years ago—and I had not thought anything could be. The play now seems deeper, sadder, more passionate, and even funnier, if that is conceivable. . . . *The House of Blue Leaves,* in case anyone needs reminding, is a satiric farce about a middle-aged zookeeper, named Artie Shaughnessy, who has a knack for writing imitations of cheap popular songs, and who is the victim of a number of American dreams, which finally destroy him. The place is his living room in Sunnyside, Queens; the time is October 4, 1965, the day Pope Paul VI flew to New York to appear before the United Nations General Assembly to plead for an end to war—perhaps specifically the war in Vietnam (and perhaps, by blessing Artie's sheet music, to ease his way to Hollywood and an Academy Award). Artie lives with his wife, who has recently gone mad and is nicknamed Bananas; he wants to put her in a sanitarium (the house of the title), run off to California with Bunny Flingus, his downstairs neighbor and mistress, who is eagerly abetting him, and then get a job with his best friend, a prominent movie director. Bananas resists the hospital, because she is terrified of shock treatments. As I remarked in my original review, "this play could be considered a whole series of shock treatments, and often I was as horrified at myself for laughing (which I did a lot) as I was at what I heard and saw on the stage." The plot is wild and

arbitrary and always outrageous. The other characters are a movie star, deafened by an explosion during the making of her latest picture, who is the director's girlfriend; the Shaughnessys' son, AWOL after twenty-one days in the Army, who arrives with a homemade bomb, his target being the Pope; three goofy nuns, who have been watching the Pope's motorcade from the roof of the Shaughnessys' apartment house; and, finally, the great director himself. The bomb misses the Pope, but it does go off, taking its toll of the assembled company.

Guare's marvellous comic writing, in which every word plays, and his ferocious high spirits glow more than ever in these drab days. . . . (pp. 66, 68)

> *Edith Oliver, "Old and Improved," in* The New Yorker, *Vol. LXII, No. 6, March 31, 1986, pp. 66, 68.*

Edwin Wilson

Seen a decade-and-a-half after it originally appeared, *The House of Blue Leaves* combines the wild mayhem of such well-known '30s farces as *Room Service* and *Three Men on a Horse* with the black humor of Harold Pinter and Eugene Ionesco.

Artie Shaughnessy, the hero of *Blue Leaves,* is a comic counterpart of Willy Loman of *Death of a Salesman*—"he has the wrong dreams, all, all wrong." A zookeeper by profession, Artie dreams of becoming a successful songwriter: the legendary Tin Pan Alley type who suddenly hits it big and is whisked off to Hollywood.

Artie feels that he is held back by bad luck and by his mentally unbalanced wife, whom he calls Bananas. He is encouraged in his fantasy by his mistress, Bunny Flingus, who lives in an apartment below, and by his connection, as a childhood friend, with Billy Einhorn, a prosperous film director. Artie is certain that if he ever gets to Hollywood, Billy will set him up in pictures.

The action occurs on the day in 1965 when the pope is scheduled to visit the United Nations. His motorcade is supposed to pass by Artie's apartment on Queens Boulevard on its way to Manhattan. In the Shaughnessy household all hell breaks loose: Artie's anti-establishment son plans to assassinate the pope; three zany nuns hoping to watch the motorcade invade the apartment; Bunny and Artie try to commit Bananas to a home so they can strike out for Hollywood; Billy's girlfriend, a luscious blond starlet who has become deaf while making a war movie, shows up unexpectedly. (Not being aware of the starlet's infirmity, Artie auditions one song after another for her; and she, not wanting to reveal her secret, pretends to hear every note.) . . .

Artie's tragedy is that his dream can never come true because he is not very talented. In one marvelous scene Bananas asks him to play one of his compositions, "I Love You So I Keep Dreaming." Immensely flattered, he throws himself into a rendition of the number. Then she asks him to play "White Christmas." Of course, it's the same tune, except that Artie had never realized it before.

What makes the play simultaneously entertaining and devastating: One moment we are lost in laughter and the next some cruelty or painful reality cuts across the action. What was madcap folly instantly becomes serious, and we are suddenly reminded of the absurdity, the agony and the unpredictability of modern life.

> *Edwin Wilson, "A Smash Revival," in* The Wall Street Journal, *April 9, 1986, p. 31.*

Robert Brustein

After years of feeling marginal—he once called himself the oldest promising playwright in America—John Guare is about to experience a vogue. Two of his plays are currently being revived in New York—*Bosoms and Neglect* and *The House of Blue Leaves*. . . . Guare is now destined to become the subject of newspaper features, magazine tintypes, TV talk shows, radio interviews, and all those other celebrity rituals that constitute the American version of ancient puberty rites and walkabouts. Or perhaps they're the gentile adult version of Jewish bar mitzvah parties where relatives and guests circulate around the confirmation boy applauding his speech, admiring his blue suit, and pinching his cheeks, before leaving him, bewildered, isolated, forlorn, amid the stacked plates and soiled tablecloths.

John Guare is young enough to enjoy these rituals and seasoned enough to be prepared for the inevitable end of the party. He knows success is always accompanied by backlash, if not whiplash, and he will keep his good nature when the ballroom empties out. He will also keep his admirable devotion to the stage and his unwavering commitment to play writing, which have been courageously maintained in the face of unkind evaluations and sour reviews of the type I am about to offer [on his *The House of Blue Leaves*].

I think I once compared John Guare to a big shaggy dog whose paws get all tangled up in its efforts to befriend you. In *The House of Blue Leaves,* this kindly creature seems to be standing on your shoulders and licking you all over the face. . . . Whatever the reason, the intervening years have turned *The House of Blue Leaves* from a provocative off-Broadway comedy into an eager-to-please middlebrow commodity.

I realize that "middlebrow" is no longer a term in the critical lexicon, but how else to describe the divided tone of this calamity-packed laugh riot? *The House of Blue Leaves* is black comedy seen through rose-colored glasses. It ends with a shock, when the trapped husband, Artie Shaugnessy, throttles his dippy wife, Bananas, in the midst of her puppy impersonation. (Why didn't Torvald think of this when Nora started her squirrel bits?) But it's tough to accept a tragic climax after having been encouraged all night to regard murder, madness, physical affliction, adultery, and assassination as occasions for gags. Yes, I know about [British dramatist] Joe Orton, but Orton never deviates from his remorseless japery. More like Peter Nichols with *Joe Egg,* Guare wants it both ways here—to exploit the absurdities of his maimed characters and then to draw down the mouths of their comic masks. But you don't establish dramatic empathy after two hours of farcical alienation.

"Alienation" is probably too lofty a word to describe a style that mixes arch one-liners ("Orion—the Irish constellation") with droll characters and whimsical situations, and turns the audience into a laugh track. Zookeeper Artie is a would-be songwriter who sometimes speaks in couplets. His consuming ambition is to compose movie music for his boyhood chum, the Hollywood director Billy Einhorn. Artie's guilty concern for the mildly insane Bananas (she occasionally tries to commit suicide by slashing her wrists with spoons) is the obstacle to this ambition. ("You wish I was fatter," she says, "so there'd be more of me to hate.") His peroxide tootsie, Bunny, doesn't offer much in the way of consolation by refusing to cook for him. ("We've gotta save some magic for the honeymoon. . . . I want it to be so good, I'm aiming for 2,000 calories.") On this particular day, the pontiff is coming to visit New York, and the couple's psychotic son, Ronnie, is planning a papal assassination. Like his nonfictional Turkish successor, Ronnie botches the job and blows up a couple of hip nuns instead, along with Billy Einhorn's girlfriend, the deaf starlet Corinna. (Bananas has mistaken her hearing aid transistors for lithium and swallowed them.) Billy decamps with Bunny, leaving Artie frustrated enough to strangle Bananas. And the play ends, as it began, with Artie in a blue spot, crooning songs.

It's too bad that Bananas gets killed at the end, because the dramatis personae of *The House of Blue Leaves* are cute enough, and the plot sufficiently contrived, to be recycled for a TV sitcom (the ultimate fate of Lanford Wilson's *Hot L Baltimore*). Billy consoles Artie for his blighted career by telling him he has "the greatest talent in the world—to be an audience—anybody can create." This flattering nod to the noncreative consumer, unequaled on the stage until Salieri's tribute to mediocrity in *Amadeus,* is the assumption underlying mass culture, and it spells the difference between art created out of need and kitsch created out of need for endorsement. (pp. 27-9)

The play is better constructed than the later work of Guare, who has a lot more feel for New York local color than for Nantucket or Civil War history, the subject of his more ambitious *Lydie Breeze* cycle. One also has to respect the playwright's effort to locate humor and vitality in the desperate careers of the dispossessed and uncelebrated, though it's not always clear how detached he is from their one articulated aim, which is to get on a plane to Hollywood. Dammit, I like John Guare, I really do, and I'm glad he's having his moment in the sun. I like him a lot more when he gets his paws off my chest and romps freely around the yard. (p. 29)

> *Robert Brustein, "A Shaggy Dog Story," in* The New Republic, *Vol. 194, No. 18, May 5, 1986, pp. 27-30.*

Michael Malone

[*The House of Blue Leaves*] is the discovery of the season, the new hot ticket, although the play is neither new nor previously neglected. Sixteen years ago, *Blue Leaves* won the New York and Los Angeles Drama Critics Circle awards; since then, college, community and stock theaters have frequently performed it. But this year it has received eight Tony nominations, including one for the best play of 1986. (p. 798)

In a way, *Blue Leaves* is about prizes, about yearning for them. Its characters are all dreamers; they dream of fame and of the famous. They want what the famous have: laurel and loot, stardust and a place in the sun. This unending American dream (American tragedy)—that we all could have been, should have been, contenders for the only spot there is, the number-one spot—brings Artie Shaughnessy to the El Dorado Bar Amateur Night as the play opens, to sing his heart out ("I wrote all these songs. Words and the music") in hopes of a blue spotlight. In the clichés of his lyrics we hear that dream. "I'm looking for Something." "I'm here with bells on. Ring! Ring! Ring!"

Then . . . behind the Shaughnessys' humdrum Queens apartment crammed with its tawdry gewgaws and totems of fame, in rhythm with the blare of Strauss's "Thus Spake Zarathustra" (better known perhaps as the soundtrack from *2001,* or as Elvis Presley's concert theme song), the glittering lights of Manhattan's skyline appear. The audience laughs; no doubt we're supposed to. But those bright towers of big-time success are as near and as far from Artie Shaughnessy in Queens as they were from Willy Loman in Brooklyn. As Guare has written about this play and its genesis in his Catholic boyhood in Queens, "How do you run away to your dreams when you're already there?" He holds his characters' failed aspirations and their absurd worship of celebrity up to a lampooning, madcap mockery that some have called cruel, but his contempt is reserved for the culture, not the creatures who have fed on its junk food of TV and tabloids. Indeed, the sadness of *Blue Leaves* centers, by Guare's account, on the cruelty of our national dream of success: "Everyone in the play is constantly being humiliated by their dreams, their lives, their wants, their best parts. . . . I'm not interested so much in how people survive as in how they avoid humiliation. . . . avoiding humiliation is the core of tragedy and comedy and probably of our lives." For the truth is that Artie Shaughnessy is never going to win prizes, any more than Chekhov's three sisters are ever going to get to Moscow, any more than Williams's crippled Laura will ever find a gentleman caller or Willy Loman ever follow his brother Ben into the jungle that's "dark but full of diamonds" and walk out a rich man.

Blue Leaves is dark and full of diamonds, and I hope it wins all the prizes it can. It's a marvelous, maniacal tragicomedy, full of waggish merriment, razor sharp in its mordant wit but never cutting out the hearts of its characters, or turning away from their keen aches. Here, as in plays like *Landscape of the Body* and *Bosoms and Neglect* (also revived this season), Guare has the nimbleness to run up and down the scaffold of gallows humor, cap and bells on his head, the comic sock on one foot, the tragic buskin on the other, without tripping into either burlesque or bathos. According to him, the impetus for this tightroping came from seeing Laurence Olivier perform in *Dance of Death* and *A Flea in Her Ear* on successive nights. "Why," he decided, "shouldn't Strindberg and Feydeau get married (or at least live together, and *The House of Blue Leaves* be their child?" (pp. 799-800)

Blue Leaves takes place on a day in 1965 when the Pope drove through Queens on his way to the United Nations to help stop the war in Vietnam. (On that actual day, Guare—in an irony worthy of his drama—had finally achieved his nun teachers' dream of touring the Vatican.) While crowds gather on the sidewalks, more excited than they've been since the premiere of *Cleopatra,* Artie dreams of his son, a recruit bound for Vietnam, becoming Pope and making his dad Saint in Charge of Hymn-Writing. Bunny, Artie's deliciously tacky mistress, a strutting compendium of hackneyed sentiments and Dale Carnegie optimism, urges him to wake up, to go get his songs blessed by the Pope, go get his wife put in a mental institution and, most emphatically, to get the two of them to Billy, Artie's old friend, a movie big shot in California. There they will have a new life where dreams can come true. Then and only then will she cook for him; until they're legally wed, he will have to content himself with sex, and with looking at photos of her dishes in a scrapbook hidden under the couch.

The scrapbook is hidden there from Bananas, Artie's mentally disturbed wife, who wanders eerily through the house she has been too frightened to leave since her suicide attempt several months ago. Its windows are now barred by an iron gate, because, like the mother in Guare's *Bosoms and Neglect,* like the mother in O'Neill's *Long Day's Journey,* like the mothers and wives in so many American plays and in so much of American life, Bananas bears the psychic burden of her family's failures; she feels the pain, screams the truth and for doing so has to be sedated with pills or sent away to an institution, the house of blue leaves (the leaves were really bluebirds that flew off and left the boughs bare). . . . Bananas transcends the pathos of her delusions and stands at the play's center, quiet as grief, heartbreaking as honesty. She moves quietly in and out of Guare's hilarious, absurdist parade of deaf starlets, monstrous moguls, terrorist sons and a trio of madcap nuns who roar on stage like the Marx Brothers in habits. Bananas stands there with the lucidity of madness and asks us to laugh and cry with her at all their—all our—lost dreams. Artie cannot escape her truth even by destroying her. Nor can we, no more than dreamer Tom in *The Glass Menagerie* (fled to cities that "swept about me like dead leaves, brightly colored, torn from branches") could escape the vision of his lost sister. The triumph of *Blue Leaves* and of its performers is that we cannot forget the sorrows that blue spotlights disguise. It is that knowledge that makes Guare not just the older but the wiser brother of tour de farce writers like Christopher Durang. If, as the successes of *Blue Leaves* and Orton's *Loot* suggest, audiences are now prepared to welcome this darker, zanier humor into the theatrical mainstream, then our theater is fortunate to have ready in the wings not only a master of laughter but a poet of compassion. (p. 800)

Michael Malone, in a review of "The House of Blue Leaves," in The Nation, *New York, Vol. 242, No. 22, June 7, 1986, pp. 798-800.*

Clive Barnes

John Guare's intermissionless and partly impressionistic new play, *Six Degrees of Separation,* at times resembles a symphony in three movements.

At first, the play appears to be a modern, sophisticated New York drawing room comedy, East Side, WASP-y and brittle. You might say we are wandering in A. R. Gurney territory. Then, in a change of pace and mood, it almost disconcertingly moves into something like a detective story genre, Channel 13, British TV, highbrow-style.

Finally, in a third movement which brings the whole evening together, Guare manages to suggest some epiphany of the human soul—and the result is astonishing. Uplifting, puzzling, yet surely telling at least some of us something about ourselves we hardly knew and only dimly perceived.

We sometimes—and there are two sides to every picture—like, envy and even admire glorious fakes. And we can feel a kinship to their fakery.

An entrepreneur-style art dealer, Flan and his wife Ouisa are entertaining a wealthy South African merchant tycoon who they hope will finance the millions needed for a speculative purchase of a Renoir to be sold at a tidy profit to the Japanese. Before they can go out to a smart, vastly overpriced dinner, their small gathering is interrupted by a personable young and bleeding black man, who claims to be a close friend of their children at Harvard.

And just guess who has come to dinner? The young man shyly claims that he is the son of Sidney Poitier—the next morning he is to meet his father, who is coming to town, he says, to cast a forthcoming movie of *Cats.*

Sam, Ouisa and the South African Geoffrey are charmed by this newcomer, Paul, who says all the right things, makes all the right moves, and seems to know them and, particularly, their children all better than they do themselves. The tiniest little details. It is almost too good to be true, and it is. Too good, rather than true.

But, dazzled and seduced out of their minds, they want to believe—Paul even cooks dinner for them, bathing in their admiration. Indeed, Geoffrey is so taken with this young "Poitier" that before he leaves he euphorically agrees to advance Flan the three million bucks he needs to clinch his Renoir deal.

Flan insists that Paul stays the night—and advances him 50 dollars to get to his father in the morning. But later that night Flan and Ouisa hear a noise—they go to the spare room and catch Paul *in flagrante delicto* with a male hustler. Consternation and collapse—Paul and his unwelcome concubine are ejected, and the saddened couple look around to see if they have been materially robbed as well as emotionally violated.

However, they soon find that their young visitor has pulled the self-same scam on a couple of their friends—once more claiming to be the son of Poitier and seeming to be a well-informed friend of their children. He is a fake. Now the issue becomes how did Paul pull off this immaculate deception and—perhaps more interestingly—why?

Robbery did not seem to be the motive. Nothing was taken—except a little odd change that had been freely given him by his blissfully duped victims.

Not unexpectedly, Guare cannot truly and convincingly explain the mechanics of the scam—or rather his explanation is difficult to swallow—and the playwright fills out his canvas with a brief, none too acceptable, tragi-comic subplot. But then in the play's magnificent final phase, the emphasis is placed not on the how, but the why of the deception. The why and the final result.

The title—*Six Degrees of Separation*—comes from some scientific contention, which I admit I had never heard before, that everyone on earth is separated from anyone else on earth by only six genetic links. I find this difficult to believe as a fact—which means it is probably true—but as a metaphor of man's universality, it is potent and here relevant.

> *Clive Barnes, "Duped to the nth Degree," in* New York Post, *June 15, 1990.*

Frank Rich

Ouisa Kittredge, the Upper East Side hostess at the center of John Guare's *Six Degrees of Separation,* delights in the fact that it only takes a chain of six people to connect anyone on the planet with anyone else. But what about those who are eternally separated from others because they cannot find the right six people? Chances are that they, like Ouisa, live in chaotic contemporary New York, which is the setting for this extraordinary high comedy in which broken connections, mistaken identities and tragic social, familial and cultural schisms take the stage to create a hilarious and finally searing panorama of urban America in precisely our time.

For those who have been waiting for a masterwork from the writer who bracketed the 1970's with the play *House of Blue Leaves* and the film *Atlantic City,* this is it. For those who have been waiting for the American theater to produce a play that captures New York as Tom Wolfe did in *Bonfire of the Vanities,* this is also it. And, with all due respect to Mr. Wolfe, *Six Degrees of Separation* expands on that novel's canvas and updates it. Mr. Guare gives as much voice to his black and female characters as to his upper-crust white men, and he transports the audience beyond the dailiness of journalistic storytelling to the magical reaches of the imagination.

Though the play grew out of a 1983 newspaper account of a confidence scheme, it is as at home with the esthetics of Wassily Kandinsky as it is with the realities of Rikers Island. The full sweep of the writing—90 nonstop minutes of cyclonic action, ranging from knockabout farce to hallucinatory dreams—is matched by [the] ceaselessly inventive production. . . .

The news story that sparked *Six Degrees of Separation* told of a young black man who talked his way into wealthy white Upper East Side households by purporting to be both Sidney Poitier's son and the Ivy League college friend of his unwitting hosts' children. In Mr. Guare's variation, the young man, who calls himself Paul Poitier, lands in the Fifth Avenue apartment of Ouisa and her husband, Flan, a high-rolling art dealer. Paul is a charming, articulate dissembler on all subjects who has the Kittredges in thrall. He is also a petty thief who invites a male hustler into the guest room he occupies while waiting for his "father" to take up residence at the Sherry-Netherland Hotel.

Much as this situation, a rude twist on *Guess Who's Coming to Dinner,* lends itself to the satirical mayhem Mr. Wolfe inflicted on white liberals in "Radical Chic," Mr. Guare has not written a satire about race relations. Paul, the black man whose real identity the Kittredges never learn, becomes the fuse that ignites a larger investigation of the many degrees of separation that prevent all the people in the play from knowing one another and from knowing themselves.

It is not only blacks and whites who are estranged in Mr. Guare's New York. As the action accelerates and the cast of characters expands, the audience discovers that the Kittredges and their privileged friends don't know their alienated children, that heterosexuals don't know homosexuals, that husbands don't know their wives, that art dealers don't know the art they trade for millions. The only thing that everyone in this play's Manhattan has in common is the same American malady that afflicted the working-class Queens inhabitants of *House of Blue Leaves*—a desire to bask in the glow of the rich and famous. Here that hunger takes the delirious form of a maniacal desire to appear as extras in Sidney Poitier's purported film version of *Cats,* a prospect Paul dangles in front of his prey.

"Among the many remarkable aspects of Mr. Guare's writing is the seamlessness of his imagery, characters and themes, as if this play had just erupted from his own imagination in one perfect piece. 'There are two sides to every story,' says a comic character, a duped New York Hospital obstetrician, and every aspect of *Six Degrees of Separation,* its own story included, literally or figuratively shares this duality. . . ."

Yet these people hunger for more as well, for a human connection and perhaps a spiritual one. It is Paul, of all people, who points the way, by his words and his deeds. In a virtuoso monologue about *Catcher in the Rye,* he decries a world in which assassins like Mark David Chapman and John W. Hinckley Jr. can take Holden Caulfield as a role model—a world in which imagination has ceased to be a means of self-examination and has become instead "something outside ourselves," whether a handy excuse for murderous behavior or a merchandisable commodity like van Gogh's "Irises" or an escapist fashion promoted by *The Warhol Diaries.* Intentionally or not, Paul helps bring Ouisa into a reunion with her imagination, with her authentic self. His trail of fraud, which ultimately brushes against death, jolts his hostess out of her own fraudulent life among what Holden Caulfield calls phonies so that she might at last break through the ontological paralysis separating her from what really matters.

Among the many remarkable aspects of Mr. Guare's writing is the seamlessness of his imagery, characters and themes, as if this play had just erupted from his own imagination in one perfect piece. "There are two sides to every story," says a comic character, a duped New York Hospital obstetrician, and every aspect of *Six Degrees of Separation,* its own story included, literally or figuratively shares this duality, from Paul's identity to a Kandinsky painting that twirls above the Kittredge living room to the meaning of a phrase like "striking coal miners." The double vision gives the play an airy, Cubist dramatic structure even as it reflects the class divisions of its setting and the Jungian splits of its characters' souls.

Mr. Guare is just as much in control of the brush strokes that shift his play's disparate moods: In minutes, he can take the audience from a college student who is a screamingly funny personification of upper-middle-class New York Jewish rage to a would-be actor from Utah of the same generation and opposite temperament. Though Mr. Guare quotes Donald Barthelme's observation that "collage is the art form of the 20th century," his play does not feel like a collage. As conversant with Cézanne and the Sistine Chapel as it is with Sotheby's and *Starlight Express,* this work aspires to the classical esthetics and commensurate unity of spirit that are missing in the pasted-together, fragmented 20th-century lives it illuminates.

That spirit shines through. Great as the intellectual pleasures of the evening may be, it is Mr. Guare's compassion that allows his play to make the human connections that elude his characters. The people who walk in and out of the picture frames of [the] set are not satirical cartoons but ambiguous, full-blooded creations. There's a Gatsby-like poignance to the studied glossy-magazine aspirations of Paul, a Willy Loman-ish sadness to the soiled idealism of [the] art dealer. As the one character who may finally see the big picture and begin to understand the art of living, . . . [Ouisa] steadily gains gravity as she journeys flawlessly from the daffy comedy of a fatuous dinner party to the harrowing internal drama of her own rebirth.

"It was an experience," she says with wonder of her contact with the impostor she never really knew. For the author and his heroine, the challenge is to hold on to true experience in a world in which most human encounters are bogus and nearly all are instantly converted into the disposable anecdotes, the floating collage scraps that are the glib currency of urban intercourse. In *Six Degrees of Separation,* one of those passing anecdotes has been ripped from the daily paper and elevated into a transcendent theatrical experience that is itself a lasting vision of the humane new world of which Mr. Guare and his New Yorkers so hungrily dream. (pp. C1, C3)

Frank Rich, "Schisms of the City, Comically and Tragically," in The New York Times, *June 15, 1990, pp. C1, C3.*

John Simon

Herewith the ingredients of John Guare's new, 90-minute comedy, *Six Degrees of Separation.* I list them in alphabetical order, but can't vouch for the completeness of the list.

Art sales, millions of questionable dollars in; Cézanne's paintings, unfinished patches in, as symbol; doormen, humanity of; doormen, loathing of rich tenants by; guilt, Jewish; guilt, parental; guilt, white liberal; gullibility, lower-class; gullibility, upper-class; homosexuals, brazenness of; homosexuals, humor of; homosexuals, pathos of; imagination, as source of vulnerability; imagination, as weapon; Kandinsky, two-sided painting by, as symbol; marital unfulfillment, comedy of; marital unfulfillment, wistfulness of.

Also: naked man, popping out on stage, daring effect of (cf. *Lisbon Traviata*); pink shirt, as status symbol; pink shirt, as sunburst, poetic but not status symbol; Poitier, Sidney, alleged paternity of, used as confidence trick; resentment, children's toward parents, undisguised; resentment, parents' toward children, semi-disguised; resentment, whites' toward blacks, disguised; rich people, ludicrousness of; rich people, secret pain of; separation, six degrees of between everyone and everyone else; sociopathic con man, devilish cunning of; sociopathic con man, poor lost soul of underneath.

Further: South Africa, problem of; suicide; theatrical aspirations, of kids coming to New York from Utah, absurdity of; theatrical aspirations, of kids coming from Utah to New York, pathos of; uncertainty, as device in penultimate scene; uncertainty, as device in ultimate scene.

There you have it: 35 degrees of manipulation, cunningly executed, seemingly seamlessly joined, interlarded with clever one-liners, alternating comic situations with mildly disturbing ones, drenched in social significance, sprinkled with poignancy. *Six Degrees of Separation* is a play about everything, with something in it for everyone, and with enough Cézannian empty patches into which you may project your own particular thing in the unlikely case that Guare overlooked it.

The play is not uninteresting: Cleverness, however dishonest, provided only that it is diabolical enough, never bores. Take this, from a South African millionaire: "One has to stay there to educate the black workers, and we know we've been successful when they kill us." Liberals can laugh at this for liberal reasons; conservatives, for conservative reasons; blacks, for black reasons. Again, the con-man anti-hero who pretends to be Poitier's son tempts his white victims with the possibility of bit parts in *Cats,* the movie, which his father is directing. Says . . . [Ouisa], one of the victims, "It seems the common thread linking us all was our overwhelming need to be in the movie *Cats.*" What joke is more ego-enhancing than one enabling us to laugh superiorly at a show we inferiorly relished? (p. 58)

John Simon, "Open for Inventory," in New York *Magazine, Vol. 23, No. 25, June 25, 1990, pp. 58-9.*

Jack Kroll

John Guare's *Six Degrees of Separation* begins with a scene of pure urban hysteria. Ouisa Kittredge and her art-dealer husband, Flan, flap about their ritzy New York apartment in a frenzy: they've discovered that they've been hoodwinked by a young black man, Paul, who's passed himself off as the son of actor Sidney Poitier. Claiming to be short on cash while awaiting the return of his "father," Paul has talked himself into the hospitality of Flan and Ouisa, who later discover their guest copulating with a male hooker. Frazzled with fear and horror, the couple throw Paul out. It turns out that Paul has pulled a similar scam on other upscale New Yorkers. Events escalate into a surreal comedy that highlights the confusion between illusion and reality in the increasingly chaotic metropolis.

Guare has based his piercing play on a true story from the early '80s. The figure of the con artist has fascinated American writers from Herman Melville's *The Confidence Man* to David Mamet's film *House of Games.* In Melville's novel, a savage satire on American moral complacency, the confidence man assumes several shapes, including that of a poor black man. Melville was making a statement about pre-Civil War America. Guare is talking about race and other disconnections that sunder the city in 1990.

Since this is John Guare (*The House of Blue Leaves, Bosoms and Neglect*) the play takes off on a careening ride from disorienting comedy into unexpected pathos and tragedy. Even greater than the gulf of misunderstanding that separates white from black is the gap across which parents and children regard one another with appallingly hilarious hostility. A daughter threatens her parents with an elopement to Afghanistan; a son goes bananas when his parents give a favorite shirt (it showed off his "new body") to Paul. What at first seem like the scary but bloodless crimes of a clever hustler take on darker aspects that lead to the suicide of one of Paul's young dupes.

Paul is a major creation: he's a figure of dizzying ambiguity, weirdly innocent, sexually seductive, socially unsophisticated, startlingly insightful. In an impassioned speech he talks of the death of the imagination, that faculty which, he says, is "God's gift to make the act of self-examination bearable." . . . [Guare makes] every shift of Paul's sensibility believable and disturbing. It's as if this apparition from the shadows embodies all the fragmented potential that his privileged victims have perverted. Flan, for example, has real insight into the nature of creativity, but his energies are directed to big scores in the madly inflated art market.

It's Ouisa who's awakened by the amoral Paul to the emptiness of life in the fast lane to nowhere. "He did more for us in a few hours than our children ever did," she says wonderingly to Flan.

Jack Kroll, "The Con Games People Play," in Newsweek, *Vol. CXV, No. 26, June 25, 1990, p. 54.*

Howard Kissel

John Guare's *Six Degrees of Separation* remains the most exhilarating theater in town.

Guare's play is based on an actual incident of a young black man who insinuated himself into the homes—and lives—of well-to-do, prominent New Yorkers.

In his brilliant 1970 essay "Radical Chic," Tom Wolfe noted that among wealthy liberals, dwelling in a world of unreal luxury, there was a deep yearning for the grubby, *real* world of their ancestors. This yearning stemmed partly from feelings of guilt about their money. It explained the desire of a trendy art dealer to give fund-raising parties for the Black Panthers.

These days, the anguish of the limousine liberals has intensified. It's harder for them to take themselves or their now neglected ideals so seriously. Their children, the heirs of their "revolutionary" aspirations, hold them in contempt. The real world itself, grubby or not, has become bewildering. So they have taken refuge in their artifacts, their (forgive the use of a pornographic word, but I have no choice) *lifestyles*.

Hence, they are flattered when the young black man, Paul, asks them,

> Why has imagination become a synonym for style? I believe the imagination is the passport we create to take us into the real world . . . the imagination. That's God's gift to make the act of self-examination bearable.

By sharing his ideas with them, Paul assuages their guilt almost as effectively as the Panthers did by accepting their canapés.

Paul undergoes his own crisis. He loses his cynicism about his prey; he sentimentalizes them, and that proves disastrous.

Every scene, every character in *Six Degrees* captures the bizarre, self-destructive mood of New York today. Guare's brilliance is that he can make this disturbing portrait hilarious.

Even more impressive, he has turned this jumble of confused, frenetic voices into a kind of music. The kids' whining, their parents' calculated archness, Paul's chameleon-like responses to their moods and needs—Guare shapes these voices, controls their rhythms so precisely that the play has the style, the irresistible momentum of musical theater.

> *Howard Kissel, " 'Separation' Gets It All Together," in* Daily News, *New York, November 9, 1990.*

Frank Rich

"How do we keep the experience?" asks an anguished [Ouisa], fighting back anger and tears near the end of *Six Degrees of Separation*. . . .

[The Upper East Side matron] has just had the experience of her life: A young black man, posing as the son of Sidney Poitier, bamboozled his way into her home, family and heart and then, just as abruptly, vanished. Ouisa is not the same person she was before she met the impostor, who called himself Paul. The encounter has jolted her out of her insular sophistication, sending her through "new doors opening into other worlds." But now she fears her cathartic reawakening may be slipping away to become merely another New York dinner-party anecdote "with no teeth and a punch line you'll mouth over and over for years to come." And if Ouisa has learned anything from Paul, it is that she wants to hold onto experience, to connect at last to the people around her, to stop being one of "these human jukeboxes spilling out these anecdotes."

Returning to *Six Degrees* nearly five months after its premiere, I worried whether it, too, might have been reduced by time to glib anecdotal status. Certainly this play, like any other hot ticket on the New York cultural scene, has been masticated by le tout Manhattan. People dined out on Mr. Guare's smartest lines all summer. The real-life con man whose 1983 scams inspired the play resurfaced in the press, and so did his prominent victims. The work's meaning has been debated by all manner of pundits, its creators have been exhaustively interviewed, its title has passed into the language. To be a full-fledged New York phenomenon, *Six Degrees* lacks only a strong critical backlash, and surely this, too, will come.

But not here. Watching *Six Degrees* again, with full knowledge of where its laughs are and where its bodies (three of them) are buried, I found it as funny and moving and provocative as ever—still a fresh experience, not last season's calcified hit. . . .

[The] bond that inexorably develops between Paul and Ouisa . . . [is] a connection at once emotional, intellectual and erotic linking two such seemingly disparate characters as a poor, gay, young black man of unknown identity and a rich, WASP-y, middle-aged wife with a pedigree. The emphasis helps focus the play, perhaps because above all else, above even its hilarious jokes about money and art and the musicals of Andrew Lloyd Webber, *Six Degrees* is an unlikely, chaste, covert love story in which Paul and Ouisa reach out for each other as surely as do those hands in Ouisa's beloved Sistine Chapel. The real if buried plot of *Six Degrees* deals not with Paul's fraudulent identity but with the authenticity of spirit that allows him and Ouisa to break through those degrees of separation that isolate people in a dehumanizing metropolis overpopulated by all kinds of phonies. . . .

Running only 90 minutes in one act at a break-neck pace, *Six Degrees* is extraordinarily dense with ideas and feelings that can be picked apart and analyzed individually after the fact but that somehow coalesce into an elegant composition on stage.

If there is one image that dominates, it can be found in the play's final words—"It's painted on two sides." The line refers to a Kandinsky canvas that twirls above the action in the Kittredge home, but it emblemizes the two-sided metaphors of a play that pointedly defines schizophrenia as "a horrifying state" where what is inside the psyche "doesn't match up with what's out there." In the fractionalized New York of *Six Degrees,* the bust town that followed the boom town of [Tom Wolfe's] *Bonfire of the Vanities,* families, classes, races and sexes are all divided, just as each individual is divorced from the imagination that might yet be his means to introspection and salvation.

As that Kandinsky canvas hangs above *Six Degrees,* so does Kandinsky's artistic principle, recited early on, that there can be a "harmony of form" in a painting only if the choice of each object is dictated by "a corresponding vibration in the human soul." Mr. Guare yearns against all odds for the same redemptive harmony from his New Yorkers. The set for his play is a series of doorways—some at ground level leading to the rooms of a Fifth Avenue apartment, others above opening to the characters' dreams, all of them bordered by the gift frames of art. What prevents this searing comedy from becoming another disposable New York anecdote is that, for all the perfection of Mr. Guare's own art within those frames, it is ourselves, imperfect and bloodied and as hungry as Ouisa for that transcendent vibration, whom we meet once we walk through those doors.

> *Frank Rich, " 'Six Degrees' Reopens, Larger but Still Intimate," in* The New York Times, *November 9, 1990, p. C5.*

Bessie Head

1937-1986

(Born Bessie Emery) South African novelist, short story writer, and historian.

Head is known for fiction that explores the sources of racial and sexual inequalities in southern Africa. A writer of mixed Scottish and South African descent who spent most of her life as an exile in her adopted land of Botswana, Head wrote from the perspective of an outsider attempting to understand her environment and her social position. She addressed problems of sexual and racial discrimination in Africa by emphasizing the similarities among all forms of prejudice, stressing such themes as the disintegration of rural traditions, the corruption of authority, and the equally powerful forces of good and evil. Critics admire Head's insightful observations on humanity and often praise her attempts to examine not only the effects of prejudice, but also the causes.

Head was born in a South African mental hospital. Her father was a black stable worker and her mother the daughter of an upper-class Scottish family who institutionalized her when she became pregnant. Quickly removed from her mother's care, Head was raised first by Afrikaner foster parents who rejected her because of her dark skin color and later by missionaries who introduced her to various cultures and religious beliefs. She worked as a reporter and teacher in South Africa for several years and was briefly married before leaving Botswana with her son in 1964. After suffering a nervous breakdown, which became the focus of her autobiographical novel, *A Question of Power,* Head dedicated herself to writing and maintaining a seedling nursery for vegetables.

Throughout her career, Head emphasized the need for Africans to abandon power struggles. She stated that until she moved to Botswana in 1964, she "had never encountered human ambition and greed before in a black form." In South Africa, her experiences with domination had been primarily with the white system of apartheid; in Botswana, however, she found that similar structures of oppression towards women and other social groups existed in tribal communities. Her first novel, *When Rain Clouds Gather,* was an attempt to suggest an alternative to the desire for power. This book focuses on Makhaya, a young South African who leaves his country only to become an outcast in Golema Mmidi, a refugee community in Botswana. With the aid of a former British colonial administrator dedicated to African concerns, Makhaya works for agricultural reform in an area where the main source of income, cattle farming, has become unproductive. Through the rejuvenation of crops, the village develops a new sense of self-sufficiency, responsibility, and community. Critics generally lauded this novel for avoiding the angry generalizations of many protest novels and for its vivid descriptions of agricultural techniques and the Botswanan landscape. Many of the stories in Head's later

book, *The Collector of Treasures,* reiterate the futility of power struggles. In the story "Deep River," for example, an heir to chiefdom relinquishes his power to avoid conflict. In this and other tales, Head implies that the overall harmony of a community should take precedence over the violence or hatred resulting from power struggles.

In her later works, Head identifies oppression and discrimination as major tools for those in power. While much of southern African literature emphasizes inequalities between whites and blacks, Head's fiction explores the sources of discrimination by examining the desire for control among all groups. Many commentators also identify her as a feminist for her attention to the forces that restrict women's freedom. In *Maru,* two village leaders, Maru and Moleka, fall in love with Margaret, a young Masarwa schoolteacher. Margaret unabashedly admits her association with the Masarwa people, or bushmen, who have traditionally been considered inferior to other black Botswanans. As both men vie for her affections, they begin to understand the plight of the Masarwa people, and a union is ultimately created between the two groups through Maru's marriage to Margaret.

Head called her autobiographical novel, *A Question of*

Power, "a private journey to the sources of evil." Elizabeth, the protagonist, is a South African refugee in Botswana who experiences temporary insanity. In dreams and fantasies she encounters both local and mythical figures representing the extremes of good and evil who cause her to assess the nature of her femininity and Africanness. This psychological work explores the roots of female oppression and questions the existence of God, as when Elizabeth concludes that there is "only one God and his name is Man." *A Question of Power* was hailed as a powerful novel encompassing profound theological and personal issues. While some initial reviewers contended that the hazy distinction between Elizabeth's real and imaginary lives rendered the book excessively complex, most critics now laud as successful Head's representation of a woman's struggle to come to terms with her madness and social situation.

In addition to her fiction, Head wrote two studies on Botswana, both of which combine local folklore with historical information. *Serowe: Village of the Rain Wind* recounts tales of the Bamangwato nation from the nineteenth and twentieth centuries, while *A Bewitched Crossroad: An African Saga* focuses on African tribal wars in the early nineteenth century. Critics admired both works, noting the universal relevance of their generalized social observations. Paddy Kitchen characterized *Serowe* as "a story which readers will find themselves using as a text from which to meditate on many aspects of society." Head's interest in the traditions and background of her adopted homeland are evident in her fiction as well as her historical works. Throughout *The Collector of Treasures,* for example, Head juxtaposes evolving moral and personal values with long-held local beliefs. Christopher Heywood observed of Head's concern for tradition: "On the surface, the novels of Bessie Head offer a vision of an Africa reformed by progress and co-operation. . . . In their inner workings, however, they offer . . . the vision of a future which has accepted and modified but not betrayed the traditional African past."

(See also *CLC,* Vol. 25; *Black Literature Criticism,* Vol. 1; *Black Writers; Contemporary Authors,* Vols. 29-32, rev. ed., Vol. 119 [obituary]; and *Contemporary Authors New Revision Series,* Vol. 25.)

PRINCIPAL WORKS

NOVELS

When Rain Clouds Gather   1968
Maru   1971
A Question of Power   1973

OTHER

The Collector of Treasures and Other Botswana Village Tales   (short stories)   1977
Serowe: Village of the Rain Wind   (historical chronicle) 1981
A Bewitched Crossroad: An African Saga   (historical chronicle)   1984
Tales of Tenderness and Power   (short stories)   1989
A Woman Alone: Autobiographical Writings   1990

Charlotte H. Bruner

[Head's novels *When Rain Clouds Gather, Maru,* and *A Question of Power*] all deal with the reorientation of the exile to a new, somewhat hostile society. The autobiographical basis evident in the experience of her lead characters gives credence to her fictionalized and hence, generalized, exile-portraits. The progression from the position of affirmation of *When Rain Clouds Gather,* her first novel, to the uncertain, thin hope of survival through individual inner strength of her latest, *A Question of Power,* mirrors Bessie Head's own unrewarded struggle for acceptance in her new community.

It is significant that her first exile figure, Makhaya, in *When Rain Clouds Gather* is a male. He achieves satisfaction in meaningful work with Gilbert, the English engineer, as they initiate land reclamation in Botswana. He achieves marital satisfaction and intellectual companionship with Paulina, a passionate and vigorous woman who leads the village women in making agricultural experiments. His success is paralleled for the village, Golema Mmidi, itself. This tiny community triumphs over its evil overlord through group action. The villagers, in common concern, defeat the chief's persecution of Paulina. Makhaya shares in this fulfillment. So, despite the poverty, the unremitting labor, the tragedy of a child shepherd's death, Makhaya—and the reader—achieve affirmation. This affirmation has its basis in shared human concern. Bessie Head described her purpose—a positive one—in so structuring this novel: "the possibility that Africa can produce a lot of idealistic young men, the need for broad planning for the people to solve centuries of exploitation and poverty . . . I would deliberately create heroes and show their extreme willingness to abdicate from positions of power and absorb themselves in activities which would be of immense benefit to people."

Bessie Head is not only an exile, she is a woman writing in exile. In her second novel, *Maru,* her personal identification with the fictionalized woman's position, suggested earlier in her characters of Maria and Paulina in *Rain Clouds,* is clear. In *Maru* the first central female character, Margaret Cadmore, is an Englishwoman teaching in Africa. She adopts and educates an abandoned Bushman child and gives the child her name. The second Margaret Cadmore becomes the main protagonist of the novel. This Margaret is light-skinned—a suspicious color—just as Bessie Head in South Africa is identified as "coloured." Neither character nor creator is a member of the Black majority—of South Africa, of Botswana, or of the African continent itself. In an interview in 1975, Bessie Head stressed her feeling of closeness to her own white mother, for whom she is named.

> I was born on the sixth of July, 1937, in the Pietermaritzburg Mental Hospital, in South Africa. The reason for my peculiar birthplace was that my mother was white, and she had acquired me from a black man. She was judged insane, and committed to the mental hospital while pregnant. Her name was Bessie Emery and I consid-

er it the only honor South African officials ever did me—naming me after this unknown, lovely, and unpredictable woman.

The second Margaret Cadmore, in **Maru,** then, like her creator is named for her spiritual mother, is light-colored, is discriminated against by color-caste. She could have passed herself off as white, but chose not to evade her Bushman heritage. Even so, she is still alienated from the black majority. Like her fictional mother and her actual creator, this Margaret is gifted, sensitive, and a teacher. Head's concern for the woman's position, shown earlier in **Rain Clouds,** here dominates her second novel. The three women characters, the two Margarets and their colleague and friend, Dikeledi, emerge as fully developed characters and dominate the novel. The two males, Maru and his counterpart Moleka, are shadowy. Their portraits shift, combine and recombine and almost merge together, like a schizophrenic lover. Is Head suggesting here a mirror-image, half-force, half-mind? Finally Maru, manipulating others with a power of will, compels a resolution of their lives. He himself renounces his leadership position in the village and takes Margaret off to idyllic bliss, far away, to live out their dream in isolation. This bliss, however, means that Margaret renounces her earlier goals to improve conditions for her people through example and education.

Thus the cross-caste marriage of Margaret and Maru sets a precedent. The idea of this union may serve as an example to the Bushmen. "When the people of the Masarwa tribe heard about Maru's marriage to one of their own, a door silently opened on the small, dark, airless room in which their souls had been shut for a long time . . . their humanity awakened." Margaret's example, however, is a passive one. Her name as marriage partner is not even mentioned. She, with Maru, really deserts the school, the village, and constructive social action. In summation, Margaret's story is inconclusive. She has achieved the education and the prestige of a teaching position. But she cannot maintain these in an alien setting. Sought by two men of opposing personalities, who only together suggest a complete man image, she ultimately abandons her community work to disappear with Maru to a single cottage off somewhere, with daisies at the door—in a never-never land dream world where a couple (but not a village like Golema Mmidi) may endure. Nor can this couple now through group interaction work for a social good, as did Makhaya and Paulina in **When Rain Clouds Gather.**

Bessie Head's own alienation in exile in Botswana is complicated by her having no present husband but one dependent son. In her application for citizenship in 1977, after living in Botswana as stateless for thirteen years, she writes, "I have one son aged fifteen years. I began to worry about his future; there are no openings for him for further education and employment in Botswana as a refugee . . . " Earlier in the same document she had explained, " . . . the refugees who get trapped in Botswana are mostly family people with children who mostly need to feel wanted and useful." Her three novels and two short stories, **"Witchcraft"** and **"The Collector of Treasures,"** constitute together a portrait of the exile, disoriented, seeking refuge in an inhospitable land from which no new

escape is feasible. Her insights as a woman, an intellectual, a mother, a single parent, an outsider who has borne a history of disorientation even as a birth label, all enhance this portrayal.

Head's writing shows a particular sensitivity to children. She puts children in all her fiction. In the first novel [**When the Rain Clouds Gather**], the toy farm of Paulina's little daughter delights the reader; the pathos of Paulina's son's solitary death saddens. In [**Maru**], Margaret Cadmore, Dikeledi, and Elizabeth all teach children.

> The children were a teacher's heaven. Children's literature and writing was often the most magical world, and yet there were harsh environments like this where all magic was dead or had not even begun to live. Everything was touched by this harshness. They ate no breakfast in the early morning, and by midday their mouths were white and pinched with starvation. Other children had soft mounds of butter where their cheeks ought to be, and dimpled smiles. The children she taught were stark, gaunt, thin, like the twisted thorn-bush.

In **A Question of Power,** Head develops some maternal-filial relationships more fully: the frustration in trivial argument within the strong mother-child attachment, the bewilderment of a child with an ill parent or one who is not herself.

> Her head was throbbing with pain from a sleepless and feverish night. She grabbed a pile of his clothes off a chair and said irritably: 'You'd like to be slaughtered, hey? Shut your mouth, you damn little nuisance.'

> He took all his moods from her and imitated her in every way. A day which started off like this could throw him off balance completely. Suddenly, he seemed to sense something funny in the air and mimicked in a shrill voice: 'You'd like to be slaughtered, hey? Shut your mouth, you damn little nuisance.'

The anguish of a parent unable to provide food and shelter and education underlies the confrontation, of course. It is a commonplace that parents frequently strain for patience, understanding, in dealing with children. In the conditions of exile, the tensions may break. Bessie Head's own problems of adjustment are obviously complicated by her feeling for and responsibility for her son. "My only truly autobiographical work is **A Question of Power,**" she writes, "the other books drew on personal experience but not so directly."

The woman's position as sole provider increases her tensions; this autobiographical theme is consistent in Head's work. In the first novel, Paulina's cattle herd is her only security for herself and her two children. In the second novel, both Margarets support themselves as teachers. In the third, when Elizabeth loses her teaching job, she experiences a

> crushing depression. . . . She pushed her leaden feet towards the small boy who sat under the tree. 'If I die, would you like to die, too?' she asked, crazily.

'What is to die?' he asked, interested. . . . 'It's like going away," she said. 'There isn't anyone to cook food or wash clothes. The house gets empty.'

'Where do we go to?' he asked, a little anxiously.

'I don't know,' she said.

In the story, **"Witchcraft,"** Mma Mabele has to have her job to support her family. She survives a mysterious affliction and alone provides for her children, on sheer will power. "There is no one to help the people, not even God. I could not sit down because I am too poor, and there is no one to feed my children." Dikeledi in **"The Collector of Treasures"** must provide for her three sons while her husband, although a well-to-do government official, denies child support. Hence, the woman, with limited employment status, as sole provider undergoes additional strain and psychic stress if she is an exile without support of husband, friends, or a known community.

A Question of Power reflects a variety of emotional crises resulting from stress upon this sensitive writer. Even the name of the lead character, like the nursery rhyme refrain—Elizabeth, Betty, Betsy and Bess—evidences the self-identification of the writer with her lead character. Head takes the reader through Elizabeth's emotional breakdowns which immediately follow her exile and then recur later and provoke her dismissal from her teaching assignment. "Something was going drastically wrong with her own life. Just the other day she had broken down and cried . . . 'I'm not sure I'm quite normal any more." Shortly thereafter, Elizabeth receives the school board report: "We have received a report that you have been shouting and swearing at people in public. Such behavior is unbecoming to a teacher. We are doubtful of your sanity, and request that you submit to us a certificate of sanity from a medical officer within fourteen days of receipt of this notice." The hospital suggested is too far away, the situation humiliating, the other teachers hostile. The conditions of conforming to accepted social patterns in what is basically still a conservative man's world in a Black African society almost defeat her. "She fell into a deep hole of such excruciating torture that, briefly, she went stark, raving mad." Her hallucinations deny her sexuality and her Africanness.

In an interview, Bessie Head speaks out for herself without fictional disguise. "I forcefully created for myself, under extremely hostile conditions, my ideal life. I took an obscure and almost unknown village in the Southern African bush and made it my own hallowed ground . . . My work was always tentative . . . it created new worlds out of nothing." In **"Witchcraft"** she writes, "If life is like this, all people are afraid of each other." Then, feelingly, of her lead character, here Mma Mabele, she continues, "her ability to observe that life was all wrong and a deep sensitivity to feel pain and desist from repeating errors was all that stood between her and the misery that was soon to engulf her life." Charles Larson says [in *English around the World,* May, 1974]: "In her concern with women and madness, Bessie Head has almost single-handedly brought about the inward turning of the African novel."

In *A Question of Power,* the male image creates the threat, provokes the female upset. The male images in hallucination and thought-transference extend to include several males, real and unreal, who blend and shift, somewhat as do those of Maru and Moleka earlier in *Maru.* The male images in *A Question of Power,* Dan, the two Sellos, and others, change roles from protector to abuser, taunter to lover, African to Africa, god to evil. They threaten Elizabeth's sexuality, attract, repel, wearing down her resistance until a spark explodes, destroying her sanity. Often the male image becomes Africa, which she wants to identify with but cannot. "A persistent theme was that she was not genuinely African; *he* had to give her the real African insight." The image of Dan is frequently hostile and threatening. "The social defects he heightened in himself, then set himself up before Elizabeth as the epitome of the African male. It began to make all things African vile and obscene." "The evils overwhelming her were beginning to sound like South Africa from which she had fled. The reasoning, the viciousness were the same, but this time the faces were black."

Charles Larson says, "The burden of exile, mixed with guilt feelings about the colour of her skin . . . produce a kind of sexual frigidity, and for a time Elizabeth becomes mad. All of this the reader sees through Elizabeth's distorted mind. At the end of the story, with her devils exorcized, Elizabeth turns to the land for comfort and solace." This persecution-rejection theme persists and deepens throughout Head's work. In actuality, the Botswana government, consistently refusing her requests for citizenship, like most government bodies is dominantly male, and continues to deny her. Can she ever belong, or do her skin color, her genealogy, her intellectualism, her artistic sensitivity forever disbar her for her differentness?

Except for her son, the portraits of male figures become increasingly threatening in Head's work. The short story, **"Witchcraft,"** published in 1975, is much like a small crystallization of the novel, *A Question of Power.* The plot may even be foreshadowed by a passage in the novel: "People who have suffered from the wanton cruelty of others prefer the truth at all times, no matter what it might cost them . . . there was also the village level of life, witchcraft and all the hidden terrors of darkness." The question of power, of one's inner strength to survive, to find solace in the simple and bare existence of poor village life continues to be a lead theme. In her interview with *Ms.* Head says, "In South Africa the white man took even the air away from us—it was his air and his birds and his land. In Botswana, I have a little bird outside my window every day."

Mma Mabele of **"Witchcraft,"** however, is not an exile like her creator. She is a villager and her persecutors are men from her own area. The father of her child ran off when he discovered she was pregnant. Others made advances to her, but, being denied, spread rumors against her. "She was called 'he-man!' and it was meant to imply that something was not quite right with her genitals, they were mixed up, a combination of male and female." She ignores her detractors but, once she gets a good job, torment begins. "It turned from this sunlit world to an inner world of gloomy brooding and pain." The Tswana doctor identifies her persecutor: "It is Molema who is injuring your life. He has spread such a bad word about you in the village that I am ashamed to repeat it. . . . " Mma Mabele refuses traditional cures and yet she survives to take care of herself and her daughter. The story has the same basic plot as that of the novel, but the predominant focus is on Man, the Malefactor.

In June of 1977, Bessie Head published a short story, **"The Collector of Treasures."** Here the woman protagonist, Dikeledi, imprisoned for life for murdering her husband, finds friendship, relief and peace in the segregated female society of a prison. Dikeledi recounts the provocation for her crime to her cellmates who are serving similar sentences. In expository author-comment, Head here reiterates some themes from earlier works: the non-human status of women in South Africa, the domination of the continent and its various governments through history by the macho-male brute.

> The ancestors made so many errors, and one of the most bitter was that they relegated to men a superior position in the tribe, while women were regarded, in a congenital sense, as being an inferior form of human life. . . . Independence produced marvels indeed. . . . the man . . . arrived at this turning point a broken wreck with no inner resources at all . . . hideous to himself . . . That kind of man lived near the animal level and behaved just the same . . . that kind of man was in the majority in the society.

Other themes of racial persecution and skin color barriers here subside in emphasis before the male-female confrontation theme. The absolute dichotomy in male characterization of earlier works (the brother chiefs, Sekoto and Malenge, in **Rain Clouds,** Maru and Moleka of **Maru,** Sello in the brown suit and Sello in the monk's robe in **A Question of Power**) here appears as the bestial pimp husband, Garesego Mokopi, and his opposite, Dikeledi's true friend, Paul Thebolo, who "was a poem of tenderness."

Foresaken by Garesego and befriended by Paul, Dikeledi had succeeded for awhile in providing a tranquil life for herself and her three children. "She had always found gold amidst the ash." She had created what comfort and affirmation she could create in a difficult environment. She is a "collector of treasures," of bits and pieces of kindness and understanding that occasionally come her way—a warm smile, a simple compliment to her industry. She is capable in handiwork. "She had soft, caressing, almost boneless hands of a strange power—work of a beautiful design grew out of these hands." She was the "woman whose thatch did not leak." She achieved eight years of relative calm, as single parent, with the support of the understanding Thebolos.

During this interim period, she guards her security, cherishes her personal treasures. She tries to ignore outside threats to her quiet life, rumors of government change, communist takeover. She rejects activism, like Bessie Head herself who said in an interview, "I am a useless kind of person in any liberation movement or revolution: I can't stand them or the people who organize them. I could

dream dreams a little ahead of the somewhat vicious clamor of revolution and the horrible stench of evil social systems." Dikeledi's enclosed private world, however, is jeopardized when she needs money to further the education of her eldest son. She is forced by poverty to seek her deserter-husband for financial aid to cover Banabothe's secondary school fees. Garesego threatens to return to her. Refusal would be unavailing. "Black women don't have that kind of power." But she has to resist. "She had filled her life with treasures of kindness and love she had gathered from others and it was all this that she wanted to protect from defilement by an evil man." She prepares to receive him after the children go to sleep. Now with the "strange power" of her hands she effects a solution: she castrates and murders Garesego after he has carried out his threat to return home to rape her. The fictional resolution is the last stage in a progression of the male/female conflict denouements in Bessie Head's plots: from the happy marriages possible to Gilbert and Maria and to Makhaya and Paulina in her first novel to the cottage fantasy union between Margaret Cadmore and the better side of the Maru image in her second, to the hope for survival of the single-parent household in **A Question of Power** and **"Witchcraft."** Now, the sadistic murder of the macho-male brute concludes the sequence.

Bessie Head's character Dikeledi does ultimately find friendship, accord, cooperation, understanding, but only in the sequestered world of prison. The imposed routines, the established meal procedures, the handicraft work program provide for the unisexual society "treasures" that the world outside cannot provide. However, the reader recalls that this woman's world of alienation found by Dikeledi, whose name means *tears,* is achieved in anguish, through violence and mutilation. Another sensitive woman exile, Simone Weil, has written, "With exiles who are ever thinking of their country—and those who forget it are lost—the heart is so irresistibly turned toward the homeland in distress that few emotional resources are left for friendship in the land they happen to be living in. Such friendship cannot really germinate and spring up in their hearts unless they do themselves a sort of violence. But this violence is an obligation on their part." Perhaps to Bessie Head, born in a hospital prison in South Africa, this retreat is a kind of return to the womb. "It is my mother's tears that I am named after," says Dikeledi. Prison, mental or physical, is not the usual sanctuary sought by the exile, of course, but the sequestered women's cell in the "high security" institution provides for Dikeledi protection from the violence, alienation, sadistically provoked disorientation she perceives in the outside world. (pp. 263-74)

Charlotte H. Bruner, "Bessie Head: Restless in a Distant Land," in When the Drumbeat Changes, *edited by Carolyn Parker & others, Three Continents Press, 1981, pp. 261-77.*

Bessie Head   (interview with Linda Susan Beard)

[The following excerpt is taken from an interview conducted on May 13, 1982.]

[Beard]: *You chose exile from South Africa. One of the most complex facets of your life must have been your reactions to exile.*

[Head]: You know, it is such a complicated answer. Such a complicated answer. First of all, I never had feelings of sentiment about South Africa. The country, the life that had emerged there, the fact that we had the experience of white domination—it was such a choking, throttling, death-like kind of world. In contrast, there's a certain aspect to my life in Botswana which is full and rich. The difference is that for the 27 years I lived in South Africa, I had the experience of a Black South African—the poverty-stricken, slum-dweller; the feeling that there was no way in which you could look around and breathe and feel the air. There was nothing there. . . .

I came to Botswana when it was still the British Bechuanaland Protectorate moving into independence. That was '64. . . . What is very significant is that Botswana was, for 80 years, under British control, but with a completely different historical experience. The British presence was barely visible. In the village where I lived in Serowe, there was a very tentative kind of administration. The Black population was 30,000, and whatever white faces you saw in the village amounted to about 50. The Black presence, the Black historical treasure really, or things that people have been able to keep for themselves, was very dominant. (p. 44)

I think what I'm really trying to say is that there has to be a very serious assessment made of this colonial experience. It has so many variations, to a certain extent. If British colonialism tended to be different, it was because the gains were not too high. A country like the old Bechuanaland Protectorate presented the British with a vista of a land that was dry and unproductive, and they were completely disinterested in it. I do not think they would have lacked interest had the country offered them resources because British colonialism tended to be very commercial. But, what was valuable for me, with my South African Black background, was to find a society where the African experience is continuous and unbroken.

Is that the reason, in **Collector of Treasures,** *that you focus on characteristics of traditional life?*

Well, you know, a book grows with you. You make certain decisions about the next book and why you're going to write it. What I could say about *The Collector of Treasures* is that it was like a kind of resumé of 13 years of living entirely in village life. And village life is particularly enchanting. In actual fact, all of the stories are based on real life happenings. The village is like this: it's *very* peaceful and everyday. There's one story, **"Life,"** which describes the rhythm almost as monotonous. One day is just the same as another, but human beings are so similar all over the world. Suddenly, a great drama explodes. Now you wake up and take your shopping basket and walk down the road and people say: 'Oh, have you heard. . . . ' So that most of the stories have this odd combination of gentleness and violence. The reason is that most of the stories came to be written because they actually happened. They may be decorated and interpreted and

so on, but you go out and people say, 'Have you heard. . . . ' And then, because it surrounds a dramatic death, a murder, or a very painful court case, you get to know all the details. In a village, it's so vivid. It's so vivid.

In reality, all I simply did was record stories that had happened and had been told to me and described to me. Most of the stories there are based on reality; they're not inventions. They happened; they are changed. They are decorated; they are interpreted. But there's a basis there in fact, in reality. (pp. 44-5)

Do you feel at home [in Botswana]?

You know, I'm a writer and something of me goes into my books. But then I feel, from my own experience, that I've never been able to write about South Africa. I feel that writing, in some way, is based on a feeling that roots are present in the society. I don't think that writers, who sort of grow into an environment that is fairly secure, concentrate so much on this sense of continuity of roots; I do as a South African. In that sense, I've always been drawing on something in this society: the feeling that the roots go deep and that the historical sequence was not broken and disturbed by the British. And I think it made sense of my life. There's that aspect. And then, when the book is eventually assessed, a person says, I notice I do it myself, that it still comes down to you, your talent, what you are putting into it so that it's original. But then you also draw on your environment. It's so many subtle combinations. If it had only been me and my choices, as I have said, life would have always been beautiful and simple, but other things beyond your control intrude on you as a human being.

How accurate is it for a reader to take **Question of Power** *as an autobiographical journal? Is Elizabeth, Bessie?*

There's no way in which I can deny that that was a completely autobiographical novel taking a slice of my life, my experience, and transcribing it verbatim into novel form. It *was* maybe the way in which I interpreted experience. It *was* an experience I went through and, if the book can be faulted, it is because of the interpreter. It was the type of experience that needed interpretation and analysis. If there is a fault in it, it is possibly because the interpretation sounds confused.

What about the autobiographical content of **Maru**?

The two are very closely linked, but **Maru** has much more inventiveness. I used certain personal material. I would state, for instance, that my beginnings and background can be found in the girl Margaret Cadmore, but I wouldn't really say that **Maru** is as autobiographical as *A Question of Power.* Bits were borrowed, but otherwise **Maru** is inventive fiction. Central to my decision to write it was the astonishing similarity between racial prejudices. You see, in South Africa, the white man says of us (and it's so painful and bitter to read it—it's even in historical records), "They don't think. They don't know anything." And then they treat you that way. When they see a Black person, they automatically either look through you or above your head because you're a non-thinking "it" or something. But when I came to Botswana, the Botswana people's reaction to a tribe they oppressed, the Masarwa, was similar. You find, you know, that racial prejudice is so standardized. What was so shocking and surprising was to hear them use terminology white people used toward Black people in South Africa. Botswana said to me: "Oh, the Masarwa, they don't think; they don't know anything." How human beings can do that to human beings beats me! I thought, well, it's not that hard for me to put myself into the shoes of the Masarwa. *Maru* is not like *A Question of Power,* but it's borrowed elements from my own life.

I thought I may as well say that I could be a Masarwa. I then portrayed parts of my own early experience because I was reared by missionaries and the early beginnings were very much my life under missionaries. So, instead of saying Bessie Head, South African, I only had to say Bessie Head, Masarwan. It came to the same thing. *Maru* was bits borrowed with observations and learnings.

Does Serowe: Village of the Rain Wind *indicate a new direction in your writing?*

Everybody says, "Oh, is she going to write another *Question of Power*?" You feel such a sense of continuity because you produce the work. If I take on a job it's because I love it. That's all. It isn't change—just that one job is finished. You've done as much as you could. It's just your own sense of continuity and direction. (pp. 45-6)

Why is it difficult for you to write about South Africa?

I think it is because I was so sensitive to my environment. On one hand, I am a very highly individualistic person and I'm sure my books have borne that out. On the other hand, there's this strong individualist apparently above environment and everything. And then, on the other hand, I feel comfortable blending in with my surroundings. And I never felt happy, I never felt happy about South Africa. I think I was so sensitive to that question of dispossession. (pp. 47)

> *Bessie Head and Linda Susan Beard, in an interview in* Sage: A Scholarly Journal on Black Women, *Vol. III, No. 2, Fall, 1986, pp. 44-7.*

Michael Thorpe

[This essay focuses upon] Bessie Head's short-story collection *The Collector of Treasures* (1977); her novels have been admirably appraised elsewhere. The stories lend themselves especially well to an understanding of Head's aims as a writer. Their subtitle, *and Other Botswana Village Tales,* indicates her kinship with the village storyteller of the oral tradition. Hers are rooted, folkloristic tales woven from the fabric of village life and intended to entertain and enlighten, not to engage the modern close critic. They are subtly didactic: it seems apt to apply to them Wordsworth's prefatory comment on the moral purpose of his *Lyrical Ballads* that "the feeling therein developed gives importance to the action and situation, and not the action and situation to the feeling." Like earlier established and better-known African writers such as Ngugi and Achebe, Bessie Head (b. 1937) wishes to present, in a human and humane light, African life before as well as after the white man's coming. She seems, however, more

deeply troubled than they by the contradictions within customary life, the difficulty of reconciling what she roundly calls "the insane beliefs of a primitive society" with the mutual care and concern she has also found in a village community.

Bessie Head on her life and work

"The least I can ever say for myself is that I forcefully created for myself, under extremely hostile conditions, my ideal life. I took an obscure and almost unknown village in the Southern African bush and made it my own hallowed ground. Here, in the steadiness and peace of my own world, I could dream dreams a little ahead of the somewhat vicious clamor of revolution and the horrible stench of evil social systems. My work was always tentative because it was always so completely new: it created new worlds out of nothing; it battled with problems of food production in a tough semidesert land; it brought all kinds of people, both literate and semiliterate together, and it did not really qualify who was who—everyone had a place in my world. But nothing can take away the fact that I have never had a country; not in South Africa or in Botswana where I now live as a stateless person."

—*Bessie Head, in* Ms., *November, 1975*

The stories invariably contain authorial comment, sometimes quite lengthy analysis of "the people" or "the society" they explore. In fact, the narrator seems often to be telling the story as an exploration, as a way to develop or even question her own understanding. There is no settled or dogmatic view of her society; the author's hard-won values, rather than the people's, ultimately hold sway. She is thus a teacher, not solely "to help my society regain belief in itself" [as Chinua Achebe asserted in his *Morning Yet on Creation Day* (1975)], but as a reformer, insistently reminding her audience and herself of the intractability of evil.

Head's complex standpoint seems to stem in part from her unusual relationship to Botswana society. She is herself a "Coloured" South African who came to Botswana after a brush with the Afrikaner authorities in 1964. For many years she lived simply with her son in the village of Serowe, a woman and an alien exile. She was not readily accepted in a male-dominated society where—a reiterated theme—"women are just dogs." The anguish of her early years there, including a breakdown and a painful readjustment to life, is movingly rendered in her admittedly autobiographical novel *A Question of Power* (1974). Nevertheless, unlike many South African exiles who have become divorced not only from their own country and people but from Africa itself, she has determinedly rooted herself in Botswana and become a creative interpreter of its life. In but not of it, sympathetically attached but inevitably distanced, she is perhaps unique among black African writers in her relationship to the society of which she writes.

Hers is a dual relationship. On the one hand Head performs the task of rehabilitating the precolonial past in order to show—again in Achebe's words—"that African people did not hear of culture for the first time from Europeans." On the other she anxiously questions that society's shortcomings, seeing them as not merely the consequence of colonial victimization, but part of the universal enigma of human folly.

Even in her stories set in the past one finds a characteristic ambivalence. The piece that opens *The Collector of Treasures*, **"The Deep River: A Story of Ancient Tribal Migration,"** and her most recently published story, **"A Power Struggle,"** are presented not as "history" but as fictionalized versions of what little she has learned from "our traditional historians," versions infused with her own preoccupation with power and its relationship to the individual, whether ruler or ruled. [Thorpe adds in a footnote that one such "'traditional historian' is the 104-year-old Ramosamo Kebonang, whom Head interviewed for *Serowe, Village of the Rain Wind.*"] Both stories describe a dispute over succession to tribal kingship: in each case the rightful heir chooses exile rather than compromise or conflict. One protagonist, "in a world where women were of no account," stands by his dead father's "third junior wife" and her son, whom he himself has fathered; rather than split the tribe, he simply leaves. The other, when challenged openly for the succession by his brother, "refused at crucial points to assert his power. . . . If power was the unfocused demoniac stare of his brother then he would have none of that world" (**"A Power Struggle"**). He too leaves, but little by little many of the people follow him, abandoning the murderous brother. In both stories an ugly Hobbesian universe is fleetingly illuminated by the noble dissent of an exceptional individual whose action forces people "to show their individual faces"; in each, one finds Head's delicate ambivalence: "Theirs was not a tender, compassionate, and romantic world. And yet in a way it was" (**"Deep River"**). Each story has a quasi-mythical pattern: brother and brother, good and evil are opposed; the people may choose. Their choice, or rather their capacity to choose, is vitally important. **"A Power Struggle"** closes with these words:

> This thread of philosophical beauty was deeply woven into the history of the land and the story was repeated many times over so that it became the only history people ever knew. But when the white strangers came this history ended as a new order was imposed on life. The people's kings faded from memory to become myths of the past and no choice was left between what was good and what was evil.

In *Serowe* Head describes the tradition of migration as one "established over the centuries to avert bloodshed in a crisis and underlying the basic nonviolent nature of African society as it was then. This gives the lie to white historians who, for their own ends, damned African people as savages."

The remaining twelve stories in *The Collector of Treasures* concern the present; they read, once one becomes aware of Head's concerns, like subtle inducements to her African readers to learn again to choose between good and evil. While evil is easily recognizable as a constant—witchcraft, human sacrifice, the abuse of women—the sto-

ryteller shows her hand most plainly in her efforts to provide models of the good. She is writing, to use Alan Paton's refrain in *Cry, the Beloved Country*, for "the broken tribe," its pride and value almost fatally eroded by the years of colonial subjection. [**"The Collector of Treasures"**] is bisected with a long excursus characterizing "two kinds of men in the society." While the lesser is responsible for "the breakdown in family life," his type is explained in historical terms that invite understanding: when independence arrived, "it provided the first occasion for family life of a new order, above the childlike discipline of custom, the degradation of colonialism"; but a man arrived at "this turning point, a broken wreck with no inner resources at all. . . . He spun away from himself in a dizzy kind of death dance of wild destruction and dissipation." Dikeledi, the story's protagonist, is married to such a man and can only yearn from a distance for Paul Thebolo, "another kind of man in the society with the power to create himself anew. . . . He was a poem of tenderness." Thebolo and his wife befriend her, and she enjoys, for herself and her children, the "kindness and love" they bestow. When her husband returns and, jealous of Thebolo, forces himself back into the house, she castrates him and accidentally kills him. It is an act of self-sacrifice and self-violation to which, we can believe, Dikeledi has been driven, out of tender care and protectiveness toward her children, an act committed with hands which—as is seen in the story's opening prison scene—are "soft, caressing, almost boneless hands of strange power—work of a beautiful design grew from those hands." In her society this precious power has been wrenched to perform an atrocious act, but Dikeledi remains a tender, virtuous being. The two truths are reconcilable only within the bounds of Head's story, but that story also is typically a parable of good and evil, of the interwoven but by no means wholly "beautiful design." Beauty is immanent and can be brought forth in unexpected places if only Head's storytelling art is heeded.

It is not until the last page of the closing story, **"Hunting,"** that Head describes Thato, a woman blessed with a caring husband "incapable of hurting life" and gifted, like herself, with the unerring heart of a good storyteller. This is Bessie Head's gift: one hopes that, like those of the grandmother in the pathetic story **"The Wind and a Boy,"** her stories might awaken "a great tenderness." Frank but unsentimental appeals to the heart give the tales one voice: the key words are heart, love, tenderness, compassion, sensitivity, care—and power, a force for good and not only for evil. Of Mompati, the garrulous village shopkeeper in **"The Village Saint,"** we are told, "It mattered that some living being cared intensely and vividly and gloriously about his fellow men." And if we believe in this man and this story, it is partly because in others Head does not shrink from the harsher truths: in a later selection a woman, almost driven mad by the "evil source" of witchcraft, recovers despite the prejudice and ignorance of her fellow villagers and becomes a bleak witness; "There is no one to help the people, not even God," she says. "I could not sit down because I am too poor and there is no one else to feed my children." There is also that most terrible yet most compassionate of her stories, **"Looking for a Rain God."** In a time of doubt and desperation an old man is inspired by "an ancient memory . . . buried by years and years of prayer in a Christian church" of "a certain rain god who accepted only the sacrifice of the bodies of children." While their elders struggle with this terrible memory and cure, the children play, mimicking the masterful ways of grown-ups: "You stupid thing! How could you have lost the money on the way to the shop! You must have been playing again!" The story continues, "after it was all over," to narrate the horrified fellow villagers' suspicions; the killers are arrested and condemned for "ritual murder, . . . but all the people who lived off crops knew in their hearts that . . . they could have killed something to make the rain fall." This, characteristically, is the voice of understanding, not condemnation.

However, while Head recognizes the two truths—or two sides—there is no moral ambivalence. This is seen most clearly in **"Jacob: The Faith-Healing Priest,"** where the narrator is a firm guide to values: "There is much to be said about the love and sharing to be found within tribal societies and much of this is true—but true too is Jacob's uncle," who, since the children are not pure Botswana by birth, treats his orphaned nephews as "an inferior species." So true are both he and Lebojang, the corrupt, faith-healing priest, that "Jacob" has the force of a parable of goodness more desired as an ideal than upheld as a living reality. There is, nevertheless, a seeming ambivalence toward "the people." They are often shown as weak, credulous dupes of their society's evil power-brokers, but the evil is *in* them too. From story to story the viewpoint fluctuates: "People were never fooled by façades," yet they put faith in the corrupt Lebojang; "What was harmful to them they rejected," but not before they have yielded all too willingly to its fascination; "Custom demanded that people care about each other," but several stories portray the isolated individual, misunderstood and shunned, exposed to "the general dirt of the village." Such contradictions, inherent in life itself, in the gap between "custom" and practice, the ideal and the reality, contribute to the sense these stories convey of a living struggle for true values and worthy action. Like Doris Lessing, who refuses in her African stories to treat white color prejudice as a unique white evil, Head seeks to combat "the atrophy in the imagination that prevents us from seeing ourselves in every creature that breathes under the sun."

The narrator's or, rather, storyteller's teaching never becomes abstract. Character and relationship are the stories' substance, steadily reinforced with organic imagery and description. Images of harmony and tenderness predominate: "a stream of holiness," the lives of those who love "flow together"; "the bundles of neat tears" shed by Johanna, who finds joy at last as Prophet Jacob's wife; the "soft, caressing almost boneless hands of strange power" of Dikeledi. There is also the image from common life raised to poetic intensity, as in this passage on the link between the "good story-teller" Thato and her husband:

> It had been such a new and intoxicating experience watching the tractor turn up the land; the perfume of the newly-wet earth arose and floated everywhere and the man's work was compact and professional, just the way he had been taught in the agricultural demonstration school

he attended. By late afternoon he had ploughed up all their land. . . . By night, an unmoving image had haunted her dreams of a man's head turned sideways in fixed concentration as he closely watched the contours and furrows he created behind him. She had cried a little to herself; he had seemed a creature too far removed from her own humble life. There were so many women like her who could work and plough and life wasn't going to offer them any spectacular rewards.

This description, evoking an image of order and tranquility, comes near the close of the collection; Thato herself, however, tells stories of the "incredible muddle and nonsense people made of their lives every day. . . . Nothing could sort out the world. It would always be a painful muddle." In Bessie Head's telling there is pain enough, but it is pain relieved constantly by the clear light of a compassionate, understanding heart. In the moral confusion of the post-colonial, post-missionary period she is one of a precious few African writers who have restored to her people, through visionary candor, the "choice between what [is] good and what [is] evil." Her stories merit the authority and force of that "law" or traditional custom which, she has said, "is written in the heart of the good." (pp. 414-16)

Michael Thorpe, "Treasures of the Heart: The Short Stories of Bessie Head," in World Literature Today, *Vol. 57, No. 3, Summer, 1983, pp. 414-16.*

Nancy Topping Bazin

Media reports about international women's meetings and even sessions at the National Women's Studies Association conferences, too often perpetuate the myth that third world women hold women's issues in low priority. It is important, therefore, to note that two of the best novels by contemporary Black African women writers focus upon the growing feminist consciousness of their protagonists. Nnu Ego in Buchi Emecheta's *The Joy's of Motherhood* (1979) and Elizabeth in Bessie Head's *A Question of Power* (1974) both move away from innocence into an understanding of the patriarchal culture in which they live. They gain this understanding through experiences so overwhelming and horrifying that each woman barely survives. However, the two protagonists emerge from their ventures with strength, wisdom, and clarity of vision they did not previously possess. (p. 32)

Nnu Ego's journey into feminist consciousness is through marriage and motherhood. Bessie Head's protagonist in *A Question of Power* arrives at the same destination through a bout of madness. In her mad nightmare world, Elizabeth struggles against and survives patriarchal efforts to manipulate her spiritual and sexual being. She is able to regain her sanity only by recognizing that she must not respond passively to those who wish to dominate her. But Bessie Head's protagonist goes beyond the rejection of domination as a principle that determines attitudes and behavior to the articulation of an egalitarian philosophy. Whereas Buchi Emecheta's focus is upon personal experiences and social customs in a patriarchal African culture, Bessie Head's concern is with the spiritual or philosophical significance of patriarchal behavior.

The title *A Question of Power* clarifies further what this novel is about. To Bessie Head whose daily life was shaped by the racist practices of South Africa and the sexist attitudes of the men she lived with, the question of who has the power is indeed important. Like Virginia Woolf, Zora Neale Hurston, and Doris Lessing, Bessie Head views the need of the male to see himself twice as big as he really is as one of the chief causes of unjust, undemocratic, and unkind behavior. In *A Question of Power* the male need to dominate and feel superior to others is represented by two men, Sello and Dan. They come to life and into power through the mad imaginings of Elizabeth. They are so real to her that she talks with them and feels her life literally threatened by them. It is because Sello and Dan use every power they have to try to destroy Elizabeth psychologically that she is mad. To regain her sanity, she must defeat them.

Elizabeth learns that Sello has already "killed several women," and he has molested his own child. Moreover, he is the creator of the powerful Medusa, who inhabits Elizabeth's mad world. His Medusa is really "the direct and tangible form of his own evils, his power lusts, his greeds, his self importance." Medusa, manipulated by Sello, tortures Elizabeth until she almost obliterates her: "It wasn't Elizabeth's body she was thrusting into extinction. It was the soul; the bolts were aimed at her soul. It seemed to make death that much slower, that much more piecemeal. The narrow, mean eyes of Sello in the brown suit stared at her over Medusa's shoulder."

Sello and Dan try to kill Elizabeth's spirit. They do this primarily through manipulating her feelings about sexuality and through using sexuality to degrade her. To undermine Elizabeth's sense of herself as a woman, Sello uses Medusa, and Dan uses his "seventy-one nice-time girls." Medusa with a smile offers Elizabeth some secret information:

> It was about her vagina. Without any bother for decencies she sprawled her long black legs in the air, and the most exquisite sensation travelled out of her towards Elizabeth. It enveloped from head to toe like a slow, deep, sensuous bomb. It was like falling into deep, warm waters, lazily raising one hand and resting in a heaven of bliss. Then she looked at Elizabeth and smiled, a mocking superior smile: You haven't got anything *near* that, have you?"

Sello displays before Elizabeth his own attraction to Medusa. He "issued a low moan of anguish. He seemed to be desperately attached to that thing Medusa had which no other woman had. And even this was a mockery. It was abnormally constructed, like seven thousand vaginas in one, turned on and operating at white heat."

Elizabeth is attracted to Dan's overwhelming masculinity: "He made a woman feel like an ancient and knowledgeable queen of love." But Dan displays his power not just over her but over all women. He sadistically parades his many women before her and his message to her is that she

should be jealous: "I go with all these women because you are inferior. You cannot make it up to my level." But, of course, just at the moment when she decides she dislikes him and wants "to pull her mind out of the chaos," he says: "If you leave me I'll die, because I have nothing else."

One of the key images in Elizabeth's madness is Dan "standing in front of her, his pants down, as usual, flaying his powerful penis in the air saying: "Look, I'm going to show you how I sleep with B . . . She has a womb I can't forget. When I go with a woman I go for one hour. You can't do that." His women include Miss Wriggly-Bottom, who "had small round breasts and a neat, nipped-in waist. She walked in time to a silent jazz tune she was humming and wriggled and wriggled her bottom." There was also Miss Sewing Machine who "liked her penny-button tickled." He added to the display "Miss Pelican-Beak, Miss Chopper, Miss Pink Sugar-Icing, whom he was on the point of marrying, Madame Make-Love-On-The-Floor where anything goes, The Sugar-Plum Fairy, more of Body Beautiful, more of The Womb, a demonstration of sexual stamina with five local women, this time the lights on, Madame Squelch Squelch, Madame Loose-Bottom—the list of them was endless." Elizabeth took heavy doses of sleeping tablets to block out his all night activities with these "nice-time girls." For Dan sometimes tumbled these women into bed right beside Elizabeth ("They kept on bumping her awake"), and he encouraged them to use her personal possessions to clean up: "He was abnormally obsessed with dirt on his women. They washed and washed in her bathroom; they put on Elizabeth's dresses and underwear and made use of her perfumes."

Of course, if Dan finds that any of his seventy-one "nice-time girls" are too sexual, then he panics and turns against them. He views women as dirty if they are more sexually potent than he. He could not stand the sexual potency of Madame Loose-Bottom or the hysterical, feverish orgasm of Body Beautiful. Because the pelvis of Madame Squelch Squelch was like "molten lava," going with her made him throw up. One night he decided Miss Pelican-Beak with her long, tough vagina was "too pushy," so he broke her legs and elbows and re-designed her pelvis to make it more passive. Then he left her for Miss Chopped. Thus, his hatred for women was not all directed at Elizabeth. But she takes his behavior personally: "Why, why, why? What have I done?" Indeed it drives her further into madness; she becomes dysfunctional and must be hospitalized.

Both Sello and Dan use male homosexuality to make Elizabeth feel excluded. Dan tells Elizabeth it is a "universal phenomenon." He makes Sello appear before her with his boyfriend, and he says, "They do it all the time." The displays of homosexuality like the displays of heterosexuality are meant to degrade her. These nightmares are extensions of her experiences with her husband: "Women were always complaining of being molested by her husband. Then there was also a white man who was his boy-friend. After a year she picked up the small boy and walked out of the house, never to return."

Elizabeth's recognition of the similarity between racist and sexist attitudes is clear. She knew that white people "went out of their way to hate you or loathe you"; similarly, Dan hits her with a "torrent of hatred" every day. She finds the misogyny of some African males to be untempered by "love and tenderness and personal romantic treasuring of women." She calls both racists and sexists power-maniacs. "What did they gain, the power people, while they lived off other people's souls like vultures?" Medusa serves as an image for domination; she represents these attitudes: "Who's running the show around here? I am. Who knows everything around here? I do. Who's wearing the pants in this house? I am."

On a philosophical level, Elizabeth is saved from permanent madness by her faith in a value system different from Dan's and Sellos and by a different concept of God. In practice, she is saved by working in a garden with a woman friend Kenosi, who admires and respects her. Her work relationship with this woman provides her with a feminist model. Ultimately, Elizabeth rejects the patriarchal model of thinking and behaving in favor of a feminist mode of thinking and behaving. This rejection of a philosophy of domination in favor of an egalitarian philosophy is reflected in her comments about God.

Elizabeth rejects a god in the sky, because "God in heaven is too important to be decent." Her ideal is to bring holiness down to earth. The gods are, in fact, those "killed and killed and killed again in one cause after another for the liberation of mankind." She saw the gods as "ordinary, practical, sane people, seemingly their only distinction being that they had consciously concentrated on spiritual earnings. All the push and direction was towards the equality of man in his soul, as though, if it were not fixed up there, it never would be anywhere else." She concludes that "there are several hundred thousand people who are God." Her prayer is, "Oh God . . . May I never contribute to creating dead worlds, only new worlds."

Elizabeth concludes that this can occur only through a struggle against greed and arrogance and an excessive concern for self. Sello admits, "I thought too much of myself. I am the root cause of human suffering." At one point Elizabeth and Sello "perfected together the ideal of sharing everything and then perfectly shared everything with all mankind." But it is through the horrors of her contract with Dan in her hallucinations that she has learned the most:

> He had deepened and intensified all her qualities. . . . he taught by default—he taught iron and steel self-control through sheer, wild, abandoned debauchery; he taught the extremes of love and tenderness through the extreme of hate; he taught an alertness for falsehoods within, because he had used any means at his disposal to destroy Sello. And from the degradation and destruction of her life and arisen a still, lofty serenity of soul nothing could shake.

The aim must be to tap into one's powers, and she places her emphasis on the soul: "If it's basically right there, then other things fall into place. That's my struggle; and that's black power, but it's a power that belongs to all mankind and in which all mankind can share."

Although her language is sometimes sexist, Bessie Head's philosophy and ethics parallel those of feminist philosopher/theologians such as Rosemary Ruether, Naomi Goldenberg, and Elizabeth Dodson Gray. They too reject the hierarchy in traditional religions and cry out for a more egalitarian world view. Feminist theologians speak out against the male God in the sky and the lingering Christian view that the world was created specifically for Man and that he has the right to use nature and women as he pleases. Nor is it surprising that the political philosophy in feminist utopian fiction is most akin to anarchism, for women are tired of being ruled, manipulated, and exploited by authoritarian figures. So, too, is Bessie Head's protagonist.

Throughout Elizabeth's madness, there existed the possibility of being healed and made sane by working in a vegetable garden with Kenosi. Kenosi had about her a quiet strength and purposefulness that appealed to Elizabeth. As they worked together, "Elizabeth clung to the woman. There seemed to be no other justification for her continued existence, so near to death was she." She found in the uneducated, hardworking Kenosi a "knowingness and grasp of life" that made her beautiful. Most important of all, Kenosi needs her. Kenosi tells her, "you must never leave the garden . . . I cannot work without you." Her relationship with this woman keeps in sight the possibility of something quite different from the patriarchal relationships she has in the nightmare world: their "work-relationship has been established on the solid respect of one partner for another." Kenosi enables Elizabeth to maintain her belief that egalitarian relationships are possible. Sello's comment to Elizabeth about her relationship with Dan also helps to save her: "Elizabeth, love isn't like that. Love is two people mutually feeding each other, not one living on the soul of the other like a ghoul!"

Elizabeth withstands the cruelty and torture of Medusa and the two men who inhabit her madness through not giving in to their view of her as nothing. At one point she tells Sello that he is making a mistake, for she is God too. Although they almost totally annihilate her sense of self, their misogynist behavior only serves to confirm her faith in the opposite of everything they represent. Throughout her struggle against these symbols of the patriarchal power system which people her hallucinations, she continues to articulate her faith in goodness, love, equality, and inner strength.

The movement toward mysticism found in feminist philosophy is obviously present in Elizabeth's as well. Elizabeth has been tested by the nightmare of madness created by Sello in his role as spiritual mentor. Once she has passed through this hell, her knowledge of evil helps her to rediscover an impersonal, mystical love. She is transported into a state in which there are "no private hungers to be kissed, loved, adored. And yet there was a feeling of being kissed by everything; by the air, the soft flow of life, people's smiles and friendships." This "vast and universal love" equalizes all things and all people. Elizabeth emerges from her hell with a confirmed belief in such love and a "lofty serenity of soul nothing could shake." At the end of the book she recognizes that humankind's fundamental error is the "relegation of all things holy to some unseen Being in the sky. Since man was not holy to man, he could be tortured for his complexion, he could be misused, degraded and killed."

Bessie Head chooses to focus on sexism rather than racism in *A Question of Power.* This forces her African readers, more familiar with racism, to see the similarities between the two and their common root in the philosophy of domination. Men degrade, manipulate, and abuse women in Elizabeth's nightmare, basically because they fail to perceive sacredness in them. Elizabeth advocates a philosophy that insists upon the sacredness of all life because of her subjection to this patriarchal behavior. This is typical of the evolution of feminist thought. That is why feminists speak of ecological and peace issues as well as equal rights; and that is why they speak of equal rights not only for women but also for the poor, the handicapped, and the racially oppressed. (pp. 34-6)

> *Nancy Topping Bazin, "Venturing into Feminist Consciousness: Two Protagonists from the Fiction of Buchi Emecheta and Bessie Head,"* in Sage, *Vol. II, No. 1, Spring, 1985, pp. 32-6.*

Joyce Johnson

Whether African nationalism should commit itself to the use of violence or to the Gandhian philosophy of non-violent positive action is a question which has been debated by black African leaders. This question, Bessie Head reminds us in *A Question of Power,* is only one aspect of the perennial and universal problem of how mankind should attempt to restrain evil or to maintain order in a society. [Johnson adds in a footnote: "At this level, Head is concerned with a question which preoccupied Leo Tolstoy, for example. The two main principles of the social order, Tolstoy observed, were 'the virtue of love, and what is opposed to love, namely the restraining of evil by violence.' "] Man's use of violent or non-violent methods, Head suggests, points ultimately to a conception of God. The advocate of non-violence imagines a compassionate God exercising his power through love; the advocate of violence imagines an autocratic and whimsical God imposing his will from above, through coercion. In *A Question of Power,* Head examines the way in which man's ideas of God is expressed through social action. In exploring this theme she conveys insights into the ways in which oppressed individuals and societies respond to domination by others.

The theme of the novel is mediated through the experience of a young woman who has been demoralized by oppression and views the world as largely hostile. She comes under the influence of two charismatic figures, one who promotes the brotherhood of man and non-violent resistance to evil and oppression and one who resists evil with violence and is himself transformed into an evil power. The novel depicts their attempts to dominate the woman and her struggle to develop an independent moral position. The philosophy of non-violence, as Head presents it, is associated with Mohandas K. Gandhi, whose name is linked with the struggle for Indian nationalism and the earlier agitation for Indian rights in South Africa. The

philosophy of violence is associated with those African nationalist leaders who not only resorted to violence as a means of achieving national independence but also used it to perpetuate types of oppression which they originally fought against. There were, in fact, leaders who saw Gandhian methods as incompatible with the African spirit.

In *A Question of Power,* the heroine, Elizabeth, is a coloured woman from an urban South African environment who goes with her young son as a teacher to Botswana. Elizabeth's black African father had been a stable hand in the household of her English mother's family. Elizabeth is not only the product of two racial groups and two social classes, but is also a representative of an urban syncretic culture which has moved away from the traditional ways. She feels socially isolated in the largely tribal Batswana village of Motabeng to which she goes. "Definitely as far as Batswana society was concerned," she reflects, "she was an out-and-out outsider and would never be in on *their* things." Elizabeth is in an unsettled state because she has for years been searching for a guiding philosophy and has been subjecting herself to rigorous self-questioning. An important aspect of her life in South Africa has been her association with Indians. She had married a coloured ex-convict because of his professed interest in Hindu philosophy. Influenced by Eastern ideas and inclined to shrink from overt political action, Elizabeth questions which is the right response to oppression and humiliation—the way of tolerance and non-violence along which Gandhi had tried to lead the Indians or the way of violence recommended by militant black activists. This question, which arises directly out of Elizabeth's experiences as a coloured person in South Africa, is answered through her experiences as an exile in Botswana.

Elizabeth's feelings of isolation and her habit of introspection lead to a mental breakdown during her first year in Botswana. She is helped by the white South African philanthropist Eugene, who finds employment for her in a local self-help scheme. Her involvement in this scheme, together with her responsibility to her son, exert a partially steadying influence on her as she struggles to recover her mental balance. Her recovery is due largely to an effort of will. Elizabeth subsequently has a second mental breakdown and again her involvement with persons working in the self-help scheme and the demands made on her by her son keep her in touch with everyday reality. Further evidences of the kindness of persons in the community help to restore her mental well-being and she finally develops a sense of harmony with her environment. As the novel ends, Elizabeth is confident that she has found a philosophy for directing her life.

In telling Elizabeth's story, Head draws a parallel between the situation of the individual who has suffered from the forces of prejudice and social oppression and that of a society which has been exploited by external forces. The disaffection in the society, as it seeks to adjust from one set of circumstances to another, is compared with the mental conflict taking place in the persecuted individual. Head implies a further comparison between the individual who is seeking a guiding philosophy and the society which is attempting to define its goals. She interprets Elizabeth's inner conflict by relating it to symbolic paradigms in African, Eastern and Western mythologies from which she also derives motifs which advance the plot and metaphorical structures which link the individual and social dilemmas examined in the novel. There is not, as Lewis Nkosi has suggested [in his *Tasks and Masks* (1981)], any confusion in bringing the various sources together, for Head refers to key points which link the meanings of the myths from different traditions. The myths referred to in the novel are generally related to mankind's quest for self-knowledge and self-mastery. In alluding to these myths, Head links the experiences of the individual in a particular society—which she treats as symptomatic of those of a whole society—with the social evolution of mankind. In the rest of this paper, we shall examine Head's attempt to integrate themes of personal, social and universal significance.

The novel is written in two parts, each dealing with an occasion on which Elizabeth suffers a mental breakdown. The breakdown in each instance may be attributed to the abnormal social situation in which she lives. Elizabeth harbours feelings of anger and resentment because of the oppression and humiliation to which she has been subjected and because of her isolation in the community to which she goes. In that community there is a deep-rooted belief that "if a man is alone with his thoughts, he may think of some mischief he can do." Elizabeth's consciousness of her isolation also gives her a feeling of guilt. Her internal anger and resentment and her sense of guilt are like evil powers guiding her thoughts and undermining her capacity to form healthy social relationships. In describing Elizabeth's mental breakdown, Head has created an image of the disintegration of an organism whose parts have ceased to function effectively. This metaphor of the disintegrating organism may also describe the society which is immobilized because of disaffection among its ranks.

Elizabeth's inner conflict is depicted in a series of dreams which take on an increasingly nightmarish quality as her mental state worsens. In both African and Western traditions, the dream is regarded as an expression of inner conflict. The form which Elizabeth's dreams take may be directly related to the African context. In Africa, as Monica Wilson has observed [in her *Religion and the Transformation of Society* (1971)]:

> long before Freud analysed the dreams of his Viennese patients, it was understood that dreams were an expression of inner conflict, before Erikson spoke of the loss of identity, African villagers talked of those with majestic authority, casting a shadow (*nesitunzi* in Xhosa) and those torn within casting no shadow.

The concept Wilson describes is presented in a concrete image in the novel. Elizabeth is haunted by two familiars who dominate her thoughts. She identifies them with black African men whom she has seen in the village. Her actual knowledge of the men is scant. One is Sello, a crop farmer and cattle breeder who is generally admired by the villagers. In Elizabeth's dreams, he alternates between the roles of prophet and ordinary man. His appeal is spiritual and Elizabeth associates him with the power of the creative imagination. The other is Dan, who is an entrepreneur and politician who is "greatly admired for being an African nationalist in a country where people were only concerned about tribal affairs." He is one of the very few cattle millionaires of the country: "He ordered a fantastic array of suits from somewhere, and he was short, black and handsome." He radiates force and energy and Elizabeth identifies him with power which is direct and uncompromising. Elizabeth's inner conflict is thus projected onto figures outside herself. The forms which these apparitions take suggest how she sees herself in relation to the black African community. As a marginal individual who has been assimilated neither by the black nor the white community, Elizabeth is, in contrast to these figures who "cast a shadow" over her, a powerless individual "torn within" and "casting no shadow."

In *A Question of Power,* Head also uses the metaphor of the dream to establish different levels for interpreting Elizabeth's experiences. Elizabeth's dreams may be explained as disturbances arising out of her situation as an unattached coloured woman in a predominantly black African community. In her former life in South Africa, Elizabeth had mixed mainly with Indians and with other coloured people. In Botswana, she is plagued by the feeling that she does not really like black Africans. At the personal level, her dreams involving two powerful black African figures may be seen as a kind of wish fulfilment in which she associates freely with persons from whom she feels isolated in her everyday existence. Elizabeth's disturbed mental state, however, has resulted not only from a problem of identity but also from her conflicting reactions to cruel social pressures. The process by which Sello and Dan attempt to dominate her provides a concrete image for the process by which she clarifies her responses to these social pressures. Elizabeth's dreams also transcend her own personal experiences. In the first place, the social problems which disturb her are related, generally, to the experiences of the coloured minority in South Africa. In the second place, she sees in her dreams figures who existed before her time and individuals with whom she has had no personal contact. Within the framework of the dream, Sello and Dan are freely associated with important personalities who are linked with the controversy surrounding the use of non-violent or violent methods of social change. They come to represent two opposed philosophical viewpoints which Elizabeth must confront before reaching her own position.

Three levels of significance may thus be distinguished in Elizabeth's dreams. At the personal level, they relate to her situation as an unattached woman in a strange society. At the social level, they relate to her position as a member of a powerless minority in an ex-colonial African society. Finally they relate to her effort as an individual to make sense of the world in which she lives, for her personal and social problems plunge her into a chaotic state out of which she struggles to find her way.

The first section of the novel describes Elizabeth's encounters with Sello. One night three months after her arrival in Motabeng, Elizabeth becomes aware of a figure entering her bedroom and sitting on a chair near her bed. Elizabeth is not sure if she is awake or asleep and "after that the dividing line between dream perceptions and waking reality was to become confused." The apparition visits her for several nights before she actually develops a visual impression of him. His dress and manner are significant and suggest that he is one who has been subjected to spiritual and physical ordeals:

> He wore the soft, white, flowing robes of a monk, but in a peculiar fashion, with his shoulders slightly hunched forward, as though it were a prison garment. He stared straight at Elizabeth in a friendly way and said in a voice of quiet affection: "My friend."

Elizabeth associates the apparition both with Sello, an African living in Motabeng, and with a universal saviour figure:

> He looked like a man she had seen about the village of Motabeng who drove a green truck, but the name she associated in her mind with the monk-robed man was that of an almost universally adored God.

Sello's two aspects are later distinguished when he also appears as an ordinary man in a brown suit. On the one hand, he is godlike and creative and, on the other, human and vulnerable.

The God who is uppermost in Elizabeth's mind, on Sello's first appearance, is Buddha and later she makes a clear identification of Sello with Buddha: "Elizabeth turned and looked at Sello. He averted his face. It was Buddha, and the only face she had acquired apart from Sello." The apparition represents, in a concrete image, Elizabeth's acquisition of a guiding philosophy. In his monk's robes, Sello is the incarnation of a great teacher and the embodiment of a way of life. His physical appearance, as is made clear at various points in the novel, is a "venture" or "visible body" assumed by the spirit or creative force. Head alludes to the Buddhist idea of the great teacher who, having earned the right to enter Nirvana, voluntarily gives it up and takes on a visible body in order to continue his work among mankind. Sello can thus represent a particular individual exerting moral or intellectual force in a society at a particular time and a timeless spirit existing throughout human history. In the latter aspect, he is associated in the novel not only with heroes of religious myth but also with particular individuals who have worked for racial equality or better social conditions in Africa. On some occasions, for example, Sello's presence merges into that of an Asian who preaches Gandhian ideas of tolerance and respect for the poor to Elizabeth. On one occasion, Sello "walks into" a figure who is referred to as "the Father" and who may be identified with the South African philanthropist Patrick Van Rensberg, who organized various projects in Botswana. Historical figures like Gandhi and Van Rensburg, Head suggests, continue to live in spirit, for their ideas continue to support the struggle for a more equitable society.

Elizabeth is also aware of her own twofold existence. Like Sello she is an ordinary individual within a particular time and place and the vesture of an enduring spirit. Our understanding of the novel is complicated by the fact that Elizabeth retains her personal identity and is at the same time transformed into a universal human type. This transformation is again conveyed in concrete images like that of Sello moving into Elizabeth's person or of the Mystic Madonna, Sello's spiritual counterpart, entering Elizabeth's person. Elizabeth thus becomes Sello's companion on his spiritual journey. Their journey represents the efforts by the different individuals in different societies who attempt to achieve a balanced relationship with their society and to create harmony in their personal lives.

Sello's appearance launches Elizabeth on a series of enlightening conversations which take place over a period of approximately four years. The major part of this period is, however, dominated by Dan and relates to the second part of the novel. At first, Elizabeth hopes that Sello's teaching will help her to control the unhealthy impulses developing within her and provide a guide for her future actions. In the early stages of their relationship, Sello introduces Elizabeth to a spectacular array of personalities and memories of the past which represent his work as "the prophet of mankind." He directs her thoughts to those who have fought spiritual battles for the sake of mankind and attempts to teach her an ideal of brotherly love. Sello reveals to Elizabeth the process of social evolution during which mankind has moved away from a situation in which the few entirely manipulated power to oppress the many to one in which ordinary people were beginning to realize their own capabilities. Elizabeth, whose life has been dominated by the "vehement vicious struggle between two sets of people with different looks," finds Sello's message difficult to accept. She is primarily aware of the reversals in the pattern of progress and cannot develop any sustained faith in Sello's promise of a beautiful future.

Elizabeth falls into despair when Sello goes on to reveal his own inner conflict. Since Sello's way is the way of truth, he can hold nothing back, even if the revelation will further destroy Elizabeth's faith in him. Thus he brings her face to face with "the Medusa," a representation of the forces which undermine his spiritual powers. Mention of Medusa recalls the classical myth of the Gorgons which, as Erich Neumann has observed, are "images of the great pre-Hellenic Mother Goddess" in whom the opposed principles of life and death are combined. In keeping with this idea, Medusa, in *A Question of Power,* represents forces which have both creative and destructive potential but which may become totally destructive if not brought under control. Thus she is associated with "the poor of Africa" and more particularly with the stubborn and reactionary elements in tribal society which threaten to divide the new nation states in Africa. "Tradition, with its narrow outlook," Head has observed elsewhere, "does not combine happily with common sense, humanity and a broad outlook." In relation to the society, Medusa is a representation of attitudes and behaviour which stem from intolerance and irrationality. [Johnson adds in a footnote that the "Gorgon is also a standard metaphor for something which is perceived as harmful to society."] She also represents the qualities in the individual which threaten to weaken his moral purpose. Elizabeth reflects, for example, that Medusa is "the direct and tangible form of [the individual's] own evils, his power lusts, his greeds, his self-importance."

In relation to Sello, Medusa represents not only those personal weaknesses which he is unable to control but also those external forces which tempt him to lose faith in his own purpose. The latter are forces set in motion by the agents of intolerance and irrationality. Medusa dominates the Sello of the brown suit while Sello the monk looks on helplessly. Like Sello, Elizabeth is attacked by Medusa, who may again be seen as a projection both of Elizabeth's own weaknesses and of the hostility directed at her by persons of narrow outlook. The areas of Elizabeth's life which are particularly vulnerable to Medusa's attacks are her spiritual life and her social relationships with black Africans. Medusa tempts her to abandon her search for spiritual satisfaction, to lose all self-control and to give way to hateful thoughts about black Africans. She appears to Elizabeth mainly in two guises: she is on the one hand the embodiment of sexual temptation, and on the other the embodiment of negative social attitudes.

In many of Elizabeth's dreams, Medusa's sexual powers are contrasted with her own. The contrast is brought out strongly, for example, in a scene in which Medusa exposes her vagina to Elizabeth. . . . Elizabeth reflects that the vagina was "not such a pleasant area of body to concentrate on, possibly only now and then if necessary." The point of this exchange was missed by Lewis Nkosi, who has concluded that the author has the "profoundest conviction" about the "insignificance of sex." In the novel, as in the mythological sources on which Head draws, however, sexual excess is a metaphor for other types of excess and the emotions attached to sexual passion are opposed to the forces of reason and to the pursuit of spiritual perfection. Clearly what Medusa symbolizes in the dreams in which she flaunts her sexual powers is the life centred on the sensual rather than on the spiritual. Reference to mythology further clarifies the significance of the contrast between Elizabeth's and Medusa's sexual powers. As Erich Neumann has observed, the vagina is symbolic of the hell or the underworld that the mythic hero must survive:

> The opening of the vessel of doom is the womb, the gate, the gullet which actively swallows, devours, rends and kills. Its sucking power is mythologically symbolized by its lure and attraction for man, for life and consciousness, and the individual male who can evade it only if he is a hero, and even then not always.

In her encounters with Medusa, Elizabeth thus experiences temptations similar to those against which Sello has constantly struggled in his attempt to put personal spiritual growth and social duty above selfish desires.

The main effects of the negative social attitudes which Medusa represents are to make Elizabeth feel excluded from the community of black Africans and to increase her insecurity as a member of the coloured minority. Because she is associated with the "poor of Africa," Medusa claims to be morally superior to Elizabeth. "I am greater than you in goodness," she tells Elizabeth. Her concern for the poor is expressed in such a way as to remind Elizabeth that she is an educated middle-class coloured woman, and her concern about traditional values is also a means of excluding Elizabeth from the African community. She claims that Elizabeth is not a genuine African and tells her, for example, "Africa is troubled waters . . . I'm a powerful swimmer in troubled waters. You'll only drown here. You're not linked up to the people. You don't know any African languages." Suffering and poverty, Head thus suggests, generate their own forms of arrogance, self-importance and exclusivity. In associating Medusa with the tribal past, she shows that, although reference to the past may give impulse to the future development of the society, it also causes divisions in the society to persist. The divisions appear, for example, in the prejudice shown against those from outside the tribe and the hostility directed at those who cannot always support the popular viewpoint. In raising the issue of Elizabeth's ethnic affiliation, Head refers specifically to questions which often arose in many post-independence societies as to who was or was not genuinely African.

The breakdown in Elizabeth's mental life becomes apparent to those around her soon after Medusa appears. With Medusa's hissing and insistent voice reminding her that she is coloured and challenging her that she does not really like black Africans, Elizabeth loses control in a shop and abuses a Batswana clerk. She spends a brief period in hospital, after which she becomes attached to a co-operative farming scheme, for she loses her job as a teacher. In her effort to escape Medusa's power, Elizabeth constantly searches for reassurances of the existence of goodness among those with whom she comes into contact. The routines related to the farming project, her concern for her son and the kindnesses of a few persons give her life a degree of stability which helps to counter Medusa's influence. She recovers her sanity temporarily.

At the end of the first section of the novel, Elizabeth has come to resent Sello's earlier influence. She has found him to be an increasingly ambivalent personality, and has lost faith in the type of goodness which seems coterminous with passivity. Sello's revelation of his own vulnerability has destroyed her confidence in his ability to help her to transcend her own weaknesses. Elizabeth escapes from Medusa's power largely by abandoning those attitudes which make her vulnerable to Medusa's mockery. Contemptuous of Sello's failure to control Medusa, Elizabeth detaches herself from him and is ready to explore a new direction. She has gained confidence from fighting her way out of her state of mental collapse. She concludes that she cannot rely on pre-existing moral rules but must find her own rules to meet the exigencies of her particular situation. Characteristically Head conveys this awakening of new energy in Elizabeth in a nature image:

> The dawn came. The soft shifts and changes of light stirred with a slow wonder over the vast expanse of the African sky. A small bird in a tree outside awoke and trilled loudly. The soft, cool air, so fresh and full of the perfume of the bush, swirled around her face and form as she stood watching the sun thrust one powerful, majestic, golden arm above the horizon.

Thus Elizabeth moves away from Sello's influence towards Dan, who is consistently associated with the radiating force of the sun. The first section ends with her words of commitment to the "new day" heralded by this rising sun: " 'O God,' she said softly. 'May I never contribute to creating dead worlds, only new worlds.' "

In the second section of the novel, which describes Elizabeth's encounters with Dan, Head examines a concept of power which is based on violence. Unlike Sello, Dan does not weaken his own purpose by agonized soul-searching and is not prepared to compromise. Elizabeth is overwhelmed by the intensity of feeling which he brings to a cause, and at first identifies with his passionate commitment: "She immediately thought: 'Ah, I'm just the same. I don't care what I do for a cause, for someone I love, for my convictions.' " Altogether Dan is Head's portrait of the popular nationalist leader, "an heroic father-figure" and leader of the single party.

In his early encounters with Elizabeth, Dan carefully masks his violent nature. He presents her with his card with the inscription, "Directorship since 1910" which is, ostensibly, evidence of his experience and ability to direct affairs. Head probably refers to the Act of Union of South Africa of 1910, which deprived coloured people of their voting rights and seemingly established a common cause between coloured and black Africans. Thus in presenting his card to Elizabeth, Dan may be reminding her of a shared experience and a basis for collaboration. To begin with, then, Dan has no need to harangue or to make a public display of himself and even appears to be humble. The vision of love which he offers Elizabeth is the opposite of Sello's, for the "heaven" into which he invites her has no place for others:

> There was a heaven there where the light had shaded down to a deep midnight blue. A man and a woman stood in it, wrapped in an eternal embrace. There were symbols of their love. . . . There was nothing else, no people, no sharing. It was shut-in and exclusive, a height of heights known only to the two eternal lovers.

The exclusivity of Dan's commitment, Elizabeth later discovers, makes him a tyrannical lover. Her encounters with him seem to represent two different periods in the nationalist leader's career. The relationship which was established in the early period when the leader shared a common cause with the ordinary people rapidly develops into one in which he becomes more authoritarian, and invokes the mystique of the African personality. As Elizabeth observes to the Peace Corps worker, Tom, when the period of fascination with Dan is over, "Any heaven, like a Black-Power heaven, that existed for a few individuals alone was pointless and useless. It was an urge to throttle everyone else to death." She observes further that the leader who tries to create a "heaven" for a select few will also turn his power against his own followers, because his feeling of dominance makes him contemptuous of those without power.

Dan's contempt for the powerless becomes clear in his later relationship with Elizabeth. Once he has her in his power, he abandons his pretence of caring. Like Medusa, he reminds her that she is not a "genuine" African:

> A persistent theme was that she was not genuinely African; *he* had to give her the real African insight. People in her daily life were vividly reintroduced through imagery at night. In almost every way she had slighted somebody. In almost every way she had to be aware of Africans as a special holy entity and deep mystery he alone understood. He too was a deep mystery she would never fathom. He could so subtly play on the earlier themes Sello had introduced to her mind about the poor, their central importance, and yet he twisted and perverted these themes with a merciless cruelty.

In giving Elizabeth "the real African insight," Dan looks at the record of human behaviour mainly to uncover weakness: his is "the tough personality, facing the facts" in an essentially hostile world. He discredits those opinions which conflict with his own and is contemptuous of Sello's tentative efforts to create social harmony. Elizabeth's involvement with Dan cuts her off both from the experiences of people in other societies and from her own private thoughts which she cherishes as an individual. Under Dan's influence she comes to see normal human relationships in a twisted way and can even believe that Sello is a pervert and child molester.

Dan's power is symbolized in the novel by his ability to dominate and use women. In her portrait of Dan, Head seems to be commenting on the kind of thinking which exalts sexual virility as a value in itself. Dan's sexual excesses are a counterpart to Medusa's exhibitionism in the first section. His affairs with various women whom he parades before Elizabeth are meant to demonstrate his own power, to mock at her powerlessness and to keep her in a state of emotional turmoil. Dan's women may be seen as representations of political factions and interest groups with which the nationalist leader may be allied from time to time. They are chosen both from the "early vision of the beautiful people" and from the "nice-time girls" of the contemporary period. In describing them, Head alludes to grassroots groups such as peasants and agricultural workers, urban proletarian groups including displaced and unemployed workers and bourgeois nationalist groups. [Johnson adds in a footnote that "Miss Loose Bottom's symbol, for example, is a clump of "wild grass," obviously a reference to the "grass roots." Miss Sewing Machine, for whom Elizabeth has some sympathy, seems to represent a workers' group. Body Beautiful, Madame Squelch Squelch, Miss Chopper and the Womb suggest behaviour and attitudes identifying local social and political factions."] Head does not always identify a woman with a particular group, for one affiliation does not preclude another, as is the case with occupational and tribal affiliations, for example. In some instances, too, she seems to be referring to alliances with foreign agencies—liberal opinion in Europe and America, commercial interests and former colonial powers. [For example, Miss Pink–Sugar Icing, Miss Pelican Beak and Miss Sugar Plum Fairy.]

In the second section of the novel, the sexual act is clearly a metaphor for secret, underhand and corrupt political and business transactions. This metaphor also suggests a comparison between Elizabeth and the visionary coping with "the demons of lust" and Dan and an evil power presiding over a hell or underworld. Unlike Sello, Dan has descended into this underworld not to fight the evil forces there but to dominate them and use them to increase his power. As in the first section of the novel, the vagina is a symbol of the underworld. In Dan's many encounters with his women, it is compared with "the gullet which actively swallows, devours, rends and kills." Evil though he is, Dan is himself a victim of his own power, spinning "away from himself in a dizzy kind of death dance of will, distraction and dissipation." [Johnson adds in a footnote that in "the short story **'The Collector of Treasures,'** Head distinguishes two types of men. One is like Sello, 'with power to create himself anew,' the other is like Dan, 'a man with no inner resources at all' who 'spun away . . . dissipation.' "]

Under Dan's constant attack, Elizabeth's belief in goodness is once more destroyed. Her second mental breakdown is preceded by an incident in which she strikes a white woman who has been kind to her. This proof of the extent to which she has absorbed Dan's teaching causes Elizabeth to despair and she contemplates killing her son and committing suicide. No longer able to distinguish between nightmare and reality, she puts up a notice on the wall of the village post office accusing Sello of being "a filthy pervert who sleeps with his daughter." The village policemen intervene at this point and she is taken to the local hospital. Later she is transferred to the mental institution.

During her second mental breakdown, Elizabeth's anger at Dan is expressed in a hatred of everything African. She is helped by a doctor who pretends to share her feelings about Africans. She is able to overcome her anger and returns home from the hospital, although she is aware that she has not fully regained control of her emotional life. In her home, she is once more aware of Sello, who had withdrawn his presence for more than a year. Although Dan also returns to subject Elizabeth to further excruciating torture, Elizabeth inclines once more to Sello's teaching. The kindness of the neighbour who cared for her son during her illness, the constant concern of Tom, the Peace Corps volunteer, and the generosity of the real Sello, who refuses to bring charges against her, cannot be ignored as testimony to the existence of goodness.

As Elizabeth recovers, she is able to discuss her nightmares with Tom. She explains her illness as due to her loss of the sense of goodness and her strong awareness of greed and arrogance around her. She compares Sello's teaching with a small light in a world of darkness, which had been obscured by an overwhelming evidence of evil, and he sees her personal conflicts as a reflection of an ongoing struggle between incompatible forces struggling for dominance in society.

As Elizabeth's nightmares finally recede, the wife of Buddha emerges from her person and is reunited with Sello who once more assumes the aspect of Buddha. Divested of this other self, Elizabeth reflects on her recent experiences:

> She'd travelled a journey with a man who had always deserted her in a pursuit after the things of the soul. He'd achieved his Nirvana and she'd toppled him out of it, she'd stained his hands with blood. . . . Maybe, the work she and Sello

had done together had introduced a softness and tenderness into mankind's history. The flowers, the animals, the everyday events of people's lives had been exalted by them. . . . They had perfected together the ideal of sharing everything and then perfectly shared everything with all mankind.

In this final appearance of Sello, Elizabeth's experiences are again linked with all human aspiration towards an ideal society. [Johnson adds: "The intellectual with a moral conviction, Head suggests in the second sentence of the quotation, is constantly being pulled into a new confrontation with reality. Elizabeth is the representative of humanity calling him back once more out of his 'ivory tower' to confront life."] Sello is again associated with the qualities of mind and spirit which underlie the hope for progress towards a more equitable and humane society. Elizabeth, who had formerly rejected Sello's idea of good as coterminous with passivity, now realizes after her encounter with Dan, how easily good can be transformed into evil if it employs the methods of violence. The resolution of the novel, however, affirms Elizabeth's commitment to society rather than a withdrawal from it. Once again, she is her proper self—the coloured woman from South Africa and an exile in Botswana who has undergone a traumatic social experience at a particular period in history. Her other self, the representative human type who is caught up in the constant struggle between incompatible social forces, retires to the background, leaving Elizabeth the particular individual to carry on within her specific social context.

In retrospect, Elizabeth sees the period of her mental breakdown as one in which she has gained enlightenment and learned to control her rebellious instincts. Elizabeth's ability to control her inner conflict suggests that the forces which promote social harmony will ultimately be stronger than the narrow loyalties which threaten to divide the society. Violence, Head has attempted to demonstrate, does not create harmony, and exclusivity is not a good basis for lasting social unity. The power of love, vulnerable as it is, she shows, is superior to that of hate. For Head, useful political action is consistent with a clear moral position, and clarity of mind cannot co-exist with anger and hate. Head thus declares herself a disciple of Gandhi and, at the same time, affirms the old Buntu ideal of "commitment to the person." (pp. 198-209)

> *Joyce Johnson, "Metaphor, Myth and Meaning in Bessie Head's 'A Question of Power',"* in World Literature Written in English, *Vol. 25, No. 2, Autumn, 1985, pp. 198-211.*

Ebele Eko

Times have changed since the sixties, and a new breed of black women writers in Africa and America are giving creative birth to a new breed of female protagonists. One of their deep concerns, a point which Hoyt Fuller has stressed [in *The Black Aesthetic* (1972), ed. Addison Gayle, Jr.], is to help destroy degrading images and myths and recreate for black women images that liberate and build up self-identity. The myth of black mother-daughter confrontation, to which [the Fall, 1984 issue of *SAGE: A Scholarly Journal on Black Women*] has been devoted, is one such. (p. 139)

In the remote Botswana village of Dilepe, Margaret Cadmore in Bessie Head's *Maru* . . . has to face a crisis of choice. She is alone, a new teacher in a strange village; her white foster mother has retired and gone back to England. She has been brought up like an English girl, with Western manners and impeccable English. Everyone who meets her assumes she is a coloured, a status not without prejudice in Botswana but certainly much better than that of the Masarwa, who are considered the lowest of the low, condemned to perpetual servitude to Botswana people. Against that background, Margaret Cadmore's firm and cool declaration in answer to her colleague's simple question, and later to the headmaster's inquiry, "I am a Masarwa," sends waves of shock the length and breadth of Dilepe village. With her one-sentence identification, Margaret confronts herself, her past, her upbringing, her future, and her society. She defies all assumptions, bursts out from the walls of her white foster mother's protection, and stands proud, aloof, and vulnerable.

Compared to Anowa and Kiswana [protagonists of Ama Ata Aidoo's *Anowa* and Gloria Naylor's *Women of Brewster Place*], Margaret is like a lamb thrown to ravenous wolves. Pete, the school principal, Morafi, a cattle chief, and Seth, another totem in the community, all band together against the woman whose identification with Masarwa slaves has sent "thrills of fear down their spines" because they all own slaves. Margaret is seen as "a problem"; her statement is " 'a slap in the face'," and their response is therefore a vicious counter-offensive. Pete organizes Margaret's pupils to taunt her into resigning. " 'You are a Bushman'," they chant to their teacher's face. Quiet but resolute, Margaret, with the aid of her friend Dikeledi and Maru, the brother, thwarts all of Pete's attempts to have her disgraced and dismissed. (pp. 142-43)

Margaret Cadmore can be seen as her foster mother's programmed alter ego. The missionary gives the orphan her own name and proceeds systematically to fill her mind with "a little bit of everything." Much of her personality—her common sense, logic, resourcefulness, and resilience—filters into Margaret, enabling her to survive in the closed and prejudiced environment of Dilepe, much like the one the missionary had worked in. Her charm, her education, and her talent are all a heritage from her mother. Even their artistic abilities are similar:

> The styles of both artists were almost identical, almost near that of a comic-strip artist in their simplicity, except that the younger disciple appeared greater than the master.

Despite the success of Margaret's environmental upbringing, she does not lose her identity as a Masarwa. It is this that gives originality to her art and upholds her commitment to common people. In a startling and ironic way, Margaret, whose mother has prepared her to help her people, fulfils that destiny not only through her symbolic paintings but also by her marriage to Maru, heir to the Dilepe chiefdom. (p. 145)

For African Totems of Botswana, who know their roots but cling selfishly to oppressive traditions and prejudices, Margaret Cadmore's embarrassing defiance causes an even greater political upheaval and challenge. Her quiet and placid surface hides a resilient and creative woman who is able to withdraw within herself from the fierce storm of love that she unleashes. Her strong influence on all the characters in the novel is decisive. The scheming Totems, Pete, Seth, and Morafi, who oppose her vehemently, are hounded out of town because of her. Maru, the heir, and Moleka, his powerful and sensuous friend, both fall in love with her at first sight, despite near-suicidal implications for their status in society. Margaret turns two best friends into fierce rivals, vying for her sake to outdo each other in their generosity towards their Masarwa slaves, forced for the first time to come to grips with issues like Masarwa humanity, social responsibility, and the future of their community.

The sudden change in Moleka, that untamed human energy associated with solar images, may better illustrate the significance of Margaret's influence. At their very first meeting, the reader is told that:

> Something in the tone, those soft fluctuations of sound . . . had abruptly arrested his life. . . . He had communicated directly with her heart. It was that which was a new experience and which had so unbalanced him.

He thinks, " 'I have come to the end of one road and I am taking another'." For Moleka, as for Margaret, the result of their meeting is psychologically crucial. Margaret secretly falls in love with Moleka, and this love, which tames Moleka, unleashes and feeds her creative embers, giving life to her artistic vision in a vital and lasting manner. Through her canvas, Margaret reaches out to common people and things, touching them with her art. Women engaged in their daily common chores, a white goat and her black kid, the makorba tree, the village huts and scenery: these are the subjects of Margaret's paintings. The desire to please the one she loves is the driving force that puts an authentic stamp on her art.

Ironically, it is her influence on Maru, the man with a vision of a new world order, that proves socially and politically far-reaching. Maru, who, like Moleka, had blatantly exploited the young women of Dilepe, quickly comes to a new beginning upon meeting Margaret. For the sake of her love, he readily renounces his chiefdom, abandoning "the highway of life" for the dusty and lonely footpath that leads to a horizon of possibilities. Just as Margaret infuses life and vitality into the women she paints, symbolically freeing them from all bondage and exploitation, even so Maru dreams of a possible world with freedom and equity. Just as art recreates for Margaret her fragmented sense of self, even so Maru sees in Margaret's love a potent force for recreating his dissipated energy and the fragmented vision of his life. The beauty and possibility of these dreams are symbolized by the sunny daisies Maru envisions lining the footpath of the home he has prepared for his Masarwa bride. The disturbing fact that Maru's dream kingdom is physically far from Dilepe may be explained as part of the dream-like quality of his vision, a quality that their dramatic departure and wedding share. As the heartbroken Margaret lies dying emotionally from the shock of her friend Dikeledi's marriage to Moleka, Maru appears and carries his bride away to his "magic kingdom," transforming her melancholy into love and joy. Fortunately, her occasional tears convince both the reader and Maru that her love for Moleka has not simply evaporated.

Nonetheless, Margaret's marriage to Maru, like a climax to a musical performance, ushers in a quiet revolution of its own, the political awakening of the Masarwa:

> When people of Masarwa tribe heard about Maru's marriage to one of their own, a door silently opened on the small, dark airless room in which their souls had been shut for a long time. . . . As they breathed in the fresh, clear air their humanity awakened. . . . They started to run out into the sunlight, then they turned and looked at the dark, small room. They said: "We are not going back there."

Margaret Cadmore's resourcefulness and personal achievements help to destroy the myth of Masarwa inferiority. Her cultural pride gives identity to her people, and challenges the myth of racial superiority. Her calm defiance forces those around her into self-examination. Above all, her symbolic marriage suggests the unlimited potential of love even in the most racist and oppressive of societies. It offers her people a choice. (pp. 147-49)

> *Ebele Eko, "Beyond the Myth of Confrontation: A Comparative Study of African and African-American Female Protagonists," in* Ariel: A Review of International English Literature, *Vol. 17, No. 4, October, 1986, pp. 139-52.*

Charles Ponnuthurai Sarvan

Bessie Head's novel *A Question of Power* raises the problem of how one can write about inner chaos without the work itself becoming chaotic. (There are similar difficulties in, for example, writing about tedium without becoming tedious; about meaninglessness without losing meaning.) One is reminded of Mary Turner in Doris Lessing's *The Grass is Singing;* of Oskar in Günter Grass's *The Tin Drum (Die Blechtrommel);* of Malcolm Lowry's *Under the Volcano;* of Saul Bellow's *Herzog* and, closer in time and distance, of Zimbabwe's Dambudzo Marechera and his *Black Sunlight.* Both Marechera and Head write about the cruelty done to individuals and the damage they consequently suffer. They are hunted and haunted writers whose works are an attempt to understand and come to terms; a wrestle to win through, out and above. Pauline Smith wrote that human beings sometimes have to endure the unendurable: Bessie Head writes of the human 'capacity to endure the excruciating'. Appropriately, the novel is set in a village called Motabeng, 'the place of sand'. Motabeng suggests a lack of certainty and firmness. Like life and the world, all is loose, shifting and changing. Yet we search for little rocks and patches of firm ground in the sand; for permanence within the wider impermanence; for value within the ultimate valuelessness. (p. 82)

The central character in *A Question of Power* is Elizabeth, and the novel covers a little more than a year in her life (around 1970) a time when she experienced a nervous breakdown and was committed to an asylum. The hallucinatory is real to Elizabeth and therefore presented as factual. The reader is placed within her world, and experiences something of Elizabeth's bewilderment and strain. Such a subject was foreshadowed in *Maru* where the characters, whilst being individuals, also represent forces. That novel confronts the mystery and power of man, the extraordinariness within the apparently ordinary. People were 'horrible' to Maru because he could see into their thoughts and feelings, see their very bloodstreams and hear the beating of their hearts. The novel goes beyond psychology and dreams to the psychic and the supernatural. Not only are Maru and Moleka aspects of one person, but within the half of Maru there are further divisions such as between his compassion and idealism on the one hand, and his cruelty and cunning on the other. The interest in psychic states, Margaret's nightmares, her awareness of something within her 'more powerful than her body could endure' all prepare us for the fracture which is the subject of *A Question of Power.* 'But there was a depth of secret activity in him like that long, low line of black, boiling cloud. There was a clear blue sky in his mind that calmly awaited the storm in his heart . . . '. To say that *A Question of Power* is about one 'fall' or breakdown is to oversimplify the novel. The work describes a series of defeats and successes and, in this way, more truthfully represents the pattern of human life. 'The dawn came. The soft shifts and changes of light stirred with a slow wonder over the vast expanse of the African sky.' But dawn and night alternate and in the experience of some, the nights are more frequent and longer.

In South Africa, the Africans 'live the living death of humiliation'. Elizabeth 'had also lived the back-breaking life of all black people in South Africa. It was like living with permanent nervous tension . . . '. The simple joys of being a human being are denied to non-whites. As a new pupil, Elizabeth is told by the European principal of the missionary school: 'Your mother was insane. If you're not careful you'll get insane . . . They had to lock her up, as she was having a child by the stable boy . . . '. Escaping from the cruelty and madness of that country, Elizabeth comes to Botswana. The British 'protectorate' of Bechuanaland was granted internal self-government in March 1965 and in the following year became the independent state of Botswana (30 September 1966). If one includes Namibia which is presently occupied by South Africa, one could say that the country is almost surrounded by South Africa. On its north, Botswana was flanked by a white settler government until replaced by an independent Zimbabwe on 18 March 1980. Thus the Botswana of Bessie Head's novels is very much under the shadow of apartheid South Africa.

As a Coloured, a descendant of African and European parents, Elizabeth finds herself in a racial no-man's land. The majority of European 'experts' and volunteers take the inferiority of the black man for granted and 'don't see the shades and shadows of life on black people's faces.' Elizabeth resents this but is herself half-European, and with her South African colour conditioning, is in danger of sharing racial opinions and attitudes. 'You don't like the African hair. You don't like the African nose . . . ':

> 'You don't really like Africans. You see his face? It's vacant and stupid . . . You have no place here. Why don't you go away . . . ' She sprang to her feet . . . and shouted: 'Oh, you bloody bastard . . . Botswana!'

Committed to an asylum, Elizabeth is asked to join the other inmates in keeping the place clean, but she refuses, demanding different treatment because 'I'm not an African'. However, [according to Head in a letter to Sarvan], Elizabeth's real desire is for acceptance by Africans as an African:

> I dearly loved Robert Sobukwe and the politics he expounded in the years 1958-60 . . . Sobukwe's view was Pan African and generally included all things African, with an edge of harshness in it that forced one to make an identification with being African and a sense of belonging to Africa . . .

Despite having lived simply in a village for many years and participating in communal work, Elizabeth remains 'an out-and-out outsider' to the people of Motabeng. One of the tormenting voices within her jeers at her because she doesn't know an African language; taunts her with not being 'genuinely African'. ' "We don't want you here. This is my land. These are my people. We keep our things to ourselves . . . " '

Past experiences make Elizabeth reluctant to repose confidence in others. She is afraid of disappointment; afraid of the sudden revelation of violence or ugliness. Yet by nature she is given to spontaneity, impulsive affection and trust. So too, the natural sensuality within her is repressed: much of her nightmare is overtly sexual. Elizabeth believes that, in extreme contrast to herself, the Africans are a potent and promiscuous people.

> The social defects of Africa are, first, the African man's loose, carefree sexuality; it hasn't the stopgaps of love and tenderness and personal romantic treasuring of women. It is just sex . . . the women have a corresponding mental and physical approach.

Bessie Head herself seemed to share this view, [as she indicates in a letter to Sarvan]:

> The clarity of Doris Lessing's political thought arouses profound respect . . . [But] I disliked the image of a woman continually in bed with men she despises. It's just a waste . . . I cannot endure the waste of trifling love affairs.

Tom, the American, has another perspective: 'This is one of the most unobscene societies in the world. Men just sleep with women, and that's all there is to it.' But Elizabeth associates sex with sadism, dirt, child molestation, incest, homosexuality and intercourse with animals: 'everything was high, sexual hysteria.' Elizabeth's obsession with sex and her attitude to it are conditioned by her childhood. Growing up in a 'beer house' frequented by prostitutes and drunken (often violent) men, it is not surprising

that Elizabeth has a distaste for sex and that she represses the instinct within her. Her husband was promiscuous, forcing his attentions on women and sexually consorting with men. He confirmed rather than mended attitudes formed in the 'beer house' and sex became 'hell' to Elizabeth.

In her deep distress, Elizabeth does not have the sustaining strength of religious belief. *The Bible* 'meant damn-all' and, like Makhaya in **When Rain Clouds Gather,** Elizabeth 'cared not two bits about an old man in the sky.' Evil appears to be the stronger force and 'patterns of goodness were too soft, too indefinable to counter the tumultous roar of evil.' And so we come to the novel's title: it is a question of power. Power is associated with evil and opposed to love. The contraries are Satan and God; evil and good; power and love. But passion has power and is also therefore a force to be controlled. 'Salvation' is to be sought through a more spiritual love, and relationships that are beneficent. 'Love is two people mutually feeding each other, not one living on the soul of the other, like a ghoul.' But the spiritual is *not* to be sought in God but in man:

> And love was like a girl walking . . . with the wind blowing through her hair. And love was like a girl with wonder in her eyes. And love was like a girl with a flaming heart and impulsive arms . . .
>
> They pray, so falsely: from the heart of God let love enter the hearts of men, thus removing the things of the soul to some impossibly unseen, mystical heaven.

Since power is evil, politics which is concerned with power, is also rejected in favour of a political laissez-faire.

The excruciating nature of Elizabeth's experience makes this novel, the record of a 'nightmare soul-journey', a very difficult work to read. To portray individuals at a mental extremity is a very difficult task. Elizabeth's inability to sleep and the fact that when she does, it is only to be tormented by nightmares, leave her exhausted physically and mentally. In the mornings, Elizabeth often finds herself on the floor, having rolled off the bed in her nightmare struggles. Desperate for sleep, she is afraid to close her eyes because of the voices and visions which take over. Her little son makes a paper aeroplane and says, 'I'm afraid of the edge' for he believes the plane will tumble off the edge of the world. Elizabeth has half-fallen off the edge and is struggling to climb up. Her world is inhabited by beings who are more real to her than the men and women she encounters in Motabeng, beings such as the destructive Dan Molomo ('the king of sex'); the Father; a half-mad Asian and Sello. Sello himself consists of two beings, one a monk and passive; the other a figure of evil. Towards the end of the novel, Sello and Dan seem to coalesce and become one, suggesting that they are aspects of Elizabeth herself.

Elizabeth wins through by using weapons and defences of her own. The work she engages in is meaningful: her first employment is as a teacher. The children she taught were thin as the 'twisted thorn-bush' but they were eager to learn. The school was the 'only sane centre of purposeful . . . and hopeful activity in this desolation'.

Dismissed by a malicious and petty headmaster, Elizabeth takes to market gardening. Earlier, she had been troubled by the thought that she did not have an adequately developed and active social conscience:

> At this gesture, a group of people walked quietly into the room. They were the poor of Africa . . . They said nothing, but an old woman out of the crowd turned to Elizabeth and said: 'Will you help us? We are a people who have suffered.'

Now Elizabeth feels that in growing vegetables, in learning and imparting better techniques, she is making a modest but valuable contribution towards the needy of this world. On the farms, she meets not only agriculturists from different parts of the world but plants alien to the country, yet thriving. The work has a 'melody', a harmony, and if 'a complete stranger' like the Cape Gooseberry could 'settle' down, why couldn't an exile like Elizabeth eventually find sanctuary, a home? Agriculture can be a solitary activity but Elizabeth works on co-operative, experimental projects. This means that she is working *with* others.

Though not a Christian, there is a strong spiritual, almost mystical element in Elizabeth: the influence of Hinduism and Buddhism. Love is not of god but of man and for man. God is but another word for that nobility, understanding and compassion of which man is capable. Love is the realization of grandeur potentially there within human beings; love is the 'gentle remodelling' of broken personalities.

In this way, through a lifting response to nature—even to its austere beauty—through physical labour, co-operative work, through human fellowship, a belief in the goodness of man, through understanding, compassion and love for one's fellow beings, Elizabeth overcomes those forces which sought to annihilate her, [according to Head in a letter to Sarvan]:

> I felt that I would go through this experience again were I re-born . . . My desperate terror then was that if I recorded the evil and the same story was about to happen in some other life, I would read *A Question of Power* and it would save me from such suffering . . . My novels and I never came in from the cold. They remained in the village building up pathetic little rural industries and co-operatives in the hope that they would expand the world and open new doors. The books stayed with the people who were in the cold.

But Elizabeth does come in from the cold, though not totally and finally. She resolves the question of identity: to identify herself with Africans was, after all, to identify herself with mankind. Black power is 'a power that belongs to all of mankind and in which all mankind can share.' She who suffered exclusion will not, in her turn, exclude anyone. Elizabeth throws away the tablets with which she had intended to commit suicide and, 'as she fell asleep, she placed one soft hand over her land. It was a gesture of belonging.' 'Power' has been understood; identity accepted and extended but, of course, the 'Question(s)', as ever, remain. The novel is the work of an honest, sensitive and courageous writer. (pp. 83-8)

Charles Ponnuthurai Sarvan, "Bessie Head: 'A Question of Power' and Identity," in Women in African Literature Today, *Vol. 15, 1987, pp. 82-8.*

Charles Larson

Bessie Head's achievement at the time of her death in 1986 was honorific: black Africa's preeminent female writer of fiction, a title that can only be taken ironically. Classified as Coloured in the country of her birth (South Africa), she fled to Botswana in 1964. The safe haven she had expected to find there became the terrain for her subsequent mental breakdown. Stateless and suicidal as an exile in an unfamiliar environment, she nevertheless came to be regarded by the people of her adopted country as their most famous writer. Yet if the inner peace Bessie Head had sought all her life was largely illusory, she wrote stories (at least in the final years of her life) that were not only humane but genuinely hopeful about the human condition.

However, that humanity is nowhere reflected in the autobiographical overview she gives of her life at the beginning of *A Woman Alone.* Instead, this brief transcript reads like a horror tale, filled not only with the most appalling acts of inhumanity but also with one of the most agonizing accounts of loneliness one is likely to encounter. . . .

The contents of [*A Woman Alone* and *Tales of Tenderness and Power*] reveal Bessie Head both at her best and at her weakest. As a group, the stories in *Tales of Tenderness and Power* are not as finished as those in an earlier collection called *The Collector of Treasures* (1977). Still, three stories are particularly distinguished. In the first of these, called **"The Lovers,"** Head addresses the African concept of community as the traditional force which inhibits individual action. An adolescent girl who questions arranged marriages is warned by her mother, "If you question life you will upset it." The power of the feminist perspective is elevated to a new dimension at the end of the tale when the reader discovers that the story is not contemporary but set more than a hundred years ago.

As if to demonstrate that much of Head's writing was not autobiographical, two stories in the volume take us far away from the author's immediate world. **"The General"** satirizes political abuse by African leaders: "A man's enemies have a way of snowballing: especially when there are heaps of bodies in detention camps." However, no other story that Head wrote equals the vision of unity depicted in **"The Prisoner Who Wore Glasses."** In six terse pages, she brilliantly describes the subtle and shifting relationship between a political prisoner and a warden in a South African jail. The subtext is quite clear: Apartheid is tantamount to incarceration, yet a system of survival may in time be worked out because of the superior patience of the detainee over the detainer. The story is also one of Bessie Head's few overt presentations of conditions in South Africa under the apartheid she had experienced until her flight into exile. . . .

The most revealing selection [in *A Woman Alone*] is the essay that concludes both volumes, and in which Bessie Head indirectly describes herself as a "dreamer and storyteller," as someone "drunk with the magical enchantment of human relationships." In this essay Head articulates her final sense of acceptance, of connectedness to her adopted home in Botswana:

> Every oppressed man has this suppressed violence, as though silently awaiting the time to set right the wrongs that afflict him. I have never forgotten it, even though, for the purposes of my trade, I borrowed the clothes of a country like Botswana . . . Possibly too, Southern Africa might one day become the home of the storyteller and dreamer, who did not hurt others but only introduced new dreams that filled the heart with wonder.

> *Charles Larson, "Bessie Head, Storyteller in Exile," in* Book World—The Washington Post, *February 17, 1991, p. 4.*

FURTHER READING

Chetin, Sara. "Myth, Exile, and the Female Condition: Bessie Head's *The Collector of Treasures.*" *The Journal of Commonwealth Literature* 24, No. 1 (1989): 114-37.
>In-depth study of Head's storytelling techniques in *The Collector of Treasures.*

Fradkin, Betty McGinnis. "Conversations with Bessie." *World Literature Written in English* 17, No. 2 (November 1978): 427-34.
>Interview with Head on her lifestyle and career.

Head, Bessie. "Writing Out of Southern Africa." *New Statesman* 110, No. 2839 (16 August 1985): 21-23.
>Discussion by Head about Africa and her personal background and influences.

Heywood, Christopher. "Traditional Values in the Novels of Bessie Head." In *Individual and Community in Commonwealth Literature,* edited by Daniel Massa, pp. 12-19. Malta: The University Press, 1979.
>Contends that an acceptance of the Southern African traditional past underlies Head's vision for reform.

Ola, Virginia U. "Women's Role in Bessie Head's Ideal World." *Ariel* 17, No. 4 (October 1986): 39-47.
>Discusses the social position and movement toward self-discovery of female characters in Head's novels.

Tucker, Margaret E. "A 'Nice-Time Girl' Strikes Back: An Essay on Bessie Head's *A Question of Power.*" *Research in African Studies* 19, No. 2 (Summer 1988): 170-81.
>Examines the structure of *A Question of Power* for "the ways in which it poses questions about time and traditional narrative," and also "the images in the text that Elizabeth learns to read, thereby dismantling the dualities that comprise time."

Vanamali, Rukmini. "Bessie Head's *A Question of Power:* The Mythic Dimension." *The Literary Criterion* 23, Nos. 1 & 2 (1988): 154-71.
>Examines "the nature of the myths which Bessie Head uses in special and unique ways to establish a special signification for her narrative [in *A Question of Power*] and the relation the myths hold to the universal question of good and evil."

Bohumil Hrabal

1914-

Czechoslovakian novelist, short story writer, scriptwriter, autobiographer, essayist, and poet.

One of Czechoslovakia's most prominent contemporary writers, Hrabal is lauded for his surrealistic narratives that feature fragmented but poignant characterizations and focus on ordinary individuals who must cope with forces beyond their control. Throughout his work, Hrabal uses hyperbolic language, extended monologues, and shifting points of view to suggest that reality is an illusion. Although much of Hrabal's writing was banned by authorities in Czechoslovakia until 1976, his works are generally considered apolitical because of their exploration of the individual psyche rather than specific ideologies. Hrabal states: "It has never occurred to me, not even in my dreams, to change, or even desire to change, the political situation in which I live. I never wished to transform the language or the world; . . . I always wanted to change myself, to change the one I had within my hand's reach, me."

Hrabal was born in Brno and raised in Nymburk, a small town on the banks of the Elbe river. His father, a brewery agent, used to take his young son with him when "he made the rounds of the taverns." These childhood experiences exposed Hrabal to the idiosyncrasies of Czechoslovakian vernacular and the concerns of common people, both of which would figure prominently in his works. In 1934, Hrabal entered Charles University in Prague, but his studies were interrupted at the outbreak of World War II when the Nazis closed all Czechoslovakian universities. During wartime, Hrabal worked as a lawyer's clerk, insurance agent, and traveling salesman. According to Hrabal, the war had profound effects on both his life and the tone of his work: "When the war ended, I saw in myself and around me so much beautiful horror and experienced so much pain in love that even today I sleep badly from it all." While Hrabal eventually earned a law degree in 1948, he was unable to practice law because of radical changes in cultural policy following the establishment of communist government in 1949. Instead, he found work in steel and paper-recycling factories, and then, after a serious accident, as a stagehand at a theater in Prague.

Hrabal began writing poetry and prose in the 1930s. His early works, which Hrabal describes as "total realism," were not published until 1956, when two short stories were released in a limited edition. It was only when governmental restrictions began to ease in the 1960s that Hrabal began to gain attention and was able to publish his short story collection *Perlička na dně*. His work was banned, however, when the Soviet Army crushed the liberalization movement that rose during what is called the Prague Spring of 1968. It was during this time that he wrote some of his most celebrated works, including *Obsluhoval jsem anglického krále* (*I Served the King of En-*

gland) and *Příliš hlučná samota* (*Too Loud a Solitude*). The original versions of these books were circulated in the underground system known as *samizdat* and were only officially published ten years after they were written. The Czechoslovakian government agreed to lift the ban on Hrabal's work in 1976 when an interview with Hrabal was printed in *Tvorba*, the official communist newspaper. Hrabal did not fully embrace communist ideology in this interview, nor did he reject it. This apparent neutrality resulted in Hrabal being one of the few writers permitted to publish his works in Czechoslovakia during this time. Although Hrabal's works were censored by government officials after the ban was lifted, his texts have been published in their original versions since the communist regime collapsed in 1989.

One of Hrabal's earliest and best known works is *Ostře sledované vlaky* (*Closely Watched Trains*). This novel, set in Nazi-occupied Czechoslovakia, chronicles the life of a young railroad employee. Feeling it necessary to prove his manhood, he attempts to blow up a German ammunition train but is killed in the attempt. Immensely popular in Czechoslovakia, *Closely Watched Trains* was adapted to film in 1967 and won the Academy Award for best foreign language film. The screenplay, coauthored by Hrabal and director Jiri Menzel, was praised by several critics, including Bosley Crowther: "The charm of [this] film is in the quietness and slyness of [its] earthly comedy, the wonderful finesse of understatements, the wise and humorous understanding of primal sex." During this period, Hrabal also wrote the short story collection *Automat svět* (*The Death of Mr. Baltisberger*). Comprising fourteen stories based on tales Hrabal heard in the taverns of Prague, *The Death of Mr. Baltisberger* is considered experimental and surrealistic due to Hrabal's use of elusive protagonists, idiosyncratic language, and episodic narratives. These techniques led some critics to compare Hrabal's work with those of William Faulkner and James Joyce. In *Postřižiny,* which also garnered widespread acclaim throughout Europe, Hrabal employed a female protagonist for the first time and addressed the changing role of women in modern society. *Postřižiny* is an allegory of the political changes that took place in Eastern Europe after World War I, including the dissolution of the Austrian-Hungarian empire and the formation of the Czechoslovakian Republic.

Hrabal's best known works, *I Served the King of England* and *Too Loud a Solitude,* did not became available in English translation until 1989 and 1990, respectively. In *I Served the King of England,* Hrabal traces the rise of his protagonist, Dítě, from a fifteen-year-old busboy at the Golden Prague Hotel to an influential hotel owner. Unhappy despite his success, Dítě renounces all of his material possessions and volunteers to do forestry work in a secluded area of Czechoslovakia. An absurdist tale of the protagonist's desire for wealth, *I Served the King of England* concurrently explores how individuals acquire the self-understanding necessary to survive in a chaotic world. *Too Loud a Solitude,* also allegorical, focuses on a man who is forced to adapt to a situation beyond his control. The narrator of this work, Haňt'a, has spent thirty-five years compacting wastepaper in an isolated, underground recycling factory. Because he loves books and literature— "I pop a beautiful sentence in my mouth and suck it like a fruit-drop"—Haňt'a secretly rescues literary works that have been deemed undesirable by government officials. He also occupies his time by imagining encounters with such historical figures as Jesus Christ and Chinese philosopher Lao-tze. Although some critics faulted the protagonist's elliptical musings for being inaccessible and obscure, others laud Hrabal's imaginative treatment of the effects of censorship. In *Too Loud a Solitude,* as in all his works, Hrabal presents literature as a humanizing force and emphasizes its moral and philosophical impact on the cultural life of both repressive and democratic societies.

(See also *CLC,* Vol. 13 and *Contemporary Authors,* Vol. 106.)

PRINCIPAL WORKS

NOVELS

Taneční hodiny pro starší a pokročilé 1964
Ostře sledované vlaky 1965
  [*Closely Watched Trains,* 1968]
Postřižiny 1976

Morytáty a legendy 1978
Krasosmutnění 1979
Každý den zázrak 1979
Příliš hlučná samota 1980
  [*Too Loud a Solitude,* 1990]
Harlekýnovy milióny 1981
Kluby poezie 1981
Obsluhoval jsem anglického krále 1982
  [*I Served the King of England,* 1989]
Svatby v domě 1987

SHORT STORY COLLECTIONS

Perlička na dně 1963
Pábitelé 1964
Inzerát na dům, ve kterém už nechci bydlet 1965
Automat svět 1966
  [*The Death of Mr. Baltisberger,* 1975]
Slavnosti sněženek 1978

SCREENPLAYS

Perlička na dně 1965
Fádní odpoledne 1965
  [*A Boring Afternoon,* 1968]
Skřivánci na niti 1969
Ostře sledované vlaky 1967
  [*Closely Watched Trains,* 1968]
Postřižiny 1980

AUTOBIOGRAPHY

Kdo jsem 1989

George Gibian

In Prague, in the spring of 1974, Bohumil Hrabal told me that he wanted to have peace and quiet for a few years, so that he could finish his program: to write five more books. Then he would go about trying to get the books published in Czechoslovakia (or, if necessary, abroad), but until then, all he wanted was not to be bothered, and to be left free to write.

In January 1975, Hrabal published in the Prague magazine *Tvorba* a brief "Conversation," which marked some degree of acceptance of him by Czech literary officialdom, and also some degree of the reverse. It was probably this gesture which led to the publication of one of his two completed works (of the five which constituted his writing plan). Both deserve attention for their outstanding literary qualities.

The one now published is a long tale, titled ***The Haircutting (Postřižiny,*** 1976). (*Postřižiny* is an old term for the cutting of a child's hair.) The other is a novel, Hrabal's first, called ***I Waited on the King of England (Obsluhoval jsem anglického krále),*** so far circulating only in typescript. Both works are uproarious. They remind us of Irish tall tales, with a dash of the Joyce of Molly Bloom—and a lot of Jaroslav Hašek's *Good Soldier Schweik.* Both (implicitly in ***The Haircutting,*** explicitly at the end of ***I Waited on the King of England***) make assertions on how people ought to live. One is a celebration; the other a story of a journey towards new ideas about life, towards self knowledge.

The Haircutting is a hymn of praise to a woman of the pre-1918 era, in real life Hrabal's own great aunt. Like most of Hrabal's previous works, *The Haircutting* is full of colorful, wild stories, told in rich folksy idiom in the first person by the chief character. Hrabal's hyperbolic leanings are also strongly in evidence everywhere. The mood of the story, however, is unusually gentle. It would be too much to call it the *Grandmother* (Babička) of the 1970's, but something of the pastel, tender qualities of Božena Němcová's nineteenth-century Czech classic can be felt in Hrabal's story.

"This relic of old Austria," as the barber calls her hair, and the cutting of it, designated by the quaint, old-fashioned term *postřižiny,* is an important turning point in the story, the beginning of its conclusion. The new short hairdo, which the heroine calls the "Josephine Baker one," is "her soul, her portrait" now. A new age has come, and she submits. She changes along with it, just as she has adapted to all the previous misfortunes and fortunes through which she so gloriously cantered.

The haircutting, which the title of the story prepared us to await, marks the end of one kind of woman, and the beginning of a new one, whose story we are not going to be told, at least not for the time being, not in this work. It signals the coming of a new regime, a new country, a new style. Czechoslovakia replaces Austria-Hungary, and everything is being shortened. The heroine notices that shorter working hours are being discussed, shorter dogs' tails are coming into fashion (and she proceeds, with her usual exuberant vitality, to shorten her dog's tail—with overly ample bribes of cream puffs from the sugar-bakery to distract the dog's attention while his tail is placed on the block); and her hair, too, will be shortened. Like so many of her other reactions in the story, her decision to change her coiffure is both absurd and correct, irrationally arrived at, yet brilliantly appropriate. The pattern of which she has become aware, the general abbreviation setting in, is located in quite disparate, logically incongruous, ungroupable categories: dogs' tails, the hours worked by laborers, speeding up of communications by radio. Yet her leap to the conclusion that it is also time for her hair to be cut in order to stay in keeping with the new general principle of things, is warranted: the grand extravagance or "length" of the old Austrian Empire is out; a new moderateness is in. Unconsciously, she is being moved by a structuralist perception which Lévi-Strauss might envy. It is the first demonstration of radio (a band playing in Prague listened to by assembled school children and the general public in the small town hotel) which suggests to her the shortening of distances, requiring an analogous shortening of skirts, as well as table and chair legs; ever positive, she acts before she tells us the reasons—making preparations for the shortening of her dog's tail before she betrays to the reader what she is doing. She is attuned to nature, to life, and to the patterns governing things in general.

It is not to her future life, symbolized by short hair, but to the rendering of her past life, to which her long hair was appropriate, that the entire story is devoted. The embodiment of *élan,* she, is married to Francin, the incarnation of caution and moderation. Later she finds an ally, or companion and playmate (literally but not erotically), Uncle Pepin. Her life is dominated by one triangular relationship (with Pepin and Francin), and one reciprocal relationship (with her audiences). The structural principle of the story is a series of picaresque episodes. Outstanding among these are those which we might term "larks," feats or *aresteias.*

The long-haired heroine exudes *joie de vivre.* She responds vehemently to anything in her surroundings, animate or inanimate, human or natural, which can be stimulus to fun. She is gargantuan in her readiness to leap to anything vital. "Blood and saliva," she repeats, and those two fluids might well be her dominant humors. She is naïve, and child-like. Among the numerous incidents in which she displays her proneness to respond, two are outstanding: climbing the brewery smokestack, and the slaughtering of pigs. She organizes life into a series of episodes of kicking up one's heels—eagerly following an opportunity for fun. She places trust in herself: "I was young, and that put me above everything, no matter what I did, I always asked myself first, and I always said yes to myself, and that inner yes-saying of mine, that sign of my teacher, who was somewhere here near my heart inside me, this yes-saying crossed over into my blood and my hand reached out and I took a drink with gusto." Above all, she says "Yes" to life. The first words of the story are "Mám ráda," ("I like" or "I love"). The anaphoric use of the phrase introduces the work as an autobiographical declaration of love for life. At home in the world of the senses and of nature, she is her own teacher, one who counsels agreeing, consenting, accepting life, which to her consists primarily of enjoyment of beauty and sensuous pleasures. Horses look at her, she says, "as if they were communicating with me." Their manes have the same golden color as beer (and as her own hair). In one of the most lyrical passages of the book, she compares her own zestful drinking of beer to a song.

She likes danger and adventure. She is *homo ludens;* her husband, on the other hand, is *homo timidus.* Their partnership is one of opposites. Deficient as he is in animality and vitality, he is all the more sensitive to symptoms of those qualities in her. He responds to, and is disturbed by, the way she eats cherries. When she husks ears of corn, "with flames playing in her eyes," he fears a bystander might misunderstand her manner of doing this as a "favorable omen for his desire." A proper lady (*slušná žena*) doesn't behave like that, he repeatedly admonishes her.

The contrast between husband and wife is most explicit when they give each other treatments with a quack radiation machine. The various colors of rays are supposed to benefit people with different constitutions and illnesses. The two spouses agree that she needs blue light, to lessen her excess of vital spirits; and he uses red rays because they are supposed to remedy his deficiency in animation. Husband and wife complement each other. He is prudent, she reckless; he lives within the bureaucratic and social worlds of conformity, she outside them; he is earnest, she is playful; he is physically nondescript, she is beautiful and attractive. She has a "wild animal's health, a love of accidents, of the unexpected, and of marvellous encounters"; Francin loves the foreseen. Yet they admire each other. He asserts his traditional male dominance—in minor and innocuous ways—and she submits, formally, but hardly affected by his admonitions.

Their life flows in two channels, and, highly ritualized, it brings contentment to both. The arrangement is epitomized in the ceremonial which they enact whenever Francin returns from Prague. He brings presents; she goes through the motions of guessing what the present might be, shutting her eyes upon request, admiring the gifts, thanking her husband, flattering him, admiring. Each has his role; both are happy. The wife clearly is the more admirable creature, but she is fond of, and humorously tolerant of, her husband.

The relationship between her and Pepin, the uncle, who arrives later in the book, is more that of two allies, a parallel rather than a contrasting pair, such as she forms with her husband. The uncle is also an enjoyer of life, and he supports her. Together they play pranks, suggest ideas to each other, egg each other on. Her husband restrains, the uncle excites her. He is still more child-like than she; and he is a crazier version of her.

She has a very clear relationship to herself, and to her audiences. Both are narcissistic, but without any pejorative connotations. She loves to be watched, and she watches herself. She enjoys an audience, and there are spectators galore, enthralled, amused, and always appreciative of her. When there is no spectator (or sometimes even when there is), she becomes her own audience. She is amused by herself and appreciates herself, just as she is a supreme appreciator of the world, of life around her.

The outstanding object of admiration, of course, is her hair. She is aware of the fact that her hair is beautiful and that people are watching it with delight, or that if they were present, they would so watch it. Her faculty of being pleased with herself is naïve and lovable. It is not conceit, but straightforward and happy acknowledgement of a basic fact: her beauty and loveliness, and other human beings' positive response to it. To her, the world is a place provided richly with wonderful treats, her hair being one. The idea of there being anything wrong with taking delight in oneself and in others does not occur to her.

She is quite innocent also in reflecting on specific instances of admiration. People are always turning to stare at her. Francin is so flustered on one occasion that he drops a sparkplug; another time, a motorcyclist passing her when she is riding her bicycle wearing a short skirt turns around to look after her, goes off the road, and crashes in a cherry orchard. "I took that to be a favorable omen," she thinks to herself, perhaps not completely ingenuously.

The heroine appreciates the world in which she lives; and if others appreciate her, that is regarded by her as completely within the proper course of events. A remark by a priest could be taken as the motto for the entire story: "A woman's rounded knee is the second name of the Holy Ghost." The book is rich in instances of someone (usually she) doing something with gusto. A characteristic comment by her is, "When I eat, I don't eat, I devour." When she drinks beer, men stop and watch. She wants other creatures (not only herself, not only other human beings) to enjoy the sensuous gifts of this world; we have seen that she overwhelms a dog with creampuffs when she is about to dock his tail.

Hrabal describes her as if she were a goddess of *joie de vivre,* and she herself displays mythopoeic leanings. When Pepin is singing, she sees him not as a plain man who is roasting malt in a brewery, but as "some kind of a god out of a primeval myth of the globe." Placed throughout the work are sudden brief stabs, comparing details of her life to religious motifs. Cutting her hair is described as a sacrilege, like spitting out the Holy Host after Communion. Her hair is spoken of as a priest's vestment. After the slaughtering of the pigs, the profusion of blood is called "something sacred," and the slaughtering itself, and the flesh and blood of the pigs, is compared to Holy Mass.

The interpolated story (one of many in the book) of Dr. Gruntorád, who in his youth caught his wife with an officer, is also a myth, not just a small town anecdote. The officer escapes through the window; as he jumps on his horse, he sticks a willow twig which he had been carrying in his boot into the ground; the twig grows into a huge willow which covers the whole house.

The heroine enjoys life to the hilt; she admires others who do likewise. She prizes, in common with Hrabal's other heroes and heroines, the ability to feast at life's banquet. Béda Červinka, when he has bought vegetables advantageously, celebrates by stopping in a series of taverns, for various kinds of drinks, and she thinks highly of him for this display of knowing how to live.

For once in Hrabal we have a heroine, and perhaps it is not stretching the point to connect her prominent feature of appreciating others and herself and the good things in life with her being a woman. This feminine protagonist's sensibility is a hymn in praise of life.

The waiter-hero of Hrabal's *I Waited on the King of England* is a Czech country boy, by the name Dítě (child), illegitimate, brought up by his grandmother, who starts as the lowliest little *pikolo* (the bottom of the waiters' hierarchy of Czech restaurants) and by successive stages before, during, and after World War II, moves from one hotel to another, becomes a hotel owner, builds a masterpiece of a hotel, then, after 1948, volunteers for forest brigade work in the border regions of Czechoslovakia, and solitarily maintains a section of a forest road, alone except for the company of a few animals.

The book is episodic and picaresque; it is also a *Bildungsroman.* There are interpolated stories, anecdotes, tall tales. The flavor and texture of the book are similar to Hrabal's other works; many of the themes are variations or repetitions of earlier ones. However, the length of the book, the changes undergone by the chief character, the varied settings in which the action takes place, and the transformation of the hero's ideals and values, are all new departures for Hrabal. This is indeed his first sustained long piece, his first novel, and his most ambitious work so far.

A brief preface to the novel calls our attention to images. Hrabal describes how he typed the book in the heat of the summer sun, forced by the events of the past years to leave the text "in its first rushes," as he puts it cinematographically, hoping some day to take it up again and then, in order to avoid "wiping off the first spontaneity of the images," to take a pair of scissors, and "to cut out of it those images which with the passage of time will still have freshness. If I should not be alive any longer, let some of my friends do it. Let them cut out a little novella or a longer story out of it."

Images are indeed the component parts out of which this most visual book is written. The scenes are brief, very dramatic, intensely described. The young boy arranging flowers around a naked girl's body; his dead wife curled around the suitcase full of stamps; an apricot tree which falls over a man who swears while his wife and daughter laugh at him as he lies imprisoned by the branches of the tree; a hired man chopping wood and only clearing his ear with his finger as a bullet flies over him; the layout of the various hotels, especially the one designed and built by Dítě; a half naked, drunk girl being driven by a general into Prague, standing up in the open car with a raised sabre, shouting "On to Prague!" looking like a painting of the Marseillaise: this is a world of set pictorial scenes. Hrabal's heroes move from one to the next, like in an old-fashioned peepshow, struck by the power of each image.

The directness of the images ties in with another feature of the book—its oral style. The syntax is that of oral narration. Series of sentences, linked by often repeated conjunctions ("and" or "so"), direct addresses to the reader, non-literary forms of words, oral diction, all give a sense of direct listening, of being in the presence of a story teller in a tavern. Repeated formulas in addition produce the effect of ritualization. The various parts of the story are introduced with the sentence, "Pay attention to what I will now tell you" and concluded with, "Is that enough?" When stories of cruelty and violence are told, when improbable events take place, the narrator repeatedly uses the tag, "the incredible became reality."

The hero's name is revealed to us only half way through the story—we are informed that his grandfather's name could be spelled Ditie, which gives a German flavor to it. But in Czech the name means "child." This is a naïve, direct, innocent protagonist, who wanders through life with a few explicit maxims to guide him, thinking little (except at the end), but appreciating beauty and creating through images. This child-like creature becomes a witness, testifying to how things are and what their essence is.

There is a remarkable congruence between the waiter's inner world (his desires, his ideas about life) and the world around him. He is not plunged into a world where he meets antagonistic people, foreign values, people different from himself. On the contrary, he is surrounded by exemplars of just what he would like to be himself. There are exceptions; the Germans whom he begins to encounter just before the occupation of Czechoslovakia, and the vari-

ous specimens of violence and cruelty which are scattered sporadically throughout the book, are antagonistic to him. But the majority of people whom he meets teach him something positive. His recurrent reaction is, "What a beauty," or "That must have been beautiful, I should like to see that."

Most of the teaching is through models; he is a great observer. No wonder that the most frequent leit-motifs are "I waited on the King of England" and "I waited on the Emperor of Abyssinia," because the hero (and most of the characters around him) belong to a particular subgroup of the watcher, the voyeur-observer: they are servants. His chief mentor, Zdeněk, many other headwaiters and bosses, and he himself, are waiters, or later, even as hotel owners, still people who wait on others, whose business it is to cater to others' wishes, whose excellence is determined by their skill in first guessing what the customer desires, what will please him (he may or may not even be himself aware of it), and then, in being outstandingly capable of performing the task.

Expertise is a quality highly valued by the hero (and, we know from Hrabal's other works, by the author himself), and to be a champion of waiters, able to divine what is desired as well as to perform it, is an accomplishment which in the hero's view gives him prestige, makes him 'taller,' justifies his existence. One of his bosses initiates him into the game of guessing. When a customer enters the restaurant, the headwaiter and Dítě place bets on the customer's nationality and region, whether or not he has any diseases which might affect his preferences in food, what he will order. The expert waiter, looking from the distance, can call in the correct order before the hero has even had time to walk to the kitchen. Zdeněk's explanation of his extraordinary abilities is that he had waited on the King of England. Having risen so high in the hierarchy of waiting, to have been so privileged, testifies to his uncanny skill. Contact with the king, in the relationship of waiter to master, stands as a shorthand formula for unique powers. It is cause as well as proof. Waiting on the King of England has increased, for ever after, the waiter's preternatural abilities. Zdeněk on one occasion glances at our hero, who is wearing a secretly borrowed tie. He immediately knows that it is not Dítě's own tie, but one he has taken without permission. Dítě is silent, but he can guess that Zdeněk had guessed, and Zdeněk says only, "I know because I waited on the King of England." Dítě himself, later, in dynastic succession, attributes his powers to the fact that he had waited on the Emperor of Abyssinia. The servile relationship leads to mastery, art, triumph.

The narrator's small stature plays an important role. From the outset, he wants to be tall. He is going through life hoping to master the set of steps needed to feel big. He is variously downcast or elevated, searching for the proper knowledge, hoping to be initiated, just as he was successively introduced to other skills and masteries. The world in which we live, he assumes, is rich in secrets, which it is possible to come to know. There are keys to find and to turn. A lay gnosticism is tacitly assumed to govern this planet. Only at the end of the book does the question of being small or tall lose significance for Dítě.

There were other admonitions which sank deeply into his awareness. His father taught him that the important thing is to have something to live for, to have a beautiful and noble goal. Dítě recalls this piece of advice when serving as *pikolo,* and decides that his noble goal which will make life meaningful is to go to the local brothel. So he proceeds to earn and save money in order to go to the prostitutes, about whom he had overheard many stories from the local patricians at the restaurant. Hrabal is of course ironic. The boy's decision that his father's precept, to have a beautiful and noble goal, means he ought to be making enough money to go to the whorehouse, is comic. Yet it is not altogether and exclusively ironically presented. The boy's action is a plausible way of reaching a worthwhile goal, even if different from what the father meant.

Dítě had been taught that happiness came through hard work. However, watching the reveling stockbrokers at another hotel, he decides that money brings happiness, not work. Nobody could enjoy himself better than these men, who show no sign of guilty conscience, playing with pretty prostitutes during their afternoons and evenings at Paris Hotel. Dítě decides to follow this empirical lesson and to become rich.

The entire book is a succession of efforts by the narrator to reach his goals; there is always the ideal of having something to live for. The father's admonition merges with another one which is drilled into him, "Money will open all the doors for you." Successively the waiter adopts the aims of growing into an excellent waiter, like Zdeněk; of becoming a millionaire; and of owning his own hotel, the best anywhere. Above all, more than being and doing those things, he wants to be recognized as being and doing them. After the Communist takeover in 1948, in a frenzied sequence, he rushes around trying to be treated as a millionaire. Frustrated through being taken off the lists of millionaires by the intercession of his good angel protector Zdeněk, who is trying to help him, Dítě begs guards in a concentration camp for millionaires to let him in.

There are always snags and obstacles on his path to being acknowledged as great by others. To the Germans he is only a Czech, to other millionaires he is just an upstart, to the Czechs during the occupation he is a traitor who joined the German side. His conscious goal of making it, then, is doomed to a series of frustrations. He achieves the positions which he expected would bring him acceptance and prestige, only to find himself denied, shortchanged. His aim of having an aim, the desire to feel tall, to be like those other men whom he chose as models, persists. The fulfillment eludes him. Each goal turns out to have been a chimera, with more chimeras ahead in the future, each appearing real and solid only until he reaches them. But there is a second order of values which the waiter does possess from the beginning till the end. They are functions, not of having done something or achieved a position, but of vision, deriving from his ability to see (and implicitly, to create). Spectator that he is, he turns into someone bearing witness: that is what his creativity consists in.

Dítě's great achievement is that he responds to beauty spontaneously, directly, strongly. When as a fifteen year old boy he goes to a prostitute, he arranges petals of peo-

nies which happen to be in the room on her naked stomach and thighs. She is enraptured and tells him that nobody else had paid such a high tribute to her beauty. With the German girl Lise who becomes his wife he follows the same practice of placing blossoms around her stomach and private parts. His strong response to her is the reason for her choosing to marry him, a lowly Czech. When he kisses her after the wedding ceremony, the extraordinary strength of their attraction for each other, the sexual link between them, is sensed by all the German bystanders. Through witnessing it, they come to understand what seemed paradoxical to them, Lise's marrying a Czech. Dítě realizes all this himself. "His love, play, and playfulness," were qualities he possessed and they lacked.

Dítě not only has the ability to enjoy life tremendously, he also loves to see others extravagantly enjoying life: people who throw their money around; who can organize a happening in the woods (a band hiding in the trees until a given moment when they surprise the person being celebrated by playing one of his own compositions); the president of Czechoslovakia chasing a French beauty, running from one heap of hay to another; a salesman who obtains attention by tossing a handful of change out the door of a restaurant and on to the town square; these, and all the other innumerable instances of exuberance, abandon, self-forgetfulness, are to Dítě symptoms of being in contact with "spittle and juice and blood"—of being truly alive, of living the right way.

The admired quality is displayed by a waiter who carries a record number of plates; but the same waiter, upset by a sneezing customer, drops all plates, and is so enraged and humiliated that he performs epic feats of destruction. Hrabal, through Dítě, expresses admiration for the beauties of excess. In fact, Dítě delights in any going beyond the boundaries of reasonable measure. Those epic incidents, like the petals of peonies on the girl, are *celebrations*.

Appreciation of Gargantuan feasts pervades the book. Most admired, it seems, are scenes which have some weird twist: a hotel where everything is permanently ready, the waiters and bosses expectant, but guests not arriving; an Abyssinian feast with camels and antelopes obtained from the Prague Zoo and roasted over a bonfire, at a top Prague restaurant; a concentration camp for millionaires where there are no walls, yet all the forms are obeyed, while everyone is living it up, visited by wives and mistresses, going to Prague with passes, a kind of Abbey of Thalème where everybody does as he wishes in reality, while in appearance they are guards and prisoners in a punitive detention institution.

The grand, sweeping gesture—someone going to the limit, to the extreme—these are the patterns which particularly engage Dítě's sympathies. There is the story of a man who once, asked by his wife to deliver a message to a woman friend, finds that the door is opened for him by a woman of such attraction, that without anything being said, and while the woman still continues to embroider, they proceed immediately to make love on the floor. The man then goes on purposefully for eighteen years making and saving money, so that at the end of that period, he can take care of his wife and child, leave them, and marry the woman whom he had thus once met.

An act the heroism of which lies not in its duration, but in the grandeur of the gesture, is that of the prostitute who visits the restaurant in which fifteen year old Dítě works, the day after he had spread peonies over her. She orders grenadine. Dítě, nervous, spills it on her dress (which is decorated with a peony pattern). The headwaiter begins to shout at Dítě, but the girl defends the waiter and asks that they cease belaboring him. The headwaiter, surprised, replies that Dítě had ruined her dress. She says she will show them how little she cares about her dress, pours many more bottles of grenadine over her hair and dress, and walks out the door. On the square, when the grenadine dries, bees swarm over her hair and dress, attracted by the sweetness of it.

Hrabal is fascinated by that which is absurd, topsy-turvy, and welcomes any intense sensuous enjoyment. He conceives of nature as surrounding man with God's plenty. Expertise of any sort is one of the forms of zestful life in this book. An illustration of this is the episode with pine-trees ("resonant pine") which have branches vibrating at a proper number of cycles, suitable for making musical instruments. They hold promise of sensuous and artistic delight, and they are very unusual, odd specimens: both qualities delight Hrabal. The episode hinges on the serendipity of expertise or connoisseurship. Dítě had worked with a resonant pine lumber unit. Therefore when he once finds himself in a little building which someone years ago had boarded up with huge wide slabs of wood, he recognizes them as resonant pine, becomes aware of their rarity, and notifies the factory manager. Almost anyone else would have looked at the lumber without knowing what he was looking at. Dítě could really see, his expertise enabled him fully to understand the import of what was before his eyes, just as one who had waited on the King of England could see, and recognize, whether someone was wearing a sneakily borrowed necktie, or a customer was Serb or Montenegrin, in good health or suffering from a sick gallbladder. At the end of the book, Dítě sees the "chocolate factory" girl, to whom an ex-professor of French literature was teaching French literature and philosophy, and Dítě's "sight" or "vision" enables him to tell she will love the professor, but will not stay with him, and will bring him sorrow.

The most far-fetched examples of the ability to "know" are those of being able to distinguish in the taste of wine the smell of locomotives of hundreds of trains which passed the vineyards, and of fires made by vineyard workers warming up their lunches. Similarly, when Dítě later buys mirrors from houses abandoned by Germans in 1945, by looking into them, he can detect the smell of the Germans who used to look into those mirrors—again a detail suggestive of magic fairy tales.

From the start, the lessons he is taught by older waiters are linked to his final ability to understand, to "see." He is told to see and hear everything, but to hear and see nothing. The experienced, knowledgeable, initiated waiter, who drills into him that requirement, means merely that he must be attentive, keep his eyes and ears open in order to wait upon the customer's wants, but remain discreet. As the book progresses, however, the exhortation to a merely practical discretion grows into the ability quietly to "see," to understand, basic, deeper things in life—to become one of the initiated—to penetrate the substance of life.

A capacity for enjoying the pleasures and beauties of life, then, is associated with Dítě's ability to "see," which in turn is linked with his being able to create: he is indeed a kind of artist sharing the divine ability to "make." He speaks, early in the book, of "creating like God, like Shakespeare." Beginning with the passive ability to respond, to enjoy, he moves on to the ability to detect: to see what not everybody would see—the beauty of a woman's body, the significance of a scene, the future emotions and relationships of people, and then goes on to create, to make up, stories and relationships. His deed is spreading the petals over the girl; his creation is imagining with what kinds of flowers he would garnish her in the various future seasons and months. He is an artist who admires other artists—people who arrange something: impresarios-creators-or "stage managers" who stage things in life, arrange, order events to express an idea, perhaps unintentionally and unconsciously. He is the one who grasps the significance of it.

What is the answer he finds at the end of the book, in solitude, with a few animals in the border regions of the country? Dítě had progressively been changing his opinion of himself. The novel is the story of the growth of the hero's self-view. Trying to achieve happiness through the mediancy of other people (by being respected by others, because of his money or beautiful hotel), he learns, was a vain effort. The concentration camp, with its upside down conditions, is just one of the illustrations of the absurdity of life. Dítě finds he cannot rely on others. He has to come to terms with himself, alone: he has to learn to know himself. The lessons taught by the ex-professor of French literature to the girl, overheard by Dítě, the dadaism of Jarry, and the existentialism of Desnos sink deeply into him. He withdraws to the woods—away from people—yet not completely isolated (he does maintain roads for society—and occasionally appears in the nearest village tavern, where he is much sought after because of his art of story telling). The fact that he has changed, found himself, is confirmed in the "examination" by his angel, Zdeněk, who appears one day, silently watches him from the distance, evidently perceives the change in him, and leaves without having spoken to him. The professor had said that only he who can move into anonymity, who can free himself from his false self, is a true man. Zdeněk's looking at Dítě wordlessly from the forest confirms that he has succeeded. The second lesson Dítě learns from the professor is that a superior man expresses himself better than others. He now wants to write; he decides to depict all the "pictures" which are tied to the thread of his life.

The pastoral idyll, with a shepherd dog, donkey, goat, and cat, and the earlier feeding of pigeons which swarm as though to kiss him when he appears with their grain, remind us of the Garden of Eden, the Terrestrial Paradise. He feels this is like a message from the Heavens, to the effect that they had found pleasure in him—he has been approved. He would rather have this than three hotels and ten million in cash. He is happy he lost the heel of a shoe where the last two stamps of Lise's treasure were hidden. He is in nature, under the sun, away from people. His seeing is still keen. Somebody else would see nothing; he delights in what he sees (abandoned, formerly German-occupied houses, smashed furniture and chests.) He has become somewhat more spiritual, if this is not too solemn a way to summarize the point of a lightly phrased finding: that he who always loved women from the waist down now loves the chocolate factory girl more from the waist up.

The novel is a journey from false ideals (money, ownership of hotel) to personal, individual self-reliance. He starts with a doorwoman (concierge) whom he tips 200 crowns wanting to kiss his hand, and ends honored for himself, his ability to tell stories, to present ideas about life, alone, except for his loyal animals who depend on him.

Haircutting is a woman's journey from harmonious existence bathed by warm, colorful life, with long hair, expressing the essence of that age, to a similarly harmonious life, with short hair, in a new age, with shorter rhythm, but still equally attuned, submissive to it and accepting of it. *I Waited on the King of England* is the hero's journey from seeing into others, to seeing into himself.

The essence of life, Dítě concludes, is to interrogate oneself. One must think about death—how will I behave when the hour comes? Man needs to be amused. To enjoy oneself is a divine need. He wants poetry to be enjoyment for the people. He tells people in the tavern about beauty, about how one must love, seek the meaning of life, win peace and calm, not run away from basic questions, not postpone the confrontation.

The philosophy comes strangely from Dítě's lips; the stress on enjoyment, however, rings true and ties together what the entire book had been leading up to.

Acting on impulse, making a sweeping gesture, particularly when moved spontaneously by love, sex, beauty, these points are admiringly and vividly presented by Hrabal over and over, and they impress the reader. When it comes to the philosophical points at the end of the book, the need for anonymity, thinking about death, living for oneself, writing—we understand them, we nod to them, but they do not grow out of the whole material of the book; they are not the dominant impression, but rather a belated diversion of the energy of the book into the channel of intellection. The vitality sweeps us along; the conceptualization makes less of a mark.

I Waited on the King of England is a book in which the absurd becomes the marvellous. Dítě states that modern French poets "were discovering human miraculousness." Hrabal, in his robust stories, is celebrating the discovery of true humanness, of the marvellous in people, of how the incredible became fact.

Dítě says towards the end of the novel, "I saw that all people are obscuring for me what I wanted to see and know, all are only amusing themselves as I used to amuse myself,

all are putting off that which some day they will have to question, if they are lucky to have time to do it before they die . . . what it came down to is that in the tavern I found out that the essence of life is in interrogating about death, how will I behave when my time comes, that death, no, that interrogation of oneself is a conversation under the angle of vision of infinity and eternity, that the solving of that death is the beginning of thinking about beauty and in beauty, because to savor the senselessness of one's journey which in any event will end in a premature departure, that enjoyment and experience of one's confusion fills a man with bitterness and hence beauty," and concludes, "man is indestructible, spiritually and physically, he only changes, metamorphoses."

Hrabal's waiter and hotel owner is an oral poet, who tells us in his cascade of words of his mostly sensual, *terre à terre* experiences, in which, through his carnal experiences and his self assertion, the little man who wants to be big journeys, like Thomas Mann's Felix Krull, from hotel to hotel, bed to bed, starting from a very narrow (but always honest) view of life, and ending with a universal, spiritual outlook.

There is also a dark side to Hrabal's new works. *I Waited on the King of England* contains more of it than *The Haircutting,* as we might expect. There is a great deal of cruelty in human relations. Men are sadistic to each other and to animals; the war years are particularly full of violence and atrocities, but even during peace time, human beings, as Hrabal sees them, are drawn to murder and torture.

Not only enjoyment and beauty, but horror and brutality inhabit Hrabal's world. Their presence balances the stress on hedonistic and esthetic enjoyments. Hrabal's paean of praise of life is also paralleled, and at times undercut, by his grotesquerie. The absurd elements which coexist side by side with, or even within, in the midst of, Hrabal's idyllic scenes, give his works their special flavor. They certainly keep him from ever coming even close to seeming maudlin, sentimental.

"Since about 1962 I started publishing one book after another, not without great apprehension, and suddenly I had readers—hundreds of thousands of them who read my texts as readily as they read the sports pages. And so I go on writing."

—Bohumil Hrabal, 1986

Imagination unifies it all: the power of fantasy of the characters and of the author—typified in the conclusion to *The Haircutting,* where a lover of local architectural beauties becomes lyrical over beauties which no longer exist—buildings which used to be there but have long ago been torn down. To appreciate through fantasy something which is not really physically any longer present is the purest and greatest exercise of the imagination.

The Haircutting can be read as a pleasant story of the old days of Bohemia, as a portrait of a simple, delightful, vivacious woman in a small Czech town, or as a series of anecdotes. It is all those things, and it stands squarely in the oral tradition of Slav story telling. Its immediate literary ancestors clearly are Jaroslav Hašek and Jakub Deml. But *The Haircutting,* while amusing and delightful on all those counts, is more than that: it is also the presentation of an ideal. The story is most unpretentious; it is quite possible to read it with the utmost pleasure, on the most superficial level alone, and there is not much wrong with leaving it at that, too. But, without any heavy-footed moralizing or portentous generalizing, *The Haircutting,* through its series of anecdotes, all the exuberant fun, the robust humor, the artful naïveté, nevertheless insidiously implies something greater; there is a unity to its episodic structure and to its small number of characters. Together they compose a hagiographical eulogy. Amidst the anecdotes and the men around her, in the incidents of a brewery steward's wife, the woman with the marvellous hair is a model of the feminine, secular, robust, earthly saint.

In both works, vitality, sensuality, physical, hedonistic exuberance are exalted, but then, ultimately, transcended (in *I Waited on the King of England* by the desire to be alone, think about death, find fulfillment through writing; in *The Haircutting,* through the heroine's cutting her hair short, according supremacy to being in harmony with the pattern of the age), yet in both works, that accumulation of hymns in praise of physical desire, play, enjoyment, is more powerful in the reader's memory than the attitudes to which those hymns are made to yield. The stepping stones remain in our minds; the goals survive in our minds more faintly. (pp. 74-90)

> *George Gibian, " 'The Haircutting' and 'I Waited on the King of England': Two Recent Works by Bohumil Hrabal," in* Czech Literature Since 1956: A Symposium, *edited by William E. Harkins and Paul I. Trensky, Bohemica, 1980, pp. 74-90.*

Peter Z. Schubert

On 8 January 1975 the Prague weekly *Tvorba* (Creation) published a "conversation" with Bohumil Hrabal that ended yet another ban on that author. Although the most popular and most widely read Czech writer of the sixties, Hrabal could not publish in Czechoslovakia until this self-criticism. His official silence (he still circulated his works through the Czech *samizdat*) was interrupted by publication of the collection *Postřižiny* (Haircutting; 1976), and *Slavnosti sněženek* (Snowdrop Festivities; 1978) followed. The latter book has just been published in Germany under the title *Schneeglöckchenfeste.* The selections in "Snowdrop Festivities" do not differ from Hrabal's earlier works. The fifteen stories, of which the shortest is six pages, the longest twenty-six pages, could be a part of his *Perlička na dně* (Pearl of the Deep; 1963) or *Pábitelé* (The Palaverers; 1964), were it not for the locality, Kersko, a little township in the woods, the framework of the *Schneeglöckchenfeste.*

Hrabal's fascination with the absurd has been commented on before, and these stories are a further testimony to that fact. Practically all of them are written in what might be termed a soft surrealism or a developed poetism wherein the absurd becomes natural. The style does not harm the protagonists. As their charcteristic features are magnified, the picture is distorted, but the heroes become more interesting. Another quality noted in Hrabal's work is his linguistic experimentation; be it the rambling sentences in some of the stories or the peculiar language of the protagonists, this experimental tendency is present here, and [translator] Petr Šimon has done his best to render it all into German. Some of the themes remind the reader of Hrabal's earlier works. For instance, the joy the heroes derive from dressing sheep and processing the parts is reminiscent of a similar scene, the pork feast in *Postřižiny.* "Leli" is to a point an echo of *Taneční hodiny pro starší a pokročilé* (Dance Lessons for Adult and Advanced Pupils; 1964), and both reflect the philosophy of Ladislav Klíma. This, however, would call for a more detailed analysis.

The Schweikian anecdote on the book jacket overemphasizes this vein in Hrabal's work. On the whole, *Schneeglöckchenfeste* is representative of Hrabal's writing, and since his other six books published in German were all successful, there is no reason to doubt this one's prospects. It is a pity that only two titles by this author have appeared in English: namely, *Closely Watched Trains* and *The Death of Mr. Baltisberger.* Moreover, the former has seen four editions already. Although not Hrabal's best, *Schneeglöckchenfeste* is "a Hrabal," and that is the best recommendation.

> *Peter Z. Schubert, in a review of "Schneeglöckchenfeste," in* World Literature Today, *Vol. 56, No. 2, Spring, 1982, p. 365.*

W. A. Iggers

How do you review [*Closely Watched Trains*], an old, beloved classic? Hrabal is one of the greatest and most inventive Czech prose writers living today. Underlying the humor in his most typical works—or perhaps all of them—is a sense of the tragic fate of that country. Hrabal's language is innovative and very much rooted in tradition, his humor is both linguistic and situational; there is a constant tension between situations and attitudes which bear a family resemblance to specifically Czech interhuman relations on the one hand, and the intellectual observer who seeks to view them from the outside on the other.

This story—not quite a novella—is truer to life than most works which follow the rules of their genres. Miloš, the protagonist who in the end heroically blows up a German ammunition train, is actually preoccupied with his own very personal problems, just as most people are during a period of protracted national disaster. Sex, in the Czech context, while important, is not omnipresent. The girl's stamp-covered buttocks express anal as much as sexual humor, and Miloš, who asks old Mrs. Lanská to go to bed with him, is not a corrupt young lecher but a clumsy, naïve kid who wants to follow what he believes to be the wise advice of his elders.

The conclusion recalls the scene in *All Quiet on the Western Front* where the French and the German soldiers in the trenches meet and see each other's humanity. There is no sentimentality here: instead, the impact of the tragedy involved in a situation where the reader who cannot call killing right but does not find it easy to call it wrong is affected by the matter-of-fact realism of Miloš's exclamation that the opponent should have "sat on his ass," which takes him back to a context of minor misdeeds in everyday life. The book, which addresses itself to the important question of Czech heroism and/or cowardice during the *German* occupation, is timelier than ever and therefore forbidden.

> *W. A. Iggers, in a review of "Closely Watched Trains," in* World Literature Today, *Vol. 56, No. 2, Spring, 1982, p. 372.*

Igor Hájek

The Hrabal phenomenon is a bibliographer's and literary historian's dream—or nightmare. In the 1950s, while working first in a steel foundry and later in a waste-paper warehouse, Bohumil Hrabal, holder of a law degree, wrote some poetry and a lot of prose that deviated so much from the Stalinist canon (by completely ignoring it) that he felt it wiser to hide his work than to submit it to a publisher. Only when the Khrushchevite thaw at last touched Czechoslovakia in 1956 was a volume of his stories accepted for publication. The printers were slow. By the time the book was set and the proofs read two years later, the political climate had changed again and the set was dispersed. The budding author had to wait for his début until 1963, by which time he was forty-nine. But there was no trace of middle-aged staidness in his writing. His first book, *Perlička na dně* (A Pearl at the Bottom), subtitled *Hovory* (Talks), was an immediate success. Like the five that followed until 1968, it provoked extraordinary reactions in both readers and critics, some ecstatic, others apoplectic. It was also during the 1960s, when the arts in Czechoslovakia flourished under a less restrictive régime, that Hrabal became known in the West, mainly because of the film based on his most conventional book, *Closely Observed Trains.* It was then believed that he belonged to the reform movement.

True, his work, devoid of any ideology, was not quite what the Party demanded of writers, but despite clear sympathies for their efforts he had little in common with the liberalizers. Still, he had to pay a high price after the Prague Spring had been suppressed by Soviet tanks: in 1970 two of Hrabal's books (with print runs of 26,000 and 35,000 respectively) were pulped, and like dozens of his colleagues he was put under a publication ban.

Most of Hrabal's work published in the 1960s had been written during the previous decade and hardly anything was added in the hectic years of belated acknowledgement and popular success. Renewed ostracism paradoxically granted him the opportunity to concentrate again on literature. In the early 1970s new works started to circulate in typed copies either among friends of the author or as *samizdat,* the most remarkable among them the "novel" *Obsluhoval jsem anglického krále* (*I Waited on the King of England*). The ban was lifted in 1975 following an ambiguous interview published in the Party weekly *Tvorba*—which some of his admirers regarded as a moral compromise with the neo-Stalinists, motivated by an overwhelming desire to see his work in print.

The lifting of the ban was far from unconditional, however. Versions of his books published officially in Prague in the late 1970s and in the 1980s differ conspicuously from the original typescripts. Comparisons can be made because throughout this period typed copies of his work continued to circulate in Czechoslovakia and some were printed (without a publisher's name) in the West. The disappearance or alteration of certain references to persons and events which could give rise to objection can be attributed to censorship, but there are other, more noticeable changes which suggest that the author himself had been rewriting his prose to make it acceptable for publication.

Not all of it. When the Prague Jazz Section, two of whose officials were recently sentenced to jail for just such activities, published a limited edition of *Obsluhoval jsem anglického krále* for its members in 1982, it did not differ from the known manuscript. But there was nevertheless trouble with the secret police, who made the author sign a Kafkaesque statement that the book—for which he had written a special preface—was published without his knowledge.

The sorting out of the textual chaos of manuscripts, typed copies, *samizdat* editions, official publications and editions printed in the West, is only one by-product of Susanna Roth's *Laute Einsamkeit und bitteres Gluck,* the first monograph in any language devoted to Hrabal. She also provides an outline of the writer's personal history, pointing out with justification that structural analysis alone cannot do justice to a work shaped by external pressures, or to his idiosyncratic style. . . .

A work not covered by Susanna Roth's study is Hrabal's three-volume autobiography, which he wrote between 1982 and 1985, and which brought about his most serious conflict with the authorities. Under pressure from the secret police, Hrabal renounced his work and subsequently had a nervous breakdown.

The third part, *Proluky* (Vacant Sites) . . . spans the period from the publication of Hrabal's first book in 1963 to the mid-1970s. The narrator, surprisingly, is not the author, but his wife. This exquisite device has allowed him to be scathingly frank without embarrassment: seen through the sarcastic eyes of his wife, Hrabal appears as a tormented, frantic braggart addicted to the intoxicating flow of talk and beer; a clown playing up to the grimly serious Heinrich Böll on his visits to Prague; a wreck writhing in the agonies of hangovers and gallstone colics; a bundle of nerves sleepless with anxiety before a public appearance and living in terror of the secret police—and all the time pretending, faking and creating a zany imaginative tale out of his life.

Mrs Hrabal's comments on the incomprehensible success

of her husband's books which read like raw, half-finished notes towards something real and serious, contain the gist of his poetics. He has always claimed that he learned to write much as a gypsy acquires the skill of playing the violin. Indeed, there seems to be a touch of magic in the way he plays his instrument with total disregard for all the rules.

The wrath of the overseers of Czech literature had been aroused because in his autobiography he not only disregarded the rules concerning unmentionable names and events, but also dared to describe a police raid on a party to celebrate his sixtieth birthday. Yet earlier this year, under the influence of the fresh wind from Moscow, Bohumil Hrabal was, after fifteen years in semi-wilderness, offered membership of the "normalized" Writers' Union. With luck this will protect him from further harassment so that he can live out the remaining years of his restless life in the spirit of a saying of his beloved Uncle Pepin: "The world is maddeningly beautiful. Well, it isn't really, but that is how I see it."

> *Igor Hájek, "A Late-Flowering Rule-Breaker," in* The Times Literary Supplement, *No. 4409, October 2-8, 1987, p. 1067.*

Julian Barnes

Small heroes are designed to be picked up and bounced around; they provoke everything from playfulness to sadism in fellow-characters, and even in their creators. John Irving's stunted Owen Meany, for example (linear descendant, even to the initials, of Günter Grass's Oskar Matzerath), was last month being tossed humiliatingly around like a football by Sunday school classmates. On the other hand, these shorties do tend to spot things the rest of us miss.

The narrator of *I Served the King of England,* a waiter in pre-war Prague, is similarly diminutive, manipulable and sharp-eyed. He ducks to his superiors' commands, boings off laundresses' breasts, flips and spins to please and obey. At one point he—or at least his simulacrum, an inflatable tailor's mould of his torso—even takes off and floats right up to the ceiling. And, in a broader way, the narrator bounces along through his own life story like a balloon: jolly, slightly irritating and surprisingly unsquashable. As the tale develops, however, it becomes clear that he is boinging not just off laundresses' breasts, but also off large and prominent bits of twentieth-century Czech history.

The novel begins, though, in sunny, comic-erotic mood. The hotel in which the waiter learns his trade is peopled with baroque nobs and crafty travelling salesmen, glad tarts and feisty gypsies. One part of his training consists of a series of bets with a head-waiter: the two of them examine an incoming customer and speculate on what he or she is going to order. The head-waiter guesses right every single time. How does he know? 'Because I served the King of England' comes the catch-all reply. The diminutive waiter aspires to such knowledge, but the nearest he can get to reliable authority is when serving triple-stuffed camel to the Emperor of Ethiopia at a burlesque banquet.

The war comes, and the novel, while never losing its gleefulness, darkens. The waiter works at an Aryan breeding station and falls for a German gym teacher. Their marriage offers a microcosmic version of the larger experiment: love turns quickly into 'National Socialist intercourse', and their son Siegfried is backward and maniacally aggressive. After the war the waiter's fortunes briefly revive, as he achieves his ambition of owning a hotel, then dip with the Communist takeover of 1948. He ends the book as a road-mender in a distant province, at first side by side with other political undesirables, then alone except for the companionship of animals. He lives with and for memory.

There is (as far as I can see) no concealed line-by-line political infrastructure; rather, the novel reflects the last half-century of Czechoslovakia in its wider moods and tonal fluctuations, from colourful bustle to greyish solitude. Of course, there are satirical parallels to draw if we wish. In one robust scene (post-1948), a football referee is rehearsing in the woods by himself, blowing his whistle and sending off imaginary players. A party of lunatics on day release happen along and turn into the crowd, roaring, clapping and jeering. Everything is there except the players and the ball. What shall we make of this? A sly metaphor of Communist rule? Perhaps; though Hrabal has already moved on.

And like his narrator, he doesn't employ conventional motion: he bounces and floats. His mode is a sort of dancing realism, somewhere between fairy-tale and satire; the narrative likes to hop jauntily into the air and glide along for a page or two, returning to earth before you can tire of the trick. Hrabal is a most sophisticated novelist, with a gusting humour and a hushed tenderness of detail. He is now in his seventies, and perhaps glancingly known in this country for the book filmed as *Closely Observed Trains.* His fellow-Czech Milan Kundera has called him 'our very best writer'; and we should read him.

> *Julian Barnes, "Order of the Day," in* The Observer, *June 18, 1988, p. 45.*

Karen von Kunes

[Hrabal] had been one of Czechoslovakia's most popular authors prior to 1969 but was not allowed to publish in his country for several years thereafter. His new, long-awaited novel was accepted with eagerness. . . . (p.684)

In *Postřižiny,* as in other works, Hrabal depicts indulgent, buoyant, self-centered, atypical, and unheroic characters who strive for a certain joie de vivre, but here he places them at the boundary of two eras: the dying Austro-Hungarian empire and the newly emergent Czechoslovakia. The heroine's lock of golden hair, "this relic of old Austria," is a symbol of womanhood of the "good old times." The plot is unexciting, but the stories are vivid and powerful in their unconventionality: hyperbolic devices and the expressive language of the common man mixed with tender lyric passages celebrating the heroine's vivacious exuberance perpetually attract the reader's attention. To accentuate the mood of the story, Hrabal has chosen an old-fashioned title for his work: *postřižiny* is used to refer to the cutting of a child's hair. Indeed, his heroine is full of almost animal vitality and nonconformity, enjoying pranks and unexpected adventures like an astounded child. Her spirit is nurtured by Pepin, her husband's brother, who, like her, is an infantile connoisseur of life. At the same time, however, she succumbs to her husband's world of traditions and restraints with joy and delight.

At the story's conclusion the fifty-year Austrian regime is over, and accordingly the cutting of the protagonist's hair celebrates the new Czech system. (pp. 684-85)

> *Karen von Kunes, in a review of "La chevelure sacrifiée," in* World Literature Today, *Vol. 62, No. 4, Autumn, 1988, pp. 684-85.*

Richard Lourie

There are books you dislike and books you simply don't like. The former are easier to deal with since they have inevitably roused a passion, or abraded a value. The latter are usually cases of an author having failed to enchant through the sheer authority of his tone. The reader is left outside the page like an unenthralled moviegoer stranded in his seat.

At first, I was taken right in by *I Served the King of England,* a novel by one of Czechoslovakia's leading writers, Bohumil Hrabal. Born in 1914, Mr. Hrabal was politically active during Alexander Dubcek's Prague Spring, for which he paid a price after August 1968. He is probably best known in this country for *Closely Watched Trains,* a film based on another novel of his. This latest is a picaresque allegory of 20th-century Czechoslovak history as lived and narrated by a short hotel waiter by the name of Ditie, meaning child. Rising from one hotel to another, each a stage of his country's history, he marries a Nazi during the war, and in the postwar years at last realizes his dream of becoming a millionaire, only to see his wealth vanish under Communism. We follow him on his long journey from crude ambition to wisdom and solitude. That journey starts with a wrench. "When I started to work at the Golden Prague Hotel, the boss took hold of my left ear, pulled me up, and said, You're a busboy here, so remember, you don't see anything and you don't hear anything. Repeat what I just said. So I said I wouldn't see anything and I wouldn't hear anything. Then the boss pulled me up by my right ear and said, But remember too that you've got to see everything and hear everything."

> **"The hero [of *I Served the King of England*] journeys from crude ambition to wisdom."**
>
> **—Richard Lourie**

The narrative quickly begins building an atmosphere that seems a quintessential Czechoslovak mixture of the

bawdy, zany and mundane. But all too soon the spell is broken. Shortly after beginning his career, Ditie witnesses a knife fight among rival gypsies in the hotel restaurant. Also present is the director of the local music school, who is so engrossed in a book that "with a smile on his face, [he] went right on reading while the gypsy storm whirled around him, and they bled over his head and his book, and twice they stuck their knives into his table." Since this behavior is so utterly at variance with anything we would expect to encounter in reality, the author must here enchant his reader into suspending his disbelief. This is the moment when the author establishes his authority.

Or doesn't. This reader was ejected from the narrative at this point, neither able to believe, nor made to believe, that the director of the music school could have been so swept away by his reading that knives, blood and gypsies would have left him unfazed. From then on, I was never quite hypnotized by either of the story's two worlds—one built of flesh, food and money, the other a more lyrical place where, to paraphrase the leitmotif of the book, the unbelievable comes true.

The business with the gypsies is not an isolated incident, but rather a sign of trouble to come. Though the hero's discovery of the pleasures of sex and money, and the secret relationship between them, is fine and vivid, his sudden shifts of allegiance—first to the Germans during World War II and then away from them—are whisked out of nowhere, neither foreshadowed by character nor pricked by incident. We have to take Ditie's word on it, and we don't.

To some extent, this may be a problem of translation, though not in the narrower sense of the word. Indeed, Paul Wilson's rendering, with rare exceptions, seems both talented and true. Here, the problem of translation may be more cultural than strictly linguistic. Perhaps there are gradations of the improbable from one culture to another. What's an enjoyable tall tale to one may be tediously farfetched to another. It's also possible that the exact choice of words in the original had flecks of tone that would lullably a Czechoslovak reader into a state where disbelief is more easily suspended. Cultural differences may account for some of the problems but the real difficulty is structural. *I Served the King of England* is really a fairy tale, and fairy tales are never told in the first person: only an omniscient narrator has the godlike authority to make us forget reality.

The book does have its stretches, moments, images. Ditie's grandmother makes a pitiful living retrieving the soiled clothing tossed out the window by the clients of a bathhouse: "Sometimes shirts that got thrown out would suddenly spread their arms like a traffic cop at an intersection, or like Christ." Or, a night scene which has a "damp countryside as blue as carbon paper." But moments and images do not make a book, and certainly not a novel that can distract a reader from the hum of his own mind, let alone gypsies and knives.

> *Richard Lourie, "Upwardly Mobile in Prague," in* The New York Times Book Review, *March 19, 1989, p. 13.*

Christopher Lehmann-Haupt

As Ditie, the narrator of Bohumil Hrabal's extraordinary and subtly tragicomic new novel, begins to recount his adventures as a tiny 15-year-old busboy at the Golden Prague Hotel in the 1930's, the reader naturally anticipates the chapter in which Ditie will fulfill the promise of the book's title, *I Served the King of England.*

Not that there's any hurry. Mr. Hrabal—who has never before been published in English, though he is known throughout Europe for his novels, story collections and screenplays (including those for *Closely Watched Trains* and *A Boring Afternoon*)—has a charming narrative style. Little Ditie has a slyly amusing way of recounting how he discovered the truth of what Mr. Walden, a hugely fat salesman of salami slicers, has told him—that "my boy, if life works out just a tiny bit in your favor it can be beautiful, just beautiful."

Not only does Ditie find money and sex "just beautiful," he even takes pleasure in the first tuxedo he buys when he gets his waiter's papers. It is made for him by a tailor using a custom-made "inflated figurine" as a model of his torso. When Ditie picks up his new suit, he asks to see his model.

> It was a magnificent sight. Up near the ceiling hung the torsos of generals and regimental commanders and famous actors. . . . A draft from an open window made the torsos move about like little fleecy clouds in an autumn wind. . . . It looked so small, my torso. I almost wept to see a major general's torso beside mine, and Mr. Baranek the hotelkeeper's, but when I thought of the company I was in I laughed and felt better.

Still, the scene where Ditie will presumably wait on royalty is something to look forward to. So it comes as a surprise to learn that it isn't Ditie who "served the King of England." It's a headwaiter who trains Ditie and always seems to know exactly how much money a guest has and what he will order. When Ditie asks him, "How do you know all this?—he answered, pulling himself up to his full height, Because I served the King of England."

Ditie's own great moment comes in a marvelous scene where he serves the Emperor of Ethiopia. The main course is prepared by Haile Selassie's cooks: barbecued camel stuffed with antelope, turkey, fish and hard-boiled eggs. A government counselor, "a well-known epicure," was so enraptured with the dish that he "ran out of the hotel shouting and dancing and cheering and beating his chest, and then he ran back in again and there was a song in his voice and a dance of thanksgiving in his legs."

To the extent that there are symbols in Mr. Hrabal's concretely illustrative prose, the image of serving royalty represents Ditie's worship of rank. That tendency is purged from him when he falls in love with a German woman named Lise Papanek, who admires him for his resemblance to the Germans who are about to invade Czechoslovakia. Though Ditie feels remorse that his countrymen are being executed by the Germans while he is proving to an SS doctor his qualifications to impregnate someone of Aryan Teutonic blood with "a New Man," he marries Lise anyway. They have their "New Child" but he turns out to be brain damaged, and his only interest in life is hammering nails into the floor.

After the war, with Lise dead and the child institutionalized, Ditie finally reaches the pinnacle of his profession. He builds a hotel through the sale of valuable stamps that Lise had confiscated from deported Jews, and becomes a millionaire. But everywhere in his hotel he hears the sound of nails being pounded into the floor. "So I decided that the money from the stamps was cursed, that it was money taken by force from someone who might have been killed in the process, or maybe the stamps had belonged to a rabbi with miraculous powers, because those nails were really being pounded into my head, and with each blow of the hammer I felt the nail puncturing my skull. . . ."

In any case, after 1948 no Czechoslovak is allowed to be a millionaire anymore. Ditie loses his hotel and is sent by the authorities to the mountains to look after "sections of road where no one wanted to be." By then, mentioning that he had served the Emperor of Ethiopia has become "a way of making fun of myself, because I was independent now and beginning to find the presence of other people irksome. . . ."

In the end, Ditie finds keeping the roads clear of snow a symbol of his life up to this point. The task prompts him to become a writer. During the day, "I would look for the road to the village, but in the evening I would write, looking for the road back, and then walk back along it and shovel aside the snow that had covered my past, and so try, by writing, to ask myself about myself."

In his concluding acknowledgements, Paul Wilson, the translator, notes that Czechoslovaks say Bohumil Hrabal's work is "untranslatable" and that this book "is my response to that challenge." Not knowing Czech, I have no way of judging how Mr. Wilson has handled what he calls "the more puzzling intricacies of 'Hrabalovstina'—Hrabal's special way of using Czech. . . ." But there's little evidence of much difficulty. Mr. Hrabal's gift seems to be for dramatizing humble details, whether they concern dirty laundry or those inflated tailor's torsos with the cords tied to them, "the way they do to babies in the maternity wards so they won't get mixed up, or the way they tag the toes of corpses in the morgues of the big Prague hospitals."

Those details are always concrete. At the beginning of his story, Ditie describes food and drink, and the flowers with which he once liked to decorate the naked laps of beautiful women. Toward the end, he remembers a trunk full of false teeth, and the fear in the eyes of animals afraid of being left alone, and his experience of tasting in the water from a spring below a hill "the dead buried long ago in the graveyard up there." And as he progresses from the living to the dead, one understands that Mr. Hrabal has told both the story of a nobody and a history of Czechoslovakia, and found in their commonplace details everything that matters in life.

Christopher Lehmann-Haupt, "A Small Life in a Large Evil World," in The New York Times, *March 27, 1989, p. C18.*

James Naughton

The hero and "I" of [*I Served the King of England*], an undersized under-waiter, once served the Emperor of Ethiopia during a royal visit (on the menu, a roast camel stuffed with an antelope with a turkey inside, and inside the turkey, fish, stuffing and solid garlands of hard boiled eggs), and he worshipped the Hotel Paris's head waiter, who knew what all his customers wanted before they spoke, because he had waited on the King of England (not served in his army—which the English title might at first suggest). But the prominent Czech author Bohumil Hrabal, now in his seventies, has not been over-abundantly served by English translators: all we have had in book form are the (variously titled) *Closely Watched Trains* (1968, better known from Menzel's film) and the stories in *The Death of Mr. Baltisberger* (1973). *I Served the King of England* existed in 1971, was published in Cologne in 1977 and in Prague in a limited edition in 1982, and has been translated into French, German, Italian, Swedish and Serbo-Croat.

To describe it as a *Bildungsroman* would be to invite misconception, even if I emphasized at once the black or absurd comedy in which it abounds. This diminutive frankfurter-seller, witness to business men's orgies and frequenter of their prostitutes, servant to pregnant German blondes swimming naked, oblivious to his presence, at an Aryan-breeding establishment, later crown-millionaire hotelier, but before this apotheosis wartime collaborator (through falling for a German gym-teacher who filched the stamp collections of Jews, thus providing him with his capital): this picaresque hero undergoes a *Bildung,* true, in which he moves on from ordinary craving for sex, heaps of money, flamboyant hotel-ownership and aristocratic spotted ties to retreat into solitude as a road-mender in a depopulated former German-Bohemian rural wilderness. Here he decides that the basis of life is in asking about death; that dealing with death is the beginning of thinking about the beautiful, because savouring the absurdity of that road which we always leave prematurely, the appreciation and experiencing of that ruination, fill us with bitterness and therefore beauty. But the history of this waiter, Dítě (meaning "Child"), is a flood of meandering garrulous narration, with dreamlike, film-like sequences, hyperbolic, grotesque and farcical analogues of familiar historical fact. No sober account, this, of how it might actually have been, yet still it projects through its debunking prism the shallowness, absurdity and cruelty of how it indeed was. The unbelievable becomes reality, to take the narrator's reiterated phrase. The fantasizing and story-telling deliver at the same time a body blow of total irreverence to the solemn mythopoeia of monumental historiography.

President Masaryk is visited by a French lady for a tumble at a country hotel and ends up with her in a playhouse, sitting on a little chair, among the toy drums and skipping ropes and teddy bears and dolls. A murderer is released from prison and returns home to find his village—the historical Lidice—obliterated by the Nazis; only the stump of a walnut tree is left, used by his dad to swing next door to have it off with the neighbour's wife (the son murdered the father for this, out of love for his mother). Our hero marries his German girl, his semen having been tested to see if he's Aryan enough. The Nazi wife produces a cretinous son, who spends hours pounding nails into floors with a noise like bombing raids, which pursues him after the war, when the wife is dead, from a bombing raid, and the son abandoned to a home for the mentally retarded. His grandmother used to catch dirty underwear and shirts tossed out of a bathhouse by travelling salesmen; a missed one would "fall akimbo, like a white bird shot out of the sky, down into the black gurgling waters . . . ". Lyricism is never far from the undertow of *memento mori.*

The only (reluctant) quibble with the skilful, flowing translation of this book is that the language has become tidier, less omnivorously improvisatory in manner than Hrabal's.

*James Naughton, "The Waiter's How It Was,"
in* The Times Literary Supplement, *No. 4493,
May 12-18, 1989, p. 519.*

D. J. Enright

Whereas George Orwell was down and out in Paris, Bohumil Hrabal's narrator and hero [in *I Served the King of England*], Ditie by name, is upwardly mobile in the hotel and restaurant world of Prague. Ditie loves his labors. In some respects his experiences resemble those of Thomas Mann's *Hochstapler* Felix Krull, who did nicely for himself while working at the Hotel Saint James and Albany in Paris.

Though his story is picaresque in its episodic nature and its wanderings, Ditie is not a swindler or a picaro on the grand scale; he is merely ambitious, ambitious to be rich, and prepared to work devotedly in furtherance of this aim. His book is a fairy tale: a poor boy, mocked for his short stature, goes out into the world, succeeds here and suffers reverses there, has many adventures on the way, and at last achieves true happiness. It isn't necessary to be big, you just have to feel big. Unlike most fairy tales, this one is suffused with irony, and not—in parts obviously not—suitable for children.

Ditie's first job, as busboy at the Golden Prague Hotel, is to sell hot frankfurters at the railway station. He soon perceives that when frankfurters cost one crown eighty apiece, and the passenger gives you a twenty-crown bill or even a hundred, if you fumble about in your pockets looking for change, the odds are that the train will have moved off before you can hand the change over. It's not your fault if you make a nice little profit. This pays for Ditie's visits to an amiable establishment called Paradise's, where the girls teach him skills that will come in handy later on. He also discovers that "money could buy you not just a beautiful girl, money could buy you poetry too."

Moving to the Hotel Tichota, Ditie picks up more useful knowledge from the proprietor, a hugely fat man confined to a wheelchair, who nonetheless whizzes around the premises and is aware of what everyone is up to. Observation, in particular of merry orgies, confirms that, contrary to folklore, it is the rich who are happy, not the poor and honest. When rich people retire to the washroom to vomit during a banquet, it is a sign of good breeding. Suspected of conspiring to steal a gold statue of the Bambino di Praga, Ditie is sacked, but "I was always lucky in my bad luck."

His next job is at the beautiful Hotel Paris, where he is taken up by the headwaiter, Mr. Skřivánek, a person who knows everything, who can virtually read minds, simply because once (he explains) he served the King of England. Old gentlemen hold voyeuristic sessions in the hotel, sipping champagne and studying connoisseur-like the folds and curves of a young female body; and it is left to Ditie to finish the job after they have left. Once a week, for those few minutes, he would feel "tall and handsome and curly-haired."

But the great event at the Hotel Paris is a state banquet given for the Emperor of Ethiopia and his entourage, held there because only the hotel has sufficient gold cutlery for three hundred guests. The Emperor's cooks prepare a native specialty: hard-boiled eggs and stuffing and fish are placed inside twenty half-roasted turkeys, the turkeys inside two antelopes (acquired from the zoo), the antelopes inside a barbecued camel, and then the whole is basted with mint leaves dipped in beer. The dish is so carved that in every portion there is a slice of camel and antelope and turkey and fish and stuffing and hard-boiled egg. Noticing that the Emperor has no wine, Ditie kneels to him and fills his glass, for which he is rewarded with a medal and a blue sash "for service rendered to the throne of the Emperor of Ethiopia."

Ditie's happiness is shattered when he is suspected of having stolen one of the gold spoons. He rushes off into the woods to hang himself, stumbles in the dark against the pendent body of someone who has already hanged himself, faints, and is rescued by the all-knowing headwaiter. The missing spoon has been found halfway down the drain of the kitchen sink. Unmistakably a fairy-tale denouement. But when he falls unpatriotically in love with a Sudeten German girl, Lise, he is fired in earnest.

This stands him in good stead when the German army arrives, and his next job is serving milk to young females and wine to young males at an establishment run by the Bureau for Racial Purity, a "breeding station" for a refined and noble human race, by means of "no-nonsense intercourse, as the old Teutons used to do it." Ditie's reputation there is as high as was Mr. Skřivánek's in the Hotel Paris, perhaps higher, since to have served the Emperor of Ethiopia would probably outrank having served the King of England. Ditie is regrettably undersized, but he can claim a conceivably Teutonic grandfather, and at least has blond hair. Hence the Good Waiter Ditie is permitted to marry Lise, who is now an officer in the nursing corps and a high-ranking member of the party. "With a mighty thumping of rubber stamps I was given a marriage license, while Czech patriots, with the same thumping of the same rubber stamps, were sentenced to death." The testing of his semen is related with what may be considered an appropriate lack of taste. Appropriate also, no doubt, is the fact that from the couple's regulated and unenjoyable acts of "National Socialist intercourse" the only issue is a cretinous child christened Siegfried.

It is another instance of being lucky in his bad luck that Ditie should be arrested in error by the SS, beaten up, and thrown into prison just as the war is coming to an end. His battered face declares him an anti-Nazi fighter, although as an undeniable sexual collaborator he gets a six-months' jail sentence.

Lise is killed in an air raid, but Ditie recovers the suitcase she has packed with valuable stamps, once Jewish property. With the proceeds he buys an abandoned quarry outside Prague, and builds himself a unique "landscaped" hotel there, visited by such celebrities as John Steinbeck (who tries unsuccessfully to buy it) and Maurice Chevalier. As he intended, he has become a millionaire. In 1948 the new regime confiscates the hotel, all property rights having devolved to the people, and there follows a hilarious episode in an easygoing internment camp (earlier a Catholic seminary) for former millionaires, who are supposed to serve one year for every million they have made, and who look down on Ditie as not a proper, prewar millionaire but a wartime profiteer. Hearing that the camp is to be shut down, the inmates arrange a last supper. The circle begins to close: Ditie puts on his tuxedo, and the medal and the blue sash, and waits on them, but there is no joy in it, and guests and guards alike end by gazing at a painting of the Last Supper and then kneeling in the chapel.

Facing a choice between going to prison and joining a labor brigade, Ditie takes up his last job, mending a remote road in the mountains that nobody uses. He settles in an abandoned inn, together with his friends or "guests," a cat, a goat, and a horse, and meditates on death and eternity. The brook in which he washes his face tells him that years from now "somebody somewhere will wash his face in me," just as someone somewhere will strike a match made from the phosphorus of his body. Whatever traces of irony still linger quickly fade away, and out of the book for good. First the fun and games, and then self-arraignment, repentance (not too strenuous), and spiritual rebirth.

To maintain the country road is to maintain his own weed-infested life, to open up his past, the past life which now "seemed to have happened to someone else." Given strength by the Emperor's medal, he sits down in the evenings to write out his story, this largely and surprisingly humorous European *Bildungsroman* or, as he puts it, "this story of how the unbelievable came true." (p. 37)

D. J. Enright, "Czech Mates," in The New York Review of Books, *Vol. XXXVI, No. 8, May 18, 1989, pp. 37-9.*

E. J. Czerwinski

Best known in the United States for the film based on his 1965 novel ***Ostře sledované vlaky*** (Eng. ***Closely Watched Trains***), Bohumil Hrabal is revered in his country for his ability to conjure up worlds for his heroes and heroines that seem in fact more real and much cozier than the inescapable normal world his readers inhabit. He has developed an easily recognizable "Hrabalian" style that owes little to any other writer: it is personal, dense, poetic, folkish, psychologically uncomplicated, bordering on fantasy. He manages to charm us with simple things: nature, love, friendship, the unreturnable past, memories, faded dreams, and lost hope.

In *Svatby v domě* (Weddings in the House) Hrabal tells his story from a woman's point of view, an attempt fraught with danger for any male author. Not for this septuagenarian, however, who manages to capture the fear and timidity of a young woman engaged to be married to a doctor and whose first fiancé "had run off just before their wedding to marry someone else." Hrabal evokes the young bride's disillusionment and newfound happiness so delicately and unobtrusively that we forget it is he who is telling the story.

"Weddings" is a poem in prose. The story is as old as man, but the novel has a freshness and originality that only emphasizes its modernity. Not cosmopolitan like Kundera nor as worldly as Škvorecký, Hrabal is nonetheless their literary equal. His vision of the world is as panoramic as that of his compatriot Arnošt Lustig, but it has absolutely none of the pessimism. He tells it as he sees it: man has an infinite capacity to overcome and go on living.

There is no reason *Svatby v domě* should be barred from publication in Czechoslovakia. In fact, it deserves to be translated into every language. We must hear more from Bohumil Hrabal. Anyone who can write a passage such as the following belongs on every bookshelf: "I knelt before him and began washing his feet, one after the other; all at once, I understood that in fact this washing of a foot, this in fact was the most beautiful thing between us, that he humbled himself before me, just as I had humbled myself before him." And one humbles oneself before Hrabal's talent. (pp. 129-30)

> *E. J. Czerwinski, in a review of "Svatby v domě," in* World Literature Today, *Vol. 63, No. 1, Winter, 1989, pp. 129-30.*

"Among [Czechoslovakian] writers what is unique about Hrabal is his capacity for joy."

—Milan Kundera, 1986

Publishers Weekly

One of Czechoslovakia's most popular authors, Hrabal (*I Served the King of England*) was never a dissident, nor are his books polemics; he is noted for his visceral, fabulistic prose and bizarre sense of humor. Hanta, the narrator of [*Too Loud a Solitude*], this absorbing novella, is a gentle alcoholic who has spent 35 years compacting wastepaper. In his messy, subterranean world, the refuse of human life accumulates: bloody butcher paper, office correspondence, yellowed newspapers and, most importantly, books. Able to quote Kant, Goethe and Seneca, he is both

"artist and audience" as he destroys or selects for his own enjoyment the printed matter others have discarded. Hanta's unusual occupation—in a country which until recently suffered severe literary censorship—is an ironic backdrop as he reflects on the women he has loved or imaginary encounters between historical figures such as Jesus Christ and Lao-tze. This fable about the modern-day equivalent of book-burning, although a showcase for Hrabal's dazzling writing talent, often slides into parody, under the weight of its obtrusive morality.

> *A review of "Too Loud A Solitude," in* Publishers Weekly, *Vol. 237, No. 30, July 27, 1990, p. 222.*

Arthur Allen and Margaret Talbot

The allegorical quality of *Too Loud a Solitude* jumps out at you on the first page: "For thirty-five years I've been compacting wastepaper and books, smearing myself with letters until I've come to look like my encyclopedias—and a good three tons of them I've compacted over the years." The novel was written in the early '70s, so presumably this most popular of Czech writers is referring to the destruction of Czech culture since 1938, the year the Great Powers gave Hitler the Sudetenland. "Inquisitors burn books in vain," he writes. "If a book has anything to say, it burns with a quiet laugh, because any book worth its salt points up and out of itself." This too is the kind of hopeful utterance one expects (expected?) from a persecuted Central European writer. The formula is all very neat and familiar—except that Hrabal actually worked as a scrap-paper compactor and seems to have enjoyed it. Like the Cold War, *Too Loud a Solitude* is an allegory that gets unexpectedly complicated.

As an editor at a Prague publishing house in the '50s, Josef Skvorecky brought his obsolete galley proofs to a basement where Hrabal, in grubby overalls, would examine them with interest then, according to Skvorecky, "launch into fluid discussions of literature." Hant'a, the narrator of *Too Loud a Solitude,* is a similar compound of high and low culture. Happily pulping everything from butcher paper to Goethe, he considers his job a vocation. The harangues of his overbearing boss each time Hant'a stops the compactor to "rescue" a worthy book, the screams of the barmaid when a mouse jumps out of his sleeve, and the gypsy girls who blithely pull up their skirts in exchange for a slice of bread make the book pleasantly picturesque. But Hant'a's ruminations on waste disposal—between swigs of beer and amid swarms of flesh flies—are intricate and cerebral. Jesus and Lao-tze become the personifications of the great life forces of the universe, "Jesus as a romantic, Lao-tze as a classicist, Jesus as the flow, Lao-tze as the ebb . . . Jesus as the embodiment of love for one's neighbor, Lao-tze as the height of emptiness." Hant'a seems to favor the way of Lao-tze, seeing his "regressus ad originem" in the great works that he returns to their compacted essences. This battle between love and emptiness is also present in the frighteningly comic tale of the "great rodent war over the rights to all the refuse and fecal matter," which Hant'a learns about from friends who are "former members of our Academy of Sciences who have been set to work in the sewers."

So the narrator goes, reflectively grinding paper into neat bales of pulp. But then he learns of a new pulping *factory,* where the workers—a Brigade of Socialist Labor—wear "orange and baby-blue gloves and yellow American baseball caps," and a machine compacts whole runs of books with monstrous efficiency, "the entire printing of a book going straight into the pulper before a single page could be sullied by the human eye, brain, or heart. . . . Then I knew the good old days had come to an end, the days when a worker shoveled in his own wastepaper, went down on his knees in one-on-one combat." After he's fired by his modernizing boss, Hant'a commits suicide by throwing himself into the compactor.

Many of the themes here are recognizable from the annals of Central European literature: a snubbing of petty officialdom worthy of Hasek and Kafka; a curious blend of spun-sugar fabulism and bathroom humor that might thrive in the medieval beerhalls of Prague. Like Kundera, Hrabal deploys sexuality self-consciously and from an overwhelmingly male point of view. Sex is the chaotic life force that burbles beneath the surface of repressed societies. Unlike Kundera, Hrabal finds all this frantic coupling relentlessly funny. His novel *Closely Watched Trains* was a '60s hit in Czechoslovakia not because of its political defiance (though pacifist and anti-heroic, it's a tale of resistance to the Nazis), but because its bawdy sexuality burst through the Victorian dictates of Socialist Realism.

Other motifs in *Too Loud a Solitude* seem like Hrabal's special domain. Hant'a, for example, is no brown-shirted book-burner but an eccentric autodidact. For him, destruction is an act of revelation. The books he will salvage "shine forth" from the maw of the hydraulic press "just as a beautiful fish will occasionally sparkle in the waters of a polluted river that runs through a stretch of factories."

At the least, Hrabal's work is a vaccination against the tendency to read all recent literature from "the other Europe" as one-dimensional allegory for communist dictatorship. What he accomplishes *beyond* that is hard to say. His books are like hard nuggets of compacted culture—untranslatable jokes, national nightmares—and they can be indigestible for the non-Czech reader. Czechs refer to his distinctive language—heavily larded, apparently, with down-and-dirty vernacular speech—as "Hrabalovstina." In the end, Hrabal's sensibility, with its peculiar amalgam of whimsy and misanthropy, may be even more resistant to translation than his prose.

> *Arthur Allen and Margaret Talbot, in a review of "Too Loud a Solitude," in* VLS, *No. 89, October, 1990, p. 8.*

John A. Glusman

"There's this tradition in Czech literature," said Czech emigre novelist Josef Skvorecky, "that books are sacred." Sadly, the political systems that have dominated Czechoslovakia for most of its history—Nazism from 1939-1945 and Communism from 1948-1989—showed little respect for that tradition. Books considered antithetical to the authorities were burned, banned and censored. If they survived intact, it was only underground, where they circulated in samizdat form. Kafka wasn't even published until the late 1950s, and Jaroslav Seifert's Nobel Prize acceptance speech couldn't appear at all in his native land. Authors were harassed if not imprisoned, and many—like Vaclav Havel, who worked in a brewery—were relegated to the most menial of jobs. As Bohumil Hrabal, author of the novel *I Served the King of England* and the . . . story *Ostre sledovane vlaky* which inspired the film *Closely Watched Trains* put it: It was a world in which "the unbelievable became true."

In many ways the hero of Hrabal's comic yet affecting novella, *Too Loud a Solitude,* embodies the conflicts waged between the official state culture and the alternative, or "second culture" as the underground was called in Czechoslovakia.

Hanta is a man who loves books, but whose job for the past 35 years as a paper-compactor has been to destroy them. No ordinary garbage man, he's an articulate, beer-swilling bibliophile who salvages classics from the trash-heap of history. "I pop a beautiful sentence into my mouth and suck it like a fruit-drop," he confesses, saving for himself those rare tomes that catch his eye: Homer, Erasmus, Kant, Hegel, Schiller and Goethe. Indeed, his house groans under the weight of thousands of books, "weighing down on me," Hrabal writes as if parodying Harold Bloom and *The Anxiety of Influence,* "like a two-ton nightmare."

Hanta may be alone and on the last rung of the social ladder (he imagines sewer-rat wars being fought in a kind of dialectical frenzy just beneath his feet) but he's far from lonely. He has his bottle, which induces visions of the future; the company of hundreds of cellar-mice, for whom old paper is "like a well-aged cheese"; and occasional visitations from Lao-tze and Jesus. One of Prague's "fallen angels," he reads books "in the blissful hope of making a change" in his life.

It was World War II that turned Hanta's head, made him understand, like his forerunner Ditie in *I Served the King of England,* "the beauty of destruction." Under Nazism lives were discarded as casually as Hanta tosses a copy of Nietzsche's *Ecce Homo* into his basement bellows. "Not until we are totally crushed," he says with morbid prescience, "do we show what we are made of."

Inevitably Hanta, who shares Kant's wonder at "the starry firmament above me and the moral law within," becomes an anachronism in a society run by the new socialist machine. Just five years from retirement, he's superseded by a giant compactor operated by the Brigade of Socialist Labor, which "piled books to the brim before a single page could be sullied by the human eye, brain or heart . . . It was inhuman, this work they were doing."

The author of his own solitude, Hanta refuses to lose his paper-strewn paradise to the soulless efficiency of the State, and chooses, like Socrates and Seneca before, to close the book, so to speak, on his own life.

Written in 1975, *Too Loud a Solitude* was immediately seen as a thinly veiled critique of the current regime. In fact, the character of Hanta is based partly on Hrabal's own experiences as a trash compactor in the mid-1950s. While Hrabal's prognosis for Czechoslovakia is understandably grim, it's a measure of his talent that *Too Loud a Solitude* transcends its historical context to assume universal significance. Not until Czechoslovakia's "velvet revolution" of 1989, when, to borrow Hrabal's phrase, "the unbelievable" again "became true," was *Too Loud a Solitude* finally published in unexpurgated form.

Ultimately, *Too Loud a Solitude* is concerned with literature as a humanizing influence and the role of both tradition and individual talent in upholding the freedom of discourse that forms the foundation of every democracy. With the playful imagination of Chagall and a delight in the absurd that recalls Gunther Grass, Hrabal has fashioned a wise, witty and wistful tale that lives up to Hanta's own dictum: "Any book worth its salt points up and out of itself." (pp. 8-9)

> *John A. Glusman, "Czech Bookman's Progress," in* Book World—The Washington Post, *October 21, 1990, pp. 8-9.*

The New Yorker

For thirty-five years Haňt'a, [the protagonist of *Too Loud a Solitude*], has been compacting trash in a cellar in Prague, the beneficiary of what he calls an "unwitting education": he has rescued thousands of valuable books from the jaws of the hydraulic press. His thoughts are full of Kant and Hegel as he assembles bales of waste, always on the lookout for more literature, surrounded by rowdy mice and swilling pitchers of beer. He is interrupted now and then by his crotchety, abusive boss, by two sexy gypsy girls who come bearing loads of trash on their backs, and by a nervous philosophy professor who relies on him for reading material. Haňt'a's dreary but book-rich routine goes awry when he is suddenly replaced by two strapping young men from the Brigade of Socialist Labor, who guzzle milk as they toss both wastepaper and rare books into the press with disinterested, cheerful efficiency. [Hrabal's] tale of Haňt'a's "farewell to small joys," which dates from the seventies, remains lighthearted even as it contends with serious matters like the ills of Communism and the rewards of intellectual freedom, and it offers a nimble answer to the chicken-and-egg question of which comes first, the text or the reader.

> *A review of "Too Loud a Solitude," in* The New Yorker, *Vol. LXVI, No. 36, October 22, 1990, p. 143.*

Sven Birkerts

The reader making a first approach to Bohumil Hrabal's *Too Loud a Solitude* has every reason to be looking for the scarlet "a" of allegory. After all, Mr. Hrabal is a Czechoslovak, the book was first published 14 years ago, when no one could have foreseen the 1989 revolution, and the premise is that this is the account of a man who makes his

wages crushing printed matter into bales for recycling. We expect Man versus State, letterpress versus hydraulic, and so on.

The novel turns out to be almost nothing of the sort. And indeed, anyone familiar with the dark and obliquely humorous imagination of Mr. Hrabal, the author of *Closely Watched Trains* and *I Served the King of England,* will know that he could no more bear the predictability of such a formula than he could stomach the inane conformism demanded by a socialist bureaucracy. *Too Loud a Solitude* is an irresistibly eccentric romp, quick with the heart's life and about as schematic as a drunken night on the town.

Mr. Hrabal's narrator, Hanta, may appear to be one of Turgenev's "superfluous" men, but in his thoughts and passions he is a giant. He is a conflagration on legs, so full of rancor and love that the page can scarcely hold him. Nor does Mr. Hrabal give him much of a plot to inhabit. The voice is all, and so long as we listen we are inside a world unlike anything we could conjure for ourselves.

Hanta is a career man, a flunky who for 35 years has worked a big compressing machine in a basement thick with flies and alive with the skittering of rodent populations. He drinks copious quantities of beer, in part so that he can bear his load, but also to lubricate his visionary faculties. For Hanta is a thinker, a tragic seer, a brother to the tippling Chinese mystics of old. He cannot shift a buttock without engaging some new notion or discovering some cosmological resonance. He is forever reading—stealing moments on the job and carting home pilfered volumes. His private joke with the universe is that he sanctifies every bale he makes either by plastering the outside with some artistic reproduction or by concealing in its innards an open volume of Kant, Erasmus or another of his favorites.

And what does he think? *How* does he think? Here is Hanta on the devastation of great libraries:

> I had begun to understand the beauty of destruction, and I loaded more and more freight cars, and more and more trains left the station heading west at one crown per kilogram, and as I stood there staring after the red lantern hanging from the last car, as I stood there leaning on a lamppost like Leonardo da Vinci, who stood leaning on a column and looking on while French soldiers used his statue for target practice, shooting away horse and rider bit by bit, I thought how Leonardo, like me, standing and witnessing such horrors with complete composure, had realized even then that neither the heavens are humane nor is any man with a head on his shoulders.

And here he ponders Jesus and Lao-tze, who appear before him in his basement:

> "I saw Jesus as a playboy and Lao-tze as an old gland-abandoned bachelor; I saw Jesus raising an imperious arm to damn his enemies and Lao-tze lowering his arms like broken wings; I saw Jesus as a romantic, Lao-tze as a classicist, Jesus as the flow, Lao-tze as the ebb . . . Jesus as *progressus ad futurum,* Lao-tze as *regressus ad originem.*"

Michael Henry Heim's translation seems expert, but what is true of most translated works is doubly true with Bohumil Hrabal: you really have to *be* there, inside the world of the book, to get the full effect.

Late in the novel Hanta pays a visit to a new compacting plant and sees an enormous apparatus staffed by teams of bronzed young workers. He watches whole printings of books pass straight from press to pulper with no one even batting an eye: "No, they just went on working, pulling covers off books and tossing the bristling, horrified pages on the conveyor belt with the utmost calm and indifference."

To Hanta, a man of the old dispensation, this is the *coup de grâce,* the end of life as he cares to struggle with it. Soon after, he will act upon this recognition.

The close of this short novel does carry a certain allegorical burden. But the equivalences are so immediate and so relevant—not just for Czechoslovaks, but for all of us—that we make them without exertion. This is what life will look like when the circuit breakers of the printed word no longer impede the larger, necessarily more impersonal circulation of social energy. Mr. Hrabal's is a cry of expiring humanism, and *Too Loud a Solitude* is a book to salvage from the deadly indifference that is more effective in killing the letter than the most sophisticated compacting machine.

> *Sven Birkerts, "Books into Trash," in* The New York Times Book Review, *December 9, 1990, p. 11.*

John Banville

Once upon a time novelists, especially American novelists, liked to list on the backs of their books the various jobs—lumberjack, soda jerk, chucker-out at a brothel, etc.—they had held in the days before success and creative-writing fellowships came their way. Such a list was the sign of a hard apprenticeship served in the real world, the badge of manliness—of authenticity. Yet when we read on the back flap of *Too Loud a Solitude* that Bohumil Hrabal, having been conferred with a degree in law, "worked as a stagehand, postman, clerk, and baler of waste paper," we are fired with indignation.

The circumstances, of course, are different. It is unlikely that Hrabal willingly took all of these jobs. We know from recent history, and indeed from novels (in *The Unbearable Lightness of Being* the brain surgeon is compelled to become a window cleaner), how these things are, or were, in the East. It is a bitter irony that in a so-called socialist state such as Czechoslovakia, work was used by the authorities as a means of punishing and humiliating a fractious intelligentsia.

Bohumil Hrabal was born in 1914. He is the author of the novel *Closely Watched Trains,* which may be better remembered for the fine film that was based on it. *I Served the King of England,* a sort of updated *Felix Krull,* appeared in English last year. A translation of a censored version of *Too Loud a Solitude* was published in the US in 1986; now, in this excellent version by Michael Henry

---

> **An excerpt from the *samidzat* version of Hrabal's autobiography, *Kdo jsem***
>
> My literature and my texts are nothing other than my own remembrance of things past; the search overwhelms me, but at the same time, it amuses me; in my texts, I put much emphasis on entertainment, on how entertained I am by the difficulty of this quest. All my slowness is unintentional; I do not try to write what I know, but to reach what I do not know; so I am not yet doing what I want to do, but what I do not want; it is necessary, I know, to piss in the wind, to be burnt by what cannot be extinguished. I am standing before my tribunal, and my internal trial is a great inquisition; it is simultaneously an indictment and a defense; I am both my prosecutor and defense attorney. My manner of writing bears within itself the premature crossing of parallel lines, the interrupting of my own conversations, because it is impossible to go forward in a mechanical way; I can move forward only by the interjection of outside events into the internal monologue. In this manner, my writing is my path, day after day, month after month, year after year, but not *ad infinitum*—only to keep me in a state of creative tension up to the moment when as the last hour dawns I will perhaps receive the check, my bill, in this gigantic tavern which this world is for me. Up to now, the innkeeper has let me run up my tab; I am living on credit; all of my expenses are inscribed in the frame of the open door through which I observe the wondrously beautiful world; I transcribe from it only what I believe to be my extenuating circumstances; although I realize, all too well, that I am fooling myself, that what I think might reduce my guilt for living will get me, will nail me, and will establish my total culpability . . . In the meantime, my writing is my punishment for wandering between crime and innocence, for constantly postponing the final judgment and settlement of accounts, for becoming, at least partially, what I have always wanted to be, an accursed poet. Now, at my trial, I subpoena what lies deep in my non-consciousness; I am horrified at myself; aware of my past, I wring my hands over myself; I cannot grant myself absolution; I am courageous at least in that I proffer, by and in my texts, my feelings of guilt. At the same time, I am cracking a smile. It is my gallows humor . . . my Prague irony.

Heim, we have the full text. The book is easier to follow than *New World Avenue,* yet also more mysterious. The protagonist, Haňt'a, has, as he tells us repeatedly, at the opening of almost every chapter, been a compacter of waste paper for thirty-five years. A whole culture, it seems, has come and gone between the grinding jaws of his hydraulic press.

> I see heaven-sent horns of plenty in the form of bags, crates, and boxes raining down their old paper, withered flower-shop stalks, wholesalers' wrappings, out-of-date theater programs, ice-cream wrappers, sheets of paint-spattered wallpaper, piles of moist, bloody paper from the butchers', razor-sharp rejects from photographers' studios, insides of office wastepaper baskets, typewriter ribbons included, bouquets from birthdays and namedays long past.

This is indeed Franz Kafka's Prague.

Along with the city's detritus there falls into Haňt'a's basement a flood of books, books of all kinds.

> In the flow of old paper the spine of a rare book will occasionally shine forth, and if for a moment I turn away, dazzled, I always turn back in time to rescue it, and after wiping it off on my apron, opening it up wide, and breathing in its print, I glue my eyes to the text and read out the first sentence like a Homeric prophecy. . . .

As we would expect, therefore, Haňt'a's story is peppered with quotations from the mighty dead: "My education has been so unwitting I can't quite tell which of my thoughts come from me and which from my books. . . ." So it is that Kant and Hegel, Jesus and Lao-tse pop up on every other page. The method is not as heavy-handed as it might have been, thanks mainly to Hrabal's refusal to take it all too seriously—or too solemnly, at least. The book is funny, in its desperate, knockabout way. Along with Haňt'a's incessant reading goes excessive swilling of beer, and the tone throughout is at once strident and woozy, so that the reader has the impression of being trapped in that basement room as the press grinds and the drunken operator rummages through the tatters of a ruined culture.

Hrabal did his stint as a dissident in the black days of the 1950s and 1960s. There is detectable in the frantic, breakneck pace of *Too Loud a Solitude* a sense of the predicament of a man caught between two worlds, between light and dark, the street and the basement, speech and silence. Toward the close of the book the public world invades his lair:

> That morning when I got to work, who should I find in the courtyard but two of the Socialist Labor youngsters in their orange gloves, nipple-high blue overalls, suspenders, green turtle-necks, and yellow baseball caps, as if on the way to a game. My boss took them triumphantly down to my cellar and showed them my press, and in no time flat they had covered my table with a sheet of clean paper for their milk and made themselves at home, while I just stood there humiliated, stressed and strained, knowing all at once, knowing body and soul, that I'd never be able to adapt. . . .

Haňt'a is to be relieved of his job and sent to the Melantrich Printing Works, where "I, who couldn't live without the prospect of rescuing a beautiful book from the odious waste, I would be compacting immaculate, inhumanly clean paper!" The prospect is too terrible, too arid, and he determines that instead of going to Melantrich he will follow the example of Seneca and Socrates "and here, in my press, in my cellar, choose my own fall, which is ascension."

> A corner of the book is lodged under a rib, I groan, fated to leave the ultimate truth on a rack of my own making, folded in upon myself like a child's pocket knife. . . .

However, despite these hints of a great theme lurking beneath the surface of Haňt'a's story, *Too Loud a Solitude* seems to me chiefly an allegory, conscious or not, of the writing life. Haňt'a in his dark pit compacting the world's

words into manageable bales, his head buzzed about by flies and sonorous phrases, is a splendid and oddly convincing picture of the literary artist frantically at work.

> I pushed my twin beds together and rigged a kind of canopy of planks over them, ceiling high, for the two additional tons of books I've carried home over the years, and when I fall asleep I've got all those books weighing down on me like a two-ton nightmare.

Yes indeed. (pp. 15-16)

John Banville, "Laughter in the Dark," in The New York Review of Books, *Vol. XXXVIII, No. 4, February 14, 1991, pp. 14-17.*

James Naughton

We still have some catching up to do on the best of Bohumil Hrabal. **I Served the King of England** made it to England in 1989, but a French edition existed in 1981. The Czech original of **Too Loud a Solitude** dates from 1976, **Une trop bruyante solitude** was published in Paris in 1983, and this version first appeared in the American annual journal *Cross Currents* in 1986.

Haňt'a, the *Ich*-narrator of this tightly packed but lyrically expansive novella, presses refuse paper and books in a cellar, drinking beer to lubricate his consumption of *livres trouvés*. The press and its bales form a metaphorical leitmotif for the book, which is hard to encapsulate. Haňt'a's job demands to be read as régime-enforced book-burning, but books and heads, says Haňt'a, are destroyed in vain: ideas come from without. Destruction, moreover, is intrinsic to the world: the heavens are not humane, nor is the mind. A tender butcher, Haňt'a terms himself, whom books have taught the joys of devastation. His brain, the mind, is its own compact bale, populated by ideas, images and literate culture, educated involuntarily on this flotsam, infused with Infinity and Eternity, Kant, Hegel, Jesus, Lao-tze, and living in this too loud a solitude.

Like Leonardo da Vinci who watched as soldiers shot up his statue, the narrator watches libraries go in waggons to oblivion. His mother dies, is cremated, her bones ground on a mill: crushing books, he hears the crunch of bones. His bales are art-works, wrapped perhaps in a Rembrandt self-portrait, man on the brink of eternity. Mice perish in the press, and cruelty and tenderness are compacted with typical Hrabalesque comic horror. At home, books pile up over the bed in tons, a sword of Damocles menacing with nemesis. Haňt'a plans to make art-bales in his retirement, just like his uncle, who plays with a signal-box and steam-engine in his orchard.

In cellar boiler-rooms, or sewers, outcast donnish figures are employed; a Hegelian struggle of rats rages down in the sewers, an eternal conflict of forces, atoms, dialectic of history. Haňt'a, too, is rat-like and sordid: he revisits the womb of time, as a clean smart youth, at a dance with a girl, Manča, who got shit from the lavatory on her dangling ribbons, and later a turd on her ski. While processing blood-soaked paper, thronging with meat flies, he sees Jesus, youthful, ever-ascending, in a *progressus ad fu-*

turum, and Lao-tze, the old man, resigned, descending along the Tao, in a *regressus ad originem.* The world goes to and fro, like the walls of his press, with its green and red on-off buttons, like the dresses of the two gypsy girls who visit him (from one of whom he refuses sex).

In the novel, all these themes start to intermingle, in shifting, dreamlike metamorphoses. When his uncle died, he was left to decay for a fortnight and Haňt'a made an oozy bale out of him, adorned with scrap metal. At night he dreams of a tiny gypsy girl who slept with him long ago. They flew a kite, sending a paper message on the twine, a quasi-message to God. Then the girl disappeared—sent by the Gestapo to her death; he recalls the cheering faces seen in piles of Nazi brochures. But human compassion and love are something more than inhumane heaven.

A gigantic new press has opened. Clean, milk-imbibing Socialist workers in yellow baseball caps merrily engage in mass-destruction, eager visiting schoolchildren too. Manča, a non-reader, has found a sculptor to create her art-apotheosis, as a white angel, while Haňt'a is losing his job. He sees an Apocalyptic Press crushing Prague and himself into a puny bale, and Seneca, author of *De tranquillitate animi,* slashing his wrist in his bath. Drunk on black beer, Haňt'a, Seneca-like, chooses suicide in his own press. The final truth extorted on his own rack is a vision of the gypsy girl and kite; he, become the kite, reads her forgotten name on the paper message.

It is important to note, however, that both printed Czech versions of **Too Loud a Solitude** (Cologne 1980 and Prague 1989) have a different ending from this one. Haňt'a's face is on the message. He cries out, from his Paradise garden, and is accosted by the two gypsy girls, who go off with their two men, creating an open, back-to-earth

closure. Otherwise, the translation is eminently idiomatic, neat and rhythmically adroit, though no one will match the gritty, gripping, boundless verve of Hrabal's own idiom. What sort of close fidelity should the reader expect? The water "both magic and plain" is really "living and dead"; "Aladdin's lamp" is "Cinderella's nutshell" (with her finery packed inside); "karma" is basically a gas water-heater. But here I quibble and fiddle, while only meaning to advocate, in a nutshell, some more quintessential Hrabal.

James Naughton, "Burning the Books," in The Times Literary Supplement, No. 4591, March 29, 1991, p. 19.

FURTHER READING

Heim, Michael. "Review of *La petite ville où le temps s'arrêta.*" *World Literature Today* 60, No. 4 (Autumn 1986): 654-5.

>   Examines the political and artistic implications of the French edition of Hrabal's autobiography.

Thomas, Alfred. "Closely Observed Selves." *Times Literary Supplement,* No. 4573 (23-29 November 1990): 1272.

>   Positive review of the 1990 edition of *The Death of Mr. Baltisberger.*

Robert Jay Lifton

1926-

American psychiatrist, nonfiction writer, essayist, critic, and editor.

Considered one of the pioneers of "psychohistory," Lifton is best known for his studies of the Holocaust, the Chinese Cultural Revolution, and the Vietnam War. Psychohistory, an interdisciplinary study that applies psychological methodology to the interpretation of significant world events, originated with psychologist Erik Erikson. Lifton expanded the theory by concentrating on how historical processes influence individuals rather than on the motivations of aggrandized historical figures. Defining such concepts as "psychic numbing," "Proteanism," and "doubling," Lifton integrates rigorous scientific research with ethical ideology in order to understand humankind's most destructive behaviors. While admitting his work is "grim and often painful," Lifton believes in the significance of his studies: "[If] you're to be a genuinely moral or spiritual person, you have to be able to imagine evil, because evil is real in our world. . . . I think we can extricate ourselves from that evil only by first allowing our imaginations to take it in so that we can then transcend it by wise decisions."

Lifton began his psychological research in Korea, where as a United States Air Force psychiatrist he studied former prisoners of war upon their release from captivity. According to Lifton, these soldiers often seemed "dazed, lacked spontaneity, [and] spoke in a dull monotonous tone with markedly decreased affectivity." This observation led Lifton to develop the concept of "psychic numbing," a reaction to severe threat that results in loss of feeling and decreased sensitivity. Describing this phenomenon as "affective anesthesia," Lifton asserts it is a means by which to "protect oneself from death and from inner death." Lifton elaborates this theory in *Thought Reform and the Psychology of Totalism: A Study of "Brainwashing" in China,* a compilation of interviews with Western missionaries, doctors, teachers, and businessmen who had been incarcerated for two to three years in China during the 1966-68 Cultural Revolution. In this work, Lifton investigates how the people's desire for an omnipotent leader can make them vulnerable to "brainwashing" propaganda. Studying political issues in Asia inspired Lifton to delve into the psychological consequences of the atomic bombing of Hiroshima, which Lifton describes as "history's greatest single act of man-made destruction." Very few scholars had attempted to study the effect of this event upon the people involved. *Death in Life: Survivors of Hiroshima,* winner of the 1969 National Book Award, is a comprehensive analysis of interviews with seventy-five *hibakusha* ("explosion-affected persons") who survived Hiroshima. In this work Lifton explores the survivors' sense of "death guilt" over the fact that they lived while so many others died and provides psychological insights into the destruction caused by nuclear weaponry.

With *Revolutionary Immortality: Mao Tse-Tung and the Chinese Cultural Revolution,* a study of the causes and strategies of China's Cultural Revolution, Lifton offers a unique conceptual framework for understanding the paranoia and urgency associated with revolutionary ideologies. A study of both Mao Tse-Tung and mass psychology, *Revolutionary Immortality* explains how the fear of death and desire for immortality can influence humanity's behavior. *History and Human Survival* and *Home from the War: Vietnam Veterans—Neither Victims nor Executioners* also examine the implications of death and war. A collection of sixteen essays, *History and Human Survival* comprises four sections that explore such topics as the contradictions of war, psychological differences between men and women, and how people survive catastrophic events. Although Lifton addresses theoretical aspects of war in this volume, he had not analyzed the effects of armed conflict on individuals until *Home from the War,* a study of Vietnam veterans who met weekly with the author for two and a half years. Drawing upon conversations with more than 350 veterans, Lifton chronicles such differing reactions to the Vietnam War as drug addiction, low self-esteem, and idealization of the military. While critics accused Lifton of presenting a simplistic view of conflict due to his lack of combat experience, most concurred that *Home from the War* addresses America's guilt over Vietnam and deconstructs the myths of war.

Lifton departs from his focus on specific world events with *Living and Dying, The Life of the Self: Toward a New Psychology,* and *The Broken Connection: On Death and the Continuity of Life.* In these works he examines how people adjust to death and aggression, and how they in turn create a sense of continuity in a disordered world. *Living and Dying,* written primarily for young adults, provides an accessible and realistic study of loss by comparing death with the termination of childhood and the beginning of adulthood. Lifton states: "[Adolescence is] itself a death and rebirth experience." In *The Life of the Self,* Lifton introduces his concept of "Proteanism," a response to rapid social change that emphasizes transition, acceptance, and rejuvenation. Taking the name from the Greek god Proteus, who was capable of changing forms, Lifton uses his idea of Proteanism to propose a new psychological paradigm that combines Sigmund Freud's studies of instinct and defense mechanisms with Erik Erikson's theories of identity formation.

Lifton studies the moral, social, and psychological implications of genocide in *The Nazi Doctors: Medical Killing and the Psychology of Genocide,* a book which attempts to understand why doctors assumed such a vital role in the Holocaust. Based on ten years of research and extensive interviews with eighty former concentration camp prisoners and twenty-eight Nazi doctors, this work traces the historical development of euthanasia from its beginnings as a method of "treatment" for retarded persons to a philosophical justification for the annihilation of Jews. Lifton identifies *The Permission to Destroy Life Unworthy of Life,* a work published in 1920 by two distinguished German professors, as a crucial theoretical argument used by Nazis to later support their program of genocide, and attempts to explain how the Nazi doctors could equate mass killing and gruesome medical experimentation with healing and renewal. Lifton uses the term "doubling" to elucidate the doctors' ability to separate their personal and professional lives and therefore distance themselves from the implications of their behavior. Although critics agreed that *The Nazi Doctors* was a much-needed inquiry into the psychological factors of the Holocaust, they also suggested that by studying the motivations of the doctors Lifton was attempting to exonerate them of their actions. Admitting that "I was by no means without fear of what I was getting into," Lifton nonetheless maintains that "we do the victims of the Holocaust most honor by learning what we can from it that it might serve the future." In *The Genocidal Mentality: Nazi Holocaust and Nuclear Threat,* coauthored with Eric Markusen, Lifton further explores the ramifications of his concept of "doubling" by linking Nazism with nuclear genocide. Defining nuclearism as "an exaggerated dependency on nuclear weapons for strength, protection, and safety," the authors state that people have been able to passively embrace the arms race by distancing themselves from the psychological and social implications of hypothetical nuclear weapon strategies. Despite the difficulties involved in exploring such profound political issues, Lifton continues to confront the

most horrifying events of the twentieth century in order to propagate a more abiding sense of social responsibility. Lifton observes: "In every age man faces a pervasive theme which defies his engagement and yet must be engaged. In Freud's day it was sexuality and moralism. Now it is unlimited technological violence and absurd death. We do well to name the threat and to analyze its components. But our need is to go further, to create new psychic and social reforms to enable us to reclaim not only our technologies, but our very imaginations, in the service of the continuity of life."

(See also *Contemporary Authors,* Vols. 17-20, rev. ed. and *Contemporary Authors New Revision Series,* Vol. 27.)

PRINCIPAL WORKS

NONFICTION

Thought Reform and the Psychology of Totalism: A Study of "Brainwashing" in China 1961
Death in Life: Survivors of Hiroshima 1968
Revolutionary Immortality: Mao Tse-Tung and the Chinese Cultural Revolution 1968
Home from the War: Vietnam Veterans—Neither Victims nor Executioners 1973
Living and Dying [with Eric Olson] 1974
The Life of the Self: Toward a New Psychology 1976
The Broken Connection: On Death and the Continuity of Life 1979
Indefensible Weapons: The Political and Psychological Case against Nuclearism [with Richard A. Falk] 1982
The Nazi Doctors: Medical Killing and the Psychology of Genocide 1986
The Genocidal Mentality: Nazi Holocaust and Nuclear Threat [with Eric Markusen] 1990

ESSAY COLLECTIONS

History and Human Survival: Essays on the Young and the Old, Survivors and the Dead, Peace and War, and on Contemporary Psychohistory 1970
Boundaries 1970
Six Lives / Six Deaths: Portraits from Modern Japan [with Shuichi Kato and Michael Reich] 1979
The Future of Immortality and Other Essays for a Nuclear Age 1987

C. Martin Wilbur

[*Thought Reform and the Psychology of Totalism: A Study of "Brainwashing" in China*] must evoke our deepest pity for the victims of "thought reform" as practiced on a massive scale in China. The horrible instrument of "brainwashing" is examined in clinical detail and the whole process laid out for our inspection and understanding.

Dr. Robert Jay Lifton, a psychiatrist and Associate of the Center of East Asian Studies at Harvard, spent more than five years studying "thought reform." His basic source was twenty-five Occidentals and fifteen Chinese who had experienced "reform" and were willing at various stages of their recuperation to discuss the intimate details of the experience with him. To these case histories Mr. Lifton brings not only his psychiatric knowledge but insights from the social sciences and the results of his eager study of Chinese culture and history. He has "constantly groped for new ways to bring psychological insights to bear upon historical sources, and to do so with a humanistic focus." With a minimum of jargon and a maximum of provocative concepts, he has produced a fascinating study.

In analyzing the stages of "thought reform," which in the case of the Occidentals was carried on in prison and lasted several years, Dr. Lifton uses the striking symbolism of a drama of death and rebirth. Under intense psychological pressure and physical torture the victim is manipulated to his breaking point. Such an unremitting assault is launched upon his basic identity as to reduce him to the status of infant or subhuman, helplessly manipulated by his "trainers." The situation is like that of an ordinary man "placed in a hospital for the criminally insane where he is accused of horrendous but vague crimes which he is expected to recognize and confess; where his assertion of innocence is viewed as a symptom of his disease, as a paranoid delusion; and where every other inmate-patient is wholly dedicated to the task of pressuring him into a confession and a 'cure.'" He is totally cut off from the essential succor of affectionate communication and relatedness and brought to the "basic fear" of total annihilation.

Suddenly—when no more pressure can be endured and when annihilation must be near—comes leniency and the opportunity to escape through "reform." Here begins rebirth, when the prisoner becomes motivated to help the Chinese officials achieve what they are trying to do to him. He has the compulsion to confess, and begins a total soul purge. His reeducation begins, and the victim regains the status of human being. His confession, worked and reworked, finally satisfies the official view of his crimes. Only then is he allowed to resume his original identity, but now as part of a confluence of identities: the evil criminal, the repentant sinner, the student of Communist doctrine, plus the man originally imprisoned. This is his rebirth.

For the prisoner to survive physically and psychologically he must avoid being totally overwhelmed by this compulsive environment, yet he must submit to some degree of influence as the price of survival. To retain no trace of the influence of "thought reform," Dr. Lifton believes, is an ideal impossible to achieve.

What were the long-term results of "thought reform"? The author followed up his studies done in Hong Kong in 1954-55 by visiting with most of his cases about four years later. "Thought reform" was a failure in that it did not permanently win the Occidental victims over to the Communist view of the world. Yet all did retain unconscious influences. None could completely cast off the picture of the world and of himself that had been induced, and all retained fears of total annihilation and deep feelings of guilt.

Turning to his Chinese cases, Dr. Lifton offers a revealing analysis. It centers around an excursion into modern Chinese history and the psychological conflicts inhering in the rapid cultural changes of the past fifty years, conflicts particularly intense for intellectuals. His interpretation of the attractions of Marxian doctrine and the Communist movement for this group in terms of psychological quest is the most persuasive explanation I have read. I found many other refreshing insights into modern Chinese history. Dr. Lifton also offers a reasonable and interesting explanation for the questions: (1) How did the Chinese Communists develop this system of "thought reform" (their unique gift to Communist techniques of control) and (2) how did they become such master psychologists?

This book will become, I think, a classic in social-science literature because the problems with which it deals so well extend far beyond Communist China in the early Nineteen Fifties. The concluding chapters are on "Totalism and Its Alternatives." The discussion of "Ideological totalism"— the coming together of immoderate ideology with equally immoderate individual character traits—puts this phenomenon into the perspective of similar movements in our own past.

Dr. Lifton sees the source of ideological totalism in the ever-present human quest for the omnipotent guide—be it supernatural force, political party, philosophical ideas, great leader or precise science. This quest may originate in patterns of security-seeking carried over from childhood. During periods of cultural crisis and rapid historical change the totalist quest for the omnipotent guide leads some men to seek to become that guide. The author presents eloquently the alternative to "thought reform" that our liberal tradition offers for changing the lives of men.

As I set this book down, the deepest question I carried away was this: How can two societies, the Communist Chinese and our own, hope to communicate with each other when their basic assumptions about man and truth stand so far apart?

> *C. Martin Wilbur, "Common Clay in Communist Hands," in* The New York Times Book Review, *February 5, 1961, p. 3.*

The Times Literary Supplement

It is a pity that the term "brainwashing", which has never been used by the Chinese communists, has found its way into popular use, since it implies something of a devilish and mechanical technique rather than the relentless effort at religious conversion which it more nearly resembles. Some of its exponents may be cynical, skilled technicians, as colourless as an examination crammer; most are zealots for the cause they are serving. Certainly all the foreigners and Chinese whom Dr. Lifton interviewed in Hongkong [for his *Thought Reform and the Psychology of Totalism: A Study of "Brainwashing" in China*] found that a formal confession was rarely accepted; they had to go back and try again and again until it was believed that their thinking had been thoroughly reformed.

Dr. Lifton had already made a study of "brainwashed"

prisoners of war in Korea before going to Hongkong in 1953 to carry on his study of Chinese methods of thought reform. He divides his foreign subjects, all of whom had spent two or three years in prison, into those who emerged from the experience obviously confused, those who were apparent converts and those who seemed successfully to have resisted the assault on their beliefs; apparent, explains Dr. Lifton, because all the resisters carried with them the grains of conversion and the converts could never quite escape a surviving core of doubt. Yet almost all of them, to whatever category they belonged, confessed to feeling some benefit from the experience.

The foreigners Dr. Lifton interviewed, at length and over a period of months, responded with something like a confession of their own. The Chinese, who had not been imprisoned but had undergone much the same process of superintended self-criticism, were removed from him by cultural difference and the traditional unwillingness of all Chinese anywhere to expound their deepest feelings. Yet they too eventually responded and by giving us a family history of his cases, Chinese and foreign, Dr. Lifton presents a rounded psychological study of all of them. It was a brilliant stroke to tour Europe a few years later to see how the patients had recovered from the experience, and not perhaps surprising to find that a Jesuit, who fell originally into his category of apparent converts, was the only one still firmly holding to his Marxist faith three years later.

The exhaustive analysis of the personal reactions of all these men and women is absorbing, especially in the group therapy imposed on a mixed party of priests and businessmen, but even more important is the light thrown on Chinese conditions by the foreigners as well as the Chinese. Dr. Lifton defines totalism as the coming together of immoderate ideology with equally immoderate character traits resulting in the subordination of human experience to the claims of doctrine. With great perception and quite without any political bias the intensity of Chinese persuasion is exposed. There is a valuable political lesson in all this. Now that the differences between China and Russia have opened up for all the world to see, the different roots of communism in each country need to be examined and it is at the point of doctrinal persuasion that the difference is most marked.

In a brilliantly argued chapter on the fate of filial piety Dr. Lifton shows how the old China merges into the new. He doubts whether the enthusiasm that is galvanizing this vast population can be equated with western communism: that is to say that China's present zeal in grinding doctrine into the face of the Chinese is not merely greater than in the first decade of Russian revolution but springs from deeper psychological roots in the civilization that is being transformed. When Mr. Khrushchev visits Mao Tse-tung he is like a shrewd and boisterous Anglican meeting the most uncompromisingly fundamentalist of nonconformists. The doctrine they share is not enough to bridge the gulf.

This is not the only sense in which China stands out as *sui generis* in this book. The foreigners who emerged from exhausting confinement and self-criticism were most of them

actively interested in China, inescapably engaged by the civilization even when they were Christian proselytisers. Their experience was thus the more lacerating. In stepping into Chinese culture they had in some sense stepped out of their own. China, it might be suggested, has a cultural totalism of its own which no other civilization can match and which only those who have made a reconnaissance inside it can know. As a study of the psychological issues raised by thought reform in China Dr. Lifton's book is humane and many-sided in its understanding; for the light it throws on the Chinese revolution it is scarcely less valuable.

"Converts for Communism," in The Times Literary Supplement, *No. 3102, August 11, 1961, p. 496.*

William Henry Chamberlin

Any close escape from death is likely to leave in an individual a more or less profound and prolonged trauma. This is multiplied many times over when the death escaped takes the form of near annihilation of a whole community, killing tens of thousands and obliterating buildings and landmarks familiar since childhood.

There were many awesome experiences of this type during World War II, increasing in scope and intensity as air bombing grew in scope and destructiveness. The bombings in Spain, even the devastation of parts of London during the Blitz, pale beside the fire bombings of Hamburg, Dresden and Tokyo. But the nearest approach to total annihilation fell to the lot of the Japanese city of Hiroshima, first target of a weapon of unparalleled destructiveness, the newly discovered nuclear bomb.

A Yale research psychiatrist, Robert Jay Lifton, on the basis of years of study in Japan, has set himself, in **Death in Life,** the task of examining the physical and psychological reactions of the Japanese who survived the virtual obliteration of their native city on Aug. 6, 1945.

The Japanese have a special word, *hibakusha,* to designate survivors of the two atomic blasts, one directed at Hiroshima, the other at Nagasaki. Mr. Lifton, who concentrated his study on Hiroshima—interviewing community leaders, politicians, clergymen, medical personnel, scholars, writers and artists—believes the unique nuclear attack exerted a profound effect not only on the survivors but on the Japanese people generally.

From being one of the most martial peoples in the world, with a code derived from the *samurai,* or knights, of medieval Japan, a code that emphasized the obligation of the Japanese always to accept death rather than surrender, the Japanese have become one of the most pacific. It is not, in the main, sympathy with communism or hatred of America that sends Japanese students demonstrating into the streets when a defense pact with the U.S. is under discussion or an American nuclear-powered aircraft carrier visits a Japanese port. It is the memory of what the ultimate weapons of modern war can inflict.

Mr. Lifton found a mixed reaction among some of the *hibakusha.* They could see the force of the argument that, in the modern world, a country without its own nuclear weapons is helpless in the face of such giants as the U.S., the Soviet Union and Red China. But the risk of a nuclear confrontation seems to them overwhelming.

Most Germans, slowly and unenthusiastically, have come around to the view that a Germany allied with other Western powers in NATO is preferable to a Germany without any means of self-defense. In a somewhat similar situation the Japanese seem much less sure. The atomic bomb may well weigh heavily in this difference in national psychologies.

As the author shows, part of the shock of the impact of the nuclear bomb on Hiroshima was due to its unexpectedness. The city had not been attacked from the air and there seemed no reason to expect that Aug. 6 would be different from any other day. Suddenly came a great flash of light, then the sound and force of the blast, finally the multicolored mushroom cloud rising high above the city.

The sequel to what as an aesthetic spectacle was not without beauty, as some Japanese witnesses testified, was appalling. The official estimate of the number of killed is 78,000; some estimates are much higher and in the confusion that followed no accurate body count was possible. The bomb exploded squarely in the center of a city built mainly of wood and created an area of total destruction extending two miles in every direction.

Those survivors nearest the site of the blast were interviewed by Mr. Lifton. They could usually recall a sudden flash, an intense sensation of heat, being knocked down or thrown some distance and finding themselves pinned under debris or simply awakening after a period of unconsciousness. The most striking psychological feature (and the author is primarily interested in psychological reactions) was the sense of a sudden and absolute shift from normal existence to an overwhelming encounter with death. Mr. Lifton sees a basis for comparison with the later reactions of survivors of Nazi death camps.

Another psychological discovery, in many cases, was a sense of guilt or shame at having survived when so many, often including relatives and close friends, had perished. The author treats this phenomenon as follows:

"The survivor can never, inwardly, simply conclude that is was logical and right for him, and not others, to survive. . . . If they had not died, he would have had to; if he had not survived, someone else would have."

There was also the aftermath of various diseases, due to radiation, often leading to slow and painful death. While the book is perhaps too repetitive and cumulative, too oriented toward technical psychological problems to hold the attention of the lay reader as a simpler narrative might have, it is an impressive warning of what a resort to modern nuclear weapons with their far greater destructive power, might be expected to produce.

William Henry Chamberlin, "Hiroshima, the Survivors and Guilt," in The Wall Street Journal, *February 7, 1968, p. 16.*

Josh Greenfeld

Deciding whether the 20th century hit its nadir at Auschwitz or at Hiroshima is like trying to choose between heart disease and cancer; a grim case can be made for either. But since the attempt at the final solution was the work of an enemy who was defeated and the atomic bomb played a role in the American victory, we have tended to direct our morbid attentions more to the brutal slaughter in Europe than to the nuclear holocaust in Asia. In fact, we can all recall the first chilling newsreels that came out from behind the barbed wire immediately after the war, and books about the death camps have become a publishing staple. But aside from the first mushroom cloud pictures, the electronic and Gutenberg fallout from Hiroshima to reach these shores has been surprisingly meager. . . . It has been as if to the victors belong the spoils—and merciful amnesia.

Even the cold statistics of Hiroshima are as vague as someone else's dream, or nightmare, compared to that awful but familiar figure of six million. The exact number of deaths caused by the bomb will never be known. The estimates vary from 63,000 to 240,000 deaths; the quasi-official figure usually settled upon by Americans is 78,000; the Japanese estimate 200,000.

In addition, there are the *hibakusha*—the atomic bomb victims of Hiroshima who are still alive. Of Japan's 290,000 *hibakusha,* 160,000 were exposed to the effects of radiation when the bomb fell on Hiroshima.

But statistics alone would tell only a small part of the continuing story. They deal, after all, only in body count. Perhaps the greatest damage done by the atom bomb has been in the almost unchartable areas of the mind and the spirit, in the psychic after-effects it has left not only upon its direct victims, but upon the rest of Japan and indeed the whole world.

In *Death in Life* Dr. Robert Jay Lifton, a Yale University professor of psychiatry, using all the tools of his trade, has at last attempted to gauge those effects, to study clinically the A-bomb's residue of psychic damage and to extrapolate from that unique experience some theories applicable to all human behavior. His method was to interview 75 Hiroshima *hibakusha,* half selected at random and half from leadership rolls. He reports these interviews completely, analyzes and interprets them professionally, and draws general theories from them most persuasively. The result is that *Death in Life* is at once a scientifically conclusive and metaphysically germinal work. It may well be one of the most important books to be published this year.

Lifton and his subjects begin at the beginning. It is all here again: the hot August morning in the garrison town of Hiroshima; the sense of having been a lucky city for having hitherto escaped bad bombings; the two air-raid alerts during the night and a third siren at 7:10 A.M. Then an all-clear sounded at 7:32 and, reassured, the people of Hiroshima started their day. A history professor recalls, for example:

> The sky was serene, the air was flooded with glittering morning light. My steps were slow along the dry, dusty road. I was in a state of absent-

mindedness. The sirens and also the radio had just given the all-clear signal. I had reached the foot of a bridge, where I halted, and was turning my eyes toward the water . . .

Then the blinding flash, the burning heat, the dead silence, the ear-shattering boom, the clouds rising, the monstrous mushroom. And eyes dripping from sockets, skin dropping from bone, steel buildings melting away and "deathly" silence.

The bomb had fallen, or rather burst above, a downtown area that contained 60 per cent of Hiroshima's population. To have even a 50 per cent chance of escaping death or injury even while indoors one had to be at least 1.3 miles from the hypocenter. For even as little as one second of exposure survivors of the bomb have suffered life long effects.

Physically, for example, incidents of cancer, leukemia and gastrointestinal disorders are inordinately high among *hibakusha*. Socially, in the highly stratified Japanese society they bear the mark of losers and so cannot make "good" marriages or secure "good" jobs. Psychologically, on one level *hibakusha* suffer from all manner of psychosomatic ailments: they fatigue easily, never feel quite well and are alarmed by minor indispositions; on a deeper level they have never recovered from—or mastered—their death immersion and all of its attendant anxieties.

In general, Lifton believes, we pay too little attention to the importance of the presence of death in shaping normal human behavior. Indeed, he argues, that "death anxiety, death guilt, and the threat to symbolic immortality are fundamental not only to the periods of depression we all undergo, but also to the entire general phenomenon of prejudice and victimization."

What actually happened at Hiroshima, Lifton says, is a dreadful world experience that has not yet been formulated. Not having mastered that massive encounter with death, we, like the *hibakusha* themselves, are in a sense victims of psychic numbing and residual death imagery; we too are haunted by survivor's guilt and fear of nuclear contagion. And if we cannot understand the psychic after-effects of the atomic bomb in its most dramtic form, we can hardly hope to understand the workaday psychic mutations we ourselves have undergone—a psychic closing-off which allows us to watch Vietnam battles on our TV screens and permits us even to postulate the use of new atomic weaponry.

Hiroshima was an "end of the world," (Lifton concludes) and yet the world still exists. Precisely in this end-of-the-world quality lies both its threat and its wisdom. In every age man faces a pervasive theme which defines his engagement and yet must be engaged. In Freud's day it was sexuality and moralism. Now it is unlimited technological violence and absurd death. We do well to name the threat and to analyze its components. But our need is to go further, to create new psychic and social forms to enable us to reclaim not only our technologies, but our very imaginations, in the service of the continuity of life.

Josh Greenfeld, "In the Shadow of Mega-

death," in Book World—The Washington Post, *March 24, 1968, p. 6.*

Jerome D. Frank

Our age is witnessing mass slaughter of innocents on an unprecedented scale, attendant on wars, revolutions and the convulsive births of new nations; and no end is in sight. These upheavals have left millions of survivors; yet we know very little of how their experience has affected their subsequent lives. Robert J. Lifton's [*Death in Life: Survivors of Hiroshima*] is the first study in depth of the "psychohistorical" effects of such holocausts, using as a prototype the atom bomb attack on Hiroshima on Aug. 6, 1945, which bears a close enough resemblance to more old-fashioned forms of mass murder to be relevant to them.

Like many of these, it caused extensive, indiscriminate loss of life and destroyed the fabric of a community. But it was unique in its total unexpectedness, its instantaneousness, the tremendous physical devastation it caused and, above all, in its introduction of the entirely new psychological stress of delayed after-effects. Unlike familiar forms of death through disease, old age and military combat, for which victims and survivors are prepared and which are part of the accepted order of things, the Hiroshima bomb abruptly shattered the survivors' sense of the coherence of life and their feelings of continuity with their own past and their fellow man. . . .

Lifton views the impact of Hiroshima primarily through the eyes of the victims. He lets them describe in their own terms the initial shock of their abrupt immersion in death, followed by psychic numbing, guilt at surviving, and many other reactions of the post-disaster period, and then their long-term efforts to cope with the massive disruption of their lives. He describes styles of leadership developed by some survivors, the creative efforts of others to digest their experience through novels and other art forms, and the struggles of all to achieve a "formulation" that restores their shattered symbolic universe, thereby enabling them to regain some sense of the meaning of existence and mastery over their environment.

"A-bomb disease," that cruel combination of psychological and biological stress created by the genuine or imagined delayed effects of radiation, is treated in detail. Its victims feel that their bodies contain a mysterious poison that may emerge and strike them down at any time. They feel endlessly vulnerable in that the cessation of one threat seems always to be followed by the emergence of another—first, leukemia, then a variety of cancers, then possibly premature senility.

Since the early signs of genuine radiation sickness are vague and protean and mimic those caused by emotional stress, every minor new complaint creates forebodings and gives rise to conflict in the victims between their desire for special attention and resentment of it as a reminder of their status. The agencies that are supposed to help the victims find themselves in an analogous conflict, between their desire to assist and their fear of creating hypochondriasis and undue dependency. Lifton explores fully the role of the mass media in fanning the fears of "A-bomb disease" and the survivors' unflattering image of the United States Atomic Bomb Casualty Commission as an attacker doing research on his victims.

At one level the book is a beautifully written, moving and vivid account of a shattering human experience. At another, it lays out the elements of a general theory of the psychology of survivors—those who have come in contact with massive death in some bodily or psychic fashion and have themselves remained alive. To this end, Lifton in the final section compares the survivors of Hiroshima with those who survived Nazi death camps and the black plague in the Middle Ages, and draws some interesting parallels between victims of disaster and other stigmatized minorities, such as Negroes in the United States.

Lifton does a good job in creating a conceptual framework to encompass highly ramified, complex and inchoate psychosocial phenomena, especially when his concepts are primarily descriptive and stay close to the data. These are usually apposite and illuminating. He is less successful when he strains for overarching explanatory principles, which often seem to be freighted with mystical overtones and to be more pretentious than profound.

To take one example among many, the readily understandable guilt of any survivor over failing to rescue a fellow victim, especially a member of his family, he transmutes into a pervasive "death-guilt" based on "an unconscious perception of social balance which makes him feel that his survival was made possible by others' deaths . . . such guilt . . . may well be that most fundamental to human existence." One cannot help wondering whether in such passages the author may not be mistaking his own conscious fantasies for his subjects' unconscious ones.

But such reservations are trivial in the face of an impressive, trail-breaking contribution in describing and conceptualizing the experience of surviving a taste of man's nuclear war on his own species—an experience which may fall to the lot of everyone alive today. Perhaps its most significant message is that the long-term psychological crippling of survivors, and the profound social disruption caused by a nuclear attack, are at least as severe a threat to the continued existence of organized society as the extent of biological and physical destruction. As such, the book is especially recommended to nuclear strategists who like to calculate just how many megatons of nuclear explosives the United States can absorb and still survive.

Jerome D. Frank, "After the Event," in The New York Times Book Review, *March 31, 1968, p. 10.*

Eliot Fremont-Smith

The enormous national convulsion in China, the Great Proletarian Cultural Revolution, as it was called, which rolled up in the summer of 1966 and apparently exhausted itself in the early months of [1968], seemed to underscore certain half-truths and myths in the West about Communist China and our perception of her. Essentially, these are two: first, a sense of ignorance about what is going on in that country (probably exaggerated, but based on an indis-

putable historical oddity, the virtual absence of either diplomatic or journalistic contact between the United States and China for 20 years); and, second, a pervasive notion that even if we had normal access to normal "facts" and day-by-day events, China would still remain inscrutable.

It is only natural to attempt to explain events in modes and contexts with which we are familiar and, if certain events cannot be so explained to our rational satisfaction, to assume that their causes are irrational, or at least are beyond the cognizance of present reason. Thus, in some part, our own demonology about modern China. The obvious failure of either the "psychotic leader" or political "power struggle" diagnoses to provide an adequate explanation of the extraordinary upheaval of the Chinese Cultural Revolution has left us without much to fall back on, save the "inscrutability" of the East or the "madness" of a whole society.

Now, in what is one of the year's most important books, [*Revolutionary Immortality: Mao Tse-Tung and the Chinese Cultural Revolution*] Robert J. Lifton offers a new conceptual framework for our understanding not only of the Chinese convulsion, its causes, its surprising potency and its consequences, but of revolution in general and the strange urgency, which can become absolutely paramount, of revolution never to proclaim itself successful, never to say its job is done and its goals attained.

It has been suggested before that the totalistic revolutionary vision is by necessity and by nature paranoiac, that it posits continuing threats long after visible enemies have been vanquished. In China, the revolution was "won" 20 years ago, and Mao Tse-tung's regime has not been in serious jeopardy by overt internal revolt since then. Yet, it has consistently talked and periodically acted as if it were in danger of being internally overthrown at any minute.

Mr. Lifton suggests that the danger is real after all. What is new is that he names the enemy: it is Death—the death first of all of the revolutionary vision, and secondarily (though now becoming imminent) of Mao, the 74-year-old leader in whom that vision has been personified. The Cultural Revolution thus was a "power struggle," but not so much (if significantly at all) between factions vying for the failing leader's mantle—an explanation that falters on the fact that Mao himself instigated and propelled the struggle—as between the Maoist regime and vision and its possible mortality. In this view, the Cultural Revolution may be seen as an effort to render eternal, if not Mao himself, at least his revolutionary works.

Mr. Lifton, an authority on psychological patterns in East Asia and author of *Thought Reform and the Psychology of Totalism: A Study of "Brainwashing" in China* and the recent *Death in Life: Survivors of Hiroshima,* has in his new book made a signal contribution to the understanding of the relationship of individual psychology to historical change, and especially of the vicissitudes of human continuity. He shows how the sense of individual continuity has been absorbed and organized into larger groupings and how it has been expressed in the Chinese instance through the "immortalization of words" in the remarkable entity known as the Thought of Mao Tse-tung, through the reliance upon revolutionary will to achieve technological goals (as in the "Great Leap Forward" of 1958), through the cyclical swing of activism and purity, and through a "nostalgic preoccupation with newness" and with a revitalization of the spirit of the epic Long March of 1934-35.

Revolutionary Immortality is, I would judge, an essential study of Communist China; more than that, it is an original, intellectually exciting, gracefully written and wholly accessible essay on an aspect of human individual and mass psychology as it operates in contemporary revolutionary circumstances around the world. (p. 45)

> Eliot Fremont-Smith, "Strife against Death," in The New York Times, September 30, 1968, p. 45.

John K. Fairbank

Psycho-history, applying the insights of psychoanalysis to historic situations, is a demanding multi-discipline. A good historian draws upon all the social sciences; a good analyst begins with a medical education. Thus a psycho-historian needs many years of training; even so he will be better off with a touch of native genius. Ideally, he also needs a good subject, a leader whose personal life is knowable but who stands in history bigger than life, who has infused a multitude with his own cast of mind—a Luther, a Gandhi, a Lenin, a Mao Tse-tung—someone who has led his followers through tumultuous events shaped by human psychology, both theirs and his. . . .

In approaching Mao's cultural revolution of 1966-68 in [*Revolutionary Immortality*], Lifton avoids a full-scale psycho-biography, or a study of Mao's individual psycho-pathology, in favor of psychological themes that link the leader and his Chinese multitude, especially the theme of "eternal survival" or "symbolic immortality" for Mao and the revolution.

Behind the desperate-seeming excesses of the Cultural Revolution, Lifton sees first of all a death anxiety, over the anticipated end of Mao and the possible "death of the revolution." Looking back a decade, he sees the failure of the Great Leap Forward of 1958, that Heaven-storming effort at instant industrialization, as the proximate cause of this anxiety. In the aftermath of the Great Leap and the chaos it produced, the temporary liberalization of the Chinese Communist program saved the regime; but it separated Mao, who was then put on the shelf, from his more pragmatic colleagues like Liu Shao-ch'i. Thus Mao, making his comeback, still visionary, eventually embarked on his quest for the rebirth of the revolution through the Red Guards of 1966. Lifton sees in this movement a theme of using the pure vitality of youth to destroy everything old and impure. Purity and power were merged in the Red Guard movement, as they already had been merged in the politicized and indoctrinated People's Liberation Army under Lin Piao. With the schools closed in 1966-67 and youth on the march, the "redness" of orthodoxy now triumphed over technological "expertness." Mao was now deified by making his Thought immortal ("the immortalization of words"); and Lifton notes especially Mao's "*insistence upon all-or-none confrontation with death,*" the de-

mand that one be ever ready to risk all, as a way of transcending death.

Mao's psychological development has led him on and on. His early courage and vision, his "revolutionary romanticism," his close identification with the rural masses, his national pride, even the vision of immortal transcendence in his poems, all have contributed to what Lifton now sees as the "*tragic transition from the great leader to the despot,*" the old man now unsure of his revolution's immortality, now obsessed with its survival. "Hence Mao's plunge into psychism, into a one-sided focus upon intra-psychic purity at the expense of extrapsychic reality." Psychism of course is the enemy of technology. It claims that voluntarism, "revolutionary will," can substitute for technology. This psychistic fallacy assumes "the interchange-ability of psychic state and technology. *Technology is sought but feelings are cultivated.*" This is a dead end.

Lifton concludes by noting the psychological limitations that have inevitably checked Mao's totalism. He sees these in three sectors: the "hostility of suffocation" on the part of followers as they develop an inner antagonism to the great leader; the break-up of the closed system of "idea-tight milieu-control" by outside influences; and diminishing returns on the domestic reform front as outward compliance substitutes more and more for inner enthusiasm. The results are evident in the alienation of youth, in "revisionism," and in the decline of Mao's charisma. He gets into the vicious circle of all tyrants on the way out: the more his followers waver, the more he demands of them, and the more violently he does it.

After reading this Maoist study, of which the above is a very pale reflection, one may ask, What then is the contribution of psycho-history? Does it require a psychiatrist to tell us that Mao the dictator has gone off the deep end and his people are becoming fed up with him?

On the whole, I think the answer is yes. We do need the insights of professional psychology to develop and sophisticate our everyday common-sense impression. The picture revealed by the psycho-historian is not unfamiliar to us in outline, but it is much sharper in focus, more specific and more reliable. Because it is tied in so firmly with the rest of our knowledge, Dr. Lifton's essay is a brilliant study, without peer in the copious China literature. Whether it results from Lifton's being so well trained or from his being merely a genius (probably both), it puts much-studied events in a new framework of psychological interpretation, without grinding an axe or disregarding cultural, political and other factors. A scholar less sophisticated in the complexities of China and psychology could have made this study both grandiose and misleading. Instead, it is done with balance and precision, and in terms that seem sufficiently meaningful to a layman.

No doubt other themes than immortality could be used in studying the psychology of Mao and the Chinese Revolution in other phases. Possibly other terms than "immortality" could be substituted for it at several points in the argument here. At any rate, one would like to see a whole seminar of 15-year-trained psycho-historians studying the great Chinese dynastic founders, the peasant rebellions, the bureaucratic reform movements. Dr. Lifton has opened a wide door. When will he train others to enter this new and multifaceted field of scholarship? How can we ensure Robert Lifton's scholarly immortality?

John K. Fairbank, "A Psycho-History of Mao Tse-tung," in Book World—The Washington Post, *October 20, 1968, p. 5.*

Lifton on nuclear weapons:

Nuclear weapons have already damaged us more than we know. . . . They have created within us an image of historical extinction and caused us to feel severed from both past and future. They also impose upon us every variety of psychic numbing—of emotional and intellectual anesthesia—so that we need not feel and cannot grasp their brutalizing effects upon human beings. This numbing not only interferes with our capacity to cope with the weapons themselves but extends into all of our perceptions of living and of dying. Rather than an age of anxiety, ours is an age of numbing.

Still worse, the weapons create in us an aura of worship. They become grotesque technological deities for a debased religion of nuclearism—gods sought by everybody as part of an all-too-human tendency to confuse the power of apocalyptic destruction with the capacity to protect, or even create, life. We then talk of nuclear stock piles, nuclear arsenals, of a beneficent nuclear umbrella or of an equally beneficent system of antiballistic missiles. We perpetuate an illusion of security by means of step-by-step logic—but this is the logic of madness. . . .

Christopher Lehmann-Haupt

Some superficial gripes first. *History and Human Survival* is a collection of pieces. Its contents come from a bewildering variety of sources: *Daedalus, The New Republic, The Journal of Nervous and Mental Disease, The Atlantic Monthly, Partisan Review, Psychiatry, The New York Review of Books, The New York Times Book Review, Trans-Action,* among others. Testimony to Mr. Lifton's diversity, but such a diverse gathering would have to be superbly organized to justify itself as an organic whole, and, in the case of *History and Human Survival,* it is not, as the catch-all subtitle suggests ("Essays on the Young and Old, Survivors and the Dead, Peace and War, and on Contemporary Psychohistory"). The book begins with what is most conclusive and familiar in Mr. Lifton's work and proceeds slowly to underlying principles. There are unsuccessful attempts to disguise some of the pieces' original purposes, as in cases where the titles of books under review are never given, or in the inclusion of only one side of a debate. Much of the book is difficult to read, both because the author's prose can be grindingly academic and because his focus is often on death and apocalypse, and the psyche plain fights it. Whatever the reason, the mind wanders.

Is *History and Human Survival* therefore to be skipped? One might as well ignore the dawn. Why? Because in the course of his 16 essays, Mr. Lifton succeeds in imposing

his highly original and bracingly challenging perspective on most of the gut issues of our time. And however one reads him (I would recommend back to front) one gradually discerns an unusual image coming into focus.

The image is that of an artistic, synthesizing intelligence patiently maneuvering to reconcile far-flung opposing forces—past and future, East and West, life and death, male and female, old and young. The book in itself (it would better have been titled "Holocaust and Human Survival" or "History and the End of It") is a synthesis of Lifton's past and future, with material covering the ground of his published works (especially his National Book Award winner, *Death in Life: Survivors of Hiroshima*) and his forthcoming book on death symbolism (*The Broken Connection*).

The book's most challenging and interesting essays set out to reconcile what we think of as increasingly opposed. **"Woman as Knower"** is an extraordinarily complex and ambitious attempt to concede woman her "liberation" without mindlessly denying her unique psychobiological nature (Betty Friedan, meet Dr. Spock). **"The Young and the Old—Notes on a New History"** relocates the generation gap and thereby concedes youth its revolution without annihilating the middle-aged (Mark Rudd, meet William J. McGill). **"Protean Man"** suggests that for modern times there is a certain stability in lack of identity (Michael Brody, meet Michael Brody).

Elsewhere, Mr. Lifton explains the unusually violent identity shifts in modern Japanese youths, and proposes new images of immortality to replace those destroyed by Hiroshima. Everywhere, Lifton excavates the foundations that support conflicting structures. Only Vietnam and the arms race lie beneath his reach, and evoke his cool outrage.

The technique that enables him to synthesize so is the grandest synthesis of all, and, in a sense, the crux of all these essays. That technique is the discipline, or art, of psychohistory—inspired by Freud, pioneered by Erik Erikson, and, since 1965, debated and monitored by a small discussion group (including Erikson and Lifton) that meets for a few weeks annually.

Psychohistory, as the word makes clear, attempts to reconcile the disciplines of psychoanalysis and history. A simple matter, it would seem on the face of it, considering that no idividual is free of history and no history is free of individuals. But as Lifton points out, the two have been traditionally opposed to the degree "that psychoanalysis seeks to eliminate history; and history seeks to eliminate psychological man."

And despite its influence on Lifton and the success with which Erikson has applied it in such books as *Young Man Luther* and *Gandhi's Truth,* Lifton betrays a certain guardedness when discussing the future of psychohistory. "We still meet regularly, but have been reticent to publish as a group," he writes in his introduction to a review essay, **"Psychoanalysis and History."** "For this some have criticized us, but I think the reticence well founded. Were I to write this review now, I would emphasize still more the pitfalls of bringing together psychology and history. . . ." Apparently, the psychohistorians have caught heavy fire from the practitioners of traditional disciplines.

For my money, Mr. Lifton is too worried about the acceptability of his stepchild to the academy. What mars these essays most of all is their schematic rigidity, their attempts to play by the rules, their lack of artistry, and their lack of a personal style—of what Lifton refers to in his introduction as "disciplined subjectivity." Why hold back? After all, as he himself writes: "We need new concepts, new modes of observation, new relationships to what we are observing. Like everyone else these days, we need a new language and even a new life-style in order to connect with, no less interpret, the world we inhabit." Why then deny this vision a little poetry?

> *Christopher Lehmann-Haupt, "History, Meet Psychoanalysis," in* The New York Times Book Review, *February 6, 1970, p. 35.*

Irving Kristol

Every American decade seems to discover a new mirror image of itself and to invent its own special psychological experience. In the 1950's we saw ourselves as David Riesman's "other-directed" man and William H. Whyte's "organization man." In the 1960's, our elder sons and daughters saw themselves—mediated through the vision of Erik Erikson—as having an "identity crisis." Now, in the 1970's, it seems that our younger children are in uneasy pursuit of themselves as "protean man," and it is to the searching essays of Robert J. Lifton we must turn for current instruction as to what it all means.

These essays, written over the past 10 years, are now published under the title, ***History and Human Survival***. Their diversity is indicated by the long subtitle Mr. Lifton has scrupulously provided: "Essays on the Young and Old, Survivors and the Dead, Peace and War, and on Contemporary Psychohistory." The actual topics behind this general statement include inquiries into the psychology of Japanese youth, the state of mind of the survivors of Hiroshima, the relation of psychoanalysis to history, the feminine psyche today, the spiritual origins of the generation gap, and so on. But there is nevertheless an authentic unity to the collection—the basic theme emerges clearly as it gradually emerged in Mr. Lifton's own mind. . . .

Mr. Lifton sees the Bomb, especially, as having a pervasive effect on the human psyche of the new generations. It has, he argues, produced an impairment of our vital sense of "symbolic immortality"; it has violated "the universal need for imagery of connection antedating and extending the individual life span, whether the idiom of this immortality is biological (living on through children and grandchildren), theological (through a life after death), natural (*in* nature, which outlasts all), or creative through what man makes and does)." This sense of an ending to human history gives rise, in turn, to a "psychohistorical dislocation": our past has become obsolete, our present has become meaningless, our imagined futures have become fanciful.

The further consequences of this historical breakdown

permeate all of our works and days. It is notably visible in the arts, where a sense of aggressive absurdity suffuses the willful disintegration of all traditional forms. It is to be seen in the New Politics, of course: we are reminded that the original Port Huron statement of the S.D.S. proclaimed that " . . . we may be the last generation in the experiment with living." And it is most startlingly apparent in the emergence among the young of a new psychological type: "protean man," as Mr. Lifton brilliantly names him, constantly and casually inventing new identities for himself—"putting on" these identities—as he flees from the smell of death that emanates from hollow institutions and decaying values.

The idea of "protean man" is one of those insights that have only to be expressed to carry conviction. Yes, that is very much the sort of thing that young people are up to; and this is indeed a crucial respect in which they differ from the rest of us, whose identities will never know such freedom for self-transformation. The effortless ease with which they dress up in odd remnants of ideology, and the equal facility with which they revert to stark ideological nudity; the determined unseriousness that puts them beyond reach of their teachers; their absolute refusal to be pinned down by circumstance or reason—all this is plainly there.

Is it a viable psychological type, this "protean man," or is it a pathological mutation? Is it creative response or nihilistic desperation? Mr. Lifton is optimistic. He sees in the protean style a functional, cunning method for remaining humanly open "to the extraordinarily rich, confusing, liberating, and threatening array of contemporary historical possibilities." It would be so nice to think he is right that one is tempted to forget that some thousands of years of human history stand ready to wager he is not.

> *Irving Kristol, in a review of "History and Human Survival: Essays on the Young and Old, Survivors and the Dead, Peace and War, and on Contemporary Psychohistory," in* The New York Times Book Review, *August 2, 1970, p. 2.*

Richard Locke

[Robert Jay Lifton's ***Home from the War: Vietnam Veterans—Neither Victims nor Executioners***] brings together many of his interests over the past 20 years: war and peace, America and the Far East, young people, patterns of survival, change, and the sense of human continuity he calls "symbolic immortality."

At its most modest level ***Home from the War*** examines the psychological effects of the Vietnam war on a group of veterans. It is based on Lifton's experiences in an informal discussion group that met weekly over the past two-and-a-half years in the New York office of Vietnam Veterans Against the War. This "rap group" consisted of Lifton, two professional colleagues and an average of 12 veterans who worked through their feelings about the war, about the American society that created it and about their own personal lives. A total of 35 veterans and 6 professionals participated in the three-hour sessions; for this book Lifton also draws on conversations with more than 350 veterans he met during antiwar efforts and lectures around the country.

According to Lifton the veterans expressed " a sense of violated personal and social order, of fundamental break in human connection, which they related to conditions imposed upon them by the war in Vietnam." They felt they had been plunged into a universe of meaningless death and evil; the war became for them "an exercise in survival rather than a defence of national values." The official justifications were quickly seen to be counterfeit. The men did not feel like noble warriors helping honest allies to repel foreign invaders; they felt they were invaders themselves, hired killers brought in to shore up a country of "thieves and whores," whose venality and military incompetence made mockery of hopes of "Vietnamizing the war."

The enemy was unpredictable, elusive and often indistinguishable from one's allies. Drawing on an old American racial adage, the men concluded "the only good gook is a dead gook." All Vietnamese became subhuman, potential scapegoats, victims whom one shot to keep death at arms' length. Feeling betrayed and victimized themselves, the men were prey to intense confusion, anxiety, self-protective "psychic numbing," anger and guilt—both for killing people without reason and for surviving without reason while their buddies died. The men were trapped in what Sartre called "an atrocity producing situation." Mylai was a typical and inevitable result, not an anomaly.

Given this stituation, the soldiers reacted in different ways. Many pulled the trigger with a vengeance and flung themselves into "the John Wayne thing"—acting out the fantasy of being the supermasculine American killer-hero familiar since childhood. Others thought this stupid: they adopted what Lifton approvingly describes as the free-floating "Protean" youth style, becoming more open, getting into rock music, smoking pot, mocking their superiors and putting down the system. Others became heroin addicts or refused orders or "fragged" their officers—threw live grenades at them. Others took refuge in worshipping the tools of war, in filtering their experience through technical jargon, in trying for high "body counts" to bolster their military self-esteem, in looking forward to the next automated gadget that would wipe out the enemy once and for all.

A small minority came to acknowledge that the "gooks" were human and struggled to unlearn the habits of American machismo, to become more sensitive to their own feelings, to other people and to the war in all its ramifications. These men went on to dedicate themselves to antiwar activities in line with new, restorative ideological commitments.

In the group, Lifton and his colleagues combined informal psychotherapy with a political, cultural and ethical analysis of the veterans' Vietnam experiences. The therapists used an approach that deliberately violated what they felt was a false standard of professional objectivity. Lifton was openly sympathetic to the veterans' political efforts, and he claims that he was as frank about his own personal conflicts and problems as the men were, and that he was himself transformed by the experience.

Lifton views this book as his form of activism, as a contribution to the antiwar effort. He calls it a work of psychohistorical "advocacy research" combining open political and ethical commitment with intellectual rigor. He strongly condemns the psychiatric profession in Vietnam for acquiescing to Gen. William Westmoreland's directive that psychiatrists should play a "personnel management consultation-type role" in the war—"adjusting" their patients enough to return to their duties and thus encouraging their participation in an intrinsically alienating, immoral, hypocritical enterprise.

Lifton makes clear that the members of his "rap group" were hardly representative Vietnam veterans: they were all antiwar activists, they were almost all white, they had all seen combat. But Lifton did not intend his study to be "comprehensive" (like his Hiroshima book), nor did he want simply to report on the dynamics of the group or to discuss individual cases. Rather, he was interested in finding "feelings and images of war in general," in understanding the "psychomythology of war making."

He believes these veterans have a cultural significance far beyond their numbers. By confronting their Vietnam experiences, confessing their guilt, acknowledging the "warrior within themselves," and then "bearing witness" to America's vile actions in Vietnam, they are engaged in a "radical subversion of the warrior myth," which has been responsible for the endless cycle of human warfare, and are replacing it with an "immortalizing cult of peace and peace-makers." The veterans' ordeal "parallels that of priests and shamans, the predecessors of biblical prophets"; each is a "new kind of hero-prophet who turns his fleshly knowledge of violence into a rejection of that violence." Consequently the book "deals with what is probably man's oldest and most fundamental theme, that of death and rebirth, suffering and realization."

It is Lifton's belief that the rap group was an experiment with a new form of social institution more viable than any of our present ones, which are, he asserts, hopelessly counterfeit and on the verge of collapse due to the erosion of our society's foundations—the shared beliefs and fantasies that give all men a sense of "symbolic immortality." For Lifton the Vietnam war is America's death knell. What he calls the "fulcrum" for the psychological and social change that will resurrect us is the guilt the antiwar veterans felt about their activities in Vietnam. With an ease that does injustice to the veterans' suffering, Lifton asserts that we are all guilty of Vietnam and know in our heart of hearts that American society is doomed—or ought to be.

Lifton is trying to persuade us that we are living in mortal sin. Some of us may not feel the guilt, but that is because we have been numbed. And even if we say we are guilty and repent, we may be only feeling "static" or "self-lacerating" guilt, a kind of neurotic repetition-compulsion, "a *mea culpa*" that leads nowhere but to frustration and rage.

Lifton argues that what we have to feel—with a very few of the very best of the Vietnam veterans (by no means all of the members of the rap group)—is what he calls "animating guilt," a sense that one has violated ultimate moral boundaries; that one must analyze the personal and social forces that led one into sin; that one must come to terms with these facts and then not merely go and sin no more but expose to all mankind the falsity of guiltlessness, the hypocrisy and deathliness of the current social order; and finally that one must exhort one's fellow man to confess his sins and convert to "Protean" nonviolence. What form the new social order will take is left deliberately vague; first the revolution, then the theory—as Danny Cohn-Bendit said in Paris in 1968.

Unfortunately, Lifton has organized his book in such a way that we are seldom in touch with the individual men on whom this vision of the future rests. He quotes them selectively; we never get a clear portrait of a veteran's personal experience as it developed. The inner process of each man's acts of self-restoration, the details of his own particular growth from a brutalized middle-American "grunt" to an active Vietnam Veteran Against the War are ignored in Lifton's sweep. (In a chapter on My Lai, one of his best, Lifton draws on interviews with one soldier there who didn't shoot; but Lifton is too interested in generalizing to render this man's experience in more than a few pages.) The veterans' early lives and backgrounds are never mentioned in any detail, their actual duties in Vietnam are barely described. We never understand precisely how these veterans are like or unlike those of previous wars in America, or elsewhere, nor how they are like and unlike other American youths of recent years.

Lifton is too quick to idealize his veterans and to identify himself with them. He was not himself a soldier in Vietnam, slaughtering civilians, filled with death anxiety, trapped in an immoral and psychologically untenable position by the Government, struggling with survivor guilt; yet in his sympathy for their suffering and in his support of their political beliefs, he has drawn onto his own shoulders a moral and psychological burden that is theirs to bear. He can describe their guilt, he can articulate his own, he can argue that we all have shirked our political and moral duty, but he should not take assertion for argument or write as if the veterans' moral authority were his.

And he certainly should not pretend that this is psychohistory. The book lacks the sensitive precision that gave tragic power to much of his first work, *Thought Reform and the Psychology of Totalism,* where he was scrupulously attentive to individual experience and moved from the particular to the general with great care. In his new book he refers to "psychobiologic universals," to "the biologically rooted psychoformative process of perpetual symbolization," and to some "mythic or formative zone of existence in which basic psychological images and transformations take shape." But he never offers us the evidence to support these vague and grandiose conceptions.

He spends a few pages disparaging aspects of orthodox psychoanalytic theory, but never properly confronts the issues. He often seems to imagine that men act like puppets manipulated by giant cultural fantasy figures—the Warrior, the Hero, the Survivor—but never shows us exactly how such figures determine individual thought pro-

cesses. He merely asserts they do, and then proceeds as if it's fact. This isn't an extension of psychological theory, it's parlor psychoanalysis.

Lifton also exaggerates the veterans' similarities to survivors of Hiroshima or the Nazi concentration camps. There is a major difference between the physical or social fact of being a survivor and being a survivor in a symbolic sense. The veterans indeed were filled with a form of survivor guilt, but still—unlike the victimized civilians of Vietnam—they did the shooting. To ignore this is to distort their experience, to minimize the work that went into their self-reclamation, and to obscure the process of their psychological and moral change.

Lifton's missionary zeal in ascribing guilt to us is ultimately self-righteous—the more extreme the charge of guilt, the more moral credit redounds to the judge. But there are always various degrees and kinds of culpability and Lifton does not clarify them. It is understandable that the veterans should feel guilt for their atrocities, or for atrocious impulses, or for being alive when their buddies are dead; it is moving and encouraging to learn that some of the veterans managed to escape from a self-perpetuating cycle of rage and guilt and were able to confront their feelings and experience in ways that gave them new energy and purpose. But Lifton is too often using them as symbols to confirm his cultural prejudices and to bully us into his reductive psychology and vision of the future. There is a moral arrogance in this book and it is Lifton's, not the men's.

The subject of *Home from the War* might well have yielded insight into the relationship of politics, ethics and psychology. This is a noble intellectual goal and few today have Lifton's energy and courage to attempt it. But in this book imaginative research is debased to moralistic propaganda, high assertion substitutes for nuanced argument, and psychohistory becomes no more than intellectual new journalism. (pp. 23-4, 26, 28, 30)

> *Richard Locke, "Home from the War," in* Book World—The Washington Post, *June 24, 1973, pp. 23-4, 26, 28, 30.*

J. Glenn Gray

Is it possible that Vietnam will prove a turning point for Americans? Are we likely at last to turn away from the warrior ethos and toward a more life-affirming one? Robert Lifton, the Yale research psychiatrist who has reported in previous books on survivors of Hiroshima and on China's revolutionaries, seems to think so [in *Home from the War*]. From his extensive work with the Vietnam Veterans Against the War, more especially his participation in numerous discussions about the war over the last few years, he has discovered in this small group "a quality that has to do with a tranformation of the human spirit."

These antiwar warriors feel great guilt about their war experiences and with Lifton's help have been struggling to come to terms with it, both psychologically and by active resistance to American war policy. They want to extirpate in themselves the John Wayne image of the fighting man in search of glory and immortality, and rediscover themselves as capable of a stable private life and a nonlethal "integrity" that are unlike the military conception of the heroic life. They have a "survivor mission," according to Lifton, to expose to us civilians the meaninglessness and hideous evil of their war. They also mean to defy the tendency of veterans to cherish their war experiences in organizations that are always politically conservative, and usually reactionary.

As a war-resister and activist himself, Robert Lifton tried to combine psychiatric therapy with ethical and political counsel in his work with the VVAW group. This interesting and valuable book is Dr. Lifton's account of their struggle with their memories of brutalities committed and witnessed, their resolve to be revolutionary opponents of a war they had earlier participated in. Robert Lifton is here clearly trying to break out of psychiatric conventions by taking full account not only of his patients' subjective lives but also of historical, political, and ethical factors. Since he believes that psychological experience is not self-contained, he thinks of himself as a "psychohistorian" and has tried to make use of what he calls "extrospection" as well as introspection. It is abundantly evident that Lifton is a "committed" man. He is transparently honest, sometimes painfully so.

In this book Lifton makes use of a theory, worked out in previous studies, which emphasizes the opposition of death and the continuity of life, a conceptual scheme he thinks more appropriate to contemporary experience than the traditional psychoanalytical preoccupation with sexual instinct and repression. For him fear of death is the overriding fact of life. It must be said that such a model has served him well in treating the Vietnam veterans in this book. In the absence of any larger values to defend, for most of them the war became simply a struggle for survival. As he puts it,

> One could make no inwardly convincing association between death and a higher principle. Individual survival, always the predominant preoccupation in war, became in this war the *only* purpose or cause one could call forth to justify one's actions. Nor could the attempt at logical explanation of why one person died and not another, so characteristic of death immersion in general, ward off the sense of total absurdity. Subsequent deaths one witnesses are no more acceptable, though more effectively managed by numbing— but one never really recovers from that first survival.

However, a reader is forced to wonder if the fear of death was—and is—as great for the Viet Cong and North Vietnamese. It certainly does not seem so. Their willingness to sacrifice their lives in the service of a political faith or in the interest of "liberating" South Vietnam seems more typical than the behavior of our soldiers. In the Second World War fear of their own death could hardly be said to have been the sole or even the dominant anxiety for soldiers of the Allies or the Axis powers.

Lifton takes Freud to task for subordinating death anxiety to the fear of castration. Both are common on the battlefield, as any veteran can testify. But there are other fears equally pervasive, I think. For example, fear of letting down one's comrades, of showing oneself a coward, fear of disgrace and dishonor, of not proving to be a man in ways that have little to do with any notions of glory and immortality. Just why we must accept a single cause to explain the complexity of human responses, or one always more fundamental than the rest, puzzles me. Robert Lifton is so absorbed in the experience of this group of veterans that he tends to forget how untypical they really are. His preoccupation with the theme of death seems too much rooted in the current moment and his overemphasis makes it difficult to understand other peoples and other times. Whatever its causes, the exaggerated fear of death has reached fantastic proportions in contemporary America, ironically enough at a time when life is "not very much to lose."

Lifton gives a fascinating and sophisticated account of a group of young Americans who were overchallenged by an evil experience and who now seek to cope with their horrible memories. Having participated in slaughtering and mutilating their opponents, and often innocent civilians as well, they have come to recognize with nearly paralyzing force that they have transgressed acceptable human boundaries. He quotes at length their conversations in these extensive sessions and his sympathetic description of their plight is painfully instructive.

Lifton's conviction is that the veterans' consciousness of guilt must be transformed rather than done away with. Static guilt must be made over into what he calls animating guilt, which involves a rediscovery of oneself as a human being capable of growth. This idea is adapted from Martin Buber but it is older, based on the principle that acceptance of guilt can open us to others and to a sense of our indebtedness to them and to society. In German the world guilt, *Schuld,* is the same as the word debt, and it is not difficult to perceive the connection between assuming responsibility for one's debts or wrongdoing as a way of becoming more self-aware and sensitive to others.

In a society like ours which relies so much on talk, it is often assumed that the best way to accomplish this transformation is in groups. One must expose one's guilt feelings to others and hear their reactions; nothing must be held back. It is as though one could atone for one's sins by a public confession. To his credit as a psychiatrist Lifton knows that this is only a beginning. After the confessions of these guilt-scarred veterans, he urged them to action, and he also participated in their public protests. For him the political-ethical and the psychological-therapeutic are inseparable.

Even so, the reader may often ask whether it is necessary to require these veterans in group sessions to turn their guilt feelings into conscious acceptance of guilt. Is not the process of changing unproductive guilt into "animating guilt" a much longer and more solitary process than is here envisaged? Will not atonement for guilt affect the character of one's life years after the guilt-inspiring deeds have been committed? I suspect that the VVAW are unlikely to grow very much by their antiwar activities alone. As one of them says poignantly in these pages: "Our life is being against the war. When the war ends then *we* end as people." Such recognition indicates the limitations of their struggle. Building a life on solid accomplishment is more difficult than being an antiwar veteran and confessing one's guilt in public.

This is in no way meant to denigrate the work these men did in helping to awaken American society to the immense evils of Vietnam. I agree with Lifton that "there is a very real sense in which those few are doing symbolic psychological work for all veterans, and indeed for all of American society." If the American involvement in the Vietnam war ever ends, we may hope that they will discover other tasks that have meaning for them, without, however, ceasing to remind Americans of the evil nature of the war. No doubt it will require years for many of them to feel that life is worth living once more, and it may unfortunately be even longer before millions of their fellows will be able to accept the disgrace and dishonor that the war has brought upon us as a people.

Lifton is probably overoptimistic in believing that the value of Vietnam for our society may lie in a turning away from the warrior ethos with its irrational enthusiasms and subtle poisons. It is surely more realistic to expect little from these few men, even if our society were suddenly to become stable for a decade or two, itself an unlikely prospect. He concedes that American pilots did not experience anything like the guilt that a few of the ground troops did, though they killed and maimed many more than "grunts" could have. As some of them express it: "Look, we're just bus drivers." Or "I don't *feel* like a war criminal. What I was doing is just like screwing fuses into sockets." One of Lifton's sources remarks about these pilots: "The issue of guilt becomes meaningless. Conscience and morality are irrelevant. One does not set out to kill and therefore, psychologically, one does not."

A few, pitifully few, of these airmen are able to break through the deadly abstraction of technological warfare. But during the recent return of the prisoners of war, most of them pilots, there was no indication that many were burdened with guilt feelings. More and better military technology is soon to come, of a sort that will make its operators even less sensitive to the human consequences of their deeds. Those who have been strong enough to get through the recent book *Voices from the Plain of Jars* will have a chilling premonition of this sort of "warfare." No psychic numbing is necessary, or as Lifton puts it, numbing itself is "automated."

In one of his most successful chapters, "The Counterfeit Universe," Robert Lifton deals with what appears to be a widespread sense of unreality among Vietnam veterans. They felt that they were engaged in unreal combat, playing at being soldiers, committing and witnessing absurd acts of evil without conviction and without even believing they were identified with it. Home again, these veterans find the same bogus and malignant quality in American life, even in their own inner selves. Lifton quotes Philip Kingry to this effect: "The war isn't just an excuse. *It* was *everything.* I am a lie. What I have to say is a lie. But it is the most true lie you will ever hear about a war."

In combatting this virulent disease, which I agree is widespread in contemporary America, the Existentialists' rem-

edy of seeking authenticity and confronting the Absurd (always capitalized) begins to taste like very thin gruel. Though Lifton draws upon such remedies freely, he does not succeed in making clear how one can be "authentic" in a society or universe that makes no sense at all. At the end of his book he falls back on the principles of perpetual rebellion against murder and the solidarity among men that Camus claimed to be the result and justification of rebellion. I fear that such romantic defiance appears as futile to the post-Vietnam generation as it seemed appropriate for a short time during the Second World War in France.

The search for reality seems nowadays to be taking a religious direction, rather than one toward Existentialist atheism. If one were inclined to prophesy, one might predict that the last quarter of our century will witness a proliferation of religious faiths, many of them as unwelcome to the old as are current religious tendencies. Traditionally, religion has been a search for reality when all else fails, and particularly when the dominant ethic disintegrates, as appears to be the case today. For those of us who teach in American colleges the signs are already numerous enough.

In spite of his psychiatric training and his failure to mention religion explicitly, Robert Lifton frequently sounds like a rabbi. In his chapter "On Healing," he describes the three steps necessary for a transformation of the self. First there is "Confrontation," which consists in a "questioning of personal integration or integrity brought about by some form of death encounter." The guilt that follows causes the second stage of "Reordering." The third stage is "Renewal," that is, the self's attainment of a form for its newly won integrity. Though all of this is put in the secular language of psychiatry, it requires little imagination to see that it follows the classic patterns of religious conversion.

Earlier, in discussing the veterans' rage against military chaplains and psychiatrists in Vietnam, Lifton himself calls attention to the kinship between psychiatry and religion. "Chaplains and psychiatrists are not only spiritual counselors; Americans also perceive them, rightly or wrongly, as guardians of the spirit, as guides to right thinking and proper behavior (in this way psychiatrists resemble chaplains more than they do other physicians)." I confess, perhaps naïvely, that this idea had never occurred to me. In World War II we had little chance to see psychiatrists but it would never have entered our heads to put them in the same category as chaplains. However, in spite of Freud's allegiance to the scientific world view, there may be a continuity here that had escaped my attention. In any case Lifton's moral earnestness, passion for justice, and concern for healing sick souls clearly connect him with this ancient tradition. Hence he may well find a religious revival, if it comes, infinitely easier to adjust to than will most of his professional colleagues.

Though understandably sensitive to the veterans' scorn for "shrinks," he ascribes their dislike to the fact that therapists have become mere technicians. He is probably right in his strictures against many psychiatric practices. In any event a layman like myself is inclined to be sympathetic to Lifton's determination to link psychiatry to ethics and to the larger situation in which the neurotic finds himself. The kind of healing that concerns him seems ultimately closer to a noninstitutional religious faith than it does either to the biological sciences or to philosophy. On this matter he will doubtless discover much disagreement with the profession. (pp. 22-3)

J. Glenn Gray, "Back," in The New York Review of Books, *Vol. XX, No. 11, June 28, 1973, pp. 22-4.*

Jane Shapiro

Living and Dying was written primarily for adolescents which is to say people who seem different from the rest of us in their keener struggles to come to some acceptable terms with life and its terrors. Lifton and [and co-author Eric] Olson's attitude toward young people is especially generous, even respectful about people's willingness to deaden themselves in their dead-earnest skirmishes with an overwhelming, tricky world. *Everybody has reasons:* usually good ones. Of course one monstrous reason has been set aside, exactly as if it could be forgotten: We die.

One of Lifton's bird cartoons introduces each chapter. In his preface Lifton calls the birds "an antidote for 'grand visions,'" for pomposity, expressing his "sense of the absurd truth that lies beneath just about everything." The birds, he says, "will mock what we write—will in fact mock the subject of death itself, which I believe to be the ultimate source of mockery per se. Kurt Vonnegut once said, 'You can't be funny unless you get close to death, to fear.' Turning that around I would say that you can't get 'close' to death and elemental fear without becoming a little 'funny' in the process."

Lifton and Olson begin by quoting Toynbee: "Death is un-American." Death, they argue is our "lost season": the idea of death has become entirely unacceptable because today it is associated with images of gratuitous holocaust: at the same time we have lost sustaining faith in institutions which once organized and gave meaning to our lives: common ideas, which Lifton and Olson explicate with uncommon lucidity, elegance, and directness. We live without compelling ritual, we cannot mourn, and we make ourselves insensible rather than admit that death—now become a potentially absurd death which mocks our lives—happens at all. In this sense "we need the theme of death to re-constitute our lives": so we can quit bumping ourselves off.

The second chapter, "Death and the Life Cycle," opens with a wonderful quote from Theodore Roethke: "So much of adolescence is an ill-defined dying./ An intolerable waiting./ A longing for another place and time./ Another condition." In early childhood, the authors say, the child's "inner imagery" of life and death is organized around three sets of opposites: connection and separation; movement and stasis; integrity and disintegration. The reinforcement of imagery of life's connectedness, movement, and integrity nourishes the child's trust and hope even in the face of death: "A child seeks" (not to have death's reality denied but) "to grasp the idea of death while having the idea of continuity affirmed."

Adolescence is "itself a death and rebirth experience": the child dies, the adult is born. Struggling more than other people to avoid deadness and affirm life, adolescents are stuck with the question of how to open oneself to growth while defending oneself against pain and the anxiety of loss, "which is a form of death anxiety." The struggle for everybody, against heavy odds, is to nurture imagery and symbols which give a firm sense of significance to one's life, thus to achieve "symbolic immortality"—this through an awareness of biological or cultural continuity; through a sense of one's link with nature; through religious "re-orientation," but of a kind which avoids the alluring lie that people don't actually die; through creative work, or "works" in the world. The authors suggest the interface of anxiety about death and discomfort when our work goes badly:

> Ordinarily, when one's work is progressing well, there is little conscious concern with its immortalizing effect. But when the products of creative effort do not seem sufficient to embody one's sense of self, then the question (previously unconscious) of the value and meaning of one's life and work begins to become a conscious concern.

The authors recommend their fifth mode of symbolic immortality, which they call "experiential transcendence," a sense of timelessness and ecstasy, of losing oneself, which can re-order the symbols by which one lives, bringing new vitality or a creatively altered viewpoint. It is a state "felt as involving extraordinary psychological unity, intensity of sensual awareness, and unexpressible illumination and insight," and it informs our sense of biological or religious continuity, of connectedness with nature or of the meaning of work. One enters into "mythic time," in which the perception of death is minimized and the threat of extinction is no longer foreboding. One feels oneself alive in a "continuous present" in which ancient past and distant future are contained." Lifton and Olson see heavy drug use as a maladroit form of the search for this kind of transcendence, a search related not just to idle or gratuitous experimentation but to "the unfolding of that which is oldest and deepest in the self."

The authors look at the ways people have tried to master death anxiety, particularly in a brilliant section on prejudice and victimization. Their discussion of the nuclear age begins with a striking description of the first bomb explosion, and suggests that the uniquely modern perception that one may die unreasonably and without leaving a trace has led to impairments in all our old methods of securing that warm feeling of symbolic immortality. They describe the survivor mentality Lifton examined in his studies of the survivors of Hiroshima: a state of mind characterized by "guilt, numbing, and a continuing effort to give form and meaning to radically disrupted lives"; but in dilute form our lives are like that. Indeed, "in cultivating and making clear to ourselves our own status as survivors," they say, we more fully confront our world and our age.

Appropriately enough, the book ends with a compelling section on the psychology of the hideously traumatized young Vietnam veterans, and of what Lifton and Olson are calling their "Protean" style of life, their "continuous experimentation in an attempt to re-animate themselves and their world." Oddly, it is our style as well.

Jane Shapiro, in a review of "Living and Dying," in The Village Voice, *Vol. XIX, No. 32, August 15, 1974, p. 26.*

William Braden

Death and survival have been the focus of Lifton's previous studies of Chinese thought reform, the Chinese Cultural Revolution, Hiroshima survivors and Vietnam antiwar veterans. In [*The Life of the Self: Toward a New Psychology*] he codifies his views in the concept of "Proteanism." He asserts we live in a "Protean environment" of rapid social change that "makes survivors of us all." He sees "the emergence of a Protean psychological style of flux and flow of the self, or self-process."

Lifton has chosen an apt metaphor. He tells us the Protean style is "named after the Greek god Proteus, a notorious shape-shifter." Proteus in fact was a prophetic sea god who could tell you anything you wanted to know. But he would try to squirm out of it by assuming a variety of forms, and to make him talk you had to seize him and hold him fast. Webster defines him as "one who easily changes his appearance or principles."

Lifton writes with a pen dipped in quicksilver, and the Secret Service would have a hard time wrestling his jargon to the ground. He proposes a "formative principle" and a "formative depth-psychological paradigm" involving "increasingly articulated focus on *form per se*" in "an interminable series of experiments and explorations of varying depth, each of which may be readily abandoned in favor of still another psychological quest." He advocates "continuing search" for forms and images that fit "this historical moment." The "resulting principle of a *formative* (or psychoformative) *process,* characterized by evolving images and psychic forms," offers a "formative-symbolic" perspective that represents "an ongoing *process of symbolization,* rather than of particular symbols." The emphasis in formative theory "is always on continuum and transitional process," and this emphasis "can lend to descriptions and explanations framed in formative terms a fluid, at times amorphous, quality in contrast to the crisp distinctions of classical Freudian theory." Finally: "Only by creating, maintaining, and breaking down and re-creating viable form are we capable of experiencing vitality—and in that very sense we may say that form equals life."

I think this means the workings of the mind are complex and dynamic. They also are not purely intrapsychic but are influenced by the immediate environment and by historical forces.

Lifton is chasing Zeno's arrow. And he's trying to avoid Bergson's cinematographic fallacy. He is saying that life is a movie, and you can't understand it by stopping the projector and studying the series of individual still shots on the film strip. You can't freeze-frame life—as it is frozen into an electronic portrait at the conclusion of so many television dramas.

That's fine. It's wise to recognize the squirming facts exceed the squamous mind. And there is merit in efforts not to be "clearer than the truth." One could also do worse than emulate Erik H. Erikson's pioneering attempts to add a psychohistorical dimension to psychoanalysis. And indeed, Lifton adds: "I am not suggesting that there is not psychological baseline beyond historically specific imagery." But there isn't the suggestion of a clue as to where that baseline might be, and Lifton is simply institutionalizing chaos and faddishness. Psychic chic.

The emptiness of it all becomes obvious when Lifton tries to use his formative principle to deal with death anxiety and the "need for a sense of symbolic immortality." Among the palliatives he offers are communes, women's liberation, rural-return and "significant work experience." (The latter would hardly satisfy Woody Allen, who has stated: "I don't want to achieve immortality through my work. I want to achieve it through not dying.") Worse yet, Lifton appears to think death is good for you. Death is "a formative or constitutive symbol, an element of creativity and renewal." To be brushed by death "can be a source of insight and power." One can emerge "with deepened sensibility and extended vitality and reach." Maintaining a psychic place for death "enhances that which is most human, the imagination."

That's silly and pathetic. Lifton in his abstractions does not take death seriously enough, or life either for that matter.

This is the kind of attitude Ernest Becker was talking about when he said that science in responding to death is essentially bourgeois—"an affair of bureaucrats"—and that "whatever man does on this planet has to be done in the lived truth of the terror of creation, of the grotesque, of the rumble of panic underneath everything." And the only way to transcend these, if at all, is "in the timeworn religious way: to project one's problems onto a god-figure, to be healed by an all-embracing and all-justifying beyond."

Proteus won't do. Lifton should keep psychiatry out of the temple—or do what Freud did, and bite the bullet.

Finally, the religious answer to death has not been immortality—in the sense of life that continues in endless time. The answer has been eternal life in an already Now that is both inside and outside of time. Lifton in one brief passage seems to be aware of the difference, but skips over it, and seems unaware that his god of flux is the very antithesis of that holy eternal. (pp. L1, L4)

William Braden, "Mortality Chic," in Book World—The Washington Post, *May 16, 1976, pp. L1, L4.*

Robert Michels

Twenty-four hundred years ago Pericles spoke at the public funeral of the first Athenians who had fallen in the Peloponnesian War. Athens was at the acme of its golden age, the cultural, political and economic center of civilization, and Pericles extolled its virtues: "We cultivate refinement without extravagance and knowledge without effeminacy;

wealth we employ more for use than for show, and place the real disgrace of poverty not in owning to the fact but in declining the struggle against it." Yet to a modern reader it is disquieting to note that the majority of the Athenian population was disfranchised, slaves and foreigners, and 27 years later Athens was defeated and the decline of Greek civilization began.

Today another war is, perhaps, drawing to a close. As we bury our dead and embrace our returning warriors, triumphant heroes and maimed survivors alike, we search for the meaning of it all and long for a modern Pericles who can give us the feeling that our struggle embodied the highest values of our society. Yet the quest is an uncomfortable one: our disenfranchised are more effective than the Athenian slaves in making their presence known, and many of our intellectual leaders predict that the decline of our own civilization is impending if not imminent.

Robert Jay Lifton, a psychiatrist and psychohistorian, suggests that we might escape that fate if we look at the truth about ourselves and our war rather than numbing ourselves to the painful awareness of death, guilt and inner corruption. . . .

The structure of [*Home from the War*] is complex and sometimes confusing, but his basic argument is simple and clear. The war in Vietnam is an evil created by Americans and those whom we have sent to fight it are placed in an intolerable ethical conflict. Most returning veterans have numbed their sensitivities to death, guilt and inner anguish in order to defend themselves from this conflict. "One can say that guilt becomes the fulcrum on which the psychological destiny of the Vietnam survivor turns."

Leading a "rap" group of Vietnam Veterans Against the War, Lifton was able to participate in their resensitization to pain and guilt, transforming what he calls their "static," numbed or self-lacerating guilt to "animating" guilt, with consequent reversal of their "counterfeit universe" and a "flow and action of change and growth." Lifton's language is poetic, and his work is perhaps more in the tradition of poetry than of either psychiatry or history, as he finds not only his data but also his explanatory concepts in the inner experience of man rather than in the world of facts, causes and effects.

His viewpoint is not only antiprofessional, it is essentially anti-intellectual, and he relies far more on rhetoric than on logic. The rhetoric, however, is often effective, and those who agree with his major conclusions will read the book with great interest. His argument, however, has some problems. All war is hell, and there is little to suggest that the experiences of being killed or surviving are very different in just or unjust wars. Lifton argues that the "central fact of the Vietnam War is that no one really believes in it," but the very statement converts the question from an ethical to a psychological one; the issue is not good or evil, but rather conviction or doubt. Many Americans believed in Vietnam; is Lifton's argument irrelevant for them? Some farsighted ones doubted World War I, and even World War II (which Lifton describes as "more psychologically defensible"). My own suspicion is that such questions seem rather abstract and far removed to most

men in foxholes with bullets overhead. Lifton wants to say something about the relationship of survivor guilt to the inherent ethical meaning of the crusade, but he comes dangerously close to saying that war is bad and it is not pursued with sufficient enthusiasm. He does not speak against all war, and seems fairly sympathetic to the Vietcong and North Vietnamese. Is the good or evil of war to be determined by political scientists or perhaps public opinion pollsters? Would a study of the North Vietnamese show different findings, and if it did would it help us to decide who was right?

This problem is a special case of Lifton's view of truth as a form of inner experience. The rap group members *felt* something, and therefore it was so. We are not told what it would mean if the Nixon cabinet or the Pentagon command had a rap group, an experience of inner conviction and true-witness, and then proceeded to bomb the hell out of North Vietnam. If the criterion of truth is experiential, and we discard "objective" and "scientific" tests, then who is to decide which truth shall prevail? Whether Lifton likes it or not, the inner conviction of most of our citizens favored the war, or at least was neutral, and it was a small minority of Vietnam veterans who joined political movements and found their way to his rap groups.

Those who don't share Lifton's bias about the war are unlikely to read very far, and few will be converted. However, even for those who do there are some disturbing questions. He is bothered by "military psychiatry," and argues that "for the psychiatrist, as for everyone else (but in many ways even more so), there is no getting away from an evaluation of the group one is to serve and, above all, the nature and consequences of its immediate and long range mission." This is indeed a crucial issue, and the traditional medical model has dealt with it by insisting on a broad professional ethic which is independent of particular political or even moral judgements. The doctor treats the sick, whether saint or sinner, capitalist or communist, Vietcong or American. Lifton seems to disagree: the psychiatrists who treated the acute psychoses of the American soldiers were helping an immoral war and therefore wrong. Perhaps, but what then of the soldier with appendicitis? Further, when Soviet psychiatry is used to suppress political heretics, which Lifton condemns, is that not the logical result of arguing that the professions must be seen as tools for the achievement of good causes, rather than as functioning relatively autonomously from the specific social-political context? If the American psychiatrist was wrong to rehabilitate the shell-shocked soldier in Vietnam because it was an unjust war, then Lifton's only criticism of the Russian can be that his cause is also wrong, not (as I would argue) that the profession of medicine should not be an agent of any political cause, right or wrong.

There is little reassurance in Lifton's example of how a psychiatrist ought to "convey antiwar values in (his) work." The result of writing reports on behalf of young men seeking to avoid military service and "giving strong emphasis to whatever findings could contribute to a psychiatric deferment" is not that fewer people go to war, but only that different ones do, poorer, blacker and less sophisticated about psychiatrists. Is this more anti-war, less immoral, this "marriage of professional discipline to imaginative spontaneity, the coming together of ethic and technique" which he advocates?

Although his psychology is overly romantic, and his psychiatry reads like that of a man who writes books rather than treats patients, Lifton has grasped a poetic truth in his vision of the experience of war and its impact on the souls of those who return from it. Perhaps most vivid is its impact on him as he shares their experiences in the rap group. As a modern day Pericles, he warns us not to bury our dead without first experiencing their death. He echoes Thomas Mann in *The Magic Mountain:* "A man's dying is more the survivors' affair than his own."

> Robert Michels, "Dead Souls," in Book World—The Washington Post, *June 24, 1973, p. 3.*

Timothy J. O'Connell

As each generation needs to rewrite history in light of its own concerns, it also needs to reconsider the psychological model of man it employs. Freud's model of man as driven by instincts, defending himself against sexual and aggressive impulses and often ending up neurotic, has had a tremendous impact on how modern man sees himself. Convincing though it was, Freud's model gave scant attention to societal forces.

It was Erik Erikson, writing in the mid-20th century, who systematically incorporated these societal forces in his view of man. Erikson's working model is that of man trying to achieve his identity by responding to developmental and environmental pressures throughout his life. Only by understanding the times a person lived in could one hope to understand the person. Responding to his own times and their historical events, Robert Jay Lifton, research psychiatrist at Yale University, has offered an updated model of psychological man [in his *The Life of the Self: Toward a New Psychology*].

Lifton has worked extensively with survivors of Hiroshima and veterans of Vietnam. Accordingly, he affords death and continuity central importance in his model. Lifton uses death in a symbolic as much as a literal sense. Symbolically, it refers to psychic numbing, a sense that one is out of touch with his own center, much like the loss of feeling experienced by Mersault in Camus's *The Stranger.* New and old experiences no longer fit together; the connection between immediate and ultimate meaning is broken.

Lifton elaborates on the types of experiences that produce psychic numbing. The first is the experience of separation. Here the infant's physiological urge to be connected with its nurturing parent becomes in later life the adult's effort to be connected with people, groups or historical forces. Any serious separation from these desired goals evokes dread. If this dread is dramatic enough, like the experiences of those at Hiroshima or in Vietnam, or pervasive enough, like Mersault's, it leads to psychic numbing.

Disintegration represents a second form of dread. It stands at the opposite pole from a feeling of harmony and order and reflects a sense that one's inner forms and images no longer adequately convey his relationship with the world and no longer provide him with a reliable plan for action. Attendant on this loss of direction is a weakening of moral and ethical commitments.

The third form of dread stems from stasis, or lack of movement. For the child, the physiological sense of movement involves moving a part of his body. For the adult, physical movement itself can symbolize progress, change and growth. When an individual has a deep sense that he is stagnating, that he is in the same place all the time, doing the same things, he becomes psychically numb.

Getting beyond this numbing involves establishing a sense of continuity, which can be gained when one faces the terrors death brings, and emerges with a sense of wholeness, a sense that past and present, near and far, fit back together. Continuity is achieved through the formative process of creating, maintaining, breaking down and recreating the image of one's experience, what Lifton calls his formative paradigm.

If his paradigm becomes popular, Lifton realizes he will be transforming how people think about psychological problems. Different causes will be cited—loss of meaning whether by separation, disintegration or stagnation, rather than repressed sexuality or developmental crises. Different solutions tried—seeking psychological continuity rather than psychoanalysis. This change in perspective will be subtle, but real. A sense of the extent of this change might be had by contrasting the view adults have of their parents with the view they had as children or adolescents. Then parents were providers, interpreters of experience, the source of values and the target of criticisms. Later parents are seen as other adults, with their own dreams and insecurities, who respond to pressures with understandable compromises and limited resources. And this change in perspective leads adults to feel and act differently toward their parents. Similarly, given Lifton's model, psychiatrists and those in other helping professions would think and act differently about their task.

The Life of the Self is an imaginative rethinking of some basic human experiences. It is a persuasive and suggestive book, and it provides an impetus for the reader to do his own rethinking. In this sense it is an effective paradigm or model. In the larger sense of paradigm—of being a fundamental shift in perspective—it leaves something to be desired. It sketches an overview, but fails to provide the detailed analysis necessary to support such a drastic shift in approach. The book's argument in this sense remains more suggestive than compelling. On a different level, I think the book suffers from a lack of clarity of presentation. Not that Lifton's style is dense or cumbersome; it is not. But the book lacks a succinct exposition of its central ideas. I found myself leafing back and forth for explanations of terms and trying to keep pace with the too frequent references to other parts of the book. But, if one has the inclination and patience for it, the novel perspective and provocative ideas make the effort worthwhile. (pp. 126-28)

> *Timothy J. O'Connell, in a review of "The Life*

of the Self: Toward a New Psychology," in
America, *Vol. 135, No. 5, September 11, 1976,*
pp. 126-28.

Terrence Des Pres

Sex is out and death is in. To judge from the rash of books on dying, the symposia on death, the academic allure of thanatology, there is more interest in the emergency ward than in the bedroom. Sensationalism accounts for some of this, but the dedication of genuine care is also part of it. The bearing of death upon life has not, until recently, been fully considered; and Robert Jay Lifton is surely correct when he argues that psychoanalytic theory has been especially remiss in its attempt to manage man's awareness of death.

In *The Broken Connection: On Death and the Continuity of Life.* Dr. Lifton attempts to set the record straight. His quarrel is directly with Freud, and his revisionary treatment of "the death instinct" includes the regret that even in a book as penetrating as *Beyond the Pleasure Principle* Freud "had to ward off the potentially transforming influence of death on *theory.*" Where the master left off, Dr. Lifton takes up. His aim, he boldly declares, is not only to create a "new psychology," but to transform basic Freudian categories—guilt, anxiety, neurosis—into the "death-oriented psychology" they imply.

Dr. Lifton is concerned foremost with the psychic process of symbolization, in particular the way we negotiate the finality of death by creating, symbolically, a counter-sense of continuity. This, broadly speaking, is what he means by "symbolic immortality," a state of mind best understood by considering "the symbolizing process around death and immortality as the individual's experience of participation in some form of collective life-continuity." Such is Dr. Lifton's program. He agrees with Freud that symbolic experience is as potent as anything concrete, but not that symbolism is the language of repression, as Freud thought, nor that the sense of immortality is reducible to illusion merely.

Against Freud, Dr. Lifton argues that our need to balance death with images of permanence is not a betrayal of psychic integrity but the very essence of it. The important insight, here, is that "the quest for symbolic immortality is an aspect of being human." As an observation, this is a truism; as the starting point for a theory of human nature, it is a principle with enormous potential. The self is a symbolic construct; and the heart of the matter may be, as Dr. Lifton suggests, that as human beings we cannot function in health and harmony unless we feel connected to something larger than ourselves that is undiminished by personal death. Whether through family or institutions, through religion, art or identification with nature's cycle, we require rootedness in a community of life we feel will not end.

Connectedness is all. The "broken connection," in Dr. Lifton's scheme, is any impairment of our capacity to connect, any experience or situation which, by breaking our relation to images of continuity, causes internal disruption. This, I take it, is the new meaning of "trauma," a

meaning much needed in this age of genocide. The underlying assumption is that disaster in the world engenders a corresponding disruption in the soul. And if Dr. Lifton is right, then mankind has reached a terrible impasse, a predicament brought on by the existence of nuclear weapons and the possibility of global obliteration, the mere *knowledge* of which mars our images of continuity, undermines our trust in life and, by mocking all claims to a future, drives the self toward terminal trauma.

Dr. Lifton offers no solutions (who can?), but he is compassionate, almost eloquent, in his analysis of the damage done by what he calls "the nuclear image." And his ability to draw psychological principles from a historical situation so dire and unprecedented is remarkable. Dr. Lifton does know what is lacking in Freudian theory, and he is deeply aware of the ruinous impact of nuclear threat. To bring the two together—Freud and the Bomb—is a very considerable feat.

And yet *The Broken Connection* is not, as it ought and deserves to be, a major book. The issues are there, the urgency and serious insight, but all is marred by the repetition of old ideas, by a nearly comic use of jargon and, perhaps worse, by Dr. Lifton's habit of inventing new words.

Dr. Lifton seems to believe that by employing the word "psychobiological" he has healed the mind/body split; or that by substituting the term "inchoate image" for "instinct" he has taken the determinism out of Freud's "death instinct." But nowhere does he demonstrate the "psychobiological" basis of his "new psychology," and his development of "the inchoate image" is shaky indeed. Having replaced the terms "idea" and "perception" with "image" and "image-feeling," Dr. Lifton goes on to suggest that we think of the image as a "plan" and that rather than resort to instinct we might better comprehend human motivation as something "contained in the genes and expressed in imagery of various kinds from birth onward." The "inchoate image" is thus a "built-in psychological guide," and if the newborn infant "expects" to be fed and "knows" how to go about feeding, then, in Dr. Lifton's view, this is proof of "the newborn's inchoate organismic inclination toward receiving the nurturing it requires."

Jargon and clotted prose aside, how do such formulations differ from current concepts of instinct? They don't. Nevertheless, Dr. Lifton is convinced that his move "from instinct to image has special importance," because thereby we get around Freud's "biomysticism" and arrive at "a psychology that is evolutionary in spirit, genuinely biological in its focus on image-making." There is no objection to Dr. Lifton's desire to ground symbolization in biology. What keeps us from full appreciation of his theories is his use of language. Bad writing produces bad ideas, and I have quoted at length to demonstrate this weakness in *The Broken Connection.*

Freud is "rationalist-iconoclastic," Jung is "mythic-hygienic," while Dr. Lifton's own approach is "formative-symbolizing." Depression turns out to be "mimetic death" or "negativistic stasis." Dr. Lifton's extreme reliance on words of his own making goes deeper than a poverty of language: it is the index of a stubbornly centripetal vision. Among the many sources he quotes, his own books predominate. He cites his own brief work with survivors of the Buffalo Creek disaster but ignores Kai T. Erikson's masterly study of the same event, *Everything in Its Path.* When he introduces "nuclearism" to suggest that the Bomb has created a new religion, a demonic awe and numbed submission, there is no mention of Thomas Pynchon's novel *Gravity's Rainbow,* surely the greatest book on that subject, and this despite Dr. Lifton's liberal use of literary examples elsewhere, including an entire chapter on Yukio Mishima to make a minor point.

At least 70 percent of **The Broken Connection** is a recapitulation of ideas that Dr. Lifton has been promoting, book after book, for more than a dozen years. Psychic numbing, survivor guilt, death immersion, totalism, symbolic immortality—this is Dr. Lifton's litany, and we have heard it all before. In his favor it must be said that by concentrating his repertory of favorite terms within the framework of his contest with Freud, **The Broken Connection** offers a sort of summit perspective, a theoretical coherence toward which the whole of his earlier work has tended.

Dr. Lifton's followers will be pleased to see his central terms in unified force. His critics will be troubled by the ease with which he slides from specific cases to generalities. Where, for example, a survivor was once a person who had come through an actual event of overwhelming destruction—men and women who endured Hiroshima or the death camps—Dr. Lifton now argues that we are all survivors. We need not have spent years in Auschwitz but simply have experienced a "death equivalent," something on the order of childhood separation from a parent or a bout with a depression with its attendant feeling of deadness. This sort of argument approaches the intellectual night, as Hegel puts it, in which all cows are black.

Yet despite its shortcomings, **The Broken Connection** is a passionate book, at grips with the largest issues of our time. Behind Dr. Lifton's obsessive return to a fixed set of terms and his penchant for inventing new ones, there is real vision, a fund of wisdom at odds with the array of conceptual contraptions which, for reasons unclear, Dr. Lifton feels constrained to employ as his chosen mode of discourse. It is as if, then, his aim were truly to create anew the constellated drama of our inner life, to warn us of our peril, to defend our humanity against increasingly inhuman circumstance. (pp. 9, 32, 34)

> Terrence Des Pres, "Death and Continuity," in The New York Times Book Review, *November 4, 1979, pp. 9, 32, 34.*

Steven Weiland

Robert Jay Lifton's interest in the extreme situation is reflected in **Death in Life** (1967), a study of the survivors of Hiroshima, and other books and essays on the psychological meaning of cataclysmic events. In **The Broken Connection** he incorporates original ideas about surviving into an elaborate theory of "death and the continuity of life." Lifton proposes nothing less than a new psychoanalysis built on a "new psychological paradigm" which advances

Freud's model of instinct and defense and Erik Erikson's of identity and the life cycle. It is based on a lost theme—death and continuity—which has been, he claims, neglected by orthodox psychoanalysts who separate death from the general motivations and interests of life. In his analysis of "the broken connection" Lifton proposes general principles applicable to the origins and maintenance of death imagery and the struggle for continuity, to the working out of the individual life cycle, to several varieties of psychological disorder, and to aspects of recent history. He is interested especially in the consequences of what he calls "the nuclear image," imagery of extinction unique to post-World War II individuals and societies. "My press," he says, "is toward integrating principles that can have meaning for psychological work and general living in our time."

Lifton also defines his place in the psychoanalytic tradition by distinguishing his formulations of the symbolizing process from those of Freud and Jung. The former, he claims, insisted on confronting death as simply the annihilation of the self, the latter only in terms of the psychological importance of mythic imagery of immortality. Lifton insists on our power to build death- and immortality-related symbols derived from individual desires for participation in some form of "life-continuity." Denial of death can never be total, "rather we go about life with a kind of 'middle knowledge' of death, a partial awareness of it side by side with expressions and actions that belie that awareness. . . . We in fact require symbolization of continuity—imaginative forms of transcending death—in order to confront genuinely the fact that we die." Lifton takes this drive to be a core area of the self. It is, he claims, "a corollary of the knowledge of death itself, and reflects a compelling and universal inner quest for continuous symbolic relationship to what has gone before and what will continue after our finite individual lives. That quest is central to the human project, to man as a cultural animal and to his creation of culture and history. The struggle toward, or experience of, a sense of immortality is in itself neither compensatory nor 'irrational' but an appropriate symbolization of our biological and historical connectedness." The quest for symbolic immortality is conducted, according to Lifton, in five general modes: biological, theological, creative, natural and through experiential transcendence. We need, he says, a more deliberate image-making psychology based on a "unitary principle" which integrates death and death imagery with the processes of life.

In this new paradigm, imagery of death and continuity is organized also around three fluid psychological axes: connection-separation, integrity-disintegration and movement-stasis. These are the framework for the formulation of our "death equivalents," the private and public translations we make of our knowledge of death and desire for continuity into usable vehicles for life. Hence these pairs are also designated "life parameters," indicative of Lifton's determination to blend our stubborn but unacknowledged awareness of death, the "unchoate image," into our plans for life. Images and symbols formulated to reflect our sense of life's endings are the proof, he claims, of the necessarily realistic and elastic psyche. Genuine psychological development means increasing symbolization, the ability to store and combine images in increasingly complex relation to space and time. And awareness of our own death stimulates and then sustains this image-making capacity on behalf of psychic survival and vitality.

In order to display the practical implications of this new psychological emphasis Lifton offers a catalogue of the emotions as their psychological boundaries are shaped by the incorporation of death imagery. Guilt, for instance, recast by Lifton in relation to its death equivalents, becomes the experience of feeling responsible, through action or inaction, for separation, stasis or disintegration. Guilt carries its own death imagery and an equivalent and dependent power for psychological balance. It has, according to Lifton, a critical evolutionary function in making us more fully accountable for the lives of others. The following passage typifies Lifton's blending of traditional psychoanalytic and historical themes with his new emphasis on the necessity of death imagery in maintaining individual health and the human community:

> From the standpoint of our death equivalents, life consists of a series of survivals, beginning with birth itself. Human culture requires accountability for these 'death immersions' and survivals—and the older, stronger person (parent or nurturer) cannot bear *all* of that responsibility. Individuation itself demands that the young organism share that accountability—indeed develop a capacity for a debt to the dead in the specific manner available to the child, through taking on some responsibility for the death equivalents. In that sense, early guilt susceptibility is by no means merely a matter of socialization. It has to do with the development of the highest order of guilt and conscience, with the capacity to participate in the functions of guilt both in terms of immediate social balance and ultimate evolutionary responsibility. Guilt threatens either when it predominates in its disintegrating potential or when its absence permits inwardly unchallenged destructiveness.

Repairing "the broken connection" means transforming the other emotions—love, anxiety, anger, rage, violence and depression—according to their relation to a newly self-conscious awareness of death and its psychological demands. The ultimate test of the process is its worthiness in enabling individuals to survive radical disorder. Like [Bruno] Bettelheim, Lifton is a psychoanalyst of the "extreme situation" and surviving. In *Thought Reform and the Psychology of Totalism* (1961), a study of brainwashing in China, and *Home from the War* (1973), a study of Vietnam veterans, as well as in *Death in Life*, he has sought to illustrate the transforming potential of recent history on the inner lives of individuals and groups. Lifton rejects the simplistic pseudo-Freudian methods of much psychohistory and its tendency to see history as the individual psyche writ large or to reduce history to instinct. These and other forms of psychohistory "ultimately eliminate history in the name of studying it." Lifton approaches historical questions, of course, from the point of view of his own psychological model: "We can understand much of human history as the struggle to achieve, maintain and affirm a collective sense of immortality under constantly changing psychic and material conditions." History for Lifton is a "symbolizing treadmill" while it is the "vehicle of our collective renewal." It moves along a spectrum defined by the categories of individual and group psychology. . . . (pp. 120-23)

It was Lifton's observations, in the 1960s, of the enduring impact of the nuclear attack on Hiroshima that first suggested this historical aspect of the new psychological paradigm. There he "came to understand that, in order to reconstitute their immediate lives, survivors had to reconstruct something on the order of a larger psychological universe, had to reimagine a relationship to human connection, to historical process, or to what I came to call their symbolization of immortality." The victims were unique in their calamitous historical circumstances yet typically human in their need for symbolization. Their "struggles were bound to be extreme in relationship to atomic survival but they were by no means limited to it. In studies involving long-term adaptations and innovations rather than sudden disaster or direct death encounter, I found that ultimate questions were crucial to everyday experience." Hiroshima, then, demonstrated to Lifton certain general principles of psychological interpretation. It was only the most recent and extreme historical instance of the "breakdown of man's sense of symbolic unity and impairment of his sense of immortality."

The final section of *The Broken Connection* presents yet another set of psychological coordinates, this time for use in understanding historical aberrations. "Dislocation," "totalism," "victimization" and "violence" appear usually in sequence in a society unable to find symbolic forms within which to locate itself. Lifton terms such circumstances "historical desymbolization," the inability to believe in "larger connections." It is manifested in apathy, unrelatedness and a general absence of trust or faith. In one of the best chapters in the book he describes the steps from victimization ("the creation of a death-tainted group of victims against which the victimizers can contrast their claim to immortality") to mass violence as they have occurred in several cultures at different times. The particulars of his argument reveal how social and historical imperatives can be absorbed into individual psyches. Take, for example, this bit of dialogue between an Eta (one of the historically social outcasts of Japan) and an American anthropologist:

> Are you the same as common people?
> No. We are dirt, and some people think we are
>   not human.
> Do you think you are not human?
> (A long pause) I don't know.

Psychohistory for Lifton would explain the origins and structure of such feelings recognized, as events are, as the material of history.

Living human beings exhibit a unique form of psychic dislocation as a result of the threat of nuclear extinction—represented in the "nuclear image," which according to Lifton is the chief motivation behind our own death imagery. "We live," he says, "in a world so dominated by holocaust—past, contemporary and anticipated—that we may look upon ourselves as, in some degree, embodiments of these horrors. This is the vague and yet disturbing 'identity of the doomed' in which we partake." Fear of extinction, however, is only one side of our debilitating "nuclearism." The other is our misplaced confidence in nuclear domination. "Nuclearism is a general twentieth-century disease of power, a form of totalism of thought and consequence particularly if paradoxically tempting to contemporary man as another of his technological replacements for his waning sense of the reliability and continuity of life." The pressure, however, of the first kind of nuclearism is what lies behind *The Broken Connection.* In the "Epilogue" Lifton insists again that "imaginative access to death in its various psychic manifestations is necessary for vitality and vision" but adds that "our present difficulty is that we must extend that imaginative access to include massive death and the possibility of total annihilation." Lifton's is a sometimes grim and always realistic psychology tempered, however, by his belief that adjustment, even renewal, can be summoned from neglected dimensions of the self.

An excerpt from *The Nazi Doctors*

While it has been estimated that 350 German doctors were involved in specific criminal acts [during the Holocaust], that figure may be, as one early observer recalled, no more than the "tip of the iceberg." A few doctors, in various ways, resisted the Nazi projects, but German physicians *as a profession* offered themselves to the regime.

During the course of my research, I gained the impression that, among Germans as well as among survivors and scholars throughout the world, this involvement of physicians in killing was viewed as the most shameful of all Nazi behavior. No wonder that it still haunts German medicine, and has only recently begun to be confronted by contemporary German physicians. Yet it must be confronted, and not only by physicians. For this vision of killing in the name of healing was at the heart of Nazi mass murder. More than that, such a malignant vision seems to be part of virtually all expressions of genocide.

Nazi "euthanasia," in fact, provides a key to an understanding of genocide as inclusive murder of the victim group in order to "cure" one's own. Since the disease one seeks to eliminate is ultimately death itself, the curative process can be endless. That murderous cure must be combated, interrupted, prevented everywhere.

Lifton's ambitious psychological and historical paradigm suffers from dependence on new psychoanalytical jargon, convoluted syntax in the explanations of its critical elements, and frequent repetitions. The stylistic shortcomings of *The Broken Connection* often obscure the impact of Lifton's very important findings. By contrast, Freud's ability, displayed several times in his career, to summarize his theories with great clarity accounts in part for the durability of his work and certainly for its appeal to non-psychoanalytical audiences. *The Broken Connection,* except for a few chapters, lacks the accessibility of Lifton's . . . best work and will probably not, therefore, reach the wide audience Lifton desires and deserves. He has pro-

posed in *The Life of the Self* (1976) that his theory is the true complement to Freud's and Erikson's. Proving that claim—and Lifton's is a truly comprehensive view of man—will probably require the presentation of his ideas with more of their characteristic grace and clarity. (pp. 123-25)

Steven Weiland, "Psychoanalysis: Back to and Beyond Freud," in Michigan Quarterly Review, *Vol. XX, No. 2, Spring, 1981, pp. 115-33.*

Anthony Storr

A large number of doctors are known to have played an important part in running the concentration camps of Nazi Germany and in organizing the infamous activities which went on in them, from cruel medical experiments to actual extermination. Robert Jay Lifton, who is already renowned for his books on Hiroshima, Vietnam, China and Japan, has spent nearly 10 years researching [*The Nazi Doctors: Medical Killing and The Psychology of Genocide*]. He interviewed 80 former Auschwitz prisoners, most of them doctors, who had worked on medical blocks; 28 Nazi physicians, five of whom had worked in concentration camps; and a variety of other professional persons who had been prominent Nazis. As a Jew himself, Lifton acknowledges the difficulty he had in empathizing with the Nazis whom he interviewed. It is a tribute to his skill as a psychiatric interviewer that he has gone a long way toward explaining how it was that members of a profession dedicated to healing came to participate in brutality and murder.

Lifton has amply demonstrated that doctors played a vital role in extermination camps such as Auschwitz. They were responsible for selecting which prisoners should be kept alive for slave labor and which should immediately be killed. The old, the ill, the pregnant and those who were too young to work were generally gassed at once. At its peak, Auschwitz killed and cremated 20,000 Jews in the space of 24 hours. Doctors supervised the gassing, certified death and, in the early days, were required to issue false certificates attributing death to a variety of natural causes. When prisoners were flogged, doctors were required to certify their fitness to receive corporal punishment. Their advice was also sought when epidemics of typhus and other diseases broke out. The usual practice was to kill all those suffering from the disease and then sterilize their living quarters. Before the technique of gassing victims with Zyklon-B became established, doctors became expert at killing prisoners with injections of phenol. Research into methods of sterilization was actively encouraged. Doctors castrated males and injected caustic substances into the uteri of females with the object of permanently blocking their Fallopian tubes. Even more horrible experiments were carried out on the eyes of children. Prisoners were also deliberately infected with tuberculosis and typhus; exposed to extremes of cold; or starved to death, so that doctors could study the reactions of the body to these stresses.

It is only if one studies Nazi racist ideology and the gradual acceptance of the Nazi program of eugenics that one can understand the participation of physicians in such activities. Although other nations, including the United States, have passed laws compelling sterilization of the criminally insane and other undesirables, this policy was carried to extremes in Nazi Germany. Within a few months of Hitler's coming to power, an extensive sterilization program was instituted. Doctors were compelled to report cases of mental handicap, schizophrenia, manic-depression, epilepsy and a variety of supposedly hereditary defects, like some forms of blindness, deafness or even alcoholism. Huge numbers of men and women were compulsorily sterilized. The program soon went further. "Mercy killing" was instituted for an ever increasing number of persons supposedly living "life unworthy of life" (*lebensunwertes Leben*). There were some objections by relatives to the mysterious deaths of so many mentally ill people, and a few psychiatrists were brave enough to resist what became a vast slaughter of their patients, but the killings went on. It was not long before the policy of eliminating the unfit was extended to the Jews. According to Nazi racist theories, it was interbreeding with inferior races that had led to the decline of the Aryan *Volk,* and killing was obviously more effective than sterilization in preventing any further contamination.

Lifton points out that a high proportion of German doctors joined the Nazi party. At a late point in the regime, 45 percent of doctors were Nazis, more than twice the percentage of teachers. Because many of the most prominent doctors were Jewish and because Jews constituted about 13 percent of all German doctors, fears that Jews would dominate the medical profession were common. Anti-Semitism amongst doctors was so powerful that, Lifton writes, within two months of Hitler's becoming chancellor, some doctors contacted their Jewish colleagues on the pretext of arranging consultations, had them picked up in cars and then arranged that they should be taken to remote places where they were beaten and left bleeding.

Once a doctor had been recruited to work in an extermination camp, the atmosphere was so different from that of ordinary life that a high degree of collaboration became inevitable. One of the Nazi doctors whom Lifton interviewed, who was at first very unhappy in Auschwitz, said of the camp: " 'One could react like a normal human being in Auschwitz only for the first few hours.' " After that, " 'you were caught and had to go along.' " This same Ernst B. acquired a reputation for being kinder to prisoners than the majority of Nazi doctors, managed to evade selecting prisoners for the gas chambers and, when arrested and tried after the war, was acquitted because of the number of ex-prisoners who testified on his behalf. Nevertheless, this exceptional doctor greatly admired the most notoriously cruel of all the Nazi doctors, Josef Mengele, defended his horrible experiments and rejected the accusations of brutality which were recognized by all the prisoners who encountered him.

Lifton accounts for this discrepancy in perception by supposing a psychological mechanism of defences which he calls "doubling." By this, he means "the division of the self into two functioning wholes, so that a part-self acts as an entire self." Lifton contrasts this mechanism with other rather similar psychiatric concepts like splitting and dissociation, but I have to confess that he does not make the difference entirely clear to me. Doubling is supposed to be distinct because it involves two different selves acting as whole persons. But 19th-century physicians, like Morton Prince, who used the term dissociation, describe their cases of multiple personality as exhibiting personalities which were completely different and yet operated as autonomous wholes.

Lifton gives an excellent account of how what was originally a eugenic program turned into mass extermination. Although what the Nazi doctors did is indefensible, one cannot read this book without gaining enhanced insight into why they did it.

But I missed any explanation of why Hitler's ridiculous ideology, absurd ideas of race, distorted notions of genetics and all the rest of the Nazi hotchpotch of nonsense appealed so strongly, not only to the downtrodden and alienated, but to so many intelligent and highly-educated professional people. Lifton neglects or underestimates the importance of myth underpinning Nazi ideology. Long before the First World War, men like Guido List, Lanz von Liebenfels and Rudolf von Sebottendorf were promulgating crazy myths of Aryan superiority which Hitler took over and adapted to his own purposes. How is it that whole nations can embrace paranoid delusions? Perhaps Lifton's next book will explore this problem further. Meanwhile, we must salute another admirable account of how men behave in extreme situations. (pp. 1, 14)

Anthony Storr, "Hitler's Perversion of Healing," in Book World—The Washington Post, *October 5, 1986, pp. 1, 14.*

Richard Eder

There was a time when the world was widely regarded as flat, and it was thought dangerous to sail to its extremities for fear of falling off into some dreadful chasm. Nowadays, with round certainty, we go pretty much where we please and manage to come back.

In terms of moral rather than physical geography, the roundness of our planet was thrown seriously into question by the Nazi Holocaust. It is no longer universally taken for granted that our understanding should properly navigate wherever it can. There are those who argue that efforts to understand or explain the perpetrators is to risk, not condoning them, certainly, but reducing an unparalleled horror into a mediated one.

"I was by no means without fear of what I was getting into," Robert Jay Lifton writes at the beginning of [*The Nazi Doctors*] the monumental study of the doctors who were so intimately involved with the death camps. The argument was put to him that "psychological study in particular . . . ran the risk of replacing condemnation with 'insights.' "

The risk, if it was one, was more than justified. *The Nazi Doctors* is a full, sometimes unbearable account of the horrors that went on. That is not its point nor its originality but these horrors, in which Lifton immersed himself during years of research and interviewing—and in which we, as readers, now find ourselves immersed—make possible the book's real achievement.

This can be encapsulated in a phrase. Lifton interviewed 28 former Nazi doctors including five who worked in the death camps; and he also interviewed about 80 Auschwitz survivors, including many who worked as prisoner-doctors along with a German medical staff. One survivor asked him what kind of men the Nazi doctors were.

"Neither brilliant nor stupid," Lifton sums up his reply, "neither inherently evil nor particularly ethically insensitive, they were by no means the demonic figures—sadistic, fanatic, lusting to kill—people have often thought them to be." And the survivor interjects: "But it is *demonic* that they were *not* demonic."

This is the book's major thesis, as Lifton traces the gradual brutalization of German medical practice. It went from involuntary sterilization, to state-ordered euthanasia of deformed babies, to the elimination in hospitals of a gradually widening range of adult mental patients and incurables—being Jewish soon qualified—to the death camps themselves.

Simply to write about the doctors, and their varying degrees of regret and almost invariable degree of rationalization, would have more or less documented one more aspect of the banality-of-evil theme. But to place the doctors against the unflinching account of what they did is to go beyond banality and to juxtapose inextricably the survivor's "demonic" and "not demonic."

The book is an ordeal, it is only fair to note. I felt physically ill as I went through the last couple of hundred pages of Lifton's deadly reporting. It was, of course, much worse for him to confront the two dozen doctors, now in their 70s and 80s and respectable civilians, with the record; and to hear them talk about it. (He had nightmares afterwards; and his survivor-friend, hearing about them, remarked: "Good. Now you can do the work.")

The arrangements were made through a prominent German medical figure, and the doctors were flattered to be asked, as colleagues, to collaborate with the eminent American Prof. Lifton. Once a Herr Doktor always a Herr Doktor. There was anxiety, of course; but it was held in check by a peculiar psychological manipulation. Though often frank, detailed and even regretful, the doctors did not place themselves emotionally inside their accounts. They talked in the third person. "The narrator, morally speaking, was not quite present," Lifton writes.

Nazism regarded itself as a great biological and spiritual cleansing and healing of a nation contaminated by decadence, weakness and the Jewish presence. "The health of the Volk" justified everything; and when you say health, you naturally think of doctors.

The Nazis did; and many doctors were honored to be in the front ranks of the biological warriors. It was only when confronted by what they would actually have to do—inject phenol in newborn babies and select out the weaker among the concentration camp inmates for gassing—that more complex reactions set in.

Some gave brutal evidence of relishing their role. A few resisted, despite their Nazi convictions. Some of the book's most fascinating accounts are of such men as Gottfried Ewald, who in the '30s refused to participate in the euthanasia program and campaigned openly against it; and Dr. Ernst B.—Lifton withholds the surnames of those he interviewed—who, alone among the Auschwitz medical staff, made a point of taking no part in the gas chamber selections.

Survivors unanimously credit Dr. B. with a humanity that approached the heroic; and yet, as Lifton discovers in his interviewing, Dr. B. essentially admired Nazism and considered Josef Mengele as the most decent man in Auschwitz. Lifton's is not a simple journey; a number of surviving prisoners had at least mixed feelings about the man later known as "The Angel of Death."

The great majority of doctors were somewhere between a Mengele and a Dr. B. They took part in the gas chamber selections, supervised the administration of the gas pellets and helped organize the cremations. At night, they would get drunk and, in drunken companionship, curse "this dirty business." And some would participate in the grotesque experimenting on living inmates.

To the doctors, of course, they were not living; they were the pre-dead. Every prisoner in Auschwitz was marked to die, they reasoned. There was nothing they could do about it. To experiment was at least to get some good out of the advance cadavers. To select the old and weak for the gas chambers was to spare them starvation, and to give the younger people a little better chance to survive.

So much for rationalization. Some of the most painful parts of the book are the voices of these old doctors talking about reasons.

Lifton suggests various explanations for the ability of men who regarded themselves as healers to administer death. There was, of course, the ideology of social cleansing; for us, at least, a special case, and a remote one.

But there were other factors, closer and more troubling. Bureaucracy, which breaks down a deadly purpose into smaller, relatively innocuous parts. Technology, which divorces the act from its results. (Killing Jews by shooting them produced a high incidence of nervous complications among the special squads assigned the job. Gassing was much calmer.)

Disassociation is hardly unknown in our own country. "I am only doing my job" is infuriating, but it is not genocide. Professional blinkers may allow a nuclear physicist to develop death weapons out of the pleasure of scientific achievement and independent of any moral questioning, but it is not genocide. Yet with his German doctors, Lifton shows us the uncomfortable linkage between such recognizable attitudes, and utterly unrecognizable actions.

I wish he had explored such implications at greater length. I also felt that the final, theoretical section of the book tends to be murky, jargon-prone and repetitive of concepts that had already been woven into the material, and more deftly.

Even as Lifton records the valor of a few figures in standing against the general dehumanizing, he treats them severely. Of a young doctor, just out of medical school, who took part in the euthanasia program for one month and then quit, he asks why he stayed that long. It is a valid question, though one can certainly see the answer.

But that, finally, is the point. We can see the answer. We might say we can almost see ourselves giving the answer. (pp. 3, 6)

Richard Eder, "The Nazi Doctors: Medical Killing and the Psychology of Genocide," in Los Angeles Times Book Review, October 12, 1986, pp. 3, 6.

Mark Caldwell

The Nazi Doctors is not about sadism but something worse—slaughter not as an aberration but as a slight extension of a respected professional group's normal behavior. (p. 52)

It's inevitable, given his subjects and his theories, that Lifton should confront the death camps, but it's also traumatic. Lifton is a Jew, and the interviews he conducted with surviving Nazi physicians were, he admits, thick with veiled lightning, full of repressed hints that, pursued, would have led to explosions. In an afterword, he confesses to "relief at the idea of Nazi doctors no longer inhabiting my study, uneasiness concerning the limitations of my work, anger toward Nazi killers in general and Nazi doctors in particular."

His irresolution is understandable. For Hiroshima's survivors, guilt is subjective, a consequence of events beyond control: trauma is harrowing, yet appropriate as a response to cataclysm. But the Nazi extermination camps were essentially different, according to Lifton: they were a perversion not merely of normal behavior but of something at least putatively virtuous—medical ethics. The Auschwitz killing machine originated in the Nazi biomedical vision, in the manifest racism of early 20th century eugenics. The Jews, Nazi thought had it, were not metaphorically but literally a disease, a source of pollution in the Aryan gene pool. Whatever madnesses later arose, excising them was thus a radical but necessary cure, the natural and proper domain of the doctor. "National Socialism," the slogan proclaimed, "is nothing but applied biological purification."

In his early chapters, Lifton traces this obsession with race therapy from sterilization to selective euthanasia (for the "consenting participant") to the routine killing of deformed infants. By 1940, the "Reich Committee for the Scientific Registration of Serious Hereditary and Congenital Diseases" had begun registering newborn children with deformities, printing up a small form for each. Three doctors had to endorse it, with a plus sign—what could be more neutral?—indicating "treatment" (killing the child). A minus sign meant life. Killing had been medicalized. A language and an apparatus had been invented for murder; unless you already knew what they meant, they would have seemed innocuously professional. Nice for you, not to know the dirty secret; nicer yet for the doctor, not to be trapped in words or actions that betrayed the truth.

Lifton tracks the steps by which such behavior ramified, engulfing the helpless in a web of imperial medicine, from deformed infants to senile adults to sufferers from tuberculosis. At first the victims were often allowed merely to starve, but injections rapidly caught on as the preferred method, being more "medical," buttressing the illusion that the killing was therapy, for the *Volk* if not for the individual. By 1942 Zyklon-B gas, supplied by I. G. Farben (a major beneficiary of Auschwitz slave labor), had become the preferred killing agent. The name was fancy parlance for a brand of hydrogen cyanide, previously a rat poison and insecticide, but at Auschwitz stored in the camp pharmacy and dispensed under the strict control of the doctors. Murder passed as euthanasia, draconian but nevertheless sound medicine.

Auschwitz at its peak gassed 20,000 a day. But for its loyal staff of physicians, this became little more than a painful but necessary part of medical routine, exterminating the doomed slaves so the healthy ones could work more efficiently for the benefit of the Aryan race. It was, they thought, humanitarian; they were shocked by the imputation that they held life cheap. "Indeed, overt suicide," Lifton observes, "such as running into the electric fence, was considered a serious violation of discipline and often exhaustively investigated."

How could doctors live with such harrowing contradictions? They're bound, Hippocrates says, to heal; first, do no harm. The question may sound naive, but Lifton rightly insists on pursuing it. His book culminates with portraits of three Auschwitz physicians: Josef Mengele; Ernest B., still alive, who had a reputation as the most humane of the camp doctors; and Eduard Wirths, the head physician, whose reputation was mixed—compassionate where possible, but never in violation of the strictest SS orthodoxy.

The common thread Lifton finds among these and less well-known men is a phenomenon he calls "doubling"— the ability to form an Auschwitz self, a stunted doppelgänger, sending new inmates to their deaths at the arrival ramp, performing grisly pseudoscientific experiments, all in accord with a studiously unexamined conviction that it was mere medical routine. Better yet, it expressed sound Nazi scientific principles, and was all the more admirable for the nerve it demanded. You walled off and denied this Auschwitz self; you pretended it didn't exist, and the rest of you could behave with compensatorily exaggerated humanity. "Uncle Mengele" petted his favorite Gypsy twins and brought them little toys when he came to perform experiments on them. Yet when he questioned an X-ray diagnosis of two of his other favorite inmate children, he had them killed at once and dissected them to settle the doubt. Wirths, who fought mightily to assure that all life-and-death decisions were made by the medical staff ("Let the syringe be in *my* hand. If anyone kills, let it be me" is how Lifton renders his motive), wrote drooling letters home to his wife, announcing that all his Auschwitz work is "for you, my life, my heart, for you and the children."

Why is this so disturbing? Not only because it represents an admirable professional code willfully perverted into a rationale for murder, but also because, being "professional," it's so easily sequestered from the rest of the personality, which remains numb to the guilt being amassed by its murdering double. Lifton finds in the Holocaust a particularly painful instance of a universal moral dilemma. Is evil imposed from outside us, a corrupting visitation; or does it come from within? Is it something we can escape from, or is it woven into human nature and therefore inevitable?

Lifton's theory of doubling, though he can't quite face the fact, locates corruption inside every one of us: professional behavior is inseparable from character. Yet to think of Auschwitz as merely natural beastliness is to insult the victims. Worse, we acknowledge the possibility that it might happen again. Worse yet, we admit that, since it's not off the moral map, you or I might, under the right circumstances, participate. The thought leaves us defenseless, and Lifton's slightly panicky reaction is understandable: "We are *not* all Nazis."

Yet claiming that Nazi psychology was a unique aberration also poses dangers. Isn't that *collective* doubling—pretending that the thing that murders isn't us, hence rendering those crimes easier to commit? Lifton's psychological analysis, inherently ethical, turns ambiguities into dilemmas. That's appropriate to the subject. Nothing is solved by **The Nazi Doctors,** though simply for raising such questions, it deserves the highest praise. (pp. 52, 54)

> Mark Caldwell, *"Unnatural Practices,"* in The Village Voice, *Vol. XXXI, No. 41, October 14, 1986, pp. 52, 54.*

"My aim has been to use psychological understanding as a means of exposing evil, maintaining both a psychological and moral perspective at all times. I've made no attempt to replace moral judgment with forgiveness."

—Robert Jay Lifton, 1986

Neal Ascherson

[It] is only now, after reading Professor Lifton's [**The Nazi Doctors**] that I have begun to understand the fundamental question, How could they?—the subjective process in the minds of these doctors which allowed them to assimilate killing to the commandment of healing. But the importance and stature of **The Nazi Doctors** is much greater than that remark suggests. This is not only one of the most important works on medical ethics yet written. It also breaks through the frontiers of historiography to provide a convincing psychological interpretation of the Third Reich and the crimes of National Socialism. No one will be able, in my view, to write perceptively about those times in the future without referring to this interpretation,

without bringing into the center of the analysis the dynamic which Lifton calls "the biomedical imperative."

Rudolf Hess said in 1934 that "National Socialism is nothing but applied biology." It was an appeal to which a large part of the German medical profession responded with a sense of dazzled, revolutionary liberation. Medicine was no longer just one profession among others, or one of many branches of applied science and research. It had become *the* profession, the central intellectual resource of the New Order. Doctors acquired a status that engineers, nuclear physicists, even generals could not approach. Doctors were "biological soldiers." Medicine was breaking away from mere "Christian" or "Judaic" compassion for the individual, and from the passive, remedial job of healing the sick. From now on, medical science would address itself to the "positive" task of actively shaping the future of the human race, to cultivating and pruning genetic stock for the future, to using "biological laws" in the service of a new understanding of the wholeness and interdependence of all life.

Lifton establishes the chronology, the steps that led eventually to doctors—not professional SS officers, but doctors of medicine—performing the supreme sacral rite of National Socialism: the selections on the ramp at Auschwitz. There were five such steps. The first was coercive sterilization. The second was the killing of impaired babies and children. The third was the so-called "euthanasia" program, the killing of impaired adults—cripples and the mentally handicapped—in the gas chambers of special institutes and adapted hospitals. Then came the extension of "euthanasia" to impaired or racially undesirable inmates brought from the concentration camps. Finally came the mass extermination of entire racial groups in the *Einsatzkommando* operations and then in the death camps.

The ideas of "racial hygiene" or coercive eugenics were circulating widely in the early years of this century, and not only in Germany. By 1920, for example, some twenty states in the United States had laws for the compulsory sterilization of the "feeble minded" and criminally insane. But in Germany, such thoughts were fatally to converge with new concepts about euthanasia. In Anglo-Saxon societies, as Lifton remarks, euthanasia implied on the whole the right of a person to choose death. In Germany, however, it had been argued since the late nineteenth century that the state as the supreme social organism retained the right to impose death on some of its subjects in the interest of the collectivity, the sacrifice of lives in war being only the most obvious precedent. An influential book published in 1920 by Karl Binding and Alfred Hoche, *Die Freigabe der Vernichtung lebensunwerten Lebens,* put forward the concept of "life unworthy of life," which was to become central to Nazi thinking and practice. The authors, a professor of law and a professor of psychiatry, declared that the destruction of "unworthy life" was in itself a healing process—a treatment for the social organism; they discussed the "ballast existence" of human beings reduced to empty shells and prophesied "a new age. . . . [There has been] an overestimation of the value of life as such."

Hitler and the other Nazi leaders seized upon such literature, adding it to their mental brew of racialist dogma, collectivist theory, and paranoia about *"Volkstod"* (the dying out of the Germanic race). In 1933, the first year of Nazi power, a compulsory sterilization law was applied to a list of mental and supposedly hereditary afflictions, including schizophrenia, hereditary blindness and deafness, and even inherited alcoholism. The program was intended to sterilize nearly half a million people in its first phase, though Lifton believes that it was applied only to 350,000 at most. A national index of persons with hereditary taints was established, and the infamous Racial Institutes for Hereditary Biology and Racial Hygiene were set up.

"Euthanasia"—Professor Lifton rightly uses quotation marks, for this was state killing, and the word is one of the earliest and ugliest of Nazi euphemisms—began in 1939. It was preceded by the Knauer case, the birth in Leipzig of a gravely malformed child whose parents appealed to Hitler for the right to end its life. Hitler's accord, with an assurance that any possible legal proceedings against the doctors concerned would be quashed by the *Führer,* led to the establishment of a commission under Hitler's personal physicians to register "life-unworthy" children and organize their killing.

Here for the first time doctors were dealing with the reality of "biological soldiering": killing as healing. The deceptions were for the benefit not only of parents but of the medical staff as well. Although parents who refused to surrender their children to these institutions were coerced and threatened, there was much talk of "latest methods for healing"; children were perfunctorily "treated" for some time before being given lethal sedative overdoses, and doctors laid much emphasis on the research value of autopsies.

Already gratuitous cruelty was appearing. The extremes were represented by the abominable Dr. Pfannmüller at one such institution in Bavaria, who introduced "the natural method": death by starvation. A member of a party of visitors describes how he pulled a dying child from its bed, and exhibited it "like a dead rabbit," explaining that only a few more days were needed. "The picture of this fat, grinning man, in his fleshy hand the whimpering skeleton . . . is still vivid in my mind." Pfannmüller exemplified a syndrome on which Lifton lays much emphasis: the association of sadism with omnipotence fantasies which came to affect many Nazi doctors.

The killing of adults "unworthy of life" began with an order from Hitler in October 1939, after the outbreak of war. "Patients considered incurable" were to be medically killed. But Lifton, in a memorable passage, warns against the temptation of interpreting this as only an aspect of war preparations and emergency measures:

> Rather than medical killing being subsumed to war, the war itself was subsumed to the vast biomedical vision of which "euthanasia" was a part. Or, to put the matter another way, the deepest impulses behind the war had to do with the sequence of sterilization, direct medical killing, and genocide.

The program to kill "unworthy" adults, known as T4,

after the Berlin address of its headquarters at Tiergarten 4, was a huge affair. Directed by a large medical and ancillary bureaucracy, it was conducted at six main centers in Germany and Austria. Gas chambers were introduced for the first time, as the mental hospitals of the Reich disgorged their "incurables," and there was a complex cover-up system of reassuring letters to relatives and of falsified death certificates. Jewish children had already been killed in the earlier program, and a number of Jewish adults were now sent to T4 centers from the camps—Jews alone required no medical paperwork or phony diagnosis to be murdered.

It is well known that T4 was halted in 1941, as a result of the only serious civilian protest in the history of the Third Reich. The facts leaked out: public demonstrations took place and Count von Galen, the Catholic bishop of Münster, delivered the famous sermon in which he declared the entire program to be a blasphemy against God: "poor unproductive people if you wish, but does this mean that they have lost their right to live?" Less familiar abroad is the resistance, religious and professional, put up by a few physicians. Professors like Karl Bonhoeffer and Gottfried Ewald, both psychiatrists, resisted, and so did several Protestant pastors involved in running mental hospitals. Paul-Gerhard Braune, the only objector who was arrested, wrote directly to Hitler condemning the very concept of "life unworthy of life" and warning that unless the "intolerable" program were halted, the moral foundations of the nation would be undermined.

In fact, T4 only paused, to continue for the rest of the war on an "informal" basis in which the central bureaucracy was dissolved and the medical staff of the killing institutions were left to carry on the work at their own discretion. The next step had already been taken. Early in 1941, the T4 leaders had agreed to allow Himmler to use their facilities for an operation to rid the concentration camps of "excess" population: "asocial" and invalid inmates.

This was the penultimate step to the death camps. The operation, known in office jargon as "14f13," for the first time merged the SS empire of the camps with the biomedical purging of society. The doctors were now working closely with the SS; gas chambers were in use; the victims were being selected on grounds that no longer had much to do with any objective health criteria but a great deal to do with racial origin and political attitude. It was for 14f13 that the euphemism "special treatment" (*Sonderbehandlung*) was first introduced to denote killing. Doctors in white coats appeared in the camps. Collective diagnosis was applied to Jews, and Lifton quotes some of the labels used: "Inflammatory Jew hostile to Germans," or "Anti-German disposition. Symptoms: well-known functionary of the KPD [German Communist Party]," or "Diagnosis: fanatical German-hater and asocial psychopath. Principal symptoms: inveterate Communist."

It was not long, however, before camp commandants were dispatching indiscriminate parties of victims chosen by their own guards for "special treatment" in the T4 gas chambers, simply to reduce overcrowding. By now, T4 staff were extracting gold teeth and fillings from corpses and forwarding them to headquarters in Berlin. It is no wonder that Lifton calls 14f13 the "medical bridge to genocide." (pp. 29-30)

The basis of Lifton's method in this book is an extensive series of interviews. He spoke to twenty-nine men "significantly involved" in Nazi medical programs, including doctors implicated in T4 and employed at Auschwitz. He also interviewed a dozen old Nazis described as "non-medical professionals," and eighty Auschwitz survivors from the medical blocks, many of whom were in the tragic category of "prisoner-doctors" working under the supervision of masters like Eduard Wirths, the chief physician, or Josef Mengele. (p. 30)

This enterprise has already proved too much for some critics, for whom the idea of a Jewish academic tactfully, even at moments tenderly, addressing questions about their psychological stresses to men who did ramp duty at Auschwitz is—simply—unbearable. Such objections seem to me quite wrong. There is an overriding need to know the process by which highly educated and intelligent people contrived to justify to themselves their participation in acts like those. The alternative is to leave—for instance—Mengele protected behind generalizations about "the beast in all of us" or even "the banality of evil," observations which hide him and his colleagues from examination as surely as the bulletproof screen shielded Eichmann at his trial.

The second part of Lifton's book is a study of individual behavior at Auschwitz, primarily of the Nazi doctors but also of the prisoner-doctors. Lifton introduces this section by remarking that the place might well have been named the "Auschwitz Center for Therapeutic Racial Killing," and emphasizing that Nazi ideologues indeed regarded it as a rather special and secret kind of public health venture. The doctors there referred in jest to "Therapia Magna Auschwitzensis"; shortened to "TM," the abbreviation came to be their unofficial euphemism for the gas chambers. That was the approach that rendered it necessary that doctors, not other camp officials, should supervise the selection process.

Their responsibilities were arduous. They included not only selection on the ramp and supervision of the killing process, but selections within the camp, direct killing by injections (mostly by phenol), certifying death at individual executions, signing false death certificates, overseeing tooth extraction from corpses, controlling epidemics, performing abortions, observing floggings, offering advice on cremation and other means of corpse disposal, and—very important—general advice on controlling the influx of prisoners into the camp itself, which of course affected the proportion of arrivals sent straight to their deaths.

Here, as Lifton says, the healing-killing paradox was at its most acute. Hard as it is to understand, the medical staff took seriously their obligations to maintain "standards of health" at Auschwitz. However, the price of protecting the inmates' health (if that is the right expression: their average life expectancy was about three months) was to keep up a high killing rate among new arrivals at the ramp, and often to recommend the gassing of whole blocks of the

camp which had become infected with typhus or other diseases, or were otherwise unmanageable.

There also remained the other, broader aspect of healing-killing: the necessities of the biomedical vision which required the curing of the Nordic race by ridding it of Jews and other "poisonous" elements. The doctors, in short, were invited to see their task as a supreme expression of medical responsibility, its value only emphasized by the fact that most doctors initially found it difficult to carry out—and some found it impossible. However, once these physicians had convinced themselves that they were still acting as doctors and not as slaughterhouse foremen, their sense of omnipotent rectitude could become extreme. The tale of the Polish children gassed to protect camp morals is one example. Another is the fact, cited by Lifton, that suicide by prisoners was regarded as a most serious offense and was followed by a careful official inquiry.

By contrast, the prisoner-doctors, most of whom were Jewish, faced their own dilemmas with open eyes. Essentially, they were all dead men and women on furlough; for any reason or none, at any moment, a prisoner-doctor could be dropped back into camp or gas chamber. Nonetheless, they did what they could to save lives, to help the sick in the medical blocks, and to restrain or mitigate the "hobby" programs of research which individual Nazi doctors were carrying out on prisoners. In order to do these things, they were obliged also to enter the awful paradoxes of Auschwitz. They provided lists for selections to the medical block doctors, knowing that the more reliable they were in assisting the death process, the more effectively they could persuade their masters to let them help others. In matters like the distribution of medicine—ten aspirins a day for a block containing thousands—they were again choosing candidates for survival by rejecting other claims to live. As Lifton says, in Auschwitz a rare syringe was worth more than a human life.

Curious, conditional bonds sometimes arose between these prisoner-doctors and the SS physicians; born of expediency, these bonds—as between terrorists and their hostages—could acquire some depth. The ties could be confessional, professional (doctors talking to doctors), sexual, or even scientific, for some of the prisoner-doctors, although appalled at the brutality of the experiments on prisoners, became almost in spite of themselves emotionally committed to their success. A few SS doctors, like the man named here as Ernst B., not only took pains to keep their prisoner-helpers alive and well-fed but even arranged forbidden meetings with their relatives in the main camp.

The extraordinary prisoner-doctor Hermann Langbein, who was in touch with a resistance group in the camp, managed to establish a sort of ascendancy over Eduard Wirths, the chief Auschwitz doctor. As his secretary, Langbein was able to extract concessions from Wirths, to encourage him in his power struggle against the SS political office, and even to dissuade him from resigning in a moment of despair. In three categories, however, the prisoner-doctors killed voluntarily. They killed vicious *kapos*, as indicated by resistance cells; they killed dangerous maniacs on the medical blocks whose behavior threatened to get the whole ward "selected"; most reluctantly, they also aborted babies or killed them at birth, in order to save their mothers from the gas chamber. As Dr. Olga Lengyel, one of the prisoner-doctors, said: "I marvel to what depths those Germans made us descend."

Two psychological terms are advanced by Professor Lifton to interpret the adaptation of the Nazi doctors. These are "numbing" and "doubling," and they have, of course, a validity which can extend far beyond the crimes of the Third Reich into any situation where human beings consent to behave in ways that contradict a previously internalized moral code—including war itself.

"Numbing," a term Professor Lifton has formulated in earlier work, is fairly self-explanatory. Selection duty on the ramp was accompanied at Auschwitz by an almost literal numbing: the doctors drank heavily in what became a carefully observed group ritual, and encouraged shaken or reluctant newcomers to get drunk with them. More generally, the doctors protected themselves against impulses of pity or horror by a battery of mental devices. Racial ideology was the most important. Lifton suggests that the doctors tended to regard Jews not simply as "subhumans" beyond normal human consideration but as people who were in practice already dead by virtue of their presence in the camp. Experiments on living prisoners could thus be experienced by the doctors as a form of autopsy, and some of the contradictions that so horrified outsiders—for instance, careful antiseptically performed surgery on patients, who were then at once killed off—were evaded.

Josef Mengele provided numerous examples of such "extreme numbing," but so did the doctors of the T4 program, including leading figures like Karl Brandt, an admirer of Albert Schweitzer and a man whom many contemporaries remembered as noble and upright: many decent Germans were bewildered by the revelations at his trial after the war. At the lowest level, "numbing" was only an extension of self-protective attitudes always present in the medical profession: the hardening to horror required in any casualty ward, or the "sawbones" humor common among surgeons. At the "euthanasia" center of Hadamar, a drunken party with music and mock sermons was held in the cremation room to "celebrate" the ten thousandth victim.

"Doubling" is a more complex idea. Lifton is defining the construction of a second "Nazi" or "Auschwitz" self. He is not, he insists, talking about the lasting dissociation of "dual personality," but about a temporary dissolving of psychic glue as "a means of adaptation to extremity." The second self accepted an entirely different set of criteria within the extreme circumstances. "Conscience" at Auschwitz meant performance of duty, loyalty to the doctors' and SS groups, the "improvement" of camp conditions (i.e., making Auschwitz function more efficiently). At the same time, the prior self continued to exist, to be entered on leave when a doctor returned to his family: or when Rudolf Höss, the commandant, went home at night to his luxurious house and played lovingly with his children.

"Doubling" was a difficult feat, nonetheless. The strains

were evident in Eduard Wirths, the chief camp doctor, a man formally responsible for all deaths in the medical blocks and co-responsible for the regular decisions on how many from the incoming trains were to be gassed and how many to be admitted for slave labor to the camp. Wirths was opposed to random brutality; he improved conditions in the medical blocks and reduced the rate of killing by injection because it was deterring prisoners from reporting sick. Yet this "aura of moral scrupulousness" did not prevent him from carrying out his own revolting experiments on typhus infection or cervical cancer. His letters home show a tormented personality who surrounded his wife and children with—as Lifton puts it—"a quality of absolute purity and goodness." He wrote that his duties must be performed for the sake of "my children, my angel," a German mission on behalf of that absolute purity of his other life. When Wirths was arrested in 1945, a British officer observed that he had shaken hands with a man who had caused the deaths of four million people. At that moment, Wirths understood that his "doubling" had collapsed, that the consequences of what the "Auschwitz self" had done were about to flood his prior self and his family with disgrace. That night, he managed to hang himself.

Lifton conducted a long and fascinating series of interviews with "Ernst B.," an Auschwitz doctor who had refused—successfully—to conduct selections and who was remembered with gratitude by many surviving prisoners and prisoner-doctors as a man who had worked consistently to save lives, improve conditions, and obstruct some of the worst medical experiments of his colleagues. Here Lifton found himself in the midst of confusing debris left over from both "selves." For much of the time, "Ernst B." was candid and open about Auschwitz, admitting to shame and guilt. At other moments, however, he would veer into a harder, "Nazi" line. The Third Reich had used "primitive methods, but there was something that was right." He consistently defended his doctor colleagues, refusing to take the easy and partly justifiable course of dissociating himself entirely from them. Most curiously, he stood up strongly for Mengele, and tried to persuade Lifton that Mengele had been a man of high integrity, that he was never cruel, and that his experiments on prisoners constituted "real scientific work." (pp. 30-2)

Neal Ascherson, "The Death Doctors," in The New York Review of Books, *Vol. XXXIV, No. 9, May 28, 1987, pp. 29-34.*

Sheila Tobias

The subject of Robert Jay Lifton and Eric Markusen's book, ***The Genocidal Mentality: Nazi Holocaust and Nuclear Threat,*** is "nuclearism," which the authors define as "an exaggerated dependency on nuclear weapons for strength, protection, and safety." Nuclearism, they claim, is inherently contradictory because the weapons are themselves "instruments of genocide." While they reserve their harshest criticism for scientists who design the weapons and military strategists who rationalize their production and deployment, by inference we are all guilty since we have all "passionately embraced" the weapons as a "solution to death anxiety and the threat of extinction." Thus, the reader is both subject and object of the book.

The authors specialize in identifying "group themes," or the "psychological environments" in which certain groups operate. In this case their focus is on two groups: the progenitors of and the present day participants in "nuclearism." Their premise is that genocide cannot be conducted (or even contemplated) without the cooperation of both groups. And so the book explores in some detail how "disciplined professionals" are euchred into the service of monstrous policy, and why onlookers merely look on. More generally, the authors begin to tackle a question that should haunt historians long after this era is over. They ask how a nation as free, democratic and pragmatic as ours purports to be, can have contemplated (in some quarters, systematically planned) the destruction of the world?

They say the answer lies in the evolution of a "genocidal mentality" that began with the development of the first atomic bomb at Los Alamos in 1945, spread to think tanks where nuclear strategy was invented and refined and eventually infected the entire population. Meanwhile, lulled by "cycles of nuclear normality," the rest of us were "psychically numbed" into passivity while we waited for whatever was to be.

Enter the Nazi doctors. The search for "group themes" brings Dr. Lifton and Mr. Markusen to the central and surely the most controversial thesis of their book: there is a fundamental sameness between Nazism and nuclear genocide, and the "disciplined professionals" in the service of both can be compared. Mindful of the criticism this thesis is bound to elicit, the authors list the many differences between the two. But, they submit, there is also much in common. Both are in the "genocide business," both are able to put their humanity on hold through psychological "doubling" when they indulge their working selves and both are convinced of the rightness and urgency of their mission. While "nuclearism," the authors are quick to point out, "has nothing to do with race or any clear-cut social or political principle . . . like the Nazi biomedical vision, nuclearism as an ideology is charismatic, overarching, anchored in 'logic,' and inherently genocidal." The main difference, it seems to me, is that unlike Nazi genocide—and for reasons the authors fail to explore—nuclear genocide simply hasn't happened, although we and the Soviet Union still have thousands of warheads aimed at each other, and other nations also have nuclear weapons.

After the thesis is set up, each succeeding chapter begins with the retelling of some event, the description of some behavior or simply the defining of some working principle on the part of professionals in the employ of Adolf Hitler, and then proceeds to analyze some "comparable" activity on the part of their American "counterparts" in the nuclear establishment. The reader begins to feel queasy. For in this analysis the Pentagon is accused of a "near worship of weapons" that is equivalent to Nazi claims of "scientific racism."

But the military is by no means the worst offender. American science and a generation of American scientists are also "Nazi-like" in their unthinking attachment to their technologies. The authors remind us that *some* engineer designed the Nazi gas chambers, *some* chemist the infamous Zyklon B gas, and that the historian Benno Müller-Hill, whom the authors quote, viewed Auschwitz as a "monument of science and technology." But this in no way demonstrates that a majority of physicians, engineers and scientists—German or American—would have participated in the wholesale gassing of Jews, or that Müller-Hill was correct. To go from Auschwitz to America's defense establishment strains credibility and diminishes what is valuable about the book: its reminder of a not so distant way of thinking and its warning that as long as such weapons continue to exist, we are not out of the woods.

In their insistence on a "psychohistorical treatment" of the nuclear era, the authors can deal but clumsily with the complexities of both strategic and moral issues. The problem is that they are writing about politics without dealing with politics, and the context and the nuances are blurred. For example, counterforce nuclear warheads targeted at an enemy's military facilities instead of at highly populated industrial centers may seem more moral because civilian damage would be limited. But counterforce doctrine encourages the acquisition of many more weapons than would be required for simple deterrence; and, because such weapons might not lead to Armageddon, they inspired the idea of limited nuclear war.

In another simplification, Los Alamos becomes just another "killing institution," comparable to Nazi death camps, and the "high" that scientists experienced there in the 1940's only a fascination with power or, in some perverse way, with destruction. What the authors dismiss is the urgency our scientists felt racing, as they knew they must, against German physicists and engineers for the prize. Theirs was no mindless commitment. They fully expected to be consulted about how, where and whether the bomb would be dropped. Then and now, weapons scientists are more diverse than these authors would have us believe. Their own interview with Hans Bethe, a Los Alamos physicist who left and then returned to weapons work, is revealing. It was politics (the outbreak of the Korean War), more than a sense or absence of morality, that dictated what he would do.

Still, the authors' questions produce insight. National policy that is incoherent and even dangerous may begin in individual behavior that becomes a systemwide tendency (for instance, what they call "nonresponsibility"). Collective "dissociation," the authors believe, accounts both for how Nazi doctors could block out the killing they were involved in and how American nuclear strategists could have invented the policy of "mutual assured destruction."

Since, in the authors' view, any attempt to respond to the nuclear threat, that is any nuclear strategy, is just another variant on "nuclearism," we should not be surprised that Dr. Lifton and Mr. Markusen cannot acknowledge *deterrence* (what they see as the epitome of "dissociation") as a reasonable and ultimately successful strategy for avoiding nuclear war. Nor can they concede that arms control, however puny its outcomes, has been a useful way of managing a deadly arms competition during periods of intense rivalry and tension. And certainly they would never admit, as some historians may conclude, that in the end the hydrogen bomb kept the peace.

With the cold war winding down, we might have expected Robert Jay Lifton, who has contributed so much to our understanding of the nuclear era, to offer a reassessment of the nuclear threat, one that would explain how the two superpowers managed not to annihilate each other, and possibly the entire planet, during their 40-year nuclear standoff. It is disappointing that this book does not include a reassessment. Critics will find in it "old think"—the Doomsday incantations and finger-pointings of yester-year—and an annoying tendency to offer us names of syndromes ("heroic scientism") in place of explanation. But in their zeal to analyze the psychological environment that blinds human beings to the moral consequences of their actions, they mean to rattle our cages and our complacency even as the first real nuclear disarmament begins. That is a rattling we need.

> *Sheila Tobias, "The Seeds of Our Own Destruction?" in* The New York Times Book Review, *May 27, 1990, p. 19.*

Ian Buruma

The point of [*The Genocidal Mentality: Nazi Holocaust and Nuclear Threat*] is not just to draw parallels between the fathers of the nuclear bomb and the Nazi scientists, but to "draw from the Nazi project lessons that might head off the ultimate nuclear Auschwitz." This is strong language, but then [Robert Jay Lifton and Eric Markusen] are dealing with a strong subject, and who can quibble with their aim? There is nonetheless a problem with this kind of language, for terms like "Auschwitz" are so loaded with extreme emotions (which is of course precisely why polemical writers use them) that they can short-circuit reasonable discourse. The same is true of a phrase like "genocidal mentality." What is a genocidal mentality? Himmler clearly had it; indeed, he said as much himself, and was rather proud of it. But did Douglas MacArthur? Possibly. Curtis LeMay? Probably. Oppenheimer, Truman, Edward Teller? I should say not. But are we talking about personalities or about a wider phenomenon? Is genocide purely a matter of numbers? If so, how many people does one have to kill or want to kill before qualifying as genocidal? Genghis Khan, Charlemagne, Mao Zedong, Air Marshal Tedder, were they all genocidal? Is indiscriminate killing genocide, or does it have to be aimed at a specific category of people? Unfortunately, the term is employed rather loosely in the book at hand. At one point the authors refer to "earlier American genocidal behavior in relation to black slavery. . . . " Is genocidal the right word?

Still, about the genocidal intent of the Nazi Holocaust there can be no doubt, nor about the catastrophic effect of a nuclear war. There is of course quite a difference. This fact is skated over a bit hastily in the book, although the point is made:

> The Nazis killed designated victims—primarily

Jews, but also Gypsies, Poles, Russians, mental patients, and homosexuals. In contrast, the stated nuclear intent is to prevent war, and the killing would take place only with a failure of that structure of deterrence.

The question of intent strikes me as crucial.

But what concerns Lifton, a psychiatrist, and Markusen, a sociologist, is the "cast of mind" of the people involved in projects that led to or could lead to mass death. As a psychiatrist Lifton has interesting things to say about the evasions, double binds, and delusions that make it possible for people to live with the idea of killing and still sleep at night. This book tells you in theory what the BBC showed recently in a fine documentary about the surviving crew members of the Enola Gay visiting Hiroshima. None of them had been there before (on the ground, that is), and each man reacted in his own way. One looked close to tears throughout and said nothing. One man blustered his way through by slapping bomb survivors on the back and bellowing banalities. Yet another kept asking questions, as though trying to solve a personal riddle. But all found visible relief in discussing the technicalities of the bombing raid; the exact location of the epicenter, the precise colors of the cloud, the altitude of the plane, the weather, the air temperature—anything, in short, that would take their minds off the effect of their bomb on human beings. This showed not that these men were especially callous or wicked, but, on the contrary, that they were ordinary men with ordinary human emotions.

Lifton and Markusen explain how the camaraderie of the laboratory, and obsessive, even fetishistic concern with scientific work can lead to moral numbing. The point they want to make is that men in nuclear labs are capable of committing genocide with the same disregard for humanity as Nazi doctors on the ramps and in operating theaters of death camps, all in the name of scientific progress. These ordinary men, absorbed in their work to the exclusion of all else, end up doing the devil's work. Germans call this *Fachidiotie,* literally "job madness." It was not for Dr. Mengele and his colleagues to question why there was an Auschwitz. It was simply there, and they did their work. In the same way, Lifton and Markusen say, the bombs are accepted as a given, and the scientists work away at finding ever more efficient ways to do humanity in. Until they, and indeed all of us, wake up and reject the evasions and double binds, and look the full horror of nuclearism in the face, we are all doomed to be victims of a nuclear Auschwitz. This psychological breakthrough can only be achieved through a so-called species mentality, a feeling of solidarity with the entire human race. That, in sum, is the argument.

There is indeed something chilling about *Fachidiotie,* but is it really a modern phenomenon? The book begs the question: Has the potentially devastating nature of nuclear weapons fundamentally changed the cast of mind of the weapon makers, or is their *Fachidiotie* comparable to the professional dedication of master swordsmiths, gun makers, or carvers of bows and arrows? The great Japanese sword maker Kanemoto spent his entire life finding better ways to hammer and fold many layers of finely forged steel to produce the perfect weapon. Did he worry much about the effect of his swords on a soft human throat? He might have done so, but I doubt it. A Nazi doctor is quoted in the book as saying that killing people in Auschwitz was "a purely technical matter." So it was, to him, but were the legendary samurai heroes who tried out new swords on commoners to test the sharpness of their blades much less technically minded?

"The near worship of weapons emerged," write the authors, "as did the claims of scientific racism, from collective attitudes involving science and technology that have taken shape over the past two centuries." Scientific racism may indeed be a modern invention, though I wouldn't be too sure even about that, but worship of weapons certainly is not. Javanese daggers are objects of a religious cult, as were samurai swords, not to mention King Arthur's Excalibur. Weapon fetishism, rightly connected by Lifton and Markusen with sexual potency and the power over life and death, presumably began with the caveman's club. John Wayne would have understood it. And just think of that wonderful scene in *Apocalypse Now,* when Playboy Bunnies dance for the boys in Vietnam, twirling guns between their thighs. It might have seemed a little crude to the great Alexander's troops, but they would have got the point.

The problem with Lifton and Markusen is that they, like many other intellectuals, ascribe far too much to that elusive thing they call modernity. *Fachidiotie,* Auschwitz, the A-bomb, are, in their view, all uniquely wicked products of the modern mind, along with industrialization, total war, and so forth. Science has gone mad; the machine has taken over; morals and humanity count for nothing: life is meaningless. It is an old complaint, going back to the ancients. Nietzsche simply put it in modern terms: the vacuum after God's death. This theme has exercized most critics of the Enlightenment: the dry inhumanity of rationalism, man's slavery to science. As the East German playwright Heiner Müller recently put it in an interview, "When one thinks of the historical catastrophes in our century, it seems plausible that the fetishization of progress is based on an accelerating death wish." Müller believes that "Auschwitz is the altar of capitalism," that "without religion, there are no more arguments against Auschwitz," that "the A-bomb is the scientific substitute of the Last Judgement." Heiner Müller is not a right-wing Christian fundamentalist, but a true believer in socialism.

What is easily forgotten is that great technological inventions, of which splitting the atom was one, were usually regarded in their time as the devil's work. Gunpowder was, and so were the first railway trains, not to mention the combustion engine and those infernal flying machines, and, who knows, maybe even the wheel. Many people in the world still believe that a camera can rob them of their souls. As far as the ability to destroy is concerned, the leap from swords and arrows to guns was arguably as great as the leap from incendiary bombs to A-bombs. If there has been a fundamental shift in our collective cast of mind, turning us all into numbed accomplices and victims of the genocidal mentality, when exactly did this shift take place? During the Thirty Years War, or in the trenches of

Flanders, or was it the carpet bombing of Hamburg that did it? Or was it Hiroshima, after all? To assume that it was Hiroshima is to accept the A-bomb as a *deus ex machina,* or at least as *sui generis.* The trouble with any *deus* is that he stands in the way of a human solution or human responsibility. (pp. 16-18)

It is no accident that almost every writer who touches the Bomb uses religious imagery, for that is how the Apocalypse is traditionally discussed. To do otherwise, to use technical, rationalist, political language, is to stand accused of nuclear madness. If Lifton and Markusen had chosen to compare American nuclear physicists to their real colleagues in Nazi Germany instead of to the death-camp doctors, they would have been struck by an interesting irony here. For rationalism and amoral abstraction were exactly what Nazis regarded as "Jewish thinking."

Our rational faculties have brought about unimaginable technological progress and sophistication, while our emotions are still stuck in a most primitive state. We shake hands on the moon, but are still prepared to kill and die for the tribe, the great ideal, the great leader. [Arthur] Koestler: "Prometheus is reaching for the stars with an empty grin on his face and a totem symbol in his hand." Here is the nub of the problem: devotion demands sacrifice; the totem of one tribe demands the blood of another. From King Herod's massacre of the innocents to Saddam Hussein, the genocidal mentality is as old as mankind. And prayer, in one form or another, is still the preferred method of many, perhaps most, people of staving it off.

Lifton and Markusen's book bears this out: it is a *cri de coeur,* so to speak, of the religious mind. Paradoxically, it is also an indictment of the use of religious language and imagery in nuclear affairs. The authors call reliance on nuclear weapons a secular religion, "in which grace and even salvation—the mastery of death and evil—are achieved through the power of the new technological deity." They quote Oppenheimer citing the *Bhagavad Gita* when he saw the effects of the A-bomb: "Now I am become Death the destroyer of worlds." But like many critics of rationalism and modernity, they themselves seek to achieve a spiritual solution to secular problems. They believe that only through the great universalist religions and the "modern secular syntheses, . . . notably those of Marx and Freud," can the species be saved from Armageddon. (p. 18)

Ian Buruma, "The Devils of Hiroshima," in The New York Review of Books, *Vol. XXXVII, No. 16, October 25, 1990, pp. 15-19.*

FURTHER READING

Carnesale, Albert. "Bombs Away: The War against Nuclear Weapons." *Book World—The Washington Post* (20 February 1983): 9.

Asserts that *Indefensible Weapons* presents a simplistic

and confusing view of the social and political consequences of nuclear weapons.

Coles, Robert. "The New Being." *The New Yorker* XLVII, No. 38 (6 November 1971): 191-98.

Discusses the themes of Lifton's *Boundaries.* These include America's increasing dependency upon machines and industry, the worldwide repercussions of diminishing natural resources, and continuing hostility between social classes and races.

Gibney, Frank. "A Japanese Way of Death." *Book World—The Washington Post* (1 April 1979): E4.

Examines the strengths and weaknesses of Lifton's *Six Lives/Six Deaths: Portraits from Modern Japan,* a study of cultural, religious, and psychological factors that have influenced how the Japanese perceive death.

Goldstein, Laurence. "Imagining the End." *Michigan Quarterly Review* XXVI, No. 3 (Summer 1987): 578-91.

Laudatory review of Lifton's *The Future of Immortality and Other Essays for a Nuclear Age* in which Goldstein states that Lifton's clinical experiences provide him with the knowledge to move beyond "speculative generalizations."

Goodman, Paul. "Stoicism and the Holocaust." *The New York Review of Books* X, No. 6 (28 March 1968): 15-19.

In-depth examination of *Death in Life: Survivors of Hiroshima.* Focuses on Lifton's research methodology, the scope and accuracy of his psychoanalysis, and the theoretical foundation upon which his concept of "survivor's guilt" rests.

Gordon, James S. "The Death Immersion." *The New Republic* 169, Nos. 4-5 (28 July–4 August 1973): 29-31.

Relates the psychological theories in Lifton's *Home from the War* to prevailing negative views of the Vietnam War in the 1970s.

Lahr, Anthea. "Descrying Protean Man." *The Nation* 211, No. 15 (9 November 1970): 470-72.

Examines the religious and psychological scope of *Boundaries,* in which Lifton explains how individuals seek meaning in a disordered world.

Podhoretz, Norman. "Vietnam and Collective Guilt." *Commentary* 55, No. 3 (March 1973): 4, 6.

Maintains that Lifton's theory of America's collective guilt over the Vietnam War is simplistic because it "holds individuals responsible for actions which they themselves never committed."

Sanders, Scott. "For a Non-nuclear Future." *The Progressive* 47, No. 2 (February 1983): 54-5.

Praises *Indefensible Weapons* for having the insight "to glimpse . . . that liberating image of a non-nuclear future."

Starr, Paul. "Professionalism Gone Mad." *The New Republic* 195, No. 21 (24 November 1986): 34-7.

Laudatory review of *The Nazi Doctors* in which Starr asserts: "We may never understand why the Holocaust happened, but Lifton has helped us to understand how it worked—at least how it worked psychologically for the executioners."

Stoesz, Willis. "Death and the Affirmation of Life: Robert Lifton's 'Sense of Immortality.'" *Soundings* LXII, No. 2 (Summer 1979): 187-208.

Academic analysis of Lifton's numerous studies concerning death, immortality, and identity. Stoesz states: "[Lifton's] way of construing psychosocial process . . . provides a starting point for understanding both the depth and the richness which life may have in the face of death."

Storr, Anthony. "Confronting Death in Modern Life." *Book World—The Washington Post* (23 December 1979): 9.

Discusses Lifton's portrayal of death in *The Broken Connection.*

"Permanent Ferment." *The Times Literary Supplement,* No. 3,502 (10 April 1969): 385.

Praises Lifton's "psycho-historical" approach to the Chinese Cultural Revolution in his *Revolutionary Immortality* while faulting the book's "slightly dogmatic tone."

Woodcock, John. "Futureless Man." *The New York Times Book Review* (16 January 1983): 18-19.

Praises as valuable and profound Lifton's theory "that images of massive annihilation wrought by technology now provide a major context for our lives and profoundly disturb our psyches and social relations."

Èduard Limonov

1943-

(Born Èduard Savenko) Russian novelist and poet.

Limonov is best known for his semiautobiographical novels, which concern his adolescence in Russia and his experiences as a Soviet émigré living in the West. Before leaving the Soviet Union with his wife in 1975, Limonov worked as a tailor and distributed his poetry through the *samizdat,* an underground system for publishing suppressed literature. Eddie, the protagonist of *Eto ia— Edichka* (*It's Me, Eddie*), *Podrostok Savenko* (*Memoir of a Russian Punk*), and *Istoriia ego slugi* (*His Butler's Story*), is loosely modeled on Limonov's own personality and experiences. In these works Limonov examines the problems facing those who are unable to assimilate themselves to the culture in which they live. Edward J. Brown noted: "The essence of Limonov's work, whether set in the West or in the Soviet Union, is its vivid articulation of the mute misery and hatred felt by those on the bottom for the scrubbed and fancy world of those on top. From their point of view, as Eddie puts it in *It's Me, Eddie,* 'There isn't a hell of a lot of difference between here [America] and there [the Soviet Union]'."

Set in New York in the mid-1970s, *It's Me, Eddie* chronicles Eddie's first two years as an émigré. Occasionally supporting himself with odd jobs, Eddie lives on welfare in a hotel near Times Square in Manhattan. After his wife leaves him for a wealthy lover, Eddie wanders the streets of New York, cynically commenting on American life while seeking out homosexual encounters. While some reviewers dismissed the novel as self-indulgent, others observed that Eddie's alienation accurately reflects experiences and feelings of some emigrants. Patricia Carden commented: "One doesn't have to think [*It's Me Eddie*] gives a balanced picture or even that it is fair to acknowledge that it is the most powerful book about this wave of Russian emigration yet to be written. Limonov has fully embraced the experience of his failure, and by doing so has turned it into success." Critics also noted Limonov's refutation of what he considers the idealized views of Western democratic institutions expressed by Soviet dissidents Andrei Sakharov and Alexander Solzhenitsyn.

Memoir of a Russian Punk examines Eddie's adolescence in the Soviet Union in the late 1950s. Taking place during a two-day holiday celebrating the forty-first anniversary of the Russian Revolution, the novel centers on Eddie's attempts to acquire enough cash to take his girlfriend on a date and includes details of rape, murder, and robbery. While many reviewers found both the character of Eddie and the incidents portrayed repelling, some noted Limonov's realistic depiction of social conditions in the Soviet Union. A critic for *Publisher's Weekly* noted: "In this absorbing novel, Limonov expertly captures the horrifying boredom of working-class Soviet urban life, and uses just the right hip, offhand tone to describe Eddie's adven-

tures in the demi-world of teenage gangs and small-time hoods." In *His Butler's Story,* Eddie supports himself working as a butler for a wealthy American businessman, whom he frequently compares to F. Scott Fitzgerald's character Jay Gatsby. Some critics compared these two works unfavorably with *It's Me Eddie;* Maggie Paley, however, commented in a review of *His Butler's Story* that "[Limonov] does have charm. It's the charm of the scamp, the self-confessed opportunist who admits his own depravity and asks if anyone else is really any better."

Limonov's other works include *Russkoe* and *Troe,* two volumes of poetry; *Dnevnik neudachnika,* a memoir; and *Molodoi negodai,* an autobiographical novel set in Russian literary circles in the 1960s.

PRINCIPAL WORKS

NOVELS

Eto ia—Edichka   1979
  [*It's Me, Eddie* (abridged edition), 1983]
Podrostok Savenko   1983
  [*Memoir of a Russian Punk,* 1990]

Molodoi negodai   1986
Istoriia ego slugi
  [*His Butler's Story,* 1987]

POETRY

Russkoe   1979
Troe   1981

OTHER

Dnevnik neudachnika   (memoir)   1982

Donald M. Fiene

Èduard Limonov, an obnoxious, anarchistic, criminally-inclined underground poet in Moscow until 1975, when he was allowed, or forced, to emigrate by the Soviet government (he is not Jewish), did not change his spots when he landed in New York and began the traumatic process of coming to terms with the New World. He thumbed his nose at Western materialism, praised his native Russia for its greater capacity for love, and made a whole new set of friends and enemies while falling head over heels in love with Manhattan.

He went on welfare, worked as a busboy, moved furniture, and did other odd jobs; living in a cheap hotel off Times Square, he got to know hookers and winos—the street people, the night people; many of his new friends were blacks, orientals, Hispanics. Of course he knew many *émigrés,* and he also met a few American intellectuals—poets, painters, and pseudo-revolutionaries. Shortly after he arrived, his young wife Elena, who had immediately taken a job as a model, acquired a wealthy lover and divorced him. This drove him nearly to suicide. He then found that he had lost his sexual confidence: he sought out homosexual lovers, including a dangerous black youth—a complete stranger—whom he propositioned in a West Side alley at four in the morning. Later he was able to carry on affairs with women, but the homosexual urges remained. Through all of this he roamed the canyons of Manhattan, looking and observing with the wondering, loving eye of a child—or poet—and, simultaneously, with the critical, cynical eye of a "spoiled intellectual." He wrote constantly in his diary, and finally he decided to rework the diary into a book.

Èto ja—Èdička is a deadly honest and highly readable account of Limonov's first two years in New York. Its explicit descriptions of heterosexual, homosexual and Lesbian lovemaking, using every slang and taboo word in the language, make it unique in Russian literature (it has become highly controversial in *émigré* circles). However, for thirty-year-old Èdička, the narrator of this autobiographical, existentialist novel, it is love (or his lost love), rather than sex, that he seeks in the sordid streets of New York. He evinces an almost Christ-like love for all the lonely and wretched people of the city, reminding one both of Raskolnikov and Holden Caulfield. (p. 443)

It is typical of Limonov to address his readers as Americans, and without doubt the ideal reader for this book (which, by the way, already happens to be a best-seller in France) is a native American who knows Russian. It would in fact make an excellent text for students in advanced Russian-language classes, who would be both amused and edified by Limonov's virtuoso display of neologisms, Anglicisms, and richly musical profanity. One continually encounters transliterations from the English (which must be very distracting to the Russian reader who knows no English): "Aj vont ju." "Maj hauz iz oll strits of N'ju-Jork." "Faken šit." One of his favorite verbs is *povyebyvat'sja,* a variation on *ebat'* not listed in Drummond and Perkins's *Short Dictionary of Russian Obscenities*—which all students reading Limonov should nevertheless be advised to buy. It would not, of course, be necessary to study all the dirtiest parts of the novel word for word in class.

Limonov's confession may win notoriety for its sexual explicitness, but it will gain lasting fame for its true literary purity and power. (p. 444)

> *Donald M. Fiene, in a review of "Èto ja—Èdička," in* The Modern Language Journal, *Vol. LXV, No. 4, Winter, 1981, pp. 443-44.*

Herbert Gold

Edward Limonov's "fictional memoir" [*It's Me, Eddie*]—he strives to make it seem like a confessional wail—has been the subject of what could fairly be described as a minute portion of "international literary controversy." The publisher announces issuance of the book on "July 4, Independence Day"; "profound irreverence, outrageously bawdy, Russian *enfant terrible,* underground poet, bisexual omnivore in Fun City"—kind of an old-fashioned good deal if the dictionary of slang is still your main kick.

The writer is a Russian poet who scraped through the emigration machine, thanks to a Jewish wife; at least that's how he portrays himself. The character Eddie lives on New York City welfare, occupied with his horniness, jealousy of his unfaithful spouse, contempt for his fellow exiles, deep reverence and love and respect for his white suit and his talent for vodka. He scuffles along, here a little Orwell down and out in the busboy trade, there a little Cervantes charging the windmills of his discontent, one heck of a lot of Henry Miller all over the place.

The eye of Limonov on America is cool: "I scorn you. Not all of you, but many. Because you lead dull lives, sell yourselves into the slavery of work, because of your vulgar plaid pants, because you make money and have never seen the world." Rushing to my ancestral vaults, I dreaded the expectation of plaid pants, but I seem to have sold them to an optometrist during the Cuban missile crisis.

The disaster of America drives our hero into making love with a man or two, traveling to Brooklyn for true abasement and noticing with scorn the Hare Krishnas and mothers with baby carriages in Washington Square. This guy is a real Bohemian learner. "Life itself is a meaningless process," he discovers. "That's why I have always sought a lofty occupation in life. I wanted to love selflessly. I was always bored alone with myself. I loved, as I now see, extraordinarily, powerfully and terribly, but it turned out that I wanted an answering love. It's not good when you want something in return."

The punk poet reveals the truth in time for Independence Day. For a time there he was a bold terrorist, but it turns out he only needed a cozy stay at an est seminar. On the final page, however, he threatens to join the Palestinians or hijack a plane or rob a bank—"to lay down sweet Eddie's life for a people, for a nation."

Mooning passersby from his welfare hotel has let him down. "Tears of agitation well up in my eyes, as always when I'm agitated, and I no longer see Madison Avenue below. It dissolves and runs. . . ." Well, we're near the end and who can expect careful writing? This is Rastignac calling. This is Corporal *All-Is-Crud*. This is the latest little irreverence pill.

"Henrymillerism" without humor makes for sneering thuggery—not the most delightful literary stance. A Henry Miller clone should also borrow a clear eye for bourgeois foolishness, a romantic and lyrical sexuality, a gift for rapid storytelling. The epithet "a contemporary *Tropic of Cancer* set in New York" means punk junk unless there is style, energy and an underlying vision of joy and sorrow. Here, Edward-Eddie complains that he is not a Jew. He suffers like a Jew, yet does not get the benefits of being a Jew. Prose needs great liveliness to make this argument helpful and attractive. When Eddie-Edward declares that those on welfare in New York "are treated by the hotel the way blacks were treated before Emancipation," he is securely in the realm of solipsism, maudlin self-pity and charmless nonsense. (p. 5)

> *Herbert Gold, "A Raunchy, Ribald Russian Refugee," in* Los Angeles Times Book Review, *August 14, 1983, pp. 2, 5.*

Richard Deveson

If you want reports on oral sex (blow by blow) with pimps and hustlers in darkened playgrounds or stairwells on the West Side of Manhattan, then Edward Limonov is your man. He will also do you solo work or vodka-and-cocaine-accompanied heterosexual duets. And he uses four-letter words even more frequently than he describes the objects or actions they refer to. Despite this, or because of it, 'little Eddie' (to use his own words) is (ditto) 'one of Russia's greatest living poets'.

Clearly, on the one hand, Limonov is expecting us to dislike him. If we do, then we have only proved ourselves to be the 'gentlemen' in grey suits, commuting into New York from Connecticut and New Jersey, whom he in his turn despises. On the other hand, he also seems to be expecting us to feel for him in his recurrent anger, confusion, self-pity and despair—and this, with reservations, we surely can. *It's Me, Eddie* is a 'fictional memoir' that describes a chaotic spring and summer in New York in the 1970s, some time after the author has emigrated from Russia. His wife has left him to pursue a series of doomed, sleazy affairs. He's living in a welfare hotel and has much cause to feel miserable. And anyone who can get down on paper,

as he can, so much of the turmoil of his inner and outer worlds almost automatically wins a reader's sympathy.

His worlds, though: Limonov's *Weltanschauung* is as romantic and simple as his version of Russian émigré life is one-dimensional. 'Love' and the abolition of work will cure all ills. The underworld is moral because it has no vested interests. Everyone else is corrupt, America and Russia both—all those men in suits. Poets are honorary underworld, and wear high-heeled multi-coloured boots in which they conceal long-bladed knives. Even the prejudice that Russians are impulsive, generous, brutish and drunk half the day and all the night won't find its refutation here. But then Limonov doesn't want to be 'calm and just'. 'Fuck justice—you can have it; I'll take injustice . . . '

> *Richard Deveson, "Lashing Out," in* New Statesman, *Vol. 107, No. 2764, March 9, 1984, p. 25.*

Zinovy Zinik

The Russian original of Edward Limonov's [*It's Me, Eddie*] reads like a desperate letter hastily informing former schoolmates and pals back in his Soviet home town about what to expect should they join the Soviet emigré community in New York. The Soviet populace had never completely lost sight of this legendary metropolis. Maxim Gorky labelled New York "the city of the yellow devil", ie, gold; Mayakovsky described it as a place where the avenues go from South to North while the streets run East to West, and Esenin complained that in New York nobody except Jewish girls read his poetry. Back in the Soviet Union, Limonov and his friends didn't believe these ludicrous statements and disregarded them as cheap Soviet propaganda. His generation could afford to regard the Soviet régime with indifference and disdain, without any sense of complicity or guilt. And off they went at the first opportunity—following the direction of the New York streets—from East to West, to the land of freedom and liberty, of which they had became aware in the 1960s, from rumours leaking through the Iron Curtain. Behind the Iron Curtain they did indeed find the Statue of Liberty and Radio Liberty but otherwise, as Limonov's characters discover, Gorky, Mayakovsky, Esenin and the rest of the Soviet classics were perfectly right. And it was the anti-Soviet classics, Sakharov and Solzhenitsyn, who were wrong, who "turned us against the Soviet world without ever having set eyes on the Western world", as Eddie insists.

Eddie Limonov arrives in New York to discover that the West of the Soviet dissidents' dreams is as bad as the East of the Western sovietologists' concoction. Mankind worships the yellow devil on both sides of the Atlantic and ignores Limonov's poetry. Full of disrespect for the aims of any society unless the way it achieves those aims fulfills his own personal criteria, this *samizdat* poet and amateur trouser-maker confesses to the reader how he, rejected by officialdom on both sides, condemns the hypocrisy of civilization and discovers for himself a new brotherhood among the oppressed and dissatisfied.

The way to such a brotherhood lies through innumerable

sexual encounters with both men and women, and it is the ability of a partner to reach orgasm that forms Eddie's criterion for spiritual freedom. Eddie's own search for freedom is soured by the looming presence of his former wife, the irresistible and whorish Elena, who left him to pursue the false dream of the Western world they once shared. The sadomasochistic image of Elena becomes obtrusively symbolic of Limonov's relationship with Russia. The printed Russian word is still as puritanical as it was in the nineteenth-century and still lacking in erotic vocabulary. It cannot accommodate the abundance of unprintable expressions or the enthusiastic investigations of sex in Limonov's book. Given this, and the indiscriminate Russian transcription of those American words that have become a part of the Russian emigré vocabulary, the original of Limonov's book sometimes reads like a bad translation into Russian. S. L. Campbell's translation into American English returns this "first draft" type of writing to the happy family of beatnik literature, Kerouac, Bukowsky *et al.* But it remains exotic for an English reader, because the protagonist of this having-it-off drama is a Russian dissident. Instead of a saint-like figure, however, tormented in Stalin's prisons and psychiatric hospitals, who, having been expelled from his motherland, exposes the hypocrisy of socialism and warns the Western world of left-wing conspiracy, we have Limonov, who compares the CIA to the KGB and proclaims bisexuality as a salvation from tyranny and oppression. Mayakovsky, whom Limonov clearly admires, once stressed the stereotype of the morally invincible bolshevik: "If a weeping bolshevik were exhibited in a museum, gawpers would stare at this rarity from dawn to dusk." Limonov has decided to exhibit a weeping dissident; and gawpers have not hesitated to come and stare.

This debunking of the dissident legend was intended, first and foremost, to shock the emigré community. Limonov's characters belong to a semi-underground welfare *demimonde,* recently augmented by thousands of immigrants from the USSR. The atmosphere of welfare, with its dependence on government administration, its distribution of subsidies, funds and grants has revived in the emigré world the deeply implanted Soviet instincts for innuendo, censorship, intolerance and protectionism. If it is true that every nation gets the government it deserves, then every emigré imitates the régime he has escaped. Most of the recent emigrés from the Soviet Union left the country voluntarily—they were allowed out on the understanding they would never be allowed in again. Those who have realized that their daring leap had ended in failure try to picture their Soviet past as gloomily as possible, so as to brighten their own feelings about the present. It is this hypocrisy of emigration that Limonov vigorously tries to expose. But Eddie's complete dependence on those same psychological categories that he attempts to dismiss, and the purely Pavlovian response the emigré world provokes in him, have turned his writing into ventriloquism. In that sense the English subtitle of the book—"A fictional Memoir"—refers to the fictional, or perhaps even defective, memory of the author. According to his own statements, the author Edward Limonov is identical in his views and way of life with Eddie. His book is a documentary, an eye-witness account, and its purely ethnographic value is diminished by being falsely called a fiction.

In Western literature Limonov's memoir would easily have found its place among the humorous "true confessions" of voyeurs and tramps. Unfortunately, the Russian literary tradition does not allow for Limonov's sort of deviation from the high road of "great prose"; and when a writer fails to slot in somewhere between Pushkin and Nabokov he is rejected. Still, one can find predecessors even for Limonov: in the "dark age" of Russian letters of the 1880s and in the naturalistic writings of the precursors of Socialist Realism—writers such as Uspensky and Skitalets, who captivated the minds of the Russian intelligentsia with their indignant exposure of the "lower depths" of society. It was a period of crisis in literary aesthetics and of the birth of "progressive" literature. Crises in aesthetics always lead to an increased stress on social ethics—to the condemnation of civilization and a preoccupation with social injustice, identification with the oppressed and ethnic minorities. It leads to demands for sincerity in literature, sincerity by any means, including Jean-Jacques Rousseau's description of childish acts of exhibitionism. And it was he who was the first to proclaim: "I may be no better, but at least I am different." Edward Limonov is a loyal follower of that tradition today.

> *Zinovy Zinik, "East-side, West-side," in* The Times Literary Supplement, *No. 4224, March 16, 1984, p. 267.*

Patricia Carden

Edward Limonov has been in the West since 1975, and . . . he has managed to make his mark against all odds. He came without the substantial reputation of other writers who had been published in Russian there, in English here, before they left the Soviet Union. Limonov had had only the provisional success of acclaim in an underground bohemia: his work had been circulated in typescript in Moscow and he had read at private gatherings. If he is now having a success in Europe, where his novel *It's Me, Eddie!* (*Eto ia—Edichka*) is appearing in a number of languages, it is a testimony both to his talent and to his will to escape the ghetto of the emigre writer and to appear in his own right, simply as "Limonov, writer."

Curiously, Limonov has attained his place outside the narrow confines of the emigre journals and publishing houses by writing the quintessential novel of the third wave emigration, the book that any writer aspiring to immortalize the experience of his generation will have to beat if he wants to lay claim to being its chronicler. From its opening pages when its obstreperous, yet ingratiating, hero introduces himself to us as he sits naked on the balcony of his welfare hotel, eating sauerkraut from a pot and taking the sun while secretaries in the surrounding Madison Avenue office buildings look down on him, we know that this book will be in a new key. The wistful, bumbling intellectual gentleman who was the first emigration's stereotype fades away—no Pnin this.

Limonov's vivid novel of life among the down-and-outers of the Russian emigration is a classical story of love betrayed: his wife has abandoned the emigre poet down on his luck for the classier seductions of life among the beautiful people. Having been cast to the very bottom, the poet embarks upon a quest for love. The quest is also a tour of places and people, for Edichka's vision is double—turned both inward to his own pain and outward on the world around him with an intense and searching curiosity. In his wanderings he encounters the cast of his *comedie humaine:* models, photographers, fashionable painters, the dissolute practitioners of the urban "glamorous" life; earnest and garrulous members of the Workers' Party who think they will accomplish a revolution by holding meetings and handing out leaflets; provincial American businessmen attending conferences at the Hilton; black toughs living on the street. From the kaleidoscopic life of the city, he returns periodically to his Russians, the unsuccessful ones who cannot integrate themselves into a culture they do not understand, whose language often as not they do not speak, who form the new lumpenproletariat of the city.

As the autobiographical narrator of his own story, Limonov utters a cry against the betrayal of illusions by the social structures of both the vast and indifferent countries that it has been his lot to endure.

> This civilization is a paradise for mediocrities. We thought that the USSR was a paradise for mediocrities and that it would be different here if you had talent. The fuckers. There it was ideology, here it's commercial considerations. About the same. What difference does it make to me what the reasons are for the world not wanting to give me what is mine by right of birth and talent. The world calmly gives it—the place I have in mind, a place in life and recognition—to businessmen here and to Party workers there. And there's no place for me. What is this, world? You mother-fucker. Well, I'm waiting and waiting, but I'll get fed up. If there's no place for me and many others, then what the fuck do we need with such a civilization?

He also blames, on the one hand, Russian dissident leaders like Solzhenitsyn and Sakharov, whom he sees as acting simply to secure a voice for the intelligentsia in the way things are run, and on the other, the American government, which, in his opinion, has acted demagogically in bringing thousands of Russians to the West, only to strand them once they are here.

Behind Limonov's disaffection we recognize a more general stance that has become familiar in the modern literature of Europe and the Americas. By identifying himself with the dispossessed, he presses into a territory already claimed by Céline, Norman Mailer, Jean Genet and many others. We have moved to ever more extreme definitions of the writer's situation: as outcast, as criminal, as, in Norman Mailer's phrase, "white negro." What is required is to be outside the law, outside *a* law. Jean Genet explains [in *The Thief's Journal*] that he left Germany in the thirties because there *everyone* was outside the law, a "race of thieves." "If I steal here, I perform no singular deed that might fulfill me, I obey the customary order; I do not destroy it. I am not committing evil. I am not upsetting any-

thing. The outrageous is impossible. I'm stealing in the void."

Disaffection can be turned into a permanent sense of exile, protected and cherished, the stuff of the writer's identity. Limonov creates his own myth of a permanent criminality and a permanent exile.

> From childhood I refused to serve; silently, stubbornly, the kid shaped his course. I want to go to the river and I go—whether it's snowing or raining—I go to the river. Despite his parents' curses the kid went. If I want to rob a store, I don't sleep nights, I roam at will, I rob it alone— in spite of the fact that this adolescent was nearsighted and that he was just fifteen years old.

The abandonment of successive pasts has marked Limonov's life and work. As a child he left his pretty bourgeois home to join drifters, *khuligany,* and outcasts. He turned from his *déclassé* comrades to become a poet. He left his provincial southern city to go to Moscow and enter the writers' bohemia, supporting himself outside the official society by sewing clothes for friends. Everywhere he turned the sense of exile into artistic possibility. So when he found himself in America in a situation where he was not wanted, where his writing was not valued, where there was no work, where his woman had left him, he was prepared to embrace the experience and turn it to artistic profit—to take on the role of exile, outcast, loner, and to redefine it as artist.

In 1969, after coming to Moscow and experiencing his first severe crisis of displacement, Limonov wrote an extended prose-poem, **"Three Long Songs,"** which contains many of the elements that will go into *It's Me, Eddie:* the sense of exile as living at risk; fear of failure, fear of death, transformed into the motive for seizing life; weakness and inconsequence transformed into self-advertisement. Limonov's search for strength has been intimately connected to his preoccupation with human mortality. In spite of its fierce commitment to life, his work is death-obsessed. The first of the **"Three Long Songs"** is structured by a series of fundamental, simple questions like those asked by a child. The poet wonders, "Why did my friend Proutorov die and I am still alive? Tell me, when will I die? Will it really be when necessary?" And again he writes: "I really don't want to die. Why will I depart alone? And why will others remain?" Finally, the fear of death expresses itself in an elemental form:

> Back to childhood as fast as possible. Shelter me, papa and mama. All morning I lay naked on my stomach on top of the blanket. I thought with horror of the terrifying grave. I fell asleep and in my sleep cried out,
> Mama, I don't want to go into the grave!
> Mama, I don't want to go into the grave!
> I haven't seen Mama for a year.

Among the Russian gilded youth a cult is made of death and madness:

> I was educated in the cult of madness. A "schiz"—shortened from schizophrenic—that's what we called odd people, and it was considered praise, the highest evaluation of a person.

Eccentricity was encouraged. To say of a person that he was normal was to offend him. We sharply distinguished ourselves from the crowd of "normals." Where did we get it from, we provincial Russian boys and girls, that surrealist cult of madness. Through art, of course. A person who hadn't spent his time in a sanatorium wasn't considered worthy. A suicide attempt in the past, almost as a child, that's the kind of credentials that I, for example, brought to this company. The very best recommendation.

[*Eto ia—Edichka*]

The simple alternatives of living or dying are presented in **"Three Long Songs"** in a Hamletian formulation:

To shake off all flesh and let the soul . . .
Or
To shake off all soul and let the flesh . . .

And what of the body? Could it be released into a heroic sexuality that would tear the veil of poor, reduced existence?

Where is laughter, this one, that one, this one. Where are these laughters? Where are these wails? These rollings about the floor? These crawlings on the ground. Why don't I rip my clothes from myself and set fire to them? When will there be the dance of savages? When will they stop being ashamed? When will it happen that they will extend an invitation to me and I will simply spit, stomp and seize the breast of someone else's wife not hiding it, and the husband from the other side?

In the poem the body's alternative is extended into sexual fantasies, or memories. Who knows? It is not significant. They return us to the refrain:

Oh, this life of fearful flesh!
It knows no laws. It knows no laws.

Sexual curiosity expressed openly shapes Limonov's work from start to finish. It would be bad faith to say in his defense that the sexual interest in his work is not prurient. Like Lawrence, like Joyce, like Genet, like all the poets of sex and desire, his interest in sex is of all kinds, both exalted and prurient.

Limonov's curiosity about death and sex extends into what we might call "the politics of curiosity." The natural curiosity of the child, which is the writer's stock-in-trade, inevitably leads—as the curious questioner presses his "why?"—to parents' or society's putting up barriers. Curiosity is the first and most fundamental violation of the common law that makes the child, the writer, into a criminal. The parents' "No, no" to the exploring child is the first provocation of frustration, and as Limonov writes in **"Three Long Songs"**: "There are no noes for me, only yeses."

The stress on consciousness in modern literature comes from a sense that freedom of action in any public form is illusory. While some writers have accepted that notion with resignation and regret and turned wholly to the inner life, others have fought against it, either by striving to take part in the world of action and politics or by asserting that writing itself is a forceful activity which makes a difference

in the world by creating a new consciousness. Limonov has taken both these active stances. He demonstrated against the *New York Times* for supporting the policy of Jewish immigration without taking account of its consequences for the people who are then stranded in a new country with little help. His work propagandizes an extreme freedom of consciousness which begins in repudiating the work-a-day world of nine-to-five and ends in rejecting any national distinction as a pernicious differentiation which leads to dissention rather than the unity of humanity. His major disappointment in America comes from its failure to elevate the artist and acknowledge his importance to society.

The politics of curiosity and desire, arising out of the question, "What would it be like if . . . ?", leads to the elaboration of fantasies. Limonov manipulates the syntax of fantasy with a sure hand. A characteristic passage occurs in his latest long work, *Diary of a Loser* (*Dnevnik neudachnika*):

There's a summer civil war.

In the city, things are inflamed as in a dream.

And the leader of the insurrection, half-Latin American, half-Russian, Victor, and Rita, a woman with straight hair, and the dove-elk homosexual Kendall—all came in the morning to my room and stood in the door and Victor threatens me with the muzzle of an automatic because I betrayed the world revolution for the thin, spidery arms of President Alberti's fifteen-year-old daughter, Celestina, for her rosy dresses and marine smiles, for her little childish cunt and her eternally-pierced earlobes, for the hedgehogs in her daddy's garden, for the hedgehogs and the snails on the gate. All of that brought me to this morning, and my best buddy in the conflict and former lover Victor is speaking terrible words in a low voice, hysterical Kendall in a fine jacket won't look, and Rita's concentrated face.

And in the bed little Celestina cried for a long time, shaking her naked breasts, while her father—the President—was entering the capital with a tank corps and the loyal western suburbs were trembling and comrades were being shot in the courtyards.

The fantasy contains much that is characteristic of Limonov: the world of childhood interpreted as a world of natural and free eroticism; appreciative curiosity about things people find in natural reality (the hedgehogs and snails); the free and natural vanity of self-display; the aspiration to heroism, only to betray it in imagination.

The narrative fragment (this is the whole of it, and the book is made up of other such fragments) is a many-layered amalgam compounded from the film, from the sensationalist press, and from pornography. In the new age our fantasies are film strips and we see ourselves played by our favorite stars. It is said that John F. Kennedy fantasized he would be played by Cary Grant, not knowing that his life would have a denouement beyond Grant's expressive capacities. The pop-culture elements are shaped seriously by their underlying homage to a literary tradition: the voices of Lorca, of Orwell, of Malraux, of Régis deBray, sound here. The archetypal events of the Spanish Civil War and the Cuban revolution are evoked: Che lives! The stifling and yet freeing repetitions of history in each revolutionary movement—Palestine Liberation Front, Red Brigades—are laid down on top of each other until all that remains is the mythic outline.

The fragment is, in fact, the skillful summary of a genre. It is maximally economical and evocative. The opening two lines—"There's a civil war in summer. In the city things are enflamed as in a dream"—are formulaic. They are meant to specify for us the proper context of cinematic fantasy. The characters are familiar stereotypes, subtly adjusted to the situation. The leader of the insurrection is rightly Latin-American, but also Russian. The inventor of the fantasy has the right to play all the roles: Limonov is not only the betrayer of the revolution in bed with the President's daughter, he is Victor, too. He both shoots and is shot. He enjoys the traditional power of the *victor* as well as the modern power of the traitor. Victor and traitor are inseparably tied in the economy of Limonov's consciousness. The manipulation of tense moves us skillfully backwards and forwards in time, bearing us away into the present tense of dream and then withdrawing us into the historical fatality of past tense.

Limonov's fantasies are fantasies of power, evolved out of the materials of a mythologized history. A self-conscious, open, ironic and yet serious megalomania is the stuff of the personal Limonov has fashioned for himself as a writer. In 1977 he published in Shemyakin's anthology *Apollon* a work written in Moscow before his immigration entitled **"We Are the National Hero."** This collage of prose fragments elaborates a fantasy in which he and his wife Elena arrive in Paris and are greeted by the President of the French Republic as "national hero" and "national woman," the perfect representatives of Russianhood. The "we" of the title is the kingly singular—"we/I am the national hero." Limonov combines the Soviet mania for giving prizes and honorific titles with a modern fairytale of celebrity. We hear in the narrator's voice both the frank megalomania of Mayakovsky and the Futurists and the wry self-deflation of Kharms and the Oberiuty. The group of concrete poets with whom Limonov has allied himself (its manifesto appears in the same issue of *Apollon*) openly expresses its tie to the Futurists and the Oberiu and even goes so far as to insult the Acmeists and the Symbolists, as if the new generation of experimental writers were forced to relive the history of Russian modernism. In a sense they are doing so, as contemporary Russian taste recapitulates the past stage by stage.

When Limonov wrote **"We Are the National Hero,"** he was in many respects living the very life of his fantasies. He existed outside conventional society as a hero of the marginal, unofficial world of artists. He had not only received recognition as a striking new voice among the young poets, he had not only married a beauty, herself a poet, he had even turned his work to profit by thwarting the system that refused to publish his work. He was the first of the underground writers to set up his own private

distribution system and charge money for his typewritten volumes. Limonov was indeed a kind of counter-culture prince. The sense of an exuberant flowering is recorded in **"We Are the National Hero,"** where, whatever self-irony intrudes, Limonov genuinely and with a kind of surprised self-admiration records his own success.

The work also records the anxiety of the king for a day who is all too afraid that the momentary realization of his fantasy may prove to be an illusion. There are bemused asides and deflations. Limonov fantasizes that Antonioni asks him to star in a film. At the same time he marvels that he with his little squinty eyes has been selected instead of his beautiful wife Elena. Celebrity has an element of chance. No matter how confident one is of one's talent, of the deservedness of one's success, the suspicion lingers— have they got the wrong person?

Limonov's doubts were soon to be made real. The police fixed up false papers and dumped him in the immigration—good riddance to a troublemaker. Limonov came to experience the deflation of his celebrity in earnest:

> Here in New York I lose additionally, because I am a Russian writer, I write in Russian words, and it turns out that I am spoiled by underground fame, by the attentions of underground Moscow, artistic Russia, where a poet—well, that's not what a poet is in New York, but for several centuries a poet in Russia has been everything—something like a spiritual leader; for example, to become acquainted with a poet there is a great honor. Here a poet is trash . . .
>
> [*Eto ia—Edichka*]

Limonov's megalomaniacal self-proclamation and his sober realism are not unrelated postures. When celebrity is so provisional, at the mercy of forces beyond the individual talent, fantasy becomes a weapon against destruction.

In conversation Limonov has used the word "coquetry" to describe his poetic strategy. If Rousseau justified writing his confessions on the grounds that no one before had written completely honestly about himself and that therefore the very laying bare of the self would be of interest, the new confessional literature bases its claim to our attention on a different foundation: the writer has dared more than we, he has penetrated into areas of experience— perverse sexuality, crime—that the rest of us will not enter; he has crossed the social boundaries and mingled with people of other races and with the rejected scum of society. Genet captures the self-appointed task when he says that the goal is to take all that has been rejected and despised by society and turn it into a thing of the highest beauty. The writer has to shock to prove the validity of his claim on the reader's attention, but he must court the reader, too, and hope to win him over to his point of view. Most of all, he must capture and retain attention by asserting, "It's me, it's me, *It's me, Eddie!*"

Hence the complexity of narrative voice in Limonov's most complex novel. His harshness towards himself and others is implicit in the confessional mode. What good is confession if it cannot win our pity, and yet how to avoid falling into sentimentality? Harshness opens the door to pity, even self-pity. They belong to the same universe of feeling. Moreover, cruelty can be presented as an evidence of capacity to feel. It demonstrates the narrator's knowledge of the worth of the emotional sphere. It shows that sincerity of feeling stands at the top of the scale of values. Feeling is so important that any holding back or falsity traduces it. In Limonov's book the body is the constant locus of sensations, the mind their register. The moral consciousness works unceasingly to distinguish the true from the false.

All this is to say that Limonov is an authentic representative of his genre. But does he have any further claim on our attention? Does the Limonov phenomenon mean nothing more than that Russia, too, has its dreaming, bookish boys from the provinces posing as toughs and demanding that we look at them? In his impressive programmatic work **"Three Long Songs"** Limonov reports another fantasy:

> Why not disappear from everyone, leave a note and one's things on one bank. And hide others for oneself. Come out on the other bank. Dress and walk away. When will that happen?

Limonov has come out on the other bank. There was always a sense in which the experience of Moscow unofficial cultural life was easy for all its dangers. It was psychologically easy, because it removed the person from ultimate responsibility for his own success or failure. It was possible to say, Well, it's the fault of our repressive regime, which cannot recognize great poetry, great art, great scholarship. Limonov's book is about coming out in many senses—coming out into the frank recognition of his own homosexual propensities for one. But more important, it is about coming out of the shelter of the ready-made nest of the Muscovite counter-culture. Limonov does it crying out with anguish, but he does it, and therein lies his book's power. One doesn't have to think it gives a balanced picture or even that it is fair to acknowledge that it is the most powerful book about this wave of Russian emigration yet to be written. Limonov has fully embraced the experience of his failure, and by doing so has turned it into success. (pp. 221-28)

Patricia Carden, "Edward Limonov's Coming Out," in The Third Wave: Russian Literature in Emigration, *edited by Olga Matich and Michael Heim, Ardis, 1984, pp. 221-29.*

Olga Matich

The émigré writer Edward Limonov (b. Èduard Savenko, 1943, Deržinsk, USSR) belongs to the Russian avant-garde tradition. Systematic subversion of literary and cultural norms and social radicalism characterize both his poetry and prose, before emigration and after. Bent on uncovering a "truer" or more essential life than Russian literature revealed before him, Limonov seems compelled to break away from the literary canon and the post-Stalin preoccupation with the past. He rejects the cultural elitism of much of literary modernism and the privileged status of all high culture, including the literary language. As an avant-garde provocateur, Limonov has challenged the boundaries between genres and between art and writing placed outside the pale of literature. In the context of traditional Russian literature, Limonov's poetry is seen by some as bordering on prose, and his prose is regularly dismissed as substandard, crude, and pornographic.

Limonov's writing, especially his poetry, can be associated with the futurist tradition of Xlebnikov, Majakovskij, and the Obèriu authors. Like them, he shapes and distorts the language and forces it into new patterns of expression by stripping it bare of romantic and linguistic convention and verbal refinement. The result is unmetaphoric and at times ungrammatical language, which is cinematically laconic, resembling Xlebnikov's naive or primitive verbal vignettes. "Contemporary poetry has moved away from the fundamental principle of all poetry," writes Limonov [in **"Gruppa 'Konkret'"**] "from the concrete event, from things, it has become emasculated, abstract, and rhetorical, 'literary.' We want to return to poetry its concreteness, the concreteness of Catullus and the medieval lyricists, of Deržavin and folk poetry."

Whereas Limonov's poetic voice may be compared to Xlebnikov's, his literary pose and statement are akin to Majakovskij's. Posing as an attention-seeking egotist, Limonov serves as a literary provocateur, whose literary politics are those of an unceremonious taboo-breaker. Instead of a polite and cultured poetic persona, Limonov introduces a lyrical protagonist who resembles a street person with roots in the post-Revolutionary new man. In the words of Aleksandr Donde, he is a folk poet, a city kid, one of the gang. Although his hero is not treated in accordance with the Soviet proletarian model, he is a proletarian hero in the manner of Celine and Genet. Like a Genet criminal, who identifies with the anarchic revolutionary energy and violent impulses of the oppressed, Limonov's protagonist lives outside the law, celebrating his own sexuality. As a poet, on the other hand, he is aesthetically refined and sensitive in the sphere of emotions.

Dislocation and exile are the underside of Limonov's self-affirmation and subversive literary position. Beneath the various masks of self-indulgent narcissism and iconoclasm is a persona that squarely faces separation, isolation, even extinction; a sensitive and eccentric loner, Limonov's protagonist is tough, like the people he comes from, and upward bound, like his literary prototype in the nineteenth century.

Limonov began his literary career as a poet in Xar'kov, where he grew up and first established himself in the local artistic underground. He came to Moscow from the provinces in 1967, but his poetry had nothing in common with the provincial writing that is regularly absorbed into the literary mainstream (e.g., village prose, ethnic writing). Although he was never officially accepted, he was ignored by political dissidents, who expect writers to be socially responsible and politically anti-Soviet. in contrast to other *samizdat* authors, Limonov rejected all noble literary and political gestures, selling typescript volumes of his poetry, which he manufactured himself, at five rubles apiece. This and making clothes provided his primary sources of income.

The heyday of Limonov's literary success at home came between 1967 and 1974, when the underground recognized him as an important new voice in Russian poetry. He became the idol of Moscow's exclusive counterculture, which reinforced his bohemian lifestyle and cultural marginality. Capping what at that point must have appeared to be a charmed life, he married the acclaimed Moscow beauty Elena Ščapova. What more could an ambitious young provincial poet want? The exhilaration of success and the self-indulgent megalomania accompanying it are best expressed in Limonov's prose-poem **"My nacional'nyj geroj."** Written shortly before he emigrated in 1974, it is a mock-heroic fantasy about Limonov and Elena conquering the Western world. Childish and toylike in its fairytale images of success, it contrasts sharply with the reality of the poet's reception in the West, depicted in Limonov's first novel *Èto ja—Èdička* (1979).

Even though he continues to write poetry (*Russkoe,* 1979; *Troe,* 1981), Limonov has developed into a prose writer, and it is in the area of fiction that he has made his controversial reputation since emigrating. Marginality is still his literary hallmark, and it has resulted in an even greater sense of personal isolation in the Russian émigré literary community than at home. Life on the outside of society, or exile, has been aggravated in Limonov's case by a preference for peripheral or eccentric experience and socially and culturally unacceptable values. A recent statement—that he regrets his association with Russian literature—is typical of his self-proclaimed marginality; it also reflects the desire to transcend his own limitations and expand his experience. Offensive to most Russian readers, the claim implies that his writing is outside of the Russian literary canon, and if not, he hopes that soon it will be. In a sense, he is emigrating once again, not from the provinces or the Soviet Union, but from Russian literature—with its particular brand of morality, civic responsibility, and sexual taboos. Geographically Limonov began his émigré career in New York, but moved to Paris in 1980, where he has greater publishing opportunities.

Limonov's most subversive and controversial text is undoubtedly *Èto ja—Èdička.* "It is the quintessential novel of the third wave emigration," writes Patricia Carden [see excerpt above] "the book that any writer aspiring to immortalize the experience of his generation will have to beat if he wants to lay claim to being its chronicler." The majority of conservative Russian readers have perceived the novel as filthy pornography and a pro-Soviet provocation. Unabashedly autobiographical, the novel portrays a bohemian Russian émigré poet down on his luck in New York City, living on the fringes of the American jungle. It is a painful story of dislocation and exile, of lost love and general dispossession. Like Majakovskij's lyrical hero in *Oblako v štanax,* Èdička loses his muse and beautiful wife Elena to the rich and powerful of this world, or so he perceives them. Whereas poets are universally admired and influential in Russia, in the United States they are invisible, and invisibility is a condition the narcissistic Èdička can't handle. Stripped of his loved ones, his social prestige, and his American dream, the young poet sinks into an almost infantile state, and this while being initiated into the harsh realities of his new existence. Èdička resembles Ralph Ellison's invisible man faced with the realization that he is alone in a hostile world, its victim, and not the imaginary champion Limonov portrayed in **"My nacional'nyj geroj."**

Although *Èto ja—Èdička* has scandalized and outraged traditional Russian readers, the image of the novel's hero is dialogic in Baxtin's sense, and is meant to evoke an ambivalent response. Èdička, who has tried to make good in the big new world, is the Russian poet Èduard Limonov as well as the little boy from working-class Xar'kov. He is simultaneously provocateur and victim, solipsistic and compassionate, amoral experimenter and old-fashioned moralist, child and adult. Even the novel's title is dialogic and is informed with several double meanings (megalomania/invisibility, adult/child, art/life). It is spoken by a self-indulgent narcissist, by a frail little boy whose life has almost been extinguished, and by a tough young adult saying matter-of-factly *Èto ja—Èdička.* Consisting of a complete declarative sentence, *Èto ja—Èdička* is actually a mini-poem which contains the kernel of the novel as a whole. The title's bipartite mirror-like structure and repetitive sounds reflect the novel's all-pervasive narcissism and the author's poetic background. Limonov's favorite metaliterary theme, the relationship between art and life (fiction and autobiography), is also found in the title. By analogy with Flaubert's famous "Emma c'est moi," "èto ja—Èdička" equates the hero with the author, directing the reader to consider various possible interpretations of the title.

The action of the novel takes place after the hero's fall from the high pedestal of **"My nacional'nyj geroj"** to the rock bottom of a cheap New York hotel. In the manner of the picaresque, Èdička ties together a series of unrelated New York adventures and new experiences by his desperate attempt to overcome and exorcise the loss of Elena. At first he tries menial labor; then, growing braver, he seeks homosexual love; finally, he feels ready again to try relationships with women, whom he, of course, fears most. All the men and women with whom he becomes friendly or intimate are victims and outsiders like himself or at least identify with the underdog. Even Elena, Èdička's Natal'ja Gončarova, is victimized by the new men in her life and is unsuccessful as a fashion model. Carol, Èdička's first new woman-friend, is a member of the Socialist Workers Party, and Sonja, his first lover after Elena, is a silly Jewish émigré from Odessa. Although Rosanne is a sophisticated American academic, she is neurotic and has recently lost her teaching job. The two black men with whom Èdička makes love are bums and criminals, whereas the well-off homosexuals he meets are of no real interest to him.

Igor' Smirnov has convincingly demonstrated that the novel's narrative progression is structured according to the laws of narcissistic writing: the ending is a mirror reflection of the beginning. [The critic adds in a footnote: "The English translation of *Èto ja—Èdička* is abridged: the chapter 'Leopold Sengor and Benjamin' has been cut, which destroys the symmetrical narcissistic structure of the novel."] In the "Epilogue," Èdička is still angry and trapped, without love, living on welfare (Smirnov), as if the therapeutic journey had not produced the desired cure. Evidence for his childlike behavior abounds in the novel, although not all of it is necessarily narcissistic. Èdička is the name for a child, and like a toddler who has just learned how to talk, he often speaks about himself in the third person, even though the novel is an *Ich-Erzählung*. Preoccupied with his body and bodily functions, he sometimes describes his sexual experiences in a language resembling baby talk; his speech is generally primitive and naive.

Besides narcissism, the novel's structure is also based on the neurotic compulsion to repeat, as reflected in Èdička's strategically placed regressive behavior in the middle and end of the book. "Where She Made Love," the seventh, middle chapter, depicts the return of Èdička the voyeur to the place where Elena first betrayed him. After struggling to free himself from Elena, the patient regresses and is compelled to return to the scene of the crime in order to relive the painful experience, after which the healing process must begin all over again. If we read the compulsion to repeat from the perspective of the therapeutic model, Èdička has overestimated his newly acquired strength; he cannot sustain it when confronting his relationship with Elena. It is as if two psychological dynamics are operating concurrently: one the healing process whose goal is Èdička's liberation, the other the hero's neurosis—his obsessive narcissism and compulsion to repeat.

In the second half of the novel, which mirrors the first, Èdička again struggles to free himself from his nemesis. As in the first half (in the chapter "Chris," to be discussed below), he has a homosexual epiphany in "Luz, Alyoshka, Johnny, and Others." In the second to last chapter ("My Friend New York"), the hero seems to be coming to terms with himself and the world. Remembering his childhood, while observing the children in Central Park on a warm spring day, Èdička removes his many literary masks for a moment and relaxes perhaps for the first time. He is actually happy with himself, for he has not betrayed any of his sacred values: his distant childhood, his soul, his love, and his lifelong hero's journey. But the moment does not last: "All I want, gentlemen, . . . is a bullet in the head, because I'm tired of holding on, to tell the truth, and scared I will not die a hero." In the final chapter ("The New Elena"), the compulsion to repeat the past overwhelms the hero again, and he once more plays out the role of Elena's painfully devoted knight, after which there can be no catharsis but only anger and a self-destructive return to the beginning. The neurotic model has the final word.

Limonov not only bares his hero's existential crisis, but also undermines its emotional impact, thereby contributing to the novel's dialogic structure and effect. As an antidote to the hero's invisibility, he counteracts the depths of Èdička's suffering by assaulting the reader's sense of decorum and propriety. His most strident attack is on the Russian reading-public's sexual taboos and on the intelligentsia's "dissident" political values. *Èto ja—Èdička* is the first Russian novel to make unrestricted use of obscenities (*mat*), a stylistic register proscribed in Russian literature, and to explicitly describe a wide variety of sexual behavior: heterosexual, homosexual, autoerotic, fetishist, voy-

euristic, transvestite, and others. Limonov's offensive sexual politics are reinforced by an equally iconoclastic political stance. Unlike most members of the post-Stalin generation, who have been thoroughly disillusioned with leftist ideology, Èdička is attracted to such radicals as Trockij, Mao Tse Tung, Che Guevarra, and Qadaffi. Sympathizing with the dispossessed of this world, he identifies with New York blacks, Latinos, and various other social outcasts, which include welfare recipients and bums. Although Èdička's politics are anarchist, not Leninist, and include a large dose of the aesthetics of violence and provocation, the Russian reader, force-fed on official Soviet culture, may have perceived him as yet another version of the Soviet proletarian or revolutionary hero, and has rejected him on this basis as well. Èdička's so-called pro-Soviet activities also serve to counteract his sense of invisibility and dispossession. At the same time, they are provocations, and it is both as the victimized invisible man *and* the eccentric provocateur that Èdička submits a cycle of poems to the Soviet journal *Novyj mir*. After all, Russians like poetry and may finally publish him.

Besides exploring unacceptable political behaviors, Èdička also deflates Russia's dissident icons Solženicyn and Saxarov, making no distinction between them. Like a naive child or a simpleton provincial, he blames them for having seduced him and others into emigrating. In an intentionally irreverent conflation of sexual and political taboo-breaking, Èdička makes love to his wife to the accompaniment of a Solženicyn interview on television. His systematic attack of Western mores and institutions, which he considers just as dishonest and cynical as their Soviet counterparts, is consistent with his radical politics. And ever the angry Russian and defensive émigré, he is highly critical of the Americans he meets—of their petty rationalism, prudence, and lack of material and spiritual generosity.

The Russian writer before and after the Revolution has been expected to represent unambiguously the ideals of community and social responsibility. Contrary to the traditional literary hero, Limonov's protagonist stands for Nietzschean transgression and a Wilde-like dandyism and eccentricity: "I have always worn nothing but high heels, and I ask to be laid in my grave, if I have one, wearing incredible shoes of some kind, high heels without fail," says Edward tramping the streets of New York in search of love and adventure. His blatant self-love also contradicts the Russian literary norm, although the dark side of his narcissistic self can be traced back to Dostoevskij's underground man and his progeny. Like the original underground man or his twentieth-century counterpart Kavalerov in Oleša's *Zavist'*, Èdička indulges in the negative emotions of self-pity, envy, and resentment, blaming the world for his problems and failures. "Where is my money?" he demands intermittently in a state of solipsistic frenzy. The self-assured egotist and dandy alternate with the frightened yet obnoxious adolescent, both of whom find little sympathy in the Russian reader.

Because Èdička's image goes against the grain of tradition and social propriety, Russian readers have tended to overlook the hero's honesty and kindness, which make him lovable and are just as much a part of the persona as dandyism and self-love, anger and hatred. "What the fuck is anything worth in this world without kindness?" asks Èdička many times over. Contrary to the Russian literary norm, the two sides of his character are compatible; provocation and moralism coexist and do not conflict. Refusing to draw the boundary between good and evil or right and wrong along traditional lines, Èdička accepts himself as he is, without the self-doubt or self-hate that has traditionally accompanied "underground" behavior.

All Èdička's "positive" and "negative" character traits and literary masks are clearly evident in the central cathartic episode in the novel: the homosexual encounter with the black stranger Chris, a scene that blends the author's militant attack on the reader's moral and social sensibilities with a sympathetic presentation of the hero's pitiful, victimized state. Whereas homosexual love with a dangerous black man in a dark corner of New York City is offensive to most of Limonov's readers, Èdička's misery evokes sympathy. Abandoned by his beloved wife, Èdička desperately seeks human contact and warmth in the streets of modern Babylon; he finds it for a brief moment in the strong, protective arms of Chris in a deserted womb-like playground. "I was like a dog that had found its master again. I would have bitten the throat of a policeman or anyone else for him." Vulnerable and degraded little Èdička is looking for a parent or someone to belong to. He also wants to reverse sex roles and become Elena, in his eyes desirable and powerful. But the sensualist and iconoclast in him finds a different order of pleasure in this his first homosexual experience. Attracted to the primal physical power of male sexuality, he is also drawn to the atmosphere of danger inherent in the situation, which he maximizes by imagining that Chris leads a criminal life.

The homosexual episode can also be read as the high point in Èdička's struggle for psychic health to the extent that the reader believes the hero has been liberated from his compulsive preoccupation with Elena. This, the novel's central epiphany, is modeled on the Dionysian and Christian myth of death and resurrection. Like the suffering god, Èdička with his preference for heterosexual love dies in order to be reborn a free man. In preparation for the exorcism he performs a transvestite ritual analogous to the Dionysian masquerade, symbolizing the androgynous character of the god. The ritual aspect becomes even more explicit with the transformation of the local street prostitutes into "priestesses of love." After getting drunk, he seems to lose consciousness ("time became a dark sack") in what is of course a symbolic death. When he comes to, he is in some kind of temple, playing with his phallic knife in an obvious profane yet devotional gesture, which foreshadows the encounter with Chris. Just before they meet, Èdička expresses a clear-cut death wish, which precedes the ultimate plunge into the Dionysian nether world: "I had essentially lost the instinct for self-preservation; I feared no one and nothing in the world because I was prepared to die at any moment." What he is not conscious of is the mythological subtext of his apparent desire to die, and only after these symbolic events does he enter the underworld sandlot where he experiences the ritual of rebirth and revitalization. The event itself is all but a mirage:

Èdička never sees Chris again, nor is he able by day to find the sacred sandlot.

Perhaps the ultimate provocation for the reader is the blurring of the line between *Dichtung* and *Wahrheit*. The hero of this novel and of all Limonov's narrative writing is Edward Limonov himself, and, as in so much post-Stalin unofficial writing, the narrator depicts actual events and real people. But in contrast to the high civic pathos of recent autobiography and history, the literary life story of Èdička is pointedly lacking in all redeeming moral or historical value. Superficially, Limonov's autobiographical writing can be labeled sordid exhibitionism or self-advertisement; on a literary level, however, the conflation of author and hero subverts our academic notions of appropriate or learned reader-response, and calls into question the jealously guarded separation of fiction and reality. Limonov seems to provoke a reader-response on the level of gossip and prurient curiosity, comparable to the effect of yellow journalism, but then, from his authorial position, he may judge us for confusing life and art. In accordance with his literary program of debunking social and moral pieties, he deflates the reader's elitist and moral self-image. As part of an ongoing dialogue with his reader, Èdička asserts his heterosexuality in a recent short story: "Since my book *It's Me, Eddie* has come out, many people in the international Russian community think I am a homosexual. Once . . . I had to punch this wise guy in the face . . . for calling me a dirty queer" (**"On the Wild Side"**). The retort is, of course, no more straightforward or reliable than the account of Èdička's behavior in the novel, for it is again the persona's voice and not that of the author. In yet another conflation of reality and fiction, the character assumes the role of authority by discussing the author's novel and his personal life.

The dilemma of reader-response is further reinforced by the confessional mode of *Èto ja—Èdička.* As a genre, autobiography is frequently confessional, focusing on the narrator's hidden, sometimes sinful, story. The educated reader knows that since Rousseau exhibitionism and depravity have been the staple material of literary confession. When the hero of Camus's *La Chute* cannot think of true stories about his own baseness, he invents them. Dostoevskij reminds us that for confession to have the proper cathartic effect it must expose all of the soul's dark recesses—and then some. It is the genre par excellence for depicting tawdriness and man's wicked, disreputable nature. As Ferdyščenko in *Idiot* retorts, "You want to hear about a man's worst deed and demand that it be brilliant. A man's worst deed is always dirty." Like Ferdyščenko, Limonov provokes the sanctimonious reader to register his outrage at Èdička's confession, only to remind him that his response is inappropriate to the genre.

Although modern literary confessions are associated with the aesthetics of provocation, they have also retained their moral function of probing the essence of life. Èdička, whose coming of age in Xar'kov is described in Limonov's **Podrostok Savenko** (1983), is also a seeker of truth, but not in the abstract or ideological sense. By unceremoniously stripping life of its many social and moral conventions, the author focuses on primal truths: "It's a question of bread, meat and cunt," says Èdička about the meaning of life, pursuing the harsh realities honestly, like a twentieth-century streetwise stoic.

As a perennial outsider and occasional outcast, Èdička sees through the many masks, deceptions, and taboos; as a post-Genet natural man, he affirms the absolute value of egoism and personal survival, especially when threatened. His rage and spite are of the Dostoevskij variety, but, unlike the twentieth-century literary descendants of the underground man, Èdička has retained a natural innocence and fundamental morality untainted by Freudian consciousness. Attracted to each and every variety of untried and forbidden experience, Èdička is not a sadist; he hates those who have hurt him and has no respect for established institutions, including the intelligentsia with its pious elitism. Limonov admires originality, unconventional courage, and personal strength, yet is invariably sympathetic toward the underdog. Both *Podrostok Savenko* and the story **"On the Wild Side"** are typical in this respect: laconic moralism is combined with a continuing assault on literary taboos.

Although Limonov seems to have rejected his affiliation with Russian literature, the primary subtexts of *Èto ja—Èdička* are Russian, and his literary anthropology is clearly Dostoevskian. The title of the first chapter "Otel' Vinslou i ego obitateli" (The Hotel Winslow and its denizens) is a variation on *Selo Stepančikovo i ego obitateli,* which is referred to ironically in the same chapter (one of the Russian immigrants in the hotel has written his dissertation on Dostoevskij's novel). On the very first pages, we learn that like Raskol'nikov Èdička lives in a tiny, cheap room high above the street, and that he has problems both with his landlady and the cleaning woman. In an attempt to escape physical and emotional claustrophobia and anxiety, he endlessly walks the streets of Manhattan, where he has numerous chance encounters with other social outcasts. When Èdička addresses the reader for the first time, Limonov replicates the underground man's dialogic discourse:

> I think it's clear to you by now what a character I am, even though I forgot to introduce myself. I started running on without announcing who I was; I forgot. Overjoyed at the opportunity to drown you in my voice at last, I got carried away and never announced whose voice it was. My fault, forgive me, we'll straighten it out right now. I am on welfare. I live at your expense, you pay taxes and I don't do a fucking thing. Twice a month I go to the clean, spacious welfare office at 1515 Broadway and receive my checks. I consider myself to be scum, the dregs of society, I have no shame or conscience, therefore my conscience doesn't bother me and I don't plan to look for work, I want to receive your money to the end of my days. And my name is Edichka, "Eddie-baby." And you gentlemen can figure you're getting off cheap.

This is also the voice of a 1970s Raskol'nikov, who perceives himself as superior to the well-fed conformists around him and is resentful of their "undeserved" prosperity and comfort. Although Èdička would have killed the pawnbroker without any moral compunctions, he also

has moments when he cannot transgress society's norms. He equates himself with Raskol'nikov, but he admits to his neighbor at the rooming house that there are times when he cannot kill "his old lady" (*staruška*). Also like Dostoevskij's hero, he has a loving and generous side and identifies with the city's underdogs—its insulted and injured. He gives money to poor people on the street, talks to prostitutes, and has a humble, shy girlfriend by the name of Sonja. Contrary to Dotoevskij's novel, however, there is no tragic conflict in *Èto ja—Èdička* between the Nietzschean superman and narcissist and the compassionate person. They simply coexist as they would in the unrepressed natural man. The psychoanalytic subject of *Èto ja—Èdička* can also be compared to that of *Prestuplenie i nakazanie:* both heroes have been reduced to childlike narcissism by their respective psychospiritual crises, and the two novels' narrative structures reflect the conflict between the heroes' self-destructive compulsion to repeat and healthy self-healing behavior. In Dostoevskij the positive Christian model triumphs in the end—not so in *Èto ja—Èdička.*

Limonov's treatment of urban poverty and alienation can be traced back to the Natural School and the physiological sketch as mediated by Dostoevskij. Èdička's prototype is thus the little-man hero, especially in his Dostoevskian reinterpretation. In the second chapter, "I Am a Busboy," Limonov presents the feelings of a "real" waiter *from within* rather than from a traditionally superior authorial position. His hero's plight also resembles that of Makar Devuškin (*Bednye ljudi*), who loses Varvara to the dishonest but incomparably more prosperous Bykov, yet continues to play the role of a devoted lover. At the end of the novel, Èdička lovingly buys Elena's intimate apparel for her trysts with his rivals, just like Makar at the conclusion of *Bednye ljudi.*

The literary prototype of Limonov's protagonist has also passed through Gor'kij's and Majakovskij's school of proletarian self-assertion and the social realities of proletarian revolution. As already mentioned, *Èto ja—Èdička* is a contemporary variation of *Oblako v štanax* in that it combines revolutionary rhetoric and violence, personal megalomania and literary taboo-breaking with vulnerability in love. In *Oblako v štanax* and *Flejta pozvonočnik,* Majakovskij's best-known poems about love, the lyrical hero is rejected by the women he loves in favor of a better-established husband or lover. "It's odd how fate persistently links little Eddie with the sexual legends of another great poet," says Èdička in reference to Majakovskij. Although Limonov's father was an officer in the MVD and his mother was educated, Limonov's lyrical hero comes from the lower classes, like Majakovskij's persona. He refers to himself as a "plebeian boy," a "mongrel" and a "punk," as "a ridiculous little Ukrainian" no longer capable, according to Elena, of transcending his social limitations. But even in his depressed state, he remains true to the futurist aesthetic and the power of the oppressed, "spitting in the face of public taste" and established authority.

Limonov's much discussed subversion of the Russian literary language in *Èto ja—Èdička* can also be subsumed by the little-man theme. Èdička speaks the newly formed language of the uncultured immigrant, whose Russian has been influenced by English on the lexical as well as the syntactic level. "The specifically American aroma of connotation and association," introduces a "satirical, humorous, and thematically appropriate effect of 'estrangement'." In the larger context of Limonov's avant-garde position, however, Èdička's "émigré Russian" reflects an anti-elitist deflation of the literary language. There is no apparent distinction between Èdička's language and that of Limonov, as if the writer has been supplanted by a hero speaking his own substandard language. When the traditional distance between author and character disappears, so does the author's superiority. Limonov's occasional lack of literary taste can be attributed to the blurring of literary boundaries and the modern ascendancy of the voice of the little man.

If the story of Èdička is a contemporary version of *Zapiski iz podpol'ja* and *Oblako v štanax,* the fable of Èdička and Elena can be read as a modern tale of courtly love. In **"My nacional'nyj geroj"** the exalted poet and his "Elena prekrasnaja" (Fair Elena) are presented as the perfect couple merged into one, a fact underscored by the *royal we* of the title. The association of Elena with Helen of Troy is in part ironic in *Èto ja—Èdička,* although in the hero's perception she is still the ancient goddess of love. Elena is a middle-class parody of the knight's fair lady and belongs to the same literary lineage as Emma Bovary and Nabokov's Lolita. Her values, like Emma's, are mimetic—they have been formed by imitating popular role-models from the silver screen and fashion industry. She wants to be like the girl model from the *Story of O,* and, like Lolita, she is a victim of American popular culture. Even if Elena is only a cheap version of the poet's "beautiful lady," Èdička is a chivalrous knight, who continues to see his fallen angel as a contemporary Dulcinea and refuses to betray the immortality of love. In other words, he is an incorrigible romantic: "I had hoped—had thought—as whores, adventurers, prostitutes, what you will, but together all our lives" is Èdička's relentless refrain. The intensity of his love can be compared to Humbert Humbert's obsession with Lolita, who is created by the hero, much as Èdička invents Elena. Both women attempt to escape their "captors," as did Nastas'ja Filippovna, Elena's Dostoevskian prototype.

The romantic plot of the novel has, in fact, much in common with the central love story in *Idiot.* Characteristically, Èdička is both Myškin and Rogožin, and Elena is his modern Nastas'ja Filippona. Like Rogožin, Èdička comes from a "milieu where love and blood stood side by side"; his feelings for Elena are animated by both hurt and hatred and an instinctual or primitive fetishism. If he cannot possess her, he will destroy her or himself. Èdička's love is also related to the story of Christ and Mary Magdalene:

> "Treat Elena . . . as Christ treated Mary Magdalene and all women who sinned," thinks Èdička to himself. "No, treat her better. . . . She is unwise and evil and unhappy, but you feel that you're wise and good: love her, don't scorn her. . . . Help, and expect nothing in re-

turn. . . . Love does not demand gratitude and gratification. Love itself is gratification."

The Myškin-like behavior of Èdička is selfless and all-forgiving, nurturing and intuitive. Like Dostoevskij's hero, he likes children and exhibits feminine characteristics. But in contrast to Myškin's Christ-like sentiments, Limonov develops fully the dark, masochist side of Èdička's humility and benevolence.

Further light is thrown on Èdička in Limonov's recent short story **"Dvojnik."** Like the novel, it is a narcissistic text representing a self-contained universe, which consists of Edward and Father John—his mirror image. But it deviates from *Èto ja—Èdička* in that the story's confessional hero is the pederast priest, and not Limonov's autobiographical hero, who in the course of the story assumes the parental roles of father-confessor and detached observer. It is as if the autobiographical Edward had distanced himself from the hero of the New York novel, who inhabits a separate body in this story. Father John is very similar to Èdička: he unites in himself human generosity (priesthood) and sexual preferences that his society views as perverse (pederasty). Like Èdička's image, the image of Father John is provocative and taboo-breaking, combining "perverse" sex and religion. At the same time the author clearly accentuates his hero's "higher" morality (he is a "true" priest) and his victimization by those he loves (cf. Èdička's love for Elena), thereby mediating the reader's outrage.

In relation to the Russian literary canon Limonov's stance in *Èto ja—Èdička* is clearly iconoclastic, although his protagonist is a modern version of Dostoevskij's hero and Majakovksij's poetic persona. Limonov subverts the prose canon at all its levels: moral, political, cultural, literary, and linguistic; yet he is "moral" and "old-fashioned" in his conception of love, friendship, and human suffering, and in matters of literary form, he is a realist. In his ongoing dialogue with the reader, Limonov also makes use of conflicting voices, ranging from outright provocation to a plea for the reader's love and acceptance. *Èto ja—Èdička* features the gamut of the author's voices, whose dialogic or polyphonic chorus helps us see the deeply "moral" nature of his "immoral" hero. (pp. 526-37)

> *Olga Matich, "The Moral Immoralist: Edward Limonov's 'Èto Ja—Èdička'," in* Slavic and East-European Journal, *Vol. 30, No. 4, Winter, 1986, pp. 526-40.*

Edward J. Brown

Once again, Edward Limonov, the powerful and problematic Soviet émigré writer, has offered up a piece of self-proclaimed autobiographical fiction about his life "in freedom." And once again, he has employed every device of obscenity and scatology at his command to undermine both the pieties of American life and the approved public image of the Soviet émigré. In 1979, Limonov's *It's Me, Eddie* outraged many of his fellow exiles, who found it slanderous and pornographic. One prominent critic declared, "If freedom means the freedom to write that book, then I am against freedom." Others, however, expressed their support for the book and declared its author one of the most important of the writers to have left the Soviet Union in the so-called third wave and almost the only one to articulate in his fiction a certain experience of exile.

Limonov's two novels about his life in America (*It's Me, Eddie* and *His Butler's Story*) explore the disorientation and unhappiness that are frequently the lot of those who have "chosen freedom." Between the strait-laced Solzhenitsyn in Vermont delivering jeremiads against "pluralism" and other evidences of "degeneration" in the West, and Eddie Limonov slaking his omnisexual appetites on the underside of New York City, while inveighing against the "vel'fer" that supports him, there is not really a great distance. Both articulate feelings that exiles generally disguise or suppress: nostalgia for the homeland, together with genuine contempt for American institutions and an appalling lack of interest in learning about how those work.

According to his more or less fictional biography, Limonov was an adolescent thief, a psycho, a tailor and an underground poet before leaving the Soviet Union in 1974. Two novels set in the Soviet Union, *The Adolescent Savenko* and *The Young Scoundrel*, . . . are apparently based on his life in the Soviet criminal world, on his sojourns in jail and in a mental institution, and on his career as a dissident poet in a flourishing cultural underground. As with the pair about his life in the United States, these books view the clean world from the underside. *Savenko* explores the psychology of a Soviet adolescent who moves from his working-class family into the criminal world; nothing in the book mitigates our horror at the simple motivations for theft, rape, mutilation and murder. The novel also gives us, as though incidentally, a vivid look at life in a working-class suburb of Kharkov: the reek of vodka and violence, the ugly housing and the scramble to get it, and especially the way in which corruption in the "law-abiding" sector feeds the criminal underground. In *The Young Scoundrel,* Eddie has blossomed into an unpublished poet moving among the disaffected intelligentsia of Kharkov, who spurn Soviet respectability in a way that foreshadows Eddie's lavish contempt for the New York establishment. The essence of Limonov's work, whether set in the West or in the Soviet Union, is its vivid articulation of the mute misery and hatred felt by those on the bottom for the scrubbed and fancy world of those on top. From their point of view, as Eddie puts it in *It's Me, Eddie,* "There isn't a hell of a lot of difference between here and there [the Soviet Union]."

Limonov has assured us—mistakenly, I think—that the practice of deducing the author's biography from his fiction is quite sound in his case. He says that he writes only about himself, "since he has studied that character better than any other," and insists that there are no "purely invented" situations in his books; he does admit that he has simplified many things, and eliminated others, thus acknowledging the novelist's work of selection and structuring. But because Limonov identifies himself with the "Eddie," sometimes "Eddie-baby," of his narratives, and provides only flimsy cover for the real people who appear in them (this has cruelly embarrassed some of them), a reader is likely to assume that Limonov and his tormented narrator are one, that the author is as morally vacuous as his central character. Such a conclusion involves a serious critical misunderstanding. Limonov is not the luckless dropout whose character he so vividly creates in his fiction. In fact the real Limonov, as far as we can tell, was actually a good tailor and poet and has managed his affairs quite well in emigration. The Eddie who fantasizes shooting up his rich master's house with an AK-47 or who, in the final pages of *His Butler's Story,* takes careful aim at the repulsive Secretary General of the United Nations, offers a fictional statement as to how slugs and underdogs feel about the world of those who have made it. The latter scene is a powerful realization not of Limonov, of course, but of the Lee Harvey Oswalds of the world.

In *His Butler's Story* Eddie is a Russian poet obliged to work as butler, general handyman and factotum in the palatial East River residence of Steven Grey, a WASP multimillionaire whose fabulous income derives from many enterprises. Steven's house guests range from the Shah of Iran and a variety of American and foreign moguls to a visiting Soviet poet—Yevgeny Yevtushenko with, as Eddie assures us, his C.I.A. impresarios, very thinly disguised—who provide him with the cachet of high culture. The image of Steven Grey, seen from the viewpoint of a proud and penniless Russian poet, is a creation of great literary power. Huge, oppressive, abusive and totally self-centered, Steven arouses in Eddie an insufferable physical revulsion. But Eddie not only hates him, he also envies him his jet-set connections, his money and limitless sexual opportunities.

Eddie needs to prove to everybody "just what sort of person it was they were neglecting." He is in constant communication with contemptible editors and publishers who keep rejecting his poetry and prose, but his principal activity is the pursuit of happiness through sexual adventures described in explicit and disgusting detail. Limonov's sexual scenes are emetic rather than aphrodisiac. Neither transports of love nor the pleasures of simple ravishment can be found anywhere in this book. Of his principal sex object in the novel, Jenny, Eddie says, "I made love to her but I didn't want to." And it turns out that she never wanted to either, but did it because she loved Eddie and thought he liked it. Then there is a "little twat named Mary Ellen," whom he didn't want to fuck, and a number of others whom he did, but without conviction and almost without pleasure. There are some who flit in and out as fantasies or nymphets, but the novel is simply an account of Eddie's "struggle against the world and everybody in it," and Jenny and the rest are only episodes in his contest with Steven and the others who control that world. The German translator of *It's Me, Eddie* distilled the ichor of that book and this one too as the single English obscenity which served in the title of the German edition: *Fuck Off, Amerika.*

Limonov breaks the widespread stereotype of the Soviet émigré as a man of the political right. In his role as Eddie he is a man of the left, not ashamed to work as a trucker, a tailor or a busboy, and he associates with the unhappy and underprivileged and with the radicals who claim to speak for them. He makes friends with blacks who are unacceptable to his fellow Soviet émigrés. As a matter of fact the American novels embrace humanity in a way that is altogether original and refreshing in a writer of Limonov's provenance. Soviet émigrés are as a rule people who have escaped or been expelled from a failed utopia; they are frequently skeptical at best about the liberal hopes still very much alive in Western democracies. In helping to define that émigré pattern by escaping from it, even though by way of *épatage* and obscenity, Limonov's novels have performed an important service.

In almost everything he has written Limonov's style is marked by the effective use of two kinds of linguistic anomaly. Foreign words—American, of course, but spelled out in Cyrillic letters—variegate the Russian text of Limonov's novel and function as the linguistic mark of Eddie's strangeness in a world of vel'fer, biznessmen, leeving-rums and dyning-rums, Dzhenni's rashen-boi-frend, Tsentral-Park, Khadson-reever and Eesreever. One of my problems with this otherwise excellent translation is that these words are presented in their proper English spelling, and thus an important lexical mark of the narrator as a contemptuous alien presence in "Amerika" has been lost. Other Russian émigré writers also use transliterated English words in their Russian text, but with a quite different function. Vassily Aksyonov uses such concoctions as "khash-poppies," meaning a kind of footwear, but the effect is less alienating than exotic. Perhaps the nearest analog to Limonov's verbal device is Henry Miller's use of French phrases in *Tropic of Cancer* as a mark of the narrator's ironic detachment from the Paris scene. Limonov's use of English in his Russian text suggests, also, the newly arrived émigré who will never lose his native accent nor make the new ideas and concepts his own.

The other persistent lexical feature in Limonov's writing is the exceptionally rich and varied use of obscenities, which also carries a heavy charge of revulsion from the normal American world, from, as he would put it, the varied collection of fuck-offs with whom he is obliged to deal in his brave new country. These two features of style, "barbarisms" and obscenities, call attention to the verbal texture itself: as a Jakobsonian linguist would put it, they are iconic rather than arbitrary, or transparent, "signs." And Limonov gives us, incidentally, a perfect model of the Russian language in its rich inflectional power when he uses the vulgar words for the male organ of generation and for the act of copulation as creative linguistic pivots, deriving from the original root form multiple parts of speech through the use of prefixes, infixes and suffixes. Much attention has been given to the linguistic features of Limonov's work, and it does seem likely that the Russian literary language will have been affected by his virtuosity. Russian, in this century, especially since the triumph of Soviet puritanism in the 1930s, has lagged far behind the West in the breaching of linguistic taboos, with the result that Limonov's writing contains a higher shock potential in its Russian context than any translation could possibly convey. In everything he has written Limonov gives new life to literary Russian by opening it up to a powerful vocabulary from the regions of proscribed speech.

Limonov does obeisance to Henry Miller in this book, and there's no doubt that his novels owe something to Miller's. Eddie is compulsive and often miserable in his pursuit of sex and he is uncertain as to what kind gives him satisfaction; in fact, his passionate accommodation of a beautiful young black man in a vacant lot near 51st and Broadway (in *It's Me, Eddie*) contrasts sharply with his sexually frustrating encounters with women. But for Miller's character the sexual smorgasbord includes both mystery and occasions for poetry. And Miller's nihilism is more philosophical than Limonov's: The chaos he mirrors is in the nature of things; the whole world is a kind of cancer eating itself away. Limonov's world is particular and concrete. He seldom budges from that Amerika—or Kharkov—in thought or image. Miller's view of catastrophe is cosmic; Eddie's is local and confined. But the problem I've alluded to above concerning the confusion of author and central character is foregrounded in the work of both writers. Limonov himself has illuminated his relationship to Eddie in ["**Hero Negative**"], his recently published poem in the *Times Literary Supplement* (June 26, translated by G. S. Smith):

> This is my hero negative
> He's always here along with me
>
> I drink a beer,—he drinks a beer
> He lives in my apartment room
>
> He goes to bed with girls I do
> My dark-skinned member hangs from him
>
> This is my hero negative . . .
> And we may see his elegant back
> Around the city of New York
> On any one of those dark streets.
>
> (pp. 313-14)

Edward J. Brown, "Eddie-Baby on the Town," in The Nation, *New York, Vol. 245, No. 9, September 26, 1987, pp. 313-14.*

Maggie Paley

A comedy of manners is a rude sort of book pretending not to be. It uses a high-minded tone and, usually, a polished style to expose to public scrutiny the base elements of human nature that manners were created to hide. Perhaps this is why Edward Limonov, the Russian émigré author and protagonist of *His Butler's Story* (which his publisher calls a fictional memoir), addresses his readers every once in a while as "gentlemen." Although his book is about the habits of the rich, he seems, this courtesy aside, to love being rude so much he can't bother to be rude elegantly.

Protagonist Limonov is an angry, desperate man, an anarchist with worldly ambitions who rises through sexual means from Manhattan welfare client to live-in butler in an East Side townhouse. There he engages in a competition (almost totally one-sided) with his millionaire master, Steven Grey, whom he refers to as Gatsby. "If you compare Gatsby and me, then who's better, who's more talented, who's more needed by the world? . . . I produce books. . . . He oversees the manufacture and sale of ever newer things that . . . undoubtedly serve the cause of enslaving man's body and spirit. Whereas my activity is directed towards the liberation of that body and spirit, towards the awakening of human consciousness."

Though Limonov hates Steven, he admires Steven's easy way with money and power. *His Butler's Story* is the story of Limonov's transformation from a fearful servant into a servant who feels ready to take his place among masters. "I know that sooner or later they'll accept me under the name of writer—it's inevitable. They won't be able to withstand my strength, and I'll descend on them and . . . their women will be wild about me and my masculinity and wickedness."

The author uses this premise, or experience, to say the worst about everyone and everything. He hates the underclass for being weak and stupid and the ruling class for being insensitive. He hates women—whom he describes in terms of female sex organs—for using men. He considers the other Russians in New York to be snobs or boors. He has no use for political systems, Communist or capitalist. He believes in revolution as a "phenomenon of nature." Yet he's made no plans to foment it. He'd only want to die fighting for freedom, he says, if he were well enough known to have his death announced on the front page of *The New York Times.*

Mr. Limonov—who now lives in Paris and wrote an earlier memoir, *It's Me, Eddie*—does have charm. It's the charm of the scamp, the self-confessed opportunist who admits his own depravity and asks if anyone else is really any better.

His Butler's Story, which was first published in France and has been translated from the Russian by Judson Rosengrant, is often painfully funny. But sometimes author Limonov feels too sorry for protagonist Limonov, and brags about his sexual prowess and his freedom from received ideas. At these moments his tone slips; he's engaging in special pleading, and becomes suspect as a witness.

His prose style in translation in both books is disappointing, too, sprinkled with curse words and clichés, as if being slangy were a license for being careless. (He's careless, also, for giving the nickname Gatsby to Steven Grey, who, having had money in his family for several generations, doesn't qualify as an *arriviste.* The Great Gatsby is apparently the figure Limonov would like to be if he had the money.)

Yet even at its worst *His Butler's Story* crackles with energy. Though Edward Limonov's judgment may be faulty, he's to be congratulated for his audacity, his insistence on saying what most people are afraid to say, his sheer, beautiful nerve.

> *Maggie Paley, "Sneering His Way to the Top," in* The New York Times Book Review, *July 5, 1987, p. 2.*

Publishers Weekly

It's 1958 in the factory city of Kharkov. Krushchev is in power, the communist economy seems firmly entrenched and Eddie-baby, the streetwise hero of the author's two previous semi-autobiographical novels (*His Butler's Story; It's Me, Eddie*) is on a collision course with the law. At age 15 Eddie is already a borderline alcoholic—gathering nightly with the rest of the neighborhood at grocery store #7 to drink fortified wine—and a thief. His skintight clothes, his arrogance and misplaced use of his gifts—Eddie-baby is a poet after the fashion of Rimbaud—have caused his disillusioned parents to cut off his pocket money. In this absorbing novel [*Memoir of a Russian Punk*], Limonov expertly captures the horrifying boredom of working-class Soviet urban life, and uses just the right hip, offhand tone to describe Eddie's adventures in the demi-world of teenage gangs and small-time hoods. The graphic street violence which punctuates the narrative seems almost shockingly mundane as Eddie, attempting to steal a few rubles to take out his girlfriend, participates in gang rape and murder. Limonov leaves us with hope that Eddie, blessed with intelligence and a cocky assurance will, unlike his friends, eventually make a successful life for himself.

> *A review of "Memoir of a Russian Punk," in* Publishers Weekly, *Vol. 237, No. 41, October 12, 1990, p. 46.*

Anna Shapiro

Homer nods, but must he absolutely nod out? Edward Limonov is not Homer exactly, but his 1983 "fictional memoir" about Russian émigré life in New York, *It's Me, Eddie,* was poetry—an account that improbably gave eloquence and lyricism to living on welfare, screwing vagrants in deserted lots and unloved women in cushier surroundings, menial labor and, above all, unrequited love. The love was for a glamorous unfaithful wife, but equally for the countries and all their millions who had no use for Eddie and his poetry. The book was also very funny. Without humor, poetry or love, on the other hand, his new novel, *Memoir of a Russian Punk,* is about sordidness, violence, lust and an unconvincing pride. It is not without interest, however, some of a documentary kind, being set in Kharkov, the "Detroit of Russia," detailing life among the proles in a fashion idealized not by exaltation of the working class but rather by rebellion as an end in itself.

Eddie-baby, as he is tiresomely called in almost every sentence, is 15, the very age of rebellion. Unlike Marlon Brando's Wild One, he does not need to ask "What've you got?"—he's got plenty to rebel against, from the "trashes," the military police, who do indeed trash anyone unwary enough to cross their path, to his parents, as is usual at that age, who represent claustrophobic, upward-aspiring conformity. Eddie's father is in fact a trash—an officer in the secret police, conducting prisoners to execution or Siberia.

The documentary interest, of course, is in the exotic details and, conversely, in the striking but unexpected similarities between Eddie's world and what is very recognizable and familiar to us. Much of the book is taken up with initiating the reader into the values of Eddie's gang, which are indistinguishable from their counterparts' in working-class Britain or a tough neighborhood of Queens or New Haven. Eddie's great accomplishments are to have tailored his velveteen pants to illicit skinniness and gotten a Polish haircut; to have run a forgery scam and burgled a cafeteria; to have participated with his pals in beating up and robbing a trash, among other acts. His great secret shame is that he is still a virgin. The incidents in this novel of incidents revolve around Eddie's efforts to accumulate 125 rubles over two days in order to take his girlfriend, Svetka, to a fancy party. Great contempt is reserved for workers, and if there is any revolutionary agenda, it is for the abolition of work. The gang's chief occupation is in drinking enormous quantities of *biomitsin,* vodka, home-brew or whatever liquor they can conveniently get their hands on. Some of the kids smoke pot and at least one shoots morphine.

It is no longer shocking to Westerners to hear of class distinctions in Russian society, although those are invariably presented as dividing the apparatchiks from everybody else. But everybody else is busy making distinctions too. Eddie's well-read mother shares the gang's disdain for workers, but in the mode of an intellectual in Levittown yearning for the Upper West Side. "The military and other educated people all moved to the center of town . . . and noisy working-class families—the proletariat, or as [Eddie's friend] contemptuously calls them, the 'hegemonic element'—quickly moved into the vacuum they had left. . . . Eddie-baby's mother started to pine." Eddie's father makes no use of his military connections, so the family remains stuck among the proles. As in this country, the distinctions within a range that might encompass, say, a plumber and a professor are less of income than of inclination.

It comes as no surprise that Western anything will have chic, but what's hilarious is that what's really cool in 1958 in Kharkov is Glenn Miller and Bobby Darin. Very exotic, too, in at least this reader's experience, is a several-paragraph examination of the hero's foreskin, complete with a discovery of the smegma it gathered, "rather like Roquefort cheese." This is by far the book's most vivid passage, and its afterimage weirdly lingers through what follows, including a rape or two (you keep imagining that damn cheese). Rape of girls and women is entirely taken for granted, even by the girls—who are depicted as liking it. The absolute rock-bottom class is simply female.

The climactic scenes, so to speak, are a gang rape accompanied by the murder of the women's male escort, and Eddie's rape of Svetka—after which she invites him to spend the night. The gang's rampage is reminiscent of nothing so much as the infamous Central Park "wilding," and no genius for description is required to make you feel nauseated, teary and angry, especially at Svetka's apostasy. What is disturbing beyond the events themselves is the tone in which they are presented. The voice of Limonov's earlier memoir is notable for a modesty that allows him to capture sensations others would choose to ignore, or fail

to notice altogether. This boastful, underdescribed installment on Eddie's earlier youth partakes of its adolescent values, asking the reader to be impressed or admiring of his posturing along with him.

A Westerner is tempted to see the novel as a parable, less about mother than mother country, in which it is the homeland that gets raped; but I hope this observation is a symptom of reviewer overachievement, such parallels being glib and making of literature a lesson plan. More likely it is an attempt to come to grips with a certain dreariness endemic to life. The British love to write about this dreariness, but when they do, it is with a crispness and clarity that make it almost bracing. When Eastern Europeans like Limonov do it, it is as if the leaden sky will never yield to sunshine. This does not seem to be a product of anything so temporary as political regimes; it looks constitutional. (pp. 98-9)

> *Anna Shapiro, "East Side Story," in* The Nation, *New York, Vol. 252, No. 3, January 28, 1991, pp. 98-9.*

FURTHER READING

Brown, Edward J. "Exiles, Early and Late." In his *Russian Literature Since the Revolution,* rev. and enl. ed., pp. 353-54. Cambridge: Harvard University Press, 1982.

> Briefly discusses *It's Me, Eddie.*

Lardner, Susan. "Sorrows of Edichka." *The New Yorker* LIX, No. 37 (31 October 1983): 140, 142-44.

> Review of *It's Me, Eddie.*

Matich, Olga. "Russian Writers on Literature and Society." *Humanities in Society* 7, Nos. 3-4 (Summer-Fall 1984): 221-234.

> Includes responses by Limonov and other Russian writers to six questions concerning their experiences with Soviet and Western literary establishments before and after emigrating.

Rosengrant, Judson. Translator's Postscript to "Love, Love, Love," by Edward Limonov. *Humanities in Society* 7, Nos. 3-4 (Summer-Fall 1984): 193-94.

> Discusses Limonov's use of obscenities and transliterated English.

Shukman, Ann. "Taboos, Splits, and Signifiers: Limonov's *Eyo ya—Edichka.*" *Essays in Poetics* 8, No. 2 (September 1983): 1-18.

> Examines Limonov's violation of Russian literary conventions and cultural norms.

David Markson

1927-

(Full name: David Merrill Markson) American novelist, essayist, short story writer, and editor.

Markson is regarded as an inventive literary stylist in the manner of James Joyce, William Gaddis, and Malcolm Lowry. His prose, a mixture of the colloquial, the erudite, and the archaic, encompasses neologisms, puns, and wry humor, and many critics have commented that his compressed, highly allusive fiction verges on poetry. Although often viewed as a writer more concerned with technique than content, Markson is noted for his sensitive exploration of such topics as love, male-female relationships, and the creative process. Commentators generally agree that as his career has progressed, Markson's work has become more technically sophisticated and metafictional. Joseph Tabbi observed: "[Markson is] among the few working novelists decisively to have carried the modernist tradition into the present, postmodern literature; a writer who, without claiming any particular knowledge of, or even affinities with, the more programmatic expounders of postmodernism, in recent work exemplifies many of the period's most vital developments."

While a graduate student at Columbia University, Markson wrote his master's thesis on Malcolm Lowry's classic novel *Under the Volcano* (1947). The two writers eventually became friends, and Lowry's influence is particularly evident in Markson's novel *Going Down,* which, like Lowry's work, is set in Mexico, where Markson and his wife lived for two years in the late 1950s.

Throughout the 1950s and early 1960s, Markson worked intermittently on *Going Down* while supporting himself by publishing crime fiction and erotica. Although considered "entertainments," Markson's detective novels—*Epitaph for a Tramp* and *Epitaph for a Dead Beat*—display the wit and stylistic verve that characterize his later, more serious works. Markson attained critical and commercial success with *The Ballad of Dingus Magee,* a ludicrous parody of the Western novel written in the complex manner of works by William Faulkner.

The financial rewards from *The Ballad of Dingus Magee* allowed Markson to explore the more personal, literary mode of *Going Down,* which he published in 1970. Set in the fictional Mexican village of Mictlán, *Going Down* is a Gothic murder mystery revolving around a ménage à trois among American expatriates: Fern Winters, an artist with a withered left hand; Steve Chance, a reclusive poet; and Lee Suffridge, the sexually voracious wife of an alcoholic painter. Written in a pastiche of styles derived from Joyce, Lowry, Faulkner, and Virginia Woolf, *Going Down* was faulted by some critics for pretentiousness. Perle Epstein, however, praised the novel as "a very contemporary, very literate record of despair; all of it in fact seems to be taking place in darkness, in shadows, in the rain, or in the secret criminal places of the heart."

Markson's next novel, *Springer's Progress,* is considered his most extravagant and allusive work. Using pithy sentences infused with wordplay and literary jokes, Markson chronicles the passionate extramarital affair between Lucien Springer, a middle-aged man, and the much younger Jessica Cornford, a promiscuous editor and novelist who tries to help him end his severe writer's block. When Springer finally begins writing, his novel emerges as the actual story the reader has been following. Sheldon Frank described *Springer's Progress* as a Joycean "celebration of carnality and creativity—an everything-goes, maniacally wild and funny and painful novel." Also recognized as a stylistic tour-de-force, Markson's recent novel, *Wittgenstein's Mistress,* is essentially an interior monologue by Kate, a former painter who believes she is the last living person on earth. Markson leaves ambiguous the notion of whether Kate is actually insane or the only survivor of a global catastrophe. In sober paragraphs consisting of one or two sentences, Kate relates her thoughts, memories, and observations on culture in an attempt to make sense of her past and present. In this work, Markson dramatizes Austrian philosopher Ludwig Wittgenstein's theory of the inadequacy of language to accurately represent reality. Sherrill E. Grace commented: "[Despite] the highly self-conscious, metafictional, plotless nature of Kate's narrative, David Markson has created that miracle of words on paper, the illusion of a living voice, a human being, and one who matters."

(See also *Contemporary Authors,* Vols. 49-52 and *Contemporary Authors New Revision Series,* Vol. 1.)

PRINCIPAL WORKS

NOVELS

Epitaph for a Tramp   1959
Epitaph for a Dead Beat   1961
The Ballad of Dingus Magee   1966
Going Down   1970
Springer's Progress   1977
Wittgenstein's Mistress   1988

OTHER

Malcolm Lowry's "Volcano": Myth, Symbol, Meaning
(criticism)   1978

Christopher Lehmann-Haupt

Mr. Markson begins [*Going Down*] with these words: "Accept the illusion. Night. Mexico. The immense, rife stillness of a village in the Mictlán hills. . . . " One is suspicious at once. Why should Mr. Markson have to tell us to "accept the illusion"? Perhaps he doesn't trust us? Perhaps he doesn't trust himself?

A clue appears further down the opening page. We read, of a girl clutching a machete, that "her face, her eyes, are vacant, without expression." Both "vacant" and "without expression"? It begins to seem as if either Mr. Markson doesn't trust the power of language to create illusions, or even that he may not be interested in creating one.

The latter turns out to be the case. True, Mr. Markson has a story to tell—one that involves two women and a man shacked up in a house in Mexico and practicing in the interest of sex some of the more acrobatic contortions since the invention of pretzels. And his plot is carefully contrived to begin with a murder whose victim, perpetrator, background and consequences are not completely clarified until the end.

But all that is seen as through plaster of Paris, darkly. The hero of *Going Down* is Mr. Markson's prose style—a lumpy spackle mixed together out of echoes from Joyce, Faulkner, Woolf and Malcolm Lowry; allusions to everybody's collection of Modern Library classics; ineffable emotions leaking out of incomplete sentences; and strings of phrases that use different words but express the same banalities over and over again.

It may be that Mr. Markson is up to something here. On the other hand, it is equally possible that he is not. My reasoning runs as follows: If the prose style of fiction doesn't serve to illuminate the action it's describing, then it's ei-

ther incompetent or it's meant to call attention to itself. It may be doing so because the "action" rests in the style itself, as in the writing of W. H. Gass or Nathalie Sarraute, for example. Or it may be doing so in order to comment on other styles, as in *Ulysses* and *The French Lieutenant's Woman.* Or it may be doing so to call attention to the persona of the narrator, as in *Huckleberry Finn.*

The prose of *Going Down* is by no means incompetent. It draws one's attention inexorably to the narrator, who turns out to be no one but the author himself. The illusion it creates is of a novelist, with nothing to say, trying to tell a story he doesn't believe for a minute. That is the only illusion I am able to accept.

> *Christopher Lehmann-Haupt, "Mexico Underdone and Done to Death," in* The New York Times, *April 24, 1970, p. 33.*

Perle Epstein

[When in *Going Down* David Markson] enjoins him to "accept the illusion. Night. Mexico . . . " it is as though the reader is confronted by an immense empty white canvas upon which very suddenly and without any warning, a technicolor series of characters, catastrophes, breakdowns, and dire spiritual mutilations is flashed. Or rather—spilled. For the language is liquid, undulating in story line, and, in many places, reads much more like a dark prose poem than a novel. The setting is Mexico, then New York, and finally Mexico again. But really it is only a mentally experienced Mexico and a Greenwich Village patterning the backdrop of a suffering mind that can be identified as "place." This—despite the dedication to and very faint echo of the ghost of Malcolm Lowry—is a very cerebral book whose landscape might as easily have been the Southern California cliffs or the barren ridges of the moon. Not to be compared with Lowry's drunkard's Mexico of bleak cantinas, beer-bellied police, and hallucinated gargoyles, despite its own preoccupations with the eerie symbiotic life-death pattern of that sinister yet irresistible land.

One by one, through the eyes of a local half-Mexican interne, an American hack writer and gossip, and finally through the tormented vision of one of the three leading protagonists herself, the bits and pieces of lives and relationships, the everyday and the legendary past are glued, stitched, and interpolated to form a collage of a book, whose essential scheme rests on the tragic dispersal by murder of a poetic menage a trois. The analogy to painting is not a random one; references to painting and painters abound throughout; one of the women in the triangle is a serious painter herself whose senses of art and life become so interwoven as ultimately to destroy her mind; the other woman, Lee, is the wife of a once great painter now wasting drunkenly in the Vermont woods; and the death of Steve, the central figure in the triangle, a bizarre suicide occurring in a church, is in itself a veritable Pieta.

The novel is a very contemporary, very literate record of despair; all of it in fact seems to be taking place in darkness, in shadows, in the rain, or in the secret criminal places of the heart. It is a skillfully handled book, very libidinal (indeed shades of Henry Miller loom higher throughout than do those of Malcolm Lowry) but with a distinctive quality and tone that place David Markson among the better Gothic novelists who—except for Poe—are not so much in the American tradition as formed by the likes of the Brontes, Thomas Hardy, and the Romantic poets who celebrate the dark and dreadful night of the soul. Here, too, a gaunt, haunted, even perhaps slightly demented hero stalks alone, unheeding, through the lives of all those unlucky enough to meet up with him. Byronic (see especially "Manfred" and "Cain"), a poet manque, a parricide, Steve Chance returns to the little Mexican town of his lonely youth and, for a while at least, establishes a successful relationship with two women who, in turn, establish a relationship of sorts with each other. The town looks on, shrugs, gossips, and finally goes on about its business.

But the heart of the story really takes place within the raw, hyper-sensitized stream of consciousness of Fern, a beautiful blonde painter whose hand is withered from birth and who acts as a kind of Magdalen to Steve, her demonic Christ, whom she literally removes from the cross at the end of the book. Numberous allusions—theological, Christian, Judaic, pagan, literary, artistic, musical—coat the story, thickening references, character names and places, meanings. The recurrent myth of the dying fisher king runs throughout, accompanied by extrapolations from the lives of painters. Verbal puns are sown like seeds everywhere. Some of them take root and are picked up later, some of them are superfluous, others are strained and without humor.

Sometimes the intellectual dialogue falls heavily, as here, after the beheading of one of his mistresses, when Steve sits (his leg bleeding and festering from a dog's bite) talking with her husband who has just bribed him out of a Mexican jail and here asks him what he expects to do now: " 'Do?' he said ultimately. 'What? Go wander again in the land of the forest sages, out of the southerly Ganges, hand in hand with Mahavira? Prove the Trinity in such a way that no rational intellect might thereafter deny it exists, like Raymond Lully? Seek out the grave of Tulsi Das? Or Kabir? Quo vadis, Stephanos—?' " A pretty overblown peroration, even for a *brilliant* man in shock.

Yet the same technique, when cast onto the inner ramblings of sad, neurotic Fern, the painter, is supremely successful. She emerges as a truly sympathetic character; her suffering (unlike Steve's) can be pinned down, followed, and is for that reason perhaps more convincing. So too the Mexican portion of the book—particularly that which probes the mind and feelings of the silent maid Petra, who bears Steve's child. All descriptions from the woman's point of view, in fact, are amazingly sensitive, apt, and finely written. It is oddly in describing the men—particularly the central figure—that the writing drops, stumbles, or seeks its way out through the imposition of a consciously "literary" symbolism. Moreover the novel is marked by too much grim despair, and except for one sad-funny incident involving a horse named Oedipus, is lacking in the humor that might relieve this somewhat.

Despite these minor lapses, however, the foundation of the book is solid, particularly in its time/place/character construction, which is admirable and entirely under the author's control—like the fine pencil draughtsmanship that so frequently underlies the paintings of genius that haunt the novel itself.

> *Perle Epstein, in a review of "Going Down," in* The Village Voice, *Vol. XV, No. 22, May 28, 1970, p. 6.*

Maureen Howard

[*Going Down*] is an outrageously empty book written in a series of pretentious styles—fake Faulkner, fake Hemingway, fake Markson. It is about a crowd of dreary aging dropouts who fortunately for the good old U.S.A. all go to Mexico to carry on their silly lives which cannot possibly have any meaning for us. *Going Down* (hopefully the lending libraries will think it means traveling South of the border) is about a *ménage à trois,* two eager women and a diffident stud, who climactically get themselves into positions too impossible even for the dreamlike terms of good pornography. Undiluted male fantasy, *Going Down* has Steve Chance (really) as its hero, a surly reluctant lover. The characters in Markson's book do talk like faded Shakespearean actors playing Boucicault. Steve Chance cries out unbelievably to a hostile dog in the street, "Well, the devil. . . . Be cursed instead, then, mendicant fool. . . . " Their muddled but high-toned thoughts constantly invoke Renoir, Vivaldi, Corelli, Judas, Christ, Oedipus, Melville, Sisyphus and Mr. Kurtz, to name but a few. The offense is that this novel is written out of some nether landscape in the writer's world that reveals itself to be empty, like Steve Chance who finds himself to be empty of all but the basest desires. It is a world that should not be tolerated outside of the confines of some passé artists colony. (pp. 567-68)

> *Maureen Howard, "The Way We Live Now,"* in Partisan Review, *Vol. XXXVII, No. 4, 1970, pp. 564-69.*

Sheldon Frank

I had every intention and expectation of strongly disliking *Springer's Progress.* Who, I pondered, needs another novel-within-a-novel about a relentlessly womanizing, self-obsessed, middle-aged, married New York writer who hangs out at the Lion's Head bar and, in the midst of an eternal writer's block, falls in love, yes, falls in love, with a sensitive, intelligent, spectacularly beautiful young woman? Hadn't I read this somewhere before? Many, many, many times?

So I was annoyed by the first page when Springer sprang into clear view; stayed irked for a few more pages; then forced myself to admit defeat. Markson had done it; he had pulled it off, had written an exuberantly Joycean, yes, Joycean, celebration of carnality and creativity—an everything-goes, risk-taking, maniacally wild and funny and painful novel.

The novel lives because of the sheer, impossible-to-describe-in-a-family-newspaper outrageousness of Lucien Springer, a Leopold Bloom in overdrive, and because of the brilliant, telescoped, multilayered, pun-besotted language. It has its flaws—the young woman remains a kind of cipher, too opaque to be convincing. Why does she behave the way she does? I want to know, and Markson won't say. And their problems in achieving climax (for her) are predictable and limply described.

In these troubled times, when one is rarely sure that sex is worth all the hassle, Markson has done the near-impossible. He has made carnal knowledge sound like fun again—not wholesome fun, mind you, not something squeaky-clean and therefore a bore—but the glorious, sweaty, brain-breaking, aren't-bodies-wonderful-in-all-the-spectacular-things-they-can-do kind of fun, the only kind that counts.

> *Sheldon Frank, "Minor Minor and Major Minor," in* The New York Times Book Review, *August 7, 1977, p. 14.*

Sheila Weller

With *Springer's Progress,* David Markson creates a microcosmic world in which the man is the striver and the women are the achievers; in which women aren't penalized for their success and the man isn't threatened by it. In addition, he's given us—in the person of blocked New York novelist Lucien Springer—a male hero who, though down on his luck and given a bit more to carousing than work, of late, is immensely endearing.

As Springer meditates on his torpor (with no small amount of wit), the three women of his past and present show him how the other half lives. Salty, classy, and wise, they're all superbly adjusted to their own accomplishments and sympathetic toward him without being indulgent. Dana, his wife of 18 years, has just hit her stride as an agent. Maggie, his pre-Dana lover, has remained a close friend and become a lionized poet. Jessica, an ambitious young editor and aspiring novelist, is a crony from his literary saloon (in this book, as in real New York life, women do professional shmoozing at bars just like men do); they enter what can be called without euphemism a sexual friendship, since it's far too psychically wholesome to be called an "affair."

Here, for the first time in anything I've ever read by a male *or* female author, is a genuinely self-assured single woman who can have a relationship with a married man without hang-ups or overinvestment, without giving up her other lovers, without canceling dates with her female and male friends.

Here, too, is that rarely depicted married woman who reacts to her husband's crisis infidelity in a way that defies the cliché of the martyred, hysterical "cheated-on" wife. For when Springer guiltily confesses his relationship with Jess (after it's over), Dana doesn't feel jealous or vulnerable. Rather, her own self-esteem gives her the munificence to understand that her husband's act had much less to do with the permanent state of their union than the temporary state of his ego.

Yet Springer's ego is one of the best things about this book. As deflated as it is by his recent failings at work and as much as it might need bolstering by an outside liaison, it *never* gets in the way of his admiration for the talents of the women around him. He's proud that Dana is so revered—even in the very circles where his own current problems are known. He enjoys the awe that Maggie elicits when they visit a bookstore together. And when he finishes reading the manuscript of Jessie's first novel, how does he react—this much older man whose own once-considerable reputation in the field has been rapidly corroding? "Jess, it's magnificent," he exclaims. Then he wryly adds that between her, Maggie, and Dana, "I plan to surface one day as the most envied bedroom footnote in American literature." Now how can you *not* be cheered by the fact that levity *is* possible in the traditionally sacrosanct realms of the male ego?

How nice it is, too, to hear men and women talk with the tough, jousting humor of lovers who are first of all pals (Springer: "Now where could you put cigarettes around here so I couldn't find them?" Dana: "How about inside your typewriter?"). And how nice to hear two people actually laugh during sex. Finally, how refreshing it is to see a man spurred on by women's accomplishments as Springer is, when, at book's end, he finally gets his own writing under way again. (pp. 36, 38)

> *Sheila Weller, "Can a Man Write a Feminist Novel?" in* Ms., *Vol. VI, No. 9, March, 1978, pp. 35-6, 38.*

Amy Hempel

Get it? Ludwig Wittgenstein, the Austrian philosopher, was homosexual. And while [*Wittgenstein's Mistress's*] title indicates a cultural romp ahead, the reference is earned in another respect. Many of Wittgenstein's mind-numbing tautologies had to do with the limits of language. Boiled down into one boldfaced line for philistines and slow learners, his concerns could be reduced to this question found in a reference work for philistines and slow learners: How can a man, by uttering a sequence of words, *say* anything, and how can another person understand him?

And what if there is no other person?

The narrator of *Wittgenstein's Mistress,* David Markson's fourth novel, is a woman nearing 50 who addresses formidable philosophic questions with tremendous wit and desperation as the last person left on earth. Her status owes nothing to science fiction and everything to Samuel Beckett. Billed as a metaphor for "ultimate loneliness," her status, if *imagined,* is that much more compelling—then she must be mad! . . .

The narrator, Kate, used to be painter. Quite logically, then, she has been making her home in the Metropolitan Museum (having long since stopped writing with white paint in intersections, "Somebody is living in the Metropolitan Museum"), in the Louvre, in the Tate Gallery, but not, when in Spain, in the Prado—"It was too badly lighted." Her world is a ghostly landscape, where she was once nearly hit by an empty cab as it rolled down a hill in London.

Over the years—she thinks it may have been 10—that she has been alone, she has divested herself of books, kerosene for lamps, vehicles and more—"It is a day for some music, actually, although I have no means of providing myself with any."

But "the things one knows"! And remembers. The intellectual baggage one can't get rid of is what her mind continues to turn over. After years alone, she sounds sane enough; for example, "If there were no more copies accessible anywhere of *Anna Karenina* . . . would its title still be *Anna Karenina?*"

And upon finding that a poster had long ago fallen from the wall of a nearby house: "Where was the poster when it was on the wall in my head but was not on the wall in the other house?"

Still later, "But then what is there that is not in my head? So that it is like a bloody museum, sometimes. Or as if I have been appointed the curator of all the world."

History recalled, the world's and her own, is increasingly qualified. The disclaimers are: to tell the truth, by which I mean, however, then again. Back and back she goes, challenging what she thinks she knows, arguing with herself in a way that brings to mind the old line, "I'm schizophrenic, and so am I."

And just when the reader may be thinking, All *right* already, *get a grip,* Mr. Markson's self-reflexive narrator does the job nicely for us: "I am not particularly happy over this new habit of saying things that I have very little idea what I mean by saying, to tell the truth."

Often, the last person on earth's attempts to remember and clarify sound like a mildly disputatious old couple. . . . In other words, Mr. Markson has managed to make a 240-page monologue come across as dialogue.

By the end, the narrator's skewed deconstruction is a desperate business, at once vivid and vague, escalated into revisionist frenzy.

Mr. Markson has matched the haunting premise of his novel with writing that is in direct alignment with it. For *Wittgenstein's Mistress* is a remarkable technical feat. It is a novel that can be parsed like a sentence; it is that well made. The sentences proceed directly one from another—what could make more sense? And what could be harder to find?

Early in the book, the narrator accidentally burns her beach house to the ground. "I still notice the burned house, mornings, when I walk along the beach," she says. "Well, obviously I do not notice the house. What I notice is what remains of the house. One is still prone to think of a house as a house, however, even if there is not remarkably much left of it."

Mr. Markson has shown that that goes for a life as well.

Amy Hempel, "Home Is Where the Art Is," in
The New York Times Book Review, *May 22,*
1988, p. 12.

Joseph Tabbi

Once in a while a writer, if he is lucky, may find himself working so close to his talents that a single, unmodified style will see him through a book. William Gaddis found such a style with *JR,* and allowed the narrative simply to range through the many voices heard throughout corporate America. Books like this impress us by their consistency, and by their ability to generate totally convincing fictions within narrow constraints. David Markson has created such a fiction—at once limited in scope and open to countless possibilities—in his latest novel, **Wittgenstein's Mistress.** A playful deconstruction of the modes of post-modern thought and writing, it is a book that comes to seem not merely "original," but necessary in its stylistic accomplishment.

Markson's narrative, which the jacket copy describes as "a series of irreverent meditations on everything and everybody from Brahms to sex to Heidegger to the Trojan war," is broken down entirely into sparse, apparently structureless musings over "inconsequential perplexities." Paragraphs are never longer than a sentence or two, and they follow one after the other, from start to finish, uninterrupted by chapter breaks. As each line builds on and revises the others, the text begins slowly to take shape, and we may start to appreciate the radical instability of a world in which "thought in its absoluteness" (to quote Kierkegaard from the book's epigraph) "replaces an apparent reality."

Obviously the book was conceived on the model of Wittgenstein's *Tractatus.* It is true that the narrator—a woman who has convinced herself that she is the only person left on earth—lives in a world that consists entirely of "facts," although facts like these are hardly logical entities, and there is nothing especially formal about how they are put together. On the contrary, what impresses us most is how, over the long haul, this narrative logic of the aleatory and the accidental can be made to generate brilliant and often hilarious effects.

The woman, who has been a painter presumably of some standing in New York City, has put art, fashionable downtown acquaintances, sex, ambition, and a dream of fame behind her; what remains is reduced to the barest essentials: the house she lives in by the beach, the clothes she wears, or doesn't wear and puts out to dry, the books, the paintings and boxes that are stored in the house, remembered and (often as not) misremembered names, arcana, and anecdotal history—such are the "harmless items" that absorb her attention. The rest is emotional and intellectual "baggage" that she would just as soon be rid of, having made the decision before she ever sat down to the typewriter that no deeper trace from before her time "alone" should come into her narrative. . . .

These remnants, as it turns out, can be surprisingly insistent, and they recur throughout the novel with the force of desperate evasion. Unlike as this book may be from anything else that Markson has written, there is one antecedent that sheds light on the psychology of **Wittgenstein's Mistress.** It had been Lucian Springer's habit in Markson's last novel, **Springer's Progress,** to retreat from rebuff into "idiosyncratic fragments of art history." Pangs of jealousy, cancelled dates, money problems, any cause at all for social, sexual, or literary professional anxiety, and Springer would find himself "pondering that Michelangelo wore his boots to bed." *Wittgenstein's Mistress* is replete with such fragments, which if they are no more consequential (and at times even funnier) than Springer's, derive in this case from a much deeper disaffection.

It is not until the very end of the book, when the narrator comes back to her typescript after a six or seven week break, that she begins to speak in any detail of her past. Having succeeded more or less in keeping "out of her head" while she was writing ("time out of mind" being the recurrent phrase Markson uses for the woman's madness and erratic memory), she now allows fragments of her previous life to interrupt her thought. Here we learn that her son's death at age seven may have been due in part to her own and her husband's negligence: she also speaks for the first time of her infidelities, and of what it had meant to her mother that she was an artist. These revelations are still sparse, however, and they would appear to be involuntary on her part: "the truth of the matter being that I did not intend to repeat one bit of that just now, actually." Moreover, they are inaccurate, she having apparently mixed up the names of Simon, her son, and Lucian, her husband (that is, unless her husband's name is Adam). The bizarre clarity of her language has been marred, and as the confusion of names deepens, we are made to feel the nightmarish insistence of what she has tried to repress.

Twice in the novel the woman quotes the line from Wittgenstein about the world being all that is the case (although, true to form, she has never read a word of Wittgenstein's). A lean, philosophical Molly Bloom, she remains nonetheless, and despite all past infidelities, a faithful mistress. Her world *is* all that is the case, and in having experienced the truth of this opening line of the *Tractatus,* she has arrived by the book's end at an equally private, equally painful interpretation of the closing line: "whereof one cannot speak, thereof one must be silent."

Markson on *Springer's Progress*

[*Springer's Progress* is] a novel about the creative process, or one variant thereof—about what triggers it, how it's pursued, about what goes on in the writer's *head.*

Then again it's about more than that as well. What it's about most of all is plainly and simply language. Language. Words, and word*play.* Meanings, and additional meanings. Sentence structures. Rhythms. Sounds. Wit. Resonances. About being infinitely more concerned with the *how* things are said than with the what, in spite of the considerable "what" I've already noted.

And/or with any socioeconomic dimensions of same.

From the essay "Reviewers in Flat Heels: Being a Postface to Several Novels," 1990.

A minimal fiction, then, but not to be confused with other

novels that have been marketed under the heading of "minimalism." Markson is the one working novelist I can think of who can claim affinities with Joyce, Gaddis, and Lowry, no less than with Beckett. He's familiar, that is, with the many possibilities for encyclopedic *inclusions* within the novel. Which is only to say that despite the spare form of the novel, Markson knows exactly what it is he's leaving out, and why.

Joseph Tabbi, "The Baggage in One's Head,"
in San Francisco Review of Books, Summer,
1988, p. 32.

Richard Gehr

They said you shouldn't trust anybody, and they were right. I probably wouldn't have completed this sad, occluded novel [*Wittgenstein's Mistress*] if not for the gushy and guilt-inducing quotes from Gordon Lish, Ann Beattie, and Walter Abish that accompany it. As the book itself demonstrates, art and ideas can drive you crazy, yet by ignoring them you risk isolation, with similar results. So I dutifully plowed onward, just in case.

In its mostly uncompromising way, *Wittgenstein's Mistress* details such insanity and loneliness. It offers the nervous ramblings of a middle-aged madwoman, perhaps a painter (although her condition puts all such personal details into question), who believes herself to be the last person on earth. Alone with her fading, permutated memories of art, music, literature, and history, she free-associates incessantly until her core of malaise is confronted.

Hermetic and aphoristic like Wittgenstein's own writing, *Mistress* sifts through its narrator's mind as if it were a memory palace or a Borgesian labyrinth. Every object has its nametag, from Helen's Trojan War to Sappho, Giotto, Brahms, Pascal, Heidegger, de Kooning, Gaddis, Silkwood, Baez, and on and on. As she retrieves this cultural debris ("One morning not too long ago all I could think about was the word *bricolage*"), the tags get exchanged, frayed, and misplaced so that, for example, Rilke becomes the author of *The Recognitions.* She becomes frustrated, her disorientation compounds. . . .

One might appreciate Markson as he messes around with such aspects of linguistic philosophy as nominalism (one of the characters is a little too pointedly named Adam), deconstruction (in the sloppy, just-taking-things-apart sense of the term), and linguistic utilitarianism. Such logocentric notions as the possibility of literal communication are offset by the narrator's slippery interior experience, a gushing of information paralleled by her ongoing menstrual flow.

Not totally worthless, I suppose, if you're in the mood for this kind of Beckett-meets-Robbe-Grillet inventory of the character's internal phenomenology. (A contradiction in terms? Sue me.) Unfortunately, Markson cops out at the end, when the narrator appears finally to recall the real experience (her child's death) that drove her over the edge. It's then she considers the possibility of writing a novel "about somebody who woke up one Wednesday or Thursday to discover that there was apparently not one other person left in the world." Unable to handle the memories, she—and, alas, we—tumble back into her desolate archives.

Once upon a time, I could proudly say I never metafiction I didn't like. Now I agree with Jimi Hendrix, who noted simply that "Loneliness is such a . . . drag."

> *Richard Gehr, "Tractatus Bricolagicus," in* The Village Voice, *Vol. XXXIII, No. 27, July 5, 1988, p. 50.*

Michael Cannizzaro

One morning in New York City, Kate, the narrator of David Markson's [*Wittgenstein's Mistress*], wakes up in an empty world. For no apparent reason, she finds herself the last animal left on earth.

After moving into the Metropolitan Museum and staying for "two winters," she embarks on a series of journeys, "looking for anybody, anywhere at all." With the world's resources at her fingertips, she travels through America, Mexico, across the Bering Strait to Russia, and even takes a symbolic trip from Troy to Greece.

Kate has her moments of hope, as when a drifting ketch's spinnaker catches wind and it swoops past her as she crosses the Aegean Sea, or when she sees herself reflected in the window of an art supply shop near the Acropolis. But she finds no one.

The novel begins as Kate starts her journal about a decade later, long after she has stopped looking and has settled on the south shore of Long Island near Southampton. With a crisp string of thoughts rapped out in compact paragraphs on her typewriter, Kate sets out to make some sense of her life. The result is a one-woman show, a monologue whose staccato pronouncements somehow mesh into a fluid, conversational and self-aware narrative that seems more like a dialogue.

While Kate intimates that she has been a lover to more than a few men, the novel's title implies that a different mistress reigns here. The mistress of the solitary Austrian philosopher Ludwig Wittgenstein would seem more likely to be the imagination, which he considered the unmarriageable lover and controller of language.

Wittgenstein's Mistress is not science fiction: Kate never finds or offers a reason for her apparent isolation, and the narrative even carries the hint that it could all be in her mind. As she readily acknowledges, the world she woke up to that morning would confuse anyone, but her confusion seems only slightly related to her strange situation. . . .

Time forgotten is what Kate wrestles with throughout the book, flirting with madness and challenging all she thought she knew along the way. Her mirthful and dogged narrative style (as rendered by Markson) harkens back to Laurence Sterne's Shandean digressions, with the reader held willing hostage to the vagaries of the narrator's imagination, and the digression becomes the point.

Kate's moments of confusion are disarming, and her attempts to resolve them are often comic and revealing. At one point she considers a painting that appears to represent the beach house she lives in. Wondering who a figure at a window in the painting might have been, she decides that she shouldn't be bothered, because the figure is actually nothing but an abstract brushstroke. Confusion follows as she chases her logic to its extreme:

"If I have concluded that there is nothing in the painting except shapes, am I also concluding that there is nothing on these pages except letters of the alphabet?"

She does not, continuing to write in part because she cannot dispatch the baggage of her mind as easily as she unloaded over the years such material baggage as heaters, phonographs, automobiles, powerboats and guns.

The beauty of Markson's achievement is that the novel is written with such precision and care that Kate's "mental baggage," so organically introduced, falls into place. It is this insistence of memory that Kate eventually finds annoying. But with a deadpan slap at the notion of fiction as escape, she proposes a remedy:

"Quite possibly I might have to start right from the beginning and write something different altogether.

"Such as a novel, say."

> *Michael Cannizzaro, "Journey through an Empty World," in* Book World—The Washington Post, *July 17, 1988, p. 11.*

Joseph Tabbi

[In the excerpt below, Tabbi provides an overview of Markson's career.]

In a decade increasingly characterized by "minimalist" novels and academic assaults on the literary canon, Markson remains one of the most allusive of novelists, a writer who continues to demand from his readers a knowledge at least of the central modernist texts. He does this not out of any conservative desire for a return to classroom "standards"—Markson is not an academic or political novelist—but rather from a belief in the sheer pleasurability of creative recognition in the reading of literature. In fact, Markson probably could not have begun to write as he does had he not himself recognized possibly the only two elder contemporaries who fully shared his literary preoccupations. In 1951, only four years after the book's appearance, he managed to file a master's thesis on Malcolm Lowry's *Under the Volcano* [*Malcolm Lowry's "Volcano": Myth, Symbol, Meaning*], and when *The Recognitions* came out in 1955, Markson was virtually alone in perceiving what William Gaddis had achieved. Markson's own subsequent achievement, though less encompassing than theirs, withstands comparison. And if he remains largely unknown even among readers who have come to believe in the importance of Lowry and Gaddis, this is largely the result of the same refusal by reviewers and even most academic critics to honor those contemporaries and near-contemporaries who have never ceased to work in the tradition of classic modernism.

Such neglect, while helping to perpetuate the academic myth of a radical break between classic modernism and the present, might well obscure some very real continuities with the modernist past. For Markson is, with Gaddis, among the few working novelists decisively to have carried the modernist tradition into the present, postmodern culture; a writer who, without claiming any particular knowledge of, or even affinities with, the more programmatic expounders of postmodernism, in recent work exemplifies many of the period's most vital developments. For this, if not for his conceivable status as our last literary modernist, Markson's creative development and career as a novelist merit attention. (pp. 91-2)

Reading [*The Ballad of Dingus Magee*] for the first time more than twenty years after its publication, one is impressed by an ease and naturalness in the writing, a result, presumably, of the craft Markson had mastered writing commercial fiction. Indeed, he began the book with the intention of completing still another genre novel, but even as he found himself turning the entire myth and stereotype of the Western on its head, he discovered he could have every bit as much fun with the literature he knew, from Cervantes to the American Transcendentalists ("Emersonian horse pee" is how Markson's preacher dismisses them and their doctrines) to the Oedipus myth and *Tom Jones* ("A feller has to face life without a mother to guide him," concludes Dingus, "he's jest nacherly doomed to tickle the wrong titty, 'times"). The satire is sure, and never once slows the progress of an unholy tall story, "Being the Immortal True Saga of the Most Notorious and Desperate Bad Man of the Olden Days, his Blood-Shedding, his Ruination of Poor Helpless Females, & Cetera . . . " as the subtitle bills it.

Markson's skill in this novel is most evident in the tightness of the plotting, where even the smallest detail will contribute to the story's development, and the most incidental remark, perhaps no more than a bit of exaggerated ranch talk, will later become the source of an idea. At one point, for example, Dingus will say of the sheriff, C. L. Hoke Birdsill, that he "couldn't hit nobody if 'n he was shooting smack-bang down a stone well," and that is exactly where our hero eventually finds himself—at the bottom of a well under the sheriff's erratic fire. The craft in this case doesn't mean a thing; it is simply there for us to enjoy if we have the wit to perceive it. In the later novels, however, where language continually generates action, and action generates language, such reflexive references become essential to Markson's meaning, though few readers, in the event, were prepared to see them.

[*The Ballad of Dingus Magee*] was well spoken of critically, and successful enough commercially to enable Markson to drop all thoughts of Westerns and detective stories, to travel and live for two years in Europe (mainly England), and finish the long novel he had been holding on to since Mexico. . . . Yet even as his art had deepened, in four years the extent of his reputation had narrowed, and the publication in 1970 of *Going Down,* which should have consolidated and advanced the position he achieved with his debut, essentially ended his career as a commercially viable writer.

Markson cites some of his more wrongheaded reviews in a very witty essay . . . , **"Reviewers in Flat Heels";** they are the result, he perceives, of a mistaken desire to latch on to "something with sociopolitical-economic import" in books whose primary commitment is to style and *language*—the artistry and craftsmanship of the novel—and to a body of allusions whose purpose is to reach into "the very pulse and continuity of culture." He must have known what was coming, having once copied out the worst reviews of Gaddis's *Recognitions* "as a kind of talisman, to steel myself for what I anticipated with *Going Down.* " And, in the event, his worst hopes were realized. For just as the word "erudite" had been thrown around by unthinking reviewers to scare away readers of *The Recognitions,* the same reviewers, or their sons and daughters, were to come down hard on the self-consciously literary aspects of *Going Down,* preferring to label the work "pretentious" and "derivative" without bothering to examine how references to art and literature *functioned* in Markson's novel, as if Gaddis had never written, and the creative use of allusion had ended with Joyce and T. S. Eliot.

Markson has, certainly, his debts, primarily to Faulkner and Joyce, and incidentally to any of a hundred other writers and poets from whose works he quotes. But what he has taken he has transfigured, and to call him derivative is to miss the point of his borrowings. It is true that *The Ballad of Dingus Magee* was written, as Leslie Fiedler has pointed out, in "straightfaced Faulknerian prose," and Markson admits that the style was intentional, a way of showing that "that same complex syntax" is possible in the popular comic novel—the sixties novel of black humor—and not only in the high literary comedy of the Snopes novels. Faulkner himself borrowed no less, and may have worked similarly in adapting narrative techniques from Joyce and Conrad to the melodrama of *Sanctuary,* for example, or to parts of *Absalom, Absalom!* The originality is not only in what an author brings of himself to the work, but equally in what he *makes of* his sources.

The method came naturally to Markson, even in the crime novels [*Epitaph for a Tramp* and *Epitaph for a Dead Beat*], where he introduced a fine beat dialogue and numerous "literary" quotations into the genre. Here, as in *Dingus,* and, more subtly, in the next two books, he is so very obviously having *fun* with the "tradition" that it is easy to miss the original effects he achieves by combining high-modernist styles and the staple subgenres of popular fiction: the Western, the crime story, the Gothic murder mystery (in *Going Down*), and the erotic romance (*Springer's Progress*). This is not mere imitation, much less parody, but a transformation of received styles in the service of new subject matter. A creative counterpart and possible corrective to the academic institutionalization of European modernism that was in full force around the time (mid-to-late 1950s) when Markson was coming of age as a writer, it is a way of exporting the modernist aesthetic—its modes of expression and representation—from the academy within which it was in danger of being circumscribed into the domain of the popular novel.

Though it is much more than an entertainment, and was meant to equal "the best" writing Markson knew, *Going*

Down is written very much *in* a popular mode, however much the major reviews and a limited distribution prevented it from reaching a very wide audience. Begun . . . nearly ten years before ***Dingus,*** drafted through 1960 to the summer of 1961, set aside, worked on intermittently, and reduced by half during a final year's revision in New York in 1969, the published text is highly accomplished, aiming at an indivisibility of surface and symbol such as Lowry achieved in *Under the Volcano.* "The early drafts," Markson told William Kennedy a few weeks before publication, "were probably more commercial, less literary, less complex" than the novel as published. Yet Markson also "always wanted it to be dramatic," and many of the revisions were evidently made not just to increase complexity or achieve greater density of language, but to *tighten the plot,* removing excess background and uncontrolled narrative, and achieving a pace and sequence that is rare in high-modernist fiction. (pp. 92-5)

Set mostly in the imaginary Mexican village of Mictlán, a locale as unitary and stagelike as Lowry's Quauhnahuac or Conrad's Sulaco, the novel is never far from the conventions or spirit of the Gothic romance, its characters, settings, and oppressive atmosphere. (Even the name, Mictlán, is the Aztec equivalent of the underworld, perhaps the most basic of many meanings of "going down.") The opening chapter is deliberately lurid, beginning with an authorial injunction that we "accept the illusion," and then presenting a beautiful woman soon to be disrobed, "a girl quite lovely and fair, whose left hand is deformed." In that hand the girl carries a machete, which we soon find out has been used, though not by her, in the killing of another woman.

Our interest captured, it is then the perfectly conventional work of the novel to build backwards to the origins and commission of the murder, saving partial revelations for the ends of chapters, and giving dramatic force to characters and events that may have at first seemed incidental. In the process, Markson manages a convincing depiction of the village in both its native Mexican and expatriate American life, but, as in the truest melodrama, he will push beyond surface realism towards the excess of representation and heightened ethical oppositions that give the novel its depth and significance.

It is within this tradition of the melodramatic imagination, which claims Conrad and Dostoyevski more centrally than Lowry, that we may best understand the main character in ***Going Down,*** the recluse and lapsed writer Steve Chance. Arrogant, preoccupied, and aloof in the town from all but two local Indians, Chance carries himself, in the eyes of another expatriate American writer, "like some brooding, disinherited prince." He is remote even from the two women he lives with, Fern Winters and Lee Suffridge, the first an artist who despairs of ever capturing "that haunted, Raskolnikov face of his." No one in the novel can quite get through to Chance, yet these very allusions, and dozens more like them to Marlowe's *Doctor Faustus, The Possessed,* and *Wuthering Heights* (to name only those works nearest in tone to Markson's novel), are meant to make his remoteness intelligible, or at least recognizable, to the reader.

Markson inside the volcano at Toluca, Mexico, 1959.

In all his besieged intellectuality, Chance is not wholly without self-irony, and neither are the women so totally captivated by him sexually that they accept his pretensions completely and without question. Fern suspects, for example, that he changed his name from Chazen to Chance "out of some counterfeit adolescent notion of the existential—", though in fact the name may have simply come from "an old-time baseball player." "Why," she asks him, "do you read all that mystical occult theological whatever horseshit if you do not have any shred of belief in [it]?" His answer, "Order, maybe," gives us the modernist project in a nutshell, which becomes, in him as in Eliot, the source of an "ultimate disaffection." His own tentative and concealed attempts to order the world through writing amount to nothing in the end. His manuscript is discovered by the unlettered peasants Manolo and Petra, whose lives he has tragically disrupted; its pages are used by them for toilet paper.

I doubt that Markson means by this closing irony simply to subvert Chance and his modernist ideals (though it is true that, in the next two novels, he would pull in the reins on his own largest, most Chance-like ambitions). It is instead more likely that the irony is meant to save the book from precisely the pretentiousness its detractors would insist on finding in it, and to reveal how tenuous are our attempts to impose a merely *literary* conception of order on the world. Chance is impatient with the women for confusing "sensuality as a spiritual ordeal . . . or carnal indulgence as a way to," presumably, salvation. After making love to each, debauching them, even, by the terms of a middle-class morality they never completely put behind them, he taunts them with the thought of "how amazingly little it lacerates your exquisite souls." But what is his own obsession with order if not a displaced religious impulse, one that in fact denies the power of the earthbound, the sensual? The tragedy of the novel, which is precipitated when Manolo discovers Chance, and not himself, to be the father of Petra's newborn child, is essentially the tragedy of this denial. (pp. 95-6)

It is hard to say what led Markson to the unexampled style of **Springer's Progress,** which at times approaches the telegraphic in its terseness, while demanding at every moment the kind of attention that readers normally reserve for poetry. Written in paragraphs no more than a sentence or two in length, with each line questioning or building on the preceding lines, the novel creates a surprisingly inward-looking consciousness, appropriate to, but much more than the self-absorbed musings of a "muchly vodka'd" author-hero in search of a subject. Lucien, or "Loosh," Springer, his head filled with "all sorts of quirky, disjunct quotations" from the work of other writers, has discovered that there is "no small degree of quaint truth you can compress into one line." Every line is duly crafted, loaded with the ore of Markson's fine learned wit; and with frequent elisions to speed the prose along, Springer gets his story told, a tale that is equally the story of the telling.

Here is Springer at his writing desk, long out of use, probing the beginnings of a current love affair for possible narrative interest:

> This girl, this horsy Jess Cornford with the Winslow Homer blouses and the sexy, cartilaginous neck, lead someplace?
> Springer given any thought to fictional names for these people either, meanwhile? *Cojones,* later, least of his worries.
> Lurking anent the ladies' latrine? Eye out for this wench who's just ducked inside, this clodhopper Cessica Jornford?
> He commencing to hear a tone now in any case? Close enough to the crotch? Or's he still not sure just who's Loosh?
> *Shlemiel* of shreds and patches. Obliquitous *borracho* jackanapes, *aussi.* Yet mayn't the straggler be pilgrim of sorts still, however oft by his pecker untracked?
> Indeed, someone like Bunyan worth a borrowing after all? As I walked through the wilderness of this world?
> Wanting a more Springerishly connotative verb, though. As I wandered? Traipsed? *Shlepped?*
> There's Springer, sauntering through the wilderness of this world?
> That take him anywhere?

Where it took him, of course, was back to the first sentence of the novel we are reading. All the details cited here con-

cerning Springer's gait and Jessica's appearance have been worked into the opening, excepting improvements in word choice and comic "refinements" of manner ("the ladies' latrine" becoming "the maidens' shittery," etc.). At last Springer has found the style that has already carried us this far, almost to the end of the book, and from here the writing proceeds apace. Springer writes this first draft so quickly in fact that within pages the events of the narrative are about to catch up with events in his life, and there is still no resolution to either in sight. As he puts it to a writer friend, "about four hours at the desk tomorrow and I'll be caught up to this very phone call. And then what? Can anybody in history ever have written anything this way?"

"Anne Frank," is the friend's wry rejoinder, though a more fitting precursor would perhaps be John Barth in *Lost in the Funhouse* (a book Markson had not read). The self-reflexive narrative in **Springer** may be less ingenious (in all but its language) than in Barth, but Markson's is never so programmatic, and always his reflexiveness is controlled and to the point. Springer's progress has been, after all, "to complete the book we are reading"—a gambit that Richard Hauer Costa finds "too easy," but which is nonetheless extremely funny, and flawless too in its execution. Markson would seem independently to have mastered Barth's trick of making an asset out of his own narrative limitations. The movement here into the book's composition *is* its resolution, and Markson takes this movement to its only logical (and grammatically ambiguous) conclusion: "Being continued." (pp. 97-8)

[The question Markson poses in his study of Lowry's *Under the Volcano*] initiates a line of thought that would eventually lead to his own next novel, about a woman who has convinced herself that she is the last person on earth, **Wittgenstein's Mistress** (1988). . . .

He had the basic situation already in mind in the early eighties, when he wrote the short story **"Healthy Kate."** The story is, among other things, a meditation on the exactions of high art when it is practiced without recognition, by a woman painter "on that rung or two below major" with whom the author may have felt a measured identification. In going from the story to the novel, however, the woman's professional and social anxieties, and to a lesser extent even her private grief at the loss of a seven-year-old son, were removed to the background, leaving Markson free to explore a more extreme and impersonal consciousness, the ultimate unreality of the self alone.

By making his central figure an artist, Markson was also able to give freer play than before to allusions, always important in his work, to the visual arts. He had made art and art history majors, respectively, of Fern and Lee in **Going Down,** and he had also made it Springer's habit to retreat from rebuff into "idiosyncratic fragments of art history." Pangs of jealousy, canceled dates, money problems, any cause at all for social, sexual, or literary professional anxiety, and Springer would find himself "pondering that Michelangelo wore his boots to bed." **Wittgenstein's Mistress** is replete with such fragments, with references as well to music, philosophy, and Greek myth, all of which, if they are no more consequential (and at times even funnier) than Springer's, derive in this case from a much deeper disaffection. (p. 100)

The most crucial place in **Going Down** where these . . . references appear is a conversation that Fern remembers having with Lee, in which Lee, describing the emptiness implicit in her promiscuity, tells Fern that she finally understood Giacometti by imagining her own life *"pared down and down until only that sliver remained."* About to lose hold herself, Fern returns that much more obsessively to the art, music, and scraps of literature she knows, a way of maintaining sanity that is finally no more successful for her than her lover Steve's own quest for "order."

In **Wittgenstein's Mistress,** a good deal of the process of paring down has gone on *before* the novel begins, the woman, Kate, having left behind all manner of devices and personal "baggage" so that she has only her own thoughts to arrange. The result is again, as in **Springer,** a narrative that revises and builds on itself line by line, though the tone this time is subdued, and the stylistic conceit—propositions, and comments on propositions—now derives from a fanciful reading of Wittgenstein's *Tractatus.* Kate's world reduces to the barest essentials: the house she lives in by the beach, the clothes she wears, or doesn't wear and puts out to dry, the books, the paintings and boxes that are stored in the house, remembered and (often as not) misremembered names, arcana, and anecdotal history—such are the "harmless items" that absorb her attention, and they fall into place with an accidental certainty as solid to her as the relation among "facts" in Wittgenstein's philosophy.

Given the extreme reduction of the narrator's style and life situation, Markson might appear to be working within the "minimalist" vein that has characterized a good deal of American fiction in the eighties, particularly the fiction written by writers a generation or more younger than he. (Indeed, both the diminishments and refinements that distinguish **Wittgenstein's Mistress** from **Going Down** are readily placeable in literary-historical terms, within the larger movement from the modern to the postmodern in literature.) Yet Markson in this novel retains a cultural ambition that much of the recent minimal fiction lacks, an ambition that reveals itself in Kate's realization that "there is baggage after all, for all that I believed I had left baggage behind." This is "the baggage that remains in one's head, meaning remnants of whatever one ever knew," and it is Markson's particular achievement in this book to show, within the most empty culture imaginable, just how crucial these remnants remain. (pp. 101-02)

[Markson] has called **Wittgenstein's Mistress** an autobiographical book, not in any external details (no character was ever so removed from the world of careers and reputations), but in the cultural weight that Kate bears as the last person left on earth. This weight has always been at the center of Markson's art, giving it a depth and cultural continuity that is ever rarer in contemporary writing. (p. 102)

Joseph Tabbi, "David Markson: An Introduction," in The Review of Contemporary Fiction, *Vol. 10, No. 2, Summer, 1990, pp. 91-103.*

Edward Butscher

[Butscher is an American educator, critic, poet, and novelist who has written books on Sylvia Plath and Conrad Aiken. In the following excerpt, he discusses literary allusions in Going Down.*]*

In his first novel, **The Ballad of Dingus Magee** (1966), Markson had manipulated the legends of the Old West and their ballad formulas to exploit a postmodern vantage, the distances broadened by self-conscious burlesque. In **Going Down,** his most ambitious and successful fiction, a delicious effort to "misread" [Malcolm] Lowry's grand novel in Harold Bloom's generational-strife sense of the term, the method is similarly overt, if more subtle in application. The formulas involved tend to simulate melodrama and private-eye twists. Information is held back, time and interior voices shifted out of sequence, violence always in the offering and linked to sexual extremes.

Below all, romantic as Conrad's jungle hell, unravels a conventional tale of three desperate human beings engaged in Mexico's ancient dance of death, estranged from themselves, each other, and their "civilized" society back home. The Gothic first chapter, which has Fern Winters, an attractive young woman with a withered hand and ego, wandering around an old Mexican cemetery late at night, a bloody machete in her good hand, not only sets the scene in quick, precise strokes but establishes the necessary bifocal vision. Its last paragraph, addressed to the half-American doctor assigned to the town as part of his internship, encapsulates the novel's governing *film noir* mode: "She sobs once in the darkness. Then she says, 'I'm sorry. Sometimes it takes me a while to make my point. But it is a weapon. And it has been made use of, I'm afraid.' "

Though it stirs familiar juices cooked by countless Saturday matinees of yore, intermingling mystery and blood shed in a potent sexual brew, there is no way this can be taken straight. Yet the reader is caught on the sensationalist hook, pulled into the narrative flow even as he is being kept at a dangling remove by the firm postmodern frame. The cemetery is where Eric Chazen, an American poet, described by his ambivalent son as a "poor man's Traherne," is buried, having died in Mictlán twelve years earlier. The son, Steve Chance—all names bear double burdens in the English manner—is the Conradian protagonist, although part of the general enigma, hazy and indistinct, given to melancholic silences and unfinished sentences, roaming "around like some brooding, disinherited prince," to quote Harry Talltrees, a member of the town's small American colony.

The third figure in the trinity of main characters is Lee Suffridge, tall, handsome, "athletic-looking" wife of Ferrin Priest, the painter who had taken Steve in for a few years after his father died, leaving him an orphan (at age sixteen) in a foreign land. Symbolic and emotional incest thus underlies the ménage à trois that moves into the poet's last residence twelve years later—another turn of the Faulknerian screw driving the fictional vessel Markson has built with the cunning of a Daedalus.

How deliberate is the construction, where naked blueprint

and artifice merge, can be seen in the sardonic duality of the novel's title. ***Going Down*** describes both the spiritual decline of the main trio and the sexual act rending and binding them together: a devouring of one another with the only kind of intensity (physical, instinctual) they are still capable of summoning in their final battle against death's tightening grasp. Besides serving as negation's familiar antidote, the vividly limned sexual episodes also reify the "motif of shared identities" Markson's thesis [***Malcolm Lowry's "Volcano": Myth, Symbol, Meaning***] isolated in *Under the Volcano* and linked to that novel's "quest for salvation."

Not content with echoing and challenging Lowry's admired achievement, as well as with thematically paralleling [Conrad] Aiken's death-journey plot in *A Heart for the Gods of Mexico,* where two men accompany a dying woman friend (at her expense and request) on her last fling, Markson boldly textures his text with a series of relentless literary allusions. Even Fern, a painter, thinks in terms of literature, her internal monologues occasionally, preciously close to a naive English major's reveries. The effect throughout is to further widen the reader's intellectual remove from event and personae, underscoring the alienation, the absent or disappearing self, modern constructs frequently configure. Steve's articulation of its poisonous reality drips an entire library of erudition, which is, to be sure, his Loki-like punishment too: "The Eliot kind of thing, I suppose, the ultimate disaffection. Or *Sisyphus.* When you become aware that the worst of it is that nothing hurts at all."

Where to go but to the inferno? The first literal "going down," Steve and Fern engaging in "sixty-nine," begins the final descent, pun-true and doubled, that will lead into Steve forcing the two women to go down on him and on one another, using their need of him (their ruined savior) to shove them to the edge—of perversion, degradation, ego boundaries. Orality must prevail, a reflection of Mexico's archaic reality, because it is the psyche's surest sign of an embattled retreat under traumatic pressures, the self's last-ditch defense.

Although Steve is the ostensible antihero focus of ***Going Down,*** it is really Fern's book, beginning and ending with her. She is "saved" from suicidal despair in Greenwich Village by Steve, who then disappears and returns with Lee, but her consciousness dominates the early chapters. She will survive her two sex partners, albeit as a victim of another man, and hence complete a cycle of sorts, though the last chapter fittingly unwinds in the mind of Manolo Ortega, which intimates the linear and regressive triumph of Mexico over the neurotic outsiders.

In the fourth chapter, Fern's stream of consciousness reveals that her fate was predetermined by nature and nurture, by her deformed hand and fantasized loss of her father. The latter helps explain the classic Electra complex behind her infantile dependence on the clay-footed Steve Chance and stresses the sly juggling of Freudian and mythic dynamics that Markson manages to sustain in his rewriting of Lowry—Lee plays Phaedra to Chance's Hippolytus. As a result, the mystery at the matrix of ***Going Down,*** Lee's murder, for which Fern seems guilty and

Steve takes the blame, orchestrates another variation on the multiple identities theme, cuckolded Manolo having mistaken the short-haired, manly built Lee for Chance (she was wearing his jacket) in the darkness. Attic tragedy and Toltec rite conflate into Oedipal destiny.

Markson's interweaving of pathological and mythic paradigms in his multilayered literary carpet allows for a wide variety of responses, interpretations, transactions, if you will, that hoist literature's oldest question on Berkeley's phallic-sadistic petard: Who am I? The brilliance of the novel, which never loses sight of melodrama's conservative narrative thrust, remains cued to a postmodern conspiracy between reader and author to subvert Coleridge's suspension of disbelief. No impulse, no reference, no tragic inevitability is free of quantum intrusions, the taint of awareness—"Shem and Shaun," literature masturbating literature. And so, the town's cantina must be "Think on the Dead." And so, Harry Talltrees owns an old horse named Oedipus that his wife Marcia ("virtually as docile as the horse") rides into a lake, drowning it and reminding Lowry readers of the horse that killed Yvonne at the climax of *Under the Volcano,* a horse described as a "Jungian archetype" by Markson's study.

And so it goes. Eric Chazen was actually Isaac Chazen, sacrificing his son's identity to his narcissistic needs, transforming Steve into another Bloom, the eternal outsider, a Jewish Steppenwolf, though he also wears Lord Jim's halo of saintly damnation, Meursault's passive indifference. Fortunately, the plot's reversals and naturalistic drive carry the allusions with a minimum of interference, however committed to a reflexive stance, as in the comic relief provided by Manolo's come-uppance at the hands of Tinkle, his previous victim—the women in the novel suffer under their men, but they generally endure, another example of Markson's covert undermining of our expectations.

Indeed, the very richness of ***Going Down*** has probably contributed to its shameful neglect by the critical establishment. No single essay can do justice to either its fierce American honesty anent the existential crisis of modern consciousness or its sophisticated handling of literary modalities. If I have touched upon a few of the more intriguing aspects of its prismatic depths, that will have to suffice until Markson encounters his own percipient thesis-writer. (pp. 188-91)

> *Edward Butscher, "David Markson's Volcano: 'Going Down',"* in The Review of Contemporary Fiction, *Vol. 10, No. 2, Summer, 1990, pp. 187-91.*

Evelin E. Sullivan

[In the excerpt below, Sullivan examines the development of Lucien Springer in Springer's Progress.*]*

What to do with Lucien Springer [protagonist of ***Springer's Progress***]? Hang him from the yardarm with a sign pinned to his chest: *Thus to all Libertines?* Lock him in a cold shower until his "leaky hots" are chilled? Tell his wife about his exploits and watch him try to drink himself to liver failure on zero income after she throws him out?

Or shake our heads and say: God love the man for a poor sot who feels what anyone who's ever been hopelessly in love has felt from the dawn of the ages? And feels it funnily and engagingly?

Surely the latter, despite the open-and-shut case against him. Yes, Springer is contemptible: does he, married man that he is, not drop his trousers at the minutest come-hithering twitch of a skirt? Does he not lie to his wife? Does he not sponge off her, drink like a fish, conduct a "slushy" affair with a woman a little older than half his age? Yes, he does. But when all is said and done in and out of Jessica Cornford's disaster area of a bed (what with sheets stained by the "coital collage" of untold other lovers), Springer deserves redemption because he is the Everyman of unrequited love, the pilgrim destined never to reach the ultimate goal of permanence that lies at the heart of all love—this despite the jubilant ending of orgasmic Jessica and conquest of her Himalayan posterior.

As Everyman unhappily in love, Springer presents all the stereotypical responses to that pained condition. At the same time, his responses are uniquely his: those of a literary man equipped with a prodigious memory for anecdotes and quotes, a highly sexed (some may say oversexed) man, a self-conscious witness and whimsical commentator on the debacle of a beloved who refuses to be his one and only, and who, once love enters the picture, does not respond to his ardor with climaxes commensurate to that ardor. Finally, Springer is a writer of the most liberated, inventive, exhilarating prose this side of Joyce, as we discover when we find him break through his writer's block, to write the book we have in hand. Thus he is that happiest of fictions, the character who is representative at the same time he is unmistakably individual.

What's it like to be in love when love is unrequited? Springer reminds us. He thrills when he is with Jessica, loves her laughter, her banter, her smile, her eyes, "shimmering softly and wise," her "cartilaginous" neck, her "columnar" thighs, her "Praxitelean" bottom. He suffers when he is away from her, feels himself "dying by chunks and pieces," especially when he knows or suspects her to be with another man. . . . He thinks of her all the time, counts the days when she is out of town, orchestrates chance meetings at the saloon that is their hangout. He calls Jessica day and night, his stomach full of butterflies, hangs up when she answers sleepily, coins choice imprecations when she tells him she's with a friend or tells him she won't be able to see him tomorrow, nor the next day—one of her steadies being in town or requiring her ministrations. He hides a photo of her in his bottom drawer. He wants to hold her in his arms, to make love to her in every conceivable way. He wants to wake up in the morning with her next to him, wants to have a child with her. He wants, finally, that elusive thing, the shared bliss of the mutual orgasm. And tries. And tries. (pp. 195-6)

Springer's difficulties in this arena—which can be summarized by: he, too soon; she, not at all—and his gnashing of teeth at foiled trysts and usurpers in Jessica's bed make for some of the novel's funniest passages. But the lover as writer (or the writer as lover) "verbally vested and etymologically equipped" provides a literary feast throughout.

His reflections, couched in diction ranging from Latin and Shakespearean to Yiddish, in alliteration, literary allusions, shameless puns, vile doggerel, Homeric epithets, and what have you, give the book's prose an exuberant vitality; the scenes of love triumphant or frustrated that Springer, the consummate fictionalist, keeps imagining are hilarious. In fact, *Springer's Progress* is one of those books that sooner or later make the commentator ask with more than a measure of unease: wouldn't everyone be better off if I kept my mouth shut and simply quoted twenty uninterrupted pages, so that we could all sit back and enjoy ourselves? Or risk asphyxiation from laughing? Or just fall off the chair with a howl when, in the middle of a vivid depiction of oral sex, we find Springer contemplating Polonius's advice to his son: "Be thou familiar but by no means vulgar"? (p. 197)

We also get a humorous sketch of the artist (Springer, not David Markson—the extent to which the novel is "truly" autobiographical is not the topic here) as recorder of his own experiences and as inventor and thief in the glimpses we catch of the book we are reading as it is/was purportedly being written. *Springer's Progress* is not a novel whose pivotal concern is the process by which it is being generated, but it shows how personal experience can become the stuff for artistic expression; at the same time, it demonstrates that the connection between experience and a work of art is a complicated one. An obvious case in point is the question of revision: Springer confesses that, although he's been known to rough out a workable full novel in two weeks, there are "groanings to come." We witness a few of these groanings. For instance, the moderately amusing first-draft choice of "the ladies' latrine" anent which Springer is found lurking as the curtain goes up becomes the unforgettable "maidens' shittery" in the book. No leap of the imagination is required to surmise that, similarly, Springer's actual frustrated sexual encounters were less witty and erudite than they appear on paper. The verbal brilliance that dazzles the reader throughout the novel, and that appears not only in Springer's ruminations but in dialogue—some of it conducted while Springer is, ahem, in the throes of passion—calls attention to the literary craftsman par excellence finding or inventing the exact right (read: comical, evocative, poetical, etc.) expression to transform his experiences into a work of art.

(We should note that the novel does not invite us to undertake the mental contortions necessary to explore the premise that the autobiographical novel Springer begins to think of writing on page 98, and then begins writing on page 201, is in fact the novel before us. For instance, when the writer tells Lipp Pike on page 211 that he is within a day or two from writing about Pike's earlier humorous claim that Pike will be reading the obituaries to find out whether Springer murdered Jessica in a fit of jealousy, we are not asked to explore the dizzying implications of finding that Springer has yet to write what we've already read, and is "currently" having a conversation that, according to the narrative flow of the novel that he's writing [and that we're reading], he won't have for several days yet.)

Authorship is invention. It is also adaptation, and, in *Springer's Progress* as often as not, unabashed, triumphant thievery. Theft begins at the beginning: the first sentences of *A Tale of Two Cities, The Great Gatsby*, the *Iliad, Under the Volcano*, etc., etc., are contemplated as potentially ripe for plunder. Bunyan's "As I walked through the wilderness of this world"—the first words of Christian's departure for the Celestial City—are chosen, after the verb is changed to one more "Springerishly connotative": "There's Springer, sauntering through the wilderness of this world." Of course, the title comes from the same source. A compendium of stolen phrases—many quoted verbatim, many hilariously adulterated, all marvelously appropriate—would fill a small volume. Shakespeare and Exodus, Malcolm Lowry and Pascal, Lewis Carroll and The Pledge of Allegiance, Swift and Descartes, Malory and Ecclesiastes, Berkeley and Joyce, *und so weiter*, are all fodder for erudite Springer's musings on love, sex, writing, and the pursuit of happiness in all three areas. Thus a literary writer's book becomes the literary reader's delight, with part of the fun being the pleasure of recognizing the discrepancy between source, or original intention, and Springerish adaptation. Coitus, ergo sum? Indeed. And Springer, if not Markson, ought at the very least to be drawn and quartered for the outrage.

Springer's Progress is a comical book, as anyone endowed with a minimal sense of humor will attest. It is, in fact, a wildly funny book. But unlike Markson's other wildly funny book, *The Ballad of Dingus Magee, Springer's Progress* hides a deep sadness. In *Dingus Magee*, dire curses and vows of revenge abound, and the air is filled with flying lead, but the novel's comic vision is that of a world without loss or death, and hence without sadness. In *Springer's Progress*, sadness is brought on by awareness of the impermanence of earthly things: beauty, passion, bodies, lives. Maggie Oldring's death—the death of an old love, a companion, reminder of Springer's youth—is only the most obvious sign of the condition. Other signs are everywhere. Jessica's beauty is rending. "You're so impossibly lovely at this instant I hurt from it," Springer tells her. The "flexure of a lifted calf's enough to spawn grief." "*Lacrimae rerum* indeed, so fetching she looks." Why hurt? Why grief? Why "the tears of things"? Because, as Virgil goes on, "mortality touches the heart." Because that loveliness, that beauty, belongs to the world and to the fleeting moment. No aesthetic response to a living creature is without the sting of awareness that life is transitory. Beauty decays, loveliness passes away, nothing we grasp and cling to remains.

Springer yearns for permanence, for the endless summer on a Mexican beach, for undying love, for a life in Jessica's arms. " 'Oh, Jess, I don't want to leave here at all!' Clutching her again then, Springer's miracle. Embrace this girl and he's come home from somewhere far." "Beside him's naked Jessie again, Springer's come back from that faraway place." Springer longs for lasting passion; the innate changefulness of life declares his wish vain.

But Springer's yearning for permanent togetherness with Jessica also has a concrete ironic counterpoint in his marriage. That marriage of eighteen years began under conditions every bit as promising as his instant passion for Jessica: an hour after he got to Dana's apartment they were in bed. No more than two hours later they decided to get married. As he tells Jessica: "Point is, you're the only one anything even remotely approximating that's ever happened with since." Clearly, this recollection is meant to convince Jessica of just how important she is in his life, but just as clearly it is laced with irony, although, for once, self-analytical Springer is oblivious to that subtlety. Those feelings he had for Dana, that intensity, that wildfire of passion, are no longer. The implications are obvious: give Springer a few years, and this new love of his will at best be an old flame or someone he loves the way he loves his wife: "dearly" but also "just incidentally" as he disingenuously tells Dana.

The same irony appears in the question of children. Springer's poetic musing on the child he would like to have with Jessica—"Child one'd have with this creature indeed, sky full of portents at the nativity"—is contradicted by his unwillingness to spend time with his children and his irritability (or at least playful exasperation) at interruptions: "Jesus, will you guys ever be old enough to understand what my work is all about? Can't you see I'm *thinking?*" (In fact, he's contriving intellectual acrostics on Jessica's name.)

Irony and sadness. The formerly adored wife becomes an obstacle to happiness; cherished children are ignored. Young women of twenty-five turn twenty-six and, as Jessica does, bemoan the onset of old age. Middle-aged women of forty threaten to put their heads in the oven at the first hot flash; middle-aged poets kill themselves when they find they have inoperable cancer. Breasts sag, sexual prowess wanes, lovers die. The woman whose cantaloupe bottom Springer grasps in rapture, the woman to whom he cleaves, for whom he burns and freezes, so deep is his longing, will be with another man the next night. And if she were to forswear all her other lovers and promise to be wholly his, he'd lose the keenness of his passion, or he would in a year or two lose her to other men, or to one of the hazards of life. Or time, Pope's subtle thief of life, would steal him from himself away, to leave her grieving.

The end of *Springer's Progress* is jubilant: First Jessie comes and comes and comes—nine consecutive times! Then Springer is successful at a somewhat higher elevation, where he previously failed. Finally, he has a brainstorm and, awash in mirth, finds the much-sought ending for his novel: "To be continued." ("Being continued" in the final version.) *Nihil obstat* anywhere.

But another ending is described earlier, and that ending, the funeral of Maggie Oldring, qualifies the exultant final pages and forces us to think beyond them. Being continued? Yes, but towards what end? We know the answer; it's a variation on the unchanging theme of loss. . . . Lovers, poets, youth, passion, life—all pass. *Lacrimae rerum*. (pp. 198-201)

Evelin E. Sullivan, "Love and the Married Writer: 'Springer's Progress'," in The Review of Contemporary Fiction, *Vol. 10, No. 2, Summer, 1990, pp. 195-201.*

Evelin E. Sullivan

[In the following excerpt, Sullivan analyzes the protago-nist's methods of recall in Wittgenstein's Mistress.]

Wittgenstein's Mistress is the last record of life on earth and the novel of ultimate loss. At the time at which Kate becomes the last person "ever to write down any real history," all of the people mentioned in that history are either verifiably dead or are dead according to the fictional prem-ise that has her alone in the world. Although a list of the former, beginning with Homer and ending with Bertrand Russell, would be far lengthier than a list of the latter, which would include such fortunately alive people as Katharine Hepburn, Peter O'Toole, Joan Baez, and Wil-liam Gaddis, the novel forces the reader to think of all life on earth but one as extinct. That, as a result, we find our-selves in the awkward position of being dead is an ironic wrinkle. As readers of *Wittgenstein's Mistress,* we may imagine ourselves like those shades encountered by Aene-as in Hades who are saddened by the regret of unforgotten past.

The difficulty posed by a dead reading public is not some-thing David Markson's novel addresses. But there is a level at which we must take the fictional premises literally or lose essentials: we must believe that Kate is truly the last person on earth—otherwise, we are left with an insane woman, who may or may not have access to a typewriter, but who in any event imagines being alone, imagines hav-ing traveled looking for people, imagines having rolled tennis balls down the Spanish Steps, having thrown alarm clocks into a river, having found in a van soccer shirts with the name Savona across the chest—and who imagines to be now living in a beach house, washing her clothes in a spring, musing over books in the basement, preparing for winter by dismantling a neighboring cottage for its wood, typing the sentences we are reading, and so forth. Which would doubtless be an interesting novel but not the one under discussion.

If Kate were offered to us as a madwoman in an ordinary world, we would read her pages differently from the way we read them if we take them to be written by a sane woman in an extraordinary world. Much of *Wittgen-stein's Mistress* is concerned with questions of how the brain perceives reality and stores what it perceives by con-necting fragments of experience into patterns. The many playful references to philosophers who have grappled with the questions of how reality is perceived, recorded, and en-coded in language give a strong clue that *Wittgenstein's Mistress* explores precisely those questions. As an investi-gation into the workings of thought and memory, the book would be invalid if the mind through which we follow this investigation were diseased. This is how an insane mind works, would be the caveat we would have to apply to ev-erything we read. (Some may argue that Kate is clearly mad and may point out that her world cannot be "real," and that the absence of bodies or of other evidence of the presumed global catastrophe by which all life but one van-ished from the earth are marked impossibilities. My coun-terargument is simply that those concerns are not the point of the book.)

With Kate sane and the last woman on earth, we get a view of a mind resurrecting from its memory a lost world composed of historical (or public) and private past. In a sense, this world is no different from the lost world of any-one's past. We all could lock ourselves into a room and at-tempt to reconstruct from memory what we know of the world. For each of us, the results of this exercise would be shaped by private perspective and experiences and would be subject to errors of memory, wrong assumptions, and idiosyncratic connections between historical and pri-vate past. The world of art, music, literature, and "Long Ago" reality (i.e., reality before she found herself alone) that Kate describes is uniquely hers in the sense of Heideg-ger's mental universe in which one's physical and histori-cal environment are uniquely one's own. The "history" she writes is thus her personal history, although we readily corroborate much of it. Yes, there was a Leonardo da Vinci who painted a fresco called *The Last Supper.* Yes, a man named Odysseus appears in a book called the *Iliad,* written down centuries after its story was told by a man (or woman) named Homer. But Kate the artist's lost world is her personal world. The world of a mathemati-cian or botanist or sailor would be different. In addition, Kate has lost her mother and son to illness, and both deaths are reflected in the historical anecdotes she records. As we gradually discover, the mental choices she makes are subconscious and are linked to those deaths. Under the same conditions, the choices made by any one of us would be dictated by things that have moved us in our own lives, and would be different from those made by her.

For Kate, the lost world of the past is a more serious con-cern than it would be for someone writing such a "histo-ry" in voluntary sequestration, since she cannot step out of her reveries into a world full of life. That she lacks this option makes her loss complete. We agree with her that "There is a great deal of sadness in the *Iliad.* . . . Well, all that death. Wrist deep in that, and in loss, so many of them so often being. But too, with all of it so long ago, and forever gone." We agree, but we can look at our own teem-ing world and can say with Tennyson's Ulysses, "Though much is taken, much abides." This luxury is not granted to Kate, and much of the novel's sadness resides in her memories of having looked with longing for anything alive, a person, a cat, a sea gull, anything at all that would make her not alone. "How I nearly felt in the midst of all that looking," is how she describes those moments when she thought she heard someone call her name.

Ultimately though, Kate's solitary present becomes less important than the connections in her mind between his-torical anecdotes, some "true," some garbled, and be-tween historical and private past. At the points where these connections involve the deaths of her son and moth-er, Markson's book achieves its greatest poignancy and be-comes enormously sad. These points also determine the narrative development of a novel that seems at a first read-ing almost without such development.

That connections are the key to *Wittgenstein's Mistress* becomes clear as we follow Kate's reflections from Helen of Troy to Cézanne to cats to Lawrence of Arabia to Brahms to baseball to *Anna Karenina* to a wealth of other things. In fact, not a single item mentioned in *Wittgenstein's Mistress* could not be connected with any other item in the novel, and for a far more important reason than the obvious one that anything found in a book is connected to anything else in it through strings of intervening words. In *Wittgenstein's Mistress,* the connections exist because every bit of information or memory or notion residing in Kate's mind is connected to everything else in her mind through mental associations, which link remembered history and myth with personal memories and notions. Thus, the historical Lawrence of Arabia, about whom she knows next to nothing, is connected with a book in German about Lawrence, which she finds in the basement of her cottage, with the film *Lawrence of Arabia,* and with urinating. Although she points out that she "can think of no connection between making a pee and Lawrence of Arabia" and that she is not suggesting "that there is any particular connection between taking a pee and Lawrence of Arabia," the connection is clearly that she relieves herself in the dunes.

This example illustrates that one of the novel's main ideas, that of the connectedness of everything residing in a single mind, is by no means something the reader will unearth only through painstaking study of the text. The word *connection* or its verb appears in the book at least thirty times, and Kate frequently compliments herself on making connections. (pp. 240-42)

The idea of connections appears also whenever Kate points out that something reminds her of something else—although she does not always remember what she is reminded of—and in certain questions she asks herself: "And what have I been saying that has now made me think about Achilles again?" In each of these instances, the text provides the answer, often simply because what she has just thought about is obviously connected to what she is "now" thinking about (she mentions her sprained ankle two sentences before she asks herself what made her think of Achilles), but many times the answer comes later as well, a little more than a page later in this case: "Actually, all I had been thinking about in regard to Achilles was his heel. Although I do not have any sort of limp, if I have possibly given that impression." Sometimes the answer is found many pages later, in a mirror image of identical phrasing. . . . (pp. 242-43)

The lists Kate keeps making and adding to are another way in which things are shown to be connected. Thus we find, in addition to her list of teachers and their pupils, lists of people who went blind, who went mad, who died in poverty. "So many lists keep on growing, and are saddening," she observes.

All of these connections exist because everything in the novel comes from Kate's consciousness and from her concern for detecting relationships. But connections also make for the novel's art and for its great success in creating a self-contained world. Kate was an artist, and she traveled through Greece, Italy, France, Russia, and elsewhere, and lived in art museums before she settled down on the beach. Neither her past, nor the fact that she recalls thinking of the art, history, and literature connected with each place she visited, and keeps musing on these subjects

now, is accidental. If we step out of the novel's internal world and consider it as a work of art, we see that everything in it, from the upside-down van in the Mediterranean, to the painting of a beach cottage, which may or may not have someone standing at a window, to the torn-out and burned pages of a book of Greek tragedies (or of a life of Brahms), to a mountain of broken bottles at a landfill site, to everything else in the book, is connected to recurring ideas of the representation of reality in art, the mental baggage of history and experience, the problems of memory, sense perception and language, and the sadness of loss. The most amazing achievement of Markson's novel is that virtually every sentence in it—every notion, event, anecdote, observation—refers to these ideas. The overall effect is the sense of flawless unity and completeness that strikes us about the very greatest works of art.

On a sentence by sentence level, connections shape the text because of the way Kate's mind moves from subject to subject by associations. A corollary to this motion is the inordinate difficulty of quoting self-contained sections of the novel, one's urge being always to back up to find the beginning of a train of thought, a beginning that is ultimately the first sentence of the book. The lack of conventional paragraphs, or of blank vertical space, or of separate chapters that indicate the passing of time or grouping of ideas, are obvious symptoms of the connectedness of things. Other symptoms are the abundance of links between sentences. "Although . . . Well . . . I say still . . . On the other hand . . . Or . . . Well, or . . . As a matter of fact . . . In fact . . . " are phrases that begin consecutive sentences.

But connections through mental associations do more than propel Kate's writing forward: they also stop it at places where the apparent seamlessness of the text is belied by statements telling us that a span of hours or days, or, towards the end, of weeks has elapsed between sentences. After mentioning portraits of her mother and father, and snapshots of her son, Kate writes: "But quite suddenly I do not feel like typing any more of this, for now." Her next entry reads: "I have not been typing, for perhaps three hours." She has meanwhile been at the spring and in town. After musing on *The Last Supper,* Cassandra, the boat basin, her going by boat to Byzantium, her first beach house burning to the ground, the question of how far the flames would have been visible on the ocean, her forgetting her jar at the spring, her peculiarity of referring to her jar as a pitcher, her feeling tired or perhaps depressed, she goes on,

> In any case, doubtless I was already feeling this way when I stopped typing. Doubtless my decision to stop typing had much to do with my feeling this way.
> I have already forgotten what I had been typing when I began to feel this way.
> Obviously, I could look back. Surely that part cannot be very many lines behind the line I am typing at this moment.
> On second thought I will not look back. If there was something I was typing that had contributed to my feeling this way, doubtless it would contribute to it all over again.

We, of course, know the reasons for her depression: her thoughts of her mother and son. Here and elsewhere, Kate's grief about her mother's death of cancer and her son's death of meningitis surfaces and causes her to pause. And in the end this grief is what prompts her to stop writing altogether when she finds that all thoughts, however "harmless," resurrect it. Associated with both deaths are certain memories. In her mother's case there is the "tiny pocket sort of mirror" at her mother's hospital bedside table. Her father took away the mirror to save her mother from seeing what the disease was doing to her. Kate found it later in a drawer full of snapshots. There is baseball, which her father watched days on end when her mother was dying. There is her mother's statement: "You will never know how much it has meant to me that you are an artist." In the case of her son's death, associated memories are Simon's inability to think of a name for his cat, her driving up to Simon's grave on a hillside with a land rover, seeing in the rearview mirror of a car the blaze she had set in the house in which she had lived with her son and husband, and her unfaithfulness to her husband.

These associations are what link Kate's private past to the historical past she recounts throughout the book. (pp. 243-45)

Wittgenstein's Mistress addresses the question of how memory works. Our memory is one of relationships, temporal and familial; of comparisons of similarities and differences: before this came that, after that came this; this looks like that, that sounds like this; I've never seen, heard, read, experienced, anything like this. Our memory is also shaped by slips, omissions, gaps, which occur at those points where memory becomes painful and subconscious defenses jump up. . . .

Throughout the book, Kate moves by mental associations from topic to topic: who was whose student, who knew whom, who lived in the same city as who, was likely to have exchanged pleasantries with whom, died of the same disease as who, had eccentricities similar to whose? And what related item does this, that, or the other thing bring to her mind? As Kate finally realizes, what anything and everything brings to her mind are things too painful to think about. She tells of having written "I love you" on her mother's pocket mirror after her mother had told her how much it had meant to her that Kate was an artist. (p. 245)

[In] the end she decides that the only way she can go on writing without being reminded of her son's and mother's deaths is by starting from the beginning and writing something different altogether, such as a novel. She quickly changes her mind, however, when it occurs to her that "your ordinary novel is basically expected to be about people too." Since, as she has found, any musings about people eventually return her to depressing thoughts, a novel cannot be the answer unless, "on third thought it just might change matters if I were to make it an absolutely autobiographical novel . . . that would not start until after I was alone, obviously."

What sort of novel would it be? It would begin with the heroine's waking up one Wednesday or Thursday to discover herself alone in the world. She would go mad, then would look for other people in all sorts of places; finally she would stop looking and would be left with very little to do but burn an occasional house to the ground and scribble make-believe Greek writing in the sand with a stick. But, she concludes, even that novel without people would be impossible to write without her getting into the heroine's head after all. And remembering. And becoming depressed. The result is that in the end she stops writing altogether, her next to last sentence being a reference to the castle on the hill in La Mancha: "To the castle, the sign must have said." It is a telling reference, since it is linked in her mind to Simon's grave on the hillside. And even her very last sentence—"Somebody is living on this beach"—with its bare statement of fact, and no link to the past, and no overt connection to anything disturbing, is far from harmless: It is an echo of the first idea mentioned in the book, which, if pursued, would lead to the second idea, and to the third, and so on—to thoughts of loss and grief. (p. 246)

*Evelin E. Sullivan, " 'Wittgenstein's Mistress':
And the Art of Connections," in* The Review
of Contemporary Fiction, *Vol. 10, No. 2,
Summer, 1990, pp. 240-46.*

FURTHER READING

The Review of Contemporary Fiction 10, No. 2 (Summer 1990): 91-254.

　　Special issue devoted to John Barth and Markson. Includes essays and personal reminiscences by critics, an interview with Markson, and fiction by him.

W. Somerset Maugham

1874-1965

(Full name William Somerset Maugham) English novelist, short story writer, playwright, critic, and essayist.

Maugham is one of the most prolific and popular authors in world literature. During a career that spanned sixty-five years, he attained great renown, first as a dramatist, then as the author of entertaining and carefully crafted short stories and novels. Maugham's productivity has sometimes hindered his critical reception, leading commentators to assess him as a merely competent professional writer. A number of his works, however, most notably the novels *Of Human Bondage* and *Cakes and Ale; or, The Skeleton in the Cupboard,* and the short stories "The Letter" and "Rain," are acclaimed as masterpieces of twentieth-century literature.

Maugham was born to English parents at the British Embassy in Paris, where his father was employed as a lawyer. His mother died in 1882, and when his father died two years later Maugham was sent to live with a childless aunt and uncle in England. While attending King's School in Canterbury from 1885 to 1889, his inherent shyness, exacerbated by a pronounced stutter, led him to avoid social activities and devote himself to his studies. Although his guardians wanted him to attend Oxford, Maugham persuaded them to allow him to study at the University of Heidelberg in Germany. By the time he returned to England in 1892 Maugham had privately decided to become a writer. Nevertheless, knowing that his guardians would disapprove of a literary career, he began medical training at St. Thomas's Hospital in London. Maugham earned a medical degree in 1897 but never practiced; that same year he published his first novel, *Liza of Lambeth,* set in the milieu he had observed during his training in obstetrics, when he was often called into London's poorest neighborhoods to attend births. This novel manifests some of the elements that characterize Maugham's fiction, including reliance on personal experience and adherence with existing literary traditions. George Gissing and Arthur Morrison, contemporary novelists of the time, had popularized realistic accounts of life in the slums, assuring Maugham of a readership; his depiction of an illicit extramarital relationship aroused sufficient controversy to stimulate further interest in the novel.

The decade following the appearance of *Liza of Lambeth* is often termed the period of Maugham's literary apprenticeship. From 1897 until 1907 he published novels, short stories, a play, and a travel book, receiving increasingly favorable reviews in English literary periodicals. In 1907 his play *Lady Frederick* met with considerable success, and Maugham quickly attained celebrity as a dramatist. In 1908, four of his plays—*Lady Frederick, Jack Straw, Mrs Dot,* and *The Explorer*—ran simultaneously in London theaters. Over the next twenty-six years, twenty-nine of Maugham's plays were produced, many of them among

the most well-received of their time. Maugham conscientiously employed contemporary conventions of popular dramatic comedy, portraying sophisticated society with satiric intent. His dramatic plots hinge on secrets, with suspense heightened by the possibility of revelation. Misplaced objects, mistaken identities, and barbed verbal exchanges abound. Climaxes are generally achieved with the reversal of a central character's fortune; the denouement follows quickly as the combined result of the revelations and reversals that have been effected. Maugham's dramas are topical, written to satisfy a contemporary preference for drawing-room comedies patterned after the French well-made-play; rather than alter his characteristic approach to drama he ceased writing plays during the early 1930s as the tastes of the theatergoing public changed.

At the onset of World War I Maugham joined the Red Cross and went to France as an interpreter. There he met Gerald Haxton, and the two became lovers and remained close companions for the next thirty years. During the war the British government recruited Maugham as an intelligence agent and subsequently involved him in covert operations in Switzerland and Russia. Despite the ongoing relationship with Haxton, in 1917 Maugham married Syrie

Barnardo Wellcome, with whom he had had a child two years earlier. They divorced in 1929. During the years between the World Wars, Maugham lived lavishly and wrote prolifically. He bought an expansive villa in southeast France, which remained his home thereafter, although he traveled widely; his visits to Italy, the United States, the South Seas, and the Caribbean provided the settings for the works that appeared between the World Wars, including the novels *The Moon and Sixpence* and *Cakes and Ale;* the plays *Our Betters* and *The Circle;* and the short story collections *The Trembling of a Leaf: Little Stories of the South Sea Islands, The Casuarina Tree,* and *Ashenden; or, The British Agent.* Maugham fled France during the Nazi occupation, and went to the United States, where he lectured and oversaw the Hollywood production of several motion pictures based on his stories and novels. Haxton, who had accompanied Maugham, died in 1944. In 1948 Maugham returned to France. Although accounts of his later years portray Maugham as somewhat mentally unstable and given to irrational outbursts, he retained a sardonic wit. "Dying is a very dull, dreary affair," he told his nephew, Robin Maugham. "And my advice to you is to have nothing whatever to do with it." He died in 1965 at the age of ninety-one.

Despite his prolificacy, Maugham's renown rests chiefly on only a few works. The most often studied of these is *Of Human Bondage.* Based on an early unpublished manuscript called "The Artistic Temperament of Stephen Carey," Maugham's semiautobiographical coming-of-age novel is commended for its penetrating psychological portrait of its protagonist. Some commentators note that *Of Human Bondage* suffers from excessive length and too-inclusive use of naturalistic detail, but these faults are generally attributed to the novel's basis in a youthful manuscript, and critics have praised the novel as a classic bildungsroman, as well as an acute study of the obsessive love relationship that dominates the protagonist for years and nearly ruins his life. Maugham's most critically esteemed novel is *Cakes and Ale.* In this lively and entertaining story, the second wife of a venerable literary figure attempts to ensure that an official biography will portray her husband and herself auspiciously, while disparaging the man's first wife. *Cakes and Ale* was controversial because it was believed to be based on the life of Thomas Hardy, but commentators subsequently discerned a devastating parody of the novelist and critic Hugh Walpole, on whom Maugham based his characterization of the second-rate litterateur Alroy Kear. *Cakes and Ale* also includes, in Rosie Driffield, Maugham's most sympathetic and fully dimensional female character. *The Moon and Sixpence,* an account of a painter passionately devoted to his art, based on the life of Paul Gauguin, and *The Razor's Edge,* which chronicles a young American's quest for meaning and purpose, are also highly regarded by critics.

Maugham has received his greatest recognition for his short fiction. He emerged as a preeminent short story writer in the 1920s, and many commentators maintain that he consistently achieved excellence in this genre, concurring with Anthony Burgess that "the short story was Maugham's true *métier,* and some of the stories he wrote are among the best in the language." Maugham's most successful short stories—which include "Before the Party," "The Book-Bag," "Mackintosh," "P. & O.," "The Pool," "Mr. Harrington's Washing," "The Letter," and "Rain"—exploit the oppressive atmosphere of British colonies, featuring petty intrigue, marital infidelity, and sometimes violent death against a background of the rigidly stratified colonial communities in India and the Far East. In "The Letter," for example, the wife of an English plantation owner in Singapore shoots and kills a man she claims forced his way into her room and tried to rape her while her husband was absent. Her lawyer, however, discovers a letter she wrote to the murdered man arranging a tryst on the night of his death. In "Rain" a medical quarantine isolates a number of travelers, including Sadie Thompson, a prostitute, Dr. and Mrs. Macphail, and the Davidsons, a missionary couple, in a remote port of Pago Pago. Mr. Davidson becomes obsessed with reforming the flamboyant prostitute, and he bullies her into a cowed, terrified state by wielding the threat of a prison term. One night he is found dead, having cut his own throat. Sadie Thompson is angrily defiant, and the words she hurls at Dr. Macphail—"You men! You filthy, dirty pigs! You're all the same, all of you. Pigs! Pigs!"—suggest that what passed between her and the missionary was not entirely spiritual in nature. These two stories are among the most frequently anthologized in world literature; both have undergone several stage and film adaptations. Maugham's Ashenden stories, based on his experiences in the secret service, are credited with originating a style of sophisticated international espionage fiction that has remained popular for decades. His stories resemble his dramas in structure: plots hinge and pivot on some secret; suspense is heightened by the possibility of revelation; and tension builds on strategically timed entrances and exits, lost and found properties, and verbal combat. In fact, Maugham often transformed short stories into plays and rewrote unperformed dramas as novels or short stories, and this ease of adaptation attests to the unity of Maugham's literary construction.

Maugham himself stated that his place in literature was "in the very first row of the second-raters"; many critics concur with this assessment. Maugham's prolificacy, together with the generally even quality of his work, fosters the impression of an adept literary workman turning out competent but unremarkable fiction. While many commentators agree that this is a fair evaluation of much of Maugham's work, some have suggested that it required more than mere competence to sustain Maugham's long and successful career. They cite his consummate achievements in the short story form and suggest that Maugham's many works of fiction include a number of the finest English novels and short stories of the twentieth century.

(See also *CLC,* Vols. 1, 11, 15; *Contemporary Authors,* Vols. 5-8, rev. ed., 25-28, rev. ed.; *Dictionary of Literary Biography,* Vols. 10, 36, 77, 100; and *Something about the Author,* Vol. 54.)

PRINCIPAL WORKS

NOVELS

Liza of Lambeth   1897

The Making of a Saint   1898
The Hero   1901
Mrs Craddock   1902; revised edition, 1937
The Bishop's Apron: A Study in the Origins of a Great Family   1906
The Magician   1908
Of Human Bondage   1915
The Moon and Sixpence   1919
The Painted Veil   1925
Cakes and Ale; or, The Skeleton in the Cupboard   1930
The Narrow Corner   1932
Christmas Holiday   1939
Up at the Villa   1941
The Hour before Dawn   1942
The Razor's Edge   1944
Then and Now   1946
Catalina   1948

SHORT FICTION COLLECTIONS

Orientations   1899
The Merry-Go-Round   1904
The Trembling of a Leaf: Little Stories of the South Sea Islands   1921
The Casuarina Tree: Six Stories   1926
Ashenden; or, The British Agent   1928
Six Stories Written in the First Person Singular   1931
East and West: The Collected Short Stories   1934; also published as *Altogether*,   1934
Cosmopolitans   1936
The Mixture as Before   1940
Creatures of Circumstance   1947
The World Over   1952
The Complete Short Stories of W. Somerset Maugham   1953 [this collection includes *East and West* and *The World Over*]

PLAYS

A Man of Honour   1903
Lady Frederick   1907
The Explorer   1908
Jack Straw   1908
Mrs Dot   1908
Penelope   1909
Smith   1909
Grace (Landed Gentry)   1910
The Tenth Man   1910
Loaves and Fishes   1911
The Land of Promise   1913
Caroline (The Unattainable)   1916
Caesar's Wife   1919
Home and Beauty (Too Many Husbands)   1919
Our Betters   1919
The Unknown   1920
The Circle   1921
East of Suez   1922
The Constant Wife   1926
The Letter   1927
The Sacred Flame   1929
The Breadwinner   1930
For Services Rendered   1932
Sheppey   1933

OTHER

The Land of the Blessed Virgin: Sketches and Impressions in Andalusia   (travel book)   1905
The Gentleman in the Parlour   (travel book)   1930
Don Fernando; or, Variations on Some Spanish Themes (travel book)   1935
The Summing Up   (autobiographical sketch)   1938
Books and You   (essays)   1940
Great Novelists and Their Novels   (criticism)   1948; also published as *Ten Novels and Their Authors,* rev. ed., 1954
A Writer's Notebook   (journals)   1949
The Vagrant Mood   (essays)   1952
Points of View   (essays)   1958
Looking Back   (autobiographical sketch)   1962
Purely for My Pleasure   (essays)   1962

Theodore Dreiser

[*Considered among America's foremost novelists, Dreiser was one of the principal American exponents of literary Naturalism. He is known primarily for his novels* Sister Carrie *(1901),* An American Tragedy *(1926), and the Frank Cowperwood trilogy (1912-47), in each of which the author combined his vision of life as a meaningless series of chemical reactions and animal impulses with a sense of sentimentality and pity for humanity's lot. In the following excerpt, Dreiser enthusiastically reviews* Of Human Bondage.]

Sometimes in retrospect of a great book the mind falters, confused by the multitude and yet the harmony of the detail, the strangeness of the frettings, the brooding, musing intelligence that has foreseen, loved, created, elaborated, perfected, until, in this middle ground which we call life, somewhere between nothing and nothing, hangs the perfect thing which we love and cannot understand, but which we are compelled to confess a work of art. It is at once something and nothing, a dream, a happy memory, a song, a benediction. In viewing it one finds nothing to criticise or to regret. The thing sings, it has color. It has rapture. You wonder at the loving, patient care which has evolved it.

Only recently I finished reading Mr. W. Somerset Maugham's **Of Human Bondage.** It was with some such feeling as this that I laid it down.

Here is a novel or biography or autobiography or social transcript of the utmost importance. To begin with it is unmoral, as a novel of this kind must necessarily be. The hero is born with a club foot, and in consequence, and because of a temperament delicately attuned to the miseries of life, suffers all the pains, recessions, and involute self tortures which only those who have striven handicapped by what they have considered a blighting defect can understand. He is a youth, therefore, with an intense craving for sympathy and understanding. He must have it. The thought of his lack and the part which his disability plays in it soon becomes an obsession. He is tortured, miserable.

In pursuit of his ideal from his earliest youth he clings to both men and women in a pathetic way, a truly moving spectacle. The story begins at the home of his mother in or near London. She is dying, and among the last things she does is to feel the deformed foot of her son, with what thoughts we may well imagine. Later in the home of his uncle, William Carey, vicar of Blackstable in Kent, we find him suffering for want of sympathy and concealing his shyness and desire behind a veil of assumed indifference. By Carey and his wife he is fostered in a somewhat stern way until his schooldays at Tercenbury begin. There he is tortured by unfeeling playmates, unconscious of the agony which his deformity causes him, until he is ready to leave for a higher school, and presumably prepare himself for the ministry.

Study, and an innate opposition to the life, decide him to leave and go to Heidelberg, Germany, where apparently he remains for a year and rids himself of all his early religious beliefs. A little later he returns to England uncertain as to his career, and enters the office of a chartered accountant in London, for which privilege he pays. If anyone has ever given a better description of English clerkly life I am not aware of it. After a year he gives this up, finding himself unsuited to it, and essays art, the suggestions and enthusiasms of certain friends impelling him to it. Two years of the Latin Quarter, Paris, and the fierce discussions which rage around the newer movements in art make it clear to him that he is unsuited for that field, and with a sense of defeat he gives it up. A few months later he enters a medical school in London with a view to becoming a physician. It is here that his loneliness and his passion for sympathy drive him into a weird relationship with a waitress in an A B C restaurant in London which eventually eats up the remainder of his small fortune of twelve hundred pounds. Finally, penniless and destitute, sleeping on park benches for days, he is compelled to enter a London shop as a clerk. . . . (p. 202)

Curiously the story rises to no spired climax. To some it has apparently appealed as a drab, unrelieved narrative. To me at least it is a gorgeous weave, as interesting and valuable at the beginning as at the end. There is material in its three hundred thousand and more words for many novels and indeed several philosophies, and even a religion or stoic hope. There are a series of women, of course—drab, pathetic, enticing as the case may be—who lead him through the mazes of sentiment, sex, love, pity, passion, a wonderful series of portraits and of incidents. There are a series of men friends of a peculiarily inclusive range of intellectuality and taste, who lead him, or whom he leads, through all the intricacies of art, philosophy, criticism, humor. And lastly comes life itself, the great land and sea of people, England, Germany, France, battering, corroding, illuminating, a Goyaesque world.

Naturally I asked myself how such a book would be received in America, in England. In the latter country I was sure, with its traditions of the *Athenaeum* and the *Saturday Review,* it would be adequately appreciated. Imagine my surprise to find that the English reviews were almost uniformly contemptuous and critical on moral and social grounds. The hero was a weakling, not for a moment to be tolerated by sound, right-thinking men. On the other hand in America the reviewers for the most part have seen its true merits and stated them. Need I say, however, that the New York *World* finds it "the sentimental servitude of a poor fool"; or that the Philadelphia *Press* sees fit to dub it "futile Philip" or that the *Outlook* feels that "the author might have made his book true without making it so frequently distasteful"; or that the *Dial* cries, "a most depressing impression of the futility of life"? "No brilliancy of style," mourns the Detroit *Times.* "Young folks are warned off," urges the Portland *Oregonian.* (As if that young person could be induced to examine so profound and philosophic a work!) "Certainly the story cannot be said to be in any sense a wholesome one, and it would require a distinctly morbid taste for one to enjoy it thoroughly." (Note the "thoroughly"). This from the New Orleans *Times-Picayune.* "One longs after reading these novels where spineless men and women yield without a struggling to the forces of evil"—but I cannot go on. It is too trite. You must judge for yourself how the reviewer on the *Saturday Evening Post* of Burlington, Ia., felt about it.

Despite these dissonant voices it is still a book of the utmost import, and has so been received. Compact of the experiences, the dreams, the hopes, the fears, the disillusionments, the ruptures, and the philosophisings of a strangely starved soul, it is a beacon light by which the wanderer may be guided. Nothing is left out; the author writes as though it were a labor of love. It bears the imprint of an eager, almost consuming desire to say truly what is in his heart.

Personally I found myself aching with pain when, yearning for sympathy, Philip begs the wretched Mildred, never his mistress but on his level, to no more than tolerate him. He finally humiliates himself to the extent of exclaiming, "You don't know what it means to be a cripple!" The pathos of it plumbs the depths. The death of Fannie Price, of the sixteen-year-old mother in the slum, of Cronshaw, and the rambling agonies of old Ducroz and of Philip himself, are perfect in their appeal.

There are many other and all equally brilliant pictures. No one short of a genius could rout the philosophers from their lairs and label them as individuals "tempering life with rules agreeable to themselves," or could follow Mildred Rogers, waitress of the London A B C restaurant, through all the shabby windings of her tawdry soul. No other than a genius endowed with an immense capacity for understanding and pity could have sympathized with Fannie Price, with her futile and self-destructive art dreams; or old Cronshaw, the wastrel of poetry and philosophy; or Mons. Ducroz, the worn-out revolutionary; or Thorne Athelny, the caged grandee of Spain; or Leonard Upjohn, airy master of the art of self advancement; or Dr. South, the vicar of Blackstable, and his wife—these are masterpieces. They are marvelous portraits; they are as smooth as a Vermeer, as definite as a Hals, as brooding and moving as a Rembrandt. The study of Carey himself, while one sees him more as a medium through which the others express themselves, still registers photographically at times. He is by no means a brooding voice but a definite, active, vigorous character.

If the book can be said to have a fault it will lie for some in its length, 300,000 words, or for others in the peculiar reticence with which the last love affair in the story is handled. Until the coming of Sallie Athelny all has been described with the utmost frankness. No situation, however crude or embarrassing, has been shirked. In the matter of the process by which he arrived at the intimacy which resulted in her becoming pregnant not a word is said. All at once, by a slight frown which she subsequently explains, the truth is forced upon you that there has been a series of intimacies which have not been accounted for. After Mildred Rogers and his relationship with Norah Nesbit it strikes one as strange.

I feel about this book, as I look back on it now, much as old Cronshaw in the story felt about the rug which was to clarify for Carey the meaning of life:

> As the weaver elaborated his pattern for no end but the pleasure of his aesthetic sense, so might a man live his life, or, if he was forced to believe that his actions were outside his choosing, so might a man look at his life, that it made a pattern. There was little need to do this or there was little need to do that. It was merely something that he did for his own pleasure. Out of the manifold events of his life, his deeds, his feelings, his thoughts, he might make a design, regular, elaborated, complicated or beautiful; and though it might be no more than an illusion that he had the power of selection, that did not matter; it seemed and so to him it was. In the vast warp of life, with the background to his fancies that there was no meaning and that nothing was important, a man might get a personal satisfaction in selecting the various strands that worked out the pattern. . . . What happened to him now would be one more motive to add to the complexity of the pattern, and when the end approached he would rejoice in its completion. It would be a work of art and it would be none the less beautiful because he alone knew of its existence, and with his death it would at once cease to be.

And so it is, Mr. Maugham, this life of Philip Carey as you have woven it. One feels as though one were sitting before a splendid Shiraz or Daghestan of priceless texture and intricate weave, admiring, feeling, responding sensually to its colors and tones. Or better yet it is as though a symphony of great beauty by a master, Strauss or Beethoven, had just been completed and the bud notes and flower tones were filling the air with their elusive message, fluttering and dying. Mr. Maugham, as I understand it, has written eleven conventional books and as many plays. It may be that for years, as the paragraph quoted suggests, he has lived willing that the large knowledge which this book reveals should remain unseen and even perish with him. For all of that he is none the less a great artist. Vicariously, it seems to me, he has suffered for the joy of the many who are to read after him. By no willing of his own he has been compelled to take life by the hand and go down where there has been little save sorrow and degradation. The cup of gall and wormwood has obviously been lifted to his lips and to the last drop he has been compelled to drink it. Because of this we are enabled to see the rug, woven of the

tortures and the delights of a life. We may actually walk and talk with one whose hands and feet have been pierced with nails. (pp. 202-04)

> *Theodore Dreiser, "As a Realist Sees It," in* The New Republic, *Vol. V, No. 60, December 25, 1915, pp. 202-04.*

Maugham on *Of Human Bondage*:

[*Of Human Bondage*] is not an autobiography, but an autobiographical novel; fact and fiction are inextricably mingled; the emotions are my own, but not all the incidents are related as they happened and some of them are transferred to my hero not from my own life but from that of persons with whom I was intimate. The book did for me what I wanted, and when it was issued to the world (a world in the throes of a terrible war and too much concerned with its own sufferings to bother with the adventures of a creature of fiction) I found myself free forever from those pains and unhappy recollections. I put into it everything I then knew and having at last finished it prepared to make a fresh start.

From his *The Summing Up*, 1938.

Raymond Mortimer

[*Mortimer was an English critic who succeeded Desmond MacCarthy as literary editor of the* New Statesman and Nation *and later joined MacCarthy as a book reviewer for the* Sunday Times. *In the following excerpt, he reviews Maugham's collection of short stories* Altogether *(published in the United States as* East and West*).*]

Mr. Somerset Maugham thinks that the critics have not given him a square deal, so the thirty stories in [*Altogether: The Collected Stories of W. Somerset Maugham*] are sandwiched between a preface by the author and a reprinted article by Mr. Desmond MacCarthy. The reviewer will find in the preface a warning of what he ought not to say, and in the article, which is almost wholly laudatory, an example of what he ought. The stories themselves are most of them told by a disillusioned man of the world who remains superbly objective in face of cruelty, treachery and murder, but for whom the highbrow is something he resents even more than he does the missionary: something to be treated with not only detestation but contempt. (Indeed **"The Creative Instinct"** seems to me the weakest story in the volume, in spite of its charming plot, because the author's hatred of highbrows has goaded him into unconvincing caricature.) It is odd that Mr. Maugham, who is, I suppose, the most successful living writer, should let his calm be ruffled by the criticisms of persons he believes to be so petty, gullible and insincere.

> Is one mocked by an elf,
> Is one baffled by toad or by rat?
> The gravamen's in that!

But if one is a highbrow it is little use pretending not to be, even to escape Mr. Maugham's contempt; and so I shall parade the cloven hoof by trying to criticise his stories by the highest standard I know.

In his preface Mr. Maugham implies, I think justly, that the critics have been cold to him largely because his stories derive rather from Maupassant than from the more fashionable Tchehov. (His remarks on these writers reveal him as a most acute critic.) Actually the stories of Tchehov have been too indiscriminately praised: many of them are mere jottings, and both he and Maupassant wrote too much. Mr. Maugham lives much more conscientiously up to his own highest level. To illustrate his methods he transcribes in his preface the working notes, made from observation, on which the story **"Rain"** was constructed. "They are written in hackneyed and slipshod phrases without grace," he says, "for nature has not endowed me with the happy gift of hitting instinctively upon the perfect word to indicate an object and the unusual, but apt, adjective to describe It." In view of this statement it is interesting to find that in the story itself most of these "hackneyed and slipshod phrases" are repeated without alteration. Mr. Maugham complains that reviewers call his work "competent," and supposes that he is damned with this faint praise because of the definiteness of form in his stories. Lord knows there has rarely been a less incompetent writer, but I think it is true to say that he does not hit, either instinctively or on reflection, the perfect word to indicate an object. It would be difficult to find examples of clumsy writing in Mr. Maugham's late work (though he sometimes trips into such surprising *clichés* as calling a woman "exquisitely gowned"), but it would be equally difficult to find passages in which the words had a life of their own. Possibly a fresher, less business-like style would slacken the pace of the stories by side-tracking the reader's attention from the design to the texture, but I do miss vividness in Mr. Maugham's descriptive passages. After reading many—too many—stories with a Malay setting, I have no clear impression of the atmosphere of Malaya: I have merely become bored with the sarongs and padangs and kampongs which serve for local colour. On the other hand, Mr. Maugham describes persons prodigiously well by the phrases he puts into their mouths. In a scrap of dialogue we have their social background, their pretensions, and the passions they seek to conceal. As a result, when re-reading these stories I have been surprised not by their excellence as stories (which I remembered) but by the suspense in which they held me, although I already knew how they would end. In this respect he beats Maupassant, whose stories depend too often on surprise. For in Maupassant the characters are created for the plot: in Maugham the plot is created by the characters. **"Honolulu"** is one of the very few stories which are just stories: and afterwards in **"P. & O.,"** where he uses a similar plot, the interest has shifted from the action to the reaction which it has upon the spectators' characters. Very often the point is the revelation of some wholly unexpected trait, a "degrading" passion in an ambassador or a society beauty, or the ability to murder in apparently commonplace persons, as in **"The Letter," "Before the Party,"** and **"Footprints in the Jungle."** Mr. Maugham delights in uncovering the heel of Achilles—that is why he is called a cynic—and there are no wholehearted heroes or villains in his work. His extraordinary knowledge of human beings is like that

of an experienced confessor, and as a result of it he is never shocked. This comprehension of the essential piebaldness of human character gives his stories a peculiar virtue. As examples of his method take **"Mackintosh"** and **"The Outstation"**: in each case two incompatible men are isolated, with the result that one becomes accessory to the other's murder. The murders, though their circumstances are arranged with admirable skill, are merely logical deductions from the confrontation of characters, and the interest of each story lies chiefly not in the violent conclusion but in the subtly stated premises. And in both of them the reader's sympathies are made to waver delicately in the balance by the calculated mixture of qualities in each of the antagonists. Mr. Maugham has developed in the narrow room of the short story a richness of characterisation hardly previously found except in the novel.

Ultimately these stories are the work of a comic writer. "Life is really very fantastic," he says in one of them, "and one has to have a peculiar sense of humour to see the fun of it." Mr. Maugham has this himself. Most of the stories "end unhappily," but they are devised to excite irony rather than pity. Almost the only character treated with tenderness is the scoundrelly old Walker at the end of **"Mackintosh,"** and here the tenderness seems to me just off the note—in fact, to be sentimentality. Yet Rosie in *Cakes and Ale* proves that Mr. Maugham can be tender. In fact, his last two novels show that he is a writer of promise. *Of Human Bondage* is so far his most solid achievement, because of the passion behind it; and I suspect it is a better book than *The Old Wives' Tale,* for instance, or any other of the realistic novels of the decade before the war. But in the meanwhile Mr. Maugham, who is not a natural writer, I think, in the sense of having a gift for handling language as a *matière,* has learnt a great deal about writing; and in *The Narrow Corner* he put his acquired skill to new uses, so that it is probably true to say that his last book was also his most perfect.

Mr. Maugham lacks the gift which is not necessary to immortality but which alone can make it certain: he does not possess a poetic vision of the world. But he has the good taste not to pretend to it, and does not offer us electroplate in lieu of silver. There are few purple passages in his work, and it would be better if there were none. Though the critics have praised him less than he deserves, the public have appreciated him more than he could reasonably expect, for he has done nothing to placate them: his irony and amorality are the qualities which usually they most dislike. He would wish the critic, I gather, to praise his stories for their shapeliness, and indeed each of these thirty is a model of construction. But I humbly recommend them for what seems to me rarer and more important than shapeliness, for the first and essential literary virtue, a virtue which they possess in the highest degree and the lack of which stamps some supposed masterpieces of form as fraudulent—the power to seize and hold the reader's attention. (pp. 243-44)

Raymond Mortimer, "Re-Reading Mr. Maugham," in The New Statesman & Nation, *Vol. 8, No. 183, August 25, 1934, pp. 243-44.*

Edmund Wilson

[Wilson, considered America's foremost man of letters in the twentieth century, wrote widely on cultural, historical, and literary matters. He is often credited with bringing an international perspective to American letters through his widely read discussions of European literature. In the following excerpt, originally published as a review of Then and Now *in the* New Yorker *on June 8, 1946 (and subsequently revised), Wilson offers a negative assessment of Maugham's career.]*

It has happened to me from time to time to run into some person of taste who tells me that I ought to take Somerset Maugham seriously, yet I have never been able to convince myself that he was anything but second-rate. His swelling reputation in America, which culminated the other day in his solemn presentation to the Library of Congress of the manuscript of **Of Human Bondage,** seems to me a conspicuous sign of the general decline of our standards. Thirty or thirty-five years ago the English novelists that were read in America were at least men like Wells and Bennett, who, though not quite of top rank, were at least by vocation real writers. Mr. Maugham, I cannot help feeling, is not, in the sense of "having the métier," really a writer at all. There are real writers, like Balzac and Dreiser, who may be said to write badly. Dreiser handles words abominably, but his prose has a compelling rhythm, which is his style and which induces the emotions that give his story its poetic meaning. But Mr. Maugham, whose language is always banal, has not even an interesting rhythm.

Now, unless I am looking for facts, I find it extremely difficult to get through books that are not "written." I can read Compton Mackenzie, for example, of the second rank though he is, because he has a gift of style of a not too common kind. But my experience has always been with Maugham that he disappoints my literary appetite and so discourages me from going on. His new novel, *Then and Now*—which I had sworn to explore to the end, if only in order to be able to say that I had read a book of Maugham's through—opposed to my progress, through all the first half, such thickets of unreadableness, that there were moments when I thought I should never succeed.

Then and Now is an historical novel: it deals with Niccolò Machiavelli and tells the story of his mission, as envoy from Florence, to the headquarters of Caesar Borgia, when the latter, in his campaign of domination, appeared at his most effective and most menacing. The way in which this promising subject is handled suggested, I was shocked to discover, one of the less brilliant contributions to a prep-school magazine. Here are Machiavelli and Borgia confronting one another:

> Although he had but briefly seen him at Urbino, Machiavelli had been deeply impressed by him. He had heard there how the Duke Guidobaldo da Montefeltro, confiding in Caesar Borgia's friendship, had lost his state and barely escaped with his life; and though he recognized that Il Valentino had acted with shocking perfidy he could not but admire the energy and adroit planning with which he had conducted the enterprise. This was a man of parts, fearless, unscru-

pulous, ruthless and intelligent, not only a brilliant general but a capable organizer and an astute politician. A sarcastic smile played upon Machiavelli's thin lips and his eyes gleamed, for the prospect of matching his wits with such an antagonist excited him.

This narrative from time to time is obstructed by the introduction of thick chunks of historical background that sound as if they had been copied out—so compressed and indigestible are they, so untouched by imagination—from some textbook in the history classroom:

> In June of the year with which this narrative is concerned, Arezzo, a city subject to Florence, revolted and declared itself independent. Vitellozzo Vitelli, the ablest of Il Valentino's commanders and bitter enemy of the Florentines because they had executed his brother Paolo, and Baglioni, Lord of Perugia, went to the support of the rebellious citizens and defeated the forces of the Republic.

etc., etc. As will be seen from the above sentence, in which, if we glide over the comma, we are at first misled into supposing that Baglioni was executed, before we find that he went with Vitelli, the writing is amateurish. The book is full of ill-composed sentences, bulging with disproportionate clauses that prevent them from coming out right, or confused by "he"s, "him"s and "his"s that apply to different antecedents: a kind of thing that an English master would have been sure to blue-pencil in the young student's themes. The language is such a tissue of clichés that one's wonder is finally aroused at the writer's ability to assemble so many and at his unfailing inability to put anything in an individual way:

> But Il Valentino appeared to be well pleased. It looked as though he were prepared to let bygones be bygones and restore the repentant rebels to his confidence. . . . But whatever sinister plans he turned round in that handsome head of his, the Duke was evidently not ready to resort to more than veiled threats to induce the Florentines to accede to his demands. . . . The Duke gazed at him thoughtfully. You might have imagined that he was asking himself what kind of a man this was, but with no ulterior motive, from idle curiosity rather. . . . The truth, the unpalatable truth, stared him in the face. . . . He had taken him on this trip from sheer good nature, he had introduced him to persons worth knowing, he had done his best to form him, to show him how to behave, to civilize him, in short; he had not spared his wit and wisdom to teach him the ways of the world, how to make friends and influence people. And this was his reward, to have his girl snatched away from under his very nose.

This dullness is only relieved by an occasional dim sparkle of the Wildean wit that made comedies like **Our Betters** amusing without investing them with that distinction which, in Wilde, is the product of style: "If only she knew as much about life as he did she would know that it is not the temptations you have succumbed to that you regret, but those you resisted." But even this kind of thing would not be beyond the competence of a schoolboy.

About halfway through the book, however, we find that what the author has been doing, in his tiresome piling up of dead incident, is introducing the elements of a plot. This plot is pretty well contrived; it could hardly have been worked out by a schoolboy, for it shows a practiced hand, and it carries us through the rest of the book. We find here, furthermore, that the scheming of Caesar to accomplish his political ends is connected, not merely through ingenuities of plot but also by moral implication, with Machiavelli's scheming to make a conquest of the wife of a friend. Machiavelli as well as Borgia is cynical about human motives; Machiavelli (though politically a patriot working for republican Florence) is aiming in his personal relations at power for the sake of power, just as Borgia is. And the victims of both are equally cynics, equally double-dealers. The upshot of the whole affair is that Machiavelli, returning home with a certain admiration for Borgia but in a rage over the duplicity practiced on him by the young wife and her allies, meditates upon his experience and finds in it the material for *Il Principe,* his treatise on Realpolitik, and for his comedy, *La Mandragola.* This, too, shows more knowledge of the world than a schoolboy would have been likely to acquire, but that schoolboy, grown-up and much travelled, having somehow been diverted from his normal career of law, medicine, diplomacy or parliament, might have produced such a novel as **Then and Now;** did, in fact, produce it.

The defenders of Somerset Maugham will tell me that he is "old and tired" now, and that historical novels are not his forte—that it is quite unfair to judge him by **Then and Now,** which is one of the least of his books. I know that he has done better stories, but I am not sure that it *is* quite unfair to judge his quality by **Then and Now.** This quality is never, it seems to me, that either of a literary artist or of a first-rate critic of morals; and it may be worth while to say this at a moment when there seems to be a tendency to step up Mr. Maugham's standing to the higher ranks of English fiction, and when Mr. Maugham himself has been using his position of prestige for a nagging disparagement of his betters. Though Mr. Maugham's claims for himself are always carefully and correctly modest, he usually manages to sound invidious when he is speaking of his top-drawer contemporaries. In an anthology which he edited a few years ago, *Introduction to Modern English and American Literature*—a mixture of good writing and tripe that sets the teeth on edge—we find him patronizing, in what seems to me an insufferable way (and with his customary buzz of clichés), such writers as Henry James, James Joyce and W. B. Yeats. "His influence on fiction," he writes of James, "especially in England, has been great, and though I happen to think it has been a bad influence, its enduring power makes him an important figure. . . . He never succeeded in coming to grips with life. . . . This story ("The Beast in the Jungle") reads to me like a lamentable admission of his own failure." Of *Ulysses:* "I have read it twice, so I cannot say that I find it unreadable, but . . . like many of his countrymen, Joyce never discovered that enough is as good as a feast, and his prolixity is exhausting." Of Yeats: "Though he could at times be very good company, he was a pompous vain man; to hear him read his own verses was as excruciating a torture as anyone could be exposed to." Well, it is quite true of Henry

James that his experience was incomplete and that he wrote about his own deficiencies, and that Joyce is sometimes too prolix, and it may be true that Yeats was sometimes pompous. It is also true that Mr. Maugham partly sweetens his detraction with praise. Yet, from reading this *Introduction,* you would never be able to discover that all these writers belong to a different plane from that of Michael Arlen and Katharine Brush, whose work is also included—to a plane on which Somerset Maugham does not exist at all. Mr. Maugham would apparently suggest to us that all novelists are entertainers who differ only in being more or less boring (though he grants, with a marked lack of enthusiasm, that Henry James supplied, "if not an incentive, at least an encouragement to those who came after him . . . to aim consciously at giving fiction the form and significance that may sometimes make it more than the pastime of an idle hour"). We get the impression of a malcontent eye cocked up from the brackish waters of the *Cosmopolitan* magazine, and a peevish and insistent grumbling. There is something going on, on the higher ground, that halfway compels his respect, but he does not quite understand what it is, and in any case he can never get up there.

There are cases in which Mr. Maugham is able to admire more cordially the work that is done on this higher plane, but even here his way of praising betrays his lack of real appreciation and almost always has a sound of impertinence. So, in his speech at the Library of Congress, we find the following remarks about Proust:

> Proust, as we know, was enormously influenced by the now largely discredited philosophy of Henri Bergson and great stretches of his work turn upon it. I suppose we all read with a thrill of excitement Proust's volumes as they came out, but now when we reread them in a calmer mood I think what we find to admire in them is his wonderful humor and extraordinarily vivid and interesting characters that he created in profusion. We skip his philosophical disquisitions and we skip them without loss.

Now, it is perfectly obvious here that Mr. Maugham does not know what he is talking about. Some aspects of Bergson's philosophy are still taken very seriously by first-rate philosophers of certain schools; and even if Bergson's whole system were regarded with universal disapproval, that might not affect the validity of the artistic use that Proust has made of one of its features. This feature—the difference between "time" and "duration": how long something takes by the clock and how long it seems while it is going on—is itself only one of the features of Proust's metaphysical picture, which in general has more in common with the implications of relativistic physics than with the Creative Evolution of Bergson. It is this play on the relativistic principle in the social and personal fields that gives Proust his philosophical interest and that makes his book, I suppose, the greatest philosophical novel ever written. In *A la recherche du temps perdu,* the philosophy so pervades the narrative that it is difficult to see how you could skip it: if you jumped over the "disquisitions," you could still not escape from Proust, in a thousand intimations and asides, expounding his relativistic theory; and since the unexpected development of the characters, the astonishing reversals of relationships, all the contrasts and paradoxes that provide the main interest of the story, are dramatizations of this theory, it is difficult to understand how a reader can "admire" the former and yet disregard the latter. The inability of Mr. Maugham to grasp what there is in Proust helps to explain why he has not been able to make his own work more interesting.

• • • • •

Admirers of Somerset Maugham have protested that this article was unfair to him and have begged me to read his short stories. I have therefore procured *East and West,* the collected volume of these, and made shift to dine on a dozen. They *are* readable—quite entertaining. The style is much tighter and neater than it is in *Then and Now*—Mr. Maugham writes best when his language is plainest. But when he wants to use a richer idiom, this is the kind of thing you get: "Be this as it may, Ashenden in the last twenty years had felt his heart go pit-a-pat because of one charming person after another. He had had a good deal of fun and had paid for it with a great deal of misery, but even when suffering most acutely from the pangs of unrequited love he had been able to say to himself, albeit with a wry face, after all, it's grist to the mill." These stories are magazine commodities—all but two of them came out in the *Cosmopolitan*—on about the same level as Sherlock Holmes; but Sherlock Holmes has more literary dignity precisely because it is less pretentious. Mr. Maugham makes play with more serious themes, but his work is full of bogus motivations that are needed to turn the monthly trick. He is for our day, I suppose, what Bulwer-Lytton was for Dickens's: a half-trashy novelist, who writes badly, but is patronized by half-serious readers, who do not care much about writing. (pp. 319-26)

> *Edmund Wilson, "The Apotheosis of Somerset Maugham," in his* Classics and Commercials: A Literary Chronicle of the Forties, *Farrar, Straus and Company, 1950, pp. 319-26.*

John Pollock

[*In the following excerpt, Pollock assesses Maugham's principal methods of characterization, drawing examples from his published fiction.*]

Somerset Maugham's place in literature will be fixed in years to come. At least a generation must go by before anything like certainty can be achieved about a writer of eminence. Often the favourite of to-day is the outcast of to-morrow, and by no means seldom does the pendulum of critical judgement swing back later from unjust depreciation. There are even now signs that George Meredith is coming again into his own. My view about Somerset Maugham is that he will be set among writers at the top of the first class, both as novelist and as playwright, really great authors being apart and above. I do not think he can be classed with Fielding, Thackeray, Voltaire, Balzac, Tolstoy, or Gogol; still less with Shakespeare, Goethe, Marlowe, Sophocles, Euripides, Racine, and Molière. As a short-story writer he comes certainly very close to those three masters Kipling, most tremendous of all, Guy de

Maupassant, and Henry James, but it may be questioned whether, as a branch of art, the short story permits of development enough to enable true greatness to show itself.

This is by the way. I wish merely to show that Somerset Maugham is worthy to have his methods carefully considered, which might not be the case with an author, however good, of the second class like, say, George Eliot, Joseph Conrad, or Alphonse Daudet. It must always be of interest to see how a first-class writer, Anthony Trollope or Anatole France for instance, works. It is Somerset Maugham's method, or at least one part of his method, that I propose to study here, because it is the part that can best be studied with as little delay as possible after his death.

In the second half of his preface to *First Person Singular* Somerset Maugham deals with the question of how does an author come by his characters, and describes in a few incisive pages how traits from real persons among his acquaintance are used to create imaginary portraits. He refers to the notes of Henri Beyle, the letters of Flaubert, and the journal of Jules Renard as evidence that this is the general practice of authors. 'I think, indeed,' he writes, 'that most novelists, and surely the best, have worked from life. But though they have had in mind a particular person this is not to say that they have copied him nor that the character they have devised is to be taken for a portrait.' And he goes on to assert that to present an exact copy would be to defeat the author's aim, which is verisimilitude. 'Nothing,' he says, 'is so unsafe as to put into a novel a person drawn line by line from life. His values are all wrong and, strangely enough, he does not make the other characters of the book seem false, but himself. He never convinces.' Somerset Maugham's purpose in so discussing a novelist's method was to rebut the charge made against him of 'portraying certain persons so exactly that it was impossible not to know them,' in other words of painting word-portraits of real people. His method, he implies, was the method he has just praised, which was, as he might have said to strengthen his case had he thought it worth while, a method employed among others by Thackeray. The Marquis of Steyne is a famous example; George Warrington in *Pendennis* was in some respects drawn from Tennyson's great friend, George Venables, Wenham from J. W. Croker, Sir Pitt Crawley from Lord Rolle, and traits in Dorington, my father's godfather, went to make up the character of Major Pendennis. Meredith drew for Beauchamp on Admiral Maxse, and for *Diana of the Crossways* on Mrs Norton.

Somerset Maugham's own account of the manner in which he built up his characters from observation may be accepted without question. It is borne out by internal evidence. Only, as in Somerset Maugham the power of observation was developed to an unusually acute degree, so do his studies of character in which strokes are drawn from living models tend to resemble those models more than is usually the case with other novelists and more perhaps than Somerset Maugham himself intended or, when challenged, would concede. In one case, he tells us, he did paint a deliberately literal portrait. That is the character of Mortimer Ellis, the 'celebrated' bigamist, in that enchanting story called **"The Round Dozen."** He suggests that we ought all to know who the original was, but I confess that I do not; neither do the few knowledgeable people I have asked. Mortimer Ellis is so vivid and so plausible a character that Somerset Maugham may be supposed, without realizing it, to have added certain features from his imagination, otherwise he would be offering a flat contradiction of his own thesis that 'a person drawn line by line from life . . . never convinces.' In reality his imagination was so keen, if perhaps more keen than wide, that he could hardly have avoided doing so. It is only because his faculty of observation was so uncommonly prominent that he has sometimes been thought deficient in imagination.

Without a powerful imagination, working almost always in the sphere of psychological analysis, Somerset Maugham could never have created the gallery of life-like characters we have from his pen. It is evident that in constructing them he worked as a rule on the lines he described. The method closely resembles that of a painter working from models on an imaginative subject. The degree in which imagination is blended with observation may vary *ad infinitum;* but, however important may be the former in the resultant mixture, it is rare that the model is not recognizable. (pp. 365-67)

Somerset Maugham used two lines of approach to his subjects. In one, he took what may be called the outer psychological values of a real person and wrought them into an imaginary portrait by embodying them in a series of incidents which had no relation, or only a very slight relation, to those of his model's actual life. In the other, he took the fundamental values and put them into fictitious persons who had otherwise no relation at all to his models. This again he would vary by taking real incidents and putting fictitious persons among them, so that his characters took upon themselves a strong colour of being observed from life. An instance of this is his story called **"The Letter,"** which he turned into a still more famous play. Here he took an incident from real life that had, years before, been the subject of a *cause célèbre* in the Far East. It had happened long before Somerset Maugham's visit to the spot, therefore he could not have known any of the persons concerned. But he fitted characters of his imagination to the facts with such skill and force as to create astonishment and no little pain in the minds of those who had been personally acquainted with the protagonists in the real drama. In general, however, he so mixed his variations of method and so embroidered his characters with imaginary touches that readers, unless possessed of special knowledge, might not realize the personages in the story to have been drawn from life. It is therefore a matter of literary and historical interest to track down some of the models from which Somerset Maugham worked. The list that I can give is doubtless far from complete. Nevertheless it contains some striking figures.

A very good specimen of a canvas containing such an admixture of traits observed in real men and women and of imaginary characters and events is to be found in *Ashenden; or, The British Agent.* Here we are at once confronted with a figure drawn from a living model: that of Ashenden himself, the narrator, who is clearly a self-portrait of the author. In the war of 1914-18, Somerset Maugham was engaged in our Intelligence Service in Switzerland and his note-book served as a basis for the stories. He says so openly. Events are seen through the eyes of the narrator, that is, his own. Apart from the fact that the key is given by Ashenden being a novelist, delicious little touches here and there produce an intimate note that surely reveals a bit of Maugham's own mind. Take this passage: Ashenden is in his bath. He 'sighed, for the water was no longer quite so hot, he could not reach the tap with his hand nor could he turn it with his toes (as every properly regulated tap should turn), and if he got up to add more hot water he might just as well get out altogether.' This is a reflexion so personal that no imagination however vivid could invent it. Ashenden is doubtless not wholly Somerset Maugham, but Somerset Maugham sat as his own model for 'the British Agent.' To clinch the matter, Ashenden reappears later as the narrator and unfashionable novelist in *Cakes and Ale,* with the Christian name of Willie, which was Maugham's own, and gives us therein much interesting insight into Maugham's mind. Later again Maugham explicitly admitted his identity with Ashenden.

The entire book, *Ashenden,* gives the impression of being studded with similar scraps of reality, jotted down here and there from Maugham's actual experiences. It is a fairly safe wager that R., the enigmatic colonel who is Ashenden's chief, would be recognized by others in the same service. On the other hand many of the characters, the hairless Mexican, for instance, Miss King, the Hindu conspirator and his cabaret love, and Mr Hamilton, that priceless American, seem to bear the hallmark of invention: they are far more types than living individuals, however cunningly the types are individualized. It is not till late in the book that two of its personages other than Ashenden himself stand out with startling actuality. In the story called **"His Excellency"** there can be no question to those who knew him but that the model for the ambassador was Sir George Buchanan. Somerset Maugham does not directly mention Petrograd as the scene of the story, though he implicitly admits it in his preface to be so, but even were this not the case the portrait of Sir George Buchanan would be unmistakable. Here we have a striking example of Somerset Maugham's more usual manner of dealing with his models. All the facts narrated in the career of his ambassador are invented: the strange romance that his Excellency reveals in his life had plainly no counterpart whatever in that of Sir George Buchanan, although the minor romance which interrupts the career of the diplomat in the story called Byring had with equal certainty a basis in fact. But this apart, the psychological portrait of Buchanan, as he appeared at all events to visitors like Ashenden, is a masterpiece. That of his Excellency's wife, on the other hand, is totally unlike Lady Georgina Buchanan, who was so impressive a personality that the neglect of her by Somerset Maugham as a model clearly shows his intention not to copy reality, but merely to borrow traits from it. (pp. 367-69)

Somerset Maugham's photographic power of observation was so acute that he could hardly look at anyone without features and characteristics being imprinted on his mental retina, and stored up for future use in one or another fictitious personage. This must be the reason why so many of the characters created by him, even without his wishing it, and apart from the cases where he deliberately used models, call up to the reader's mind such and such a man or woman in real life. Actors who saw in *Theatre* an unfriendly hit at the stage were much mistaken. No personal malice was intended; Maugham simply used actors and actresses as all with whom he came in contact, as the raw material for fiction. Those shocked by *Theatre* might have taken comfort from *The Three Fat Women of Antibes,* in which hilarious tale the still exquisite, but fat and greedy, Arrow Sutcliffe was unquestionably studied by Maugham from the rich, beautiful, but always massive American actress, Maxine Elliott. . . .

Friendliness to his models was not usual with Somerset Maugham, who doubtless found asperity to give a heightened tone to his portraits. This may have been the main cause of the outburst that greeted *Cakes and Ale,* which contains some of the most remarkable of them. An impulsive American lady even wrote a whole book, so indignant was she at Maugham's treatment of Thomas Hardy in *Cakes and Ale.* The author was thoroughly justified in denying that Edward Driffield was a portrait of Thomas Hardy and Alroy Kear a portrait of Hugh Walpole. They were not portraits in the same sense as Reginald Eves's oil painting is a portrait of Hardy; once more all the facts about the men in the book are invented; and Rosie, who Maugham tells us haunted him for years, is wholly a creature of his imagination. What Somerset Maugham did was to make psychological studies of his models and then let the characters behave as he conceived they must in hypothetical circumstances. (p. 371)

Somerset Maugham's second line of approach to his models, namely by taking their fundamental values and putting them into fictitious persons, is perfectly illustrated by his treatment of himself in *Of Human Bondage.* No one could ever doubt that the hero of his book, Philip, represents Maugham himself; and this is admitted in the preface to the volume in the collected edition of 1937. It is a spiritual autobiography. But the spiritual truth is set in trappings of slender verisimilitude. Philip's experiences at school must be reminiscences of Somerset Maugham's own youth; those at the hospital are evidently drawn from life; but the master thread on which this long chaplet of pearls is strung is not a bit of reporting. This is Philip's club foot. Somerset Maugham was not a cripple. Then how does this dominant motive, absent from the author's life, fit into an autobiographical novel? Very simply. Philip's crippled leg in the book is Somerset Maugham's stammer in real life. The author's infirmity was transmuted by him into a totally different sort of infirmity, graver physically, but morally perhaps not more galling than his. From Philip we know of the dreadful mental pain suffered by Somerset Maugham as the result of his infirmity, just as in Philip's torment in the linen-draper's shop we can read Maugham's detestation of the drudgery entailed by his medical practice in Lambeth. (373-74)

Another glimpse of Somerset Maugham's soul comes to us, I submit, in that brilliant short story, **"The Human Element."** Here, unless my shot is off the mark, Maugham projected something of his own feelings into the character

of Lady Betty Welldon-Burns, daughter of a duke and electric leader of the bright young people in London, who retires to the Isle of Rhodes to live maritally with Albert, formerly 'the second footman at Aunt Louise's.' This drama is kept on the plane of high comedy and we are allowed to feel its deeper repercussions only in the despair of Humphrey Carruthers, the cultured Foreign Office clerk who vainly tries first to win, then to save, Lady Betty. 'What destroys me,' says Carruthers, 'what makes me so frightfully unhappy, is to think of her unspeakable degradation. . . . I admired her courage and her frankness, her intelligence and her love of beauty. She's just a sham and she's never been anything else.' In his rôle as narrator Somerset Maugham makes answer.

> I wonder if that's true. Do you think any of us are all of a piece? Do you know what strikes me? I should have said that Albert was only the instrument, her toll to the solid earth, so to speak, that left her soul at liberty to range the empyrean. Perhaps the mere fact that he was so far below her gave her a sense of freedom in her relations with him that she would have lacked with a man of her own class. The spirit is very strange, it never soars so high as when the body has wallowed for a period in the gutter.

It is difficult not to see here an apologia for Maugham's own way of life that cut him off for some years and in some degree from regular intercourse with men of his own station and from completely normal society. This partial and self-imposed ostracism, accentuated by Maugham's firm refusal ever to attach himself to a literary clique, seems to be reflected in Lady Betty's withdrawal from the great world, to live with her own thoughts and her own tastes on a far-off Greek island. Maugham was too big a man to fall in with the artifices of London literary snobs. They distrusted and envied his success; they feared his biting pen. His place was achieved by himself alone, against all adventitious aids. But to achieve it he had to withdraw within himself, and his professional aloofness was redoubled not only by his infirmity but by the ordering of his life that was in no way flaunting or tinged with proselytism but, though discreet and purely personal, none the less put him at odds with received British ethical standards. (pp. 374-75)

John Pollock, "Somerset Maugham and His Work," in The Quarterly Review, *Vol. 304, No. 650, October, 1966, pp. 365-78.*

Maugham on his critical reception:

In my twenties the critics said I was brutal, in my thirties they said I was flippant, in my forties they said I was cynical, in my fifties they said I was competent, and now in my sixties they say I am superficial. I have gone my way, following the course I had mapped out for myself, and trying with my works to fill out the pattern I looked for. I think authors are unwise who do not read criticisms. It is salutary to train oneself to be no more affected by censure than by praise; for of course it is easy to shrug one's shoulders when one finds oneself described as a genius, but not so easy to be unconcerned when one is treated as a nincompoop.

***From his* The Summing Up (*1938*).**

R. Barton Palmer

[*In the following essay, Palmer contends that the narrative strength and artistic excellence of* Cakes and Ale; or, The Skeleton in the Cupboard *are due to the novel's autobiographical basis.*]

The prevailing academic View of W. Somerset Maugham has changed little since David Daiches [in his *The Present Age in British Literature,* 1958], pronounced him "an accomplished professional writer" whose fiction lacked "any original vision of humanity or any great distinction of style." Unlike true artists, Daiches suggested, Maugham wrote to make money and, striving to sell books, failed to produce anything deserving serious critical attention: "Maugham's writings are offered as entertainment rather than as profound and original interpretations of the human situation. Even the fair number of academic studies devoted to his writing in recent years has failed to persuade the vast majority who share Daiches' views. The explanation, I think, is simple. Like Daiches, even those sympathetic to Maugham have emphasized his professionalism. Maugham himself would certainly be pleased by this, since the professional writer was the public role he cultivated. But this image is only partly correct. Maugham was not simply a successful hack who appealed to ephemeral middlebrow tastes. He was instead a writer whose urge to communicate artistic truth conflicted with and was finally overcome by a stronger desire for financial gain and popular acclaim. And this struggle is recorded in a most illuminating way in the autobiographical *Cakes and Ale,* a novel whose importance for the understanding of Maugham and career has been sadly neglected. Though *Cakes and Ale* treats, in short, the problem of Maugham and writer, the novel (and Maugham's deepest intentions in it) have been misconceived from its initial publication, ironically because Maugham the professional did his best to make it seem a simple entertainment.

When it appeared in 1930, *Cakes and Ale* achieved overnight notoriety. Largely set in an Edwardian Bloomsbury and peopled with a host of venal or mediocre *litterati,* the novel announced itself as a playfully malicious *roman à clef,* whose satire was aimed at certain well-known men of letters as well as, more generally, at the commercialism of the literary establishment. No small furor erupted upon *Cakes and Ale's* publication. Those who felt attacked (principally Hugh Walpole) and their supporters (chiefly the admirers of the recently dead Thomas Hardy) protested the vilification to an "incredulous" Maugham who denied all. The scandal culminated, rather laughably, in the appearance of *Gin and Bitters,* an amateurish spoof by an obscure American writer that accused Mr. Maugham of pillorying in print those who had shown him friendship or hospitality. At the time, Maugham claimed that both Alroy Kear, the self-promoting author of meager talent, and Edward Driffield, the burnt-out grand old man of letters, were composite characters drawn from many sources. But readers and critics alike found unmistakable the resemblances to Walpole and Hardy. In the preface to The Modern Library edition published twenty years later, Maugham finally admitted that, in the case of Walpole at least, he had had some deliberate fun. We can therefore conclude that Maugham envisioned the scandal his novel

was to arouse. He was unquestionably too astute an observer of the literary scene to think that a biting caricature of one of England's most popular novelists would cause less than a sensation. He was also, doubtless, not surprised when, boosted by this publicity, *Cakes and Ale* sold briskly. The serious critics, however, like Mark Van Doren writing in *The Nation,* appraised *Cakes and Ale* less highly than the book-buying public. Thinking it another exercise in the acerbic humor for which Maugham, as a popular West End playwright, had long since developed a reputation, Van Doren found it a "witty" but "very slight" effort.

But only partly was it Maugham's aim to debunk commercial belles lettres and attach the *eminences grises* whose fame he perhaps begrudged (while naturally insuring for himself some healthy royalties in the process). Only the novel's background is peopled with satiric portraits of the famous and prominent. The main character is the successful writer Willie Ashenden, a Maugham *persona,* whose struggles to escape fake intellectualism, pseudo-art, and social narrow-mindedness are the book's main subject. Maugham's wicked humor, however, made it difficult for even perceptive critics like Van Doren to see what he was about. As a result, when the novel was re-issued in a Penguin edition (1948), Maugham felt it necessary to explain what should have been obvious to anyone possessed of a passing acquaintance with his work: "After so many years I did not see why I should not get closer to the facts. The Uncle William, Rector of Blackstable, and his wife Isabella, became Henry, vicar, and his wife, Sophie. The Philip Carey of the earlier book became the I of *Cakes and Ale.*"

The novel, as Maugham reveals, draws upon the autobiographical material treated earlier in *Of Human Bondage* (1915), but, more important, incorporates certain technical changes to make its presentation more authentic ("closer to the facts"). The new names for his uncle and aunt signal a different emotional tone. And by making his *persona* the main character and narrator, Maugham is able to structure the story in a more successful fashion. This new treatment, Maugham hints, was made possible by the fifteen years or so that had elapsed since he had finished *Of Human Bondage,* a period of time that afforded him reflection on his early life and his fictional treatment of it. The relationship between the two works, however, has been largely disregarded. Writing in 1938 about "The Maugham Enigma," Malcolm Cowley singles out *Of Human Bondage* as Maugham's only really competent work and identifies the novel's strength as its authentic material. Cowley finds Maugham's other novels inferior because they possess neither the sincerity nor the depth of feeling in *Of Human Bondage.* Disregarding the autobiography in *Cakes and Ale,* Cowley proclaims that, after 1915, Maugham would "never return to the material that was closest to his heart." Maugham thus becomes a writer whose one first-rate book stands out from the incredible volume of simply competent work that he produced. This view prevails among those critics who, unlike Daiches, find some value in Maugham's fiction.

Cakes and Ale, like *Of Human Bondage,* also avoids inauthenticity because it draws on Maugham's experience. Moreover, the novel proves that the composition of *Of Human Bondage* was no accident (i.e. Maugham's one lapse into art from a determination to make money by producing strictly what the public wanted). In *Cakes and Ale* we get a glimpse of Maugham the artist, doing his best to improve the power and structure of his fiction. Perhaps because he was writing about what he knew best, his own self, Maugham likewise avoids that unsympathetic and unengaging treatment of human foibles that mars much of what he was to write. In *Cakes and Ale* Ashenden finally excuses the faults of hypocrites, snobs, and pretenders with genuine charity, largely because he was himself one of their number. The novel shows, in short, that Philip Carey and Willie Ashenden, seekers after truth and goodness, are honest projections of Maugham's own self, or, at least, of the best part of that self. I do not deny, of course, that Maugham was always tempted by commercial success to produce work that fattened his bank account but hardly advanced his reputation. His battle (finally, of course, a losing one) was much like Willie Ashenden's: a struggle to free himself from a drive for success that would deny happiness and true creativity.

In the novel Maugham the professional is represented by Alroy Kear, the middlebrow novelist who so assiduously courts public recognition and critical approval. Although on a superficial level Kear is simply a caricature of Hugh Walpole, like so much in the novel he also reflects Maugham's personal experience. In the 1948 preface, Maugham observes that there is in him "a great deal of myself." The unflattering portrait, he goes on to explain, constitutes both self-analysis and self-criticism: "For I have a grim capacity for seeing my own absurdity and I find in myself much to excite my own ridicule." We are right to take this statement at face value because the resemblances between Kear and Maugham are close. Like Kear, Maugham at the time was conscious of his public and anxious to increase both his reputation and the sale of his books. Not only did he write pot boilers; he also produced publishers' blurbs, introduced collections of others' works, and penned critical prefaces for anthologies.

If Kear suggests what Maugham was at the time, Edward Driffield, suggests what he imagined he might become. A novelist of modest talents who becomes the grand old man of British letters through the promotion of others and, chiefly, through his longevity, Driffield, his sources of creativity cut off by the social climbing of his second wife, outlives his ability to write. In 1950 Maugham recognized that he was progressing toward that same "sad, absurd and transitory eminence." Like Maugham, Driffield writes well when he sticks to his own experience. Ashenden's criticism of Driffield's fiction not surprisingly echoes the views which Cowley and others have advanced of Maugham's. Dismissing as barely competent all but one of Driffield's novels, Ashenden discovers that *The Cup of Life* (the only book that, as the title indicates, possesses authenticity) draws its power from a painful episode in

Driffield's life. Speaking about *Of Human Bondage,* Maugham revealed that, in the midst of a successful career as an author of light comedy, he found himself forced to write about his early life in order to rid his mind of an unhappy childhood's oppressive memories. Like Driffield, Maugham came to know the cathartic power of fiction. And like Ashenden, he recognized the artistic value of an imagined reality firmly based on felt life. If Kear and Driffield, then, are indeed caricatures of Walpole and Hardy, they, and Ashenden, are reflections of Maugham himself. The novel's satire is thus not only a source of amusement, but also a way of clarifying Ashenden's rejection of commercialism and creative impotence.

Cakes and Ale's first section traces Ashenden's refusal to join Kear in a project that will serve not the interests of truth, but rather Kear's desire to profit by falsifying it. Kear wants Ashenden's help in writing a biography of the recently deceased Edward Driffield. Like Kear's fiction, the book is calculated to give the public what it wants, not the real novelist, whose creative power will always be masked by the puzzling incongruities of his actual existence, but the figure that literary society demands, free from complexity, contradiction, and indecorousness. Kear's memorial will do in death what the second Mrs. Driffield, Kear's backer in the project, was never able to do for her husband in life, convert him into the very image of respectability. The literary enterprise Kear promotes is thus from the outset identified with a life forced into the unnatural mold of reasonless convention. His collaboration with the second Mrs. Driffield suggests the connection between social hypocrisy and pseudo-art that is one of the novel's main themes. Ashenden, however, believes that the biography would be better if it drew Driffield "warts and all." Kear fears the public reaction to the truth: "It would be rather amusing to show the man with his passion for beauty and his careless treatment of his obligations, his fine style and his personal hatred for soap and water, his idealism and his tippling in disreputable pubs; but honestly, would it pay?"

As a self-proclaimed "gentleman," Kear knows that lies are easier to believe than the truth and cause the teller less embarrassment. Ashenden refuses to help. The remainder of his narrative, however, consists of Ashenden's reminiscences of his connection with Driffield and his two wives during childhood, early adult life, and finally middle age. *Cakes and Ale* thus becomes the book that Kear would not write; a remembered truth ordered by the imagination. But those memories, while they do round out the character of Driffield, do more to complete Ashenden's self-description. He recalls those events that have formed his sensibilities and outlook. Finally, the other characters, including Driffield, are important only insofar as they have contributed to this sentimental education.

Besides Driffield, the most important of these is Rosie, the first Mrs. Driffield who helps Ashenden shed the narrow-minded bourgeois conventions of his upbringing and introduces him to sexual joy. Like many of the characters and much of the action, Rosie is based on a living original. But she had nothing to do with Maugham's experiences as a young man, nor did he connect her, in the early stages of invention, with the story he meant to write of an older writer whose talent had run out. Her appearance in the novel results from the synthesizing effect of Maugham's imagination, from the same kind of process which in the novel causes Ashenden to recall and relate the experiences which he does.

In this respect *Cakes and Ale* differs once again from Maugham's first fictional version of his early life. *Of Human Bondage* faithfully follows the chronology of that life, except that it ends with Philip's marriage to Sally Athelny, the good woman whom Philip admires but cannot love. This finale to his search for identity and happiness is, however, unsatisfactory, not so much because it is the product of pure imagination, but because it is what Maugham termed a "wish fulfillment." Sally, in other words, is the *dea ex machina* Maugham hoped could end Philip's struggles (and his own) for emotional stability and reconciliation to society. Thus *Of Human Bondage* ends with Philip institutionalizing his commitment to live in a world whose values he has hitherto rejected. We can see no way that Sally can deliver Philip to happiness except by imposing a new "bondage," that of family responsibility, upon him. Rosie, however, is conceived as Willie's means of escape. She helps him as a child to rid himself of the foolish snobbery that is the legacy of his uncle and aunt. And when he meets her again as a young man, she becomes a source of genuine sexual love. Though she finally deserts him to run off with another man, Rosie remains for Ashenden, as he grows older, that true and good image which inspires his art. Kear's book will ignore her important influence on Driffield's creativity because her flagrant though harmless promiscuity hardly fits the narrow conventions of the life Kear intends to write. She is the "skeleton in the closet" (the novel's subtitle) who would spoil the ersatz propriety of his biography. Ashenden's infatuation with her, however, is hardly romanticized. His last and chance meeting with her is with a Rosie grown wizened and plump, now more a Wife of Bath than a Beatrice. But that meeting reinforces his acceptance of a life without illusions or pretense.

Thus *Cakes and Ale,* because of Rosie, is in a sense an even more imaginary kind of autobiography than *Of Human Bondage.* But it is also "closer to the facts," that is, more representative of the mature view of life that Maugham in his middle years had come to hold. The harshness and misery of his youth (which are unrelentingly portrayed in the earlier book) are redeemed by what he had learned, much later, could redeem them. The social airs and the meanness of his uncle and aunt are in *Cakes and Ale* balanced by the bohemianism and generosity of Driffield, Rosie, and her lover, Lord George. Likewise, Willie's love for Rosie, which grows beyond irrational passion and jealousy, contrasts with Philip's desperate obsession with the unworthy Mildred. Maugham's second attempt at a portrait of his young artistic self makes us understand not only how a bourgeois society lays its traps for the man who would live and write what is true. We are also made to understand how the artist escapes from and is simultaneously reconciled to that society, finding the strength to deny as well as affirm the world that made him. The story of Philip Carey is given at last its proper end.

And that story is given as well its proper form. Because it follows strictly the chronology of his experience, *Of Human Bondage* lacks a proper *mythos* (the end ever receding into the present, the novel can only finish with what, we have seen, is the unhappy device of the wedding). In addition, because Maugham follows James in using a third person point of view limited to the awareness of the main character but (unlike James) does not dramatize fully the workings of Philip's mind, his characterization of Philip is largely external. But the story of Philip's development is a story of inner change, of spiritual and emotional growth only roughly represented by the workings of the plot. Maugham's switch to first person-main character narration, however, makes him stay closer to Willie's sensibilities. Perhaps because first person narration is so common in Maugham's other work, the use of the narrator in *Cakes and Ale* has been much misunderstood. The *persona* of Maugham's other fiction projects the curious complexities of human character, particularly the admixture of the admirable and foolish, onto the exotic people he meets or is told about. He accuses himself, however, of nothing more blameworthy than the obvious failings of self-indulgent urbanity. He observes but does not participate. Unaffected by the human sorrow and strangeness he describes, he engages no more than our polite interest. In *Cakes and Ale,* however, Willie Ashenden tells his own story. He indicts the narrowmindedness of the prim and proper Blackstable of his youth most strongly in the portrait he draws of his own self. If first person narration is often a device that allows Maugham to distance himself from the story he tells, he does not so use it in *Cakes and Ale.*

He himself recognized that the first person narrator, though obviating the problem of proper focusing that the omniscient method entails, tends "to appear pallid in comparison with the persons he is concerned with." This effect is naturally quite appropriate for those stories in which the narrator figures as a raconteur not a participant. It presents a difficulty only when, as here, the narrator is indeed the central character. In *Cakes and Ale,* however, the narrative materials are unified only by association; the narrator can thus function both as character and commentator. The initial section, set in the present, is dramatic. Ashenden relates the encounter with Kear that leads, first, to his rejection of the financially prudent whitewashing Kear has in mind and, second, to the reminiscing that, as he verbalizes it, becomes both a biography of Driffield and an autobiography. Ashenden's character, in other words, is developed by contrast with Kear's; the rest of the novel demonstrates how Ashenden became the man he is. This structure avoids the problem of the ending which a chronological approach to experience necessarily faces. Ashenden's character, as we first perceive it, is in effect a *stasis;* only the remembered actions constitute an evolution. The reading and re-reading of Proust that absorbed Maugham in the years after the composition of *Of Human Bondage* most likely influenced him deeply and inspired him to restructure his own story as a journey of the mind in search of self. In *Cakes and Ale* Maugham is thus able to escape the tyranny of simple chronology, which in *Of Human Bondage* so complicates his telling of Philip's maturing.

We can therefore endorse Maugham's own view that *Cakes and Ale* is "closer to the facts." But the important point is not that it is the better novel, but rather that Maugham wrote it in response to an inner compulsion to make more truthful and satisfactory what cannot, *pace* Daiches, be termed other than his "original interpretation of the human situation." And the novel also, perhaps surprisingly, reveals why it is as a "professional" writer that Maugham is largely remembered today. Unlike Joyce, he did all he could to insure that *Cakes and Ale* would be read as an exercise in wit not as a *bildungsroman*. The attacks on Hardy and Walpole, as he undoubtedly foresaw, aroused a controversy that boosted the novel's sales. At the same time, however, the prefaces to the later editions can hardly be read otherwise than as appeals to make his readers take the novel more seriously.

The key to understanding Maugham's actions, of course, is found in the novel itself. The conflict between Willie Ashenden, the artist committed to truth who scorns social hypocrisy, and Alroy Kear, the writer who assiduously and unscrupulously pursues popularity, reflects the struggle in Maugham's own self. In *Cakes and Ale,* however, Willie's victory is relatively easy, accomplished by a gentlemanly rejection of Kear and his project. Maugham himself was never able to sustain Willie's position for long. *The Summing Up* (1938) treats once again, but this time as memoirs, the events of Maugham's early life. Like *Cakes and Ale,* the book is filled with evident self-satisfaction, but, one feels, this self-satisfaction Maugham can achieve only because, speaking as a public figure, he avoids the conflicts that beset him as a writer and man. Only in *Cakes and Ale* does Maugham thoroughly reveal his own desire to escape the double trap of pandering to his readers and living the life expected of a literary figure. Finally, however, he could not avoid (and of this his contemporary reputation is an eloquent witness) the paths which lead Alroy Kear and Edward Driffield to the uncertain celebrity so thoroughly exposed in *Cakes and Ale.* Only behind the *persona* of Willie Ashenden could Maugham as a writer sustain the philosophical balance of *The Summing Up,* whose meditations on the psychic and physical trauma of childhood are meliorated by an espousal of Truth, Beauty, and Goodness, those unchanging values which make life bearable. Only as a Willie freed for a time from the Alroy Kear within could he produce a novel with the compassion, the artistry, and the optimism of *Cakes and Ale.* (pp. 54-62)

> *R. Barton Palmer, "Artists and Hacks: Maugham's 'Cakes and Ale'," in* South Atlantic Review, *Vol. 46, No. 4, November, 1981, pp. 54-63.*

Joseph Epstein

[*Epstein is an American educator and critic. In the following excerpt, he provides an assessment of Maugham's career and reputation.*]

> The critic I am waiting for is the one who will explain why, with all my faults, I have been read for so many years by so many people.
> —W. Somerset Maugham

"Four powers govern men: avarice, lust, fear, and snobbishness." Somerset Maugham didn't write that; Hilaire Belloc did. But Somerset Maugham, I think it fair to say, believed it. Avarice, lust, fear, and snobbishness are Maugham's great subjects; they are everywhere in his work, as theme, as motive, as background. Small wonder that they would be, for the same dark quartet—avarice, lust, fear, and snobbishness—were also the four reigning qualities in Somerset Maugham's own triumphant, lengthy, and finally rather sad life.

Cyril Connolly once called Somerset Maugham the "last of the great professional writers." He meant it as an honorific. It has not always been taken that way. One small step down from the professional writer is the hack; one large step up is the artist. A great many more critics have been willing to drop Maugham a step than have been willing to raise him a step. Maugham was always highly conscious of this; and one could string together a quite long necklace composed of the BB's he shot over his lifetime at highbrow critics, small-public writers, intellectual-magazine editors, and others who accorded his work less respect than he thought it deserved. "But you must remember the intelligentsia despise me," Maugham in late life told his nephew Robin Maugham. "Take that magazine that's indoors. What's it called? *Encounter?* Well, all the writers on *Encounter* despise me completely. I read it just to find out what's going on and what people are interested in. But I must confess I find it terribly boring." Not the least interesting item in that snippet of conversation is that, whatever his professed views of *Encounter,* Maugham nevertheless subscribed to and read it. He was a man who didn't miss much. (p. 1)

Somerset Maugham never worked at any other job but that of writer over the course of his ninety-one years. He never descended to journalism, or worked as a publisher's reader, or took on literary or any other kind of odd jobs. He lived on the £150 income from his small inheritance, not an impressive sum even then. Nor did success come quickly. He published a first novel, *Liza of Lambeth,* at twenty-three, which, though it garnered decent reviews, earned no serious income. He had book-length manuscripts rejected. He wrote plays that were produced but enjoyed only brief runs and others that were not produced at all. At one point he moved to Paris, where he lived, frugally, among English and American expatriate writers and painters, among whom was the businesslike Arnold Bennett, who suggested that Maugham share a mistress with him and a third party. But there was nothing of the bohemian about Maugham, who was an Edwardian under and atop the skin and who, though he took a serious interest in the avant-garde art of his day, wished to avoid the garret style of life that often produced it. It was only in 1907, at the age of thirty-three, that Maugham was able to strike the success going with a comedy of manners entitled *Lady Frederick,* which ran for 442 performances in London. The music of that gong was something he had longed to hear, for Maugham was a money writer; as he would later aver, "Money was like a sixth sense without which you could not make the most of the other five." Henceforth all that he wrote turned to gold, piles and piles of gold.

Granted that accounting may be no proper part of literary criticism, the amounts of money Somerset Maugham earned by his pen are too impressive to be ignored. As a successful playwright, Ted Morgan asserts [in *Maugham,* 1980], Maugham "bridged the quarter century between Oscar Wilde and Noël Coward," which is chronologically accurate but leaves Shaw out of reckoning. Nonetheless, during these years Maugham always had a play or two running in London and New York theaters and at one point had four plays running concurrently in London's West End. (He generally took no more than three or four weeks to write a play.) No writer to this day has had more novels, stories, and plays turned into movies. (pp. 3-4)

While widening his social horizons, money broadened his subject matter; it made him worldly in a way that a writer who struggles ceaselessly for a living can never quite hope to be. As the Maughamish character named Ashenden says in the story entitled **"Giulia Lazzari,"** "just as the advantage of culture is that it enables you to talk nonsense with distinction, so the habit of luxury allows you to regard its frills and furbelows with a proper contumely." (p. 4)

Maugham thought of himself, interestingly, as a professional humorist, which in his stories he calls himself more than a few times, and in one of his Ashenden stories, **"The Traitor,"** he speaks of "the pleasant comedy of life." He meant this, I believe, in the sense in which one speaks of the human comedy. He put his case in *The Summing Up,* where he wrote: "A sense of humour leads you to take pleasure in the discrepancies of human nature; it leads you to mistrust great professions and look for the unworthy motive that they conceal; the disparity between appearance and reality diverts you and you are apt when you cannot find it to create it." If the humorist sometimes misses truth, beauty, and goodness, he is nonetheless tolerant, for he has no interest in moralizing but is "content to understand; and it is true that to understand is to pity and forgive."

While there was nothing of the aesthete about Maugham, nor any aesthetic difficulty about his work, few modern writers have been clearer about their own aesthetic program and, with the exceptions of Paul Valéry and Henry James, perhaps none has thought more trenchantly about the aesthetic questions raised by literary creation. Maugham thought, for example, that the artist is not justified in wishing to be judged by his intention; for him the crucial moment in the aesthetic transaction is that of communication—that moment when the work of art addresses the viewer or listener or reader. He thought talent to be made up of a natural aptitude for creation combined with a strong outlook on life shorn of the prejudices of the current day. "Sometimes," he wrote in *Don Fernando,* "there will be found a man who has this facility for writing to an extraordinary degree and to this joins an outlook on life which is not only peculiar to himself, but appeals to all men, and then he will be called a genius." Once, when asked the secrets of his own craft by a Chinese professor, he replied: "I know only two. One is to have common sense and the other is to stick to the point."

Maugham may also have been among the best read of

modern writers. He never travelled any distance without a laundry bag filled with books, and he read, as one would imagine, with penetration. He adored the Russian novelists and admired Stendhal. The French called him the English Maupassant, which pleased him greatly. He thought Kipling and Chekhov, along with Maupassant, the ablest of the world's short-story writers. He had mixed feelings about Henry James, on the one hand thinking him amusingly absurd and finding himself unable to believe in the motivations of the characters in his fiction and on the other hand remarking, in his essay **"Some Novelists I Have Known"**: "the fact remains that those last novels of his, notwithstanding their unreality, make all other novels, except the very best, unreadable." But generally he expressed his own personal preference for the straightforward over the ornate, for among prose writers he preferred Dryden and Hazlitt and Arnold and Cardinal Newman over Dr. Johnson and De Quincey and Carlyle and Pater. Here he joined the majority in preferring those who are most like himself.

One cannot read much in Maugham without recognizing that his own straightforward prose style came into being as a result of conscious artistry. He was a careful student of prose, which he wrote about extremely well in an essay on Edmund Burke as well as in *Don Fernando* and in *The Summing Up.* As a beginning novelist, he wrote under the influence of Pater and Oscar Wilde and other of the late Victorian decorative-prose stylists. He soon enough realized he had no talent in this line and set out to write more plainly, taking Swift as his model. (In later life he claimed he would have done better to have studied Dryden.) His own gifts, he recognized, were not poetical: lyricism was not his cup of tea, nor charming metaphors and cogent similes his sugar and milk. What he did have was clarity, logic, and an appreciation for euphonic language. On the subject of the formation of his own prose style, he wrote; "I knew that I should never write as well as I could wish, but I thought with pains I could arrive at writing as well as my natural defects allowed. On taking thought it seemed to me that I must aim at lucidity, simplicity and euphony."

Maugham's was a strong and a serviceable style. His prose tended to be more elegant when he was writing essays than when he was writing novels and stories. He himself remarked, in his essay on Edmund Burke's prose, that the most settled styles in the history of English prose belonged to essayists, divines, and historians, and that too settled—that is, too polished—a style might even redound to the disadvantage of the writer of fiction, who is primarily a teller of stories and whose prose needs to remain supple enough to capture so many shades of mood and to insinuate itself into the thoughts of various and often vastly different characters. "But perhaps it is enough if the novelist contents himself with avoiding the grosser errors of grammar," Maugham wrote, "for no one can have considered this matter without being struck by the significant and surprising fact that the four greatest novelists the world has seen, Tolstoi, Balzac, Dostoyevsky and Dickens, wrote their respective languages very carelessly. . . ." Here one can add the name Dreiser, the prose in whose powerful novels on occasion didn't even achieve the level of care-lessness.

Not that Maugham was ever close to being in the Dreiser class. (Dreiser himself, truth to tell, wasn't that often in the Dreiser class.) I have recently read what must amount to some four thousand pages of Maugham's prose and found myself seldom brought up by infelicities. In his ear-lier work he occasionally lapses into cliché; more than once he refers to the heart of one of his characters, in the heat of passion, going "pit-a-pat," when, for such a phrase, once is at least ten times too often. In *Of Human Bondage,* Sally Thorpe, the Dickensian sugarpuss heroine whom Philip Carey eventually marries, says to Carey, "You're an old silly, that's what you are," which causes one to blush, not for Carey but for Maugham. In the same book Mildred Rogers, the waitress who has enthralled Carey, is described as "weak as a rat," when rats are not generally thought weak at all but rather sinewy and tena-cious. Finally, in *The Razor's Edge* Maugham, who be-lieved that a writer of one nation has little chance of un-derstanding the people of another nation, has his male American characters use the words "gosh" and "gee" more often than Oogie Pringle on the old "A Date with Judy" radio show. Still, for roughly four thousand pages, that isn't bad.

As a stylist what Maugham had was lucidity, fluency, and economy. In a sheer storyteller, which is what he was, these are the paramount qualities. Often his stories seem almost to tell themselves; such ostensible artlessness, of course, can only be conferred through the exercise of high art. Maugham wrote every morning from 9:45 to 12:45, and he wrote quickly and revised little. He received no ed-iting from his publishers, Heinemann's in England and Doubleday in the United States, for he wanted none. As an author he was the equivalent to what in sports is known as a franchise player; with his huge sales, he could make a publishing house single-handedly, and publishers know not to fool with success of the kind such an author brings. In 1935, though, that curious figure Eddie Marsh, who had been a private secretary to Churchill, Asquith, and Jo-seph Chamberlain, offered to inspect Maugham's manu-scripts for lapses in precision and errors in usage, which he did do for fourteen of Maugham's books until his, Marsh's, death in 1953 and for which Maugham felt great gratitude. Maugham learned a good deal from Marsh, as he seemed to learn from everyone and everything, and as he grew older his prose grew more confident and more precise.

As a writer of fiction, Maugham's ambitions were Balza-cian. He believed an important writer needed to produce an ample body of work, and from that body deserved to be judged by the best of it. He claimed to have small pow-ers of imagination, which caused him to fall back on in-dustry to make up for it. "I have had one advantage," he wrote, "I have never wanted a subject. I have always had more stories in my head than I ever had time to write." He may not have had large powers of imagination but his powers of observation were of the first order. He plagia-rized from life, frequently putting people he knew or had heard about in his stories and novels. (As a result of his

writing many stories acquired in his travels in the Malay States, he was said to be considered very much non grata in the British clubs and outposts there.) "I have painted easel pictures," he wrote, "not frescoes." But when he was done he could fill many a gallery.

Why did Maugham write so much? Because, he might have answered, writing is what a writer is supposed to do, and besides, what else was he, who was rather easily bored, to do with his mornings? While at a certain point he no longer needed the money his pen brought in—a pen designed specifically for him, incidentally, with a thick collar that permitted a surer grasp—most assuredly he liked to see it come cascading in. He had, as the small busi-nessmen used to put it, a high nut, with the expenses of maintaining the princely establishment that was Villa Mauresque, paying (always resentfully) alimony to his wife, and travelling in the grand style; doubtless, too, as someone whose young manhood was perforce lived frugal-ly, he had no wish as a middle-aged and older man to dip into interest. But above all he appears to have written as much as he did because he loved to write, to go about with the characters from a story in his head, to work through the technical details of composition, to attempt to bring it all off as nearly perfect as possible. Whatever his mo-tives, working day after day he produced an immense body of writing, although not all of it was of even quality and some of it was pretty poor stuff.

Enter the critics. "This novel, as unmitigated a specimen of fictional drivel as has appeared under respectable au-thorship within living memory, might be fitly dismissed as the latest triumph of servant-girl's literature were it not for the phenomenal value that still attaches to Maugham's name among modern authors." That explosive sentence is the opening line from a 1941 review by Morton Dauwen Zabel in *The Nation* of Maugham's novel *Up at the Villa* [see Further Reading]. In its anger this review does not drop off precipitously from this first line. It goes on to at-tack Maugham for being "hostile to artistic risk," for "his career in the fashionable drawing-rooms and international cocktail sets of Europe," and for his derogations of Henry James; and the review ends by noting that "if the title of 'greatest living English novelist' is to be thrown around any further, it is time it landed in the right quarter. The greatest living English novelist is E. M. Forster." *Up at the Villa,* true enough, is a very poor novel; Maugham himself told Glenway Wescott that he was ashamed of having written it. But the poorness of the novel doesn't quite explain the vehemence of Zabel's review. Whence the anger in that review? Why the personal attack?

Edmund Wilson was even rougher on Maugham, saying that he was "second-rate" and that "his swelling reputa-tion in America"—the year was 1946—showed "a con-spicuous sign of the general decline of our standards." The occasion for Wilson's attack was another poor Maugham performance, *Then and Now,* his novel about Machiavelli. The quality of this book, Wilson pronounced, "is never . . . that either of a literary artist or of a first-rate critic of morals; and it may be worthwhile to say this at a moment when there seems to be a tendency to step up Mr. Maugham's standing to the higher ranks of English fiction, and when Mr. Maugham himself has been using his position of prestige for a nagging disparagement of his betters." Who, one may ask, might these betters be? They turn out to be the great modernist writers—Joyce and James and Yeats and Proust—of whom Maugham had, in Wilson's view, a far from adequate appreciation. For example, in a talk at the Library of Congress, Maugham had said:

> Proust, as we know, was enormously influenced by the now largely discredited philosophy of Henri Bergson and great stretches of his work turn upon it. I suppose we all read with a thrill of excitement Proust's volumes as they came out, but now when we reread them in a calmer mood I think what we find to admire in them is his wonderful humor and the extraordinarily vivid and interesting characters that he created in profusion.

Wilson counters that this is, in effect, philistine—true, one doesn't encounter all that many Proust-reading philistines—and that Proust's use of Bergson is crucial to his novel's being "the greatest philosophical novel ever written." I think Maugham was more correct than Wilson, but what we have here is a serious conflict of intellectual temperaments—that between a writer and a reader, which Maugham was, and a pure critic, which Edmund Wilson was. In his publication of this piece in *Classics and Commercials,* Wilson stepped up the vehemence of his attack on Maugham in a postscript in which he called him "a half-trashy novelist, who writes badly, but is patronized by half-serious readers, who do not care much about writing."

Maugham found admirers among men of letters and writers; among his supporters were Cyril Connolly, Virginia Woolf, Desmond MacCarthy, Evelyn Waugh and V. S. Pritchett; and Orwell wrote of him, "I believe the modern writer who has influenced me most is Somerset Maugham, whom I admire immensely for his power of telling a story straightforwardly and without frills." But among what he termed "highbrow critics" Maugham's name has never been an approved one. He knew this, and, though he pretended to be above it, one finds running throughout his work a sputtering volley of shots against "intellectuals," "highbrows," "the intelligentsia," and "critics of the intelligentsia," Maugham is partly to blame for incitement to critical riot against his own work.

Why did they detest Maugham so? Were they jealous of his success, the vast audience and riches his writing earned? Perhaps this entered into it, but more important, I suspect, was that his writing was an affront to them. He was apolitical and he wrote dead against the grain of modernism, with all its difficulty, preferring instead to write as plainly as possible about complex things. Say what one wishes against them, no one can accuse the modernist writers of not keeping critics gainfully employed. In an idle fantasy I sometimes think of these writers—Joyce and Eliot and Yeats and Kafka and the rest—mounted on motorcycles in a parade up the Champs-Élysées, a critic or two sitting in a small sidecar attached to each cycle, beaming with pleasure at being allowed along for the ride. But Maugham kept no sidecar; each of his books, to switch

metaphors rather abruptly, might have carried a small message, à la the Surgeon General's warning on cigarette packages, "No explanation, explication, or exegesis required. Read on without prolegomenon."

But one doesn't have to attack the modernist writers because one admires Somerset Maugham; nor need one think oneself half-serious for admiring him. Maugham remains intensely, immensely readable. Why? One recalls his revealing the secrets of his craft to the Chinese professor: "One is to have common sense and the other is to stick to the point." The point Maugham stuck to throughout his long career was the investigation of that magnificent, comic, admirable, outrageous, depressing, impressive, grim, gracious, grudging, great, and elusive thing called human nature. Human nature was Maugham's enduring subject, and for fiction there is none greater. If you are interested in it, you have to be interested in the writing of Somerset Maugham. As for his common sense, it was pervasive; the test is that he was an artist who knew that there are things in life greater than art. "I think," he wrote in *A Writer's Notebook,* "there is in the heroic courage with which man confronts the irrationality of the world a beauty greater than the beauty of art." Because he was able to insinuate such sentiments, subtly, dramatically, into his work—see, for an example, the story entitled **"Sanatorium"**—Maugham shall always be a writer for readers who care for more than writing alone.

And yet it is difficult to convey a precise impression of the quality of Maugham's work through naming two or three of his best books. He was right about himself in thinking that he was a writer of the kind for whom the body of his work is greater than the parts taken individually. Of his novels, I find only one, *Cakes and Ale,* completely successful. It is, I think, his masterpiece, a rich comedy about the literary life, its exactions and its delights and its fraudulence. It contains a dazzling portrait of the type of the literary widow and an even better account of the young literary hustler in the character of Alroy Kear, modeled, as it turns out, on Hugh Walpole—a man, as Maugham later averred, "easy to like, but difficult to respect." The literary widow, the literary hustler, the utterly self-absorbed artist, these are types that do not disappear, and Maugham was the first to mount them, like so many butterflies, on a narrative of seamless velvet.

Of his own books, Maugham said he liked *Cakes and Ale* best but tended to agree with the common opinion that held *Of Human Bondage* to be his most important work. In this latter, largely autobiographical book Maugham worked on a larger canvas than he ever would again; it is the sort of novel where one can introduce, for the first time, a major character as late as page 421. I first read *Of Human Bondage* when I was twenty and now I have re-read it approaching fifty, and it still seems to me immensely interesting. I tend to think of it as the best nineteenth-century novel written well into the twentieth century. It was publicly promoted at its publication by Theodore Dreiser in a review in *The New Republic* that made its reputation in America [see excerpt above]. Good as much of the book is, it nonetheless seems badly flawed toward its close by Maugham's need to resolve the action, to put an end to his young hero's troubles in a way that is not only conclusive but happy, and happy in the rather sappiest Dickensian mode.

I shall not run through all of Maugham's books that I have read or re-read, but I do think *The Razor's Edge* is in some ways representative of both Maugham's gifts and deficiencies. This is the novel, it will be recalled, about the quest of a young American named Larry Darrell for the ultimate truths about the meaning of life. In the character Isabel Maturin, Maugham created an extraordinarily vivid and hence persuasive portrait of a grasping American rich girl who wants *merely* everything. In Elliott Templeton, the wealthy expatriate American snob, Maugham has created a character of whom it is not ridiculous to say that, after the Baron de Charlus, he may well be the most interesting snob in modern literature. "I don't in the least mind pigging it at the Ritz," he announces at one point. Elliott Templeton is one of those characters whom you don't wish ever to leave the page, in the way one wants certain charming character actors never to leave the stage. Almost everything about *The Razor's Edge* is brilliant—except, alas, Larry Darrell's quest. This may be because goodness, which young Darrell is tiresomely meant to represent, is usually less interesting than its reverse; it may be because ultimate truths about the meaning of life are never quite convincing; it may be because Somerset Maugham's powers of idealization had long since withered. But *The Razor's Edge* resembles nothing so much as a ring with a large rhinestone at the center and with smaller but perfect gems all round it.

One is unlikely to encounter Maugham's books in a university curriculum. In my youth his work, because he was an international bestseller, was ubiquitous, and if one was at all bookish one was likely, when young, to have read *The Razor's Edge* and *Of Human Bondage;* or if one thought of oneself as artistic to have found self-justification in reading *The Moon and Sixpence,* his not very good novel modeled on the life of Paul Gauguin. Today I think the best introduction—or re-introduction— to Maugham is through his short stories. So many of these seem so good that it may be unjust to single out a few. But among the four volumes of stories now available in Penguin editions, **"Mr. Harrington's Washing"** is a work of comic genius; **"The Pool"** may be the best story ever written on the subject of going native; **"The Hairless Mexican"** is spy fiction raised to the highest power; and **"Lord Mount Drago"** is but one of his many stories that provide a cunning anatomy of snobbery. Maugham's nonfiction also bears looking into. At the top of his form he was a very capable essayist—see the volumes entitled *The Vagrant Mood* and *Points of View*—and *Don Fernando,* the book on Spanish culture, contains many clever and wise things. My sense is that it is best to read Maugham's stories and nonfiction first, and let them lead one back to the novels, where one is likely to discover that Maugham is one of those novelists who can be profitably read when young but who get better as one gets older.

Maugham would probably be best served by a single volume on the order of the "Viking Portable" series, except that, in his case, the volume, to suit his ample talent, would have to be of a thickness beyond portability. Such a volume, if I were its editor, would include all of *Cakes and Ale,* the better part of *The Summing Up,* the portrait of Elliott Templeton from *The Razor's Edge,* the essays on El Greco, Burke's prose, and Kant's aesthetics, and nearly everything he wrote on prose style. What would make the volume bulge, proving a severe test of the binder's art, would be the number of short stories that would have to be included. The short story really was Maugham's best form, and he published more than a hundred of them—among serious writers, perhaps only Chekhov wrote more. Some of his stories are thin, especially those that attempt to point an easy moral or have a trick ending, but the vast majority are very sturdily made. Those set in the Malay States, taken together, conduce to give as complete a picture of the British abroad as do Kipling's stories of India. Maugham's stories about the artistic life—**"The Alien Corn," "The Creative Impulse"** chief among them—are also too good not to be included.

Often Maugham's stories seem akin to reading La Rochefoucauld with illustrations—not drawings of course but illustrations from life. Maugham resembles La Rochefoucauld in taking avarice, lust, fear, and snobbishness for his subjects. Yet unlike La Rochefoucauld, Maugham's dark views about human nature are often stood on their head by evidence of courage, honesty, and integrity, almost always of an unexpected and complicated kind. Maugham is that odd phenomenon: a moralist who is never surprised by immorality. As he puts it in **"The Pool,"** "I held my breath, for to me there is nothing more awe-inspiring than when a man discovers to you the nakedness of his soul. Then you see that no one is so trivial or debased but that in him is a spark of something to excite compassion." (pp. 6-12)

Joseph Epstein, "Is It All Right to Read Somerset Maugham?" in The New Criterion, *Vol. IV, No. 3, November, 1985, pp. 1-13.*

Maugham on fictional characterizations:

I have been blamed because I have drawn my characters from living persons, and from criticisms that I have read one might suppose that nobody had ever done this before. That is nonsense. It is the universal custom.

From his *The Summing Up,* 1938.

John Whitehead

[*Whitehead, an English critic, is the editor of* W. Somerset Maugham, a Traveller in Romance: Uncollected Writings, 1901-1964 *(1984), and coeditor, with Anthony Curtis, of* W. Somerset Maugham: The Critical Heritage *(1987). In the following excerpt, Whitehead discusses plot, symbol, and structure in* Of Human Bondage.*]*

On qualifying as a doctor Maugham at once abandoned medicine for good and, with one novel already published and a second awaiting publication, set off for a long sojourn in Spain, determined to make his living by his pen. His next book was a collection of six short stories (including **"A Bad Example"** and **"Daisy"**) which Unwin's published under the title *Orientations* in 1899. (p. 30)

Besides these juvenile stories, none of which was ever included in any of the collected volumes of his stories, Maugham was spending his time in Spain writing an autobiographical novel, which he called "The Artistic Temperament of Stephen Carey". Since neither Unwin's nor the other publishers to whom he submitted the manuscript would pay him the advance he was asking, he put it aside until, forty years later, he presented it to the Library of Congress in Washington on the condition that it is never published. Some account of it, however, needs to be given . . . because it is in effect the first draft of the novel he published in 1915 under the title *Of Human Bondage.* (p. 31)

The novel, of about 90,000 words, was written in notebooks which were later bound into two volumes, and additionally there are several foolscap sheets tucked into a pocket at the end of the second volume continuing the story, probably at the suggestion of one of the publishers who read the manuscript, so as to give it a happy ending. Stephen Carey is first shown as a child playing with a toy theatre. His nurse comes in to tell him his mother has died, and going into her room he opens a cupboard and buries his face in the dresses hanging there, so that he can smell her scent. Orphaned, he goes to live at Woodlake with his Uncle John (who is not a clergyman) and Aunt Nellie, who have a daughter May, four years younger than Stephen. He is sent to Regis School, Tercanbury, where, because he is no good at games but wins many prizes for his work, he is bullied by the other boys. Unlike Philip Carey in *Of Human Bondage* he does not have a club-foot. While at school he tests the existence of God by praying to be made a better cricketer, a prayer that is not fulfilled; and his loss of faith is completed at Rouen (where he is sent to learn French) in conversation with an American, Francis House, with whom he discusses Religion and Patriotism. After two years he returns to England to become a solicitor's articled clerk and eventually qualifies as a solicitor. Also in the firm is Stanley Parsons, a man of the world under whose guidance Stephen develops a taste for smart clothes and snobbishness. He has an affair with May's governess Miss Wilkinson and for a brief period lives with her in London; his dismay at learning she is forty years old he expresses in the words: 'What a situation for a young man with an artistic temperament!' For he is a romantic youth who plays Wagner on the piano and is given to Byronic reveries. When Parsons leaves the firm he is replaced by Greene, with whom Stephen discusses Art and Literature.

Rose Cameron is a waitress at a teashop they frequent, with whom Stephen falls madly in love, and they spend a weekend together. She is thin and in bad health, and told by her doctor she is not strong enough to work becomes engaged to a commercial traveller Todd, who also frequents the teashop. Todd does not marry her, and when he abandons her, now pregnant, Stephen beats him up with cries of 'you cad!', 'you cur!' Stephen's relationship with Rose drags on miserably, he being too high-minded

to accept her offer to come and live with him. After a serious illness he returns to Woodlake and is nursed by May—now a 'Greek goddess'—who falls in love with him. Although he feels no more than affection for her, he likes the idea of the wealth she will inherit, and they become engaged. At this point he received an importunate letter from Rose asking him to see her, and May encourages him to go, wanting him to get Rose out of his system; but despite himself he again succumbs to her inexplicable charm and wakes up in a cheap Shaftesbury Avenue hotel with Rose asleep beside him. Instead of a farewell letter he leaves her a banknote.

It appears that Maugham originally intended to end the novel on a note of gloom with Stephen realizing that he has destroyed his chance of happiness and can never return to May. The foolscap sheets, however, carry the story a stage further to the point where Stephen returns to Woodlake intent on marrying May, thus securing his future as a landowner and a member of parliament. Maugham's intention in writing the novel, as reflected in the title, was to portray the development of an 'artistic temperament', by which he meant 'a Byronic soul', and its model appears to have been Goethe's *Wilhelm Meister*. There are enough references in the books he wrote at this period to support the view that he thought of Byronism in relation to himself, a term he used in reference to the mysterious moodiness of Childe Harold; and it is significant that when he came to rewrite the novel as *Of Human Bondage* he gave to its autobiographical hero the unmistakably Byronic appendage of a club-foot. One critic who has read the manuscript of 'Stephen Carey' dismissed it as loosely constructed, sloppily written, badly exaggerated and embarrassingly immature and crude [Robert L. Calder, *W. Somerset Maugham and the Quest for Freedom,* 1972]; so Maugham's later feeling of gratitude to the publishers who rejected it is understandable. (pp. 31-3)

. . . . .

Although Maugham gave his long autobiographical novel *Of Human Bondage* no other formal structure than its division into one hundred and twenty-two chapters, it does fall naturally into five parts of roughly equal length. It was essential in the first part of the novel to establish Philip Carey's boyhood and early youth in the reader's mind on a credible basis, so as to provide a foundation firm enough to support the topheavy edifice to be raised on it in the parts to come. That Maugham succeeded in this, if somewhat precariously, is borne out by the fact that the chapters dealing with Philip's lonely childhood under his uncle's reluctant guardianship in the vicarage at Blackstable, his unhappy time at Regis School, Tercanbury, and his gradual intellectual awakening at Heidelberg, make a more vivid and lasting impression on the reader than anything else in the novel apart from the crucial relationship with Mildred. The two themes implicit in this part concern Philip's gradual loss of belief in God, from which he concludes that he lacks 'the religious temperament', and his growing to sexual awareness at Heidelberg through discovering that Fraulein Cäcilie is having an affair with the Chinese student Sung: an awareness that remains theoretical owing to his inability to reconcile his romantic dreams with the reality represented by the whores he sees in the city's brothel quarter. Limping his way through these early years, he comes to recognize his club-foot as symbolizing some special handicap barring him from the easy routes to normal human happiness. As has been seen, the unpublished ur-novel from which *Of Human Bondage* developed placed no such disability on its hero, and it is worth pausing before following Philip on his later adventures to enquire what Maugham intended the club-foot to signify.

In fact it has more than one symbolic function to perform. In relation to Philip as a child, his lameness, as has often been suggested, may well be the fictional equivalent of the stammer that afflicted Maugham all his life. Another function, already foreshadowed in the ur-novel, becomes explicit when Philip at Heidelberg reflects on his inexperience with girls:

> His imagination and the books he had read had inspired in him a desire for the Byronic attitude; and he was torn between a morbid self-consciousness and a conviction that he owed it to himself to be gallant.

In other words, the club-foot (though affecting the left rather than, as in Byron's case, the right foot) was meant, in part, to symbolize Philip's 'Byronism', by which Maugham appears still to have meant the quality that makes a man 'seductive by the complexity of his emotions, by the persistence of his mysterious grief'. When the present examination of the novel reaches a point at which Philip has progressed towards some understanding of his own nature, a third reason will be suggested why it suited Maugham's purpose for his hero to be a cripple.

Philip eventually owes his sexual initiation to the 40-year-old daughter of a clergyman-friend of his uncle, the grotesque Miss Wilkinson who is staying at the vicarage on his return to Blackstable from Germany; an event for which she awaits him in her bedroom one Sunday afternoon wearing a black petticoat with a red flounce which only reached the top of her boots and a calico camisole with short arms. The account of their brief affair is succeeded by the twelve Paris chapters describing Philip's life as an art student, for which the reader has been given only the most perfunctory preparation. They contain three incidents which are developed later in the novel. A fellow student returning from a visit to Spain has wonderful things to say of a painter new to them whose pictures he had seen in Toledo. On a painting holiday in the forest of Fontainebleau, with another student and his girl-friend Ruth, Philip's jealousy is qualified by a 'deformity of vision that exaggerated the revolting', that is, the girl's flat chest, decayed teeth and corns. Thirdly, he meets Cronshaw, a failed man of letters given to drunken philosophizing. But for the most part the Paris chapters (which primarily relate the harrowing story of Fanny Price, the ugly student who hangs herself when convinced she will never be a first-rate painter) are extraneous to the main narrative and lead merely to Philip's lame conclusion that, since he lacks 'the artistic temperament', he should abandon painting.

At the beginning of the third part, approaching the novel's mid-point, when Philip is attending his first lectures as a medical student at St. Luke's Hospital in London, Maugham makes heavy weather of describing the view of life Philip has arrived at consequent upon his loss of religious belief and a study of Hobbes, Spinoza, Hume and Darwin, which he formulated in the following slogans: might is right; good and evil have no meaning except insofar as some actions are to the advantage of society while some are not; follow your inclinations with due regard to the policeman round the corner; sin consists in being found out; throw out conscience, the traitor within the gates. Philip is in this frame of mind when he meets Mildred Rogers, a waitress at the teashop the students frequent in Parliament Street. And with her entrance—tall and thin with narrow hips and the chest of a boy, her skin a faint green colour from anaemia, like 'the petals of a yellow rosebud when you tore it to pieces before it burst'—the novel suddenly returns to life. In the first phase of their relationship the pattern is established in which Philip's abject yearning for her, frustrated by her indifference, sends him alternately to the extremes of anger and of self-pity. In his obsession with her, for which he has to be content with an occasional condescending kiss, his medical studies suffer, and only her announcement that she is going to marry Miller, another customer at the teashop, restores him temporarily to his senses. By now he has discovered that he hates doctoring, for he lacks 'the scientific temperament', and wants to see the world.

> As soon as I've got through my hospital appointments I shall get a ship, I want to go to the East—the Malay Archipelago, Siam, China, and all that sort of thing. . . .

Three chapters intervene in which—under the ministrations of Norah Nesbit, a married woman separated from her husband who writes penny novelettes, looks after Philip's health and linen, and 'satisfies his appetites'—he begins to pass his medical exams again. Reality returns to the novel with Mildred, abandoned by Miller, pregnant and still unmarried; at once Philip knows he is as passionately in love with her as ever, and the second phase of their relationship begins. He instals her in two rooms in Vauxhall Bridge Road, and from the first there is something unhealthy about their association. After he has helped her unpack her clothes she watches him kneel to unbutton her shoes and, wanting to put on a tea-gown, gets him to undo her dress, turning round unconcernedly as though he were a woman. He rejects her offer to go to bed with him as a return for what he is doing for her, because the thought of her and Miller disgusts him; but he talks of their taking a little honeymoon ('You are naughty', she says) after the baby is born. But soon after the baby has been farmed out to a foster-mother in Brighton Mildred falls in love with Griffiths, one of Philip's fellow students, and Philip reaches his nadir when he insists on lending them money so that she can go away with Griffiths for the weekend and get over her infatuation for him; but she fails to return.

Again, with Mildred's departure tension slackens, and there follow twelve chapters (Chs. 78-89) in which Maugham is content to trundle the narrative along, tidying up loose ends, giving a documentary account of Philip's experiences at medical school, describing the lingering death from cirrhosis of the liver of Cronshaw, whom Philip puts up in a spare room in his own lodgings, and introducing the Athelney family, unconvincing characters brought in to round off the novel.

Thorpe Athelney had lived eleven years in Toledo and is obsessed with Spain. Not only has he given his six (illegitimate) daughters Spanish names and filled his London house with Spanish furniture and pictures, but he is also given to conversing about Don Quixote, Calderón and the mystical writers of Spain and its Golden Age. He brings out photographs of El Greco's paintings, on studying which Philip feels himself on the brink of discovery, reading in them something of mysterious significance, a message it was important for him to receive but given in an unknown tongue which he could not understand. Before the mystery can be elucidated, he comes upon Mildred one Sunday evening in a feathered black straw hat and a black silk dress, soliciting in Piccadilly; and the last phase of their relationship begins. In a hired room in a shabby street behind the British Museum where she takes him he listens to her story and, relieved to find he no longer loves her but moved by a deep pity, he asks her to come and live in his spare room with the baby. They form a curious *ménage*. She is not a servant, for she takes her meals with him, but when she makes clear she wants him to sleep with her he is firm in his refusal, angering her: 'Oh, very well, it's just as you choose. I'm not one to go down on my hands and knees for that, and chance it', slamming the door. The fact is that—as with Miss Wilkinson, Ruth, Fanny Price and Norah—he now feels only repulsion for her. In Brighton where they go for a holiday after he has had an unsuccessful operation on his club-foot their relationship suffers a marked deterioration, partly because she feels insulted when he drags her and the baby from one boarding-house to another until one can offer them separate rooms ('I might be poisonous', she says); and partly because they are bored with each other. He muses on going to Spain when he qualifies, still feeling that El Greco held a secret of peculiar moment for him. On their return to their lodgings in London there is an ugly scene when she tries to force on him a change in their relations—

'You disgust me.'

'Me? I disgust you?'—

and she hurls a torrent of abuse at him, culminating in the insult she knows will hurt him most: 'Cripple!' Next day returning from the hospital he finds she has smashed his belongings and gone.

And with her departure the novel ceases to interest, though for twenty-six more chapters it meanders its way to a happy and quite unbelievable ending. Having lost his small capital in a risky investment, Philip lives rough until rescued by Athelney, who gets him a job as shopwalker at the linen-draper's where he works. When his uncle the vicar dies the money he inherits enables him to resume his medical studies and, on qualifying, he acts as locum to a doctor on the Dorset coast. During a hop-picking holiday with the Athelneys in Kent he seduces Sally, one of the daughters, and abandoning his plans for travel in Spain and the East for the life of a country doctor becomes engaged to her.

Whilst down and out Philip at last understands what Cronshaw had been trying to teach him about the Meaning of Life: that it has no meaning, so man must impose his own pattern on it purely for his own pleasure. And in this last part of the novel, before becoming engaged to Sally, for the third time he daydreams of Spain, of wringing from El Greco 'the secret which he felt the mysterious painter held for him'; and it must now be asked what Maugham intended the reader to make of this mysterious secret, for he offers no explanation. Earlier it has been suggested that Philip's club-foot may have had some symbolic function to perform besides standing in for Maugham's stammer and (harking back to the ur-novel) underlining the hero's 'Byronism'. Such an additional function would have to account for the final insult—'Cripple!'—flung at him by Mildred. The clue to what Maugham had in mind but shied away from making explicit in *Of Human Bondage* he withheld for twenty years and then, in an essay in *Don Fernando* (1935), revealed it by propounding the view that El Greco had been a homosexual. In making his hero's limp bear this symbolism he was following the example of E. M. Forster, who gave the hero of *The Longest Journey* (1907) a similar symbolic handicap; and when Maugham had to abandon the original title *Beauty from Ashes* because someone had recently used it and chose that of one of the books of Spinoza's *Ethics,* the bondage referred not to Philip's thraldom to Mildred, as has been generally assumed, but to his hero's thrawn nature. In this, surely, lies the key to Philip's otherwise inexplicable attitude towards the women with whom he became involved, especially to his extraordinary relationship with Mildred.

In the last part of the novel she makes a final appearance when Philip in response to a letter calls on her in a shabby lodging-house in Fitzroy Square. She is back on the game, suffering from venereal disease (for which he prescribes medicine), but rejects his call that she should give up the life she is leading because she is a danger to others. 'What do I care? Let them take their chance. Men haven't been so good to me that I need bother my head about them.'

For all its length *Of Human Bondage* is not Maugham's masterpiece, but inside it a shorter and better novel is wildly signalling to be let out. Excluding extraneous matter, this would comprise the childhood, schooldays and Heidelberg chapters; the account of Philip's relationship with Mildred whilst a medical student; and, its end coinciding with his dawning realization of his true nature, his decision to set out for Spain in order to wrest El Greco's secret from him. As it is, besides whatever therapeutic service it performed for the author in laying the ghost of the past that had been tormenting him, it can properly be seen as an impressive tombstone marking the end of the first phase of his writing career. (pp. 72-8)

John Whitehead, in his Maugham: A Reappraisal, *London: Vision Press, 1987, 224 p.*

Archie K. Loss

[In the following excerpt, Loss surveys Maugham's dramas.]

In *The Summing Up,* at the beginning of his discussion of the important elements of drama, Maugham remarks that a prose play is "scarcely less ephemeral than a news sheet." The note of prophecy in this remark, in relationship to his own plays, was not lost on Maugham, because it is his plays that gave rise to it: he gave up writing for the stage because he determined that such work had little lasting value. It had served a purpose in his career—that of establishing him as an author of prominence—and it had definitely rewarded him well, but in the end Maugham never felt totally at home in the theater and abandoned it after 1933 without regret. Were he alive today, he would not be surprised to find that most of his plays have been relegated to the library shelf, with only a few showing signs of more-permanent life. [In a footnote, the critic adds: "Of all the plays, *The Circle* and *The Constant Wife,* both of which are representative of Maugham and of their types, show the best signs of permanent life. . . . "]

Maugham's approach to the drama was the same as his general approach to the writing of fiction: that of the craftsman and professional who knows what he must do in order to satisfy the requirements of the genre in which he is working and the tastes of his audience. Elsewhere in *The Summing Up,* Maugham notes that a play represents a collaboration between the author, the actors, and the audience (also, he adds somewhat reluctantly, the director), but clearly the most important of these elements, in his analysis, is the audience: "All the best dramatists have written with their eye on it and though they have more often spoken of it with contempt than with good will they have known that they were dependent on it. It is the public that pays, and if it is not pleased with the entertainment that is offered it, stays away."

While the great innovators of the modern drama—Ibsen, Chekhov, Strindberg, Pirandello, and Brecht—certainly never lost sight of the fact that they were writing for an audience, they also just as certainly did not write with the tastes of the audience foremost in their minds. Rather, they molded the public to their view of drama, creating their own audience, even when this involved a great deal of personal travail. By contrast, Maugham was a popular dramatist who wrote plays to suit the requirements of the commercial theater. He did variations on a commonly appreciated theme—primarily comedies that turned upon the question of whether someone would marry (or stay married) or not—and reserved innovation, to the extent that he practiced it, for his last few plays, by which point he no longer cared whether he retained his audience or not.

If this sounds deprecating, it should be kept in mind that throughout history, most of the world drama conforms to Maugham's dictum that the audience is the most important element in the theatrical mixture. It should also be kept in mind that in the particular form in which Maugham specialized—a form derived from sophisticated drawing-room comedy of the English school—he clearly excelled. For some twenty-five years his work was among the best the English stage had to offer.

Maugham began writing for the Edwardian stage and ended his career during the Great Depression. His work reflects the changing tastes of audiences during this transitional period in British drama. Much of that work is comedy, and much of that comedy turns upon the question of marriage. Furthermore, almost all of the plays are focused upon female characters. Beginning with Maugham's first real success as a playwright, *Lady Frederick* (1903; first produced 1907), his plots center on his heroines' relationships and on decisions in their personal lives. The whole plot of *Lady Frederick* turns on the question: whom will Lady Frederick, a woman of somewhat doubtful reputation, marry? In *Penelope* (1908; 1909), the protagonist remains tied to her unfaithful husband, who shows by the end of the play that he loves her once again. *Our Betters* (1915; 1917) asserts the importance of marital fidelity less directly, but no less conclusively, when Bessie, the American girl whose sister has become the mistress of a wealthy Englishman, decides against marriage with an English lord because she has seen her sister decline as part of the English aristocracy. *Caesar's Wife* (1918; 1919) sees Violet, in the manner of Penelope, reunited with her husband by the end of the play. There are exceptions—for instance, in *Caroline* (1915; 1916) the main character, as the subtitle of the play suggests, remains "unattainable," her husband missing or dead—but in general these plays support the notion of love through marriage, a convention of the Edwardian, not to mention the Victorian, stage.

The Circle (1919; 1921) differs thematically from most of these plays, yet at the same time it typifies in most respects Maugham's whole approach to drama. It is also, of all his plays, the one most completely alive today.

The title of *The Circle* tells much about its subject and theme, for a circle consists of a single, continuous line whose end is its beginning. As a geometric form, it is perfect; as a symbol, it suggests action that repeats itself. Indeed, the action of *The Circle* is a repetition of events that happened previously, but with a difference that makes them, as the original subtitle of the play suggests, "modern." Elizabeth and Teddie do not simply repeat the experience of some thirty years earlier of Lady Kitty and Lord Porteus; they do it their way, in the modern manner. Their decision becomes their own, as Porteus suggests in one of the key speeches of the play: "No one can learn by the experience of another because no circumstances are quite the same."

Elizabeth is married to Arnold Champion-Cheney, MP, but is in love with the much less wealthy, much more aggressive Edward Lutton, a planter who hopes to make his fortune in the Federated Malay States. Elizabeth must ultimately choose between the loveless security of her relationship with Arnold, and the much more exciting, though much more insecure, alliance with Teddie. For Arnold, the situation is especially painful, because his mother, Lady Kitty, left his father for Lord Porteus and has not been back to see him since.

As the play opens, all the parties to the earlier elopement appear on the scene at the stately family home of the Champion-Cheneys, including Arnold's father, who chooses to visit at the very time Elizabeth has extended an invitation to Lady Kitty and Lord Porteus to spend some time there. His presence completes the equations among the characters important to the complications of the plot: Elizabeth with Lady Kitty, Teddie with Lord Porteus, and Arnold with his father. As Elizabeth and Arnold are trying to adjust to the tension aroused by these visitors, Elizabeth realizes that she is the object of the affection of Teddie Lutton. In the scenes that ensue, Arnold at first completely resists Elizabeth's declared intention to leave him, then, prompted by his father (who speaks from his own experience), tries to make Elizabeth feel so guilty about what she is doing that she will desist. Ultimately, however, the affection that Elizabeth feels for Teddie is great enough to overcome any scruples she may have, and, aided and abetted by the lovers of an older generation, she and Teddie escape into the night to begin their own adventures together.

If the final scene of the play suggests the similarity between Elizabeth's decision and Kitty's, much else in the play suggests how different the two women are. In that difference lies much of the point, and poignancy, of Maugham's comedy. At first Elizabeth imagines Kitty to be a romantic figure who surprised her husband by running off with his best friend. This impression is tarnished by the reality of Kitty grown old and the revelation of how difficult it has been for her and her lover through the years. Still, Elizabeth's approach to leaving Arnold is markedly different from Kitty's way of leaving his father; in the difference one sees why Kitty can't live without lipstick, while Elizabeth never uses it. Elizabeth, when she realizes that she is in love with Teddie, confronts Arnold with the fact very openly and candidly; it is Arnold who is devious in dealing with the situation. Furthermore, what Elizabeth responds to in Teddie is *his* openness and candor. "It's you I love, not what you look like," he says to her. "And it's not only love; love be blowed! It's that I *like* you so tremendously." Unlike the older Kitty—and unlike the women of many of Maugham's earlier plays—Elizabeth is incapable of behaving in a devious manner.

Elizabeth and Teddie also form an exception to the typically unequal heterosexual relationships in the work of Maugham. Elizabeth gives up a great deal to run away with Teddie, but at the same time she gains a measure of self-respect and independence that is significantly lacking in her married relationship. Teddie promises her little, but it is clear that she feels what she has with Arnold is suffocating her: "I don't want luxury. You don't know how sick I am of all this beautiful furniture," she tells Kitty early in act 3. "These overdecorated houses are like a prison in which I can't breathe." It is Lady Kitty, however, who strikes the ultimate note of realism on the subject when she says, "Woman will only be the equal of man when she earns her living in the same way that he does." Kitty is willing to risk that necessity, for Teddie promises her nothing.

Between Arnold and Teddie there is a contrast just as deep as the one between Elizabeth and Lady Kitty. Arnold is interested in old furniture and a political career; he is as conservative in his viewpoint on life as presumably he is conservative in his politics. Marriage completes his personal circle, and his desire to keep Elizabeth from leaving has as much to do with his personal ambition (and his sense that history should not repeat itself in his family) as it does with his affection for her. It is clear in fact that the affection of Arnold and Elizabeth for each other has long since cooled to the level of familiarity without ardor.

Teddie on the other hand is interested not in marriage but in Elizabeth herself. He is bold enough to have gone to the colonies to make his fortune, and the ultimate outcome of that venture, like the ultimate outcome of his relationship with Elizabeth, remains very much in question. Teddie is a positive version of Edward Barnard, who, in Maugham's short story of this same period, went to the South Seas and decided not to return. Teddie may not return either, for, like Elizabeth, he seems to find the English environment stultifying. Unlike Edward Barnard, however, Teddie may be successful in making his fortune.

If the tendency of Maugham's earlier comedies was toward a decision in favor of marriage, *The Circle* reflects the general tendency of British comedy of the twenties toward less conventional outcomes. Elizabeth and Teddie are not part of the Bright Set to emerge in the later twenties in the work of Noel Coward and others who became famous for representing the style of life of postwar British youth (for one thing they are too old to be counted in this category), but their decision to run off has about it the same no-nonsense toughness associated with the characters in Coward's work. Like Constance and her husband in *The Constant Wife,* Teddie and Elizabeth work out their own version of destiny. In doing so, they are at the same time more open and more bold than Lady Kitty and Lord Porteus, their immediate predecessors in such a venture in the play.

In many respects, however, the characters of *The Circle* are of a piece with those of Maugham's earlier comedies, as the play in which they occur is in many respects characteristic of Maugham's established brand of comedy. The characters of *The Circle* (with the exception of Teddie) are both titled and wealthy. Money is important to them, but as a means to maintain their way of life, not as an end in itself. The male characters are not, for the most part, financiers or men on the way up the ladder. They are at the top, or near it, and trying to stay there. Their careers, if they have visible ones, are in the respectable professions or in politics, but their careers are not of first importance in these plays: the focus is rather upon their personal relationships, the comedies reaching their points of crisis over decisions to marry or not to marry, to leave one's spouse or stay. Although the wives and mistresses of these plays are concerned with romantic intrigues and assignations, as well as with the right hat or gown, they are on the whole more important than the males. The focus of the plays is on their reactions and development, and they determine the course of events more than the male characters do. Maugham's comedies, in short, reflect in their characters as in their structure most of the qualities of the English drawing-room comedy.

The fundamentally aristocratic nature of the characters and the emphasis of the plays upon their personal affairs are both characteristic of this kind of comedy. So is the tendency—not overbearingly strong in **The Circle,** but certainly noticeable—toward aphorism in the writing: "It's very unfair to expect a politician to live in private up to the statements he makes in public" (Mrs. Shenstone to Elizabeth in act 1); "I always reserve to myself the privilege of changing my mind. It's the only one elderly gentlemen share with pretty women" (Arnold's father to Elizabeth in act 1); "The tragedy of love isn't death or separation. One gets over them. The tragedy of love is indifference" (Lady Kitty to Elizabeth in act 3). These and other lines like them typify the dialogue of Maugham's comedies and of drawing-room comedy in general. It is less important what the characters have to say than how they say it, and such statements form an important part of the thematic underpinning of the play, on which its action, however related to the wisdom they suggest, is built. Maugham was especially noted for his skill at this kind of dialogue, which audiences and critics alike expected in this comic form.

The plot line of drawing-room comedy is frequently complicated but it must always be clearly and neatly resolved by the end of the final act. The pleasure is in seeing how, with all the complications, the playwright gets us there. In Maugham's comedies the twists of the plot are not extraordinarily complex, but, as in **The Circle,** one does not know until the end of the play what the outcome will be. In this respect as well as in others Maugham's comedies are related to the *pièce bien faite* (the well-made play) of the French tradition, an influence that one would expect to see reflected in the work of an author much indebted in other ways to French literature.

The well-made play follows the pattern of exposition, complication, and resolution, with the climax of the play, the ultimate point of revelation, coming at the very end, often in the final line. Augustin-Eugène Scribe defined the genre. Victorien Sardou's *Tosca,* made familiar by Giacomo Puccini's opera, is a good example of it, and so, in British drama, is Arthur Wing Pinero's *The Second Mrs. Tanqueray* (1895). As serious drama, the well-made play takes the form of melodrama. As comedy, it tends toward farce. If Maugham's work does not follow precisely the pattern of such plays, it nevertheless shares with them a sufficient number of characteristics to make analysis in such terms informative. His serious dramas all have the marks of melodrama—certainly one reason for their popularity—and many of his early comedies are in fact best described as farces. In the end, however, it is English drawing-room comedy, more than the French tradition, that provides the model for Maugham's comedies.

The master of English drawing-room comedy was Oscar Wilde. In such plays as *Lady Windermere's Fan* (1893) and *The Importance of Being Earnest* (1899) (his greatest dramatic achievement) he used the form (with appropriate touches of the *pièce bien faite*) to create a new comedy of manners, reviving a type of play not significant in England since the eighteenth century. So individual was Wilde's achievement in the form that it was to a large extent inimitable, but it did encourage the popularity of drawing-room comedy in the nineties; such comedy later became a staple of Edwardian theater. By the time Maugham began to write plays, it was only natural, given his desire for commercial success, that he should write plays of this kind.

Of the other comedies of Maugham it is probably **The Constant Wife** (1926) that would best hold the boards today. In this stylish comedy (Maugham's next-to-last effort in this particular vein) Constance Middleton and her husband John take the flippant view of marital fidelity soon to be immortalized in Noel Coward's *Private Lives* (1929). After a series of complications derived from John's affair with another woman, Constance—now with the independent means that Lady Kitty in **The Circle** tells Elizabeth are essential to a woman's independence—has her own fling, but leaves with the understanding, reached at the end of the final act, that she can return. "You are the most maddening, wilful, capricious, wrong-headed, delightful and enchanting woman man was ever cursed with having for a wife," John says in the final speech. "Yes, damn you, come back." Constance, unlike Elizabeth, wants independence and marriage at the same time and manages to achieve both.

If Maugham is noted today chiefly for his comedies, one must not forget that he wrote more serious plays as well. **Our Betters** and **The Circle** are both comedies with an edge of seriousness that nearly carries them over the line. Other plays begin in that other terrain. Part of Maugham's impatience with theater came from his feeling that he would have to continue writing what his audience had come to expect of him, which for the most part meant comedies. This growing impatience led him to his decision to stop writing plays altogether.

Having made that decision, Maugham was equally determined that he would write four more: "I had been thinking of them all for a good many years; I had done nothing about them because I did not think they would please. . . . I wrote these four plays in the order in which I expected them to be increasingly unsuccessful." The first two—**The Sacred Flame** (1928) and **The Breadwinner** (1930)—turned out to be fairly successful. The last two—**For Services Rendered** (1932) and **Sheppey** (1933)—did not succeed. The intentions of their author were achieved. As a group these plays are interesting for what they tell about Maugham as a dramatist not aiming to please—that is, not writing with any particular concern for the financial success of his play.

Each of these plays attempts to do something different from what Maugham was best known for as a playwright. In **The Sacred Flame,** a play about the tragic circumstances surrounding the death of a pilot paralyzed in World War I, Maugham tried to escape from what he saw as the increasing tyranny of naturalistic dialogue in prose drama. "In certain passages," Maugham writes of the play in his introduction to the **Collected Plays,** "I tried, quite deliberately, to make my characters use not the words and expressions that they would have used in real life on the spur of the moment and in the give and take of conversation, but words and expressions that they might have used if they had had time to set their thoughts in order." Thus Mrs. Tabret to Stella in act 2: "I could never bring myself to teach my children what I couldn't myself believe. When they were little and I used to sit in the evenings in our house and look at the multitudinous stars sweeping across the blue sky of India and thought of what we are, so transitory and so insignificant, and yet with such a capacity for suffering, such a passion for beauty, I was overwhelmed by the mystery and the immensity of the universe." Or Nurse Wayland, at a moment of high emotion, again to Stella, in act 3: "No. No. My love for that poor boy was as pure and as spiritual as my love for God. There was never a shadow of self in it. My love was compassion and Christian charity. I never asked anything but to be allowed to serve and tend him." Rather than finding this dialogue more expressive than the customary dialogue of the day, critics found it stilted (not to say stale), and Maugham did not attempt it again.

The Breadwinner, Maugham's last comedy, takes the situation of ***The Constant Wife***— that of a wife who realizes that her marriage is no longer working and wants to do something about it—and applies it to the husband. Charles Battle (the last name suggests something of his spirit, and the first calls to mind another Charles, also a stockbroker, in ***The Moon and Sixpence***) realizes that his marriage has gone flat and his relationship with his children has become pointless, so he leaves both rather than prolong the institution of marriage that he no longer values. Like the decision of Charles Strickland, Charles Battle's is irrevocable, and the end of the play sees him leaving for his new life.

For Services Rendered is Maugham's statement on the effects of World War I, at least insofar as they can be felt by a small group of characters in a provincial English town. In 1929 R. C. Sheriff's *Journey's End* had been an immensely successful portrait of life in the trenches, and in the next year, Noel Coward's *Cavalcade,* a chronicle of an English family during the years from 1899 to 1929, dealt with the effects of the war on the people back home. In ***For Services Rendered*** Maugham shows that for those who stayed at home the rewards of service were neuroticism or madness, with Eva's cracked rendition of the national anthem, at the end of the final act, an ironic commentary on the complacency of her father and mother (and also perhaps a comment on the use of the same anthem, in a patriotic context, at the end of *Cavalcade*).

Sheppey, the final play of Maugham's last four, deals with the familiar situation of the man of modest means who comes into money—in this case by way of a winning ticket in the Irish Sweepstakes. What effect will this small fortune have on the lower-middle-class barber who gives his name to the play? All the money seems to inspire in Sheppey—whose daughter has the same selfishness that is seen so often in children in Maugham's plays (an anticipation perhaps of Maugham's later attitude toward his own daughter)—is the desire to give it away to the poor and needy, the downtrodden and distraught. In a play that begins as a straightforward, low-keyed piece of naturalism with comic overtones, Sheppey's second-act conversion

comes as too much of a surprise, but even so, the appearance in the final act of Death, come to claim him as her own, has a gripping dramatic effect and indicates the distance Maugham has come from the sort of play that made him famous. The final scene of ***Sheppey*** represents a return to one of the earliest forms of drama, allegory, and reflects Maugham's unhappiness with the strictures of realistic theater. "I sighed for the liberty of fiction," he writes in ***The Summing Up,*** "and I thought with pleasure of the lonely reader who was willing to listen to all I had to say and with whom I could effect an intimacy that I could never hope for in the garish publicity of the theater."

What was Maugham's achievement in the theater? He produced in his thirty-two plays probably the most significant body of work in English drama after George Bernard Shaw and before Noel Coward, yet comparison with the achievement of the first of these playwrights, at least, can only be damaging to Maugham. Nowhere in Maugham's work for the theater does one see the brilliance, the wit, or the intellectual energy that make Shaw's work, particularly after the turn of the century, so compelling a part of theater to this day. By comparison, Maugham's work seems pale, dated, and trivial, even when, as in the very best of it, all of its elements work. Shaw used theatrical effect—especially in his earlier plays, but also in such later ones as *Androcles and the Lion*—in the service of ideas, a procedure that energized otherwise conventional forms and made them seem, if not new, at least renewed by his touch. Maugham on the other hand more often used theatrical effect for its own sake to engage the audience and never produced any drama that was in any sense intellectually compelling. One could argue indeed that the more he tried to produce such work, as in his last plays, the less he succeeded as a dramatist. Maugham frankly sought in drama something to which Shaw paid far less attention, and often eschewed: popularity with the audience.

Coward, like Maugham, actively sought to be a popular dramatist. Like Maugham, he took various commercial forms of drama, serious as well as comic, and eventually made them his own, including the form of high comedy at which Maugham excelled. All of Coward's plays show a strong sense of theatrical effect and artifice and an equally what audiences looked for. Coward's work, however—in particular his comedies—has managed to maintain its popularity to this day while Maugham's for the most part has not. Coward's comedy may reflect the style of a period, but it also speaks to us in our own; Maugham's comedy speaks for its time, but not so well for ours.

The difference between the work of these popular dramatists perhaps tells us more than their similarities, at least insofar as Maugham's achievement is concerned. The difference lies in Coward's greater individuality as well as in his greater separation from Edwardian forms. In structure and content most of Maugham's dramatic work conforms to the conventions of a bygone era; Coward's is much looser in structure and tone ("the average talk," Maugham was to describe Coward's dialogue, "with its hesitations, mumblings and repetitions, of average people"), hence in a sense more modern. It is also, in a way

Maugham's never is, more individual: Coward not only wrote for the theater, but also wrote parts for himself in his best plays. For this reason, as well as for their tone, Coward's comedies achieve an individuality that Maugham's never manage and in fact never aim for. Maugham remains outside his work for the theater and, though it may at times share certain themes or attitudes with his fiction, it is in the end far less individual. When one thinks of Maugham's "voice," it is of the fiction—or nonfiction—that he wrote, not the plays.

At the same time one must give Maugham his due as a dramatist. Even at this late date, in plays like *The Circle* and *The Constant Wife,* one can appreciate what he does with a now-extinct comic form. (pp. 83-96)

> *Archie K. Loss, in his* W. Somerset Maugham, *Ungar, 1987, 139 p.*

Gore Vidal

[*Vidal is an American novelist, short story writer, dramatist, and essayist. He is particularly noted for his historical novels and his iconoclastic essays. In the following excerpt from an essay occasioned by the publication of Robert Calder's biography* Willie: The Life of W. Somerset Maugham (1990) *and several new editions of Maugham's works, Vidal offers a lively, acerbic assessment of Maugham's life and works.*]

Maugham spent his first twenty-six years in the nineteenth century and for the subsequent sixty-five years he was very much a nineteenth-century novelist and playwright. In many ways he was fortunately placed, though he himself would not have thought so. He was born in Paris where his lawyer father did legal work for the British Embassy, and his mother was a popular figure in Paris society. Maugham's first language was French and although he made himself into the premier English storyteller, his prose has always had a curious flatness to it, as if it wanted to become either Basic English or Esperanto or perhaps go back into French. . . .

Maugham's career as a writer was singularly long and singularly successful. The cover of each book was adorned with a Moorish device to ward off the evil eye: the author knew that too much success overexcites one's contemporaries, not to mention the gods. Also, much of his complaining may have been prophylactic: to avert the furies if not the book-chatterers, and so he was able to live just as he wanted for two thirds of his life, something not many writers—or indeed anyone else—ever manage to do. (p. 39)

"Few authors," Mr. Calder tells us [in *Willie: The Life of W. Somerset Maugham,* 1990], "read as widely as Maugham and his works are peppered with references to other literature." So they are—peppered indeed—but not always seasoned. The bilingual Maugham knew best the French writers of the day. He tells us that he modelled his short stories on Maupassant. He also tells us that he was much influenced by Ibsen, but there is no sign of that master in his own school of Wilde comedies. Later, he was awed by Chekhov's stories but, again, he could never

"use" that master because something gelled very early in Maugham the writer, and once his own famous tone was set it would remain perfectly pitched to the end.

In his first published novel, *Liza of Lambeth* (1897), Maugham raised the banner of Maupassant and the French realists but the true influence on the book and its method was one Arthur Morrison, who had made a success three years earlier with *Tales of Mean Streets.* Mr. Calder notes that Morrison,

> writing with austerity and frankness, . . . refused to express sympathy on behalf of his readers so that they could then avoid coming to terms with the implications of social and economic inequality. Maugham adopted this point of view in his first novel, and was therefore, like Morrison, accused of a lack of conviction.

In general realists have always been open to the charge of coldness, particularly by romantics who believe that a novel is essentially a sermon, emotional and compassionate and so inspiring that after the peroration, the reader, wiser, kinder, *bushier* indeed, will dry his eyes and go forth to right wrong. This critical mindset has encouraged a great deal of bad writing. The unemotional telling of a terrible story is usually more effective than the oh, by the wind-grieved school of romantic (that is, self-loving) prose. On the other hand, the plain style can help the dishonest, pusillanimous writer get himself off every kind of ideological or ethical hook. Just the facts, ma'am. In this regard, Hemingway, a literary shadow self to Maugham, was our time's most artful dodger, all busy advancing verbs and stony nouns. Surfaces coldly rendered. Interiors unexplored. Manner all.

For someone of Maugham's shy, highly self-conscious nature (with a secret, too) the adoption of classic realism, Flaubert with bitters, was inevitable. Certainly, he was lucky to have got the tone absolutely right in his first book, and he was never to stray far from the appearance of plain storytelling. Although he was not much of one for making up things, he could always worry an anecdote or bit of gossip into an agreeable narrative. Later, as the years passed, he put more and more effort—even genius—into his one triumphant creation, W. Somerset Maugham, world-weary world-traveler, whose narrative first person became the best-known and least wearisome in the world. At first he called the narrator "Ashenden" (a name carefully chosen so that the writer would not stammer when saying it, unlike that obstacle course for stammerers, "Maugham"); then he dropped Ashenden for Mr. Maugham himself in *The Razor's Edge* (1944). Then he began to appear, as narrator, in film and television dramatizations of his work. Thus, one of the most-read novelists of our time became widely known to those who do not read.

Shaw and Wells invented public selves for polemical reasons, while Mark Twain and Dickens did so to satisfy a theatrical need, but Maugham contrived a voice and a manner that not only charm and surprise in a way that the others did not, but where they were menacingly larger than life, he is just a bit smaller (5'7"), for which he compensates by sharing with us something that the four histrionic masters would not have dreamed of doing: inside gossip. It is these confidences that made Maugham so agreeable to read: *nothing,* he tells us with a smile, *is what it seems.* That was his one trick, and it seldom failed. Also, before D. H. Lawrence, Dr. Maugham (obstetrician) knew that women, given a fraction of a chance, liked sex as much as men did. When he said so, he was called a misogynist.

In October 1907, at thirty-three, Maugham became famous with the triumphant production of *Lady Frederick* (one of six unproduced plays that he had written). Maugham ravished his audience with the daring trick of having the eponymous lady—middle-aged with ardent unsuitable youthful admirer—save the boy from his infatuation by allowing him to see her un-made-up at her dressing table. So stunned is the lad by the difference between the beauty of the *maquillage* and the crone in the mirror that he is saved by her nobleness, and right before our eyes we see "nothing is what it seems" in spades, raw stuff for the theater of those days.

By 1908 Maugham had achieved the dream of so many novelists: he had four plays running in the West End and he was financially set for life. (pp. 39-40)

In 1915 . . . *Of Human Bondage* was published. Maugham now was seen to be not only a serious but a solemn novelist—in the ponderous *American* manner. The best that can be said of this masterpiece is that it made a good movie and launched Bette Davis's career. I remember that on all the pre-Second War editions, there was a quotation from Theodore Dreiser to the effect that the book "has rapture, it sings." Mr. Calder does not mention Dreiser but Mr. Frederic Raphael does, in his agreeable picture book with twee twinkly text, *Somerset Maugham and His World.* Mr. Raphael quotes from Dreiser, whom he characterizes as "an earnest thunderer in the cause of naturalism and himself a Zolaesque writer of constipated power." Admittedly, Dreiser was not in a class with Margaret Drabble but—constipated?

The Maugham persona was now perfected in life and work. (p. 40)

One reason, prurience aside, why Mr. Calder tells us so much about Maugham's private life (many kindnesses and charities are duly noted) is that Maugham has no reputation at all in North American academe where Mr. Calder is a spear-carrier. The result is a lot of less than half-praise:

> His career had been largely a triumph of determination and will, the success in three genres of a man not naturally gifted as a writer.

Only a schoolteacher innocent of how literature is made could have written such a line. Demonstrably, Maugham was very talented at doing what he did. Now, this is for your final grade, *what* did he do? Describe, please. Unfortunately, there aren't many good describers (critics) in any generation. But I shall give it a try, presently.

At seventy-two, Maugham went to Vevey, Switzerland, where a Dr. Niehans injected aging human organisms with the cells of unborn sheep, and restored youth. All the great and not-so-good came to Niehans, including Pius XII—in a business suit and dark glasses, it was said—an old man in no hurry to meet his Jewish employer. Thanks perhaps to Niehans, Maugham survived for nearly fifteen years in rude bodily health. But body outlived mind and so it was that the senile Maugham proceeded to destroy his own great invention, W. Somerset Maugham, the teller of tales, the man inclined to the good and to right action, and above all, to common sense. By the time that old Maugham had finished with himself, absolutely nothing was what it seemed and the double self-portrait that he had given the world in *The Summing Up* and *A Writer's Notebook* was totally undone by this raging Lear upon the Riviera, who tried to disinherit daughter while adopting [his secretary-companion Alan] Searle as well as producing *Looking Back,* a final set of memoirs not quite as mad as Hemingway's but every bit as malicious. With astonishing ingenuity, the ancient Maugham mined his own monument; and blew it up.

For seven decades Maugham had rigorously controlled his personal and his artistic life. He would write so many plays, and stop; and did. So many novels, and stop; and did. So many short stories. . . . He rounded off everything neatly, and lay back to die, with a quiet world-weary smile on those ancient lizard lips. But then, to his horror, he kept on living, and having sex, and lunching with Churchill and Beaverbrook. Friends thought that Beaverbrook put him up to the final memoir, but I suspect that Maugham had grown very bored with a lifetime of playing it so superbly safe.

. . . . .

It is very difficult for a writer of my generation, if he is honest, to pretend indifference to the work of Somerset Maugham. He was always so entirely *there.* By seventeen I had read all of Shakespeare; all of Maugham. Perhaps more to the point, he dominated the movies at a time when movies were the lingua franca of the world. Although the French have told us that the movie is the creation of the director, no one in the Twenties, Thirties, Forties paid the slightest attention to who had directed *Of Human Bondage, Rain, The Moon and Sixpence, The Razor's Edge, The Painted Veil, The Letter.* Their true creator was W. Somerset Maugham, and a generation was in thrall to his sensuous, exotic imaginings of a duplicitous world.

Although Maugham received a good deal of dutiful praise in his lifetime, he was never to be taken very seriously in his own country or the United States, as opposed to Japan where he has been for two thirds of a century the most read and admired Western writer. Christopher Isherwood tells us that he met Maugham at a Bloomsbury party where Maugham looked most ill at ease with the likes of Virginia Woolf. Later Isherwood learned from a friend of Maugham's that before the party, in an agony of indecision, as the old cliché master might have put it, he had paced his hotel sitting room, saying, "I'm just as good as they are."

I suspect that he thought he was probably rather better *for what he was,* which was not at all what they were. Bloomsbury disdained action and commitment other than to Art and to Friendship (which meant going to bed with one another's husbands and wives). Maugham liked action. He risked his life in floods, monsoons, the collapse of holy Russia. He was worldly like Hemingway, who also stalked the big game of wild places, looking for stories, self. As for what he thought of himself, Mr. Calder quotes Maugham to the headmaster of his old school: "I think I ought to have the O.M. [Order of Merit]. . . . They gave Hardy the O.M. and I think I am the greatest living writer of English, and they ought to give it to me." When he did get a lesser order, Companion of Honour, he was sardonic: "It means very well done . . . but."

But. There is a definite but. I have just reread for the first time in forty years *The Narrow Corner,* a book I much admired; *The Razor's Edge,* the novel on which the film that I found the ultimate in worldly glamour was based; *A Writer's Notebook,* which I recalled as being very wise; and, yet again, *Cakes and Ale.* Edmund Wilson's famous explosion at the success of Maugham in general and *The Razor's Edge* in particular is not so far off the mark:

> The language is such a tissue of clichés that one's wonder is finally aroused at the writer's ability to assemble so many and at his unfailing inability to put anything in an individual way.

Maugham's reliance on the banal, particularly in dialogue, derived from his long experience in the theater, a popular art form in those days. One could no more represent the people on stage without clichés than one could an episode of *Dynasty:* Maugham's dialogue is a slightly sharpened version of that of his audience.

Both Wilde and Shaw dealt in this same sort of realistic speech but Shaw was a master of the higher polemic (as well as of the baleful clichés of the quaint workingman, rendered phonetically to no one's great delight) while Wilde made high verbal art of clichés so slyly crossed as to yield incongruent wit. But for any playwright of that era (now, too), the *mot juste* was apt to be the well-deployed *mot banal.* Maugham's plays worked very well. But when Maugham transferred the tricks of the theater to novel writing, he was inclined to write not only the same sort of dialogue that the stage required but in his dramatic effects he often set his scene with stage directions, ignoring the possibilities that prose *with* dialogue can yield. This economy won him many readers, but there is no rapture, song. Wilson, finally, puts him in the relation of Bulwer-Lytton to Dickens: "a half-trashy novelist who writes badly, but is patronized by half-serious readers who do not care much about writing." What ever happened to those readers? How can we get them back?

Wilson took the proud modernist view that, with sufficient education, everyone would want to move into Axel's Castle. Alas, the half-serious readers stopped reading novels long ago while the "serious" read literary theory, and the castle's ruins are the domain of literary archaeologists. But Wilson makes a point, inadvertently: If Maugham is half-trashy (and at times his most devoted admirers would probably grant that) what, then, is the other half, that is not trash? Also, why is it that just as one places, with the right hand, the laurel wreath upon his brow, one's left hand starts to defoliate the victor's crown?

A Writer's Notebook (kept over fifty years) is filled with descriptions of sunsets and people glimpsed on the run. These descriptions are every bit as bad as Wilson's (in *The Twenties*) and I don't see why either thought that writing down a fancy description of a landscape could—or should—be later glued to the page of a novel in progress. Maugham's descriptions, like Wilson's, are disagreeably purple while the physical descriptions of people are more elaborate than what we now put up with. But Maugham was simply following the custom of nineteenth-century novelists in telling us whether or not eyebrows grow together while noting the exact placement of a wen. Also, Dr. Maugham's checklist is necessary for diagnosis. Yet he does brood on style; attempts to make epigrams. "Anyone can tell the truth, but only very few of us can make epigrams." Thus, young Maugham, to which the old Maugham retorts, "In the nineties, however, we all tried to."

In the preface, Maugham expatiates on Jules Renard's notebooks, one of the great delights of world literature and, as far as I can tell, unknown to Anglo-Americans, like so much else. Renard wrote one small masterpiece, *Poil de Carotte,* about his unhappy childhood—inhuman bondage to an evil mother rather than waitress.

Renard appeals to Maugham, though "I am always suspicious of a novelist's theories, I have never known them to be anything other than a justification of his own shortcomings." Well, that is commonsensical. In any case, Maugham, heartened by Renard's marvelous notebook, decided to publish his own. The tone is world-weary, modest. "I have retired from the hurly-burly and ensconced myself not uncomfortably on the shelf." Thus, he will share his final musings.

There is a good deal about writing. High praise for Jeremy Taylor:

> He seems to use the words that come most naturally to the mouth, and his phrases, however nicely turned, have a colloquial air. . . . The long clauses, tacked on to one another in a string that appears interminable, make you feel that the thing has been written without effort.

Here, at twenty-eight, he is making the case for the plain and the flat and the natural sounding:

> There are a thousand epithets with which you may describe the sea. The only one which, if you fancy yourself a stylist, you will scrupulously avoid is *blue;* yet it is that which most satisfies Jeremy Taylor. . . . He never surprises. His imagination is without violence or daring.

Of Matthew Arnold's style, "so well suited to irony and wit, to exposition. . . . It is a method rather than an art, no one more than I can realize what enormous labour it must have needed to acquire that mellifluous cold brilliance. It is a platitude that simplicity is the latest acquired of all qualities. . . ." The interesting giveaway here is Maugham's assumption that Arnold's style must have been the work of great labor. But suppose, like most good writers, the style was absolutely natural to Arnold and without strain? Here one sees the hard worker sternly shaping himself rather than the natural writer easily expressing himself as temperament requires:

> My native gifts are not remarkable, but I have a certain force of character which has enabled me in a measure to supplement my deficiencies. I have common sense. . . . For many years I have been described as a cynic; I told the truth. I wish no one to take me for other than I am, and on the other hand I see no need to accept others' pretenses.

One often encounters the ultimate accolade "common sense" in these musings. Also, the conceit that he is what you see, when, in fact, he is not. For instance, his native gifts for narrative were of a very high order. While, up to a point, he could tell the truth and so be thought cynical, it was always "common sense," a.k.a. careerism, that kept him from ever saying all that he knew. Like most people, he wanted to be taken for what he was not; hence, the great invention W. Somerset Maugham. (pp. 41-2)

Posterity? That oubliette from which no reputation returns. Maugham:

> I think that one or two of my comedies may retain for some time a kind of pale life, for they are written in the tradition of English comedy . . . that began with the Restoration dramatists. . . . I think a few of my best short stories will find their way into anthologies for a good many years to come if only because some of them deal with circumstances and places to which the passage of time and the growth of civilization will give a romantic glamour. This is slender baggage, two or three plays and a dozen short stories. . . .

But then it is no more than Hemingway, say, will be able to place in the overhead rack of the economy section of that chartered flight to nowhere, Twentieth Century Fiction.

I would salvage the short stories and some of the travel pieces, but I'd throw out the now-too-etiolated plays and add to Maugham's luggage **Cakes and Ale,** a small perfect novel, and, sentimentally, **The Narrow Corner.** Finally, Maugham will be remembered not so much for his own work as for his influence on movies and television. There are now hundreds of versions of Maugham's plays, movies, short stories available on cassettes, presumably forever. If he is indeed half-trashy, then one must acknowledge that the other half is of value; that is, *classicus,* "belonging to the highest class of citizens," or indeed of any category; hence, our word "classic"—as in Classics *and* Commercials. Emphasis added. (p. 44)

> *Gore Vidal, "Maugham's Half & Half," in* The New York Review of Books, *Vol. XXX-VII, No. 1, February 1, 1990, pp. 39-44.*

FURTHER READING

Aldington, Richard. *W. Somerset Maugham: An Appreciation.* New York: Doubleday, Doran & Co., 1939, 34 p.
> Includes the title essay by Aldington; "Sixty-Five," an essay by Maugham; a primary bibliography; reprinted excerpts from favorable reviews of Maugham's books; and an index of short stories.

Auden, W. H. "Notebooks of Somerset Maugham." *The New York Times Book Review* (23 October 1949): 1, 22.
> Review of *A Writer's Notebook* in which Auden comments on Maugham's self-assessments.

Bates, H. E. "Katherine Mansfield and A. E. Coppard." In his *The Modern Short Story: A Critical Survey,* pp. 122-47. Boston: The Writer, 1941.
> Includes an assessment of Maugham as a proficient but not innovative short story writer in a discussion of post-World War I English short story writers.

Barnes, Ronald E. *The Dramatic Comedy of William Somerset Maugham.* The Hague: Mouton, 1969, 190 p.
> Analysis of Maugham's dramatic comedies, focusing on the relation of technique to content.

Braendlin, Bonnie Hoover. "The Prostitute as Scapegoat: Mildred Rogers in Somerset Maugham's *Of Human Bondage.*" In *The Image of the Prostitute in Modern Literature,* edited by Pierre L. Horn and Mary Beth Pringle, pp. 9-18. New York: Frederick Ungar Publishing Co., 1984.
> Deplores the characterization of Mildred as a victim "sacrificed . . . to the development process of the protagonist."

Burgess, Anthony. "Somerset Maugham: 1874-1965." In *The Listener* LXXIV, No. 1917 (23 December 1965): 1033.
> Obituary tribute in which Burgess declares that "the short story was Maugham's true *métier,* and some of the stories he wrote are among the best in the language."

Burt, Forrest D. *W. Somerset Maugham.* New York: Twayne Publishers, 1985, 157 p.
> Critical overview of Maugham's career, focusing on his principal works.

Calder, Robert. *Willie: The Life of W. Somerset Maugham.* London: Heinemann, 1989, 429 p.
> Scholarly biography prepared with the assistance of Maugham's companion-secretary Alan Searle.

Connolly, Cyril. "The Art of Being Good." *The New Statesman and Nation* XXVIII, No. 705 (26 August 1944): 140.
> Review of *The Razor's Edge* that includes the assessment: "Maugham is the greatest living short-story writer, and so one expects his handling of plot to force one into a breathless, non-stop reading from the first page to the last, and his character-drawing and observation to be in the fine tradition—but one would not expect to be so captivated by the brilliant fluency of the writing. Here at last is a great writer, on the threshold of old age, determined to tell the truth in a form which releases all the possibilities of his art."

Cowley, Malcolm. "The Devil a Monk Was He." *The New Republic* 110, No. 18 (1 May 1944): 609.
> Review of *The Razor's Edge* assessing Maugham's por-

trayal of his protagonist's spiritual quest as unconvincing.

Curran, Trisha. "Variations on a Theme." In *The English Novel and the Movies,* edited by Michael Klein and Gillian Parker, pp. 228-34. New York: Frederick Ungar Publishing Co., 1981.

> Examines the 1934 and 1964 film adaptations of *Of Human Bondage.*

Curtis, Anthony. *Somerset Maugham.* Windsor: Profile Books Ltd., 1982, 47 p.

> Summary of Maugham's career.

Curtis, Anthony, and Whitehead, John. *W. Somerset Maugham: The Critical Heritage.* London: Routledge & Kegan Paul, 1987, 470 p.

> Reprints important first reviews of Maugham's plays and books. The editors provide an insightful introduction that surveys Maugham's life and career.

Dobrinsky, Joseph. "The Dialectics of Art and Life in *Of Human Bondage.*" *Cahiers Victoriens & Edouardiens* 22 (October 1985): 33-55.

> Examines Maugham's exploration of the relationship between art and life in *Of Human Bondage.*

Dodd, Lee Wilson. "Set of Six." *The Saturday Review of Literature* VIII, No. 13 (17 October 1931): 206.

> Review of *Six Stories Written in the First Person,* stressing Maugham's competence in matters of plotting, style, and execution.

Greene, Graham. Review of *Cosmopolitans: Very Short Stories,* by W. Somerset Maugham. *The Spectator* 156, No. 5625 (17 April 1936): 720.

> Suggests that while the stories in the collection are not among Maugham's best, they reflect Maugham's "supreme competence, the dry amusing reserve of a man who has the highest admiration for the interest, rather than the goodness, of human nature."

Innes, Christopher. "Somerset Maugham: A Test Case for Popular Comedy." *Modern Drama* XXX, No. 4 (December 1987): 549-59.

> Considers underlying serious themes and astringent social satire in Maugham's popular comedies.

Kanin, Garson. *Remembering Mr. Maugham.* New York: Atheneum, 1966, 313 p.

> Reminiscence by the screenwriter, novelist, and short story writer who, together with his wife, actress Ruth Gordon, maintained a friendship with Maugham for the last twenty years of Maugham's life.

Kronenberger, Louis. "The Story-Telling Art of Mr. Maugham." *The New York Times Book Review* (12 August 1934): 2.

> Review of *East and West* commending Maugham's technical skill but regretting the lack of variety among his short stories.

Maugham, Robin. *Somerset and All the Maughams.* London: Longmans, 1966, 274 p.

> Reminiscences by Maugham's nephew providing genealogical information and insights into Maugham's character.

Mavor, Elizabeth. "Maughamisms." *London Review of Books* 7, No. 13 (18 July 1985): 22.

> Review of *A Traveller in Romance* noting some of Maugham's characteristic themes.

Moore, Harry T. Review of *Seventeen Lost Stories,* by W. Somerset Maugham. *The Saturday Review* 52, No. 47 (22 November 1969): 87.

> Considers these early stories, originally published between 1898 and 1908 and not previously collected, revelatory about Maugham's development as a fiction writer.

Morley, Christopher. "Gin and Quinine Tonic." *The New York Times Book Review* (8 October 1950): 3, 24.

> Review praising *The Maugham Reader,* comprising novels, short stories, plays, essays, and an autobiographical sketch, as "a generous load of the most continuously readable storyteller of our lifetime."

Nichols, Beverley. *A Case of Human Bondage.* London: Secker & Warburg, 1966, 153 p.

> Account of the Maugham's marriage by a longtime acquaintance of both Maugham and his wife, written to refute Maugham's vilification of Syrie Wellcome Maugham in *Looking Back.*

Pritchett, V. S. Review of *The Mixture as Before,* by W. Somerset Maugham. *The New Statesman and Nation* XIX, No. 486 (15 June 1940): 750.

> Examines some essential characteristics of Maugham's fiction, noting in particular his cynicism, moralism, and class-consciousness.

——. Review of *A Writer's Notebook,* by W. Somerset Maugham. *The New Statesman and Nation* XXXVIII, No. 970 (8 October 1949): 401.

> Commends the interest and readability of Maugham's published notebooks.

Sunne, Richard. "Current Literature: Books in General." *The New Statesman and Nation* 2, No. 35 (24 October 1931): 516.

> Asserts that Maugham's inability to effectively portray character has prevented him from receiving wide critical regard.

Zabel, Morton Dauwen. "A Cool Hand." *The Nation* 152, No. 18 (3 May 1941): 534-36.

> Review pronouncing *Up at the Villa* "as unmitigated a specimen of fictional drivel as has appeared under respectable authorship withing living memory," and charging that Maugham has written nothing but slick commercial fiction since *Cakes and Ale.*

Kate Millett

1934-

(Full name: Katherine Murray Millett) American nonfiction writer and autobiographer.

Millett is widely acknowledged as a pioneering figure of the contemporary feminist movement. Since 1970, when her nonfiction work *Sexual Politics* became a standard text for study of sexual inequality in Western culture, Millett has been considered one of the movement's most articulate spokespersons. Her works explore topics relating to sexuality, sociology, and psychology from scholarly, personal, and artistic perspectives. Many also examine in greater depth the social and sexual dilemmas associated with growing up female in America.

Millett was born into an Irish-Catholic family in St. Paul, Minnesota. Her father deserted his wife and three daughters when Millett was fourteen, and her mother's subsequent search for employment awakened Millett's feminist consciousness to the realities of sexual discrimination. Although she possessed a college degree, Millett's mother was offered only menial work until she found a job selling insurance. Even then, however, she was not given weekly wages as were the men in the company, but had to earn her entire salary on commission. In interviews, Millett recalled that the commission amounted to only six hundred dollars during the first year and the family "lived on fear largely." Despite these financial hardships, Millett managed to attend the University of Minnesota, graduating *magna cum laude* and Phi Beta Kappa in 1956. Always rebellious, Millett was becoming increasingly unconventional and disdainful of Catholicism when a wealthy aunt, disturbed by her niece's eccentricities, offered to send her to Oxford University for graduate study. Millett accepted and earned first class honors in English literature in 1958.

Upon returning to the United States, Millett decided to pursue art as a career and supported herself by teaching kindergarten in Harlem, New York. In 1961, she traveled to Tokyo to study sculpting. There she met Fumio Yoshimura, an artist who returned to the United States with her two years later. Their marriage in 1965 helped Yoshimura avoid deportation, and, while Millett is a professed lesbian, they remained married for twenty years. During the 1960s, Millett also taught English at Barnard College and became passionately involved in the flourishing civil rights movement, joining the Congress of Racial Equality and the National Organization for Women, where she served as chairperson of the education committee. Her ardent participation in these progressive causes displeased the Barnard administration and she was dismissed from her teaching duties after less than a year. Soon after this, Millett began her doctoral thesis for Columbia University. Aimed at illuminating the ways in which literature and philosophy conspire against sexual equality, the thesis, *Sexual Politics,* earned Millett a Ph.D. with distinction and became a national best-seller as well.

Sexual Politics is widely regarded as the first major literary criticism written from a feminist perspective. In various sections of this work, Millett explores the political oppression of women and documents the feminist revolution and reactions against it. She also castigates the patriarchal literary ideas of D. H. Lawrence, Norman Mailer, and Henry Miller, while citing the French homosexual writer Jean Genet, whose works sought to reverse cultural stereotypes of both men and women, as a genius of social criticism. Reaction to *Sexual Politics* was varied and often extreme; numerous male critics chastised the feminist movement in general, and many were taken aback by Millett's militant, caustic tone. One reviewer offered the simile that reading *Sexual Politics* was like "sitting with your testicles in a nutcracker." Jonathan Yardley illustrated the general male reaction when he stated that "[Millett] is several cuts above the feminist movement's screechers." Some female commentators cited such flaws as biased views and excessive analyses. However, the majority of reviewers instantly recognized *Sexual Politics* as significant criticism and lauded Millett's intelligent commentary and successful blend of rationality and humor.

In a British review of *Sexual Politics* a year after its American publication, the feminist writer Germaine Greer discussed the "dues" Millett had paid for writing the " 'bible' of women's liberation." Millett instantly and involuntarily became a celebrity feminist who was forced to take public responsibility for both the positive and negative aspects of the liberation movement. She lost any semblance of a private life and had to cope with verbal abuse and physical attacks from those who disagreed with her ideas. Millett incorporated these experiences into an autobiographical work, *Flying,* which discusses her life after *Sexual Politics,* her attempts to practice the philosophies she had promoted in the book, and her unconventional but successful marriage to Yoshimura. Numerous critics found Millett's admission of her lesbian sexuality—and the public and private commotion that resulted—to be the most intriguing part of *Flying.* She acknowledged her lifestyle in 1970 during a speech at Columbia University, when an audience member asked her outright if she was a lesbian. Although it was an era when gay life-styles were often kept private, Millett stated the truth about her sexuality and was met with both encouraging and discouraging responses. Some of the dissenting public felt that *Sexual Politics* lacked authority because it was written by a lesbian. On a more personal level, Millett's mother was horrified and embarrassed by her daughter's "confession." In subtle retaliation, Millett dedicated *Flying* to her mother.

Sita, Millett's next autobiographical work, is based on a journal she kept throughout 1975 recording her relationship with Sita, a middle-aged university administrator and mother. After a three-year affair, Sita loses interest in Millett and begins to date men again. Unable to forget the past, Millett follows her to California but finds the woman preoccupied with various male lovers. Millett accounts in minute detail every aspect of the affair and its collapse, a flaw in many critics' opinions, but a technique others saw as an intensely realistic perception of an unraveling relationship. Although often considered to be her weakest book, *Sita* nevertheless garnered praise for its frank depiction of an alternate life-style and is viewed as a breakthrough work in lesbian fiction. Nancy Manahan asserted: "*Sita* is an important book because it presents realistically a subject that has been neglected, sentimentalized, or deplored in most literature—lesbian relationships. It contains, as does *Flying,* some of the first prose which presents in an author's own voice her experience of lesbian sexuality. In addition, *Sita* explores in unprecedented depth the old themes of power and powerlessness and offers a model for emotional self-revelation of a kind traditionally found only under the cloak of fiction."

Millett departed from the personal prose of *Flying* and *Sita* to write the sociological study *The Basement: Meditations on a Human Sacrifice.* Composed in a stream-of-consciousness style, the book concerns the 1965 murder of Sylvia Likens, a sixteen-year-old girl who was tortured to death in Indianapolis, Indiana. Sylvia's parents, unable to provide for their children, paid a woman named Gertrude Baniszewski to board Sylvia and her younger sister. Four weeks after the sisters moved in, Sylvia's mutilated body was found in the basement of the Baniszewski home. Gertrude, three of her seven children, and two neighborhood boys were found guilty of her murder. Millett meticulously researched the case over fourteen years, and concedes in the beginning of *The Basement* that she was obsessed: "Finally, I can touch you with my voice, finally it's time, Sylvia Likens. In how many sad yellow hotel rooms have I spoken to you, writing these words before me on the wall as I lay back on some bed and staring at the painted plaster, beginning this in my mind. Emboldened for an hour. And then a coward again at home never getting anything on paper. Waiting till the time came. For fourteen years you have been a story I told to friends, even to strangers, anyone I could fasten upon and late at night. Since the first moment I heard of you, came across something in a magazine, the outline of your ordeal." Millett adopts various personas in telling the story, including Gertrude, the neighbors, and Sylvia herself, at turns focusing on the curious conspiratorial silence of those involved and the terrible vulnerability of women in modern society. Many critics praised the simultaneously realistic and empathetic tone of the work; Gertrude, for example, is both a hideous and pitiful voice, a woman who spends her money on televisions and stereos instead of food for her children and who was beaten and deserted by her husband. Although several critics disagreed with Millett's theory that Sylvia was killed chiefly because she was female, the vast majority found *The Basement* a gripping study of human cruelty and submission, labelling it Millett's most powerful work to date.

Millett returned to autobiographical writing with *The Loony-Bin Trip,* a chronicle of her 1980 mental breakdown that occurred when she voluntarily stopped taking Lithium, a prescribed drug used for treating manic-depression. Millett chose to go off the drug after seven years because it diminished her creativity; while Lithium balances the massive mood swings of manic-depressives, it also slows thought processes and represses brain activity. However, as *The Loony-Bin Trip* recounts, the negative effects of the manic personality soon returned, and Millett's friends and family tried to commit her to an institution. Evading their well-meant intentions, Millett traveled to Ireland and was involuntarily committed to a Catholic asylum by police after exhibiting strange behavior at the airport. Eventually she was released with the help of friends. Throughout *The Loony-Bin Trip* Millett stresses the belief that individuals are declared insane when they deviate in any way from conventional norms. Her detailing of life in an institution, both disquieting and darkly comic, has been favorably compared to Ken Kesey's *One Flew over the Cuckoo's Nest.*

In addition to these works, Millett has written *The Prostitution Papers,* which gathers stories from feminist lawyers and prostitutes, and *Going to Iran,* an account of the fight for women's rights in Tehran. She wrote and directed *Three Lives,* a documentary film about the unusual lives of a trio of women, one of whom is Millett's sister Mallory, an actress who is also active in the feminist movement. Millett also owns a seventy-five acre Christmas tree farm in New York, which she uses as a summer retreat for women artists.

(See also *Contemporary Authors,* Vols. 73-76, rev. ed. and *Contemporary Authors New Revision Series,* Vol. 32.)

PRINCIPAL WORKS

NONFICTION

Sexual Politics   1970
The Prostitution Papers   1971
The Basement: Meditations on a Human Sacrifice   1979
Going to Iran   1981

AUTOBIOGRAPHY

Flying   1974
Sita   1977
The Loony-Bin Trip   1990

OTHER

Three Lives   (documentary screenplay)   1971

Jonathan Yardley

Kate Millett is a professor at Barnard, a sculptor of some note, and a radical feminist. As the latter, she is evidently a seminal figure of sorts in Women's Lib: two years ago she shocked the gentlemen of Morningside Heights with *Sexual Politics: A Manifesto for Revolution,* a brief document which summarily dismissed our whole array of sexual customs and demanded their drastic revision. According to the feminist booklet *Notes From the Second Year,* in which the manifesto is reprinted, *"The Columbia Spectator*—and the Columbia Radio station as well—took one look and refused to have anything more to do with it, despite the fact that it was written by a faculty member to whom they had promised the space and time."

Yet for all her undeniable radicalism, Millett (I eliminate the "Miss" in deference to her sexual egalitarianism, though the omission certainly comes hard) is several cuts above the feminist movement's screechers. . . . *Sexual Politics* is too long, too discursive, too arbitrarily organized, and its lapses into doctrinaire silliness are maddening, but on balance it is an impressive, sober, provocative study which commands serious attention from male practitioners of the "sexual politics" it so devastatingly defines—not to mention women who lumpishly consent to their own subjugation.

Sexual Politics is nitty-gritty Women's Lib. Men willing to meet the book on its own uncompromising terms will find the experience lacerating, and it is my guess that any sensitive housewife who has never given much thought to her status will be persuaded that she has been an exploited ninny. Though Millett is demonstrably not a manhater and does not appear to be a clitoral absolutist, her tone is so unflaggingly militant (and irreverent) that only the true-blue feminist will read the book without discomfort. But Millett's militancy, even when overstated or misdirected, is to good purpose, as is that of Women's Lib generally; it forces the reconsideration of entrenched and invidious, but widely evaded, sexual/social assumptions.

One senses that the book began as an examination of sex-ism in contemporary literature and ballooned into the "ambitious, often rather overwhelming, undertaking" that Millett self-applaudingly calls it. It opens with "instances of sexual politics" in the work of D. H. Lawrence, Henry Miller, Norman Mailer and Jean Genet; it ends with extensive chapters devoted (with some fine wit and perceptive criticism) to each of the four. The choice is clever but ultimately damaging to her cause. Attacking Lawrence, Miller and Mailer for sexual posturing is the literary equivalent of shooting whales in a barrel, and citing Genet as prophet of the new order . . . has limited appeal since Millett glosses over the problems inherent in a homosexual viewpoint.

In its middle sections, *Sexual Politics* is concerned with defining its title, revealing the guises in which sexism is masked, exposing its deleterious effects and sketching its history. The book is essentially about female subjugation in the United States, and is wisely assessed within that framework. All its meanderings finally arrive at the consideration of sex in this country as "a status category with political implications," politics being broadly defined as "power-structured relationships, arrangements whereby one group of persons is controlled by another," "a set of stratagems designed to maintain a system." It is, or comes very close to being, a conspiracy theory, a view of history in which a diabolical patriarchy systematically holds women in a state of submission and dependency. Conspiracy is as far-fetched in this case as it was at Chicago, but the evidence that women are treated as a subordinate class, or caste, is considerable:

> What goes largely unexamined, often even unacknowledged (yet is institutionalized nonetheless) in our social order, is the birthright priority whereby males rule females. Through this system a most ingenious form of "interior colonization" has been achieved. It is one which tends moreover to be sturdier than any form of segregation, and more rigorous than class stratification, more uniform, certainly more enduring.

To be sure, we have been depicted as a nation of Momists, we celebrate Mother's Day and fete debutantes, we congratulate ourselves upon the memory of Jane Addams and the presence of Margaret Chase Smith; but the true situation is another matter. We (white) men view women much as, Millett claims, we view blacks: "inferior intelligence, an instinctual or sensual gratification, an emotional nature both primitive and childlike, an imagined prowess in or affinity for sexuality, a contentment with their own lot which is in accord with a proof of its appropriateness, a wily habit of deceit, and concealment of feeling." Isn't our societal "worship" of woman merely a stratagem to lull her into submission, an extraordinary piece of sexual politics "a game the master group plays in elevating its subject to pedestal level?"

The claim is an example of the brand of partial truth in which Millett excels. Her talent for coating the implausible with a veneer of the plausible is impressive indeed: "Achievement in the arts and humanities is reserved, now, as it has been historically, for males"—a ludicrous statement containing just enough truth to lend it respectability.

Most of the time her aim is better. It is more true than not that "women are a dependency class"; that their "relation to the economy is . . . typically vicarious or tangential"; that "the military, industry, technology, universities, science, political office, and finance—in short, every avenue of power within the society, including the coercive force of the police, is entirely in male hands." . . . (pp. 26, 30-1)

It is also true, though the question is more complex than Millett will allow, that men tend to regard women as sexual objects who exist for male gratification. Henry Miller

> has given voice to certain sentiments which masculine culture had long experienced but always rather carefully suppressed: the yearning to effect a complete depersonalization of woman into cunt, a game-sexuality of cheap exploitation, a childish fantasy of power untroubled by the reality of persons or the complexity of dealing with fellow human beings and, finally, a crude species of evacuation hardly better than anal in character.

That seems rash overstatement only so long as one conveniently ignores a psychology which produces pornography, which reduces women to "pieces of ass," which considers female orgasm an irrelevant by-product, if it occurs at all, of male pleasure, which embraces a *machismo* that "inextricably" intertwines sexuality and violence.

One would think the girls would have marched on City Hall ages ago, but Millett explains that paternalism stays in office by "passing itself off as nature"—that "masculine ascendancy" is justified by its exponents as being naturally, indeed divinely, ordained. Either we men are great salesmen or women are great suckers, but no matter, Millett presses on. "Masculine" and "feminine" are not the complex natural distinctions we had assumed them to be, but "elaborate behavioral constructs for each sex within society, obviously cultural and subject to endless cross-cultural variations." "Sex is biological, gender psychological, and therefore cultural." Ignore our penises and our vaginas and we should all be the same; in a perfect world, no one would know the difference between Joe Willie Namath and Raquel Welch.

As biologist and anthropologist Millett obviously has her shortcomings, but her point that history has not been kind to the female must be conceded. As historian, she points out that women were generally held in thrall until the early 19th century. In a long, interesting section on sexual revolution and counter-revolution, she argues that the rebellion against male dominion began around 1830 and was "officially inaugurated" with the formation of the Women's Movement at Seneca Falls, New York, in 1848. The revolution lasted a hundred years, she contends, and accomplished a great deal by way of legal and economic gains, but foundered because it failed "to challenge patriarchal ideology at a sufficiently deep and radical level to break the conditioning processes of status, temperament and role"; it was "reform rather than revolution."

"The Counter-Revolution: 1930-60," Millett believes, was led by Lawrence ("the most talented and fervid of sexual politicians") and Freud (possessor of "unflagging enthusiasm for glorifying the inestimable male organ," fabricator of penis envy), who recognized the threat to male suzerainty and moved to thwart it. That judgment seems to have less to do with the actual movement of history than with the psyches of Lawrence, Miller and Mailer—"some of those who helped to build these (sexist) structures—writers who, after the usual manner of cultural agents, both reflected and actually shaped attitudes." The impact of all three cannot be denied. But neither can we ignore their inflamed sexuality and their obsession with celebrating it. To select them as somehow representative is to evade the problems one encounters in more complex, and I think more honest, male writers who have sought to depict sexual relationships. It is no flattering comment on the thoroughness of *Sexual Politics* that the century's three most important American writers, Faulkner, Fitzgerald and Hemingway, each the prisoner of terribly complex, ambiguous and fascinating sexual attitudes, are mentioned in passing or not at all. Millett is right: "the adventure of literary criticism is not restricted to a dutiful round of adulation, but is capable of seizing upon the larger insights which literature affords into the life it describes, or interprets, or even distorts." But neither is it restricted to the analysis of those writers who happen to confirm a critic's preconceived notions even when their accuracy as social mirrors is, to put it most kindly, questionable.

If Millett had been willing to be less ambitious and more flexible, *Sexual Politics* would be a better book. It is too much of a literary-anthropological-sociological-historical-psychological grabbag to be a clear success in part or in sum, and its regressions into Women's Lib rigidities diminish its many splendid inquiries into sexual attitudes. Like Women's Lib it is most useful when it explores the daily forms of sexual discrimination, least when it wanders into biological theorizing. It most deserves our attention when it asserts that "the great cultural change which the beginnings of a sexual revolution represent is at least as dramatic as the four or five other social upheavals in the modern period to which historiographical attention is zealously devoted." If the book is received properly the rewriting of history may begin; for we *have* ignored the history of women, and demeaned it, just as we ignore and demean its makers.

A final caveat: as a male who is trying to kick sexism but has no particular expectation of doing so, I welcome the taunts and challenges of Kate Millett, but I am not sure they bear the seed of a final answer. That a society without sex, or without gender, is a desirable goal, seems to me unlikely. A nation finally rid of the canard of the ethnic melting pot should not rush to create a sexual melting pot. Our discriminations and cruelties are bitter ones, but our differences are healthy; we need to eliminate discrimination, not difference. A woman who has the refreshing arrogance to claim, as Millett does, that "the female possesses, biologically and inherently, a far greater capacity for sexuality than the male, both as to frequency of coitus, and as to frequency of orgasm in coition," should be the last person to urge that such unique attributes be eliminated in a wave of "unisex." But then maybe Women's Lib is more complex than even the radical feminist realizes. (pp. 31-2)

Jonathan Yardley, "Women's Lib Gets Rough," in The New Republic, *Vol. 163, No. 5, August 1, 1970, pp. 26, 30-2.*

Clara Claiborne Park

I am enough of a Christian to find ego-sacrifice a virtue, and to recognize, as Kate Millett does not, that Christianity revolutionized patriarchal Judaism by incorporating into its value system, for men as well as women, the servile—or feminine—virtues of humility, tenderness, and self-sacrifice. . . .

I am also enough of a realist to wish that this thorough, scholarly, and very important treatment of how literature helps society educate girls in the behavior which it will then adduce as evidence of their inferiority showed some sign that its author had ever observed the differences betweens cocks and hens. But she could not have written this book if she had accepted biological determinism, or reached the mature woman's acquiescence in a role which (like any other) presents advantages and disadvantages mixed. To give to criticism something genuinely new—a self-respecting woman's reading of some of our most influential literature—she had to preserve the angry sensitivity of a young girl.

Sexual Politics explores the literary record of the ascendency of "the oldest ruling class in the world." As she traces the vocabulary of sexual power in texts ranging from the *Oresteia* to Henry Miller and Mailer, it is hard not to be convinced that no deck has ever been more thoroughly stacked, and that the same impulse that recognizes "black is beautiful" must respond to "feminine is intelligent, responsible, and strong."

This is a richly informative book. Though she indulges herself in a heavy irony which women may find more amusing than men, she has no space for polemic. She has too much to tell us. Here are Rousseau on the education of women ("to please men, to be useful to them"), Sojourner Truth as flaming feminist (abolitionism and the women's rights movement are historically linked), the responses of Ruskin, Tennyson, Engels, Mill to what they variously conceived as the threat or the promise of women's liberation. Interesting new readings of Hardy's *Jude* and Meredith's *Egoist* bring to life the great forward movement that led to the vote—where, as Millett demonstrates, it stopped. She goes on to examine the literature of the reaction—no room for Hemingway among the cultists of virility, but fascinating treatments of Lawrence, Freud, and a sampling of current sociological and psychological texts.

Millett works through textual analysis; the book is worth buying for the quotations alone. The opening chapter, indeed, will draw in many an unsuspecting reader, consisting as it does of an anthology of ripely pornographic passages. That these are regularly permeated with hatred and contempt for the woman conquered, brutalized, and "enjoyed" is so amply demonstrated that a female reader can only wonder at the acquired thickness of skin that enabled her, once, to read Miller and Mailer without flinching. With Lawrence she is sympathetic but searching; she

notes, among many other things, the contrast between the awed admiration of the male organ (as in Lawrence, Miller, and Freud) with the very little they find to say in praise of the female apparatus.

As they accumulate, the quotations become embarrassing; the wish-fulfillment and power-fantasy are so evident that masculine righteous indignation gets drowned in feminine tenderness for the weak. By nature or by nurture, women tend to do their woman's thing, to try to figure out what men and children need, and give it to them. One adds to one's chivalrous pity for Lawrence and Mailer, and the superiority they find so necessary, a gnawing concern for the male readers of *Sexual Politics,* who have never committed acts of brutality and work hard to maintain a wife in comfort.

This book will antagonize most men and some women. But it is important that it be read so that we may come to understand that "colonial or feminine mentality of interiorized oppression which must conquer itself in order to be free."

Clara Claiborne Park, "The Wrong Lessons About Life," in Book World—The Washington Post, *August 9, 1970, p. 5.*

Barbara Hardy

On the delicate skin of the Rokeby Venus in London's National Gallery are the slashmarks made by the suffragettes. The aggressive women, the odalisque represented, the model, the painter celebrating such form and flesh, and the consumers of such high pornography are all victims of corrupted sex. Like race and class, sex is a subject we cannot simply write "about," for it is our sex that writes. Aloofness is no merit, being inappropriately tolerant. Corrupted lovers all, we find it hard to keep heart and head in the right place.

Kate Millett's [*Sexual Politics*] is thus a rare achievement. Its measure of detachment is earned by learning, reason and love, its measure of involvement is frankly set out. It is a piece of passionate thinking on a life-and-death aspect of our public and private lives.

We are plunged in at the deep end, in a not unappreciative commentary on a scene of sex in and just out of the bath, from Henry Miller's *Sexus,* rapidly followed by a more complexly brutal passage from Mailer's *An American Dream.* [A third extract is from Genet's *The Thief's Journal*]. Permissive fiction proffers rich materials. The pornographic element now so assimilated by imaginative literature as to confound the legal distinctions of censorship has exposed far more than beds and bodies. Its freedom shows truths and fantasies about sex hitherto disguised. Moreover, the act of sexual description is itself aggressive, indulgent, attractive, repulsive. These scenes are crucial. The power-politics of a patriarchal society creates the complacent zest of Miller's hero as he subdues his women, and creates too the desperate arrogance of Mailer's Rojack.

The texts Kate Millett has chosen have to transcend pornography, too. They are rich in the revelation of complexities of corrupt reason, ethic, language and sensuality. (p. 8)

[They give] a taste, a method and a theme, leading persuasively into a historical and intellectual history of sexual politics, taking in art, anthropology, physiology, psychology, politics and economics. Genet's novels and plays are at the center of the plea for change. It is unlike the Victorian plea for a change of heart in being much more firmly and optimistically related to current signs of a change of consciousness.

But this close and original analysis of individuals serves a larger cause. This is a book that analyzes revolution in order to serve revolution. It has to look at individual cases both because it is concerned with culture and because its subject is human consciousness. Yet it cannot be solely concerned with individual expression in art and language. It needs to demonstrate more broadly the nature of the patriarchal society and the nature of that revolution which started to overthrow patriarchal laws, values and relations. This sexual revolution partly succeeded, was arrested and temporarily defeated, but is once more active. Kate Millett shows why and how.

The revival, as she observes, is only about five years old, and the contemporaneity makes analysis slide away from precision. But the earlier stages are susceptible to conventional historical analysis. History is sensibly condensed where it has already been fully documented, as in the fields of education and the women's movement. In generalization and vivid historical particulars (like the marvelous speech of Sojourner Truth at a woman's rights convention in Akron, Ohio, in 1851), she writes history in order to bring out two truths. One is the relation between class war and sex war. Despite some progress in education and legislation, the great Victorian sleight-of-hand is brought out. Men divided and ruled, used intimidation, flattery and provoked envy in order to persuade the ladies that woman's weakness and maternal function needed protection and worship, not civil rights, and while exposing and exploiting working-class women without benefit either of chivalry or coverture. Yet out of economic exploitation came slow advance.

The second truth concerns the nature of the revolution and its halt. She compares it not with the French or the Russian revolution, but with such gradual though radical changes as the industrial revolution or the rise of the middle classes, explaining its slowness and its sporadic nature by the comparison. For the sexual revolution gained considerable advances in education and, more slowly, in legislative change, but is only now beginning to move habits of mind, feeling, and relationship. She argues plausibly, for instance, that women were freer in the twenties than in the last four decades, though superficial technological emancipation—most obviously through contraception—masked stasis and even retrogression.

It is in order to expose the inadequacy of the revolution and the strength of the counterrevolution that she makes her analysis of literature. The writers and thinkers give the evidence of the slow and complex erosion of patterns of feeling. You need sympathy and toughness to analyze

such complexities, and Kate Millett manages brilliantly, whether she is looking at Tennyson's better-than-nothing struggles in "The Princess" or [John Stuart] Mill's excellent analysis, slightly underplaying economics, but superior to [Friedrich] Engels in a courageous appraisal of the future of the family. (pp. 8, 10)

Freud is admired for his work on the unconscious and on infantile sexuality, but seen as ironically basing observations about female character on pathological cases, social victims. The ghost of penis-envy is finally laid, beautifully and good-temperedly, and the author generally refrains from too many laughs at penis-pride; when she occasionally succumbs, she is not strident or complacent. The book's humor is part of its warmth and tenderness, and in striking contrast, I thought, to the chill humorlessness of those other two great feminists, Simone de Beauvoir and Doris Lessing.

My very few disagreements were provoked by the sensitivity of the book itself. The insights about Genet's creative descent seemed to suggest something similar in Dickens, who is rather passed over. It is not Dickens's Nancy in *Oliver Twist* who is most like Genet's Divine in *Our Lady of the Flowers,* but Edith Dombey; a marvelous instance of the honor of open degradation. Her double revenge on both her husband-capitalist and her seducer-manager is not only a rare female triumph in the Victorian novel but a fine case of political and sexual teasing. Not sustained, true, but like those moments in Tennyson, better than nothing.

Kate Millett's analysis of D. H. Lawrence is devastating and almost acceptable. There do seem to be one or two things left out concerning Lawrence's exceptional recognitions, breaks and blurs in his fable of power. The artist is not to be trusted, or the man, but there are times when the tale, fuller than its fable, expands beyond the stereotype which Lawrence's sickness needed. In *Sons and Lovers* he uses Miriam and Clara as instruments, true, but there are glimpses at Miriam's family difficulties, seen with some sympathetic sense of the need for masochism. There is one great scene when Paul visits Clara and we feel in one significant stroke the woman's sense of degradation by maleness and by labor conditions. Even the victory of Ursula over Skrebensky in *The Rainbow,* though it is part of the Lawrentian phallic fable, is also perhaps a realization of the other side, or inner story, of *vagina dentata?* Lawrence evidently failed to seduce Frieda, and that failure forced into the novels such things as Ursula's intransigence in *Women in Love* and her vital indictment of Loerke. When she tells Loerke that his sculpture of the girl on the horse comes out of sadism, is indeed an aggressive thing, she is surely making the kind of recognition which is the stuff of Kate Millett's own argument. (pp. 10, 12)

To say this is not to try to score points in literary criticism but to raise issues of genuine difficulty. In *Lady Chatterley's Lover* Connie's tears over the peasant chicks don't seem all that funny to me, and both her conception-urge and her sense of abandonment and release do not seem to be identifiable all that clearly as submission, shared as it is by men also, and at least belonging to that area of sexual experience where it is impossible to speak of nature. But as the author's last words remind us, we may be able one day to separate the private life from the political, but as yet we only speak as prisoners.

Sexual Politics is a remarkable document because it analyzes the need and nature of sexual liberation while itself displaying the virtues of intellectual and emotional openness and lovingness. (p. 12)

> Barbara Hardy, "de Beauvoir, Lessing—Now Kate Millett: 'Sexual Politics'," in The New York Times Book Review, September 6, 1970, pp. 8, 10, 12.

Mary Jean Irion

One factor that works against success in the women's liberation movement is the voice of its enthusiasts; their tone tends to become harsh and shrill, thereby alienating listeners. But Kate Millett (at least in this book) sounds good. **Sexual Politics** talks in clear, straight, powerful language about the need to reconceive Western society on grounds of sexual equality rather than of patriarchy. In its passion for justice, the book may occasionally shout, but it never raves. Here are reason and humor at work on what is surely one of our greatest challenges: to make sex a liberator rather than a constrictor of persons and society. (p. 1487)

The first section opens with a discussion of the works of Henry Miller and Norman Mailer, whose descriptions of the brutal use of women are quoted—i.e., male domination begins in bed. However extreme and fictional the cases are, my trust in artistic integrity warns me not to discount them as false; they may well be dramatizing real evil in the midst of our loves and decencies. To whatever extent such exploitation is true, Millett's moral outrage is justified.

It is to the thinking of Jean Genet that Millett turns for guidance; together they make the important point that "sexual caste supersedes all other forms of inegalitarianism: racial, political or economic"; and that "unless the clinging to male supremacy as a birthright is finally foregone, all systems of oppression will continue to function simply by virtue of their logical and emotional mandate in the primary human situation."

There follows an overview of patriarchy that explains how the system works. Patriarchal ideology creates the complicated temperaments we call "masculine" and "feminine" from the simple biological givens of male and female; it exaggerates difference, prescribes roles for each sex, and finally grants unequal status. Contrary to popular belief and much spurious "proof," any overall male superiority results from society's, and not nature's, loading of the dice. Patriarchy is an unholy mindset maintained by institutions, the chief of which is the family. Women's lower caste is often subtly disguised by class differences, by chivalry and by a degree of economic and educational progress; but the fact is that maleness is consistently, arbitrarily, irrationally preferred because of the patriarchal system itself. This ranking of the sexes occasions "a variety of cruelties and barbarities" that spreads across society. The whole complex is sanctioned by myth and religion, with the result that most women believe themselves to be naturally inferior. The very basis of our life together needs reworking.

Part Two of the book traces the history of the sexual revolution (1830-1930) in its political, polemical and literary manifestations. Here John Stuart Mill is featured; Friedrich Engels, Charlotte Brontë, Thomas Hardy and others are appreciated; and John Ruskin's poeticizing of antifeminism is held up for thorough and delightful scorn. Millett then shows how a counterrevolution developed (1930-1960) in both theory and practice. Gains far-reaching, but unsound, were lost; and during this regression both Nazi Germany and Soviet Russia have illustrated that close ties bind authoritarianism to patriarchy. The women's liberation movement was also silenced by some theories of Freud and those who followed him; and progress is still being notably retarded by the poetic but nonetheless objectionable attitudes of Erik Erikson. A criticism of functionalism finishes the historical survey.

Throughout this two-thirds of the book, I was generally in agreement with the author. While I hardly accept Kate Millett whole and unquestioned, I like the way she thinks, works, writes. She yields exquisite sense, and I hope she will not surrender that for sensationalism.

However, I am less confident about Part Three, "Literary Reflection." While I cannot dispute her findings nor condone the male power and cruelty displayed in the works of D. H. Lawrence, Henry Miller and Norman Mailer (who are cited as counterrevolutionaries), something is wrong in Millett's art criticism. She has come at these works head-on, full force, with but a single aim: to dig out the man-woman theme. To ram at quality fiction with straight reason, following no curve that allows for symbol and allusion and the profound depths that they contribute, is to distort the work and to reduce the authors to far less than they are. It is possible to assign to a writer's words a too literal interpretation (Jonah did too live three days in the fish's belly; it says so right here); or to assume that an author approves of whatever he describes; or to fail in sympathy for artists who sometimes—for reasons they themselves little understand—have to live right into their own symbols at awesome personal cost; or to support one's theory imperfectly with a scattering of evidence from authors' ill considered statements and from actions in their lives.

Where Millett has erred I am not sure; but in Part Three some injustice has been done to art. Even in the snatches quoted from the works of the above three men, there is a power that has nothing to do with their maleness nor the sex of their characters and everything to do with a swing at depth which Millett herself neither reaches nor reaches for. The artists she blasts confirm in me an old conviction: that we must go even deeper than sex and patriarchy if we are to save ourselves. Some fundamental, conceptual problem of man's relationship to nature is at bottom; and not until religion, science and art working together can transform the power struggle between man and universe to oneness will we achieve a man-in-world view which may free us from the domination complex.

While some work for adjustment between cosmos and humanity, others work for adjustment between men and women, others for adjustment between strong and weak nations, others for adjustment between white and black people. It is all of a piece toward peace; hostility is unnecessary and destructive. *Sexual Politics* has a flaw, then. But what hasn't? This book says important things. It deserves a wide—and a wide open—hearing. (pp. 1487-88)

Mary Jean Irion, "Millett's Message," in The Christian Century, *Vol. LXXXVII, No. 49, December 9, 1970, pp. 1487-88.*

On *Sexual Politics*

"I hope I pointed out to men how truly inhuman it is for them to think of women the way they do, to treat them that way, to act that way toward them. All I was trying to say was, look, brother, I'm human."

—Kate Millett, 1970

Germaine Greer

Now that Women's Liberation has become a subject upon which each publishing house must bring forth its book, much as it must upon such pressing topics as contract bridge or the techniques of modern marketing, the struggle for the liberation of women is being mistaken for yet another battle of the books. Each publishing house backs its own expertise to identify the eventual bible of the women's movement, characterising it as a religious cult in which one publisher will corner the credibility market, sending the world's women rushing like so many lemmings after a book. The hapless authoresses of the books in question find themselves projected into the roles of cult leaders, gurus of helpless mewing multitudes. In fact, one becomes the 'high priestess' of Women's Liberation in the same way as one becomes the undisputed queen of contract bridge. The penalty is to find oneself reviled by one's sisters as a self-styled leader, a lady don who cannot know the perils and endurance of the front upon which the battle must be fought.

Kate Millett has had the misfortune to write what her exploiters have indeed called the 'bible' of Women's Liberation, and she has paid her dues, regardless of how much she has earned as a result of the operations of a marketing system which was irrelevant to her motivation in writing a book at all—paid her dues in destruction of privacy, in bearing abuse when she let slip ingenuously that she was (as we all are) bisexual, and in bearing responsibility for a movement whose achievements she can never claim, whose failures she must speak for.

Her book, *Sexual Politics,* is basically a literary and pedantic enterprise. The vanity of *littérateurs* is to suppose that they are of immediate political relevance, so that Norman Mailer can state because he is attacked in Kate Millett's book that he is certainly the 'primary target' of the women's campaign. The Writer is immensely tickled at the notion, and has been casting about vainly for an opportunity to vanquish single-handed all the spokeswomen for liberation at one sitting, or, failing that, to be ignominiously whipped by a majority of two or three to one. So far the women have refused to be drawn. Failing his emblematic confrontation in Carnegie Hall, Mailer has nevertheless managed to publish his anti-liberation arguments in an article, "The Prisoner of Sex", in *Harper's:* with the result that the editor Willie Morris has resigned and his resignation has been accepted almost before it was made. His staff have come out with him and massive subscriptions have been lost.

The ultimate result of the pother will be advantageous to women. Kate Millett herself cannot have hoped for such a clear and absurd statement of the male supremacist position. The mayhem which broke out in the offices of *Harper's* is only a foretaste of the destruction that the male animal will inflict upon the world when his supremacy is finally challenged. How could the Mailer male subside into venerable old age sans punch, sans prick, sans what he thinks is everything? Isn't it more likely that he too will blow the back of his head off in one last killer come? (If you think that's mannered expression, I caught it from "The Prisoner of Sex".)

When Caruso was in his agony, his screams are said to have been utterly beautiful; outside in the street passers-by stopped to lend ear to the arabesques of pure pain. Even in extremity Mailer writes well: the deadly appeal of violence-sexier-than-sex flashes and bangs in a last seductive display. But Aquarius knows absurdity: painfully grinning, the prisoner marches in a dead straight furrow carved by phallic relentlessness, clear out of sight. Nothing would irritate this battered warrior-child more than a woman's compassion, but we will weep for him nonetheless.

Unfortunately "The Prisoner of Sex" is not uniformly absurd. Where Mailer takes issue with Millett he is powerful, as well he might be, for *Sexual Politics* is not, however much a feminist might wish it was, a good book. It has become perforce an important book, because the media machine that seized upon it was merely capitulating to the pressure of curiosity in the female community itself. In response to the pressure of this demand Kate Millett has offered us her PhD thesis, which is gargantuan and assails enough issues to earn 50 PhDs in any more rational system. She is first, then, a victim of the academic game, which leads her to adopt an impersonal tone of unassailable authority and expertise, and that for her is dishonesty. She builds great chains of abstractions, forging a logical system behind which she might shelter from the hard gaze of her fellow academics. Nothing in her book is as subversive as the unguarded and simple story she tells in Midge McKenzie's film, *Women Talking,* an ordinary story of a little girl taking a lift home from a stranger. That little girl, too polite and innocent to protect herself from outrage, has grown into a warm and funny woman but no trace of her, no sound of her voice, can be found in the dreary pedantic wastes and portentous pertness of *Sexual Politics.* One can only hope that the academics whom Kate Millett so humbly and sweetly thanks in her preface will eventually realise what their straitjacket discipline has produced in the way of deformed birth.

In delineating her theory of sexual dominance as a political phenomenon in all societies regardless of biology or economics, Kate Millett almost succeeds in making liberation itself seem an absurdity. While it is clear that women will not find freedom in any revolution in which they do not represent their own interests, it seems true that women have arrived at a position where liberation is a possibility. But if, as Millett seems to argue, the fucked is always female and always inferior, the patterns of exploitation seem ineradicable. It is not unheard of for liberationists to argue that sexual intercourse must cease: if we take Mailer's mystique of the pristine will on the edge of doom into account there seems to be some *ad hoc* justification for this position. It is, after all, a case of the polarisation in political movements which is coming to characterise radicalism in the impatient USA. Any theory which denies enmity and vengeance is dubbed liberal with a sneer, even though it should prove more radical in its vision of change than the pseudo-empiricism and fatuous fightin' talk of those who pride themselves on the purity and hardness of their line. (As long as unwillingness to seek out and destroy the unwitting enemy is the mark of a liberal, I'm it. Let them realise what an anarchist is when it's too late, by all means.) (pp. 355-56)

Sexual Politics is a curiously constructed work. Like the other writers of female liberation, Kate Millett is driven by a desire to be exhaustive, to anticipate criticism, although she tacitly accepts the major criticisms of her schematisation in her preface. She has adopted the difficult mode of arguing from literature to ideology to behaviour, a topsy-turvy passage for any social theorist, especially a Marxist. The connections between the sections of her book are vital but tenuous. The book begins with instances of sexual politics paraphrased rather ruthlessly from the works of Mailer, Miller and Genet, and it swings back to the same area for its final third. The intervening sections are in a way to explain the values subsumed in the criticism and, hopefully, to justify them.

The opening section is the most familiar, since it appeared in the *New American Review* as long ago as August 1969. It partakes of a deficiency in criticism which is very like that which marred an essay which even my convent school had the sense to reject, in which I explained that I had abandoned my reading of *Le Rouge et le Noir* because Julien Sorel was such an unworthy fellow. The writer is identified with his persona and accused of the crimes of his characters although it is he who has exposed them. The vigour and appeal of the depiction is not the artist's fault but very much more an indication of the centrality of the individual fantasy to the culture in which he is writing. A criticism on this basis would have made sense, but Kate Millett is so genuinely incensed that she sneers and bellyaches at the authors, who are not after all the enemy, any more than books are the battlefield. The writer is a curious

animal, drawn closer to the realm of bi-sex than those who take up more normal masculine professions. Mailer's description of the thraldom of Lawrence's imagination to the masculinity he could never attain is masterly: perhaps a woman will find power and pity enough to delineate the same vain striving in Mailer himself, beset by his fattening bottom and the difficulty of the 'adventurous juncture of ego and courage' which is a 'firm erection'.

The opening literary skirmish is followed by an attempt to state the theory of sexual politics, the heart of the book, which would have been better off as the whole book in 300 pages instead of 26. It is laboriously written, condensed into a style as flexible and sensitive as a Panzer tank. This is the part of the book which will have to serve as a textbook for the movement, although the maximum effort will have to be expended in translating it back from theoretic jargon into the language of experience.

The description of the sexual revolution and its counter-revolution returns to the familiar fields of literary polemic. The selection of material and the analyses are alike influenced by the theory outlined in the preceding chapter. The historical terrain is thereby flattened, and the conflict emerges as an eternal sameness. The schema is unnecessary because the ebb and flow of revolution is more rhythmic and complex than the requirements of Kate Millett's thesis: even the most sympathetic reader is vexed by the desire to dissent. (p. 356)

> Germaine Greer, "Lib and Lit," in The Listener, *Vol. 85, No. 2191, March 25, 1971, pp. 355-56.*

The Times Literary Supplement

Sexual Politics is a much more wide-ranging and sharply intelligent account of the past and present sex-war situation than preliminary publicity and early reviews might suggest. Kate Millett's stance is bristlingly militant, but she is not so much a fighter in the ranks of Women's Lib as a propagandist and theoretician, at once publicizing the horrific actions of the Other Side, and analysing the ideas of sexual revolutionaries (John Stuart Mill and Engels) and their reactionary opposites (Ruskin and Freud). She writes sometimes with the ferocious joviality of a Wyndham Lewis, more often in a language so choked with righteous wrath that it is hard to catch her exact meaning. "Women should be on top", might be her slogan, and it is characteristic of her book that, although she deals with education and political organization as well as literature and psychology, it is difficult to consider anything she says except in sexual terms.

Her argument is confusingly presented, but when summarized appears sensible and for the most part not especially novel. From a date that she puts roughly as the publication of Mary Wollstonecraft's *Vindication,* which she sees as "the first document asserting the full humanity of women and insisting upon its recognition", the attainment of women's rights has been part of the social revolution. Others have seen these rights in terms of more votes, better pay, a share in government, but although Kate Millett glances at these things she regards them only as brief stopping stations on the way to full emancipation. . . .

The revolutionary aspect of her thesis is that she wants to destroy altogether what she calls the "patriarchal structure" by which men run the world in their own interests. She praises the early attempts in the Soviet Union to set up a "new psychic structure . . . to replace that of patriarchy", and her ideas would seem to envisage a condition of ideal communism or anarchism, although this is never explicitly said. They include free marriage, divorce and abortion, and "most material of all . . . liberation from the controlling economic power of the husband". Economically and emotionally Kate Millett finds women subject to men, and she would like to correct this situation. Indeed, at times it seems that she would like to reverse it.

This argument is behind rather than contained in her book, for she writes hardly at all about the ways in which women might achieve such "full humanity" and does not consider whether many of them would want to replace the family by a "new psychic structure". She does not deal with the revolution so much as with the easier theme of the counter-revolution, seen chiefly in terms of sexual attitudes in the work of Jean Genet, D. H. Lawrence, Norman Mailer, and Henry Miller. To be fair, she deals with some Victorian literature as well, making a lively analysis of Tennyson's "Princess", and using a comparison between Mill's essay on *The Subjection of Women* and Ruskin's lecture "Of Queen's Gardens" to point up differences of attitude with much polemical skill. Her attack upon Freud's doctrine of penis envy, although monstrously partial, is also carried out with enjoyable verve and irreverence. More than a third of her book, however, is given over to an account of the four writers mentioned, and their attitude towards sex is in practice largely its theme.

This attitude is found in its most extreme form in the work of Genet, whose pimps abuse and do not protect their slaves, and are merely amused when they are beaten or even killed. The "girl queen" receives in return only the promise of "an intensity of humiliation which constitutes identity for those who despise themselves". For women, in the eyes of these male novelists, humiliation equals satisfaction, or at least it is the only satisfaction they are likely to get. What they describe, according to Kate Millett, is a fantasy world of male domination and feminine subjection. If we murmur that Genet is a homosexual writer and that his queens are boys, the brisk reply is that his "homosexual, criminal world . . . mimics with brutal frankness the bourgeois heterosexual society". In relation to these writers plenty of evidence is offered to support the case, and Miss Millett would no doubt find irrelevant the observation that dozens of other novelists do not play this particular kind of sexual politics. What she has to say about them is often very funny, a fact which has not been much remarked:

> Sexual congress in a Mailer novel is always a matter of strenuous endeavour, rather like mountain climbing. . . .
>
> An erection (in *Lady Chatterley's Lover*) provides the female with irrefutable evidence that

male supremacy is founded upon the most real and uncontrovertible grounds. . . .

It should be added that she shows at times a ponderous lack of humour, as in the straight-faced remark, "Coition can scarcely be said to take place in a vacuum"; and at others a disagreeable condescension, as in the observation that Ruskin "was by no means a stupid man".

One carries away two impressions from *Sexual Politics:* of intelligence and of confusion. Kate Millett is a social and not a literary critic, but on the social plane her attack on Lawrence, Mailer and Miller is well-ordered, sustained and damaging. Genet is treated more tenderly, perhaps because however much he mimics heterosexual society his insulted victims are after all not women. The Victorian material she has gathered is skilfully used, and her account of recent developments in psychoanalysis is interesting though incomplete. There is no question about the alertness of her responses and the toughness of her mind.

Yet there is no doubt either about her confusion. She never discusses the point basic to her argument, that the complete emancipation to which she looks forward could not take place except in a totally different social order from any existing in the world at present. The sexual revolution she envisages could take place only as part of a social revolution which she never mentions, and even in such a social revolution the emancipation of women is by no means inevitable. . . . And her dismissal of the biological grounds for believing male aggression and feminine passivity to be mutable only within fairly narrow limits is distinctly sketchy. It is, after all, men who penetrate women and not (except in *Myra Breckinridge*) the other way round.

"A New Vindication of the Rights of Women,"
in The Times Literary Supplement, *No. 3606,
April 9, 1971, p. 410.*

Jane Wilson

"No apology justifies what I have done" writes Kate Millett at the beginning of her preface to *Flying*, an autobiographical work of dazzling exhibitionism and of such ingrown confusion that this same preface does not appear until page 81. In attempting to explain herself to the lagging and disoriented reader, she offers first an ominous moral muddle in the proposition that it might ever be possible to *justify* an action by apologizing for it. As the book proceeds, it becomes clear that she believes absolutely in such a possibility. But in *Flying* it is not mere justification that Millett seeks. She is after absolution as well, empathy, approval and admiration, and her demanding neediness hounds the reader from the beginning to the end of this marathon essay in self-absorption. She knows quite well what she is doing. There are few likely hostile thoughts about her work that have not been anticipated by the author. An arm raised to send *Flying* in flight across the room may be arrested by a sudden aside from Millett announcing "disturbing visions of disgusted reader throwing the book on the floor. How dare I take up his time? I see his annoyance with brilliant clarity."

It had occurred to her, she says, "to treat my own existence as documentary." The time of her life that she is most concerned to detail, almost as a cautionary tale, is that following the publication in 1970 of *Sexual Politics,* a period of conflict, unrequited love and personal misery which culminated in what sounds like a classic depression. To go with her "documentary" metaphor—the result is a *cinéma vérité* endurance test, with warts and boredom unedited. The focus is haphazard, some of the reels appear to have been projected in an arbitrary sequence, and there are problems with the soundtrack in that characters other than Millett are frequently inaudible. However, she stands ready beside the screen, providing an avid running commentary on the action, exhorting the audience to laugh, cry and suffer at appropriate moments, rousing it from somnolence during arid stretches, and apologizing always for the disparity between her intention and its performance. Whenever the movie gets really out of whack, she steps out in front to forestall catcalls with a plucky comedy routine mocking herself and her pretensions. Her nerve never fails her.

If it is difficult to recognize *Flying* and *Sexual Politics* as products of the same mind, it must be because one was written as an academic thesis and the other as a cry of pain. *Sexual Politics,* with all its faults, was an original and useful book in that it imposed a moratorium on reiterated, dead-end feminist complaint against the male chauvinist pig in the street. Millett's oblique approach to the problem of women's liberation—concentrating on the incidence of sexism in literature, as opposed to life—made cooler and somewhat more productive discussion possible. It is also dramatically increased the number of potential participants in the ongoing seminar. Where once personal experience of sexist discrimination had been the paramount credential, it was now possible to enter the fray armed only with a working knowledge of the perfidy of D. H. Lawrence or Norman Mailer.

Millett's book defined areas and supplied helpful examples, so it became a best seller, and she, as night follows day, became a celebrity. Whereupon, as she recalls, "My decent anonymity was blasted into a ruin of interviews, articles, attacks, a banal paper war of thunderous volume if minute proportion." As a 35-year-old unsuccessful sculptor living scruffily in the East Village, she was at first excited by the publicity. But soon she became angry. She is a forceful woman who, on the evidence in *Flying,* is accustomed to controlling, manipulating and on occasion exploiting the people around her, so she was literally maddened—"Has anybody ever gone mad from the media before?"—when she came up hard against the fact that she could not control the image of herself that was projected by the press and on television.

This being the case, and finding herself constitutionally unsuited to life as a talk-show exhibit and peripatetic spokeswoman for Women's Lib, why did she not simply quit the scene? Once recognized as an articulate member of the movement, she somehow ceased to be a free agent. In her uncomfortable new spokeswoman status she was urged on by her sisters to do her duty in speaking out on

their behalf, while also being browbeaten and harassed for her arrogance and "élitism" in presuming to do so.

It is possible that she felt an extra obligation—she evidently discussed *Sexual Politics* with a number of women in the movement while she was writing it. Just before it was published she was hysterically attacked for signing her own name to the work by some former friends who asserted that it should appear as the work of a Women's Lib collective. Though she attends plenty of meetings and marches in *Flying,* she seems often to be weary of the whole business. "How does one get out of the movement?" she asks. "Where is the exit? I can't be Kate Millett any more. It's an object, a thing. A joke at cocktail parties."

The most painful result of the publicity that engulfed her when *Sexual Politics* was published was a cruel "coming out," a forced public admission of her lesbianism at a meeting of the women's movement at Columbia University. This was in 1970, before such intimate communiqués were commonplace and at a time when Gay Lib and the Radical Lesbian bloc were intent on claiming their own and making unseemly waves inside Women's Lib. Millett vividly recalls the scene at which she was obliged to identify her proclivities, one way or the other:

> Teresa Juarez's voice loud butches me from a floor mike center of the room, a bully for all the right political reasons. Five hundred people looking at me. Are you a Lesbian? Everything pauses, faces look up in terrible silence. I hear them not breathe. That word in public, the word I waited half a lifetime to hear. Finally I am accused. "Say it! Say you are a Lesbian!" Yes I said. Yes. Because I know what she means. The line goes, inflexible as a fascist edict, that bisexuality is a cop-out. Yes I said yes I am a Lesbian.

She was, and is, married to the Japanese sculptor Fumio Yoshimura, a union undertaken in friendship and affection to thwart the plans of immigration officers. They share a studio in the Bowery, a farm in Connecticut and, from time to time, a bed. Millett writes of heterosexuality as of a relaxing creature comfort in the same category as a warm bath or a mug of hot chocolate at bedtime. She is delighted by the ingenious and convenient mechanics of the whole procedure, which make mutual satisfaction possible without any particular inventiveness being required of either partner.

But she is a lesbian—and her mother back home in St. Paul was disgraced before friends, neighbors, colleagues and relatives by the public and undeniable announcement of this fact in *Time* magazine. She describes her mother's reactions—"It's dirty, filthy, disgusting"—and she returns time and again to her mother's inability to accept a deviant daughter. And then, pathetically, she dedicates to this same stony mother a book filled with explicit descriptions of lesbian sexual encounters. (pp. 2-3)

The best part of *Flying* is about a visit to England where she is to edit a "talking heads" movie she has made about some friends in the women's movement. Celibacy and work are the order of the day. She is the house guest of an unhappily married couple on the verge of bankruptcy whose lives are being blighted by their seriously retarded child. Their problems are so patently worse than hers that, for a while, the level of her self-pity is wonderfully reduced. Distance from her New York beat shakes her out of familiar patterns and lends perspective.

Walking about in the London rush-hour crowds she sees herself as "an American dyke intent on creating myths out of a handful of Lesbians in New York City, and a few other friends, while the real world, the employed and the responsible, have a routine and a reality to accomplish." It is in London that she gets what she describes as a "peculiar warning" from a friend who tells her "You must not think all life is to produce. It is also to live. You cannot forever package it into art. This cheapens it to product." She pauses to remark that the admonition will always haunt her, and then bowls on inexorably to discuss a friend's frigidity.

From the moment that Millett decided on the "documentary" form of *Flying,* she must have lived her life in order to write about it. The book is littered with complaints about the exhaustions of the task, about the damaging effect that her constant reportorial stance is having on her relationships. At times the unexamined life must have seemed eminently worth living. But she presses on, the weight of her vigilance bearing down on everything that she and her friends say, do and are, driven on by her need to order and control, to present at last her chosen image of herself.

At the end of the book, pretending flippancy, she gives an extraordinarily self-indulgent sketch of

> a fantasy self in Mexican shirts, thinking she's glamorous and hoping women will love her, bit of a character, always carries a large disheveled bag, drives an outlandish old car, is tickled when people discuss it. They indulge her. The great fault in her character, this insatiable thirst for affection. Does things people are not going to love her for. And then insists on being surprised when they hate her instead.

If this, or anything resembling it, is the self that she intended to present, Millett has failed as dismally as ever she did with the media. After 500 pages of her life "packaged into art," the reader is well acquainted with a much sadder, more complex and less innocent figure. (p. 3)

> *Jane Wilson, "Sexual Apologetics," in* The New York Times Book Review, *June 23, 1974, pp. 2-3.*

Muriel Haynes

It is getting crowded these days on the island of Lesbos. One imagines Sappho's shade bewildered by her new disciples. Who can blame her if she murmurs, echoing Marx: deliver me from the sapphists. Something has surely gone awry to set off this chorus of suffering and guilt, this niagara of tendentious prose. Kate Millett's autobiography [*Flying*], for example, a leviathan of self-justification that demands of the reader an analyst's endurance, is a monologue that lasts for 546 pages.

In *Sex Pol,* the nickname by which Millett affects to dis-

parage her first book, **Sexual Politics,** she went beyond the indictment of patriarchy to suggest a sexual utopia. Repression by cultural stereotypes would yield to acceptance of human variety and its possible choices. *Flying* is an unflinching record of her uneasy struggle to practice what she preaches in the trying circumstances of her sudden fame as a leader of the feminist movement. "It had occurred to me," she explains, "to treat my own existence as documentary." So began The Book, a domineering project of self-bugging. It is a therapeutic effort to recover her balance during the difficult year in which, with fear and anguish, she repudiated her false image of "nice married lady" in order to proclaim her lesbianism.

Almost accidentally, in the early days of sisterhood, Millett resumed the sexual relationships with women that began in her school days. These affairs were variously unsuccessful. Agonizing over her rejection by Celia, she is tempted to return to the straight path: "It doesn't work out with women . . . it only works with Fumio" (her Japanese sculptor husband). But she is bound to make it work to vindicate her romantic theories about multiple relationships, sex as the completion of friendship, love freed from possessiveness. The details of her program are rather daunting for their emotional ambition no less than for sexual energy. Fumio, patiently forbearing, sums it up: "You are living exaggerated life."

The Book, like a *doppelganger,* nags Millett's days and nights with its tyrannical presence. Notebook in hand, she scribbles it all down—conversations, quarrels, political meetings, memories, sex in many places with many people. She reports it almost as it is happening, seemingly verbatim, with tireless respect for minutiae. Any embarrassment is the reader's, unless perhaps belatedly for those who approved the use of their own names. The Book sits at Kate's table, sleeps in her bed(s) and sometimes bullies its characters. "Do you know you're in a book?" she asks a friend warningly, who replies: "Of course. Everybody knows you're writing a book, you never shut up about it." Yes. If only she could stop talking!

Acting as one's own Boswell requires a sense that one is eligible for legend. We balk at that, yet why is Millett so likable for all her solipsism? An intelligent, gutsy, loving woman, full of self-hate and a passionate longing for acceptance, her genuine suffering reflects the damaging confusions of American culture in transition. Intellectually she early rejected her Roman Catholic upbringing, but the guilt of mortal sin lingers on. "Are you queer?" she used to ask herself in the mirror. Condemned by her mother, only her mother can grant absolution. She tells Mrs. Millett about The Book. "You're not going to put the awful stuff about lesbianism in it?" She is and she will dedicate it to her, what's more, to prove her mother's love can take her as she is. (p. 28)

Forestalling her reviewers, Millett protests The Book is not literature. She writes with verve and Irish wit; there are brilliantly colored scenes. She can catch character with exactitude. Yet, *Flying* is an assemblage of raw materials that might have been transmuted to literature if the need for catharsis *now* hadn't prevented the play of "that particular detachment" esteemed by Henry James and that he found "so terribly wanting in autobiography, brought, as the horrible phrase is, up-to-date." (p. 29)

Muriel Haynes, "Sexual Energy," in The New Republic, *Vol. 171, Nos. 1 & 2, July 6 & 13, 1974, pp. 28-9.*

Rene Kuhn Bryant

Now, try to pay attention and follow closely and we'll see if we can sort this whole thing out somehow. Kate is a teacher but she doesn't teach because she is really a sculptor. But she doesn't sculpt because she has to go to so many meetings and make so many speeches. She has to go to so many meetings and make so many speeches because she wrote a book four years ago. A lot of people took that book very seriously, starting with Kate, and decided she was the theoretician of the women's liberation movement. That's quite a responsibility. Now she has written another book about how she feels about what happened after she wrote the first one. Only it's a little hard to write a book when what you are really doing is making a documentary film on women's lib and the film is being shot in New York but processed and edited in London because it's cheaper to do it that way. Anyway, it's plain to see where the title [*Flying*] comes from, isn't it?

Where were we? Oh, yes, the women's liberation movement. This is the really tricky bit but we'll take it slowly. Taking a deep breath, Kate tells us she is a lesbian. But she is married to Fumio who, in addition to being her husband, is, she assures us, her "best friend." She's also in love with Celia. Celia, however, has broken off with Kate and is now living with Ann, and Kate finds that fairly anguishing. Meanwhile, Vita and Fred have *both* "come out," and that means that, temporarily at least, Vita can be Kate's lover and, since she's tidy and organized and a good speller and typist, her secretary as well. Unfortunately, before long Vita begins to get on Kate's nerves because she reminds her of her mother, so that arrangement doesn't work out so well after all. But also meanwhile, in a march on Albany, Kate has met Claire who, thousands of paragraphs later, turns out to be the love of her life—so far, anyway. And meanwhile still, there are Naomi and Miriam and Nell and Zoe and Jill and Rachel and Rhoda and, I mustn't forget, of course good old Fumio.

But suddenly the urge to parody collapses in the face of the towering, overpowering egotism and destructive narcissism of this book. The Empress stands revealed as quite naked and extremely ill-favored at that. Exasperation succeeds bemusement, as it is borne in on us that we are being asked to accept cant and claptrap as serious political analysis.

To those earnest followers of social change who regard the militancies of women's lib as a force for eventual good, as devoted simply to such worthy and unselfish objectives as ensuring equal pay for equal work, for example, *Flying* should prove a stunning revelation. For Kate Millett and perhaps for the majority among the activists, women's lib is the vehicle through which private psychosis is metamorphosed into public purpose and not only glorified but sanctified. To suppose anything else is to allow oneself to become a co-conspirator in the vast con game known as Gay Liberation.

It is all to be seen here in an endless outpouring of shallow, witless comment that is ungainly and graceless in its structure, gratingly obvious and banal in its observations, inchoate when it is not incoherent, blundering in its posture, and intolerable in its pretentiousness. Consider, for instance, these passing bows to Angela Davis and Bernadette Devlin:

> Then redecorated (at a protest meeting on South Africa and Rhodesia, of course) with Angela buttons. Angela in her grandeur reduced to a smudge. Angela real as prison and the world flaunting her courage, riding on that wind of heroism while an actual woman is in handcuffs behind real bars somewhere taking the rap for our emotional effusions. . . . And now I remember I still have not composed my letter to Devlin, roasted on the box and in newsprint this week. Having a baby on her own. Lady interviewer turns the knife, "Won't that mean your career?" Mick Bernadette, her face only human and beautiful parries thrust while I groan for her, stuck in the soft spot of scandal once myself.

And so on and on and on and on. But these are the better moments of the book. The worse are reserved to explore the fatal fascination Miss Millett holds for herself. . . . [On] page 535 she queries frantically: "Will I be caught here? I wonder. Trapped in this book forever?"

If it is only all those hundreds of thousands of words later that such a possibility finally crosses her consciousness, think of the claustrophobia long since induced in the reader. She may, indeed, be trapped in her own verbiage but we, at long last, can escape and make our way back to civilization. (pp. 989-90)

Rene Kuhn Bryant, "Drowning in Claustrophobia," in National Review, *New York, Vol. XXVI, August 30, 1974, pp. 989-90.*

Letters to Ms.

[*Ms.* Editor's Note]: *In the December, 1974, Ms. "Forum," Elinor Langer discussed "the absence of a genuinely critical tradition in the Women's Movement," and focused on the confessional genre, citing Kate Millett's* Flying *as a recent, important example of the form. Langer argued that "confession protects. By pretending that we are presenting 'life,' not art, we avoid criticism. . . . "*

Kate Millett replied in the January, 1975 "Forum," that she had "never seen Flying *as a 'confession,' " but rather as symbolic of a turning point in women's literature. "In beginning to express . . . we go forward from that starting line where we stood and argued our humanity." She concluded, "the shame is over."*

An unusual number of readers contributed thought-provoking letters to this debate. The dialogue continues with some of the readers' responses, printed here.

How irresponsible of *Ms.* to give space to Elinor Langer's poorly thought-out, snobbish lambasting of Kate Millett's book. Certainly you have no time to waste in the worn-out game of Let's Get Kate Millett.

First of all, *Flying* is *not* confessional writing. Confession implies penitence, the desire for forgiveness, for absolution; the realization of a mistaken way of life and the moment of change. *Flying,* for all its painful self-examination, is an affirmation of Kate Millett.

Above all, *Flying* is honest. Too often and for too long women have written self-deception, the happy-ever-after tales of housewives and husbands. True Confessions of the mistaken notions of their strength and power, the returning to the feminine role, the absolution of society. The magazines of the fifties reeked of it, the magazines today still do. I wish that Elinor Langer would actually *read* confessional writing. And not the stream-of-consciousness writing she thinks it is, but the real honest self-accusations of women who test their cocoons, who test their sexuality, and creep back.

Nowhere in *Flying* did I feel that Kate Millett was exhibiting herself—the freak, the queer—although that was certainly part of the experience of her book. There is plenty of pain in *Flying,* but there is plenty of pain in the life of a woman. It is not phony, nor put there to protect Millett against criticism.

Langer seems enraged by the "heavy pornography" of the book; which just proves that beauty—and smut—is in the eye of the beholder. The sexual writing in *Flying* is beautifully and tenderly done. It is also very often lesbian. Perhaps here we have the real root of Langer's rage, her impotent anger that Millett does not, indeed, "confess" her lesbianism but celebrates it.

Millett through her honesty and courage has suffered greatly from the flexing of muscle within the Movement. It is time we gave her the great credit due her and stopped playing stupid games . . .

> Kathleen Cima
> Monroeville, Pa.

• • •

I do not understand how Langer can say that *Flying* "can remind us of the absence of a genuinely critical tradition in the Women's Movement." If anything, the Women's Movement is distinguished by its critical and analytical writings, and certainly Millett is a major figure in that tradition.

Despite what I have read about *Flying* in various reviews, I find it honest, compelling, full of crucial information on how women relate to each other, technically quite astonishing. I am particularly distressed over Langer's repeated accusation that the work is "pornographic." For a woman to write about erotic meetings with other women in a literal way is not to write "pornography." It is not necessarily to demean women and to pander to male fantasy. The fact is that Millett does not at any point cheapen her own sexuality or that of her sisters. I was unhappy that Millett feels such guilt at being "queer"—not that she writes about it,

but that she herself feels it. Many women her age, however, do feel precisely what she puts down before us. She does what an artist, a feminist artist, must do—she vividly creates the conflicts, pains, and joys of a life lived bravely.

I find nothing "pitiful" about *Flying* as a work. Millett does not "(take) up the imagined charges of past and future 'enemies' and transform them into self-hate." There is nothing "imagined" about the charges of her past and future enemies; whatever "self-hate" she delineates belongs to us all and is an active dynamic in the Women's Movement—what Flo Kennedy calls "horizontal hostility," the self-hatred of the oppressed.

I don't think that it is legitimate to use *Flying* as the emblem of the confessional form, and then to repudiate the form. These are two separate questions. The form could be valid, and yet *Flying* could fail. But Langer does not like the *form itself*: she rejects journals and diaries en masse, so long the treasured private writing places for so many distinguished women who could not bear the brutality of the public place dominated by men. Langer wants us to reject this woman's tradition—and *Flying* with it—and do serious work: critical, analytical, hard-headed, serious work—"male" work, that is, using the forms that have a certain kind of male approval. But *Flying* is serious work—it is the study of a particular time in a particular woman's life, and it touches themes that concern us all.

To use *Flying* as an emblem for the rejection of a particular literary form is terribly unfair. Rainer Maria Rilke said that works of art should be critically judged by those who love them. If, before one begins, one has no sympathy for the project itself, then how can one see where it is good, where it is bad, where it is useful, where it is not? Adversary criticism ill serves women: the kind of bludgeoning it requires will destroy those who give us the most . . .

> Andrea Dworkin
> New York, N.Y.

• • •

I read *Sexual Politics,* then I read *Flying.* Langer is correct—the former is literary, brilliant, politically incisive; the latter, confessional, pitiful, emotional. *Sexual Politics* is an intellectual exercise; *Flying* is human intimacy. I will forget the words of the remote PhD. I will not forget the woman. Thanks, Kate.

> Martha B. Barrett
> Havertown, Pa.

• • •

I think it's unfair to deal with Elinor Langer's description of *Flying* as pornographic as merely an example of homophobia, as Millett has done. Lesbians can be pornographic too, when they contemplate their vaginas and call it love. *Flying* is pornographic because it is egocentric, not because it is lesbian.

If any book can be seen as representative of the era from which it comes, it seems to me *Flying* is indicative of a generation of women who saw sexual liberation as the *sine qua non* of revolution. I've seen many of these same people disillusioned, and even bitter lately. To have been flying in 1969-70 was one thing; to defend it as exemplary today is another.

Relationships between women are extremely difficult under male supremacy, and in the years since *Flying* took place, perhaps they've become even more difficult. I have, to use Langer's analogy, seen many quivering lower lips in the Movement of late, and I think a few stiff upper lips may be necessary for its survival. Living in the past does not seem the best survival tactic.

It seems sad to me that Millett evidently does not see her book as a social document. As one of the participants in the foot-stomping days she describes . . . , I feel shut out by the narrowness of her vision. Many of us have suffered in the Movement; *all* our mothers have had to come to terms with our choices. A movement which began with a collectivist ideal has ended up with an individualist one.

Still, if Millett truly believes all the things she's said, she deserves a lot of credit. She may be, as Doris Lessing said, a very courageous woman. I only wish she would share that courage with us in a broader sense. I do not relish the thought that leading figures in the Movement stand around talking about their nervous breakdowns, as she describes. I think there's a need for strength rather than self-pity. Portraying oneself as a basket case provides inspiration for no one.

The development of a critical tradition in the Movement is the best thing that could happen to us. Not only might we learn to overcome our fear of criticism, but it might help stem the tide of rip-off books about women.

Millett seems unable to believe that anyone should spurn her gift of love, *Flying.* But then she should know better than most that an act of love is a mutual one, a meeting of mutual needs rather than individual ones. *Flying* may be spurned like an old love, not because one doesn't care any more, but because one has changed, moved on, outgrown it, come down for a landing.

Sandy De Wine
New York, N.Y. (pp. 10-13)

Kathleen Cima and others, "Letters," in Ms., *Vol. III, No. 12, June, 1975, pp. 10-13.*

Annette Kolodny

Kate Millett's *Flying* was not kindly received by the reviewers when it appeared in 1974. Although one might be inclined to dismiss René Kuhn Bryant's attack, which appeared in the *National Review,* as motivated by her politics and by her overt hostility towards both Millett and Gay Liberation, nevertheless, her description of *Flying* as only "an endless outpouring of shallow, witless comment" repeated the sentiments of many a more sympathetic reviewer, as did her distaste for the way in which the book documented its subject "minute by remorseless minute, if not second by interminable second" [see Kuhn Bryant's excerpt]. Muriel Haynes, writing in the *New Republic,* for example, made much the same observation when she called the book "a leviathan . . . that demands of the reader an analyst's endurance" [see Haynes's excerpt].

But the most surprising response was undoubtedly Elinor Langer's "Forum" article, in *Ms.,* which dismissed the book on the grounds that "confession is not disciplined autobiography" [see *Ms.* excerpt for responses].

Responses like these—all by female reviewers—belie the currently fashionable notion that women will naturally be receptive or sympathetic to another woman's writing. Supporting that notion, of course, is the assumption that women share certain rather specific areas of experience which men and women do not (as a result both of biological and cultural factors), and that they will therefore automatically recognize and understand the content of another woman's work. Yet *content* in these reviews never really seemed to be the issue. Bryant objected to the book's detailed all-inclusiveness as "inchoate when it is not incoherent," and Langer rejected a narrative format in which "free association has supplanted thought." For Murial Haynes, the *form* was unfinished, representing only an "assemblage of raw materials."

Typical as they are of the many other critical responses to greet *Flying,* these remarks suggest that while women may well be desirous of greeting and encouraging the recently increasing outpouring of women's writing, they are, in reality, no better able to deal with some of the new and different forms that writing is taking than is the more traditional male reviewing establishment. Nor is it difficult to understand why. Kate Millett obliquely addressed the point in her response to Langer's article. Declaring "the shame is over," and insisting that, henceforth, it would no longer be possible to constrain or constrict the kind of information incorporated into women's writing, she was suggesting, if only by implication, that women might well begin to produce books with contents we have not previously seen before and, as a result, that such contents might themselves demand forms or evolve into artifacts we are hard put to label. Millett herself claimed to have written "not quite an autobiography," and responded to critics by insisting that her book "refuses and eludes any literary category, just as it was meant to."

Muriel Haynes, perhaps, most clearly put her finger on the problem when she insisted that the "assemblage of raw materials" presently comprising the text "*might* have been transmuted to literature" (italics mine) had Millett only been capable "of 'that particular detachment' esteemed by Henry James." It is a prescription that comes not only out of Henry James, of course, but out of the entire accepted canon of Western autobiographical writing—a canon, for the most part, of male manufacture. . . . It is only with the discoveries, rediscoveries, and reprintings of the last few years, in fact, that Agnes Smedley's autobiographical novel, *Daughter of Earth,* or Anaïs Nin's diaries have been made widely available; and only now do Susannah Moody's journals begin to appear on course lists, along with Elizabeth Cady Stanton's *Eighty Years and More.*

Until just recently, then, the standard studies of autobiography have offered us a genre—spanning St. Augustine and Peter Abelard through Rousseau and Goethe in Europe, or homey Ben Franklin through Henry Adams and Lincoln Steffens in the United States—in which successive generations of male writers have been able to refine and define their lives according to variously accepted norms of importance, personal and/or cultural. Omissions and deletions have constituted the very art of the form, resulting, as William L. Howarth argues [in "Some Principles of Autobiography"], in a highly self-conscious and intentional "self-portrait—one far different from (the) original model, resembling life but actually composed and framed as an artful invention." (pp. 541-43).

Since the publication of Millett's *Sexual Politics* in 1970 and, shortly thereafter, Germaine Greer's *The Female Eunuch*, women have come more and more to protest the fact that they themselves appear to be "an artful invention"—in most recent years, having been defined, framed, restricted, and simplified (for their own purposes) by everyone from Norman Mailer to Madison Avenue advertising executives. It would, then, be reasonable to expect that when a woman who had herself been a leader in this protest decided to set down her own life's story, she might well disavow, or at least alter, the male tradition. A woman who devoted her Ph.D. thesis to the study of the inadequate and inauthentic presentation of women in literature would hardly be satisfied with presenting her own life as that "literary simplification of an extremely complex reality" which Wayne Shumaker summarizes as the heritage of male autobiography [in his *English Autobiography: Its Emergence, Materials, and Form*]. Indeed, it is the very complexity of their reality that women today are trying so desperately to map. Moreover, the fine distinctions between public and private, or trivial and important, which had served as guides for the male autobiographer have never really been available to women. Traditionally taught that what was "important" for them lay wholly in the private sphere, having no public consequence, women internalized a picture of themselves that itself precluded the kind of self-attention which might generate autobiography.

With purposes very different from that of the male autobiographer, then, intent upon collecting *all* the "tidbits of thought, memory, grasshopper trivia," and without access to any significant countertradition of female autobiography from which to learn, Millett produced a text which in no way resembles that disengaged, self-critical, self-distanced, and self-scrutinizing brand of autobiography we have been taught to read and critics have come to expect. But then any demand that women write the same kind of formal, distilled narrative we usually get from men implies a belief that women share the same kind of reality as men; clearly, this is not the case. All of which brings into question not only the way in which most critical reviewing is practiced, but the theoretical formulae upon which that practice is based. Treated, however, as an ongoing reading experience, rather than measured against a Procrustean bed of received expectations to which it was never intended to conform *Flying* reveals its own internal organizing principles, as it explores the many-layered associative intertwinings of consciousness, memory, and image.

Although the structuring chronology of *Flying* covers roughly the eighteen months following the publication and success of *Sexual Politics,* that time frame is stretched—through flashback, flashforward, and free association—to encompass virtually her entire life. In the first chapter, appropriately entitled "Fugue State," Millett introduces us to many of the thematic motifs and narrative threads which, as the book continues, will be repeated, expanded, and explored in a variety of contexts. In what are almost tiny film clips of association and reference, we learn that she is about to return to the United States after five weeks in London; that she has been involved in making a film; that she is struggling to write still another book—but that it isn't coming along, and that, partly as a result of this, partly as a result of other (as yet unnamed) things, she fears going "over the ledge before winter's out." There are flashbacks and anxious anticipations: memories "from the Connecticut summer days when they sold the first copies of *Sex Pol,* and anxiety at meeting those who will greet her at the end of the flight, at Kennedy airport.

Through all the apparent confusion of names and places, the purposefully confused time sequences, and the jumbled chronology of events and feelings, the reader desperately searches for some kind of organizing principle or some thread of continuity by which to negotiate what Millett herself calls "a bridge between the voice talking in my head and prose as I'd known it." If it is indeed to prove what she promises—a "documentary" of her existence—then the book must offer the reader some cohering picture to which all the disparate images can be related. Will the narrative concentrate on love relationships, we wonder, or on the story of love's demise? (pp. 543-45)

By page 7, then, the reader is primed and ready for that coherent "something remembered from childhood," an episode which at once validates and explains her reading anxiety by giving thematic expression to what, until this point, had been a repeated stylistic device. Simultaneously, this episode blares forth, in the sharpest possible relief, several of the central thematic motifs whose fuguelike variations will permeate the pages to follow. For, the story remembered from childhood, the story of a little girl sexually attacked by a strange man in a strange car in the middle of a snowstorm, is a story of multiple and simultaneous experiences of loss, all of them happening over and over again in the eternal now of memory impinging upon present experience.

In what is perhaps one of the best and most vividly sustained sequences in the book, Millett shares with us the child's growing terror, her denial, and, finally, her anguished admission that, "This is real now. It's danger." Reliving every detail through a child's present-tense language, we, as readers, bolt with the girl running for safety, "running with the air blue in the snow," only to be shattered with the child's climactic discovery: "I have lost it." At first, pausing with the period break, the reader assumes that what has been lost is the girl's virginity—a quite natural assumption following the detailed description of attempted sexual assault. The following sentence, however, identifies the loss: "My turtle. The brace to keep my teeth straight." Instead of trivializing the situation, or allowing us some momentary relief from tension, however, the sentences relentlessly insist that *all* loss, to a child, is serious:

"I have lost twenty-five dollars. . . . Mother said they could never afford to buy another." In quick succession, then, the loss of the brace is compounded by a loss of health (as she gets pneumonia), the loss of a father (the parents separate), the threatened loss of family ties ("Will I still get to see Aunt Christina now?"), and the even more threatening loss of Nancy, "my best friend": "If I have to drop out of Derham (private parochial school) 'causeit costs money I can't ever see Nancy again."

Only in the final paragraph of the sequence is the worst admitted: the loss of innocence that we'd feared all along. But even here, as she lies in bed thinking, recovering from pneumonia, multiple experiences get compounded—the memory of the man in the car, the strange responses of others to her love for Nancy, the pubescent sexual awakening, and all the weighty baggage of a Catholic upbringing:

> Lying in bed sick I think about the man. The blue car. I touch myself and my head gets hot. It's a sin. A sin to have gotten in his car. I have been touched by him. Did I lose my virginity? What does it mean really? Not a sin if I escaped. Even if I ran away, was it a sin? But a sin to lose the turtle. Sometimes I want him back. He could put the thing in me. Then I would know what it is. If he put it in me I would stop itching. . . . Think about the basketball game at St. Thomas. Be one tonight, it's Friday. . . . Nancy'll be there too. Ashamed again, thinking that. 'Cause people act funny about us when we say we're in love. Before Thanksgiving vacation we told the seniors and they laughed, kind of scary, like when you've made a mistake. The nun heard and she got mad. Sally's boyfriend heard us talking on the phone and said a magic word to Mother. Lesbian. It takes so long to get well. Already it's eight weeks. Doctor Flannigan says six more. There's nothing to do but remember. Over and over. This secret. The blue Mercury. His face sort of blurry. The terrible purple thing. Then running. It keeps happening. If I yell no one hears me, the house is empty. Will he find out where I live, get me, tell on me? Face hot, sweating, is it the fever? I wonder. It's a sin and thinking is a sin. How do I stop it from happening?

Such writing insists that we abandon the illusion that experience is discrete and isolate or that time is linear, with neatly separated points of reference. The linear chronology we had been trying to piece together since the opening pages, and our consequent anxiety over our inability to find order in all that apparent chaos of narrative, now all coheres around a recognition that experience is itself chaotic; and that, through every page that follows as through every one we have so far read, Millett will explore (among other things) the recurrent confusions and consequent flights from danger, as well as that continuing sense of loss, which is at once one loss and all losses, that makes up the daily reality of vulnerable little girls in our society.

So, in spite of the fact that her text makes no pretense to artistic purpose or to conscious artistic structure, the opening "Fugue State" actually functions as such, by introducing not only the first major example of the flying imagery (the flight from danger) and some of the major sty-

listic devices to be employed throughout; but, more important, by delineating, if only in piecemeal fashion, the many-layered and interrelated thematic motifs which will flesh out and adumbrate the book's action or story line. These include the concern for personal and cultural change—the seeking of a *vita nuova,* as it were; the difficulty of understanding or making sense of personal experience; the involvement with various love-partners; the need to find more suitable parent figures and to make peace with an unaccepting, and even rejecting, personal mother and father; and, finally, that which seems to have been the book's motivation as well as its most compelling theme, "A quietly desperate search for self." . . . Determined that "steps had to be taken," she embarked on this combination confession, memoir, and autobiography, hopeful that it would move her closer "towards recovering my being."

What we might call the "story" of that recovery involves the various activities of the year and a half following *Sexual Politics'* success: her various speaking engagements and love affairs, the trip to London to edit her film, the film's debut in New York, and repeated shuttles between the Bowery, Connecticut, her farm, and, finally, Provincetown. But while a reader may feel compelled to sift some kind of sequential ordering out of the myriad trips and relationships, the narrative itself is not organized either by chronology or sequence; episodes from the past are recalled with similar frequency in each of the book's first four parts. If there is any underlying structural or organizational principle, then, it lies in the repeated elaboration and adumbration of certain key thematic motifs—many of them linked to the "flying" imagery. The overall synchronic effect of this kind of structure further reinforces our sense of what it means to be "wondering . . . always if I am going forward or backward." It is, in short, a structural device by which to project and examine her fear that, "inch by inch growing older we become what we came from and left."

By wrenching events out of their original causal or chronological order, relating them by memory and free association to other events that have only private, or even idiosyncratic, associational continuities, Millett allows them to take on new shapes and to suggest significances they might not otherwise have held. Thus, the private iconography of her emotional symbology is revealed, while, at the same time, the otherwise everyday and familiar no longer evades notice by virtue of its very familiarity. (pp. 545-48)

The book is divided into five parts: "Vertigo," "The New Life," "Blick. The English Notebook," "Trajectory," and "Landfall"—in that order. Part 1, "Vertigo," moves from the opening "Fugue State" to a whirling presentation of people and events, jumping back and forth between present and various pasts. It incorporates many more shorter sections—vignettes, brief character sketches, memory fragments, etc.—than do any of the following parts, and gives us, also, the impetus for the book's beginning, and provides an appropriate context for the "flying" imagery frame. . . . In contrast, the urge to write the book appears to be, at least in part, an attempt to get at meaningful beginnings and to order what follows. "Starting in the spring last year, just a year ago in New Haven, I slept with a woman for the first time in eight years," she explains. "Starting in the spring. . . . Naomi suggested I begin the book there starting when it all started again." The precision of this one, single, isolate event stands in sharp contrast to her confused memory of "the dark of those speechifying days, arriving in airports, met by some little knot of greeters," and her consequent resort to the, by now, most familiar use of the flying imagery—flight as escape from danger or entrapment. . . . (p. 549)

The title of Part 2, "The New Life" (an intentional reference to Dante's *Vita Nuova*), is both serious and ironic, for it invokes the "new life" promised by the women's movement at the same time as it details her frantic attempts to make another kind of "new life" for herself through her love for Celia—a woman who, in a later chapter, will reject her. If any single attitude may be said to pervade this part, it is ambivalence: ambivalence as to her proper role in the making of the film, ambivalence about her own complicated sexuality and its implications, ambivalence about consciousness-raising groups and the problems of individualism and elitism in the women's movement as a whole, and ambivalence about the value or meaning of the Columbia University demonstrations of 1968 (itself another isolated example of stunningly effective writing). What we also see, in this part, is how much the writing of the book is itself another kind of flying, a verbal *rite de passage* into that "new life" she envisions both for herself and for society at large. Forcing her to come to grips with her own ghosts and deepest fears, the very process of writing seems to promise both a way of laying those ghosts to rest forever while, at the same time, initiating her into at least the precarious possibility of being able to "trust paradise. Daedalus never melted," she reminds herself at the end.

Thematically and psychologically, Part 3 coheres around the ordered imprinting of meaningful images. Her attempt to help "pattern" Winnie, the brain-damaged child of the friends with whom she stays while in London, and her concern to make a good print of her film, both stand as external projections of her private attempts to discover her own authentic images and "be who I am." (pp. 549-50)

In order to facilitate the various processes of renovation and "transformation" which she envisions in this section, however, there is the obligatory and almost archetypal descent to the underworld. For the initial fact of arriving . . . in London has meant, not liberation, but entrapment—as the use of the flying imagery makes clear. Winnie's presence is that of "a tyrannical force in the basement. Dominating every moment." As a result, Millett initially sees herself, and Winnie's parents, as a threesome "all . . . caged in this house. I flew in, arriving solitary, free as a bird on my wings. And they talked to me, said they were trapped. And now it's all three of us, the rescuer too is stuck." To get unstuck, the rescuer seeks aid from the powers of the underworld: in this case, a meeting of gay activist groups in a sleazy London basement. Full of literary allusions to all such previous mythic descents, this sequence shows her successfully gathering volunteers to help pattern Winnie, and then concluding: "I have gone

to the underworld, through its labyrinths and waiting, its uncertainty. Asked. And received. From my own people." (pp. 550-51)

With the descent to the underworld, change and transformation become associated with the tapping of yet unused sources of power, while, through the flying imagery, they become synonymous with the experience of liberation and unfettered freedom. The previous uses of that imagery—as flight from the present, flight from the past, and flight from danger—are now transformed so as to include flight *towards* something and the idea of flight as freedom. (p. 551)

Purposefully reminding us of Doris Lessing's *Golden Notebook* in its title—"Blick. The English Notebook"—Part 3 is highlighted by a luncheon conversation with Lessing. A telling and central portion of the book, Lessing's remarks validate precisely what Millett is attempting in her narrative: that is, the revelation and exposure of the private, normally unacknowledged portions of women's existence; and, as such, a profound transformation of the old rules of narrative discourse.

" 'Let me tell you what it (*The Golden Notebook*) meant to me,' " Millett says to Lessing:

> "In a detail you may find ridiculous. It's the moment your heroine shall we say," we smile, "finds herself in a toilet at the outset of her period. In St. Paul we call it the curse." We smile again. "And the blood is running down her legs while she struggles with toilet paper. Kleenex. That sort of thing. In a book! Happens every month of adult life to half the population of the globe and no one had ever mentioned it in a book."

Confirming Millett's reading response in her own reply, Lessing both validates the experiment Millett is attempting in the narrative we are engaged in reading and, also, reinforces our sense that for women to explore their private worlds demands of them a willful—and often anxious—breaking of previous codes of silence and a determination to push aside the accepted boundaries of narrative content. For, as Lessing explains, " 'The very passages that once caused me the most anxiety, the moments when I thought, no, I cannot put this on paper—are now the passages I'm proud of. . . . Through letters and readers I discovered these were the moments when I spoke for other people. So paradoxical. Because at the time they seemed so hopelessly private.' . . . "

To the literary critic, this is a significant exchange, not simply because change and the nature of self-transformation are what *Flying* is all about, but because it is what *Flying* is doing. It is a point most reviewers, however, seem either to have missed or ignored, assuming that Millett's problem was a neurotic compulsion for public confession, rather than the more serious one of finding an appropriate language by which to describe certain kinds of previously unacknowledged experience. Certainly Millett posed the problem clearly enough when she admitted to Lessing " 'feeling so vulnerable, my god, a Lesbian. Sure, an experience of human beings. But not described. Not permitted. It has no traditions. No language. No history of agreed values.' 'But of course people wish to know,' " Lessing countered, " 'And you cannot be intimidated into silence. Or the silence is prolonged forever.' "

With Part 4, titled "Trajectory," Millett has returned to New York, her film now edited and ready for screening. She pictures herself in this section as a continuously moving body, navigating both emotional and geographic pathways. As the flying imagery is explored and expanded, so, too, is the vocabulary of filmmaking. . . . Subdivided into two parts, "Ascent" and "Descent," Part 4 is at least figuratively plotted (and I use that word in both its literary and navigational meanings) by her ebullient anticipation at seeing Celia Tyburn again, followed by the pain and guilt of Celia's abrupt rejection. "Ascent" and "Descent" here, then, mark a flight of the emotions.

While the emotional and sexual involvement with the *person* of Celia may be concluded in this section, however, Millett's involvement with what Celia had represented—that is, the possibility for a "new life"—is not. Continuing the thematic explorations of all the earlier sections, Part 4 includes a series of self-searching questions, a new kind of personal catechism, which ends with the following: "What is your life about? About change, I think lately." . . . In short, this section is a compilation of the many and varied persons and thematic units we have met before, with nothing lost or abandoned. The point of such inclusions, of course, is that the path of a trajectory is usually plotted as occurring in several simultaneous dimensions at once. The title of Part 4, thereby, connotes its theme, its style, its content, and its structure.

Similarly with the title of Part 5, "Landfall," suggesting a goal sighted, or a journey completed. The shortest of the book's five parts, "Landfall" follows the action of a single summer in Provincetown; in fact, "Provincetown" stands as the subtitle for Part 5, suggesting that town's geographic and symbolic significance as a kind of resting place. In the course of Part 5, Millett flies from Provincetown in order to attend a panel on nonviolence in New York, and then returns to spend an idyllic time with her new lover, Claire. There is a continuing concern, throughout these activities, to accurately record everything for the book now before us. Notebooks and tape recorders intrude upon the days and hours of original living and are then consulted again, during the winter, when Millett has returned to Provincetown, in order to complete the writing, "now remembering then." Throughout, there is an almost novelistic tying-up of loose ends, a recapitulation if not an ending, as Millett muses on almost all the major "characters." . . . (pp. 551-54)

With the last airplane trip depicted in the book—to attend the conference on nonviolence—the act of flying ceases to represent only the dizzying transportation of her personal frenzy from one place to another; and even though it appears to start out that way, the initial flight from Provincetown, via Boston, to New York, actually involves the discovery of a helpful and generous father and a consequent experience of rebirth. Having missed her scheduled flight out of Provincetown, she is aided in securing a private flight by a friendly businessman, a Mr. Van Arsdale, "this new father of mine." She can "rest now," she reassures herself, "Van Arsdale has saved you." At the conference itself she will find Flo Kennedy, "the real mother of us all." This discovery of appropriate parent surrogates nicely coincides with her experience of being "reborn in an airplane"; a new life, she boasts, has been "breached in an aisle over Boston Airport."

By the time she goes back to Provincetown, flying is no longer either escape or escapade; finally, it represents a return—both to Claire and to the book which we are reading. Taking off, out of New York, she exclaims, "The plane lifts with the same uncertainty that lovers know. Yet I knew this morning. . . . Because I know I am going back. Now it is only time until I am with her [Claire]." As the plane's takeoff had served as an appropriate metaphor for the uncertainties of the emotions, so, too, its altitude marks a quality of experience she has enjoyed commanding for herself: "Fly, stay high, living it." The mere "living it" obviously isn't enough, however. With "the plane in air now," its flying (if not her own) assured, she meditates upon the meaning of the book she is trying to write about the life she is trying to live. Just as the flying is a progress from one place to another, so, too, she realizes, the book in her head is an analogous process, striving towards another kind of landfall, "a way of inventing the self. Striving toward one you can live with." With the termination of this particular journey, then, she has reached an unprecedented triumph of acceptance, both of herself and of flying, with all its multivalent associations: " 'The flight back was beautiful,' " she announces, " 'I love to fly.' "

The next important and sustained use of flying imagery again follows a statement of concern over her book—her fear that she "will fail," that she "will not get anyone right in the book." The associative connections of memory provide the perfect correlative for such creative flights and depressions, as she proceeds to recall an afternoon spent flying kites with Claire and Molly. The first two kites don't fly, but "the last kite," "the black one," does indeed take off. And, as it does, Millett appropriates its flight as an emblem of "all my hopes, my self, my future." Almost fearfully, she asks, "Will it fly?" It does—so successfully, in fact, that it snaps its own string, to "go like a meteor for heaven." Like her own erratic fits and starts, however, the kite is one moment headed for "eternity, the wonder of it free," and in the next "helpless unhooked . . . fall[ing], plung[ing] into the sea, a star broken." Reminiscent of the image of a bird with a broken wing, which anticipates Edna Pontellier's last swim out to sea in Kate Chopin's 1899 novel, *The Awakening,* the kite plunges, clause by clause, inflection dropping (exactly as in the Chopin passage), "into the sea." But, again as in the Chopin novel, the descent is not here experienced as either defeat or loss. As Edna Pontellier felt herself reborn—in some of the most beautiful imagery of that novel—as she swam beyond her power to return, so, too, Millett experiences a kind of death-and-renewal: "For an instant my heart too was with it, my self, until almost by surprise I accept its death." (pp. 554-55)

It goes without saying, of course, that there are many . . . symbolic "landfalls" in Part 5. The book itself, for example, both literally and figuratively reaches its end. As it does so, the various thematic concerns move toward resolution, while, accompanying these, the flying images undergo their most dramatic and final transformations. Flashbacks occur with decreasing frequency, as Millett attempts a reconciliation with her past, not by reliving it, but by redeeming it—in and through the present.

An episode on the last two pages makes the point clear. It records a moment between a father and another little Katie who, miraculously, lives next door on the beach.

> There is a child next door, a little girl squatting in the dirt, playing alone. Incredible but her name is Katie. She is me then when I look at her. When I was eight Mallory was three and broke my sand castle. I punched her in the stomach. Hard. For a moment she turned blue. My dear little sister bellowing because I had hurt her. Dad spanked me. A violent man then. I screamed. We never broke the circuit. This Katie has a brother and a father who walks out of this house down below me, gray haired, looking like an intellectual on vacation, not very physical fellow. . . . The father takes his son's toy and spins it. A launching rocket. But the thing is unpredictable, the plastic suddenly vicious in the air, explodes, hurling a jagged part at his eye. He is hit. Blood of the cut. He goes into the house and comes out with a handkerchief. It is hard to keep your manly dignity when a child's toy has nearly blinded you while some female in blue grasses is observing you from a balcony. But he has not lost it. Nor his temper. Gentle as his little girl rushes to him, comforting him.

Emotionally participating in the scene, Millett completes her apparently endless search for parent figures, declaring: "Now I have overwhelmed my childhood. Free of its patterns finally." Some internal balance has been restored, as the mind, through the imagination, allows the personal father to be replaced by the felt, albeit vicarious, experience of this gentle, almost archetypally benign and loving father.

But the breaking of the personal pattern, and the subsequent recording of it in these pages, however, has larger resonances for the student of American literature. Self-consciously disengaging herself from the traditional view that women who experiment with their lives are either damned or doomed, Millett rejects both the tradition and its imagery and declares herself done, once and for all, with "this last broken-wing story." Replacing it, instead, as this book closes, is the bouyant imagery of birds in flight:

> Gulls so many of them I try to count them but they split and break I cannot place and order them in the sky. Flying in a haze of wings noises cries. Chaos and serenity together.

As a closing statement, it is also an apt description of the mind we have come to know so intimately in these pages and an apt imagistic rendering of our experience of coming to grips with that mind. In other words, Millett's sense of what her life feels like to her, and our sense of what it

has meant to participate in that life through this narrative, are both, like the gulls splitting and breaking, an experience of "order forming itself and then (being) lost again." In pursuit of order, Millett has lived her life and composed this text; but because her experience could or would not easily accommodate itself to ordering, so, too, her story of that experience, like the failed counting and placing of the gulls, similarly resists order, placement, organization—in short, resists narrative form as we have come to expect it in autobiography. Hence, this narrative ends . . . with an insistence that, in some lives, if truth be told, chaos is not always reduced to order, but may exist simultaneously with it: "Chaos and serenity together." (pp. 556-57)

As a scholar trained in both the European and American literary inheritances, Millett was obviously able to take advantage of previous epic journeys to the underworld, Dante's *Vita Nuova,* and the narrative experiments of Joyce and Woolf. Such piecemeal pickings from works of other genres, however, hardly constitute the kind of coherent background from the vantage point of which most critics like to view a work, or out of which most male authors are privileged to write. Important in the Millett text, and germane to any full understanding of it, are the recurrent references to women writers and their work, the application of film techniques to language, and the comic-book heroics of Wonder Woman and Mary Marvel. Again, however, this is hardly a coherent tradition specifically relevant to the autobiographical genre itself nor, some would argue, a coherent or satisfying tradition in any sense of the word.

The result is a text which, out of necessity, resorted to daring experimentation and sheer invention—attempting to build a "bridge," as it were, "between the voice talking in (her) head and prose as (she'd previously) known it." Not that the experiment was an unqualified success. In her unwillingness to leave anything out, based on her observation that too much had already been excluded from what has been written by and about women, she gives us . . . the uncomfortable sense of wading through a "collection of the clutter in (her) mind." The writing is often self-indulgent, the narrative associations too abstruse or too idiosyncratic to be meaningful, and some of the people do indeed come across as only "tin echoes . . . feeble sketches." Little wonder Millett agonized over the book's composition, feared she would never complete it to her satisfaction, and, reluctantly, ended up in "bitter disappointment," admitting "This is not literature."

Not literature in the sense of something that will speak beyond its own time and place, perhaps. But it *was* a necessary literary experiment. In attempting to tell the story of a life in a way it hadn't been told before, and, especially, the story of so unconventional a life as her own, Millett broke many long-standing codes of silence and omission. By "telling certain truths, truths about the media and politics, about psychological and social change as they are lived, about unconventional loves and the struggle for a new ethic," Millett herself realized, "something in the fabric, the old fabric of things, was threatened, was ripped and torn." To deal with such assaults upon "the old fabric of things," our professional reviewing establishment is too little prepared.

To counter that ineptitude, the feminist critic/reviewer must ask her colleagues to accept the various ways in which the moment-to-moment content of a life may shape the form of its narrative, and, further, she must insist upon a serious examination of the resulting text—however odd its form may at first appear, and in spite of any personal misgivings one might have about the details of the life depicted. Moreover, as long as women continue to produce texts which cannot easily be accommodated to our previous notions of form and structure, it will be the special duty of the feminist critic, additionally, to insist upon restoring to the language of critical analysis its sense of reading as an ongoing process. That is, we must restore and reiterate the fact that our experience of a text is not an experience of any kind of whole or totality, as a genre definition would imply, but, instead, a series of feelings, emotions, expectations, responses, questions, revelations—in all, discrete events which, in aggregate, make up not our experience of the book, but the *history* of that experience.

Looking back over our various experiences of reading **Flying,** for example, we see that our involvement in the abbreviated phrasings, present participles, and omitted grammatical subjects of stylistically choppy sentences has been *our* way into sharing the narrator's own broken and discontinuous experience. The narrative's refusal to obey normal rules of sequence and chronology reminds us how all past experience participates in the present. And the sometimes annoying use of flashbacks, together with an idiosyncratic manipulation of free association, articulates her and initiates our awareness of those "eternal patterns we only repeat," while, at the same time, provoking us to share her determination upon "breaking through, insisting we can transcend the welts and scars of youth. . . . beat them, escape." The apparently loose or disjointed sentence style, coupled with an analogous associational structure, we see, constitutes not only our recurrent reading experiences of the book, but its major themes, as well.

The constant search for an authentic and appropriate *vita nuova* in these pages, then, is at once a personal and anxiety-filled pursuit of a more satisfying life-style and a difficult search for a narrative form through which to delineate the urgency of that pursuit. In expanding the *content* of autobiographical narrative, revealing things that have not previously found their way into women's prose, Millett was not only a self-styled political revolutionary intent upon "a transvaluation of values," but a conscious artist attempting an alteration "of the very *forms of apprehension*" (italics mine). The great male lives, distilled and apprehended through patterns of order and hierarchy, and the popular notions of women, apprehended through images of frail birdlike creatures and comic-book caricatures like Mary Marvel, both demanded rejection. Careening, in these pages, "full tilt from broken wing to superwoman," in the end rejecting and transcending both, Millett at once tries to set up alternate images of flight to depict female experience and, also, holds firm to her perception that an appropriately meaningful pattern by which to order her experience, in fact, is not available to her. What

her life did convey, and what we shared with her, was precisely that "assemblage of raw materials" which Muriel Haynes, quoting Henry James, had so deplored.

What is being revealed here, among other things, is the lack of appropriate cultural definitions for women in our contemporary society. The implications of addressing that lack are at once literary and political: for, in altering the images and narrative structures through which we compose the stories of our lives, we may hope to alter the very experience of those lives as well. By so oddly rearranging and representing the events of her own life, Millett essentially defamiliarized a great deal of quite ordinary experience—in addition to incorporating the previously unacknowledged and the unusual—and thereby opened both to new perception. To discover or invent alternate images through which to express our sense of ourselves is one way out of the broken wing/Mary Marvel syndrome; while to see in a new way what we have not seen before presents at least the possibility of a liberating vision.

In terms of literary history, it is a situation not unlike that of the eighteenth century, the first great age of autobiographical outpourings, when, as James Cox put it [in "Autobiography and America"], "the modern self was being liberated as well as defined." As more and more women today seek precisely those goals—that is, liberation and self-definition—we may expect even more startling autobiographical narratives to come. Because, as Wayne Shumaker points out, "literature cannot have exploited all the varieties of human experience, (the autobiographer) is likely to explore milieux and vicissitudes concerning which there is no literary tradition." Millett's text, I am certain, is only one of the first to assert the truth of that statement and its unique application to women's narratives in particular. (pp. 558-62).

Annette Kolodny, "The Lady's Not for Spurning: Kate Millett and the Critics," in Contemporary Literature, *Vol. 17, No. 4, Autumn, 1976, pp. 541-62.*

Sara Sanborn

[*Sita*] is the most awful book. It's so bad that it radiates a kind of embarrassing innocence, like a Victorian parlor-set or anything that solemnly expresses the most ridiculous pretensions of its time. If you like fringed lampshades or 19th-century sex manuals, you'll love *Sita.* The people in charge of these things should make sure to bury a copy in the New Mexico desert for the delight of future generations.

It seems that after publishing **Sexual Politics** in 1970 (for my money a powerful work), Kate Millett had some rough times. Bad love affairs, bad head-trips—all the things that sensitive people were occupying themselves with. Somewhere in there she met Sita, and they had an affair. Sometimes Sita was nice to Kate; sometimes she was nasty—a woman of infinite variety. They rented a house together in Berkeley and settled down to an idyllic "marriage," all wine and roses and happy romps in front of the fire. Then Kate went back East for a while to resume her work as "a New York artist." When she returns to Berkeley with the spring, she finds that Sita has filled the house with her un-savory children and their strung-out friends, and is herself carrying on with various male plug-uglies, and there is no place left for Kate. This is where the book begins: "I fell back on the bed. The nightmare change of it all."

It's going to be a nightmare, all right. After the admirable *in medias res* beginning, the book dashes back and forth like a maddened anteater. Instead of going straight back to New York ("my New York; all those mellow bohemian years grown cold as an empty plate"), Kate decides to hang around the house trying to catch Sita's eye and mooning over happier times. Then she decides to write it all down. First she thinks keeping a notebook may be good therapy; then she thinks it may be "an experiment." Finally she thinks it's something the whole reading public ought to get in on. And that's where she makes her big mistake.

Take style, for starters. You can get better writing in a supermarket paperback: "Living here together after we got the house, the two of us. How it hurts even to summon that time, how it stings the eyes." For her basic style, Millett has chosen New Journalism Rat-A-Tat-Tat, the mode in which sentences tend not to have subjects. Or for that matter predicates. Given the agonizing tediousness of what she has to tell, it's probably not a bad choice; as ad writers have discovered, the speed of telegraphese can give the illusion of an important message. (pp. 13, 20)

The style chimes perfectly with the narrative. Kate considers trying to turn her experience into fiction but finds that she just can't imagine being anyone but herself. After all, "one does not aspire to govern life, only to convey it accurately." She conveys absolutely everything, including her (well-founded) doubts about how good a job she's doing. Breakfast, lunch and dinner, it seems that Kate can't bear to leave out a single meaningful detail. After you've been reading for a while, say a week or so, the book starts to take on a certain interest, the kind I remember once finding in a soap opera when I was sick in bed with fever. Will Pia speak to Kate in the kitchen today? Will Sita come home to dinner? (Much hangs on this.)

Kate Millett seems entirely convinced of the artistic virtue of sacrificing herself, even to the point of providing the knife: "on behalf of the great generalized hostility of the world, I have here perfected the instrument of its revenge." I hate to disappoint, but I really don't care who she sleeps with. I have to admit that when I read about women "taking" each other and "entering" each other, I feel as if I'd walked in on a couple of children playing doctor, but I've been embarrassed by heterosexual reminiscences too. What bothers me is that Millett has been so overcome by self-seriousness that she thinks her personal doings are important to the rest of us, and a firm of publishers has abetted her in it. (p. 20)

Sara Sanborn, "Personal Doings," in The New York Times Book Review, *May 29, 1977, pp. 13, 20.*

On Notoriety

"Every afternoon I'm notorious for something else. They wanted to make me a sort of elder stateswoman because I wrote *Sexual Politics.* I think in America when you become respectable you become . . . a product—a little metal file cabinet: Millett, K. *Sexual Politics.* For me that would be a coffin. So I had a nice way to get out of it. I said, 'Guess what? I'm not as respectable as you think. I have a few other ideas up my sleeve, like I'm a lesbian.' "

—Kate Millett, 1977

Nancy Manahan

[In *Sita*], Kate Millett describes in excruciating detail the last months of her three-year love affair with a middle-aged mother and university administrator. The book is based on a journal Millett kept during the spring of 1975 when she moved to Berkeley to teach and to resume her place in the house where she and Sita had spent the previous idyllic spring. But Sita, no longer in love with Kate, is absorbed by her job, children, friends, and other (male) lovers.

Kate has recently been divorced and cannot gracefully let go of the woman she had counted on to be her new life partner. Instead she stays to record the minute-by-minute process of love's death: Sita's deceptions, her own helpless anger, their charged silences and false reconciliations, the "little shoots of hope annihilated in the soft closure of a door." Millett ritualistically re-tells the story of their years together, sometimes in memory of a once powerful love, more often in an obsessive hunt for where it went wrong. The author retraces the sequence of events as if to invite readers to participate in the chant-like chorus of a Greek tragedy.

Sita is an important book because it presents realistically a subject that has been neglected, sentimentalized, or deplored in most literature—lesbian relationships. It contains, as does *Flying,* some of the first prose which presents in an author's own voice her experience of lesbian sexuality. In addition, *Sita* explores in unprecedented depth the old themes of power and powerlessness and offers a model for emotional self-revelation of a kind traditionally found only under the cloak of fiction.

Nancy Manahan, in a review of "Sita," in American Notes & Queries, *Vol. XVI, No. 1, September, 1977, p. 14.*

Anne Tyler

It takes an act of courage to read this book. Think, therefore, what it must have taken to write it. *The Basement* is an exhaustive study of the weeks-long torture of a 16-year-old girl named Sylvia Likens. It is nonfiction. Sylvia Likens died on October 26, 1965, in Indianapolis. Her starved and mutilated body was found in the house of Gertrude Baniszewski, the woman with whom Sylvia and her sister had been left while their parents followed the fair circuit. Gertrude Baniszewski went to trial for the murder, along with three of her children and two neighborhood boys.

"Likens Trial Turns the Mind Away," said one of the headlines at the time. It turns the mind away still. Surely no one can read *The Basement* without feeling sick, and there is a constant temptation to drift into thoughts of something else—anything else, anything at all.

Why bother with it, then?

First, there's the feeling that it would be somehow cowardly, ostrich-like, to slam the book shut and forget it (or attempt to forget it). We'd be joining ranks with Sylvia's carefully blind and deaf neighbors, who were so anxious not to "get involved." Second, you can't travel too far into this book without stumbling over some important thoughts on the condition of being a victim.

To Kate Millett, the case became such an obsession that she spent 14 years trying to figure out how to write about it—"waiting to be good enough," she says. She opens her book by addressing Sylvia directly:

> Finally, I can touch you with my voice, finally it's time, Sylvia Likens. In how many sad yellow hotel rooms have I spoken to you, writing these words before me on the wall as I lay back on some bed and staring at the painted plaster, beginning this in my mind. Emboldened for an hour. And then a coward again at home never getting anything on paper. Waiting till the time came. For fourteen years you have been a story I told to friends, even to strangers, anyone I could fasten upon and late at night. Since the first moment I heard of you, came across something in a magazine, the outline of your ordeal.

Clearly the wait was of value. The writing is fully ripened, rich and dense, sometimes spilling out in torrents.

The subtitle of this book is *Meditations on a Human Sacrifice,* and the style does resemble the internal voice of someone deeply meditating, turning a single subject over and over to view it from all angles. Or perhaps it's more like the circular, nighttime thoughts of an insomniac. Kate Millett looks at events now through Gertrude's eyes, now through Sylvia's, now through the eyes of one of the neighborhood boys; then she steps back inside her own skin. She is occasionally, in her various disguises, too self-aware. It seems unlikely that Gertrude would be openly conscious of the sexual implications of paddling Sylvia, for instance, or that she would trouble to formulate such complex explanations for her brutality. At her best, though—as when Gertrude is just ironing, and reflecting upon the act of ironing—Kate Millett is wonderfully convincing.

Some of the shock is dulled by repetition; the book goes on far too long. But it's a flaw we can understand. This is an obsession, after all, and the author has to work it through. What keeps us with her is that we, too, have to work it through. There are questions here that need answering—not, of course, that any final answers are possible. What leads humans to such extremes of cruelty and rage? And what leads others to submit? (pp. 35-6)

The notion that Sylvia's ordeal was specifically related to her being female is [hard] to accept. Kate Millett calls the case "a nightmare, my own nightmare, the nightmare of adolescence, of growing up a female child, of becoming a woman in a world set against us, a world we have lost and where we are everywhere reminded of our defeat." But doesn't this kind of reflex pigeonholing diminish Sylvia's death? What happened in Indianapolis was a puzzle in basic human relationships—the mystery of why certain people torment and why others acquiesce. It is not a mystery limited to women. The prisoners in the German concentration camps—some obediently digging their own graves, smiling hopefully into the camera even as their executioners' rifles were cocked—were not all female. Nor were those who resisted all male.

"Sylvia would not have been subjected to her specific tortures if she were not a girl," says Kate Millett. "They were devised for her precisely because she was one. That was her crime." But actually, any of her tortures could have been practiced, with very little variation, upon a boy; and girls are not the only victims of child abuse, which is what Sylvia's case boils down to. The fact that boys eventually, at around Sylvia's age, develop the weight and muscle that often lend them confidence to defend themselves doesn't really seem an ideological issue.

It's more plausible that Sylvia was a victim of a general sense of despair on both her part and her murderers' part, largely resulting from poverty. Which is not to excuse her murderers in any way. ("Simply being poor does not necessarily lead you to the place where you torture children in basements," Kate Millett says, sensibly enough.) In addition, Gertrude seems to have felt toward Sylvia that inexplicable personal animosity—almost an allergy—that so often figures in cases of child abuse. It could have been, as Kate Millett suggests, that Gertrude killed Sylvia "for sex. Because she had it. She was it. Like a disease. Like some bizarre primitive medicine. Because nubile and sixteen she is sex to the world around her and that is somehow a crime." But no firm proof of this is ever offered.

More to the point, Gertrude was the sole support of a tumult of children, one of whom was already pregnant out of wedlock. She was asthmatic, ugly, brutalized, a battered wife long ago abandoned. It emerged in the trial that she had nine people to feed and one spoon, literally, to feed them with. Since Gertrude also had a lawyer, a series of doctors, a TV and a stereo, as well as cigarette money, Kate Millett supposes that "the question of spoons is not simple poverty, but poverty of a special kind, a kind of disorganization hard to imagine in someone responsible for seven children." Disorganization, yes, but also a straightforward aversion toward being the nurturer. When Gertrude was approached, almost at random, by Sylvia's father with an offer of $20 weekly to board his daughters, she was taking on two more open, expectant mouths—and mere money must have done little to ease her inner sense of depletion. No one can side with the defense psychologist, who seemed to absolve Gertrude purely on sentimental grounds ("she has a very great need for love and attention"), but neither should we assume automatically that she killed for sexist reasons, however convoluted.

It may seem that, in criticizing a central tenet of *The Basement,* I am criticizing *The Basement* itself. I am not. The book can stand alone, quite apart from any feminist polemics. It is an important study of the problems of cruelty and submission, intensely felt and movingly written. I don't expect to forget it, although I'll keep trying. (p. 36)

> *Anne Tyler, in a review of "The Basement," in* The New Republic, *Vol. 181, Nos. 1 & 2, July 7 & 14, 1979, pp. 35-6.*

Joyce Carol Oates

It may be argued that tragedy consoles us, in ways too deep, too complex, for us to delineate. "Tragedy," of course, implies art, and art implies artifice. Denuded of Shakespeare's language, for instance, the brutal acts of the great plays—Gloucester's blinding, Othello's murder of Desdemona, Cordelia's gratuitous death—would have a stupefying effect on us. We would be horrified, sickened and eventually numbed. Our very humanity would be eroded.

The Basement, so bluntly and so appropriately titled, is about a tragedy that has little to do with art and everything to do with horror, sickness, inhumanity. After reading even a few pages of this highly detailed account of a 16-year-old girl's death by torture, one is shocked almost beyond anger. For four weeks the girl, Sylvia Likens, who had been left by her parents to board in the home of 37-year-old Gertrude Baniszewski and her seven children, was routinely scalded, kicked, beaten with a paddle, punched, branded with burning cigarettes. In her final anguish Sylvia chewed her lips nearly in half. Her screams were heard throughout the neighborhood, and more than 25 other children saw her being beaten. No one called the police. Even people living within *14 feet* of the basement corner in which the girl died did not notify the authorities.

What *can* an appropriate response be?

This is no event out of our wretched witch-hunting past, no episode out of a cautionary German fairy tale, but a crime that took place in Indianapolis in 1965. And though much is made of the "impoverishment" of the neighborhood in which it took place—New York Street—it is really not a slum, judging from a photograph included in this book. (p. 14)

The Basement is partly an account of the trial of Gertrude Baniszewski and her family for the murder of Sylvia Likens, partly a brooding discourse by Kate Millett . . . on the nature of "feminine" sacrifice. The book is the result of the author's 14-year obsession with the case, which she first read about in *Time* magazine when she was a young instructor at Barnard College. Miss Millett was immediately captivated: "You (Sylvia) have been with me ever since, an incubus, a nightmare, my own nightmare, the nightmare of adolescence, of growing up a female child, of becoming a woman in a world set against us, a world we have lost and where we are everywhere reminded of our defeat."

Miss Millett's identification with the murdered girl is extraordinary, and one can only respect, if not fully comprehend, the depth of its power: "I was Sylvia Likens. She was me." Elsewhere, as part of a long, reasoned, admirably sustained meditation on the historical fate of women in general (which includes a discussion of clitorectomy and other genital mutilations still practiced today), she comes to the conclusion: "To be feminine, then, is to die."

There is something mesmerizing about another's obsession, at least initially. One is struck by, perhaps even alarmed by, the passion, the devotion, the tireless concern for details of all kinds: Gertrude Baniszewski had seven children of her own, including an infant son. She owned one spoon. She had no stove, only a hotplate. She had a television set, a stereo, even a lawyer. She went often to the doctor, complaining of various ailments. Her 23-year-old, common-law husband, the father of the infant, had deserted her. Her former husband, an Indianapolis policeman, was always behind on his child-support payments, but he was kind enough to leave behind his policeman's belt so that Mrs. Baniszewski could discipline their children. Both men beat her.

One soon begins to wonder, as Miss Millett did, so obsessively, *Why did they do it? Why did the neighbors allow them to do it?* And since it seems that Sylvia Likens could have escaped—it was not until the last two weeks that she was bound and gagged—the most troublesome riddle of all is why Sylvia failed to save herself.

She failed, Miss Millett believes, because she had no faith in the authorities—in police, in social workers; because her parents, who were traveling in Florida, had more or less abandoned her and her younger sister; because she had lived in 14 different places in 16 years; because she was a girl, conditioned to be passive, to be sweet: "To cooperate, to assuage, to hold out the hands to be tied. To beg quietly. Not to scream, because it will make him angry, because it will make him strike you. To mimic every gesture of submission. . . . To be 'feminine.' " Miss Millett might have compared this to the Patricia Hearst case, for there, too, in Miss Millett's words, "The victim [is] seized with the same enthusiasm, the same madness or at least the same motivations as those of her captors." It does not matter that the captors are near-idiots: Gertrude Baniszewski managed somehow to blacken her own eye with the paddle she was using on Sylvia; a teen-ager named Coy Hubbard practiced judo flips on Sylvia while his girlfriend watched, giggling; Rickie, another neighborhood boy, later gave a detailed confession to the police and recounted some of the torture incidents with "amusement."

Why did these moral imbeciles persecute Sylvia? Miss Millett has numerous ideas, all of them provocative but none really convincing. Being a "female adolescent" was Sylvia's crime, evidently, and Mrs. Baniszewski derived sadistic pleasure from torturing her. In the end, the author says, Sylvia died because she had no strategy, no imagination, for survival.

One can admire Miss Millett's courage in taking on so ugly a subject, but one must draw back from her conclusions. If to be "feminine" is to die, how can one account for the fact that some of Sylvia's most vicious torturers were female—one of them a pregnant 18-year-old? How can one account for the fact that Sylvia was high-spirited, impudent, known for "playing the clown" in school—in short, rather tomboyish, not a "good" little girl? It is never clear exactly why Sylvia must be seen as a "human sacrifice." . . . (pp. 14, 24, 26)

Miss Millett's secondhand knowledge of the case (she did not attend the trials) might have been fruitfully supplemented by traditional journalistic research: she might have interviewed Sylvia's teachers and classmates, members of the Likens family, even the torturer-murderers. . . . The powerful opening pages of *The Basement,* in which the author advances her thesis of women-as-victims, are somewhat undermined by the book's length, and by the passages in Part II that attempt to take us into the minds of Sylvia and Gertrude. Here Miss Millett's "stream-of-consciousness" monologues have the effect of flattening out and even trivializing the horror.

She seems to have sensed the risk of this sleight-of-hand: "I wonder if it's a relief, finally, or is it merely disconcerting, to come upon an author confessing to have no real hold over what a character 'thinks'? . . . After the transcript runs out, thought, dialogue, even action, I 'make it up' and admit that I make it up." But while Miss Millett in her own voice is forceful and intelligent, in her characters' voices she is disappointing. Gertrude Baniszewski isn't Stavrogin, after all. The simple truth is that she and the other murderers are unredeemably dull.

But *The Basement* is grimly compelling, not to be ignored or brushed aside. Look for no moral uplift here, no tragic consolation, no preachiness, no sense that things are final-

ly harmonious in God's great scheme. Kate Millett believes that the basement/cage is "the only viable metaphor" for life itself, particularly for the lives of women, and this book is her passionate argument. One hopes that writing this book has consumed her obsession and that she can now ascend the basement stairs. (p. 26)

> *Joyce Carol Oates, "To Be Female Is to Die,"*
> *in* The New York Times Book Review, *September 9, 1979, pp. 14, 24, 26.*

Cathleen Hoskins

Nine years ago *Sexual Politics* shot Kate Millett to star status in the reborn women's movement. Millett blasted patriarchy, the foundation—as she saw it—of Western culture, focusing on works of 19th- and 20th-century literature, dazzling us. Since then her books, such as the libertine manifesto *Flying,* have gone in directions other than academic, but have failed to touch the pant cuff of *Sexual Politics.* Her latest, *The Basement: Meditations on a Human Sacrifice,* is perhaps most curious of all: a fiercely personal, almost confessional interpretation of evil, with women as the victims.

In 1965 the starved and mutilated body of 16-year-old Sylvia Likens was found in the Indianapolis, Indiana, tenement house where she and her younger sister boarded. For weeks, the girl had been kicked, scalded and cut; the words "I am a prostitute and proud of it" had been etched into her abdomen. She had been confined to the filthy basement and refused adequate food and water or the use of the toilet. Gertrude Baniszewski, the 37-year-old woman who was paid $20 a week to look after the two sisters, was indicted for murder. Three of her teen-aged children and two neighborhood boys were also charged. It's a soul-chilling story—one of those unspeakable acts that slashes from time to time through the plumped-up pillow of civilized society. After 14 years of brooding on Sylvia Likens' death, Millett declares herself ready to explain the evil behind it. A noble but ultimately futile effort; evil remains rooted in a bafflement of reason.

The Basement is a strange mixture: Millett's obsessive musings, the testimony of trial transcripts, and the dialogue she has dreamed up for victim and killers. But what the book lacks in cool intelligence and eloquence, it makes up in ferocity and *haute voix.* Millett clearly identifies with the young victim. . . . Yet she also tries to portray the hidden logic of Baniszewski's behavior: the older woman is a victim herself, physically and psychically abused by men, poverty and repressive religion. One of the few intensely empathetic moments comes early in the book when Millett suggests that Baniszewski's trial for murder is a release from the deprivations of her past: at last there's a respectable wardrobe to wear to court each day and the polite attentions of gentlemen lawyers, a far cry from the Baniszewski house and 10 people sharing a single spoon.

Millett believes Sylvia Likens died because of her sex, because of Gertrude Baniszewski's need to break the fresh body and spirit she envied. For Baniszewski's collaborators, the torture seems to have begun as neighborhood theatrics. Though Millett insists "they killed her for sex" and repeatedly fictionalizes scenes of brutalized sexuality, her view of victimization seems remarkably, uncharacteristically simplistic. Questions such as why they did it and why did she let them do it just won't go away.

Despite perceptive, provocative moments, particularly when Millett comments on the trial transcripts, *The Basement* suffers from overdone rhetoric, heavy with the curious loathings inherent in the victim theme. Large chunks of *The Basement* are pure fiction—Millett's attempts to create the characters of Sylvia and Gertrude through dialogue and interior monologue. But characterization is the novelist's art, not Millett's. Her Sylvia and Gertrude, though vocal, never really breathe.

But to discover that Kate Millett is not another Charlotte Brontë is less distressing than to feel the pornographic edge that runs through the fiction. As we drag through the mire of Likens' torture, a mindless, titillating suspense takes hold. Suddenly, terribly, we realize that Millett's very descriptions have turned Likens into a sex object in a pornographic play and we are the captive audience. It is an obscene and unsettling effect, and yet it comes closest in the book to explaining how a hideous torture like this can happen. When Millett looked at what happened to Sylvia Likens, she saw evil, and *The Basement* will make you want to look the other way. (pp. 52e, 52f)

> *Cathleen Hoskins, "What Happens to Little Girls," in* Maclean's Magazine, *Vol. 93, No. 37, September 10, 1979, pp. 52e, 52f.*

Susan R. Ruel

Standing in a bookstore in Bloomington, Indiana, I read Kate Millett's *The Basement* from cover to cover. I could not afford to buy the book, nor am I an admirer of Kate Millett. Yet I could not put this book down.

The Basement, which calls itself a "personal, philosophical, speculative, and at times fictional account," documents the most gruesome murder in Indiana state history: the torturing to death of a sixteen-year-old girl, Sylvia Likens, by her foster mother, Mrs. Gertrude Baniszewski, with a gang of neighborhood kids in Indianapolis (1965). Using this case as an example, Millett invokes and illuminates the larger issues of women's vulnerability to male violence.

The Basement presents a complex feminist analysis of "Woman as Victim," imbuing the book with rich sociological value. It is worth reading for its intensive discussion of the key question: Why did Sylvia let them do it? The family history of the victim, who was the neglected product of the broken home of two drunken carnival vendors, is carefully investigated. Millett is too interested in seeking authentic motivations to excuse Sylvia's "passivity" too readily. Her autopsy reveals an unusually independent girl whose rebelliousness may have provoked her "punishment" in the first place. Indeed, her abuse apparently began as a form of parental discipline. Sylvia's position is complicated by the possibility that she may have been shielding her crippled little sister Jenny from beatings by assuming the role of the scapegoat.

Against a group of torturers which sometimes swells to include every kid in the neighborhood, with Gertrude Baniszewski as overseer, Sylvia hardly stands a chance. The author interprets Sylvia's final resignation as unfocused, self-condemning guilt. She was seduced into believing the excuse of her tormentors: she was a bad girl and thus deserved chastisement. Yet, as Millett documents, she did try to escape, several days before her death, only to be grabbed and thrown back downstairs to the basement.

Sylvia's case is particularly interesting in that what Millett views as a timeless misogynistic ritual is inflicted on a woman by another woman. Gertrude's aggression is traced to her experiences as the battered wife of a policeman. Yet, the gorier elements of the crime are described with the utmost delicacy and discretion: Millett's curiosity is never morbid or sensational. Instead, she draws brilliant analogies between Sylvia's torture and the African ritual of clitorectomy, practiced by female secret societies. Ultimately, the murder is analyzed not only from a feminist perspective, but also as a manifestation of the violence that pervades American society in general.

In the era of "true life novels," such as *In Cold Blood* and *The Executioner's Song,* Millett has wrung a rare and painful reality from her material. Through the author's eyes, coke bottles and cigarettes, the instruments of torture, are transmogrified from daily necessities into luminous cultural symbols. Thus, Millett explains the fact that these particular objects, "man-made . . . things of commerce and modernity . . . in every sense profane," have been converted into murder weapons. Stylistically, the author is at her best interpreting the "American [language] of the Midwestern poor, blunt and repetitive as blows, as life, day after day, without color or pity." (pp. 124-25)

[The] down home accent and stream of consciousness narrative sometimes clashes with *The Basement*'s sophisticated philosophical arguments. The rationalizations Millett puts in Gertrude's mouth, "The child has taught me my work. Lord have mercy on my soul. I walk in his ways and bear him witness," rely too heavily on clichéd pentecostalism. Certainly, in arguing that Sylvia's mistreatment began as parental discipline, Millett has revealed a crucial point. Yet, by expressing this idea in the pat formulas of camp meeting Christianity, Millett oversimplifies the motives of a murderess so cold-blooded that she alone, among those accused and convicted, never admitted that what she did was wrong.

Murkily cerebral in certain passages, . . . *The Basement* is overly personal in others, and often marred by its undue concern with the author's private reactions. Furthermore, her tone sometimes turns precious and literary, callously out of keeping with the mood of this grim case. Yet, despite these failings arising from the ambitious scope of the book, *The Basement* transcends such flaws, rises above its skewed time sequence and disharmonious blend of too many times and approaches. (p. 125)

> *Susan R. Ruel, in a review of "The Basement: Meditations on a Human Sacrifice," in* The Denver Quarterly, *Vol. 15, No. 1, Spring, 1980, pp. 124-25.*

Marilyn Yalom

Once upon a time literature had its seasons; poetry for youth, fiction and essays for the mature years and autobiography for old age. Benjamin Franklin wrote his autobiography in his sixties and seventies; Elizabeth Cady Stanton, hers at the venerable age of 80. Increasingly, this literary calendar has given way to the tell-as-you-go chronicle, of which Kate Millett's *The Loony-Bin Trip* is an unusually provocative specimen.

Millett, now 55, has already written two other autobiographies—*Flying* and *Sita*—in the 20 years since the publication of *Sexual Politics* catapulted her into international fame. As a cutting-edge feminist theoretician, a much headlined political activist, a bold writer and artist, Millett the celebrity became the colorful persona of her outrageous narratives. Not only did we come to know her, but she also brought to public attention a bevy of intimate portraits depicting her bicoastal friends—artists, civil rights activists, an ex-husband and lesbian lovers, as well as her more conventional Irish Catholic family from St. Paul, Minn. What right did she have, I wondered (recalling George Sand's judgment of Rousseau's *Confessions*), to "confess" so many others as she confessed herself?

Now her confessions have taken an unexpected turn. *The Loony-Bin Trip* tells the story of Millett's second mental breakdown, which occurred in 1980 when she voluntarily went off the drug that had been keeping her "sane" for seven years. Without the lithium prescribed for her manic-depressive condition, she experienced the "high" characterized by mile-a-minute speech, exuberant spending and grandiose illusions—odd behavior in the eyes of her lover, Sophie, and the young apprentices gathered that summer at the women artists' colony she had founded in Poughkeepsie, N.Y. The summer turns from an idyll of communal farm work, with early morning swims in a bucolic pond and late evening talks and lovemaking, to a quarrelsome dystopia. Millett skillfully records the cumulative havoc wrought by a manic person, even as she stubbornly disowns responsibility for the disintegration of her once blissful community.

Against the advice of friends and family, she takes off in the autumn for Ireland where she has speaking engagements and feminist connections. There she lands in Our Lady of Clare, in her words "a real madhouse . . . the worst bin of all . . . the end of the road." This state mental hospital is a forbidding fortress containing "thirty-five tired female captives." But the "true evil" is not the locks and bars on the doors, but the drugs that, in Millett's view, erode the will and transform one into a compliant puppet. She is determined to outwit the system, to fight against the lithium and Thorazine by hiding pills in her cheek until they can be disposed of, or by eating an inordinate number of counteractive oranges: "To remain sane in a bin is to defy its definition."

Not since Ken Kesey's *One Flew over the Cuckoo's Nest* has the literature of madness emitted such a powerful anti-institutional cry. However "high" or however suicidal—for the manic period is invariably followed by depression—Millett refuses the labels that would declare her in-sane. The entire medical model is seen as a social construct fashioned upon the criminal code and designed to treat patients as prisoners. "Having committed no crime, one can . . . lose one's liberty for an indeterminate period, even for life."

Ultimately Millett pleads for a new tolerance toward the entire range of mental activities, including madness, which she characterizes as "a certain speed of thought, certain wonderful flights of ideas. Certain states of altered perception . . . Mental activity at the margin. Or over the line."

Millett's prose is rich, her passion compelling. If it were not for the sight of thousands of severely disturbed people released from now defunct mental institutions and gracing the pavements of San Francisco, Los Angeles, New York and Washington, one might almost be persuaded by her writing that it is indeed drug-dispensing psychiatrists who cause, rather than alleviate, mental illness.

Raising questions about the etiology of madness, Millett is clearly in the camp of psychiatrists like Ronald Laing and Thomas Szasz, both cited in her book, who believe that we do not go crazy because of genetic predispositions but that we are driven crazy and declared insane when we deviate from oppressive systems. But this book's strength does not derive from that already tired political message. Rather, it is valuable as a literary representation of what it is like to go mad and to be institutionalized against one's will—"the shame, the terror of being locked up," the feel of being "cornered" and "busted," "convicted but never convinced." Like Sylvia Plath some 30 years ago, and more recently Marie Cardinal in France, Millett takes us into internal landscapes where no one goes by choice. She conveys the paranoid terror of being judged cruelly by others for what seems to the afflicted person to be a reasonable act. She has added to the madness memoir gripping hallucinations, such as her recurring identification with Joan of Arc, and wild sexual fantasies, like her loving description of a horse's genitals conflated with her father's, that flout conventional ideas about bestiality and incest.

Now that Millett has presumably exorcised the obstacle that madness presented to her creativity for almost a decade, an obstacle that "stood like a boulder in the middle of the room, demanding to be attended to," we can expect further chapters in her by no means ordinary life.

Marilyn Yalom, "Kate Millett's Mental Politics," in Book World—The Washington Post, *May 13, 1990, p. 7.*

Florence King

Remember Kate Millett? She made the cover of *Time* in 1970 after her dissection of literary machismo, *Sexual Politics,* became a blockbuster best-seller and won her the title of leading feminist spokesperson.

It didn't last. Although she was married, she soon announced that she was a lesbian, which split the women's movement and destroyed her superstar status. Thereafter came two rambling autobiographical books, and a series of liberal causes that finally got her expelled from Iran for trying to stir up the Ayatollah's docile female population.

During this time she also suffered from manic depression and was committed twice by family members. She emerged from the hospital dependent on the drug Lithium to balance her moods, only to make the ironic discovery that balanced moods are inimical to creativity. Lithium slows the thought process and represses brain activity, which interfered with her writing, while its side effect of hand tremors interfered with her sculpting and painting.

In the early 80's, Millett decided to go off Lithium and take her chances. This harrowing, often unbearable book, [**The Loony-Bin Trip**], is the story of what happened to her when she tried to buck a system and an era that have declared war on self-reliance.

Trying to go cold turkey while running an artists' colony and feminist commune on her upstate New York farm, she was thwarted at every turn by the bevy of do-your-own thing blithe spirits with whom she had surrounded herself. With the studied casualness of the sane confronting the mad, they kept asking her "Are you all right?" and "How do you feel?" until she was ready to scream.

With cheeky, college-age lesbian hippies running in and out of her office, yelling and playing rock music, she did scream: "I lost my temper while trying to write a check." Her perfectly natural outburst "proved" to the communards that she had entered a manic stage and was losing her mind. They ganged up on her and nagged her to take her Lithium, and even though she was the owner of the farm, she was rendered helpless by the sacred structure of commune life: "Impudent kid, I think again, aware that our democratic style does not really grant me any literal authority over anyone; it is all to be a product of personality, and mine is in ruins."

Soon these committed pacifists, including her own lesbian lover, a proponent of every conceivable civil right, decided to use force. . . . (pp. 43-4)

To [Millett's] terrified disbelief, her sister, her lover, and several friends tried to get around New York's involuntary commitment law ("It's done all the time") to have her institutionalized so she would be forced to take Lithium. Their excuse was that she was spending money like water—what was once the sin of waste is now a "symptom" of mania to those of little faith in anything but the religion of psychiatry.

In commitment interviews her every natural reaction conspired against her; Irish as Paddy's pig and endowed with an artistic temperament, she nonetheless had to prove her sanity by following the law of the loony-bin: "Keep your temper and never raise your voice." American cultural ignorance was another nemesis: a chance literary reference, natural enough for a writer, to a scene in a Dumas novel made the doctors think she was hallucinating, and she had to refrain from laughing too hysterically when a self-satisfied feminist psychiatrist complimented her with "You didn't decompose." She meant that Millett remained admirably calm during an examination.

Matters came to a head when Millett went to Ireland and

got involved with Bernadette Devlin, the Irish Labour Party, and the hunger strikers in Ulster. If Franz Kafka had written the screenplay of *The Snake Pit,* it would still fall short of Millett's description of what happened to her in the Auld Sod when the commitment cabal back home joined forces with the Irish constabulary to have her snatched from the airport and dumped in an insane asylum in the wilds of County Clare. Here, in a scabrous ward of moaning old women whose families no longer wanted them, she is sedated not only with Lithium but several other tranquilizers, becoming a prisoner of "the triumph of ignorance: television and narcotic fantasy," until her Irish political allies gain her release.

This is a gripping and valuable book, the kind we have been getting lately from former feminist honchos who seem to be sidling up to conservatism. Anti-porn activist Andrea Dworkin now hates the ACLU, Susan Brownmiller has turned into a starchy spinster who unabashedly "blamed the victim" in her Hedda Nussbaum novel, and now Kate Millett has declared war on the insidious mental health industry and the passivity of a citizenry that accepts prescription pills. . . .

Unfortunately, she fingers the wrong villain. She blames "fascism," "Reagan's new America," the Pope and the CIA for pioneering the authoritarianism that psychiatry has adopted, unable or unwilling to see that it is her own liberal side of the political spectrum that enshrined psychiatry in the first place, beginning with the fashionable craze for Freud in the 20's down to today's constant admonitions to "seek professional help" for the slightest upset. The perfectibility of mankind, whether through yammering on the couch or through biochemistry, is a liberal goal. The conservative takes his leaf from Seneca: "Scorn pain; either it will go away or you will." Conservatives don't believe in coddling people, but neither do we kill them with the kindness that Millett endured.

This is a personal story; she says nothing about the need for involuntary commitment among the raving homeless, many of whom were sprung from mental institutions by an erring liberalism that likes to extend freedom for groups while restricting it for individuals. Except for spready analyses of farming problems and muzzy descriptions of lesbian ecstasies ("the billy goat of our perfect shamelessness" unconsciously combines the two), Millett's writing here is highly readable and effective, marked by a self-described style of "run-of-the-mouth Americanese" that is often ingratiating.

The book's most pleasant surprise is her casual and unself-conscious repudiation of radical feminism as she watches a horse:

> Suddenly the maleness, the majesty of its maleness, opens itself to me and I love it, revere it. Remember in a burst how I have always loved it, maleness, men themselves, all things masculine. . . . I had forgotten, too, its place in things, its half of the universe. As if in the years of feminism and the need to square imbalance it had seemed necessary to negate what claimed too much for itself.

That should soothe the reviewer who said that reading

Sexual Politics was like "sitting with your testicles in a nutcracker." (p. 44)

Florence King, "Hell Is Other People," in Chronicles: A Magazine of American Culture, *Vol. 14, No. 6, June, 1990, pp. 43-4.*

An Excerpt from *The Loony-Bin Trip*

Imagine anything at all, for after all one is free to do it here. That is the purpose of this place; it was made for you to be mad in. And when you give in and have a real fine bout, they have won. And then they have their evidence as well. But the temptation in the long hours is hard to resist, and it comes over you like the drowsiness of the powders. . . .

The moments of clarity are the worst. You burn in humiliation remembering yesterday's folderol, your own foolish thoughts. Not the boredom of here, the passive futility of reality, but the flights of fancy, which would convict you, are the evidence that you merit your fate and are here for a purpose. The crime of the imaginary. The lure of madness as illness. And you crumble day by day and admit your guilt. Induced madness. Refuse a pill and you will be tied down and given a hypodermic by force. Enforced irrationality. With all the force of the state behind it, pharmaceutical corporations, and an entrenched bureaucratic psychiatry. Unassailable social beliefs, general throughout the culture. And all the scientific prestige of medicine. Locks, bars, buildings, cops. A massive system.

Joy Williams

Kate Millett wrote *The Loony-Bin Trip* between 1982 and 1985, the brief conclusion to it only recently. She spent the last five years doing something else, I presume, certainly not shaping, editing, clarifying or even confronting the awesome possibilities in writing about going crazy. Her reasons for writing the book shift, change, are vague and contradictory, but basically she wants "to spill the beans," to "explore the region from whose bourne only silent and censured travelers return," "to plead for a new respect for the human mind."

She's become an activist for crazy rights. Bring down the madhouse, build theaters with its bricks, or playgrounds. Her thesis is that craziness doesn't exist. Or if it does, so what? She believes in holidays for the mind—a little fantasy, a little imagination, a few odd connections now and then. Unfortunately, when Kate Millett's mind takes a holiday, it imagines that Kate is Joan of Arc or can fly or is enjoying nuptials with her father.

The orbit both described and traveled in *The Loony-Bin Trip* is dismaying. Shortly after the publication of *Sexual Politics,* Millett has a breakdown, is institutionalized by her mother and sisters (beyond ironic, this) is released and maintained on lithium, decides to go off the drug, behaves in ways that alarm her mother, sisters, friends and lovers (sisterhood has not been kind to her), is institutionalized again, this time in Ireland, voluntarily goes back on lithi-

um again after lurching through months of severe depression, decides to go off lithium again and so forth.

Gloomy things do happen to Millett. Her novel flops; her "show uptown" fails, the exhibit on Lesbian Erotica, the nudes and city water towers (maybe it was too far uptown, she thinks); she can't finish her book on her father ("scabrous, turgid, furtive fantastic stuff "); she can't even find the manuscript for *Deathbooks,* the notes and fragments and passages from her first bust and lock-up; no one wants to make love to her anymore or hug her anymore or listen to her anymore. She has to deal with the treachery of relatives, the betrayal of friends, the righteous malice of lovers. And according to Millett, if you come a little apart under conditions such as these, you're packed off and medicated.

You fail to show up for a lecture at Princeton and they call the white coats. You get a little cranky, a little sarcastic, you talk a little too loudly and spend a little too much money and they're trying to shove pills down your throat. You can't even escape in a taxi from the sister who wants to put you away because she's standing behind you making twirly crazy gestures and scaring off the cabbies. In an Irish airport you get a little tired, decide to wash your hair in the nice ladies' room and take a nap on the floor and you're carted off to a rest home. There you try to cheer up the other gray tranquilized women in their bathrobes, "instilling the spirit of rebellion and non-cooperation, talking back and asking questions, having opinions and complaints, getting their stories giving support," and they think you need more rest than ever.

To hear Millett tell it, her problems began, the second time, because she was a little short-tempered when she simply "demanded a little respect" from the "apprentices"—the young women who came up to her farm in Poughkeepsie to farm the land and build the studios, Amazons in a brave new "just do it" world, ploughing, sowing, building, painting, skinny-dipping or, as the author describes them, "dripping and grinning in the skins of their nakedness."

The title tells a great deal about the tone of this book—plucky, breezy, a flip bravado masking a quavery confidence. The book actually is quite incoherent; there seems a disinclination here to focus, to shape a truth. The tools Millett has as a writer are indignation, jargon and an unfortunate reliance on tape recorders, old journals and boxes of notes.

The tools she lacks are lyricism, imagination and a quest for meaning beyond cant. The material here hasn't been translated. There is no sense of the mind examining itself, of the judgment of the present upon the past. She is too shy for this business of recall—too secretive, too fearful of offending or accusing or embarassing others. All the women are named Sita or Sheila or Sophie or Sally, indistinguishable from one another.

Her hallucinations are her own, I'm sure, but they seem bleakly common, shopworn. In one unfortunate passage she spends a good part of one moonlit evening with Big Jim, a gelding she bought at a horse auction and named after her dead father. She muses on his large member and thinks about her dad. She rattles along this track for awhile and then bids good-bye. "Go, Big Jim, in the moonlight and off into the dark and again in the light, be all you are and can be."

The most integrated, sadly mesmerizing section of *The Loony-Bin Trip* is the last, the one written first, the section the author, in an afterword, dismisses as "false consciousness." Tame and terrified, in a "frenzy of sadness" and on a variety of anti-depressants, she reads junk novels 18 hours a day. Finally, she is saved by Sheetrock. Good old humble Sheetrock.

Part of an all-woman construction crew, Millett cuts and nails and tapes and muds and sands. Sheetrock kindly brings her back. "I am good at the job. And it is infinitely good for me."

But books aren't slapped together and up as guilelessly and crudely as Sheetrock, particularly books about going crazy and coming back.

> *Joy Williams, "Spilling the Beans," in* Chicago Tribune—Books, *June 3, 1990, p. 5.*

Rosemary Dinnage

It sounds paradoxical to say that anyone who has undergone the appalling experiences described [in *The Loony-Bin Trip*] by Kate Millett is lucky; but compared to the great majority of sufferers from mental illness, whose condition is aggravated rather than helped by hospitalization, she *is* lucky. Few of them return from the "loony-bin trip" with the energy or articulateness to describe what it was like; some never return at all. It is this majority that Ms. Millett understands and identifies with. As an outpatient at a public hospital in Manhattan, she writes, "In the corridors of St. Vincent's I am one with the mad. . . . One of the shabby who waste eternity staring at the lighted numbers and reading discarded newspapers, forbidden to smoke. . . . Madwomen who mumble, men who pace, nervous people who use the phone all the time to tell whomever that they are still stuck down here, won't be done for another couple hours."

Having some years earlier been forcibly hospitalized for manic depression and put on lithium medication, Ms. Millett decided in 1980 to come off the drug, "belong to myself at last." The result—as she saw it—was that friends began to pick on her, to gang up on her to persuade her to take her pills and eventually to plan to lock her away. Rightly, she does not make a final judgment of how disturbed she actually was, but tells it as it felt to her (and perhaps still does). It is the omnipresent sense of persecution that she re-creates, the fear of a trapped animal that has to placate and outwit its captors, keep an eye on the door in hope of a breakaway, silently calculate chances of rescue. But she is honest enough to include a letter from a friend that suggests that it is also difficult for other people to handle someone apparently becoming irrational and hard to recognize.

Kate Millett describes the awful helplessness of the ill person, not only in relation to what the world may do to her, but what her own mind may do to her—"Has something

happened inside my skull which will unfold quickly or even slowly but which will be my downfall? My God, if anything should happen to my mind—realizing only too late how precious it is, and now how fragile." The essence of the plight is condensed in one detail of her description of an attempted involuntary hospitalization: she signals for taxis to make her escape but, curiously, none of them stop; then she sees that her sister, farther down the road, is tapping at her temple to indicate "crazy." From this situation she does escape through knowledge of her legal rights, but some time later the frightened jokes we all make about funny farms and men in white coats come true, and she is taken from Shannon Airport in Ireland to a grim "barracks" of a Roman Catholic "rest home" in the Irish countryside.

In the end, back in the United States, it is the depressive rather than the manic phase of her illness that defeats her. After much suffering, she accepts the wretched necessity of going back on medication, and a combination of courage, hard physical work and help from friends and a doctor get her back to health—and to writing the book. Writing *The Loony-Bin Trip* must have been of the greatest value, because, as she says, "During depression the world disappears. Language itself. . . . One's real state of mind is a source of shame. So one is necessarily silent about it, leaving nothing else for subject matter." She is telling her story here for all the other people who still are shut up in this silence.

Ms. Millett argues that mania is creative and should be left to run its course, that people are far more sympathetic to the person who is depressed—even punitively so. . . .

But given—and Ms. Millett might not agree with this— that in a minimum of cases people must be in psychiatric care, must it so rarely be an asylum in the real sense of the word? Should not, for instance, psychiatric staff take antipsychotic medication for a time as part of their training in order to know what it feels like? (A psychiatrist friend of mine who was given haloperidol, one such drug, when she was "mad" now does not prescribe it.) Analysts and therapists (sometimes) manage to offer empathy and affection because they are protected by the 50-minute hour, the selection of "well-behaved" patients and the support of a prestigious profession; but within psychiatric institutions there seems often to be much less of this humaneness. I should like to see, as a parallel to *The Loony-Bin Trip,* a book by, say, a psychiatric nurse who can write as articulately as Kate Millett and can explore what it is that so often gets in the way of compassion and real human contact.

> *Rosemary Dinnage, "I Am One with the Mad," in* The New York Times Book Review, *June 3, 1990, p. 12.*

Joanne Alton Riordan

Remember the imprisonment of Rochester's wife in Charlotte Brontë's *Jane Eyre?* Or the horrors visited on the mentally ill in the old movie, *The Snake Pit?* Or the demeaning manner of the hospital personnel toward patients in *One Flew over the Cuckoo's Nest?* Are people who are considered mentally unbalanced still subjected to hospitalization from which there is no escape? Must they endure physical restraints if they "get out of line"? Are they forced to take drugs which leave them tranquilized to the point of immobility? Are these archaic methods being used on patients in the late twentieth century? Kate Millett answers these questions in her book, *The Loony-Bin Trip,* a first hand account of her struggle to recover her equilibrium as well as authority over her life, after being diagnosed as a manic depressive.

The book begins with the author's recalling the summer of 1980 at The Farm, a feminist artists' and writers' retreat in upstate New York which she has established some years earlier. There are pleasant days spent writing, painting, or sculpting, and evenings of drinks and dinners with friends, but the atmosphere begins to deteriorate. A few weeks after Kate stops taking lithium which was prescribed for her years earlier when she was hospitalized, her friends tell her she is becoming "argumentative," "difficult," "nasty." Is she acting "crazy" or merely being extremely on edge, as she thinks she is? As this is an autobiographical book, Ms. Millett can relate only what she feels and remembers about her behavior. Indeed, she doesn't think she is more difficult than anyone else is at times, rather that her moods are being scrutinized because she confided in her friends that she was no longer taking the prescribed drug. She feels she is constantly watched. She feels betrayed. This is a slightly gray area for the reader, however; we may assume that her actions were causing attention and unfavorable reactions.

The residents of The Farm call her family to obtain aid in "dealing with" Kate, and their aid consists of trying to trick her into re-entering a hospital. Aware of her civil rights, she enlists the help of her lawyer and averts hospitalization at this time.

However, during a trip to Ireland, after an argument over a minor airport rule, she is whisked from Shannon Airport to a Catholic "rest home." There, she experiences all of the nightmarish treatment still practiced at some hospitals. She is forcibly drugged with Thorazine which causes constant thirst. She is isolated. She is treated like "a defective child." Her situation is more frightening because she had told everyone she was leaving Ireland, and only one friend, Marguerette D'Arcy knows she has decided to extend her stay. Although D'Arcy tries to contact her, the authorities at the "home" don't allow her to have visitors. After several weeks, D'Arcy obtains a lawyer and together they are able to free Kate from what essentially was a prison.

Back home, she endures terrible depression and seriously contemplates suicide. She tries killing herself with gas, but the lofty barn at The Farm is too drafty, and the attempt fails. Finally, she asks her doctor to renew her prescription for lithium, and she begins a long, tough climb out of the depths of her anguish. With the help of her doctor, the medication, her friends, and her own courage, Kate regains her mental stability.

During her hospitalization in Ireland, she was determined to do something to help those who are still "imprisoned"

in institutions such as she was in, and writing *The Loony-Bin Trip,* telling the story of her own illness, fulfills this pledge.

Millett writes:

> But the madhouse lives for us all.
>
> It waited for Jonathan Swift's great mind to "break," to "crack," to be lost. I have escaped his imprisonment, but I have no more lost my mind than he did. Only my freedom. How tragic that he never recovered his, the great mind in chains for years, a dog collar around his neck. We do not lose our minds, even "mad" we are neither insane nor sick. Reason gives way to fantasy—both are mental activities, both productive. The mind goes on working, speaking a different language, making its own perceptions, designs symmetrical and assymmetrical; it works. We have only to lose our fear of its workings. I do not speak of Alzheimer's disease or any other condition where the mind's function itself appears to be hampered. I mean plain old "insanity."
>
> And I say it doesn't exist.

Kate Millett, whose earlier work, *Sexual Politics,* was a strong affirmation of her activities and leadership in the women's movement two decades ago, has written a powerful account of her trip in and out of reason mixed with fantasy. Although the first third of the book seems to concentrate too heavily on irrelevant details of her personal relationships and love affairs with other women at The Farm, these digressions do not weaken her work. *The Loony-Bin Trip* offers a new perspective on the subject of mental illness and one that is chillingly informative, one that will perhaps lead to more enlightened treatment of those who unfortunately experience the chemical imbalance that leads them to be labeled as mad, insane, crazy. (pp. 4-5)

> *Joanne Alton Riordan, "Millet on Madness,"* in New Letters Review of Books, *Vol. 4, No. 2, Winter, 1991, pp. 4-5.*

FURTHER READING

Andriotakis, Pamela, and Chambers, Andrea. "In the Name of Sisterhood, Kate Millett Finds Herself in the Eye of the Storm in Iran." *People Weekly* 11, No. 3 (2 April 1979): 36-8.
　　Chronicles Millett's experiences with women's rights demonstrations in Tehran, which led to her writing of *Going to Iran.*

Goldberg, Jeff. "The Last Interview in This Issue: Jeff Goldberg and Kate Millett." *Unmuzzled Ox* IV, No. 3 (1977): 132-33.
　　Short interview in which Millett addresses her art, the Gay Rights movement, and her public notoriety.

Lerner, Laurence. "Lawrence and the Feminists." In *D. H.*

Lawrence: Centenary Essays, edited by Mara Kalnins, pp. 69-87. Bristol, England: Bristol Classical Press, 1986.

Cites *Sexual Politics* as a chief proponent of the charges of sexism against Lawrence by modern critics. Originally a lecture delivered at the D. H. Lawrence Centenary International Summer School in July, 1985.

Millett, Kate. "All Spruced Up." *Ms.* XVI, No. 11 (May 1988): 30-1.

Discusses the Christmas tree farm and women's artist colony Millett founded in Poughkeepsie, New York.

Nord, Deborah Epstein. "Mill and Ruskin on the Woman Question Revisited." In *Teaching Literature: What Is Needed Now,* edited by James Engell and David Perkins, pp. 73-83. Cambridge, Mass.: Harvard University Press, 1988.

Examines Millett's treatment of John Ruskin's *Sesame and Lilies* and John Stuart Mill's *The Subjection of Women* in *Sexual Politics.*

Woolf, Michael. "Henry Miller and Kate Millett: Strange Bedfellows, Sexuality and Introspection." *Dutch Quarterly Review of Anglo-American Letters* 15, No. 4 (1985): 278-92.

Argues that while Millett attacks Henry Miller in *Sexual Politics,* her autobiographical works *Flying* and *Sita* reveal parallels to Miller's attitudes and narrative strategies.

——. "Beyond Ideology: Kate Millett and the Case for Henry Miller." In *Perspectives on Pornography: Sexuality in Film and Literature,* edited by Gary Day and Clive Bloom, pp. 113-28. London: Macmillan Press, 1988.

Compares Millett's *Flying* with Miller's *Tropic of Cancer* and *Tropic of Capricorn,* asserting that these works view sex as both a release and confinement of the ideological self.

Keith Reddin

1956?-

American playwright.

Reddin's plays are satires that illuminate the moral and political corruption beneath the exterior calm of everyday American life. His works often feature genial but amoral protagonists who are faced with difficult ethical choices. Although Reddin, who is also an accomplished stage and film actor, has been faulted for superfluous plotting, critics nevertheless applaud his vivid characterizations, noting that his acting experience allows him keen insight into the strengths and weaknesses of specific roles.

Reddin's first full-length play, *Life and Limb*, went largely unnoticed. A surreal black comedy set in New Jersey during the Korean War, it centers on Franklin and Effie, a couple who cope with many bizarre hardships including the loss of Franklin's right arm in the Battle of Pork Chop Hill and Effie's literal descent into Hell. Reddin's next work, *Rum and Coke*, a satire of the Bay of Pigs Invasion, received greater attention. Jake Seward, the protagonist, is a naive low-level government worker who helps prepare the C.I.A.'s raid of Cuba. The assault is viewed from the perspectives of fictional characters, including Jake and his sister, a *Time* correspondent interested in working for the chic Kennedy Administration, as well as characters modeled on such people as Fidel Castro and Richard Nixon. Reddin ridicules the efforts of the United States to control Castro and, against popular sentiment, portrays the Cuban government sympathetically. While several reviewers found Reddin's political acumen lacking in *Rum and Coke*, many praised the creativity and imagination of the playwright's retelling of what is considered one of the greatest political blunders in American history.

Reddin's next acclaimed work, *Big Time: Scenes from a Service Economy*, focuses on the conflict between personal ethics and the temptation of money through an exploration of the intertwined lives of three people. Fran, a layout artist, is romantically involved with Paul, a prominent banker. Increasingly excluded from Paul's personal life, Fran consoles herself by entering into an affair with the couple's mutual friend, Peter, a photojournalist. Both men are egocentric and, when forced to deal with personal crises, ultimately favor material wealth over resolving their problems. Fran, however, achieves the play's only moral victory when she leaves them both. *Big Time*, noted for its adroit use of such cinematic techniques as cross-cutting and short, erratic scenes, was adapted into a movie for public television in 1989.

Life during Wartime is Reddin's most celebrated play to date. A farcical look at American suburbia, the work follows the nightmarish adventures of Tommy, a door-to-door salesman of home security systems. His route takes him through a placid-looking suburb which, upon closer investigation, harbors violent, bizarre people who need more protection from themselves and one another than

from the intruders that Tommy's system would deter. Although some critics voiced irritation with Reddin's customarily guileless hero, most lauded the play's insight and intelligence; John Simon described *Life during Wartime* as an "amiable dark comedy with a mind of its own and the wit and courage to speak it."

PRINCIPAL WORKS

PLAYS

Life and Limb   1985
Rum and Coke   1985
Highest Standard of Living   1986
Big Time: Scenes from a Service Economy   1987
Nebraska   1989
Life during Wartime   1990

Edith Oliver

Life and Limb, the first full-length play by the young actor Keith Reddin, was done originally as a staged reading at the O'Neill Playwrights Conference at Waterford, Connecticut, a couple of years ago. When I saw it then, I had no idea what Mr. Reddin was driving at, and I have no idea what he is driving at now. Which doesn't mean that I didn't enjoy quite a lot of it, scene by scene. There is no question of Mr. Reddin's talent and liveliness (or of his self-indulgence). The action takes place during the years 1952-56, and the story is about a young couple named Franklin and Effie, whom we meet right before he goes off to the Korean War. They are in Atlantic City. Why? Who knows? Back at their apartment, they are joined by Effie's best friend, a Rumanian movie nut named Doina. Doina and Effie go to the movies together and think about the movies and are obsessed by the movies, and Doina drives Franklin crazy. Next time we see Franklin, he has recently lost his right arm in the Battle of Pork Chop Hill and is waiting for a plane to take him home. With him is a youngster of nineteen named Tod, a whimsical dime-a-dozen tormentor (the character has become a dramatic commonplace these days). Franklin suggests to Tod that he go into the artificial-limb business once he gets home. These are the basic facts. From here on, goodbye, coherence; the scenes—more like skits or blackouts—are often macabre or mildly disquieting. Anyway, Franklin gets a job at the limb factory with Tod, who grows ever nastier. Effie and Doina are killed when a balcony in a movie house collapses. Reappearing in Hell, they work in a laundry or dry-cleaning establishment under a sadistic boss. They also appear in a supermarket, pushing carts, where they are joined by a couple of subsidiary characters and Franklin. (I can't imagine why Franklin is in Hell.) The play ends with Franklin and Effie and Doina back in Atlantic City.

It should be apparent even from this sketchy outline that some sort of social commentary is intended, and it can be said right off that the social commentary is negligible, Mr. Reddin's ideas deriving more from literature than from observation. What he invents, in short, is more interesting, more original than what he thinks. Doina, for example, is a truly comic creation, and there are many funny lines and surprising moments. For a first try, Mr. Reddin's is certainly to be commended. (pp. 92-3)

> *Edith Oliver, in a review of "Life and Limb,"* in The New Yorker, *Vol. LX, No. 51, February 4, 1985, pp. 92-3.*

Clive Barnes

Fancy—a political comedy about that political farce, the abortive 1961 invasion, known with geographical and emotive accuracy as the Bay of Pigs, of Castro's unconvertible Cuba.

The young actor-playwright Keith Reddin has fancied it, and the result of that fancy, which he calls with sarcastic incisiveness, *Rum and Coke,* was officially unveiled last night. . . .

The facts of this baffling and baffled episode in American history not only speak for themselves they actually—in a comi-tragi way—laugh for themselves.

The miscalculation of the C.I.A.—its wild and woolly plans to discredit Castro, including the consideration of a Mafia contract on his life—and its over-estimation of the counter-revolutionary Cuban resistance, is the kind of thing that can happen to the cutest of bureaucracies, although rarely in such a public spotlight.

Reddin certainly does not believe in giving either the C.I.A. or the American government of the time an even break—his play is passionately concerned with ridiculing its attempts at controlling Castro.

Castro himself emerges as a benign father figure—a fine contrast to the driven, desperate Nixon who also appears peripherally.

Even though the harsh sentences meted out to the would-be invaders are recorded—the blame for them seems settled on the U.S. rather than Cuba.

Some of this muddled play is really funny, as its hero Jake Seward . . . gets more and more involved in the convoluted political finaglings, much to the distress of his sister, a *Time* magazine correspondent all too ready to sell out her integrity for a White House appointment.

Unfortunately, the play never manages to mark the tricky demarcation line between satire and psuedo-documentary, and the humor becomes hysteric rather than abrasive, inane rather than ironic.

Reddin—as we know from earlier plays—has talent, even if his voice currently seems too inflected with Christopher Durang's personal accent. But he needs to ease up, slow down, and let his fury match his frenzy.

> *Clive Barnes, "'Rum and Coke,' Pigs and Jokes," in* New York Post, *January 28, 1986.*

Frank Rich

In American history, as taught by the young playwright Keith Reddin, the cold war is to be found not only in the conflicts of nations and ideologies but also in the American values enshrined by hit pop songs, glossy Hollywood films and Life magazine photo spreads. *Life and Limb,* the Reddin play seen at Playwrights Horizons last year, offered a black comic vision of post-Korean War New Jersey in which the characters behaved like mutated conformists from Frank Capra movies and *I Love Lucy.*

The author's new comedy, *Rum and Coke,* advances the calendar a bit—to the years from 1959 to 1961—but tries to take a similar tack. Even as Mr. Reddin provides a detailed account of the Bay of Pigs fiasco, he fills us in on such period phenomena as Frank Sinatra's hit songs, the complete supporting cast of *The Nun's Story* (Dean Jagger included) and the contrasting fashion profiles of Mamie Eisenhower and Jacqueline Kennedy.

If *Rum and Coke* is far less provacative than its predecessor, it's not because Mr. Reddin's sensibility has ceased to be fascinating. Along its periphery, at least, the new play offers some of its author's characteristically pungent juxtapositions of Realpolitik and cultural kitsch. We're told that Cuban "freedom fighters" are so infatuated with Kim Novak that they see *Pal Joey* seven times during their training period in Guatemala. In a flashback set during Richard Nixon's riot-torn visit to Caracas in 1958, the Vice President confronts an egg-throwing mob while wishing aloud that he "was home watching Uncle Miltie or Robert Young." Indeed, in the witty set design, the garish rear fins of the Nixon limousine are themselves a grotesque cultural expression of the American ethos of an era.

Where *Rum and Coke* goes flat—defying even the levitating efforts of Les Water's stylish, well-cast production—is in its central narrative. By telling the story of Jake Seward, an innocent young government go-getter who helps prepare the Central Intelligence Agency's proxy invasion of Cuba, the playwright gets caught up in the kind of conventional historical rehash customary to television docudramas.

As we wait with growing impatience for Jake to discover the obvious, *Rum and Coke* can seem as stale as a piece of investigative journalism 20-odd years after its original publication. It's during those scattered scenes in which Mr. Reddin digresses from the public record that his distinctive imagination goes to work. Easily his most interesting character is a subsidiary one—Jake's older sister, Linda, a *Time-Life* journalist who epitomizes changing fashions in power when she decides it's less glamorous to be a star reporter towing the Luce line than a press officer in the "classy" Kennedy Administration. When Mr. Reddin takes us back to Linda's youth as a rich American teen-ager vacationing imperialistically in pre-Castro Havana, her romantic tryst with a baffled Latin boy at the Tropicana becomes a farcical microcosm of her country's whole addled relationship with Cuba.

Too much of *Rum and Coke* is devoted to an evenhanded recycling of the familiar incidents of C.I.A. hypocrisy and incompetence, as well as the journalistic self-censorship (in the "interests of national security"), that coalesced around the Bay of Pigs. Worse, Mr. Reddin usually views these events not as a virulent satirist but from the same naïve perspective as his hero, a true believer who gradually becomes a Daniel Ellsberg-style whistle blower. The play is often written as if no one had ever before exposed the debacle it describes—or explored its ramifications in the implicit context of subsequent United States adventures in Asia or Latin America.

There are also some funny bits involving the Washington intelligence bureaucrats—who smoke Castro's favorite cigars while concocting scenarios to depose him. . . . [The] men could step from *Rum and Coke* right into a film version of David Halberstam's *Best and the Brightest*.

Yet even the impassioned, omnipresent [Jake] leaves less of an impression than the cultural detritus around him—from the opening projected images of Tupperware parties and beach-party movies to the final Andrews Sisters recording of the title song. The dogged earnestness poured into *Rum and Coke* is just no match for the Pop Art renderings of history that give Mr. Reddin's best writing its kick.

> *Frank Rich, " 'Rum and Coke,' Bay of Pigs Revisited," in* The New York Times, *January 28, 1986.*

John Beaufort

Rum and Coke recalls the 1961 Bay of Pigs disaster from the vantage point of a low-level government careerist. Jake Seward typifies history's unknown fall guy. He is the Rosencrantz or Guildenstern of Keith Reddin's raucous satire.

"I'm going to do something good for America," Jake announces after he has signed up with the Central Intelligence Agency to train Cuban exiles who will broadcast propaganda and later spearhead the misguided assault. When the action predictably miscarries, Jake asks: "How could we have been so dumb?" The once-gullible Everyman knows the answers. They lie in the C.I.A.'s arrogant assumptions, foul-ups by an implacable bureaucracy, failure to supply the rebels, and most of all the absence of an indigenous Cuban underground ready to challenge Fidel Castro.

Finally convinced of impending disaster, Jake attempts to leak the facts. His chosen journalist turns out to be a C.I.A. plant. President Kennedy blunders into the Bay of Pigs, and the would-be whistle-blower goes to jail.

Rum and Coke (the American version of *Cuba Libre*) is a stage cartoon, a play of primer politics, primary colors, and primitive humor. The dialogue is often coarse and sometimes intentionally disgusting. Being an actor, Reddin knows how to write characters—and caricatures—that actors can relish.

Since its outcome is history, *Rum and Coke* faces the task of sustaining interest as a mordant footnote. In these circumstances, Jake's slow awakening tests the spectator's patience. Lively performances don't suffice when the play's development sags.

> *John Beaufort, in a review of "Rum and Coke," in* The Christian Science Monitor, *January 29, 1986.*

Edith Oliver

In the satiric *Rum and Coke,* Keith Reddin tells in mock-documentary style the story of an earnest young Yale graduate called Jake, who, on the strength of one childhood vacation spent in Cuba, is recruited by the C.I.A. in 1959 to foment rebellions against Castro in Guatemala and adjacent countries. There are twenty-one characters in the play, of whom three—Jake, his sister Linda, and a Cuban exile named Miguel, who works with Jake and becomes his dear friend—are people; the rest are types. These types, often amusing, are familiar by now: malignant C.I.A. clowns; a barbaric, rich Fascist from the Southwest; assorted eager beavers; and figures with real names, such as Richard Nixon and Fidel himself. Many of them seem to be talking in cartoon captions or second-hand synthetic speech—at times clever, at times not. Jokes abound, as do references to popular songs and movie casts of the period. The scenes that are truly strong are those involving Jake and Linda and Miguel, and one of the best is Miguel's speech—a comic masterpiece . . . in which he describes to Jake with an admiration that approaches awe the sexual inventiveness of a prostitute imported into Central America by the C.I.A. The play ends, of course, with the catastrophe of the Bay of Pigs. (pp. 100-01)

As for the adventurous Mr. Reddin, he surely has one of the most vigorous imaginations among younger dramatists today, and it seems a shame to turn it loose on Nixon and C.I.A. stereotypes. Mr. Reddin's high spirits, his kaleidoscopic inventiveness belong more to fiction than to fact. Though the factual material seems sound enough, it is prepackaged, and the cleverness of its handling, genuine as it may be, is no match for the real humor, understanding, and originality that he brings to his three completely realized characters. *Rum and Coke* seems to me several giant steps beyond Mr. Reddin's *Life and Limb,* of a year ago, but I still feel that the social commentary is negligible; his creativeness is everything. (p. 101)

> Edith Oliver, "Cuba Libre," in The New Yorker, *Vol. LXI, No. 51, February 10, 1986, pp. 100-01.*

Robert Brustein

The subject of Keith Reddin's new play *Rum and Coke* is coded in the title. Rum and Coke proportionately blended are a concoction known to senior prom circles as a "cuba libre": *Free* Cuba, a descriptive adjective misconstrued by the Kennedy administration as an imperative verb. *Rum and Coke* concerns the American effort to liberate this island 90 miles to our south from Castro Communism through an aborted invasion by Miami-based Cuban exiles backed by the C.I.A.—surely one of the most idiotic enterprises in a long catalog of absurd government adventures.

It was Philip Roth who first remarked that the behavior of contemporary Americans, whether official or civilian, had become so extreme that it was outstripping the writer's capacity for satire. The challenge to any playwright addressing an event so incredibly botched, so ludicrous in planning and execution, as the Bay of Pigs fiasco is to discover an appropriate tone. Reddin's solution mixes baffled innocence, ironic indignation, and documentary facts in proportions as sweet and potent as his titular mixed drink.

I suspect his unconscious model was Stanley Kubrick's *Doctor Strangelove,* another comedy of disaster about government agencies gone temporarily mad. While Reddin's wrath is considerably milder than the lunatic fury of that surreal farce, his scalpel has its sharp edges. In place of Group Captain Mandrake—Kubrick's personification of impotent exasperation—he substitutes a young Yale graduate named Jake Seward to witness, and to participate in, the events leading up to the Cuban invasion. Jake spent some time in Havana as a child, and later ran a radio program in Caracas, playing records and making jokes. There he met Vice President Nixon during his ill-fated visit to

Venezuela. This makes him a ripe candidate for the C.I.A., which recruits him to train exiled Cubans in broadcasting.

Under other circumstances, Jake would probably grow up to be George Bush. He has (aside from the habit of wearing white socks with his pin-striped suits) a perfect Ivy League finish combined with the capacity to rationalize the more barbarous behavior of his own government. He also has an older sister, Linda, a reporter for *Time* magazine, who functions initially as his political conscience ("What's your country? Connecticut?") until she too is co-opted by the promise of a government job. In the course of their meetings around Miami pools and restaurant tables, Linda, the liberal investigative reporter, gradually transforms physically and spiritually into an administration apologist and press secretary for Jackie Kennedy. What attracts her is the first lady's chic—"She's class; we could use a little class around here"—contrasted with the style of the previous administration, symbolized by Ike walking around on polished White House floors in golf cleats, swinging a nine iron.

Jake is first recruited for his new position by a smooth functionary named Rodger Potter and by Tod Cartmell, a Texas redneck with a ferocious hatred of Sinatra; the latter tells stories about a four-foot worm that once dropped out of someone's backside into a pan of milk ("You guys hungry? You want something to eat?"). At a C.I.A. board meeting, Jake is apprised of the plans for overthrowing Castro—planting LSD in his double corona, spraying his beard with a strong depilatory to make it fall out overnight, hiring a member of the Mob (syndicate money being tied up in Cuban casinos) for purposes of assassination. Bizarre as this sounds, it is the stuff of history, if not of *Godfather II.* But Jake nevertheless proceeds with his obligation to train "freedom fighters"—exiled Cubans stationed in Guatemala whose hatred for Castro is surpassed only by their unrequited lust. (Until the whores arrive, they have to be satisfied with Kim Novak movies.)

> "It was Philip Roth who first remarked that the behavior of contemporary Americans, whether official or civilian, had become so extreme that it was outstripping the writer's capacity for satire. The challenge to any playwright addressing an event so incredibly botched, so ludicrous in planning and execution, as the Bay of Pigs fiasco is to discover an appropriate tone. Reddin's solution mixes baffled innocence, ironic indignation, and documentary facts in proportions as sweet and potent as his titular mixed drink."

Jake's patriotism has been fueled by his personal contact with Nixon in Venezuela. Reddin intercuts scenes from this besieged meeting—where Nixon, dodging stones, admits, "People don't take to me; I'm not the life of the party"—with brief shots of Castro, complete with beret, cigar, and fatigues, teaching baseball to kids playing "Yankee invader." Later, when Jake begins developing doubts about the invasion and telephones Nixon, now a defeated presidential candidate, for reassurance, he is answered with character-building bromides and invective against Eastern Ivy League professors who watered down his original invasion plan.

Jake has qualms not about the act of overthrowing Castro, but rather about the means. He knows the C.I.A. has overestimated the extent of native Cuban discontent with their government, and without a local uprising his Cuban exile friends will be left behind on the beaches, expendable sacrifices to a callous and careless bureaucracy. He attempts, unsuccessfully, to expose the situation to Linda for publication in *Time.* But the administration has already asked *Time-Life* to kill the story on security grounds ("Hey, we're all patriotic Americans"), and anyway she's more occupied with persuading Jake to dress like a Kennedy. Eventually, he tries a Deep Throat maneuver, handing stolen memos to a newspaper reporter who turns out to be a C.I.A. contact. He is apprehended by Rodger for breach of security.

"We're fucked," he moans, and when the smoke clears, it is obvious the Cuban invaders have been fucked too. American support has faded away. Fidel stands over the survivors gloatingly, meting out sentences ranging from imprisonment to death. The opposition has vanished, but as Fidel says, "I am still here." Nixon calls it "a bigger fuckup than PT 109." Linda has lost her job; Jake faces trial. Brother and sister, both now dressed Kennedy style, reminisce over the good times they once had in pre-Castro Cuba, over its pleasures and corruptions: "It made me feel special." When the investigative report of the invasion was issued in 1961, Jake cried and threw up. "How could we have been so dumb?"

Rum and Coke ends an elegy for lost innocence and lost honor. For the young Reddin, Cuba represents a historic event as catastrophic to patriotic ideals as Suez continues to be for young Englishmen. (*Rum and Coke*'s English counterpart is David Hare's *Plenty,* another elegiac study of the subversion of personal values by official duplicity.) But although the play has a political subject, it is not strictly speaking a political work. Reddin takes no stand regarding the ethics of overthrowing Castro. What fires him is the betrayal of committed human beings in a stupidly contrived adventure. In common with previous work by this developing dramatist, *Rum and Coke* deals with historic subjects largely in an effort to humanize them, conforming to Chekhov's dictum that "writers and artists must concern themselves with politics only insofar as it is necessary to put up a defense against politics." In short, the play is a document more eloquent than most of the speeches at the recent PEN conference about the adversary relationship between the "writer's imagination" and "the imagination of the state."

Rum and Coke has its flaws, most of them confirming Roth's remarks about the inadequacy of modern satire in the face of contemporary reality. Often Reddin can invent nothing more ludicrous than the established facts, which gives his work the feel of newsprint scraped off the front page. Some of his characters—the redneck Texan, for example—are stereotypes. His portrayal of Nixon ("Maybe you don't know it, but I sweat") is conventional and facile, little better than a stand-up impersonation, and his cruel paternalistic Castro is neither fully imagined nor realized. His intercutting and flashback techniques are more cinematic than theatrical. And his tangential comic monologues—Tod's story of the four-foot worm, the exile leader Miguel's account of a Guatemalan woman smoking a cigarette "with her thing"—while providing the wildest, most virtuosic moments in the play, occasionally seem extraneous to the action.

Still, *Rum and Coke* is never less than intriguing, and sometimes very moving. (pp. 24-6)

Robert Brustein, "Highballs and Ballups," in The New Republic, *Vol. 194, No. 3711, March 3, 1986, pp. 24-6.*

John Simon

I have scant use for Keith Reddin's previous plays, but nothing about them prepared me for something as thoroughly awful as *Highest Standard of Living.* . . . [The] highly polished, virtually flawless production only underscores the emptiness, obviousness, and witlessness of this would-be absurdist, would-be satirical would-be comedy. Reddin has, in the past, received high marks (though not from me) for accosting subjects with political or social significance, sophomoric as his approach may have been. This time it should be plain as a pikestaff that although he pants after political commentary, what he offers us is two-cent iconoclasm and a rather cheaper style.

Tiresomely he rehashes the tired argument that life in Communist Russia, unfree, fear-ridden, precarious as it is, is scarcely different from life in the United States, free, easy, and rewarding as it is supposed to be. The problem with this is, first of all, that it is patently untrue; but it is the with-it thing for liberal whipper-snappers—who know nothing of life in the U.S.S.R. and not much more about life anywhere—to expatiate on. This kind of simplistic smart-asininity panders to overgrown but underdeveloped collegiate rebels of the sixties—perhaps even to some present-day campus pundits—but cannot provide enough basis for the flimsiest of comedies.

In the second place, Reddin's Moscow and New York are equally cliché-studded and sloppily observed. Thus you do not make fun of a typical Russian by representing him as one who never heard of Mayakovsky or Akhmatova; the trouble is that he has heard too much, can recite reams of both poets, and still not learn anything from them—a trouble by no means limited to Soviet Russia. Similarly, the American Secret Service types who detain the hero, expelled from Russia, for humiliating questioning would not camp around like a pair of homosexual comics; surely there would be better things about them to ridicule. And for a Columbia graduate student in Russian literature, the hero is far too ignorant of Russian literature, language, and life.

Theater of the absurd must take off from a sense of reality that is then variously exaggerated and distorted; Reddin starts with a preposterousness he can neither heighten nor develop. All he can do is repeat and repeat: **Highest Standard of Living** reiterates its feeble jokes—already dragged out way beyond the point of diminishing returns, assuming there were any returns in the first place—within each act ad infinitum. And the parallel structure—Act I: Moscow, Act II: New York—merely encourages further repetition and schematism. A Russian fan rattles off an endless litany of Little Richard song titles from his record collection. The American hero and a young Russian fanatic vie in reviling Reagan, the American befuddling his opponent by outdoing him—which might be funny if not so dragged out. The hero's confusion when the heroine, a Russian doctor he casually invited to America, actually shows up, as a defector, is interminable, both of them hemming and hawing at unconscionable length. A bunch of vicious, hammer-wielding children are brought on twice in Moscow, their equivalents appearing twice in New York. Dead bodies disappear in a twinkling in both cities; desperate people jump off boats in both. . . .

[No] prodigality of talents in the production can mitigate the crudeness of concept, banality of humor, and sweat under the collar **Highest Standard of Living** exhibits, reducing it pretty much to the lowest standard of playwriting. Keith Reddin is a very good actor; why subtract from this by becoming a very poor playwright? (p. 86)

> *John Simon, "Odious Comparison," in* New York *Magazine, Vol. 19, No. 46, November 24, 1986, pp. 86, 88.*

Edith Oliver

Keith Reddin's **Highest Standard of Living** doesn't come to much as political satire; its originality and humor are all theatrical. The show opens on the ferry from Finland to Leningrad. The hero, a young American called Bob, is aboard, eventual destination Moscow, where he plans to do graduate study of the work of the Soviet writer Mikhail Bulgakov. He meets a Russian passenger, to whom he confides his knowledge of Soviet poets by listing them in the manner of Danny Kaye chanting the names of Russian composers in *Lady in the Dark*. The passenger responds by reciting "The Shooting of Dan McGrew," complete. As the voyage ends, another passenger jumps, howling, off the boat. From then on, the action is kaleidoscopic. Bob becomes ill from food poisoning in his hotel room and is taken to a hospital (the rooms have identical red brick walls), where he is attended by an attractive woman doctor, Ludmilla, and a brawny nurse, who tells him that she works for the K.G.B. Every encounter is peculiar, not to say sinister. A man in peasant costume enters Bob's hospital room accompanied by a bear; the two are Bob's uncle and aunt, in disguise. (They have arrived with a circus.) Another nurse, whose face has been hidden behind a magazine, turns out to be Bob's mother. An old man in the next bed, dying of a surfeit of vodka, is visited by his son, who spouts a stream of Soviet propaganda and attacks the United States; Bob agrees with every word he says. Five little boys run in with hammers, and that is the end of the

old man. Bob goes to dinner at Ludmilla's apartment and invites her to defect to New York, and then to stay with him there. Bob is ordered by an American official to leave the country. Bob is attacked by the children with hammers. So much for Act I.

Act II is also brimming with incidents, but a lot of the steam has escaped during the intermission, and a lot of the fun, too. The action opens at the airport in New York, as Bob enters, his head bandaged, to confront a couple of men from the State Department (I guess). Again, all events are spooky and/or dangerous; the C.I.A. has become the counterpart of the K.G.B. In the final scene, Bob and Ludmilla, hand in hand, leap from the Staten Island ferry, but long before that the play—such as it is—has perished of a surfeit of itself. The production is ingenious, and gives some coherence to a script that is essentially jumpy, for all its high spirits. (I am not ungrateful for high spirits.) (pp. 111-12)

> *Edith Oliver, in a review of "Highest Standard of Living," in* The New Yorker, *Vol. LXI, No. 41, December 1, 1986, pp. 111-12.*

John Simon

There is a new kind of theater afoot that is heavily influenced by the movies, usually not to its benefit. Here short scenes jump nervously from location to location, often with minimal changes in scenery or lighting, or just by shifting the action to another part of a unit set. In itself, this does not make a play cinematic, or else the Elizabethans would all be proleptic cineasts. What is cinematic, however, is not getting deep inside a character but letting surfaces do most of the work, and punching scenes home with specious shock effects at the beginning or end or both. So, too, is relegating dialogue to a subsidiary position.

Such a play is Keith Reddin's **Big Time: Scenes from a Service Economy.** Reddin is a good actor but an erratic playwright, and though his choice of political subjects makes him a bit of a rare bird among our dramatists, the intellectual acumen is often closer to Big Bird's. In **Big Time,** we encounter Fran, who does layouts for a magazine and lives with Paul, the rising star of an international bank, whose constant travels and business partying tend to shut out the young woman. Frustrated, she drifts into a clandestine affair with a friend of theirs, Peter, a photojournalist. At least he seems to be an idealist—witness his pictures of bodies in Central American ditches. But he proves just as self-centered and opportunistic as Paul.

Both men suffer setbacks. Paul is fired by his bank for wheeling and dealing with a Third World government that is toppled; Peter is reduced to taking party pictures of Molly Ringwald. And both men end up shortchanging Fran, who, disillusioned with them and her job, leaves. Morally, she may be the winner; but the men bounce back in unappetizing ways, whereas she vanishes. The play is over in little more than an hour, proving that it is possible to be concise without incisiveness. There are also three minor characters, one of whom gets a long, preciously weird monologue; but with or without monologue, they manage to exude just as much inconsequentiality, in even less time, as the major ones.

There is, however, a certain slickness here. Someone who had not successfully absorbed a good deal from other such plays and movies could not have written *Big Time,* any more than someone original enough not to need such osmosis could have done so. Slickness of this kind, however, though seemingly better than clumsiness, is in fact less helped by the odd good moment; it needs rapid-fire wit to sustain it, and that is not forthcoming from Mr. Reddin's popgun. (p. 48)

> *John Simon, "Small Time," in* New York *Magazine, Vol. 21, No. 30, August 1, 1988, pp. 48-9.*

William A. Henry III

Essayists on the American mind usually find it impossible to go much longer than two or three paragraphs before making some reference to Calvinism. But it takes guts for a playwright to make John Calvin, the 16th century theologian, an actual character onstage. Scholars of popular culture frequently assert that the national soul is mirrored in the game of baseball. Yet it takes great faith—not only in his own intelligence but also in the audience's—for a dramatist to depict the making of the American imperium through the life of centerfielder Ty Cobb. The nation's theater has long excelled at the agonies and ecstasies of family life but has faltered at portraying the broad sweep of public life; its ambitions have been toward emotional, not intellectual, riches. Thus two new plays would be noteworthy for their reach, whatever their merits. But what Keith Reddin, 34, aspires to in *Life During Wartime* and Lee Blessing, 40, aims at in *Cobb* proves in each case to be well within the writer's grasp.

Reddin's play is much the more complicated of the two—and certainly the wackier. Instead of a naturalistic kitchen-sink drama, this is an everything-but-the-kitchen-sink melodrama-cum-farce, featuring fantasy sequences, flashbacks; ghosts, tall tales, quoted swatches of e.e. cummings verse and repeated incursions into a contemporary setting by a bearded and costumed Calvin. He recites his writings on predestination and free will and inveighs, sounding suspiciously like a televangelist, against the iniquities of Pop culture. The "war" of the title is not an event but a metaphor. It refers to the sense of embattlement that prompts some suburban householders to buy security systems and others to turn their homes into armories.

What fuses this apparent chaos into a coherent and haunting play is the theme that runs through all of Reddin's work, notably *Rum and Coke* (1985), *Big Time* (1987) and *Nebraska* (1989): the tandem dangers of run-amuck individualism and nice-guy uninvolvement. The central character in *Life During Wartime* is, like almost all of Reddin's heroes, a genial but morally weightless young man. When he learns that other salespeople in his home-security firm are running a sideline in burglary—for the loot and to generate additional sales—he assumes it has nothing to do with him. Tragically late, he finds that it

does. Reddin's point, no less forceful for being familiar, is that the unexamined life is not worth living.

The show leaves one wishing that Reddin were less preoccupied with writing about people so lacking in self-awareness, so ethically dead that in a crisis they shrivel rather than change. By temperament he cuts himself off from straightforward plot development. His characters rarely grow and deepen, eliminating another avenue by which plays accumulate impact. Thus this fine writer produces works that stimulate the mind but do not linger in the heart.

> *William A. Henry III, "Myth, Ambition and Anger," in* Time, *New York, Vol. 136, No. 4, July 23, 1990, p. 78.*

Frank Rich

In the roughly five years since Keith Reddin began spending more time writing than acting, he has produced a steady stream of black comedies about the underground of corruption, political and moral, that lurks just beneath the slick sitcom surface of American life. His plays, notably *Life and Limb* and *Rum and Coke,* are unfailingly intelligent and are generally produced by the finest resident theaters in and outside New York. Yet Mr. Reddin has not so far caused a serious stir within the non-profit theater, let alone with a larger public. He is perpetually on the verge.

Why? The answer can be found . . . [in] Mr. Reddin's *Life during Wartime*. . . . Its hero is a boyish naif, Tommy, who stumbles into Kafkaesque conspiracies beyond his wildest nightmares while working as a door-to-door salesman for a company that sells home-security systems. In the suburban households he visits, Tommy finds terror and violence; back at the office, his white-collar colleagues prove to be the perpetrators of a lethal shell game that has more to do with the practice of crime than its prevention.

"Let's be realistic," says Tommy's sinister boss, named Heinrich no less, at the very start of the play. "It's a dangerous world. Everyone has a weapon." Heinrich is played by an actor long associated with David Mamet, and it is in that opening speech that Mr. Reddin's problems begin. Heinrich's three sentences are Mamet lines if ever there were any, an echo heightened by the bristling . . . delivery of them. They also sound like dialogue that might have been written by Howard Korder, whose *Search and Destroy,* seen at the Yale Repertory Theater this season, had an actress . . . , themes and even the military coinage of its title in common with *Life during Wartime.*

Can Mr. Reddin beat these masters at the game of dramatizing dog-eat-dog American men in staccato, paranoia-tinged comic vignettes? Of course not. And he surely goes out of his way to court comparisons here by giving his salesmen a scene in a Chinese restaurant, the site of similar and more pungent sales conferences in Mr. Mamet's *Glengarry Glen Ross.*

But an even bigger failure in *Life during Wartime* rises out of Mr. Reddin's major departure from the Mamet pattern—his use of an innocent hero. Every Reddin play I've seen has had such a center-stage figure: a wide-eyed do-gooder who is shocked to the quick once he discovers that the business world or the government is duplicitous and rotten. The playwright's fatal error is his assumption that everyone except himself is just as unsophisticated as his protagonists. As a result, the audience is almost always a few impatient steps ahead of his heroes, waiting for that long-delayed moment when the light bulb will go on and they will at last wise up to blatant corruption all around them.

In *Life during Wartime,* the bright side of Mr. Reddin's talent—the originality that keeps one rooting for his eventual artistic breakthrough—is also apparent. Throughout the evening, a Bible-thumping John Calvin, dressed in full 16th-century regalia keeps dropping in to give his views on *Leave It to Beaver* and the acting talents of Mickey Rourke as well as to reopen for debate the doctrine of original sin. . . . It is also representative of Mr. Reddin's imagination at its most free-wheeling that a dead character in his play refuses to stay dead and that dismemberment becomes a source of surreal comedy.

> *Frank Rich, "When Innocence Collides with Menace and Mayhem," in* The New York Times, *March 6, 1991, p. C13.*

John Simon

In *Life during Wartime,* Keith Reddin has written not only his own best play but also one that any current playwright might be pleased to have written. It is amusing, literate, nicely idiosyncratic, and has something to say. . . . There are moments when Reddin strains a bit: John Calvin is used funnily as character and commentator, T. S. Eliot is quoted whimsically, but e. e. cummings may be dragged in a tad self-consciously. Still, a little excess ambition in an otherwise sound and idiomatic play is pardonable.

Tommy, the protagonist, is, like other Reddin heroes, a latter-day Candide, sucked into a very shady salesman's job where, along with home-security systems, he may be selling his soul. Certainly the cost to both him and his dear ones is enormous; but in the end there is redemption, albeit no thanks to Calvin, whose hilarious attempts to meddle in modern lives are no more satisfactory than those lives themselves.

A basically nice young fellow, Tommy could be happy with Gale, a similarly likable older woman, except that life kicks them in the teeth, largely through his fault. Still, they persevere, one on each side of the grave, even though they both fall on bizarre company: she on Calvin, he on all kinds of weirdos—criminally, paranoically, or just plain weirdly weird. But there are also some decent people around—a postal clerk, a woman antiquarian—and Tommy makes a heartening discovery or two that he passes on to us, eloquently and engagingly. . . .

[Don't] wait; be among the first to discover this amiable dark comedy with a mind of its own and the wit and courage to speak it.

Let me add, though, that I find it disconcerting that a T-shirt featuring a quotation from Calvin should misspell "principal": "The principle combat we must wage. . . ." If this were meant as a joke, the inscription would not just flash by, and such illiteracy in a literate play is shocking. Of course, you may not be troubled by such things; but in that case, you are unlikely to find the play itself worth the trouble. (p. 77)

> *John Simon, "Two from the Heart, Two from Hunger," in* New York *Magazine, Vol. 24, No. 11, March 18, 1991, pp. 76-7.*

Edith Oliver

The "wartime" of Keith Reddin's *Life during Wartime* refers not to Vietnam or the [Persian] Gulf crisis but to our own day-by-day cops-and-robbers warfare. It is a comedy of sorts—as much dramatic curiosity as play—about a young man called Tommy, who gets a job selling home-security systems. In the opening scene he is instructed in alarm systems and related matters by his new boss, one Heinrich, and then immediately falls in love with his first customer. She is a very pretty woman, considerably older than he is, and she responds wholeheartedly. We proceed, episode by episode, until, somewhere near the end, she and her adolescent son are murdered (through a fluke we needn't go into), and the comedy turns grim. Sporadically, John Calvin, the sixteenth-century theologian, enters, making appropriate moral pronouncements of an extremely gloomy nature.

Mr. Reddin is a good writer who certainly seems to know what he is up to, . . . yet I kept feeling that I should be laughing more, having a better time. Reviewing Mr. Reddin's *Rum and Coke* (about the C.I.A. in Cuba) five years ago, and, before that, his *Life and Limb,* I wrote that his social commentary was negligible but his imagination was "vigorous" [see Oliver's earlier entries]. This time, the first words that came to mind were "sterile" and "remote." Nevertheless, that imagination does break through. At one point, Tommy visits a prospect who, sternly shunting him aside, displays his own private arsenal with a pride that would do credit to Douglas MacArthur. . . . Afterthought: that Mr. Reddin has written a comedy about absolutely humorless people is one oddity among many.

> *Edith Oliver, "House of Mamet," in* The New Yorker, *Vol. LXVII, No. 4, March 18, 1991, p. 82.*

Michael Feingold

Has anyone ever explained, successfully, the American obsession with materialism? The things of this world never stop interesting us, even in that metaphysical arena, the theater, where the realest thing can never be more than a representation. It's half a century since Thornton Wilder—and he wasn't the first—yelled at our theater to "tear down that proscenium arch," yet we still love having our plays happen in a picture-perfect, fully furnished spaces. Money and the objects it buys remain our passion, no matter how angrily our playwrights throw the objects onstage as a way of telling us there's more to life than acquisition. Piling the material goods high in our imagination, the writers get implicated unavoidably in the very obsession they're attacking, but it's hard to see what alternative they might have. Trapped in the system, they're prisoners of affluence like the rest of us, sitting there watching it shrink, wondering what will be left of the U.S. when our objects go and we realize we never had anything else.

The unreal physical object in Keith Reddin's *Life during Wartime* is the suburban happy home, worshipped by many of the characters but accepted as a reality only by the hero, a romantic idealist who, in a time of skyrocketing crime rates, sells and swears by home-alarm systems. Reddin is a teasy, hit-and-run playwright: He loves to hook audiences on the sweetness of a setup, then torment them with its hideous possibilities for destruction before he's barely brought it to life. Tommy, the innocent alarm peddler, falls in love with his first customer, a smart, eccentric divorcée with a trouble-prone teenage son and a penchant for kinky questions like (while she and Tommy are making love on the floor), "What would you do if I was missing my arms?"

While Tommy has dreams of a cozy home life, his boss Heinrich has a scam: Every so often, purchasers have their homes broken into. Sales get a boost, the victims get an upgrade, and the salesmen get a piece of the burglars' take. Honest Tommy doesn't want in, and Heinrich tells him it's cool, but then intruders visit the divorcée's home, and she and her son are killed; Tommy doesn't know if Heinrich did it or not, and isn't sure, either way, what to do about it. As a reminder that this is a satire on the violence of materialism rather than a tragic romance, Reddin supplies vaudevillian interruptions by a campy TV-style monologuist—John Calvin, whose doctrine of grace made visible in worldly prosperity started Christians on the road to capitalism. Reddin's Calvin, hectoring us and the characters alternately, wants us to remember that we're all damned from birth by original sin, but he'd also like to be cast as Ward if they ever remake *Leave It to Beaver,* in his

obliviousness to the basic tenets of his own preaching, he's like a male Protestant rewrite of Sister Mary Ignatius.

"Reddin is a teasy, hit-and-run playwright: He loves to hook audiences on the sweetness of a setup, then torment them with its hideous possibilities for destruction before he's barely brought it to life."

Not that his strictures help the characters, any more than his irritating routines help the play, which is otherwise full of sharp observation and complex, discordant ironies. Reddin's non-naturalistic tricks, like the typically American lapses into violence he depicts, seem to come from a nervousness at the thought of dealing with emotional depths. Droll in theory, onstage the notion of a show-bizzy Calvin keeps dragging the play into a *Saturday Night Live* world where everything's cutely okay because nothing's really real. Finally Reddin succumbs to that world altogether, letting Tommy's torment subside into a sentimental appeasement, with a few pat speeches, about accepting risk as a natural part of life, that seem to belong in a different play, and do a disservice to the rich and disturbing material of this one. Making the brisk, edgy most of the play's tough side, [the director] treats Reddin's work with more respect than the author himself shows. . . . [The cast] all get well past Reddin's flimsy surface cleverness into the dark depths he loves to point at but rarely dives in to explore. (pp. 85, 106)

Michael Feingold, "Prisoners of Affluence," in The Village Voice, *Vol. XXXVI, No. 12, March 19, 1991, pp. 85, 106.*

João Ubaldo Ribeiro

1941-

Brazilian novelist, short story writer, and journalist.

Ribeiro has received international attention for his novels *Sargento Getúlio* (*Sergeant Getúlio*) and *Vivo o povo brasileiro* (*An Invincible Memory*), both of which he translated into English from Portuguese. Set in modern Brazil, *Sergeant Getúlio* is a stream of consciousness narrative that has been praised as a compelling portrayal of the mind of a hired gunman. The eponymous protagonist of this work is a deserter from a state militia who works for Senhor Antunes, a local politician. At the beginning of the novel Getúlio has been sent out to abduct one of his employer's enemies. In a rambling monologue, Getúlio recounts his earlier crimes and provides vivid descriptions of his torture of the man he takes prisoner. Bowing to political pressure, Antunes finds it expedient to release his opponent; Getúlio, however, refuses to comply and kills the soldiers sent to relieve him. Although a few reviewers were discomfited by scenes of brutality in the novel, many consider this work a highly relevant commentary on Brazilian society. David William Foster noted that "*Sergeant Getúlio* is an exceptionally eloquent example of the unreflective cruelty and violence of the social and political structures of Latin America within the national myths of law and order and civilized society." Some critics have further asserted that Sergeant Getúlio's sense of duty and his inability to understand the political realities that lead his boss to betray him transform him from a savage brute into a complex, tragic figure. Robert DiAntonio wrote: "Out of one man's epic quest for redemption, Ribeiro has fashioned one of the most complex and compelling Brazilian novels of the present age."

An Invincible Memory is a panoramic historical novel that examines Brazilian society from the seventeenth-century colonial period to the present. Comprising a large cast of characters and a number of interwoven subplots, the novel focuses primarily on a nineteenth-century affair between General Patrício Macário, the youngest son of an aristocratic, land-owning family, and the woman he has been ordered to capture, Maria da Fé, a guerilla fighter and descendant of a slave owned by the Macários. Through the tragic relationship between these two characters, Ribeiro explores the problems of violence and racial prejudice in his native society.

(See also *CLC,* Vol. 10 and *Contemporary Authors,* Vols. 81-84.)

PRINCIPAL WORKS

NOVELS

Setembro não tem sentido   1968
Sargento Getúlio   1971
   [*Sergeant Getúlio,* 1977]

Vila real   1979
Vivo o povo brasileiro   1984
   [*An Invincible Memory,* 1989]
O sorriso do lagarto   1989

OTHER

Vencecavalo e o outro povo   (novellas)   1974
Livro de histórias   (short stories)   1981

Peter S. Prescott

[*Sergeant Getúlio* is] a story Tamerlane would have liked, had he known how to read. A Brazilian novel, it has been adroitly translated into English by its author, who advises us that it is "a tale of virtue." That it is, if you remember that virtue's root lies in the Latin word for male and that its many meanings encompass diligence and physical force, power and the display of valor, as well as conformity to moral principles of conduct. It is also a splendid novel, a point I must make at once because, as serious fiction goes, it is as exultantly bloody as anything west of de Sade.

Sergeant Getúlio tells it as a monologue. A deserter from a Brazilian state militia, he works as a hired gun for a local politician. Having killed more than twenty people ("It's like women, impossible to remember them all. The first one is the most difficult"), Getúlio has been sent to capture and bring back one of his employer's political enemies. This he does, talking incessantly as his driver maneuvers a bullet-ridden Hudson across the desolate country. At some point, Getúlio's boss changes his mind and soldiers are sent to relieve the gunman of his prisoner, but the sergeant, a suspicious man and a superlative warrior, annihilates them. Getúlio can think only of performing his duty: "It is necessary to deliver the animal." A manhunt ensues; the violence escalates. In one memorable scene Getúlio beheads a lieutenant; in another he extracts four teeth from his prisoner's jaws with a pair of pliers, having first applied his rifle butt to the man's gums by way of anesthesia.

This is a story about loss. Getúlio, a fatalist, knows with part of his mind that it cannot end well. "The situation has changed," he is told. The world is different now: you can't behead lieutenants any longer, you can't rip out a man's teeth. "In the old times there was magic, I think," Getúlio says. He would be a bandit, but there are no more bandits. He dreams of a heroic future: "The way it is, I don't know. I don't like the world to change, it gives me an uneasy feeling, I don't know what to do."

So skillful is João Ubaldo Ribeiro that he makes us bleed for this barbarian he has created, even respect him. Getúlio is not to be blamed for using violence the way suburban matrons use detergents—as a cleansing, corrective antidote for human messiness. "Created" is the key word here. Ribeiro has created not only a remarkable man, but a distinct sensibility in which violence and a sensuous appreciation of the physical world seem effortlessly blended. He has created a diction based upon but not limited to common language—Getúlio is capable of flights of rhetoric. Most important, he has created an entire (though closely circumscribed) world which, though it exists only in his narrator's head, reminds us of a world we have known, or have heard of since the first Sergeant Getúlio set up his camp against the walls of Troy.

Peter S. Prescott, "A Good Barbarian," in Newsweek, *Vol. XCI, No. 5, January 30, 1978, p. 68.*

Luis Larios

The plot of **Sergeant Getúlio** is definitely a simple one: the protagonist takes a prisoner from Paulo Afonso to Barra dos Coqueiros, but in the pages of this short volume the reader finds a most remarkable psychological portrait of a man. Getúlio is a professional killer, but although his life has been a series of crimes and has included plenty of violence (he has murdered more than twenty people), he longs for a quiet life near the Japaratuba River. As a small child he arrived penniless in Aracaju, worked as a shoeshine boy, joined the state militia and eventually deserted and became a hired gun for Senhor Antunes, a local politi-

cian. When the story starts, Getúlio, a driver named Amaro and the prisoner are traveling in a bullet-riddled Hudson. The entire narrative is a long monologue. The sleepless Getúlio is not sure whether he is thinking or talking aloud. Nevertheless one becomes aware of even his most insignificant thoughts. Everything is seen through Getúlio's eyes, he being the protagonist-narrator.

Getúlio is a primitive personage similar in some ways to Pascual Duarte. He is totally insensitive to human suffering but kills with purpose and disdains those who murder indiscriminately: "There was great badness in him, he killed without ideas." Getúlio has a militaristic sense of morality based on loyalty and a total commitment to his mission. When Amaro and Luzinete, Getúlio's lover, are killed, for example, he does not appear to have any emotions about their deaths, even though they were the only persons to whom he seemed to be close. Getúlio finds it difficult to fully comprehend the world; he is uncomfortable with changes, and he is also totally unable to perceive or adjust to new developments. Thus when orders from his boss to free the prisoner reach him, Getúlio, a suspicious and, above all, professional man, can think only of performing his duty.

The focal point of the novel lies precisely here, in Getúlio's incapacity and unwillingness to accept changes. He is also convinced that his is the only profession he knows and, in order to survive, his performance must be uncompromising at all times. "I can't be anything else, and that means I have to do well the things I do, because if I don't how is it going to turn out?" This "strength" in his character is both his most admirable quality and the likely cause of his downfall.

The translation, done by the author, is excellent although at times far too literal. The vitality of the Brazilian idiom is unfortunately not sufficiently captured in the English version. Nevertheless, as Jorge Amado [see *CLC,* Vol. 10] writes in the foreword, **Sergeant Getúlio** is a new example of the developing literary craft being produced in Brazil.

Luis Larios, in a review of "Sergeant Getúlio," in World Literature Today, *Vol. 53, No. 1, Winter, 1979, p. 94.*

Ricardo Sternberg

A hired gunman for a political boss, Getúlio has been sent out to capture and deliver a political prisoner. However, circumstances change and political expediency now dictates that the prisoner be set free. Getúlio's boss publicly denies having given the orders and sends a message to the embarrassing mission: release the prisoner. For a variety of reasons Getúlio refuses. Surviving ambushes, he is stopped only at the outskirts of town and killed by federal troops.

This bare bones synopsis of the plot [of **Sergeant Getúlio**] leaves out what is perhaps most admirable about the book: the telling. The story is completely told in Getúlio's own voice, either aloud, ruminating to himself or, in the final pages, delirious with strain and fatigue. This "extremely rich narrative voice," as Jorge Amado [see *CLC,* Vol. 10] called it, allows the character of Getúlio and his story to emerge rooted to the particulars of Brazil's Northeastern culture. His motives for going on with the mission despite his boss' betrayal remains, for example, complex and ambivalent. His resolve derives in part from the sense of duty of a man that cannot understand the machinations of political expediency. It derives as well from the code of bravery and manhood engendered in the popular literature of *cordel* and of the *desafios*. In the magnificent last pages, for instance, Getúlio, clearly overwhelmed, assumes the bragging voice of the Bunyan-like heroes of popular literature. He imagines himself the sire of a fantastic stable of sons: "Stud Santos Bezerra," "Knocks-All-Down Santos Bezerra," and "Overcomes-Horses Santos Bezerra." (pp. 580-81)

> *Ricardo Sternberg, in a review of "Sergeant Getúlio," in* The Hispanic American Historical Review, *Vol. 59, No. 3, August, 1979, pp. 580-81.*

Peter Kemp

[In João Ubaldo Ribeiro's book, **Sergeant Getulio**] the code of murderous machismo is ecstatically acclaimed. 'In this story Sergeant Getúlio takes a prisoner from Paulo Alfonso to Barra dos Coqueiros. It is a tale of virtue,' the author's introductory note bluntly affirms. Eagerly acquiescing, the blurb declares the book to be an 'epic saga of the human spirit', its protagonist 'a classic hero, rigid in his integrity'. Recorded hosannas from Latin American literati—'this great novel' (Jorge Amado), 'a free man whom we must love and honour' (Jose Yglesias)—amplify the adulation.

Moving from this chorus of praise into the book is like stepping from church to abattoir. Butchery abounds. The narrative is strewn with bits of brain, jaw splinters, severed testicles, spilled bowels, caved-in faces. Pages are devoted to the epic hero's brutish ponderings about such matters as the best way partially to castrate his prisoner—with a knife? a pestle? red-hot iron?

Finally, he settles for tearing out the man's teeth with rusty pliers after battering his mouth. Earlier, he has stabbed a pregnant girl to death, and later he first mutilates, then hacks off, the head of a lieutenant who has called him a cuckold. 'You did the right thing,' applauds a priest, going on to deplore the 'yellowness' that now pervades the land.

Mirroring Getúlio's increasing frenzy as he combats this decline in standards, the book's language gradually collapses into outlandish howlings like 'Aboormish pustulent . . . disfrickumbered friffolill . . . Carniculated of the burragilla, retroquelent of the muckolamud'. Reading it is, one hopes, a unique literary experience. (p. 351)

> *Peter Kemp, "Messy Pasts," in* The Listener, *Vol. 103, No. 2653, March 13, 1980, pp. 350-51.*

Alan Hollinghurst

It is very exciting to find a new novel which uses genuine technical originality in the service of a deeply disturbing and unusual moral vision. Ribeiro's stupendous **Sergeant Getúlio** (which has already won prizes in Brazil) is precisely such a book. Set entirely in the thoughts of a sergeant detailed to transport a political prisoner from one town to another, it is written in a highly natural idiom which is brilliantly sustained through extremes of brutality, sadism, fantasy, self-pity, and insecure and childish self-esteem. It is as convincing as 'stream of consciousness' writing can be of the way the mind runs, slows, repeats itself—and it is never for a moment obscure.

Its vivid immediacy confines us in a world where our grasp on normal criteria of morality and understanding is weakened. We participate in the sensuousness of Getúlio's fantasies of violence and his fairy-tale visions of himself, naively elaborated to buttress his self-confidence when, at the crux of the novel, he is betrayed by his own chief. And we are unable to flinch from the imaginative conviction with which, when he is able, Getúlio puts his fantasies into action: for instance, tearing out the teeth of his prisoner, or raiding a barracks single-handed. He is the crudest kind of man of action: 'I keep moving, because when I am moving I am not thinking and when I am acting I am not even knowing, that's it.' But by the end of the book our repulsion is wholly transformed by pathos and exhilaration. His simple understanding cannot cope with the political complexity which entraps him, and a heroic integrity emerges in his actions; as Ribeiro says by way of preface: 'It is a tale of virtue.'

> *Alan Hollinghurst, "Heroic Integrity," in* New Statesman, *Vol. 99, No. 2556, March 14, 1980, p. 402.*

Adam Feinstein

The central character of João Ubaldo Ribeiro's brilliant novel **Sergeant Getúlio** has much in common with the "bandeirantes", the energetic, enterprising and brutal slave-raiders from São Paulo who, from the beginning of the seventeenth century, penetrated deep into the interior of Brazil, appropriating land and seizing Guarani Indians as slaves.

Sergeant Getúlio is escorting a prisoner back to Aracaju, the capital of a province in North-Eastern Brazil. Vicious though the Sergeant often is, he is not without warmth of feeling. The impressive juxtaposition of monstrous threats and a fever of lyricism, as Getúlio records his responses to the misty mornings by the mountains, lends him the same disturbing ambivalence that we find in Camus's Meursault. Getúlio can be very amusing. He declares naive amazement at the medical profession: "I can't understand how a man can spend his life feeling other people's parts". Yet his fundamental lack of confidence ("the worst thing is to be nobody") leads him to relish such thoughts as cutting his prisoner's head off and using it as a football.

The moments when Getúlio turns his self-obsessed attentions on to others are memorably touching. The one man he feels any true affection for is Amaro, the mysterious soldier accompanying him to the capital with the prisoner. He is fervently religious (which Getúlio admires) and has a kind of childish playfulness about him. At one point Getúlio recalls with delight his telling of a short tale: "Once upon a time there was a cow named Tory and she farted and that's the end of the story."

Getúlio's mood wanders from this simple affection to a magical sense of the world—a sense which will be familiar to readers of the contemporary Latin-American novel. In a passage towards the end of the book, he describes the exploits of certain omnipotent figures from the army: Captain Geraldo Bonfim puffs the clouds away when it rains and makes trees wilt with a single grimace; while Major Alligator is so fearful that rivers run dry in fright as he approaches.

As the foremost Brazilian writer Jorge Amado says of Ribeiro in his short introduction, "there is nothing in his rich universe to which he is indifferent". The dynamic awareness of the world in this novel makes João Ubaldo Ribeiro one of the most exciting Brazilian writers of his generation.

> *Adam Feinstein, "No Nobody He," in* The Times Literary Supplement, *No. 4029, June 13, 1980, p. 674.*

An excerpt from *Sergeant Getúlio* (as narrated by Getúlio)

I take him back or I don't take him back, that's the question. Maybe it's better to suffer one's luck no matter what it is, for it must have been written so. Or it's better to fight everything and finish everything. To die is like sleeping and to sleep is to put an end to agony, which is why we always want to sleep. It's just that sleeping can bring you dreams and then everything stays the same. For this reason it's better to die, because there are no dreams when you turn your soul loose and everything ends. Because life is too long and has disasters. Why endure old age coming slowly, tyrannifications and false orders, the pain of cuckoldry, the slowness of things, the things that can't be understood, and the ungratefulness that's undeserved, if you can dispatch yourself with a plain knife? Who can carry this weight, in this life that brings only sweat and fights? The ones who endure it are those who are afraid of death because no one has ever come back from there, and this is what weakens the wish to die. And then you go on putting up with bad things so as not to have to try others that we still don't know. And it is by thinking that you become yellow and the will to fight fades when you think about it and when you remember this you forget about what you were going to do and end up not doing anything at all. Priest, most reverend, in your prayers remember my sins.

David William Foster

Ribeiro belongs to a group of recent Brazilian writers who have been able to take advantage of the relaxation of the stringent censorship imposed by the military take-over in 1964. As a consequence of this cultural thaw, they are able to write about Brazilian society with a frankness and explicitness which reflects in large measure a virtual explosion of pent-up rage and despair. Augusto Boal, Luiz Fernando Emediato, Edilberto Coutinho and Robert Drummond are some of the writers who, along with Ribeiro, have written along these lines. The English translation of Ribeiro's *Sergeant Getúlio,* published in 1978, revealed a very different form of Brazilian fiction than the magical realism of João Guimarães Rosa or Dalton Trevisan or the existentialism of Clarice Lispector. *Sergeant Getúlio* is an exceptionally eloquent example of the unreflective cruelty and violence of the social and political structures of Latin America within the national myths of law and order and civilized society.

Livro de Histórias represents quite another facet of Ribeiro's writings. Eschewing the tragic tones of *Sergeant Getúlio,* it is essentially a comic collection of vignettes on the strategies of provincial life for maintaining autochthonous identity in the face of pressures from the "center," whether Rio or foreign culture, and the mythopoeic drive to "explain" immediate reality and experience. Thus the stories may be seen as local-color burlesques of the pretensions of sophisticated or polite society or, on a deeper level, as the accounts of the need of marginal individuals (in this case allegedly provincial hicks) to explain things as they see them. The results in either reading are stories in which a putatively naïve narrator provides a mordantly hilarious version of dominant motifs in Brazilian culture, such as masculine sexuality, soccer, religion, individualistic bravado and the like.

> *David William Foster, in a review of "Livro de histórias," in* World Literature Today, *Vol. 56, No. 2, Spring, 1982, p. 316.*

Robert DiAntonio

The traditional nature of the mythmaking process has always been comprised of a confluence of sociological, artistic, and philosophical elements. In *Sergeant Getúlio* (1971) João Ubaldo Ribeiro, like his primitive counterpart, utilizes epic formulae and mythological correspondences to posit his chthonian vision of the modern world. Although the contemporary Brazilian novel is as variegated in substance and narrative technique as that of any national literature, there exist intriguing thematic parallels throughout many works of that country's most respected writers. The grotesque motif born of the tension of innocent victims confronting torture is so pandemic that it is now recognizable as a full-fledged archetype. Often history relies on the novelist to aid in documenting in palpable and human terms the political failings of an era. George A. Panichas has stated [in the introduction to *The Politics of Twentieth-Century Novelists*]: "To a large degree history, not literary aesthetic, dictates sensibility and belief in twentieth-century literature." Ribeiro's novel masterfully fuses very real sociopolitical concerns, the aesthetic experience, and his role as modern-day mythmaker. It is truly a protean masterpiece; an elegantly wrought study that is, on balance, one of the most distinguished pieces of modern Brazilian fiction. Peter S. Prescott [see excerpt above] calls the work a "splendid novel," and writer-critic Erico Veríssimo observes: "It is something unique. It derives nothing from any other book." The supreme compliment comes from the internationally acclaimed novelist Jorge Amado: "Among the works of fiction published in Brazil in the last decade, few have been as important as João Ubaldo Ribeiro's *Sergeant Getúlio* . . . "

The present analysis focuses upon *Sergeant Getúlio* from the primary perspective of its inherent artistic integrity, its accommodation of mythic topoi, and the cogency of its vision of one man's journey to redemption.

Charles I. Glicksburg, in analyzing the zoological metaphor in modern literature, observes [in his *The Self in Modern Literature*] that this metaphorical metamorphosis " . . . drives home the absurdity of investing human life with a divine purpose or any purpose at all; it reinforces the suspicion that the emergence of consciousness is in the service of instinct, an emanation of the blind energy of Nature." There exists no character in contemporary fiction who has so incarnated this "blind energy of Nature" than has Ribeiro's Sergeant Getúlio. No other work of modern fiction so strongly concentrates on analyzing this "consciousness in the service of instinct." This work stands in marked contrast to the narrative innovations and authorial playfulness that form such an integral part of the contemporary Brazilian novel. Ribeiro's style and focus could well be termed neo-Dostoevskian. His novel's central conciousness is a modern-day underground man, an exmilitia sergeant working for a local political boss. Ribeiro's narrator, Getúlio, in the fashion of Dostoevsky's unnamed civil servant in *Notes from Underground,* tenders his jaundiced views on life from manhood to hair cream to sex and torture, all within the context of an extended monologue, a protracted soliloquy that acquires mythic and anthropomorphic dimensions. Jon S. Vincent's reading of *Grande Sertão Veredas* illustrates the interplay between the "autobiographical account . . . of the narrator" and the nonregistered speech of "the interlocutor." An analogous narrative structure exists in *Sergeant Getúlio* with Amaro, his driver, being his silent sounding board.

The epic dimensions of this book can be derived from the Odysseyan journey that Getúlio embarks upon, becoming a symbolic Grail Quest. There are present many prefigurations of traditional epic formulae: the journey itself, the hyperbolic nature of Getúlio's feats of violence, the larger-than-life aspect of the hero's being, the threshold crossing, the legendary quality of his reputation, his trials against overwhelming odds, and the continual use of his name as an incantation. "My name is a verse: Getúlio Santos Bezerra. . . . " "I am the Bogey Dragon. Eater of hearts." " 'Your name is a verse,' Luzinete said, 'and you are never going to die'."

The work's many mythic and epic correspondences strongly suggest that the novel is archetypically rich, transcending a purely sociological reading. Ribeiro has created a unique epic hero who is not the embodiment of a nation's hopes and ideals but who is a hellish emanation of will, the violent will of the *sertão,* the backlands. As such, the novel's vision can be considered sociomythic, perhaps reacting to a political reality that needed to be addressed in aesthetic terms.

The plot line, in its simplicity, is expressed immediately by the author: "In this story Sergeant Getúlio takes a prisoner from Paulo Afonso to Barra dos Coqueiros." Then the flat value judgment is added: "It is a tale of virtue." Getúlio is hired to bring back a political enemy of one of the local politicians. He captures the man, and they cross Sergipe province in an old bullet-ridden Hudson, driven by Amaro. Throughout the journey Getúlio freely offers his inverted sense of morality and his puerile views of politics and life. "A profession is a profession. I don't like doctors. I never shot a doctor. Or did I? I can't remember. . . . Gravedigging, what a miserable profession. All men from Paraíba are gravediggers. Paraíba is Brazil." "I went over to help hold the girl, so that he could hit her once or twice. She deserved it. A woman who has seen a man in such a state is a whore. Or will be. Punishment does good."

In broad terms, then, *Sergeant Getúlio* can be seen as an allegory of confrontation between civilization and the last stages of Brazilian barbarism. This work, however, is more a multilayered confrontation that, on the first level of meaning, dramatizes the tension between victim and oppressor. This novel's victim is the true innocent. The prisoner is totally dehumanized by Getúlio. He is debased verbally, physically, and mentally. Getúlio fixates upon this sacrificial lamb and projects all his hatred upon this "creature," this "pox." He pulls out his teeth, ties him to trees, and berates him constantly. "The creature was gagged behind us groaning because of the pain on his gums, since the pliers were not the kind specifically for pulling out teeth and they were rusty and slippery, so that the extraction was delayed and the gums almost came off with the teeth. . . . " "Help me tie this thing to a tree. We're not going to untie him for his needs." The victim is dragged across the *sertão* like a package to be delivered. Only the village priest has any compassion for the man. He is, however, impotent to stop the Sergeant's cruelty or his mission; he can only alleviate the prisoner's suffering momentarily by placing a compress dipped in holy water on his bloody mouth.

> **"Ribeiro has created a unique epic hero who is not the embodiment of a nations hopes and ideals but who is a hellish emanation of will, the violent will of the *sertão*, the backlands."**

Symbolically, the victim is the true innocent at the mercy of a ruthless political system that is as unfathomable as it is unjust. From this perspective, the prisoner's life can be viewed in Kafkaesque terms as an absurd nightmare. The prisoner is the quintessential Job figure with punishment after punishment heaped upon him by an irrational captor. " 'Do you happen to know a fancy word for pulling out teeth? Would you be so kind as to open your little daisy of a mouth quick? Dammit, damn you!' Then I turned my weapon around, pounded twice on the creature's lips and pulled out four teeth with the pliers, and stopped." As Getúlio, Amaro, and the prisoner continue on their journey, government soldiers, led by a young lieutenant, come to cancel the mission. Getúlio is bound by his personal code of honor to deliver the "pox." It seems it is now politically expedient even for Getúlio's boss to rescind his vendetta. This Getúlio refuses to do:

> Besides, the chief told me to go look for this creature and I went, I caught him, brought him along, broke him and I am going to take him, even if the chief can no longer support me I will have taken the man and delivered him. It is necessary to deliver the animal. I deliver him and I say: Mission accomplished. . . . I will take this trash with me no matter what, I will get there and deliver him. Even if I burst. I want to see who is man enough in Aracaju to tell me I can't do it, because I am Getúlio Santos Bezerra and my equal has not yet been born.

His sense of mission cannot be influenced, and it is against these government soldiers that Getúlio's most violent act is committed. In a mythological accommodation of Perseus' beheading of Medusa, Getúlio coldly cuts off the lieutenant's head:

> It's impossible to cut off a frog's head without cutting the whole rest of the body for lack of a neck, but as for the lieutenant, as soon as I had finished the beheading I was able to tie his head to the end of a piece of rope and swirl it around my own head . . . saying, "Look at his head, look at his head, whoever persists will end up like this too," and then I jerked the rope and threw the head in the middle of the force. . . .

This act of inhumanity and defiance was triggered by an insult to Getúlio's manhood. " 'Maybe,' the lieutenant said. 'But when you are in the company of a sergeant who is a cuckold and a deserter with a queer for a driver, I cannot very well believe that.' " Throughout the extended monologue the reader perceives that part of the reason for Getúlio's anger emanates from his having been betrayed by his wife. "The pain of being a cuckold, a deep pain in the chest, something draining your strength from inside. I don't even know how to say it. A woman is not like a man." He tells of past tendernesses but quickly implies that he killed his wife and his unborn child for a supposed act of infidelity. "But I said nothing and when I plunged the iron, I closed my eyes. She made no sound. She fell there, with her hands on her belly."

Much of *Sergeant Getúlio*'s tone is somber and humorless; the horror of disquisitions on methods of murder and torture seems endless, evoking a strong feeling of reader disgust. Getúlio's being is permeated with *Schadenfreude*. This perverse delight is Getúlio's overriding passion. In his choice of a woman he selects his mirror image, Luzi-

nete, a larger-than-life reflection of himself. "She is one devil of a big woman, two armlengths of a woman from top to bottom, seventy-five kilos of genuine woman well measured. . . . " She equals his thirst for brutality and impels him to complete his mission. "Luzinete said, 'And why don't you finish all those accursed people once and for all and go on with your mission?' " She is as accepting of violence as a natural state as he is. Her death and that of Amaro leave Getúlio truly alone.

Ribeiro's tale is marked as well with strong psychological concerns. The work is framed only by Getúlio's perceptions of reality, and, as such, these perceptions are at times lyrically poignant and, at others, mask the rambling convictions of a madman. Getúlio is now obsessed with completing his mission. Although his tales of violence may be compelling, the effect of his extended monologue is that Getúlio is a true grotesque of nature, a bestial aberration:

> Over twenty people to my credit, imagine, it's like women, impossible to remember them all. The first one is the most difficult, but after that you learn not to look at the face so as not to bungle the job. When you're too close it's no good. They grab at you, they pull your jacket down.

Symbolically, he has now turned on the same political system that had so frequently used him in the past.

One of the keys to an understanding of this "tale of virtue" is that the reader is able to see through the constant and twisted philosophizing, perceiving a being, like Dostoevsky's unnamed narrator, whose imagination impels him to exaggerate the slightest insult or feeling of inferiority. Unlike his Russian counterpart, Getúlio, however, never considers the consequences of his actions. He is as impulsive as his parallel consciousness is inert. Both men are totally out of step and at variance with the tenor and tenets of their times.

The antiintellectualism of Getúlio is largely attributable to envy and incomprehension. He is amazed that his companion Amaro is able to remember the words to popular songs and prayers. He loathes the prisoner because he has had a high school education. Getúlio dwells upon that fact throughout the novel:

> You went to high school, you went to high school! a high school never made a man out of a bum, and don't answer because it's better for you, I'll stick your head in a straw bag and leave the rest to the wild dogs. . . .

It is an antirationalism born of a being unable to fathom the people and place around him:

> I want to take a very long look at Aracaju, nursing my anger and thinking about life and wondering what so many people are doing there, piled up on those big streets. When I speak nobody there understands, when someone speaks there I don't understand.

Getúlio is only at home on the *sertão*, for he senses his own limitations. "I memorize very little, being a man of little learning, but if I had more learning I would memorize more verses, because I enjoy them and everybody enjoys them." Of Amaro's death he observes: "If it weren't for his being a man, I would miss him." His animal nature, however, is continually underscored as he remarks of a simple checker game: "I will never figure that out. I have no patience to keep studying these pieces on this board, it heats up one's head, it has no purpose."

A comparison of the thematic stance underlying the motif of the "stone wall" in *Notes from Underground* may help to clarify the scope and significance of Ribeiro's vision. Dostoevsky's narrator remarks: "Of course, I won't be able to breach this wall with my head if I'm not strong enough. But I don't have to accept a stone wall just because it's there and I don't have the strength to breach it." Dostoevsky's underground man, in considering all the consequences of his actions, is rendered immobile and withdraws into a solipsistic realm of his own spiteful consciousness. Getúlio, on the other hand, the man of direct action, proceeds into the waiting militia. His sense of self is engendered by his life as a sergeant and the fear that that position instills in others. "The worst thing is to be nobody. . . ." This pride leads him to seek his own immortality in the completion of his near-impossible mission. Thus, he knowingly advances directly toward certain death.

In the novel's concluding chapter Ribeiro's narrative tone becomes lyrical and mythic as Getúlio's epic journey is nearing an end. The hero is being made ready for his apotheosis. Witness the psychic transformation of Getúlio's being: "I think, well then, that man you sent out is no longer that man. I used to be him, now I am I." In completing this mission Getúlio has been transformed from a man at odds with his own world to one whose sense of will and purpose is carried beyond life itself. The mythic qualities of the last chapter are formidable. "I used to be him and now I am I. I will say this with my eyes on his eyes and will leave you there tied and toothless, and with my ash face and with my woman in the moon. . . ." In this anthropomorphic transfiguration, Getúlio becomes one with the earth of the *sertão:*

> This I have, this whole land I have, because I was given birth by the land through a hole in the ground and I came out in the middle of hot smoke and she will bear others like me, because this land is the greatest breeder in the whole world.
>
> And I being I, being I, when I was a boy I ate clay and entered the ground eating clay, shitting clay and eating again. . . .
>
> My ash face, my hair of earth, my leather boot, my iron gun, huh creature? aren't we all the same? not much so now because I am I, Getúlio Santos Bezerra and my name is a verse which is always going to be versed and if there is a moon out it glows and if the sun is out it burns the face. . . .

Within this cosmic at-one-ment with the life force of nature Ribeiro disorders prosaic reality as he metamorphosizes Getúlio into a primitive emanation of pure will that endures in the dry lands of the Northeast. "I live everywhere. I live walking. Ay, aaaaaaaaay, aay, aay, ay, ay, aaaaaaaaay, aaaay, ay, a clay bull, ay a clay bull. . . ."

Getúlio's being remains only as a resonant image of a totally new mythic configuration. "I am now covered with clay like this and I eat of the clay as though it were food, because of the brown taste." The violent will of this hellish creature is now transfigured into the clay of the backlands. He is the eternal clay bull.

The novel ends with a montage of verbal exclamations, words run together, but Getúlio's will persists, as do his final thoughts. "claybull claya-ay a-ay a-ay ayapan nierfull of clay and life I am I and will and who was ay mywiltedo rangetree ay hey I will and carry out and do and." Considered within this mythic perspective, Getúlio's dream of populating these dry lands of Sergipe with an army of violent sons serves as a prophetic warning. "I would give them real male names and after that we would take these lands around here and we would organize some troops with more men and we would be masters of the world here. . . ." Narratively, his dream becomes a Brazilian tall tale of vengeance. This theme of one man's anger—"I get angry inside, it seems I have a need to be angry"—is subjoined to the motif of the innate anger and violence of an animistic *sertão.* An apocalyptic warning is tendered on the final words of Chapter Six. "You see the kind of son I have? Invincible." It is at this juncture of the novel that Ribeiro masterfully commingles the art of the modern-day mythmaker with, in Jorge Amado's words, "a persistent concern with exposing both individual and social problems."

João Ubaldo Ribeiro's modern hero Getúlio has broken through the barriers of his own deformed soul to find redemption in death. Freed from its purely Christian connotation, the archetype of redemptive suffering [presented in *The Novelist and the Passion Story* by F. W. Dillistone] is applicable to Getúlio's death in the service of his successfully completed mission. He is transfigured and redeemed through his willingness to accept death " . . . in the process of a transcendent value, a worthy end. . . ." Only by means of this willed death can he be reborn within the soil of backlands, rejuvenating it with his force and vitality. He is finally able to state: "I can cry now, because I feel like crying. . . ." Getúlio's spiritual commingling with the clay of the Brazilian *sertão* perpetuates his will, a forceful will that is needed for future political and social change. He affirms: "I am alive in Hell. . . ." He is now eternal, forming a coalescence with all that is bestial and chthonic. Like Jerome S. Bruner's observation in "Myth and Identity," Ribeiro, through the conscious use of mythological correspondences, "externalize[s] the daemon where it can be enmeshed in the texture of aesthetic experience. . . ." As Amado concludes: "Among the mass of books published in Brazil in the last ten years, ***Sergeant Getúlio*** stands out as one of the few works contributing to the development of a literary art that is genuinely Brazilian. Out of one man's epic quest for redemption, Ribeiro has fashioned one of the most complex and compelling Brazilian novels of the present age. (pp. 449-57)

> *Robert DiAntonio, "Chthonian Visions and Mythic Redemption in João Ubaldo Ribeiro's 'Sergeant Getulio'," in* Modern Fiction Studies, *Vol. 32, No. 3, Autumn, 1986, pp. 449-58.*

Thomas Christensen

João Ubaldo Ribeiro's monumental saga, *An Invincible Memory,* chronicles the history (or legend) and soul (or souls) of Brazil—from its settlement in the 17th Century, through its independence from Portugal and the founding of the republic in the 19th Century and on into the present. It is many stories in one, one story of many—for as a blind 19th-Century storyteller argues to his outlaw audience in a clandestine outback settlement, "no story has an end."

Ribeiro's story does have an ending, if not an end, and one or two beginnings. But what it most clearly possesses is a heart and a center: the tragic love between General Patricio Macario and the revolutionary teacher, bandit and beauty Maria da Fe. Their lives span the years of the Brazilian empire, when a line of the Portuguese royal family declared Brazil an independent state, and of the republic that succeeded it.

The legacy of Brazil's colonial heritage was a society sharply divided by race and class, between a small group of land-owners and a large pool of slave labor and disenfranchised freedmen. Slavery was not abolished in Brazil until near the end of the century; and the context for, and in large part the subject of, Ribeiro's sweeping story is the struggle for freedom—a struggle that, the novel suggests, continues today.

Ribeiro views the conflict in sharp contrasts of black and white, good and evil. His heroic lovers reflect the best qualities of the Brazilian people from both classes of society. Patricio Macario, youngest son of one of the leading land-owning families of Northern Brazil, is strong, proud and manly, but his features manifest a black strain in the family lineage. This appalls his father—who has had papers forged to document a longed-for aristocratic British ancestry, and who refuses to acknowledge his mulatto mother—and he banishes Patricio to the army.

The mother of Patricio's lover, Maria da Fe, was a slave on the estate owned by Patricio's father. Maria's father was a colonial baron who brutally raped her mother. Later on, when Maria and her mother are attacked by a group of white men and her mother is killed defending herself, Maria becomes a guerrilla fighter. Patricio's unit is sent to capture her, but the woman general outmaneuvers them. Patricio is captured. The two become lovers, but it is an impossible love, because Maria is committed to the cause of freedom. Patricio retreats to a life of solitude and dies on his 100th birthday in 1939; Maria gradually fades into the immortality of folk legend.

Patricio is considered white, though his features are black; Maria is black, but her father was the colonial baron. Ribeiro's message is clear: The Brazilian people are one, and the divisions that split them are sham.

But Ribeiro's tale is more complicated than that. His saga of perpetual recurrences is fueled by a notion of reincarnation in which the same souls journey to and from their celestial "Souls' Perch" to repeatedly inhabit the bodies of the living.

Maria is inhabited by the soul of the first Brazilian outlaw,

Caboco Capiroba, an Indian with a fondness for the flesh of Dutchmen, whom he captured and raised as cattle. To further complicate matters, Maria is Capiroba's natural descendent, his great-great-great-great-great granddaughter, and Patricio is inhabited by the soul of Capiroba's favorite daughter, Vu. Patterns such as these, echoing through the centuries and casting their spiraling recurrences on Brazilian history, are revealed through voodoo rituals.

Patricio and Maria's story, though central to Ribeiro's novel, is only one among many, for Ribeiro is skillful at constructing stories and conveying character. *An Invincible Memory* will be compared to the complex novels of Gabriel García Márquez, Isabel Allende, Mario Vargas Llosa and other Latin American writers. But despite such flourishes as his "Soul's Perch" conceit, Ribeiro is a more traditional novelist, rooted in the conventions of realism.

Ribeiro's best quality is a genius for satirical characterization that recalls the 19th-Century novels of Balzac and Dickens, or even earlier works by Smollett and Fielding. Dickensian caricature is Ribeiro's basic unit of construction, and, like Dickens, he excels at villains and eccentrics. (Ribeiro has translated his own novel, and to judge from his unfaltering command of English, he must be familiar with English literary tradition.)

While worthies such as Patricio and Maria tend somewhat to clichè, most characters, even minor ones, are individualized, sharply drawn and memorable.

There is the colonial baron Perilo Ambrosio, whom we meet lost in a reverie of hams and sweetmeats, suddenly skewering his sister's hand with a greasy spit when she reaches for a morsel he particularly covets; the raffish Black Leleu, Maria's protector, is "all natty and dapper, with widebrimmed slouch hat, stylish paltot, more than spruce pantaloons, plastron-type necktie, ruffled handkerchief, shirt of fine linen, undertrousers of the best calico, pair of shiny bluchers hanging from his fingers, knee-high socks with floss-silk garter thrown over his shoulders—and the worst intentions!"; and the cigar-smoking, rum-drinking witch Rufina—so fat she has to pass through doors sideways—who introduces Patricio to voodoo.

It is in evoking such characters that Ribeiro is most compelling. His social argumentation, which recalls John Dos Passos as well as Amado, is meant to be stirring, and indeed, one's blood often boils at the outrages he details. But it is Ribeiro's novelistic talent, rather than his call to social action, that makes *An Invincible Memory* a remarkable literary achievement.

> *Thomas Christensen, "Brazilian Saga," in* Chicago Tribune, *April 9, 1989, p. 6.*

Mary Morris

João Ubaldo Ribeiro's novel *An Invincible Memory* is about the forging of the Brazilian national identity—the incongruous merging of the various elements of its indigenous, Dutch, Portuguese colonialist and African slave populations into one unified spirit that calls itself Brazilian. As such, the novel attempts to trace the history of

Brazil from the arrival of the early Dutch settlers in the 17th century (with some fairly hilarious Rabelaisian passages regarding their cannibalism) to the country's recent struggles with right-wing dictatorship and state-sponsored terrorism. It is an often miserable history, as Brazil endeavors to become itself during its colonial periods, its fight for independence in 1822, the freeing of its slaves and its critical war with Paraguay, which began in 1864. In this panoramic, epic sweep, *An Invincible Memory*—fluently translated from the Portuguese by the author himself—tries to give its readers not merely a story, but the history of a people.

The second novel of a former journalist and teacher, the book is written in a nonlinear, episodic style. Mr. Ubaldo Ribeiro plays a kind of historic hopscotch; there is a general forward movement that ultimately carries us toward present-day reality. (For example, consecutive episodes are dated June 10, 1821; June 9, 1827; Feb. 26, 1809; June 11, 1827.) The complex plot is generational and virtually universal in its scope, with characters who represent the members of the Brazilian class system, such as the patron-colonial ruler, the slave, the mulatto. Its patchwork skips from date to date, character to character. If this sounds confusing, it is, unless one is well versed in Brazilian history. (Given the complex format and cast of characters, a simple genealogical or chronological chart would certainly have helped the North American reader, as it does in such works as, say, the Louise and Aylmer Maude translation of *War and Peace* or the Gregory Rabassa translation of Gabriel García Márquez's *One Hundred Years of Solitude*.)

The novel's many subplots spin off like the spokes of a wheel. To take one example, a baron of the empire lives in the coastal town of Bahia, where he is in charge of the fishing industry. He has tremendous wealth, many slaves and so forth. The way he became a baron and a hero in the battle for independence is an important element of the book. He secretly killed one of his slaves, smeared himself with the slave's blood and declared himself to have been wounded in combat. Another slave happened to witness this killing, and the baron ordered his tongue cut out at the root so that he could never reveal what he saw.

The baron prospers and grows powerful, and one day he rapes a young slave who is actually an African princess named Vevé. He believes the slave girl has been killed or sent away after the rape, but she remains and delivers his child nine months later, a beautiful, green-eyed girl who will become known as Maria da Fé. Concurrent with the birth of this child, some of the baron's slaves begin a revolutionary faction called the Brotherhood of the Flour House. After Maria, as a young girl, witnesses the brutal murder of her mother (who was trying to protect her daughter from rape by eight white men), she joins the brotherhood and becomes a major revolutionary force herself.

What João Ubaldo Ribeiro handles very well, and in a moving fashion, is the episodes about slavery and its remarkable cruelty. The severing of the slave's tongue, the rape of Vevé, the terrible life that the slaves lived—all are effectively rendered in this novel. The book persuasively

portrays a country in collision, deeply troubled by its class struggles. The mulatto Amleto, for example, passes for white and denies his own mother (who is black) and will not even permit her to attend the baptism of her grandchild, even though she offers to pose as a house servant.

While the novel does have these poignant moments, their impact doesn't carry through the whole. In part, the structure—its splices in time, its mosaic of small incidents and subplots—never lets the reader sink very deeply into any one story. But the real problem is the characters themselves. Rather than being fleshed-out, organic outgrowths of the story, they are stereotypes, inventions in the service of an idea: the horrid baron, the rebelling slaves, the conflicted mulatto, the monsignor who makes endless speeches espousing the church's viewpoint, never really come to life on the page.

For instance, when Patrício Macário—a rather mediocre military man whose destiny it is to fall permanently and impossibly in love with the great revolutionary Maria da Fé—finds himself face to face with the son he never knew existed, the offspring of his star-crossed love, he says, "What do you do, my son?" And the son responds: "I'm a revolution maker, my father. Ever since my mother's time, even before that, we've been looking for a conscience of what we are. And before that we didn't even know we were looking for something, we just rebelled. But as time passed we accumulated wisdom through practice and thought, and today we know we are searching for this conscience and are finding this conscience."

While admirable for its ambitious scope and its vision of history, the microcosmic world of the novel topples under the weight of its heavy language and stereotypical characters. There is no Buendía family, as there is in *One Hundred Years of Solitude,* whose quirks and foibles carry us along. No Alba, as in Isabel Allende's *House of the Spirits,* who narrates her story in such a way that our hearts break in the final pages. Instead, we have a novel of ideas told by a student of history rather than a story told by a real storyteller.

Mary Morris, "E Pluribus Brazil," in The New York Times Book Review, *April 16, 1989, p. 18.*

Nicci Gerrard

An Invincible Memory is a triumph of Joao Ubaldo Ribeiro's magnificently baroque prose over his vast subject and incomprehensible plot. A saga of two families, one aristocratic and the other enslaved, it covers four hundred years of Brazilian history, from the arrival of the Portuguese in Brazil to present day. As if this were not testing enough, Ribeiro scorns chronology and leaps backwards and forwards in time (now 1647, now 1827, now myth) and to and fro in geography.

His huge cast of characters looms momentarily out of the teeming confusion before again being swallowed up. And yet whenever the path seems to have dwindled away entirely, Ribeiro reaches out from the marshy riches of history and mythology with a phrase or anecdote and rescues our interest. *An Invincible Memory* hurls itself in all directions. Carnival meets war and cannibalism crosses with tenderness; savage details pin fictional chaos into place; jokes have the habit of turning into mirthless harangues. It is by turns a messy epic and an epic mess.

Nicci Gerrard, in a review of "An Invincible Memory," in The Observer, *November 5, 1989, p. 54.*

Irwin Stern

Praised by Jorge Amado, João Ubaldo Ribeiro, the author of *O sorriso do lagarto* (The Lizard's Smile), has earned a reputation both in Brazil and abroad owing primarily to two earlier novels: *Sargento Getúlio (Sergeant Getulio)* deals with violent banditry in the backlands of his native state of Bahia; *Viva o povo brasileiro* is a panoramic historical novel about Brazilian life and the ongoing quest for definition of a national identity.

O sorriso do lagarto dwells on very recent Brazilian life. Specifically, the author analyzes the alienation and foibles of upper-class Bahians who live on an (allegorical?) off-shore island and are emotionally, intellectually, and geographically (but happily) isolated from the Brazilian reality. Ana Clara and her husband Angelo Marcos are on bad terms. She is a stereotypical empty-headed socialite who begins each sentence with "I," and he is a bisexual, macho philanderer and corrupt politician. Ana Clara continues in the marriage for a traditional reason: financial security. To shake off this yoke, she embarks on a pseudocareer as a popular novelist and gossip/advice columnist (read only by herself, her husband, and a friend) under the nom de plume of Suzana Fleischman. Ana Clara subsequently falls in love with a local biologist turned fisherman, João Pedroso, who, by accident, discovers a bizarre secret project in genetic manipulation taking place in Bahia. Pedroso is secretly murdered by the offended husband, and Ana Clara, feeling abandoned by Pedroso, goes mad and believes that she is indeed Suzana Fleischman.

Into his formula novel the author superficially introduces many themes of contemporary Brazilian life: endemic corruption; the upper class's alienation with anything Brazilian and adoration of everything foreign; the ecological and atmospheric problems of a nation in development. The plot develops on many potboiler levels: a mystery story, a murder novel, a soft-porn tale, a science (-fiction) novel. Of tangential note in the plot are the role of the religious cults in Bahia, although not specifically the Afro-Brazilian *candomblé* or *macumba,* and the repeated racist and regionalist offenses uttered by the characters. Most of these characters are shallow stereotypes; only João Pedroso offers some depth of personality. Stylistically, he has a tendency to repeat his material word for word. Some of the dialogues in the novel are boring and long. Ribeiro's continued linguistic innovation, his comic moments, and references to local traditions (e.g., the title comes from an obscure tale about what may happen when you see a smiling lizard) and color are, however, entertaining.

O sorriso do lagarto is a satiric view of some aspects of Brazilian society in the final years of the 1980s. It takes to task many Brazilian personality quirks and long-standing national dilemmas. I get the impression that Ribeiro has been watching too many soap operas, both Brazilian and of the "Dallas" variety, or perhaps he hopes that the novel's possible success will result in one. Though not a serious work, it does satisfy its own objectives and indeed may find a place among a similar ilk of best sellers.

Irwin Stern, in a review of "O sorriso do lagarto," in World Literature Today, *Vol. 64, No. 2, Spring, 1990, p. 286.*

Luiz Fernando Valente

Originally published in Brazil in 1984 and recently translated into English by the author, *An Invincible Memory,* João Ubaldo Ribeiro's fourth novel, consists of a series of subplots centering on dozens of characters from different social classes whose personal and family histories intersect in often unexpected ways. Rather than telling a linear story, Ribeiro chooses to carry the reader back and forth between such locations as Bahia, Rio de Janeiro, Lisbon, and Paraguay over a time span of more than three centuries, providing only small amounts of information at a time and leaving a lot of gaps in the narrative to be filled later.

In the process of creating this vast panorama and telling this most entertaining story, Ribeiro comments on various aspects of Brazilian life. His main targets are the pretentious upper classes, whose members he satirizes for their tendency to ape European tastes and fashions, for the questionable origin of their wealth, for their haughty contempt of the lower classes, and for their obsession with concealing any tinge of black blood in the family line, a particularly difficult task in a society where miscegenation is a daily fact of life. The oppressed lower classes fare much better, for, as the original Portuguese title of the novel ("God Save the Brazilian People") suggests, Ribeiro regards them as the strongest and most authentic element in Brazilian society. Not surprisingly, the only truly heroic character, Maria da Fé, is a mulatto woman, born of her slave mother's rape by the insufferable Baron of Pirapuama. Da Fé, who combines traits of Joan of Arc with those of Bahia's own heroine Maria Quitéria, acts in defense of the dispossessed and epitomizes the Brazilian people's legendary capacity to endure.

An Invincible Memory appeared in Brazil in the last few months of the ten-year transition from military to civilian rule that was completed on 15 March 1985. With the elimination of censorship and the gradual return to normal political life, this period was marked by an open discussion of the national past and a renewed interest in the origins of the national character. It was also a time of optimism and confidence in the future of Brazil, a feeling which has been eroded by the deteriorating economic situation of the last three years. Ribeiro's novel is a typical representative of the atmosphere of that period, for it contests the official version of Brazil constructed by the military regime's propaganda and attempts to write an antihistory that questions and demystifies all the treasured national myths, including that of Brazil as a multiracial society free from prejudice, and that of Brazilians' inherently nonviolent nature. However, the work is also a proud affirmation of the Brazilian nationality. This aspect is best represented by a memorable passage of truly epic inspiration, in which the *orishahs,* the gods of the Afro-Brazilian religion of *candomblé,* intercede on behalf of Brazil during her bloody war against Paraguay.

The few flaws in the translation, such as an occasional instance of awkward syntax or stilted diction, should be attributed to the fact that English is not Ribeiro's native language. They are hardly noticeable once one becomes engrossed in the reading of his excellent novel. ***An Invincible Memory*** is a monumental achievement by one of the best contemporary writers from Brazil, a welcome and overdue addition to the growing list of first-rate Brazilian fiction available in English translation. (pp. 288-89)

> *Luiz Fernando Valente, in a review of "An Invincible Memory," in* World Literature Today, *Vol. 64, No. 2, Spring, 1990, pp. 288-89.*

Oliver Sacks

1933-

(Full name Oliver Wolf Sacks) English neurologist, non-fiction writer, and essayist.

A neurologist who has been praised for his compassionate and personal approach to both the physiological and psychological effects of illness, Sacks is a proponent of the rehumanization of medicine. He advocates a holistic approach predicated on the belief that health is a consequence of the complex interrelationship between mind, body, and lifestyle. Recognizing that individuals respond in dramatically different ways to disease, Sacks asserts that patients must be permitted to take an active role in determining an appropriate cure for their specific illness. Frequently lauded for presenting case histories that are both accessible and interesting to nonspecialists, Sacks dismisses much current medical literature as "unfruitful, unreadable, inhuman, and unreal." He is perhaps best known for his nonfiction book *Awakenings,* adapted into an award-winning film in 1990, which traces the effects of an experimental drug on patients stricken with "sleeping sickness." In *Awakenings,* as in all of his works, Sacks provides objective scientific data without disregarding the needs of individual patients. Sacks explained: "The patient's essential being is very relevant in the higher reaches of neurology, and in psychology; for here the patient's personhood is essentially involved, and the study of disease and identity cannot be disjoined."

The son of two physicians, Sacks was born in London, England. He attended Oxford University, where he received both his undergraduate and medical degrees. He decided to emigrate to the United States in 1960 after visiting California. While attending the University of California from 1962 to 1965, Sacks, an avid motorcyclist, provided medical services to a local chapter of the Hell's Angels. In 1965 Sacks became a researcher after winning a fellowship from the Albert Einstein College of Medicine in the Bronx, New York. His responsibilities included such meticulous work as extracting myelin from earthworms. However, after losing a vial of the substance, breaking numerous slides, and dropping hamburger in a centrifuge, Sacks was dismissed. Dr. Robert T. Terry, his supervisor at the time, later stated: "He was an absolute disaster. While we all liked Oliver and respected his intelligence, it was apparent that his future was not in laboratory work." Sacks openly admitted his numerous errors: "They said, 'Get out. You'll do less harm with people.'"

In 1966 Sacks became a staff neurologist at Beth Abraham Hospital for Incurables in the Bronx. There he discovered a group of patients suffering from a range of debilitating symptoms, the worst of which was a coma-like "sleep." These patients, Sacks later discovered, were survivors of the 1916-27 *encephalitis lethargica*—or "sleeping sickness"—epidemic that had afflicted nearly five million people. Before Sacks's treatment, about half of the patients

were functional; the others, he wrote, were "as insubstantial as ghosts, and as passive as zombies." The book *Awakenings* is an account of Sacks's attempts to help these people. Recognizing the similarities between the symptoms exhibited by his patients and those afflicted with Parkinson's disease, Sacks decided to administer L-DOPA, a drug proven effective in treating Parkinsonism. L-DOPA initially produced dramatic results; patients who had been "asleep" for more than forty years suddenly awakened. However, aggression and difficulty in adapting to a changed world proved too disorienting for many in the group. Some died; others reverted back to their trance-like states. Of the twenty patients Sacks chronicled in *Awakenings,* many showed moderate long-term improvement but only three were able to adapt to the drug and live relatively normal lives. In addition to its straightforward narrative and striking clinical observations, *Awakenings* is also considered an honest and moving portrayal of the devastating effects of illness on the everyday lives of individuals.

In *A Leg to Stand On,* Sacks explores illness entirely from a patient's viewpoint, tracing his recovery from a serious leg injury sustained while mountaineering in Norway. After ignoring a sign that read "BEWARE OF BULL,"

Sacks fell off a cliff while fleeing from the animal. Although surgery repaired severely torn tendons and ligaments, his leg remained immobile. Disturbed by his slow recovery, the sensation that the leg was no longer his own, and his surgeon's dismissive manner, Sacks was prompted to write an account both psychologically introspective and openly critical of the depersonalization of the medical establishment. Sacks further examines illness from the patient's perspective in his next volume, *The Man Who Mistook His Wife for a Hat and Other Clinical Tales,* a collection of case histories about various perception, memory, and language defects. One of Sacks's essays concerns a forty-nine-year-old man who suffered from Korsakov's syndrome, a disorder in which long-term memory remains intact while short-term memory is virtually nonexistent. This patient, believing he was still a teenager, had no memory of events after 1945. While Sacks demonstrates the variety of abnormal conditions that can arise from brain damage, he also explains ways in which people learn to survive and find meaning and fulfillment in their lives despite their disabilities. Highly praised for both its emotional and philosophical insights, *The Man Who Mistook His Wife for a Hat* further illustrates Sacks's belief that medicine must not ignore humanistic elements. Michiko Kakutani explained: "Blessed with deep reserves of compassion and a metaphysical turn of mind, Dr. Sacks writes of these patients not as scientific curiosities but as individuals, whose dilemmas—moral and spiritual, as well as psychological—are made as completely real as those of characters in a novel."

After gaining widespread acclaim for *The Man Who Mistook His Wife for a Hat,* Sacks published a revised and enlarged edition of his first work, *Migraine: Evolution of a Common Disorder.* Although the book was not widely reviewed when first published in 1970, the second edition, titled *Migraine: Understanding a Common Disorder,* was praised for its holistic approach to an ancient affliction often misunderstood by both doctors and patients. Recognizing that the symptoms of migraine headaches often vary with each episode, Sacks focused not on the cures but on explanations of the psychological sources of migraines. In his next work, *Seeing Voices: A Journey into the World of the Deaf,* Sacks departs from his focus on neurological and physical disorders to investigate the nature of language and communication. *Seeing Voices* comprises three essays: a history of deafness, an examination of sign language, and an account of the 1988 student revolt at the predominantly deaf Gallaudet University in Washington, D.C., at which the students, angered by the appointment of a non-deaf president, staged a sit-in until their demands for a new president were met. Sacks asserts in this work that because the syntactic structures of sign language differ from those of oral communication, the ways in which the deaf perceive the world also differ. While Sacks is not deaf and wrote *Seeing Voices* as an "outsider," he nonetheless offers intriguing insights into the complexities of various language systems and recognizes the deaf as a unique and vigorous community.

In 1991, Sacks and more than a thousand other staff members at the Bronx Psychiatric Center lost their jobs due to state budget cuts. He has continued his clinical studies at Beth Abraham Hospital and is a volunteer professor at the Albert Einstein College of Medicine. Sacks states that he loves the clinical life because it calls "equally to the scientific and the emotional," and his work reflects his emphasis on the variability of human perception and the importance of adaptation when confronting illness. Contrary to physicians who believe their primary responsibility is to focus on the physiology of disease, Sacks asserts that doctors must be empathetic and sincere in their interactions with patients: "What must finally be given is understanding—and courage: an attitude that is life-affirming in the face of disease."

(See also *Contemporary Authors,* Vols. 53-56, rev. ed. and *Contemporary Authors New Revision Series,* Vol. 28.)

PRINCIPAL WORKS

NONFICTION

Migraine: Evolution of a Common Disorder   1970
   [revised and enlarged edition published as *Migraine: Understanding a Common Disorder*], 1985
Awakenings   1973
A Leg to Stand On   1984
The Man Who Mistook His Wife for a Hat and Other Clinical Tales   1985
Seeing Voices: A Journey into the World of the Deaf   1989

Richard Gregory

Experiences so strange that they are difficult to conceive are not limited to travels up the Amazon or to the Moon, but can occur within the confines of the human head, wherever that head happens to be—even in people kept, unable to move for decades, in hospitals for the hopelessly incurable. At first thought, a ward of elderly people stricken by Parkinson's disease, so crippled that they are incapable of more than waggling a finger and occasionally blinking their eyes, is a scene of such Hammer Horror that we may reject the situation, and be thankful that they are shut away from our concern. What would happen if such people could be suddenly awakened—to move, to express their feelings, to speak their thoughts? Would they be articulate adventurers emerging from a long life of dreams? Would we find raging conflicts in them—or, perhaps, such peace that they had nothing to report from all those years?

The patients described in [*Awakenings*] are a group of survivors from a world-wide epidemic (fortunately of rare occurrence) which started in 1916 and by 1927 had had nearly five million victims. A third of these died, in the deep coma of sleeping-sickness, *encephalitis lethargica;* some are still alive, more or less impaired, perhaps some hundreds remaining in deep sleep. What Dr Sacks did was truly dramatic. He tried, with the drug L-DOPA, to wake people who had been asleep for thirty or forty years—and he succeeded. He is a neurologist, working at a hospital for incurables near New York. He was the first to try L-DOPA on patients who had been in torpor for long periods. He emphasises—and I would like to repeat this here—that the dangers of the drug, for it has its dangers, by no means apply to normal cases of Parkinsonism.

Parkinsonism was described in James Parkinson's celebrated and beautifully written *Essay on the Shaking Palsy* in 1817. There is far more to Parkinsonism than uncontrollable tremor, clumsiness and sudden inability to move. There may be episodes of hurrying, as though pushed along by inner forces, sometimes affecting speech and thought. There may be the converse: living in slow motion. One of the most characteristic, and apparently most frightening, symptoms is sudden stopping-in-the-tracks—being on the instant transformed to a statue, perhaps animated by a tap on the shoulder, a word, or some movement in the field of view. There are patients who cannot walk except upstairs ('If only the world were all stairs,' one of Sacks's patients said) and others who can dance, keeping time to music, yet cannot initiate their own steps for walking.

Upon the drug L-DOPA taking effect, the awakening was typically sudden. Within minutes, to the astonishment of the nursing staff, after more than thirty years of total torpor the patient would wave his arms, get up and walk, talk volubly—and as though he were still in the Thirties. This long sleep and sudden awakening to a new strange world are so myth-laden, so evocative of our childhood fear of the dark, and of sleeping perhaps never to awake, that these experiences, though so alien, have an immediate power to grip the imagination. It is hardly an exaggeration to say that through this book we live with the dead, brought back from the past. We immediately share their astonishment (far deeper than the shock to the nurses) at hearing themselves talk, and being able to affect the people and the things around them. They sense a rush of energy, after their long lethargy, which may carry them into mania and uncontrollable violent movements—into a rushing flood of speech, sometimes with the same words repeated over and over again. How much are their uncontrollable movements—saluting, pill-rolling, handflapping, each highly individual—a pulling of the strings of the puppet physiology of motor control? How far are they frantic attempts to reestablish lost internal connections? Or are these gestures ineffective attempts to communicate by waving at the world? Sometimes these strange tics have a ferocious intensity. They may throw the sufferer out of his chair; in some cases they may 'dance' around his body, almost as though induced by unseen moving flames. It is hardly surprising that such symptoms used to be regarded as the manifestations of devils, as dire punishment for sin. The triumph of the discovery of viruses is surely not only the devising of countermeasures, but, more profoundly, the development of the recognition that it has freed us from the metaphysics of guilt.

Have these people benefited from the 'miracle drug' L-DOPA? Unfortunately, the awakening is maintained only by keeping them balanced on a tightrope between their former torpor and the bizarre manifestations of overstimulation of brain cells which probably succumb irremediably to the drug. (This kind of Parkinsonism seems spe-cially sensitive to L-DOPA, so that its effect may be more damaging than in the more usual cases, for which—as is well-known—it is often maintained over many years with great success.) Curiously, it is sometimes the most deeply impaired patients who have the most sudden awakening, in Dr Sacks's experience, and who may make the most extensive initial recovery. How far this is maintained he believes to be more than a matter of chemistry: it is a question of how far they come to develop their own controls and strategies to deal with the structure of their illness. Dr Sacks has interesting things to say about the 'side-effects' of illness and of drugs. His reaction to such progressive illnesses as Parkinsonism is not that of Canute, commanding the tide to halt, but is a matter of learning to swim with it. Although the effects of L-DOPA are at first so dramatic, and so hopeful, these people nearly always succumb to a rising sea of neurological complications. They have a growing sense of things going wrong, then they become engulfed in their sea of troubles—but generally with a greater awareness and ability to live in peace in their submerged world.

What are the implications of our strange human ability to remain dormant for half a century, and emerge for a time reborn, with memories, abilities and personality virtually intact? There is much here to stimulate and to puzzle psychologists. Most suggestive, perhaps, is the similarity of the symptoms to those found in people suffering stress. These patients are extremely sensitive to stressful situations: they are thrown off the tightrope they have to walk by what to most of us would be welcome stimuli to thought or action.

Dr Sacks regards the experience of his patients as philosophically interesting, but, somewhat curiously, he has less to say on this in the book than in his earlier article in the *Listener* of 26 October 1972. It is now generally agreed to be a mystical and untenable view that—as Aldous Huxley argues in *The Doors of Perception*—drugs reveal truth. Huxley's view was that the brain is a kind of filter between us and reality, hiding rather than creating truth: so drug-induced damage was thought by him to reveal hidden truths as the brain's efficiency was reduced. But if we regard the brain as creating truth (perhaps much as facts and generalisations are established in science) by storing and relating the sensory data of experience, then drugs should be expected to produce error. The symptoms of brain disease may be highly revealing for our understanding of people, and of how the brain functions: but are the reports of Dr Sacks's patients epistemologically helpful? His position on this is not entirely clear, though he does make some evocative suggestions.

The book is an extraordinary compound of clinical observation and, one feels, deep understanding of the plight of these people. The technical jargon of neurology is used: but Dr Sacks has embellished it with a rich prose that only occasionally goes into the purple. One senses in the author a passion to communicate his discoveries with all the power of his intellect, knowledge and deep compassion—so that we may 'awake'. (pp. 869-70)

Richard Gregory, "Raised from the Dead," in

The Listener, *Vol. 89, No. 2309, June 28, 1973, pp. 869-70.*

Anthony Storr

When brains are damaged or disordered, personality may seem to disappear. In cases of schizophrenia, psychiatrists are familiar with the fact that someone who has been totally withdrawn and perhaps mute for years may, under stress of physical illness, recover his "normal" personality, and speak and behave as he did before mental illness overtook them. In *Awakenings,* Oliver Sacks, an English neurologist working in New York, describes a similar resurgence of lost or buried personality in cases of post-encephalitic patients treated with a new drug, L-DOPA. The virus which, from 1916 to 1927, caused *encephalitis lethargica* killed about a third of those who contracted the infection. Of those who survived, many who were children became destructively delinquent. The adults affected showed a bewildering variety of neurological disabilities, of which one of the commonest was "Parkinsonism", a disorder characterised by tremor, rigidity of muscles, and difficulty in initiating voluntary movement. Many patients were more or less stuporose, paying little attention to their environment, and quite unable to engage in normal activities. However, the variability of their symptoms suggested that whatever part of the brain had been attacked by the virus was damaged rather than totally destroyed. In the 1960s, it was discovered that the part of the brain most damaged by *encephalitis lethargica* used a special chemical transmitter called dopamine. Moreover, it was also discerned that post-encephalitic patients were particularly short of this chemical substance. L-DOPA, a precursor of dopamine, was first given to these sufferers in 1967.

The results were startling. Patients who for forty years had hardly uttered a word began to speak almost normally. Others who had not been able to walk began to do so. In almost every case, an "awakening" occurred in which the patient's previous personality reappeared and began to manifest itself. Tragically, these returns to life have been but transient phenomena. It appears that the damaged brain cells were stimulated by L-DOPA, but in most cases could not sustain the activity which the drug potentiated. No patient entirely "recovered"; and many slipped back into immobility, silence, and despair.

It is clear that L-DOPA re-established channels of communication between one part of the brain and another which the virus had all but destroyed. Sacks, one of those rare neurologists who also has had experience of psychoanalysis, gives moving descriptions of his patients, and alleges that, even when a person is grossly disabled on account of brain damage, he still retains his characteristic personal style and dignity. If we begin to think of personality in neurological terms, it is clear that the particular individual neural network which constitutes its anatomical substratum must be formed very early in life, as indeed psychoanalysis would lead us to suppose. It seems probable that further research upon the chemical basis of memory, and a greater understanding of how particular lines of communication within the brain are facilitated by use

and habit, will bring neurological and psychological descriptions of personality closer together. (p. 90)

Anthony Storr, "A Linking of Disciplines: Prospects in Neuro-Psychiatry," in Encounter, *Vol. XLI, No. 5, November, 1973, pp. 85-92.*

The Times Literary Supplement

In April 1916, Constantin von Economo reported a series of patients with an influenza-like disease which he had investigated thoroughly and for which he proposed the name *encephalitis lethargica*. Von Economo's work was confirmed and extended. It soon became apparent that the disease at first occurred sporadically, though there had been previous outbreaks, that it was characterized by quite severe symptoms and lasted for many months or even years. The most conspicuous features of the chronic form of the syndrome were tremor, rigidity, immobile face and loss of associated movements.

The resemblance of this condition to Paralysis Agitans, a disease which had been described by James Parkinson, was striking. So close a likeness could be confidently attributed to a similarity in its pathological basis; this was found in the "substantia nigra" of the brain. Degeneration of the cell system which manufactures the neurotransmitter "dopamine" led to intensive study of dopamine metabolism and its therapeutic possibilities. It was found that this substance dopamine was much decreased in the "striate body" of patients with Paralysis Agitans. It seemed logical to correct this decrease by introducing dopamine into the brain. But dopamine does not cross the blood-brain barrier. Its immediate precursor, levodopa, is not open to this objection. When large doses were administered to people with the Parkinson Syndrome and the subject became the point of departure for a wide range of clinical and laboratory studies, the therapeutic effect was striking enough for it to be called a miracle drug.

[In his book *Awakenings*] Oliver Sacks stands a little aside from such enthusiasm: "It is curious to hear sober physicians, and others, in the twentieth century, speaking of miracles and describing a drug in millenial terms." In a familiar trope he affirms that we all have an intuitive feeling that once we had something infinitely precious which we lost: "One day, perhaps, we will suddenly find it. And this will be the miracle, the millennium."

Dr Sacks is a neurologist in charge of patients with the post-encephalitic syndrome, who have been brought together at a hospital in a New York suburb. He compares it with its counterpart, the Highlands Hospital in London. They were both opened after the First World War and house patients with very severe post-encephalitic conditions, but the regime and spirit of the two hospitals are vastly different. At one there is strict administration, rigidly committed to efficiency and rules; familiarity with the patients is strongly discouraged. At the other it is the reverse; and patients tend to be mercurial, sprightly, impetuous and hyper-active—with vivid and ardent emotional reactions.

Dr Sacks has selected twenty patients for detailed description; he reports their tribulations with compassion and understanding, and with much grace of style. His indictment of the language of conventional scientific publications is wholehearted. They are "the ugliest exemplars of assembly-line medicine". Instead of perpetrating such drab, soulless productions, Dr Sacks dramatically conveys his sense of vast forces all round one: post-encephalitic disease lending to "the dark heart of being".

The picture he draws is no slap-dash performance but a well-conceived tour de force.

> *"The Tribulations of Lethargy," in* The Times Literary Supplement, *No. 3745, December 14, 1973, p. 1535.*

A. Alvarez

For just over a decade, from 1916-27, a new sickness spread from Europe to the rest of the world. It showed itself in innumerable ways before it was finally diagnosed as *encephalitis lethargica.* The more common name was "sleeping sickness," and it ravaged the lives of nearly five million people. A third of them died, some recovered completely, but the largest number fell into a kind of living death, as unmoving, unspeaking and apparently insentient as zombies. They were, in fact, aware of what went on around them and inside them, since their "higher faculties" were spared, but they remained profoundly indifferent and unrousable, silent witnesses to their own suffering.

In 1927 the sleeping sickness disappeared as mysteriously as it had come, leaving the survivors stranded like empty hulks in hospitals for the chronically ill. Others, who had seemed to have recovered, relapsed without warning years later, as if they had unexpectedly stumbled into some black hole in their being. Nearly all of them exhibited in one form or another the tremors, tics, vacant starings and frozen postures of Parkinson's disease. All seemed lost beyond hope of recovery. "Most of the survivors," says Dr. Oliver Sacks [in *Awakenings*], "went down and down, through circle after circle of deepening illness, hopelessness and unimaginable solitude"—unimaginable because, at the center of their black and speechless world, they continued to think and feel in the silence.

Fifty years later a so-called "miracle drug" was developed, laevo-dihydroxyphenylalanine or L-DOPA, under the influence of which patients who had slept away half a century, as impassive as rocks, were suddenly awakened into urgent life. For a period they spoke and moved fluently, and were passionately aware of the world around them, as though trying to make up by their intensity of response for all the years of life their sickness had swindled them out of. Dr. Sacks says of one of them:

> I thought of prisoners released from jail; I thought of children released from school; I thought of spring-awakenings after winter-sleeps; I thought of the Sleeping Beauty; and I also thought, with some foreboding, of catatonics, suddenly frenzied.

Alas, in this case and in nearly every other, Dr. Sacks's sense of foreboding was justified. In a tragically brief time,

most of the patients to whom he administered L-DOPA developed frantic, uncontrollable physical and mental compulsions, as though the drug which had released them from their physical prisons had also released psychic energies they couldn't cope with, and the force of life now erupting through them was beyond their depleted capabilities. When the drug was finally withdrawn for their safety's sake, they relapsed again into Parkinsonism even more acute than they had suffered before.

[The bulk of *Awakenings*] is made up of 20 case-histories selected from the 200 patients whom he treated with the drug. What is extraordinary about *Awakenings* is not the short-lived "miracles" induced by L-DOPA but the subtlety and penetration with which he describes the inner world of his patients and ponders upon their predicament and its relation to the whole question of illness. In simplest terms, he writes exceptionally good prose:

> Some of the "things" which gripped her under the influence of L-DOPA—in particular, her gnawing and biting compulsions . . . and certain obsessive ideas and images—could not be dismissed by her as "purely physical" or completely "alien" to her "real self," but, on the contrary, were felt to be in some sense *releases* or *exposures* or *disclosures* or *"confessions"* of very deep and ancient parts of herself, monstrous creatures from her unconscious and from unimaginable physiological depths below the unconscious, pre-historic and perhaps prehuman landscapes whose features were at once utterly strange to her, yet mysteriously familiar, in the manner of certain dreams. And she could not look upon these suddenly exposed parts of herself with detachment; they called to her with Siren voices, they enticed her, they thrilled her, they terrified her, they filled her with feelings of guilt and punishment, they possessed her with the consuming, ravishing power of nightmare.

The excellence of the prose matters, I think, for a number of reasons: it makes a technical book on a mercifully rare disease compulsively readable; more important, it brings the individual cases vividly alive to the lay reader, making him understand something of the enormity of their suffering; most important of all, it shows that they must have been even more alive and urgent for the author, since it is impossible to write so sharply about anything one has not understood intensely from the inside.

In a way, the doctor's style is part of his purpose. He believes that most current medical literature is "unfruitful, unreadable, inhuman and unreal" because the abstract, polysyllabic jargon it deploys reflects a correspondingly inert, mechanical way of thinking which considers only the symptoms of illness and the ways they can be eradicated, ignoring altogether the person who is ill and the manner in which his illness is an essential part or expression of his nature. "Diseases," he says, "have a character of their own, but they also partake of our character." To demonstrate this he leans less on medical authorities than on the methods of the existential psychoanalyst Ludwig Binswanger, and he quotes freely from Donne, Leibnitz and Sir Thomas Browne, Eliot, Joyce and Lawrence to show that "what we need so much—and not only in medicine—is an anatomy of wretchedness, an epistemology of disease." He is against the idea of a miracle drug which will restore us dramatically to some lost Eden of health for the same reason that he is against other miracles: because sickness, like all forms of evil, is not something special and alien, no science fiction invader from outer space; it is simply an essential part of human nature.

> **"What is extraordinary about *Awakenings* is not the short-lived 'miracles' induced by L-DOPA but the subtlety and penetration with which [Sacks] describes the inner world of his patients and ponders upon their predicament and its relation to the whole question of illness."**

Given his existential and psychoanalytic bias, it is a pity he touches only briefly on an important aspect of the disease he otherwise describes with such profound sympathy: institutionalization. He remarks that life became harder for his post-encephalitic patients when their once easygoing hospital was reorganized into an authoritative, rigid "total" institution. Yet he spends not much more than a footnote discussing how much a "coercive" institution encourages and sustains a coercive sickness like Parkinsonism, despite the fact that much of his evidence points that way.

One patient, for example, exhibited no symptoms at all whenever she spent a day out on the town with her sister who once remarked to the doctor, "She goes mad in your madhouse because she is shut off from life." Similarly, one of Dr. Sacks's most spectacular successes, one of the few who got well and stayed well, was a cobbler who, when L-DOPA finally unshackled him from his terrible immobility, was able to take up his old craft again in hospital. It is as though life in what another patient called the "human zoo" of the hospital were so deprived of purpose and dignity that there was no place for all the newly recovered vigor the drug released; more appropriate, perhaps, certainly safer, to remain immured in the prison of chronic sickness.

If I am disappointed that Dr. Sacks refrains from following up this point, it is only because his brilliant and humane book seems otherwise to raise all the essential questions, even the least expected. More important, it raises them in an alert, dissatisfied, questing way which seems to imply that, as in life, the questions matter intensely while the answers themselves are always as provisional and untrustworthy as miracle drugs.

> *A. Alvarez, "Miracle and Madness," in* Book World—The Washington Post, *July 7, 1974, p. 2.*

Galen Strawson

A Leg to Stand On is a most interesting book. But it is also a most unfortunate book, and an unworthy sequel to *Awakenings,* Oliver Sacks's remarkable account of the treatment of the victims of sleeping sickness (*encephalitis lethargica*) with a drug called L-DOPA. Professor Sacks is certainly not unaware of the fact that the emotions recorded in *A Leg to Stand On* are in certain respects ludicrous and disproportionate. He speaks of his "ego-charged frenzies", and there are important trace elements of irony in his self-portrayal. But these are quite insufficient to counter the general and debilitating flood of verbal and emotional extravagance.

Introducing the book as a "neurological novel . . . but one which is rooted in personal experience and neurological fact", Professor Sacks thereby specifies the other main thing that is wrong with it: it lays claim both to the special impact of factual truth and to the special licence of fiction. These two things work against each other, however. One's general disposition to treat the whole thing as true renders the element of fabulation extremely tiresome; while the fact that the story is fictionally boosted undermines one's confidence in its accuracy, and thereby seriously weakens its impact as a drama of real life. The fiction undercuts the claim to truth; the claim to truth causes one to lose patience with the fiction. This is not to say that truth and fiction can never be mixed, only that Sacks has not done it well. In the end one is not quite sure one can believe anything he says, either here or elsewhere—his highly polished case histories of strange neurological disorders bear all the same marks of dramatic enhancement.

A Leg to Stand On opens with Sacks bounding self-congratulatorily up a Norwegian mountain in a shifting mist. Rounding a boulder, he comes upon a massive, milk-white bull. It turns to look at him, and he takes this very badly:

> The huge white face seemed to swell and swell, and the great bulbous eyes became radiant with malignance. The face grew huger and huger all the time, until I thought it would blot out the Universe. The bull became hideous—hideous beyond belief, hideous in strength, malevolence and cunning. It seemed now to be stamped with the infernal in every feature. It became, first a monster, and now the Devil.

What follows? His fear, his flight, his fall; a severe injury to the left leg—"the entire quadriceps (muscle) ripped from the patella" or knee cap; a struggle down the mountain in a great flurry of allusion to God, Tolstoy, Ecclesiastes, Death, Kant, Goethe, Nietzsche, Pavlov, Harvey, Mozart, Leibniz, Joshua and Auden; rescue, hospitalization in London, surgery, convalescence, physiotherapy and final return to health.

Sacks's main subject, however, is the complete loss of all feeling and motor control in his leg for over two weeks after his operation. *"I knew not my leg. . . . It was absolutely not me. . . . I had lost my leg".* He experiences for himself something he has previously encountered only in books and in his patients—a sense of radical alienation and emotional dissociation from his own leg, a feeling that it is repellent in so far as it is still there, combined with a strong sense that it is not really there at all.

Intellectually he knows it is still there. Exteroceptive sense confirms its lumpish presence: he can see it and touch it. But interoceptive (or proprioceptive) sense draws a most alarming blank—no leg, no leg at all. He lacks any kinaesthetic awareness of the leg as something that moves and is movable at will: he is no longer in touch with it *via* that precise, fully automatic, internal "somatognostic" awareness which we ordinarily have of the position of our limbs, and which seems to be so intimately bound up with our entirely unreflective ability to move them at will that, very often, to lose the one is *eo ipso* to lose the other.

This awareness is something that we take so much for granted that we don't really notice it until we lose it. But when we lose it, even partially, we are utterly confounded. It appears from Sacks's experiences that one's sense of the reality of one's body is so deeply founded on one's internally mediated awareness of it that loss of this awareness overrides all the reassurances of sight, touch and intellect in the most remarkable and emotionally disturbing way. One of Sacks's patients apparently woke in the night to find what he took to be a severed human leg in his bed. A hospital prank in the poorest taste—he threw it out of the bed. And went with it, for it was in fact his own. . . .

Something of the same existentially unnerving sort happens to Sacks; "neuro-ontological extinction" of the leg, and a corresponding dent in the self. One of the most surprising things about Sacks's loss of control is that it is not caused by any injury to the brain—by some right hemisphere dysfunction, some damage to the somatosensory cortex—but by a peripheral injury. It is injury to the leg itself which causes it to be erased from the body-image in such a dramatic fashion.

As the nerves heal, Sacks's will re-extends itself into his leg. Slowly he learns to walk again, despite some startling hallucinations in which his leg, wildly telescoping and concertina-ing, is "now . . . a thousand feet long, now a matter of two millimetres . . . now . . . fat, now . . . thin . . . now . . . tilted this way, now . . . that". He rediscovers what A. R. Luria called the "kinetic melody" of his leg. Rapturously convalescent, he learns from other patients that symptoms like his own are not uncommon, but that hospital doctors, strong on physiology, anatomy and aetiology, short on sympathy, time and imagination, pay them little heed. . . .

The doctors—those unfeeling, banausic mechanicals—record an "Uneventful Recovery" for Sacks. "What damned utter nonsense!" says Sacks. And indeed he lives the whole episode with a gaudy intensity that borders continually on the hysterical, soaring and plummeting on the Brobdingnagian rollercoaster of his emotions. Part of this is unsurprising. Alone on a misty mountain, one is an easy prey for unreasonable fears. Hospitalized with an illness of uncertain outcome, one is naturally subject to violent fluctuations of mood. But Sacks outfluctuates us all, swooping from sudden terror to infinite relief, from total panic to uttermost peace—on every page there are rapidfire epiphanies, surprise, wonder, trembling, awe, horror,

bliss and joy. What manner of man is the Sacks of *A Leg to Stand On,* shuttling between infinities of this, that and the other? Is this really the real Sacks? The dominant impression is of a voracious sensuality, a Jurassic, only half-genial *Lebenslust,* a truly enormous Ego like an implacable milk-white bull. At other times *A Leg to Stand On* reads like the breathlessly inspirational enchiridion of a glory-be preacherman:

> The moral obscurity and darkness was lifted, as well as the physical darkness, the shadow. . . . Now the road lay open before me into the land of light and life. Now, unimpeded, I would run this good road, swifter and swifter, into a fulness and sweetness of life, such as I had forgotten, or never known. My spirits had been rising since that wonder-walk on Wednesday, and now, on Saturday, I was flying with joy—a joy which was to last, and deepen, for six weeks, which transformed and transfigured the world, and made of everything a new wonder and festivity.

Sacks has a great many interesting things to record. It is a pity that he has chosen to do it in this way. He is an inventive and subtle distinguisher, and in his sober moments he puts his powerful vocabulary and quickly associative intelligence to very good use. His range and interests invite a comparison with William James. But he suffers badly in the comparison. On page after page of Sacks's gushing, immoderate words, one looks in vain for some of the wit, decorum and brilliant lightness which James brought to his most routine writings—his 1887 paper on "Consciousness of Lost Limbs", for example.

Galen Strawson, "Riding the Rollercoaster," in The Times Literary Supplement, *No. 4238, June 22, 1984, p. 686.*

Michael Neve

Oliver Sacks is the Jules Verne of the neurological interface. Knowledgeable about science, he also wishes to summon a host of readers to a great adventure, a journey to the centre of the body and ways of knowing about bodies. As with Verne's skilful use of half-understood scientific symbols, the project that Sacks has come to make his own has brought into public view a gallery of exotic events and phenomena that, precisely in their strangeness, remain memorable to the untrained reader. People have slept, and have been awoken. Others have mistaken people for hats and failed to recognise their nearest and dearest. News has come, too, from inside, and not just outside, other people. People, people who have to be thought of as patients, have been pushed to the side of their own lives; they have lost parts of their body, and started to lose themselves. The neurological sciences, as written up by Sacks for a wide audience, have opened up the abyss: under the impact of certain physical injuries, individual men and women become gaps in their own nature.

From the appearance of *Awakenings,* in 1973, one aspect of the reception of Sacks's work has been striking, and it bears on the nature of *A Leg to Stand On,* which is a piece of autobiography. This is that Sacks's writings have particular attractions for literary society, and indeed for practitioners of literature. It is not just a matter of the exotic world itself, a world of lost creatures, or suddenly saved souls, that distinguishes the books and articles of Doctor Sacks. . . . Sacks's standing with literary people is not just due to the regard in which W. H. Auden is known to have held him. Like Verne before him, Oliver Sacks has produced a metaphorical vision, indeed, in some readings, a neurological version, of fiction. The interest of ***A Leg to Stand On*** is that it is a story about something which happened to Sacks himself, and about which he has now chosen to write. The aspiration to the condition of literature that his previous neurological case-studies sometimes showed signs of is now to be realised from his own experience. Bearing in mind all the ground rules that medicine will have given him—the commitment to careful, even mundane observation, the sceptical business of listening and feeling—Doctor Sacks is now to write about himself: and that, as everybody knows, is a damned hard business.

Before asking whether this conjunction of the medical and the literary has worked or not, whether we can actually *believe* the story, it is necessary to see how Oliver Sacks thinks of the history of neurology, of its happy and unhappy phases, and how he sees his own work fitting into it. To put it very crudely, he greatly admires the pioneering work of the 19th-century American physician S. Weir Mitchell, who witnessed considerable amounts of physical damage in the years of the American Civil War. What is attractive to Sacks about a man like Mitchell was his freedom from the straitjacket of scientific specialism, a freedom that allowed him to write medical short stories, on themes of amputation, say, or phantom limbs, in places like the *Atlantic Monthly*. Mitchell was a literary doctor, free to speculate, to imagine, before the age of scramble. In the 20th century, there are two crucial further developments: the work of Henry Head in the 1920s, in England, and then the great Russian advances of later decades, culminating in the work of R. A. and A. R. Luria in the 1950s. Sacks sees the work of Henry Head as having a classic style, detached, cool, interested in the science of function, but without being too concerned about the patient's experiences, or the totality of events that might have made up the whole story of a neurological event. Head would listen to his patients, but would not, so Sacks alleges, include the patient's story in his neurological model. The move toward a unified explanation, one that would seek to integrate a science of observing with a science of doing, was essentially a Soviet achievement, born out of the need to redeem victims of war injury. This initiative Sacks calls neuropsychology, stressing its commitment to 'performance', as laid out by the Lurias, Leontev, Bernstein and others.

Sacks is suggesting, then, that neurology itself has had its own gaps. In ways that historians of neurology might well find interesting but highly selective, he is proposing an absence, an existential space that ought to have been filled, but wasn't, and which has held the science back. The full involvement of patients themselves, in the practical task of recovering the self that has been damaged or lost, is the largest of these missing parts. To complete the progress that the Russians started, Sacks calls for 'a neurology of the self, of identity', a task of neurological completion

which he (unconvincingly) proposes was resolved in the history of philosophy when Kant dealt with Hume's philosophy of identity and restored 'the self' to an existence that was not fleeting or transitory.

These are large, even rabbinical claims and hopes. They are intensely human, since they seek for nothing less than the discovery of the lost person that is 'oneself', the damaged double removed by injury and then gone from sight and from touch. Almost any reader [of ***Awakenings***], as indeed any television viewer of Sacks's L-DOPA patients, will start out longing for this completion to work out. This is a matter of resurrection, not only of the individual medical case, but of neurology itself, since Sacks's own science, in his version, has been missing a limb, as I have been saying, has had a gap in its own nature. (p. 3)

What 'happened' to Oliver Sacks to make him become one of the patients at the neurological interface that he believes now exists? Basically, he behaved like a silly twit. He went on a holiday in Norway, in the peak of health, and went walking in the mountains. He was (like all prophets) alone, and had not bothered to tell anyone his whereabouts. He came to a field, which had a huge sign saying 'BEWARE OF THE BULL!' He ignored it, came face to face with a large white bull (which appears to have resembled the Devil), panicked and ran. In flight, he fell, twisted his left leg, and had considerable difficulty getting himself back down the mountain. Fortunately, a night in the open was avoided when two passing Norwegians picked him up.

The main part of Sacks's tale follows from this incident, an incident that, as it were, turns one into the Doctor's mother, making one want to give this burly man a hug and tell him not to go to Norway and have no one know where he is. This sense of protectiveness towards a man bent on resolving all the mysteries of human knowledge is reinforced when we learn that he has 'fifty books' in his rucksack and no change of clothes.

Dr Sacks becomes 'a patient': he is taken from Bergen to London, troubled by what damage has been done to his leg, and already starts to feel a certain hostility to unimaginative doctors. The journey to the centre of Oliver Sacks has begun, going from the Mountain, to the Hospital, to the Operation, to the Abyss: 'I phoned up my family and friends, to let them know what had happened, and was happening, and to say that if I should, by malchance, die on the table, I wished and willed them to make suitable extracts from my notebooks, and other unpublished writings, and publish these as they thought fit.'

The story of his 'becoming a patient' is partly the story of losing a sense that his left leg existed, but is partly also a story of being 'unmanned by medicine'. It would be wrong to make too much of the Freudian possibilities at this point, but Sacks's hostility to the male surgeon, 'a Mr Swan', and a conception of medicine (from the patient's viewpoint) as unfeeling and masculine, are noticeable. Once the operation was over, Sacks tried to use his leg muscles again—'to tense the quadriceps', to feel again that earlier power that took him to Norway, that took him to the bull. And it is gone. It's being gone also allows Sacks to reconnect himself to his internal account of the history of neurology, since he has become a sufferer from Babinski's and/or Pötzl's syndrome, with its painful (and comic) signs, where patients fail to recognise one side of their body, feel that parts of it belong to somebody else, or suggest that a nurse take away an arm that has become a nuisance.

Now at this point, in the maternal way that the distressing if overblown story makes one come to feel, the advice might be: 'Ollie, sit tight.' But this would be useless, since, Verne-like, the journey must get stranger. Limbo awaits, introduced by a suitable quotation from the Book of Job. There is no longer a way round the fact that if Sacks's account of himself has now degenerated, into, most noticeably, literary ostentation and generalised exaggeration, then this matters. By not adhering, with some care, to the delicacy of the necessary linguistic account, by insisting on the glamorous nightmare of his experience, at the expense of its odd mixture of strangeness and mundanity, Sacks is jeopardising the very connection between outer and inner, surgical and perceptual, neurological and metaphysical, upon which the claims for his 'existential neurology' must rest. And, at least for me, the middle parts of *A Leg to Stand On* are indeed thus jeopardised, by a painful combination of unbelievable anecdote, cultural name-dropping and simple craziness. It surely *must* be crazy for a distinguished doctor to ask us to believe the following prominently displayed quotation: ' "Every disease is a musical problem, every cure a musical solution." Novalis.'

The doubts about Sacks's sentences set in quite early on in his story, back at the fjord in Norway. At one point he writes: *'I could no longer hear myself'* (his emphasis). Now, in no doubt very ordinary, clumsily intuitive ways, I simply don't believe that that is possible, not even for Oliver Sacks. It is of course all too possible not to recognise sounds that seem to be to do with—even to be uttered by—oneself. And there must be a self that hears the silence, in silence. But, in ways that matter because these are issues that matter, Sacks is typically asking us to believe the mega-thing, the Absolute proposition, the complete disappearance.

The middle parts of the book, which might in a modest, Chekhovian manner have described distressing things (a foul migraine, with eerie results, a perfectly understandable despair) instead appear in an unbelievable 3D. He is sinking; he is in the abyss; and yet 'I kept reading *Dr Faustus* at this time, especially its passages on Hell—and Music.' (When?) It is all John of the Cross, Nietzsche, Eliot, John Donne, Leibniz, Kant and, of course, music. The determination to exaggerate leads to two dreadful things: the reader, irony of all ironies, starts to disbelieve the writer. And worse, the truthful tension that must hold, between the organic experience and the psychological experience, between the science and the subject, starts to fail, and a dreadful thought enters, as the second thing: that a man who is having a bad time, who one wants to get well, is making this stuff up. By the time we read another, later sentence, a strange sadness is creeping in. Sacks writes: 'Not the least part of the terror was that I experienced no terror.'

But his body comes to the rescue, quietly and without fuss. The leg comes back, and, secretly and delightfully, the memory of how to walk comes back as well: this marks a 'turning-point' similar to that of Zazetsky, in Luria's *The Man with a Shattered World*. Sacks remains upset that, as seen from outside, by the clinical gaze, his recovery has been deemed 'uneventful'. He himself feels reborn, back from the Abyss: but it is typical of the philosophical thinness of his account that he never discusses how the outsider's gaze is meant fully to comprehend the cinematic grandeur that he himself has experienced. No doubt doctors are guilty of a weary lack of interest in much of a patient's inner experience, and the use of 'uneventful' is a tired shorthand for that. Sacks makes one shift uneasily, by again going too far the other way, when, during convalescence, he decides that *all* the patients he is among (about whom he is strangely uninteresting) are 'much wiser than the doctors who treated them'.

The story effectively ends with an incident that is instructive in its simplicity. Oliver Sacks goes to see an orthopaedist in Harley Street after his convalescence in Kenwood, a 'Mr W. R.' (who might, one guesses, understand the mysteries of the organism). 'Mr W. R.' recommends that Sacks goes swimming but has mischievously (and yet carefully) arranged for the lifeguard at the pool to take Sacks's stick from him and push him into the water. This outrages Sacks, but completes his return to a full body-image, since he 'kept up a fast crawl for four Olympic lengths', and only stopped then, he says, because the lifeguard yelled 'Enough.'

The possibility that Oliver Sacks's 'existential neurology' is simply a way of talking about important things in unbelievable ways lingers in the mind. There must be many other experiences—strange and neurological, to be sure, but which can be shaped and understood in less grandiose ways, and which might put to use a different combination of Henry Head's classicism and the neuropsychology of the Lurias. By writing about himself as he does here, Sacks swamps the various dimensions—surgical, neurological, psychological—in his zeal for a unitary hypothesis. Such distinctions are important: otherwise he might, for example, end up mistaking his patients for himself, seeing himself as the historical apotheosis of all their experiences. When he himself 'becomes a patient', he is so determined to solve the riddle of neurological history that his story is less well observed, and less potent, than one might have hoped.

The vexed relationship between subject and object that existentialism concerns itself with remains distressingly unclarified after *A Leg to Stand On.* Florid, fictive, without sufficient respect for the worldliness of pain and illness— let alone the need to be careful about what you say—the book takes its place among the more harmless products of medical egomania. I am very glad that Oliver Sacks got better, and I also wish that his autobiographical tale did not seem so full of the loneliness that comes with intellectual messianism. (pp. 3-4)

Michael Neve, "It's Got Bells On," in London Review of Books, *Vol. 6, No. 11, June 21-July 4, 1984, pp. 3-4.*

Jerome Bruner

[Sacks's *A Leg to Stand On*] is about a horribly injured leg, his own, what he thought and learned while living through the terrors and raptures of recovering its function. But it is also a book about the philosophical dilemma of neurology, about the philosophy of mind, about what it might take to create a "neurology of the soul" while still hanging on to your scientific marbles.

The metaphor around which both Sacks's drama and his reflections revolve is the scotoma, and I had better say a word at once about these holes in experience, these pieces of self that evaporate, that escape the control of intention. For Sacks—for all that he concentrates on his disconnected leg—is writing about experience, self, intention, about their injury and restoration.

The visual scotoma—that is, a gap in the visual field—provides a good model of the metaphor. When a piece of occipital cortex is penetrated and/or invaded by a tumor or a toxic agent, there develops in a corresponding part of the visual field a "hole," a dead area. Often the patient does not know he has it, complaining instead of "dimness" on that side. It is easy to miss a scotoma, for central processes often complete seen figures parts of which fall in the dead area. Sometimes the part of the world that falls into this hole suffers "neglect" altogether and is ignored completely. Occasionally involvement of the tempero-parietal area of the cortex produces a very strange version of a visual scotoma. The patient reports nothing there and shows the usual hole: if you present an object or picture to the "hole" the patient reports seeing nothing. But now ask him to guess which of several things it might have been. Even if he swears he cannot see anything, he will almost invariably guess correctly. The phenomenon is called "blindsight" and it is now under intense study with the few unfortunate cases who exhibit it.

Current theories hold that this form of awareness, unadorned by consciousness, is mediated by the intact old part of the brain, the optic tectum, that in its evolutionary history aimed the frog's tongue at the natural fly and the trout's lunge at a rising nymph. It may, in fact, be the same mechanism that accounts for "subliminal" information that people seem to gain from a very rapidly presented display that they also claim not to be able to see. Scotomata "blind" us, but the better way of saying this is that they cause the world to disappear where they occur: they create an existential, ontological hole rather than a cookie-cutter hole. But that needs modifying too. For there are some lighter scotomata where, if "neglect" (that telltale word of neurologists) is overcome by "hyperattention," if we try *very* hard to see, then things come back into view and the hole is filled. Holes in the world, in short, pose very puzzling problems for the neurologist—and for the philosopher. After his injury, and after the surgery had rejoined the quadricep to the femoral nerve in his left leg, Oliver Sacks had a scotoma, a hole in the world for his leg. He could not feel it or move it. What he saw stretched out there below him was alien, "not-him," nonexistent.

The circumstances of the injury have the quality of a fable, worthy of the kind of analysis developed by the folklore specialist Vladimir Propp. Sacks tells it with consummate skill. A fortyish, robust, and reflective English neurologist on holiday sets off to walk the six-thousand-foot mountain that surmounts the Hardanger fiord. He departs in the misty dawn from the village in whose church he has heard the Mozart *Requiem* the night before, hoping to reach the top by noon and be back down the steep mountain path before night sets in. Halfway up he reaches a path to the gate of which there is tacked a sign in Norwegian, BEWARE THE BULL! "A bull? Up here?" On he trudges, blessing Nature for strong legs trained by years of pushing himself at sports. Higher now, he threads his way among the great boulders, and as he rounds one, he comes upon the seated bull. (pp. 39-40)

The Englishman panics, turns, and plunges headlong back down the treacherous and slippery path, unsure whether the thudding steps he hears are his own or those of the bull pounding after him. Then the slip, and he is at the bottom of a short, sharp cliff, his left leg twisted grotesquely beneath him, his knee in unimaginable pain. It flashes in his doctor-mind that somebody has been seriously injured, and in the next instant he realizes it is himself. The leg is dead, no tone, no motion. He pulls himself together and diagnoses: "Muscle paralyzed and atonic—probably nerve-injury. Unstable knee-joint—seems to dislocate backwards. Probably ripped out the cruciate ligaments." He is alone in a desolate, unpopulated part of the world, with a totally useless leg, near the top of a mountain at an altitude and latitude where the temperature drops well below freezing at night, even in August. And then begins the fight for life.

He carries a stout umbrella for a walking stick on all his rambles; it is there by his side. He rips his anorak into strips, splints the umbrella to his paralyzed and numb leg, and starts down the long mountain—backward, on all threes, gulping in pain, dragging himself through a glacier-cold swollen stream on whose stepping stones he had fearfully leapt on the way up, feeling his consciousness ebbing from cold and shock. Down, down, until at seven the sun disappears. "*I could no longer hear myself.* . . . This must be the beginning of the end."

Suddenly a shout: a man and a boy with rifles, a reindeer hunter and his son. He is saved, brought down the mountain, put in a local hospital, then flown to London and placed under the care of a noted orthopedic surgeon. Now the physical, spiritual, and philosophical ordeal begins.

The doctor has become a patient; he is operated upon by the brisk surgeon and is assured that the tendons have been reconnected to the quadriceps muscle, that all is well. But the leg is still paralyzed dead and lacking not only in the ordinary sensation but in the deep sense of "proprioception" that makes it possible to know that the leg is even there, let alone knowing where it is. No effort of will can reach it and nothing at all comes through by way of sensation. A scotoma where there was once a leg, an existential nothing.

For days on end he lies in his small room, taunted by nightmares of his lost capacities, failing persistently to reconnect his will to his leg in spite of the games-mistress urgings of his physiotherapist. No way to find the leg in the scotoma, no way of getting hold of it to move it—it is untethered, gone. He becomes convinced that there is *"not just a lesion in my muscle, but a lesion in me."* He recalls Wittgenstein's remark in his last book, *On Certainty,* to the effect that certainty is grounded in our certainty about our bodies, a certainty that comes from the capacity to *act.* He falls into a state of desolation. The brisk surgeon, grandly on rounds with his entourage of interns, inspects the casted leg and holds up his hand to interrupt patient Sacks as he recounts his troubles. "There's nothing the matter. . . . You're completely mistaken. There's nothing wrong with the leg." And so into limbo with the scotoma. Twelve empty days.

First came stabs of lightning pain, then one morning freshly awakened, there is a flash, an impulse to move the left leg, and with the impulse comes a spasm of movement, "half jerk, half act." Will had connected again with action, but it was not spontaneous action, rather like "convulsions of will." What was lacking was the music, the wholeness of an act. "Something spontaneous must happen—or nothing would happen at all." Cajoled, bullied by the therapists, he takes his first step, dares it, does it—and remembers how to walk. "All of a sudden, I remembered walking's natural, unconscious rhythm and melody; it came to me, suddenly, like remembering a once-familiar but long-forgotten tune . . . ," like Zazetsky in Luria's *The Man with a Shattered World* who makes the sudden discovery one day that writing is not, after all, those lines and letters but requires "giving yourself over" to its natural flow.

The long road to recovery follows, through convalescence, "not to be seen as a smooth slope, but as a series of radical steps, each . . . the quality of miracle." With his scotoma, his "frame of reference" had shrunk, the visual depth of things beyond his narrow range squashed flat somehow. *It* returns, and with each return an insane optimism about what is now possible, leading most often to damaging overexertions. In the process he slowly recovers from the role of the patient, dependent for when to rise and when to walk (as John Donne long ago put it) upon a doctor's word and will. For recovery also required a moral recovery from the "stationless status" of the helpless patient.

Throughout the book runs the theme of spontaneous "natural" action, of connecting self with natural act through intention. A consultant in Harley Street (seen because Sacks cannot get his uncast knee to act naturally in walking) asks him what sport he likes best. "Swimming." "Good," and he phones a swim bath, gets Sacks to go right over, where the tipped-off lifeguard laughingly pushes him into the pool with a "Race you!" Four laps of the Olympic pool; Sacks climbs out and walks naturally for the first time since the injury. He has found the music for his knee (as W. H. Auden tells him later, quoting Novalis: "Every disease is a musical problem, every cure a musical solution"). (pp. 40-1)

This is a moving, at times perhaps over-emotional book, its descriptions sometimes evoking the late Erving Goffman, sometimes even Conrad. It is a masterful instance of what Alexander Luria lovingly and longingly used to refer to as "romantic science." But for all that, it is also instruc-

tive to the philosopher coping with the ontology of intention, with those problems that Elizabeth Anscombe dealt with a quarter-century ago in her classic, *Intentions,* and that John Searle (among others) deals with today in the battle against an image of man on the model of the brainy automaton whose recursive loops enable "him" readily to reflect on his own action, indeed to reflect on his reflections, and to represent it all in memory store, but never to intend *in sensu strictu,* never to generate the form of spontaneity whose thwarting throws the machine into a stage of existential anguish. Sacks has written a book about a leg, his leg; but it is a story about the nature of selfhood—a narrative comparable to Conrad's *The Secret Sharer.* (p. 41)

> Jerome Bruner, "Hole in the World," in The New York Review of Books, *Vol. XXXI, No. 14, September 27, 1984, pp. 39-41.*

"There is only one cardinal rule: one must always listen to the patient."

—Sacks, 1984

Daniel X. Freedman

Some eight years ago, Oliver Sacks, a poetically gifted neurologist, climbed atop an isolated Norwegian mountain and, in sudden pell-mell flight from a rampant bull (a great white beast, no less), sustained a wrenching leg injury. He underwent successful surgical repair in his native London and—at the story's center—a profoundly perplexing postoperative course. In *A Leg to Stand On* he shares his reflections on the phases of peripheral nerve injury and recovery and on therapeutics.

In part, this short book is a sketchy prologue to a vision. The author wishfully foresees a warmly humane, existentially rooted medical science, a veritable "neurology of self." In its readable fact, it is an adventure in self-discovery, vividly detailed in brief, persuasively instructive accounts of illness and the fundamental rudiments of self. To other physicians, Dr. Sacks remarks that "being a patient forces one to think." But even the severest of afflictions is unlikely to evoke the kaleidoscopic range, depth and verve of reflection that Dr. Sacks conveys with deftly dramatic eloquence.

Cheerfully acknowledging his unordinary perspective, Dr. Sacks notes that his vacation rucksack contained few clothes but 50 books, and from this lively library of personal companions, he offers numerous apt snippets. His injury ripped the attachments of the tendons and macerated the muscle of the left thigh to the knee and leg. The attendant neuromuscular damage deprives him of the power to "call to myself," to command even the slightest motion. There was no knowledge even of passive movement or of the location of the useless leg—not the faintest feeling to confirm the very existence of what he could see but not believe. Touching it, he finds a doughy pulp and can no longer imagine or recall how to move it.

What neither feels, moves nor can even know that it does (or does not) is a lacuna in body image. He struggles to convey, beyond this conceptual defect, the gap in body ego—the sensing, acting and self-reflecting self. The sixth sense of proprioception (once called "muscle sense"), by which the body possesses itself and knows and ceaselessly confirms itself, is gone. The vital organic foundation of reality is removed. Astonished, Dr. Sacks finds not only a lesion of muscle but "a lesion in me," an uncanny and involuntary "experiment in identity" striking at the usually unstated origins of being.

Seeking validation of this internal amputation, Dr. Sacks is curtly dismissed by his surgeon as "unique," but in a convalescent home, and subsequently in his practice, he discovers otherwise. An amputee suffering from phantom limb (still feeling the pain, position, substance or movement of a leg that is gone) eagerly hears Dr. Sacks' description of his own "negative phantom"—a leg that, while present, could not be known. The patient inventively wonders if he could not have usefully borrowed the doctor's defect; perhaps a local anesthetic prior to amputation might have obviated the brain's blind persistence in supplying a leg that isn't "there."

And if these organically mediated distorted mirrors of self and reality were not enough, Dr. Sacks notes Anton's syndrome, by which, with a lesion in the right posterior brain, a perfectly healthy limb is discerned as "not me," with the patient blandly requesting that it be removed along with the breakfast tray. The perceptual oddities he suffers with migraines are also described. These may well have sensitized him for the "neuro-existential" explorations of his professional life.

Dr. Sacks carefully perceives the return of feeling and movement, at first in sudden, totally involuntary twitches which, nevertheless, generate a quasi-voluntary feeling as in the knee-jerk reflex. Later, the problem is how to get the now episodically movable but still unguidable leg to walk, to calculate and painfully implement the intricacies of freely flowing, confident motion. There are gropings, and then a sudden spontaneous gathering in which the disparate elements, the sensations of volition and the sense of estrangement, totally vanish—simply in effortless doing. The return of command, of uncalculated certainty, an "I," arrives in one swoop by unsummoned "grace" manifest in sheer action. Thus, he observes and celebrates the basis of motion, its musicality, the role of spontaneity and, in a few lines, even a theologically evocative view of grace.

Reflecting on the nature of convalescence, recovery and healing, he perceives they are not one act but many, not a process but made up of surprising and often unexpected events. But a healer is essential; an "intermediary" is necessary for a patient to ascend from one level of convalescence to the next. Without such a healer or enabler, the nervous system, he asserts, will neither mature nor heal. And what of healers? While Dr. Sacks is still suffering some limitation of knee motion, a truly knowledgeable surgeon who discovers his love of swimming literally tricks him, arranging for the reticent patient to be pushed into a pool, whereupon total movement returns. Action is the key to therapy. Dr. Sacks believes unexpectedness and spontaneity can somehow evoke natural action, an approach reminiscent of that of the Zen master. He also obviously knows the value of openness, of listening and connecting. With his friend W. H. Auden's help, he finds that music can "center" his patients. Thus, he summarizes his credo: the need to "center" the patient—to find and evoke "a living personal center, an 'I,' amid the debris of neurological devastation"—a credo applicable to the entirety of medical practice.

This search for how the living organism can gain organization and self-possession has been a far more central and elaborated topic in the literature of existential and psychoanalytic psychotherapy than in neurology, where, if practiced, it is rarely preached. Dr. Sacks, a professor of neurology at the Albert Einstein College of Medicine, has long focused on the rehabilitation of severely neurologically impaired patients, a topic more developed in Eastern Europe than in the West. Known mainly to readers of *The New York Review of Books* for his evocative biographies or "neurographies" of odd disorders, his 1973 book, *Awakenings,* illumines the inner world of long-immobilized, motorically frozen postencephalitic patients kindled into motion and emotion by L-DOPA.

Obviously, physicians might also gain from the awakening *A Leg to Stand On* attempts. But in his search for things as they are, unspoiled by concepts, Dr. Sacks also eschews the details of neural mechanism. In his frank disappointment with his scientific heroes for being unable to escape the cold confines of science even though they were warm men, he does not convince one that their science is thereby less valuable.

It is not surprising that when substance and appearance, reality and image, are so dramatically challenged by disease, fundamental philosophical questions of origins, certainty, epistemology, noumena and phenomena, ontology and intentionality come to mind. It has always been so for profound students of the behaving brain, who in touching the tissue are also touched by the wonder of its evolution but specifically probe to learn more about how we are organized to experience what we do. Dr. Sacks's rucksack does not contain much reference to those developments, or to several pioneering students of body image. But while this is not a fully presented picture of the field, one can still readily share his ringing hope that in therapeutics the violated self and the kind of anguish he experienced can become a full subject of understanding—"like grief."

So, in *A Leg to Stand On,* one finds fascinating subject matter and a man perhaps more interesting than his topics. During his period in limbo, Dr. Sacks was visited by his 82-year-old aunt who gave him Joseph Conrad's "The Rover," and remarked, "You're definitely a rover. You seem to have one strange adventure after another. I wonder if you will even find your destination." And so can the reader wonder. Yet, for his patients, one senses that the right destination of this healer—so open, so mindful and full of music and action—has been found. (pp. 11-12)

Daniel X. Freedman, "Where the Rest of Him Was," in The New York Times Book Review, *November 11, 1984, pp. 11-12.*

Israel Rosenfield

> An extraordinary sensation of cold and heat, of pains in several parts of the body; syncopes, and vaporous convulsions; catalepsy and tetanus; gas in the stomach and intestines . . . vomiting of black matter; a sudden and abundant flow of clear pale urine . . . palpitations of the heart; variations in the pulse; *periodic headaches;* vertigo and nervous spells . . . depression, despair . . . madness, nightmares or incubi.

Thus Robert Whytt, an 18th-century English physician, described migraine. Known since the dawn of recorded history, migraine is a complex disorder whose symptoms do not necessarily include what is generally considered its cardinal sign—headache. Oliver Sacks, the author of the classic study of the treatment of Parkinson's disease, *Awakenings,* and a memoir about the effects of serious illness, *A Leg to Stand On,* published *Migraine: The Evolution of a Common Disorder* in 1970. In [the] expanded, updated and resubtitled edition of the book, Dr. Sacks describes the various manifestations of migraine and their relationship to emotional and physical well-being.

Migraines, Dr. Sacks notes, typically begin with a period of emotional and physical excitement. Rage or euphoria may be accompanied by discomfort—tingling sensations in the hands or feet or disturbances of vision or hearing. These symptoms are transformed into a state of "engorgement," a bloated feeling associated with anxiety, restlessness and tension. A headache usually follows, though apathy, nausea, depression and weakness dominate during this phase. Then there is a rapid purging of the system (vomiting or sneezing) and emotional outbursts. Finally, the crisis ends; the individual becomes euphoric, alert and aroused.

Each stage of a migraine attack, from the initial excitement through the lassitude and depression to the subsequent revival and general alertness, may manifest itself in various ways; and the time span of the entire crisis varies greatly as well. The syndrome, Dr. Sacks writes, is a "paradoxical combination of inner violence, and outer detachment—analogous to the dreaming of paradoxical (rapid-eye-movement) sleep, or the concealed agitations and hallucinations of psychotic stupors."

Migraine attack is characterized by emotional and physical indecision, as the following case illustrates. "This 32-year-old man," Dr. Sacks writes,

> was an ambitious and creative mathematician whose life was geared to a weekly psychophysiological cycle. Toward the end of the working week, he would become fretful, irritable, and distractable, 'useless' at anything save the simplest routine tasks. He would have difficulty sleeping on Friday nights, and on Saturdays would be unbearable. On Sunday mornings he would awaken with a violent migraine.

There may be "odd, dancing, twitching" movements, tics or disturbances of speech. Visual, auditory and tactile information may be misrepresented or distorted. The nervous system cannot decide what information is important and what is not. Feelings of strangeness and absurdity are accompanied by a distorted sense of space and time.

Most striking are the visual hallucinations that may accompany some forms of migraine attacks—the migraine auras. Auras were recognized almost 2,000 years ago, when the term was used to describe the "cold vaporous" sensations that begin in the hands or feet and travel up to the head, warning of an imminent epileptic seizure. The Greeks believed that the nerves were hollow and that vapors (in Greek, *aura*) traveled through them. Since the 19th century the term has been used to describe similar symptoms that precede migraine attacks—disorders of vision and speech and intense emotional states. Long before it was understood that such disturbances were related to migraine, the nun Hildegard of Bingen (1098-1179) recorded a series of visions that, Dr. Sacks notes, were "indisputably migrainous": "I saw a great star most splendid and beautiful," she wrote in the manuscript codex *Scivias,* "and with it an exceeding multitude of falling stars which with the star followed southwards. . . . And suddenly they were all annihilated, being turned into black coals . . . and cast into the abyss so that I could see them no more."

The falling stars in Hildegard's vision are typical of the showers of lights that cross the visual field and burn out during some migraine auras. Hildegard invested her vision with mystical significance, providing, as Dr. Sacks writes, "a unique example of the manner in which a physiological event, banal, hateful, or meaningless to the vast majority of people, can become, in a privileged consciousness, the substrate of a supreme ecstatic inspiration."

What physiological and psychological purposes might be served by such disruptions of normal perceptual functioning?

Dr. Sacks views migraine as a disorder of arousal (the state of general alertness in response to environmental stimuli), and it is this insight that explains the psychophysiological purpose of migraine attacks. Animals respond to situations of threat or danger by fighting or fleeing or, equally dramatically, becoming passive and immobile. Typical of the last strategy is the opossum's playing dead. Humans too may freeze, faint or swoon in the midst of emotional and physical crises. Dr. Sacks quotes Darwin's description of this strate: "A strong tendency to yawn . . . death-like pallor . . . beads of sweat stand out on the skin. All the muscles of the body are relaxed." And migraine, Dr. Sacks argues, is part of the human repertory of passive reactions to danger. The complexity of human social activities often necessitates passivity—neuroses, psychosomatic reactions and the varieties of migraine—when the individual confronts essentially unsolvable problems.

In some, though not all, migraines, the crises may be chronic, and a whole complex of emotions may be compressed into a brief migrainous episode. The migraines may be more tolerable than the emotional problems they symbolize. For example, Dr. Sacks treated a 24-year-old man who suffered from migraines

> every Sunday afternoon. The use of ergot compounds effectively aborted these attacks, and after three months of therapeutic care, he suddenly ceased to experience even the premonitory migraine auras. Some weeks after this he returned to me angrily complaining that his long-defunct attacks of asthma had returned, and that they came, in particular, on Sunday afternoons. He regretted the change, finding his migraines preferable to, and altogether less frightening than, the asthmas.

The treatment of migraines associated with menstruation may also be undesirable, since tensions and anxieties may then be released in migraine attacks throughout the entire month rather than concentrated in a brief, particularly violent premenstrual attack. The periodic (monthly) attacks may bind into brief episodes emotional problems of such complexity that their resolution may be beyond therapy or even alteration of life style. The preferred treatment is none at all. At least some migraines may serve psychological purposes analogous to those served by dreams and neurotic symptoms.

Migraine, then, is an example of the nervous system's retreat in the face of the unresolvable. In a desperate effort to find a way out, it reorganizes its forces and tries to view the world in new ways. That all this usually fails is an indication of the limits of our mental and physical capacities. But there are economical ways of failing, and the nervous system appears to have found one in migraine attacks. The migraine sufferer comes out of his attack euphoric and with a new sense of being. After an attack, the mathematician mentioned earlier "would feel a profound refreshment, a tranquillity, and a surge of creative energy which would carry him to the middle of the following week."

When Dr. Sacks' book appeared 15 years ago, it was the first major study of the disorder since Edward Liveing's *On Megrim, Sick-Headache, and Some Allied Disorders: A Contribution to the Pathology of Nerve-Storms* in 1873. Written by one of the great clinical writers of the 20th century, the new edition of *Migraine* intended specifically for the general public, should be read as much for its brilliant insights into the nature of our mental functioning as for its discussion of migraine.

> *Israel Rosenfield, "Like Dreams or Stupors," in* The New York Times Book Review, *July 7, 1985, p. 8.*

Joel Yager

Since an estimated 10% of the population suffers from some form of migraine, it's likely that you or someone you know have suffered from this enduring affliction. [In the expanded and updated version of *Migraine: Understanding a Common Disorder*], Oliver Sacks, a professor of clinical neurology at the Albert Einstein College of Medicine in New York City, offers an erudite, literary and thoughtful medical treatise on migraine for lay persons and physicians, emulating some of the best in classic medical writing. His writing is informed by history and culture as well as science, filled with good critical evaluation of the field, and capped with a punch line that is far-reaching in its implications. Yet he is likely to arouse some antagonism within current neurological circles: He takes a somewhat anti-technological stance in his understanding of migraine and its treatment. For in contrast to many modern neurologists, Sacks comes across as either a classicist or a visionary—far behind—or far ahead of—his time.

In previous books Sacks showed that he could present neurological stories in an engaging way, talking about people rather than bundles of damaged neurons. The present work, in the same tradition, is based on his considerable clinical experience: Dr. Sacks has examined more than 1,200 patients with migraine, observing with a keen eye, getting to know his patients well, over time, and learning the ins and outs of this complex malady.

And complex it is! One strong message here is that migraine is not simply a headache, but a collection of highly variable physical and psychological signs and symptoms that differ from patient to patient, and often within the same patient over time. The common migraine that consists of severe, usually one-sided, throbbing headache and nausea is often accompanied by disorders of vision, sleep and arousal, mood, fluid imbalance, bowel dysfunction, and myriad other plagues. The "classic" migraine, which occurs in less than 1% of people, includes a premonitory aura, usually a perception of twinkling lights. But it may involve other unusual sensations, strange impairments of consciousness or abnormal movements. Sometimes the auras, nausea or other symptoms, occur without headache, and these phenomena, too, are regarded as migraine.

Indeed, so many manifestations of migraine are possible that the boundaries between what constitutes migraine (as "migraine equivalents") and what constitutes other neurological and psychiatric disturbances such as epilepsy and hysteria are blurry. Perhaps Sacks can be excused for viewing the world through migraine-colored lenses; he sees migraine in places where others might not.

There are scores of clinical stories: Here are cyclic migraines that follow an internal clock, going off every month in premenstrual rhythms; here are previously persistent migraines, mysteriously interrupted for years by imprisonment in a concentration camp only to return upon release; here are migraines that run in families, and those prompted by exhaustion, or arousal, or heat, or cold, or alcohol, or noise, or music, or the monosodium glutamate (MSG) in Chinese food.

Or by an unhappy life. For although Sacks dispels the myth of a single "migraine personality," he shows how migraines can become learned responses, triggered by cues of distress and conflict, becoming habitual when life circumstances remain problematic.

How to make sense of this? In Sacks' view, migraine is best understood as a way we protect ourselves from a variety of noxious stimuli—whatever our personal poisons seem to be. At its simplest, migraine, it would seem, is one of nature's ways of telling us to slow down, or to speed up, or to avoid exhaustion, or alcohol, or noise, or MSG. Beyond its ability to force physical recuperation by requiring the victim to lie down in a quiet place to sleep it off, migraine may serve other complex psychological functions: For some it may provide a way to be sick and signal the need for help; for others it may bind rage, conflict and anxiety that would be even more disabling if unbound; for others it may be a way of getting even, or of being self-punitive.

In short, migraine is a psychophysiological reaction that may have very different meanings for different individuals. Note that while this is helpful, it doesn't explain why only *some* people protect themselves, or regress in this painful fashion. We still lack a comprehensive understanding of the hows and whys of migraine.

Sufferers who read Sacks' section on treatment will know what they're getting, or what they're missing, from their physicians. In contrast with many modern physicians whom he sees as "pestering" active interventionists, through experience, Sacks has learned the virtues of patience, of trying to assess the meaning of the migraine for the individual patient and of offering simple tried and true remedies that go *with* the patient's biology instead of fighting it. His therapy requires a lot of asking, listening and discussing—psychiatry and neurology both. He is not at all averse to using available medications, and he uses them well, but he has no illusions that any one medication will ever provide a "magic bullet" for migraine. He has learned that some patients do better keeping their migraines than trying to abort them, because the down side of attempts to short-circuit the attacks, such as prolonged depressions and malaise, may be worse than the few bad hours of headache.

One important caveat. This book is supposed to have been written primarily for lay people. Although there is a glossary to help the reader through some of the technical language, many may find the going tough. It's also regrettable that Sacks neither expanded nor updated this excellent list of suggested readings since the first edition: The most recent was published in 1968.

But, all in all, if migraine concerns you, this book is worth browsing through, and if you can deal with the technical words, it's worth reading thoroughly. You might also give copies to your physicians and ask them to explain the hard parts. You'll all be better for it.

> *Joel Yager, in a review of "Migraine: Understanding a Common Disorder," in* Los Angeles Times Book Review, *October 13, 1985, p. 10.*

J. K. Wing

Sickness, says Oliver Sacks, is a quintessential human condition. Whether it is or not, disease does present us with a distorting mirror in which we can view our "normality" from a different perspective. The result is particularly alarming when the disease affects a person's identity or, odder still, one part of a person's identity, the other parts remaining apparently intact.

In an earlier book, *Awakenings,* Oliver Sacks showed himself able to describe with sympathy, clarity, honesty and wit the extraordinary post-encephalitic complications that afflicted survivors of the epidemic of sleeping sickness that raged during the 1920s. These were mostly severe and unusual forms of symptoms seen in ordinary Parkinson's disease. On the one hand a zombie-like passivity or lack of will to act that could result in catatonia or a decades-long "sleep". On the other, irresistible motor urges that might follow some unexpected stimulus such as a fire-alarm, setting the individual "suddenly and startlingly alive for a minute". Such flashes were rare. Segregated in institutions, the sufferers were forgotten until it was discovered that the transfer and metabolism of the neurotransmitter dopamine were defective in those parts of the brain affected in Parkinson's disease. *Awakenings* is about the responses, often bizarre, sometimes tragic, always intensely moving, of twenty patients treated with L-DOPA, a drug that partially substitutes for dopamine, which enabled some of them to begin another kind of life.

Dr Sacks wrote the stories of these patients with a driving passion and a literary skill that led W. H. Auden to acclaim the book as a masterpiece and Harold Pinter to write a play, *A Kind of Alaska,* based on the story of one of the patients. Sacks's new book [*The Man Who Mistook His Wife for a Hat*] could not reasonably be expected to achieve a similar intensity or unity, because it consists of a set of diverse case histories loosely connected by one of the themes that was powerfully developed in *Awakenings*—loss of or damage to personal identity.

The title-story is about a distinguished musician who developed a visual agnosia. He could not recognize faces, or facial expressions, or complex objects presented visually. He had no visual imagination or visual memories or visual dreams except for simple images. Hence his mistake when, looking for his hat, he reached for his wife's head instead. He was totally unaware of his disability. (Neurologists have a word for this, too—anosagnosia. Who is more damned, asks Sacks: the man who knows, or the man who does not?) A massive tumour in the visual parts of the brain left this man's musical talent intact. He was able to play and to teach music until the tumour ended his life.

The first part of the book is all about deficits. There are nine brief stories; each concerning a person who somehow has to come to terms with a disability that other people cannot imagine themselves having. One such is the grey-haired sailor who lost his memory through alcoholism and lived in a world that, to him, was perpetually 1945, when he was nineteen. Another is the man who, following a stroke, thought his hemiplegic leg belonged to someone else and fell out of bed while trying to get rid of it. Then there is the man who cannot understand the meaning of words but who can follow the pitch, assonance and emotional expression of speech with enjoyment and a degree of comprehension. By contrast, there is the man who has a tonal agnosia; he understands words but, to him, Oliver speaking Hamlet would sound stale, flat and unprofitable.

In the second section, Sacks presents stories about excesses, such as those suffered and enjoyed by Witty Ticcy Ray. He suffered from Tourette's syndrome, which is characterized by "tics, jerks, mannerisms, grimaces, noises, curses, involuntary irritations and compulsions of all sorts, with an odd elfin humour and a tendency to antic and outlandish kinds of play". How can the ego withstand this bombardment, asks the doctor: can identity survive? Having a strong personality, Ray puts his tics to good use as a drummer in a jazz band on Saturdays, but suppresses them with the drug "Haloperidol" during the week. Lesser characters, or those with more severe forms of the disease, like the woman in the story called **"The Possessed"**, might be overwhelmed and become almost indistinguishable from their disease. The miracle is that, in most cases, the afflicted people not only survive but achieve their own personal identity.

Perhaps the most remarkable stories are told in Part Three, which is called "Transports". An Indian girl of nineteen developed a localized and removable brain tumour. After operation she was well for ten years but then the tumour recurred; malignant, invasive and inoperable. She started to have *grand mal* fits but as the tumour spread to the temporal lobe these changed to turns of a different kind, she became dreamy and saw visions of places that she had known as a child. The form of the temporal lobe seizure, which tends to be somewhat stereotyped and limited, was developed into an experience of dying like a dream of going home. A completely different experience was related by a medical student who had experimented with a variety of "mind-bending" drugs like cocaine and amphetamine. One night he dreamt he was a dog living in a smell-rich world. On waking, he found that he was, in fact, surrounded by a universe where smell was the chief sensation. He could distinguish his friends, the streets of New York, each individual shop, by smell. After three weeks he returned to "normal".

In the final section, Sacks provides an insight into the world of people who are born, or become, simple-minded but who nevertheless have special talents that most of us would envy; the so-called *idiots-savants* and the autistic children grown up who can draw or play music like angels. There are better accounts of these matters elsewhere but Sacks does manage to convey, as few authors do nowadays a sense of continuity between the neurological and the psychiatric that has tended to be lost since the development of two separate professions.

While the author is involved in his stories his virtues are paramount: excellent prose, a literary imagination, a talent for clinical (though not technical) exposition that is out of the ordinary; above all, a capacity to see through the eyes of people who have entered new worlds and must achieve new identities if they are to survive as truly human beings. His attempt to provide an overall philosophical framework is less satisfactory, because too far removed from the practicalities and limitations of medicine so well expressed by Dr Rieux in Camus's *La Peste*. It might have been better to have considered each case in the light of what it could tell us about normal as well as abnormal neurological and psychological functions. One is also uneasily aware (it was not so obtrusive in *Awakenings*) that Sacks's patients all talk as he does. He cannot quite give them their own accents and idiom.

These are small matters. What really holds the book to-

gether is the author's recognition that a large part of medicine has to do with the problem of living with disability; whether it is schizophrenia or Tourette's syndrome or diabetes or an amputated limb or just one's own unique personality.

J. K. Wing, "Distorting Mirrors," in The Times Literary Supplement, *No. 4323, February 7, 1986, p. 146.*

Brina Caplan

Mostly, it doesn't matter that our physiology consists of cranky evolutionary compromises and is liable, like all overdesigned machinery, to glitches, discontinuities or outright breakdowns. We're jerry-built, but we're lucky: over time, lots of redundant function has been built into the works. Even that delicate system, the brain, has plenty of backup circuitry; so, usually, it's a wheeze or a thump, then everything's back in action. Sometimes, though, things go wrong in a big way. And when there is a major disorder in the mechanisms of the brain, more than our functional well-being is at risk. A personality does not rule the body like some *deus ex machina;* instead, selfhood inheres mysteriously in a physiology of fibers and cells, a biochemistry of charges and fluids. Disease processes in the brain threaten our ability to be ourselves—perhaps, to be any selves at all. The soul of the machine may recover from a neurological "event" only to find itself radically distorted or reduced to something alien, strangely enhanced or fatally lost.

How individuals respond to finding or losing themselves in the context of such crises has been neurologist Oliver Sacks's subject in three earlier books. . . . Now he's collected a variety of case histories and clinical vignettes under the title **The Man Who Mistook His Wife for a Hat,** once again presenting us with the profoundly creative yet disintegrative world of neuropathology. Sacks offers brief, orienting essays before taking us through four domains: Losses, Excesses, Transports and The World of the Simple. Within each domain, men and women struggle individually with a common problem: how to reconcile being both a faulty mechanism and a thematic, complex and enduring self.

Sacks tells stories. "We must deepen a case history to a narrative or tale," he says. "Only then do we have a 'who' as well as a 'what,' a real person . . . in relation to the physical." His stories concern not only his patients but also, in an informal way, the physicians of medical history—Dr. James Parkinson making clinical observations in the streets of eighteenth-century London, or Civil War physician Weir Mitchell puzzling over the way wounded soldiers experienced "phantom limbs." The evolution of neurology clearly delights Sacks. He expresses deep admiration for the rigorous, technical order brought to the field by the nineteenth-century neurologist Hughlings Jackson, whose work, incidentally, Freud also admired. At the same time, he has a case to make against classical, "Jacksonian" neurology, at least against its present-day application to patients. Give a person a neurological examination, he warns, and you're likely to wind up with no persona at all, just a list of functions and deficits. Too often, neurology ends in impersonal diagnostic disassembly. Yet neurological illness is the most deeply personal of experiences, challenging the patient's very identity.

The corrective, Sacks argues, is what his beloved mentor, Russian psychoneurologist A. R. Luria, called romantic science, a science which respects the meaningfulness of lived experience. Perhaps as body-machines we're as modular as Sonys, with identical interchangeable parts, but our lives have a thematic integrity that cannot be made uniform. One of Sacks's stories concerns two old women, both forced by cerebral strokes to hear and rehear unconsciously retained melodies. For one woman that meant a constant mind-numbing barrage of sound, but for the other, the loud music called to mind the joy of being a small child in the arms of her singing mother. This involuntary memory reassured her about a loving childhood, which in old age she doubted had been hers. "Biologically, physiologically," Sacks tells us, "we are not so different from each other; historically, as narratives—we are each of us unique."

Through his title story Sacks shows how grotesquely diminished the world becomes when apprehension of uniqueness is lost. The case in point is that of a musician-educator, Dr. P., referred for examination because he's been making laughable errors in visual discrimination. He reportedly had greeted parking meters in the street, mistaking them for passers-by. Although he could produce a lengthy analysis of the form of a glove or a rose, when shown the objects themselves he could not identify either. In reaching around for his hat, he took hold of his wife's head, as though it were the object he sought. Yet he felt nothing was wrong, and examination showed his intellect to be considerable and intact. Without difficulty he named the complex geometric shapes Sacks handed him. "Don't bother with the others," he told Sacks during testing, "I'll get the eikosihedron too." A disorder in the area of the right half of the brain concerned with visual processing had effectively marooned him: "Visually, he was lost in a world of lifeless abstractions . . . . he construed the world as a computer construes it, by means of key features and schematic relationships. . . . in an 'identiti-kit' way—without the reality being grasped at all."

Sacks uses Dr. P.'s impoverished vision as a symbol for another kind of blindness, self-imposed by the professions that study human understanding. The cognitive sciences—neurology, psychiatry, psychology—can make it seem as if knowing abstractly is the only kind of knowing worth anything. But, Sacks contends:

> Our mental processes, which constitute our being and life . . . involve not just classifying and categorising, but continual judging and feeling also. If this is missing, we become computer-like, as Dr. P. was. And, by the same token, if we delete feeling and judging, the personal, from the cognitive sciences, we reduce *them* to something as defective as Dr. P.—and we reduce *our* apprehension of the concrete and real.

Sacks is pushing a Romantic argument against the grain of custom. We are culturally disposed to value the abstract over the concrete; impersonal deduction over personal apprehension and feeling. Developmental psychologists from Freud through Piaget and Kohlberg have described the changes between infancy and adolescence in terms of the child's increasing ability to rise up the ladder of abstraction, away from the immediately felt toward the generalized and universal. To be sunk in specific perceptions is to hit bottom on any of these developmental scales. The "concrete thinker" is seen as stupid, retarded, self-limited, maybe schizophrenic.

With a Romantic spirit worthy of William Blake or D. H. Lawrence, Sacks urges us to look again at basic levels of perception we tend to ignore or to dismiss. Like Wordsworth, he asks us to respect an ability to see vividly in the moment even though such seeing is a form of perception that adults share with children and certifiable idiots. Perhaps the most challenging notion in *The Man Who Mistook His Wife for a Hat* lies here, in Sacks's Romantic assertion that concrete thinking is not secondary. It is not just the passive foundation on which abstract intelligence raises, stage by stage, the higher orders of wisdom. Concrete thought can also build a worthy architecture of understanding. "The particular," he says in discussing his autistic artist-patient José, "if one is particular enough, is also a road—one might say nature's road—to reality and truth."

In this regard Sacks tells how he came to reassess his initial professional view of a young retarded patient, Rebecca, as a result of seeing her in another context. When formally tested, he reports, Rebecca "had come apart, horribly," amounting to "a mass of sensorimotor impairments and breakdowns, limitations of intellectual schemata and concepts" all loosely bound by the anger, shame and anxiety of repeated and inevitable failure. Later, however, outside in the spring-stirred garden, Rebecca could speak in bursts of concrete images, movingly if haltingly. "An idiot Ecclesiastes," Sacks admits to thinking. In places where she had unconditional acceptance—at home with her grandmother or at her synagogue—she did not look foolish. At times when her emotions were deeply touched, she was composed. Then "there was no sense of handicap or incapacity, but a feeling . . . of being a soul, deep and high, and equal to all others."

It's a Romantic proposition that emotion provides the center for human consciousness. Sacks brings that proposition to life, case by case. His patient Martin, for example, has reached his 60s but seems at times a stunted "snotty child" and at other times an aging curiosity. With perfect ("eidetic") memory, Martin could provide exact information on the music, staging and performance details of 2,000 operas. Much of this perfect recollection, Sacks says, was flat and automatic, as though the data occupied an otherwise blank screen. That was not always so, however; what Martin knew could also have the deepest resonance of love and loss. Sacks explains that Martin's father, a retired opera star, spent the last years of his life

> playing his great collection of vocal records on the phonograph, going through and singing all his scores—which he did with his now thirty-year-old son (in the closest and most affectionate

communion of their lives), and reading aloud Grove's dictionary [of music and musicians]—all six thousand pages of it—which, as he read, was indelibly printed upon his son's limitlessly retentive, if illiterate cortex. Grove, thereafter, was "heard" *in his father's voice*—and could never be recollected by him without emotion.

In his account of The World of the Simple, Sacks shows us the power of personal perception to seize a moment, stabilizing it, like a photograph or a painting, in some personally meaningful pattern. Such patterns are doubly powerful in that they both interpret reality and express the soul of the perceiver. In fact, D. H. Lawrence advised people to quit thinking altogether and spend a generation or two learning properly how to feel. Sacks slips every now and then into Lawrence's sort of overwriting, but he does not reproduce any of Lawrence's anti-intellectual prejudices. Clearly, he appreciates the higher cortical functions that bring us neuropsychology or metaphysics or *The New York Review of Books,* his sometime publisher. This world too is his.

Indeed, Sacks's habit is to understand worlds rather than to dismiss them. And his argument with the cognitive sciences is an appeal that they widen their range of vision to include the worlds of the personal within their research and practice. What he's arguing for is a set of neglected values: empathetic, emotional, individual, storylike. To ignore those values, he suggests, means constructing a science of cold, rigid design. If coldness and rigidity are qualities suited to a mechanic's tools, which can pry into machinery, they produce equipment inadequate for understanding—much less treating—human beings. (pp. 211-13)

> *Brina Caplan, "Orders of Wisdom," in* The Nation, *New York, Vol. 242, No. 7, February 22, 1986, pp. 211-13.*

Charles Rycroft

Dr. Sack's aim in **The Man Who Mistook His Wife for a Hat** is . . . to tell stories or tales about his encounters with patients, in order to demonstrate that it is possible to be objective and subjective at the same time, that the gulf between the psychical and the physical can after a fashion be bridged, and that disorders of the nervous system (mostly, fortunately, very rare ones) can eliminate or, less frequently, exaggerate aspects of the sense of identity which those of us who have intact nervous systems take entirely for granted.

For instance, in health we assume without question that when we see a familiar thing or person we will be able to recognize it or him, and it is only in rare moments of reflection that we appreciate that there is, indeed, something remarkable about the fact that we effortlessly convert visual sensations into images that we recognize, that have meaning for us. However, Dr. P., the subject of Dr. Sacks's title story, who had a lesion in the visual cortex, could no longer effortlessly convert sensations into recognizable objects. When shown a glove, he described it as "a continuous surface infolded on itself. It appears to have

five outpouchings," and only when, by accident(!), he got it on did he exclaim, "My God, it's a glove!" And when at the end of his consultation he sought to put on his hat, he instead seized his wife's head and tried to put it on his own. "His wife looked as if she was used to such things," and later gave Dr. Sacks a coherent account of how her husband coped with the everyday details of living.

> He does everything singing to himself. But if he is interrupted and loses the thread, he comes to a complete stop, doesn't know his clothes—or his own body. He sings all the time—eating songs, dressing songs, bathing songs, everything. He can't do anything unless he makes it a song.

Dr. P. was a doctor of music, not of medicine, and in ways that are vividly described by Dr. Sacks he had learned to use melody, sound, and rhythm as an integrating guide that gave meaning to his actions.

But perhaps a clearer example of the dependence of the sense of identity on an intact nervous system is that of Christina, in the clinical tale **"The Disembodied Lady."** In health we always know where our bodies are and what position or posture we are in, and we know this without having to look and see where we, our trunk, our head, our limbs, are. The knowledge is just part of our (often only) subliminal self-awareness. It is, however, dependent on a specific sense, the proprioceptive sense, which was discovered in the 1890s by the British neurologist, Charles Sherrington, who called it "our secret sense, our sixth sense" and named it proprioception because of its indispensability for our sense of ourselves. Nerve endings in all the movable parts of our body (muscles, tendons, joints) send a continuous but unconscious flow of information about their position, posture, and tone which keeps us in touch with our bodies. And, although we are readily able to imagine that we might go blind or deaf or lose our sense of taste or smell, it is hard to imagine that we might lose all sense of our bodilyness, of owning our own bodies.

Yet this is what happened to Christina who, while in the hospital for routine surgery, developed an acute infection of her nerves (a polyneuritis) which selectively and permanently destroyed her proprioceptive nerve fibers. As a result she became and remains disembodied, lacking all instinctive sense of her body, its position, its solidity, and has had to learn how to use vision to monitor her posture and her movements. And although she has, it seems, been remarkably successful in doing so, she still feels that her body is "dead, not-real, not-hers—she cannot appropriate it to herself." As she herself says: "I feel my body is blind and deaf to itself . . . it has no sense of itself."

But I must not tell Dr. Sacks's tales for him. To do so would be to take away the sense of surprise and shock on which so many of them depend. It is enough for me to say that readers of **The Man Who Mistook His Wife for a Hat** will meet a gallery of patients who have suffered a major neurological disaster which has left them lacking some essential quality of being that the healthy take for granted or, more rarely, possessing some gift that seems bizarre rather than enviable: a middle-aged ex-sailor who believed himself to be nineteen and for whom time had stopped in 1945; a man who found a severed human leg in his bed which is really his own, unsevered leg; a man who tilted like the Leaning Tower of Pisa until, at his own suggestion, he was supplied with a spirit level attached to his glasses; a ward full of brain-damaged patients who all found President Reagan talking on television hilariously funny; a ninety-year-old woman whom tertiary syphilis, contracted seventy years previously, rendered frisky and skittish; a young man high on amphetamines who dreamed he was a dog and for the next three weeks lived in a doggy, olfactory world; mentally defective twins who amused each other by swapping six-figure prime numbers—and many others.

Some of these tales sound tall and Munchhauseny, but in fact they have been chosen to exemplify precisely how damage to specific parts of the nervous system can deplete, distort, or exaggerate those functions on which the sense of identity depends—and to show how, despite massive damage to the brain, the self continues to exist and assert itself. As one reads them one comes to appreciate why Dr. Sacks chose as his epigraph William Osler's remark that "to talk of diseases is a sort of *Arabian Nights* entertainment."

Readers of these tales will learn a lot about Dr. Sacks too. He clearly has no inhibitions about using his own flamboyant behavior and appearance—one of his patients likened him to an archimandrite priest—as a diagnostic and therapeutic tool. In doing so he is continuing or perhaps reviving an ancient tradition among physicians, which was particularly common among neurologists in the days before medicine became applied technology. He is a born storyteller who has no qualms about affecting surprise and endowing himself with the gift of total recall for the sake of liveliness of presentation. And he has a number of abiding preoccupations—not only with identity, but also with the role played by music, religious ceremonies, and nature, particularly in gardens, in helping patients (and, by implication, all of us) to maintain integration and to achieve what Osler called Aequanimitas. One hopes that he will develop this theme further in a later book.

He has heroes too, both his "suffering, afflicted, fighting" patients and his forerunners in neurology: Hughlings Jackson, Charles Sherrington, Henry Head, Kurt Goldstein, and A. R. Luria, who are, I think, better known and less forgotten than Sacks assumes. Finally, it must be said that, despite the liveliness of Sacks's writing, parts of this book will be heavy going for nonmedical readers. Unexplained anatomical and physiological terms abound but there is no glossary of technical terms and no index. (pp. 11-12)

Charles Rycroft, "The Sixth Sense," in The New York Review of Books, *Vol. XXXIII, No. 4, March 13, 1986, pp. 11-12.*

Paul Baumann

At first glance the neurological casualties in Dr. Oliver Sacks's *The Man Who Mistook His Wife for a Hat* may remind you of all those peculiar folks on your freshman year college hall, but as it turns out, things are not quite that bad. Of course the gentleman referred to in the title—

suffering from severe visual agnosia—makes life around the house seem a little like a *Honeymooners* skit, with Ralph and Norton giving the girls a very hard time indeed. And that's only the beginning. In another case, Jimmie, the forty-nine-year-old "ancient mariner," is caught in a time warp that would make Rod Serling proud. People find strange legs—their own, usually—in their beds, while others suffer from olfactory overload or the paradoxical effects of neurosyphilis's return in old age. In other words, the eye hath not seen, nor ear heard, what the good Dr. Sacks has in store. (p. 182)

Sacks possesses the gifts of a speculative philosopher and the subtler, rarer skills of an old-fashioned doctor who was taught how to take a history. He knows a good story when he treats one, and propounds a conundrum with the same vigor of expression, eye for detail, and vivid sense of character that made Sir Arthur Conan Doyle, another English physician-writer with a profound regard for the spiritual properties of intelligence, a master storyteller. Sacks shares with the creator of Sherlock Holmes a fascination with what we might call cerebral mysteries. In fact, when Sacks introduces his patients and their fantastic problems, he all but turns to an invisible companion after each clinical description and says, "And what, Dr. Watson, do you make of that?" "Extraordinary," comes the reply. "A singular case, Holmes." And so it is with *The Man Who Mistook His Wife for a Hat:* a collection of singular cases, written in a singular felicitous style.

The case histories collected here concern Sacks's investigations into what he calls the neurology of self, and illuminate the nature of mental processes and the false certainties that beset our common notions of defective intelligence. In accomplishing this, Sacks displays a theoretical audacity not unlike Freud's and the moral perspicuity of a Robert Coles or George Orwell.

Sacks is concerned with neurological impairments affecting the right hemisphere of the brain. Our most basic understandings of reality, Sacks says, are affected by this comparatively little known area of the mind. The sense of what is real—as inexplicable as it is rudimentary—is apprehended in concrete, personal, and what Sacks calls iconic terms. In these neurological transactions, the right hemisphere differs fundamentally from the left. On the left side the mental processes are abstract, conceptual, and schematic—what might be regarded as the higher functions. But the brain-as-computer model does not apply to the right hemisphere, where knowledge is shaped and retained in a more organic and sensorial way.

On the right side mental operations are cast in a symbolic mode and depend on what Sacks calls our narrative sense of ourselves. Neurological afflictions, like hyper-amnesis and hyper-gnosis, "testify to the essentially 'melodic' and 'scenic' nature of inner life, the 'Proustian' nature of memory and mind." Moreover, the experiences of his patients suggest that at least some neurological incapacities offer "portals" through which the nature of being and the mysterious origins of the self can be glimpsed.

A patient's struggle to maintain his identity in the face of neurological chaos is what interests Sacks. The spirit, the soul, the self, cannot be merely calculated or systematically diagrammed. Meaningful existence is the product of the spirit's struggle for coherent expression. Being deprived of the ability for such expression can be a form of damnation, a kind of neurologically imposed perdition. "Experience is not possible until it is organized iconically; action is not possible unless it is organized iconically. 'The brain's record' of everything—everything alive—must be iconic. This is the final form of the brain's record, even though the preliminary form may be computational or programmatic. The final form of cerebral representation must be, or allow, 'art'—the artful scenery and melody of experience and action."

Even when the conceptual apparatus of the left hemisphere is shattered, the neglected powers of the right brain can be cultivated—through story, music, and art—in a way that liberates the mentally impaired from the prison of their physiological incapacity. Stories, and especially music, provide the context, the sequencing of events, the schematic framework that the injured mind cannot provide for itself. Despite their classification as mental defectives, the so-called simple-minded possess a "quality of mind" rich in meaning, memory, aesthetic and symbolic power. Sounding very much like [psychologist] Bruno Bettelheim on the ontological efficacy of fairy tales, Sacks reminds us that only story and symbol give a truly empowering and purposeful "sense of the world" and our unique place in it.

Sacks's larger ambition is to develop what he calls an "existential neurology" or "romantic science" that will shed the rigid computational paradigms of traditional neurology and open itself up to the dynamic "powers" of the mind. "Our cognitive sciences are themselves suffering from an agnosia," he says of the emphasis contemporary neurology places on abstract reasoning alone. Turning with renewed curiosity to the concrete, personal, and symbolic powers of the mind will help restore the true complexity of the human subject to the center of scientific investigation.

"The patient's essential being is very relevant in the higher reaches of neurology," Sacks asserts. That person can only be fully understood when we "deepen a case history to a narrative or tale." The truth about existence, Sacks writes, is that "to be ourselves we must have ourselves—possess, if need be repossess, our life stories. We must 'recollect' ourselves, recollect the inner drama, the narrative, of ourselves. A man *needs* such a narrative, a continuous inner narrative, to maintain his identity, his self." It is that narrative that doctor and patient use to stave off neurological catastrophe, and that even those untouched by such trauma must use to fashion an identity.

In *Time and Myth: A Meditation on Storytelling as an Exploration of Life and Death,* theologian John S. Dunne made similar claims for the role story plays in rendering the world meaningful and the self whole. All identity is maintained in the face of chaos, he suggested, and the individual is lost unless "the story of the world . . . finally becomes the human thing that mediates between man and the unknown . . . " It has apparently become Sacks's happy task to insist that science finally speak in a language that can accommodate such truth, for Sacks tells us that we must first know the world as symbol, if we are to know it at all. Even Holmes would have been baffled by that mystery. (pp. 182-83)

Paul Baumann, "Cerebral Mysteries," in Commonweal, *Vol. 113, No. 6, March 28, 1986, pp. 182-83.*

"It seems to me that reading and writing are entirely natural and I've never known anything else. What I *do* find strange— and a bit frightening—are those people in medicine who are semi-literate and not at ease with words. I'm also bothered with the deterioration of language and thought which goes with it, which I think occurs in a lot of medical writing now. Medical writing was often natural and beautiful a half-century or quarter-century ago. Now it is filled with jargon—in an attempt to be precise, but in fact it backfires and is as imprecise as it is unbeautiful."

—*Sacks, 1987*

Peter S. Prescott

Oliver Sacks belongs to the tribe of Sir Thomas Browne: the physician who is as skilled in writing as he is in medicine, whose inclination is to look beyond the disability at hand to see what it can teach us about the human condition. Sacks is a neurologist. Fifteen years ago, in *Awakenings,* he wrote of his work with victims of Parkinson's disease and sleeping sickness. This led him to questions about enforced cultural isolation and the extraordinary measures some people must take to regain the full humanity that the rest of us take for granted. . . .

[With *Seeing Voices: A Journey into the World of the Deaf*] he has done it again, examining similar problems while observing as nearly as a hearing person can the relatively closed world of the congenitally deaf. The deaf are not ill, of course; they are nobody's patients. But they are impaired and their education into language—even into useful thought—may prove rigorous and prolonged. For Sacks, the condition of the deaf points to broader concerns: the nature of language, the awakening of intelligence and the proper governance of a community.

His book is divided into three essays: a history of the deaf; an examination (and celebration) of the complexity and richness of Sign, the true language of the deaf; and an account of last year's uprising at Gallaudet University, which for the first time placed a deaf president in charge.

If history begins when people learn how to leave a record of their lives, then the deaf had no history until the mid-18th century, when a French priest, the Abbé de l'Epé, took the trouble to pay attention to the signals they made with their hands. Up to then, the deaf had been considered not only impaired but mentally incompetent: they were thought "dumb" in both senses of the word. The abbé learned their language and by applying it to pictures and words taught the deaf to read. For the first time, the deaf could acquire an education and make their thoughts known to the hearing world.

Without language, Sacks writes, we can't become fully human. "Intelligence, though present and perhaps abundant, is locked up so long as the lack of language lasts . . . Nothing is more wonderful, or more to be celebrated, than something that will unlock a person's capacities and allow him to grow and think." This is exactly what Sign, a true language, complete, complex and rich in ways the hearing cannot quite imagine (it works, for instance, in space as well as time, as our spoken language does not), has accomplished for the deaf. True Sign—as opposed to the pseudo-languages that link gestures to the sounds and grammars of heard languages—is "capable of expressing not only every emotion but every proposition . . . as economically and effectively and grammatically as speech."

Sacks's enthusiasm for Sign is contagious. His excitement over the ways in which the deaf have overcome their tragic past is reflected in his narrative, which proceeds on two fronts: a text and a running sequence of large-type footnotes containing digressions, additions and documentation in a breathless I-can't-wait-to-tell-you-this-too manner. *Seeing Voices* is a searching book; if it isn't quite as affecting as *Awakenings,* it's because Sacks is an outsider here, not himself involved with the struggles of those whom he observes.

> *Peter S. Prescott, "Beyond the Hearing World," in* Newsweek, *Vol. CXIV, No. 14, October 2, 1989, p. 72.*

Paul West

The born-deaf are very different from you and me, not least because, even now, they attract to themselves as a group the alliterative clincher "dumb," with all it implies of mental inadequacy. No wonder we get indignant on their behalf, deploring, as Oliver Sacks does, the insult added to injury, though bothering no more than he to pursue the matter into etymology, which tells us that "surd" in our word "absurd" means "deaf" in Latin. Clearly there is an atavistic link between not hearing and not making sense. Someone born deaf cannot make sense of the world, and as an entity does not make sense to other humans; because he or she lacks language, others only too readily shade their evaluation over from *cannot speak* to *cannot think*—the two dumbs that make a person all thumbs.

Dr. Sacks is the author of luminous and articulate books about the role of neurological deficit in the art of being (or remaining) human, most recently a collection of essays, ***The Man Who Mistook His Wife for a Hat.*** He writes as a physician who had seen the deaf in "purely medical terms—as 'diseased ears' or 'otologically' impaired"— until he happened to read Harlan Lane's *When the Mind*

Hears: A History of the Deaf (1984). He then began to think of them, ethnically, as a different or separate linguistic nation, but those who interest him most are the pre-lingually deaf, who number perhaps a quarter of a million in the United States and compose some thousandth of the world's children. As soon as Dr. Sacks realizes they can attain a rich appreciation of written English, do not complain about or sense silence and have acute responses to vibration, he is off on his "journey" to their slandered terra incognita. He soon discovers that they have open to them only three options: lip reading (and the attempt at traditional speech); signed English, which corresponds to English word by word; and American Sign Language (A.S.L.), or Sign, a virtually separate language that, as he says, does not resemble signed English. There are indigenous sign languages all over the planet, with much the same spatial structure. It is these sign languages, all having "some generic resemblance to ASL," that excite him because they strike him as dynamic, original and iconically expressive. As he says, there is no universal sign language "but there are, it seems, universals in all sign languages, universals not of meaning, but of grammatical form."

Thinking of analogies for languages that have no written equivalent, he recalls the learned, never spoken language of the elite Chinese bureaucracy and points out that Sign is not uniform and ecumenical, but has British, American, Chinese, Mayan and Australian aboriginal counterparts, and many others. Worldwide, signers have the same almost Dionysian, histrionic compulsion to make the otherwise ineffable visual. Enthralled and appalled, as he says, Dr. Sacks comes out vehemently against both the so-called oral method and the signed English that together rule the educational roost, in favor of this idiosyncratic metalanguage, reminding us that "a monolingual Japanese would be lost in Arkansas, as a monolingual American would be lost in rural Japan. But a deaf American can make contact relatively swiftly with his signing brothers in Japan, Russia, or Peru—he would hardly be lost at all. . . . By the end of a day, a grammarless pidgin will be established."

It sounds like paradise. Indeed, Dr. Sacks, whose heart is in the right place, yearns for Sign to be an immediate "language of the heart." He notes that the born-deaf, who show little disposition to speak, go to Sign with relish. Deaf children of deaf parents using Sign, he says, "make their first signs when they are about six months old and have considerable sign fluency by the age of fifteen months." Sign, he contends, is a fundamental language of the brain, and he wonders rather angrily why it is not used in schools but is "still largely restricted, as seventy years ago, to a colloquial and demotic use," even at Gallaudet, the university for the deaf in Washington.

I write these words as if I had followed Dr. Sacks' presentation, but I can't be quite sure, as his first chapter is a ramshackle job, consisting of an expanded book review both unrevised and cluttered with some 28 footnotes that drag the eye at first down, then across, and on to yet another page while the presumed major discourse lies unread higher up. In a disarming self-vindication, Dr. Sacks says, "I should add that I have never found it possible to tell a story, or pursue a line of thought, without taking innumerable side trips or excursions along the way, and finding my journey the richer for this," to which, wouldn't you know it, he appends a footnote saying, "The many (and sometimes lengthy) footnotes should be regarded as mental or imaginative excursions, to be taken, or avoided, as the reader-traveler chooses." Dr. Sacks, who writes of his book's "successive drafts," should have done his own work of incorporation and ordonnance, especially when dealing with a subject as grave, complex and fraught with emotion and controversy as this. The book has notes and references appended, but a glossary would have been useful, especially for someone puzzled by Dr. Sacks' use of "sign" and "Sign." Perhaps he is simply the man who mistook a book review for a book.

I wonder, too, in what ghetto of plain, minimal English he formed the notion that signing "has a playful quality, a style, *quite different from that of speech* [my italics]. Signers tend to improvise," he says, "to play with signs, to bring all their humor, their imaginativeness, their personality, into their signing, so that signing is not just the manipulation of symbols according to grammatical rules, but, irreducibly, the voice of the signer." The same would be true of almost any personable, plausible talker with normal hearing. Oral style, that emanation from the personality, is possible for all. Dr. Sacks seems to me to scant the immediacy and spellbinding qualities of everyday speech. I have a quarrel, too, with the book's drawings, all four of them culled from other works, in which they must have been as indecipherable and inexplicit as they are here. Could they not have been redrawn? The only telling one reveals how well deaf Chinese children reproduced a Chinese pseudocharacter that hearing Chinese children could hardly draw at all.

The second of Dr. Sacks' three chapters, or sections, is his best, bedded in footnotes as it is. Here he gets into language and the brain, tossing off data with ease and casualness. Unless pushed, a deaf child will have only 50 to 60 words at the age of 6, whereas the average hearing child has 3,000 (interestingly enough, the Dictionary of American Sign Language lists the same number of root signs). What signers do amounts to "movement parsing." Signing seems to reallocate areas of the purely auditory left temporal lobe for visual processing, which, as Dr. Sacks says, is extraordinary proof of the nervous system's plasticity. He leaves us with Helen Neville's vision of the brain's microstructure "as having, at first, a great neuronal redundancy and plasticity, and of this being subsequently 'pruned' by experience." Language grossly alters the brain.

From this heady stuff to the 1988 student strike at Gallaudet University, in which deaf undergraduates demanded and got a deaf president, is a logical move. Dr. Sacks' third and final chapter makes his point with a thump. He saw it all, even a young woman signing to her dog right there on the campus that invented the football huddle. You have to know that, at Gallaudet, "only a minority of the faculty . . . is deaf " (except in the mathematical faculty), that even those teachers who sign use signed English rather than American Sign Language and that, in general, "there are very few deaf teachers of the deaf; and ASL, for

the most part, is either not known to, or not used by, hearing teachers." Now, if the boot were on the other foot. . . . Dr. Sacks' main virtue is that he makes you want to switch roles all the time.

I have often thought that the deaf are true symbolists, trying always to reunite two things severed (sound and sense) or to go beyond that old dichotomy into a realm in which the strained face of near-superhuman concentration no longer tweaks itself toward some prodigy of speech but softens with delight, as when Dr. Sacks sees a thousand-odd Gallaudet students milling around, "signing freely," in the great plaza in front of the Capitol. How wonderful to have such a language of their own; how discomfiting not to be able to use it in dealing with hearing people.

How wonderful it might be if we all learned A.S.L. at an early age. But in the meantime, is it better for deaf children to learn only Sign or just speech and lip reading? Surely, some holistic compromise makes more sense; at least you'd think so until you realize the enormous burden imposed on a child who has to learn speech, lip reading and signed English while homing to A.S.L. There is a world of difference between this grievous overload and wanting a hearing child to be bilingual. Dr. Sacks, whose heart is in the right place, wants the deaf to have all they need, but most of all, their own natural and private language. He brings afresh to our attention a problem that is never easily going to be solved. (pp. 17-18)

> Paul West, "Say It with Signs," in The New York Times Book Review, *October 8, 1989, pp. 17-18.*

Simon J. Carmel

[*Carmel, born deaf, is an American anthropologist and educator who specializes in deaf folklore and culture.*]

Is the sign language of deaf people an authentic form of human language among the thousand spoken languages of the world? Or is it merely gestures and pantomime without grammar? How do deaf people acquire a written or sign language without hearing a spoken language? Is deafness a medical or pathological view, or a cultural and social view? And why did deaf students suddenly revolt against the appointment of a new university president at Gallaudet University in Washington, D.C., last year?

In his latest book, **Seeing Voices: A Journey into the World of the Deaf,** Oliver Sacks admits that three years ago he knew nothing about the enriched realm of deaf adults and children, their world views or their visual language. When Sacks started to read books on the deaf, he was so enraptured that he began a journey into their silent world. He began to learn the history of deaf people and their completely visual language, "Sign," a language different in mode from his own. (Sign refers to American Sign Language [ASL], as well as to all indigenous signed languages, such as French Sign, Chinese Sign, and so on.) Sacks's journey took him to deaf people and their families; to schools for the deaf; to the unique Gallaudet University of the deaf; to Martha's Vineyard, where at one time everybody (the hearing as well as the deaf) spoke Sign; to towns like Fremont, California, and Rochester, New York, where there are special social areas for the deaf community; and to the researchers on Sign. He was forced to look at language, at the nature of talking and teaching, at child development, the development and functioning of the nervous system, and the formation of communities, worlds, and cultures in a way that was wholly new to him. After his journey, he was left with mixed feelings. For instance, Sacks was appalled to learn that many deaf people never acquire good language or thinking. He learned that deafness is not only a biological phenomenon but also a cultural one. And he found that many deaf people have acquired language of an entirely different kind that serves as the medium of a community with a rich culture. Sacks was aware of the "medical" status of deaf people, but he learned that they are also an "ethnic" group with a distinct language, sensibility, and culture.

The book is divided into three segments. The first was written in 1985 and 1986 when Sacks was asked to review a book on the history of deaf people, Harlan Lane's *When the Mind Hears*. The second part was written last, and Sacks places it at the heart of the book because it is based on his most personal view of the subject. The book's third part was stimulated by the revolt of the students at Gallaudet University in March 1988 and was first published in the *New York Review of Books* on June 2, 1988. However, it was revised and enlarged for this book. Sacks emphasizes that, although he is a professor of neurology at Albert Einstein College of Medicine in New York, he is an outsider, with no special knowledge or expertise in the field of deafness: "I am not deaf, I do not sign, I am not an interpreter or teacher, I am not an expert on child development, and I am neither a historian nor a linguist."

Although Sacks claims that deafness is "one of the most desperate of human calamities," the book's first part reveals that hearing people are vastly ignorant about deafness. Sacks raised the subject of deafness with many hearing people and usually received the same responses: "Deafness? Don't know any deaf people. Never thought much about it. There's nothing *interesting* about deafness. . . . " He admits that before he read Harlan Lane's book, he would have made the very same comments.

In the past three centuries, languageless deaf people have aroused the curiosity and compassion of philosophers and educators alike. In the eighteenth century, Abbé Sicard, a director of the National Institution for Deaf-Mutes in Paris, asked,

> *Why* is the uneducated deaf person isolated in nature and unable to communicate with other men? *Why* is he reduced to this state of imbecility? Does his biological constitution differ from ours? Does he not have everything he needs for having sensations, acquiring ideas, and combining them to do everything that we do? Does he not get sensory impressions from objects as we do? . . . *Why* then does the deaf person remain stupid while we become intelligent?

In another view, the sixteenth-century Italian physician Girolamo Cardan proposed that "it is possible to place a deaf-mute in a position to hear by reading, and to speak by writing. . . . Written characters and ideas may be connected without the intervention of actual sounds." The notion that understanding ideas does not depend upon the hearing of words was revolutionary in the sixteenth century.

Abbé de l'Epée, the founder of a French school for the deaf, changed the ideas and theories of philosophers by using the indigenous sign language of the deaf. He could not bear to think of the souls of deaf people living and dying unheeded. The abbé acquired their language and then taught them to read, opening the world of learning and culture to them. He founded his school in 1755 and trained a hundred teachers for the deaf who, in turn, established twenty-one schools for the deaf in France and the rest of Europe. His school became the National Institution for Deaf-Mutes in Paris. Many celebrated philosophers and other public figures came to observe de l'Epée's and Sicard's class demonstrations and saw that deaf people were no longer the outcasts of human society.

This period was a kind of golden age in deaf history because with the rapid establishment of deaf schools, usually manned by deaf teachers, deaf people emerged from neglect and obscurity and began to appear in positions of eminence and responsibility—as writers, engineers, philosophers, and intellectuals. In 1816, Laurent Clerc, a deaf student of Abbé Sicard, was brought to the United States by Thomas Gallaudet to assist in establishing the American Asylum for the Deaf in Hartford, Connecticut. Deaf literacy and deaf education increased in the United States, as it had in France and throughout other parts of the world. By 1869, 41 percent of the teachers of the deaf in the U.S. were themselves deaf.

In 1864 Congress passed a law authorizing the Columbia Institute for the Deaf and the Blind in Washington, D.C., to become a national deaf-mute college, the world's first institution of higher learning specifically for the deaf. Its first principal was Edward Gallaudet, the son of Thomas Gallaudet. Columbia Institute was later rechristened Gallaudet University; it is still the only liberal arts college for deaf students in the world.

Most unfortunately, by 1870 the philosophy of oralism started to suppress the use of Sign by and for the deaf. And for the past century, teachers and parents of deaf children have felt that the goal of deaf education should be teaching deaf children how to speak. Edward Gallaudet was an open-minded man, who in the late 1860s visited deaf schools in fourteen European countries. He found that the majority used both sign language and speech and that these schools obtained superior results. Gallaudet felt that speech skills could not be the basis of primary instruction—this had to be achieved early by Sign. In contrast, the "radical" reformers wanted to overthrow the "old-fashioned" sign language schools and introduce "progressive" oralist schools. At the infamous International Congress of Educators of the Deaf held in Milan, Italy, in 1880—where deaf teachers were excluded from the vote—oralism won the day and the use of Sign in schools was "officially" outlawed. Deaf students were forbidden to use their own "natural" sign language.

One of the most salient consequences of the Milan conference was that hearing teachers, not deaf teachers, now had to teach deaf students. In 1850, approximately 50 percent of teachers for the deaf were themselves deaf. That number fell to 25 percent by the turn of the century and to 12 percent by 1960. More and more, English became the language of instruction for deaf students, taught by hearing teachers, among whom few knew any sign language at all.

Sacks discovered that oralism and the suppression of Sign have resulted in a dramatic deterioration in the educational achievement of deaf children and in the literacy of deaf people generally. Congenitally deaf students suffer from "information deprivation." The content of deaf education is poor or insufficient compared to that of hearing children because hearing teachers spend so much time teaching deaf children speech that there is little time for transmitting information, culture, complex skills, or anything else. During the 1960s historians and psychologists, as well as parents and teachers of deaf children, started asking, "What has happened?"

A century after the Milan conference, deaf people are still largely deprived of their own, indigenous sign language. Sacks points out that profoundly deaf people show no native tendency whatever to speak. Speaking is a labor of years. In contrast, they show an immediate and powerful tendency to Sign, which as a visual language is completely accessible to them. This is most apparent in the deaf children of deaf parents using Sign, who make their first signs when they are about six months old and have considerable fluency by the age of fifteen months. Sacks emphasizes that language must be introduced and acquired as early as possible; in the case of profoundly deaf children, only by Sign. Therefore, deafness must be diagnosed as early as possible, and the children must be exposed to fluent signers—their parents or teachers. Once signing is learned, deaf individuals have a free flow of information and can acquire reading and writing, and perhaps speech. There is no evidence that signing inhibits the acquisition of speech.

In the second part of his book, Sacks speaks of isolated deaf people who failed to acquire any language whatever. In the absence of any real language or communication, do these individuals lack intellectual abilities and emotional and social development? Sacks wonders in what ways hearing people have become complete human beings. He raises several questions: "Is our humanity, so called, partly dependent on language? What happens to us if we fail to acquire any language? Does language develop spontaneously and naturally, or does it require contact with other human beings?" Sacks explores different issues focusing on human beings deprived of language, including those suffering from aphasia, which has been a central preoccupation of neurologists since the 1860s.

There is a striking autobiographical sketch by the early nineteenth-century French deaf teacher Jean Massieu. Until the age of fourteen, when he became a pupil of Abbé Sicard, he was languageless; later he became fluent in both Sign and written French. Massieu wrote about what his preeducation mind was like: "I saw cattle, horses, donkeys, pigs, dogs, cats, vegetables, houses, fields, grapevines, and after seeing all these things remembered them

well." He also had a sense of numbers, even though he did not have names for them. He explained, "Before my education I did not know how to count; my fingers had taught me. I did not know numbers; I counted on my fingers, and when the count went beyond ten I made notches on a stick." When he entered the school for the deaf in Paris, Massieu developed a tremendous, violent hunger for names, just as Helen Keller did when she first understood what "water" stood for and then desired to know the names of all objects surrounding her.

No scientific or linguistic attention was given to Sign until the 1960s when William Stokoe came to Gallaudet University to teach English to deaf students. At that time sign language was seen not as a proper language but as a kind of broken English or pantomime of gestural symbols. In 1960 Stokoe published *Sign Language Structure,* and in 1965, *A Dictionary of American Sign Language* with his deaf research colleagues Dorothy Casterline and Carl Croneberg. Stokoe was convinced that signs were not pictures but complex abstract symbols with a complex inner structure. His book was a double revolution: a scientific one calling attention to the system of sign language and its cognitive and neural levels, and a cultural and political one that helped deaf and hearing people become aware of sign language as a true communal language within the deaf world. Later, scientists at the Salk Institute in San Diego, California, studied the ways in which a sign is changed to express different meanings through grammar and syntax. They showed that the single most remarkable feature of Sign is its unique linguistic use of space. At every level, Sign has lexical, grammatical, syntactic, and spatial systems. In 1978, Sign researchers demonstrated that very finely detailed differences in a sign movement could distinguish some nouns from related verbs.

Many hearing people had thought that deaf people in different countries had a universal sign language that enabled them to communicate with one another without difficulty. Sacks points out that there are many hundreds of indigenous signed languages all over the world that have evolved separately and independently wherever there are groups of deaf people. Although a universal sign language does not exist, there are "universals in all sign language, universals not of meaning, but of grammatical form." Therefore, a deaf American can make relatively swift contact with his or her counterparts in Japan, Russia, or Peru. Their understanding will usually be established within minutes, accomplished mostly by gesture and mime.

In closing his second part, Sacks emphasizes that a language's "character" is essentially cultural, for it expresses the way a people think and feel and aspire. In the case of Sign, the distinctiveness of the language, its character, is biological as well, for it is rooted in gesture, in iconicity, in a radical visuality that sets it apart from any spoken tongue. But it is also, and equally, an expression of personal and cultural identity. For in the language of a people "resides its whole thought domain, its tradition, history, religion, and basis of life, all its heart and soul."

The third part of the book describes the student revolt at Gallaudet University, which began on a Wednesday morning in March 1988, and the author's analysis of the inevitable factors that led to it. In its 124 years of existence, Gallaudet University had never had a deaf president. The students had been actively campaigning for one ever since the last hearing president had resigned. A presidential search committee selected the six final candidates—three hearing and three deaf. The board finally chose Elisabeth Ann Zinser, one of the hearing candidates. The board's announcement, in addition to the chairman's comment that "the deaf are not yet ready to function in the hearing world," caused outrage. On March 8, a thousand students closed the university and barricaded the campus entrance doors. Later, the faculty and staff came out in support of the students and their demands.

Sacks reflects on an earlier visit he made to Gallaudet, in 1986-87, an experience that was both astonishing and moving. After attending philosophy and chemistry classes in Sign and observing the wonderful social scene in the student snack bar, with hands flying in all directions, Sacks realized that Sign might be "a complete language—a language equally suitable for making love or speeches, for flirtation or mathematics." These experiences changed his previous "medical" view of deafness to a "cultural" one—deaf people forming a community with its own language and culture. He also sensed an unspoken tension between faculty and administration. There were many teachers who signed, and some were deaf. But only a small number of the faculty members at Gallaudet were deaf in contrast to the numbers during Edward Gallaudet's day.

At the time of the uprising, Sacks was overwhelmed when he gazed around the campus "filled with passionate Sign, with passionate soundless conversation." At that moment he sensed that the students deserved one of their own, that no one not deaf, not signing, could possibly understand them. The students would be cut off from any president who was not one of them. They were tired of hearing the "You can't" syndrome for so many years. They really needed a deaf president who understood the deaf and the need for education, culture, language, and leadership. Sacks witnessed the "transformation" of the communal mind of the Gallaudet deaf community. The deaf students suddenly were no longer passive, scattered, and powerless. The transmission of deaf culture came not only through Sign but through their schools as well. These schools acted as foci for the deaf community, passing down history and culture from one generation to the next. Sacks sees that deaf individuals have their "identity" as a "people" with their own culture, like the Jews or the Welsh. The deaf have had a long struggle to break the old-fashioned concept of "pathologizing" deaf people.

In the past, some doctors tended to see "the deaf merely as having diseased ears and not as whole people adapted to another sensory mode." Deaf people felt this to be an offensive value judgment by hearing people—a way of saying, "We know what is best for you. Let *us* handle things." Deaf people felt they were being dictated to, being told whether or not they could use Sign, being judged as to their capabilities for education and jobs. They were being treated as children.

In contrast, the students at Gallaudet showed a high com-

petence in managing the March revolt. They contacted the press and television for interviews and issued press releases around the clock. They successfully gained the world's ear. Later, Dr. Zinser, having reexamined her assumptions and views, saw things in a new light and resigned. On Sunday evening, March 13, a new chairman of the board and a new president, both deaf, were appointed.

At the end of the book, the author presents, for his curious readers, a good selected and annotated bibliography. But there is a tiny flaw in Sack's book—there are too many lengthy (albeit informative) footnotes. And I am somewhat bothered in regard to Sacks's meetings with researchers and other individuals. I don't know if he has a tendency to "patronize" deaf people, but he does mention that he spoke in depth with a number of hearing researchers and experts on deafness. Although he did speak with a few deaf people, he does not mention whether he ever had the same in-depth discussions with any well-known deaf people like community leaders, sociologists, teachers, actors, writers, and so on. There are important deaf people who could be of great help to anyone, including Oliver Sacks, who wishes to understand the history, language, and culture of deaf people. Of course, I am fully aware of Sacks's limited use of sign language, but he could have conversed with deaf people via a TDD (telecommunication device for the deaf) or with help from an interpreter hired for personal interviews. Above all, I must admit that Sacks's book is most informative and stimulating, and I must praise his intense research and crystal-clear understanding of the deaf world. So I strongly recommend that his book be read by those individuals who want a better understanding of the cultural, educational, historical, linguistic, psychological, and sociological discipline of deafness. (pp. 88-92, 94–5)

Simon J. Carmel, "Journey into a Silent World," in Natural History, *Vol. 98, November, 1989, pp. 88-92, 94-5.*

FURTHER READING

Auden, W. H. "The Megrims." *The New York Review of Books* 16, No. 10 (3 June 1971): 25-6.

> Laudatory review of the 1970 edition of *Migraine* in which Auden analyzes Sacks's physiological and psychological theories concerning the origin of migraine headaches.

Harding, D. W. "Need and Greed." *New Statesman* 86, No. 2216 (7 September 1973): 318-20.

> Suggests that while *Awakenings* is "humanly moving and scientifically fascinating," Sacks's focus on the metaphysical aspects of sickness contradicts the curative aims of the medical profession.

Kohn, Marek. "Interview: Oliver Sacks." *New Statesman* 112, No. 2905 (28 November 1986): 19-20.

> Interview in which Sacks discusses religion, neuro-

science, and the problems involved in objectively and accurately recreating case histories.

Lesser, Wendy. "Drink Me: *Alice* and *Awakenings.*" *The Threepenny Review* VII, No. 2 (Summer 1986): 10-12.
Discusses the thematic and symbolic similarities between Sacks's *Awakenings* and Lewis Carroll's *Alice in Wonderland.*

Perlmutter, David M. "The Language of the Deaf." *The New York Review of Books* XXXVIII, No. 6 (28 March 1991): 65-72.
Positive review of *Seeing Voices* in which Perlmutter also discusses the history of the deaf, and the grammar and syntactic structure of American Sign Language.

Wax, Amy L. "Papa Knows Best." *The American Scholar* 54, No. 3 (Summer 1985): 419-24.
Comparative study of the themes of "silence and abandonment" found in Sacks's *A Leg to Stand On* and Jay Katz's *The Silent World of Doctor and Patient.*

Edith Sitwell

1887-1964

(Full name Dame Edith Louisa Sitwell) English poet, novelist, critic, autobiographer, biographer, and editor.

An eccentric, controversial figure in English letters, Sitwell was best known for her experimental verse that evidenced her deep interest in the sound and rhythm of language. In her youth, she rebelled against what she perceived as unimaginative and sentimental poets popular at the time, and, with her brothers Osbert and Sacheverell, created a literary circle whose satirical, experimental poetry foreshadowed the Modernist period in literature. Early contemporaries condemned Sitwell's poetry as pretentious, inaccessible, and vacuous, yet she later garnered considerable accolades when she moved away from strident experimentalism toward verse that explored universal human experiences through religious, mythical, and natural imagery. While Sitwell's position in English letters remains controversial, her poetry is increasingly valued for its spontaneous vitality and moral vision.

Sitwell was the first child of Sir George and Lady Ida Sitwell, an unhappily married couple who disliked their daughter's awkward physical appearance and willful manner. Their insensitivity, however, was offset by Sitwell's strong attachment to her younger brothers, Osbert and Sacheverell, and by the rich history and cultural milieu of the family estate, Renishaw Hall. She was educated by governesses, and developed an affinity for such diverse poets as Alexander Pope, Charles Baudelaire, and Arthur Rimbaud. At the age of twenty-six, Sitwell moved to London, where she lived with her former governess, Helen Rootham, and gained prominence as the sharp-witted editor of *Wheels,* an annual anthology of verse she founded with her brothers that offered an alternative to what she termed the "dim bucolics" of the Georgians. She also received notice for her unconventional readings of experimental verse that emphasized tonality of language over meaning. For example, she set the poems of her 1922 volume *Façade* to music by William Walton and recited them through a megaphone while sitting behind a curtain. Despite the negative reaction of some critics to her work, she and her brothers eventually became the hub of a literary circle that included Gertrude Stein, T. S. Eliot, and Aldous Huxley. Sitwell's manner of dress—flowing gowns, turbans, amulets, and silver nail polish—generated as much attention as her unconventional poetry, and she became a sought-after subject of painters and photographers.

During the 1920's, Sitwell's linguistic experimentations gave way to poems reflecting her moral, social, and political concerns. The long piece *Gold Coast Customs,* which draws a parallel between African rituals and the corruption of the British aristocracy, was among the most successful of these works. In the following decade, however, Sitwell abandoned poetry and began writing prose in order

to support herself and Helen Rootham, who had been diagnosed with cancer. *I Live Under a Black Sun,* Sitwell's only novel, is based on the life of Jonathan Swift and chronicles his relationships with his lifelong companion, Stella, and a young woman, Vanessa, with whom he fell in love. The narrative structure is considered experimental because of Sitwell's shift from Swift's era to the early twentieth century and her juxtaposition of biographical and fictitious elements. This technique was frequently faulted as awkward and ineffective, but Sitwell's celebration of nature and exploration of the tragedies of war were lauded for being powerful and insightful. During this period Sitwell also produced numerous biographical works, including *Alexander Pope, Victoria of England,* and *The Queens of the Hive.* While these volumes were extremely popular among the general readership, they were later castigated by critics for lack of research, unoriginal material, and questionable psychological analyses. In *Aspects of Modern Poetry,* an influential collection of criticism in Great Britain, Sitwell expounds her theory of poetry, and praises such poets as William Butler Yeats, T. S. Eliot, and Ezra Pound. *Aspects of Modern Poetry* is also noted for its harsh commentary on those critics and poets Sitwell considered her "enemies" due to their negative assessments of her work.

In 1938, Sitwell met and fell in love with Pavel Tchelitchew, a surrealist painter. Although their relationship was complicated by Tchelitchew's homosexuality, they maintained a close friendship for over twenty years and Sitwell became Tchelitchew's primary subject and patron. Following Rootham's death and the outbreak of World War II, Sitwell returned to verse with the acclaimed volumes *Green Song* and *Street Songs,* which solidified her standing as a major figure in the British literary community. During the 1950s, she received an honorary degree from Oxford University and was created a Dame commander of the Order of the British Empire. At this time, Sitwell's religious beliefs also intensified, and in 1955 she was received into the Roman Catholic Church.

Sitwell's first volumes of poetry, *The Mother and Other Poems, Twentieth-Century Harlequineade,* and *Clowns' Houses,* draw upon nursery rhymes and the Italian *commedia dell' arte* to evoke the exoticism in gardens, clowns, maids, and mandolin music. Critics generally regarded the poems of these collections as artificial, but a few detected an admirable strain of rhythmic and tonal experimentalism that was given full expression in *Façade.* Sitwell described the poems of this collection as "[abstract] patterns in sound." Their phonetic novelty as well as Sitwell's unorthodox choice and association of images baffled or infuriated many reviewers, yet *Façade* aroused much needed attention toward revolutionary trends then emerging in poetry generally associated with Modernism. Critics were more receptive to her ensuing verse, which largely abandoned the linguistic oddities of *Façade* in favor of a more romantic, elegiac style. In the collections *Bucolic Comedies, Troy Park,* and *Rustic Elegies,* Sitwell frequently recalls both the enchanting and stultifying aspects of her childhood at Renishaw Hall.

In *Gold Coast Customs* Sitwell uses several elements of her experimental verse to link the violent funeral customs of the African Ashanti nation to the debauchery of a British matron and her social circle. The poem's vivid imagery, convulsive rhythms, and moral tenor have led critics to rank it among Sitwell's most successful works. Her political and social awareness resurfaced in *Street Songs* and *The Green Song and Other Poems.* Written in response to the devastation of World War II, the pieces in these collections express hope for spiritual rebirth as they lament humanity's drive toward self-destruction. "Still Falls the Rain," "Night and Dawn," and "Serenade" are considered among the most memorable poems of the war period, as is *The Shadow of Cain,* a book-length piece concerning Hiroshima and the horror of the nuclear age. The poems of Sitwell's later years reflect her renewed Christian faith as well as her growing perception of herself as a poet-philosopher—in her words "the golden woman grown old"—whose personal losses and feeling for the suffering of others has afforded her a transcendent wisdom. As evidenced in the poems of *The Canticle of the Rose* and *Gardeners and Astronomers,* Sitwell combined Christian and mythological symbols with images from nature to celebrate what she deemed the eternal beauty that exists beyond the evil of the physical world.

Sitwell was in the process of completing her autobiography, *Taken Care Of,* when she died of heart failure in 1964. Glenway Westcott called this work "a set of remembrances and reflections, loosely connected in several categories: sorrowful early home life, portrait sketches, [and] a few slight diatribes." Most critics, however, consider much of this volume a vindictive discourse on two writers Sitwell disdained—D. H. Lawrence and Wyndham Lewis. After describing Lawrence as "a plaster gnome on a toadstool," Sitwell went on to admonish *Lady Chatterley's Lover* for being worthless and obscene. Although cynical and bitter in tone, *Taken Care Of* provides insights into Sitwell's poetic theory and structural techniques.

Sitwell's career has undergone much reevaluation through the years. In light of her eccentric personality and literary friendships, several critics reinforced F. R. Leavis's early estimation that Sitwell belongs "to the history of publicity rather than poetry." However, others regard her as a formidable figure in the development of twentieth-century English poetry. Dilys Powell asserted: "The fact remains that she was one of the writers who bridged the gap between the sterile years of the early war and the post-war years of excited experiment; that she helped keep interest in poetry alive when it was near extinction." Her vivid imagery, linguistic innovation, and commitment to a deeply spiritual worldview place Sitwell among the most original and inventive poets of her time.

(See also *CLC,* Vols. 2, 9; *Contemporary Authors,* Vols. 9-12, rev. ed.; *Dictionary of Literary Biography,* Vol. 20; and *Poetry Criticism,* Vol. 3.)

PRINCIPAL WORKS

POETRY

The Mother and Other Poems 1915
Twentieth-Century Harlequinade and Other Poems [with Osbert Sitwell] 1916
Clowns' Houses 1918
The Wooden Pegasus 1920
Façade 1922
Bucolic Comedies 1923
The Sleeping Beauty 1924
Troy Park 1925
Elegy on Dead Fashion 1926
Rustic Elegies 1927
Gold Coast Customs 1929
Collected Poems 1930
Five Variations on a Theme 1933
Selected Poems 1937
Poems Old and New 1940
Street Songs 1942
The Song of the Cold 1945
Green Song & Other Poems 1946
The Shadow of Cain 1947
The Canticle of the Rose: Selected Poems 1920-1947 1949; also published as *The Canticle of the Rose: Poems 1917-1949* [revised edition], 1949

Façade and Other Poems, 1920-1935   1950
Poor Men's Music   1950
Selected Poems   1952
Collected Poems   1954; enlarged edition, 1957
Gardeners and Astronomers   1955
The Outcasts   1962;   also published as *Music and Ceremonies* [enlarged edition], 1963
Selected Poems of Edith Sitwell   1965

OTHER

Poetry and Criticism   (criticism)   1925
Alexander Pope   (biography)   1930
Bath   (social history)   1932
The English Eccentrics   (social history)   1933; revised and enlarged, 1957
Aspects of Modern Poetry   (criticism)   1934
Victoria of England   (biography)   1936
I Live Under a Black Sun   (novel)   1937
*A Poet's Notebook   (criticism)   1943
Fanfare for Elizabeth   (biography)   1946
*A Notebook on William Shakespeare   (criticism)   1948
The Queens of the Hive   (biography)   1962
Taken Care Of   (autobiography)   1965

*These works were published as *A Poet's Notebook* in 1950.

Edmund Gosse

The verse of Miss Edith Sitwell has been before the public for about a dozen years. At all events I became conscious of it in 1915, when a thin grey pamphlet arrived from Oxford, containing five short pieces of a tentative character. In these there was nothing to startle or to scandalise; they were accomplished exercises owing not a little to the study of Shelley. Only the final one, the fierce and tender denunciation by a mother's ghost of the son who has murdered her for her gold, had a certain individuality. Miss Sitwell then became a contributor, during four seasons, to one of those friendly miscellanies in which talent which cannot find individual outlet makes a collective appeal for attention. In *Wheels,* as this medley was called, for 1916, a piece entitled **"Gaiety"** gave the careful reader an impression of something new intelligently attempted.

Next year, this sensation was emphatically increased by **"The Satyr in the Periwig."** The advantages of a social miscellany are great at the outset of a career, but they turn after a while into disadvantages, and Miss Edith Sitwell was wise to sever her connection with *Wheels* and to publish her selected poems in an independent volume as **Clowns' Houses** in 1918. Such are the short and simple annals of this author's early career from a bibliographical point of view, but they give no hint of the hubbub which the verses themselves have continued to awaken, nor of the passions they have roused in critical bosoms.

The central instinct which drove Miss Sitwell into metrical expression was, I presume, a sense of the need she had of escaping from boredom. She found herself stifled in a literary atmosphere where almost every human being,

even every boy and girl at a board school, could exhale what was called "decent poetry." The torpor of style pressed upon the whole generation; she saw no great fixed stars, but a Milky Way. She felt an irrepressible desire to introduce fresh emotion, and above all to divest words of their traditional value. She deprecated the modern excessive cultivation of logic; she proposed to herself to be preposterous and prodigious. Her imagination was fantastic, and it expressed itself naturally in unfamiliar terms. In a moment I may return to the historical aspect of this attitude of mind, which gave her early critics a great deal of needless solicitude.

While being thus true to her own nature, however, she did not escape the temptation to be *outré* and extravagant. I do not think that in future years she will look back upon the highly entertaining little volume called **Façade** (why not "Façade"?) as doing full justice to the seriousness of her purpose. The reviewers wished to blaspheme, and here she laid herself out with liberality to collect their curses. She wrote "Long steel grass, the white soldiers pass," and the critics went simply off their heads. Nothing stimulates the Muses so much as persecution, and no doubt Miss Sitwell has been appreciated sooner than she would have been had she not so wilfully laid herself open to attack. Moreover, she is "ever a fighter," and evidently enjoys the fray. But fortunately she has not been willing to satisfy her ambition by a mere ebullience of eccentricity, and her later writings have shown her to be detained no longer by the pleasant exercise of putting out a defiant tongue at her enemies. **The Sleeping Beauty** displayed a development of style which is more than confirmed by **Rustic Elegies.** Miss Edith Sitwell has only to cease being a mere "grotesque" for her poetry to become an important factor in our current literature.

Less than justice is done to Miss Sitwell's talent by those who insist on the harlequin element in her verse. By quoting extreme examples of her mannerism, it is easy to represent her as nothing better than a mountebank, screaming for personal attention without having seriously deserved it. This is entirely unfair both to her theory and practice, but it is encouraged by her admirers when they thrust upon us such extravagant pieces as the too-familiar scene of the Bishop eating his ketchup in presence of "the flunkeyed and trumpetting sea." I am ready to admit that it would be easy and entertaining to justify this and many other slightly perverse examples of a system that is pushed beyond the borders of wisdom. Of the so-called **Bucolic Comedies** of 1923 there are many which will, in all probability, lose their strangeness and ultimately prove as acceptable as many of the recognised poems of the past.

But in order that they should do so it is essential that their author, by the development of her powers, should justify readers of the next generation in returning with indulgence to her early poems. If Miss Sitwell were not prepared to advance beyond, let us say, the giddy bravura of "Beelzebub called for his syllabub," we should have to confess that, amusing as her impromptus were (I adore "Beelzebub and his syllabub"), they had in them no quality of permanence. When we had laughed once or twice at the sheer audacity of them, there would be an end of it.

But if we find their author, without resigning her ambition, rising to more serious matters, with greater skill, then we not merely appreciate her advance, but we learn to look back upon her experiments and find a new value in them. In short, we make of the author what she contrives to make of herself.

In this spirit I invite a candid reader to examine **Rustic Elegies** with an open mind, and without prejudice for or against the lady's previous productions. The book is formed by a group of three very elaborate and artificial studies in lyrical satire, all composed with extreme and sometimes finicking minuteness by a writer who pretends to have a contempt for art, but who is to her most diminutive finger-tip an artist and nothing but an artist. The opening poem is the best which Miss Sitwell has yet published—the most coherent, the most articulate—and we therefore do her no injustice if we examine it. **"Elegy on Dead Fashion"** is a sustained piece of some 500 verses, dealing, as in a vision, with the mental and social peculiarities of the much-discussed Victorian Age. If the publication of Lady Augusta Stanley's "Letters" had preceded it, **"Dead Fashion"** might have been taken as a commentary on that special revelation of the period of crinoline.

But in Miss Sitwell's picture Windsor melts into a vaporous landscape by Watteau, disguised as Winterhalter:

> The nymphs are dead like the great summer
>   roses;
> Only an Abyssinian wind dozes:
> Cloyed with late honey are his dark wings'
>   sheens;
> Yet once on those lone crags nymphs bright as
>   queens,
>
> Walked with elegant footsteps through light
>   leaves
> Where only elegiac air now grieves,
> For the light leaves are sere, and whisper dead
> Echoes of elegances lost and fled. . . .
>
> One wood-nymph wore a deep black velvet bon-
>   net
> With blackest ivy leaves for wreaths upon it,
> Shading her face as lovely as the fountains
> While she descended from deep-wooded moun-
>   tains.

The quietness of these verses may conceal from those who have welcomed Miss Sitwell most joyously in her megaphonic moods the fact that the essentials of her style remain unchanged. Another dip into the same lucky bag:

> Beside the Alps of sea, each crinoline
> Of muslin and of gauze and grenadine,
> Sweeps by the Mendelssohnian waterfall,
> O'er beaver-smooth grass, by the castle wall,
>
> Beside the thick mosaic of the leaves.
> Left by the glamour of some huger eves
> The thick gold spangles on those leaves are seen
> Like the sharp twanging of a mandoline.

We shall be greatly lacking in ingenuity if we permit these lines to leave no definite impression on the mind. The difficulties they present are of a kind which incessantly present themselves in the poetry of Miss Sitwell, and which claim intelligent appreciation. Whether she always succeeds or not, her aim is apparent, namely to extend the range of impressions produced by words without losing essential beauty. The employment of images taken from dress, from personal adornment, from objects of common use, is in direct opposition to the restriction of poetic language insisted upon by the Romantics; it recurs to the practice of the seventeenth century, when it was considered poetic to describe the trees in winter as "periwigg'd" with snow. Hence, into an elegy wholly sentimental and pensive are abundantly introduced such epithets as "swan-skin" for strawberry-leaves, while Artemis shoots her arrows through greenhouses of vegetable marrows, and Psyche pines away, a kitchen-maid.

The Wordsworthians saw Nature in dim and Ossianic forms, released from the garnishing of everyday life; to Miss Sitwell the foreground is crossed by dream-figures in crinolines symbolical of 1850, which carry baskets of velvet nectarines over trellised mountain-bridges. The use of words is consistent with this defiance of the old poetic formulas. The wind is "dark-winged" and wines are "plumed as birds of paradise"; the rain falls in "gauze ribbands"; wild cherries "sing their madrigals." These extensions of the significance of words produce an odd effect for the moment, but they never seem, when they fulfill their purpose, to obscure the poet's symbolic intention, and until they do that, I see no reason why we should allow them to annoy us. I ask that literature should give me pleasure; I do not dictate to writers by what route they shall approach me.

The second piece in **Rustic Elegies** is called **"The Hambone and the Heart."** Rabelais tells us that Panurge was born of the loves of a ham and a bottle, but Miss Sitwell is not inclined towards anything Pantagruelist. She tells, or hints, a story of recurrent tragedy, and she writes it with the image of a screaming clown, brandishing a hambone in one hand and a human heart in the other. **"Prelude to a Fairy Tale"** seems to open with a first draught of **"Elegy on Dead Fashion,"** and this impression is deepened by the recurrence of marked phrases from that poem. For instance, the strawberry plants have "swan-skin" leaves, and even the pool a "swan-skin" surface. I do not quite perceive what merit resides in the couplet,

> the hot wind, that little Savoyard,
> Decked them with wild flowers à la montagnard,

but I am quite sure that we do not need to find it repeated three times in one slender volume. Indeed, my main quarrel with Miss Sitwell is not that she uses violent and grotesque imagery, as she has a perfect right to do, but that she does not perceive that to recommend such extraordinary innovations as she projects, her *technique* should be faultless. This it is as yet far from being. She can write verse of exact and poignant beauty, but her ear must be defective, or she would not allow so many sudden deviations from rhythm to disturb her serious verse. This defect also seems to be passing, and she has written nothing more mellifluous than the six final stanzas of **"Elegy on Dead Fashion."** Yet, even here, it is strange that she should permit the dislocated syntax of the couplet "How day rolls down" to pass unamended.

An extraordinary mixture of sensitiveness and bravado

marks Miss Sitwell's attitude towards the art she cultivates, and makes it extremely difficult to estimate the value of her writing. She seems as though at any moment she might break out into exquisite music, but is held back by a crochety dryness of voice, an invasion of the bull-frog into the domain of the nightingale. The main charge brought by indignant reviewers against her verse, namely, that it indulges in analogies preposterously borrowed from senses which are in no æsthetic relation (the "creaking" of light, "blunt stalactites" of rain, the "sour, unripe" wind), has no point for the student of literature, who has only to recollect Blake, Calderon, Donne, and even Shakespeare to see how daringly poets in rebellion against convention have renewed their surface by violent sensorial innovations. Nothing is forbidden to an experimenter, except failure. If Miss Sitwell does not produce the impression she aims at, her practice must be condemned, and not her theory. It would take me too far afield to explain why in certain cases, in spite of her daring and skill, she fails to hit the bull's-eye. Perhaps the reckless acrobatism of Laforgue has been something of a snare to her. But she has no need of spangled tights and a trapeze. She is full of talent and ambition, and the one thing (so it seems to me) which she lacks to carry out her vocation to the full is a firmer instinct for sober and delicate technical precision. I would have her aim relentlessly at being less funny and more human. (pp. 255-61)

> *Edmund Gosse, "Miss Sitwell's Poems," in his* Leaves and Fruit, *William Heinemann Ltd., 1927, pp. 253-61.*

Desmond Shawe-Taylor

When Miss Sitwell was born the nine Muses clubbed together and presented her with a lovely big paint-box. "There!" they said: "that will do from all of us; we're hard up at the moment, and we can't help it if people think us mean." But the paints were so varied and so brilliant that nobody dreamt of calling them mean: least of all Miss Sitwell. Far from it. When she grew up she used her paint-box to the most admirable purpose. Her poetry was so crammed with scintillating colour that everybody was dazzled and delighted. Her world was bright as a seedman's packet, it was full of parrot-hued fruits and maroon parasols, even the dim distance was as blue as the Marquis of Bristol's coat; while over all shone perpetually—for there is no dull weather in Sitwell-land—the enormous and gold-rayed rustling sun. In her glittering verse, which bore a clear (and welcome) resemblance to the post-war décors of the Russian Ballet, we all splashed happily, and only the wise old fogeys could be heard murmuring that, like a weaker Monet, it was more remarkable for colour than for form or substance. Then Miss Sitwell dropped poetry, and applied herself to such sober (if decorative) topics as Bath and Queen Victoria. *Nec caelum, nec animum:* in between the massive quotations all the old scenery kept reappearing, like the backcloths in a touring opera company; no matter where we were, we had the fruits, the dew, the parasols, the crinolined waterfalls, and the great gold suns. We began to grow tired of that paint-box.

Her first novel, [*I Live Under a Black Sun*], is based upon

the story of Swift, Stella and Vanessa; and now at any rate it might be supposed that she would break new ground. The very first paragraph dashes our hopes; it appeared that once more she was only anxious, like her brother, to "create opportunities for the kind of writing that comes easiest" to her. Easy come, easy go. She can turn out—and has turned out—stuff like that first paragraph by the yard:

> Through the forest of white damson trees with the constellations of sharp and of soft flower-stars and of dew falling upon their hair and brushing their lips, with the oceans of flower smells and of light lapping about them, two young people were walking hand in hand. The airs were green among the branches, and you felt that the forest stretched for ever, far beyond this spring and the song of birds.

The Foreword tells us that, while the author has "drawn copiously upon the works and letters of Jonathan Swift," "not only the details of that story, but also the framework, have been changed." The changes are considerable, the most important being that the story is transferred to modern times. I am not clear why Miss Sitwell did this; was her purpose similar to that of the Shakespeare in Modern Dress producer? It was certainly a self-denying decision: she is at home in the eighteenth century, whereas I cannot see that the contemporary setting (or as much of it as may be descried through the jewelled veil of her words) helps to elucidate that classic and extraordinary tale.

Jonathan Swift becomes Jonathan Hare; Stella, Anna Marton; Esther Vanhomrigh, Esther Vanelden; and the mysterious triangle works itself out in a manner that would be fairly interesting were we not distracted by kaleidoscopic scenery and occasional misfits: the stylistic gulf between the words put into the mouth of Hare-Swift and the original letters, quoted almost without alteration, is widened by the retention of such phrases as: "To be frank, unless the Government sends for me, I have no intention of ever seeing England again." How often are country clergymen sent for by the Government in these days? The story is further weakened by an elaborate below-stairs sub-plot, and the second chapter plunges us into a bombing outrage on a mysterious "Governor"—an episode whose only apparent connection with the story is remote. Although the final section of the book paints approaching madness with some power, the whole thing must, I fear, be relegated to the category of the ill-conceived. Miss Sitwell is a delightful poet, but she is decidedly not a novelist.

> *Desmond Shawe-Taylor, in a review of "I Live Under a Black Sun," in* The New Statesman & Nation, *Vol. 14, No. 345, October 2, 1937, p. 491.*

The Times Literary Supplement

In a foreword to [*I Live Under a Black Sun*], her first novel, Miss Sitwell explains that it "is founded upon the story of Jonathan Swift, Stella and Vanessa. But not only the details of the story, but also the frame-work, have been changed." One major change is that of period, for the story is set in the twentieth century, and includes the European War. Otherwise it follows, under various pseudonyms, the broad outline of Swift's career and of his relationship with Stella and Vanessa. Accompanying the story of Swift is the story of Susan Daw, a gardener's daughter whose lover is killed in the War, who runs away from home and after many vicissitudes marries the German who killed him, and at length finds employment in Anna's (Stella's) household in Ireland.

The book is very uneven. Miss Sitwell's prose, overburdened with startling similes and metaphors, gives the early part of the story the unreality of a fairy-tale, an unreality which is increased by the alteration of period. The general impression, perhaps deliberate, is of no period in particular. There is something of the eighteenth century, for there are passages from Swift's works and correspondence which bring their own associations; and something of the twentieth, for there are references to railways and taxicabs and ragtime. But there has necessarily to be a good deal of vagueness and evasion in describing what is going on in this mixed world; and it is perhaps for this reason that Swift, who was so intimately involved in the affairs of his day, remains, as Jonathan Hare, an unsubstantial, half legendary figure throughout most of the book. We see him through the eyes of others, and learn of him by report, but his immediate life is seldom before us. He is a shadow by comparison with several minor characters, such as Sir Henry Rotherham, Miss Mintley, Susan Daw's father, Mr. Debingham and Mrs. Vanelden. There is something eccentric about all these characters, and Miss Sitwell is adept in the presentation of eccentricity: verbal fancy is here related to its subject, and succeeds. The passages describing London from the beggar's point of view are also admirable, for reality here is indeed the substance of nightmare; and it is significant that it is only towards the end, when the horror of madness is already upon him, that Jonathan begins to emerge as a tangible creature. The closing chapters are perhaps the best in the book.

Miss Sitwell's implied explanation of Swift's attitude towards Stella is that he knew madness lay in wait for him, and therefore would not bring their intimacy to its normal conclusion; though, at the same time, it was vital that he should have someone to believe in him and submit to him without question. This assumption gives the story of Jonathan Hare a perfectly logical development; but it leaves unsolved the enigma suggested by the life and work of Jonathan Swift. A solution was perhaps no part of Miss Sitwell's intention—her book is not, after all, a Life of Swift. That is another and a stranger story.

> *"Jonathan Swift Returns," in* The Times Literary Supplement, *No. 1861, October 2, 1937, p. 713.*

William Soskin

Miss Edith Sitwell's fancy has found a focus in and about eighteenth century England in a number of her recent, most excellent works. She has projected her hypersensitive imagination into a study of the work of Alexander Pope. She has made a ceremonious and satiric study of the city of Bath and its social whirls. She has come now, [with *I*

> "The world I see is a country world, a universe of growing things, where magic and growth are one . . . a world of rough, fruitful suns, and the age of the innocence of man . . . At other moments, as a contrast to this world, one of heavy, brutish darkness."
>
> *Sitwell, from her* "Notes on My Own Poetry," *(1930).*

Live Under a Black Sun], on the most modern man of the era and, in a sense, the most difficult patient for biographical surgery—Jonathan Swift.

Miss Sitwell has not attempted to tread or even skip lightly where others have marked out a biographical road to the tragic Dean. A number of British writers have applied modern psychological formulae to Swift in recent years, with highly sensational but unrewarding results. The most thorough study of the man is contained in Ricardo Quintana's biography, *Swift*. The most rounded, humane account combined with an expertly just literary estimate is to be found in Carl Van Doren's biography. But Miss Sitwell has gone beyond conventional studies and histories, to a consideration of the personal tragedy involved in Swift's extraordinary relationship with Stella and Vanessa; and she has found herself so intricately caught in the web of masochistic emotion, in the abnormalities and intensities of their passions, that she has chosen to write a novel rather than a biography, a poetic novel which frees her immediately from the meaningless and cumbersome obligations involved in the more official biographical form.

Usually the fictional reconstructions of history undertaken by modern romantic novelists are outrageous costume-dramas in which character and genuine dramatic motives are buried under avalanches of Egad! and Forsooth! Miss Sitwell has quite daringly transcended all such ungainly nonsense, probing straightway to the core of the problem and translating that drama into significant modern terms. Indeed, there is no indication that her story of Jonathan "Hare" and the lovely Anna, who is Stella, and the pathetic Essie Vanelden, who is Vanessa, is not laid in a present day setting.

The horrible world of stinking men who tortured Swift's olfactory sense and choked him, the mobs of infected human beings, hulks of emptiness swaying their mammoth bellies and hiding the Nothingness in their hearts, are certainly as revolting today as they were in Swift's time. The Ireland that gossiped and swirled with rumors and slander about Swift and Stella is surely not greatly altered in these matters. The London of that era, despite the best efforts of the Boswellians and coffee-house school of criticism to make it seem more polished and courtly than the present age, was probably no more worldly than the London of Anthony Eden. Swift, one realizes, might very well have lived today with his literary and philosophic points of view readily applicable. And Miss Sitwell therefore violates no proprieties in transferring her hero to the 1930's.

Beyond the consideration of Swift as a sensible actor in modern society, there are further assets in Miss Sitwell's device. She has thought of young Jonathan Swift, who even in his youthful romances knew the odor of mortality rising from the most beautiful woman, as a man who could not possibly endure normal love. He conceived of womanhood as a terrible creative force, a gross symbol of Nature that was willing to destroy all previous life and forms of creation in order that it might create.

Miss Sitwell makes due recognition of the physical facts of Swift's life that seemed to explain his constant communion with death and his refusal to make a normal, acknowledged marriage out of his life with Stella. Jonathan watches the slow disintegration of his father—the dizziness and the paralysis and the eventual insanity—and he realizes that he is doomed to a similar fate by a similar process of degeneration. It is not hard to understand, then, why the reality of his life is destroyed, why he loves ghosts of women rather than women.

In the flush of his greatness and the sweep of his literary success Jonathan finds temporary surcease from his agony in the disastrous flirtation with little Vanessa. This must have been the most difficult of Miss Sitwell's problems in the composition of the novel—this making a reality of the friendship between the fragile, childlike girl and the older, brilliant, hard man who lets his defenses down to bask in the delicately warming light of her love. So subtly is the crescendo negotiated—from a curious fascination on the girl's part to a flight of vanity, to an awakening of love, to a feverish pursuit of the man who flees when he senses flesh-and-blood passion, to a hysterical martyrdom and a thirst for vengeance which leads Essie to destroy Jonathan's marriage—that the fantastic unreality of the actual, biographical truth is effectively destroyed.

It is hard to believe in Jonathan's mental integrity during the struggle between Essie and Anna and during his deceitful concealment of his feeling about each of the women—but Miss Sitwell has so thorough and sympathetic an understanding of Jonathan's hardest, most cruel impulses and so great an admiration for his relentless philosophy, that she carries us along with her. She is merciless to the women of the story; yet she pictures their pitiable defeats with carefully contrived heart-break, poetically effective and never trite. Essie, for example, when she is finally faced with Jonathan's determination to be rid of her, remembers

> a small dog she had seen once in the city—a little untidy dog running through the streets between crowds of tall, remote people, looking piteously and imploringly up in each face as he passed. He would never again find anyone whose face he knew, or whose voice he knew and who would speak to him kindly. His master has lost him on purpose . . . and now he would go on running forever, until his feet were worn to shreds, he would lie down in the unfriendly night under the

shadow of a doorway or a railway arch, perhaps, or in the yet more uncaring air, and he would steal a bit of food here, a bit there, out of dustbins. But then would come a day, and then another, when he could find nothing to steal, and when he would be too worn out and bewildered by that endless running through the streets, that search for his master . . .

Parallel with the story of Swift, Stella and Vanessa in this novel, Miss Sitwell has told another story that seems to touch the biographical drama only accidentally. It follows the plight of a young girl, Susan, who runs away from home when her lover goes to war, who tramps the mean streets of London like a hungry bottom-dog in a universe of beggars. It is the world of which Swift wrote, when he watched from the continent of darkness: "A child just dropt from its dam, may be supported by her milk for a solar year with little other nourishment . . . which the mother may get . . . or the value in scrap; by her lawful occupation of begging . . . A young healthy child well-nursed is at a year old a most delicious, nourishing and wholesome food . . . "

Eventually Susan finds employment as a maid, and then she drifts to the grave of her lover who has been killed in action. There she meets a German who has come to pray at the grave of the man he had killed in battle. His own life has been ruined by the war and the senseless hatred of statesmen. When he murdered on the field of battle he achieved some sort of transfiguration that made him know all men were equally guilty, equally pitiable, "small creatures afraid of the darkness, yet pulling it down upon our world."

The inclusion of this allegorical story will probably puzzle readers. But there is nothing obscure about Miss Sitwell's purpose. The blackness and the death-like scene of her modern story of Susan is an effective modern echo in social terms, of the similar blackness and sterility involved in Swift's individual fate.

It is a tribute to the intelligence of the author's pattern and to its effectiveness, that both stories can exist within the single volume. In the end she makes the purpose of the dual drama overwhelmingly clear, for she leaves Swift dying in his chair, the crumbs of bread which he often fed to a pet mouse fallen to the floor. As Swift dies, the mice in the house fight for the feast. "The civilization of mice, upheld by war, was being made safe for posterity. Rather than share the piece of bread that had fallen from the giant's hand, they were willing to be wiped out. Squealing and shrieking among the dust, they rushed to destroy each other."

There are no adjectives to describe the darkness of this novel, its pity and its terror. Miss Sitwell proves that her icy delicacy can achieve more than the violent onslaughts, the tumult and shouting of the large-scale propaganda novelists.

William Soskin, "Novel on Jonathan Swift," in New York Herald Tribune Books, *February 27, 1938, p. 4.*

Maurice Bowra

With the publication of *Street Songs* in 1942 and *Green Song* in 1944, Miss Edith Sitwell has not only won an almost unique place for herself among the poets of this war but abundantly fulfilled the highest hopes which her admirers have had of her. This great flowering of her genius is her reward for years of devoted and patient labour at her art. From her first beginnings she possessed an instinctive sense for the true essence of poetry and a sensibility so fine and delicate that it can detect all the subtle echoes and associations which float round the sounds of human speech. She set herself a hard task when she made up her mind to restore to English poetry the richness of texture which had been largely lost in the Edwardian and Georgian epochs. For this reason much of her early work was experimental. She experimented with rhythms, with the values of vowels and consonants, with new kinds of imagery and with unaccustomed themes. Of this preparatory work, in many ways so brilliant and so fascinating, she is herself a stern critic. When she published her *Collected Poems* in 1930, she omitted many pieces that others would wish to be included. But she had her own good reasons. She was content only with her best work; the rest was experimental and must be excluded. Yet even in this remarkable volume she had not found the full range of her gifts. Though *The Sleeping Beauty* showed of what enchanting fancy and haunting melody she was capable and *Gold Coast Customs* showed what tragic power and prophetic fury were hers, it was not until the Second World War that she fused all her different gifts into a single kind of poetry and combined in noble harmony her delicate fancy, her uncommon visual sense, her tender sympathy, her heroic courage in the face of a shattered world and her deep religious trust in the ultimate goodness of life.

In these two latest volumes Miss Sitwell has brought her technique to perfection. Her verse moves with unfailing ease and flexibility. She has so mastered its intricacies that it seems to respond without effort to any demands that her changing moods may make of it, to be equally effective in long, rolling lines or in the brief tune of a song. Her rhymes come so easily that we hardly notice them, though they make their essential contribution to the final, musical result. Her vocabulary, which looks so unpretentious, has been purified and published by long, discriminating selection. When she permits herself an unusual word, such as 'pyromaniacs' or 'ombrelle,' it comes with all the greater effect because of the simplicity of its surroundings. But the central triumph of this art is that Miss Sitwell has succeeded in her first aim of restoring its texture to poetry. Her work is first and always poetry and makes its chief appeal to the imagination through the ear and the inner eye. There is no padding, no hackneyed phraseology, no attempt to cover imprecision of thought or feeling by vague, vast words, no lapse into unimaginative flatness or lifeless echoes from other poets. The subtly varying rhythms respond with exquisite tact to the movements of the poet's sensibility. Each word is chosen with a keen appreciation of its sound-values. It would be pleasant to dilate on almost any verse in this poetry and to show what consummate skill has gone to its creation. An example, taken at random, must suffice:

> And with them come gaps into listening darkness:
> The Gun-men, the molochs, the matadors, man-eaters,
> Hiding in islands of loneliness, each one
> Infections of hatred, and greed-plague, and fear.

The half-concealed alliterations, the occasional monosyllables, like 'gaps' and 'fear,' placed with so powerful an emphasis, the grating sound of such words as 'molochs' and 'greed-plague,' the rise of the whole verse to a crisis of emotion, the imaginative precision with which the different powers of destruction are chosen and named, all these are the fruits of a technique so accomplished that it never asserts itself or attracts our attention. The result, clean and direct and powerful, shows no traces of its workshop and merely makes us feel how impressively and nobly Miss Sitwell writes.

This perfected technique is used to convey experiences of tragic grandeur and intensity. Miss Sitwell is a seer, a prophetess. Just as in *Gold Coast Customs* she denounced the hideous emptiness and bestiality of modern life, so now she sees with anguish and torment the devastation wrought by the war. Though the years have brought her patience and detachment, and though she no longer feels herself an active figure on the human stage, she responds with all the warmth of her compassionate heart to the carnage and desolation round her and shows what they mean to her, what wounds they have dealt to her and with what vision and courage she has sought an answer to the ugly questions which they raise. In **"Green Flows the River of Lethe-O"** she tells of the spiritual journey on which she has gone. Once she tried to stand apart from the empty frivolities of the world, but something inside her took control and turned her to another road:

> I was Annihilation
> Yet white as the Dead Sea, white as the Cities
> of the Plains.
> For I listened to the noontide and my veins
> That threatened thunder and the heart of roses.
> I went the way I would—
> But long is the terrible Street of the Blood
> That had once seemed only part of the summer
> redness:
> It stretches for ever, and there is no turning
> But only fire, annihilation, burning.

It is of this 'Street of the Blood' that Miss Sitwell now writes. Blood is her symbol for life, for all that beats in the heart and flows in the veins, that stirs emotions and affections and brings men closer to one another from their separate solitudes. This blood, split so wantonly, becomes a symbol of all that happens to mankind in war, of the sacrifices and the redemption, the penalties and the consolations which rise from the madness of mutual destruction. The seer who tried to stand outside life has been dragged inexorably into it and found herself forced to share in the common human lot. This experience has been an inestimable gain to her. Her natural sympathies have found a full scope for their exercise; her creative gifts have been unified in a new strength and humanity and grandeur.

While Miss Sitwell faces her own lot and losses with an uncomplaining endurance, she is deeply outraged by the sufferings of others, especially of the young. In **"Serenade"** she shows with poignant insight the lot of the young lover who knows that his love is under sentence of death and can never be fulfilled. The horror of such a situation, in which every hope or pleasure is darkened by the imminence of destruction, comes out with strange magnificence in Miss Sitwell's classical octosyllabics, with their ironical echoes of passionate Elizabethan love-songs and their conclusion that the only hope of happiness for such lovers is in the grave. The lover knows that his love-making is little more than a pretence because he can never fulfil his promises to give himself up entirely to his beloved. His heart and mind must always be full of that death which hangs over him and distracts his thoughts:

> And so I love you till die—
> (Unfaithful I, the cannon's mate):
> Forgive my love of such brief span,
> But fickle is the flesh of man,
> And death's cold puts the passion out.
>
> I'll woo you with a serenade—
> The wolfish howls the starving made;
> And lies shall be your canopy
> To shield you from the freezing sky.

Therefore the only offer that he can honestly make is

> Then die with me and be my love.

Miss Sitwell picks up words from Marlowe's "The Passionate Shepherd to his Love" and alters them to a new and terrible significance. Just as the world at war is an inverted, topsy-turvy counterpart of what it has once been, so the modern lover's position is itself inverted. His only prospect is death, and he turns to the thought of it as once lovers turned to the thought of life. Miss Sitwell's tenderness has been deeply wounded by the barbarities of war and finds its outlet in this tragic paradox.

In **"Lullaby"** a similar spirit informs a vision of the levelled, devastated world that lies before modern children. To this Miss Sitwell gives a peculiar power by the myth which holds it together. She imagines that the world has returned to a state of primeval chaos. Its inhabitants are odious monsters. The bombing aeroplane has become a pterodactyl which lays steel eggs in the heart of mother-earth and then fouls its nest; the mother, symbol of the old, lost tenderness and humanity, is dead, and her place is taken by the Babioun, whose very name, taken from Ben Jonson, suggests a monstrous, hideous ape, and who becomes a foster-mother to the orphan child and sings over it a sinister, blood-curdling lullaby. The purport of this song is that the child can look for nothing in the future but a deadly, meaningless, hopeless uniformity, a world in which all distinctions have been obliterated and there is no pleasure in possession or in creation:

> Hear my ragged lullaby,
> Fear not living, fear not chance;
> All is equal—blindness, sight,
> There is no depth, there is no height;
> Do, do.

The poem reflects the mood of despair which many knew in the dark early years of the war when nothing seemed likely to survive the universal destruction, and all the labo-

rious constructions of civilisation looked as if they might perish in the night of blood. Miss Sitwell secures a specially poignant effect by using the form of a lullaby. The refrain of 'Do, do' which the Babioun sings over her foster-child recalls with ironical contrast such delicate lullabies as that of Miss Sitwell's *The Sleeping Beauty:*

> Do, do,
> Princess, do,
> Like a tree that drips with gold you flow
> With beauty ripening very slow.

The form which was so well suited to the atmosphere of an enchanted dream is transferred with powerful effect to a hideous nightmare.

The irony of these two poems reflects the conflict which the war has created in Miss Sitwell. It is her challenge, her defiance to circumstances so malign that she cannot see an end to them, and yet she refuses to admit that they defeat her. It rises from her heroic attempt to understand a world which has apparently lost all order and reason, and it is characteristic of her that what awakes this mood is not her own plight but the plight of others. At times she passes beyond it to a more truly universal outlook, to an embracing, prophetic vision. In **"The Night before Great Babylon"** she gives her poetic account of a world on the edge of destruction. It begins with an evocation of lovers who need nothing but each other and find in their mutual love a complete and satisfying universe. But a wind comes and brings rain. The woman feels safe in the protection of the man, but her trust is soon shown to be an illusion:

> But a wind came tall,
> The wind in his grey knight's armour,
> The wind in his grey night armour—
> And the great gold Sun was slain.
> 'What is the wind that doth blow?
> It is cold, and begins to rain.'
> 'Not only the rain is falling.'

In this apparently simple poem, with its little story of lovers in Babylon and its compelling, evocative imagery, Miss Sitwell conveys the menace of coming doom as it strikes on the self-contained world of human affections. She attempts nothing grandiose or spectacular and relies for her main effect on the contrast between two perfectly chosen events, the young woman rapt in her love and the sudden burst of wind and rain with the unnamed horror that comes with them. The last line of the poem, so simple in its presentation and so rich in imaginative suggestion, catches the moment of transition from the old secure world to the new world of unforseen horror.

The imagery of rain is developed with enormous power in **"Still Falls the Rain,"** which has claims to be the most profound and most moving poem yet written in English about the war. It was inspired by the air-raids of 1940, but it has nothing transitory or merely contemporary about it. It is an intense, highly imaginative and tragic poem on the sufferings of man. The rain which falls in **"The Night Great Babylon"** now realises all the fears that are there held of it had become a real rain of destruction from the sky. Real and horrible enough it is, it has a great metaphysical and symbolical significance. It is an example and a sign of the suffering which man inflicts upon himself, or rather which human depravity inflicts on the innocent human heart. The opening lines show that this new abomination is a kind of crucifixion:

> Still falls the Rain—
> Dark as the world of man, black as our loss—
> Blind as the nineteen hundred and forty nails
> Upon the Cross.

The rain falls impartially on rich, on poor, on just and unjust. All are equal beneath it. It is like the blood which flows from the wounded side of the 'Starved Man,' of the Christ who is in every man, and it comes from the wounds which mankind has dealt to itself:

> The last faint spark
> In the self-murdered heart, the wounds of the
> sad uncomprehending dark,
> The wounds of the baited bear,—
> The blind and weeping bear whom the keepers
> beat
> On his helpless flesh . . . the tears of the hunted
> hare.

Yet this suffering, so hideous and yet in some ways so inevitable and underserved, is not hopeless or irretrievable. The falling blood is like the blood of Christ and brings redemption even to those who have inflicted the wounds. When the dawn comes,

> Then sounds the voice of One who like the heart
> of man
> Was once a child who among beasts has lain—
> 'Still do I love, still shed my innocent light, my
> Blood for thee.'

In the destruction wrought by the air-raids is transformed into an example of man's wickedness and punishment and redemption. He brings his own sufferings upon himself, but through them he may be redeemed. So Miss Sitwell passes beyond the horror of the present moment to a vision of its significance in the spiritual history of man and through her compassion for him finds a ray of hope for his future.

Miss Sitwell understands the war-stricken with more than an ordinary woman's insight. In such a time there are many who feel that the struggle is too much for them and turn with longing to the thought of death. Miss Sitwell knows what they think and enters so naturally into their minds that she seems almost to identify herself with them and to speak on their behalf. From the depths of her compassionate and imaginative soul she knows what this longing for death means and why men and women have it. In **"Spring"** she tells how the lost and the hungry cry out to death as to a fellow outcast who shares their sufferings: in **"Street Song"** she speaks through the lips of those who wish for death because it delivers them from the apes and tigers incarnate in man:

> The holy night of conception, of rest, the consol-
> ing
> Darkness when all men are equal,—the wrong
> and the right
> And the rich and the poor are no longer separate
> nations,—
> They are brothers in night.

But though she understands this longing not only with her head but with her heart, she does not ultimately share it or admit that it is right. In **"Spring"** the cry of the outcasts is answered by the call of the warm earth in spring to forget their misery; in **"Street Song"** the longing for peace and rest is resisted by the intellect or, as Miss Sitwell calls it, the Bone, which doubts the reality of these cries and asks if they are something else:

> Who knows if the sound was that of the dead
> light calling,—
> Of Caesar rolling onward his heart, that stone,
> Or the burden of Atlas falling.

It is possible that the cry is really from the depths of the human heart as some brutal tyranny pursues its relentless way; but is no less possible that the present agony is some little understood process of change in the world. And when such a doubt is present, it is wiser to wait and do nothing. So too in **"One Day in Spring"** Miss Sitwell tells of a man whose wife is dead and who in his sense of irreparable loss believes that he has ceased to love her as he should or as he once did. For him too there is an answer. The love which he once had is not dead. It is born again with each year. In the end the forces of life triumph over those of death, and the most haunting and insistent doubts are dispelled by the warmth of the sun in the spring.

This assertion of positive values in the face of corruption and destruction is fundamental to Miss Sitwell's poetry and gives to it a special coherence and harmony. Against **"Lullaby"** and **"Serenade"** we must set such poems as **"Harvest"** and **"Holiday."** We shall then see how Miss Sitwell passes through the harrowing doubts and despairs of war to a constructive outlook. This outlook is religious. Sometimes she uses the symbols of the Christian faith, in the Crucified whose wounds are on every human hand, in the Holy Ghost who speaks at night 'in the whispering leaves,' in the angels who sing through the earth. But behind this there is something, that is not narrowly or specifically Christian, unless it be a kind of Christian pantheism. For Miss Sitwell the earth is more than the garment of God; it is a manifestation of God himself. In the rebirth of natural forces and the comfort and strength which it brings to man she finds a real display of something unquestionably divine. Just as in her poetry she extends the significance of actual things and events by seeing in them a symbolical significance which reaches into vaster and less familiar spheres, so in her religious beliefs she sees in the physical world not only something powerful and life-giving in itself but the symbol of something else still more powerful and more life-giving. She does not distinguish between the importance of things in themselves and their importance symbolically, because for her this importance is one and the same. The physical world is separated from the spiritual by artificial barriers, and for some the distinction may be meaningless. With her acute and lively senses Miss Sitwell sees in the events of physical nature the manifestations of a spiritual power, and this is the inspiration of her faith and the object of her worship.

An example of this outlook can be seen in Miss Sitwell's treatment of light. Light is an ancient symbol for the dazzling radiance of God and has many implications for the faithful. But the light of which they speak is usually the 'celestial light' which Milton summoned to irradiate his soul. For Miss Sitwell celestial and physical light are one; the sun is a power both in the physical world and in the spirit. It is—

The Sun whose body was split on our fields to bring us harvest, and it is also a divine power which resolves the discords of life and imparts an order to everything:

> to him, the heat of the earth
> And beat of the heart are one,—
> Born from the energy of the world, the love
> That keeps the Golden Ones in their place
>   above,
> And hearts and blood of beasts even in motion.

Just as in spring the sun revives decayed life and creates hope in men and women, so in the spirit something similar happens when 'the Intelligible Light' works its miraculous transformations and turns all to gold. And this identification of the physical with the spiritual is true not only to the intellect but to the heart. The warmth which we receive from the sun in spring, and the sudden burst of hopes and affections which its brings, are not purely physical sensations. In our complex natures body and soul are so intermixed that they cannot ultimately be distinguished, and what affects the one affects the other. That is why in **"Holiday"** Miss Sitwell shows how the whole natural and human scene is transformed by the power of light:

> Beneath the flowering boughs of heaven
> The country roads are made of thickest gold;
> They stretch beyond the world, and light like
>   snow
> Falls where we go, the Intelligible Light
> Turns all to gold, the apple, the dust, the unripe
>   wheat-ear.

And this visible transformation is only part of a greater transformation which affects the human consciousness no less than the countryside. The same power brings men closer to one another, makes men and women fall in love, sanctifies the commonest human feelings, and banishes despair and doubt. This miraculous change can only be called divine, and that is why Miss Sitwell, true to her convictions, associates it with symbols of Christian belief, and shows how—

> the workless hands
> Where the needs of famine have grown the claws
>   of the lion
> Bear now on their palms the wounds of the Cru-
>   cified,

or finds in so simple an act as the gift of a crumb to a starving bird a symbol of the breaking of the Body of Christ.

The depth of these convictions gives a peculiar strength to such a poem as **"How Many Heavens."** Starting from the words of John Donne that 'the Stancarest will needs have God not only to be in everything but to be everything,' Miss Sitwell pursues her own line of thought and tells how her blood responds to the growing grass, as if it were the display of a divine power. Then she tells how she finds God in the flame and the shadow, in the stone, the straw, and the light, and comes to her exalted conclusion:

> He is the sea of ripeness, and the sweet apple's
>   emerald's lore.
> So you, my flame of grass, my root of the world
>   from which all Spring shall grow,
> O you, my hawthorn bough of the stars, now
>   leaning now
> Through the day, for your flowers to kiss, my
>   lips shall know
> He is the core of the heart of love, and He, be-
>   yond labouring seas, our ultimate shore.

The divine power, which is revealed in natural things and through them restores the heart of man, is in the end love. That is why it is a source of healing and of strength, why it sustains men against their blackest misgivings and redeems them from their brutal faults. It is this love for which the poet prays in **"Invocation,"** though it may seem for the moment to be almost beyond her call:

> Now falls the night of the world: O Spirit mov-
>   ing upon the waters
> Your peace instil
> In the animal heat and splendour of the blood.

It is this which in **"Green Song"** blesses all things 'in their poor earthy dress' and makes men conscious of their forgotten faiths and delights and duties. It is this which in **"An Old Woman"** brings comfort to a woman in her old age and makes her see that there is an easy answer to many questions which have troubled her and a consolation for the losses which have been hers. It is this which brings comfort to those who have lost their beauty, their youth, their children, their wives, to the haunted and the hunted, the misfits and the outcasts, the victims of social injustice and of pitiless carnage. Whatever wounds mankind may inflict upon itself, whatever it may suffer from decay and destitution, it can in the end be healed by finding itself in harmony with the powers of nature and with the light and the love that inform them.

This is Miss Sitwell's answer to the dark questions raised by the war. Though in many of the poems she does not refer directly to it and even seems to have dismissed it from her thoughts, it is never really far from her. It raises the problems which she has to solve and it provides the bitter experience of suffering which makes her heart and mind so alert and so quick to understand the agonies of others. Her own conflict has been between the heart and the mind, between the blood and the bone. While her tender heart has drawn her into the storm of human afflictions and tossed her about in their chaos, her mind has wished to keep its distance and its detachment. In **"Heart and Mind"** she suggests that this conflict can never really be ended until the end of the world. Yet she herself has done much to resolve it. Her heart has forced her mind to take note of the sufferings of men and to widen its understanding until beyond the immediate horrors of the present it can see a not impossible future when human sympathies will revive and heal old wounds. It finds even in the destruction of life a means for its redemption. And she herself is perhaps conscious of such a solution. For in **"Song,"** after telling how she has lost her old world and found an empty substitute for it, she concludes:

> For withering my heart, that summer rose,
> Came another heart like a sun,—

And it drank all the dew from the rose, my love,
And the birds have forgotten their song
That sounded all summer long, my dear—
All the bright summer long.

Her new heart, which has withered so much in her, and
robbed her of her old songs, is none the less like a sun and
gives its life and strength to her. (pp. 378-87)

> *Maurice Bowra, "The War Poetry of Edith Sitwell," in* The Cornhill Magazine, *Vol. 161, No. 965, July, 1945, pp. 378-87.*

Sitwell on poetry:

There is a general misapprehension of the aims and of the neccessities of poetry; and this misapprehension has arisen in part from the fact that many respectable persons, but very few poets, are encouraged to write it. The task I have given myself is a dangerous and formidable one; since whatever I say must of its very nature injure the personal susceptibilities, and make evident the lack of sensibility towards poetry, of some of our more eminent bores. This general blighting and withering of the poetic taste is the result of the public mind having been overshadowed by such Aberdeen-granite tombs and monuments as Matthew Arnold. Added to this misfortune, we are now afflicted by the shrill moronic cacklings of the Sur-Realists—laying never so much as an addled egg—and the erotic confidences of rich young ladies, suffering less from an excess of soul than from an excess of distilled spirits. All, or most of these persons, have theories or battle-cries. These theories are all very well in their way, but they do not produce poetry.

> **Sitwell in her introduction to her** Alexander Pope *(1930).*

Stephen Spender

A recent adverse critic of Miss Sitwell's poems quotes Gerard Manley Hopkins catechizing Browning for monstrousness in his use of imagery. Hopkins held "that Browning was 'not really a poet, that he has all the gifts but the one needful and the pearls without the string; rather, one should say raw nuggets and rough diamonds.' His turning of concave into convex" (when he compared heaven in *Instans Tyrranus* to a shield protecting the just man from tyrants) "was a 'frigidity,' an 'Untruth to nature'."

Emboldened by the example of Hopkins, Mr. Geoffrey Grigson quotes examples of "monstrosities," "untruths to nature," in the recent poems of Edith Sitwell. For example,

> . . . bird-blood leaps within our veins
> And is changed to emeralds like the sap in the
>   grass.
>
> And you are the sound of the growth of spring
>   in the
> heart's deep core.
>
> And I would that each hair on my head was an
>   angel

O my red Adam.

O heed him not, my dew with golden feet
Flying from me.

And so on and so on. The list could be added to indefinitely until it includes practically everything that Miss Sitwell has written: because this is her way of writing, and if one can criticize it for not being close to nature then criticism is easy game, and there is little more to be said.

Mr. Grigson, of course, quotes Dryden, to show the kind of consistent parallel development of the interior movement of poetry with the external organic movement of nature, he thinks a poem should contain.

This kind of criticism starts off with an assumption which—despite Hopkins on Browning—should be the conclusion rather than the beginning of an argument. One has only to glance at Shakespeare and take a by no means extreme example from *Hamlet*. One line will do:

> To crook the pregnant hinges of the knee.

Enough to point out that Dryden would not have written this line and that it is difficult to see how Hopkins could have approved of it. When we come to recent poetry, the thought of the Romantics, of Rimbaud, of the Symbolists, the Imagists and the Surrealists should give us pause before we decide that imagery must be true to nature. On the face of it, such an assumption looks like a prejudice which may be held with great fervour by those who prefer one kind of poetry to another. But there is no basis on which the "nature" school can argue that the inventors of an artificial type of imagery do not write poetry.

It is interesting, though, to approach Miss Sitwell's poetry from the side of her imagery. For it is in the development of her imagery that her growth as a poet and as a human being living a spiritual life in her poetry are most apparent. And it is in a study of her imagery that one has the firmest grasp of the experience of life that her poetry does express. Her imagery may not be photographically representative of nature, but it is true to a very real experience.

Basically, Miss Sitwell's imagery is of a kind which one must call artificial. But the development of her poetry has been to infuse ever more observation of society and even of nature, more emotion, more experience into this imagery, which still has a hard clear quality like transparent stone. It is exactly this forcing, as it were, of blood into stone which makes her later poetry so remarkable.

In the early poems, the artificiality is so striking, that in a characteristic passage such as the following, without having to be Mr. Grigson one can see that this is not "like nature":

> At Easter when red lacquer buds sound far slow
> Quarter-tones for the old dead Mikado,
> Through avenues of lime-trees, where the wind
> Sounds like a chapeau chinois, shrill, unkind,—
> The Dowager Queen, a curling Korin wave
> That flows for ever past a coral cave,
> With Dido, Queen of Carthage, slowly drives
> (Her griffin dog that has a thousand lives)
> Upon the flat-pearled and fantastic shore

> Where curled and turbanned waves sigh "Nev-
> ermore,"
> And she is sunk beneath a clear still lake
> Of sleep,—so frail with age she cannot
> wake. . . .

This is a world of artifice kept at a certain distance from nature—a distance which is perhaps measured and indicated by the phrase "red lacquer buds" which is just like and just unlike enough to make one realize that Miss Sitwell's world is real and unreal at the same time. One steps backwards and forwards from the almost-real, the almost-true, to the fantastic and completely artificial. This happens not only on the plane of observation but also on that of feeling. The feelings most often provoked by these early poems are enchantment, humour and pity. The writing is at once sophisticated and very simple, with a simplicity bordering at times almost on the primitive and the childish.

I first read these early poems of Miss Sitwell when I was sixteen. At this time I was enchanted by them and my own early efforts were often their imitators. Later I valued them for lines which still seem to me of a ravishing beauty. . . . (pp. 11-13)

Turning back to these poems again, I am amazed at the consistency of quality with which they are imagined. They create pictures, hard, angular, toy-like, brightly coloured and vividly seen, extremely self-contained, which are unlike any other poetry. There persists through them the personality of the poet which one gets to know well, though one seems to know it in an external way, much as one knows her world from the outside. One knows when she laughs, when she is mercilessly satiric and when she melts with pity, but one does not feel oneself in contact with the very springs of her emotion.

It appears to me that the first quality which one requires of poetry is that it should create. If a poet even creates a few images, a few haunting lines, that is already something. Next one asks that creativeness should be sustained and that there should be a consistency of mood and purpose within a poem, however violent the superficial changes of manner. A poem which has been completely created in detail and as a whole, exists in the mind of the reader as a kind of object, a single impression, like any other remembered experience. And as with other experiences one compares poems and finds that they have qualities which differ from each other, and that some make a profounder impression than others. All the same, once a poem has been accepted as a definite experience, only prejudice can dismiss it by inventing some reason for refusing to examine it seriously.

Miss Sitwell's early poems seem to me, firstly, definitely to be works of art which have been fully created. On the other hand those universal qualities do not go into them which make one turn to them constantly as illuminations which seem to have a living relationship to all the most vital passages of one's life. In a good sense, they are "fashionable," beautifully made and highly idiosyncratic works which one delights in in certain moods but which one does not always want. They are likely, with much other poetry, to go out of fashion and then to be rediscovered again.

The great difference between the early and the later poetry is that in the later poems, the whole inner personality of the poet and a lifetime of experience, have entered. But between the early and the late work, there is a bridge, supplied by the astonishing poem called *Gold Coast Customs* (A poem, by the way, greatly admired by W. B. Yeats, partly perhaps because he also was a poet of fantasy and artifice.).

Gold Coast Customs is a poem in which the ceremonies of a tribe of the Ashantees are juxtaposed with a picture of fashionable party life in civilized countries. It is a commonplace, of course, that all customs are barbaric. But the intensity of vision which is haunted by the insistent connection between the civilized and the barbaric is very rare. For, essentially, to see this connection of the pursuits of a civilization which one is taught to regard as civilised with a so-called barbarous civilization, is essentially to see the mocking shape of barbarity and death under all the pretences and all the aims of all existence, whether in Europe or in Africa.

In *Gold Coast Customs* Miss Sitwell's artificiality is used to new purpose, with astonishing effect. It achieves the synthesis which can place one kind of civilization beside another. The barbaric and the civilized both become slightly unreal within the medium of her manner, and the result is that they become identical. The artifice of *Gold Coast Customs* throws that of the early poems into a new light. One begins to see the sense of artificiality not as something superifically imposed on the poet's experience but as part of her experience of life itself. She is obsessed by the feeling that human behavior is artificial. It is this which gives her fantastic approach to reality its consistency, which is an inner consistency of her whole personality.

In her later work there is a wholeness due partly to the development of her own personality, partly to a deepening of sympathy with the suffering of other people during the recent years of anguish and war. Her poems have at the same time broadened far beyond any personal idiosyncrasies and become more deeply personal. **"Serenade: Any Man to Any Woman"** begins

> Dark angel, who are clear and straight
> As cannon shining in the air,
> Your blackness doth invade my mind
> And thunderous as the armoured wind
> That rained on Europe is your hair. . . .

The invasion of France has already become absorbed into this poet's strange world: and perhaps only a world as personal as Miss Sitwell's is capable of absorbing so directly, and then recreating, such an immediate and violent experience.

Two impressions predominate in her mature later work. One is the music, and the other the imagery. The music is, as it were, a horizontal movement which in its long, measured beat has a certain appeal also to the eye. The imagery gives a sense of verticality. It suggests upright figures, the sun in the height of the heavens, the pillar of fire, trees, etc. There is more to it, though, than this. There is also a prostrate imagery of death, earth enclosing bodies in its dust, kings who have died long ago. Miss Sitwell's extraordinary control of her medium is due to her power of keeping impressions separated from each other. She is like a painter who uses very simple colours, but who makes them all glow and who gives them a structural purpose: or, again, she is like a composer who is extremely conscious of the use of intervals and of notes widely separated from each other. This effect of the separation of music from imagery and of image from image can only be attained by the simplest means used with the greatest intensity and clarity of purpose. By invoking the same images again and again, by using very often the same rhymes, Miss Sitwell makes us thoroughly acquainted with the notes of her instrument, on which she produces her prodigious hymns.

> We are the darkness in the heat of the day,
> The rootless flowers in the air, the coolness: we
>   are the water
> Lying upon the leaves before Death, our sun,
> And its vast heat has drunken us . . . Beauty's
>   daughter
> The heart of the rose and we are one.

Here one has the long, horizontal, measured beat, manipulated with faint disturbance—the disturbance of a comma or of three full-stops—to indicate the restlessness above the calm of a summer evening. The imagery itself all suggests things standing or things prostrate, the rootless flowers, the sun.

Although it is easy enough to describe Miss Sitwell's effects, it is not easy to say why they are successful. The subject matter is very general, dealing with death, love and life in their most universal aspects. And the epithets are very simple: the sun, the rose, water, gold, are invoked again and again. Nevertheless, these generalized ideas and simple images exist within a world which remains always entirely Miss Sitwell's own. They are convincing because the whole of her personality is projected into her poetry, and her mature personality brings with it the preoccupations of Europe at this time. Miss Sitwell exists in her poetry as Lorᴄ‾ exists in his ballads, and as Van Gogh in his painting and his letters. The light, the ripeness, the death and the anguish of these later poems, are as accurate a picture as we have of an interior life of the spirit in our time. This poetry comes from a great isolation allied to a widening sympathy: such an isolation as we remark in the later work of Yeats and of T. S. Eliot, which is perhaps the only way for the poet in our time.

A poet's use of imagery can only be criticized in the light of his artistic purpose: and one can understand this not by quoting single lines out of their context, but by considering the use of imagery in an entire poem. Here, then, let us consider a poem entitled **"Anne Boleyn's Song."** (pp. 14-17)

This poem is an excellent example of the quality which I have called stone-like, made transparent with a passion as of light shining through it. The inner theme of Miss Sitwell's later poems is often transformation—the transformation of life into death, of warmth into coldness, of love into hatred. This sense of transformation is something which takes place within the images themselves. One must judge these images not as being derived from natural pro-

cesses but from unnatural ones—chemical changes of one substance into another, identification of opposites one with the other. There is a tendency in this poem to transform human feeling into something at first inhuman and then altogether cold and mineral. The blood of the queen first suggests bird-blood and then emeralds. This process of metamorphosis is interwoven with the associations of Spring, birds in branches and green leaves. The polar opposites, heat and cold, sun and earth, life and death dominate the poem. One is reminded of some lines of Yeats which describe the experience of all these poems:

> Once out of nature I shall never take
> My bodily form of any natural thing,
> But such a form as Grecian goldsmiths make
> Of hammered gold and gold enamelling
> To keep a drowsy Emperor awake;
> Or set upon a golden bough to sing
> To lords and ladies of Byzantium
> Of what is past, or passing, or to come.
>
>   (p. 19)

Stephen Spender, "Images in the Poetic World of Edith Sitwell," in A Celebration for Edith Sitwell, *edited by José García Villa, New Directions, 1948, pp. 11-19.*

Arthur Waley

"The Way that can be told is not the Eternal Way", says Lao Tzu, and the same is true of Poetry. Critics today try to get round this by treating poetry as a social product and showing the connection between the poet and his material surroundings. This is fun for the critic, who enjoys knocking the mystery-man off his perch and making him line up for once in the common queue, and it is not at all uninteresting for the reader. But it is sociology, not poetics, and though the poet is perfectly fair game for the sociologist, the sort of thing this method tells one would apply just as much to bad poets as to good. The psychological method, which might at first seem to be more applicable, lets us down in just the same way. It throws no light on quality. It can show just how Shakespeare's Oedipus-complex is reflected in *Hamlet:* it cannot explain why other dramatists' Oedipus-complex did not lead to equally good results.

Theoretically, discussions about the poet's mythology and technique are open to the same objection. In practice, however, it does not work out quite that way. Take, for example, Miss Edith Sitwell's poetry. Technique is of course only a vehicle; it is not poetry itself any more than a perambulator is a baby. But I do not know any instance of a bad poet having technical skill at all comparable to that of Miss Sitwell, and although the enormously wide range of her subject-matter could not by itself make her a good poet, I think one may at least say that the skimpy range of the Georgian Nature Poets (who held the field when she began to write) made it unlikely that they would produce anything but a crude and over-simplified form of poetry.

That is why I have chosen in this note chiefly to discuss

her technique and material, fully aware that in doing so I am merely skirting the periphery of her art.

She herself has written very fully about one aspect of technique—the deliberate choice of words not merely for their meaning but also the for the emotional effect of their sound. For example, of a poem that expresses the furry, growling, bear-like quality of primitive nature she says: "It is built on a scheme of harsh 'r's'," and shows just how. She has indeed, as regards her own verse, gone into this subject so thoroughly in the preface to her *Selected Poems* (1936), that there is not need to discuss it here. Metrically, she has on the whole been traditional. She has never written the sort of free-verse which uses prose rhythm and is indeed merely prose printed as though it were poetry. On the rare occasions when she altogether discards rhyme she uses the ordinary blank-verse line (as in that very beautiful early fragment, **"The Madness of Saul"**) or something fairly close to it. Her usual forms have till recently been the traditional four-stress or five-stress lines of standard English poetry, with latterly a tendency to six-stress lines such as

> I who was once a golden woman like those who
> walk . . .

In the most recent poems (**"Eurydice"**, for example) many seven and eight-stress lines occur and the versification has become much looser. Lines sometimes have a recitative cadence and even assume the dimensions of small paragraphs, as in **"Green Song"**.

> With the bird-notes of Doom in the egg, and
> Fate in the bud that is flushed with the world's
> fever.

This is, of course, an eight-stress line, and the use of such lines gives scope for immense variety of cadence, created by different distributions of the pauses. I think that the ear, used to shorter divisions, takes a little time to accommodate itself to these sustained periods. It is too, so far as I have noticed, only since about 1940 that Miss Sitwell has taken to using Sprung Rhythm, one feature of which is to allow two fully stressed syllables to stand side by side, without an intervening light-syllable or syllables to buffer them, as in the poem from *Street Songs* called **"Tears"**:

> The rocks of great diamonds in the midst of the
> clear wave,

which occurs in a scheme of six-stress lines. Or again in **"Most Lovely Shade"**:

> Deep in the dark secret of the rose.

This is of course quite a different thing from the distribution of a stress over two syllables, as in the line from **"The Peach Tree"**:

> Until your long dark fluid hands unfold

where the stress is shared by "long" and "dark," each getting half of it.

Slightly apart, in Miss Sitwell's metrical development, stand a few early poems that were evoked by popular tunes. **"Polka,"** for example, is a libretto rather than a poem:

> 'Tra la la la—
> See me dance the polka;
> Said Mr. Wagg like a bear,
> 'With my top hat
> And my whiskers that—
> (Tra la la) trap the Fair.'

I have only quoted the opening lines. One has to read them to a polka tune, and that deprives them of complete independence as poetry. But the commonly held idea that all the poems subsequently set to music by William Walton in *Façade* were inspired by music or (alternatively) were written to be set to music is quite false. Nothing, for example, could be more a poem in its own right than **"Sylph's Song"**—the one which begins:

> Daisy and Lily
> Lazy and silly
> Walked by the shore of the wan grassy sea . . .

There has been a lot of trouble about Miss Sitwell's use of metaphor and simile. One can best explain this by saying that it is the opposite of Dante's. Dante looks for the likest possible concrete parallel. The graves of the sectaries in Hell are like the graves outside Arles; the hoods worn by the hypocrites are like those worn by the monks at Cologne (and if you don't happen to have been to Arles or Cologne, Dante seems to say, there's nothing to be done about it). Sometimes he stays so close to what he is illustrating that he seems almost to be going in circles, as when he says that what he felt on hearing Beatrice's voice was like what Pyramus felt when he heard Thisbe's. If one had asked Dante, "And what *did* Pyramus feel?", he would presumably have had to answer, "Just what *I* felt", and so left us just where we started. Miss Sitwell, on the contrary, always gets far enough away from her starting-point to make sure that her metaphor or image throws light on her subject from a new angle. No one today is likely to quarrel with her (as they did in the twenties) for making cross cuts from one sense to another (calling light "shrill" or the like). "Where the language of one sense is insufficient", she has told us, "to convey a meaning, a sensation, I use another, and by this means I attempt to pierce down to the essence of the thing seen". When she says in **"Metamorphosis"**

> I looked out from my window where the urban
> Leaves seemed turkeys, (Sultans in a turban),
> Across the lake where, cupolas and gables,
> The ripples seemed deserted Georgian
> stables . . .

one is perfectly satisfied by the ripples-stables image. The motion of the water pulls its flatness into arcs and curves, just as the prevailing straightness of Georgian line is broken by cupola and gable. But I think something else happens too. The strangeness of the comparison, its apparent remoteness from the thing imaged, acts like a sudden, sharp rap on the table of the senses and startles them into vivid apprehension. Sometimes, however, when the poet does not aim at sudden illumination, her images and allusions are gently led up to, somewhat as the musician "prepares" a modulation. Thus near the beginning of *The Sleeping Beauty* the mention of Fortunatus, who according to Medieval legend had a purse that never ran dry, leads up to the "Figs, each like a purse of gold"; further on, the mention of the Mikado prepares us for the likening of the spell-bound Dowager-queen to the arrested wave on a screen by the Japanese painter Korin. If Miss Sitwell's poetry were a network of such allusions it would be uphill work for the average modern reader. But it is not. They are only occasional, and the classical references (which are by far the most numerous) are of an everyday kind. Daphne, Corydon, Amaryllis, Philomel, Proserpine are not recondite figures, and the reader to whom they are unfamiliar can easily find out about them (as presumably Miss Sitwell had to do herself).

When **Street Songs** appeared in 1942 immense surprise and gratification were expressed at the fact that Miss Sitwell had noticed the war, mobilized herself and written poems about the air-raids. Reviewers wrote as though she had hitherto dealt only with an enchanted world, half-nursery, half Mont Parnasse, had shut herself away behind the 'gilded trellises' of wit and phantasy. This was of course a strange line to take about some one who had written long ago such humanly tragic poems as **"Metamorphosis"**, **"The Hambone and the Heart"**, **"The Lament of Edward Blastock"** and **"Gold Coast Customs"**, three of which poems (or considerable parts of them) were included by W. B. Yeats in the *Oxford Book of Modern Verse* (1936), and were therefore particularly accessible. But the new enthusiasm was certainly not misplaced. **"Still Falls the Rain"**, **"Lullaby"**, **"The Youth with the Red-gold Hair"**, **"The Night Before Great Babylon"**, **"The Swans"** (all from **Street Songs**) are some of the finest poems that Miss Sitwell has written. Where I think she is not completely successful is in some of the recent poems about Death. The material she uses is too restricted and too imperfectly mythologized. Think for a moment of the wealth of allusion, of the constant changes of atmosphere—classical, contemporary, Spanish, fairy-tale, Georgian—in her poems of Life, contrasted with her narrow world of Death, in which the denizens do not even seem (like Emily Dickinson's dead) to "Talk between the rooms", but appear to be locked away each in a private skeletal anguish. Personally I am inclined to agree with the maxim in Hilaire Belloc's nonsense-rhyme:

> There is a good deal to be said
> For being dead,

and am much more sorry for the living. That, however, is only a difference of opinion and not a criticism of Miss Sitwell's Death poems. But I do think that the comparative poverty of her Death mythology has definitely had a handicapping effect on many of her recent poems, making as it does for a too frequent repetition of the same words and images. Recently Miss Sitwell, as though she too felt that she needed the help of an accepted mythology for her Death poems, has used the story of Orpheus and Eurydice. It is a poem that begins magnificently:

> Fires on the hearth! Fires in the heavens! Fires
> in the hearts of Men!

But I feel that the references to Proserpina, Osiris and Adonis work as ethnological parallels rather than as flowerings of the Orpheus myth itself. Moreover the name of Proserpina is bound up in one's mind with the very sensible arrangement that was ultimately made about her: she

was to spend the winter in Hades and the summer on Earth, a compromise by which we still benefit. Miss Sitwell leaves her tragically lying "in the silent Tomb"—where after all she was having an affair with her winter-husband, Pluto. For these and other reasons I do not feel that the mythology is integrated into the poem so successfully as, for example, in the early poem about Apollo and Daphne, that begins:

> Heat of the sun that maketh all men black,—
> They are but Ethiopian shades of thee—
> Pour down upon this wild and glittering fleece
> That is more rich than feathers of bright birds,
> The ripening gems, the drops of the still night.

And here I must apologize for quoting so little of Miss Sitwell's poetry. But this is a note of her methods, not an anthology. So I cannot give whole poems, and she does not deal in "good lines" (any more than music does in "good bars") not even in "fine passages." Everything fits into everything else and every value depends on its ambience. As though to prove this Miss Sitwell once took the lines:

> Beautiful carriages from Champs Elysee
> Filled with maidens on cushions easy

which had been quoted to her as a specimen of the "worst poetry ever written" (they are attributed to a lady called Georgina Farrer) and embedded them, with full acknowledgements, in her poem **"Lady Immoraline"** where, provided with suitable surroundings, they cut a very reputable figure. (pp. 83-9)

> *Arthur Waley, "A Note on Edith Sitwell's Poetry," in* A Celebration for Edith Sitwell, *edited by José García Villa, New Directions, 1948, pp. 83-9.*

M. C. Bradbrook

Today, the 7th of September, Dame Edith Sitwell celebrates her 75th birthday. On the 7th of September 1533 a lady even more spontaneously mistress of the grand style in rhetoric was born at Greenwich Palace. In **The Queens and the Hive,** the young girl introduced in a now reissued earlier work, **Fanfare for Elizabeth,** sits waiting for her accession, a jewelled image of regal greatness.

> We see a thin-waisted gold body, like that of the Bee Priestesses, with a high ruff and sleeves like the thin wings of these; we see a gown that seems descended from the Minoan or Cretan civilizations . . . Her appearance was that of the Plantagenet race. Her ugly face, so full of fire, so full of intellectual power, wisdom and vanity, was the face of the Plantagenets . . . She was born at the time of the martyrs' fires under King Henry. At all moments of greatness, her Promethean fire burned in her speech, which was of transcendental grandeur . . . She inherited, in her blood, a dark strain of animality from her mother and from the Minotaur, her father.

The great tale unfolds, through all its famous moments—of dalliance, of martial splendour, when at Tilbury in Armada year the Queen 'wore a silver corslet over her white velvet dress and held a truncheon in her hand' while the great speech rang out. The story moves on to the moment when Essex burst into her room to find 'the magnificent ruin stood before him—Carthage and Palmyra in disarray—the sunset-coloured wig, and all the tires and towers, and crowns, fallen away'; on, to the last 'golden speech' to her people, to the last hours at Richmond.

A pattern of gorgeous images—gold, blood, flames, death—woven with a Tudor boldness worthy of the theme, is shot through with inflexions of irony and sympathy. Behind the mask a woman appears. Behind the lion's courage, the terror that was with Elizabeth from childhood, when the repeated knell of her mother's death, Katharine Howard's death, the deaths of statesmen and of martyrs, called out a hollow echo which never ceased. Dame Edith would appear to think that the Queen's unexpected illnesses, like the sudden bursts of rage or vindictiveness that troubled her accustomed magnanimity, rose from this suppressed fear. When religious persecution revived,

> the present writer is not surprised that, according to the prayer for the Queen's recovery from a dangerous illness in the same year, 'God had abashed her soul with divers troubles and terrors of mind'.

At the end, 'she saw one night her own body exceeding lean and fearful, in a light of fire', as a few years before her cousin Lord Hunsdon had seen a vision of six friends already dead, who summoned him to join them. Leicester was one, 'all in fire'.

In Dame Edith's mirror of history, other queens dwindle to reflexions of Elizabeth. Mary Tudor is an effigy, 'the waxen form of the Queen whose child was Death', lying, her 'red hair spread on either side of her like spent flames'. Mary Stuart, ever unconsciously seeking Death as a bridegroom, chose first a 'Waxworks King', Darnley, out of hatred for Elizabeth, then a murderer. Some lesser ladies are dealt sharp buffets, such as their own mistress might have bestowed. Penelope Devereux is 'false, sly, arrogant and alternating between insolence and cringing'. Her brother, Essex, is allowed bravery and loyalty to his friends, if not to his benefactress, whose affection Dame Edith believes not to be 'the unpleasant infatuation of an old, vain woman for a young man,' but chiefly maternal in character.

Any re-creation of history by an artist demands a natural sympathy with the subject and gives a work which is of a highly individual kind. A taste for the gorgeous, the macabre, for *fêtes galantes* in Tudor costume, and for the splendour of words permits Dame Edith to paint with the loaded brush. She has studied the classic lineaments of Sir John Neale's portrait, the feminine version of Elizabeth Jenkins, but has made something quite new. She has also absorbed a Tudor attitude towards her sources. Although their variety has its charm, the diminutive outriders of her narrative labelled as footnotes might have been replaced by a list of authorities. (pp. 292-93)

> *M. C. Bradbrook, "Dames Coincident," in* New Statesman, *Vol. LXIV, No. 1643, September 7, 1962, pp. 292-93.*

Ronald Bryden

Icons are not portraits. They are not intended, as portraits are, to be human. They are tinted images of beings held sacred or in some way supernatural, designed to express not their personality but their power. This is conveyed by extreme formalising of the features, by exaggeration of them into relief with putty, enamel or *papier mâché*, as well as by gilding, haloing and ornate, begemmed framing. Icons are symbols in the strictest sense: emblems intended to transmit an impression not of life but a *mana* in which they participate. Thus they themselves become sacred, and objects of reverence. Icons may be given things—candles, money, incense; may be dressed up, like dolls, with coronets, costly fabrics and pendant jewellery. In Byzantium, where they originated, it was sacrilege to pull an icon by the nose.

The difficulty many modern readers, myself particularly, find with the work of Dame Edith Sitwell is, I think, a matter of definitions. We have come, since the Renaissance, to define poetry and art as in some sense a rendering of reality. Since Romanticism, of course, 'reality' has been extended to include subjective impressions, moods and imagery of the mind, which admits both surrealism and abstraction; but we have lost touch entirely with the mediæval tradition of art as a representation, sacred in itself, of sacredness. To this older definition Dame Edith's creations belong. She is a maker not of art as we know it, but of icons.

At least, I can find no other explanation of the two prose volumes she has devoted to Elizabeth the First. Like *Fanfare for Elizabeth,* its predecessor, *The Queens and the Hive* cannot be classified as historiography. History may be written to explain the past or to recall it—to single out, as Gibbon attempted, the thread of causality from the flux of circumstance; or to recapture, as Carlyle endeavoured, that flux entire, recreated as a chunk of living experience. *The Queens and the Hive* does neither. It makes no effort to explain: events swim up like dreams from the subconscious, unpredictable and ineffable as pantomime transformations. Characters perform evil because they 'carry a darkness within them'; they behave magnanimously because they look like 'pale, thin flames.' The Armada looms inexplicably from the mists of Biscay as if conjured overnight out of Philip of Spain's ambitions; as if Professor Mattingley had never written.

This of course may be a theory of history: that events have no explanation, can only be reanimated in their complex meaninglessness. This seems at first Dame Edith's belief and intention; why else the rhapsodic, costume-novel style?

> Robert was the husband of another woman. Still, she must have told herself, often, 'It will always be like this . . . we shall always be young, happy . . . Tomorrow will never come.'

Why else, but to recreate the murky tangle of time, to recapture how it felt without trying to make sense of it, revive impossible rumours and superstitions—that Catherine of Aragon's heart, after her death, was found black and swollen with poison, that Catherine de Medici had a child decapitated to consult its head as an oracle?

But such a quest would imply an attempt to reach a reality still undiscovered, to go behind the standard versions. There is little sign in Dame Edith's text of original research: the majority of her references are to familiar accounts—Hakluyt, Neale, Miss Jenkins, Stefan Zweig, Froude; particularly Froude, from whom she quotes copiously. Such original documents as she cites are notable more for sonority than for illumination. No, it becomes clear that Dame Edith's intention is to heighten, not reinterpret, the traditional picture: her documents are the *papier mâché* to achieve this, What she has to add is the gilding, the jewellery of Style. Adjectives encrust her figures richly—'glittering,' 'pale,' 'fox-coloured,' 'lion-coloured' (the very pigmentation of hair is made heraldic). The words 'gold' and 'golden' spatter her pages like references to champagne in the *Daily Express.* There are such rococo curlicues as the spelling, each time it appears, of Robert Dudley's title as 'Leycester.' The salient impression left by her Armada chapter is of the clothes, the silks and white satin worn by the Spanish grandees.

What results, in fact, is the traditional legend of Elizabeth formalised, mythologised, glazed with language. Presumably this is the intention Dame Edith describes when she speaks, in the preface to her ten new poems, of poetry as 'the deification of reality.' It is not an intention or method which can command much sympathy today or, as displayed in the poems—an image or event (the photograph of a Korean orphan, the wedding of the Duke of Kent) embossed with mythological reference, framed in a cosmic analogy, festooned with more or less arbitrary symbols—startle, shall I say, with a sense of felt life. But applied to Tudor history it may be, in a special way, illuminating. For the Elizabethans, history *was* the legend of its monarchs; they had no importance as persons, only as myths vaguely embodying the nation's sense of itself. Kings in a sense were national deities, historians their icon-makers.

And so presumably (to try and deal with one's remaining difficulty with Dame Edith) the poet-historian who makes these sacred artifacts shares in a reflected sacredness. He is not himself only, but a vessel of power: not only poet but totem, a mask of Poetry. In a sense, the poet himself is a kind of icon; and icons, as we began by saying, are not meant to be human. . . .

> *Ronald Bryden, "Iconography," in* The Spectator, *Vol. 209, No. 7003, September 14, 1962, p. 374.*

Marya Zaturenska

Those who have read Dame Edith Sitwell's colorful *Fanfare for Elizabeth,* written more than a decade ago, have long wished for a sequel. That book, written in Dame Edith's own inimitable style (the Swinburnian-Sitwellian), read as if indeed written to the sound of trumpets. There was never a dull page. Dame Edith left Elizabeth as a young girl on the threshold of tragedy and danger, already learned in that wisdom that never left her. It was an education that served the future Queen in good stead, an education that her spoiled, beautiful rival the Queen of Scots never had. Now in *The Queens and the Hive* we have the sequel.

It is still the fashion to call Swinburne unfashionable. The fact is that he was one of the last great English poets, whose unique lyric force rang in the blood, whose lines, powerful as the sea he so often invoked, remain in the memory. For he was in the great tradition of the Elizabethans and the dark and subtle Jacobeans, with which he and Dame Edith have a natural affinity.

Dame Edith has always been partial to Swinburne, and it is no discredit to her to say that she does for Queen Elizabeth what Swinburne did for Mary Stuart. Both of them have created a Queen in their own image, the reflection of their own original personalities. For Dame Edith's prose is one with her poetry; one must either love it or leave it. Like her poetry, it has been called baroque Gothic: it is like nobody else's. It is thrilling, readable; we hear the sound of her voice, the cadences ring.

Is it history? The average solid historian may shudder. Dame Edith knows the facts, though she uncovers no new ones; but with brilliant poetic perceptions she throws light on things that seemed dark before. There are moments when she identifies herself so thoroughly with the great Queen, that we feel that the Queen herself is talking, and telling us things that must be true. There are moments when Dame Edith's Elizabeth seems like a character from Isak Dinesen's *Seven Gothic Tales,* but all is color and movement, and we keep reading on.

The Hive of the title, we are told, is the power and glory of England; the Queens are Mary Tudor, Mary Stuart and, at the center, the great Elizabeth. Needless to say it is Elizabeth who dominates. Dame Edith's other portraits, say of Philip II, the two Cecils, are sharp, brilliant, a little more real than life. Her passionate admiration for Henry VIII is somewhat hard to take for non-English readers. Only Sir Walter Raleigh among Elizabethans seemed to understand the essential horror of that brutal figure. Yet, then, there must be something essentially English in Henry's character that made him both loved and feared so that men died unjustly on the scaffold, still reciting their love and loyalty to him. Both Mary Tudor and Queen Elizabeth, in spite of their cruel treatment at his hands, never failed to express their love and admiration for him.

Dame Edith has fine wild prejudices, which she always tempers with justice. Her portrait of Mary Tudor is excellent. She shows her generous, genuinely pious, essentially more honest and truthful than Elizabeth, but wrecked by early experiences, going down in history as "bloody Mary." Elizabeth, whose reign was also darkened by religious persecution (and one also thinks of the horrors she allowed to be perpetrated in Ireland), has become a glorious symbol in English history, a kind of ikon. But history, as some cynic said, is written by the winning side; and in England it was Protestantism that won—thanks perhaps to Elizabeth and her able advisers. Mary Tudor allowed Elizabeth to live in spite of all the pressure put upon her to put Elizabeth out of the way—and so saw all her work undone. Elizabeth, we feel, would have been tougher.

Whatever the truth of the matter may be, Queen Elizabeth has a devoted champion in Dame Edith, who portrays her in her true glory. Her physical image of her alone is striking:

> Her appearance was that of the Plantagenet race. Her ugly face, so full of fire, so full of intellectual power, wisdom, vanity, and a strange fascination was the face of the Plantagenets. She had the great hauntingly beautiful eyes of Anne Boleyn, but the high, thin, and arched nose, whose nostril seemed as if breathing fire, the long carved eyelids, the long and faultlessly beautiful hands were the Plantagenet nose, eyelids, and hands.

Dame Edith does not underestimate the influence of the Earl of Leicester on Elizabeth. He was the only man Elizabeth always loved, and he was more than a magnificent stuffed shirt. Elizabeth was too intelligent not to see through a stuffed shirt when she saw one. Leicester was able, devoted, truly loyal. All the pathos of his wasted life appears when the Queen (after all hope of marrying him was gone) turned on him with ferocity after he made a belated marriage with one of her cousins on the Boleyn side. But Elizabeth's great love was for her country and her people, and that love was understood and returned.

Sitwell on her poetic imagery:

If some of the images in [my] poems appear strange, it is because my senses are like those of primitive peoples, at once acute and uncovered—and they are interchangeable; where the language of one sense is insufficient to convey a meaning, a sensation, I use another, and by this means, I attempt to pierce down to the essence of the thing seen, producing or heightening its significance by discovering in it attributes which at first sight seem alien, but which are actually related—by producing its quintessential color (sharper, brighter, than that seen by an eye grown stale), and by stripping it of all unessential details. The apparent strangeness comes, too, from the fact that all expression is welded into an image, not removed into a symbol that is inexact, or squandered into a metaphor.

Sitwell in her introduction to a 1937 edition of Selected Poems.

Compared to Elizabeth, Dame Edith's Mary Stuart is a shadowy, violent ghost. She is very much like the heroine of Swinburne's poetic dramas. Yet somehow one feels that these poets have caught essential truths that are strangely convincing. It is impossible to doubt the authenticity of the Casket letters (incriminating correspondence supposedly involving Mary in the murder of her husband, Lord Darnley) after reading this book. Dame Edith also gives an illuminating clue as to why Mary Stuart lost the affection of the only able man around her, the one who could have saved her. This was her bastard brother, the Earl of Moray—usually the villain of the Mariolators.

The Queens and the Hive is an exciting and original reconstruction of history that will give pleasure to select readers for many years to come.

> *Marya Zaturenska, "Told to the Sound of Trumpets," in* The New York Times Book Review, *November 18, 1962, p. 34.*

The Times Literary Supplement

Dame Edith Sitwell's posthumous short autobiography, brisk, digressive, written very much in a speaking style, might be considered as a kind of last rally against a certain kind of critic she had long been at war with. There is nothing in the tone of [***Taken Care Of,*** a] scrappy and lively and gossipy book, written though it was with a swollen hand and in conditions of physical pain, that suggests the slightly forced solemnities and the formal and not wholly sincere reconciliations of a death-bed. There is rather eldritch laughter, cackles of wild gaiety. There is no reconsideration of claims, recantation of attacks, or, indeed, failure of loyalites. There is a fine rashness and simplicity about the book; one thinks of some grand ship of the line going down in flames, but with its flags still flying, and its deck-guns firing to the last. Even the ranks of *Scrutiny,* perhaps, could scarce forbear to cheer. To use a distinction Miss Pamela Hansford Johnson has made about her, the paying off of old scores here is perhaps vicious (like a cat that scratches when its fur is stroked the wrong way) but not spiteful. Dame Edith could not hate people. Those who attacked her or bored her also made her laugh; and she conveys her helpless amusement, her sense of funniness, even where she cannot convey where exactly, for her, the joke lies.

A writer in these columns, for instance, said about another very distinguished woman poet, one at the opposite pole from Dame Edith in that this other woman poet is noted not for her ornateness but for her transparency of diction: "The frailty of these poems is their distinction. At their very best, they seem to be just on the verge of being not there at all." One could perhaps think of happier ways of phrasing a sound critical perception. Dame Edith pins this unfortunate reviewer to her page and then relates how she remembers the poet in question (with a tactfulness towards her own sex she does not name her, but it was in fact Miss Kathleen Raine) saying to her: "The mind is a vortex." So, to be sure, the mind is. But Dame Edith then quotes a wonderful piece from Dickens:

> "Mind and matter," said the lady with the wig, "glide swift into the vortex of immensity. Howls the sublime and softly sleeps the calm ideal in the whispering chambers of imagination. To hear it, sweet it is. But then, out laughs the stern philosopher, and saith to the Grotesque 'What ho! Arrest for me that agency. Go bring it here!' And so the vision fadeth."

This is shockingly unfair but both Miss Raine and her reviewer would have to admit that it is extremely funny.

Dame Edith was not good at abstract argument; but she was wonderfully good at detecting possible false notes and at bringing out the ludicrous side of persons or attitudes of which she disapproved. A passage about Dr. Leavis, similarly, is introduced with surprising effectiveness by a quotation from Plato; and the passage ends with some quotations from Dr. Leavis's famous chapter on Milton, and with some lines from *Paradise Lost* analysed by him. Dame Edith's comment is, "It is sad to see Milton's great lines bobbing up and down in the sandy desert of Dr. Leavis's mind with the grace of a fleet of weary camels." Again, this is strikingly unfair; but for visual aptness and grotesque humour, for the quality which in poetry Dr. Leavis himself calls "enactment", it could hardly be bettered.

Dame Edith, similarly, had none of the qualities of the modern academic critic of poetry. Her taste in poetry was for the sort of poetry she practised; for colour rather than line, flamboyance rather than strictness, fullness rather than measure. We have seen that Miss Raine, a linear, strict, measured poet, did not please her. In her preface she has a strange combined swipe at the poets, roughly speaking, of the Movement school and at a poet who has many affinities with Miss Raine, Edwin Muir:

> I have pointed out, also, the depths to which po-
> etry has fallen, and the non-nutritive qualities of
> the bun-tough whinings of certain little poetas-
> ters—but I have been careful, for instance, not
> to refer to the late Mr. Edwin Muir (Dr. Leavis's
> spiritual twin-sister).

A certain plain and careful sobriety which marks Edwin Muir's critical prose, as it marks his poetry, would no doubt have been displeasing to Dame Edith. In the chapter in which she is gunning for the Movement, particularly for Mr. Robert Conquest, Mr. D. J. Enright, Mr. Roy Fuller, and Mr. Kingsley Amis (though she had a taste for the comical-satirical-picaresque in fiction, and enjoyed Mr. Amis's novels as she had enjoyed the early novels of Mr. Anthony Powell), she concludes:

> I understand that these poets aim at purity and
> clarity, with the result that each of their poems
> resembles a glass of tepid lemonade in which a
> couple of teaspoonfuls of Matthew Arnold have
> been dissolved.

The house of criticism has many mansions and, in heaven, Dame Edith will perhaps share one with Swinburne and Landor. None of these three critics is fair and balanced, each has a taste which is in some degree narrow and eccentric. Each can praise memorably, and attack with humorous fury. Each also is a performer, what Wyndham Lewis, one of Dame Edith's other targets here, called a "personal-appearance artist".

Dame Edith combined two characteristics of the aristocrat, a frank delight in personal display, and a certain fundamental reticence. She does not go in detail in this book, for instance, into the unhappiness of her childhood or into her conversion to full Christian belief. She says little about her deep personal affection for her brothers. She disliked the middle-class habit of what may, perhaps, most aptly be called "unbosoming". Thus, having described the appearance and manners of D. H. Lawrence vividly and with sympathy, she adds tartly:

> Though courteous and amiable, he was deter-

mined to impress us that he was a son of toil (that was the great romance, apart from his marriage with Mrs. Lawrence, in his life) and he seemed to be trying to make us uncomfortable by references to the contrast between our childhood and his. But this was not our fault. Our childhood was hell, and we refused to be discomfited.

Taken Care Of is not an elaborate, ornate, subtly composed tapestry like Sir Osbert's autobiographies. It is abrupt, informal, tangential. Yet the very slightness of structure and directness of attack means a lack also of disguise. Here is a very strange and rich personality, to be taken or left. The humour, the sharpness, the good heart come out in this little anecdote about Dylan Thomas: "On another occasion he came to luncheon with me, and, as he arrived, said to me. 'I am sorry to smell so awful, Edith. It's Margate.' I said, 'Yes, of course, my dear boy, it's Margate'."

"With All Guns Firing," in The Times Literary Supplement, *No. 3293, April 8, 1965, p. 268.*

Stephen Spender

Edith Sitwell was scarcely justified in calling [*Taken Care Of*] her autobiography. The early part provides a useful appendix to Sir Osbert's massive autobiography, in which she provides her own account of her childhood, and her own portrait of Sir George and Lady Sitwell. This is by far the best part of the book, a story of suffering told in strokes as incisive and cruel as those irons in which the little Edith was put for the purpose of improving her figure, and which resulted in atrophying her muscles. When she sticks to childhood she provides a model of writing which exactly reflects a model attitude. Looking back at herself as a small girl, she has dispassionate unflinching vision, no self-pity, and she can be extremely funny.

For the rest, the book is very scrappy. There are interesting reminiscences of the three Sitwells in their early days in London, a great many anecdotes, some of them funny, occasional brilliant observations, and overwrought revenges, reading like rather tired set pieces, on people against whom the Sitwells bear grudges—D. H. Lawrence, Wyndham Lewis, and a great many people who sought interviews with, or wrote letters to, Dame Edith, asking advice about their poetry. To balance this, there are sympathetic accounts of Virginia Woolf, Aldous Huxley, Gertrude Stein, Pavel Tchelichew and others. There is a glowing chapter, flattering to them, (and indirectly flattering to Dame Edith for having appreciated them so much) on Dylan Thomas and Roy Campbell (praise of one, surely, rather cancels out praise of the other, whichever you happen to like). The warmest and most deeply felt passages in the book are about her brother Osbert, and about her governess, Helen Rootham, whom Edith nursed through her desperate last illness.

One has the impression that Edith Sitwell delayed writing her autobiography too long. Very few of her pen portraits are sustained, the childhood memories and the love for her brothers are still real, but the heart has gone out of those literary feuds which, at the time when she was still entertaining her friends, made up so much of her conversation.

Yet in spite of many reservations, this is an interesting book, because Edith Sitwell was extraordinary. A portrait—not exactly a self-made portrait but one done almost in spite of herself—does emerge. One feels that a friend, caring for her reputation might have advised her not to publish this book in which nearly all her attacks on enemies seem to rebound on herself. Yet he would have been wrong to do so, because in the end the portrait revealed makes one care much for her. Her defenses are often down, but as a result one sees a real and courageous, agonized person. If they were kept up, one would probably be more disconcerted by the unreality of many of her attitudes.

The most striking fact about Edith Sitwell is that she was one of those whose childhood was so shattered that to a great extent she retained through life the attitudes of an only-just-escaped prisoner. She was not only sensitive, but her sensitivity had been battered at the most sensitive moment of her life. The consequence of this was that she divided other people into two kinds: those who were potentially as brutalized as she had been herself, and the brutalizers and persecutors who had no feelings whatever.

In her book one is struck again by her oscillation between two attitudes: cruel caricatures of others because they take over the role of the tormentors of her childhood, and identification with them. The result is that she is very unreliable about people she does not like, incapable of seeing beneath their external behavior into the motives behind it which might make them appear human. Her attacks on Lawrence and Wyndham Lewis are so exaggerated as to be almost harmless. As anyone who went to Edith Sitwell's parties will remember, she was extremely kind in practice though sometimes cruel in conversation and in her attitude to particular *bêtes noires*. In real life she allowed herself to become surrounded with "lame ducks" to whom she was endlessly generous. At the same time she could make you feel disloyal to others—if they happened to be your friends—by her attacks on them. In reading her autobiography, it seems rather surprising that she retained perfectly intact so many of her childhood attitudes about people whom she had known when she was extremely young. A London boarding house where she stayed as a girl, seemed to her, sixty years afterwards, inhabited entirely by monsters whom she regarded without any sympathy. Here is one of them:

> This enormous woman, with her thick and muffled face and neck, when she was fully painted and equipped for the sad and hopeless business of the day, looked, when static, like an effigy of one of the Deadly Sins (swollen by some meaningless importance), the figurehead of Greed or Envy, carried at the head of some purposeless procession. Her vast size gave her an unwieldy, lumbering gait, a shambling walk, so that she seemed always to be in at least four places at once. So, bobbling and plunging as if she was a long line of sea-elephants facing the surge of waves, she faced the poverty of her days.

From other passages in the book, one knows that if someone had remarked to Dame Edith that the "poverty" which she herself saw as the key to this person's behavior might have suggested, fifty years after the event, a more sympathetic attitude, she would have replied that she had been dreadfully poor herself, and tortured at Renishaw.

The best piece of literary judgment in this book is a discussion of some marvelous lines of Pope. Perhaps Edith Sitwell's greatest piece of luck as a writer is that she discovered Pope before she did the Romantics. Her strength as a poet is that she inhabited a world of sometimes cruel, sometimes piteous caricature. Her book makes one sympathetic to her poetry; we see it as the work of a mannered caricaturist with a somewhat 18th-Century touch, portraying an aristocratic world in which men kill animals and one another and women go puffed up in their monstrous crinolines, a world in which some spirit suffers poignantly underneath and the poet is "a little outside life," indeed a cripple.

The 18th-Century analogy cannot be pushed far, because Edith Sitwell lacked intellectual force. She flashes occasionally, that is all, and a good deal of the time she is merely tiresome. All the same the flashes do come from a real and genuine person imprisoned in unreal and falsifying circumstances. It is difficult to think that the world of space travel into which we are now moving will produce another Edith Sitwell. To have known her or to discover her in her work is to be extremely grateful for her. (pp. 19-20)

Stephen Spender, "Three Little Sitwells and How They Grew," in The New Republic, *Vol. 152, No. 17, April 24, 1965, pp. 19-20.*

Geoffrey Grigson

How are we to explain or explain away (since it is going to need some explaining away for our posterity) the eminence or the acceptance or the at times reverential praise of the poems of the late Edith Sitwell? The poems will fall apart. They strike me, when I look at them again, as a tumble of imitation reliquaries. Of her early poems—the reliquaries are the later ones—some had the tinkliness of a broken musicbox, some exhibited the arch simplemindedness, not always pleasant-mindedness, of a neo-Victorian bouquet of wax and silk under the jags of a dome. Then the war, the bombs, the Great Bomb, and the reliquaries, inside of which there might—or might not—be the scraps of some body of holiness.

I was skeptical when these earnest poems began to appear and to be praised. The psalm sounded—O praise Miss Sitwell in the holiness of her pity and imaginative insight—and swelled; and even old skeptics were converted. But not this skeptic, who looked inside, and found precisely the nothing he expected to find, on past form. It was—I shall vary the exposition and call upon St. Adelbert of Prague and the luminescent fish once caught in the Danube—a fishy to-do. When that saint had been dismembered, it happened that his little finger fell or was thrown into the river: the fish swallowed the finger, the finger shone through the fish. But out of these Sitwellian reliquaries there shone, at any rate to my critical sense, no interior light even of that coldest luminescent kind. Crosses were inscribed or carved on the lid, inside there was not even the little finger of St. Adelbert.

As before, as so often in the Middle Ages, the best thing about these reliquary poems—"golden" having been Miss Sitwell's key word—was their externality of gold leaf, or tinsel. All the light, all the sparkle came from outside, and reflected from the gilt, had its source in simpletons, sophisticated and unsophisticated, English and American, who were still in need of relics to worship; which is part of the explanation of Miss Sitwell. And another part, confirmed by [**Taken Care Of**], this miserable autobiography, is that Miss Sitwell was one of her own most servile adulators.

She relates, to begin with, that she had a most unhappy childhood; which is no doubt true. If she is to be believed, her father and her mother alike were true scions of English aristocracy at its most vacuous, ignorant, insolent, and vulgar, which—such has been our aristocracy's frequent eminence in these faults—is not saying a little. England's aristocrats have scarcely been the makers or safekeepers of English civilization. "My parents were strangers to me from the moment of my birth." Just as well, from the way she describes them. She needed to be straightened in an iron frame. She was ugly. She was bullied, she was violent, and she was lonely. (p. 11)

One might sympathize rather more, if the consequent and compensating vanity, the unbelievable self-adulation was not reflected backwards on to the account. "Perhaps I, at four years old, knew the incipient anguish of the poet I was to become." Arthur Rimbaud "in some ways my closest spiritual relation." "Fields of yellow jonquils that, in my later life, were like the spirits of my early poetry." " 'What are you going to be when you are grown-up, little E?' . . . 'A genius,' I replied"—which is thrown to the adulating reader with the unexpressed because unnecessary assurance that a genius she became. Her first love was a peacock, her second an owl, she writes; and there are two ways of interpreting either bird.

One might sympathize rather more if the adult who grew into her "Plantagenet features" contrived to replace hatred with charity, if contumelious insults were not flung back as well into the past years, at her parents, at her relations, at the servants, at the doctors, at her teachers. "He looked like a statuette constructed of margarine" (orthopedic surgeon). "An alleged beauty . . . The upper part of her body consisted of an enormous pink ham which served her as face" (friend of her mama's). "Endowed with a treble ration of shining protuberant teeth . . . always bared ingratiatingly" (the kindly maiden lady who tried to teach her to paint).

One might respect her more if the frenetic insults were not, page after page, thrown around as well as backward, if a self-extrication or transformation were visible such as Coleridge detected in Wordsworth, who out of a black nature made himself a deservedly happy man because he had learnt "the intrinsic value of the different objects of human pursuit." Everything returns to the egoistic measure. As

when she was young, as when she was middle-aged, so in old age every response was conditioned by the beginning. She met at one time D. H. Lawrence and Frieda Lawrence, who evidently presumed neither to like her nor to admire her. How appallingly coarse, insolent, and arrogant the deferred revenge! Lawrence looked "like a plaster gnome on a stone toadstool in some suburban garden." How dared he be so beastly to *Sir* Clifford Chatterley—himself (during the First World War) having remained "safely at home, fornicating and squealing, shrilly, about the oppression from which he had suffered." How appallingly and savagely she replies, thinking it worth printing the reply, to a slightly cuckoo if unsolicited letter from a harmless unknown!

Nastiness combines with triviality as one characteristic of this book, unameliorated by "success." "Were I not too kind to laugh at the cruel disappointment and envy suffered by certain poor little unsuccessful writers"—poets forty years younger than herself who wrote of her poems without enthusiasm—"I might be amused by the fact that although I am now seventy-seven years of age, the unsuccessful are still thrown into what is practically an epileptic fit brought on by envy and malice at the mere mention of my name."

"Were I not too kind . . ." In England it is now customary to say, Ah but Edith was so kind in private life. One's concern is with her public life, the writing she exhibits; and in this book this writer, exclaiming because some people had abused her friend the poet Roy Campbell for "his verbal savagery about the Spanish Reds," urges that they did not know what those Reds had threatened to do to his wife and children ("Roy did not appreciate these threats. Some people are most unreasonable!") only a very few sentences after she had in effect praised this same Roy Campbell—for what? For threatening a Cambridge don (I suppose F. R. Leavis) with assault: "I'll walk into your College and tear the clothes off your back, and by the time I've done with you your wife and children won't know you." The cause of this physical threat: critical disapprobation of Miss Sitwell's poems. Such was her taste for vicarious violence where she was offended.

Add to the charges which condemn this book, sneering, malice, megalomania, arrogance and the rest, a very considerable stupidity, already apparent in some of the scraps I have quoted; and to stupidity, what is, after all, the most obvious characteristic of this writer: she was in everything she wrote an amateur, a poseur of art. Frequently she has to break off (can this life have been so meager?) to instruct her servile readers in the virtues, not of poetry, but of her poetry, servile once more to herself. A poem is quoted. A poem is explained, once more, as so often in her previous work, in the familiar jejune chatter of the texture of her vowels, consonants and vocables. That "the words ending in the letter D are placed so close together makes, in this particular case, a slight leap into the air."

> Though *head* is immediately linked up again in the next line with *egg*, yet because it had no previous related sound, there is no effect on rhythm.

Comparing her experience "during the first inception and creation of a poem . . . with all humility . . . to the experience of the saint," this amateur poet thought that she must break now and then into writing her account of herself poetically. Now Dame Blake, now Dame Traherne, and now Dame Rimbaud, she proffers a sneezing parody of their vision—"In these countrysides, the people know that Destiny is reported, and has features like a hen. There have I seen pig-snouted darkness grunting and rooting in the hovels. The very clouds are like creaking wooden chalets filled with emptiness," etcetera, in a general air of cheap and frigid untruth. The senses were weak and invented lies, like a child (simple ones, too—the hands of Wyndham Lewis were not "thick" and "meat colored" but of a singular delicacy. Dylan had no "look of archangelic power," or of William Blake).

There are quotations in this book. Excluding quotations from herself, they are the best of it—though often used to indicate a parity between quoter and quoted. The aptest one, included for the differently megalomaniac purpose of ridiculing the idea that her genius, the genius of the tumbled reliquaries, could be ridiculed, she took unwisely from the poet D. J. Enright. "Writers who detach tragedy from the persons who suffer it," Mr. Enright declared in the *New Statesman*, "are generally to be seen soon after wearing someone else's bleeding heart on their own safe sleeve—an odious transaction and an odious transaction is what Dame Edith Sitwell's atomic poetry seems to me to be." And to me. But that was a condemnation too subtle and complete for this (poetically and publicly) impossible person to have understood. Yet in the end the disgrace lies more upon her febrile and snobbish supporters than on herself. (pp. 11-12)

> Geoffrey Grigson, "Nothing Like a Dame," in The New York Review of Books, Vol. IV, No. 8, May 20, 1965, pp. 11-12.

"I have never minded being laughed at. All original artists *are* laughed at. But sometimes I laugh back and that is not appreciated."

—Edith Sitwell, (1961).

Denise Levertov

Taken Care Of, the autobiography of Edith Sitwell, would seem to be of clinical interest only (except to gossips) as a record of the largely paranoic ramblings of a poor old woman blighted by a most horrible childhood, if it did not contain a few pages that show the one peculiar good that managed to develop in this warped being.

Edith Sitwell appears to me to have been a monster, in a quite strict sense—"any plant or animal of abnormal shape or structure, as one greatly malformed or lacking some parts." But her ability to distinguish the affective properties of verbal sounds—the logic of melopoeia—was developed to a most extraordinary degree. This faculty is in itself a valuable phenomenon, and she was able to transmit its findings to her readers in some of her poems and in much of her critical writing, such as *A Poet's Notebook, A Notebook on William Shakespeare,* a book on Pope, some of her notes for *The Atlantic Book of British and American Poetry,* etc. But an autobiography asks the reader to look at the author as a human being; and it is hideous, shocking, painful, to witness the degree to which this one gift of hers was unaccompanied by any proportionate presence of other related properties. Pages 28-31, 39-46, 142-144, 168-169 (and an occasional sentence elsewhere) contain those passages of technical analysis which will be valuable to any poet and to most serious readers. An example: "From the thin, glittering, occasionally shadowed, airy, ever varying texture of that miracle of poetry [*The Rape of the Lock*] the instinct was instilled into me that not only structure, but also texture, are parents of rhythm in poetry, and that variations in speed are the result, not only of structure, but also of texture." She proceeds to develop this idea, in a passage too long to quote here. Or again, " . . . if you use one three-syllabled word, it has a greater speed than the three one-syllabled words which might have been used as its equivalent." This is Edith Sitwell the poet.

She had, as I've said, a horrible childhood. I cannot take her word for what her parents were really like, because it is simply not credible that the idiot she describes her father to have been could have written *Tales of My Native Village,* a book of great charm and interest—however much it may idealize the 13th century—but whatever their reality, her father and mother certainly failed to give their plain, precocious, ill-tempered daughter the most rudimentary sense of being loved. Moreover, she was, it seems, subjected to all sorts of ill-advised orthopedic tortures, designed to act variously on her back, ankles, feet, and—surely hardest to bear of all—her nose: " . . . a band of elastic surrounded my forehead, from which two pieces of steel (regulated by a lock and key system) descended on each side of the organ in question, with thick upholstered pads at the nostrils, turning my nose very firmly to the opposite way which Nature had intended, and blocking one nostril, so that breathing was difficult. This adornment . . . was worn only during my long hours in the schoolroom (unlike the other devices) as it was thought it might arouse some speculation—even, perhaps, indignation—in passers-by if worn in the outer world." Her nurse, her father's valet, a peacock (which later came to prefer the society of a peahen, to the poor child's grief), a puffin and an owl were the sole friends of her infancy, at least until her brothers were old enough to become her companions. A large *number* of friends is not a human necessity; but one cannot but feel sharply how *faintly* these particular relationships must have supplied love. Even the devotion and kindness of Davis, the nurse, must have fallen far short of the warmth so desperately needed.

Still it must be acknowledged with compassion that under the circumstances it is remarkable that Edith Sitwell made anything of her life at all. But compassion cannot give artistic interest to her unconscious revelations of her own warping. One sees how rejection by her parents made her defensive in a way that no doubt led to her eventual paranoia, but the actual displays of that result are only sad; and that strain of vulgarity in her that was so ready to scream "Vulgar!" at others is not quite accounted for, however charitable the reader wants to be, by an unhappy childhood: rather, by a lack of intelligence. For that exquisite sensibility to the sensuous and emotive qualities of English words must not be mistaken for general intelligence.

It must be added in fairness that this book was written when Edith Sitwell was ill, and completed shortly before her death. There are several minor instances of a certain confusion of thought. She even makes a startling and, to the reader of the early chapters, painfully pathetic reference to "the fun, liveliness and happiness" of her youth. The "ineffable happiness" she knew as a young child, in the vivid sense of nature's splendor she had then and knew intermittently throughout her life, can hardly be described as "fun"! She makes only bare allusion to events that must have been of great importance to her development, or her failure to develop. Speaking of the deterioration of her friendship with Helen Rootham (the translator of Rimbaud's *Illuminations*), who had been her governess and with whom her first years of emancipation from parental domination—beginning only in her late twenties—had been spent, and spent apparently more happily than any other extended period of her life, she says: "But then, suddenly, *life rotted.*" (My italics.) She does go on to tell of Miss Rootham's psychological changes and to refer to her eventual illness and death—which was "very terrible"; but she does not give the reader more than a shadowy, and as if it were involuntary, hint, of whatever dreadful conflict justified, as no doubt it did, those words—"Life rotted."

She frequently inserts, among mean diatribes, disclaimers: "I trust that I have hurt nobody." "I have never, in all my life, been so odious as to regard myself as *superior* to any living being, human or animal." (Surely only someone who *does* feel superior feels a need to deny it!—and at the same time, what honest person can deny having *at some moments* in his life felt superior to some other being?) "In private life I am an exceedingly mild person." Etc. Yet literary battles—and slights—of long ago still roused her to a fury of malicious attack, always self-defensive, in which she describes her enemies as "squealing" and as being "floozies." (pp. 618-19)

The human poverty self-revealed in all but a few pages of *Taken Care Of* does, after all, throw light on an aspect of her work. Her later poems, with their tragic themes, obsessive symbols and seemingly compassionate point of view, have never moved me, as did the light, crisp, early work—which she herself describes precisely as showing in some poems, "a violent exhilaration, [in others] a veiled melancholy, a sadness masked by gaiety." I see now—reading her words of cheap contempt for anyone who has criticized her, of vulgar self-praise, her passages of heavy sarcasm (in the style of Mrs. Wilfer in *Our Mutual Friend*)—that though she also had, in her fierce and loyal affection for a few persons and for many books, moments when she did envision "the warmth of love that makes all men brothers" (she is alluding to her wartime poems), it must have remained largely a theoretical experience, which was not only constantly at variance with the spite

and pettiness in her but was also a projection that helped prevent her from acknowledgment of that spite. All the world's evil comes from "them"; "they" are the crucifiers; Edith Sitwell identifies consistently with the poor, the long-suffering, the crucified. It is this that, quite naturally, makes the later poems seem false, lacking in the very depth they seem to claim so fervently for themselves. They are overextended, and any such overextension inevitably shows up in the language and rhythm, the very substance, of a poem.

This is not true of the grim **"Lullaby"**—

> Though the world has slipped and
>   gone,
> Sounds my loud discordant cry
> Like the steel bird's song on high:
> "Still one thing is left—the Bone!"
> Then out danced the Babioun . . .

That rings true, clangs with the dull unresonating tone of agony. But when, for instance, in **"Dirge for the New Sunrise (August 6, 1945)"** she wrote:

> Bound to my heart as Ixion to the
>   wheel,
> Nailed to my heart as the Thief
>   upon the Cross,
> I hang between our Christ and the
>   gap where the world was lost
> And watch the phantom Sun in
>   Famine Street,

but then continued, a few stanzas later:

> But I saw the little Ant-men as they
>   ran
> Carrying the world's weight of the
>   world's filth
> And the filth in the heart of Man—

something has gone wrong, to my ear. A rhetoric is masking with its extraneous riches a thinness of substance, and the substance is thin because the total person is not really backing the words. I'm not saying that any artist's vision of nobility must at all times be supported by impeccably noble behavior in his day-to-day life!—but that no artist can accuse the human race of its sins while reserving himself from full implication in them, and still move us deeply. We are moved at a deep level only by words that come from a deep level; we are moved only partially by words that express only a partial involvement of their author; when such partial involvement, partial realization, seems to claim for itself a totality, an omniscience, we are moved to a lesser degree than we would be if the partiality were admitted.

Such poems, examined carefully, can be instructive, especially in our present phase of "Camp" art, with its terror of "sincerity." Edith Sitwell was certainly not consciously "insincere." Nevertheless, her art was compartmentalized; she didn't back it up with her human totality of emotions and intelligence. It remained an outgrowth of her monstrous sensibility. Therefore as long as it dealt with expressions of sensibility, as in the early work, it satisfies; it is an operation of its own universe of discourse. But when in her latter years she pressed forward ("sincerely") into the realm of morals, of eschatology, of absolutes, it fails *in its very language and rhythms,* because the necessary blood supply, as it were, is denied it.

Perhaps those contemporary artists who squirm at the very idea of sincerity, of earnestness, are failing to distinguish adequately between the conscious sincerity which in its very single-mindedness tends to deny the terrifying multiple possibilities of each individual, and which is therefore not enough to sustain life in a work of art—a sincerity which is indeed a form of hypocrisy—and the largely unconscious, all-embracing sincerity of great artists whose whole being stands doggedly in back of their work. (p. 619)

Denise Levertov, "Monster with Melopoeia," in The Nation, *New York, Vol. 200, No. 23, June 7, 1965, pp. 618-19.*

Jean MacVean

It is interesting to look at Edith Sitwell's work with a fresh eye. It has always met either with admiration or dismissal, some of it hostile. She herself fought for it, and for that of others, with the utmost tenacity, and, occasionally, with ferocity. She used, to some effect, the sharpened weapon of her wit.

Yeats, an admirer, saw in her early poems a double vision: 'A perpetual metamorphosis that seems an elegant, artificial childhood, created through separated metaphor, amid crowds and scenery that suggest the Russian Ballet and Aubrey Beardsley's final phase,' and, 'a nightmare vision, like that of Webster, of the emblems of mortality.'

Yeats, writing in 1936, was, of course, not referring to the poet's later work created from her anguish over the war and her often painful love for the homosexual Russian painter Pavel Tchelitchew. In her later poems she developed a visionary style of almost Blakean intensity.

Of her early poems, she herself wrote:

> The world I see is a country world, a universe of growing things, where magic and growth are one . . . a world of rough, fruitful suns, and the age of the innocence of man . . . At other moments, as a contrast to this world, one of heavy, brutish darkness.

This was, in fact, an oversimplification, as her delightful poem ***The Sleeping Beauty*** shows. The *mise en scene* is Londesborough, the home of Edith Sitwell's maternal grandmother, in all its eighteenth century luxury and opulence. The gardener, a recurring character in this poet's work, tells the story. The wicked fairy is closely modelled (and with some relish) on Lady Londesborough. Her other grandmother, devout Lady Sitwell, was fond of 'poor little E.' who danced and sang hymns for her. In her garden, the poet would have found some of the flowers of the poem: 'White periwinkles, little pensionnaires / With muslin gowns and shy and candid airs', 'lilies of the valley whose buds blond and tight / seem curls of little school children that light / The priest's procession, when on some saint's day / Along the country paths they make

their way,' and, 'Forget-me-nots, whose eyes of childish blue / Goldstarred like heaven, speak of love still true.'

To the poet, however

> The sweet flowers seem for a fading while
> Dear as our first love's fading smile—
> Till they bruise and wound the heart and sense
> With their lost and terrible innocence.

And there is the lament:

> When we were young, how beautiful life seemed!
> The boundless bright horizons that we dreamed,
>
> And the immortal music of the Day and Night
> Leavening the echo of their wonder and their might
>
> Deep in our hearts and minds. How could the dust
> Of superstitions taught in school rooms, lust
>
> In love's shape, dim our beauty? What dark lie
> Or cruelty's voice, could drown the God-made harmony?

The world of this beauty, who seems 'as she glimmers round the room, / Like a lovely milk-white unicorn' is both magical and elegant, with a background of eighteenth century sophistication: the fairies (modelled perhaps on the ladies at Loughborough, where a portrait of Queen Anne stood 'upon a perfumed dressing table') arrive in sedan chairs; yet they co-exist with nymphs, satyrs, naiads of classical myth, and with the homelier world of the gardener, old Poll Troy, the housekeeper, and the numerous housemaids 'like the thickest-berried / Cherrytrees in their ruched gown'. There are also 'smiling dim as satyr-broods / Horned as moons, that haunt our deepest woods' . . . 'the country gentlemen, so countryfied / That in their rustic grace they try to hide / Their fingers sprouting into leaves; we see / Them sweet as cherries growing from a tree.'

The sleeping beauty is not re-awakened. Instead the gardener warns:

> And oh, far best . . .
> Like fruits to lie in your kind bed,
> To sleep as snug as in the grave
> In your kind bed, and shun the wave,
> Nor ever sigh for a strange land
> And songs no heart can understand.

The beauty in the dark wood is, then, the dangerous impulse of poetry, the first revelation coming to the unloved child in the beautiful, but haunted, house at Renishaw. 'What do you want to be when you grown up?' 'A genius.'

The Sleeping Beauty also reflects the life at Renishaw with its deep woods and great gardens. These surroundings and the exotic tapestries in the house itself grew into Edith Sitwell's imagination. Never exposed to school or relationships with other children save those of the family and their friends, she was 'in my earliest childhood, when not being bullied, ineffably happy under those strange suns that illuminated only *my* life, and were unknown by others . . . But I had not yet reached those years of my later childhood, when, like Arthur Rimbaud (in some ways my closest spiritual relation) I could say, as he said in *Une Saison en Enfer, 'une voix étreignait mon coeur gelé'* [**Taken Care Of** (1965)].

Her parents found this strange child both plain (the Plantagenet features and deep-set eyes) and violent.

In 1922 *Façade,* that technically accomplished group of poems set to music by William Walton was, at first, very naturally, misunderstood. The poems, which were abstract, as was much of the art of the period, contained images both unfamiliar and shocking to the established Georgian poets ('the reynard-coloured sun', 'the wan, grassy sea', 'a swan-bosomed tree', 'the fire furry as a bear'), and were often funny, poetic *jeux d'esprit.* 'The audience is meant to laugh' [**Taken Care Of**].

> 'Do not take a bath in the Jordan,
> Gordon,
> On the holy Sabbath, on the peaceful day!'
> Said the huntsman, playing on his old bagpipe,
> Boring to death the pheasant and the snipe—
> Boring the ptarmigan and grouse for fun—
> Boring them worse than a nine-bore gun.

Some were melancholy, as **"By the Lake,"** inspired perhaps by Verlaine's "Dans le vieux parc solitaire et glacé" from *Les Fêtes Galantes.* Here

> And all the ropes let down from the cloud
> Ring the hard, cold bell-buds from the trees—
> codas
> Of overtones, ecstasies, grown for love's shroud.

In some the poet was experimenting to obtain the rhythms of dance measures, such as waltzes, polkas and foxtrots. She defined rhythm as 'one of the principal translators between dream and reality . . . It is, to the world of sound, what light is to the world of sight . . . My experiments in *Façade* consist of enquiries into the effect on rhythm and speed of the use of rhymes, assonances and dissonances, placed at the beginning and in the middle of lines, as well as those at the end, and in most elaborate patterns' [**Collected Poems** (1930)].

Attacked as frivolous, Edith Sitwell claimed for her early poems the status of butterflies, as defined by the naturalist John Ray, 'whose use is to adorn the world and delight the eyes of men, to brighten the countryside, serving like so many golden spangles to decorate the fields' [**Collected Poems**].

Edith Sitwell had an acute ear. Music was an important part of life at Renishaw, even more so when Helen Rootham arrived as her governess. Helen was a talented pianist and had also a considerable knowledge both of music and of French poetry. Verlaine, Rimbaud and Baudelaire are all influences on Edith Sitwell as well as the music of Stravinsky, Debussy, Chopin, Schumann and Brahms. She was a Symbolist poet at a time when such Russian poets as Gumilev, Mandelstam and Akhmatova were rejecting symbolism.

In **"Colonel Fantock"** Edith Sitwell wrote more intimately of her early life and that of her brothers:

> There is a land, austere and elegant,
> The castle seemed an arabesque in music;

We moved in an hallucination born
Of silence, which like music gave us lotus
To eat, perfuming lips and our long eyelids
As we trailed over the sad summer grass
Or sat beneath a smooth and mournful tree.
. . . I was like one dead, like a small ghost,
A little cold air, wandering and lost.

This is a compassionate poem with its understanding of the unfortunate Colonel Fantock, his confidence destroyed by some careless words.

The nightmare vision diagnosed by Yeats is very apparent in the first version of **"Metamorphosis"** in 1929.

> O Dead, your heart is gone, it cannot weep!
> From decency the skeleton must sleep;
>
> O heart, shrink out of sight, you have no flesh
> For love or dog or worm to court afresh,
>
> Only your youthful smile is mirrored lone
> In that eternity, the skeleton.

Gold Coast Customs in the same year represents a great change in Edith Sitwell's work. Its title was suggested by a custom in Ashantee, a century or so earlier, when the death of an important person was followed by ceremonies in which slaves and poor people were killed so that the bones of the dead could be washed with human blood.

The poem was almost prophetic:

> . . . Do we smell and see
> The sick thick smoke from London burning?

This appalling custom became a metaphor for the poet for what was happening in the contemporary world. The theme of the poem is the spiritual breakdown between the wars. It has a rocky, feverish movement and symbolically places the scene in the primeval mud where the blindness of the slums, the African swamps and 'that foul plague-spot,' Lady Bamburger's heart, all merge. The horror expressed in this poem is that of someone who has suddenly become aware of the facts of nightmare, but it ends with a vision the poet was to develop during and after the Second World War.

> When the rich man's gold and the rich man's
> wheat
> Will grow in the street, that the starved may
> eat,—
> And the sea of the rich will give up its dead—
> And the last blood and fire from my side will be
> shed.
> For the fires of God go marching on.

Edith Sitwell wrote no more poems until after the war had broken out. The tone of her work, as heralded by *Gold Coast Customs* had completely altered. She abandoned the rocking movement of that poem and developed a longer, and steadier, line. She ends **"An Old Woman"**:

> Wise is the earth, consoling grief and glory,
> The golden heroes, proud as the pomp of
> waves,—
> Great is the earth embracing them, their graves,
> And great is the earth's story.
> For though the soundless wrinkles fall like snow
> On many a golden cheek, and creeds grow old

And change,—man's heart, that sun,
Outlives all terrors shaking the old night:
The world's huge fevers burn and shine, turn
   cold,
The golden lovers walk in the holy fields
Where the Abraham-bearded sun, the father of
   all things,
Is shouting of ripeness, and the whole world of
   dews and splendours are singing
To the cradles of men, beasts, harvests, swinging
In the peace of God's heart.

This is, of course, poetry in the grand manner and has to
my ear a noble and majestic sound.

To audiences at her wartime readings, it offered a transcending of the 'terrors shaking the old night', particularly
when a V-1 passed noisily overhead and the poet read
steadily on.

"Still Falls the Rain," set to music by Benjamin Britten,
was suggested by the air raids of 1940. It has an implacable, fateful beat, but the poet re-created out of the on-
slaught the voice of the suffering Christ:

Then sounds the voice of One who like the heart
   of man
Was once a child who among beasts has lain—
'Still do I love, still shed my innocent light, my
   Blood, for thee.'

There is only despair, however, in **"Lullaby,"** a black aspect of the world presented to the child of war, still relevant today to children suffering from adult brutality.

Red is the blood of Poland, Spain,
And thy mother's breast, who has grown wise
In that fouled nest. If she could rise,
Give birth again
In wolfish pelt she'd hide thy bones
To shield thee from the world's long cold
And down on all fours shouldst thou crawl
For thus from no height canst thou fall—
Do, do.

•   •   •

The Judas-coloured sun is gone,
And with the Ape thou art alone.
Do,
      Do.

In **"The Song of the Cold,"** Edith Sitwell mourned 'the
cold in the heart of man.' It is a poem about death in its
many forms.

. . . for this is the Cainozoic period
When we must learn to walk with the gait of the
   Ape and Tiger:
The warmth of the heart is dead, or has changed
   to the world's fever—
And love is but masked murder, the lust for pos-
   session,
The hunger of the Ape, or the confession
Of the last fear, the wish to multiply
Their image, of a race on Oblivion's brink.

Would she now see, in the present crude distortions of the
meaning of sex, the same fear—'of a race on Oblivion's
brink'?

In **"Tears"** she grieved for

. . . Venus whose body has changed to a meta-
physical city
Whose heartbeat is now the sound of the revolu-
   tions,—for love changed
To the hospital mercy, the scientists' hope for
   the future,
And for darkened Man, that complex multiplici-
ty
Of air and water, plant and animal,
Hard diamond, infinite sun.

"Holiday," however, is a poem of resurrection:

Dives and Lazarus are brothers again:
They seem of gold as they come up from the city
Casting the grave-clothes of their lives
Where the ragged dust is nobly born as the Sun.
Now Atlas lays aside his dying world,
The clerk, the papers in the dusty office;
And lovers meet their bright Antipodes
To whom they are borne by the young siren seas
Of blood . . .

In this poem, there is a kinship with the work of Stanley
Spencer, as if for both artists the darkness of war stimulated its opposite: a vision of transcendence.

For a poet with such acute sensibilities and insight as
Edith Sitwell, the atomic bomb was a further and more
terrible revelation of the 'Cainozoic period.' Out of this
came **"Dirge for the New Sunrise"** with this lovely stanza:

There was a morning when the holy light
Was young. The beautiful First Creature came
To our water-springs and thought us without
   blame.
Our hearts seemed safe in our breasts and sang
   to the Light—
The marrow in the bone
We dreamed was safe . . . the blood in the veins,
   the sap in the tree
Were springs of Deity.

All values however were threatened on 6th August, 1945,
when:

—The ghost of the heart of Man . . . red Cain
And the more murderous brain
Of Man, still redder Nero that conceived the
   death
Of his mother Earth, and tore
Her womb, to know the place where he was con-
   ceived.

'Before the time came for *The Shadow of Cain* to be written,' wrote Edith Sitwell, 'various of my poems spoke of
the change from the worship of the holy life-giving gold
of the wheat, to the destructive gold of Dives—the change
from the warmth of love that makes all men brothers to
the state in which men only call their fellow men 'Brother'
in order to act the part of Cain.'

Nadezhda Mandelstam, writing of Russian life in 1932,
said: 'The century saw intensive efforts to rehabilitate
Cain. Someone even explained that Cain, as a man with
new ideas about husbandry, had no option but to kill the
backward shepherd Abel . . . Children in the lower classes at school had to learn . . . always to be ready to de-

nounce their own fathers. Our best educators followed in the footsteps of Cain,' [*Hope Abandoned* (1974)].

Edith Sitwell's *The Shadow of Cain* opens, like some majestic opera, in 'the ancient Cold' during 'huge migrations from some primeval disaster in the heart of Man'. It reflects the Second Fall, a turning away from love to a primeval cold like a new Ice Age when there is only a memory of warmth. In this vision the lost hordes have almost forgotten the power of communication and return to the inhuman world of the huge prehistoric animals. The point of extreme cold is, nevertheless, a point of extreme meaning. They reach the door of birth and death and are confronted by the three primal realities: birth, struggle and death, revealed through lightning. It seemed as if a new spring might be possible, that a cosmic love might return.

> But there came a roar as if the Sun and
> Earth had come together—
> The Sun descending and the Earth ascending
> To take its place above . . . that Primal Matter
> Was broken, the womb from which all life
>   began.
> Then to the murdered Sun a totem pole of dust
>   arose in Memory of Man.

This atomic disaster uproots the dead Lazarus, the man of poverty, representing 'the gold in the husk of the world', the sacrificed man, to whom the terror-stricken hordes come for redemption, as once they came to Christ. Dives, too, is revealed 'like a leprous Sun,' to be cured only by the true gold. There is an alchemical significance in this poem and indeed the poet quotes Paracelsus in her notes:

> Gold is the most noble of all, the most precious and primary metal . . . And we are not prepared to deny that leprosy in all its forms, can be thereby removed from the human frame.

Then the frightened survivors accuse Dives: You are the Shadow of Cain. Out of the split sepulchre and the womb comes the judgment:

>   when
> The last clamour of the Bought and Sold
> The agony of Gold
> Is hushed . . . when the last Judas-kiss
> Has died upon the cheek of the Starved Man
>   Christ, those ashes that were men
> Will rise again
> To be our fires upon the Judgment Day!
> And yet—who dreamed that Christ died in vain?
> He walks again on the Seas of Blood, He comes
>   in
> The terrible Rain.

It is interesting that this great poem was recognised and praised by a Marxist critic, Jack Lindsay, who wrote of this and some of Edith Sitwell's later work: 'The figures of Cain, Dives, Lazarus and Christ are basic symbols of the human condition and the forms of social struggle that make up history.' He noted her themes of 'elemental death and renewal.'

> The battle of men is realised, not as something projected on to the detached screen of the Universe, but as a storm of potencies which reaches everywhere . . . A form of pantheism? Yes, but

not quite according to the definitions in the manuals of philosophy . . . the philosophic affinity is rather with Marx . . .

Edith Sitwell was never a Communist. The revolutionary spirit shown in her work was not precisely that in which Lindsay believed. There is a wide gap between alchemical transformation and Marxist philosophy. Nevertheless Lindsay penetrated the poet's meaning more deeply than many critics of the time.

The Shadow of Cain represented for the poet herself a way of reconciling the two forces she had always perceived so clearly: those of extreme light and those of extreme dark. She had succeeded, as Blake would have put it, 'in redeeming the Contraries.'

In one of her last poems, **"A Song of the Dust,"** she comes to terms with death in these beautiful lines:

> Beyond the ripening stillness
> I heard the thunder of the growth of vines
> And the great thunders in the veins of youth
> And now the amethyst stars of the night dew
> That fall upon our hair lifted like vines
> By the wind of night, hold all tomorrow's heat
> And the violet heart of oceans in each sun,
>
> And morning comes to the heart and the heart's
>   warmth, its fevers,
> Rapacity and grandeur—comes to the dress
> Of flesh inconstant as the splendours and the ru-
>   bies
> Of the day's heat, the pity and glory of the rain-
>   bow.
>
> And still the uncombatable song rose to the light
> From all the heights of Being, and from the
>   depth of the last abyss:
>
> If every grain of my dust should be Satan—
> If every atom of my heart were Lucifer—
> If every drop of my blood were an Abaddon
> —Yet should I love.

Edith Sitwell was greatly honoured in her lifetime. Three universities made her a Doctor of Literature, she became a Dame of the British Empire and in 1957 was one of three vice presidents of the Royal Society of Literature. In 1962 to celebrate her 75th birthday there was a gala performance of *Façade* at the crowded Royal Festival Hall. The inevitable reaction was, however, approaching. New poets were appearing with very different voices. Critics began to complain of a repetition of symbols and images in her work, attacked her grand manner and praised the new under-statement, accusing her of empty rhetoric.

Reading her work today, however, is to enter a world of great originality and beauty. There are many 'butterflies' which will continue 'to delight the eyes of men.' In addition, no other poet has been able to deal with the implications of the nuclear age against such a vast backcloth. Rising above the chauvinism of politicians, Edith Sitwell saw immediately that the crime was that of humanity against itself and against its mother, the earth, 'and tore / Her womb, to know the place where he was conceived.' (pp. 57-67)

Jean MacVean, "Another Look at Edith Sit-

well," in Agenda, *Vol. 21, No. 3, Autumn, 1983, pp. 57-68.*

FURTHER READING

Bogan, Louise. "Edith Sitwell." In her *A Poet's Alphabet,* edited by Robert Phelps and Ruth Limmer, pp. 372-77. New York: McGraw-Hill, 1970.
    Collects three reviews of Sitwell's work written by Bogan for the *New Yorker* magazine.

Brophy, James D. "Electric Eel." In his *Edith Sitwell: The Symbolist Order,* pp. 3-17. Carbondale: Southern Illinois University Press, 1968.
    Overview of Sitwell's critical works in which Brophy asserts that "besides the evisceration of authors and critics who annoy her, [Sitwell] reveals considerable appreciative understanding of the organic integrity of poetry."

Cohen, J. M. "Books and Writers." *Spectator* 185, No. 6385 (10 November 1950): 472.
    Laudatory review of *A Book of the Winter, The Canticle of the Rose,* and *Facade and Other Poems.*

Coles, Mervyn D. "The Poetry of Edith Sitwell." *Contemporary Review* 195, No. 1118 (February 1959): 120-23.
    Contends that Sitwell filters her personal emotions through universal images of nature.

Connolly, Cyril. "Edith Sitwell." In his *Previous Convictions,* pp. 331-34. London: Hamish Hamilton, 1963.
    Contends that while Sitwell's poetry is somewhat flawed, it has "the purest poetic intention" of any twentieth century verse.

Deutsch, Babette. "Creative Sensibility." *The Nation* 145, No. 1 (3 July 1937): 20-1.
    Review of *Selected Poems* that addressed claims by other critics that Sitwell's poetry is inaccessible.

———. "Twentieth Century Sense and Sensibility." *Accent* XV, No. 2 (Spring 1955): 149-52.
    Favorably contrasts Sitwell's *Collected Poems* with W. H. Auden's *The Shield of Achilles.*

Driberg, Tom. "Queen Edith." *The New Statesman and Nation* XLVII, No. 1195 (30 January 1954): 131.
    Letter to the editor in which this member of parliament condemns the anonymous attack on Sitwell in the article entitled "Queen Edith."

Forster, E. M. "Review of *The English Eccentics.*" *Spectator* 150, No. 5,473 (19 May 1933): 716.
    States the theme of *The English Eccentrics* is "that eccentricity ranks as a high national asset, and that so long as it is respected there is some hope that our country will not go mad as a whole."

Glendenning, Victoria. *Edith Sitwell: A Unicorn Among Lions.* New York: Alfred A. Knopf, 1981, 393 p.
    Biography of Sitwell.

Hassan, Ihab H. "Edith Sitwell and the Symbolist Tradi-

tion." *Comparative Literature* VII, No. 3 (Summer 1955): 240-51.
    Uses Sitwell's work to demonstrate the influence of late nineteenth-century French verse upon British modernists.

Lindsay, Jack. "The Poetry of Edith Sitwell." *Life and Letters* 64, No. 149 (January 1950): 39-52.
    Contends that Sitwell is "the first fully *English* writer" since Dickens.

Mégroz, R. L. *The Three Sitwells: A Biographical and Critical Study.* London: The Richards Press Limited, 1927, 333 p.
    Analysis of the Sitwells' early lives and careers.

Mercier, Vivian. "Another Look at the Sitwells." *The Hudson Review* VII, No. 3 (Autumn 1954): 445-53.
    Review of works by the three Sitwell siblings in which Mercier refutes laudatory estimations of Edith Sitwell's poetry.

Moore, Harry T. "Sharp Slaps for Some." *New York Times Book Review* (2 May 1965): 6.
    Contends that despite its bitter and critical tone, *Taken Care Of* is "rewardingly full of entertaining observations and piquant insights."

Muir, Edwin. "Edith Sitwell." In his *Transition: Essays on Contemporary Literature,* pp. 147-59 New York: The Viking Press, 1926.
    Examines how Sitwell's romantic poetry transforms "the dynamic into the static" and "the audible into the visible."

Nemerov, Howard. "Poets in the Dark." *The Kenyon Review* XII, No. 1 (Winter 1950): 165-72.
    Brief review of *The Song of the Cold* in which Nemerov contends that Sitwell has wrongly substituted emotional intensity for technical precision.

"Queen Edith." *The New Statesman and Nation* XLVII, No. 1194 (23 January 1954): 96-7.
    Satirical indictment of Sitwell's exalted status in English letters.

Pearson, John. " 'In Full United Swing'—The Sitwells Remembered." *Listener* 100, No. 2588 (30 November 1978): 731-32.
    Collection of impressions and reminiscences concerning the Sitwells by their friends and colleagues.

———. *Facades: Edith, Osbert, and Sacheverell Sitwell.* London: Macmillan London Limited, 1978, 534 p.
    Biography of the Sitwell siblings.

Scott-James, R. A. "Modern Poets." In his *Fifty Years of English Literature, 1900-1950,* pp. 210-39. London: Longmans, Green and Co., 1951.
    Contains a brief overview of Sitwell's career.

Symons, Julian. "Miss Edith Sitwell Have and Had and Heard." *London Magazine* 4, No. 8 (November 1964): 50-63.
    Appraisal of Sitwell's career that focuses upon fluctuating opinion of her in fashionable literary circles.

"The Artist as Biographer." *Times Literary Supplement* No. 3, 163 (12 October 1962): 785-86.
    Contends that Sitwell's psychological approach in her two biographical works about Queen Elizabeth was "certainly off the mark."

Walton, Eda Lou. "Allegory of Swift." *Nation* 146, No. 16 (16 April 1938): 448-49.

   Examines the historical, fictitious, and allegorical elements of *I Live Under a Black Sun.*

Westcott, Glenway. "A Face to Laugh, A Face to Cry." *Book Week—New York Harold Tribune* (2 May 1965): 3, 8-10.
   Laudatory review of *Taken Care Of.*

Williams, Charles. "Edith Sitwell, Osbert Sitwell, Sacheverell Sitwell." In his *Poetry at Present,* pp. 175-93. Oxford at the Clarendon Press, 1930.
   Asserts that the disconcerting atmosphere that pervades Sitwell's verse sets it apart from the work of other poets.

Derek Walcott

1930-

(Full name: Derek Alton Walcott) West Indian poet, playwright, critic and journalist.

Walcott is a highly respected author whose poetry and plays often focus on the opposing African and European influences of his colonial West Indian heritage. His poetic language reflects this cultural division, employing both the formal, structured language of English verse and the colorful dialect of his native island, St. Lucia. While embracing the literary tradition of England, he frequently denounces the exploitation and suppression of Caribbean culture resulting from British colonization. His acclaimed poem "A Far Cry from Africa" delineates the theme of uncertain identity that has dominated his poetic career: "I who am poisoned with the blood of both, / Where shall I turn, divided to the vein? / I who have cursed / The drunken officer of British rule, how choose / Between this Africa and the English tongue I love?"

Walcott was born on St. Lucia, a small island in the West Indies. He has characterized his childhood as "schizophrenic," referring to the divided loyalties associated with his African and English ancestry and the fact that he grew up in a middle-class, Protestant family in a society that was predominantly Catholic and poor. His mother, a teacher actively involved in the local theater, strongly influenced his artistic development, and although his father died when he was still an infant, Walcott drew inspiration from the poems and numerous watercolor paintings he left behind. In an interview, Walcott explained: "[My father's paintings] gave me a kind of impetus and a strong sense of continuity. I felt that what had been cut off in him somehow was an extension that I was continuing." Walcott's childhood ambition was to be a painter, and in his autobiographical poem *Another Life,* he and his friend, the painter Dustin St. Omer, vow to record the unique atmosphere of the Caribbean through their art: "we would never leave the island / until we had put down, in paint, in words . . . / all its sunken, leaf-choked ravines, / every neglected, self-pitying inlet. . . . "

Walcott also developed an affinity for the English literature he read in school, and he began writing poetry, often imitating such writers as W. H. Auden, T. S. Eliot and Dylan Thomas. At the age of eighteen, he financed the publication of *Twenty-Five Poems,* his first poetry collection. While studying literature at St. Mary's College in St. Lucia and at the University of West Indies in Jamaica, he completed two more volumes of poetry and produced *Henri Christophe,* a historical play written in verse. A following historical play entitled *Drums and Colours* brought Walcott both critical recognition and a Rockefeller Fellowship to study theater in the United States. Upon his return to the Caribbean, he became intensely involved in Trinidad's artistic community, writing reviews and organizing the Trinidad Theatre Workshop, where several of

his plays were produced during the 1950s and 1960s. Since the 1970s, Walcott has divided his time between the West Indies and the United States, where he has taught at Yale, Columbia, and other universities.

The importance of understanding and preserving West Indian culture is prominent in Walcott's works. Many of his plays, often called "folk-dramas," are firmly rooted in the common life and language of the West Indies, and frequently evoke Caribbean dialect and legends. *Ti-Jean and His Brothers,* for example, is strongly influenced by the African art of storytelling. In this play, a humble, sensible boy named Ti-Jean succeeds in outwitting the Devil. Walcott explained his use of folklore and dialectical speech: "The great challenge for me was to write as powerfully as I could without writing down to the audience, so that the large emotions could be taken in by a fisherman or a guy on the street, even if he didn't understand every line." Walcott's *Dream on Monkey Mountain,* often considered his most successful play, won an Obie Award in 1971. Many critics interpreted the play as a metaphorical work in which the downtrodden consciousness of a colonized society is symbolized through the hallucinations of Makak, an aging charcoal maker and vendor. In an interview Walcott described the main character of the play: "Makak comes from my own childhood. I can see him for what he is now, a brawling, ruddy drunk who would come down the street on a Saturday when he got paid and let out an immense roar that would terrify all the children. . . . This was a degraded man, but he had some elemental force in him that is still terrifying; in another society he would have been a warrior."

Many critics have emphasized Walcott's portrayal of the Caribbean as a society of uncertain heritage—a "new world" in which the artist may greatly influence the development of a cohesive cultural identity. His long autobiographical poem *Another Life* celebrates the artistic opportunity presented by an ambiguous culture: "we were the light of the world! / We were blest with a virginal, unpainted world / with Adam's task of giving things their names." However, while Walcott's poetry expresses the potential for a unique identity of diversity in the West Indies, it also reveals his fear that island culture will become overwhelmed by British dominance and expanding tourism. In *The Star Apple Kingdom* he declares: "One morning the Caribbean was cut up / by seven prime ministers who bought the sea in bolts— / one thousand miles of aquamarine with lace trimmings, / one million yards of lime-coloured silk. . . ." His poem "St. Lucie" laments the loss of French patois to the national language of English: "Come back to me / my language / Come back, / cacao, / grigri, / solitaire, / oiseau." Contrasting with the enthusiasm of *Another Life,* many of Walcott's later poems depict the artist as an outcast from the West Indian community—estranged from both African and European heritage. In "The Light of the World" from *The Arkansas Testament,* he expresses his sense of alienation and futility as a poet: "There was nothing they wanted, nothing I could give them / but this thing I have called 'The Light of the World'."

Anger and resentment associated with the injustice of colonized history is another common motif in Walcott's poetry. Reviewers praised his poem "The Schooner Flight," in which Shabine, a smuggler, sailor and poet of racially mixed heritage, feels exiled by his own past: "I met history once, but he ain't recognize me, / a parchment Creole, with warts / like an old sea-bottle, crawling like a crab / through the holes of shadow cast by the net. . . ." Discussing the role of colonized history in determining Caribbean identity, Walcott stated: "At great cost and a lot of criticism, what I used to try to point out was that there is a great danger in historical sentimentality. . . . The whole situation in the Caribbean is an illegitimate situation. If we admit that from the beginning that there is no shame in that historical bastardy, then we can be men. But if we continue to sulk and say, 'Look what the slave-owner did,' and so forth, we will never mature." *Omeros,* Walcott's acclaimed epic poem, has been interpreted as a historical and literary pilgrimage into West Indian history. Reinventing Homer's *Odyssey* as he casts West Indian fishermen, prostitutes, and landlords in such classical roles as Achilles, Helen, and Hector, Walcott explores various cultures of the world, tracing their influence on the present identity of the Caribbean people. Oliver Taplin observed: "Throughout the poem, as in the mind, there are persistent reflections on the historical events that have directly and indirectly shaped the characters' lives: the brutal attacks of the slaves on Achille's African forebears, of Europeans on native Americans, of French warships against British when the Windward Islands were first colonized. . . . But Mr. Walcott recalls these scenes of death and suffering with the objective sympathy of a Homer, who tells what happened to Trojans as well as Greeks."

(See also *CLC,* Vols. 2, 4, 9, 14, 25, 42; *Contemporary Authors,* Vols. 89-92; *Contemporary Authors New Revision Series,* Vol. 26; *Black Writers* and *Dictionary of Literary Biography Yearbook, 1981*)

PRINCIPAL WORKS

POETRY

25 Poems   1948
Epitaph for the Young: A Poem in XII Cantos   1949
In a Green Night: Poems, 1948-1960   1962
Selected Poems   1964
The Castaway and Other Poems   1965
The Gulf and Other Poems   1969
Another Life   1973
Sea Grapes   1976
Selected Verse   1976
The Star-Apple Kingdom   1979
The Fortunate Traveller   1981
Selected Poetry   1981
Midsummer   1984
Collected Poems, 1948-1984   1986
The Arkansas Testament   1987
Omeros   1990

PLAYS

Henri Christophe: A Chronicle in Seven Scenes   1950
Harry Dernier: A Play for Radio Production   1951
Wine of the Country   1953
The Sea at Dauphin: A Play in One Act   1953
Ione: A Play with Music   1957
Drums and Colours: An Epic Drama   1958
Ti-Jean and His Brothers   1958
Malcochon; or, Six in the Rain   1959
Dream on Monkey Mountain   1967
In a Fine Castle   1970
The Charlatan   1974
The Joker of Seville   1974
O Babylon!   1976
Remembrance   1977
Pantomime   1978
Three Plays   1986

Derek Walcott (Interview with Edward Hirsch)

To live next door to Walcott, even for a week, is to understand how he has managed to be so productive over the years. A prodigious worker, he often starts at about 4:30 in the morning and continues until he has done a four or five hour stint—by the time most people are getting up for the day. On a small easel next to a small blue portable typewriter, he had recently done a pencil drawing of his wife, Norline, and a couple of new watercolors to serve as storyboards for a film version of **Pantomime** *(he is doing the film script); he had also just finished the draft of an original screenplay about a steel band, as well as an extended essay about the Grenada invasion (to be called "Good Old Heart of Darkness"), and a new manuscript of poems,* **The Arkansas Testament** *(Spring, 1987). At the time of this interview the cuttings for two more films were all but complete: a film version of his play,* **Haitian Earth** *(which he had produced in St. Lucia the previous year), and a documentary film about Hart Crane for public television. At times one gets the impression that the poetry for which he is primarily known has had to be squeezed between all his other projects.*

And yet while I was in St. Lucia, most of Walcott's other activities were suspended as he worked on a new poem, **"The Light of the World."** *It is a homecoming poem, a narrative lyric about returning to Castries. The poem is set on a transport—what we would call a mini-bus—and characterizes the poet's sense of feeling both separated from, and connected to, the life of the people around him. Once more he is struck by the grace as well as the difficult poverty of his people; he reexperiences the beauty of St. Lucian women and feels the weight of their daily lives.* **"The Light of the World"** *is a large poem of guilt and expiation, and it gives a good sense of Walcott's inner feelings during the time of our interview.*

Our conversation took place over three days—beginning in the late afternoon or early evening and continuing until dark. We talked at the table and chairs outside our cottages where we could hear the wind in the coconut trees and the waves breaking on the shore. A compact man in his mid-fifties, Walcott was still dressed from his afternoon on the beach—barefoot, a pair of brown beach trunks and a thin cotton shirt. Often he kept a striped beach towel draped around his shoulders, a white flour-sack beach hat pushed forward jauntily on his head. He seemed always to be either smoking or about to start.

• • •

[Hirsch]: *I'd like to begin by asking you to talk about your family background. In many ways it was atypical for St. Lucia. For example, you were raised as a Methodist on a primarily Catholic island. Your family also seems to have been unusually oriented toward the arts.*

[Walcott]: My family background really only consists of my mother. She was a widow. My father died quite young; he must have been thirty-one. Then there was my twin brother and my sister. We had two aunts as well, my father's sisters. But the immediate family consisted of my mother, my brother, my sister, and me. I remember from very early childhood my mother, who was a teacher, reciting a lot around the house. I remember coming across drawings that my father had done, poems that he had written, watercolors that were hanging in our living room—his original watercolors—and a terrific series of books: a lot of Dickens, Scott, quite a lot of poetry. There

was also an old victrola with a lot of classical records. And so my family always had this interest in the arts. Coming from a Methodist minority in a French Catholic island, we also felt a little beleaguered. The Catholicism propounded by the French provincial priests in St. Lucia was a very hide-bound, prejudiced, medieval, almost hounding kind of Catholicism. The doctrine that was taught assigned all Protestants to limbo. So we felt defensive about our position. This never came to a head, but we did feel we had to stay close together. It was good for me too, to be able to ask questions as a Protestant, to question large authority. Nobody in my generation at my age would dare question the complete and absolute authority of the church. Even into sixth form, my school friends and I used to have some terrific arguments about religious doctrine. It was a good thing. I think young writers ought to be heretical.

In an essay called **"Leaving School"** *you suggest that the artifacts of your father's twin avocations, poetry and painting, made your own sense of vocation seem inevitable. Would you describe his creative work and how it affected you?*

My mother, who is nearly ninety now, still talks continually about my father. All my life I've been aware of her grief about his absence and her strong pride in his conduct. He was very young when he died of mastoiditis, which is an ear infection. Medicine in St. Lucia in those days was crude or very minimal; I know he had to go to Barbados for operations. I don't remember the death or anything like that, but I always felt his presence because of the paintings that he did. He had a self-portrait in watercolor in an oval frame next to a portrait of my mother, an oil that was very good for an amateur painter. I remember once coming across a backcloth of a very ordinary kind of moonlight scene that he had painted for some number that was going to be done by a group of people who did concerts and recitations and stuff like that. So that was always there. Now that didn't make me a morose, morbid child. Rather, in a sense, it gave me a kind of impetus and a strong sense of continuity. I felt that what had been cut off in him somehow was an extension that I was continuing. (pp. 198-201)

Your book-length autobiographical poem, **Another Life,** *makes it clear that two painters were crucial to your development: your mentor Harold Simmons, called Harry in the poem, and your friend Dunstan St. Omer, renamed Gregorias. Would you talk about their importance to you?*

Harry taught us. He had paints, he had music in his studio, and he was evidently a good friend of my father's. When he found out that we liked painting, he invited about four or five of us to come up to his studio and sit out on his veranda. He gave us equipment and told us to draw. Now that may seem very ordinary in a city, in another place, but in a very small, poor country like St. Lucia it was extraordinary. He encouraged us to spend our Saturday afternoons painting; he surrounded us with examples of his own painting. Just to let us be there and to have the ambience of his books, his music, his own supervision and the stillness and dedication that his life meant in that studio was a terrific example. The influence was not so much technical. Of course, I picked up a few things from him in terms of technique: how to do a good sky, how to water the paper, how to circle it, how to draw properly and concentrate on it, and all of that. But there were other things apart from the drawing. Mostly, it was the model of the man as a professional artist that was the example. After a while, the younger guys dropped out of the drawing thing and Dunstan St. Omer and I were left. We used to go out and paint together. We discovered it at the same time. (p. 202)

What would you say about the epiphanic experience described in **Another Life,** *which seems to have confirmed your destiny as a poet and sealed a bond to your native island?*

There are some things people avoid saying in interviews because they sound pompous or sentimental or too mystical. I have never separated the writing of poetry from prayer. I have grown up believing it is a vocation, a religious vocation. What I described in *Another Life*—about being on the hill and feeling the sort of dissolution that happened—is a frequent experience in a younger writer. I felt this sweetness of melancholy, of a sense of mortality, or rather of immortality, a sense of gratitude both for what you feel is a gift and for the beauty of the earth, the beauty of life around us. When that's forceful in a young writer, it can make you cry. It's just clear tears; it's not grimacing or being contorted, it's just a flow that happens. The body feels it is melting into what it has seen. This continues in the poet. It may be repressed in some way, but I think we continue in all our lives to have that sense of melting, of the "I" not being important. That is the ecstasy. It doesn't happen as much when you get older. There's that wonderful passage in [Michael] Traherne where he talks about seeing the children as moving jewels until they learn the dirty devices of the world. It's not *that* mystic. Ultimately, it's what Yeats says: "Such a sweetness flows into the breast that we laugh at everything and everything we look upon is blessed." That's always there. It's a benediction, a transference. It's gratitude, really. The more of that a poet keeps, the more genuine his nature. I've always felt that sense of gratitude. I've never felt equal to it in terms of my writing, but I've never felt that I was ever less than that. And so in that particular passage in **Another Life** I was recording a particular moment.

How do you write? In regard to your equation of poetry and prayer, is the writing ritualized in any way?

I don't know how many writers are willing to confess to their private preparatory rituals before they get down to putting something on paper. But I imagine that all artists and all writers in that moment before they begin their working day or working night have that area between beginning and preparation, and however brief it is, there is something about it votive and humble and in a sense ritualistic. Individual writers have different postures, different stances, even different physical attitudes as they stand or sit over their blank paper, and in a sense, without doing it, they are crossing themselves; I mean, it's like the habit of Catholics going into water: you cross yourself before you go in. Any serious attempt to try to do something worthwhile is ritualistic. I haven't noticed what my own devices are. But I do know that if one thinks a poem is

coming on—in spite of the noise of the typewriter, or the traffic outside the window, or whatever—you do make a retreat, a withdrawal into some kind of silence that cuts out everything around you. What you're taking on is really not a renewal of your identity but actually a renewal of your *anonymity* so that what's in front of you becomes more important than what you are. Equally—and it may be a little pretentious-sounding to say it—sometimes if I feel that I have done good work I do pray, I do say thanks. It isn't often, of course. I don't do it every day. I'm not a monk, but if something does happen I say thanks because I feel that it is really a piece of luck, a kind of fleeting grace that has happened to one. Between the beginning and the ending and the actual composition that goes on, there is a kind of trance that you hope to enter where every aspect of your intellect is functioning simultaneously for the progress of the composition. But there is no way you can induce that trance.

Lately, I find myself getting up earlier, which may be a sign of late middle-age. It worries me a bit. I guess this is part of the ritual: I go and make a cup of coffee, put on the kettle, and have a cigarette. By now I'm not too sure if out of habit I'm getting up for the coffee rather than to write. I may be getting up that early to smoke, not really to write.

What time is this?

It can vary. Sometimes it's as early as half-past three, which is, you know, not too nice. The average time would be about five. It depends on how well I'm sleeping. But that hour, that whole time of day, is wonderful in the Caribbean. I love the cool darkness and the joy and splendor of the sunrise coming up. I guess I would say, especially in the location of where I am, the early dark and the sunrise, and being up with the coffee and with whatever you're working on, is a very ritualistic thing. I'd even go further and say it's a religious thing. It has its instruments and its surroundings. And you can feel your own spirit waking.

Recently, I heard you say that you were deeply formed by Methodism. How?

In a private way, I think I still have a very simple, straightforward foursquare Methodism in me. I admire the quiet, pragmatic reason that is there in a faith like Methodism, which is a very practical thing of conduct. I'm not talking about a fanatical fundamentalism. I suppose the best word for it is "decency." Decency and understanding are what I've learned from being a Methodist. Always, one was responsible to God for one's inner conduct and not to any immense hierarchy of angels and saints. In a way I think I tried to say that in some earlier poems. There's also a very strong sense of carpentry in Protestantism, in making things simply and in a utilitarian way. At this period of my life and work, I think of myself in a way as a carpenter, as one making frames, simply and well. I'm working a lot in quatrains, or I have been, and I feel that there is something in that that is very ordinary, you know, without any mystique. I'm trying to get rid of the mystique as much as possible. And so I find myself wanting to write very simply cut, very contracted, very speakable and very challenging quatrains in rhymes. Any other shape seems ornate, an elaboration on that essential cube that really is the poem. So we can then say the craft is as ritualistic as that of a carpenter putting down his plane and measuring his stanzas and setting them squarely. And the frame becomes more important than the carpenter.

Another Life suggests that eventually you gave up painting as a vocation and decided to concentrate on poetry. Recently, though, you seem to be at work on your watercolors again. What happened?

What I tried to say in *Another Life* is that the act of painting is not an intellectual act dictated by reason. It is an act that is swept very physically by the sensuality of the brushstroke. I've always felt that some kind of intellect, some kind of preordering, some kind of criticism of the thing before it is done, has always interfered with my ability to do a painting. I am in fairly continual practice. I think I'm getting adept at watercolor. I'm less mucky. I think I could do a reasonable oil painting. I could probably, if I really set out, be a fairly good painter. I can approach the sensuality. I know how it feels, but for me there is just no completion. I'm content to be a moderately good watercolorist. But I'm not content to be a moderately good poet. That's a very different thing.

*Am I correct that you published your first poem, **"The Voice of St. Lucia,"** at the precocious age of fourteen? I've read that the poem stirred up a considerable local controversy.*

I wrote a poem talking about learning about God through nature and not through the church. The poem was Miltonic and posed nature as a way to learn. I sent it to the local papers and it was printed. Of course, to see your work in print for any younger writer is a great kick. And then the paper printed a letter in which a priest replied (in verse!) stating that what I was saying was blasphemous and that the proper place to find God was in church. For a young boy to get that sort of response from a mature older man, a priest who was an Englishman, and to be accused of blasphemy was a shock. What was a more chastising thing was that the response was in verse. The point of course was to show me that he was also capable of writing verse. He did his in couplets and mine was in blank verse. I would imagine if I looked at both now that mine was better.

*Most American and English readers think of **In a Green Night** as your first book. Before you published abroad, however, you had already printed three booklets at your own expense in the West Indies. How did you come to publish the first one, **25 Poems**?*

I used to write every day in an exercise book, and when I first wrote I wrote with great originality. I just wrote as hard and as well as I felt. I remember the great elation and release I felt, a sort of hooking on to a thing, when I read [W. H.] Auden, Eliot, and everyone. One day I would write like Spender, another day I would write like Dylan Thomas. When I felt I had enough poems that I liked, I wanted to see them in print. We had no publishing house in St. Lucia or in the Caribbean. There was a Faber collection of books that had come out with poets like Eliot and Auden, and I liked the type-face and how the books

looked. I thought, "I want to have a book like that." So I selected a collection of twenty-five of them and thought, "Well, these will look good because they'll look like they came from abroad; they'll look like a published book." I went to my mother and said, "I'd like to publish a book of poems, and I think it's going to cost me two hundred dollars." She was just a seamstress and a schoolteacher, and I remember her being very upset because she wanted to do it. Somehow she got it;—a lot of money for a woman to have found on her salary. She gave it to me, and I sent off to Trinidad and had the book printed. When the books came back I would sell them to friends. I made the money back. In terms of seeing a book in print, the only way I could have done it was to publish it myself. (pp. 203-08)

You once described yourself at nineteen as "an elated, exuberant poet madly in love with English" and said that as a young writer you viewed yourself as legitimately prolonging "the mighty line" of Marlowe and Milton. Will you talk about that sense of yourself?

I come from a place that likes grandeur; it likes large gestures; it is not inhibited by flourish; it is a rhetorical society; it is a society of physical performance; it is a society of style. The highest achievement of style is rhetoric, as it is in speech and performance. It isn't a modest society. A performer in the Caribbean has to perform with the right flourish. A Calypsonian performer is equivalent to a bullfighter in the ring. He has to come over. He can write the wittiest Calypso, but if he's going to deliver it, he has to deliver it well, and he has to hit the audience with whatever technique he has. Modesty is not possible in performance in the Caribbean, and that's wonderful. It's better to be large and to make huge gestures than to be modest and do tiptoeing types of presentations of oneself. Even if it's a private platform, it is a platform. The voice does go up in a poem. It is an address, even if it is to oneself. And the greatest address is in the rhetoric. I grew up in a place in which if you learned poetry, you shouted it out. Boys would scream it out and perform it and do it and flourish it. If you wanted to approximate that thunder or that power of speech, it couldn't be done by a little modest voice in which you muttered something to someone else. I came out of that society of the huge gesture. And literature is like that, I mean *theatrical* literature is like that, whether it's Greek or whatever. The recitation element in poetry is one I hope I never lose because it's an essential part of the voice being asked to perform. If we have poets we're really asking them, "Okay, tell me a poem." Generally the implication is, "Mutter me a poem." I'm not in that group.

*There is a confident, fiery sense of privilege in your early work. In a recent poem, **Midsummer,** you write "Forty years gone, in my island childhood, I felt that / the gift of poetry had made me one of the chosen, / that all experience was kindling to the fire of the Muse."*

I never thought of my gift—I have to say "my gift" because I believe it is a gift—as anything that I did completely on my own. I have felt from my boyhood that I had one function and that was somehow to articulate, not my own experience, but what I saw around me. From the time I was a child I knew it was beautiful. If you go to a peak anywhere in St. Lucia, you feel a simultaneous newness and sense of timelessness at the same time—the presence of where you are. It's a primal thing and it has always been that way. At the same time I knew that the poor people around me were not beautiful in the romantic sense of being colorful people to paint or to write about. I lived, I have seen them and I have seen things that I don't need to go far to see. I felt that that was what I would write about. That's what I felt my job was. It's something that other writers have said in their own way, even if it sounds arrogant. Yeats has said it; Joyce has said it. It's amazing Joyce could say that he wants to write for his race, meaning the Irish. You'd think that Joyce would have a larger, more continental kind of mind, but Joyce continued insisting on his provinciality at the same time he had the most universal mind since Shakespeare. What we can do as poets in terms of our honesty is simply to write within the immediate perimeter of not more than twenty miles really.

How does your sense of discovery of new subject matter integrate with the formal elements in your work?

One of the things that people have to look at in West Indian literature is this: that what we were deprived of was also our privilege. There was a great joy in making a world which so far, up to then, had been undefined. And yet the imagination wants its limits and delights in its limits. It finds its freedom in the definition of those limits. In a sense, you want to give more symmetry to lives that have been undefined. My generation of West Indian writers has felt such a powerful elation at having the privilege of writing about places and people for the first time and, simultaneously, having behind them the tradition of knowing how well it can be done—by a Defoe, a Dickens, a Richardson. Our world made us yearn for structure as opposed to wishing to break away from it because there was no burden, no excess of literature in our heads. It was all new.

Well, then how do you see yourself in terms of the great tradition of poetry in the English language?

I don't. I am primarily, absolutely a Caribbean writer. The English language is nobody's special property. It is the property of the imagination: it is the property of the language itself. I have never felt inhibited in trying to write as well as the greatest English poets. Now that has led to a lot of provincial criticism: the Caribbean critic may say, "You are trying to be English," and the English critic may say, "Welcome to the club." These are two provincial statements at either end of the spectrum. It's not a matter of trying to be English. I am obviously a Caribbean poet. I yearn for the company of better Caribbean poets, quite frankly. I feel a little lonely. I don't see what I thought might have happened—a stronger energy, a stronger discipline, and a stronger drive in Caribbean poetry. That may be because the Caribbean is more musical: every culture has its particular emphasis and obviously the Caribbean's poetry, talent, and genius is in its music. But then again the modern Caribbean is a very young thing. I consider myself at the beginning, rather than at the end, of a tradition.

Would you say that your relationship to English poetry has changed over the years? As your work has progressed you seem to have increasingly affiliated yourself with a line of New World poets from Whitman through St. John Perse to Aimé Césaire and Pablo Neruda.

Carlos Fuentes talked in a *Paris Review* interview about the essential Central American experience, which includes the whole basin of the Caribbean—that it is already a place of tremendous fertility. The whole new world experience here is shared by [Gabriel Garcia] Márquez as it is by [Jorge Luis] Borges, as it is still by American writers. In fact, too many American poets don't take on the scale of America. Not because we should write epics but because it seems to be our place to try to understand. In places that are yet undefined the energy comes with the knowledge that this has not yet been described, this has not yet been painted. This means that I'm standing here like a pioneer. I'm the first person to look at this mountain and try to write about it. I'm the first person to see this lagoon, this piece of land. Here I am with this enormous privilege of just being someone who can take up a brush. My generation of West Indian writers, following after C. L. R. James, all felt the thrill of the absolute sense of discovery. That energy is concomitant with being where we are; it's part of the whole idea of America. And by America, I mean from Alaska right down to Curaçao.

How do you respond to V. S. Naipaul's repeated assertion—borrowed from Trollope—that "Nothing was created in the British West Indies"?

Perhaps it should read that "Nothing was created *by the British* in the West Indies." Maybe that's the answer. The departure of the British required and still requires a great deal of endeavor, of repairing the psychological damage done by their laziness and by their indifference. The desolation of poverty that exists in the Caribbean can be very depressing. The only way that one can look at it and draw anything of value from it is to have a fantastic depth of strength and belief, not in the past but in the immediate future. And I think that whenever I come back here, however desolate and however despairing I see the conditions around me to be, I know that I have to draw on terrible reserves of conviction. To abandon that conviction is to betray your origins; it's to feel superior to your family, to your past. And I'm not capable of that.

Why is the figure of Robinson Crusoe so important to you?

I wrote a poem called **"The Castaway."** I told my wife I was going to stay by myself for a weekend somewhere down in Trinidad. My wife agreed. I stayed in a beachhouse by myself and I wrote the poem there. I had an image of the West Indian artist as someone who was in a shipwrecked position. I'm not saying that's the origin of my Crusoe idea. But it's possible. The beaches around here are generally very empty—just you, the sea, and the vegetation around you, and you're very much by yourself. The poems I have written around the Crusoe theme vary. One of the more positive aspects of the Crusoe idea is that in a sense every race that has come to the Caribbean has been brought here under situations of servitude or rejection, and that is the metaphor of the shipwreck, I think. Then you look around you and you have to make your own tools. Whether that tool is a pen or a hammer, you are building in a situation that's Adamic; you are rebuilding not only from necessity but also with some idea that you will be here for a long time and with a sense of proprietorship as well. Very broadly that is what has interested me in it. There are other ironies, like the position of Friday as the one who is being civilized. Actually, the reverse happens. People who come out to the Caribbean from the cities and the continents go through a process of being recultured. What they encounter here, if they surrender to their seeing, has a lot to teach them, first of all the proven adaptability of races living next to each other, particularly in places like Trinidad and Jamaica. And then also in the erasure of the idea of history. To me there are always images of erasure in the Caribbean—in the surf which continually wipes the sand clean, in the fact that those huge clouds change so quickly. There is a continual sense of motion in the Caribbean—caused by the sea and the feeling that one is almost traveling through water and not stationary. The size of time is larger—a very different thing in the islands than in the cities. We don't live so much by the clock. If you have to be in a place where you create your own time, what you learn, I think, is a patience, a tolerance, how to make an artisan of yourself rather than being an artist.

Your recent play **Pantomime** *explores the racial and economic side of the relationship between Crusoe and Friday. In the play, a white English hotel owner in Tobago proposes that he and his black handyman work up a satire on the Crusoe story for the entertainment of the guests. Is the play a parable about colonialism?*

The point of the play is very simple. There are two types. The prototypical Englishman is not supposed to show his grief publicly. He keeps a stiff upper lip. Emotion and passion are supposed to be things that a trueblood Englishman avoids. What the West Indian character does is to try to wear him down into confessing that he is capable of such emotion and there's nothing wrong in showing it. Some sort of catharsis is possible. That is the main point of the play. It's to take two types and put them together, put them in one arena and have that happen. I have never thought of it really as a play about racial conflict. When it's done in America, it becomes a very tense play because of the racial situation there. When it's done here, it doesn't have those deep historical overtones of real bitterness. I meant it to be basically a farce that might instruct. And the instruction is that we can't just contain our grief, that there's purgation in tears, that tears can renew. Of course, inside the play there's a point in which both characters have to confront the fact that one is white and one is black. They have to confront their history. But once that peak is passed, once the ritual of confrontation is over, then that's the beginning of the play. I've had people say they think the ending is corny, but generally that criticism has come when I'm in America. The idea of some reconciliation or some adaptability of being able to live together, that is sometimes rejected by people as being a facile solution. But I believe it's possible.

How would you differentiate your work of the middle and late sixties, **The Castaway** *and* **The Gulf,** *from your previous writing?*

There's a vague period in any poet's life between thirty and forty that is crucial because you can either keep working in one direction, or you can look back on your earlier work as juvenilia, a nice thing to look at from a distance. You have to head toward being forty with a certain kind of mindset to try to recreate chaos so you can learn from it. Yet you also have the fear that your work really has been basically mediocre, a failure, predictable. You find yourself at a point at which you say, ah, so you have become exactly what you were afraid of becoming: this person, this writer, with a certain name and a certain thing expected of you, and you are fulfilling that mold. The later books attempt to work against the given identity. At this point I don't think they're deep enough in terms of their sense of sin. Their sense of guilt could be more profound. In a way a lot of these poems smooth over while seething underneath the surface. One can always put a sort of poster over the rough, you know. A smoothness of attitude over something that's basically quite null and chaotic and unsettling. A lot of the roughness is missing in these books, but then that dissatisfaction continues all one's life.

Would you talk about your experience in the Trinidad Theater Workshop which you founded in 1959 and finally left in 1976? You once stated that you wanted to create a theater where someone could produce Shakespeare and sing Calypso with equal conviction. Did the idea succeed?

Yes, I think I made that happen. The best West Indian actors are phenomenal. Most West Indian actors have gone to West Indian secondary schools. The classical training and reading they get there is pretty wide and impressive—a lot of Shakespeare, and all the great English writers. Once that happens people read much more widely than if they hadn't done the great poets. So most West Indian actors have a familiarity with the classic theater of the English language. They also have an accent, not an affected accent, but a speech that is good diction. Some of the finest Shakespeare I have ever heard was spoken by West Indian actors. The sound of Shakespeare is certainly not the sound we now hear in Shakespeare, that androgynous BBC-type, high-tone thing. It's a coarse thing—a great range between a wonderful vulgarity and a great refinement, and we have that here. We have that vulgarity and we also have that refinement in terms of the diction. The West Indian actor has a great rhetorical interest in language. In addition to that, the actor is like the West Indian writer in that he is a new person: what he is articulating has just begun to be defined. There's a sense of pioneering. For me writing plays was even more exciting than working on poems because it was a communal effort, people getting together and trying to find things. When I won a fellowship to go to America in 1958, I wanted to have, much as the Actors Studio did, a place where West Indian actors, without belonging to any company, could just come together and try and find out simple things such as how to talk like ourselves without being affected or without being incoherent, how to treat dialect as respectfully as if we were doing Shakespeare or Chekhov, and what was our own inner psychology as individuals, in a people, as part of a people. The first couple of years we had a very tough time. Very few people would come. We didn't know what we were doing; we just improvised and explored and tried things. I was determined not to do a production until I thought we had some kind of ensemble. I had no intention of forming a company. At that time, all I wanted to do was to have the actors come and begin to work together. It took a very long time. But eventually we did put on a play and for about seventeen years I had a terrific company. It also began to involve dancers and some great actors. I remember Terry Hands came once (he is now one of the associate directors of the Royal Shakespeare Company) for a performance of **The Joker of Seville** that Margaret, my then wife, suggested we do. We had this little arena, like a bullfight ring, or a cockfight ring, and we served sandwiches and coffee and oranges and so on, and the crowd by that time had begun to know the songs and they were singing along with the actors. Terry said to me, "Derek, you're doing what Brecht tried to do." Well, I felt terrific because I knew what he meant. Brecht's idea of the participation of the audience, the whole idea of the boxing ring as a stage or the stage as an arena, had happened. But after several years of falling out and fighting and coming back together, eventually, for all sorts of reasons, the thing wore down. Although I still use actors from the company singly, I no longer run the company. But seventeen years is a long time to run a theater company.

You've written that you first began writing drama "in the faith that one was creating not merely a play, but a theater, and not merely a theater, but its environment." But by the time you came to write the prologue to **Dream on Monkey Mountain** *in 1970, the feeling of pride was replaced mainly by exhaustion and the sense of innocence seems to have given way to despair. What happened?*

Well, right now I'm writing a play called *A Branch of the Blue Nile*—about actors, a small company of actors and how they fall apart. I don't know up to now—and I'll have to decide pretty quickly—if it's going to end badly. The epiphany of the whole thing, the end of it, is a question that remains.

Is the problem at all related to questions of whether the state should support the arts?

I'm fifty-five now and all my life I've tried to fight and write and jeer and encourage the idea that the state owes its artists a lot. When I was young it looked like a romance; now that I'm older and I pay taxes, it is a fact. But not only do I want roads, I want pleasure, I want art. This is the terrible thing in the Caribbean. The middle class in the Caribbean is a venal, self-centered, indifferent, self-satisfied, smug society. It enjoys its philistinism. It pays very short lip-service to its own writers and artists. This is a reality every artist knows. The point is whether you say that and then turn your back on it and say to hell with it for life. I haven't done that and I don't think I'm capable of doing it. What's wrong is this: a legacy has been left by the British empire of amateurism. What we still have as an inheritance is that art is an amateur occupation. That attitude is combined with some of the worst aspects of bourgeois mercantilism, whether it is French, Danish, British, or Spanish bourgeois. The whole of the Caribbean that I can think of has this stubborn, clog-headed indifference to things around them. The philanthropy that exists in the Caribbean is negligible. Money is here—you just

have to see the houses and the cars, and to look at the scale of living in any one of these islands—but nobody gives anything. If they do, I don't know what they give to, but that penny-pinching thing is typical of the petty-bourgeois merchant, the hoarder of money. Without any bitterness I can say that anything that I have gotten, whether earned or not, has been from America and not from the Caribbean. (pp. 209-19)

Your prologue to **Dream on Monkey Mountain** *also blasts the crass, state-sponsored commercialization of folk culture. One of your subjects in both poetry and essays has been how negatively tourism has affected the West Indies. Would you discuss that?*

Once I saw tourism as a terrible danger to a culture. Now I don't, maybe because I come down here so often that perhaps literally I'm a tourist *myself* coming from America. But a culture is only in danger if it allows itself to be. Everybody has a right to come down in the winter and enjoy the sun. Nobody has a right to abuse anybody, and so I don't think that if I'm an American anybody should tell me, please don't come here because this beach is ours, or whatever. During the period I'm talking about, certainly, servility was a part of the whole deal—the waiters had to smile, and we had to do this and so forth. In tourism, it was just an extension really of master/servant. I don't think it's so anymore. Here we have a generation that has strengthened itself beyond that. As a matter of fact, it can go beyond a balance and there's sullenness and a hostility toward people who are your guests. It can swing too far as well. But again, it's not enough to put on steel bands and to have people in the hotels entertaining and maybe to have a little show somewhere to keep them what they think is light-minded and happy and indifferent and so on. If that's the opinion that the government or culture has of itself, then it deserves to be insulted. (p. 220)

What do you have against folklorists and anthropologists? Some people think of them as an intellectually respectable lot.

I don't trust them. They either embarrass or elevate too much. They can do a good service if they are reticent and keep out of the way. But when they begin to tell people who they are and what they are, they are terrifying. I've gone to seminars in which people in the audience who are the people the folklorists are talking about, are totally baffled by their theories.

One of your most well-known early poems, **"A Far Cry from Africa,"** *ends with the question, "How can I turn from Africa and live?" However, by 1970 you could write that "The African revival is escape to another dignity," and that "Once we have lost our wish to be white, we develop a longing to become black, and those two may be different, but are still careers." You also assert that the claim to be African is not an inheritance but a bequest, "a bill for the condition of our arrival as slaves." These are controversial statements. What is your current sense of the West Indian writer's relationship to Africa?*

There is a duty in every son to become his own man. The son severs himself from the father. The Caribbean very often refuses to cut that umbilical cord to confront its own stature. So a lot of people exploit an idea of Africa out of both the wrong kind of pride and the wrong kind of heroic idealism. At great cost and a lot of criticism, what I used to try to point out was that there is a great danger in historical sentimentality. We are most prone to this because of suffering, of slavery. There's a sense of skipping the part about slavery, and going straight back to a kind of Eden-like grandeur, hunting lions, that sort of thing. Whereas what I'm saying is to take in the fact of slavery, if you're capable of it, without bitterness, because bitterness is going to lead to the fatality of thinking in terms of revenge. A lot of the apathy in the Caribbean is based on this historical sullenness. It is based on the feeling of "Look what you did to me." Well, "Look what you did to me," is juvenile, right? And also, "Look what I'm going to do to you," is wrong. Think about illegitimacy in the Caribbean! Few people can claim to find their ancestry in the linear way. The whole situation in the Caribbean is an illegitimate situation. If we admit that from the beginning that there is no shame in that historical bastardy, then we can be men. But if we continue to sulk and say, "Look at what the slave-owner did," and so forth, we will never mature. While we sit moping or writing morose poems and novels that glorify a nonexistent past, then time passes us by. We continue in one mood, which is in too much of Caribbean writing: that sort of chafing and rubbing of an old sore. It is not because one wishes to forget; on the contrary, you accept it as much as anybody accepts a wound as being a part of his body. But this doesn't mean that you nurse it all your life.

The Fortunate Traveller is filled with poems set in a wide variety of places. The title poem itself elaborates the crisis of a fortunate traveller who goes from one underdeveloped country to another. And in "North and South" *you write that "I accept my function / as a colonial upstart at the end of an empire, / a single, circling, homeless satellite." Has the Castaway given way to the Traveller? Do you still feel the old tugs between home and abroad?*

I've never felt that I belong anywhere else but in St. Lucia. The geographical and spiritual fixity is there. However, there's a reality here as well. This afternoon I asked myself if I would stay here for the rest of my life if I had the chance of leaving. The answer really is, I suppose, no. I don't know if I'm distressed by that. One is bound to feel the difference between these poor, dark, very small houses, the people in the streets, and yourself because you always have the chance of taking a plane out. Basically you are a fortunate traveller, a visitor; your luck is that you can always leave. And it's hard to imagine that there are people around you unable, incapable of leaving either because of money or because of any number of ties. And yet the more I come back here the less I feel that I'm a prodigal or a castaway returning. And it may be that as it deepens with age, you get more locked into what your life is and where you've come from and what you misunderstand and what you should have understood and what you're trying to reunderstand and so on. I'll continue to come back to see if what I write is not beyond the true experience of the person next to me on the bus—not in terms of talking down to that person, but of sharing that person's pain and strength necessary in those pathetically cruel circum-

stances in which people have found themselves following the devastations of colonialism.

What led you to assert, as you do in **Midsummer,** *that "to curse your birthplace is the final evil"?*

I think it is. I think the earth that you come from is your mother and if you turn around and curse it, you've cursed your mother.

You've written a number of poems about New York City, Boston, old New England, and the southern United States. I'm thinking in particular of the first section of **The Fortunate Traveller** *where one of the poems is entitled* "American Muse" *and another asserts "I'm falling in love with America." What are your feelings about living in the United States? Do you think you've been Americanized in any way?*

If so, voluntarily. I don't think I've been brainwashed. I don't think I have been seduced by all the prizes and rewards. America has been extremely generous to me—not in a strictly philanthropical sense; I've earned that generosity. But it has given me a lot of help. The real thing that counts is whether that line is true about falling in love with America. That came about because I was travelling on a bus from one place to another, on a long ride looking at the American landscape. If you fall in love with the landscape of a place the next thing that comes is the people, right? The average American is not like the average Roman or British citizen. The average American doesn't think that the world belongs to him or her; Americans don't have imperialist designs in their heads. I find a gentleness and a courtesy in them. And they have ideals. I've travelled widely across America and I see things in America that I still believe in, that I like a lot. (pp. 221-24)

Over the years your style seems to have gotten increasingly plainer and more direct, less gnarled, more casual, somehow both quieter and fiercer at the same time. Is that an accurate assessment of the poetic style of your middle age? I can't imagine a book like **Midsummer** *from the young Derek Walcott.*

It varies, of course. When I finished *Another Life,* I felt like writing short poems, more essential, to the point, things that were contracted. They didn't have the scale of the large book and so on. It goes in that kind of swing, in that kind of pendulum. In the case of *Midsummer,* I felt that for the time being I didn't want to write any more poems, although that sounds arrogant. I just felt perhaps I was overworking myself. I was going to concentrate purely on trying to develop my painting. While painting, I would find lines coming into my head. I would almost self-destruct them; I'd say, all right, I'll put them down . . . but with antipoetic vehemence. If they don't work, then I'll just forget it. What kept happening is that the lines would come anyway, perhaps out of that very irritation, and then I would make a very arbitrary collage of them and find they would take some sort of loose shape. Inevitably, of course, you try to join the seams. I was trying to do something, I think, that was against the imagination, that was not dictated in a sort of linear, lyrical, smooth, melodic—but rather something that was antimelodic. For a poem, if you give a poem personality, that's the most exciting thing—to feel that it is becoming an-timelodic. The vocabulary becomes even more challeng-ing, the meter more interesting, and so on. So what hap-pened was that by the very wish not to write, or to write a poem that was against the idea of writing poems, it all became more fertile and more contradictory and more complex. Gradually a book began to emerge. Inevitably you can't leave things lying around with unjoined shapes, little fragments and so on. I began to weld everything to-gether—to keep everything that I felt worthwhile. I thought—well, whether this is just an ordinary thing or not, it has as much a right to be considered as something a little more grandiose. That's what I think happened in **Midsummer.**

*How do you feel about publishing your **Collected Poems?***

You're aware of the fact that you have reached a certain stage in your life. You're also aware that you have failed your imagination to some degree, your ambitions. This is an amazingly difficult time for me. I'm absolutely terrified. It's not because I have a kind of J. D. Salinger thing about running away from publicity. It's really not wanting to see myself reflected in that way. I don't think that that's what the boy I knew—the boy who started to write poetry—wanted at all, not praise, not publicity. But it's troubling. I remember Dylan Thomas saying somewhere that he liked it better when he was not famous. All I can say is this: I do have another book about ready, and I hope it will be a compensation for all the deficiencies in the **Collected Poems,** something that will redeem the **Collected Poems.** (pp. 229-30)

> *Derek Walcott and Edward Hirsch, in an in-terview in* The Paris Review, *Vol. 28, No. 101, Winter, 1986, pp. 197-230.*

Elaine Savory Fido

[In] Third World critical circles the interconnections be-tween anti-racist and anti-colonialist perspectives and those of the womens' movements are beginning to be closely examined. This is nowhere more important than in the work of masculinist male writers in Third World so-cieties who often unthinkingly reflect mass male preju-dice/myth about women. We are aware that some of these attitudes are so widespread as to amount to a *cultural* bias in the male culture of a particular society, but they never-theless receive special reinforcement and endorsement when a talented and mainly effective writer includes them in his major work.

The argument of this paper seeks to demonstrate that not only is the work of Derek Walcott, a deservedly celebrated poet, dramatist and theatre practitioner in the Caribbean, inclusive of strong prejudices about women but that these are often associated with weakening of power in his writ-ing. It seems reasonable to assume, after all, that preju-dices, which deflect the individual from exploration and growth, will have that same effect on those areas of writing which are centred in them. Fortunately, given his attitudes to women, Walcott's creative world is a predominantly male one, in which men have close and important under-standing of one another. He also deals with racism, colo-nialism and the situation of the poor masses with intelli-gence, anger and originality. But his treatment of women is full of clichés, stereotypes and negativity. I shall seek to show how some of his worst writing is associated with these portraits of women, which sometimes lead him to the brink of losing verbal control, or give rise to a retreat into abstract, conventional terms which prevent any real treatment of the subject. (pp. 109-10)

Walcott's Caribbean region is a place of tension between the sexes. Single mothers, still very numerous, and often in economic difficulty, are still somehow perceived often by men as powerful, despite their social and economic powerlessness. Men talk about women in hostile ways (al-though the younger educated man is beginning to respond to the strength of the women's movement in the region). The degree of female autonomy, leadership and sexual in-dependence which has been forced to develop in many Ca-ribbean women as a result of male behaviour is not recog-nised as an advantage to the region, but as a reason for men to resist change being advocated by feminists. The good husbands and lovers of the Caribbean are also too often silent and invisible: the creative literature at present available for young women to read abounds with portraits of difficult male-female relations and with stereotypical at-titudes towards women, depicting them as victims of male violence or in other ways as losers or marginal figures.

Walcott's work reflects this world. Some portraits of women will first make it clear how his vision of women fo-cuses on fear/disgust on the part of the man. In a poem about Othello and Desdemona, the association of sexuali-ty and violence is very explicit, interwoven of course in this case with racial tension. The quality of the writing be-trays a failure to hold these elements together in a creative way. The overblown emotional crudity of the following passage will serve to illustrate how Walcott can rely upon images from the world of sexist prejudice and racial myth:

> And yet, whatever fury girded
> on that saffron-sunset turban, moon-shaped
>   sword
> was not his racial, panther-black revenge
> pulsing her chamber with raw musk, its sweat
> but horror of the moon's change,
> of the corruption of an absolute,
> like a white fruit
> pulped ripe by fondling but doubly sweet.

The technical competence is here stretched so taut that it collapses. In the centre of this passage, there is a tension between idealism and disgust which characterizes another portrait of woman's sexuality in **Another Life.** Here a beautiful woman is unfaithful to her husband and al-though this is indeed an immorality which might justify moral rebuke, Walcott's choice of language once more re-veals powerful resentments against a woman less than de-voted to her husband, and furthermore sexually adventur-ous, and insinuates that her son is damaged by her nature.

> Next day her golden face seemed shrunken,
> then, when he ulyseed, she bloomed again . . .
> Dressed in black lace, like an impatient widow,
> I imagined that skin, pomegranate, under silks
> the sheen of water, and that
> sweet-sour smell vixens give off.

This passage presents a tension between woman's loveliness (golden) and her sexual nature (pomegranate skin, sweet-sour smell, vixens) which create a repulsive intimacy with the woman, which is what happens also in the passage on Desdemona and Othello, and again, in the play *Joker of Seville* (where of course male infidelity is treated lightly and stylishly), Juan's attitude to women is tinged with disgust:

> For if there's nothing in that cleft,
> that little Delphic mystery,
> but God, there's very little left
> to die for, between you and me.
> Two graves, one life, the second grave
> no more than an indifferent slit
> to take another stiff.

In the portrait of Anna, youthful love of the poet-persona in *Another Life,* there is a threatening quality which Edward Baugh has considered:

> I see her stride as ruthless as that flax-bright harvester Judith, with Holofernes' lantern in her hand.

This too is a kind of idealisation, as Judith by her murder of Holofernes, proved herself a partner and heroine; but the connotations which adhere to her when she is seen from Holofernes' point of view are inescapable, complicating Anna's connotations of simplicity and truth.

This image of Anna as a murderous female (perceived via the freemasonry of maleness rather than through the role she plays in her culture by her action), comes after a description of her sexual energy in a mildly threatening context:

> For one late afternoon, when again she stood
> in the door of a twilight always left ajar,
> when dusk had softened the first bulb
> the colour of the first weak star,
> I asked her, 'Choose',
> the amazed dusk held its breath,
> the earth's pulse staggered,
> she nodded, and that nod
> married earth with lightning . . .
> I hear that open laugh,
> I see her stride . . .

The images of Anna here are idealised, romanticized (something of the famous bathos of Hemingway's "the earth moved" for orgasmic experience in his novel *For Whom the Bell Tolls* lurks in "the earth's pulse" and the "amazed dusk"), but there is a sense of the energy of this young woman being part of natural forces which could be hostile to the poet. The fear of strong female sexuality which characterizes patriarchy is present here: Anna is young and innocent but there is that about her which will be powerful, and it is this quality which creates conflict in the poet-persona.

Of all these passages, the first one discussed (from **"Of Goats and Monkeys"**) is the weakest, from an aesthetic point of view, but all the passages are relatively slack. Both the descriptions of the Captain's wife and Anna have a facile quality, produced in the former by an urgency of tone which disturbs the rhythm of the lines in a breathless hostility couched in nearly abusive language, and in the latter by a choice of conventional "poetic" words/phrases which seem to evade Anna as much as they describe her, and are woven into a conversational, all too easy, tone. In none of these passages is there that wonderful tightness of rhythm and unorthodoxy of word, image and idea which marks Walcott at his best. It is as if woman has little reality in Walcott's imagination, and that there is little between romanticism on the one hand and appalled rejection on the other in her treatment in his works.

One of the most powerful and revealing descriptions of woman as ideal which he offers comes in his prose essay which prefaces the collection of plays *Dream on Monkey Mountain:*

> The last image is of a rain-flushed dawn, after a back-breaking night of filming, in a slowly greying field where the sea-wind is like metal on the cheek. In the litter of the field among tarpaulins, stands a shawled girl caught in that gesture which abstractedly gathers cloth to shoulder, her black hair lightly lifting, the tired pale skin flushed, lost in herself and the breaking camp. She was white, and that no longer mattered. Her stillness annihilated years of anger. His heart thanked her silently from the depth of exhaustion, for she was one of a small army of his dreams. She was a vessel caught at the moment of their Muse, her clear vacancy the question of a poem which is its own answer. She was among the sentries who had watched till dawn.

The elements in this description are important. Once more there is use of conventional images, romantic aspects of woman in conjunction with romanticisms about nature. The woman is white, and Walcott's attitude to that is honest and important: her whiteness is no longer a source of anger because her passivity and service to the poet have absolved her of her colour (but what images this conjures of the passive, serving white wife being able only through her service to transcend the history of her race's guilt). Here the underlying violence in the Othello-Desdemona poem and the underlying fear of Anna in *Another Life* are explained: woman is ideal if she is an extension of the man's imagination, a servant of his will and a quiescent figure in his world. Let her set out with a stride (like Anna) towards her own goals, and she becomes dangerous. Though the passage from the preface to [*Dream on Monkey Mountain*] is overwritten and highly removed from the reality of the real woman it describes (who was in fact anything but a merely passive handmaiden of the poet), it does contain some important elements for our study. The woman described is used to aggrandize the poet's (male artist's) need for female support/inspiration for his work, and also is perceived through a romantic distancing.

Women who step out in life have often been the subject of male writers' tragic stories, stories which put the blame on the unusual spirit of the woman and not on the fecklessness of the male saboteurs of her life. Three of the most tragic victims of male-dominated societies are the male-created figures of Pasternak's Lara, and Thomas Hardy's Tess and Bathsheba Everdene. Walcott uses these in a poem which is again expressive of fear of woman:

I feared the numbing kiss
of those women of winter
Bathsheba, Lara, Tess

whose tragedy made less
of life, whose love was more
than love or literature.

Once again the poetic vision here is diffuse, the poetry pretending to a philosophical grandeur which under examination proves to be a shallow statement. The real "danger" in these women of northern fiction is that they each tried to be a real person as opposed to a male fantasy (although they are also, of course, myths as well). Once the idealism which makes woman controllable goes away, there lurks underneath a raw anger:

When I left the madhouse I tried other women
but, once they stripped naked, their spiky cunts
bristled like sea-eggs and I couldn't dive.

Walcott's work contains many images of beautiful, desirable women as *passive* creatures who await the male decision/appreciation. But these women are often described in near-cliché, pretty images which belong in popular myths of femininity. Walcott is rarely near to the originality and sturdiness of his portraits of men when he deals with women although he is sometimes negatively innovative, as with the image of the "spiky cunts." Often the woman is associated with conventional images like the moon, treated conventionally. The moon and the sea become (as in other poets ambivalent about women, like T. S. Eliot and Christopher Okigbo) convenient ways of showing abstract approval to women. When Walcott wants to describe sexual happiness, he looks for a conventionally pretty word:

K with quick laughter, honey skin and hair,
and always money. In what beach shade, what
    year
Has she so scented with her gentleness
I cannot watch bright water but think of
    her . . .

Sometimes, his writing conjures up more of the coy and calculated sexuality of a *Playboy* centrefold:

I knew when dark-haired evening put on
her bright silk at sunset, and folding the sea,
sidled under the sheet with her starry laugh,
that there'd be no rest, there'd be no forgetting.

There is one powerful female image which is not attacked, because it is perceived as a *maternal* force, and that is the goddess-moon, a symbol which has brought out the masochistic side of *macho* maleness in a number of poets (again, notably Okigbo). It is only sexually active/possible women who are required to be passive to be approved, but a mythic symbol can represent the dominating and yet sustaining aura of a mother who loves her child:

happy the earth is still changing
that the full moon can blind me with her fore-
    head
this bright foreday morning . . .

The writing here is good, because here the language blends sounds and rhythmic patterns freely and is positive and full of energy, expressing a confidence and an original vi-

sion (the moon's "forehead"). In the same poem, **"The Morning Moon,"** he says he is "still haunted by the cycle of the moon" and that "I gasp at her sane brightness." Although Walcott overworks the word "bright" in relation to his positive images of woman, the adjective "sane" lifts it in this context into something fresh. Again, in *Another Life,* the moon is a maternal force which, like Anna, is associated with the cosmic power of lightning, but here there is no rejection as a result:

The moon came to the window and stayed there.
He was her subject, changing when she
    changed . . .
His dun flesh peeled white by her lightning
    strokes!

Walcott's ultimate refinement of woman takes her out of the world altogether:

I live on the water,
alone. Without wife and children . . .

Now I require nothing,
from poetry, but true feeling,
no pity, no fame, no healing. Silent wife,
we can sit watching grey water . . .

Woman becomes art, and a certain resolution settles over the poetry.

This whole context of woman as image in Walcott's work contrasts abruptly with the creations for which he is justifiably known and admired: the male pairs who abound in his work, like Makak and Moustique, or the odd couple of *Pantomime,* and the individual male creations like the Devil in *Ti-Jean* or Afa in *Sea at Dauphin,* or the poet-persona in *Another Life* are all living beings precisely because they are complex, perceived with tolerance, wryness, compassion and a bold honesty, a blend of realism and romanticism which makes the characterization close to archetype but not in the least unconvincing. The characters seem to absorb their creator's full attention, and ours: their language is subtle, containing a true balance between opposites held together in a creative tension. The fictive personality of the Devil for example, is a marvellously entertaining character, as well as a racist white Planter and the archetype of evil. He longs to feel and is clearly condemned by his nature to be unhappy. Walcott's Devil is a serious philosophical comment on evil, on the effect evil has on the individual, and at the same time a strong socio-political comment on Caribbean racism and colonialism. He is also a witty individual. Such complex and creative perception never marks Walcott's women characters who are linear by comparison: the Captain's wife, for example, is said to be "formidable" and "obliquely masculine" and her son is terrified of life: her adventuring is therefore placed in a negative context and the possibility for a living, contradictory character is ignored. The reader is asked for a relatively simplistic emotional response.

What I am arguing here is that since Walcott is clearly capable of superb characterization and writing, it is a pity that when he depicts women his aesthetic achievement falls to a level of relative banality. His portrait of the Black woman, for example, bears no relation to the feisty, emotionally various, strong, vulnerable and generally complex picture emerging by Black women themselves:

> a black rose of sorrow, a black mine of silence
> raped wife, empty mother, Aztec virgin . . .

In **Dream on Monkey Mountain,** he offers an archetype of the White woman which owes something to Jean Genet's *The Blacks,* and which despite the obvious relevance of a symbol of whiteness being destroyed to release the hero of the play from his own psychic enslavement to self-hate, presents a stage image of justified violence against woman. Man revolts against the tyranny of his own fantasies/desires, choosing to destroy that which he cannot otherwise resist. It is important that this image of white racism is presented as a *woman,* justified object of hate and violence which lies just under the surface of the adoring lover (as we graphically saw in **"Goats and Monkeys,"** in the portrait of Othello). Clearly, the white woman was not the only oppressor in the slavery-colonial period in the Caribbean, but the White man seems less culpable in Walcott's world, for both the Devil in **Ti-Jean** and the grand failure Harry in **Pantomime** are perceived as human despite their evident capacity for tyranny. Perhaps Walcott only makes allowances for *male* evil, out of the freemasonry of maleness which regardless of race, culture or history, can unite against woman. It is also perhaps important that the White woman predominates as a symbol over the Black woman in Walcott's work, possibly because she is more distant and unknowable as a person (because of the male resistence to reality in woman, and because of racial tensions), and therefore is easier to evade as a reality than a woman of the community with which Walcott predominantly identifies, i.e. the African majority.

Women writers, critics and philosophers are at work at this time trying to undo the damage which has been done to women and to relations between women and men, by the refusal of male society to cope with the reality of woman's resources and strengths. Of course, just as the slave/servant knows the master better than the master can know her/him, so the woman knows male culture better than the man knows hers. Adrienne Rich, the poet and feminist writer, has said that woman must re-see and revise: once the ability to see properly is achieved then many things change. It is then not a minor issue that Walcott's women are so limited. Whether a woman watches **Joker of Seville** and sees women as creatures of limited perception and intelligence, or hears the honestly strong wife of Jordan in **Remembrance** called a Xanthippe and a Delilah (the old clichés of the "shrew" and the "bitch"), or accepts an unrealistic image of sexual womanhood (in the mermaid image in **"Anadyomene"**), she is absorbing negative images of her gender to no productive end. Furthermore, Walcott's creative achievement falters very often when he presents these limited images. If he explored the tensions and contradictions inherent in the images of women he chooses, perhaps some really great writing would ensue. (pp. 111-18)

> *Elaine Savory Fido, "Value Judgements on Art and the Question of Macho Attitudes: The Case of Derek Walcott," in* Journal of Commonwealth Literature, *Vol. XXI, No. 1, 1986, pp. 109-19.*

Paul Breslin

The publication of Derek Walcott's **Collected Poems 1948-1984** offers an occasion to reflect on the career of a poet widely (and justly) recognized as among the best writing in English. Although reviewers have praised Walcott lavishly, his work has attracted surprisingly little sustained criticism, and general studies of contemporary poetry seldom mention him. The North American critic, lacking detailed knowledge of Caribbean literature and history, is tempted to romanticize Walcott as an exotic, a bird of tropical splendor who shames, by his brilliant plumage, the drab language of his colleagues to the north. Although I have been unable, for the occasion of this review, to acquire such detailed knowledge either, I have found that taking a first step toward such knowledge helps enormously in understanding Walcott's poetry and in assessing his achievement. (p. 168)

Walcott's **Collected Poems** opens with **"Prelude,"** written in 1948, when he was eighteen years old. In retrospect, its title seems more appropriate than he could possibly have known when he chose it, for this poem not only hints at themes that reverberate through much of his work, it shows him already aware of an intersection between characteristic modernist attitudes and his own experience. The first three lines seem consciously aimed at the genre of Caribbean pastoral:

> I, with legs crossed along the daylight, watch
> The variegated fists of clouds that gather over
> The uncouth features of this, my prone island.

By a Cranean logic of metaphor, the island lies "prone" on its face, its "uncouth features" turned down; if it tries to get up, it will be knocked down again by those "fists of clouds." This imagery insists on the powerlessness, rather than the beauty or vitality, of the place, despite the tourists with binoculars who "think us here happy."

The diffidence of the last three stanzas reflects not only the poet's youth, but also his sense of belonging to a "lost" culture, "Found only / In tourist booklets," or "in the blue reflection of eyes / That have known cities." The poet who must become imagining subject belongs to a culture that has been defined only as the object of European perceptions, European intentions. And yet the language by which he registers this diffidence comes straight from the dominant literary tradition: "I go, of course, through all the isolated acts, / Make a holiday of situations, / Straighten my tie and fix important jaws." This is Prufrock speaking, or the Crane of "Chaplinesque." (pp. 172-73)

At eighteen, Walcott was still borrowing more than he was reimagining, but he progressed rapidly. In **"A Far Cry From Africa,"** one hears a momentary echo of Auden ("Statistics justify and scholars seize / The salients of colonial policy"), but the poem has an unmistakable unity of style. It confronts a language of moral statement, reminiscent of neo-Augustan satire, with the metaphorical daring and elided logic of modern symbolism. Thus it can accommodate lines such as "The violence of beast on beast is read / As natural law, but upright man / Seeks his divinity by inflicting pain" alongside its animistic opening: "A wind is ruffling the tawny pelt / Of Africa. Kikuyu, quick as flies, / Batten upon the bloodstream of the veldt." Thematically, too, the poem concerns the confrontation of opposites: Walcott, "divided to the vein," cannot bring himself to condone the terrorism of the Kikuyu during the Mau Mau rebellion, even though he condemns the British colonialism against which the Kikuyu fight. The precedent of modernist primitivism, which rummaged *The Golden Bough* for vanished gods in order to restore contact with the elemental forces of the earth, gives Walcott his language for the African and tribal side of the dilemma; the neo-Augustan language of moral statement gives him a language for his distance from this part of his heritage.

In such poems as **"Tales of the Islands,"** Walcott experimented with juxtapositions of dialect and standard English. We have been listening to "college boys" talking pretentiously about art and politics, and witnessing a "fête" at which "savage rites" are re-enacted "For the approval of some anthropologist," when Walcott slips into the vernacular:

> Poopa, da' was a fête! I mean it had
> Free rum whisky and some fellars beating
> Pan from one of them band in Trinidad.

Even one of the literary types gets drunk enough to descend from the acrolect while "quoting Shelley with 'Each / Generation has its angst, but we has none.'" The vernacular ironically corrects the stuffiness of the "college boys" and the self-consciousness of the anthropologist: to reconstruct the rites of the past is to serve "history," but to turn from the anthropologists to the steel band from Trinidad is to enter the living present of "tradition," for which the vernacular provides a language. But for Walcott, the choice between acrolect and basilect is not narrowly allegorical: there is a living present to be found in the great English poets as well as in the regional life. In **"Orient and Immortal Wheat,"** one finds a subtler juxtaposition:

> So heaven is revealed to fevered eyes,
> So sin is born, and innocence made wise,
> By intimations of hot galvanize.

The first two lines, with their lofty language of generalization, aim at moral universality. They recall the tradition of meditative verse in English, extending back to Marvell and beyond, and it is hard to hear "intimations" in the third line without thinking of Wordsworth's Ode. But with "hot galvanize," we are back in the landscape as well as the idiom of the islands: Walcott has before him, as material for his spiritual analogies, the cheap metal roofs of the village houses. Here, the juxtaposition does not undercut the loftiness of the previous lines, but rather confers dignity on the local landscape.

These early poems, and others such as **"Goats and Monkeys," "Laventille"** (dedicated to V. S. Naipaul) and **"The Glory Trumpeter"** force us to complicate the distinction between the Adamic and the historical that Walcott

would later make in **"The Muse of History."** In these, the path to Adamic disencumberment must be cleared by recognition and exorcism of history. In order to become Adamic, the poet must first become historical. So in **"Goats and Monkeys,"** Walcott must first see Othello as a fantasy spun out of racial fear: kissing Desdemona, Othello "is Africa, a vast sidling shadow / that halves your world with doubt"; their union mates "Virgin and ape, maid and malevolent Moor." In order to claim, at the end of the poem, that Othello is "no more / monstrous for being black," Walcott must first disentangle our perception of him from the historical burden of racial stereotype: Othello's "fury . . . was not his racial, panther-black revenge / . . . but horror of the moon's change, / of the corruption of an absolute." Othello is monstrous in his unforgiving horror of mutability—which is essentially Platonic idealism, a Greek rather than Moorish idea.

In **"The Muse of History,"** Walcott claims that "it is not the pressure of the past that torments great poets but the weight of the present"; in **"Laventille,"** however, one cannot look at the present without recognizing that the pressure of the past has shaped it:

> The middle passage never guessed its end.
> This is the height of poverty
> for the desperate and black;
>
> climbing, we could look back
> with widening memory
> on the hot, corrugated-iron sea
> whose horrors we all
>
> shared. [. . .]

The poem ends with an ambiguous image of simultaneous death and birth, as if to suggest that only through escape from this crippling past, that "withheld / us from that world below us and beyond" can the poet recover a lost Adamic freedom: "We left / somewhere a life we never found." Until then, the poet must struggle toward a difficult emergence, still wrapped in the "swaddling cerements" of a colonial history.

In most of his early poems (by which I mean those included in the *Selected Poems* of 1964), Walcott writes exclusively from a Caribbean perspective. The plane that takes him toward "the final north" at the end of **"Tales of the Islands"** heads into the unknown; there is a poem called **"Return to D'Ennery: Rain,"** but it says nothing of the place *from which* the poet has returned. **"Bleecker Street, Summer"** treats Greenwich village as pastoral, as if to requite the great world for its pastoral idealization of the Caribbean. And **"A Letter from Brooklyn"** turns out to be about a letter written *to* the poet by a woman in Brooklyn who once knew his father. **"The Glory Trumpeter,"** one of the finest early lyrics, reveals Walcott no longer entirely "withheld," as in **"Laventille,"** from the world "beyond" the Caribbean. In the closing stanza, Eddie, the trumpeter of the title,

> turned his back
> On our young crowd out fêting, swilling liquor,
> And blew, eyes closed, one foot up, out to sea,
> His horn aimed at those cities of the Gulf,
> Mobile and Galveston, and sweetly meted

Their horn of plenty through his bitter cup,
In lonely exaltation blaming me
For all whom race and exile have defeated,
For my own uncle in America,
That living there I never could look up.

Like the poet, Eddie inhabits two cultures, but is at ease within neither. He has turned his back on his West Indian compatriots to aim his horn across a literal and figurative Gulf, toward North American cities too far away to hear him; and yet the jazz he plays comes from the part of North America where Mobile and Galveston are; it is *their* horn of plenty. It is as foreign to the "young crowd" as Walcott's complex and allusive style must be to many West Indian readers. Back from America, the poet feels guilty for having become relatively assimilated, but in America he remains an outsider, the unwelcome relative of the uncle he "never could look up."

By the time he wrote **"The Gulf,"** Walcott's sense of dual citizenship had been much extended. As in the conclusion of **"Tales of the Islands,"** the poet is in an airplane, but this time he is leaving the United States, not the Caribbean. As it begins its flight, "friends diminish"; the poet is attached to the United States, as he is to the Caribbean, though still he has "no home." If the poem shows Walcott still further assimilated into the English-speaking world outside the islands, it also shows him working, in a more particularized way than previously, from the historically concrete toward the universally symbolic. **"The Gulf,"** which is literally the Gulf of Mexico beneath the airplane, becomes the vehicle for a set of parallel metaphors. It is also the detachment, further depicted in the plane's departure from the earth, of the soul in meditation: "So, to be aware / of the divine union the soul detaches / itself from created things." It is the poet's sense of a lingering "gulf" between himself and both the island culture from which he came and the larger world into which he has ventured. And finally, it turns out that in the United States, too, there is a gulf: the poem was published in 1969, when the nation appeared to be coming apart at the seams:

> The Gulf, your gulf, is daily widening,
>
> each blood-red rose warns of that coming night
> when there's no rock cleft to go hidin' in
> and all the rocks catch fire, when that black
>   might,
>
> their stalking, moonless panthers turn from Him
> whose voice they can no more believe, when the
>   black X's
> mark their passover with slain seraphim.

The apocalyptic language of this passage may seem dated, but in other respects, this poem wears well. I find most fascinating its implication that the dream of transcendence—of "divine union," a universality encompassing the divisions of black and white, Caribbean and cosmopolitan identities—arises precisely when the pressure of history becomes most acute, and seems to drive toward an impasse. Only after confronting his historical predicament and finding no way out of it can he turn from history altogether and recover, unexpectedly, the lost Adamic identity:

> Yet, somehow, at this height,
>
> above this cauldron boiling with its wars,
> our old earth, breaking to familiar light,
> that cloud-bound mummy with self-healing
>   scars
>
> peeled of her cerements again looks new.

One is reminded of the "swaddling cerements" in the last line of **"Laventille."**

Perhaps this is the time for me to say that, much as I admire Walcott's poetry, I am uncomfortable with claims to Adamic transcendence of history, to claims of elemental kinship to the earth that circumvent cultural mediation. To be sure, no poet could go on writing without the faith that poetry finally transcends the historical pressures that impinge on its making; but that "finally" is an important qualification. To skip the intervening steps is to invite the faults of bombast and bardic pretentiousness into one's poetry, and it must be admitted that they often visit Walcott's. There is a thin line between magniloquence and grandiloquence, and if **"A Far Cry from Africa," "The Glory Trumpeter,"** and most of **"The Gulf"** manage to stay on the right side of it, a great many poems, early and late, do not, or do so only intermittently. Walcott's chief gift (like Robert Lowell's) is for the brilliant phrase, the mighty line, the heart-stopping passage; the architectural virtues have come less easily to him.

All this is by way of preface to my reservations concerning *Another Life,* an autobiographical sequence in twenty-three verse "chapters" that occupied Walcott from 1965 to 1972 and takes up some thirty percent of the space in his *Collected Poems.* It tells the story of Walcott's life from childhood to his first successes as a poet and departures into the wider world. It begins promisingly, with evocative descriptions of the setting. The third chapter seems to launch the narrative proper when it describes a cast of village characters, with names from A to Z, as "the stars of my mythology," and likens them to figures in Homer. But only a few of these ever reappear in the poem, and only to take marginal roles. Instead of narrating, Walcott becomes fixated on landscape, on the sacredness of the artist's vocation, and on the intensity of his own feelings. The poem does indeed have a structure, as Edward Baugh demonstrates in his fine monograph study of it. But it is not a narrative structure: the poem is knit together by continuities of imagery, and it progresses not by narration but by a sequence of tableaux.

Another Life is a long, ambitious poem, and I can only sketch, on this occasion, my reasons for considering it on the whole a failure, albeit a noble and interesting one. To begin with, it lacks any hierarchy of intensity; reading *Another Life* is rather like listening to an organist who leaves the diapason stop on for the whole recital. . . . [Walcott] drives unrelentingly at the sublime. As a result, foreground is hard to distinguish from background, key points of arrival from incidental detail. When the young Walcott encounters the *First Poems* of the Jamaican poet George Campbell, he *tells* us that it is an important moment, from which "another life it seemed would start again"; it is the first time that he, who had wished to shed his own blackness, finds a literary depiction of black people as "sacred" rather than brutish beings. But Walcott-as-autobiographer has already been hammering away for a hundred lines or so with language like this:

> The groves were sawn
> symmetry and contour crumbled,
> down the arched barrack balconies
> where colonels in the whisky-coloured light
> had watched the green flash, like a lizard's
>   tongue
> catch the last sail, tonight
> row after row of orange stamps repeated
> the villas of promoted civil servants.

However dazzling such passages may be in isolation, they leave Walcott with nowhere to go when he wants to intensify his language to meet a special intensity in his experience. The fire that destroyed Castries in 1948, the mystical epiphany of his fourteenth year described in Chapter 7, even the suicide of Harold Simmons, art-teacher and father-figure of Walcott's youth, ought to stand out as moments of crisis, but they are all but lost in the general furor of Walcott's language.

My second difficulty with *Another Life,* related to the first, concerns its thinness of incident. One can understand that Walcott, unwilling to surrender to the "muse of history," wants to distill the essential and universally-resonant from the particulars of experience. But I am not asking for confessional detail. Even though one can barely discover, by reading *The Prelude,* that Wordsworth lost both his parents by the age of thirteen, the milieu is solidly present: one can see his Cambridge and his London, and one can at least glimpse the village life of the Lake Country. In *Another Life,* everything seems ready to turn into myth or metaphor before it is first solidly *there;* whereas Joyce plays the mythical against the quotidian in *Portrait of the Artist as a Young Man* or *Ulysses,* Walcott seems impatient with the literal. Autobiography can be highly selective in what it includes; it can fictionalize and distort; it can be disingenuous as the day is long. But it cannot afford an essential blankness of incident, and that is what troubles me in *Another Life.* The style has been asked to do all the work; the intense excitement that the style claims to feel has been severed from its occasion, for the characterization of the authorial "I" and of his first love Anna is so abstract as to prevent the tracing of emotion to motive. The passages concerning the friendship with Gregorias (Walcott's name for the painter Dunstan St. Omer) are the ones that wear best; although Gregorias has been quite consciously treated as a figure worthy of legend, we see the man at work, in despair and in triumph, and the characterization seems rooted in experience as no other in the book really is.

But I do not wish to dwell on the flaws of *Another Life;* Walcott has given us four volumes of poetry since, and I would like to close by considering two of the finest poems from these: **"The Schooner *Flight*"** and the well-nigh perfect lyric, **"The Season of Phantasmal Peace."** The first (along with the equally fine **"The Star-Apple Kingdom"**) shows Walcott able to write a long poem that sustains the level of his finest shorter works. The second was assumed bodily into the *Norton Anthology of Poetry* soon after its appearance in *The Fortunate Traveller,* and the editors, not always judicious in their canonization of new work, are to be congratulated for recognizing this poem at once.

"The Schooner *Flight*" is Walcott's most inspired experiment in dialect mixed with the Marlovian "mighty line." This time Walcott attempts autobiography at a remove, through the obviously fictional character of Shabine, smuggler, sailor and poet. Like Walcott, Shabine feels himself to be an exile: "I had no nation now," he says, "but the imagination." And yet he remains attached to the islands he leaves: "if loving these islands must be my load, / out of corruption my soul takes wings." Shabine, no less than Walcott, seeks to be purged of history; his voyage becomes a baptismal "sea-bath," a return to the primal relation of Adamic man and the history-less elements. But like Walcott also, Shabine cannot be purged of history other than by re-experiencing it. He encounters a phantom slave ship; passing Dominica, he cannot help recalling the fate of the Carib Indians: "Progress is something to ask Caribs about," he tells his friend Vince. "They kill them by millions, some in war, / some by forced labour dying in the mines." And finally, like Walcott, Shabine feels caught between white and black, between the cynicism of the colonial governments and the cynicism of the new governments that have replaced them. Racially mixed, he carries the contradictions of the region within himself: "I have Dutch, nigger, and English in me, / and either I'm nobody, or I'm a nation."

Whereas *Another Life,* undecided whether to tell what happened or to condense narration into iconic symbols, thrashes and sprawls, **"The Schooner *Flight*,"** deciding in favor of the iconic, has admirable compression. The purgational voyage of the *Flight* tests Shabine, first by the painful recollection of history and then by the climactic storm in which the captain becomes a black Christ: "crucify to his post, that nigger hold fast / to that wheel, man, like the cross held Jesus, / and the wounds of his eyes like they crying for us." The voyage sustains narrative movement, building toward the ending when Shabine, having accomplished his sea-change, is finally at peace: "I wanted nothing after that day."

The economy of means afforded by the convention of spiritual voyage is one strength of **"The Schooner *Flight*"**; another is the marvelously inventive satirical wit that Walcott unleashes here. One had seen only brief flashes of this comic talent in earlier poems; here it is fully evident:

> I met History once, but he ain't recognize me,
> a parchment Creole, with warts
> like an old sea-bottle, crawling like a crab
> through the holes of shadow cast by the net
> of a grille balcony; cream linen, white hat.
> I confront him and shout, "Sir, is Shabine!
> They say I'se your grandson. You remember
>   Grandma,
> your black cook, at all?" The bitch hawk and
>   spat.
> A spit like that worth any number of words.

If Walcott can stick it to the colonialists, he can also be hard on cant about revolution: "In the 12:30 movies the projectors best / not break down, or you go see revolution." So much for revolutionary fervor, if it can be quieted by an afternoon movie.

"The Season of Phantasmal Peace" contains not a word of dialect; if **"The Schooner *Flight* "** stands as Walcott's most successful incorporation of the vernacular, the shorter poem is the finest expression of his aspiration to universality, to being a poet of the world rather than of a particular region of it. The poem's ravishingly lofty language risks Walcott's familiar faults of bombast and overreaching, but this time, with perfect tact, the poem recognizes the limits of its own yearnings for the sublime and pulls back from the brink of excess. As the title itself tells us, the poet knows that the gorgeous vision he is about to show us is at best a transitory glimpse of an unattainable transcendence, and perhaps even a glimpse of an illusory transcendence that exists nowhere at all. The poem subtly sustains this awareness:

> Then all the nations of birds lifted together
> The huge net of the shadows of this earth
> in multitudinous dialects, twittering tongues,
> stitching and crossing it. They lifted up
> the shadows of long pines down trackless slopes,
> the shadows of glass-faced towers down evening
>   streets,
> the shadow of a frail plant on a city sill—

The grandeur of scale immediately conveyed by "all" and "huge" may tempt us to envision the net dragging the massive skyscrapers and pines free of the earth and raising them into the air, but it is only their shadows that the net can hold, not their substance.

If the revelation is ethereal, leaving the things and ourselves, "the wingless ones," still earthbound, it is also obscure:

> And men could not see, looking up, what the
>   wild
>   geese drew,
> what the ospreys trailed behind them in silvery
>   ropes
> that flashed in the icy sunlight . . .

"Drew" has the primary meaning of "pulled"; it is parallel with "trailed." But it also has a secondary meaning: whatever figure the geese "drew" in their movement through the sky, we were unable to see it; if they were trying to give us a sign from the transcendent realm they inhabit, we, from our earthly vantage point, could not read it. The net is protective, "covering this world / like the vines of an orchard, or a mother drawing / the trembling gauze over the trembling eyes / of a child fluttering to sleep." This simile prompts the recollection that, first of all, the net's protection cannot be imagined except in analogies of earthly, fallible protection; and, second, that if the protection turns out to be illusory, the "net" takes on a different meaning, more akin to its literal use: no fish wants to be caught in a net, just as no one wants to be taken in by an illusion. To be sure, the poem affirms the epiphanic moment as valuable, however brief: "for such as our earth is now, it lasted long." But it does not encourage sentimental illusions, especially if read in the context of other poems from *The Fortunate Traveller* such as **"North and South"**

and **"The Spoiler's Revenge,"** which depict earthly conflicts still very far from reconciliation.

Walcott on American poets

I think the thing about being a poet in America, or even a young poet in America is the poet is almost crying out for the society to be hostile to him—or her, I mean both him and her—to repress him, to take notice, to imprison him, to pay attention in a sense. But what happens is suddenly or quietly there is a very wide blandness that occurs, in which the poet is subtly absorbed and given a name and a trade *separate* from the society, maybe because of that naming. You are a poet, you write poetry, you get your books published, you're in magazines. And you don't go around with a cape and a rose, so you can't tell in this democracy how different being a poet would be. And I think that it is this real unnavigable but hospitable space ahead of the poet that finally makes a lot of them say, I'll just do something else. And that is another kind of death, really, that happens. It's not some big dramatic thing. It may not be like breaking your pen and fleeing into the jungle or something. But there's something that just quietly absorbs and deadens the spirit. And it's not inertia, because Americans are vigorous, industrious, honest—that's the quality of American activity—direct, forthright. Pay you what you deserve, reward you with what you get, etcetera. It's a just society, and not a cunning one. And it isn't that you want more evil, but it may be a very, very spiritually satisfied society—or apparently spiritually satisfied society. It can't be disturbed. It's like making a lot of noise in a void room. And I think that when that voice begins to sound as if it's being raised for effect or lowered so that attention can be paid to it, that middle ground is not found, you see. And then, in a way, the poet goes into a kind of isolation. He may be on the Pacific coast, or he may be alone on a farm in Iowa, or he may be in a loft in New York, or he may be teaching in Boston, but there's no *necessity* in him.

In an interview with David Mantenegro, 1990.

By concentrating on these two poems, I mean only to show the range of Walcott's recent accomplishment; there is much else in the last four volumes that is nearly as good. Despite the fact that he has sometimes been overpraised and idealized, and despite his chronic temptation to the grandiose and overwrought, sometimes more *is* more. His best poems use the full resources of English in a way that most contemporary work—clipped, prosy, and understated—does not even attempt to do. He deserves his reputation as one of the best poets writing in English, but our praise would be more sincere if it extended to imitation. Despite the gulf between Walcott's Caribbean and our workshop-ridden literary culture, he can teach us that we do not have to starve our language in the name of authenticity; he can remind us, with Blake, that you do not know what is enough until you know what is more than enough. (pp. 173-82)

Paul Breslin, " 'I Met History Once, But He Ain't Recognize Me': The Poetry of Derek Walcott," in TriQuarterly, *No. 68, Winter, 1987, pp. 168-83.*

Lachlan Mackinnon

[When] we turn to Derek Walcott's autobiographical verse-novel *Another Life* (1973) [included in his *Collected Poems 1948-1984*] we find the poet inviting himself to

> Begin with twilight, when a glare
> which held a cry of bugles lowered
> the coconut lances of the inlet,
> as a sun, tired of empire, declined.

The bugles and lances are British, but the subtle hint of decadence in "declined" also reflects Walcott's troubled view of his own mixed ancestry. . . . Walcott is steeped in literature—academic success was what first enabled him to leave St Lucia for a wider world, about which he is still ambivalent—and in his own culture, as the success of many of his "oral" poems shows.

For the young Walcott literature was doubly alienating. On the one hand, there were the objects loved by his dead father, a watercolourist,

> the stuffed dark nightingale of Keats,
> bead-eyed, snow-headed eagles,
> all that romantic taxidermy,
> and each one was a fragment of the True Cross,
> each one upheld, as if it were The Host.

On the other, there was the "new Word" which found "the natural man" in the wild. "I looked from the bus window", Walcott writes,

> and multiplied the bush with savages,
> speckled the leaves with jaguar and deer,
> I changed those crusted boulders to grey, stone-
>   lidded crocodiles,
> my head shrieked with metallic, raucous par-
>   rots,
> I held my breath as savages grinned,
> stalking through the bush.

Of this childhood, Walcott reminds us that "years must pass before he saw an orchestra, / a train, a theatre, the spark-coloured leaves / of autumn whirling from a rail line", and in it he sees power and ignominy. English literature is stuffed and inert, but the Rousseauistic side of Romanticism, reflected in popular fiction, liberates the transforming power of the imagination only to reduce, demean and miss the real. A moment of personal vision and a friendship led him to understand and name the particular, at first by painting.

> Where did I fail? I could draw,
> I was disciplined, humble, I rendered
> the visible world that I saw
> exactly, yet it hindered me, for
> in every surface I sought
> the paradoxical flash of an instant

> in which every facet was caught
> in a crystal of ambiguities.

The shift to poetry was inevitable.

The line I have quoted from *Another Life* illustrates the strengths and risks of Walcott's style, which is pitched much higher than that of any of his English contemporaries. He can achieve unusual grandeur, but can also bathetically overwrite. In a poem dedicated to Joseph Brodsky, **"Forest of Europe"** (1979), Walcott describes his dedicatee memorably as "a man living with English in one room" and says of Mandelstam that

> He saw the poetry in forlorn stations
> under clouds vast as Asia, through districts
> that could gulp Oklahoma like a grape.

Walcott's imaginative reach is compelling, but the blank assertion that "there is no harder prison than writing verse" feels a little self-indulgent, particularly from one who wonders "what's poetry, if it is worth its salt, / but a phrase men can pass from hand to mouth?" Walcott's career-long insistence on the necessity of poetry is, like Brodsky's, what we most need to hear. It is a pity that he tries to parallel Caribbean and Gulag archipelagos, because what he really has in common with Brodsky is the marginal status of exile. In the end, each lives alone with his language.

It is therefore fitting that **"The Castaway"** (1965) should be the first poem in this massive selection (Walcott has excluded a fair amount of his work) in which his characteristic tone is mastered. Two lines: "The starved eye devours the seascape for the morsel / Of a sail". The prosodic freedom works for emphasis, is a discipline. The next line, "The horizon threads it infinitely", is ambiguous, as one wonders whether the horizon threads a sail (implicitly like Penelope), the seascape or the lacerated eye. Mixed metaphors pull together into desolation. **"The Castaway"** is the first poem really to work as a whole: the earlier poems are recognizable stylistically, but veer between gross overwriting ("the profound cigarette") and fragmentation. Sonnets in particular lead Walcott to a sonorous vacuity. The struggle between the riveting, isolated phrase and overall control has dogged his whole career, a heroic effort to master tumultuous gifts.

"Schizophrenic, wrenched by two styles, / one a hack's hired prose, I earn / my exile" Walcott says in **"Codicil"** (from *The Castaway and Other Poems*). Economic independence means dependence, for Walcott as for St Lucia, and he is torn between knowing that "To change your language you must change your life" and that "I cannot right old wrongs". He understands Auden's dictum that poetry makes nothing happen, which is what elevates his work above the ultimately and tragically disabling *parti pris* nature of most [Caribbean verse]. . . . He also knows that the origin of poetry is oral (Homer is probably the author he cites most frequently) and some of his best work has been in a regional vernacular. . . . [Walcott's poem **"The Spoiler's Return,"**] uses an oral persona (Theophilus Phillip, "The Mighty Spoiler", was a calypso writer who died in 1959) to say, "I see these islands and I feel to bawl, /

'area of darkness' with V. S. Nightfall.'' The poem is not wholly successful, but the Spoiler's plea

> so back me up, Old Brigade of Satire,
> back me up, Martial, Juvenal, and Pope
> (to hang theirself I giving plenty rope),
> join Spoiler' chorus, sing the song with me,
> Lord Rochester, who praised the nimble flea

shows its ambitions. Walcott claims the heroic couplet for the dispossessed, for he knows that language is an instrument of power and must therefore be seized, and he gives his character his own confident assumption of a place in world culture.

Walcott evidently believes that to assume such a place the tradition, however defined, must live in his work. Often it does. In *Midsummer,* **"L"** (1984), he claims that

> These poems I heaved aren't linked to any tradition
> like a mossed cairn; each goes down like a stone
> to the seabed, settling, but let them, with luck, lie
> where stones are deep, in the sea's memory.

What he lays claim to is a tradition older than tradition, a poetry rooted in nature, almost Shakespearean, as in *Midsummer,* **"XXXVI."** Here, the scene is Warwickshire, for which Walcott surmises his father Warwick may have been named, and a pub with "white-haired regulars" so deaf they can't tell whether what they hear is "the drone of the abbeys" or "a chain saw working late". Then we find "four old men" in the pub garden, talking about "bows" and "wenches": Walcott remembers hearing "their old talk carried / through cables laid across the Atlantic bed", and can "drop their names / like familiars"

> because the worm that cores the rotting apple
> of the world and the hornet's chain saw cannot touch the words
> of Shallow or Silence in their fading garden.

This astonishing ending explains why the men's "maker granted them a primal pardon". It is carefully prepared for, so that it is both startling and inevitable, the diminuendo of the two lines beginning "of " playing down its bravura.

The problem is that Walcott's cosmopolitan ambition can lead to rootlessness, as he knows. The unhappy Stalinism of my phrasing perhaps reveals the poverty of this as a complaint: to have been rendered almost unrecognizable by the influence of Robert Lowell, as in much of *The Fortunate Traveller* (1981), is hardly shameful. Lowell's voice in the 1970s was as persuasively that of its time as was Auden's in the 1930s, and as compulsive. It is, indeed, testimony to Lowell's power that so fine a poet as Walcott should have suffered from the epidemic of influence, and *Midsummer* testifies to an almost complete recovery by assimilation.

Walcott's uneven prolificness is perplexing and enviable. His purest success is **"The Schooner *Flight*"**, a sequence in which he adopts the persona of the sailor Shabine. Joseph Brodsky, again, has pointed to the daring of the lines

> I'm just a red nigger who love the sea,

> I had a sound colonial education,
> I have Dutch, nigger, and English in me,
> and either I'm nobody, or I'm a nation.

As Brodsky says, "When you hear such a voice, you know; the world unravels." "Shabine sang to you from the depths of the sea", the sequence ends, and Walcott is right. As a later poem in the same volume, *The Star-Apple Kingdom,* has it, "The sea is History".

> Where is your tribal memory? Sirs,
> in that grey vault. The sea. The sea
> has locked them up.

Brodsky has argued that only "bacon-lined retinae" and racism have prevented Walcott from being acknowledged "the great poet of the English language". The variety and beauty of this volume will convince all but the most pigheaded of what many—more, anyway than Brodsky supposes—have suspected. Walcott is not entirely without peers, but he has very few. He is not a local poet, and the problem may have been that one must see his work whole to appreciate this fully. This book is a triumph which bears its scars proudly: Walcott speaks with and for humanity when he tells his first love, become a nurse, that "No woman should read verse / twenty years late. You go about your calling, candle-like", a calm moment in his discovery and revelation of *Another Life.* (pp. 1185-86)

Lachlan Mackinnon, "Nobody, or a Nation," in The Times Literary Supplement, *No. 4360, October 24, 1986, pp. 1185-86.*

Caryl Phillips

[In 1986], Derek Walcott's *Collected Poems* appeared in a 500-page volume. It seemed to me then, and his new collection of verse confirms my feelings, that it may have been a somewhat premature assembling of the poet's canon. *The Arkansas Testament* not only finds Walcott examining some of his old themes, but doing so with youthful invention.

Born in 1930 on the small Caribbean island of St. Lucia, Walcott now divides his time between Boston and Trinidad. He is part of the poetic gang of four (Josef Brodsky, Czeslaw Milosz and Seamus Heaney being the other three), the internationally displaced poets who teach in America.

His poetry draws on an awareness of the lack of any viable West Indian literary tradition or consensus of culture. He emerged from an often intellectually restricted environment and managed to master the vocabulary of the English language and to explore the rhythms of syntax, the power of metaphor and the intellectual game-playing of allusion. But the problem of a West Indian writer working in a tradition tied to British imperialism has always been present in Walcott's mind.

> The riot police and the skinheads exchanged quips
> You could trace to the Sonnets or the Moor's eclipse
>
> (*Midsummer*)

Walcott's seven previous collections have been steeped in an ambivalence toward the outside world and its relationship to his own native land of St. Lucia. The clash of Europe and colony, language and landscape, the "old world" and the "new world" of the Americas; these have been his themes. That there are always choices to be made implies a rejection of something and an inevitable sense of loss. In *Midsummer,* one felt a growing awareness of mortality, which bestowed upon his poetic journey the qualities of a pilgrimage. The volume ended shrouded in overwhelming forfeiture.

> . . . though no man ever dies in his own coun
> try
> the grateful grass will grow thick from his heart

The Arkansas Testament is a collection of 39 poems divided into two parts—"Here," referring to the author's native Caribbean, and "Elsewhere." The voice of the Caribbean half of the volume moves easily between the received European tradition and the local oral one. The author is able to employ both when necessary. This accounts in part for Walcott's distinctive tone, pitched somewhere between the rhetorical and the vernacular.

> as I watch a low seagull race
> its own cry, like a squeaking pin
> from the postcard canoes of Lə ᴾlace,
> where the dots I finished begin,
> and a vendor smiles: 'Fifty? Then
> You love home harder than youth!'
> Like the full moon in daylight, her thin,
> uncontradictable truth.

The high point of "Here" is the poem **"The Light of the World,"** a sensitive and heart-rending account of a Saturday-night bus journey from the town marketplace back to a small house on a country beach where the speaker is staying. On this serene, moonlit evening, the speaker, having walked about the town he was born and grew up in, now "lusts" peacefully after two girls on the bus and falls in "love" with a third. Here is a perfect opportunity to feel in tune with his past. But no, thoughts of discord disturb the tranquility of his communion with his people. The truth is painful, ever-present, and reduces the speaker to tears.

> I, who could never solidify my shadow
> to be one of their shadows, had left them their
>   earth,
> their white rum quarrels, and their coal bags,
> their hatred of corporals, of all authority.

The moment when he should belong is the very moment he is most acutely aware of the fact that he no longer does.

In "Elsewhere," Walcott, the poet who did not want to leave home but at the same time needed to aspirate his mind, addresses the West. He pays homage to a past master, in a eulogy addressed to W. H. Auden.

> It was such dispossession
> that made possession joy,
> when, strict as Psalm or Lesson,
> I learnt your poetry.

He dedicates the title poem **"Elsewhere"** to another "master," Stephen Spender. But with each poem, it becomes

more clear to what degree Walcott remains a West Indian, with Europe or America claiming attention only inasmuch as they cast light back upon his central dilemma. He is able to write:

> I remember the cities I have never seen
> exactly. Silver-veined Venice, Leningrad
> with its toffee-twisted minarets. Paris . . .

A man of Walcott's classical education and intellect is sensitive to the power of these centers of international culture, but one senses of Walcott that he has come to understand that (as Seamus Heaney, to whom this volume is dedicated, once wrote) the provincial state of mind, which needs the affirmation and approval of the metropolis, is not as important as the parochial imagination, which has no doubt about "the artistic validity of its own parish."

Therefore as we quarry on through "Elsewhere" with its formal invention, its classical allusions, its references to Cambodia, Chernobyl and Gorbachev, there is a suspicion that, although Walcott may be embracing cosmopolitan ideas and subjects, he does so with less emotional assurance than when he is barefoot and feeling sand trickling uneasily between his toes, and in the grip of the obsession that compels him to address the more essential questions of his origins and identity.

> **"Walcott 'the outsider' is the supreme poet of the Caribbean, because he has rejected the easy labeling that might have enabled him to make peace with himself."**

This is not to suggest that Walcott should confine himself to the Caribbean; far from it. **"The Young Wife"** is as painful and universal a poem about cancer as one is ever likely to read, and **"God Rest Ye Merry, Gentlemen: Part II"** depicts the urban squalor of Newark, N.J., with at least as much passion as the writing of its most famous literary inhabitant, Amiri Baraka.

> Johannesburg is full of starlit Shebeens.
> It is anti-American to make such connections.

The title poem of the volume, **"The Arkansas Testament,"** picks up where **"God Rest Ye Merry, Gentlemen: Part II"** leaves off. It handles "the stripes and scars" of modern American racism with dignity and urgency. Walcott checks into a $17.50 motel in Arkansas. He wakes early, needing a 5 a.m. caffeine "fix," and drives into the nearest town, Fayetteville.

> I bagged the hot Styrofoam coffee
> to the recently repealed law
> that any black out after curfew
> could be shot dead in Arkansas.

This is no protest poem. True, it concerns the history of the South; it concerns racism and the feelings of self-contempt that white ignorance often engenders in black people's souls. But it is a poem about writing, about a man's struggle to bare his soul and talent in an environment other than that which nurtured it. It is a poem about a particular type of black man; a West Indian writer, in America.

As another outstanding West Indian writer, C. L. R. James, once said, "it is when you are outside, but can take part as a member, that you see differently from the ways they see, and you are able to write independently." Walcott "the outsider" is the supreme poet of the Caribbean, because he has rejected the easy labeling that might have enabled him to make a peace with himself. *The Arkansas Testament* is witness to his ongoing struggle. Having held at bay the anger brought forth by his treatment in Fayetteville, Walcott knows that

> There are things that my craft
> cannot wield, and one is power.

He refers here to the Southern power of "Lee's slowly reversing sword," not the moral power of which his work contains an abundance. (pp. 1, 9)

> *Caryl Phillips, "No Man Ever Dies in His Own Country," in* Los Angeles Times Book Review, *April 6, 1987, pp. 1, 9.*

Anthony Kellman

Divided into two parts—"Here" and "Elsewhere"—the poems [in Walcott's *The Arkansas Testament*] contain subjective/objective declarations concerning the poet's place in his homeland (the Caribbean) and in other, more northern places where he often sojourns. Walcott's two testaments are both Old and New, underlining the book's structural parallel with the Bible. "Here" can be seen as an Old Testament—the poet's origins and past life in the Caribbean, while "Elsewhere"—a New Testament—articulates his current experiences in the United States, where he works.

What links the two geographically disparate parts of the book is the poet's sense of personal invisibility, and his disappointment, at times even despair, at the human condition. Walcott's is a continuing quest to integrate two selves fashioned by his African and European ancestries. Because he is neither and always "Here" and "Elsewhere," Walcott, time and time again, finds himself an outsider, an Everyman figure, "schizophrenic, wrenched by two styles" (**"Codicil,"** *The Castaway,* 1965).

From his sense of historical alienation in *The Castaway* and *The Star Apple Kingdom* (1979); through *The Fortunate Traveller* (1981), who is fortunate only in the sense that he is in a position to escape places when they become unbearable, but who is hounded by guilt complexes; through his penultimate collection, *Midsummer* (1984), where, in **"Gaugin,"** he concedes his regret that "I left (The Caribbean) too late," Walcott seems to be wrestling with his Janus double-sided vision. He uses this schizophrenic reality of Caribbean Man in order to testify to the failures of regional Independences to sustain artists there. In a bid to find his place / the poet's place in a world of arrogance, pride, upside-down values and racism, Walcott presents a personal Testament which is universal in its im-

plications, and which challenges the reader to be more open in terms of relationships, racial and otherwise.

As he has done recently in the openings of his books, Walcott returns, in the poem **"The Lighthouse,"** to the Caribbean, his island home, St. Lucia, where "Stars pierce their identical spots / over Castries. . . . " Apparently, nothing has changed. The domino-slamming men in the rum shops share the same ribald jokes, while "Unaging moonlight falls / on the graves." The tightly-structured meter of this long poem suggests the tenseness and apprehension the poet feels on returning home. The imagery of the poem also reflects his psychological precariousness. The full moon is described as "A coin tossed once overhead, / that stuck there, not heads or tails."

The personas in this poem, very reminiscent of V. S. Naipaul's hopeless characters, are the dispossessed: men who have become victims of historical legacies of attrition and post-Independence victimization. There are drunks; an actor "lost in the post office! Stripped / A superfluous character written out of script"; and children running down crooked streets, some falling, most taking "the straight / road from their galvanised hell."

In **"The Three Musicians,"** a parody of the tale of the Biblical wise men, three down-and-out musicians go house-to-house on Christmas Day, serenading neighbors for food and drink. These men, who "eat in silence . . . belt out two straights, / then start singing like shite," are pitied by the master of the house who "feels / that his heart will burst" at the sight of these three "kings."

Another character, the persona in **"A Letter From the Old Guard"** who has served with Lord Alexander in the Sudan, is reduced to an arthritic night watchman. It is Remembrance Day, and the elderly man reflects proudly on his days in the colonial army. Today, he has very little to show for his heroic exploits and attributes his fate to the failures of the new Independences. He states with some bitterness: "Then we get Independence all of a sudden / and something went. We can't run anything / . . . we black people."

The dots of stars that mottle the sky in **"The Lighthouse,"** suggesting ellipsis or incompleteness, are the points where the poet resumes his exploration of his island/history/self with each return. The fact that Walcott consistently makes this effort at coming to terms with his heritage is a hope in itself.

Not only does Walcott have a stubborn love for his homeland, but he is also extremely courageous in his quest for stability and wholeness, considering that his responses to the region are often tinged—sometimes laced—with terror and dread. In **"Cul De Sac Valley,"** he notes that "the forest runs / sleeping, its eyes shut," and that "Pigeon Island / pins the sea in its claws." This disturbing imagery underlines the poet's fear of Caribbean leaders bounding into the twenty-first century through the dark—(the blind leading the blind?)—and is articulated, I think, out of a sense of responsibility and concern for his homeland.

In **"Gros Islet,"** the poet's bitterness (or perhaps it is more his disappointment) reaches new intensity and outspokenness. Here, "There is no wine . . . , no cheese, the almonds are green, / the grapes bitter, the language is that of slaves." And in **"White Magic,"** white myths are praised for their authenticity, whereas the local ones are denounced as being unoriginal, based on ignorance. Walcott writes:

> . . . the deer-footed, hobbling hunter, Papa
> Bois,
> he's just Pan's clone, one more translated satyr
>
> • • •
> Our myths are ignorance, theirs is literature.

The last poem in Part 1 of the book, **"The Light of the World,"** highlights Walcott's feelings of guilt for having "left" the Caribbean. He says: "I had abandoned them, . . . left them to sing Marley's songs of sadness. . . . " Yet, he loves his people's warm neighborliness, and feels as though he "might suddenly start sobbing on the public transport" in which he is travelling. He thinks that he has abandoned them and also that they have abandoned him. Specifically, he feels that he should have given them something more tangible, but all that he can give them is "This thing I have called 'The Light of the World.' " In short, Walcott implies that what he will give his people (and perhaps this is the best possible gift that he can truly give) are his poems, his art.

There are some beautiful poems in Part 2 of this collection as well. This section's title poem, **"Elsewhere,"** examines the effects of war. It becomes a parody of a pastoral. Children waddle in streams, there are old men nearby, women squatting by a river, and "a stick stirring up a twinkling of butterflies." Above this scene, in contrast, "flies circle their fathers." **"Salsa"** is a satirical comment on the Americanization of San Juan; **"The Young Wife,"** an elegy written to a man whose wife has died of cancer; **"For Adrian,"** about an old subject—departures. All these poems are tightly structured, using Walcott's innovative ballad meter.

While there are these fine poems in this part of the book, the section, overall, is not as assured as Part 1. Too often, it seems as though Walcott has not fully assimilated the nuances of the northern cultures that he writes about. Although always skillfully crafted, several of the poems here are half-glimpsed clichéd sketches. In this section, one gets a sense of travelogue writing, mere reportage, particularly in the disappointing title poem [**"The Arkansas Testament"**].

This thirteen-page poem describes the poet's sojourn in Arkansas, a racially segregated state. He feels himself "homesick / for islands with fringed shores," and although very acute in his observations of the physical surroundings of the place, he lacks an authoritative tone. The main point of this long poem, however, and one which makes the link between the two sections, is that "I was still nothing." The poet is exiled both "Here" and "Elsewhere." In the Caribbean, he is alienated as an artist; in Arkansas, because he is a black man. Once, in a cafeteria, "I looked for my own area," he writes. "The muttering black decanter / had all I needed; it could sigh for / Sherman's smoking march to Atlanta / or the march to Mont-

gomery." The sunshine in Arkansas is cold. Fearing rejection, the poet asks: "Will I be a citizen / or an afterthought of the state?"

The fear of regional rejection drove Caribbean writers to the Metropolis in the 1950s and 60s and is still driving New Generation writers to the U.S.A. and Canada—that is, those who can leave. It is this sense of rejection at home which is at the heart of Derek Walcott's disappointment in the Caribbean. (pp. 605-07)

The hope in **The Arkansas Testament** is that while the wandering poet may be nothing, by that very nothingness he has the potential to contain and be everything. The book is also a testament to the need for people—whether Caribbean or North American—to be less parochial and provincial in their outlooks on life. As Walcott states in **"Tomorrow, Tomorrow"**:

> To have loved one horizon is insularity;
> it blindfolds vision, it narrows experience.
>
> (p. 608)

> *Anthony Kellman, "Testimony from Here and Elsewhere," in* Callaloo, *Vol. 12, No. 3, Summer, 1989, pp. 605-08.*

Sean O'Brien

Much of the splendour of Derek Walcott's poetry is to be found in his writing about the sea. The epic **Omeros** may prove to be the consummation of his love affair with water. It begins with the hero, Achille, explaining how canoes are cut down from the forest of St Lucia and ends with his return to shore and the words "the sea was still going on". **Omeros** is, in one sense, a work in praise of its capacity to do just that. The sea has "no memory of the wanderings of Gilgamesh / or whose sword severed whose head in *The Iliad.* / It was an epic whose every line was erased / yet freshly written". It "never altered its metre to suit the age, a wide page without metaphors. / Our last resort". In **Omeros,** land itself tends to become ocean, especially the island's windy forests, while desks and floors are covered with charts or the maps made by sunlight and leaf-shadow. Human identities are themselves shifted and transformed by real or imagined voyages. The act of speech itself is described in oceanic terms. When the poet is told the word "Omeros" by the Greek girl who seems the poem's shadowy inspiration, he provides its Creole etymology:

> *O* was the conch-shell's invocation, *mer* was
> both mother and sea in our Antillean patois,
> *os,* a grey bone, and the white surf as it crashes
>
> and spreads its sibilant collar on a lace shore.
> Omeros was the crunch of dry leaves, and the
> wash
> that echoes from a cave-mouth when the tide has
> ebbed.

The "Homeric coincidence" of this marine voice with an island "once named Helen", and now named for a blind saint, provokes the poem, not "for kings floundering in the lances of rain" but "the prose / of abrupt fishermen cursing over canoes".

From this account, and from the names of the central figures (Achille, Hector, Philoctete and Helen), it might be supposed that *Omeros* recasts Homeric materials directly into a Caribbean setting. If this were simply the case, Walcott's detractors could enjoy a field-day at the expense of those tendencies summarized in Stewart Brown's (largely favourable) essay "Spoiler: Walcott's People's Patriot": namely, Walcott's alleged Eurocentricity, his arrogant individualism, and his inability "because of his class, culture and philosophy to 'ground' with West Indian people". But *Omeros* is a complex work, both structurally and in its repeated examination of perennial themes in Walcott's work—identity, exile, how history is suffered and survived, and the obligations of the artist—in which he is hardly sparing to himself. It might be further objected that the rehearsal of error is luxury of a kind, and as E. A. Markham, in his anthology *Hinterland,* has pointed out, "many of Walcott's early statements have been taken not as the privileged glimpse inside a writer's mind trying to relate achievements to objectives, but as literary manifestoes". Part of the subject of *Omeros,* however, is the problem of getting past "literature" to achieve, in the words of an early poem, **"Islands"**, "Verse crisp as sand, clear as sunlight, / Clear as the cold wave, ordinary / As a tumbler of island water". *Omeros* is also informed by love and humility, the subjects of the superb **"The Light of the World"**, from Walcott's previous collection, *The Arkansas Testament,* where the beautiful unknown woman on the crowded island bus at night is surely a forerunner of Helen as she appears in *Omeros.*

The first three of the seven books of *Omeros* tell of the quarrel between the fishermen Achille and Hector, of Helen's desertion of Achille for Hector, and of their friend Philoctete, incurably injured by a cut from an anchor. Their town also contains the blind seer Seven Seas and the wise woman Ma Kilman. Helen's doings in particular are observed by Plunkett, her former employer, retired RSM and pig farmer, who, like the poem in general, identifies her with the island. In search of a history for the place he studies the naval engagement in which the French treasure ship Ville de Paris was sunk by the British and in doing so discovers the death, in the same battle, of a Midshipman Plunkett, thereby finding for himself and his wife, Maud (who spends much of her time at embroidery), the son whom life has not allowed them. The despairing Achille is also drawn to the past, diving for the treasure (guarded, it is said, by a one-eyed octopus) in hopes of winning Helen back. These events, veering between the literal and the visionary, are complemented by two comic episodes, the one broad and the other sour—the cyclone, depicted as a syncretizing knees-up for the gods, and the short-lived activities of Maljo's United Love Party, which opposes itself to the island's "identical" capitalist and Marxist factions. After the shindig which marks the flowering and imminent extinction of the ULP, Achille, in despair at Helen's absence, suffers sunstroke and undergoes a return to Africa, drawn on by the flight of the ocean-going swift to encounter his ancestor Afolabe to witness the enslavement of the tribe, the torments of the slave passage:

the fading sound of their tribal name for the rain,

the bright sound of the sun, a hissing noun for
the river,
and always the word "never", and never the
word "again".

That Walcott is trying to win back ground from the novel is apparent not only in the variety and ingenuity of the narrative, but in his or his persona's constant presence in the poem, whether invoking Omeros or encountering his dead father in the streets of the island capital. The latter episode is one of many fine set-pieces. It dramatizes the intersection of the then-and-thereness of the barber's shop and political conversation with the sense of historical scale which accompanies the arrival of a liner for coaling. Teams of local women walk "like ants up a white flowerpot": as the poet's father states, "the / infernal anthracite hills showed you hell early". The feet of the women are identified with those of verse, and the son's duty is "to give those feet a voice".

Although the personal exile begun at the close of the third book has many reverberations in the remainder of the poem, it seems uncertain whether the more extensive autobiographical material which occupies much of the fourth and fifth books is successful or wholly necessary. There is a slackening of impetus and—despite the appearance of Omeros in the guise of a tramp outside St Martin in the Fields—there are occasions when Walcott lapses into the "writing" noted by Seamus Heaney in the weaker moments of *The Fortunate Traveller* (1982). The meditative passage on Ireland, for instance, drawn from a visit to Glen-da-Lough, is reminiscent of MacNeice having a thin time. Nor am I convinced that the material concerned with the destruction of the Sioux (seen as analogous to the vanished Aruacs of the Caribbean) is fully meshed with the poem as a whole. Yet the sorrows, frustrations and insights addressed in the book's centre are a preparation for return. As the poet's father states in a further meeting in a colder climate, "in its travelling all that the sea-swift does, / it does in a circular pattern". To "have seen everything and been everywhere" is a way of renewing attachment to the sight of a "sail leaving harbour and a sail coming in", and the implied possibility of refreshed inspiration is confirmed in the opening chapter of the sixth book:

Ah, twin-headed January, seeing either tense:
a past, they assured us, born in degradation,
and a present that lifted us up with the wind's

noise in the breadfruit leaves with such an elation
that it contradicts what is past! . . . .

What remains of the central narrative is largely concerned with reconciliation and healing. Ma Kilman finds the appropriate root (grown from a seed carried by a bird from Africa) to heal Philoctete: bathed in a cauldron, he also discovers his name. Hector, tempted away from the sea, becomes a daredevil taxi-driver and dies on the road. The pregnant Helen returns to Achille, who is himself to die beyond the book's pages. Plunkett recovers from the death of Maud, whose coffin is draped with her embroidery of the island's birds. The botched modernization of the island—another familiar Walcott theme—is seen taking place. Yet as these events are resolved, their author undergoes an inquisition by Omeros, whom he encounters on the shore. This familiar compound ghost, part wooden beam, part Homeric bust, part mulatto Charon, part plain speaker, states: " 'Forget the gods . . . and read the rest. . . . / A girl smells better than the world's libraries' ". Their subsequent tour of the island involves a visit to a volcanic Purgatory rich in politicians and poets, and Walcott himself barely escapes their fate, restored to the world with a damning enquiry:

> You tried to render
> their lives as you could, but that is never enough:
> now in the sulphur's stench ask yourself this
>   question,
>
> whether a love of poverty helped you
> to use other eyes, like those of that sightless
>   stone?

Walcott has referred to his sense of himself as a member of a "guild", a contributor to a greater literary whole, and has also spoken of his pleasure at being told that he sometimes sounds like someone else. There are Audenesque moments in *Omeros,* and some of the duller passages sound like Lowell. More strikingly, the etymology of **"Omeros"**, the encounters with the poet's father and the Dantesque passages in Purgatory seem, like some of the work in *The Arkansas Testament,* to build on suggestions from [Seamus] Heaney, though these are so far expanded as to render the idea of simple indebtedness a marginal one. As throughout his work, Walcott is preoccupied here both with European-derived tradition and the claims of home. In a recently published interview with David Montenegro in *Partisan Review* he argued that

> when you enter a language, you enter a kind of choice which contains in it the political history of the language, the imperial width of the language, the fact that you are either subjugated by the language or you have to dominate it. So language is not a place of retreat, it's not a place of escape, it's not even a place of resolution. It's a place of struggle.

The struggle Walcott undertakes in *Omeros* in one sense resembles Achille's or Plunkett's: that is, to know history and overcome it, as Achille does on his return to the island, reconciled to the dead Hector, or as Plunkett, beached at the end of an empire, attempts to do. Significantly, Walcott supplies the funeral oration for Hector which Achille himself cannot make, and in so doing brings back to mind the passengers at the close of **"The Light of the World"**: "There was nothing they wanted, nothing I could give them / but this thing I have called 'The Light of the World' ". *Omeros,* then tries to speak for a people unaware of the story it tells.

Omeros is a problematic poem. For some, the very limited use of patois may condemn it. For others, although Helen may be so fundamental a literary presence as to resist appropriation, there may be something uneasy in Walcott's preoccupation with *seeing* her, and with her physical beauty, however intimately she comes to represent the island. From time to time there is also a suspicion that discursive material is being forced into verse, while the prominence given to matters of artistic conscience might seem

misplaced. But having said this, *Omeros* is an extraordinarily ambitious undertaking, clearly founded in the conviction that poetry is an urgent task and an art which should be capable of whatever the imagination requires. Walcott's powers of evocation seem inexhaustible: the virtual omnipresence of the sea never threatens to become formulaic, while the motifs of lace, the forest, the conchshell and the flight of birds gain in suggestiveness as the poem travels through its several thousand lines. The narrative episodes—in particular Achille's voyages—are compelling in themselves, and in its movements through time and memory and between the external and interior worlds the poem is satisfyingly mysterious. St. Lucia, by this account, is, as Kavanagh put it, one of the world's "important places", one that "held all . . . of paradise, / with no other sign but the lizard's signature, / and no other laurel but the *Laurier-canelle*'s". With *Omeros* Derek Walcott has thrown down an intimidating challenge to the Old World's dispirited centre. (pp. 977-78)

> *Sean O'Brien, "In Terms of the Ocean," in*
> The Times Literary Supplement, *No. 4563,*
> *September 14-20, 1990, pp. 977-78.*

Mary Lefkowitz

Toward the end of his epic poem *Omeros,* Derek Walcott suddenly interrupts his rushing narrative and asks himself whether he has not "read and rewritten till literature / was guilty as History." "When would the sails drop / from my eyes, when would I not hear the Trojan War / in two fishermen cursing?" he asks. "When would it stop, / the echo in the throat, insisting, 'Omeros'; / when would I enter that light beyond metaphor?" This apostrophe is a moving and appropriate challenge not only to the poet, but to the reader. Why are we in the present always haunted by the past, not just our past but the past of other people and peoples? Like Homer's Odysseus, we learn the answer by joining the poet on an exciting and disturbing journey "to see the cities of many men and to know their minds."

But it is the figure of the poet Homer, rather than the heroes of his poems, who serves as Derek Walcott's principal inspiration. According to ancient legend, Homer came from a humble background and had a hard and lonely life. Born the bastard son of a Greek girl living in Smyrna (modern Izmir), when he was young he traveled around the Mediterranean. But then he became blind and had to make a living as a beggar, by reciting his verse. Occasionally he was treated kindly, but more often he was driven away from the towns he visited; because he was an outsider and a hanger-on he acquired the name *Homeros,* "hostage." After much wandering, Homer finally died on the Aegean island of Ios, friendless and alone, unable to answer a simple riddle put to him by young fisher-boys.

It is this everyman's Homer, and not the comfortable court poet some people imagine Homer to have been, who inspires Derek Walcott's epic poem, and who records the past events that determine the lives of the people he describes—including that of Mr. Walcott himself and, ultimately, of all of us. This Homer is a Protean figure, infinitely knowledgeable but elusive, constantly changing shape. He is Omeros (his name in modern Greek) and also the old blind man "Seven Seas." Later he turns up as a sightless, homeless bargeman clutching a brown manuscript, only to be driven off the steps of St. Martin's-in-the-Fields church in London by a prim clergyman. He is the voice of the sea, (Winslow) Homer, and the Roman poet Virgil who guides the narrator (as he once guided Dante through hell in Dante's own epic, the "Commedia"). Omeros's authority comes from a curiosity and sympathy learned from isolation and suffering, and it is this lonely, painful knowledge that is his principal legacy to the characters in the epic, and through them to anyone who reads about their lives.

In the *Iliad* and the *Odyssey* Homer needed to recall only what happened before Odysseus' return from Troy, but now the poet must reflect on an older and larger world, with new wars and new continents. If his principal characters are Antillean people with Homeric names, one also meets here Roman emperors, Spanish conquistadors, Herman Melville and James Joyce. His mind ranges from the Antilles now to the Mediterranean in antiquity to the British Empire at its height to frontier America in the Indian wars to Boston and London last week or last year to an Africa buried so deep in the memories of its exiled children that only terrible trauma can bring them to think about it. This is, as Mr. Walcott says "a reversible world." "Art is History's nostalgia."

> "*Omeros* derives its extraordinary power not from suspense, for Mr. Walcott makes us aware in advance of what will happen, but from his ability to capture and express the thoughts of his characters and to re-create, with a remarkable clarity that compels the reader to follow and even to see them, the swift mutations of ideas and images in their minds."

But his new epic does not so much tell a story as explain the feelings and reflections of some inhabitants—past, present or, like Mr. Walcott himself, intermittent—of St. Lucia in the Windward Islands. Several characters have Homeric names, but their connection with their counterparts in the *Iliad* and the *Odyssey* is deliberately tenuous and evanescent.

Helen is as beautiful as her ancient namesake, but her face does not launch a thousand ships or bring on the destruction of her city. Achille, the "main man," son of an African slave, is strong and brave like Homer's Achilles. But instead of Patroclus Mr. Walcott gives him as companion the crippled Philoctete, who suffers, like his counterpart in the ancient story, from a wound that does not heal, and whose cure marks the end of the war. But, unlike his Greek namesake, Philoctete lives among men, enduring his pain. Achille also does not inflict his resentment on his

friends, nor does he kill Hector, even over Helen. Hector dies as the result of his own recklessness, but the poem ends not with his funeral, but with the continuing existence of the survivors who learn to live with their memories.

When, toward the end of the poem, the narrator encounters Omeros, he complains he can no longer use the gods who dominate the action of the *Iliad* and the *Odyssey*. "Forget the gods," Omeros advises, "and read the rest." In their place Mr. Walcott puts forces even more pitiless and unpredictable than the gods of Olympus: nature, the sea, violent changes of weather, lizards and iguanas and the jungle foliage that casts debris and disorder onto the landscape. When Homer's Achilles goes down to the sea, he finds his goddess mother Thetis ready to come to his aid, but Achille must trust himself to a beautiful but unfeeling Sea-Mother (*mer-mère*) who can support or destroy him.

The gods brought order to Homer's world, but in Mr. Walcott's epic, Odysseus (and all of us who like him are exiles) must return to a home whose character has changed over time, even to the point where we can no longer recognize it. Yet these references to the ancient past, brief and insubstantial as they may seem, form the foundation of Mr. Walcott's poem. They endow his new characters and situations with heroism; they suggest that their experiences, particular as they are to specific places and present times, are also timeless and universal.

Omeros derives its extraordinary power not from suspense, for Mr. Walcott makes us aware in advance of what will happen, but from his ability to capture and express the thoughts of his characters and to re-create, with a remarkable clarity that compels the reader to follow and even to see them, the swift mutations of ideas and images in their minds.

The narrative mimics the process of thinking in several ways. Since we make associations first of all by patterns of sound, there are significant puns, like *mer* and *mère* and O-mer-os, or occasional and thus all the more arresting rhymes, "House of memories that grow / like shadows out of Allan Poe." Then there are literary reminiscences, often incomplete, mutated, congested: Achille's lonely, brooding fishing voyages acquire dimension from allusion to Joseph Conrad's "Nigger of the Narcissus" or the threatened shipwreck survivor in Winslow Homer's painting "The Gulf Stream." And just when they are needed to punctuate the somber reflections, there are swift transitions to ordinary preoccupations or occasional bitter humor, as when we learn that the waiter struggling with his tray across the sand dunes of a seaside country club is called Lawrence.

Throughout the poem, as in the mind, there are persistent reflections on the historical events that have directly and indirectly shaped the characters' lives: the brutal attacks of the slavers on Achille's African forebears, of Europeans on Native Americans, of French warships against British when the Windward Islands were first colonized; of the impersonal, devastating shelling of armies in World War II. But Mr. Walcott recalls these scenes of death and suffering with the objective sympathy of a Homer, who tells what happened to Trojans as well as Greeks. No loss, individual or collective, is felt more keenly than any other's. The Romans enslaved the Greeks; the Southerners built Greek Revival houses and gave the slaves they mistreated Roman names. Sons are lost, or never born, alike to black and white.

In Homer's day, the only possible medium for epic narrative was poetry, with a strict metrical pattern based on the quantity of sounds. Mr. Walcott uses a rhythmic blank verse to call attention to patterns of sound, and to suggest likeness and contrast with sudden, dramatic metaphors and similes. Although the events of his story take place, as they must, in linear time, over several months, the narration moves in a spiral, replicating the circularity of human thought. The past can easily become present as we remember it: we can talk with the dead, and see them before us, and become the same age as, or even older than, our own parents. We can discover an ancestor who was killed in a war long ago, and begin to mourn for him.

The narrative of **Omeros** is exciting and memorable, despite the absence of the chases, duels and descriptions of violent deaths in the Greek epics. At the end, Helen returns to Hector; a war-wounded Englishman in exile finds he can talk to his dead wife with the aid of one Ma Kilman, the wise old woman who runs an establishment called the No Pain Café and who also somehow recalls the ancient African remedy that cures old Philoctete's incurable wound. In place of action there is an increasing awareness of other people's suffering. Like Odysseus and the legendary Homer himself, everyone (including the narrator and reader) learns from his or her wandering and exile, even if it is only how better to understand what has happened.

Perhaps most surprisingly of all, we discover that it is the remote past, antiquity and military history, that matters, rather than modern concerns about money or self-promotion. Mr. Walcott's epic is a significant and timely reminder that the past is not the property of those who first created it; it always matters to all of us, no matter who we are or where we were born. (1, 34-5)

> *Mary Lefkowitz, in a review of "Omeros," in* The New York Times Book Review, *October 7, 1990, pp. 1, 34-5.*

Brad Leithauser

In one of the first glimpses we have of Helen, the heroine of Derek Walcott's book-length poem **Omeros** she walks barefoot along a beach on her native Antillean island of St. Lucia, singing a Beatles song. The tune is "Yesterday," and the line she focusses on strikes a note of understated wistfulness: "Yesterday, all my troubles seemed so far away." Helen is reflecting upon the upheavals of romance—as well she might, for she, in her surpassing beauty, is a heartbreaker. An "ebony girl" in a "lemon frock," she has recently been fired from her job as a servant to a pair of British expatriates, Dennis and Maud Plunkett. Dennis, a retired major who has taken up the disciplining of a new sort of troops—he has become a pig farmer—is

silently mad about her. So are, silently or vociferously, most of the other men on the island, including a pair of fishermen whose rivalrous designs threaten to unravel the community's uneasy workaday calm.

Some forty pages farther along, we learn that the young woman's troubles were never "far away," as Walcott resurrects "Helens from an earlier time," whose lives were indentured to an inhumane colonialism. He vividly summons those forebears of hers who, working for pittances under the scorching Caribbean sun, once carried staggering loads of anthracite down from the hills to the holds of imperial freighters:

> Hell was built on those hills. In that country of
> coal
> without fire, that inferno the same colour
> as their skins and shadows, every labouring soul
>
> climbed with her hundredweight basket, every
> load for
> one copper penny, balanced erect on their necks
> that were tight as the liner's hawsers from the
> weight.
>
> The carriers were women, not the fair, gentler
> sex.

As she sings, Helen is ruefully conscious of an unwanted burden: she is pregnant and does not know who the father is. But she bears, simultaneously and unwittingly, a greater burden still. She, like all the dark-skinned islanders, carries the weight of a history of generations of cruelty and chicanery, most of which has passed away unchronicled and unrighted. Through Helen, and Helen's precursors, Walcott ventures back more than four hundred years, to that "yesterday" when the first African slaves were transported to the Caribbean.

Yet his backward-looking muse does not halt there. He equates the Caribbean and the Mediterranean—both belonging to a "sea without time"—and thereby likens his Helen to Homer's, and his squabbling fishermen to the warring Greeks and Trojans. The whole of **Omeros** (the title is Homer's name in Greek) is anchored to *The Iliad* and, in a lesser degree, *The Odyssey*. Only a page after Helen strolls the beach, Walcott forges a litany of "yesterday"s, and St. Lucia dissolves into the fields of Troy:

> And yesterday these shallows were the Scaman-
> der,
> and armed shadows leapt from the horse, and
> the bronze nuts
> were helmets, Agamemnon was the commander
>
> of weed-bearded captains; yesterday, the black
> fleet
> anchored there in the swift's road. . . .

Implicit in the undertaking of this colossal poem are a number of presuppositions, among them a root belief in the sustaining continuities of history. The links between ancient Greece and the modern Caribbean are regarded as genuine and artistically negotiable. No matter that the Greeks were empire builders and the Antilleans are portrayed as the pawns of new empire-makers, the multinational corporations. Both peoples are seafarers, and Walcott makes much of the notion that to a marine community the daily nudge and drain of the tides overrides more recent life rhythms. His characters may watch American TV programs or dance to reggae music or hot-rod down the streets, but all such trappings of modern life vanish before the larger reality of the "ocean's voice." Similarly, Walcott confederates the two cultures on the basis of their pagan convictions; they are alike in inhabiting islands flush with ghosts and natural spirits. *Omeros* opens in a state of what might be called vegetal panic: jungle trees are quaking in fear as islanders hack their way toward them in search of trunks that might make seaworthy canoes. Finally, Walcott assumes that his dark-skinned islanders cultivate a spoken language of sufficient beauty, punch, and dexterity to render it suitable for the elevated dignities of an epic poem. Needless to say, there is in this assumption a touch of the antiquated. The broad consensus among English-language poets is that the eclogue is no longer viable. The conventions that deemed it plausible for the common man, in the guise of shepherd or fisherman, to declaim in elaborately patterned verse died some time ago, perhaps when the last of Frost's rugged New Englanders traded in his Vermont sheep farm for a rent-with-option-to-buy condo in Sarasota. Fortunately, news of the form's demise has not yet reached Walcott, who presents his fishermen, taxi-drivers, domestics, and barkeeps as natural poets. To be sure, he has fun with their linguistic uncertainties—their solecisms and malaprops and misspellings. But make no mistake: he is singing a song of praise to the mettle and resilience of a tongue that has wandered far from those shores where the King's English is spoken.

It becomes evident after only a couple of pages that Walcott in *Omeros* has set himself a pair of sizable tasks, one a matter of content and the other of technique. As regards the former, he must have recognized from the outset the grave risk that the parallels between Homer's Greeks and Walcott's Antilleans would, in the long haul, grow artificial and contrived. (It is a danger he has chosen to confront head on, going as far as to name the two fishermen who battle over Helen's affections Achille and Hector.) In terms of technique, Walcott has likewise deliberately courted our eventual fatigue, by deciding to work in three-line stanzas whose rhymes evoke Dante's terza rima. In English, as opposed to rhyme-rich Italian, the rhymed tercet has proved to be of scant utility over the centuries, its currency typically restricted to the short lyric. A potential reader is therefore entitled to hesitate before embarking on an epic poem set in the modern Caribbean which draws heavily for subject upon Homer and for music upon Dante. But these are reservations likely to fade straightaway in the presence of Walcott's sure-handed stanzas. The welcome truth is that in *Omeros,* his ninth full-length book of verse, Walcott has overcome a number of seeming insurmountables. Even those readers who, like me, have admired much in his previous work may well find *Omeros* an inspiring and enlivening surprise.

Although Homer lends his name to its title and many details to its plot, *Omeros* is hardly a mere retelling or updating of *The Iliad* or *The Odyssey. Omeros* moves on a wide diversity of tides and currents, and the bulk of the book is devoted to incidents and meditations that have an exigu-

ous link, at best, to Homer's epics. Its narrative encompasses a nineteenth-century woman pioneer on the Great Plains; an eighteenth-century midshipman ancestor of Dennis Plunkett's; an aborted Antillean political campaign; a sunken treasure; a hallucinatory pilgrimage to Africa; a faith healer; and a contemporary poet—not so much a persona of the author as the author himself—who ponders modern urban life in Boston and Toronto. In dreams, in memory, sometimes in the flesh, Walcott's characters venture onto at least four continents and across at least four centuries.

Generally, what unites these far-flung souls and objects is the sea (or its agonizing absence, as when Major Plunkett relives the campaign against Rommel in the Sahara). In Greek mythology, it was of course a body of water—the navigable Styx—that conjoined the living and the dead, and Walcott has solid precedents for supposing that an epic poet should feel at liberty to travel by means of the mind's waterways from one end of creation to the other. Still, there are moments when, in aspiring to be all things to all people, *Omeros* winds up chugging like an overburdened motorboat. The Great Plains sections, in particular, seem not only narratively peripheral but thematically superfluous. They feel didactic, as though composed chiefly to highlight our nation's betrayal of the Indian. But do they—one must finally ask—add anything noteworthy? Hasn't the issue of the Old World's pillage of the New already been broached, unignorably, by Walcott's decision to center the poem on impoverished Antilleans? One recalls the lesson that, half a century ago, the Irish poet Patrick Kavanagh encapsulated in his sonnet "Epic," in which Homer's ghost materializes in order to point out that *The Iliad* was fabricated from nothing but a "local row." Even for the epic writer, Kavanagh reminds us, largeness needn't begin large; the trick is not in the scale of the tale but in the skill of the telling.

Omeros is most moving, significantly, when it stays close to home. The extended interludes in which the poet converses with the ghost of his father are indelibly drawn: spooky and graceful and loving and wrenchingly sad. Although the poet is, implicitly, an eminent man (he's the author, after all, of the brilliant feat of learning that is *Omeros*), and the father in his lifetime was, explicitly, a gifted man whose career was hamstrung by poverty and race prejudice, the place of honor throughout the meeting belongs to the father. He is at once taskmaster, supporter, and counsellor. (pp. 91-3)

And yet as rich a character as the poet's father becomes, Major Plunkett may be a still more considerable artistic achievement, in part because he begins so unpromisingly. When we first see him, in his "khaki shirt and capacious shorts," he is wiping the froth of a Guinness from his "pensioned moustache." He looks, in brief, like an all too easy stereotype and target—the English-colonial "hanger-on"—and the reader naturally worries that Walcott's rage will get the better of him. But quickly, as the lineaments of Plunkett's life come clear—his bewilderment over Britain's geopolitical decline, his flair for puns, his unfulfilled dream of a freewheeling trip around the world, his taciturn grief in the face of his wife's illness—he takes on subtler pigments and finer shadings. Indeed, the tragedy that eventually sinks him, as he careens into a stunned widowerhood, is the book's most fully realized bereavement. We feel for him. And that a man who appeared destined to provide the poem with its villain instead becomes a stirring, weighty figure testifies to the deep sympathies that inform *Omeros.* It's a bighearted book. . . .

In any poem of this length you would expect to find a range of rhyme types, if only because the customary prototype—exact rhyme—can become constraining or monotonous over time. But Walcott extends himself far beyond all foreseen deviations. A teacher of versification might well employ *Omeros* as a rhyme casebook. Here, in addition to exact masculine and feminine rhymes, one encounters triple rhymes (gentility / humility) and visual rhymes (plough / enough) and pararhymes or rim rhymes (often coming in strings: nose / canoes / noise) and anagrammatic rhymes (organ / groan) and apocopated rhymes (river / deliverer) and macaronic rhymes (come / *homme,* glory / *mori*) and light rhymes (sea / money) and rime riche (piss / precipice, Raj / mirage) and hosts of intricate couplings—each bearing its own distinctive acoustical qualities—for which, so far as I know, no terms have been coined except that grab bag designation "off rhyme." (p. 93)

Perhaps the most striking feature in his rhyming is his ready use of outlandish pairings of a sort usually reserved for light verse. When he rhymes "panther" with "and her" or "altar" with "halt. Her" or "Florida" with "worried her" or "hunter" with "front of her," we are closer to W. S. Gilbert or Ogden Nash than to Milton or Spenser. We are perched right at the teetering edge of parody—which is where he wants us. *Omeros* is no sendup of epic traditions—it is no "Rape of the Lock"—but Walcott is keenly attuned to the humble, farcical aspects of his island world, as when his hero Achille, with a touching combination of faith and ignorance, christens his boat In God We Troust.

Omeros is a poem of elusive metres. Robert Frost once observed that there are "virtually but two" metres in English—strict iambic and loose iambic. *Omeros* initially looks like an example of the latter, with interspersings of a tighter iambic line. But elsewhere the lines are loosened to a point where the iambic beat disappears, with the result that any systematic attempt to read the poem metrically—with that easy sense of place, that fluid but constant awareness of where you stand within the line, which is the hallmark of solidly metred poetry—must end in frustration. There are simply too many uncertain feet, extra stresses, ambiguous emphases, and so forth, for comfortable processing. Perhaps Walcott would have us take another approach? So many of the lines contain twelve syllables that one is tempted to conclude that he has forgone conventional metrics in favor of purely syllabic verse. However, the uncertainties that attend syllabic count in English, and the reader's difficulties in comprehending such a long syllabic line, make this interpretation problematic. The cadences are powerfully rhythmic, to be sure, and one may decide that Walcott has "captured the music of the sea," or something of the sort, and let the matter

drop there—but the lack of an orthodox metre is in fact a crucial, individuating trait. Rhyme—which could not help playing a signal role in *Omeros,* given Walcott's ingenuity with it—becomes preëminent in the absence of a clearly felt metre. Rhyme-based rather than metre-based, *Omeros* is a nonesuch among long poems.

One might go as far as to call it rhyme-driven. Over and over, rhymes are what hold the tumbling, pell-mell stanzas together, and since so many of the rhymes are unorthodox and recherché the poem's structure is forever on the verge of being lost. Even more than most verse, *Omeros* demands to be read aloud. When the prosodic underpinnings of a poem consist of rhymes like, say, "coffee" and—some twenty syllables later—"of the," you probably can't depend on your eye alone to catch the buried order that balances the hurly-burly; for this, you probably need actual, spoken echoes lingering in the air. (pp. 93-4)

Among marathoners, Mile 20 traditionally represents the point of greatest pain and trial and despair, and it is tempting to postulate that among the epic poets—the marathoners of the versifying world—a similar testing ground arrives at about the three-quarters mark. In any case, I had reached approximately that point in my reading of this more-than-three-hundred-page poem when either my own or the poet's energies flagged a little. Somewhere toward the close of *Omeros* the reader sees that its various branches are never going to wind up belonging to a single trunk; and with the knowledge that the poem will remain a thing of disparate parts comes the realization that one can in fairness formulate piecemeal judgments—can conclude, perhaps, that the passages dealing with Plunkett's ancestor could use some trimming, or that Hector's character needs to be clarified. Late in the poem, too, one may weary somewhat of Walcott's penchant for the sweeping abstract—for big, summational declarations about the nature of time or history or love. Every poetic virtue contains its hazards, obviously, and Walcott's characteristic eagerness to don a sage's getup and utter vatic grandiosities carries the risk that he may at times stumble on his robes, or his beard may slip a bit.

But they're apt to be momentary lapses, these stumblings or slippages, since Walcott wields all kinds of strengths that can bolster a sagging passage in a twinkling. He has a sure, prepossessing vocabulary, a deft and ludic wit ("she was an adamant Eve"), an intricately calibrated ear. He's a man of wonderful analogical talents, especially when he fixes his eye on the natural world. He gives the reader roosters that really crow ("their cries screeching like red chalk / drawing hills on a board"), jellyfish that truly float ("tasselled palanquins of Portuguese man-o'-wars / bobbed like Asian potentates"), swifts that genuinely fly ("this frail dancer / leaping the breakers, this dart of the meridian"). And he's better than wonderful—he's little short of miraculous—when he stirs up some weather. The hurricane he brews in an early chapter is so splendidly overmastering that a reader is left feeling dazed, windblown, waterlogged. If to read *Omeros* is to sign on for a substantial voyage during which small doubts are constantly raised and quelled, raised and quelled—well, what long poem of our time can be read without misgivings or objections? (p. 94)

So bright and immediate are many of Walcott's local virtues that one can lose sight of the lowering darkness of **Omeros.** Not until I'd set the book down, the journey completed, did it become clear what an unbroken line of woes it enfolds. Maud Plunkett is not the only one whose life ends sadly: Hector dies in an accident; the midshipman falls in combat while still a boy. And, year by year, political corruption cankers the island's soul, pollution threatens its beauty. There is a loud call of anguish at the center of **Omeros,** but the book is something more—something better—than a simple cry from the heart. It's a complex cry from the heart, for Walcott has succeeded in filtering all sorts of titanic sorrows through a limpid and ferocious intellect. (pp. 94-5)

> *Brad Leithauser, "Ancestral Rhyme," in* The New Yorker, *Vol. LXVI, No. 52, February 11, 1991, pp. 91-5.*

FURTHER READING

Atlas, James. "Derek Walcott: Poet of Two Worlds." *The New York Times Magazine* (23 May 1982): 32, 34, 38-9, 42, 50-1.
    Biographical discussion of Walcott's career.

Bedient, Calvin. "Derek Walcott, Contemporary." *Parnassus: Poetry in Review* 9, No. 2 (Fall-Winter 1981): 31-44.
    Analysis of *The Fortunate Traveller,* arguing that its sense of dislocation and lack of authority reflects a pervasive trend in contemporary literature.

Birkerts, Sven. "Derek Walcott." In his *The Electric Life: Essays on Modern Poetry,* pp. 265-72. New York: William Morrow and Company, 1989.
    Reprint of an essay that originally appeared in *The New Republic* on January 23, 1984, in which Birkerts analyses the structure of Walcott's *Midsummer.*

Brodsky, Joseph. "On Derek Walcott." *The New York Review of Books* XXX, No. 17 (10 November 1983): 39-41.
    Argues that Walcott should be perceived not just as a Caribbean poet but as an outstanding poet of universal appeal.

Brown, Lloyd W. "Caribbean Castaway New World Odyssey: Derek Walcott's Poetry" *The Journal of Commonwealth Literature* 11, No. 2 (December 1976): 149-59.
    Focuses on Walcott's theme of artistic odyssey.

Dove, Rita. "Either I'm Nobody, or I'm a Nation." *Parnassus: Poetry in Review* 14, No. 1 (1987): 48-76.
    Thorough discussion of works included in Walcott's *Collected Poems.*

Fox, Robert Elliot. "Big Night Music: Derek Walcott's *Dream on Monkey Mountain* and the 'Splendours of Imagination'." *The Journal of Commonwealth Literature* XVII, No. 1 (1982): 16-27.
    Examines the metaphorical structure of *Dream on Monkey Mountain.*

Heaney, Seamus. "The Language of Exile." *Parnassus: Poetry in Review* 8, No. 1 (Fall-Winter 1979): 5-11.
    Review of Walcott's *The Star-Apple Kingdom.*

McWatt, Mark A. "Derek Walcott: An Island Poet and His Sea." *Third World Quarterly* 10, No. 4 (October 1988): 1607-15.
    Overview of Walcott's career as a poet and dramatist.

The New Yorker XLVII, No. 19 (26 June 1971): 30-1.
    Interview in which Walcott discusses his *Dream on Monkey Mountain* and his Caribbean background.

Ramsaran, J. A. "Derek Walcott: New World Mediterranean Poet." *World Literature Written in English* 21, No. 1 (Spring 1982): 133-47.
    Focuses on the influences contributing to Walcott's development of a distinctly West Indian form of literature.

Taylor, Patrick. "Myth and Reality in Caribbean Narrative: Derek Walcott's 'Pantomime'." *World Literature Written in English* 26, No. 1 (Spring 1986): 169-77.
    Critical analysis of Walcott's *Pantomime.*

Thompson, John. "Old Campaigners." *The New York Review of Books* 23, No. 16 (14 October 1976): 33-4.
    Review of Walcott's *Sea Grapes.*

John Edgar Wideman

1941-

American novelist, short story writer, nonfiction writer, and critic.

Wideman, whom critic Robert Bone called "perhaps the most gifted black novelist of his generation," is best known for novels and short stories that trace the lives of several generations of families in and around Homewood, a black ghetto district of Pittsburgh where he grew up. His major theme involves the individual's quest for self-understanding amidst personal memories and African-American experiences in general. Kermit Frazier commented: "The characters in Wideman's fiction can escape neither collective nor personal history and memory, so they are forced to deal with them in some way—be it successfully or ineffectually." Although Wideman deemphasized specifically black issues early in his career, his later works evidence his interest in "bringing to the fore black cultural material, history, archetypes, myths, the language itself, . . . and trying to connect that with the so-called mainstream." Many critics concur that Wideman's blend of Western and black literary traditions constitutes a distinctive voice in American literature.

Wideman attended the University of Pennsylvania before being selected as the first black Rhodes scholar since Alaine Locke in 1905. In England, Wideman studied eighteenth-century literature and the early development of the novel. His first two novels, *A Glance Away* and *Hurry Home,* reflect this formal training as well as his own experiments with narrative technique. These works involve a search for self by protagonists who are confused and dominated by their pasts. In *A Glance Away,* a rehabilitated drug addict returns to his home, where he renews family and social ties while trying to avoid a relapse; in *Hurry Home,* a black law school graduate seeks cultural communion with white society by traveling to Europe, then reaffirms his black heritage in Africa. These characters find hope for the future only by confronting their personal and collective pasts. In *The Lynchers,* Wideman focuses upon racial conflict in the United States during the 1960s.

Wideman has attributed the shift toward black-oriented themes and increased use of myth and dialect in his later novels to his growing awareness of such prominent black authors as Richard Wright and Jean Toomer. In *The Homewood Trilogy,* which comprises the short story collection *Damballah* and the novels *Hiding Place* and *Sent for You Yesterday,* Wideman uses deviating time frames, black dialect, and rhythmic language to transform Homewood into what Alan Cheuse described as "a magical location infused with poetry and pathos." The interrelated stories of *Damballah* feature several characters who reappear in the novels and relate tales of the descendants of Wideman's ancestor, Sybela Owens. *Hiding Place* concerns a boy's strong ties to his family and his involvement in a petty robbery that results in an accidental killing. *Sent for*

You Yesterday won the 1984 PEN/Faulkner Award for fiction. Through the characters of Doot, the primary narrator, and Albert Wilkes, an outspoken blues pianist, Wideman asserts that creativity and imagination are important means to transcend despair and strengthen the common bonds of race, culture, and class.

The eponymous narrator of *Reuben* is an ambiguous and enigmatic figure who provides inexpensive legal aid to residents of Homewood. Among his clients are Kwansa, a young black woman whose brutal ex-husband, a recovering drug addict, seeks custody of their illegitimate child as revenge against her, and Wally, an assistant basketball coach at a local university who comes to Reuben because he fears he will be blamed for the illegal recruiting practices of his department. Wally, who may have actually murdered a white man, is possessed by an ingrained hatred that leads him to fantasize of violence against middle-aged white males. Madison Smartt Bell commented: "[*Reuben*] is perhaps most importantly a detailed and sensitive portrait of the inner life of its characters, here rendered credibly and frighteningly as a kind of endless nightmare. Aside from, and along with that, it seems to be saying something new about the old vexed question of race relations in America. The question is not whether 'hate's bad for you,' but why." Race-related strife, violence, and suffering are also prominent themes in *Fever: Twelve Stories*. In the collection's title story, Wideman juxtaposes present-day racism in Philadelphia, a city once offering freedom for slaves through the Underground Railroad, with a narrative set during the yellow fever epidemic of 1793. Commenting upon the fever as a metaphor for racism and related anguish, a black physician rejects biological explanations for the infection: "We have bred the affliction within our breasts. . . . Fever grows in the secret places of our hearts, planted there when one of us decided to sell one of us to another."

In the novel *Philadelphia Fire,* Wideman combines fact and fiction to elaborate on an actual incident involving MOVE, a militant, heavily armed black commune that refused police orders to vacate a Philadelphia slum house in 1985. With the approval of W. Wilson Goode, the city's black mayor, police bombed the house from a helicopter, killing eleven commune members—including five children—but creating a fire that destroyed approximately fifty-three houses. The book's narrator, Cudjoe, a writer and former Rhodes scholar living in self-imposed exile on a Greek island, returns to his native city upon hearing about the incident to search for a young boy who was seen fleeing the house following the bombing. This fictionalized narrative is juxtaposed with Wideman's address to his own son, who was sentenced to life in prison at eighteen years of age for killing another young man while on a camping trip. In an earlier nonfiction work, *Brothers and Keepers,* Wideman had commented upon his brother's involvement in a murder similar to that described in his novel *Hiding Place.* Combining Wideman's literary skill with his brother's street-wise attitude, *Brothers and Keepers* sensitively explores the consequences of decisions and how the brothers arrived at such dissimilar fates.

(See also *CLC,* Vols. 5, 34, 36; *Contemporary Authors,* Vols. 85-88; *Contemporary Authors New Revision Series,* Vol. 14; *Black Writers;* and *Dictionary of Literary Biography,* Vol. 33.)

PRINCIPAL WORKS

NOVELS

A Glance Away   1967
Hurry Home   1969
The Lynchers   1973
*Hiding Place   1981
*Sent for You Yesterday   1983
Reuben   1987
Philadelphia Fire   1990

OTHER

*Damballah   (short stories)   1981
Brothers and Keepers   (nonfiction)   1984
Fever: Twelve Stories   1989

*These works were reissued in a collected paperback edition as *The Homewood Trilogy* (1985).

John Edgar Wideman with Kay Bonetti

[Bonetti]: *Mr. Wideman, we know a lot about your biography from both the Homewood trilogy and* **Brothers and Keepers,** *in which you try to come to terms with your brother Robby's imprisonment for first-degree murder. But I wonder about your life as a writer. Can you tell us at what point you began to know that's what you wanted to do?*

[Wideman]: I liked to get up and tell stories in grade school and I was pretty good at it. Most of my stories were bits and pieces of the reading I'd been doing, which would vary from the kids' fiction in the Carnegie Library to comic books. I loved comic books. I guess I began to identify myself as a writer even that early. Not as a writer with a capital W; I just liked to write and I had a lot of encouragement all the way through high school. But I don't think it was until probably senior year in college that I actually began to make life decisions based on the idea that maybe I wanted to write.

Were your parents supportive in that?

My parents have always been enormously supportive. Anything I've wanted to do was okay. I was told do it well and work hard and make sure it's something you really like. That kind of support. But for my parents and really for the whole extended family I was a test case. Nobody else had gone all the way through school. Almost everybody in my parents' generation had a high school education, but nobody had gone on to college, so I was the flagship; I was out there doing things that no one else had done. My parents were smart not to try to monitor that, except by being supportive. The reasons that I went to college were basically mine. I thought I wanted to play pro basketball, and I knew in order to play pro basketball you had to play college basketball and to play college basketball you had to get a scholarship, so things sort of dovetailed and it was a lockstep kind of future that I had figured out for myself.

You were on an athletic scholarship at the University of Pennsylvania?

Well not exactly, because the Ivy League schools claim that they don't give athletic scholarships. That means that I had to qualify for an academic scholarship. In reality, if you were a good athlete they gave you a certain number of points so that if I were competing against some kid from Illinois who had the same grades and the same sort of test scores as I did, I would get the scholarship.

You went on to become a Rhodes Scholar. Were you the first black Rhodes Scholar?

There had been one black Rhodes Scholar, Alaine Locke, in 1905, I believe it was. And then the same year I was elected, 1963, another man, Stan Sanders, from the West coast was elected. So we were the first three. And Stan and I were the first two in about sixty years. (pp. 77-8)

When you went to Pennsylvania, what did you study?

I started out as a psych major, found out that meant mostly counting the number of times a rat went down a particular tunnel and got tired of that pretty quickly. I wanted to learn about Freud and Jung and all that fancy stuff about the unconscious and be able to look in somebody's eyes and tell what they were going to do and who they were going to be. That wasn't what psychology meant at the University of Pennsylvania at that time, so I flirted with anthropology for about a half-semester and then I eventually became an English major. I took some creative writing classes there—one with a man named Christopher Davis, who is a very good novelist. Also I had a chance to meet Archibald MacLeish, who came in for a three-day stint at the University. He met with the writing class and looked at samples of writing from Penn students. I was very encouraged by having someone whose name I'd seen in the lights actually look at my writing, pat me on the back and say, "Son, you're doing pretty well and keep at it." The climate at Penn at that time was even freer than when I was a teacher at Penn in encouraging the arts and encouraging writers to come and spend time on the campus. All that helped me make up my mind.

Did you write while you were at Oxford?

By the time I got to England I was fairly serious. I began to see myself as a writer and I saw the whole experience of getting out of the country as something that would forward a career in writing. I thought that was one way to get the kind of seriousness that I needed in my work. All of us grow up very confused and I thought writing was something that was connected with Europe. The matter of Europe. I didn't want to be a good American writer, let alone a good black writer. I wanted to be world class, man, and to be world class you had to be Thomas Mann and you had to be Marcel Proust and you had to walk along the Champs Elysées and you had to know about bullfights. Those were the things that were kind of stirring around in my head. I wanted to go where the action was. So going to Europe was a very conscious attempt to become part of that tradition.

Was James Baldwin much of a model for you when you were young?

Not at all. I came through school with a standard Eng Lit education. I knew that there was a man named James Baldwin, because he made the newspapers, but he was not taught in my classes and I didn't know his work. I'm not sure whether or not I read any Ralph Ellison in college but if I did, it would have been probably the only piece of writing by a black writer.

Did you read Langston Hughes and Richard Wright in the public schools?

They may have been in my high school anthology—"The Negro Speaks of Rivers" maybe for Hughes. But he certainly wouldn't have been picked out as a black writer and he probably was skipped because most teachers didn't know how to deal with it. (pp. 79-81)

Had you read Baldwin when you wrote **Hurry Home?**

I had educated myself a little bit about black literature. I had taught Baldwin by that time, I believe, so I was much more familiar with black writers.

There are some similarities: the sensitive alienated black intellectual going to Europe, taking up with some kind of strange guilt-ridden white man, looking for a black son that he's never seen, who may or may not be real.

When I wrote **Hurry Home** I was certainly trying to deal with that need to get out of the United States which Baldwin writes about quite explicitly. So sure, that was an influence and he was—as a black man wandering around in Europe trying to gain a purchase on his identity, trying to find out what he needed to write about—he was an archetype in the back of my mind, but by then I also knew about other people who had to go through the same kind of thing. Sculptors, actors, musicians. It was go to Europe, be appreciated, and then maybe they'll pay some attention back in the US of A.

You said that you had started educating yourself about black literature. What made you start doing that?

One way I got involved was my own curiosity. I had begun to read a few things. The sixties brought that whole necessity to examine one's own race and one's own background. I was part of that. By 1968 I was teaching at the University of Pennsylvania, and a group of black students asked me to start a course in Afro-American literature. I hemmed and hawed because I didn't know anything and I had my own writing to worry about and I didn't want to get involved in the work to put together a decent class and I didn't want to do it in a off-hand manner either. So there they sat in front of me and I suddenly heard myself giving them all the excuses, "That's not my field, and I don't know it, and I have my own work." I sounded like such a punk, I sounded like the very voice that had turned so many people back that I stopped short in the middle of all my excuses and said, "Yes, I'll do it, sure." It was the eye contact, it was the sense of myself sitting out there listening to me, that did it. That was a very important moment and I think my reading began to be quite serious at that point. (pp. 81-2)

You have written that you see your vocation as a writer to be that of authenticating your background, authenticating black life.

Not so much a planned campaign but the inevitable direction that my writings turned. For me writing is more and more a tool of self-expression and as I understand better who I am, I understand more about the culture of which I'm part. That's what I'm trying to get into my writing. The possibility of individual growth, coupled with the idea that a given culture can help you select or select for you a framework in which it's most natural to work and from which you draw your range of choice. In any matter, whether it's playing basketball or dancing or speaking.

And in your case it's language. "Language is power," you say at one place. Beginning with the **Homewood Trilogy** *it seems that you are trying to authenticate that language.*

It started even earlier than that; it just wasn't a central concern. I had to work my way through it. **Hurry Home** is all about mastering one's own culture and the kind of paranoia and craziness that comes when you can't make those decisions or when people keep making the decisions for you.

What do you value about the first three books?

I don't look back that often. The work that's past is gone. Some of my books are going to be reprinted and I'll be curious to see what the reaction to them is. When the books were published they were always published in small editions and had readers who were very appreciative, but not many in number. Yet through it all I knew I was doing some things the other writers weren't doing and I knew that I was doing some things that might be valuable if somebody would listen, if somebody would pay attention.

Can you name any of those things?

They're the same things we've been talking about. Experiments with language, experiments with form, bringing to the fore black cultural material, history, archetypes, myths, the language itself, the language that black people actually speak and trying to connect that with the so-called mainstream.

And yet you have said that what you felt like you were doing was translating one language into another language.

I think I had my priorities a little bit mixed up. I felt that I had to prove something about black speech for instance, and about black culture, and that they needed to be imbedded within the larger literary frame. In other words, a quote from T. S. Eliot would authenticate a quote from my grandmother. Or the quote from my grandmother wasn't enough, I had to have a Joycean allusion to buttress it, to keep an awareness that "Hey, this is serious writing and this guy's not just a solitary black voice, but he knows the things that you know, he's part of the shared culture." I felt you had to leave a signpost to make that clear. Sometimes it works and sometimes it doesn't. But the urge to do that, the urge to make my work a blend of all the different cultures that have filtered through me is still there. It's tough, it's very tough because if you really do bridge two cultures it probably happens not because that's what you want to do but because you are so thoroughly part of both those worlds that what you do comes out being a true blend.

In our classes they teach us to distinguish between the local color writer and the genre writer and the regional writer. And in every case the local color writer is the outsider trying to write about something and his outersiderness both moves and somehow lessens the work.

There's that and there's also simply the politics of writing in this country. And the politics of our national psyche which tends to see things in cartoons and tends to try to grab things without really touching them. We look for either/ors: things are either black or white, up or down, you're either rich or poor, you're a winner or a loser. Who knows where that fault in our imagination comes from: maybe it's because Americans have felt so alienated from the land, their past, that the notion of cleavage, the notion of either/or is fundamental. I personally think it comes from racial politics. In order to define yourself as an American you had to define yourself over and against something. And to define yourself over and against Eu-

rope actually meant always to put America in the derogatory light.

Toni Morrison has said that she is working for a black audience. She uses the analogy that if Dostoyevsky were writing Crime and Punishment *for an American audience it would be a totally different book. I think she was getting at the universality that comes from focusing on the particular, focusing on one place from the inside. Do you think that in focusing on Homewood you have managed to move someplace that you didn't go in the first three books?*

The notion of being grounded is a very important notion in all traditional cultures. I'm using the word grounded metaphorically: the forefathers entered this land and it was dangerous and nobody ever lived here before. But they spoke to the spirits of this land and those spirits gave them information and knowledge that they needed to start a village. The village could grow and would be sustained because the people kept alive that knowledge of the original contract, a knowledge of the rootedness. Everything flows from that ancestral bargain. And I believe that in order for my art, anybody's art, to flourish it has to be rooted, it has to be grounded, in that sense. So, yes, particularity, yes, the very unique and real ground that you fought for and bled in and created as a people. In my case that's Homewood. (pp. 88-91)

Do you have any feelings about the issue of the writer as a plunderer of other people's experience?

I remember once in college reading a story by Henry Miller. It was a story about coming home from Europe and going back to a family gathering, and he used his own name and I assumed the names of the people in his family. I was shocked. I was absolutely shocked by the candor and the frankness and even the fact that he said his father had a wart, or his mother was a crabby old bitch, that his father burped at the table, that somebody's ears weren't clean. That seemed to be telling tales, seemed to be betraying mother and father and home. I just couldn't believe that as a writer he would trespass that way and reveal that kind of information, be that intimate. So I started with a very conservative idea about what was okay to reveal and what wasn't okay to reveal, combined with the very powerful cultural imperative that you don't tell most of what you know. It would just get you in trouble.

Baldwin writes about that.

It's crucial. You can find the same proverbs among the Russian serfs.

It's the underclass, whatever that class is.

Exactly. You can't speak what's on your mind, you can't be frank with people because it will be used against you. Your language and your customs, etc. revolve around the hard, cold facts of your servitude, of the oppressed state that you live in. I couldn't ever see myself writing about my family at all. So when I wrote my first novel, I didn't name the city, the people were disguised very carefully, I didn't use things—I sort of made up most of the book. I brought in major characters from my life as a student, from my life in Europe and put them into this sort of vaguely big city atmosphere. But it wasn't until the Homewood books that I actually began to try to deal with that primal ground. It was a question of getting enough confidence in myself and knowing enough about my people so that I knew that I wasn't embarrassing myself and I wasn't embarassing them but that the truth about them, if I could ever write the truth about them, would be powerful and it would be beautiful and it would be true.

You have written, "One of the earliest lessons I learned as a child was that if you looked away from something, it might not be there when you look back. I feared loss, feared turning to speak to someone and finding no one there. Being black and poor reinforced the wisdom of a tentative purchase on experience. . . . If you let your eyes touch lightly, rely on an impressionistic touch—then you may achieve the emotional economy of faint gains, faint losses. Writing," and this is the remark that is so important, "forces me to risk ignoring the logic of this lesson." Could you expand on that a little bit?

From the writer's point of view writing is a laying on of hands. I feel that if I'm going to write well, I have to take the risk, I have to take lots of risks, risks of finding out something about something I've done or something I haven't done and having that knowledge hurt me or hurt somebody else or disorient me. All those risks are involved if you want to write well. So I had to start taking some chances that go against the grain of that wisdom. I also learned that the people who loved me and whom I cared about most were people who flew in the face of that initial wisdom of touching lightly. The people I love most and who loved me most were folks who did expose themselves, who did make themselves vulnerable, went the whole nine yards, if you will. I reacted in a personal way to the examples of my mother, and my aunts and uncles, and my grandfather and the people who, as I wrote about and thought about and learned about them, came to be the most important people in my life again. I had kind of lost touch with them and lost touch with their importance. I was looking in other places for the nurturing and the wisdom and models. But coming back to them I found that they had taken the most dramatic kinds of chances. They had united their fate with mine. And as I looked around more carefully I found that that had occurred in no other arena of my life. (pp. 93-5)

> **"From the writer's point of view writing is a laying on of hands. I feel that if I'm going to write well, I have to take the risk, I have to take lots of risks, risks of finding out something about something I've done or something I haven't done and having that knowledge hurt me or hurt somebody else or disorient me. All those risks are involved if you want to write well."**

There are people who think that writing being done in the

black American tradition during the last generation is in many ways the very best writing that's being done, that being a member of an oppressed group in society gives you an insight that leads to the creation of novels that are beautiful and socially responsible at the same time, as Toni Morrison would say.

I think that you might look at black writing and say that this is some of the best that the culture is producing and it's a splendid time for black writing. A judgment like that suggests that what's happening is new, that what's happening is rare, and that what's happen..:g has no history; but there have always been powerful black voices. Ellison between 1940 and 1960, and before him Richard Wright and Zora Neale Hurston. They've been at the forefront of fiction; we just didn't know it, we just didn't know where or how to look. The other reason I don't like to endorse that kind of Golden Epoch of Black Literature notion is that the same conditions, economic and social, that made so many black writers invisible before, could happen again. A force of circumstances could quiet the black voice, but would that mean that there weren't any good black writers any more? That people could nostalgically look back at the 60s, 70s, and 80s and say, "Boy, there were some good black writers then, but there are none now." No. It would probably mean that publishing had decided that blacks are not in vogue this year, and so all those good black voices would just be quieted. (pp. 98-9)

Many people point to Native American writing—work by Scott Momaday and James Welch and Leslie Silko, and argue that being in the underclass somehow gives you a better eye for creating these very beautiful and very big novels.

When it works, yes.

But you don't think there's anything magic about it?

It's hard work and it's discipline. The writers you're talking about are—first of all their art and genius should not be connected to the sociology of their lives because you could point to a hundred people who went through the same kinds of experiences and didn't write novels. So what's the difference. When you talk about cultures and styles even, you can't have it both ways; either you're ethnocentric or not. You're not ethnocentric if you believe that all cultures have values and you have to get inside and understand them and look at them in their own terms. You can't go around praising exotic people for being exotic, or outsiders for being outside. It's like lots of Americans will—I've noticed this, it's not original with me, but if there's an Indian woman, East Indian woman, at a party inevitably someone will come and tell me, "Did you see that beautiful woman over there, isn't she beautiful?"—a white person will say that to me. That over-compensation is pigeonholing, is cataloging, is talking about the otherness of the person, and I think we have to resist that.

James Baldwin felt that there was no way to tell the truth about the American culture without trying to get white culture to see its relationship to black culture.

Well, that's not quite clear to me, I'm not exactly sure what he was getting at or what you're getting at. I think you have to be very cautious. I believe that I have a very definite advantage in being black in America. Both insider and outsider, that's the archetypal artistic stance. Whether or not that stance becomes a discipline, produces art, has to do with countless other factors. It may be a flying start, but there are a whole lot of winos and junkies who have been alienated from their society and stand on the outside—who have the perfect angle for writing novels—but they're killing themselves, not producing art.

You've said that the best stories are those written for a specific person to read.

Yes, in a funny way I don't think a writer has a choice. How shall we write a universal story, how shall we write a story that's appealing to everyone? You might as well go to the Propp fairytale index and pick out one or two of those recurring myths and just put in characters and write them over and over again. No. You have to be aware of the particular. You have to be aware of the specific people, the specific words, the specific locales and then something grows out of that. It doesn't work the other way around. At least I've never seen it work the other way around. (pp. 99-101)

> *John Edgar Wideman and Kay Bonetti, in an interview in* The Missouri Review, *Vol. IX, No. 2, 1986, pp. 75-103.*

Walter Kendrick

At the center of John Edgar Wideman's fifth novel [*Reuben*] stands the grotesque, enigmatic figure of Reuben—which might be his first name, his last, or both. No one knows how old Reuben is; no one knows for how many years he's been dispensing cheap legal aid to the residents of Pittsburgh's black Homewood district. All they know in Homewood is that if you need to post bond or bail, if charges have been filed against you or you want to file charges, if you require a will, a birth certificate or any sort of permit, the place to go is Reuben's rotting trailer, permanently parked "in that vacant lot behind Hamilton over near the school."

Reuben can be relied upon at all seasons, but he's a bit disconcerting at first. His child-size body is too small for his long face and hands, and he carries one shoulder higher than the other:

> He wasn't built funny enough to be pitiable, but he wasn't put together quite right either. So you were careful when you spoke to him. Certain words you didn't want to say, certain lines you didn't want to cross. . . . Which made you careful. Made it hard to talk to him without your mind straying.

Kwansa Parker's mind strays when she goes to Reuben about her illegitimate 4-year-old son, Cudjoe, whose father—off dope now, newly married, and abetted by his snooty sisters—is claiming custody on the grounds of Kwansa's unfitness as a mother. Wally's mind strays, too; a former basketball star, he now recruits players for "the university" (it gets no other name) and flies frequently coast to coast, interviewing promising candidates. He goes to Reuben about a bribe-taking scandal that's about to

break and incriminate the whole sports staff, top to bottom. Wally *is* the bottom, so he worries about his future and wants Reuben to forestall disaster.

Wally's mind strays to an afternoon in a glossy Chicago men's room, where he killed a white man. No special provocation, no reason: "So it was almost with regret that he swiftly brought the knife edge of his right hand down, down on the man's neck. An ugly whoomp knocked flesh senseless as a sack of flour." Wally finished his victim off by shoving his head into an antiseptic toilet bowl.

Maybe he didn't, though. Maybe he only wanted to, still wants to; maybe the story was told to him by a next-seat passenger on one of Wally's indistinguishable flights. He tells Reuben the story twice in different guises and would tell it again, returning to it with the nagging certainty that this must mean something, though he doesn't know what. Instead of an answer, Reuben offers his own story of Flora the madam and the piano player Dudley Armstrong, how Flora's fancy house burned to the ground and Reuben saved himself, way back when. Meanwhile, Kwansa has found solace in the arms of Toodles, a lesbian prostitute whose love Kwansa never sought, though she welcomes it gladly when it comes.

These fragmentary, often blurry stories unwind in 11 discrete chapters, most labeled with their protagonists' names. Nothing links them except the presence of Reuben, who by turns plays narrator, listener, interpreter and guardian spirit. Only Reuben seems to believe that experience makes sense, or at least that it can be infused with sense by memory—that experience can be *told* in any meaningful way. Kwansa's life lurches from moment to unprecedented moment; Wally often lives the present as if it were already memory, so he "didn't have it to worry about anymore." Only Reuben regards today as the proper inheritor of yesterday. Yet Reuben is a solitary, extraordinary, marginal creature, even in a neighborhood that itself is marginal to the point of falling off the edge.

It appears, in fact, that Homewood has fallen, that in *Reuben* Mr. Wideman has given up on his old stomping ground as a source of tales worth telling. In the *Homewood Trilogy*—*Damballah* (1981), *Hiding Place* (1981) and *Sent for You Yesterday* (which won the 1984 PEN/Faulkner award)—he made the place seem inexhaustible, despite its steady decline into drugs and desuetude. Figures from the past cast grand shadows on the present, shaming the present but granting it resonance. In *Brothers and Keepers* (1984), he completed the transition, foreshadowed in the last two Homewood books, from fiction to memoir, by revealing that many of the stories he'd told were really about his brother, a convicted murderer, or else they came to him as family legends. He hadn't made them up.

Reuben, Mr. Wideman's first novel since *Sent for You Yesterday,* proclaims that he can make things up if he has to, just look. Kwansa, Wally and Toodles are types, not individuals, though they ring true enough. Reuben, however, on whom the novel depends for such coherence as it possesses, is evidently intended to be mythic, but he betrays more of intention than of myth. Timeless and cryptic, he recalls the Haitian voodoo god Damballah: Damballah is requested to "gather up the family," and on a small, desperate scale, that is what Reuben does at the end of *Reuben.*

Among the most impressive features of Mr. Wideman's earlier work was his deft mastery of language on several levels—from precise, often lyrical standard English to a raw street slang that conveyed the ungrammatical immediacy of experience reported without reflection. Especially in the *Homewood Trilogy,* the interaction of these dialects achieved a rare fusion of stateliness and heat; but *Brothers and Keepers* sealed them off in airtight compartments labeled Robby (slang) and John Edgar (standard). *Reuben* tries to unite them in a single narrative voice, but the mixture curdles.

Reuben himself speaks standard English that's usually either florid or clichéd. "We'll work out a mutually satisfactory arrangement," he tells the befuddled Kwansa, who—like most of the novel's subsidiary characters—speaks a version of street talk: "Got the paper right here. Man from the sheriff's office came to my door. That's when I knew they was serious." But the narrator tries to span the full range. This voice prefers ventriloquism to transcription; it barges in constantly, analyzing a character's feelings in the process of expounding them and too seldom letting the character speak. Kwansa mulls over a come-on from Toodles: "Kwansa had never loved with a woman, but the few times the idea crossed her mind, it was with a woman like Toodles. Not mannish. She could have a man for that. . . . Had to be somebody got something going for they ownself." The standard narrator dips into slang as if slumming: Kwansa deserves better than this.

But the principal fault lies with Reuben, a character constructed rather than observed. He feels a "long-standing fascination" with both ancient Egypt and the photography of Eadweard Muybridge, an implausible pair of hobbyhorses that converge on an obsession with halting change. The Egyptians mummified their dead to preserve them on the journey to the other world; Muybridge took stop-motion pictures of living people and animals, seeking to break motion down into its smallest components, which would not move. Whatever success the Egyptians enjoyed, Muybridge failed, as he informs Reuben in a ghostly visitation that might be a dream: "I thought I was cracking the Stone Age but I created rows and rows of cells. Tiny, isolated cubicles with a pitiful little figure marooned in each one. Prisoners who couldn't touch, didn't even know the existence of the twin living next door."

Except for the thwarted ambition, this is a good summary of *Reuben*: minimal almost to the vanishing point, its stories overlap nowhere but in the mind of Reuben, who is powerless to join them and knows it. Even the metaphors of brotherhood and imprisonment, which served Mr. Wideman well in his earlier work, turn here into figures for death, for the lack of further stories to tell. Homewood must really have fallen, or perhaps *Reuben* fails because Mr. Wideman has mined that vein to depletion and needs to move on. In a career as rich as his, one can only hope that *Reuben* marks a pause for breath.

Walter Kendrick, "A Voodoo Guide to the Marginal," in The New York Times Book Review, *November 8, 1987, p. 3.*

Noel Perrin

As everyone admits, John Edgar Wideman is one of the half-dozen leading black novelists alive today. There's just one problem with that description. He doesn't write novels. He certainly writes books *called* novels, and they contain fictional characters in fictional situations. But what they really are is myths—generally myths of the biracial society. And a good thing, too. Because if Wideman were a novelist, he would be a seriously flawed one.

Take his new book, *Reuben.* Listen to a brief account of it, and you'll see what I mean. Let's start with the title character.

Reuben is an old black lawyer in Pittsburgh—a tiny man with a pointed gray beard and a misshapen body. When he was young, he served as janitor and occasional pimp in a white-boy fraternity at what seems to be the University of Pennsylvania.

One Sunday the frat boys chip in and buy *him* a session with Flora, the beautiful, possibly part-black madam of the bordello. It's a trap. Once Reuben and Flora start making love, the boys rush in. First they flog Reuben (his back is a mass of scars to this day) and tie Flora spreadeagled to her bed. Their amusing plan is to rape her en masse and then mash her face in. "Such a fetching piece of real estate, but when we finish with it . . . no one will want her," laughs one of the boys, no doubt a future land developer.

The plan is not completed, because just as the mass rape is about to commence, flames come leaping up the stairs. Dudley, the black piano player, has set the building on fire. Flora, tied to the bed, dies a painful death; the brave frat boys jump out the window. No one is ever caught or punished.

Now consider Wally. Wally is younger and better-looking. He's an assistant basketball coach at a mostly white university, but fantasy life is what really interests him. One of his favorites is to imagine himself armed with a baseball bat striding down an endless row of posts. Each post is topped with the head of a middle-aged white male. Wally smashes each one as he passes, and does he enjoy it! Never gets tired, never gets bored. Once (the book is deliberately ambiguous here) Wally seems to have enacted his fantasy, killing a white man picked at random in Chicago. That killing, if it really occurred, is one of the two reasons he's consulting Reuben, the other being the imminent exposure of illegal recruiting practices at his university. As junior coach, Wally will be the official sacrifice.

Then there's Kwansa (born Lily). She's a young black prostitute. Five years ago she had an illegitimate child, a son whom she named Cudjoe and whom she adores. She does not farm him out to an aunt; she raises him herself.

Now the boy's father, not having lifted a finger for five years, has decided he wants his son, and steals him. Kwansa counts on lawyer Reuben to get him back. That's not how it works out, though. Kwansa's new lover, a woman named Toodles, retrieves the kid. She uses a very basic approach. She cuts the father's throat with a razor, so that he dies "spouting blood like a fountain." No more custody fights with *him*.

In short, if **Reuben** were a novel, it would be total and shameless melodrama. But it doesn't read that way at all. It reads like the myth it is. A melodrama has a plot, and lots of suspense; the tension builds. **Reuben** has no real plot—just events, told discontinuously—and it has almost no enacted scenes. Mostly you have the voice of John Edgar Wideman, narrating as a tribal storyteller might. Mesmerizing his audience. Building sound, not story. Speaking in many tongues, from black English in Wally's thoughts and Kwansa's speech to the most whitely formal of poetic styles, as in the passage beginning "Night gnaws the city."

This is a book to be read aloud. One chapter that I thought I disliked for being too pretentious in its language—that chapter I happened to read aloud to a friend, and discovered that I liked it after all. There is true magic in the language, and if you let it crash over you like waves, you may cease to care that there is no enacted story. You may even be able to cease minding that the words "nigger" (for blacks) and "cracker" (for whites) are used as conscious obscenities, meant to shock. In the end one sees that all the shocks—the murders, the fantasies, burnings, strong words—all of them amount to a kind of metaphor for the psychic damage that human beings do to each other and that is no less hurtful than spread-eagled beating, just less visible to the outer eye.

> Noel Perrin, *"John Edgar Wideman's Urban Inferno,"* in Book World—The Washington Post, *November 15, 1987, p. 7.*

Madison Smartt Bell

[The] titular hero of John Edgar Wideman's new novel [**Reuben**] is lawyer to the poor, outcast and dispossessed black citizenry of the Homewood district made legendary by Wideman's earlier work. At a glance he appears to be the sort of lawyer one would more likely find in a rural place or some small town, a tireless laborer on behalf of the legally unlucky, paid in pig's feet and promises more often than anything else. Because of his considerable age, his reticence, and some dwarfish physical peculiarities, he is a figure of great mystery in the community, a queer cross between a respected and envied member of the professional classes and some new kind of witch doctor. Ingeniously, Wideman lets a sort of communal mutter introduce him:

> *Booker, you better get your behind over to see Reuben. Hey, I heard Hazel's in a trick even Reuben can't fix. Reuben's a dog. Least Reuben do for you when none of the others will. Reuben got piles of money. Just too crazy to spend it. Reuben's crazy like a fox. Like a rat, you mean.*

Reuben is also the needle's eye through which the threads of the book's plot are drawn, and in aggregate, the stories of his clients, disclosed like his own by means of interior monologue, compose the whole story of the novel. His average client is somebody like Tucker, an old craftsman who accepts a job tearing down empty buildings, without knowing that the people who hired him are strip-and-run thieves. Typically, Reuben handles not the case of mistaken identity but the case of mistaken behavior.

Of such cases the most important is that of Kwansa Parker, who comes to us straight from the welfare system's blotter: an unwed mother, not too bright, she has known a lot of sex and precious little love. She's not a prostitute, but she brings men home and lets them give her money, and because of that she is in danger of losing her son Cudjoe to his father, now established in a comparatively stable marriage.

Kwansa looks like a textbook case of an unfit mother, but we're not allowed to think that separation from her child would be much help to either one of them:

> Her son had saved her. He was her mirror, she could find herself in his eyes, laugh because he laughed, cry when he cried. Touching him, touch lived again. When he slept, she could dream.

Wideman has pulled no punches with this characterization; Kwansa is as disorganized and hapless as they come, just smart enough to see how she is contributing to the spoliation of her own life without being strong enough to stop.

> The hardest thing of all to believe was the dream she'd carried of a better Kwansa, the Kwansa she'd find one day and throw her arms around and they'd cry and laugh like long-lost sisters, like fools in the middle of Homewood Avenue don't care who's watching, don't care what anybody got to say.

Reuben's bread-and-butter work is to pilot people like Kwansa through the maze of a social and legal bureaucracy which (more through ineptitude than malice, one hopes) tends to grind down their hope and their sense of self-worth. His relationship with another client, Wally, is considerably more complex. Wally is a retired basketball player who now works as a university athletic recruiter, and he comes to Reuben because he fears he is likely to be scape-goated in an investigation of expense account fiddling, but their conversation is mostly of other matters.

Scrap by scrap, Reuben tells Wally much of his own history: how he worked as valet, janitor, and occasional pimp for a white fraternity in Philadelphia, how the white boys tricked him into a situation where they could rape the woman he loved before his eyes, how in the aftermath of this ugly affair they caused her death, how he resolved to survive the episode, to persevere until he had learned the law, as if that learning would be the means to his revenge. Wally responds with a tale of his own: how on one of his recruiting trips he encountered a middle-class white stranger in some anonymous public restroom, and apparently for no reason (no more than is given for many lynchings, etc.) knocked him cold and drowned him in a toilet. It is never clear if Wally has actually done the murder or fantasized it or been told about [it] by someone else; what seems to matter is that the thought of it attracts or at least compels him.

A blurb on the back jacket of **Reuben** gives Wideman much credit "for placing white readers deep in black heads." In the case of **Reuben,** it must be said, this is not a very pleasant place for white readers to find themselves. A clear message is given that the fundamental atrocity committed by whites on blacks, a version of which Reuben recalls, can never be forgiven or forgotten. As it's expressed in Wally's recollections:

> Abstract hate means you don't got nothing against any particular person. You may even like or respect a particular person, but at the same time there's something about that person, "the white part," you can't ever forgive, never forget.

The notion that this abstract hate is an elemental part of the mental make-up of all or most black people is bound to be uncomfortable for white readers, though none of us can say for sure it isn't so. Moreover, the novel seems to imply that not only is there nothing we can do about it, it really isn't any of our business.

Reviewed from the standpoint of "abstract hate," the social system against which Reuben seeks to protect his clientele seems not merely inept but actively inimical, controlled as it is by racial enemies. So it becomes possible to think that every person Reuben is able to safely steer through the bureaucratic labyrinth counts as a kind of revenge for his own insults and injuries. Still, one also comes to feel that, although his humiliations persist right through the end of the novel, he has somehow got past the idea of revenge.

> Trouble is that hate's bad for you. Takes something away. Fucks with your insides. Spoils whatever you try to do, how you feel about what you've done. Whether you're dealing with white people or yourself in the mirror.

Like most of Wideman's works of fiction, this one is perhaps most importantly a detailed and sensitive portrait of the inner life of its characters, here rendered credibly and frighteningly as a kind of endless nightmare. Aside from, or along with that, it seems to be saying something new about the old vexed question of race relations in America. The question is not whether "hate's bad for you," but why. If black people do need to get around their hatred, it's not so as to accommodate to whites but to accomodate to themselves. That is what Reuben himself seems to have accomplished finally, in the sort of moral victory that has force to save the soul.

"Revenge," Wally says to him at one point. "So you did try to get back at them."

"In my fashion," Reuben says. "With love and hate . . . yes . . . it's complicated."

Well, so it is. (pp. 60-1)

> *Madison Smartt Bell, "Somehow Past Revenge," in The North American Review, Vol. 273, No. 2, June, 1988, pp. 60-1.*

Michael Gorra

[One] of the attractions of **Reuben** is the ease with which [Wideman] moves between the minds of his characters, now inhabiting the title character, a self-taught lawyer in the black Pittsburgh neighborhood of Homewood; now one or another of Reuben's clients, like the college basketball recruiter Wally, or Kwansa Parker, whose old lover Waddell has stolen their child away; now the choral voice of barroom spectator recalling the novel's concluding fight between Kwansa and Waddell:

> Sheeit. Don't tell me. I was there. Them bitches kicked his ass. First one got him in the eyes and he's hollering, don't know what hit him. He's rolling on the floor and screaming and punching the shit out the bitch but she steady raking his face with them fingernails. Yeah, man. Like razors. Could see em drawing blood. Nobody don't try to stop it, neither. Shit. Who wants to get down in that mess? Howling and thumping and biting and scratching. She's like a pack of alley cats on that poor boy's head. Nobody don't want nothing to do wit it. Not even when he finally got up on top her. Got the best of her, you know. Him being a man, you dig. But boy, she give him a go for a while. A hefty mama. You know Kwansa Parker, man. Nothing skinny bout that ho.

Wideman's pungent mastery of Black English is one of the novel's givens. So I note instead the difference between "sheeit" and "shit," the nonchalance of "Got the best of her, you know," the economy with which such phrases evoke a speaker at once unillusioned and yet surprised by what he sees. What's most surprising about this voice, however, is that Wideman hasn't used it until the end of the novel. In the sentence before this passage starts, he's been writing as an objective third-person narrator; on the previous page he's sunk his own voice into Kwansa's memory of the one time Waddell took her to a restaurant, with "a waiter dishing out food from his tray like they ain't got the sense to help themselves." Now he jump-cuts into the voice of Homewood itself, without preparation and yet without losing me, and in reading I'm dazzled by the speed and the daring and the skill.

> **"The various pieces of [Reuben] don't fully cohere; Wideman never pulls the stories of his three main characters— Kwansa, Wally, and Reuben—into a whole. But page by page this is the most exciting new fiction I read this quarter, marked by an energy and a passion that makes its story of poverty, violence, and prostitution anything but depressing."**

But that's not the only way Wideman's narrative moves around. A third of the way through the novel he offers a present-tense account of Reuben's days as a janitor at the

University of Pennsylvania, where his duties include taking the frat boys to a whorehouse in the black part of town. But it's only near the chapter's end that Wideman lets us realize this account is half reverie and half Reuben's side of a conversation with Wally, an explanation of the rage he feels toward white America. Wally shares that rage, and his description might have come from of *Notes of a Native Son.* "You live among them, thrive, love one or two, but . . . it's in your gut and there's righteous cause for it to be there, so it stays there . . . Trouble is the hate's bad for you." But he can't forget the isolation and anger he felt his first year in college on a basketball scholarship, and it may or may not have led him to kill a white man in a Chicago men's room. May or may not because the boundary here between the fantasies of the inner life and the outer world, or between one moment and another, is as permeable as in Faulkner. Faulkner is, in fact, clearly on Wideman's mind, both in his interfusion of past and present, and in the way he returns to Homewood in book after book. (This is the fourth he's set there.) Wally remembers reading "A Rose for Emily" in college, and Reuben is fascinated by Eadweard Muybridge, the nineteenth-century pioneer of stop-action photography. Wideman's use of Muybridge seems less economical and more labored than Faulkner's use of Quentin Compson's watch, but both yield a sense of the past as being at once irrevocably over and yet present as well. This is particularly true for Kwansa, who lives in memory of the time just before Waddell got her pregnant.

The various pieces of the novel don't fully cohere; Wideman never pulls the stories of his three main characters—Kwansa, Wally, and Reuben—into a whole. But page by page this is the most exciting new fiction I read this quarter, marked by an energy and a passion that makes its story of poverty, violence, and prostitution anything but depressing. Reuben starts life as a janitor, but by the time the novel begins has for years worked as a lawyer, though a member of no bar, a man known in Homewood as someone who "would take your troubles downtown. Peace bond, bail bond, divorce, drunk and disorderly . . . " He has created the terms on which he engages American life. But he gets caught in the end, arrested, exposed as a mere "do-gooder," and not a lawyer at all. Gatsby couldn't reach the green light; the territories caught up with Huck. *Reuben* joins them in demonstrating how impossible the dream of a fresh new world, if not the literature that depends on it, has always been. (pp. 407-08)

> Michael Gorra, "American Selves," in The Hudson Review, *Vol. XLI, No. 2, Summer, 1988, pp. 407-08.*

Richard Gibson

Reuben is John Edgar Wideman's first novel since *Sent for You Yesterday* (1981), the last of his Homewood trilogy. In *Reuben,* Wideman returns to the familiar turf explored in the trilogy: Homewood, a black inner-city community founded by a runaway black slave more than a century ago during the spread of the multi-ethnic urban maze of Pittsburgh.

Addressing his imprisoned brother, Robby, in the preface to the Homewood trilogy, Wideman urged him to "consider all these stories as letters from home". They are rather more like sad blues songs, and are not very cheering. Although Wideman writes about a black ghetto, he is not a social realist. Precise descriptive detail is often missing from his work, which is written in an emotionally charged and lyrical prose that plunges readers deep into the minds of his characters in a series of interior monologues.

The eponymous black hero of *Reuben* is an ageing, wizened, slightly hump-backed would-be lawyer who lives in a junk-filled abandoned trailer on a vacant lot. Despite his sharp knowledge of the law, Reuben is really no more than an astute go-between for the blacks of the ghetto and the mainly white authorities. . . .

Whereas Wideman's previous novels were complex, almost contrapuntal, tales of black suffering and survival, *Reuben* is a brief, if at times prolix, straightforward linear narrative. Wideman may be criticized for telling us little that is new about the black urban scene. He has not yet attempted to bring the expanding horizons of the new world of black Americans into his chronicle. He writes well, though, about such matters as the miseries and shame of black pimps and piano-playing "professors of music" in the one-time black houses of pleasure that serviced white men.

Reuben also displays weaknesses new to Wideman's work. The plot is slender and social complexities are reduced to monochromatic monotony. A simple black woman, Kwansa Parker, commonly considered a whore in Homewood, asks for Reuben's help in regaining custody of her only son, Cudjoe, taken from her by his brutal father. Intermittently, Reuben hears the confessions of his friend Wally, a corrupted, low-ranking university sports official, but can do nothing to exorcize Wally's guilt for a Fanonist act of violence against a white that, anyway, fails to liberate him from his feelings of oppression. Paradoxically, it is Wally who rescues Reuben when the little man's pretensions to the legal profession are questioned.

Wideman is basically a novelist of sentiment, whose heart-rending narratives are rarely touched by humour. This latest sombre tale of Homewood is told in the funeral tones of the great American tradition of high moral seriousness. The voices of his characters drift from time to time into bathos and self-pity within the sparse, disconnected sequence of static monologues that make up the book. Despite its limitations and familiarity, *Reuben* still bears many signs of the author's poetic vision and writing skill. But one hopes that Wideman soon turns again to more ample projects for his manifest talent.

> Richard Gibson, "Homewood Revisited," in The Times Literary Supplement, *No. 4453, August 5-11, 1988, p. 857.*

Clarence Major

Suffering and the quest for redemption are what most of the stories in John Edgar Wideman's second collection, *Fever,* are about.

The word "fever" becomes a metaphor for both suffering and injustice. The 19th-century black doctor treating Philadelphia yellow fever victims in the title story ["**Fever**"] rejects explanations that the fever comes from ships fleeing insurrection in Santo Domingo. "To explain the fever we need no boatloads of refugees, ragged and wracked with killing fevers, bringing death to our shores," he muses. "We have bred the affliction within our breasts. . . . Fever grows in the secret places of our hearts, planted there when one of us decided to sell one of us to another."

Although the other 11 stories are set in the present century, in one way or another they echo the sentiment of the fever metaphor. The legacy of slavery is the common denominator. But Wideman's characters—white and black—exist with irony in the stage setting of this history.

An example of this irony plays around the question of vision as enlightenment, which becomes a form of redemption in Wideman's hands. In **"When It's Time to Go,"** Sambo, a blind piano player, concludes that what is important about humanity—despite suffering and callousness—is its continuation.

Another blind character—the narrator of **"Doc's Story"**—recovers from a broken heart when he is transformed by the courage and faith of a blind basketball player.

Broken hearts come in various forms in Wideman's stories but so does the questing for recovery. An elderly Jew, whose life was saved by a black woman in a prison camp during the war, attempts to make sense of his own luck and life through an effort to communicate with the black woman who has cleaned for him for decades. A black intellectual struggles to understand the hostage crisis and the Middle Eastern conflict between the Jews and the Arabs. In the process he discovers there are many unfortunate ways in which people hold each other hostage. And the captive is always a victim of violence.

This threat of violence links the stories as much as does the theme of suffering and redemption. A quiet violence, for example, permeates **"The Statue of Liberty."** The narrator, who is white, invites a black jogger (and his white female companion) into her home for "cool drinks." When she has herself and them naked in chairs arranged in a Y with the man at the base, the violence of her erotic fantasies erupts, leaving the mysterious—almost terrifying—presence of the ghost of all human desire.

But ghosts and lost souls are everywhere in these stories. In **"Rock River,"** the ghost is the blood left on the seat of a truck where a man has been killed. The blind man of **"When It's Time to Go"** lives constantly with the magical presence of his own ghost. Fever, in the title story, makes its ghostly presence felt through "vomiting and diarrhea, helplessness, delirium" and "convulsions."

Lest I be misunderstood, this is not a pessimistic book. Even so, the reader earns an uneasy truce with the writer because any particular moral conclusion must be tempered with a final uncertainty, except over the issues of cruelty and injustice. Because the characters are so complex and richly textured, the situations rendered with such an even hand, the reader's sympathies are not one-sided.

Stylistically, the stories are impressionistic, with pointillistic touches. The constantly shifting points of view give them a cubistic touch as well. Wideman's narrative voices have strong, clear personalities. But his prose is always, more or less, the hero of his fiction. He avoids closure, to characters as well as to stories. Who, then, are his literary ancestors? I would say he loves or once loved Sterne, Joyce and Faulkner.

As with almost any collection, some of the stories are better than others. **"Fever"** itself is the most ambitious while **"Valaida,"** **"The Statue of Liberty"** and **"Hostages"** seem the most artistically successful.

The weaker ones gain, though, by association with the stronger. **"Little Brother,"** a warm-hearted, nostalgic, sentimental fiction about a dog; **"The Tambourine Lady,"** about a smart girl's world of the familiar comforts of home and church; **"Presents,"** about a boy whose grandmother represents his means to understanding, compassion and reverence, gain much for coming after much more profound stories such as **"Valaida,"** **"Hostages,"** and **"When It's Time to Go."** **"Fever,"** at the end, is a deep historical echo, coming up from the belly of time, the way "Kabnis" does at the end of Jean Toomer's *Cane*.

Even **"Surfiction"**—the least satisfying story here—does not seem too far out of place although I am convinced that it is possible to read it as an essay without the slightest bit of trouble.

There has always been a kind of thematic and stylistic ambivalence in John Wideman's work. It is hard to say precisely what it is all about, but my guess would be that he is constantly torn between a commitment to representational writing and all the other kinds of technical innovations he tries. In total, this conflict comes out as positive and correlates with the sense of moral and cultural paradox through which his characters are created.

Clarence Major, "A Sickness of the Soul," in Book World—The Washington Post, *November 5, 1989, p. 7.*

Judith Rosen

John Edgar Wideman is a man who disdains labels, who refuses to allow either his life or art to be boxed in or dismissed by descriptive terms like "black writer." The problem, he says, "is that it can be a kind of back-handed compliment. Are you being ghettoized at the same time as you are being praised?"

His writing, too, refuses to be pigeonholed. He has written one work of nonfiction, ***Brothers and Keepers,*** which was nominated for the National Book Award; three novels, including the PEN/Faulkner Award-winning ***Sent for You Yesterday;*** and two collections of stories. . . .

On this beautiful fall afternoon, we have come to Wideman's newly built house on the outskirts of Amherst not to dwell on the "time capsules of his past" but to speak of his life as a writer and the publication of his newest book, *Fever,* . . . a breathtaking collection of 12 stories written primarily over the past few years. . . .

We sit in Wideman's book-lined study overlooking the woods as he talks about *Fever,* which he regards as "his first collection per se." For him, the earlier *Damballah* . . . is closer to a novel with its discernible beginning, middle and end.

"These stories are more miscellaneous," he explains.

> The key story, the pivotal story, is **"Fever."** I see the others as refractions of the material gathered there. All the stories are about a kind of illness or trouble in the air. People aren't talking to one another or are having a difficult time talking to one another. There's misunderstanding, not only on an individual level but on a cultural level. These stories are also about ways of combating that malaise through love, through talk, through rituals that families create.

The malaise of which Wideman speaks cuts backwards and forwards into the past, into the present, because of the very ambiguity of time, of history, of fact. ("I never know if I'm writing fiction or nonfiction," he remarks several times throughout the interview when speaking of his stories and books.) And that very ambiguity accounts for much of the bite in **"Fever,"** which serves as a bridge to his forthcoming novel, *Philadelphia Fire.* . . . (p. 37)

On one hand the plague described in **"Fever"** is a historical fact of colonial Philadelphia; on the other hand it provides a powerful fictional prelude to the MOVE bombing that destroyed an entire city block in 1985.

That the story should float so freely from one period to another is, for Wideman, what makes it work: "It shouldn't be tied to any historical period, because it starts in this very room. I was looking out there, out this window, when I saw the snow, and that's where the story starts."

It is no coincidence, then, that this and other stories in the collection achieve a certain timelessness. "Stories are a way of keeping people alive," says the author, "not only the ones who tell the story, but the ones who lived before. You talk about authors being immortal, but there's not only the story, there are the people inside the story who are kept alive."

Wideman thrives on the potential for experimentation in storytelling. "How does one person tell a story that is quite meaningful to that person but is really someone else's story? What does it mean for people to carry around stories in their heads, little time capsules from the past? Yet if I'm telling it to you, it's present."

Elsewhere, in *Brothers and Keepers,* he writes about the pointlessness of telling stories in strict chronological sequence, as

> one thing happening first and opening the way for another and another. . . . You never know exactly when something begins. The more you delve and backtrack and think, the clearer it becomes that nothing has a discrete, independent history; people and events take shape not in orderly, chronological sequence but in relation to

other forces and events, tangled skeins of necessity and interdependence and chance that after all could have produced only one result: what is.

As the interview goes on it becomes obvious that time, like race, is one of the many barriers that Wideman seeks to overcome with his art.

> Stories break down our ordinary ways of conceptualizing reality. Because when we talk about what's alive and what's dead, what's past and what's future, male/female, all these dichotomies that we need in order to talk, they're not really very accurate or descriptive.
>
> On one level of language we do that kind of crude conceptualizing, labeling, and it's necessary. But language can break down these categories, free us. So that we suddenly realize that past and future are not different. That living and dead are kind of arbitrary categories.

Switching gears, he adds with a smile, "Why can't a blind man play basketball?" referring to the central image of **"Doc's Story,"** the first offering in *Fever.*

With this deceptively simple query, he opens a Pandora's box of questions about some of our most basic assumptions about what people can and cannot be, do or say. Wideman himself has consciously attempted to break stereotypes.

> If somebody told me I couldn't do something, that was often a good reason to go ahead and try to do it. And I got satisfaction out of that. On the other hand, as I get older I think I do things less because I'm oriented toward the outside, toward what somebody's thinking, than because I have some inner drive. But it often works out to the same kind of iconoclasm. Because if my goals are unusual and I accomplish them, then they'll be noticeable and will have the same effect as consciously trying to break a mold.
>
> (pp. 37-8)

Judith Rosen, "John Edgar Wideman," in Publishers Weekly, *Vol. 236, No. 20, November 17, 1989, pp. 37-8.*

Cara Hood

Fever is a collection of stories about storytelling. Ironically, at the center of each of the 12 pieces there is a tale that never completely materializes, is either partially rendered or altogether absent. **"Doc's Story"** provides one example of the theme that Wideman examines in a dozen different ways—the struggle between the desire to remember and the inevitability of forgetting. The central figure, an African-American man, tries unsuccessfully to remember Doc's story, which he has heard from the men at the basketball courts in Regent Park, and repeat it to his former lover, a white woman. Unable to retell the story as it was originally heard, he wonders, looking back on their broken relationship, "if he had known Doc's story, would it have saved them?" This concern reemerges in **"Fever,"** when the narrator admits that his stories are useless for saving anyone from the epidemics of cholera and racism besieging his hometown. Complicating the general theme, the book explores the relationship of storytelling to ideas of community, sexuality, history, race, and disease.

Like most of the other pieces, **"Doc's Story"** and **"Fever"** are set in Philadelphia, a nexus of African-American culture and history. Once a destination for African Americans traveling the Underground Railroad, the city was synonymous with freedom from slavery. However, **"Fever"**'s protagonist is present-day Philadelphia. Through the architecture that stands as a monument to its past, the narrator presents portraits of the city that collapse historical time. Philadelphia becomes at once a haven for fleeing slaves, the site of abolitionist conventions, and the stage for the MOVE bombings.

With the juxtaposition of these historical images, *Fever* conveys a public view of the political, which has not appeared in Wideman's other books. In his earlier novels and autobiography, he investigated the politics that emerge in personal relationships and through storytelling in communities sharing the African-American vernacular tradition. In *Brothers and Keepers* he explains that the book grew out of "my brother and I talking about our lives" and represents "an attempt to capture a process . . . to learn my brother's story." The narrator of *Sent for You Yesterday,* conflating blood, race, and storytelling, reveals that "I'm linked to Brother Tate by stories, by his memories of a dead son, by my own memories of a silent, scat singing albino man who was my uncle's best friend."

Fever asks what happens when a story moves out of this context—when an African-American man attempts to tell Doc's story to a white woman or when Mr. Cohen tries to describe his experiences in a concentration camp to his African-American maid. The resulting story can't be told, but—and this is the central concern of *Fever*— the reason remains purposely unclear.

Although storytelling is a universal human activity, the story is not the kind of cultural artifact that can be salvaged, collected, and reproduced, an exact replica of an original. It mutates from telling to telling. In Wideman's formulation, each story is "a circle of stories" converging and spinning away from a false center, fragments of narratives constructed from other fragments that are inaccurately remembered, recombined, misread, or mistold.

Is Doc's story impossible to reconstruct because the unnamed African-American man can't remember it, because the white woman leaves, because she wouldn't understand it anyway ("to her it was folklore, superstition"), because he is African-American and she is white, because he's a man and she's a woman? Or because, like all stories, it's fated to self-destruct and reemerge as something else? Although he poses these questions, Wideman refuses to answer them. Boundaries must be transgressed, he insists, even though they continually reassert themselves. Stories must be told even though they dissolve and are transformed in the telling.

Throughout this collection, storytelling is compared with the uninterrupted flow of blood from one body to another, undoing metaphors of prophylaxis and containment and "fiction of our immunity" that have appeared in the popular imagination since the advent of AIDS. Clara explains in **"When It's Time To Go"** that the "point of the story, I guess, if it has one, I guess, if it got to, is look down at your hands. Look at the blood in the ropes in the backs of your hands. Think of that blood leaving you and running up in somebody else's arms, down into somebody's fingers black or brown or ivory." Disease descends when these channels are blocked, the narrator of **"Fever"** insists, "when the waters that connect us are clogged with filth. When our seas are garbage. The waters cannot come and go when we are shut off one from the other, each in his frock coat, wig, bonnet, apron, shop, shoes, skin, behind locks, doors, sealed faces, our blood grows thick and sluggish. Our bodies void infected fluids."

As the author in **"Surfiction"**—which merges genres of fiction, literary criticism, and autobiography—observes about his notes in the margin of Charles W. Chesnutt's "Deep Sleeper," a story is "a pastiche," "a stew," "a rather unstable mix of genres and disciplines and literary allusion." The stories in *Fever* are examples of this. Collapsing the received boundaries defining the African-American literary tradition, Wideman brings Chesnutt into a dialogue with Barthes, Ellison with Beckett, Nietzsche with Bugs Bunny. "The train doesn't stop here. Mistah Kurtz he dead. Godot ain't coming. Ecce Homo. Dat's all, folks. Sadness. And so it goes." (pp. 7-8)

> *Cara Hood, in a review of "Fever," in VLS, No. 81, December, 1989, pp. 7-8.*

Herbert Mitgang

In **"Fever,"** the title work in [*Fever: Twelve Stories*], the novelist John Edgar Wideman ventures into new territory, turning a historical event into a fictional narrative. Even though the event he describes takes place in the 1790's, his own didactic voice as a modern black writer with something to report comes through.

Mr. Wideman calls his story a "meditation on history" and, in a note, credits several previous historical studies for providing him with background and details. The story takes place during the yellow fever epidemic that devastated Philadelphia in 1793. Among the author's aims is to show that black nurses and undertakers labored courageously to help the city's residents, white and black, overcome the calamity.

At the same time, Mr. Wideman uses the epidemic as a springboard to describe the black experience. He writes of Richard Allen, a churchman who was a leading figure in the black religious movement in the United States. Moving back and forth in time and thought from the 18th century to the present, the author has his narrator recall a trans-Atlantic crossing in chains:

> Curled in the black hold of the ship he wonders why his life on solid green earth had to end, why the gods had chosen this new habitation for him, floating, chained to other captives, no air, no light, the wooden walls shuddering, battered, as if some madman is determined to destroy even this last pitiful refuge where he skids in foul puddles of waste, bumping other bodies, skinning

himself on splintery beams and planks, always moving, shaken and spilled like palm nuts in the diviner's fist, and Esu casts his fate, constant motion, tethered to an iron ring.

During the yellow fever plague a form of blood libel is imposed on the blacks in Philadelphia; they are said to be both responsible for and immune to sickness because of the color of their skin. The sickness is labeled "Barbados fever" and a dark skin is seen as a badge of shame. "It mattered not that some of us were born here and spoke no language but the English language," the author has his narrator say. Then, he directs his wrath against his white neighbors: "My fellow countrymen searching everywhere but in their own hearts, the foulness upon which this city is erected." During autopsies to discover a possible treatment, the victims, black and white, are examined and found to have the same insides. Death knows no difference; the color bar stops in the morgue.

In one of the impassioned passages in **"Fever,"** the author speaks for his characters:

> You do know, don't you, Allen, that God is a bookseller? He publishes one book—the text of suffering—over and over again. He disguises it between new boards, in different shapes and sizes, prints on varying papers, in many fonts, adds prefaces and postscripts to deceive the buyer, but it's always the same book.

At the end, **"Fever"** fades away, like most of the short stories in the book, but the author's searching for some sort of universality of tolerance survives his overwrought language.

A central theme emerges in several of these disconnected stories: the efforts of blacks and whites to develop friendships and the difficulties, even with goodwill, of penetrating each other's worlds. Tackling the problem from a sociological viewpoint nearly a half-century ago, the economist and sociologist Gunnar Myrdal called it—in a title that remains relevant today—"An American Dilemma."

Mr. Wideman, who teaches at the University of Massachusetts, has written six novels. His fifth, *Sent for You Yesterday,* received the Faulkner Award, and his powerful memoir, *Brothers and Keepers,* was nominated for a National Book Critics Circle award. Apart from **"Fever,"** the rest of this book's stories do not add to the author's reputation. They are fragmentary in their plots, strained in writing, and not always able to persuade the reader to suspend disbelief. The characters and stories include a blind basketball player who inspires others with his grit; two adolescent sisters; a case of voyeurism; an elderly Jew trying to find his black cleaning woman; Jews and Arabs, hostages and freedom fighters; joggers and a young woman's erotic fantasy. These quick summaries do not, of course, cover everything in the author's mind.

An experimental story, **"Surfiction,"** has originality and possibilities for development. It seems to compare a student's writing and a professor's comments, with both running side by side. But, as the author writes in the story itself,

> Rereading, I realize my *remarks* are a pastiche

of received opinions from Barthes, certain cultural anthropologists and linguistically oriented critics and Russian formalists, and if I am beginning a story rather than an essay, the whole stew suggests the preoccupations of Borges or perhaps a footnote in Barthelme.

It's hard to say if this is self-parody or revelation. Whichever, these stories are not the best of Wideman.

> *Herbert Mitgang, "Dozen Tales of the Black Experience," in* The New York Times, *December 5, 1989, p. C21.*

Susan Fromberg Schaeffer

Images of blindness, of masks, of facades, of mirrors, of reflections, dominate *Fever,* this strange and powerful book of 12 short stories by John Edgar Wideman. Mr. Wideman's characters seek glimpses of their own faces in other people's eyes, in cups of coffee, in the surfaces of newly polished shoes. It is as if all of them were confused by *the face,* the mask, which is either white or black, the difference in color seeming to signify difference where no difference exists. (p. 1)

These new stories—about the nature of the attachment between an old white man and his cleaning woman (**"Valaida"**), or the sexual fantasies of a white woman watching a young black jogger (**"The Statue of Liberty"**), or the plague of yellow fever that struck Philadelphia at the end of the 18th century (**"Fever"**), or a family gathering in which a pet dog takes center stage (**"Little Brother"**)—all, in the end, ring changes upon one idea: black or white, beneath the skin we are all the same and we ought to love one another.

This idea is hardly new; almost everyone claims to believe it, yet it seems, if we can go by the evidence of newspapers and what we see around us, one of the most difficult ideas to grasp. The tragedy of this—our failing to comprehend the obvious fact of our sameness—is what obsesses Mr. Wideman in these stories. His achievement is to take this idea from the world of concepts and, through the alchemy of his prose, convert it to flesh-and-blood truth. (pp. 1, 30)

Fever is Mr. Wideman's book of suffering. What makes it so odd is its perspective, which is, somehow, not quite human but godlike, not limited by the conventions of ordinary storytelling. His narrators often seem to be looking down upon the planet with genuine omniscience; at any given moment, they know what multitudes of people are thinking. These narrators can take apart the characters they observe as a watchmaker takes apart a clock, yet it is as if they tell their stories from a great distance. They are oddly impartial; they seem to speak with the neutrality of gods, and because they see so much, the sorrow they feel is also godlike, at times overwhelming. Mr. Wideman's narratives frequently jump from one speaker to another, as the mosquito that brings yellow fever in the title story moves from one body to another. When a story does not entirely succeed, this device confuses, exasperates and causes unnecessary difficulties. But when it is successful, as it is in **"Fever,"** an almost unbearably anguished meditation on human nature in plague time, the power and sadness of the story are enormous, its vision triumphant.

The title story is almost majestic in its evocation of the goodness and evil of the human heart. An account of the plague that struck Philadelphia, it is narrated by, among others, a slave in the hold of a ship; a physician tending plague victims; Richard Allen, the founder of the African Methodist Episcopal Church; a dying Jewish merchant; and a black man who, against all reason, abandons his own family to tend the plague-stricken whites, as did many blacks at that time. The dominant voice, however, is anonymous, oracular and prophetic:

> No one has asked my opinion. No one will. Yet I have seen this fever before, and though I can prescribe no cure, I could tell stories of other visitations, how it came and stayed and left us, the progress of disaster. . . . We have bred the affliction within our breasts. . . . We are our ancestors and our children, neighbors and strangers to ourselves. . . . Nothing is an accident. Fever grows in the secret places of our hearts, planted there when one of us decided to sell one of us to another.

The fever, then, Mr. Wideman seems to be saying, is caused by slavery, which is, in turn, caused by our failure to see that beneath the skin we are all the same. **"Fever"** twice quotes from autopsy reports of plague victims, as if to tell us, if the color of the skin obscures the truth, then look beneath it: "When you open the dead, black or white, you find: the dura mater covering the brain is white and fibrous in appearance. . . . Sections are unremarkable." Look, if you have to, *literally* beneath.

In **"Valaida,"** an old Jewish man, a concentration camp survivor, wants to establish some connection with the black cleaning woman who has grown old caring for him. He finds more of a connection than he bargained for. Although the two have never talked, the description of the care the old woman has taken of his shirts makes clear what love she feels for him:

> She has laundered the shirt how many times. It's held together by cleanliness and starch. A shirt that ought to be thrown away but she scrubs and sprays and irons it; he knows the routine, the noises. She saves it how many times, patching, mending, snipping errant threads, the frayed edges of cuff and collar hardened again so he is decent, safe within them, the blazing white breast he puffs out like a penguin when it's spring and he descends from the twelfth floor and conquers the park again, shoes shined . . . welcoming life back and yes he's out there in it again, his splay-foot penguin walk and gentleman's attire, shirt like a pledge, a promise. . . . Numbers stamped inside the collar. Mark of the dry cleaners from a decade ago, before Clara Jackson began coming to clean.

These two, who have lived together wordlessly, apparently separate and indifferent, know each other well—are, in fact, as the old man is to realize, suddenly, startlingly, the same:

> He thinks of Clara Jackson in the midst of her

family. . . . He tries to picture them, eating and drinking, huge people crammed in a tiny, shabby room. Unimaginable, really. The faces of her relatives become his. Everyone's hair is thick and straight and black.

Immediately after the denial of sameness comes the hallucinatory perception of it. Under the masks, the facades, is identity of emotion and purpose.

In **"Little Brother,"** a very funny and deceptively simple story, the attempt to get beyond the face, the mask, has been made but has not succeeded. Various members of a black family sit around the kitchen table discussing Pup-pup, their pet dog that recently died, and Little Brother, their peculiar, more recently acquired dog, who refuses to come into the house and instead lives in an "apartment" built for him under the porch.

The dogs weren't capable of getting along; family members speculate that Pup-pup's jealousy of Little Brother eventually led to his death. The two dogs seem as unable to live together as the neighborhood's blacks and whites; and in the course of a drifting, associative conversation about the pets and their failure to develop a friendship, one sister, Penny, asks the other, Geral, about her friend Vicki, the only white woman in the neighborhood. Even though she knows her white friend will eventually hurt her, Geral has tried to protect Vicki, advising her how to behave, and has grown fond of Vicki's daughter, Carolyn:

> Saw [Vicki] dressed up real nice in Sears in East Liberty last week and she ducked me. I know why, but it still hurt me. Like it hurts me to think my little sugar Carolyn will be calling people niggers someday. If she don't already.

This failure is small, and is quickly passed over, but the failures of sympathy, taken together, create an agony in the narrators of Mr. Wideman's stories that is enormous. Mr. Wideman compares this agony to the pain felt by the Lamed-Vov of Talmudic legend, "the Thirty Just Men set apart to suffer the reality humankind cannot bear." These men wander the earth unable to die, and later 10 centuries at God's side will be barely sufficient to heal their pain. "I thought," says one of the narrators of the title story, "I might be one of them. In my vanity. My self-pity. My foolishness. But no. One lifetime of sorrows enough for me. I'm just another customer"—one more purchaser of the book of suffering. That John Edgar Wideman, looking at what white and black people do to one another, should not only evoke the image of the Lamed-Vov, but feel driven to compare himself to one of them, tells us everything we need to know about what it is like to look at the world and see it spinning in space, burning, not with the fever of light, but of pain. (pp. 30-1)

Susan Fromberg Schaeffer, "We Are Neighbors, We Are Strangers," in The New York Times Book Review, *December 10, 1989, pp. 1, 30-1.*

Randall Kenan

"Do not look for straightforward, linear steps from book

to book," wrote John Edgar Wideman in the 1985 preface to his **Homewood Trilogy.** "Think rather of circles within circles within circles, a stone dropped into a still pool, ripples and wavemotions." In *Fever,* Wideman has troubled the water again, refining his already elliptical and dense prose; in the process he has reinvented black English and (re)made it, elegant, suave, as elastic as ever: "Ball be swishing with that good backspin, that good arch bringing it back, blip, blip, blip, three bounces and it's coming right back to Doc's hands like he got a string on the pill," he writes in **"Doc's Story,"** a story about stories, a nigh-fantastical tale of a blind man and the man who inexplicably watches him and ponders over lost love.

Wideman began evolving the style evidenced in these stories in his **Homewood Trilogy,** most markedly in the 1983 PEN/Faulkner award-winning **Sent for You Yesterday** and further still in 1987's **Reuben.** It is his own patented stream of consciousness, sliding easily through tense and point of view; and, when it works, its power has the force of the most righteous prayer. It is as if he wrote his stories and then compressed them to a third of their original size. Eschewing quotation marks, Wideman has his speakers shift and shift and at times meld—as if into one mind, one voice.

The word haunting best describes the result. In each story some dim memory, some deep urge, some knowledge, some inescapable prophecy reaches through time or space. Voices whisper across voids; calls float over oceans.

These voices he often finds—like a child picking up pebbles on the beach—in fragments of history, news items, his own novels, even Bobby Short! Valaida Snow, the legendary trumpeter of the Jazz Era to whom the Queen of Denmark gave a golden trumpet, supplies perhaps the most chilling voice in **"Valaida."** "Tell him," she speaks from the grave, "they loved me at home too, a down-home girl from Chattanooga, Tennessee, who turned out the Apollo, not a mumbling word from wino heaven till they were on their feet hollering and clapping for more with the rest of the audience. . . . Yesteryears, yesterhours." But the story turns into a What If: What if Valaida Snow, who was interned in a Nazi concentration camp for over a year, what if she had saved the life of a 13-year-old boy who would become a survivor? Cut then within the same story to an old man disgusted and indifferent toward life trying to tell the remarkable tale of how he had one day been saved by a "colored woman" to his equally disgusted and indifferent black cleaning woman who "has put on flesh for protection. To soften blows. To ease around corners." The ironies do not merely abound, they cluster, almost fester—he, a Jew, tells her, a black woman, the story on Christmas Eve.

For irony is the tool Wideman is forever honing, sharpening, working with surgical precision. **"Hostages,"** the story of a woman whose husband is a captive of Arab terrorists, becomes an unraveling, a debunking of the concept of "prisoner." Suddenly everything is to be viewed in a new light—marriage, sickness, materialism—and to be seen as imprisoning. An immigrant in a new land; to be black in America; to be a child in the care of parents: Mostly trouble haunts these characters, trouble as in ten-sion between black and white, Arab and Jew, men and women. Wideman manages to transmute that trouble into some of his most challenging and powerful prose yet, in which everything is subject to ridicule or doubt.

Even his own fiction is fair game, as in **"Surfiction,"** where he takes on his own opaque, relentless, spiderwebby prose. It is a parody that is oddly more than a parody, a question within a question, a sly illumination—or is it yet more nasty tricks on the ever-gullible, at times contemptible, reader? He ponders: "Without authors whose last names begin with B, surfiction might not exist. B for Beckett, Barth, Burroughs, Barthes, Borges, Brautigan, Barthelme." But even in his high-minded meta-play, amid the (de)analysis of fragments of Charles Chestnutt and his own journal, we get a nugget of the old tensions and ironies, for ultimately in this quagmire of twisted logic he slips in a story as old-fashioned as Gilgamesh, about a couple fighting over a diary.

And though it may seem like wordplay, **"Surfiction"** offers insights into some of Wideman's less opaque motives:

> All goes swimmingly until a voice from the watermelon patch intrudes. . . . Recall your own reflection in the fun house mirror and the moment of doubt when you turn away and it turns away and you lose sight of it and it naturally enough loses sight of you and you wonder where it's going and where you're going in the wrinkling reflecting plate still laughing behind your back at someone.

Time and Space. Like present-day cosmologists, Wideman seems to have in mind not merely a blurring of the two concepts but their elimination. He meta-jokes about our Western cultural bias toward "clock time, calendar time," to time "acting on us rather than through us" and "that tames space by manmade structures and with the *I* as center defines other people and other things by nature of their relationship to *I* rather than by the independent integrity of the order they may represent." Wideman's true mission appears to be to replace the *I* at the center of all his stories, to make it subject to an internal order of things rather than to external structures and limitations. Unlike Ishmael Reed, his humor does not slice to the bone to the truth; Wideman's humor is sparse if not (at times) nonexistent. And unlike Amiri Baraka, his rage is far from militant; it is sublimated, almost repressed.

Nowhere in this collection is this more evident than in the title story. More a meditation than an eyewitness account, **"Fever"** centers around Philadelphia's yellow fever epidemic of the late eighteenth century. Snatching up bits and pieces of history here and there, he brilliantly creates an organism, like a New Age psychic channeler, that transports the sufferers from the 1700s to the present, and takes us back in time as well. Its scenes bring to mind images from Herzog's *Nosferatu* of a plague-ridden town debilitated, full of coffins, corpses, rats and decay: "A large woman, bloated into an even more cumbersome package by gases and liquids seething inside her body, had slipped from his grasp. . . . Catching against a rail, her body had slammed down and burst, spraying Wilcox like a fountain." Yet without warning the story shifts to the present, to the aftermath of the 1985 MOVE massacre, to the voice of a black hospital orderly. It is as if Wideman is again playing games with us, forcing us to see the past and the present as one; how we are affected by what has gone before, not only in our thinking but in our acting and in our soul-deep believing. Science (knowledge) becomes a metaphor for understanding hate; disease, a euphemism for the plague visited upon the wrongs of the unholy.

And the voices. Wideman leads us to believe the main character of **"Fever"** to be none other than Richard Allen, who founded the African Methodist Episcopal Church. His voice, initially eighteenth-century and pious, merges with a chorus of victims, singing of guilt, of racism, of ignorance. Ultimately the voices question Allen—a freedman—for staying in Philadelphia, abandoning his wife and children, risking his life by working with the virus-infected, practically enslaving himself to strange, clueless physicians. And Allen can articulate no reason for staying to combat the "unpleasantness from Egypt."

Not all of these stories sing as clearly. **"The Statue of Liberty"** seems particularly peculiar, a gratuitous walk on the prurient side, whose only purpose seems to be to shock for shock's sake. **"Presents,"** though powerful in spots, slips too close to cliché for comfort. Based on a song by rhythm and blues holy man Solomon Burke, it is a grandmother's prophecy of a child's rise to fame and fortune through music and his eventual, inevitable decline; an all-too-familiar story with no new insights. **"The Tambourine Lady,"** a light/dark-hearted play on the children's ditty "Step on a crack/break your mama's back," amuses but does not linger. **"Rock River,"** on the other hand, returns once again to the conceit of the voice of the dead reaching back, this time after a husband's suicide while his best friend attempts to console the stolid widow. In the end pleasant, life-affirming memories overtake us, but leave us with more questions than resolutions.

More successful is **"Little Brother,"** a biography of a dog in the form of a conversation between two old characters from Homewood, Geraldine and Penny, a discourse that encompasses the here and the gone, man and animal alike. In **"Concert"** a jazzman's meditations on his mother's death become an elegant musical riff. And **"When It's Time to Go"** calls up once again the all-too-easy symbol of blindness, but this time Wideman lets loose the language like a snake in a cage of rats: "Light was just singing to me, Mama, telling me I didn't need no eyes. Wasn't no such thing as eyes less you call your knees and hands and shoulders eyes cause everything you got can hear the light, or touch it and everything you got is something to see with." This tale of a blind boy whose witch mother cannot save him is also a thrice-told tale, but the language, the concentration, the shifting viewpoints, lift it above the mere or the hackneyed, transforming it into a story full of the incantatory power of a Zora Neale Hurston or a Virginia Woolf; a haunting yarn of magic and ways of being in the world.

Perhaps that is what these voices are speaking of: Ways of being in the world. Wideman wants us to see with our ears, to hear with our eyes, to smell with our hearts, to learn with our guts. Stop relying on "time" and "place,"

he says. Recognize that we are all "I." Wideman's characters all want something, desperately, something they cannot have, something inarticulate and inconceivable. This is the vision, that of a cruel world peopled by victims who go on and on unrequited, unavenged, unloved, that fuels *Fever.* A theme recurs in these stories: the mythic, Talmudic Lamed-Vov: "The Thirty Just Men set apart to suffer the reality humankind cannot bear? Saviors"; "God's hostages"; "Lamed-Vov are sponges drawing mankind's suffering into themselves"; "A thousand years is not long enough to thaw the agony each Lamed-Vov endures." Wideman sees us all as Lamed-Vov—which accounts for these ever-present, insistent, wailing voices, rippling out through time. (pp. 25-7)

> *Randall Kenan, "A Most Righteous Prayer,"* in The Nation, *New York, Vol. 250, No. 1, January 1, 1990, pp. 25-7.*

Richard Eder

The bloodiest and—relative to the level of disorder that provoked it—most violent government repression ever undertaken in an American urban black community was the helicopter bombing of a Philadelphia slum house in 1985.

The house was occupied by MOVE, a Rastafarian-like commune that had resisted repeated municipal orders to vacate. The group was armed, and some level of force was required to accomplish the eviction. It turned out to be a mini-holocaust. The bomb killed 11 commune members, including five children, and burned down 53 houses.

That horror provides the central imagery of the agonized fictional meditations and variations that make up *Philadelphia Fire.* John Edgar Wideman's novel is a blaze of rage, but what makes the blaze hotter and the book more stunning is the despair that lies under it.

Mayor Wilson Goode, who ordered the bombing, is black. He was elected in the hope that Philadelphia, with its prosperity and strong civic and cultural traditions, might be the city where black voices and white resources could come together to reverse the spiral of urban decay and racial degradation.

The cruel irony of Goode's decision provides Wideman, our most powerful and accomplished artist of the urban black world, with a theme so overwhelming and painful that it threatens to burst his throat. Sometimes it does, and his voice splinters and becomes inchoate. Sometimes, Wideman's genius for impassioned imagery triumphs and *Philadelphia Fire* delivers its message with a careening momentum and astonishing precision.

If the telling is multifarious and passionate, the theme is straightforward and harsh. There is a narrator figure who, much like Wideman—a Rhodes scholar, acclaimed writer and professor—managed to rise out of disadvantage, thanks to talent, struggle and the opportunities that the '60s briefly opened. The thought was that such individual successes would in some fashion bring a whole people along.

Instead of a rising tide lifting all boats, a few rising boats were supposed to raise the ocean. For the achievers, the hope seemed genuine, despite uneasiness at enjoying the benefits of being its chosen instrument. Such uneasiness has flavored Wideman's books, and given them edge, anger and art.

Now he uses the Philadelphia fire as the turning point, the end of the road. It stands, dramatically, for the less dramatic and more lethal turning of the last dozen years. Instead of tentatively holding out their hands, the privileged classes were encouraged to tuck them back in their pockets. And Wideman's black mayor, who thought he was to deliver his people, bombed them instead.

Whether it was a forced choice, in view of MOVE's violent resistance, and whether a white mayor would have felt empowered to make it, are debated questions. Whether any mayor would have ordered such a bombing in a middle-class white neighborhood, and if he had, whether the neighboring houses would have been so wretched and flimsy as to burn up, seems much less debatable.

Do you try to join a society that is ready to bomb you? The question splits the narrator in two. One half is Wideman, writing and teaching in western Massachusetts. The other half is a figure named Cudjoe, who represents a Wideman in transition from a belief in peaceable means to a hesitant, despairing identification with extremes. Cudjoe lives in a comfortable literary exile in Greece; news of the fire sets him on a voyage of discovery back to Philadelphia.

An image drives him. A boy named Simba was briefly spotted fleeing from the burning house, and subsequently disappeared. Cudjoe thinks of Simba—he visualizes him caught in the cross-hairs of a policeman's sniper-scope—as part of himself. And Wideman, in his own voice, reminds us of his own real son, jailed for a killing and seemingly lost to his father's world of achievement. Success is a fraud if you cannot bring your children too.

Fire tells of Cudjoe/Wideman's search. He talks to Margaret Jones, one of the "slaves" of King, the leader and prophet of MOVE. He talks to Timbo, a former classmate now ensconced in power—and bitterness—as an aide to the mayor. He talks to the young men hanging around the neighborhood basketball court. And he recalls or imagines others: a white publisher who helped him get into print, members of a violent gang of boys for whom Simba is symbol and hero, and a ragged, picaresque wanderer named J. B. who also seems to be the dead King.

It is a swirl of stories, images and voices. Some burn indelibly. Wideman has made fire his own, and there are fire figures everywhere, illuminating us and driving us back with heat and smoky confusion.

There is the clotted, dreadlocked J. B. roaming implacably through the business district, begging, singing rap songs and transfixing the city's prosperous heedlessness like a risen Lazarus. Even more memorable is Margaret Jones' account of coming under the spell of King.

An office worker with "my little bit of degree," determined to keep her place clean and rear her two children decently, she is repelled when she first sees King lounging in front of his house. He has J. B.'s dreadlocks, filth and stink. He is everything she abhors. Yet after a month or so, she is living with him. Her mother spent her life on aching feet, working as a maid and cleaning up for white folks. King's blazing defiance suddenly shows her that she is simply a better-paid maid. Her feet still hurt. "He got to me through my feet," she says. "Though he did it wrong, he did it right."

Feet are Wideman's recurring sign; the most literal image of oppression. An oppressed body discharges its burden on its feet. In an extraordinary passage, the author describes a mound of sneakers beside a city fountain where the slum kids go to cool off.

They are beat-up, "the way kids' shoes always are, but these scattered around on the wet steps, these were worse, gaping holes in the bottoms, shredded uppers, laces missing, shoes taped, patched, lined with cardboard. Cheapest concoctions of glue and foam and canvas that money could buy."

But a lot of money. The ad-driven status symbol that exploits poverty and despair while seeming to promise that you can jog right away from them. And in a tremendous extrapolation, Cudjoe:

> . . . constructs a room to match the shoes, fills it with sleeping bodies, many funky pairs of sneakers set out overnight to dry. Constructs a row house to hold the room, matches it with house after house till there is a street, then a neighborhood matching the sorry-assed shoes he's ready to lace now and thinks of miles of streets he must negotiate to reach the fountain, how pebbles and grains of glass punch through the thin soles, how after walking awhile with his brothers and sisters in tow, it's like walking barefoot on burning coals, you don't stop and wait for a light to change, you charge through intersections, daring cars to hit you. Constructs a city to hold the neighborhood. . . .

Cudjoe never finds Simba but the mayor's aide, Timbo, tells him about Simba's disciples, a gang of 15- and 16-year-olds that calls itself the Kiddie Kars Korps—or KKK. (We will think of the Ku Klux Klan and register Wideman's savage irony.) They wild around the city. Their target is adults. In scrawled flyers—did they write them? did some adult radical or police provocateur?—they proclaim that the world belongs to them; that "olds" must be killed, robbed and exiled to islands.

"Everything for the young," is their slogan, Timbo explains. "It's fair, they say, because everybody's young once. And nobody has to grow old if they don't want to." It is a bitter twist. Adults have eaten their children's seed corn and denied them decent schools and jobs, and made a profit by selling them drugs. Many of the young never will grow old, but not because they don't want to. They have no choice.

It is in passages like these that Wideman's book comes to its burning focus. Elsewhere it rambles, clumsy and sometimes indecipherable. When he writes of a Maine vacation, of Cudjoe's troubled marriage, of the book editor, his control wavers; mainly, perhaps, because his heart doesn't seem to be in it. A long section about staging *The Tempest* with a cast of slum children has a diffuseness, even a sentimentality, that overwhelms a rather academic point about Caliban as the symbol of black oppression.

Wideman holds nothing back. The unevenness, the repetitiveness, the partial chaos of *Fire* are, in a sense, the embodiment of his theme. An authentic culture is entangled and choked in a culture that is superimposed. The book can be as ungainly as Caliban or the dreadlocked King. The defect may be partly willed, but it is a defect in any case; a form that struggles to encompass its theme and often fails.

Yet the successes are indelible. Wideman offers himself as a casualty of the struggle, but he is its victor as well. (pp. 3, 8)

> *Richard Eder, "The Fire This Time," in* Los Angeles Times Book Review, *September 30, 1990, pp. 3, 8.*

Rosemary L. Bray

There is an old and bitter saying about the vulnerability that comes with being black in America: "When white folks get a cold, black folks get pneumonia." So it can't be much of a surprise that as the century winds down, amid earnest conversation about the worrisome state of the world there should be much dialogue about the political and spiritual crisis within black America. What is a surprise, however, is the passion and the yearning, the rage and the courage at work in John Edgar Wideman's complex and grief-stricken novel of urban disintegration, *Philadelphia Fire.* (p. 7)

Passion is perhaps a lost quality these days; we are too used to apathy or a hopeless, minimalist cool. It has been a long time since a writer has focused attention on the grit and greed, the despair and horror of urban life experienced, not by the wry observer or the tourist passing through, but by men and women enmeshed in its fatal web or dancing on its periphery, comforted for a time by illusions of immunity. It has been a long time, too, since anyone has written honestly, and with such power, of the sometimes funny, often brutal, frequently enraging experience of being black and male in these times. By its very nature, *Philadelphia Fire* is not an easy book, a warm book, not even a smoothly crafted book. Written in three interconnected sections—sometimes as essay, sometimes in African-American idiom, sometimes in parables reminiscent of folktale or mythology—the novel is grounded too deeply in the chaos it means to re-create to leave its readers at ease.

A variety of characters moves through this panoramic novel—from J. B., an angry and opportunistic street man, to a reimagined Caliban who might have encouraged Shakespeare to rethink *The Tempest* entirely. But central to the story is Cudjoe, a West Philadelphia writer and exile who has spent the previous decade in flight from virtually every aspect of his past. We learn in Part One that Cudjoe has flouted almost every taboo of the African-American consciousness of the 1960's—he has married a white woman with whom he has had children; he has turned his

back on the old neighborhood and gone off to embrace a brave and colorblind new world. "I lived on an island. Learned another language. Almost like a new life. Born again before born again was big business."

When we meet him a decade after his departure he has turned away again, this time from his wife and children and his writing, too, and created a newer, freer life on the Greek island of Mykonos—sailing and beachcombing, bartending and making love. Cudjoe has found a measure of peace in his exile—until, months after the incident, he reads an account of the MOVE bombing and fire in his old neighborhood. It is a shock strong enough to bring him home, to immerse him in the radically changed settings of his childhood and adolescence, to create an obsession not only with the people who died in the fire, but with the lone boy seen running from the flames. And in delineating Cudjoe's search for that singular naked child, Mr. Wideman takes his readers on a tour of urban American perched on the precipice of hell—a tour in which even his own personal tragedy is part of the view.

Upon his return to America, Cudjoe assumes the role of journalist and goes back to his old neighborhood to speak to people who might have known or seen the boy. He locates a former member of the collective, Margaret Jones—a woman just hostile enough to distrust his motives.

> Polite, accommodating to a degree, she also maintained her distance. . . . The precise space between Cudjoe's island and West Philly. Somehow she knew he'd been away, exactly how long, exactly how far, and that distance bothered her, she held it against him, served it back to him in her cool reserve.

But Cudjoe is willing to endure her quiet scorn, if it will get him what he wants most—access to the child known as Simmie, "the boy who is the only survivor of the holocaust on Osage Avenue, the child who is brother, son, a lost limb haunting him since he read about the fire in a magazine."

At first Mr. Wideman's narrative is persistent enough to make you believe it is just this simple—the search for a child, one lost boy who has escaped the flames. But as Cudjoe travels through West Philadelphia, and as Mr. Wideman injects other voices, we are irresistibly drawn to bigger questions about urban life and anyone's ability to survive it. As Margaret Jones speaks of the cult leader—the man she and others called King before he was burned to ashes—she reminds Cudjoe that "nobody cares. The whole city seen the flames, smelled the smoke, counted the body bags. Whole world knows children murdered here. But it's quiet as a grave, ain't it? Not a mumbling word."

Cudjoe returns to the basketball courts of his youth, falls in with some of the local players. In a fast game, he talks with a man whose oldest brother, Darnell, played ball with Cudjoe when he was younger. Darnell is gone now,

> "in the slam, man. Five years now."
>
> "Damn."
>
> "Dope, man. Into the dope . . . you know."

"Darnell?"

"Yeah. Surprised everybody. My big brother always a together dude. Never in no trouble. He looked out for me. More like a daddy to me, you know. Then dope, man. He just couldn't handle."

The waste, the weariness is everywhere. Other old friends have died or fallen away. A classmate from college, Timbo, assumes his place within the system he rejected years before, his fantasies of collective change withered like dry grass, exchanged for the token symbols of individual achievement—a limousine, regular tables at good restaurants. Now a powerful attaché in the mayor's office, Timbo has made his trade, and seems satisfied; for him, the fire on Osage Avenue is less a tragedy than a public relations problem.

"They were embarrassing, man. Embarrassing. Trying to turn back the clock. Didn't want no kind of city, no kind of government. Wanted to live like people live in the woods. . . . How the mayor spozed to stand up and talk to white folks when he can't control his own people? . . . Sooner or later those nuts had to go."

But there are plenty more "nuts" where they came from, including a gang of young people known as Kaliban's Kiddie Korps, whose graffiti slogan—"Money Power Things"—decorates walls all over the city.

In Part Two the lost child of the conflagration assumes a different identity—the "lost" son of Mr. Wideman himself. Jacob Wideman, at age 18, pleaded guilty in 1988 to the murder of a companion after a camping trip in Maine two years earlier. (It is not the first time Mr. Wideman's family has been confronted with such tragedy. His brother, Robert, is also serving time for murder; Mr. Wideman explored that story in an earlier nonfiction book, *Brothers and Keepers,* in 1984.)

Mr. Wideman's son was sentenced to life in prison in a plea-bargain agreement that prevented him from receiving the death penalty. The sentencing hearing was a particularly bitter affair, with the parents of the murdered child accusing Mr. Wideman of having created the "monster" that is his son.

It is an act of almost unimaginable boldness to take such personal sadness and to insert it into a novel; its presence is at first so jarring it has the feel of literary schizophrenia. Yet it is just such a splitting of identity—his own, his son's—that Mr. Wideman works to convey here, and few things are as heartbreaking as the sections in which he stumbles toward the hope of understanding what has happened to his child:

To take stock, to make sense, to attempt to control or to write a narrative of self—how hopeless any of these tasks must seem when the *self* attempting this harrowing business is no more reliable than a shadow. . . . Can this story he must never stop singing become a substitute for an integrated sense of self, of oneness, the personality he can never achieve? The son's father. Father's son.

Cudjoe's voice reassumes prominence in Part Three, where in its last pages *Philadelphia Fire* spins wildly among scenes of a memorial service for the dead of the MOVE bombing, an imagined scenario of the bombing itself and scenes involving ghosts of an Independence Day rally in the year 1805, in which black Philadelphians attending the celebrations are beaten and chased from Independence Square. The cacophony of images panics Cudjoe until the moment when, finally, he chooses not to run from the disarray surrounding him.

It is a rare and wonderful pleasure to hear a variety of complex male voices; very few writers can invoke them successfully. Mr. Wideman has captured a particular pain and anguish that is part of African-American manhood without denying the experience of women; he has created male characters that are by turns tender, vulgar, insightful, evil, compassionate, wary: in short, he has shown us men we know.

Most important of all, however, *Philadelphia Fire* uses facets of African-American life to illuminate issues at the heart of American life. In a society most people believe is disintegrating, at a time when the assignment of blame seems more important than the acceptance of responsibility, Mr. Wideman argues for a vision of life that includes virtues that may be disappearing from 20th-century culture: mercy, the ability to tolerate and accept difference, even distasteful difference. He is nowhere more articulate about these than in a section of Part Two in which he once again addresses his son in prison:

What I'm trying to do is share my way of thinking about some things that are basically unthinkable. I cannot separate myself from you. Yet I understand we're different. I will try to accept and deal with whatever shape your life takes. I know it's not my life and try as I might I can't ease what's happening to you, can't exchange places or take some of the weight from you. But I believe you have the power in your hands to do what no one can do for you. . . . We don't know what the future will bring. We do have a chance to unfold our days one by one and piece together a story that shapes us. It's the only life anyone ever has. Hold on.

(pp. 7, 9)

Rosemary L. Bray, " 'The Whole City Seen the Flames'," in The New York Times Book Review, *September 30, 1990, pp. 7, 9.*

Charles Johnson

Novelist John Edgar Wideman is easily the most critically acclaimed black male writer of the last decade. The author of 10 books, he received the PEN/Faulkner Award for his 1984 novel, *Sent for You Yesterday,* and extensive praise for *Brothers and Keepers,* his memoir of his brother Robert's imprisonment for armed robbery and felony murder. Each new work, such as his recent story collection *Fever,* is regularly featured on the front pages of the nation's various book review sections. A new, ambitious work of fiction by a writer as prolific and artistically uncompromising as Wideman is, therefore, a reason for celebration.

However, Wideman fans, of which I'm one, may be disappointed, if not downright confused, by *Philadelphia Fire,* his latest novel, which purportedly is about the May 13, 1985, assault by the City of Philadelphia on members of a black organization called MOVE. Eleven people who defied a police eviction order were killed in this widely covered incident, but Wideman's book is only tangentially about the event. It is less journalism than an impressionistic hymn to the dead in West Philly, not so much fictionalized history (or even a story) as a lyric, angry brooding on the excesses of white power, and in this sense brings to mind James Baldwin's use of the Atlanta child-murder case as a springboard for his own sociological reflections in *The Evidence of Things Not Seen.*

Divided into three parts, *Philadelphia Fire* opens with Cudjoe, a former teacher and writer (and Wideman's alter ego), learning of the MOVE disaster while in self-exile on the island of Mykonos. A drifter now, he feels himself to be "a half-black someone," a half-man who couldn't be depended upon" because "he'd married a white woman and fathered half-white kids" whom he believes he's failed. Cudjoe feels driven to find a lost boy named Simmie, "the only survivor of the holocaust on Osage Avenue." He returns to Philadelphia and begins his quest for the boy by interviewing Margaret Jones, a former member of the MOVE family.

MOVE's leader, says Jones,

> taught us about the holy Tree of Life. How we all born part of it. How we all one family. Showed us how the rotten system of this society is about chopping down a Tree. Society hates health. Society don't want strong people. It wants people weak and sick so it can use them up . . . He taught us to love and respect ourselves . . . He said that every day. We must protect Life and pass it on so the Tree never dies.

As it turns out, this is as close as Cudjoe ever gets to unraveling the philosophy and history of MOVE, or to Simmie, who Jones says "just disappeared." A dinner with his erstwhile running buddy Timbro, a "class dude" now working as cultural attaché for the city's black mayor, reveals only that Philadelphia's officials regarded the MOVE people as "embarrassing," cultists who had to be removed because they,

> didn't want no kind of city, no kind of government. Wanted to live like people live in the woods. Now how's that sound? . . . Mayor breaking his butt to haul the city into the twenty-first century and them fools on Osage want their block to the jungle.

In part two, the thin line that separates Wideman from Cudjoe ("Why this Cudjoe, then?" he asks. "Why am I him when I tell certain parts? Why am I hiding from myself?") disappears completely as this section opens with the author and his wife watching the MOVE fire on CNN. Wideman receives a call from his recently imprisoned son, broods on "the unmitigated cruelty of the legal system," and in a moving passage wonders,

> Will I ever try to write my son's story? Not dealing with it may be causing the forgetfulness I'm

experiencing . . . I do feel my narrative faculty weakening . . . What I'm doing or saying or intending engages me only on a superficial level. I commit only minimal attention, barely enough to get me through the drill I'm required to perform.

But mostly Part Two concerns Cudjoe's failed attempt to stage a production of *The Tempest,* using black kids as performers, in a West Philly park in the late 1960s. This play is, Wideman writes, "figure within a figure, play within a play, it is the bounty and hub of all else written about the fire." Wideman's "authentically revised version of Willy's con" is, at bottom, the now familiar interpretation of Prospero as a white imperialist and Caliban as the colonized, and he invites us to see the MOVE tragedy as a "lesson . . . about colonization, imperialism, recidivism, the royal [expletive] over of the weak by the strong, colored by white, many by few . . ."

An excerpt from *Philadelphia Fire*

Best to let it burn. All of it burn. Flame at the inmost heart. The conflagration blooming, expanding outward, like ripples from a stone to the corners of the universe. One little candle. The scab above Twanda's eyelid burns and festers and grows concentrically as she picks at it, sworls of white-speckled soreness on her black forehead and it leaps from her brow suddenly as a siren in the middle of the night and we know instantly it's coming for us, we're implicated as its light arcs and flashes in circles, we are infected, finished in the feral swoop of its dirty-fingered stab into the town houses where we are hiding. The gem in her forehead explodes slowly as a rose blooming, dying simultaneously because we neglect to tend it, adore it, praise it as our own.

These ruins. This Black Camelot and its cracked Liberty Bell burn, lit by the same match ignited two blocks of Osage Avenue. Street named for an Indian tribe. Haunted by Indian ghosts—Schuylkill, Manayunk, Wissahickon, Susquehanna, Moyamensing, Wingohocking, Tioga—the rivers bronzed in memory of their copper, flame-colored bodies, the tinsel of their names gilding the ruined city. Oh, it must have been beautiful once. Walking barefoot in green grass, the sky a blue haven, the deep woods full of life. Now the grit . . . ground into the soil lodges in our children's toes when they play in the park. Poison works its way through their veins to their brains. They play cowboys and Indians. Colored and white with real guns. Shots exchanged over Cobbs Creek and one player falls down forever. Real bullets bridging the racial gap, hurtling over the scrufty water and trees that separate two warring villages. The Book of Life exchanges hands. Who will read it next, kill for it next? A red ghost thin as conviction giggles its last laugh.

The final section, briefer than the others, focuses on a black derelict named J. B., a beggar who witnesses a white businessman jump to his death from the 19th floor of the Penn Mutual Savings and Loan building, takes the dead man's briefcase, and is himself set on fire by white hooligans. Then it shifts back to Cudjoe attending a memorial service for the dead of Osage Avenue. "Hey fellas, It's about youall," he thinks.

> If they offed them people on Osage yesterday
> just might be you today. Or tomorrow . . . be-
> cause that day in May the Man wasn't playing.
> Huh uh. Taking no names. No prisoners . . .
> And here you are again making no connections,
> taking out no insurance.

And there you have it: a novel in which we learn nothing new about the MOVE incident, a book brimming over with brutal, emotional honesty and moments of beautiful prose lyricism (no one can sing the spiritual side of playing basketball better than Wideman), but by no means a page-turner. In a recent interview the author, who remains one of our most important fiction writers, said he chose to write about MOVE because, "My goal is not to let it disappear into the collective amnesia." In this noble intention, at least, *Philadelphia Fire* is not unsuccessful. (pp. 6, 12)

> Charles Johnson, *"The Fire That Time,"* in
> Book World—The Washington Post, *October
> 7, 1990, pp. 6, 12.*

Mike Phillips

[The protagonist of *Philadelphia Fire*] is a writer named Cudjoe, who has been living on Mykonos and working in a bar. He's drawn back to the US by a newspaper report about the local police bombing a commune of blacks led by a dreadlocked prophet named King, "the dirtiest man I ever seen". (pp. 38-9)

If this sounds like the beginning of an offbeat detective novel, don't worry: it isn't. Cudjoe's quest is internal, and what he's looking for is largely an expiation of the guilt he feels for having rebelled against a network of Afro-American taboos. He's left the old neighbourhood, married a white woman and gone off to embrace a new, colour-blind world. Later on, he deserts his wife and children and winds up on Mykonos, "bartending and making love".

When he returns to Philadelphia, he interviews Margaret Jones, a woman who used to belong to the collective. . . . He follows this up by playing basketball in the park with some younger versions of his old friends, and then lunches with Timbo, an old classmate and now one of the mayor's aides, who sees the tragedy of the commune as a public-relations problem.

The second part of the novel abandons the narrative to become a series of reflections, delivered in the voices of different characters. One of them is J B, an angry street man; another is an old friend and colleague at the University of Philadelphia. . . .

The third part is a sort of panorama of Philadelphian history. Cudjoe moves back and forth in time, from the MOVE bombing, to a memorial service for its victims, to an independence rally in 1805, when blacks were beaten and chased from Independence Square. *Philadelphia Fire* is a literary novel in the grand contemporary, postmodern, literary style. The author is the character who is the narrator, who doesn't tell you a story, but breaks into reflection and reminiscence, reads you letters, articles, essays. Here's a kit. Build your own story.

The text moves in great swoops through time and space, the shifts signalled by the use of various idioms: Afro-American slang, high academic, sports commentary, the poetic. All of it tends to have the punning, riddling structure of rap language, which gives some of it a slightly irritating feel—"He would cast about. Cast himself a caste. A cast in his net. Catch the day. Fresh. Castanet."

Sometimes it's worse. The coy insistence on Cudjoe's scholarship is downright annoying: "Sea pitches and shivers and bellows in its chains. Green and dying. Green and dying. Who wrote that poem?" Please! But Wideman strikes a universal chord when he addresses his own feelings of sorrow, and his identification with his son: "I cannot separate myself from you. Yet I understand we are different. I will try to accept and deal with whatever shape your life takes."

Philadelphia Fire is a welter of fine writing, sociological observation, polemical address and messianic prophecy. I wish I felt that it said anything new or penetrating about its subject. What we get instead is a rehash of Ralph Ellison, Richard Wright and George Lamming, decorated with a magpie selection of classical and contemporary allusions. This is a pity, because on the evidence of Wideman's collection of short stories *Fever,* newly published by Penguin, when not writing a grand literary novel, he's a thoughtful and sensitive author, with interesting and original things to say about being American and black, especially in Philadelphia. (p. 39)

> Mike Phillips, *"Burning Bright,"* in New
> Statesman & Society, *Vol. 3, No. 136, Febru-
> ary 1, 1991, pp. 38-9.*

Mark Hummel

Dream time. *Philadelphia Fire,* as readers of John Edgar Wideman's work have come to expect, seems to be written in dream time, that funky, hazy slipping in and out of sleep, of nightmares so real they could only mean their occupant must be awake—the everyday time of being Black in America. Wideman freely mixes fiction and nonfiction, past and present, street rap and Shakespeare, which, carried to the reader through multiple narrators, conjure a novel of layered depth. As characters surface, then disappear, each connected to the decaying cityscape of Philadelphia, they lament the loss of their children and of themselves.

The characters of this novel unite in the realization that on a Monday in May 1985, the city-sponsored destruction of the MOVE house on Osage Avenue took with it pieces of their lives, and that, in their Blackness, their common heritage will be scooped up among the ashes of eleven dead men, women, and children. This factual event, the police bombing and subsequent rush of fire which destroyed fifty-three homes, sparks the fiction. *Philadelphia Fire* is the story of intersecting lives; the MOVE fire is common ground for a series of middle-aged, educated Black men who all have, in one form or another, been living behind exteriors hiding lives of pain and isolation.

We meet Cudjoe, a writer returning to his West Philly

roots from a self-imposed, invisible exile on the Greek island of Mykonos. Cudjoe, feeling a connection he cannot articulate, returns in search of a naked child reported fleeing the burning house on Osage. In returning home he must face the losses that sent him running away years before—his failed marriage and severance from his sons, his abandoned students (Black youngsters he had dreamed could stage a revised *Tempest*), his hope of a world capable of change. The child for whom he searches, Simba, is never found. Instead Cudjoe finds painful memories and shattered lives. He even finds an underground war waged by children, their apparent freedom anthems touching familiar rhythms but their words unintelligible; only graffiti messages shouting "money, power, things" are clear. We recognize the urban-renewed streets as familiar homes to our children, fighting for survival in a world of drugs, poverty, and crime, searching for identity and hope.

Those familiar with Wideman's work are accustomed to the sometimes slim divisions between fiction and nonfiction, and in the midst of this novel we encounter Wideman himself interrupting Cudjoe's story, drawn by the passing TV images of the fire in Philadelphia on the very street where he had lived years before. Like Cudjoe, he cannot distance himself from the burning, and through narrative, quotations, and letters, he finds the connections between past and present, between him and Cudjoe and the dead residents of the MOVE house. He writes to and of a son lost to a jail cell and a split self—his own lost child. The clarity with which Wideman writes through his own pain is one of the strengths of this book; stronger still is his ability to see the connection of his experience to others.

One of those others is J. B., college-educated, perhaps once idealistic, but now living on the streets of Philadelphia, an abandoned skeleton of promise, living almost entirely in dream time. J. B. brings the novel to its climax in Independence Square, where, living a daytime nightmare, he is convinced little White boys have doused his sleeping body with kerosene and ignited him. Desperate to extinguish the flames, he flails in a dry fountain. Cudjoe is there in the square, too, attending a memorial for the victims of Osage Avenue. Unaware of J. B., he shares something of J. B.'s real paranoia, questioning what may come next in a world stranger than fiction, left only with the heavy weight of words.

The potent words of **Philadelphia Fire** form a multilayered story mourning the loss of a generation—a generation of promise—and the subsequent loss of their children. This is a sad and painful book. Yet it is a book that is vital to an honest reading of contemporary America. In it Wideman shows his versatility, shifting with ease from the sweaty, out-of-breath reality of a basketball court to the dreamy ambiguity that comes with trying to make sense of a world where sons and brothers live their lives in jail, where vital teachers are furloughed, where police drop bombs from helicopters. Some of the novel's most important moments occur within the dreams of its characters, like Cudjoe's nightmare of being sprawled on a basketball court, legs amputated, while simultaneously floating above his own screaming body, witness to a child lynched from the basketball rim. He realizes the child is

me and every black boy I've ever seen running up and down playing ball and I'm screaming for help and frozen in my tracks and can't believe it, can't believe he's dangling there and the dumb thing I'm also thinking in this dream or whatever it is, is if they'd just waited a little longer his legs would have grown, his feet would have reached the ground and he'd be OK.

This lynched boy haunts Cudjoe, as Simba has, for the loss they represent surrounds him in memory and in reality.

It is important that Simba is never found, for his absence is stronger than his presence, a symbol for the lost children everywhere. He represents a world where our children are being consumed by fire. "A child lost cancels the natural order, the circle is broken." Wideman, knowing that to break the circle of generations affects all, is willing to step forward and shoulder part of the burden. Though he purposely questions the generation who came of age in the idealism and faded hope of the 1960s, this burden is one we all must share.

The dream time depths of this novel prove difficult but immensely important and always eloquent. Despite the tough questions and the deep-rooted pain, the novel is about survival. While hope is distant, Wideman asks us to hold on. And while his own words seem—to him—heavy, even cumbersome, all he has left, they bring meaning to events apparently beyond meaning.

Mark Hummel, "Mourning the Loss of a Generation," in The Bloomsbury Review, *Vol. 11, No. 2, March, 1991, p. 1.*

FURTHER READING

Alter, Jonathan. "The Case for Brotherhood." *The Washington Monthly* 17, No. 2 (March 1985): 39-41.

> Contrasts liberal and conservative attitudes toward crime and punishment and praises Wideman's questioning of the appropriateness of life imprisonment for different crimes in his nonfiction work *Brothers and Keepers.*

Bell, Bernard W. "John Edgar Wideman." In his *The Afro-American Novel and Its Tradition,* pp. 307-15. Amherst: University of Massachusetts Press, 1987.

> Overview of Wideman's novels up to and including *The Homewood Trilogy* in which Bell explores the tension between European and African-American influences in Wideman's writing.

Bennion, John. "The Shape of Memory in John Edgar Wideman's *Sent for You Yesterday.*" *Black American Literature Forum* 20, Nos. 1-2 (Spring-Summer 1986): 143-50.

> Examination based on Bennion's assertion that "the reader's struggle to apprehend the familiar and foreign elements of [*Sent for You Yesterday*] approximates the characters' struggle to apprehend their own world through perception, memory, and metaphorical reconstruction of perception and memory."

Berben, Jacqueline. "Beyond Discourse: The Unspoken Versus Words in the Fiction of John Edgar Wideman." *Callaloo* 8, No. 3 (Fall 1985): 525-34.

    Analysis of Wideman's use of interior monologue and dialogue in *Hiding Place* to juxtapose the bleak reality of his characters' environments with their escape into comforting worlds of dream and fantasy.

Coleman, James W. "Going Back Home: The Literary Development of John Edgar Wideman." *CLA Journal* XXVIII, No. 3 (March 1985): 326-43.

    Overview of Wideman's novels up to and including *The Homewood Trilogy* in which Coleman explores Wideman's treatment of family, community, and the black experience.

"John Wideman." In *Interviews with Black Writers,* edited by John O'Brien, pp. 213-23. New York: Liveright, 1973.

    Interview with Wideman in which he discusses such topics as the genesis of his first three novels, use of experimental forms, and treatment of history and race.

Plummer, William. "John Edgar Wideman." *People Weekly* 23, No. 6 (11 February 1985): 121-22, 124, 127-28, 131.

    Biographical article contrasting the lives of Wideman and his brother Robert as they are described in *Brothers and Keepers.*

Wideman, John Edgar. "The Language of Home." *New York Times Book Review* (13 January 1985): 1, 35-6.

    Wideman comments on the reasons why he has frequently returned to his childhood neighborhood of Homewood in his works.

William Carlos Williams

1883-1963

American poet, novelist, playwright, essayist, autobiographer, and historian.

The following entry presents criticism on Williams's *Paterson* (1948-1956). For an overview of Williams's complete career see *CLC*, Vols. 1, 2, 5, 9, 13, 22, and 42.

Paterson, which Williams called his "magnum opus," is considered by some critics the greatest twentieth-century American epic poem. The composition and publication of the five separate books that make up *Paterson* spanned well over a decade of Williams's career and solidified his reputation as an important figure in American literature. While many of his earlier works were short, imagist poems, *Paterson* was Williams's attempt to create an expansive, unified piece embodying his quest as a poet for an understanding of self and environment.

Several of Williams's contemporaries were expatriates, writing about the universal condition of humanity through European perspectives on history and philosophy; Williams, however, believed the artist could best understand humanity by exploring his or her personal surroundings. In *Paterson* he addresses social, economic, and sexual issues unique to his American experience. As a work of art, *Paterson* responds to poems by T. S. Eliot, whom Williams held in contempt for his abstract, elevated verse; the complex theories of Ezra Pound; and works by Walt Whitman, who strongly influenced Williams. According to Robert Lowell, "*Paterson* is Whitman's America, grown pathetic and tragic, brutalized by inequality, disorganized by industrial chaos, and faced with annihilation. . . . Because [Williams] has tried to understand rather than excoriate, and because in his maturity he has been occupied with the 'raw' and the universal, his *Paterson* is not the tragedy of the outcast but the tragedy of our civilization."

Paterson takes place almost entirely in the New Jersey city of the same name, which neighbors Williams's home of Rutherford. "Paterson," however, also refers to a fictional poet. Throughout the work, the name suggests both man and city, as well as Williams himself, and, more broadly, Everyman, or all of humankind. Williams considered the post-Depression era city an effective embodiment of modernity in all its facets, expressing humanity's deviation from its history and detachment from its immediate surroundings. In the city, he claimed, one encountered "man at his most accomplished," and here one witnessed the current state of humanity. The parallel in *Paterson* between man and city also provided a unifying image throughout the poem. Williams selected Paterson both for its geological and historical background, with which he was already quite familiar. He had done extensive historical research on the region while preparing his collection of interpretive essays, *In the American Grain*, in which he

contemplates United States history and Americans' lack of association with their past.

Paterson was published in five separate books. Williams had originally planned only the first four: "The Delineaments of the Giants," introducing the landscape of Paterson; "Sunday in the Park," in which the poet surveys the lazy residents of the city picnicking in the park; "The Library," where he reads of the 1902 tornado, fire, and flood in Paterson and envisions a similar destruction for the library's old and irrelevant books; and "The Run to the Sea," with the poet plunging into the Passaic River as it flows through the city and into the ocean. Realizing upon completion of Book IV, however, that the work could continue indefinitely, Williams added Book V, in which the poet emerges from the ocean; he was working on a sixth book when he died in 1963. Although the five books were published in an eight-year period, several critics contend that Williams began planning *Paterson* as early as 1914 with his poem "The Wanderer," part of which is included in *Paterson*.

Paterson juxtaposes poetry with prose excerpts from history books, newspapers, and personal letters to Williams from friends and such poets as Ezra Pound and the then unknown Allen Ginsberg. Some of these excerpts are quoted verbatim, while others are altered by the poet. The poem's structure strongly resembles montage techniques used by contemporary painters whose trends Williams carefully observed. The use of prose was among the most debated aspects of *Paterson* upon its release. Some critics claimed that these passages caused the work to appear disjointed and fragmentary, and many objected to the lengthy, disturbing letter by "Cressa" that closes Book II. Most now agree, however, that their inclusion was essential for Williams's adherence to his concrete environment and to the development of what he called "the American idiom."

One way in which Williams attempted to place his poem inside the American experience was through the use of vernacular speech as opposed to what he considered the essentially European poetic language used by many contemporary poets. His use of distinctly American language, or "the American idiom," was essential to conveying the American experience. Another central motif in *Paterson*, voiced in the first book, is "No ideas, but in things." By this dictum Williams intended that his poem should be grounded in the tangible world as he experienced it as opposed to relying upon abstract theories. Many critics claim that the newspaper clippings and letters that interrupt the verse in *Paterson* are meant as points of reference for the poet, who, by repeatedly confronting everyday facts, restrains himself from transcending the physical world. Many commentators have suggested that Williams's attention to the concrete stemmed in part from his lifelong profession as a physician. Williams was a general practitioner in Rutherford, and his awareness of societal realities often parallels a doctor's understanding of his or her patients' physical states. His medical career also influenced the material found in *Paterson*, which recounts several of the poet-doctor Paterson's interactions with patients, drawn from Williams's own experience.

Critics recognize *Paterson*, above all, as the poet's deeply personal quest for beauty and a means of representing his environment. On the search for what he calls "beautiful thing," Williams apposes attractive and repulsive scenes, thereby highlighting the social extremes he witnessed and remaining consistent with reality. William Sharpe contended that for Williams, "a poetry that would deal faithfully with the corruptions and fragmentation of contemporary life should present the beautiful and innocent alongside the perverted and hideous, much in the same way that the daily newspaper juxtaposes the brutal and the trivial, the sordid and humane."

Williams is recognized as a lyric innovator who, with such poetic devices as free verse and "the variable foot," influenced a subsequent generation of American poets. With the variable foot, the poet is not restricted to a predetermined length of line; this enabled Williams to adapt line breaks to the rhythms of American speech. *Paterson*'s often short, choppy lines disturbed reviewers who claimed that while this style may have been appropriate for Williams's shorter verse, it was ineffective in sustaining the reader's attention in such a long, complex poem as *Paterson*. Many other critics, however, noted a development of

sensitivity to the poetic line throughout the five books of Williams's epic. It was in the second book, for example, that he first used the triadic stanza that became a standard structural device in much of his later work.

The first three books of *Paterson* received little serious critical attention upon their release, as many critics were hesitant to comment on the poem until it was completed. With the publication of Book IV in 1951, however, *Paterson* began to gain recognition as a revolutionary and innovative poem, and Williams is credited with influencing a wave of original American poetry in the latter half of twentieth century. Critics recognize *Paterson* both as a sensitive examination of the modern condition and as a testament to Williams's later poetic and personal development.

(See also *Contemporary Authors*, Vols. 89-92; *Concise Dictionary of American Literary Biography*, 1917-1929; and *Dictionary of Literary Biography*, Vols. 4, 16, 54, and 86.)

PRINCIPAL WORKS

POETRY

The Tempers 1913
Al que quiere! 1917
Kora in Hell: Improvisations 1920
Sour Grapes 1921
Go Go 1923
Spring and All 1923
The Cod Head 1932
Collected Poems, 1921-1931 1934
An Early Martyr and Other Poems 1935
Adam & Eve & the City 1936
The Complete Collected Poems, 1906-1938 1938
The Wedge 1944
Paterson 1948-1956 (Book I, 1946; Book II, 1948; Book III, 1949; Book IV, 1951; Book V, 1958; Books I-V, 1963)
The Clouds 1948
The Pink Church 1949
Selected Poems 1949
The Collected Later Poems 1950
The Collected Earlier Poems 1951
The Desert Music, and Other Poems 1954
Journey to Love 1955
Pictures from Brueghel, and Other Poems 1962

NOVELS

The Great American Novel 1923
A Voyage to Pagany 1928
A Novelette 1932
White Mule 1937
In the Money: White Mule—Part II 1940
The Build-Up: A Novel 1952

SHORT FICTION COLLECTIONS

The Knife, and Other Stories 1932
Life on the Passaic River 1938
The Farmers' Daughters: The Collected Stories 1961

OTHER

In the American Grain (essays) 1925

I Wanted to Write a Poem: The Autobiography of the Works of a Poet 1958

Isaac Rosenfeld

There are many distinct levels in William Carlos Williams's new poem [*Paterson* (Book I)]. Three are object levels, what the poem is about: Paterson, the city; the city as man; language as bridge between the two, joining their identity. The second of these levels can be further divided into city-as-man-in-general, as this-or-that man, and as the self, the largest abstract autobiographical image of the poet. Then there are the levels of language-in-use: first prose, in the form of passages from a local history, newspaper clippings, expense accounts, letters and reminiscences; and finally the surface itself, which is Williams's familiar, and at the same time deceptively, but authentically, simple poetry. The completed poem of four parts will elaborate the image, "a man in himself is a city, beginning, seeking, achieving and concluding his life in ways which the various aspects of a city may embody. . . ." The present installment "introduces the elemental character of the place." Thus far, the curious thing about this poem, with its divisions and subdivisions, is that its lines are a true green, though they grow not as meadow but real estate.

The simplicity of Williams's lines is not strained by the need to bind so much disparate symbolic material. The pace accommodates itself to things seen, tactile qualities, an uncrowded catalogue. (p. 216)

The ease with which Williams hauls his symbolic freight is to the credit of his prose. It is in his clean idiomatic manner (I assume he has written most of it himself, instead of actually taking it from local sources), and it fixes beforehand the objects, events, and meanings that the lines of poetry draw upon. (It is rather as if the notes of *The Waste Land* had been moved into the poetic foreground, with the poem serving as commentary—or need one say *as if?*) Thus the image of Mrs. Sarah Cumming and Sam Patch, who met their deaths, respectively, by an accidental fall and a stunt leap into water, is well prepared in the prose excerpts to serve the later purpose—death by drowning as the typical metaphor of ineffable poetic language. The lines in the following passage that Williams puts in quotes illustrate the value of such a cut-back in making concrete a generalization about poetry.

> Moveless
> he envies the men that ran
> and could run off
> toward the peripheries—
> to other centers, direct—
> for clarity (if
> they found it)
>   loveliness and
> authority in the world—
>
> a sort of springtime
> toward which their minds aspired
> but which he saw,

within himself—ice bound

> and leaped, "the body, not until
> the following spring, frozen in
> an ice cake"

There is an obvious scrap-book advantage in this method; it permits running back and forth in time, leaps from man to this-man to the self, and provides a sociological or historical distillate of the city which the poetry, essentially lyrical, could never undertake to do. But the success of this attempt, a generalizing lyricism with an *ars poetica* as its motive, cannot as yet be determined. It will depend on how freely the poetry detaches itself, in the subsequent parts, from the prose conveyor belt and works out its own designs. There is already some spontaneous generation of material in the lyrical sections; thus, a reconstruction of a National Geographic snapshot of native women, which develops into a delicate passage on marriage and the communication between lovers.

Of course, devices are essential, for the lyric has short wings. But more important than the sustaining of the lines is the sustaining of the mood, which is here one of summary and wisdom: whether it can grow, circle out, and return on itself with real gain. In recent years the poet's only wisdom has been poetry; he knows all about knowing about poetry, and the earth, which Williams in his concluding lines calls "the chatterer, father of all speech," is a borax heap on which only words grow. But Dr. Williams knows many other things: child-birth, women, life along the Passaic. One can expect him to bring this knowledge to his wisdom in the forthcoming parts of *Paterson.* (pp. 216-17)

Isaac Rosenfeld, "The Poetry and Wisdom of Paterson," in The Nation, *New York, Vol. 163, No. 8, August 24, 1946, pp. 216-17.*

Robert Lowell

Paterson, Book Two, is an interior monologue. A man spends Sunday in the park at Paterson, New Jersey. He thinks and looks about him; his mind contemplates, describes, comments, associates, stops, stutters, and shifts like a firefly, bound only by its milieu. The man is Williams, anyone living in Paterson, the American, the masculine principle—a sort of Everyman. His monologue is interrupted by chunks of prose: paragraphs from old newspapers, textbooks, and the letters of a lacerated and lacerating poetess. This material is merely selected by the author. That the poetry is able to digest it in the raw is a measure of power and daring—the daring of simplicity; for only a taut style with worlds of experience behind it could so resign, and give way to the anthologist. The didactic chapters in *Moby Dick* have a similar function, and are the rock that supports the struggles of Captain Ahab.

The park is Everywoman, any woman, the feminine principle, America. The water roaring down the falls from the park to Paterson is the principle of life. The rock is death, negation, the *nul;* carved and given form, it stands for the imagination, "like a red basalt grasshopper, boot-long with window-eyes." The symbols are not allegorical, but loose, intuitive, and Protean.

Paterson, like Hart Crane's "For the Marriage of Faustus and Helen," is about marriage. "Rigor of beauty is the quest." Everything in the poem is masculine or feminine, everything strains toward marriage, but the marriages never come off, except in the imagination, and there, attenuated, fragmentary, and uncertain. "Divorce is the sign of knowledge in our time." The people "reflect no beauty but gross . . . unless it is beauty to be, anywhere, so flagrant in desire." "The ugly legs of the young girls, pistons without delicacy"; "not undignified"; "among the working classes *some* sort of breakdown has occurred." The preacher in the second section, attended by the "iron smiles" of his three middle-aged disciples, by "benches on which a few children have been propped by the others against their running off," "bends at the knees and straightens himself up violently with the force of his emphasis—like Beethoven getting a crescendo out of an orchestra"—ineffective, pathetic, and a little phony. He has given up, or says he has given up, a fortune for the infinite riches of our Lord Jesus Christ. Interspersed through his sermon, as an ironic counter-theme, is Alexander Hamilton, whose fertile imagination devised the national debt and envisioned Paterson as a great manufacturing center. Nobody wins. "The church spires still spend their wits against the sky." "The rock-table is scratched by the picnickers' boot-nails, more than by the glacier." The great industrialists are "those guilty bastards . . . trying to undermine us." The legislators are "under the garbage, uninstructed, incapable of self-instruction." "An orchestral dulness overlays their world." "The language, tongue-tied . . . words without style!"

This is the harsh view. Against it is the humorous, the dogs, the children; lovely fragments of natural description; the author's sense of the human and sympathetic in his people.

Williams is noted as an imagist, a photographic eye; in Book One he has written "no ideas but in the facts." This is misleading. His symbolic man and woman are Hegel's *thesis* and *antithesis.* They struggle toward *synthesis*—marriage. But fulness, if it exists at all, only exists in simple things, trees and animals; so Williams, like other Platonists, is thrown back on the "idea." "And no whiteness (lost) is so white as the memory of whiteness." "The stone lives, the flesh dies." The idea, Beauty, must be realized by the poet where he lives, in Paterson. "Be reconciled, Poet, with your world, it is the only truth," though "love" for it "is no comforter, rather a nail in the skull."

Paterson is an attempt to write the American Poem. It depends on the American myth, a myth that is seldom absent from our literature—part of our power, and part of our hubris and deformity. At its grossest the myth is propaganda, puffing and grimacing: Size, Strength, Vitality, the Common Man, the New World, Vital Speech, the Machine; the hideous neo-Roman personae: Democracy, Freedom, Liberty, the Corn, the Land. How hollow, windy, and inert this would have seemed to an imaginative man of another culture! But the myth is a serious matter. It is assumed by Emerson, Whitman, and Hart Crane; by Henry Adams and Henry James. For good or for evil, America *is* something immense, crass, and Roman. We

must unavoidably place ourselves in our geography, history, civilization, institutions, and future.

The subjects of great poetry have usually been characters and the passions, a moral struggle that calls a man's whole person into play. One thinks of the wrath of Achilles, Macbeth and his conscience, Aeneas debating whether he will leave Dido, whether he will kill Turnus. But in the best long American poems—*Leaves of Grass, The Cantos, The Waste Land, Four Quartets, The Bridge,* and *Paterson*—no characters take on sufficient form to arrive at a crisis. The people melt into voices. In a recent essay Eliot has given his reasons why a writer should, perhaps, read Milton; Williams has answered with an essay that gives reasons why a writer should *not* read Milton—Eliot and Williams might learn something from *Paradise Lost* and *Samson Agonistes,* how Milton populated his desert.

Until Books III and IV are published, it is safer to compare *Paterson* with poems that resemble it; not with *The Bridge,* that wonderful monster, so unequal, so inexperienced—dazzling in its rhetoric at times in the way that Keats is dazzling; but with a book in which its admirers profess to find everything, *Leaves of Grass.* Whitman is a considerable poet, and a considerable myth. I can never quite disentangle the one from the other. I would say that Whitman's language has less variety, sureness, and nerve than Williams's; that his imagination is relatively soft, formless, monotonous, and vague. Both poets are strong on compassion and enthusiasm, but these qualities in Whitman are *simpliste* and blurred.

Paterson is Whitman's America, grown pathetic and tragic, brutalized by inequality, disorganized by industrial chaos, and faced with annihilation. No poet has written of it with such a combination of brilliance, sympathy, and experience, with such alertness and energy. Because he has tried to understand rather than excoriate, and because in his maturity he has been occupied with the "raw" and the universal, his *Paterson* is not the tragedy of the outcast but the tragedy of our civilization. It is a book in which the best readers, as well as the simple reader, are likely to find *everything.* (pp. 692-94)

"I had a concept that came to me: it was to speak as a person, as a certain person; and I thought to myself: 'Well, if I am going to speak about a person it must be an actual person, but a really heroic figure as all epic poems are.' But also a fanciful poem. It must be a fanciful poem, but dealing with particular events and a particular place. And I searched around for what would be the center of the thing. Because a city is a typical thing of the modern world, it's a place where men are most operative. You may think of individual men as being perhaps from a country district, but the concept of the city, as I conceived it, was man at his most accomplished."

William Carlos Williams in an interview, *Interviews with William Carlos Williams: "Speaking Straight Ahead,"* 1976.

Robert Lowell, "Paterson II," in The Nation, New York, Vol. 166, No. 25, June 19, 1948, pp. 692-94.

Ralph Nash

[*The essay excerpted below was originally published in* Perspective, *Vol. 4 (1953).*]

The real subject here is that prose to which Williams calls attention by differentiating type. **Paterson** does contain obvious prose that is undifferentiated from the surrounding verse: the sermon of Klaus Ehrens, the conversation with old Henry, the fragmentary talk of Corydon and Phyllis, the letters from Pound, an old man's reminiscences of early Paterson. But most of the direct prose is acknowledged with italics or small type, is kept in its place, apart from the main flow of the poetry. This method is something of an innovation in technique; no major, or even relatively successful, poem has previously explored its possibilities. So the kinds of prose in **Paterson,** and their effects, have a general interest in relation to the developments of poetic technique as well as the specific interest of their contributions to the success of the single poem. This sketch will try to abstract from the poem some classification of the types of prose used and to suggest some of the effects that must be reckoned with.

Three major classes of prose can be fairly well separated. There are newspaper clippings and factual data, directly transcribed; there are Williams' own summaries of historical data, excerpted from old newspapers, local histories, etc.; and there are the personal letters. These are the types (not always easily distinguished) that recur most often. If profitable, classification and subdivision could be carried further. For example, there seem to be some transcriptions from the doctor's notebooks, and here and there a passage that sounds more like the record of a conversation than like a written letter. And for exact subdivision there are many problems. Most of the letters are surely authentic, but Phyllis' are surely fictional, and the letter about Musty I suspect is the poet's artifact. The account of Sam Patch's career evidently combines authorial summary with direct transcription of an eyewitness account; and the survey of Hamilton's plans for a National Manufactory may be direct transcription or summary or both, while the counterpoint indictment of Federal Reserve Banks might be from Williams himself, or from Pound or some other source. But these questions of fact remain minor. Most of the prose involves the use of personal letters, direct transcription of material from newspapers and books (usually local history), or authorial summary of such material.

This classification by source can be supplemented with a temporal classification that may seem to affect more directly the function of the prose within the poem. That is, the prose of Contemporary Fact and the prose of Historical Fact. Both classes, contemporary and historical, are examples of "invention" in the classical sense—the discovery of material appropriate to the meaning and the decorum of the poem.

The letters, which make up most of the prose of contemporary fact, supply corroborations of the poet's insight into contemporary obsessions and confusions. Williams re- ceives a letter that speaks of a "kind of blockage, exiling one's self from one's self," of an inability to communicate, of scorn for the divorce that would "bring to literature and to life two different inconsistent sets of values, as you do." This echoing of the themes of divorce and blockage and failure at communication—a large part of the intellectual content of Books One and Two—is a remarkable corroboration of Williams' exploration of his age. It is much more remarkable than the verbal coincidence in an image of "the rough ice of that congealment which my creative faculties began to suffer." And it is actually more relevant to the poem than are the complaints about clothes, irons, typewriters and stolen money orders, which anticipate Williams' own complaint: "The writing is nothing, the being / in a position to write (that's / where they get you)."

Another significant letter, possibly fictional, is the one about Musty. The comic picture of the housewife peeking between her laundered sheets and trying to beat off the male with a stick is also a serious commentary on the civilization's fear of fertility and its attempts to govern and control brute nature. The penitent letter, confessing that Musty has become pregnant in spite of the housewife's precautions, takes its place with many thematic references to the dog, an animal that links the urban and the pastoral world. It is a kind of link between the Dog-as-Opponent (NO DOGS ALLOWED AT LARGE IN THIS PARK; "guilty lovers and stray dogs") and the Dog-as-Companion (the Collie bitch, combed out with deliberate design as Williams must comb out the language; old Henry's feist, which the doctor caused to be killed; the favorite dog buried with Pogatticut; the black bitch who follows her master inland at the close of the poem).

The letter about Musty's "marriage" not only comments on major themes (fear of fertility, divorce, uneasiness about animals disobedient to The Law), but also it points up Williams' process in "inventing" his poem. For although the various references to dogs depend upon one another for cumulative meaning and importance, they come from diverse sources. Walking in the park, the doctor sees a man combing his Collie, hears somebody calling "Yeah, Chi-Chi," and reflects wryly on the significance of the prohibition against unleashed dogs. Later, reading about local Indian funeral customs (the dancing of the Kinte Kaye; the burial of Pogatticut), he is interrupted by Henry, whose favorite dog he had reported for biting him. Still later, again in the library, as he imagines the scene of the great flood and pictures a dead dog floating in it "toward Acheron," he remembers both the Indian funeral and Henry's bitter accusation, realizing that he himself has had to be one of the upholders of the white man's law and order, causing the death of Henry's dog, for all his sympathy with unleashed dogs. With his intense drive toward honesty, he is accusing himself of sharing the "guilt" of the ordered society in which he bears responsibility as medicine man. Against this (partial) background is thrown the blatantly sterile and stinted attitude of the housewife, whose attempt to prevent an intrusion of Nature into her backyard, however comic it may seem, is nevertheless only another facet of the general divorce of urban man from his sources, a divorce which Williams has accused himself of making between his life and art. Thus, whether authentic or an artifact, the letter corroborates a view of himself and of contemporary man, at the same time that it helps to make more meaningful one of the poet's letters and one of his readings in local history.

These two examples will serve to suggest how the letters partially function in the same way as the images, details, phrases and quotations of the poetry itself, in building up patterns of recurring motifs in a poem that shares the contemporary predilection for thematic structure. The letters also share in the special functions of the other prose. For one thing, I have classed them as Prose of Contemporary Fact. I mean this to stress their nature as blocks of material coming into the poem from outside. These letters (at least most of them) are not constructs of the poet; they are given quantities, entities in their own right, that must be fitted into the structure of the poem. One cannot speak as if Williams were a scientist, shaping his theory to fit all the facts: he necessarily keeps at least the negative power of choice and omission. But a letter (or anything else) written by someone other than the poet brings into the poem something of an air of documentation. Irrelevancies and private allusions emphasize that this is not exactly a piece of the poem, but a piece of the poet's world, an upthrust of his autobiography, an outcropping of the substratum on which his City is based. The direct presentation of these fragments, without their being shaped into the rhythms and diction of the surrounding poetry, is of course an artistic device. No doubt Williams intends it partly as a forceful marriage of his poem's world with that world of reality from which he is fearful of divorcing himself. But it has also a special effect of presenting the Poet as Recorder, relatively detached and objective, reading his morning mail as he might read a history of Paterson, acting somewhat as the scientist might in checking his guesses against the facts. Perhaps the best corroboration of this is that Williams keeps up the device of the interpolated letter, even though he has to create the letters, in the specifically dramatic objectification that makes up the pastoral of Phyllis and Corydon.

One other effect is largely, though not exclusively, a property of the personal letters. They document, very directly, the basic problem of the need for a language ("Haven't you forgot your virgin purpose, the language?"). An obvious example is the letter of DJB ("Tell Raymond I said I bubetut hatche isus cashutute Just a new way of talking kid"), but also the dead triteness of the letter about Musty and the pathetic braveries of Phyllis' slang are examples of the same kind of failure with the language. Even clearer and more damaging are the "literary" letters, those from T. and/or T.J., from *La votre C.,* and from A.P. These people sound interesting but their stylistic posturing is incredible: "In spite of the grey secrecy of time and my own self-shuttering doubts in these youthful rainy days, I would like to make my presence in Paterson known to you. . . . Not only do I inscribe this missive somewhat in the style of those courteous sages of yore who recognized one another across the generations as brotherly children of the muses . . ." However much Williams was concentrating on the contents of these letters, he could hardly be oblivious of their relevance to his underlying concern for "the language . . . the language!"

This latter aspect of the prose of contemporary fact also appears in the extracts from Historical Fact. The clearest example is the nineteenth-century rhetoric of the account of Mrs. Cumming's death: "She had been married about two months, and was blessed with a flattering prospect of no common share of Temporal felicity and usefulness in the sphere which Providence had assigned her; but oh, how uncertain is the continuance of every earthly joy." Williams' comments are explicit:

> A false language. A true. A false language pouring—a language (misunderstood) pouring (misinterpreted) without dignity, without minister, crashing upon a stone ear. At least it settled it for her.

Other passages of nineteenth-century prose reinforce this one, but need no special comment. However, it is irresistible to note the wry humor (and the constant alertness to the problem of language) in Williams' excerpt from an account of Indian ritual, immediately following a bitter passage on the artist's struggle to live and his audience's complete refusal of any struggle to comprehend ("Geeze, Doc, I guess it's all right / but what the hell does it mean?"). The passage on Indian ritual concludes:

> While some are silent during the sacrifice, certain make a ridiculous speech, while others imitate the cock, the squirrel, and other animals, and make all kinds of noises. During the shouting two roast deer are distributed.

The two roast deer mark this as the "invention" of a genius, a genius, moreover, with the high good humor of despair.

Like the letters, the prose of historical fact emphasizes the Poet as Recorder, partly through the same device of inserting unshaped blocks of foreign material, but in this case also through Williams' appearance as impersonal summarizer. The quality of this summary prose is sometimes exceptionally fine, as in Williams' account of early life in the Ramapos; in almost all instances it provides a special effect of calm and interested but detached observation. Further comment on this quality of impersonal detachment would have to involve fuller discussion of the prose rhythms, but the lack of comment here is not meant to minimize its importance. It is one of the most striking and consistent effects of the prose in *Paterson.*

Also, the various excerpts and summaries from past history are interwoven with general themes of the poem, but for brevity this function may be passed over, since it is not different in kind from that illustrated above for the personal letters.

While we are still concerned with the relation of the prose to *Paterson*'s content and structure, we may observe two rather special types. One of these is the prose passage that is simply a kind of footnote, existing as an appendage to one particular passage without much relevance to other parts of the poem. An example is the fragment from Columbus' account of his discovery of the New World, which is relevant directly to Marie Curie's discovery of the new world of atomic physics—although perhaps it is also a bit of ironic counterpoint to the atom bomb. The neatest example, though, is the case history of prevention of contagious diarrhea in the pediatric ward. This is a quiet joke, the clue to which is the last sentence: "The nurse was at once removed from duty with full pay, a measure found to be of advantage in having hospital personnel report diarrheal disturbances without fear of economic reprisal." Since Williams has just quoted Chaucer's "Thy drasty rymyng is not worth a toord," it is clear that reporting diarrheal disturbances without fear of economic reprisal is another version of the plight of the poet. An amusing footnote, but nothing more. There are only a few of these sharply limited addenda.

The other special type is the prose passage which has supplied a theme for the poem. Clearly it is of some interest to note when Williams' reading of local history has supplied him, not with additional illustration, but with a theme to be illustrated. One of the most probable examples of this (apart from the Annus Mirabilis of 1902) is Peter the Dwarf, whose deformed body could not support the enormous weight of his head (J. W. Barber and H. Howe, *Historical Collections of the State of New Jersey,* New York 1844, p. 407). The dwarf becomes for Williams a sardonic symbol of himself as poet, "hideously deformed," a kind of toad "saved by his protective coloring," threatened with decomposition into leaves and toadstools unless he comes to terms ("Go home. Write. Compose . . . Ha! Be reconciled, poet, with your world"). With this image of the dwarf-poet in his mind, coupled with the associated image of the poet as lame dog, Williams would obviously appropriate with grim delight Symonds' declaration that "The choliambi are in poetry what the dwarf or cripple is in human nature." Perhaps less obviously, he might have had his deformed monster in mind when he noted, as another symbol for the poet, the heavy crow and the smaller birds stabbing for his eyes.

Thus far I have been concerned largely with the relation of the prose to thematic content and structure, with some emphasis on the interplay of past and present in the total poem. For the difficult subject of the relations of the prose passages to the poetic technique of *Paterson,* I can only offer a few suggestions. It is evident that the prose affects the poem most strongly by its sound, by the inevitable interruption to eye and ear whenever one of the prose passages appears. This means, for one thing, that the prose is of tremendous importance to the pace and tempo of the entire poem. Nowhere is this more striking than in the eight pages of closely set type that provide a tortured, involved, garrulous, intimate, but ultimately dignified and quiet close for Book Two: "*please* [read this], merely out of fairness to me—much time and much thought and much unhappiness having gone into those pages." Such a huge chunk of extraneous prose obviously will bring the reader to a full halt: but this is exactly right at the close of a book, especially this one which marks a kind of midpoint in the poem. But inextricably connected with this effect is the fact that the long letter from C., portions of which have appeared before, has been serving as ironic counterpoint to the conversation of He and She ("I wish to be with you abed, we two / as if the bed were the bed

of a stream.") And if it were not for the extract from C's unhappy letter (an extract which begins "My attitude toward woman's wretched position in society . . . "), Book Two would close with a lyric promise of the consummation of love—"On this most voluptuous night of the year." So the problem of pace and rhythm here is closely connected with the content of C's letter, with its previous structural use, with its own prose style, and with its own particular placing in the poem. No doubt similar difficulties would surround many passages if one were to pursue the question of pace further.

The range of subject matter and rhythmic movement in the prose passages makes a kind of parallel to the range of the poetry. The prose is sometimes, one might say, "the waste farina in the sink." Yet again, as in the burial of Pogatticut, for example, it may be very close to the precisions and rhythms of the poetry. A long analysis, with many examples of rhythms, images, and details, might do something toward making explicit the degrees of prosiness, as it were. And this might in turn illuminate a part of Williams' general method in poetry, since the use of prose in *Paterson* is from one point of view only a kind of logical extension of that drive toward the direct, unadorned fact, the single stubborn *thing,* that has always been known to be part of Williams' faith. That is, how much does the prose work with the poetry, and how much against it? Do the rhythms of the prose set up defiantly a world of "fact" against which the poetry batters? For all that may be said of their contribution to the total poem, do the prose passages by their nature keep up a posture of opposition to the poetry, because of their movement and sound, and subject matter too? And if the prose does this, in varying degrees, may it not provide some measure for the same kind of thing—gradated, no doubt—*within* Williams' verse? (*i.e.,* can we at least admit that the prose is not poetry, and starting from there build up some kind of meaning and definition for the quality in Williams' verse that Wallace Stevens blandly and reasonably chose to call "antipoetic"?) In this way, the prose in *Paterson* strikes one as quite an important subject for anyone interested in Williams' general aesthetics.

Other facets of the prose as vehicle of the language have been alluded to above—the "scientific" tone of detachment, the ironic illustration of failure in communication. The last function to be noted here is a mixture of various things—prose style, subject matter, authorial attitude, sources—but it is at any rate a very important contribution to the effect of the poem. This is the function of the prose in constantly reinforcing an immediate sense of locale. Newspaper clippings, letters addressed to Paterson, excerpts from local history: all insist upon Paterson as place. Paterson the Man is no Ulysses; the sea is not his home. However much the techniques (and economics) of *Paterson* remind us of the *Cantos,* Williams is not writing of the Wanderer who knew many manners of men and saw many cities. And he is not constructing a City of the Just. It is Paterson, not Dioce. The prose passages are by no means a minor device for keeping us clear on that essential point.

To sum up. The use of prose in *Paterson* contributes to

a sense of immediacy (the use of personal letters, contemporary newspapers) while at the same time it gives a sense of distance and objectivity (the use of historical materials, the relatively dispassionate recording of personal involvements). The appearance of passages, both contemporary and historical, that in themselves document such a theme as the search for a language, accentuates in a completely valid way the continuity of that problem; and in general the appearance of both contemporary and historical "documentation" of the thematic concerns of the poem tends to give it continuity, to increase the sense of structural and contentual unity and validity. In addition, the prose passages sometimes represent ultimate sources, the origins of some of the thematic material.

As for the contribution of the prose to the techniques of presentation, the actual speaking of the poem, the inevitable key word is counterpoint. There is the counterpoint affecting pace and tempo—the intrusion of flat prose rhythms, in passages of varying length, the occasional rhythmic and vivid prose, the ironic juxtaposition of lyric affirmations and unpleasant "facts," or the opposite juxtaposition of a grimly urban scene and an excerpt from the days of a more pastoral village life. Closely related is the counterpoint of the materials of the poem: the balancing of the pure with the dirty, the resolution with the confusion, the dream with the fact, the past with the present (but cutting both ways, not neglecting the old newspapers, the murders, the suicides, the child aflame in a field trying to crawl home). And over all this—and over the tone of impersonal observation, the outright *examples* of the failure of language, and the many effects I have probably missed—is what we might call the counterpoint of poet and city. Yesterday's weather, last week's meeting, a nineteenth-century artesian well: they crop up out of past and present like the flint ("the flinty pinnacles") out of the ground, insisting on the here and now and then of Paterson as place.

This has been more a description than a judgment. We probably all need to know the poem better before anyone comes to judgment. But some major points rise naturally out of the description. I have had to speak of Williams' "invention" as being invention in the classical sense of "coming upon" the appropriate material: and I suppose it is clear that I think his powers of invention are splendid. However, the obvious thing, after granting the poet the right to "invent" his material wherever he can, is to say that he "must transform it," must shape it with the shaping power of imagination. The classical line is that it is not rhyming and versing that maketh the poet, but his power of Fiction, or of Making; and the demand for powers of "fiction" continues strongly in our time ("A fictive covering Weaves always glistening from the heart and mind"). But surely Williams does exercise his invention without going on to fictive transformation of the invented material. That is a part of the method of *Paterson,* a part of its technical innovation. Is *Paterson* a better, or worse, poem for this partial denial of the great requirement of Fiction? No doubt the question can be avoided, with our highly developed sense for the fineness of the line between sanity-or-insanity, mental-or-physical, fact-or-fiction. But avoiding it is not to my purpose, because a major point in what has

been said here is that the denial of Fiction—the widespread use of unaltered "factual" prose—is a positive, novel contribution to the meaning and the technique of Williams' long poem. (pp. 20-9)

Ralph Nash, "The Use of Prose in 'Paterson'," in The Merrill Studies in Paterson, *edited by John Engels, Charles E. Merrill Publishing Company, 1971, pp. 20-9.*

Richard Eberhart

The most startling thing about *Paterson* (Book Five) is the compulsion of the author to write it. It is a masterful part of a masterful long poem. Readers enjoyed the first four books as a completed work. They made sense as an esthetic whole and they continue to excite students with their rich sparkle of ideas. The theme was the mind and history of modern man. *Paterson* is one of the major long poems of the century, defining new territory of the American poetic imagination.

Now Dr. Williams has felt compelled to go on with the Paterson story as a living continuum of man and city, civilization and culture. The last part of Book Four was "The Run to the Sea." There was a rightness of ending the poem on an image of going back to the sea, but even then, at the very end, the poet wrote "The sea is not our home" and contrived man and dog coming out of the water. He "headed inland, followed by the dog."

Book Five is written in the same style, with prose letters and historical commentaries interspersed with the lithe and flying poetry. It is as if Dr. Williams could never rest from an endless attempt to put the whole of his vision of life onto paper. Startled to have the addition of Book Five, as if Virgil or Dante had added onto their poems in an astounding passion of illogic, we should envisage further books because this part does not necessarily conclude the subject or matter.

I would welcome further books because they would be as natural to Dr. Williams' restless, inventive mind as is this addition. He could search out further meanings, as he has done here, maintaining the apt quality of the confections in quick esthetic shifts and stances.

Since there is a touch of the comic in the fact of Book Five, a denial of the work of art as inevitable, an insistence on its flowing, protean, ever-changing nature, Dr. Williams should continue with this breath-like work. A tragedy has an end, but history does not. This is an historical poem and there is no good reason why it should not flow on as long as Dr. Williams can make it do so. The last word is never said in art. "What but indirection / will get to the end of the sphere?" He also writes: "I cannot tell it all" and "It is the imagination / which cannot be fathomed."

There is fresh writing here, with the Unicorn and the Virgin as symbols, with Sappho paired with Satyrs. There is good talk about painting and music, and about the nature of poetry. For instance, in a question-and-answer passage about a Cummings poem we have this:

Q. Well—is it poetry?

A. We poets have to talk in a language which is not English. It is the American idiom. * * * It has as much originality as jazz. If you say '2 partridges, 2 mallard ducks, a Dungenese crab'—if you treat that rhythmically, ignoring the practical sense, it forms a jagged pattern. It is, to my mind, poetry.

Q. But if you don't 'ignore the practical sense'. . . you agree that it is a fashionable grocery list.

A. Yes. Anything is good material for poetry. Anything. I've said it time and time again.

As Williams says in a prose passage, "I mean to say Paterson is not a task like Milton going down to Hell, it's a flower to the mind, etc., etc." And Book Five ends beautifully in an existential-esthetic passage as follows: "We know nothing and can know nothing but / the dance, to dance to a measure contrapuntally, Satyrically, the tragic foot."

> Richard Eberhart, "A Vision of Life and Man That Drives the Poet On," in The New York Times Book Review, *September 14, 1958, p. 4.*

Joel Conarroe

Nearly equal in importance to the wandering hero in tying together the various parts of **Paterson** is the river. Introduced (or rained down) in the "Preface," it flows throughout the five books. The proximity of the Passaic to Paterson was one of Williams' main reasons for choosing this city as the site of his poem. Following a course from above the Falls down to the sea, the industrially vital waterway was, he realized, a ready-made symbol: "This was my river and I was going to use it. I had grown up on its banks, seen the filth that polluted it . . . all I had to do was follow it and I had a poem." The movement downstream is carefully worked out from book to book: "Each part of the poem was planned as a unit complete in itself, reporting the progress of the river."

This progress as documented in the poem is very close to the actual progress of the Passaic, and the places mentioned—Notch Brook, Ramapos Valley, and Singac, for example—are New Jersey landmarks. (p. 81)

[The poem's river] has its source in the "Preface" with the words, "floating mists, to be rained down and / regathered into a river that flows / and encircles." This genesis, Williams said, is a symbol of all beginnings. Book I opens and closes with descriptions of the Falls, which crash down in the hills above the city, producing the thunder that fills Paterson's dreams. It is the noise of this pouring river that gives substance to "the subtleties of his machinations," thereby animating "a thousand automatons." The movement of the river from its source (designated simply as "From above") to the gorge, which forms the Falls, is pictured graphically in the opening descriptive sequence:

> From above, higher than the spires, higher
> even than the office towers, from oozy fields
> abandoned to grey beds of dead grass,
> black sumac, withered weed-stalks,

mud and thickets cluttered with dead leaves—
the river comes pouring in above the city
and crashes from the edge of the gorge
in a recoil of spray and rainbow mists—

Williams evokes a sense of violent movement and power by making a sharp break between the static "grey . . . dead . . . black . . . withered . . . dead" and the intense "comes pouring . . . and crashes . . . in a recoil." This is of considerable importance: throughout the poem the Falls quicken the action and give a sense of dramatic chaos, invariably related to the chaotic attempt to comb out the language. The lines following the description just quoted sketch this relationship between the Falls and the language-falls within the mind:

> (What common language to unravel?
> . . combed into straight lines
> from the rafter of a rock's
> lip.)

The connections between the flow of thought and the flow of water are then fully analyzed in a long, intricate passage. This relationship is reintroduced, with variations, throughout the poem. Its unusual importance in Book I lies in the passages dealing with Mrs. Cumming's "suicide" jump into the Falls, and with the death leap of Sam Patch. Each of these unnatural deaths is related to a failure of speech, and each is frequently invoked, in the manner of a leitmotiv, to contrast the free flow of the river with the stasis in the mind.

There are also other strategic and important descriptions of the river in this opening book. The spent waters of the Falls, for example, form the outline of Paterson's back, and the "quiet river" has carved out the Park. The Falls are central in the prose descriptions of the "monster in human form," and of Hamilton's visit to Paterson. The "monster" bass is captured just below the Falls basin. The "roar of the river" induces eternal sleep. The compact juniper trembles "On the embankment," and a frozen body is fished "from the muddy swirl." Following the description of another body, this one caught between two logs hanging over the precipice of the Falls, the river is related to the industry of Paterson:

> Half the river red, half steaming purple
> from the factory vents, spewed out hot,
> swirling, bubbling. The dead bank,
> shining mud   .

And in the final image in the book, thought, personified, clambers up the wet rocks beneath the pouring torrent, having its birth and death there.

The importance of the water imagery in this book is immense. In addition to those passages in which the Falls and river are described explicitly, there are numerous images that derive from the river symbolism and that can be understood only in relation to it. The second prose passage, for example, describes the pearls discovered by the poor shoemaker in Notch Brook, which is a tributary of the river. The girls from decayed families "may look at the torrent in / their minds / and it is foreign to them." The two half-grown girls who hail Easter are described as "disparate among the pouring / waters of their hair in which nothing is / molten—" When Paterson experiences a sudden revulsion at the poverty of his imagination he draws on a marine image: "Stale as a whale's breath." Jesus' parable of the seeds thrown among the good and stony earth is transformed into "the snow falling into the water, / part upon the rock . . . " And in the description of the conspicuous waste that existed during a time of general privation, the poet mentions "a swimming pool, (empty!)," providing a contrast between the artificial and empty pool and the natural flow of the river. The prose description of the slaughter of the eels and fish in the drained lake also suggests a perpetuation of stasis in dramatic contrast to the crash of the Falls.

Thus from the beginning to the end the Passaic is in evidence, fusing all the parts much as the word "Walking" does in Book II. Water is clearly the controlling element in this book, as "earth" is in Book II, fire in Book III, and air in Book IV. As the source of life, of "shells and animalcules" and of man, it is appropriately exploited in the section that "introduces the elemental character of the place." The river flows throughout the entire poem, but only in Book I is its relationship to the action so completely central.

Until section iii, when the Falls serves as the setting for a strong and complex sequence centering on marriage and language, the Passaic remains in the background in Book II. A "Plan for II," in the Buffalo papers, projects this book as a "loose association looking toward the 'language,' the Falls obsessing the mind." It is after the evangelist's sermon, as evening descends, that "Faitoute" strolls off to the Falls. Until this point they are mentioned only as a background detail. In section i, for example, the phrase "over-riding / the risks: / pouring down!" suggests both the Falls and the rush of Paterson's thought. Later, as the poet stands at the rampart observing the steeples and ball-park, he looks "beyond the gap where the river / plunges into the narrow gorge, unseen." The river remains unseen throughout this section.

In part ii, a prose passage dealing with Hamilton's enthu-

The Passaic Falls in Paterson, New Jersey.

siastic response to the Great Falls and to "the navigable river to carry manufactured goods to the market centers" leads into a description of the evangelist's sermon:

> Give up my money!
>
>   —with monotonous insistence
> the falls of his harangue hung featureless
> upon the ear, yet with a certain strangeness
> as if arrested in space

Here the linguistic and the economic connotations of the Falls are merged. Williams' own comment on the evangelist's speech is the simple assertion that "He does not have it (the language) though his leap is just." By now it is evident that Williams has set up an equation between the Falls and man's language, and that this equation involves man's symbolic leap in an attempt to wrest some meaning from the language of the Falls. If his speech fails, as in the case of Mrs. Cumming and Sam Patch, then death is unavoidable. In the evangelist's case there is neither destruction nor revelation, but simply a featureless suspension, a state of arrest.

With section iii, the Falls becomes the center of attention. The lines beginning "the descent beckons" suggest the descent of night, of memory, and of the Falls, as well as the more obvious descent down the mountain. With evening, love wakens, and Paterson listens to "the pouring water!" He strolls to the Falls. The passages that follow . . . all center on the role of the poet, on the divorce from learning within the universities, and on the urgent need for invention and "marriage." First of all, the poem is described in a splendid falls image: "That the poem, / the most perfect rock and temple, the highest / falls, in clouds of gauzy spray, should be / so rivaled." This passage laments that the poet, in disgrace, must borrow from erudition. The scholars of the word are described as "dangling, about whom / the water weaves its strands encasing them / in a sort of thick lacquer, lodged / under its flow." These servants of tradition, like the evangelist, remain under the flow of language, with no chance to comb out its meaning. But Paterson, the poet, "untaught but listening," strains in an intense effort to decipher the meaning of the roar:

> Caught (in mind)
> beside the water he looks down, listens!
> But discovers, still, no syllable in the confused
> uproar: missing the sense (though he tries)
> untaught but listening, shakes with the intensity
> of his listening

This attempt is integrally related to the awakening of love and to the realization of the need for marriage. The passage is followed by the introduction of the marriage theme, which is related to the use of language and to the contradictory demands made on the creative sensibility.

> Only the thought of the stream comforts him,
> its terrifying plunge, inviting marriage—and
> a wreath of fur
>
> And She —
>   Stones invent nothing, only a man invents.
>   What answer the waterfall? filling
>   the basin by the snag-toothed stones?

And He —
>   Clearly, it is the new, uninterpreted,
>   that
>   remoulds the old, pouring down .

And she —
>   It has not been enacted in our day!

>   *Le
> pauvre petit ministre,* swinging his arms,
>   drowns
>   under the indifferent fragrance of the bass-
>   wood
>   trees .

The "She," or feminine principle, questions the validity of the waterfall, preferring the actual marriage between man and woman to the figurative union suggested by the plunge into a quest for language. "It has not been enacted in our day!" is an echo of "No poet has come." And the "*Pauvre petit ministre*" refers to the evangelist who drowns, not within the crashing torrent of the Falls, but under the indifferent fragrance. This image foreshadows the idea of "indifferent men" that emerges as a major theme in Book IV.

The "debate" is followed by a fragment of a letter from Paterson's correspondent, the rejected Miss Cress who, hurt and angry, speaks without her "usual tongue-tied round-aboutness." Following this, Paterson's own anger mounts, and he sees the dwarf who warns, "Poet, poet! sing your song, quickly!" This is followed by

>   He all but falls .   .
> And She —
>   Marry us! Marry us!
>   Or! be dragged down,
>   dragged
>   under and lost

The next passage is a reference to Mrs. Cumming, who "leaped (or fell) without a / language, *tongue-tied* " (my italics), and is composed as an ideogram, resembling a waterfall. . . .

This is followed by more words from the dwarf ("Go home. Write. Compose"). The passage ends with Faitoute fleeing, "pursued by the roar." The failure to understand the implications of the roar and to realize fully the love inherent in it is further documented . . . by the shrill, neurotic letter that makes up the final eight pages of the book. It should be noted here, however, that the attempt to decipher the language of the Falls does not cease with this retreat. Rather, as Williams wrote in his plan for the book, "He flees to the library." There his quest continues on an altogether different level.

In "The Library," Book III, the river serves two specific functions, the lesser of which is to advance the movement of the poem ever closer to the sea, thereby continuing the symbolic flow of man's life from his original source outward toward the "world." (pp. 82-9)

The major function of the river in this book, however, lies in the sustained use of the roar of the Falls as a symbol of the torrent of language within the poet's mind. From this chaos some meaning must be wrested if Paterson is

> **"From the beginning I decided there would be four books following the course of the river whose life seemed more and more to resemble my own life as I more and more thought of it: the river above the Falls, the catastrophe of the Falls itself, the river below the Falls, and the entrance at the end into the great sea."**
>
> **—*William Carlos Williams***

to escape destruction. He goes to the library to find what was missing at the Falls themselves, seeking—in books, in the language of others—an interpretation. As a note in the Yale collection states, however, he "finds it not in the books but in his mind that wanders as he reads." He searches in the printed page, but his mind is "elsewhere / looking down / Seeking." The parallelism of the mind and Falls is continued, but with variations, since the library is in the city and the focus is off the river itself. The Falls now tumble and refall "unseen," and the roar in his mind, unabated, is "not of the falls but of its rumor / unabated." The tumult is only a roar of books, and at one point Paterson exhorts himself to go back to the *actual* river for an answer, "for relief from 'meaning,' " back where all mouths are rinsed. The image of the Falls' "heavy plaits" is repeated twice, thus setting up Paterson's final resolution to "comb out the language—or succumb." And the image of the Falls is given an unusual twist, in the fire passage, in the description of the "waterfall of the / flames, a cataract reversed, shooting / upward."

This description of the cataract reversed is the only reference to the Falls in section ii, in which fire is the controlling element. In section iii, however, wherein the flood dominates, the water imagery is rich and suggestive. The passages on the 1902 disaster are also a detailed expression of the flood of words within Paterson's brain. Just as the water wipes out the slums, making rebuilding essential, so also the mental inundation purges the mind and makes way for a new language: "The words will have to be rebricked up, the / —what? What am I coming to . / pouring down?" (A similar idea is expressed following the burning of the library.) Only through destruction is the new creation possible, the phoenix rising while the nest is consumed.

Section iii begins with a passage of quiet, dream-like marine images, "a drumming of submerged / engines, a beat of propellers." (Williams was aware that the city of Paterson has a long history of submarine experimentation.) This is followed by "We walk into a dream, from certainty to the unascertained," suggesting the movement from the present into the clouded past. The tension between past, present, and future is of the utmost importance in this section. It poses one of the important questions—where is one to channel his energies?—that Paterson has to answer. The description of the flood begins with the falling of the rain, surfeiting the river's upper reaches. Things begin to break apart. The water is sullied, and the lilies drown in the muddy flux. At the same time,

> The stream
> grows leaden within him, his lilies drag. So
> be it. Texts mount and complicate them-
> selves, lead to further texts and those
> to synopses, digests and emendations. So be it.
> Until the words break loose or—sadly
> hold, unshaken. . . .

It is essential to the rejuvenation of the language that the words break loose. Before there can be a new measure the old, confining one must be destroyed. If the words "hold," the language, "sadly," will not be renewed.

The floods, within the city and within man ("to the teeth / to the very eyes"), continue parallel courses. The description of the dead dog in the river, descending "toward Acheron," adds a new dimension, suggesting Paterson's own descent into the dark night of his soul. The flood slowly "lifts to recognition in a / rachitic brain" at the same time that the water is "two feet now on the turnpike / and still rising." The flood reaches its peak as the water, a "piston, / cohabitous, scouring the stones," undermines the railroad embankment. At this point the mind too is undermined. The language breaks completely apart, and the words, splattered all over the page, are arbitrarily chosen. They have broken loose. The flood then recedes, leaving things formless:

> How to begin to find a shape—to begin to
>   begin again,
> turning the inside out : to find one phrase
>   that will
> lie married beside another for delight   .   ?
> —seems beyond attainment   .

This recognition of the possibilities (and terrific difficulties) of starting from scratch heightens the belief that there can be no return to the past. "There is no recurrence. / The past is dead." The final passage in the book returns to the symbol of the Falls:

> The past above, the future below
> and the present pouring down: the roar,
> the roar of the present, a speech—
> is, of necessity, my sole concern   .

At this point, Paterson does not speak of leaping into the Falls. The cataract is the "visible part" of the cascading language, and only by making of it a replica will his disease be cured. This can be accomplished not by remaining in the library, "to spend my life looking into the past." Rather, he must find his meaning in the present "and lay it, white, / beside the sliding water: myself— / comb out the language—or succumb." This image of combing the language is related to the earlier descriptions of the Falls' "heavy plaits." It also evokes the vignette in Book II of the man deliberately combing the long hair of a new-washed collie bitch, "until it lies, as he designs, like ripples in white sand giving off its clean-dog odor." Paterson has not yet found his meaning, but he has escaped the tyranny of an exhausted language. He has also been purged and renewed for greater seeking.

In discussing the river as symbol in Book IV it is essential to note that this section is described, in the Author's Note, as "the river below the falls," and that it is titled "The Run to the Sea." The river mingles with the ocean and carries the protagonist away from his city into the "world." In a note in the Yale papers, Williams projected the book as an attempt to "show the perverse confusions that come of a failure to untangle the language and make it our own as both man and woman are carried helplessly toward the sea (of blood) which, by their failures of speech, await them. The poet alone in this world holds the key to their final rescue."

The ideas of perverse confusions and of movement toward the sea are meshed in section i, in the words of the "poetess" who lives in an apartment high above the East River in Manhattan:

> That is the East River. The sun rises there.
> And beyond, is Blackwell's Island. Welfare Is-
>   land,
> City Island   .   whatever they call it now   .
> where the city's petty criminals, the poor
> the superannuated and the insane are
>   housed   .

This is a different scene from the richly natural one through which the river runs in New Jersey, and all that is left of "the elemental, the primitive" are three rocks tapering into the water, which the woman, with her romantic bent, and in her loneliness, calls "my sheep," and which Phyllis, the prosaic realist, admits are "white all right but it's from the gulls that crap them up all day long." These gulls, which are less in evidence in the inland river above the Falls, give an unclean, predatory mood to the book. They are introduced as impersonal scavengers in the passage describing the search for the body of the young girl suicide (possibly a parody of Eliot's "Death by Water"). Phyllis' description, with its reference to the "hellicopter [sic], "some student," and "the papers," contrasts strikingly, in its clinical detachment, with the sentimental language used to describe Mrs. Cumming's suicide leap. Her response is a vivid demonstration of the irrevocable movement toward the sea of blood, of indifferent men.

The older woman's interpretation of the same scene, in keeping with her literary pretensions, is more evocative. And yet here too an utter detachment and indifference come through:

> .   a whirring pterodactyl
> of a contrivance, to remind one of Da Vinci,
> searches the Hellgate current for some corpse,
> lest the gulls feed on it
> and its identity and its sex, *as* its hopes, and its
> despairs and its moles and its marks and
> its teeth and its nails be no longer decipherable
> and so lost   .

The corpse is simply an "It," unnamed, unknown, unlamented (save by the gulls, "vortices of despair"), another river-muted victim of the failure of speech. . . . The suicide theme is repeated (and completed) in the passage describing the lunch hour, as the expressionless faces "(canned fish)" read in the papers "of some student, come / waterlogged to the surface following / last night's thunderstorm . the flesh a / flesh of tears and fighting gulls." To point up the horror of this unnatural, impersonal death by water, Williams has "Corydon" comment, in a Yeatsian manner, on the fertile waters of Anticosti, "where the salmon / lie spawning in the sun in the shallow water." (pp. 89-94)

In section iii . . . the river again comes into the foreground, finally running into the "sea" toward which it has moved throughout the poem. Williams described the movement in the book as "the river of blood (escape or *attempted* escape to New York. His return 'home')." Thus the scene shifts from New York back to the area surrounding Paterson, where one again hears the constant roar of the water. The return to the Falls seems structurally inevitable since, as has been emphasized, it is the noise of the Falls that symbolizes the language "which we were and are seeking." The movement, however, is irresistibly in the direction of the sea—not the actual sea, but rather the "sea of blood."

Thus, section iii begins with a few lines of verse, including the statements that "all but for the tides, there is no river," and "The ocean yawns!" and then plunges immediately into a description of the bloody slaying, in 1779, of Jonathan Hopper. . . . This passage is followed by the phrase "Come on, get going. The tide's in." It is evident, by the other passages following, which deal with violence, that the tide is one of blood. These passages do not appear, however, until after Paterson has bid his farewell to the river, his "adored one," which he personifies in a manner reminiscent of Thoreau and Walden Pond. . . . (pp. 94-5)

This valedictory is followed by some loose lines on the Falls and the Paterson countryside, a letter from Allen Ginsberg about River Street, and a quiet description of a sunset. Again the calm is shattered, however, this time by a newspaper clipping about the murder of a baby girl by her twenty-two-year-old father. More slack description follows, and again it is interrupted, this time by the description of the violent knife and hatchet murder, in 1850, of old John Van Winkle and his wife. The supposed killer was John Johnson.

The remaining pages are written in a violent, choppy verse, which vividly evokes the sea of blood that slowly rises. . . . Again, the reference here is not to the actual ocean, but rather "the 'sea' of Book IV is a sea of objectively (Chaucer) indifferent *men:* bring it finally back to that." It is toward *this* sea (and the date mentioned ["October 10, 1950"] suggests the Korean conflict) that men and women, by their failures in speech, are carried to their deaths. Thus in planning this section Williams wrote: "begin with the first murder and end with the spectators on the Park Cliff watching the hanging." And so it is that the book ends with the image of John Johnson hanging in full view of the "thousands who had gathered"—the sea of indifferent men.

This hungry ocean, with its siren song evoking man's death wish, this ocean of savage lusts in which the wounded shark gnashes at his own tail, dominates the entire section. The despair generated by the remainders of the "blood dark sea" is softened, however, by the vignette that

precedes the words on Johnson's hanging, the image of the swimmer who walks from the *true* ocean, sleeps, gets dressed, spits out the seed of a beach plum, and heads inland, followed by his dog. It is in this passage that hope for a future lies: "It is the seed that floats to shore, one word, one tiny, even microscopic word, . . . which can alone save us." The book ends, thus, with alternating visions of life and death, "the spiral / the final somersault / the end," as the river mingles with the ocean.

This image of the spiral, which suggests a beginning as much as an end, is reiterated in one of the few river passages in Book V. After mentioning the serpent with its tail in its mouth, Williams adds, quoting from his early **"The Wanderer,"**

> "the river has returned to its beginnings"
> and backward
>   (and forward)
> it tortures itself within me
> until time has been washed finally under:

Except for [a] few scattered references to water, however, Book V has no particular bearing on the parallel flow of a river with man's life. As Williams said, "When the river ended in the sea I had no place to go but back in life. I had to take the spirit of the River up in the air." And so at the end of the five books the "rained down" river, having started above the Falls, crashed downward, and wandered toward its source in the ocean, is finally drawn back *up,* ending, however, not where it began, in the air, but rather in the boundless world of the imagination. (pp. 95-8)

> *Joel Conarroe, "The River," in his* William Carlos Williams' "Paterson": Language and Landscape, *University of Pennsylvania Press, 1970, pp. 81-98.*

Benjamin Sankey

Williams was a good observer, and he took pains in arranging words on a page to convey an impression; but he was also a man with opinions, something of a theorist, and not always inclined to omit his theories from his verse. A characteristic feature of Williams's style—just as characteristic, perhaps, as his close attention to detail—is a habit of exploding into semiphilosophical commentary. (Often, however, a move in the direction of general argument will also be a *formal* move, intended mainly to help organize the detail.) This habit, a kind of controlled self-indulgence, carries over into **Paterson,** where one of Williams's problems is to see to it that the reader divines the import of the materials.

There is plenty of good description in **Paterson,** but there is little that is purely descriptive in intent. Just about everything mentioned participates in the poem's symbolic argument, either as an instance or a symbol, referring by the logic of synecdoche or analogy (or by the quasilogic of pun) to one of Williams's major symbolic terms. When he describes the Park and the people in it, he is also describing the American people and the American continent. "Sunday in the Park" implies an elaborate myth about the American past. When he describes the leaps and recoveries of the waters at the Falls, he is also describing the course of a man's thoughts; and so on. As the reader learns to recognize the poem's recurrent metaphors (wind for spirit and inspiration, for instance) he will also begin to notice quick allusions to these key terms in passages that are ostensibly descriptive. (When Williams notes that there is "no wind," he can be taken to mean that inspiration is lacking, say, in the preacher's sermon.) The motto "No ideas but in things" does not mean that there will be no general ideas in the poem, or that the ideas will be "implicit," but only that the ideas at stake will be grounded on things present in actual experience and actually described in the poem. The consequences of this working principle are not the same as those that would follow if Williams were also committed to "realistic" conventions for drawing meaning from the things described. In **Paterson** a description can be entirely "realistic" (an exact presentation of something the poet has seen), and its implications nevertheless managed "nonrealistically" by means of pun or allegory.

Because Williams varies his procedures for deriving meaning from detail, **Paterson** is an unusually *tricky* poem.

The language of **Paterson** can be intricate and discontinuous; it can also be very natural and clear. Generally it is clear and natural except where special exigencies of transition or metaphor tempt Williams to skip over steps in the presentation of an idea, or to move without explanation or apology to a new subject. A certain calculated obscurity is, as we have seen, part of Williams's plan for the poem; it is as if he does not wish the reader to be entirely sure of the meaning of particular passages until he has grasped the overall argument. Where the language is obscure, it will often be because Williams breaks off a sentence or introduces an ambiguous pronoun reference. (Often a change in line form or a shift to prose will signal a change of the foreground subject, though the general line of argument continues despite the shift.) Other obscurities are caused by Williams's handling of metaphor. He is willing to let the meaning of a metaphorical term be influenced by (or depend on) an oblique relation to one of the poem's main symbols; he is also willing to mix his metaphors pretty drastically, and a passage of complicated mixed metaphor with syntactic loose ends can present the reader with some problems. Yet, with all his indulgence in tricks and special usages, Williams remained [as he stated in a letter] "a stickler for the normal contour of phrase which is characteristic of the language as we speak it."

The naturalness and clarity of Williams's language can be illustrated by a descriptive passage from Book Two:

> At last he comes to the idlers' favorite
> haunts, the picturesque summit, where
> the blue-stone (rust-red where exposed)
> has been faulted at various levels
>   (ferns rife among the stones)
> into rough terraces and partly closed in
> dens of sweet grass, the ground gently sloping.

Here the purpose is to describe a scene clearly while at the same time carrying along the symbolic argument, not too obtrusively. The language is quiet and precise, but not ostentatious about its precision, ranging from the offhand public phrasing of "the picturesque summit" to a techni-

cal formulation ("has been *faulted* at various levels") and to the visual precision of "rust-red where exposed." The reader can picture the terraces caused by the faulting; at the same time, some of the words point to an abstract argument. The *rifeness* of the vegetation, for instance, indicates the unguided profusion of natural growth (an aspect of the "elemental" scene) and also the multiplicity of the poet's material (in contrast with the simplicity and unity of the supporting rock).

The lines have a structure firm enough to give force and movement to the description. The clear shape of the lines on the page makes available the runover principle, which helps to produce the relaxed but quick movement and a certain matter-of-factness of tone.

The versification of **Paterson** is reasonably varied, and it should be pointed out that the verse of **Paterson** dates from various stages of Williams's career. Some of the verse is quite early (specifically, passages from **"The Wanderer . . . "** used in Book Two with slight revision). Again, the passages of descriptive reminiscences in Book Four, section 3, are earlier than one would think; Williams seems originally to have written them as a beginning for the poem, set them aside, and then returned to them when he had (as he felt) almost completed a later version of it. (Among the latest material in **Paterson** is much of the prose: prose passages often replace verse.)

Like everything else in the poem, the versification is uneven—deliberately so, since the verse includes unfinished fragments intended to be set off against finished passages. (The typescripts show that almost everything was carefully reworked, often typed and revised and retyped many times, and that the placement of words in the line was a prominent consideration as Williams revised.) Still, though the versification is various and to an extent uneven, it should be possible to generalize a bit about the line forms employed. For one thing, the verse is "free," in the obvious sense that it is not governed by any system for counting accents or syllables or feet; there is almost no rhyme (and what little there is aims for special effects). The lines have sufficient structure to support the syntax and to allow for clear variations of movement and emphasis. (The line structure, indeed, seems conceived mainly as a principle to support and play off against the syntax.) The lines are firm enough for the runover principle to function effectively.

There are some little "songs," scattered throughout the poem, with short lines and stanza-like shapes on the page.

In general, I should say, the verse is not nearly so "prose-like" as some of the reviewers found it. There is a form—or, rather, a set of related forms—and Williams knew what he was doing with them. Whatever may be said of the overall plan of the poem, the construction of the poem's elements, and particularly the management of the line, was very careful. The success of the versification (and it seems to me largely successful) was a result of Williams's experience and tact, and of extremely attentive revision. Williams also had theories about versification, and it may be useful to conclude this account by quoting from a discussion of these theories as they relate to Williams's practice. In a review of *Pictures from Brueghel* [in *Poetry*, February 1963], Alan Stephens points out that Williams's late notion of a "variable foot" could not quite do what Williams claimed for it. " 'Measure' calls for a unit of measurement, and in our verse you can select your unit from only a few possibilities: you can count beats, or syllables, or feet constructed of definite and recurrent combinations of stressed and unstressed syllables; the identity of the line is a matter of simple arithmetic, and you will search in vain for such a basis in Dr. Williams's line." But Stephens goes on to point out that there is a traditional basis for Williams's line; and this would apply to *Paterson* as well as to the later verse.

> I believe that the identity of Dr. Williams's line has no metrical basis, but that nonetheless the line has a definable identity. The general principle is this: a line is a line because, *relative to neighboring lines,* it contains that which makes it in its own right a unit of the attention; and it is as precisely various in its way as are the shadings of accent that play about the abstract norm of the metrical foot, for it too has a norm against which it almost constantly varies, allowing for feats of focusing on values that would be otherwise indistinguishable. The norm is the ordinary unit of the attention in language—the formal architecture of the sentence. This principle, it seems to me, also underlies verse with a metrical basis—is indeed the ultimate principle of all verse; if this is so, then audible rhythm, whether produced by a formal metric or by improvisation, is not the supreme fact of the verse line (though it is of course indispensable) and Dr. Williams will have been working in the tradition all along.

Williams in *Paterson* experiments with the mixture, or alternation, of highly sophisticated "literary" procedures and the spontaneous, uncalculated. Certain features of the poem are inconceivable apart from a self-conscious literary tradition going back to Joyce and early Pound (and, through these writers, to the pre-Raphaelites, say, or to Gautier or Flaubert). But other features are inconceivable apart from Williams's temperament—his impatience, his distrust of logic, his quickness to invent procedures, to take chances without much concern about the implications of particular maneuvers. The effect of this hybrid procedure is to keep the reader fascinated and a bit dazed. (pp. 19-23)

> *Benjamin Sankey, in an introduction to his* A Companion to William Carlos Williams's "Paterson," *University of California Press, 1971, pp. 1-26.*

Mutlu Konuk Blasing

[The] constant creation of novelty implies the simultaneous destruction of the old, and Williams insists throughout *Paterson* that destruction is in fact central to the process of creation:

> Beautiful thing:
>
> —a dark flame,

a wind, a flood—counter to all staleness.

In this idea of the "beautiful thing" as "the flame's lover" we see a stylistic similarity between radical art and radical politics, which is as significant as their material and historical connections. [Harold Rosenberg writes in "The Avant Garde" in *Discovering the Present*] that the vanguards "have infused into art the passion and momentum of radical politics. Their intellectual do-or-die is among their major contributions; it has restored seriousness to the arts and prevented them from degenerating into mere crafts under the pressure of the industrial age." Williams felt the full force of this pressure, and his response has seriousness because he was able to achieve a militant *style,* which gave his voice urgency without recourse to dogma, systems, or theories.

Williams's culturally radical poetics, in which the supreme reality of history confers value on change and newness both in social systems and in the arts, informs his cultural autobiography *Paterson,* which embodies the new not only in its subject but in its structure. In the dialectical view of change that Williams's concept of the mutually regenerative relationship between art and society posits, both art and social life change by absorbing their opposition. Art changes by incorporating hitherto nonartistic realities, and each truly new work is self-transcending, for it redefines art by changing, expanding, and even vulgarizing the definition of art. In the case of *Paterson,* the nonpoetic provides for Williams's very poetics and informs the poem's subject, structure, and language. Thus *Paterson* may be seen as poetry in the process of self-definition; it redefines poetry itself, because it embodies the vulgarization of poetic subject, language, and structure *and* remains poetry. For Williams's "beautiful thing" is not perfection but life, whose "vulgarity of beauty surpasses all their / perfections!"

To begin with, the vulgarization of subject matter involves moving away from "poetic" subjects to the quotidian as subject, and Williams's subject is the urban industrial environment in all its "nonpoetic" aspects. He does not choose to write about a Brooklyn Bridge or a New York City, which might more easily be seen as heroic, if only in its conception; instead, he chooses Paterson, which points to nothing beyond itself. Moreover, Williams does not choose to make his "modern" subject heroic through sheer poetic will power, as Hart Crane does, nor does he back out of it, as T. S. Eliot does. Rather, he searches for a way to talk about Paterson on its own terms and as he knows it: "I *knew* of these things. I had *heard.* I had *taken part* in some of the incidents that made up the place. I had *heard* Billy Sunday: I had *talked* with John Reed: I had in my hospital experiences *got to know* many of the women" (italics mine). The difficulty was how to talk about all this *as a poet,* for "it called for a poetry such as I did not know." In other words, the problem became how "to *make* a poem, fulfilling the requirements of the art, and yet new, in the sense that in the very lay of the syllables Paterson as Paterson would be discovered." His stance, then, is that of a self-consciously poeticizing poet facing up to Paterson *as it is.* And this confrontation itself amounts to a transformation of the art and the place. For his announcement in *Spring and All* characterizes the poet of *Paterson* as well: "I speak for the integrity of the soul and the *greatness* of life's inanity; the *formality* of its boredom; the *orthodoxy* of its stupidity."

Williams's culturally radical poetics, in which the supreme reality of history confers value on change and newness both in social systems and the arts, informs his cultural autobiography *Paterson,* which embodies the new not only in its subject but in its structure.

The tension in the poem, then, is between Paterson and poetry or between "everyday life in the modern world" and the poet's task of reconciling "the people and the stones." The figure of the city embodies this tension, for the city is both Paterson and the Dr. Paterson who dreams it up—both fact and poetic subject, both earth and the human "speech" that shaped it into a city. And the power of *Paterson* derives from Williams's maintaining the tension between the poet and his subject, so that neither is negated by the other. . . . The image of modern life in Book 2, for example, is as chilling as anything in *The Waste Land;* the industrial city, Williams tells us, reflects the alienation—fostered by Christianity and capitalism—of its inhabitants from the earth under their feet, from what is near and real. To detach one's imagination from the local and the real and to come to see the earth as the "excrement of some sky" is, he insists [in his poem **"To Elsie"**] what "destroys" us. Williams, however, does not throw up his hands at this point and take refuge in mysticism. Not only does his vision remain inclusive and enable him to interweave what he hears, sees, and thinks and the "poems" that he writes, but he remains grounded in the earth. "That the poet, / . . . should borrow from erudition / . . . (borrowing from those he hates, to his own / disfranchisement)" is indeed a "disgrace" for Williams, and his hymn to earth or the giant of the place answers "erudite" poets as well as ministers and capitalists. . . . What makes Williams such an effective voice, then, is that as a poet he does precisely what he asks of his townspeople: he returns to the city and owns up to the social and economic realities of the local present. He knows that "We cannot go to the country / for the country will bring us no peace":

> Though you praise us
> and call to mind the poets
> who sung of our loveliness
> it was long ago!
> long ago! when country people
> would plow and sow with
> flowering minds and pockets
>   at ease—
> if ever this were true.

Once, when people still made their living from the earth, there was drama in country life, and the country might

have saved us. But [as Williams writes in **"Raleigh Was Right"**] "not now":

> Empty pockets make empty heads.
> Cure it if you can but
> do not believe that we can live
> today in the country

Left with the city, we must learn to regard cities not as abnormal growths but as part of present "nature"—as embodying the dramatic encounter of the human and the natural. We must accept what Santayana's Oliver in *The Last Puritan* cannot: " . . . cities are a second body for the human mind, a second organism, more rational, permanent and decorative than the animal organism of flesh and bone: a work of natural yet moral art."

Book 3, which this quote opens, insists that we must come to know the city as a living organic entity, since our salvation lies in city life. [In a footnote, Blasing adds that "Williams would agree with urban theorists like Lewis Mumford and Henri Lefebvre that the city is the locus of the drama of modern life. See Mumford, *The Culture of Cities;* and Lefebvre, *Everyday Life in the Modern World.* ***Paterson*** is full of the kind of chance encounters that only a city can provide, perhaps the most stunning being Williams's meeting the thin, old woman in Bk. 5. Through such encounters, one retains a sense of life as *drama,* which is precisely a sense of life as a creative and self-creative process."] Thus the poet must study the history of Paterson, even while asking himself, "Why do I bother with this / rubbish?" The written history of the city is "rubbish" because it is dead residue when compared with the city. If the written history is dead stuff, however, there is also a living history of the city. For we can regard the city itself as writing—as a text "written" by its population, past and present. The numerous analogies in Book 3 between the city and writing affirm that the present shape of the city *is* its history. Like all living organisms, then, the city embodies its history. And as a living organism, the modern city—the creation of industrialism—has the potential to withstand the destructiveness of technological society, which conceives of time as speed and of history as obsolescence. The living city stands forth as the present reality of its past and upholds the idea of time as a creative force as opposed to the concept of time as destruction.

In the balance between Paterson and poetry that Williams maintains throughout his poem, ideas about the nonpoetic environment work equally well as ideas about poetry, and Paterson and *Paterson* are never too far apart. In Book 3, for example, Williams affirms the reality of the present city and defends the act of his writing in the same move. First, he admits the lifelessness of all writing that is historical recording:

> We read: not the flames
> but the ruin left
> by the conflagration
>
> Not the enormous burning
> but the dead (the books
> remaining). . . .
>
> Dig in—and you have
>
> a nothing, surrounded by

a surface, an inverted
bell resounding, a

white-hot man become
a book, the emptiness of
a cavern resounding

As art, however, writing also has the power to transcend history and to counter the passage of time by creating a permanence:

Through this hole
at the bottom of the cavern
of death, the imagination
escapes intact.

This is possible in poetry because a poem lives or embodies its history, which it is still making each time it is read. Because poetry embodies its history in a *temporal* structure, moreover, it is capable of withstanding its own dissipation of energy; as Williams asserts, a poem does not "grow old and rot" but remains sensual. Since anything that does not change "rots," the poem survives as long as it changes. Writing is "dead" to the extent that it approaches written history and opposes itself to "spontaneous Life." In the historical account that Dr. Paterson is reading, for example, even the fire—which represents the destructive-creative force—remains unreal. And if poetry is to partake of the reality of "spontaneous Life," it must itself become as destructive as the fire. The fire of the city, which is the subject, must become *within* the poem a fire of the "library" as well. The very form of the fire-poem, then, must represent the destruction or "burning" of all past dead writing:

Hell's fire. Fire. Sit your horny ass
down. What's your game? Beat you
at your own game, Fire. Outlast you:
Poet Beats Fire at Its Own Game! . . .

Thus art lives only if it is "careless," spontaneous, and as naturally destructive as life itself:

Beautiful thing

—intertwined with the fire. An identity
surmounting the world, its core—from which
we shrink squirting little hoses of
objection . . .

Accordingly, Williams's prescriptions for the ills both of modern poetry and of modern life are the same. Like *Paterson,* the city can be a "marriage" of people and place:

What end but love, that stares death in the eye?
A city, a marriage—that stares death
in the eye

Similarly, Williams's insistence on localism in poetry has its counterpart in his demand for urban localism. Given the wholeness of his thought, this total localism amounts to a cultural revolution. Such a revolution, heralded by poets who write to the giant of the place, would not only provide for "LOCAL control of local purchasing / power" but would begin at the beginning and teach people to live *in* the world, to

WALK in the world
(you can't see anything

from a car window, still less
from a plane, or from the moon!? Come
off of it.)

Williams's thought here would seem to be revolutionary on the American model: a poet must first change the hearts of the people, and then urbanism and political and economic reorganization will naturally follow. Since destruction always accompanies creation in Williams, however, his vision of change would not necessarily exclude violence. In any case, his focus on the city enabled him to envision a cultural revolution involving simultaneous economic and cultural changes. A localist and inclusive art could lead to a regeneration of everyday life, since it had itself been generated by the social life. The sources as well as the aims of this kind of art, then, are ultimately not aesthetic but social. Choosing the industrial city as the subject of his poem, Williams came to conceive of the sources and aims of poetry in primarily social terms. Thus his poetic purpose in *Paterson* is to minister to the needs of his local parish, to give his people speech so that the "torrent in their minds" may not be "foreign to them," and to marry them to their local environment so that their daily lives may become self-expression or self-creation.

The "vulgarization" of language in *Paterson* is "of a piece" with this kind of cultural regeneration. In its language, *Paterson* moves away from Poetry or Art toward more impersonal cultural utterance, for the vulgarization of language involves the incorporation not only of slang, street talk, everyday expressions, and found language but of prose rhythms and structures and even prose itself. Williams's readers have discussed his use of nonpoetic language and prose in *Paterson* in terms of the then-current art movements, especially Cubism. Bram Dijkstra, who studies the influence of Cubism on Williams's early poetry, asserts [in *The Hieroglyphics of a New Speech*] that Williams's development from a derivative poet to a radically innovative one is the result of his moving away from literary precedents and inspiration and reformulating his art according to the stylistic concepts of the new painters. Similarly, Jerome Mazzaro, who traces the influence of Cubism on Williams's later poetry, regards his use of prose and poetry "as two different facet-planes" as analogous to the "dimensionality" of analytic Cubism. [According to Mazzaro in *William Carlos Williams,* by] the time of *Paterson,* however, Williams had arrived at a poetry closer to synthetic Cubism: " . . . for it was not until he began to incorporate items from newspapers and segments of historical documents and letters that one can say that art space begins to intrude on life space and the collage begins." Thus his incorporation of the world outside art parallels the Cubists' use of newspapers, wallpaper, pieces of cloth, and so on, which also served to transform the art space into life space. In Gertrude Stein's terms, such works wanted to come outside their frames and establish contact with their nonartistic environment.

Mazzaro's interpretation of the significance of Williams's collage method is based on a view of Williams's daily life as embodying the psychic tensions of his being at once doctor and poet. The tension between the doctor and the artist or between life and art in Williams's life is reflected in the conflict between prose and poetry in his work. Mazzaro explains how this conflict is worked out in *Kora in Hell*:

> These language experiments [prose and poetry echoing themes], in which the operative mode of a poem becomes its thematic statement, approximate attempts by the poet to devise a style consistent with the mythic patterns of his work, devoid of as much subjectivism as possible, to represent how Williams the desperate, descending hero is also Williams the ascendant, Orphean singer. The mood making the poem is also the poem made.

This reading works for *Kora in Hell* by establishing the connection between its style and its subject. Since *Paterson* is not only autobiographical but has an announced cultural subject as well, however, we must look into the cultural-artistic implications of Williams's method. The counterpointing of poetry and found prose represents a dramatic encounter of art and nonart or city art and city life, which are the two aspects of Williams's subject. For he is involved in a conversation both with his historical urban environment and with his art. And it is in the act of juxtaposing poetry and found prose that art and the environment enter into a dialectical relationship. The question now becomes whether art is absorbed into the environment, whether the environment is transformed by the art, or whether both occur at once.

Harold Rosenberg observes that in collage—an expression of an advanced industrial age—art no longer copies nature, as in the classical model, or seeks equivalents to it, as in the Romantic and symbolist ideas of parallel structures; instead, art appropriates the external world on the assumption that it is already changed into art. This is exactly how Williams understood the redefinition of poetry in his own time. He writes, for example, that Pound can effectively incorporate prose in his work because all his material is already "changed in *kind* from other statement." Thus the use of prose becomes in fact a poetic device. "All the prose" in *Paterson,* Williams claims, "has primarily the purpose of giving a metrical meaning to or of emphasizing a metrical continuity between all word use. It is *not* an antipoetic device. . . . It *is* that prose and verse are both *writing,* both a matter of the words and an interrelation between words for the purpose of exposition, or other better defined purpose of *the art* "; consequently, "poetry does not *have* to be kept away from prose as Mr. Eliot might insist, it goes *along with* prose and, companionably." In Williams's method, then, the use of prose does not define poetry by way of contrast; rather, poetry is redefined by its tolerance for and ability to incorporate prose or nonart. Art and its nonart environment, therefore, transform each other in their encounter in *Paterson.*

In this sense, the use of the collage method implies the presence of a rather overwhelming environment, and the collage is understandably a product of urban industrial society, where the difficulty is how to pull such disparate and "divorced" elements into something "fulfilling the requirements of the art":

> . . . a mass of detail
> to interrelate on a new ground, difficulty;

> an assonance, a homologue
>   triple piled
> pulling the disparate together to clarify
> and compress

Since divorce is so widespread, any synthesis of the fragments—if such a synthesis is possible at all—has to be more than literary, and Williams's collage method represents in fact a cultural synthesis. As a cultural synthesis, collage takes us beyond individualism in the arts. Daniel-Henry Kahnweiler points out, for example, that Gris and Picasso understood the essentially impersonal nature of collage, for a great number of their collages are unsigned. Yet such impersonality is only one pole of modern art, which oscillates, in Rosenberg's words, between the extremes of the selfless eye and brain and omnipotent identity. This tension is very much present in *Paterson,* Williams's collage poem. For although the overwhelming environment of Paterson casts the poet as a selfless eye, the poet also incorporates the environment into his work and thereby radically redefines his art. In this process the poet becomes so omnipotent that, in effect, whatever he says is art *is* art, and Williams would agree with Allen Ginsberg's "Beauty is where I hang my hat. And reality. And America." Indeed, the poet is so omnipotent *and* impersonal that his name and the name of his city are the same. Louis Martz notes [in "The Unicorn in *Paterson:* William Carlos Williams"] that *Paterson*—incorporating as it does history, newspapers, conversations, overheard speech, and so on—is in a sense written by the entire milling population of Paterson. The real significance of the method of *Paterson,* however, is that it represents a *cultural collaboration.* Williams's art is a kind of socialist art, for in *Paterson* the culture is creating itself in conversation with the poet, who is barely a poet: "I have defeated myself purposely in almost everything I do because I don't want to be thought an artist. I much prefer to be an ordinary person. I never wanted to be separated from my fellow mortals by acting like an artist. . . . I wanted to be something rare but not to have it separate me from the crowd." Thus in *Paterson* the verbal environment of common usage and the poet enter into a dialectical relationship, in which each continuously transforms the other and neither is allowed to establish a tyranny over the other.

Finally, since Williams is indeed more interested in the "bloody loam" than in the "finished product," *Paterson* represents a thorough vulgarization of structure, and change does in fact show through it. The vulgarization of structure involves rejecting preconceived, formal, and "structuring" structures in favor of more "historical" structures that might have a better chance of capturing

> The vague accuracies of events dancing two
> and two with language which they
> forever surpass . . .

This development in effect equates writing with action, for what becomes important for the writer is not the question of form but the discovery of a kind of writing that has a direct relationship with one's perceptions and that will attest to the authenticity of one's experience. It follows, then, that

> The writing is nothing, the being

in a position to write (that's

where they get you) is nine tenths
of the difficulty . . .

. . . So that
to write, nine tenths of the problem
is to live. . . .

Thus there must be a life to authenticate the writing, just as in the long run there must be the writing to authenticate the life. And if Henry James, for example, would emphasize the second half of this equation, Williams would stress the first. This kind of art would necessitate a certain vulgarization of structure; more autobiographical, it would be informed by orders found, not imposed.

Autobiographical writing in general is open-ended and potentially very congenial to novelty in form, structure, and language, because it is responsive to the historical particularity of the writer's experience. The historical emphasis of autobiographical writing, which in effect equates living and writing, constitutes a continuous source of novelty. The same historical emphasis underlies avant-garde art in general, and in avant-garde writing the definition of art continuously expands, because it is the writer's *attitude* toward his or her material—any material, however unartistic—that determines whether one's activity is art. As a result, the danger of the extreme avant-garde position is that its historical emphasis on the value of change can itself be undermined: if *anything* is art, it would follow that art is nothing in particular, and this position does not allow room for change. Yet the important question for all art is whether it changes. (pp. 121-33)

It is Williams's insistence on and faith in change as a social and aesthetic value that saves him from a suicidal avant-gardism, which negates change itself. He writes [in his *Selected Essays*]: "There is nothing sacred about literature, it is damned from one end to the other. There is nothing in literature but change and change is mockery. I'll write whatever I damn please, whenever I damn please and as I damn please and it'll be good if the authentic spirit of change is on it." Although he would dissociate art from the Museum or Library and would have it become inclusive and profane, he would not say that anything is art, because he affirms change as value. As a result, a curious, homemade formalism sneaks in through the back door in the form of his lifelong insistence on "measure" and the "variable foot," which nevertheless remain more or less mystical. The social emphasis of his poetry also kept him from losing sight of the social relationships and interactions that constitute art. Even avant-garde art is based on such communication. For if art is what the artist says is art, and if an artist is someone who the public says is an artist, art comes to be partly a matter of belief or faith, since the audience has to believe in the artist. As we can see from the passionate acclamations or denunciations that it inspires, avant-garde art in fact absorbs the energies of both religion and politics. If art is a matter of faith, the object created, chosen, or found by the artist becomes a medium of communication between the audience and the artist, because they understand each other when they agree to call X art. And in this act the artist and the audience or society meet, thereby defining their present, shap-

ing their culture, and making history. This idea of art as communication between two people that changes both is one way of understanding the concept of change-as-structure. Ultimately, then, Williams judged the success of a work of art by whether it communicated. He says of a Cummings poem, for example, that it is not art for him, because he can "get no meaning at all" from it. And of his own work he writes:

. . . what good is it to me
if you can't understand it?
But you got to try hard—

When art is understood as social communication, it gains seriousness, for in becoming a historical event it assumes moral significance. In return, however, art loses the privilege of being protected from time; self-consciously historical, it protects its own destruction, since it must necessarily be surpassed. Poe was one of the first literary theorists who not only understood a work of literature as a temporal construct but accepted the full implications of this view. As a temporal construct, a work dissipates its energy both within the limits of its first and last lines and in the course of its public history as a cultural product. Because it is a long poem and because Williams chooses an explicitly historical structure for his poem, dissipation of energy characterizes the movement of *Paterson*. Williams starts out confessing that he does not know where the poem will lead:

There is no direction. Whither? I
cannot say. I cannot say
more than how. The how (the howl) only
is at my disposal (proposal) . . .

By Book 4, however, it becomes clear that the progression of the poem has been more a dissipation: "What I miss, said your mother, is the poetry, the pure poem of the first parts," and he asks himself, "Haven't you forgot your virgin purpose, / the language?"

Paterson is Williams's autobiography both because it includes a wide variety of facts and details of his daily life and because its growth through destruction represents a formal repetition of the poet's own progress as well as of his current concerns. The poem, like the life it would incorporate, is a temporal structure: its very nature is temporal change. As a result, the poem also embodies the destruction that all creation entails.

Williams comes to the defense of his historical, autobiographical form and cites a number of personal, cultural, and scientific examples of progress through dissipation, which is simply another instance of creation through destruction. The father-son conflict in this section is one example. The sons—including poetic "sons" like Allen Ginsberg—will come to replace the fathers: "The best

thing a man can do for his son, when he is born, is to die."
The splitting of the atom to release energy from matter,
embryonic fission leading to birth, the breaking up of the
poetic foot to energize the "field" of the page, and the
splintering of the epic narrator's voice for the dramatic energy of interacting voices are all processes analogous to
the growth of the poem through the dissipation of energy.
All are forms of creative destruction, and their use in *Paterson* reflects personal motives. For by Book 4 it is plain
that the poem and the poet both evolve through dissipation of energy. The poem *does* leave behind the "pure" poetry of the earlier parts, Williams *is* aging between Book
I and Book 4, and the world *is* destroying itself in the Korean War. Thus the method of composition-as-
decomposition in the long, autobiographical poem not
only parallels the progress of the poet, who "composes"
and decomposes, but proves adequate to Williams's relationship to his subject-environment:

> . . .—in your
> composition and decomposition
> I find my
>   despair!

Williams's need to believe that something good will eventually come out of all the destruction is expressed in his
formula that dissonance is discovery:

> Dissonance
> (if you are interested)
> leads to discovery

This idea finds support both in the history of science, since

> A dissonance
> in the valence of Uranium
> led to the discovery [of radium,]

and in the image of love as "antagonistic cooperation"
that leads to creation. We can read this formula as his justification not only of his subject—Paterson as an environment of dissonance—but of his composite poetic, personal, and public voice and of his literary method of working
through the dissonance of poetry and prose in the earlier
books. The power and the credibility of his assertion, however, are that it emerges out of his current experience of
the drift of *Paterson,* of himself as aging, and of the Korean War. In reading *Paterson,* then, we should keep in
mind that Williams took more than ten years to write it.
For his form evolved just as his personality evolved—in
time. Strictly autobiographical writing stimulates the temporal evolution of personality by structuring it as a story.
But in *Paterson* personality and form evolve simultaneously, since the recording coincides in time with the experience that it partially creates; indeed, the two are not
easily separable:

> nothing is so unclear, between man and
> his writing, as to which is the man and
> which the thing and of them both which
> is the more to be valued

Thus *Paterson* is Williams's autobiography both because
it includes a wide variety of facts and details of his daily
life and because its growth through destruction represents
a formal repetition of the poet's own progress as well as
of his current concerns. The poem, like the life it would

incorporate, is a temporal structure: its very nature is temporal change. As a result, the poem also embodies the destruction that all creation entails. For it is the ongoing
"dissipation" of the poet and the poem that enables both
to move on. *Paterson,* then, is so steeped in Williams's
life—in his psychic, political, and scientific environment—that its structure is itself part of that environment.
The poetic "escape" of *Paterson* lies through—not outside—the nonpoetic experience, for Williams takes his
own advice:

> Escape from it—but not by running
> away. Not by "composition." Embrace the
> foulness

Moreover, *as* history *Paterson* itself can only "progress"
through literary and cultural history by dissipating its energy. Marcel Duchamp remarks about painting that "after
forty or fifty years a picture dies, because its freshness disappears." A painting dies when it no longer inspires painters and new paintings and becomes an object. Williams
also believes that the forms of art evolve in conjunction
with historical change: "Of course I'm iconoclastic. . . .
An artist has to be. A continual break down and build up
has to go on. Take the forms in which poems are cast.
Most of them are old, not suited to our times. We have to
cast about searching for new ones. . . . Pretty soon, they
will become old hat. Somebody else will have to work to
get rid of them." A poem, then, is a high-energy structure
that runs down in time, and the creation of new art involves the destruction of the stabilized old art. Jouffroy describes this kind of destruction as the change of a "permanent order" into a "provisional disorder." "Provisional
disorder" suggests that art prepares its history and steps
into it; when the provisional disorder reverts back to an
order, the work stabilizes and becomes inert, like a piece
of lead.

Paterson embodies such a provisional disorder, for it exists as a dialog between order and disorder. As we have
seen, its structure is not really a structure; its growth is in
fact a dissipation; its "poetry" is always threatening to dis-
integrate into prose or worse, as in the "poem" in which
the straight lines of print are violated; and its measure has
no measure. "The foot not being fixed," Williams writes,
"is only to be described as variable. If the foot itself is variable it allows order in so-called free verse. Thus the verse
becomes not free at all but just simply variable, as all
things in life properly are." This telling definition of that
anomaly the "variable foot" is one more expression of the
dialog between art and life that sustains Williams's poetry.
Since his forms derive from life and, properly speaking,
are not forms at all, the charge of his work is far from
dead, as his wide and steady influence attests.

Paterson is a radical poem, because change—social *and*
artistic—is both the ultimate value that the poem upholds
and the supreme reality that it embodies. Williams understood his poem as an act aimed at changing social life and
his art at the same time. The reader's confrontation with
Paterson becomes a kind of action as well, for the poem
requires not merely an intellectual response but a change
of consciousness on the reader's part if it is to become a
"poem." And in forcing the reader to follow the author's

act of self-creation through art, *Paterson* tests the limits of autobiographical writing: the poet generates his continuous self-creation in a language and form of change, which in turn lead the reader to reenact the experience of the work. As history becomes form, then, form itself becomes a historical experience, a provisional disorder, which transforms both reader and poet. And as the occasion for the reader's as well as the poet's self-creation, this kind of autobiographical art implies the creation of a new culture, for it in effect regenerates everyday life. (pp. 134-39)

> *Mutlu Konuk Blasing, "Two Poets: 'Paterson,'*
> *Notes Toward an American Revolution, Frank*
> *O'Hara and the Poetics of Love," in her* The
> Art of Life: Studies in American Autobio-
> graphical Literature, *University of Texas*
> *Press, 1977, pp. 113-156.*

James E. Miller, Jr.

Williams repeatedly asserted that [*Paterson*] constituted a search for a redeeming language. The question remains, Did he find it? . . . Of the poem's many languages, there is first and foremost the Language of Chaos: there is the unmistakably less robust Language of Beauty; and there is the more fragile Language of Redemption. As we comb out these languages we shall simplify, but they will immediately re-entangle themselves in the poem where they shall remain inviolate.

The loudest language of *Paterson* is the language of chaos, of criticism, the language which the poet finds as the reality of Paterson, the reality of America. Indeed, a first reading of the poem might well leave the impression that it is the only language because it is so dominant. The voiceless drownings of Sam Patch (who used the symbolic name of Noah Faitoute Paterson, thus enabling the poet to identify with him) and Mrs. Cumming offer a paradigm for a languageless, perishing America, suffering from "blockage" (it's there but it's damned up, blocked) and from "divorce," a failure of connecting humanly because of a failure of language. But the Patch-Cumming episodes are only the most vivid of a large cluster of related images of failure:

> The language, the language
>   fails them
> They do not know the words
>   or have not
> the courage to use them   .
>   —girls from
> families that have decayed and
> taken to the hills. no words.
> They may look at the torrent in
>   their minds
> and it is foreign to them.   .
>
> They turn their backs
> and grow faint—but recover!
>   Life is sweet
> they say: the language!
>   —the language
> is divorced from their minds,
> the language   .   .   the language!

It is not, of course, that there is no language at all: worse,

there is abundant language (or sound) that misleads and betrays:

> A false language. A true. A false language pour-
>   ing—a
> language (misunderstood) pouring (misinter-
>   preted) without
> dignity, without minister, crashing upon a stone
>   ear.

By divorce Williams does not of course have reference simply to matrimony: his notion of divorce goes much deeper, with profounder consequences:

>   a bud forever green,
> tight-curled, upon the pavement, perfect
> in juice and substance but divorced, divorced
> from its fellows, fallen low—
>
>   Divorce is
> the sign of knowledge in our time,
> divorce! divorce!
>
>   with the roar of the river
> forever in our ears (arrears)
> inducing sleep and silence, the roar
> of eternal sleep   .   .   .   challenging
> our waking—

This divorce is a severance from the fruition of life itself. In divorce "from its fellows," the bud remains "forever green." Thus Williams suggests a profound immaturity characteristic of America, with the energy and potential present but unrealized. And the divorce is clearly related to the "roar" which communicates nothing but its un-combed sound, rendering genuine human connection difficult if not impossible. Life roars by and leaves nothing in its wake but a trailing silence, "the roar / of eternal sleep," death, the final and lasting divorce.

In Book II of *Paterson,* the poet-protagonist's Sunday walk through the park brings into focus some of the causes of blockage and divorce. There is, first of all, the people— Alexander Hamilton's "great beast"—coarsened by a life of hard work. . . . Their Sunday relaxation suggests the nature of the other days of their lives—days in the factories and businesses of Paterson earning the money for survival. In what is potentially an Eliotic *Waste Land* scene, the "great beast" of the people ignoring the traditional meaning of Sunday and wasting their time in meaningless activities, drinking beer, playing ball, quarreling and napping, we encounter a vision closer to Whitman's than to Eliot's: there is sympathy and understanding and searching as Paterson walks through the park. "Cash is mulct of them that others may live / secure / . . . and knowledge restricted." A significant part of the poet's vision comes in a prose passage: "Even during the Revolution Hamilton had been impressed by the site of the Great Falls of the Passaic. His fertile imagination envisioned a great manufacturing center, a great Federal City, to supply the needs of the country. Here was water-power to turn the mill wheels and the navigable river to carry manufactured goods to the market centers: a national manufactury." Williams had been attracted to Paterson and its Passaic Falls precisely because of Hamilton's historical involvement, his vision of great material wealth, prototype of the American dream. Somewhere, back in the past, in the visionary planning of such as Hamilton, lies the cause of the wastes on display on Sunday in the park.

There is one man in the park who speaks a torrent of words: Klaus, the "Protestant! protesting—as / though the world were his own." In telling his story to the Sunday park strollers, he reveals himself the victim of the American dream—victim in the sense that he came to America, made the riches he dreamed of, and discovered in a visitation from "our blessed Lord" that he was not happy. He followed the injunction to give away all his money and found finally in his evangelism the way to happiness: "There is no / end to the treasures of our Blessed Lord who / died on the Cross for us that we may be saved." We no sooner read the "Amen" to Klaus's familiar revival sermon than we find ourselves in a prose passage describing the Federal Reserve System in the U.S., a private enterprise that creates money and lends it at high interest, forcing the people to "pay interest to the banks in the form of high taxes." Usury, a familiar theme from Ezra Pound's *Cantos,* here divulged as lying obscurely behind the ugliness of Sunday in the park: "The Federal Reserve Banks constitute a Legalized National Usury System." Klaus's torrent of words misses the economic reality. The people comprehend neither him nor the system his mythology distorts and veils. The roar goes on, unattended, uncombed.

The Library, in Book III, turns out to be the repository not of the wisdom of the past, but of the cumulative horrors of history. Accumulated newspapers reveal that the past is simply more of the present:

> Old newspaper files,
> to find—a child burned in a field,
> no language. Tried, aflame, to crawl under
> a fence to go home. So be it. Two others,
> boy and girl, clasped in each others' arms
> (clasped also by the water) So be it. Drowned
> wordless in the canal. So be it.

From newspapers Paterson turns to the books: "A library—of books! decrying all books / that enfeeble the mind's intent." It is soon clear that the books do not contain the revelation for which the poet seeks:

> The place sweats of staleness and of rot
> a back-house stench   .   a
> library stench

Paterson realizes that the books "cannot penetrate and cannot waken, to be again / active but remain—books / that is, men in hell, / their reign over the living ended." In the midst of this awareness, one of the most violent of the prose inserts relates the story of the torture and murder of innocent Indians by American colonists, witnessed by "leaders" who "stood laughing heartily at the fun." The reader muses: where are the books in this library that reveal the reality of this American pioneer past? By the time the tornado strikes, followed by the fire and the flood, the reader yearns with Paterson for the cleansing of the past to make way for a new beginning.

Book III concludes with some of the most Whitmanian lines of *Paterson.* Unlike Eliot and Pound, very much like Emerson and Whitman, Paterson learns from the Library experience—

> The past above, the future below
> And the present pouring down: the roar,
> the roar of the present, a speech—
> is, of necessity, my sole concern   .

Whitman put it this way in his 1855 Preface: "The direct trial of him who would be the greatest poet is today. If he does not flood himself with the immediate age as with vast oceanic tides . . . and if he be not himself the age transfigured . . . let him . . . wait his development." Paterson seems determined to be the Whitmanian poet:

> I cannot stay here
> to spend my life looking into the past;
>
> the future's no answer. I must
> find my meaning and lay it, white,
> beside the sliding water: myself—
> comb out the language—or succumb
>
> —whatever the complexion. Let
> me out! (Well, go!) this rhetoric
> is real!

Whitman always declared that his rhetoric was of the flesh: "Camerado, this is no book, / Who touches this touches a man."

Book IV, which was once thought to complete *Paterson,* pleased almost nobody, and even Williams felt moved to add another book. No doubt a major reason for the critical displeasure with the book is the dominance of the language of chaos, with vignettes and images of perversion, sexual frustration, violence and death. Readers have not known how to interpret the opening section, portraying a Lesbian poetess vying with Dr. Paterson for the sexual favors of a beautiful nurse. Critics have tended to be more condemnatory morally than Williams himself, who commented: "The little girl gets herself mixed up at last in the pathetic sophisticate of the great city, no less defeated and understandable, even lovable, than she is herself." Clearly Williams did not intend the episode in an Eliotic sense— sexual perversion as emblematic of moral and spiritual perversion. His sympathies for all the frustrated participants come through the long sketch, and his admiration for the girl shines brightly in the poetry. What has not been much noticed about the narrative is its mixture of languages. The poetess in the "Idyl" is a creature out of the library of Book III, her version of reality framed by poetic visions from the past, classical or modern; she forces her life into the unreal form of a pastoral, and she writes Phyllis a poem with lines that even she recognizes from Yeats. Paterson, too, sees his experience with Phyllis framed in an Eliotic vision: "Oh Paterson! Oh married man! / He is the city of cheap hotels and private entrances." As he departs from a rendezvous, he remembers that there is something he wanted to say—"but I've forgotten / what it was . something I wanted / to tell you. Completely gone! Completely." The only entirely genuine language in this frustrated triangle is the language of the down-to-earth letters that Phyllis writes to her alcoholic father, reeking with a refreshing reality that points up the phoniness of the rest: "Look, Big Shot, I refuse to come home until you promise to cut out the booze."

Book IV presents other images of chaos, images of the atomic bomb, of "the cancer, usury," and of violence. Perhaps the most impressive of these are the prose accounts (in Part Three) of several murders, one the story of a young man killing his own infant daughter when "her crying annoyed him," and another the story (1850) of one John Johnson, a sometime hired hand (an inverse of Robert Frost's), who killed his former employer and wife, and then "was hung in full view of thousands who had gathered on Garrett Mountain and adjacent house tops to witness the spectacle." What gives this passage authority is its position within five short lines of the conclusion of Book IV (and one time the end of the poem). It is, indeed, the final image of the book, and is almost like a slap in the face for readers who have smiled affirmatively as they have just witnessed Paterson wade out of the "sea of blood" and strike inland for what seems to be a new beginning. The closing lines: "This is the blast / the eternal close / the spiral / the final somersault / the end." Thus readers are not permitted a sentimental conclusion; they are reminded of the reality of violence as it exists not only in Johnson but also in the crowds come to witness, among whom the reader might even, if he looks hard enough, discover himself.

In Book V of *Paterson,* the images of chaos decrease considerably, and they are integrated almost inseparably with images of renewal—the unicorn suffers death, but transcends death. . . . Paterson does not evade evil and horror, but seems now to see it in a totality that balances: there is the man who shoots, but there is also the man who comforts—a Whitmanian figure bringing succor to the suffering (as in "Song of Myself "). The serpent with its tail in its mouth; evil begetting good, good begetting evil, evil begetting good: "the river has returned to its beginnings." Paterson goes on—

> Dreams possess me
> and the dance
> of my thoughts
> involving animals
> the blameless beasts

Whitman said: "I think I could turn and live with animals, they are so placid and self-contain'd, / I stand and look at them long and long." Paterson's dance, the dance of his thoughts and the dance that ends the poem, is a dance of acceptance that embraces (as "all we know") both the joyous and the tragic.

Paterson's Preface opens, "Rigor of beauty is the quest. But how will you find beauty when it is locked in the mind past all remonstrance." At one time, Williams had added: "It is not in the things nearest us unless transposed there by our employment." Language must be used in explorations for beauty, and much of *Paterson* is given over to its discovery and delineation, its tenuous embodiment in an elusive language. Paterson does indeed find beauty in "the things nearest us," but it is only by employment of his art that it is "transposed there."

The first extended probing for beauty comes in Book I, with minute examination in memory of an old photograph from the *National Geographic.* . . . Paterson's eye of memory moves from the youngest, most recent wife along the line to the "last, the first wife, / present! supporting all the rest growing up from her." Her breasts sag "from hard use," but on her face there is a "vague smile, / unattached, floating like a pigeon / after a long flight to his cote." After presenting the examples of Sam Patch and Mrs. Cumming (blockage and divorce), Paterson's mind returns to this enigmatic woman:

> Which is to say, though it be poorly
> said, there is a first wife
> and a first beauty, complex, ovate—
> the woody sepals standing back under
> the stress to hold it there, innate
>
> a flower within a flower whose history
> (within the mind) crouching
> among the ferny rocks, laughs at the names
> by which they think to trap it. Escapes!
> Never by running but by lying still—

Beauty locked—or lurking—in the mind? An unlikely place, this—an old African woman with sagging breasts—to begin the search for beauty. But for the African chieftain, the beauty of his first wife crouches there among the "ferny rocks" of *his* mind, and is obscurely translated through the eight successors. Paterson will seek—and find—beauty in the most unlikely of places.

In "Sunday in the Park" (Book II), Paterson spots two lovers in a "grassy den," the woman "lies sweating" at the side of a dozing man—

> She stirs, distraught,
> against him—wounded (drunk), moves
> against him (a lump) desiring,
> against him, bored
>
> flagrantly bored and sleeping, a
> beer bottle still grasped spear-like
> in his hand   .

Small boys peer down on the frustrated lovers. The woman moves nearer the man, "her lean belly to the man's backside," but he does not waken:

> —to which he adds his useless voice:
> until there moves in his sleep
> a music that is whole, unequivocal (in
> his sleep, sweating in his sleep!—laboring
> against sleep, agasp!)
>   —and does not waken.
>
> Sees, alive (asleep)
>   —the fall's roar entering
> his sleep (to be fulfilled)
>   reborn
> in his sleep—scattered over the mountain
> severally
>   —by which he woos her, severally.

Later in the day, Paterson passes by once again and notices that "the drunken lovers slept, now, both of them."

Later, after listening to the evangelist Klaus, Paterson ponders and puzzles over beauty—"These women are not / beautiful and reflect / no beauty but gross . . / Unless it is beauty / to be, anywhere, / so flagrant in desire." *Unless, unless.* Before presenting the frustrated Sunday park lovers, Paterson remembered a scene from an Eisenstein film in which an old peasant is drinking with abandon in a kind of sexual celebration: "the female of it facing the male, the satyr— / (Priapus!)" The priapus principle of life has been frustrated in the lovers in the park—but affirmed by the poet. These lovers are not re-creations of Eliot's typist and "young man carbuncular," but rather, perhaps, answers to them. Their desire is healthy and life-affirming, not sordid and meaningless. It is the beauty that the poet seeks, and he works to "transpose" it there without falsifying or sentimentalizing or satirizing. Many readers have been misled by this passage, seeing it in the context of Eliot's *Waste Land* view of sex. But Williams has made it clear, both in the poem and out of it, that he is on the side of the frustrated lovers. . . . Williams saw the "love" scene as vital to the poem: "It's easy to miss, but the whole theme of *Paterson* is brought out in this passage, the contrast between the mythic beauty of the Falls and Mountain and the industrial hideousness. . . . so in this scene love has triumphed." Beauty locked in the mind—released.

In Book III, "The Library," the quest for beauty surges to the fore, flashing in Paterson's (and the reader's) mind in the strangely vague refrain, "Beautiful Thing." But the vagueness perhaps suits the poet's purposes in appearing rather common (and undistinguished) language but suggesting reverberations that go beyond any specific attachment. The refrain has a long history in the conception of *Paterson.* It appeared first at the end of the Columbus chapter, "The Discovery of the Indies," in *In the American Grain* (1925): Columbus has sent his men off for water in the new land of his discovery, and during the two hours he contemplates this new world: "During that time I walked among the trees which was the most beautiful thing which I had ever seen." Williams inserted this passage in *Paterson* IV, ii (changing only the last word to *known*), himself calling attention to the historic and national dimension of the refrain: Beautiful Thing was there for the simple viewing, not locked away in the mind, not hidden deep within the sordid surfaces—in the beginning of the American experience. What had become of it (or what we had done to it) in the centuries since was a different matter. (pp. 142-52)

Beautiful Thing figured centrally in Williams's 1937 poem, "Paterson: Episode 17," and many of the passages of this poem turn up in Book III of Paterson. The idea and the phrase embodying it, then, seem to have been an important part of the poem's beginning. Throughout Book III, Beautiful Thing seems to be set over against the library, offering a meaning and vitality that the books of the dead past cannot match. The Beautiful Thing of the original poem is a beautiful Negro servant girl, loved and violated by many, caught in the lively moment of beating a rug. But in *Paterson* she seems raised to mythic level— "tall / as you already were— / till your head / through fruitful exaggeration / was reaching the sky and the / prickles of its ecstasy / Beautiful Thing!" In this role, she reaches back in the poem to Book I to connect with the old (first) wife of the African chieftain of the *National Geographic* picture and to Book II to connect with the girl filled with frustrated desire in the park; and she reaches

forward in the poem to connect with Phyllis of the Idyl and with Madame Curie (Book IV) and with the "whore and virgin" of Book V: the mystery of woman, the mystery of sex, the mystery of love, the mystery of creativity— themes of Whitman throughout *Leaves of Grass,* but especially in the sex poems of "Children of Adam." (p. 152)

Beautiful Thing appears (as we noted above) in numerous incarnations in *Paterson,* but perhaps receives her apotheosis in Book V in the fused vision of the virgin and the whore. "The moral / proclaimed by the whorehouse / could not be better proclaimed / by the virgin, a price on her head, / her maidenhead!" Again: "The whore and the virgin, an identity: / —through its disguises." And again: "the virgin and the whore, which / most endures? the world / of the imagination most endures." The Unicorn legend woven into the tapestries of the Cloisters invites this fusion of identities, as it brought together both religious and secular meanings, the Unicorn itself representing Christ, but also, with his phallic horn, the lover-bridegroom. Thus the poet allies himself to a long tradition in seeing the two designations—virgin and whore— based on a single identification of sexuality, evocative of fundamentally identical creative sexual energy: "every married man carries in his head / the beloved and sacred image / of a virgin / whom he has whored." And he can assert paradoxically: "no woman is virtuous / who does not give herself to her lover / —forthwith."

The seventh tapestry in The Hunt of the Unicorn series at the Cloisters, a central image in Paterson, *Book V.*

In Part Two of Book V of *Paterson* there appears what seems to be an independent poem, beginning:

> There is a woman in our town
> walks rapidly, flat bellied
> in worn slacks upon the street
> where I saw her.
>   neither short
> nor tall, nor old nor young
> her
>   face would attract no
> adolescent.

This woman could be Beautiful Thing in another guise. Her appearance is not extraordinary, but her effect on the poet is: "She stopped / me in my tracks—until I saw / her / disappear in the crowd." And he exclaims, "if ever I see you again / as I have sought you / daily without success / I'll speak to you, alas / too late!" The poem might be read as an updated version of a Whitman "Children of Adam" poem ("A Woman Waits for Me," perhaps), and the poet adds at the end: "have you read anything that I have written? / It is all for you."

Beautiful Thing, sexual-creative energy, the phallic-priapus principle, love against death: these themes intermingle and become vital in *Paterson,* culminating in Book V: "The Unicorn roams the forest of all true lovers's minds. They hunt it down. Bow wow! sing hey the green holly!" The poet admonishes himself: "Paterson, / keep your pecker up / whatever the detail!" Sexuality and creativity, like the virgin and whore, fuse, and the energy of the "pecker" is as important to creating poetry as for making love. For "to measure is all we know, / a choice among the measures / . . / the measured dance." And this "measure" is made up of the eternal satyr in man as well as the eternally tragic—"to dance to a measure / contrapuntally, / Satyrically, the tragic foot."

Paterson's search for a redeeming language turns up a language of redemption, but it is a delicate thread winding its way through the poem. In the first book the emphasis is on descent, as Paterson himself identifies with Sam Patch in his leap into Passaic Falls, ending up in a cake of ice. Paterson hovers near the edge—

> The thought returns: Why have I not
> but for imagined beauty where there is none
> or none available, long since
> put myself deliberately in the way of death?

The imagination as man's redeemer? Possibly, as we shall see in Book V. But meanwhile, the nul and the descent must be faced. Part Three of Book II opens with the admonition: "Look for the nul / defeats it all." This "nul" is "the N of all / equations," "the blank / that holds them up." It is "that nul / that's past all seeing / the death of all that's past / all being." This blankness and nullity appear to be very close to that palsied whiteness that Melville's Ishmael (in *Moby-Dick*) saw in the heart of all matter, the whiteness that "shadows forth the heartless voids and immensities of the universe, and thus stabs us from behind with the thought of annihilation."

Then Paterson suddenly breaks off from contemplation of the nul: "But Spring shall come and flowers will bloom /

and man must chatter of his doom." This is self-admonition, a turning away from abstract ideas of nullity and blankness to the apprehendable realities of spring and flowers ("no ideas but in things"). There follows the justifiably famous passage in which Williams discovered his beloved triadic line—as well as affirmation in nullity:

> The descent beckons
>   as the ascent beckoned
>   Memory is a kind
> of accomplishment
>   a sort of renewal
>   even
> an initiation, since the spaces it opens are new
> places
>   inhabited by hordes
>   heretofore unrealized,
> of new kinds—
>   since their movements
>   are towards new objectives
> (even though formerly they were abandoned)
>
> No defeat is made up entirely of defeat—since
> the world it opens is always a place
>   formerly
>   unsuspected. A
> world lost,
>   a world unsuspected
>   beckons to new places
> and no whiteness (lost) is so white as the memo-
> ry
> of whiteness   .

The vision here may be reminiscent of Ezra Pound's descent described in the "Pisan Cantos," resulting in the unanticipated new awareness on Pound's part—"What thou lov'st well remains," a reservoir of the memory that is "a kind of accomplishment," "a sort of renewal." Like Pound, Paterson finds in descent a reversal—

> The descent
>   made up of despairs
>   and without accomplishment
> realizes a new awakening   :
>   which is a reversal
> of despair.

The nul, the blank, the descent, confronted in their reality, open up new spaces for the imagination.

In contrast with Eliot's wasteland negativism, Williams's vision might be called creative despair—that which brings reversal not by sentimental avoidance but by inhabiting the new spaces revealed. It is very much like the reversal that comes in Whitman's "Song of Myself," where the poet has come (in section 33) to identify with all the miserable of the world—"Hell and despair are upon me," "Agonies are one of my changes of garments." But as he reaches the nadir of his despair ("I project my hat, sit shame-faced, and beg"), he also reaches one of those open spaces, and he experiences reversal of despair in a new awareness. He cries out "Enough! enough! enough!" as he remembers the "overstaid fraction," discovering new spiritual or imaginative energy which he can share through his poetry.

This theme of renewal through despair is echoed throughout *Paterson,* as, for example, in Book III, in the midst of the burning of the library—

An old bottle, mauled by the fire
gets a new glaze, the glass warped
to a new distinction, reclaiming the
undefined. A hot stone, reached
by the tide, crackled over by fine
lines, the glaze unspoiled
Annihilation ameliorated:

In the renewal of the bottle (found in its "new space")
there is vital reversal—

       the flame that wrapped the glass
deflowered, reflowered there by
the flame: a second flame, surpassing
heat   .

Deflowered: reflowered. Despair, reversal of despair. Descent: renewal. Paterson contemplates the example of the reflowered bottle:

Hell's fire. Fire Sit your horny ass
down. What's your game? Beat you
at your own game, Fire. Outlast you:
Poet Beats Fire at Its Own Game! The bottle!
the bottle! the bottle! the bottle! I
give you the bottle! What's burning
now, Fire?

It is the poet's language of redemption that has beaten the fire at its own game, turning destruction into creation, resurrecting (and preserving) the bottle in its new incarnation.

In Book IV, Madame Curie's discovery of radium constitutes a similar reversal—

A dissonance
in the valence of Uranium
led to the discovery
Dissonance
(if you are interested)
leads to discovery

At a critical moment in the Curie investigations, there appeared the nul, the blankness—but

a stain at the bottom of the retort
without weight, a failure, a
nothing. And then, returning in the
night, to find it
             LUMINOUS

The luminosity derives from the assumed nothing—the blank space that gave room for the new awakening.

The pattern of descent and renewal is the pattern of the central action of the poem. Paterson takes on the identity of Sam Patch fallen to his doom and encased in a cake of ice in the opening of the poem. If the doom is final, Patch-Paterson should disappear in the sea at the end of the descent of the falls as the river runs to the sea—the "sea of blood"—in the conclusion of Book IV. . . . With the recurring cry, "the sea is not our home," Paterson wades out of the "blood dark sea" at the end of Book IV and has a refreshing nap on the beach. All the imagery in the closing lines describing Paterson's action is the imagery of life—the dog who accompanies him, the girls he notices playing on the beach, the beach plums he samples (spitting out the seed, emblem of renewal), his striking out energetically inland.

The language of redemption moves to the central position in Book V of *Paterson,* inherent in the very nature and narrative of the Unicorn tapestries. The story is a story of death and resurrection. The most magnificent of all the tapestries is the last, in which the Unicorn appears alone, chained to a tree, surrounded by a wooden fence in an incredibly beautiful field of multicolored flowers. Here the Unicorn may be the risen Christ in Paradise, or he may be the lover finally secured by his lady-love, a fusion of sexual-religious symbolism that goes to the heart of Williams's purposes. . . . The risen (erect?) unicorn "has no match / or mate," just as "the artist / has no peer": "Death / has no peer." The Unicorn has been killed, yet lives. . . .(pp. 154-59)

The descent of death is the final descent: but there are new spaces even here, and a reversal of despair: the imagination finds the hole at the bottom of death through which to escape—as the resurrected Unicorn has escaped in the tapestry. . . . Immediately following this defiant assertion appears a letter from the young, then unknown poet Allen Ginsberg, setting out to dedicate his life to the poetic imagination. The letter thanks Williams for writing his introduction (to *Howl!*), and proclaims his "whitmanic mania": "In any case Beauty is where I hang my hat. And reality. And America." Williams-Paterson's Unicorn, perhaps? Redemption, resurrection, through the imagination, of Whitman's "ages' and ages' encrustations." But of course, Williams's Unicorn of the seventh tapestry is the poem *Paterson* itself. It has handsomely escaped through the hole at the bottom of death. And many readers would conclude with Robert Lowell's judgment, in proclaiming Williams as "part of the great breath of our literature, that "*Paterson* is our *Leaves of Grass.*" (pp. 159-60)

*James E. Miller, Jr., "How Shall I Be Mirror
to This Modernity? William Carlos Williams's
'Paterson'," in his* The American Quest for a
Supreme Fiction: Whitman's Legacy in the
Personal Epic, *The University of Chicago
Press, 1979, pp. 126-61.*

James DeMuth

The epic appeals strongly to American poets. One thinks immediately of Walt Whitman and Hart Crane, as well as such minor figures as Philip Freneau and Stephen Vincent Benét. The size of our country, diversity of our people, and wealth of our resources all demand epic comprehension. More importantly, our history of nation building, by turns inspiring and distressing, has been a theme of intense moral interest. It is this moral concern which William Carlos Williams dramatizes in his epic *Paterson,* a poem originally conceived in four books but later extended to five.

Williams immediately alerts his reader to the epic character of *Paterson* by calling his first book "The Delineaments of the Giants." However, unlike Walt Whitman, whose influence he repeatedly acknowledges, Williams does not style his "Giants" as the democratic people "enmasse." With Williams, the "Giants" stand for the large figures of Paterson's landscape (the city and Garret Mountain) whose potential for beauty and inspiration (embodied in the Passaic Falls, the natural wonder of the place) has been defiled by the citizens. Instead of singing the optimistic epic of the making of democratic men in our history, Williams tells the grim story of an American "Waste Land":

> . . . a thousand automatons. Who because they
> neither know their sources nor the sills of their
> disappointments walk outside their bodies aim-
> 　　lessly
> 　　　for the most part,
> locked and forgot in their desires—unroused.

If the first four books of *Paterson* are epic in scope, they are decidedly anti-epic in content; they are the unremittingly pathetic record of men sometimes willfully, more often indifferently, debasing their environment and their community.

Whereas *Paterson I-IV* is a severe indictment of Americans who in the course of their history have lost and show little interest in recovering an authentic language of cultural and spiritual integrity, *Paterson V* is a more modest, temperate, and contemplative poem. The later poem, though differing in tone, composition, and rhetoric from the earlier books, successfully culminates them by reclaiming their seemingly hopeless theme—the possibility of authentic language. Williams reconsiders in *Paterson V* the varieties of American idiomatic speech he had impugned in *Paterson I-IV* to demonstrate in his new verse their genuine, if limited, aesthetic capacity in "A WORLD OF ART / THAT THROUGH THE YEARS HAS / SURVIVED!"

In *Paterson I-IV,* Williams had sought the language which would heal the divorce of the contemporary Patersonite from his experience, environment, and history: "Life is sweet / they say: the language! / —the language / is divorced from their minds, / the language . . the language!" This language, though ill-defined and elusive in the four books of the poem, evokes the constellation of meanings Williams more commonly denoted by the term *contact.* As Williams defines the term in various essays written before and after *Paterson, contact* means the direct, sensual apprehension of reality and the imaginative comprehension of this experience in native arts—whether poetry, painting, or folk crafts—undistorted by the "false language" of derivative customs, fashions, and ideologies. The redemptive language sought in *Paterson I-IV* would be, considering the range of Williams's materials, the idiomatic speech and vernacular literature, as well as material arts and cultural rituals, expressing authentic contact; the irony undercutting the imperative search is that the language is sought among a people who, by their urban history, secular materialism, and industrial labor, have become alienated from their environment, ignorant of their aborted community traditions, and dulled in their curiosity and imagination.

That the search for a language of authentic contact should be the theme of Williams's American epic is understandable in light of our history of literary and linguistic nationalism. From its patriotic origins in Philip Freneau, Noah Webster, and William Cullen Bryant, through its more complete and conscious development in Longfellow, Whitman, and Twain, American literary nationalism has affirmed, in Emerson's touchstone phrase, the democratic language of "the near, the low, the common." (pp. 150-52)

To Williams, contact with the New World or divorce from it was the persistent drama of American history, weakening over time as the country became more urbanized. Williams's thesis of American historical experience, informing *Paterson I-IV* and governing Williams's selection of incidents from Paterson's local history, is that the dominant, urban culture (embodied in the figure of Alexander Hamilton in *Paterson I-IV*) is the "unrelated, borrowed, the would-be universal culture," while the "culture of immediacy" had only been accomplished by eccentric individuals (Sam Patch, for example) or small, isolated communities (the colonial Paterson village) which "made contact with the intrinsic elements of an as yet unrealized material of which the new country was made."

The severe contrast Williams draws between the "culture of immediacy" and the "unrelated, borrowed" urban culture is the rhetorical design of *Paterson I-IV,* defining the "divorce" which the "language" of democratic conviction and sensual contact might resolve; in presenting Paterson as a synecdoche of American historical experience, Williams repeatedly juxtaposes in ironic contrast an expression of the unified life in a primary culture (principally, Totawa and Mezo-American Indian cultures, African tribal culture, colonial Paterson culture) with a related expression of the debased life in industrialized Paterson. With a few exceptions in *Paterson IV* that I will discuss, Williams characterizes the difference between the city and the rural or primitive cultures as an absolute difference in expression; the Patersonite either speaks a vulgar and mean-spirited idiom or gushes foolish sentiments, while the primitive contrasted with him expresses the spirit of his common life in candid and devout art.

In Williams's usual portrait, the primitive exemplifies a life of "contact with the intrinsic elements" by patterning his imagination of the timeless and mythic in rituals of "the near, the low, the common." Thus, where the sentimental Mrs. Cumming, lacking the words and art to comprehend her sensual experience, stumbles over the Passaic Falls under the narcotic influence of the "beautiful, wild and romantic scenery," the nine African women in a *National Geographic* picture use the most common natural materials ("log," "mudcaked") to symbolize their sexual roles as the chief's consorts. Similarly, Ibidio women bury a fallen warrior on a bed of fresh leaves and, waving the bough from a sacred tree over his genitals, preserve his sexual vigor for the tribe's continued fertility. By contrast, the pathetic invalid Clifford keeps his sexuality by writing his friends "to send him some dirty jokes because he can't get out to hear them himself."

It is not necessary, though, to go as far afield as Africa to find rituals of primitive cultures contrasted with the spiritually barren "false language" of Paterson. "Indians!" The American Indian is always in the background of *Paterson* and is a memory Patersonites wish to exorcise: "Forget it! for God's sake, Cut / out that stuff." Indian culture is most prominently featured in Book III in three incidents from Totawa life. Aesthetics, the creation and comprehension of beauty, is the principal theme of Book III, and the Totawa are presented as men who artistically fashioned their whole lives. In the first incident, for example, the Indians are sadistically mutilated by Dutch soldiers, and one of the victims asks his tormentors "to permit him to dance the Kinte Kaye, a religious use among them before death." Not only in these terrible moments of crisis, however, did the Indian find solace in artistic ritual. Everything in his life is touched by beauty: "They made money of sea-shells. Bird feathers. Beaver skins." The Dutch, however, imagined only the commercial exploitation of Indian culture: they dug up the grave of an Indian priest, stole the funeral furs, and left the carcass to the wolves.

Williams's affirmative depictions of "primary" cultures contrast sharply with his portraits of Patersonites as heirs of a "secondary" urban culture; whereas Williams consistently represents the primitive living in a richly integrated culture, he uniformly depicts Patersonites, through his selection of newspaper clippings, letters, and odd bits of historical record, as people who have debased their cultural language through their avarice, violence, and gross materialism. Thus, in the beginning of *Paterson I,* after introducing the primordial union of Paterson and Garret Mountain, and after describing Garret Mountain's power to waken the dreams of the people ("Pearls at her ankles, her monstrous hair / spangled with apple-blossoms is scattered about into / the back country, waking their dreams"), Williams dramatically shows the avaricious turn their dreams took in 1857. In that year, David Howe discovered the "Queen Pearl" in a lot of mussels collected at Notch Brook. This discovery incited a wanton destruction of millions of mussels. In plundering Garret Mountain ("Pearls at her ankles"), Patersonites destroyed what they would possess: "A large round pearl, weighing 400 grains which would have been the finest pearl of modern times, was ruined by boiling open the shell."

Williams selects many similar scenes of defilement from Paterson's history: boys stone a huge striped bass and are commended by the *Bergen Express* and the *Paterson Advertiser;* men slaughter eels in a drained lake on the upper Passaic; police officers delight in harrying a mink through town. In Book II, the "great beast" of picnickers exhibit this callousness toward nature as an ingrained attitude. And this attitude is not a local prejudice: Paterson is the symbol of all American cities. Thus in Book IV, Williams startles us with the recognition that American cities have exhausted the sources for pastoral imagination by retelling the classical tale of Corydon and Phyllis as an unconsummated lesbian seduction in Manhattan. Corydon, the businesswoman, poetess, and lesbian of this ironic idyll, expresses the sterility of her passions in dispiriting landscape imagery. She ruefully notes that three bald rocks are "all that's left of the elemental, the primitive" in the East River. Though she gamely attempts a "pastoral" with this meager primitive ("I call them my sheep," says Corydon. "They're white all right but it's from the gulls that crap them up all day long," notes Phyllis), her poem only achieves coherence and power in the section where she describes Manhattan commerce as mechanized sexual intercourse. Corydon senses the ruined cityscape, but she can

no longer express the landscape; for her, Anticosti is simply an exotic prop for the champagne cruise seduction of Phyllis.

Paralleling Paterson's abuse of its environment is Williams's other theme of criminal destruction, the rapid and tragically irreversible dissolution of community. In Williams's grim picture of Paterson's hobbled community, even the family is dissolved. "T," for instance, writes of his macabre visit home to his ailing mother and his sister Billy. The family is convulsed in petty jealousies masking very deep hatreds which suddenly erupt when Billy attacks "T" with a poker and is threatened with death if she strikes. There are similar incidents. Fred Goodell kills his six-month-old-daughter. Phyllis fends off her alcoholic father's incestuous attacks.

All human relations are poisoned in this befouled community. As the "Giants" delineated in Book I (Paterson and Garret Mountain) are figures of an ideal union, so the real anarchy of urban Paterson is mirrored in the fractured, squalid sexuality of its citizens. Sex is either assault ("senseless rapes—caught on hands and knees / scrubbing a greasy corridor"); or the dumb lethargy of the lovers in section one, Book II—"wounded (drunk), moves / against him (a lump) desiring, / against him, bored." The poet is not exempt. The personal letters Williams reprints, save the somewhat fawning epistles from Allen Ginsberg, are all carping, bitter accusations of, ironically, Williams's haughty indifference to the real life of Paterson: " . . . writers like yourself who are so sheltered from life in the raw by the glass-walled conditions of their own safe lives," hisses the spurned poetess-lover "C" in Book II. Not the giants' marriage but "Divorce is / the sign of knowledge in our time, / divorce! divorce!"

For Williams, the major symptom of Paterson's divorce is the "false language" which the poet vainly tries to redeem. As a slight example of the ignorance and cultural envy revealed in our characteristic language choices, Williams had cited, in **"The American Background,"** our misnaming of the native redbreasted thrush as robin, that "rosy, daintier English bird." He again alludes to this example in *Paterson I* when, in one of the laments marking his search for a redeeming language ("Stale as a whale's breath: breath!"), he invokes the forsaken bird:

> Clearly!
> speaks the red-breast his behest. Clearly!
> clearly!

The red-breast's clear behest is not simply for a distinctive vocabulary but, as Williams's portraits of primitive cultures indicate, for an entire language of ritual. However, throughout *Paterson I-IV* Williams repeatedly shows the Patersonites' inability to achieve authentic expression. For example, in *Paterson III,* he associates the dead dog floating in the Passaic flood with Cerberus and then, characteristically sharply juxtaposes a citizen's plaintive cry, "Come yeah, Chi Chi!" Immune to any transcendent meaning to reality, Patersonites cherish their petty grievances: "That was your little dog bit me last year." By contrast Wyandach, brother of the slain Pogatticut, killed Pogatticut's favorite dog and "after painting his muzzle red" laid him in the dead warrior's grave.

In the final section of *Paterson IV,* though, Williams's scathing indictment of Patersonites softens. His tone, there, is often solicitously personal: "Virtue, / my kitten, is a complex reward in all / languages, achieved slowly." And some citizens now achieve the language of virtue. Williams's friend, the hotel manager, quite innocently sleeps with the naked girl he finds in his room; at a funeral, Williams remembers the dead woman generously and sympathetically. *Paterson* here touches on the character of tragedy; not "automatons" nor the "great beast" but live, complex individuals are borne on the forces debasing the city.

The tragedy of Paterson's debasement is reinforced by Williams's long pastoral on colonial and early national Paterson (Book IV, section 3). Its settlers casually and gracefully unite native products with European: "Rude furniture, sanded floors, rush / bottomed chair, a pewter shelf of Brittania [sic] / ware." They produce native artists ("a drawing / made by Lieut. Gov. Pownall [excellent work]"), ceremoniously welcome the returning Lafayette and, in their "antiquated" circus, create public entertainment perfectly proportioned to the community. They have, in short, everything that the "debased city" lacks: work is a robust activity, the business center is "the prettiest spot in town"; Fyfield's tavern is idyllically set amid delicate ponds where birds sport.

Though the sentimental quaintness with which Williams embroiders his memory of the early Paterson lessens the effect of tragic loss in its post-Alexander Hamilton susceptibility to a "false language," still the loss is real. As he had argued in **"The American Background,"** the small American community "was the culture of immediacy, the active strain, which has left every relic of value which survives today." So, in *Paterson IV,* Allen Ginsberg discovers the enduring Paterson in the area around Mill and River streets where faint relics of the lost Paterson survive. This ghost of Paterson past is not enough, though, to regenerate the present. Williams ends the poem utterly alone shouting defiance at the "hungry sea." When the man and his dog appear as another living "relic of value" of rural Paterson, the memory of John Johnson's execution intervenes with all its connotations of Paterson's dismal urban history, and Williams seals his poem:

> This is the blast
> the eternal close
> the spiral
> the final somersault
> the end.

Paterson IV ends on the rhetorical note which has sounded throughout the long poem, the ironic contrast between an image of easy, unmediated contact with "the near, the low, the common"—a man rises from the sea, sleeps on shore, dresses, and heads inland with his dog after first sampling some beach plums from a low bush—and a blunt reminder in the newspaper notice of John Johnson's hanging in April 1850 (avidly witnessed by thousands, some from rooftops) of the criminality and prurient interest in criminality degrading Paterson's history. Aptly, Williams names his conclusion "the final somersault," an image which captures the poem's rapidly turning upside-down movement through repeated ironic contrasts of primary or "contact" cultures and secondary or "divorce" cultures.

The "final somersault," though, is not the complete summary image: Williams concludes with a seemingly disjointed visual image of the poem as both a spiral and a somersault. While "somersault" points to the poem's rhetorical technique of ironic contrast, dramatizing the "divorce" which the language sought is to mend, "spiral" is an appropriate image of the poem's orderly descent through distinct levels of experience in the search for that language. In each book, the "Giants," Noah Faitoute Paterson, and his consort, Garret Mountain, descend through metamorphic changes on successively lower levels of experience to reenact the previous book's dramatic quest for a redemptive language.

Book I introduces Paterson as the elemental "Giant" drawing life from the awesome Passaic Falls to sustain the parasitic "automatons" of the modern city. Book II finds Paterson as a man, yet distinct from other men. Here he is a prophetic figure wandering alone through the Sunday picnic crowd straining "to catch the movement of one voice" that will redeem the day. In Book III Paterson is the persona of Williams (in the first two books, Williams's explicit voice is distinct from the character of Paterson). Here Paterson-Williams is a poet researching in the library and a doctor ministering to the scarred, beaten Negro woman in the basement. Though Paterson remains "I" in section 1 of Book IV, he is more deeply implicated in the degraded life of his city than in previous books. Instead of being very distanced from the common Patersonite by his professional callings of poetry and medicine, he is introduced as simply a "married man" pursuing but never consummating an illicit affair with Phyllis, a backwoods girl on the make in New York City as masseuse for the wealthy lesbian Corydon.

The career of Garret Mountain corresponds to the declining station of her lover. In Book I, Garret Mountain is an inexhaustibly fertile beauty calmly reposing in Paterson's embrace. By Book II, Garret Mountain is simply an urban park. Instead of "farms and ponds," she is now burdened with refreshment stands and toilets. The "automatons" of Book I have ominously grown to the "great beast" and now obstruct the "ceremonial of love" between Paterson and Garret Mountain.

In Book III, Paterson's consort assumes human form as the sick, abused woman in the basement who embodies, in Paterson's intense longing, the "Beautiful Thing." This phrase incarnated Williams's reverence for the beauty and wildness awaiting contact in the New World; it is the phrase of wonder taken from Columbus's diary of October 13, 1492: "I walked among the trees which was the most beautiful thing which I had ever seen." By embodying the "Beautiful Thing," the woman in the basement symbolizes the potential for a language of contact; yet, significantly and revealing for the poem's theme of divorce, she is unconscious of all that her marred beauty represents; she has wasted her beauty on a three-day drunk, ending, Williams strongly implies, in gang rape. Before her dumb pain, Doctor Paterson weeps.

In Book IV, the bond between Paterson and his love is further weakened; as they become more human, their love debases. Whereas Doctor Paterson was emotionally overcome before the nude "Beautiful Thing," the Paterson of Book IV sees only a naked woman in Phyllis, and his vision is described in terms which obviously parody the previous exalted experience:

> He drew back the white
> shirt   .   slid aside the
> ribbons   .
>   Glory be to God   .
> —then stripped her
>   and all His Saints!
>
>   .
> No, just broad shouldered

While the metamorphic changes of Paterson and his consort define the levels of experience through which the poet seeks the redemptive language, and while their decline to illicit, unconsummated lovers makes more extreme the "divorce" which the language might resolve, the spiral character of the poet's search is signalled in a characteristic scene in the final section of each book. In these scenes, just as the poet's search for a redemptive language seems to reach a despairing end, he finds, unexpectedly, a "new awakening" which turns the quest back on itself:

>   Faitoute ground his heel
> hard down on the stone:
>
> Sunny today, with the highest temperature near
> 80 degrees; moderate southerly winds. Partly
> cloudy and continued warm tomorrow, with
> moderate southerly winds.
>
> Her belly   .   her belly is like
> a cloud   .   a cloud
>   at evening   .
> His mind would reawaken:

Just as the weather report here suggests a simile to reawaken N. F. Paterson's mind, so in Book I the squalid tenements reveal "a tranquility and loveliness," in Book III the memory of "La capella di S. Rocco" arrests Paterson's lament, and, in Book IV, a swimmer emerges from the "blood dark sea" into which the Passaic, a symbol of the whole poem, is dissolving.

The "new awakening" of one book's conclusion, though, is frustrated in the "despairs" that make up the following, and Book IV ends with no gain or hope. That the "spiral" of the descent through the levels of *Paterson I-IV* should only issue the "final somersault" of ironically opposed images has been conditioned by Williams's narrow selection of incidents from the city's history; the language the poet seeks, we imagine, could resolve the conflict between primitive and urban, ceremonial and debased which has been the drama of Paterson, but Williams's selection from Paterson's history seals this possibility of redemptive language. The city's language defies the poet's search for the "gist" of a language of authentic contact because it expresses, in the newspaper clippings, personal letters, and historical incidents Williams selects, not the Patersonites' consciousness of place but only callous waste and criminal defilement.

Though *Paterson IV* announced a definite end, it remained unsettled in Williams's mind and was succeeded, seven years later, by *Paterson V*. In many ways, Williams isolates *Paterson V*. Instead of episodes from the city's local history, Williams selects images from "A WORLD OF ART / THAT THROUGH THE YEARS HAS / SURVIVED!" Except in Ezra Pound's comically paranoid letter, the political and economic themes of the earlier books are largely abandoned for "the museum." Where Williams's correspondents in Books I-IV were involved, if not locked, in the city, now many seem to be deserting Paterson: Josie writes from her very pleasant rural estate; Allen Ginsberg announces his plans to leave on a ship for an Arctic cruise; Edward is content in Spain. The only remaining Patersonite, other than the poet, is the indifferent woman "in worn slacks" ironically invoked as Williams's muse.

Paterson V's greatest distinction, though, is its freedom from the self-conscious anxiety about an authentic, honest language so evident in the earlier books. The only place this theme appears in *Paterson V* is in the reprinted transcript of the television interview of Williams by Mike Wallace. Here one senses Williams mocking his own pretensions of capturing the "American idiom" in a poem unintelligible to the bewildered Mr. Wallace and then being confronted by Wallace with a poem by e. e. cummings that is unintelligible to both of them. In any event, the problem Williams discusses is not the creation of a new language but the poetic clarification of the rhythm of our present language.

Instead of searching for a language to redeem our debased tongue, the elusive goal of the poet's quest throughout *Paterson I-IV*, Williams now persistently confronts the challenge of making art from our "shoddy" times. Where Book IV ended with a man and his dog, symbols reminiscent of the simple life in a long-lost Paterson village, Book V concludes in the immediate present with Williams confronting his cantankerous grandmother. Williams's choice of his grandmother is significant; now he is personally bound in the present and cannot so easily yield to the anguished rhetoric about the "blood dark sea" and "debased city" that marked the earlier books. Whereas Williams's nostalgic image of the swimmer in *Paterson IV*, following upon his long pastoral of colonial Paterson, had denied the modern and urban, now he wrings poetry from the modern tongue:

> She did not want to live to be
> an old woman to wear a china doorknob
> in her vagina to hold her womb up—but
> she came to that, resourceful, what?
> He was the first to turn her up
> and never left her till he left her
> with child, as any soldier would
> until the camp broke up.

Language is not now the burden of "false language" but a poetic resource. The Unicorn tapestry aptly symbolizes Williams's successful effort in *Paterson V* to weld the local and the mythic, a feat only primitives could do in *Paterson I-IV*. While the foreign is remote and idealized in *Paterson I-IV*, now Brueghel and the Flemish tapestry are immediately present and can be apprehended in modern idiom:

> The expression of her face,
>> where she stands removed from the oth-
> ers
> —the virgin and the whore,
>> an identity,
>>> both for sale
> to the highest bidder!

Furthermore, Williams drops the solemn tone he so often adopted in *Paterson I-IV* when depicting a past or distant "primary culture" and now even banters the foreign emissaries. For example, before cataloguing all the flowers in the Unicorn tapestry, Williams consoles his poet-hero:

> Paterson,
> keep your pecker up
>> whatever the detail!

This, just after Paterson had been grandly styled "I, Paterson, the King-self."

The difference in idiom between *Paterson I-IV* and *Paterson V* is revealing. In the earlier poem, Williams emphatically and frequently used idiomatic speech as a sign of the debased language. Now he forsakes his quest for the Grail of a phantom language and, instead, presents himself as simply a craftsman "trying / to get the young / to foreshorten / their errors in the use of words which / he had found so difficult." Instead of a descent to despair, the poet-craftsman of *Paterson V* ends with a modest victory:

> We know nothing and can know nothing .
>> but
> the dance, to dance to a measure
> contrapuntally,
>> Satyrically, the tragic foot.

Just as the "spiral" and "somersault" of *Paterson IV* had summarized the character of its drama and poetry, so in *Paterson V*'s conclusion, "contrapuntally" identifies the dynamic union of opposites (satyr-tragedy, virgin-whore) which is the poem's pervading theme. In *Paterson V* Williams welds refined and vulgar idioms, exalted and gross experiences to evoke an elusive "identity" in their contrapuntal play:

> The whore and the virgin, an identity:
> —through its disguises
> thrash about—but will not succeed in breaking
>> free   :
>>> an identity

In Williams's range over "THE WORLD OF ART," we find, through his sensibility, this identity thrashing about in the tension between the divine and the adulterous in Peter Brueghel's *Nativity,* between love and promiscuity in Lorca's *The Love of Don Perlimplin,* and, most fully, in the play between the sensual and the carnal in the Unicorn tapestries.

Not only in its tense, evocative imagery is *Paterson V* distinguished, but also in its poetic measure, a more subtle and confident poetics than the awkward dependence on ironic contrasts in *Paterson I-IV.* The "dance to a measure" which Williams achieves in *Paterson V* is, in his terms, the "variable foot" meter. Each line is a discrete "foot" and, though lines vary in syllable-length, all lines have the same time-duration. The pattern of syllabic accents is based on the ordinary rhythm of phrase and rhetorical stresses; it is a "talking" poetry. As such, this represents little change in Williams's art; from the beginning he had structured his poems on the rhythm of simple declarative sentences. The only real departure from this method is *Paterson I-IV,* and that poem's coherence suffers from its lack of recurrent meter.

Because *Paterson V* has a basic rhythm, Williams can vary the measure in different parts of the poem without the whole poem fracturing. While *Paterson I-IV* is frequently a shattered poem of short, varied clusters of verse interspersed with prose, *Paterson V* is built of longer units of poetry and prose, each with a distinct voice, yet all speaking a common tongue. Williams's furthest departure from variable-foot blank verse in *Paterson V* is his translation of Sappho in section 2. Here Williams uses anapestic trimeter quatrains, each stanza, however, concluding with a line of one foot. Though regular, the meter of Williams's translation is subtly varied by his shortening of several anapests, by his alliteration of consonantal clusters, and by his skillful continuation of some poetic feet from the end of one line into the opening syllable or syllables of the succeeding line ("to your swéet spéech and lóve ly / láugh ter"). Knit as it is with alliteration and internal assonance, the poem evokes musical rhythm, as befits a rendition of Sappho's unique "clear gentle tinkling voice." In contrast to the despair over worn-out language in Books I-IV, Williams here demonstrates the lyric potential of American language. However, Williams subtly makes another point. Where the despairing poet of *Paterson III* piteously laments his inability "to find one phrase that will / lie married beside another for delight," Williams now quietly implies much the same thing by limiting his delightful American verse to his translation of Greek.

This point is underscored by the following unit of poetry in which the "woman in our town / walks rapidly, flat bellied / in worn slacks." These stanzas in a wholly American idiom about an American subject are deliberately prosaic with no hint of the delightful artifices of Williams's translation of Sappho. There is no discernible accentual pattern, and the only rhythm seems to be the normal breath rhythm of speech; it is variable-foot verse with the least variety. Only occasionally does Williams "poeticize" his verse by isolating one word, thus forcing pause to what is otherwise a reading of prose. Again, this technique shows Williams's increased subtlety in *Paterson V.* Whereas he castigated our "tongue-tied" language in *Paterson II,* now by the occasionally isolated words of this verse he simply demonstrates the awkward, halting character of our speech.

Though the "WORLD OF ART" emblazoned on the opening pages of *Paterson V* seems to seal the world of Paterson, I think Williams achieved a truer image of the city in this "museum" than in the mausoleum of the "automatons'" local history. *Paterson I-IV* is laden with history but reads as fantasy. Williams too easily and frequently lapses into simple contrasts of the sacred primitives and the "debased city." Assuming that the "raw new" is destroyed ("You come today to see killed / killed, killed,"), the poet finds little to create in the present; the Passaic Falls, Williams's symbol of the uninterpreted "raw new" in Paterson, begins and ends simply a roar. In **Paterson V** Williams sets aside the futile quest of the earlier books. He accepts (humbly, as his self-image of the poet-craftsman indicates) the "American idiom" as an authentic cultural expression and probes its structure. By this acceptance, Williams opens the real world of Paterson. (pp. 152-65)

James DeMuth, "William Carlos Williams's 'Paterson': A Search for Language, a Recovery of Words," in The Library Chronicle, *Vol. 45, Nos. 1 & 2, 1981, pp. 150-66.*

Robert Coles

Not rarely, modernist writers have appeared to lose their aim or perhaps (as they certainly felt) to widen their aim: an assault upon the supposedly sterile, self-important academy might, for instance, turn into a bitter denunciation of intellectuals in general, including the very writer making the accusation. William Carlos Williams' **Paterson** starts with such a mode of social analysis and interpretation. We are to be offered "a local pride," a pointed reference to those who leave America for places such as London or Paris—or who leave small towns within our country for cultural centers, either big cities or celebrated universities. Next comes "a reply to Greek and Latin with the bare hands." It is a not very obscure effort to make a claim for a proud, contemporary, intellectual excitement, worthy of attention and approval: one of W. C. Williams' several versions of modernism—in this case, a working-class machismo appeal to folk wisdom, to the polyglot ethnic intuitions that a Paterson, New Jersey, general practitioner had come to know so well.

But Williams was not only taking on an arid classicism. He used the word *daring* provocatively as a truculent response to Eliot's Prufrock, a tough challenge to enemies in the present, never mind those lost in the ancient world. He repeats his animus in these lines, meant to raise the eyebrows of those familiar with the fifth and last section of Eliot's "Little Gidding":

> For the beginning is assuredly
> the end—since we know nothing, pure
> and simple, beyond
> our own complexities.

Then he escalates his assault even further and takes on "ideas," the entire ambitious enterprise of Theory. He treats abstract formulations as a means of removing oneself from countless human experiences, including those a poet ought to know and address in his or her writing:

> and the craft,
> subverted by thought, rolling up, let
> him beware lest he turn to no more than
> the writing of stale poems . . .
> Minds like beds always made up,
>   (more stony than a shore)
> unwilling or unable.

A harsh broadside: Williams is the antagonist, who uses Paterson, New Jersey, as a base of operations in a fiercely ambitious military campaign. A few lines further the commanding general sounds his clarion call, to be repeated again and again: "Say it, no ideas but in things." Let others become swollen-headed with thoughts, interpretations, and extended reifications. This poet and, he hoped, his readers would, in the powerful intimacy of a particular American lyrical celebration, cling tenaciously to the infinite, exuberant reality of the concrete, the everyday, the tangible and visible and audible.

> Sniffing the trees,
> just another dog
> among a lot of dogs. What
> else is there? And to do?
> The rest have run out—
> after the rabbits.

With such lines as these Williams escalated his polemics even further, presenting the artist as a street dog. Not a prissy human being, locked in a library, removed from the flesh's vitality; and speaking of human beings, not an aesthete, chasing rabbits in some far removed, all too "pretty" field. A mongrel in a factory town, out to survive today, then tomorrow: find the food, have some sex if it's available, empty the bladder and the bowels—and no highfalutin pretenses or postures. Man is an animal, and if he forgets that or denies that, he is living a big lie, and soon enough other lies get going.

Nor is Williams himself, for all his daring criticism of others, immune to the skeptical poet's eye. He poses a question that contains a devastating self-indictment, rendered decades before the subject of narcissism became yet another (narcissistic?) preoccupation of the American intelligentsia:

> Who are these people (how complex
> the mathematic) among whom I see myself
> in the regularly ordered plateglass of
> his thoughts, glimmering before shoes and bicy-
> cles?

Literary smugness, the writer's preening egotism, the poet knew, cannot be banished by a few slaps at others. Modernism meant taking chances—not only with language, images, and forms but also with the range and depth of one's self-observation. Williams uses the word *divorce* as a signal of sorts in the first book of **Paterson;** and he knows that one form of uprootedness or alienation, those fashionable twentieth-century statements, is the divorce of the social critic from the objects of his criticism: so long as I tear into a "them" with my words and speculations and grim approximations (sometimes amounting to not so flimsily disguised denunciations), I am myself safe, protected, clean, and wholesome. No, a truly radical survey of a world and its language demands a lacerating introspection and an earthy return to origins:

> A delirium of solutions, forthwith, forces
> him into back streets, to begin again:
> up hollow stairs among acrid smells
> to obscene rendezvous. And there he finds
> a festering sweetness of red lollipops—
> and a yelping dog:

Come YEAH, Chichi! Or a great belly
that no longer laughs but mourns
with its expressionless black navel love's
deceit.

In the event that anyone should fail to notice the determined nature of such a return to the elementary, to the urgently physical (again, the dog!), Williams lifts his flag of battle again (a version of it), with "No ideas but / in the facts"; and a little further on, he lances yet again the boil of his own self-centeredness: "How strange you are, you idiot!" Then, a few pages on, he fires off this blast:

We go on living, we permit ourselves
to continue—but certainly
not for the university, what they publish

severally or as a group: clerks
got out of hand forgetting for the most part
to whom they are beholden.

spitted on fixed concepts like
roasting hogs, sputtering, their drip sizzling
in the fire

Some of us who got to know Dr. Williams, even across the distance of age and residence, remember that the above could be considered an understatement of his, if placed in the overall spectrum of sentiments professed during a lifetime—especially those uttered among friends. But for his poetry, this was one of the blunter moments; the imagery intensifies rather than mollifies an argumentative statement. Clerks, as in *trahison des clercs:* the intellectual is charged with arrogance, with bullying pushiness. Moreover, there is another bill of divorcement entered in the growing annals of **Paterson**—heady professors who are removed in heart and mind and soul from others in a given community or region or nation. Lest the reader (not to mention the first reader, who wrote the words) be troubled by the self-serving nature of such anti-intellectualism (yet another "them," which affords protection to an "I," a "we") a prose segment follows immediately—in sum, a devastating portrait of the self-preoccupied, if not selfish, practicing doctor. His own idle reveries take precedence over the specific, here-and-now complaints of a vulnerable, needy, ailing group of patients, whose number and condition get spelled out: "Twenty and more infants taking their turn from the outer office, their mothers tormented and jabbering."

This was an unflinching look inward, a spell of Augustinian self-scrutiny—part of an intellectual tradition, actually, that has both a religious and a secular aspect. Williams desires membership in that tradition. He jabs at his own kind, writers and thinkers; then for good measure, he gives himself a good kick in the pants—but quickly moves to the poor of New Jersey in the Depression years, to the dreary banalities of a general culture saturated with materialism, much of it crooked: commerce and its discontents. We begin to wonder whether he is simply flailing—a poet anxious to be a wise philosopher, a shrewd observer of his fellow human beings, but unable to summon the necessary, sustained cohesion, the required largeness of outlook. When, toward the end of the first book, a line "the knowledgeable idiots, the university" appears, we notice a dangerous repetition—and wonder why, given the careful ambitiousness of this major modernist statement.

Williams begins to redeem himself in that last section of the first book with a kind of candor that transcends the constraints of bitterness and invective. Here is Augustine improved upon—the way Pascal tersely, if not poetically, managed to do in some of his *Pensées:*

Moveless
he envies the men that ran
and could run off
toward the peripheries—
to other centers, direct—
for clarity (if
they found it)
              loveliness and
authority in the world—

The references to Pound and Eliot are obvious—they both escaped, leaving the Doc to tend the patients he found stimulating and nourishing but also wearing, distracting. Anyway, he was himself unable to follow suit, able only to confront lyrically his envy—and in a startling reference a few lines further, to acknowledge the "ice bound" quality to his mind that kept him confined. Ice and glass—both are elements of a writer's imprisonment within himself: "vanity of vanities," as it is put in the famous passage of *Ecclesiastes.* Here is poignant release through scrupulous self-arraignment—the jail is an anteroom, where the glass will break, the ice melt, so that William Carlos Williams may begin to do his dancing and singing in unashamed earnest, free of the malignant self-consciousness a poet has been ascribing to everyone, it seems—as a way, of course, to acknowledge the eager intellectual who is himself.

But repeated self-accusation can be a coy form of the very egotism being condemned. After a while self-rebuke reveals its narcissistic origins, as does an overworked humility. True enough, Williams would no doubt have been the first to admit. Still, there *is* a difference between a narcissism of self-importance and a narcissism of self-criticism as a corrective for (as well as an expression of) that self-importance. The only release from such endless psychological inquiry is in others, in the outside world—hence the admonition at the very start of the second book of **Paterson:**

Outside
              outside myself
                            there is a world,
he rumbled, subject to my incursions
—a world
              (to me) at rest,
                            which I approach
concretely—

That last word is no offhand adverb thrown in as the poet rushes along to his subject matter. Again he is at it: the "approach" of *Paterson* must be distinctively at odds with the kind of comprehension congenial to other writers, cultural observers, social theorists, and yes, political polemicists or activists; all those for whom the world is a means to one or another overriding purpose—an essay or treatise or poem or book, a big conclusion, a series of definitions, a plan or objective or program.

Williams was not without the above; he embraced his own, idiosyncratic American populism. He dipped into the Social Credit movement, so influential, for a while, with his old friend Ezra Pound. Nor was Williams unable to reach out *generally* to a given population. *Paterson* is full of his social indignation, his sense that injustice rules the day, and his compassionate yearning for more equity in America. The poor were his patients, after all; and plenty of times he worked for nothing. He could be, on their behalf, enthusiastically nonconcrete:

> Minds beaten thin
> by waste—among
>
> the working classes SOME sort
> of breakdown
> has occurred. Semi-roused
>
> they lie upon their blanket
> face to face,
> mottled by the shadows of the leaves
> upon them, unannoyed,
> at least here unchallenged.

That collective "they"—and, needless to say, "the working classes": Dr. Williams is distanced, as have been countless sociologists, reformist advocates, and revolutionary organizers. True, he is usually ironic, at the very least, when he generalizes. He moves from "picnickers" to "voices! / multiple and inarticulate," and then to this line: "The 'great beast' come to sun himself." He is taking on, politically, Alexander Hamilton and his class-conscious capitalism; but he is also struggling with his own situation as the Rutherford physician/writer who lived in a quite pleasant Victorian home on Ridge Road and who was educated, traveled, and in so many ways a lucky, privileged man. He was not Hamilton's kind of aristocrat with Hamilton's social views, and not (or not yet) Harvard's kind of poet; he was still not prized, still not covered with honorary doctorates, but nevertheless on his way—and aware that he had always been, from birth on, all things considered, a singularly blessed animal (socially and economically) rather than an anonymous cell of the "great beast."

Such awareness was not denied the author of *Paterson;* rather, such awareness fuels his intermittent rage, his episodic anti-intellectualism. He cannot escape himself and does not desire to do so. He wants a cleansing change in the way people get on—a shared vision that somehow enables a successful triumph over certain of his longstanding foes, and academic snobbery was only one of them. He detested materialism and the debasement of human affairs (language, sex, the environment, learning) at the hands of modern exploitive industrialism: the story of the city of Paterson's demise. Yet he had no confidence, really, in any of the proposed twentieth-century solutions other intellectuals have found attractive: statism (be it in the name of socialism or fascism), psychoanalysis, the withdrawal into art, religion, or personal adventurism and fulfillment of one kind or another. Even his much announced inclination to the particular, as opposed to the schematic or the theoretic, was by no means an unqualified source of solace or hope to him. When, in the first book of *Paterson,* he denounces "the whole din of fracturing thought," he

quickly has to insist: "the particular / no less vague." There are few consolations offered *this* intellectual; hence, perhaps, his despair—based not only on a dislike for others but on a gnawing knowledge of his own inadequacies.

The second book of *Paterson* is full of a poet's frustration. The problem is utterly contemporary. Paterson is "debased by the divorce from learning, / its garbage on the curbs, its legislators / under the garbage, uninstructed, incapable of / self instruction." Again, the teacher is impotent: what language, what manner of education, what effort of will and analysis can turn around such an impossible state of affairs? Some of Williams' anti-intellectualism is an expression of his moody bafflement. His modesty, too, expresses his hesitancy, his doubt. He could on occasion mobilize the very impatient hauteur he criticized so strenuously in others, especially professors and critics. But in the second book, especially, he is down-and-out, skeptical, worried about everyone and everything, and not in the least able to see a way through the general impasse he has been documenting, line after line, in a lyrical social history spiraling downward without letup.

That second book ends with a long letter from a rejected correspondent of Dr. P; the correspondent is Williams himself, of course—sparing himself and his kind little. This resort to sustained prose, rendered in the form of the letter, brings to mind Pascal's *Provincial Letters* and the structure of Georges Bernanos' novel *The Diary of a Country Priest.* (pp. 331-38)

[With] *Paterson,* and in particular with the long, complaining letter that closes the second book: "You've never had to live, Dr. P—not in any of the by-ways and dark underground passages where life so often has to be tested," she tells him. Then she strikes at his vulnerable, writing self: "The very circumstances of your birth and social background provided you with an escape from life in the raw; and you confuse that protection from life with an *inability* to live—and are thus able to regard literature as nothing more than a desperate last extremity resulting from that illusionary inability to live. (I've been looking at some of your autobiographical works, as this indicates.)"

She spells out her differences with Dr. P further in a devastating paragraph that gets to the very center of Williams' felt tension, in *Paterson,* between art and conduct. Living, she stresses, is not something one plans, constructs, or *decides* to do. Life happens, "in a small way, like measles; or in a big way, like a leaking boat or an earthquake." He "brings to life," she charges, "purely literary sympathies and understandings, the insights and humanity of words on paper *only*—and also, alas, the ego of the literary man." He is the imposter who knows others of his own ilk, abandons their sinking ship through angry verbal blasts at them, and tries to masquerade as an enraged ordinary Paterson citizen—yet by his own admission, he makes "incursions." Anti-intellectualism, she implies, is a form of manipulation as well as an indication of self-loathing. The expression of anti-intellectualism is, at its best, confessional; at its worst, it is an act of illusionary self-purification. The resort to "her" letter in *Paterson* represents, it would seem, a penitential exercise; it is the poet saying: I know the aforementioned, all of it, and can only use words, once again, in the service of a self-critical truth about the writer and those who read him devotedly.

Williams, we know, was constantly attracted to autobiography. Little in his own life, including the life of his beloved Flossie's family (the Stecher trilogy), escaped the writer in him. But his anti-intellectualism seemed also to be a constant attraction—and when used, it was subject to his writer's censoring skills: intelligence, a sense of proportion, a respect for factuality, the desire to be clear, pointed, convincing. Modernism, so proximate historically with psychoanalysis and the devastating social satire of, say, Expressionist painters—never mind the probing of such political, intellectual, and literary figures as Kurt Weill, Gramsci, and Lukács—would naturally welcome Williams' socially conscious, morally earnest, emotionally relentless self-scrutiny. The intellectuals become, for Williams, a foil, a means of being all the tougher on himself. Without his vigorous explication of their sins, we would be tempted to dismiss his enunciation of his own failings, if not misdemeanors, as overwrought and unnecessary. Instead, we take him seriously with respect to himself, feel rather pained about ourselves, and are maybe even tempted to follow suit: to use that exclusively human disposition, language, as a weapon against someone, anyone, a bit like ourselves, who works in a library or a classroom.

One final function of anti-intellectualism in the modernist canon: it is a means of both connecting with and dispensing with a tradition. The Williams who assaults intellectuals is also the Williams who quotes them with evident interest and favor—as in the reference to John Addington Symonds' *Studies of the Greek Poets* given us at the end of the first book of **Paterson.** Williams did, after all, write **In the American Grain,** showing thereby that his writing makeup included the learned social historian. He was not barbarous; rather, he was a polemical enthusiast who wanted his intellectual allies to fight hard against their enemies. Modernism has been, in so many instances, a recourse to past invigorations, too brusquely and completely set aside by various "principalities and powers," so the particular, agitated modernist claims. Let the bullying interpretations be set aside, let the original voices be heard or new ones in this fresh linkage with those original ones: Williams, through Symonds, to Hipponax and his iambics, ending with a spondee or a trochee rather than the compulsory iambus. (pp. 339-40)

> *Robert Coles, "Instances of Modernist Anti-Intellectualism," in his* That Red Wheelbarrow: Selected Literary Essays, *University of Iowa Press, 1988, pp. 331-43.*

FURTHER READING

Barry, Nancy K. "The Fading Beautiful Thing of *Paterson*." *Twentieth-Century Literature* 35, No. 3 (Fall 1989): 343-63.

Chronicles the genesis of *Paterson* and Williams's plans for the poem.

Furia, Philip. "*Paterson*'s Progress." *Boundary 2* 9, No. 2 (Winter 1981): 31-49.

In-depth study of punning and verbal play in *Paterson*.

Lloyd, Margaret Glynne. *William Carlos Williams's Paterson.* Cranbury: Associated University Presses, 1980. 304 p.

In-depth overview of *Paterson*'s literary context, themes, and structure.

Mariani, Paul. *William Carlos Williams: A New World Naked.* New York: McGraw-Hill, 1981. 912 p.

Critical biography of Williams, including in-depth discussion of *Paterson*'s development and Williams's relationship with Marcia Nardi, the female poet and author of several letters included in *Paterson.*

Martz, Louis L. "The Unicorn in *Paterson:* William Carlos Williams." *Thought* 35 (1960): 537-54.

Important essay on the significance of myth in *Paterson*.

Matthews, Kathleen D. "Competitive Giants: Satiric Bedrock in Book One of William Carlos Williams' *Paterson*." *Journal of Modern Literature* 12, No. 2 (July 1985): 237-60.

Notes Williams's satiric representation of T. S. Eliot, Ezra Pound, Hart Crane, and E. E. Cummings in *Paterson,* Book I.

Peterson, Walter Scott. *An Approach to Paterson.* New Haven: Yale University Press, 1967. 217 p.

Examines patterns of conventionality and free pursuit in *Paterson.*

Quinn, Sister Bernetta M. "William Carlos Williams: A Testament of Perpetual Change." In her *The Metamorphic Tradition in Modern Poetry,* pp. 89-129. New York: Gordian Press, 1966.

Landmark analysis of the structure of *Paterson* I-IV.

Rodgers, Audrey T. "*Paterson:* 'Beautiful Thing'." In her *Virgin and Whore: The Image of Women in the Poetry of William Carlos Williams,* pp. 93-122. Jefferson, N.C.: McFarland and Co., 1986.

Studies the structure of *Paterson* as a quest for union with women, who are both sacred and profane, ugly and beautiful in the poem.

Rogoff, Jay. "Pound-Foolishness in *Paterson*." *Journal of Modern Literature* 14, No. 1 (Summer 1987): 35-44.

Focuses on excerpts from Pound's letters used in *Paterson* and Williams's reaction to Pound's views.

Schmidt, Peter. "Dada, *Paterson,* and Epic Tradition." *William Carlos Williams Review* 8, No. 2 (Fall 1982): 1-14.

Examines Dadaist influence on *Paterson,* particularly the library sequence in Book III, and *Paterson*'s status in relation to the tradition of epic poetry.

Schricker, Gale C. "The Case of Cress: Implications of Allusion in *Paterson*." *William Carlos Williams Review* 11, No. 2 (Fall 1985): 16-29.

Discusses literary allusions found in *Paterson,* particularly references to Chaucer's *Troylus and Criseyde.*

Sharpe, William. "'That Complex Atom': The City and Form in William Carlos Williams's *Paterson*." *Poesis* 6: No. 2 (1985): 65-93.

Argues that Williams successfully portrays the modern urban experience in *Paterson.*

Zabriskie, George. "The Geography of *Paterson.*" *Perspective* 6, 201-16.
    Clarifies references to the city in *Paterson* with descriptions of the Paterson's history, industry, and geography.

Literary Criticism Series
Cumulative Author Index

This index lists all author entries in the Gale Literary Criticism Series and includes cross-references to other Gale sources. References in the index are identified as follows:

AAYA: *Authors & Artists for Young Adults,* Volumes 1-6
CAAS: *Contemporary Authors Autobiography Series,* Volumes 1-13
CA: *Contemporary Authors* (original series), Volumes 1-132
CABS: *Contemporary Authors Bibliographical Series,* Volumes 1-3
CANR: *Contemporary Authors New Revision Series,* Volumes 1-33
CAP: *Contemporary Authors Permanent Series,* Volumes 1-2
CA-R: *Contemporary Authors* (revised editions), Volumes 1-44
CDALB: *Concise Dictionary of American Literary Biography,* Volumes 1-6
CLC: *Contemporary Literary Criticism,* Volumes 1-67
CLR: *Children's Literature Review,* Volumes 1-24
CMLC: *Classical and Medieval Literature Criticism,* Volumes 1-7
DC: *Drama Criticism,* Volume 1
DLB: *Dictionary of Literary Biography,* Volumes 1-104
DLB-DS: *Dictionary of Literary Biography Documentary Series,* Volumes 1-8
DLB-Y: *Dictionary of Literary Biography Yearbook,* Volumes 1980-1988
LC: *Literature Criticism from 1400 to 1800,* Volumes 1-17
NCLC: *Nineteenth-Century Literature Criticism,* Volumes 1-32
PC: *Poetry Criticism,* Volumes 1-3
SAAS: *Something about the Author Autobiography Series,* Volumes 1-12
SATA: *Something about the Author,* Volumes 1-64
SSC: *Short Story Criticism,* Volumes 1-8
TCLC: *Twentieth-Century Literary Criticism,* Volumes 1-42
YABC: *Yesterday's Authors of Books for Children,* Volumes 1-2

Author Index

CLC Cumulative Nationality Index

Nationality Index

Nationality Index

Nationality Index

CLC-67 Title Index